THE STRUCTURE OF CLASSICAL HEBREW POETRY: ISAIAH 40–55

OUDTESTAMENTISCHE STUDIËN

NAMENS HET OUDTESTAMENTISCH
WERKGEZELSCHAP IN NEDERLAND EN BELGIË

DEEL XLI

THE STRUCTURE OF CLASSICAL HEBREW POETRY: ISAIAH 40–55

BY

MARJO C.A. KORPEL

AND

JOHANNES C. DE MOOR

BRILL
LEIDEN · BOSTON · KÖLN
1998

This book is printed on acid-free paper.

Library of Congress Cataloging-in-Publication Data

Korpel, Marjo Christina Annette.
The structure of classical Hebrew poetry : Isaiah 40-55 / by Marjo C.A.Korpel and Johannes C. de Moor.
p. cm. — (Oudtestamentische studiën, ISSN 0169-7226 ; d. 41)
Includes indexes.
ISBN 9004112618 (alk. paper)
1. Bible. O.T. Isaiah XL—LV—Language, style. 2. Hebrew poetry, Biblical—History and criticism. I. Moor, Johannes Cornelis de, 1935- . II. Title. III. Series.
BS1520.K67 1998
224'.1066—dc21 98-47026
CIP

Die Deutsche Bibliothek – CIP-Einheitsaufnahme

Korpel, Marjo Christina Annette:
The structure of classical hebrew poetry : Isaiah 40-55 / by Marjo C.A. Korpel and Johannes C. de Moor – Leiden ; Boston ; Köln : Brill, 1998
(Oudtestamentische Studiën ; Deel 41)
ISBN 90-04-11261-8

ISSN 0169-7226
ISBN 90 04 11261 8

PRINTED IN THE NETHERLANDS

Contents

A practical hint to the user: If one wants to study a certain chapter of Isaiah 40–55 in somewhat greater detail, it is advisable to copy the structured text and translation from section 1 of the chapter concerned for personal use.

Preface

Exegesis starts with the delimitation of the pericope to be interpreted. Yet the principles for selecting passages are seldom made explicit and if one compares various commentaries and Bible translations, it soon becomes apparent that this lack of methodical transparency gives rise to a lot of confusion and dissent.

In this work we make use of text divisions found in ancient Hebrew, Greek and Syriac manuscripts of Isaiah 40-55 (Second Isaiah). For the first time the poetic structure of the text is largely based on controllable evidence which is roughly 500-1000 years older than the medieval Masoretic manuscripts on which all modern editions are based.

We have strived to translate in a concordant way wherever this was possible because it often appears to be enlightening in discussions of parallelism on the higher levels of strophe, canticle, sub-canto and canto. In Hebrew poetry it is not only the immediate context which determines the meaning of words, but also the macrostructural links.

Several people helped us to complete this work within reasonable time. Utrecht University and the 'Theologische Universiteit' at Kampen enabled us to devote a substantial part of our recent research to this project. We thank dr Konrad Jenner of the Peshiṭta Institute in Leiden for his permission to collate some of the microfilms in the possession of the Institute. He and Dr Marinus Koster (Bathmen) were kind enough to draw our attention to some precious publications that otherwise might have escaped us. Several generations of student assistants participated in the preparatory work. We want to mention especially Carolina Koops, Alfred Lubbinge, Hennie Marsman, Ernst-Paul Paans, Jolanda Paans-Spoelstra and Piet van der Woel.

We are grateful to Professor Marc Vervenne (Leuven) who as a member of the Advisory Board of *Oudtestamentische Studiën* was kind enough to read part of the manuscript and agree to its publication in the series.

The results of this study encourage us to undertake similar studies for some other parts of the Hebrew Bible in the future and we do hope that some of our colleagues will find it worthwhile to join us in this effort.

Marjo Korpel   Johannes de Moor

Chapter 1

Introduction

1.1 Text Division in Antiquity

1.1.1 Text Division in Hebrew Manuscripts

Exegesis starts with the delimitation of the pericope to be interpreted. Whether some verses do belong to a unit or not can make all the difference between a prophecy of doom and a prophecy of salvation. Yet the principles for selecting passages which form the part of departure for the exegete are seldom made explicit and if one compares various commentaries and Bible translations, it soon becomes apparent that this lack of methodical transparency gives rise to a lot of confusion and dissent. In the chapters Isaiah 40–55 studied in this book examples of such hotly disputed issues are the delimitation of the so-called Servant Songs and the passages in which idolatry is denounced. On the basis of literary analysis many scholars have argued that these passages are later interpolations. Others are of the opinion that they form an integral part of the context in which they have been transmitted, using exactly the same type of literary arguments, but weighing them according to their own not always clearly defined standards.

It is for this reason, we believe, that a study like H.C. Spykerboer's work on the structure of Isaiah 40–55 failed to command general acclaim. Spykerboer concluded that the polemics against idolatry and the so-called servant songs do belong to the original book of Second Isaiah which he sees as a coherent work with continuity in both its content and form.[1] However, the problem with this type of study is that structural integrity is claimed on the basis of a relatively small number of repetitive patterns which other scholars see as the result of later editorial elaboration.[2] It would be an enormous step forward

[1] H.C. Spykerboer, *The Structure and Composition of Deutero-Isaiah*, Meppel 1976. With regard to the servant songs see also T.N.D. Mettinger, *A Farewell to the Servant Songs: A Critical Examination of an Exegetical Axiom*, Lund 1983. The structure of the idol passages was studied anew by K. Holter, *Second Isaiah's Idol-Fabrication Passages*, Frankfurt a.M. 1995. He too works with a kind of literary analysis and concludes that these passages do have a function within their immediate context, but cautions that this might be attributed to the skill of a later redactor.

[2] See for some surveys of the work on structure and composition of Isaiah 40–55, A. Richter in: C. Westermann, *Sprache und Struktur der Prophetie Deuterojesajas*, Stuttgart 1981, 116-22; Steck, 173-90; Oswalt, 12-16.

if one could agree at least on the proper delimitation of pericopes, since it does make a difference whether one may legitimately invoke the 'immediate context' – whatever is meant by 'immediate'.

Even with regard to the larger units exegetes are prone to follow the customary division into chapters which goes back to Stephen Langton, Archbishop of Canterbury († 1228), who applied it to his copy of the Vulgate. This system of capitulation was taken over in the Bomberg Hebrew Bibles of 1517 and 1525 for the sake of easy reference, and has since been used by almost everybody.[3] However, it should be obvious enough that Langton's division was often totally beside the mark.[4]

It is a strange phenomenon that whereas in textual criticism there is seen a fairly general tendency to return to an attitude of respect for the textual tradition of the Old Testament, scholars generally ignore the divisions of the text found in ancient manuscripts. Most editions do not bother to register differences in this category and many a Hebrew student does not even know what a *petuḥa* or *setuma* is. It took a major effort by J. Oesch to demonstrate that the Hebrew tradition of *paragraphoi*, *petuḥot* and *setumot* dates back to several centuries BCE.[5]

Since *petuḥot* and *setumot* are found less frequently in the historical books and these dividers are evidently used to delimit sense units

---

[3] Cf. J.S. Penkower, "The Chapter Divisions in the 1525 Rabbinic Bible", *VT* 48 (1998), 350-74, who points out a number of curious divergencies.

[4] The most notorious case being his strange incision between Isa. 52 and 53, although it may have been inspired by medieval Jewish exegesis, cf. Oswalt, 376, n. 69. For other examples of erroneous divisions see E. Tov, *Textual Criticism of the Hebrew Bible*, Assen 1992, 4; J.C. de Moor, "Structure and Redaction: Isaiah 60,1–63,6", in: J. van Ruiten, M. Vervenne (eds.), *Studies in the Book of Isaiah: Festschrift Willem A.M. Beuken*, Leuven 1997, 325-46; Penkower, "The Chapter Divisions", 350, n. 2. It would be helpful if such examples were collected in the form of a comprehensive survey.

[5] J. Oesch, *Petucha und Setuma: Untersuchungen zu einer überlieferten Gliederung im hebräischen Text des Alten Testaments* (OBO, 27), Freiburg 1979. Professor Oesch was kind enough to provide us with a corrected version of his tables. In many instances we also consulted the photographs of 1Q[ab] ourselves. See furthermore Y. Maori, "The Tradition of Pisqa'ot in Ancient Hebrew Manuscripts: The Isaiah Texts and Commentaries from Qumran" (in Hebrew), *Textus* 10 (1982), 1*-50*; J.W. Olley, "'Hear the Word of Yahweh': The Structure of the Book of Isaiah in 1QIsa[a]", *VT* 43 (1993), 19-49; E. van den Berg, "Over de structuur van oudtestamentische verhalen en de indeling in petucha's en setuma's", *NedThT* 52 (1998), 89-106.

In addition to the material collected by Oesch we will use the data culled from the 4QIsa-fragments, cf. E. Ulrich *et al.*, *Qumran Cave 4*, vol. 10: The Prophets (DJD, 15), Oxford 1997. The manuscripts containing information relevant to our project are 4QIsa[b] (3rd quarter 1st century BCE), 4QIsa[c], 4QIsa[d], 4QIsa[g] and 4QIsa[h], all first century CE.

there, it must be concluded that their higher number in the prophetic books has to do with the poetic nature of this type of literature. Apparently they delimited smaller structural units there, comparable to stanzas in other literature.[6]

With regard to the division into the smaller units like cola, verses and strophes the general feeling seems to be that the Masoretic accentuation as well as their division into verses are demonstrably late and therefore totally unreliable. Indeed there is a number of notorious cases of discrepancy with regard to verse division between editions of the Hebrew Bible.[7] However, it seems to have escaped most scholars that recent finds have demonstrated that in this case too evidence dating back to the second and first centuries BCE proves the Masoretic colometry to be correct in about 85% of the cases.[8] This alone should be reason enough to take the testimony of 𝔐 much more seriously.

It is for this reason that in previous publications we have always sought to use attested traditional divisions in our analyses of ancient Hebrew and other North West Semitic poetry. Basing ourselves on this kind of evidence we have developed a number of rules which can be applied to recover the structure of these ancients poems despite the fact that in most cases they were written in continuous mode in order to economize on precious writing materials. In this book we want to elaborate this method further.[9]

1.1.2 Text Division in Greek Manuscripts

In his still very instructive survey of text-divisions in manuscripts of the 𝔊 Swete shrinks back from drawing any conclusions with regard to the markings of larger units in the manuscripts at his disposal,

> "It is clear that no induction can be drawn from the facts which are at present within our reach; nor can the various systems of capitulation be safely classified un-

[6]Yet not identical to them because unlike stanzas their length could apparently vary. It is for this reason that we have chosen to speak of canticles, see M.C.A. Korpel, J.C. de Moor, "Fundamentals of Ugaritic and Hebrew Poetry", in: W. van der Meer, J.C. de Moor (eds.), *The Structural Analysis of Biblical and Canaanite Poetry* (JSOT.S, 74), Sheffield 1988, 1-61 (38-44).

[7]Cf. Tov, *Textual Criticism*, 5.

[8]J.C. de Moor, W.G.E. Watson, "General Introduction", in: *Verse in Ancient Near Eastern Prose* (AOAT, 42), Neukirchen 1993, xv; P. Sanders, *The Provenance of Deuteronomy 32* (OTS, 37), Leiden 1996, 102-32; De Moor, art. cit. (n. 4).

[9]Inevitably the enormous increase in relevant data necessitated a thorough revision of our own previous work in this field too. *Dies diem docet*!

> til some scholar has collected and tabulated the chapter-divisions of a large number of MSS. of varying ages and provenance."[10]

Meanwhile the Greek Minor Prophets Scroll from Naḥal Ḥever, dating from the first century BCE, has demonstrated that even at this early age colometry was marked, be it not very consistently. In this case by spaces and/or somewhat larger first characters of cola. At the beginnings of Masoretic verses – in our opinion often equalling strophes – this scroll often has a somewhat wider space. Occasionally ancient Hebrew manuscripts too use this method of delimiting strophes, e.g. 1Q[a] in Isa. 50:1-11.[11] Finally, larger units were marked by bigger *setumot* and *petuḥot*, as well as *paragraphoi* (small horizontal lines) and capital letters protruding into the left margin after a closed section.[12] Mostly these larger divisions appear to agree with the Masoretic tradition. As Sanders has shown in his study of Deut. 32, it is certainly worthwhile to consult the Greek manuscripts with regard to text division.[13] But at the same time it must be observed that the working with spaces of various widths in two of the most ancient Bible manuscripts we have – 1Q[a] and the Greek Minor Prophets Scroll from Naḥal Ḥever – was a confusing method of text division which was bound to create problems. If space was tight, a scribe might easily be tempted to narrow a Setuma a little, or the reverse procedure if space was ample. As we shall see, this did indeed confuse later scribes and it will be our task to critically evaluate any major text division found in our witnesses.

For the chapters we are dealing with in this book, a Chester Beatty papyrus of the early third century seems to mark the beginning of Isa. 42:1 by indentation. The same papyrus occasionally uses single points to divide cola.[14]

---

[10]H.B. Swete, *An Introduction to the Old Testament in Greek*, rev. R.R. Ottley, Cambridge 1914, 342-65, quotation p. 354.

[11]See our analysis below.

[12]E.Tov, *The Greek Minor Prophets Scroll from Naḥal Ḥever (8ḤevXIIgr* (DJD, 8), Oxford 1990, 9-12, with earlier literature. It is worthwhile to study his plates carefully in each particular case because the differences are small and open to various interpretations.

[13]P. Sanders, *The Provenance of Deuteronomy 32*, Leiden 1996, 121-30.

[14]F. Kenyon, *The Chester Beatty Biblical Papyri: Descriptions and Texts of Twelve Manuscripts on Papyrus of the Greek Bible*, fasc. VI/1, Text, London 1937, 11-21; R.J. Hayes, *The Chester Beatty Biblical Papyri: Descriptions and Texts of Twelve Manuscripts on Papyrus of the Greek Bible*, fasc. VI/2, Plates, London 1958, Pl. 92-100.

Since our objective is restricted to the structural analysis of the Hebrew text of Isa. 40–55, we deemed it justifiable to collate only four major uncials with regard to unit divisions of the text: the *Codex Sinaiticus* ($\mathfrak{G}^{S}$) (early fourth century),[15] the *Codex Vaticanus* ($\mathfrak{G}^{B}$) of the late fourth century,[16] the *Codex Alexandrinus* ($\mathfrak{G}^{A}$) of the fifth century,[17] and the *Codex Marchialianus* ($\mathfrak{G}^{Q}$) of the sixth century.[18] In all four uncials[19] the scribes have marked major divisions by *petuḥot* and *setumot* and/or lines projecting into the left margin and usually headed by a capital letter, as is the case in the much older Minor Prophets Scroll from Naḥal Ḥever. In addition to this system the punctuator of $\mathfrak{G}^{S}$ has marked the end of larger units by a colon (:). Often a later hand has marked the *paragraphoi*, usually by horizontal lines in the margin, sometimes accompanied by various other sigla.

Although most of the interpunction of the 𝔊-manuscripts was apparently added only after the main text had been written, it is difficult to say when this was done. Deliberate addition of interpunction shortly after the execution of the main text is by no means excluded. In any case it is well-known that 𝔊 sometimes presupposes a different colometry.[20] So we deemed it worthwhile to collate at least two manuscripts with respect to punctuation, mainly because the Naḥal Ḥever Scroll has demonstrated the antiquity of colometric division in Greek manuscripts of the 𝔊.[21] For this purpose we selected the Sinaiticus and the Marchialianus where cola have been marked by a single

[15] H. & K. Lake, *Codex Sinaiticus Petropolitanus et Friderico-Augustanus Lipsiensis: The Old Testament Preserved in the Public Library of Petrograd, in the Library of the Society of Ancient Literature in Petrograd, and in the Library of the University of Leipzig, Now Reproduced in Facsimile from Photographs*, Oxford 1922.

[16] *Bibliorum SS. Graecorum Codex Vaticanus 1209 (Cod.B) denuo phototypice expressus iussu et cura Praesidum Bybliothecae Vaticanae*, Pars Prima: Testamentum Vetus, Tomus III, Mediolani 1907.

[17] F.G. Kenyon, *The Codex Alexandrinus in Reduced Photographic Facsimile: Old Testament*, Part III, London 1936.

[18] J. Cozza-Luzi (ed.), *Prophetarum Codex Graecus Vaticanus 2125 Qui Dicitur Marchialianus*, Romae 1890.

[19] For a critical evaluation of these manuscripts see S. Jellicoe, *The Septuagint and Modern Study*, Oxford 1968, repr. Winona Lake 1993, 176-88, 201-2.

[20] For some examples see E. Tov, *The Text-Critical Use of the Septuagint in Biblical Research*, Jerusalem 1981, 178-9.

[21] As a rule, we did not take into account interpunction which was not supported by either 𝔐 or at least one manuscript of 𝔖 because such an isolated testimony might rest on a scribal error or a speck of dirt.

For convenience' sake we will often refer to the position of punctuation in the 𝔊 or the 𝔖 by citing the *Hebrew* word. Obviously we had to reckon with transpositions in the Greek or Syriac text in this respect.

point between words, and more rarely by a double punctuation mark (:), mostly at the end of verses or paragraphs.[22]

It should not be forgotten that even the strongest Masoretic divider, the Soph Pasuq, was still unknown at Qumran. So not only the colometry, but also the versification of the Masoretes must be tested against other ancient traditions. Here, however, we are in a much more precarious position because verses were rarely marked in the ancient Greek manuscripts either. Nevertheless their colometric division fairly often indicates a different versification too and such cases will be discussed in our structural analysis below.

1.1.3 Text Division in Syriac Manuscripts

Also in the Peshiṭta we find a system of markers at the end of longer units, usually spaces deliberately left open, as in the Hebrew and Greek traditions, or 'diamonds' (diamond-shaped clusters of 3 to 5 points, 'rosettes'), sometimes a series of diamonds to fill out the line.[23] As has been demonstrated by several scholars, this system is older than the systems of pericopes used in the Jacobite and Nestorian liturgies. Although probably somewhat corrupted by copyists who did not understand the function of these markings anymore, it is highly likely that the system itself goes back on the Hebrew original(s) used by the Syrian translators because in many instances the markings coincide with Petuḥot or Setumot in Qumrân and 𝔐.[24] However, since

---

[22]The Vaticanus does not have interpunction in this part of the codex and the facsimiles of the Alexandrinus are too much reduced in size to be readable in all instances. We noted the difference between high and low points in the two manuscripts we selected, but discovered that the difference between a high and a low position of the point was mostly dictated by the available space. So it is a system of single points that is still recognizable in both these manuscripts.

[23]We established with absolute certainty that there is no difference in dividing weight between one diamond or more diamonds. More diamonds were added for the simple purpose of filling out the line. Other embellishments, like garlands, could be used for the same purpose.

[24]A. Baumstark, *Vom geschichtlichen Werden der Liturgie*, Freiburg 1923, 13-21; S.P. Brock, "Text History and Text Division in Peshiṭta Isaiah", in: P.B. Dirksen, M.J. Mulder (eds.), *The Peshiṭta: Its Early Text and History*, Leiden 1988, 49-80, esp. 65-78; K.D. Jenner, *De perikopentitels van de geïllustreerde syrische kanselbijbel van Parijs (MS Paris, Bibliothèque Nationale, Syriaque 341)*, Leiden 1993, 196-203; Idem, "A Review of the Methods by Which Syriac Biblical and Related Manuscripts Have Been Described and Analysed: Some Preliminary Remarks", *ARAM* 5 (1993), 255-66; Idem, "The Development of Syriac Lectionary Systems: A Discussion of the Opinion of P. Kannookadan", *The Harp* 10 (1997), 9-24; Idem, "Petucha and Setuma: Tools for the Interpretation or Simply a Matter of Layout?", H.J. Bosman, H.W.M. van Grol *et al.* (eds.), *Studies in Isaiah 24-27* (forthcoming in *OTS*).

there are also considerable differences between the Masoretic and the Syrian traditions, the Syrian markers are of eminent importance for the study of Hebrew text division. It is a pity that in this case too, as with the editions of the 𝔊, most modern editions of the Peshiṭta simply ignore these markers.

Fortunately, Brock did note the markers he found in his main witness for the Book of Isaiah, the seventh century manuscript 7a1.[25] However, because it is likely that various systems of text division were transmitted in Syria[26] we found it necessary to collate a number of other manuscripts in addition to 7a1,[27]

LEIDEN NOTATION	IN THIS BOOK
6h3	S^{a}
6h5	S^{b}
7a1	S^{c}
8a1	S^{d}
9a1[28]	S^{e}

With regard to text division we have paid special attention to the positioning of the diamonds. If we found a marking of a lection, either in the text of the manuscript itself or in the margin, we have designated it as a *paragraphos* (§) in our database, but do not distinguish it here from the 'diamonds' if the two coincide.

Moreover, the Syriac manuscripts are provided with a scansion system which became more and more elaborated as the textus receptus grew into its final shape,[29] just as is the case in the Greek and

[25]The Peshiṭta Institute Leiden, *The Old Testament in Syriac*, Part III, fasc. 1, Isaiah, ed. S.P. Brock, Leiden 1987. Our collation of the microfilm resulted in only one major difference, a diamond after 41:29 which may have been added later on because 42:1 is marked as the beginning of a lection.

Here we follow the designations of the Peshiṭta manuscripts as described in W. Baars, M.D. Koster, *List of Old Testament Peshiṭta Manuscripts*, Leiden 1961. In the designation system used by the Leiden Peshiṭta team the first digit designates the century (e.g., 6h3 dates from the sixth century).

[26]See Jenner, *De perikopentitels*, 203.

[27]Microfilms of the manuscripts involved were magnanimously provided by Dr Konrad Jenner of the Peshiṭta Institute, Leiden.

[28]We included this manuscript because it seems to represent a much older text type which might well go back to the sixth century, cf. Jenner, *De perikopentitels*, 203, n. 1; Idem, "A Review of the Methods", esp. 262-64. Also with regard to interpunction, this is appears to be true (see Ch. 16). It appears, however, that as compared to the 6th century manuscripts the scribe favoured the main division of the text according to the Christian lectionary he adhered to, omitting many traditional dividing signs ('diamonds') which he thought to be superfluous.

[29]See Th. Weiss, *Zur ostsyrischen Laut- und Akzentlehre auf Grund der ost-*

Hebrew traditions.[30] This scansion system probably started with the single point at the end of a colon (*pāsōqā*), as in the Codex Sinaiticus and Codex Marchialianus,[31] but was soon expanded with other accents, the most important of which were the *taḥtaya* and *'elaya*.[32] Because we found that the manuscripts differed rather frequently in assigning these 'lower' accents, we will refer to such accents indiscriminately as 'subordinate' accents and will take them into account only if Brock's edition based on 𝔖^{c} (7a1) indicates a subordinate accent. However, the low point being the oldest and most important divider, we registered all such points in the manuscripts we collated.[33] Unfortunately, as in the case of the oldest Hebrew and Greek manuscripts, no system for the demarcation of verses was developed in Syria, although the colometry of the Peshiṭta manuscripts often indicates that verse division must have been different. We intend to discuss such cases in detail below.

Even though the structure of Syriac and Hebrew differs considerably, the mere fact that the Syriac colometry is centuries older than the Masoretic one renders it worthwhile to take it into consideration when trying to recover the intended division of the Hebrew text into cola and verses.[34] However, we decided to collate all five manuscripts of 𝔖 with regard to punctuation because Koster noted a case where his manuscripts 5b1 and the related 10l1 had preserved a division which

---

syrischen Massorah-Handschrift des British Museum, Suttgart 1933; J.B. Segal, *The Diacritical Point and the Accents in Syriac*, London 1953.

[30]For the beginnings of Hebrew cantillation marks see e.g. M. Dietrich, *Neue palästinisch punktierte Bibelfragmente veröffentlicht und auf Text und Punktation hin untersucht*, Leiden 1968, with earlier literature. Unfortunately, variants in punctuation are not recorded in the Leiden edition of the Peshiṭta. Even in Koster's meticulous study of the Peshiṭta of Exodus such variants are registered only occasionally, cf. M.D. Koster, *The Peshiṭta of Exodus: The Development of its Texts in the Course of Fifteen Centuries*, Assen 1977, 3 sub h)c, with the restriction p. 541, n. 8. See the cases of category h)c he describes on pages 119, 135, 144, 148.

[31]The Syrian authors themselves attribute the origin of their accents to the Greek custom. Cf. Segal, *The Diacritical Point*, 58, 62-3. As a matter of fact, some early Palestinian Hebrew manuscripts use the single point instead of the double point to mark the end of a verse, cf. Dietrich, *Neue palästinisch punktierte Bibelfragmente*, 97.

[32]The former being the stronger accent. See Weiss, *Zur ostsyrischen Laut- und Akzentlehre*, 38.

[33]As a rule, however, we did not take into account points which are not supported by either 𝔐 or at least one manuscript of 𝔊 because such an isolated testimony might rest on a scribal error or a speck of dirt.

[34]Sanders, *The Provenance*, 130-1, noted the importance of the punctuation for the colometric division of Deut. 32.

is in accordance with 𝔐 whereas all others have a different divison.[35] As we shall see, it paid off to collate several manuscripts of 𝔖 in this respect.

Whereas in the case of the diamonds the obvious correspondence with the *petuḥot* and *setumot* in very ancient Hebrew manuscripts suggested that this system of delimiting larger units was derived directly from the Hebrew, this is much less certain in the case of the division by points. Since this Syriac system was probably derived from Greek manuscripts, as we have seen, it might well be that 𝔖's punctuation was taken over from manuscripts of 𝔊. However, our findings disprove this hypothesis. True, in a number of cases 𝔊 and 𝔖 agree in offering a division which is different from that of 𝔐[36], but as we shall demonstrate at the end of this book the differences are too large to warrant the conclusion of a direct dependence.

1.1.4 Text Division in Christian-Palestinian Manuscripts

Also in Christian-Palestinian manuscripts of the Old Testament, dating from the 5th–8th centuries CE, the colometric division is indicated by a system of points.[37] Since the Christian-Palestinian version was mostly derived from 𝔊, it can hardly be viewed as an independent witness. Nevertheless, we have checked the few fragments from Isaiah 40 and 50 found in the lectionaries.[38]

1.1.5 The Weight of Combined Testimony

It would seem obvious enough that if more than one of the ancient witnesses testifies to a divider, especially if these witnesses belong to different traditions (𝔔, 𝔐, 𝔊, 𝔖), it should be taken very seriously. If one wants to diverge from such a combined testimony, he has to argue the case convincingly, just as one customarily does if one proposes an emendation of the Hebrew text.

1.2 Additional Tools for Text Division

In addition to the markers found in the ancient non-Masoretic manuscripts, there is a number of other fairly objective arguments that may be used to critically evaluate the traditions with regard to text

[35] Koster, *The Peshiṭta of Exodus*, 97. We thank Dr Koster for bringing this passage to our attention.

[36] See below, p. 637.

[37] C. Müller-Kessler, M. Sokoloff, *A Corpus of Christian Palestinian Aramaic*, vol. 1: The Christian Palestinian Aramaic Old Testament and Apocrypha Version from the Early Period, Groningen 1997.

[38] Müller-Kessler, Sokoloff, *op. cit.*, 142-147.

division.[39] On every level of ancient Hebrew poetry we encounter both separating forces, like emphatic constructions and distinctive punctuation, as well as uniting forces, like parallelism and conjunctive punctuation. We established the existence of this kind of markers by analyzing texts which were fortunately divided into separate units by the ancient scribes themselves. Nevertheless, reconstructing the most probable textual division is often a matter of weighing one type of argument against the other.[40] So we do by no means pretend to present a fool-proof method of analyzing Classical Hebrew poetry. What we do claim, however, is to present a method enabling scholars to narrow down the number of possibilities and thus to make more responsible decisions with regard to text division. We shall briefly enumerate the type of arguments we believe to be admissable below. Later on we will draw the balance of the analysis of Second Isaiah as a whole.

1.2.1 Delimitation of Cola

In our opinion it is best to start structural analysis at the level of the smallest units, the feet and cola. If one starts at a higher level preoccupation with an intuitively accepted interpretation, for example that of the Masoretes, is a real danger.[41]

1.2.1.1 Separating Force: Larger Masoretic Distinctivi

It is common knowledge that the most important Masoretic delimiters of cola are the Silluq (No. 1 in the table provided with the *BHS*), Atnaḥ (No. 2) and Zaqeph Qaṭon (No. 5). The other 'heavy' distinctive (or: disjunctive) accents up to Revia' (No. 7) may occasionally be used as colon dividers, but are often also used as so-called 'servi' – minor accents used within the domain of a 'heavy' accent.[42] This

[39]We do not include methods like the counting of letters or syllables in this class of arguments because it has been demonstrated that there is too much variation in this respect in parallel traditions and ancient manuscripts. Cf. J.C. de Moor, "The Art of Versification in Ugarit and Israel, I: The Rhythmical Structure", in: Y. Avishur, J. Blau (eds.), *Studies in Bible and the Ancient Near East Presented to S.E. Loewenstamm*, Jerusalem 1978, 119-39. On the relative value of the counting of stresses see 1.2.2.2.

[40]See for some recent reviews of these basic principles, Korpel, De Moor, "Fundamentals"; J. Kim, *The Structure of the Samson Cycle*, Kampen 1993, 118-27; Sanders, *The Provenance of Deuteronomy 32*, 99-137, 258-66.

[41]So we disagree with the method applied by P. van der Lugt, *Rhetorical Criticism and the Poetry of the Book of Job* (OTS, 32), Leiden 1995, esp. 34-5.

[42]See for all this see I. Yeivin, *Introduction to the Tiberian Masorah*, transl. E.J. Revell (MasSt, 5), [Missoula] 1980; J.D. Price, *The Syntax of Masoretic Accents in the Hebrew Bible* (SBEC, 27), Lewiston 1990.

means that if any other accent than the first three mentioned is supposed to mark the end of a colon a scholar has to argue why she/he departs from the traditional versification.

Of course we do not contend that the Masoretes were always right. On the contrary, we intend to prove that in many cases they were simply wrong. In some cases we are able to suggest that the Masoretic distinctive accents rest on rabbinic exegesis which cannot be followed by modern scholarship anymore. But it is our working hypothesis that in the majority of cases the Masoretic delimitation of cola, verses and strophes rests on ancient, reliable tradition which should not be rejected without proper discussion.

1.2.1.2 Binding Force: Colon Parallelism

As Wilfred Watson has shown, there exists an important, but often neglected category of parallelism[43] which he calls 'half-line parallelism' or 'internal parallelism'.[44] In order to prevent misunderstanding, we prefer the term 'colon parallelism' – a form of parallelism like that found in the very first colon of Second Isaiah:

נַחֲמוּ נַחֲמוּ עַמִּי 1aA "Comfort, comfort my people,"

The repetition of the imperative is superfluous from a logical point of view, but it emphasizes a new beginning and at the same time provides us with a strong argument to regard this as one colon. To be sure, any kind of parallelism may recur at any other level of a Hebrew poem.[45] In this case it is certain that the same pair of identical verbs occurs in verse-line parallelism.[46] In itself, therefore, the pair might just as well argue in favour of a colon of one word (נחמו) followed by a next colon of two words (נחמו עמי). This is what we mean by 'weighing the evidence'. For it is absolutely clear on the basis of other arguments (like Masoretic accentuation, number of stressed units, etc.) that the binding force of the colon parallelism should be taken seriously in this case.

[43] We have to thank here several generations of student assistants at Kampen who patiently built up an enormous database of parallel pairs, culled not only from the Hebrew Bible but also from numerous ancient Oriental poems. In addition we made use of several computer programs enabling us to implement fast searches for pairs of roots and the words derived from them.

[44] See W.G.E. Watson, *Traditional Techniques in Classical Hebrew Verse* (JSOT.S, 170), Sheffield 1994, 104-91.

[45] All parallel pairs found in Second Isaiah, at any structural level, are listed in the Index of Parallel Words at the end of this book.

[46] See Isa. 66:13.

1.2.2 Delimitation of Verse-Lines

1.2.2.1 Separating Force: Descending Masoretic Distinctivi

As indicated above, the evidence for the existence of verse-lines in Antiquity is rather meagre, be it sufficient to prove that such a poetic unit did exist.[47] Probably this was mostly left to oral tradition for reasons of economy. The reproduction of poetry in the form of verse-lines resulted in a waste of precious writing materials.

For this reason the Masoretic tradition about the delimitation of verse-lines is our most consistent source of information for the delimitation of verses. A verse-line – as distinct from a numbered Masoretic verse! – is usually marked by a chain of distinctive larger accents[48] *in descending order* if counted according to the usual enumeration as presented on the *Tabula Accentuum* added to the *BHS*.[49] This means that whenever a distinctive accent with a higher number according to the *Tabula* occurs, one has to assume that a new verse-line has started. Of course, in this case too other considerations may lead to a choice differing from that of the Masoretes, but the basic principle should be to pay due attention to the sequence of Masoretic accents. Obviously it may be an additional argument if such sequences can be demonstrated to exist elsewhere in Classical Hebrew poetry.[50]

1.2.2.2 Binding Force: Number of Stresses

Even though no rigid metre can be found in Hebrew poetry, there often appears to exist a loose rhythmical balance resulting in equal or symmetrical patterns of stressed units (feet) in a series of cola.[51] Far from being a tool enabling the scholar to emend the transmitted text *metri causa*, the rhythmical balance may sometimes function as an additional argument in the delimitation of cola and verse-lines.[52]

---

[47] See in addition to the evidence indicated above, the Moabitic Mesha stele on which verse-lines have been marked by vertical strokes, cf. J.C. de Moor, "Narrative Poetry in Canaan", *UF* 20 (1988), 149-71 (149-60).

[48] As defined in 1.2.1.1.

[49] See W.Th. Koopmans, *Joshua 24 as Poetic Narrative* (JSOT.S, 93), Sheffield 1990, 178. Actually of course, the lower the number, the stronger the accent.

[50] We have to thank here our student assistant P.J. van der Woel who drew up a database of accentual patterns found in a great number of poems.

[51] E.g. J.C. de Moor, "The Art of Versification in Ugarit and Israel, I"; Korpel, De Moor, "Fundamentals", 6, 16; W.G.E. Watson, *Classical Hebrew Poetry: A Guide to its Techniques* (JSOT.S, 26), Sheffield 1986, 87-113.

[52] One should certainly refrain from making it one of the main arguments in analyzing Classical Hebrew poetry. In this respect it is instructive to compare our results with those of C. Franke, *Isaiah 46, 47, and 48: A New Literary-Critical Reading*, Winona Lake 1994.

For this reason we have consistently marked the number of stressed units within the chains of cola forming a verse-line. In doing so we did not resort to methods aiming at a nicer poetical balance, such as discounting particles even if no Maqqeph is present. We simply present the evidence according to the Tiberian Masoretic text.

1.2.2.3 Binding Force: Ellipsis

The omission of one or more words in a parallel colon is a frequent phenomenon in poetry. It often had to do with the rhythmical balance in a verse. As it is impossible to understand this kind of ellipsis (or, as it is sometimes called: gapping) without taking into account the neighbouring colon or cola, ellipsis must be seen as a binding force on the level of the verse-line.[53]

The on-running sentence (or: enjambment of cola) results in so-called synthetical parallelism.[54] It is possible to view this type of verse-line as a double or triple ellipsis. In any case it is clear that in such cases the cola appear to be bound by syntax.

1.2.2.4 Binding Force: Verse-line Parallelism

This is the best known form of parallelism that has been long recognized as a binding force in Classical Hebrew Poetry.[55] However, since parallelism may occur also on the levels of colon and strophe, it is sometimes difficult to determine whether the parallelism may be interpreted as a binding force on the level of the verse-line and therefore further discussion will often prove necessary.

1.2.3 Delimitation of Strophes

1.2.3.1 Separating Force: Major Division Markers

In many cases major divisions have been marked in the tradition by special markers like the Setuma and Petuḥa in 𝔐, paragraphoi, capital letters, 'diamonds', etc. (see our description above, 1.1.1–1.1.4).

[53] Cf. J.C. de Moor, "Syntax Peculiar to Ugaritic Poetry", in: J.C. de Moor, W.G.E. Watson (eds.), *Verse in Ancient Near Eastern Prose* (AOAT, 42), Neukirchen 1993, 191-205 (200-5).

[54] See for a critical evaluation of this concept S.A. Geller, *Parallelism in Early Biblical Poetry*, Missoula 1979, 375-85.

[55] See e.g. Geller, *Parallelism in Early Biblical Poetry*; J.L. Kugel, *The Idea of Biblical Poetry: Parallelism and its History*, New Haven 1981; D. Pardee, *Ugaritic and Hebrew Poetic Parallelism: A Trial Cut* (VT.S, 39), Leiden 1988; Watson, *Classical Hebrew Poetry*, 114-59; Idem, *Traditional Techniques*, 104-312. Because certain critics objected to our registering of the parallelistic use of the article and the conjunction ו, we decided to skip these in this book although we remain convinced that even such small elements may contribute to the verse-line parallelism.

Although the function of these markers is a different one, namely the delimitation of larger units which we call canticles (see below 1.2.4), it is clear that they may function at the same time to mark the beginning or end of strophes positioned at the beginning or end of such a canticle.

1.2.3.2 Separating Force: the Soph Pasuq

It seems fairly obvious that in many cases a Masoretic verse ending with a Soph Pasuq consists of more than one verse-line. So we may assume that the Soph Pasuq often marks the end of strophes. It remains to be seen what in this respect the results of our investigation will be, but it seems admissable to treat the Soph Pasuq as a strophe delimiter from the start, even though we have to keep open the possibility that it sometimes ends the last one of two or more strophes, or must be ignored for compelling other reasons. In both cases it is proper to discuss such decisions, and not to present them as self-evident choices, as has become customary.

1.2.3.3 Separating Force: Emphasis

The most important markers of the beginning and end of strophes are particles and syntactic constructions which lend 'emphasis'.[56] Especially the deliberate changing of the syntactic order of words common in normal prose appears to be an important structuring force on the level of the strophe. Often it is quite obvious that no real emphasis can have been intended. It is our contention that in poetry the changing of word-order often has no other function than to mark the boundaries of strophes. So we shall incorporate the following markers of separation in our analysis of the strophic delimitation:

---

[56]The first to apply syntax comprehensively to the analysis of biblical poetry was M. O'Connor, *Hebrew Verse Structure*, Winona Lake 1980, 2nd printing with an 'Afterword' (631-61), Winona Lake 1997. We apply a much less sophisticated method, concentrating mainly on 'emphasis'. Cf. De Moor, "Syntax Peculiar to Ugaritic Poetry", 191-200, and also T. Muraoka, *Emphatic Words and Structures in Biblical Hebrew*, Leiden 1985, who deals with poetry only incidentally (despite 167: "Poetry was not touched at all.").

For a very detailed study of word-order in Second Isaiah see M. Rosenbaum, *Word-Order Variation in Isaiah 40-55: A Functional Perspective*, Assen 1997. Rosenbaum objects to the use of the term 'emphasis' and replaces it by 'foregrounding'. It was not his aim to study the relevance of syntax for poetic structure, though he did recognize "that variant word-order could be used as a signalling device in discourse" (215). Rosenbaum only noted that this was an area deserving further study.

deictic particle(s)	interrogative pronoun	repetitive verse-line paralllelism
demonstrative pronoun	jussive(s)	swapping (subject)
imperative(s)	marker of direct speach	swapping (object)
independent personal pronoun	paronomasia	swapping (adjunct)
		vocative

1.2.3.4 Binding Force: Strophe Parallelism

Parallelism works as a connecting device on all structural levels of Hebrew poetry. It is an argument in favour of joining adjacent verse-lines into one strophe if these lines contain parallel pairs of words.

1.2.4 Delimitation of Canticles

The most important objective basis for determining the limits of the next larger unit after the strophe is furnished by the markers of major divisions in the ancient Hebrew, Greek, Syriac and Christian-Palestinian manuscripts. Yet some other arguments may serve to evaluate this type of evidence critically.

1.2.4.1 Binding Force: Canticle Parallelism

As in many other types of poetry, the next higher unit is – what we call – the canticle (others prefer 'stanza') which is the unit comprising several strophes.[57] Parallelism also functions on this level of the Hebrew poem. It serves to link the strophes belonging to the same canticle in a more or less formal way. If the parallelism is in verses on opposite structural ends of the canticle, this has a kind of embracing effect which we call *inclusion*. If it is in verses on corresponding structural positions within the canticle we speak of *responsion*. Finally, if the last verse-line of a strophe is paired by parallelism with the first verse-line of the next strophe, we speak of *concatenation* (chaining of strophes).[58] In some cases, this type of distant parallelism takes the form of a refrain.

1.2.4.2 Binding Force: Enjambment of Strophes

In some cases the delimitation of strophes can hardly be in doubt, yet the strophes are connected by the fact that the sentence runs on.

[57] In accordance with what we have called the 'Law of Expansion and Contraction' every structural unit of Hebrew poetry may be reduced to only one element, cf. Korpel, De Moor, 'Fundamentals', *passim*; M.C.A. Korpel, "Exegesis in the Work of Ilimilku of Ugarit", in: J.C. de Moor (ed.), *Intertextuality in Ugarit and Israel* (OTS, 40), Leiden 1998, 86-111. This is also true of the canticle, but this is a rare phenomenon. Cf. 'Fundamentals', 43.

[58] Obviously the decision to interpret the latter category as a device of joining strophes instead of verse-lines which belong to the same strophe will always require an explanation.

Such a case is found in Isa. 55:10-11. The encroaching of one strophe upon the 'territory' of the next one (enjambment) may be regarded as a binding force because it renders a break in the canticle impossible.

1.2.4.3 Binding Force: Thematic Unity

As a rule a canticle is characterized by a certain unity of thought or thematic consistency.

1.2.4.4 Separating Force: Thematic Discontinuity

As a corollary to the preceding, a change of theme, often formally recognizable by a change of subject, may be regarded as an indication that a new canticle has started.

1.2.5 Delimitation of Macrostructural Units

Beyond the canticle we discern even larger units comprising several canticles which we have dubbed *sub-cantos* or, if several sub-cantos are involved, *cantos*. Here, however, we cannot rely on the ancient witnesses because as far as we know such larger units were never marked by special signs.[59] We reconstruct such larger units merely on the basis of distant parallelism and thematic unity. In this respect our approach may be termed conventional and we regard the results as less reliable than the division up to and including the canticles. Yet we believe it to be worthwhile to present our analysis of the macrostructure because we do not share John Barton's rather sceptical view of Classical Hebrew literature in general,

> "There might be no unity in the text, because ancient authors and readers may not have expected there to be any. Composing a book, for them, might have been simply putting together pieces of text without any presumption that they would form a new unity, characterized by coherence and closure, even if the pieces of text had been written by the author himself."[60]

---

[59] As we shall see later on, it is noteworthy, however, that the attestation of the borderline after the last canticle of such a large structure is often exceptionally well-attested in the tradition.

We do not regard the various pericope headers as reliable testimony for these larger structures because they were often added later on and were connected with different liturgies.

[60] J. Barton, "What Is a Book? Modern Exegesis and the Literary Conventions of Ancient Israel", in: J.C. de Moor (ed.), *Intertextuality in Ugarit and Israel* (OTS, 40), Leiden 1998, 1-14 (10).

Chapter 2

The Structure of Isaiah 40

2.1 Isaiah 40: Text and Translation

פ <ס> – ס̇ – $_1\mathfrak{Q}^{a}$ – $_4\mathfrak{Q}^{b}$ – $\mathfrak{G}^{SBAQ}$ – $\mathfrak{S}^{abcde}$ ________________

A.i.1 (Isa. 40:1–2a)

נַחֲמוּ נַחֲמוּ עַמִּי	1aA	Comfort, comfort my people,[1]
יֹאמַר אֱלֹהֵיכֶם׃	1aB	says your God.
דַּבְּרוּ עַל־לֵב יְרוּשָׁלַםִ	2aA	Speak to the heart of Jerusalem
וְקִרְאוּ אֵלֶיהָ	2aB	and cry to her

A.i.2 (Isa. 40:2b–c)

כִּי מָלְאָה צְבָאָהּ	2bA	that her forced labour is fulfilled,
כִּי נִרְצָה עֲוֺנָהּ	2bB	that her iniquity has been repaid,
כִּי לָקְחָה מִיַּד יְהוָה	2cA	that she has taken from the LORD's hand
כִּפְלַיִם בְּכָל־חַטֹּאתֶיהָ׃	2cB	double for all her sins.

ס – $_1\mathfrak{Q}^{a}$ – $\mathfrak{G}^{SBAQ}$ – $\mathfrak{S}^{abcde}$ . . . .

A.ii.1 (Isa. 40:3)

קוֹל קוֹרֵא בַּמִּדְבָּר	3aA	A voice[2] of someone crying in the desert:
פַּנּוּ דֶּרֶךְ יְהוָה	3aB	Prepare the way of the LORD,
יַשְּׁרוּ בָּעֲרָבָה	3bA	make straight in the bare valley
מְסִלָּה לֵאלֹהֵינוּ׃	3bB	a highway for our God!

A.ii.2 (Isa. 40:4)

כָּל־גֶּיא יִנָּשֵׂא	4aA	Every valley will be lifted up,
וְכָל־הַר וְגִבְעָה יִשְׁפָּלוּ	4aB	and every mountain and hill will be made low,
וְהָיָה הֶעָקֹב לְמִישׁוֹר	4bA	and the rough terrain will become level,
וְהָרְכָסִים לְבִקְעָה׃	4bB	and the rocky places a plain.

A.ii.3 (Isa. 40:5)

וְנִגְלָה כְּבוֹד יְהוָה	5aA	And the glory of the LORD will be revealed.

---

[1] There is insufficient reason to interpret עמי as a vocative. It is Zion that has to be comforted (cf. Lam. 1:2, 9, 16, 17, 21; 2:13).

[2] We reject the modish translation "Hear!" (see also our note on Isa. 52:8aA). Koole's translation "A voice" (so also Luther, RSV, NIV, NJB, JPS, Segond, etc.) is better than Young's "The voice" (so also KJV). However, the conjunctive accent of 𝔐 indicates the construct state: "The voice *of* someone saying" (compare 𝔊 φωνὴ βοῶντος "the voice of someone crying"). The resulting truncated way of introducing direct speech is not uncommon in Second Isaiah (see our notes with Isa. 41:12 and 47:4).

וְרָאוּ כָל־בָּשָׂר יַחְדָּו	5bA	And all flesh will see it together,
כִּי פִּי יְהוָה דִּבֵּר׃	5bB	for the mouth of the LORD has spoken.

ס <פ> – 1𝔔^{a} – 𝔊^{SBAQ} – 𝔖^{be} . . . .

A.iii.1 (Isa. 40:6)

קוֹל אֹמֵר קְרָא	6aA	A voice of someone saying: Cry!
וְאָמַר מָה אֶקְרָא	6aB	But it is said:[3] "What should I cry?
כָּל־הַבָּשָׂר חָצִיר	6bA	All flesh is grass,
{𝔊^{A}} וְכָל־חַסְדּוֹ כְּצִיץ הַשָּׂדֶה׃	6bB	and all their loyalty[4] is like a flower of the field.

A.iii.2 (Isa. 40:7–8)

יָבֵשׁ חָצִיר נָבֵל צִיץ	7aA	The grass withers, the flower fades,
כִּי רוּחַ יְהוָה נָשְׁבָה בּוֹ	7aB	when the spirit of the LORD blows upon it ..."
אָכֵן חָצִיר הָעָם׃	7bA	Surely,[5] the people is grass,
יָבֵשׁ חָצִיר נָבֵל צִיץ	8aB	the grass withers, the flower fades ...
וּדְבַר־אֱלֹהֵינוּ יָקוּם לְעוֹלָם׃	8aC	But the word of our God will stand to eternity!

ס <פ> – 1𝔔^{a} – 𝔊^{SBAQ} – 𝔖^{abde} . . . .

---

[3]Literally "He/someone says". Emendation to a first person, with 1𝔔^{a}, 𝔊 and 𝔙, is a removal of a more difficult text which exactly for that reason deserves more trust. With Barthélemy, 278-9, contra De Waard, *Handbook*, 155. There is very little reason to think of an unnamed spirit receiving instructions in the heavenly court, as proposed by Barthélemy, 279. In our opinion the speaker is an imagined interlocutor answering the prophet's adhortation to join him in announcing the good news, just as he will urge Zion to cry out good tidings in v. 9. However, this speaker is a disillusioned man who fears that there is no reason for a joyful message now that the wrath of God has scorched the fresh vegetation, an obvious reference to the sorry fate of the youth in exile.

[4]There is very little reason to assume a rare meaning "strength" or "beauty" for חסד here (with Hulst, 148). The interlocutor has little faith in the loyalty of his fellow sufferers, including the prophet. Preparing the way for the LORD together (v. 3) might be considered a rebellious act which would require great solidarity of those planning such a move. The speaker refuses to believe that one can put so much trust in each other. This interpretation is the best solution because the most obvious antecedent of the suffix of חסדו is כל בשׂר.

[5]There is no need to regard this colon as a gloss (with Barthélemy, 279-80). We assume a lively dialogue, the prophet cutting in at this point in order to prevent his partner from blaspheming. Such lively dialogues without introduction of direct speech are a common phenomenon in Semitic literature. Cf. K. Hecker, *Untersuchungen zur akkadischen Epik* (AOAT, 8), Neukirchen 1974, 70-74; M. Dijkstra, *Gods voorstelling: Predikatieve expressie van zelfopenbaring in oudoosterse teksten en Deutero-Jesaja*, Kampen 1980, 125-6, 128-9; W.G.E. Watson, "Abrupt Speech in Ugaritic Narrative Verse", *UF* 22 (1990), 415-20; S.A. Meier, *Speaking of Speaking: Marking Direct Discourse in the Hebrew Bible* (SVT, 46), Leiden 1992, 23-42.

A.iv.1 (Isa. 40:9a–b)

עַל הַר־גָּבֹהַ עֲלִי־לָךְ	9aA	Climb on a high mountain,
מְבַשֶּׂרֶת צִיּוֹן	9aB	O Zion, heraldess of good tidings!
הָרִימִי בַכֹּחַ קוֹלֵךְ	9bA	Lift up your voice with strength,
מְבַשֶּׂרֶת יְרוּשָׁלִָם	9bB	O Jerusalem, heraldess of good tidings!

A.iv.2 (Isa. 40:9c)

הָרִימִי אַל־תִּירָאִי	9cA	Lift it up, do not fear!
אִמְרִי לְעָרֵי יְהוּדָה	9cB	Say to the cities of Judah,
הִנֵּה אֱלֹהֵיכֶם׃	9cC	Behold your God!

𝔊^{A} ....

A.v.1 (Isa. 40:10)

הִנֵּה אֲדֹנָי יְהוִה בְּחָזָק יָבוֹא	10aA	Behold, the Lord GOD will come as[6] a mighty one,
וּזְרֹעוֹ מֹשְׁלָה לוֹ	10aB	and his arm will rule for him.
הִנֵּה שְׂכָרוֹ אִתּוֹ	10bA	Behold, his wages[7] are with him,
וּפְעֻלָּתוֹ לְפָנָיו׃	10bB	and his recompense before him.

A.v.2 (Isa. 40:11)

כְּרֹעֶה עֶדְרוֹ יִרְעֶה	11aA	Like a shepherd he will shepherd his flock,
בִּזְרֹעוֹ יְקַבֵּץ טְלָאִים	11aB	in his arm he will gather the lambs,
וּבְחֵיקוֹ יִשָּׂא	11aC	and in his lap he will take them up,
עָלוֹת יְנַהֵל׃	11bA	the nursing ewes he will lead gently.

ס <פ> – 1𝔔^{a} – 𝔊^{SA} – 𝔖^{abcde} ____________________

B.i.1 (Isa. 40:12)

מִי־מָדַד בְּשָׁעֳלוֹ מֵי* יָם*	12aA	Who measured the waters of the sea[8] in the hollow of his hand
וְשָׁמַיִם בַּזֶּרֶת תִּכֵּן	12aB	and staked out the heavens with a span,
וְכָל בַּשָּׁלִשׁ עֲפַר הָאָרֶץ	12aC	and filled out a three–cup with the dust of the earth?
וְשָׁקַל בַּפֶּלֶס הָרִים	12bA	And weighed the mountains in scales
{𝔊^{A}} וּגְבָעוֹת בְּמֹאזְנָיִם׃	12bB	and the hills in a balance?

B.i.2 (Isa. 40:13–14)

מִי־תִכֵּן אֶת־רוּחַ יְהוָה	13aA	Who staked out the spirit of the LORD
וְאִישׁ עֲצָתוֹ יוֹדִיעֶנּוּ׃	13aB	and which man made his counsel known to him?

---

[6] *Beth essentiae*, with the majority of modern scholars.

[7] Preluding to the metaphor of the shepherd who took part of the increase of the herd as payment in the ancient world.

[8] Though 1𝔔^{a}'s מי ים is attractive because of the standard pair ים || שמים, it is better to keep to 𝔐 because Barthélemy, 281-2, and De Waard, 155-6, are right in pointing out that we should have מי הים then (cf. Ex. 15:19; Am. 9:6; Ps. 33:7). With Koole and others we assume that the primordial waters are meant here.

אֶת־מִי נוֹעָץ וַיְבִינֵהוּ	14aA	Whom did he consult that he would have made him understand,
וַיְלַמְּדֵהוּ בְּאֹרַח מִשְׁפָּט	14aB	and would have taught him the path of what is right,
{וַיְלַמְּדֵהוּ דַעַת}	14aC	{and would have taught him knowledge,}[9]
וְדֶרֶךְ תְּבוּנוֹת יוֹדִיעֶנּוּ׃	14aD	and would have made known to him the way of deep understanding?

$\mathfrak{G}^{SA}$ . . . .

B.ii.1 (Isa. 40:15)

הֵן גּוֹיִם כְּמַר מִדְּלִי	15aA	Behold, the nations are like a drop from a bucket,
וּכְשַׁחַק מֹאזְנַיִם נֶחְשָׁבוּ	15aB	and are accounted as particles of dust on a balance.
הֵן אִיִּים כַּדַּק יִטּוֹל׃	15bA	Behold, he lifts up the islands like powder.

B.ii.2 (Isa. 40:16)

וּלְבָנוֹן אֵין דֵּי בָּעֵר	16aA	And the Lebanon will not suffice for fuel,
וְחַיָּתוֹ אֵין דֵּי עוֹלָה׃ {<פ>ס}	16aB	and its beasts will not suffice for a burnt offering.

B.ii.3 (Isa. 40:17)

כָּל־הַגּוֹיִם כְּאַיִן נֶגְדּוֹ	17aA	All nations are as nothing to him,
מֵאֶפֶס וָתֹהוּ נֶחְשְׁבוּ־לוֹ׃	17aB	they are accounted by him less than[10] non-existent and void.

$\mathfrak{G}^{SA}$ – $\mathfrak{S}^{abde}$ . . . .

B.iii.1 (Isa. 40:18–19)

וְאֶל־מִי תְּדַמְּיוּן אֵל	18aA	And to whom you would liken God?
וּמַה־דְּמוּת תַּעַרְכוּ לוֹ׃	18aB	And which likeness would you arrange for him?
הַפֶּסֶל נָסַךְ חָרָשׁ	19aA	An idol? A craftsman casts it,
וְצֹרֵף בַּזָּהָב יְרַקְּעֶנּוּ	19aB	and the goldsmith overlays it with gold,
וּרְתֻקוֹת כֶּסֶף צוֹרֵף׃ {$\mathfrak{G}^{A}$}	19aC	and with soldering[11] of a goldsmith's silver.

B.iii.2 (Isa. 40:20)

הַמְסֻכָּן* תְּרוּמָה	20aA	He who shapes[12] the pedestal
עֵץ לֹא־יִרְקַב יִבְחָר	20aB	chooses wood that does not rot.
חָרָשׁ חָכָם יְבַקֶּשׁ־לוֹ	20bA	He seeks out a skilful craftsman
לְהָכִין פֶּסֶל לֹא יִמּוֹט׃	20bB	to set up an idol that will not topple.

<ס> – $\mathfrak{G}^{S}$ . . . .

---

[9] We regard this colon to be a later addition, see p.45. However, Barthélemy, 283, rightly argues that one should not invoke the support of $\mathfrak{G}$ here.

[10] With e.g. Barthélemy, 283-5.

[11] See M.C.A. Korpel, "Soldering in Isaiah 40:19–20 and 1 Kings 6:21," *UF* 23 (1991), 219-222.

[12] See the preceding note. For the article with a *nomen regens* see Waltke-O'Connor, §13.6b.

B.iv.1 (Isa. 40:21)

הֲלוֹא תֵדְעוּ הֲלוֹא תִשְׁמָעוּ	21aA	Don't you know? Didn't you hear?
הֲלוֹא הֻגַּד מֵרֹאשׁ לָכֶם	21aB	Has it not been told to you from the beginning?
הֲלוֹא הֲבִינֹתֶם מוֹסְדוֹת הָאָרֶץ׃ {$\mathfrak{G}^{A}$}	21aC	Don't you understand the foundations of the earth?

B.iv.2 (Isa. 40:22)

הַיֹּשֵׁב עַל־חוּג הָאָרֶץ	22aA	It is he who is dwelling on the circle of the earth
וְיֹשְׁבֶיהָ כַּחֲגָבִים	22aB	and its dwellers are like grasshoppers.
הַנּוֹטֶה כַדֹּק שָׁמַיִם	22bA	It is he who stretches out the heavens like a membrane
וַיִּמְתָּחֵם כָּאֹהֶל לָשָׁבֶת׃	22bB	and spreads[13] them like a tent to dwell in.

$\mathfrak{G}^{A}$ ....

B.v.1 (Isa. 40:23)

הַנּוֹתֵן רוֹזְנִים לְאָיִן	23aA	It is he who is bringing princes to nothing,
שֹׁפְטֵי אֶרֶץ כַּתֹּהוּ עָשָׂה׃	23aB	he makes the judges of the earth void.

B.v.2 (Isa. 40:24)

אַף בַּל־נִטָּעוּ אַף בַּל־זֹרָעוּ	24aA	Scarcely are they planted, scarcely are they sown,
אַף בַּל־שֹׁרֵשׁ בָּאֶרֶץ גִּזְעָם	24aB	scarcely their stem has rooted in the earth,
וְגַם־נָשַׁף בָּהֶם וַיִּבָשׁוּ	24bA	when he blows upon them, and they wither,
וּסְעָרָה כַּקַּשׁ תִּשָּׂאֵם׃	24bB	and the storm carries them off like chaff.

ס <פ> – $1\mathfrak{Q}^{a}$ – $4\mathfrak{Q}^{a}$ – $\mathfrak{G}^{SAQ}$ – $\mathfrak{S}^{abce}$ ____________________________

C.i.1 (Isa. 40:25)

וְאֶל־מִי תְדַמְּיוּנִי וְאֶשְׁוֶה	25aA	And to whom will you liken me, that I would be his equal?
יֹאמַר קָדוֹשׁ׃	25aB	says the Holy One.

C.i.2 (Isa. 40:26)

שְׂאוּ־מָרוֹם עֵינֵיכֶם וּרְאוּ	26aA	Lift up your eyes on high, and see:
מִי־בָרָא אֵלֶּה	26aB	Who did create those over there?
הַמּוֹצִיא בְמִסְפָּר צְבָאָם	26aC	He who brings out their army in number!
לְכֻלָּם בְּשֵׁם יִקְרָא	26bA	All of them he calls by name;
מֵרֹב אוֹנִים וְאַמִּיץ כֹּחַ	26bB	because of him who is great in forces and mighty of strength,
אִישׁ לֹא נֶעְדָּר׃	26bC	not one of them is missing.

ס <פ> – $1\mathfrak{Q}^{a}$ – $\mathfrak{S}^{be}$ ....

[13] For the translation as an actual present see M.C.A. Korpel, J.C. de Moor, F. Sepmeijer, "Consistency with Regard to Tenses" (see Abbreviations).

C.ii.1 (Isa. 40:27)

לָמָּה תֹאמַר יַעֲקֹב	27aA	Why do you say, O Jacob,
וּתְדַבֵּר יִשְׂרָאֵל	27aB	and speak, O Israel:
נִסְתְּרָה דַרְכִּי מֵיְהוָה	27bA	"My way is hidden from the LORD,
$\{\mathfrak{G}^{S}\}$ וּמֵאֱלֹהַי מִשְׁפָּטִי יַעֲבוֹר׃	27bB	and my right is neglected by my God?"

C.ii.2 (Isa. 40:28)

הֲלוֹא יָדַעְתָּ אִם־לֹא שָׁמַעְתָּ	28aA	Don't you know? Or didn't you hear?
אֱלֹהֵי עוֹלָם ׀ יְהוָה	28aB	The LORD is a God of eternity,
בּוֹרֵא קְצוֹת הָאָרֶץ	28aC	the Creator of the ends of the earth.
לֹא יִיעַף וְלֹא יִיגָע	28bA	He does not become exhausted and does not grow weary,
אֵין חֵקֶר לִתְבוּנָתוֹ׃	28bB	it is impossible to trace his understanding.

$\mathfrak{G}^{A}$ ....

C.iii.1 (Isa. 40:29)

נֹתֵן לַיָּעֵף כֹּחַ	29aA	He is giving strength to the exhausted,
וּלְאֵין אוֹנִים עָצְמָה יַרְבֶּה׃	29aB	and increases the vigour of him who has no force left.

C.iii.2 (Isa. 40:30)

וְיִעֲפוּ נְעָרִים $\{\mathfrak{G}^{S}\}$ וְיִגָעוּ	30aA	Yes, youths may become exhausted and grow weary,
$\{\mathfrak{G}^{Q}\}$ וּבַחוּרִים כָּשׁוֹל יִכָּשֵׁלוּ׃	30aB	and young men may stagger terribly,

C.iii.3 (Isa. 40:31)

וְקוֹיֵ יְהוָה יַחֲלִיפוּ כֹחַ	31aA	but those waiting for the LORD will renew[14] their strength,
יַעֲלוּ אֵבֶר כַּנְּשָׁרִים	31aB	they will grow new pinions, like eagles.
יָרוּצוּ וְלֹא יִיגָעוּ	31bA	They will run and will not grow weary,
יֵלְכוּ וְלֹא יִיעָפוּ׃	31bB	they will walk and will not become exhausted.

פ <ס> – $1\mathfrak{Q}^{a}$ – $\mathfrak{G}^{SBAQ}$ – $\mathfrak{S}^{abcde}$ ______________________________

[14]The causative meaning of the two stems should not be ignored in translations (typically Luther's "kriegen neue Kraft", probably for theological reasons). The exiles themselves have to make a new start, as in 40:3.

2.2 Isaiah 40 – Delimitation of Cola

COLON 40:1aA:

נַחֲמוּ נַחֲמוּ עַמִּי 1aA Comfort, comfort my people,

With: 𝔐 (2)
Colon parallelism: נחם || נחם; grammatical parallelism.
Discussion: Both here and in 40:25 𝔊 and 𝔖 lack a major divider.[1] The same is the case in the similar 41:21bB where יאמר also introduces the final colon and 𝔊 and 𝔖 lack a dividing point. Nevertheless we believe 𝔐's colometry to be correct. See also 45:13. The colon parallelism marks 40:1aA as a colon in its own right. From the viewpoint of content, Isa. 52:9bA כי־נחם יהוה עמו argues decisively in favour of taking עמי as the direct object of the verb נחם.

COLON 40:1aB:

יֹאמַר אֱלֹהֵיכֶם׃ 1aB says your God.

With: 𝔐 (1) – 𝔊^{SQ} – 𝔖^{abcde} – Chr. Pal. lectionaries.

COLON 40:2aA:

דַּבְּרוּ עַל־לֵב יְרוּשָׁלַםִ 2aA Speak to the heart of Jerusalem

With: 𝔐 (10) – 𝔊^{Q}
Discussion: Again the attestation of the divider is weak. However, the verse-line parallelism supports our division (see 2.3). The Masoretes misdivided the second strophe because the sentence runs on (enjambment). This necessitated their choice of a low-level divider in v. 2a.

COLON 40:2aB:

וְקִרְאוּ אֵלֶיהָ 2aB and cry to her

With: 𝔐 (5) – 𝔊^{S} – 𝔖^{abcde}

COLON 40:2bA:

כִּי מָלְאָה צְבָאָהּ 2bA that her forced labour is fulfilled,

With: 𝔐 (5) – 𝔊^{SQ} – Chr. Pal. lectionary.
Discussion: 𝔊 supports 𝔐 against 𝔖.

---

[1]Also lacking in the Christian-Palestinian lectionary, cf. Chr. Müller-Kessler, M. Sokoloff, *A Corpus of Christian Palestinian Aramaic*, vol. 1, Groningen 1997, 142.

COLON 40:2bB:

כִּי נִרְצָה עֲוֺנָהּ 2bB that her iniquity has been repaid,

With: 𝔐 (2) – 𝔊^{SQ} – 𝔖^{abcde}

COLON 40:2cA:

כִּי לָקְחָה מִיַּד יְהוָה 2cA that she has taken from the LORD's hand

With: 𝔐 (5) – 𝔊^{S} – 𝔖^{a}

Discussion: The support for 𝔐 is weak, but convincing because the continuing sentence made it difficult to discern the correct colometry.

COLON 40:2cB:

כִּפְלַיִם בְּכָל־חַטֹּאתֶיהָ׃ 2cB double for all her sins.

With: 𝔐 (1) plus ס – 𝔊^{SBAQ}, major division markers in all – 𝔖^{abcde}, major division markers in all.

COLON 40:3aA:

קוֹל קוֹרֵא בַּמִּדְבָּר 3aA A voice of someone crying in the desert:

With: 𝔐 (6) – 𝔊^{SQ} – 𝔖^{abde}, cf. Mark 1:3 par.

Discussion: All early witnesses argue against the division of 𝔐 which has a major dividing accent (Zaqeph Qaṭon, No. 5) with קורא, although the immediately following Zaqeph Gadol (No. 6) with במדבר might point to some uncertainty on the part of the Masoretes. Both divisions are defensible, but the parallelistic balance is nicer with the non-Masoretic witnesses,

IN THE DESERT – PREPARE – THE WAY – OF THE LORD || MAKE STRAIGHT – IN THE BARE VALLEY – A HIGHWAY – FOR OUR GOD.

COLON 40:3aB:

פַּנּוּ דֶּרֶךְ יְהוָה 3aB "Prepare the way of the LORD,

With: 𝔐 (2) – 𝔊^{SQ} – 𝔖^{cde}, 𝔖^{b} subordinate accent – Chr. Pal. lectionaries.

COLON 40:3bA:

יַשְּׁרוּ בָּעֲרָבָה 3bA make straight in the bare valley

With: 𝔐 (5) – 𝔖^{abcde}

Discussion: 𝔊 is absent at this point, but 𝔖 supports 𝔐.

COLON 40:3bB:

מְסִלָּה לֵאלֹהֵינוּ׃ 3bB a highway for our God!

With: $\mathfrak{M}$ (1) – $\mathfrak{G}^{SQ}$ – $\mathfrak{S}^{abcde}$ – Chr. Pal. lectionaries.

COLON 40:4aA:

כָּל־גֶּיא יִנָּשֵׂא 4aA Every valley will be lifted up,

With: $\mathfrak{M}$ (5) – $\mathfrak{G}^{SQ}$ – $\mathfrak{S}^{abcde}$ – Chr. Pal. lectionary.

COLON 40:4aB:

וְכָל־הַר וְגִבְעָה יִשְׁפָּלוּ 4aB and every mountain and hill will be made low,

With: $\mathfrak{M}$ (2) – $\mathfrak{G}^{SQ}$ – $\mathfrak{S}^{abcde}$ – Chr. Pal. lectionaries.
Colon parallelism: הר || גבעה.

COLON 40:4bA:

וְהָיָה הֶעָקֹב לְמִישׁוֹר 4bA and the rough terrain will become level,

With: $\mathfrak{M}$ (5) – $\mathfrak{G}^{SQ}$ – $\mathfrak{S}^{e}$, $\mathfrak{S}^{abcd}$ subordinate punctuation – Chr. Pal. lectionaries.
Colon parallelism: Antithetical עקב || מישור (unique).

COLON 40:4bB:

וְהָרְכָסִים לְבִקְעָה׃ 4bB and the rocky places a plain.

With: $\mathfrak{M}$ (1) – $\mathfrak{G}^{SQ}$ – $\mathfrak{S}^{abcde}$ – Chr. Pal. lectionaries.
Colon parallelism: Antithetical רכס || בקעה(unique).

COLON 40:5aA:

וְנִגְלָה כְּבוֹד יְהוָה 5aA And the glory of the LORD will be revealed.

With: $\mathfrak{M}$ (2) – $\mathfrak{G}^{SQ}$ – $\mathfrak{S}^{ab}$, $\mathfrak{S}^{cd}$ subordinate punctuation – Chr. Pal. lectionaries.
Discussion: Unicola are by no means rare in Hebrew poetry.[2]

COLON 40:5bA:

וְרָאוּ כָל־בָּשָׂר יַחְדָּו 5bA And all flesh will see it together,

With: $\mathfrak{M}$ (5) – $\mathfrak{G}^{SQ}$ – $\mathfrak{S}^{abcde}$
Colon parallelism: כל || יחדו/יחד.

---

[2] See e.g. W.G.E. Watson, *Classical Hebrew Poetry: A Guide to Its Techniques* (JSOT.S, 26), Sheffield 1984, 168–174.

COLON 40:5bB:

כִּ֛י פִּ֥י יְהוָ֖ה דִּבֵּֽר׃ 5bB for the mouth of the LORD has spoken."

With: 𝔐 (1) plus ס <פ> – 𝔊^{SBAQ}, major division markers in all mss; – 𝔖^{abcde}, major division markers in 𝔖^{be} – Chr. Pal. lectionary.

COLON 40:6aA:

ק֚וֹל אֹמֵ֣ר קְרָ֔א 6aA A voice of someone saying: "Cry!"

With: 𝔐 (5) – 𝔊^{SQ} – 𝔖^{abcde} – Chr. Pal. lectionary.
Colon parallelism: אמר || קרא.

COLON 40:6aB:

וְאָמַ֖ר מָ֣ה אֶקְרָ֑א 6aB But it is said: "What should I cry?

With: 𝔐 (2) – 𝔊^{SQ} – 𝔖^{abcde} – Chr. Pal. lectionary.
Colon parallelism: אמר || קרא, see 40:6aA.

COLON 40:6bA:

כָּל־הַבָּשָׂ֣ר חָצִ֔יר 6bA All flesh is grass,

With: 𝔐 (5) – 𝔊^{SQ} – 𝔖^{abcde} – Chr. Pal. lectionary.

COLON 40:6bB:

וְכָל־חַסְדּ֖וֹ כְּצִ֥יץ הַשָּׂדֶֽה׃ 6bB and all their loyalty is like a flower of the field.

With: 𝔐 (1) – 𝔊^{SA} (major division marker in 𝔊^{A}) – 𝔖^{abcde} – Chr. Pal. lectionaries.
Discussion: 𝔊^{SQ} and 𝔖^{a} have a point after חסדו (𝔐 accent 8) which would result in a tricolon. The strong parallelism between v. 6bA and v. 6bB argues in favour of a bicolon.

COLON 40:7aA:

יָבֵ֤שׁ חָצִיר֙ נָ֣בֵל צִ֔יץ 7aA The grass withers, the flower fades,

With: 𝔐 (5) – 𝔊^{SQ} – 𝔖^{abcde}
Colon parallelism: יבש || נבל; חציר || ציץ.
Discussion: 𝔊^{SQ} have a point after the first חציר. However, the accent of 𝔐 (10) is rather low there and 𝔖^{abcde} do not support a division at that point. Since all ancient witnesses support a division after ציץ we regard the parallelism of v. 7aA as colon parallelism.

COLON 40:7aB:

כִּי רוּחַ יְהוָה נָשְׁבָה בּוֹ 7aB when the spirit of the LORD blows upon it ...”

With: 𝔐 (2) – 𝔖^{abcde} (𝔊 absent) – Chr. Pal. lectionary.

COLON 40:7bA:

אָכֵן חָצִיר הָעָם׃ 7bA “Surely, the people is grass,

With: 𝔐 (1) – 𝔖^{abcde} (𝔊 absent).
Discussion: The delimitation of the colon is beyond doubt but we think it belongs to the next verse-line, so the Silluq of 𝔐 is a too heavy accent.[3]

COLON 40:8aB:

יָבֵשׁ חָצִיר נָבֵל צִיץ 8aB the grass withers, the flower fades ...

With: 𝔐 (2) – 𝔖^{e}, 𝔖^{abcd} subordinate punctuation – Chr. Pal. lectionary.
Colon parallelism: יבש || נבל; חציר || ציץ.
Discussion: See v. 7aA.

COLON 40:8aC:

וּדְבַר־אֱלֹהֵינוּ יָקוּם לְעוֹלָם׃ 8aC But the word of our God will stand to eternity!”

With: 𝔐 (1), major division markers – major division markers in 𝔊^{SBAQ} – major division markers in 𝔖^{abde}, point in 𝔖^{c} – Chr. Pal. lectionaries.
Discussion: 𝔊^{SQ} presuppose a divider after ודבר־אלהינו, but 𝔐's accent (8) is rather low and 𝔖 does not support a division at this point.

COLON 40:9aA:

עַל הַר־גָּבֹהַּ עֲלִי־לָךְ 9aA Climb on a high mountain,

With: 𝔐 (10) – 𝔊^{SQ}
Colon parallelism: Alliteration על and עלי.
Discussion: Even though the divider in 𝔐 is rather weak (10) and 𝔖 does not support our delimitation we decided to accept the testimony of 𝔊 because 𝔐 does have a major accent (5) after the parallel colon 9bA.

COLON 40:9aB:

מְבַשֶּׂרֶת צִיּוֹן 9aB o Zion, heraldess of good tidings!

With: 𝔐 (5) – 𝔊^{SQ} – 𝔖^{abcde} – Chr. Pal. lectionary.

---

[3]See p. 42.

COLON 40:9bA:

הָרִ֤ימִי בַכֹּ֙חַ֙ קוֹלֵ֔ךְ 9bA Lift up your voice with strength,

With: $\mathfrak{M}$ (5) – $\mathfrak{G}^{SQ}$
Discussion: Again $\mathfrak{S}$ does not support the division of $\mathfrak{M}$ and $\mathfrak{G}^{SQ}$. See 9aA.

COLON 40:9bB:

מְבַשֶּׂ֖רֶת יְרוּשָׁלִָ֑ם 9bB O Jerusalem, heraldess of good tidings!

With: $\mathfrak{M}$ (2); $\mathfrak{G}^{SQ}$ – $\mathfrak{S}^{abcde}$

COLON 40:9cA:

הָרִ֙ימִי֙ אַל־תִּירָ֔אִי 9cA Lift it up, do not fear!

With: $\mathfrak{M}$ (5) – $\mathfrak{G}^{SQ}$ – $\mathfrak{S}^{acde}$
Discussion: No ancient witness supports a division after הרימי.

COLON 40:9cB:

אִמְרִי֙ לְעָרֵ֣י יְהוּדָ֔ה 9cB Say to the cities of Judah,

With: $\mathfrak{M}$ (5) – $\mathfrak{G}^{SQ}$ – $\mathfrak{S}^{a}$

COLON 40:9cC:

הִנֵּ֖ה אֱלֹהֵיכֶֽם׃ 9cC "Behold your God!"

With: $\mathfrak{M}$ (1) – $\mathfrak{G}^{SQ}$, major division marker in $\mathfrak{G}^{A}$ – $\mathfrak{S}^{abcde}$ – Chr. Pal. lectionary.

COLON 40:10aA:

הִנֵּ֨ה אֲדֹנָ֤י יְהוִה֙ בְּחָזָ֣ק יָב֔וֹא 10aA Behold, the Lord GOD will come as a mighty one,

With: $\mathfrak{M}$ (5) – $\mathfrak{G}^{SQ}$ – $\mathfrak{S}^{e}$
Colon parallelism: אדני || יהוה.

COLON 40:10aB:

וּזְרֹע֖וֹ מֹ֣שְׁלָה ל֑וֹ 10aB and his arm will rule for him.

With: $\mathfrak{M}$ (2) – $\mathfrak{G}^{SQ}$ – $\mathfrak{S}^{abcde}$ – Chr. Pal. lectionary.

COLON 40:10bA:

הִנֵּ֤ה שְׂכָרוֹ֙ אִתּ֔וֹ 10bA Behold, his wages are with him,

With: 𝔐 (5) – 𝔊^{SQ}
Discussion: The verse-line parallelism supports 𝔐 and 𝔊.

COLON 40:10bB:

וּפְעֻלָּתוֹ לְפָנָיו׃ 10bB and his recompense before him.

With: 𝔐 (1) – 𝔊^{SQ} – 𝔖^{abcde}

COLON 40:11aA:

כְּרֹעֶה עֶדְרוֹ יִרְעֶה 11aA Like a shepherd he will shepherd his flock,

With: 𝔐 (5) – 𝔊^{SQ} – 𝔖^{abcde} all subordinate punctuation.
Colon parallelism: רעה || רעה.

COLON 40:11aB:

בִּזְרֹעוֹ יְקַבֵּץ טְלָאִים 11aB in his arm he will gather the lambs,

With: 𝔐 (5) – 𝔊^{SQ} – 𝔖^{abcde} all subordinate punctuation.

COLON 40:11bA:

וּבְחֵיקוֹ יִשָּׂא 11aC and in his lap he will take them up,

With: 𝔐 (2) – 𝔖^{b}, 𝔖^{acde} subordinate punctuation.
Discussion: 𝔖 supports 𝔐 against 𝔊.

COLON 40:11bB:

עָלוֹת יְנַהֵל׃ 11bA the nursing ewes he will lead gently.

With: 𝔐 (1), major division markers – 𝔊^{SQ}, major division markers in 𝔊^{SA} – 𝔖^{abcde}, all with major division markers – Chr. Pal. lectionary.

COLON 40:12aA:

מִי־מָדַד בְּשָׁעֳלוֹ מֵי* יָם* 12aA Who measured the waters of the sea in the hollow of his hand

With: 𝔐 (7) – 𝔊^{SQ} – 𝔖^{abcde} all subordinate punctuation – Chr. Pal. lectionary.

COLON 40:12aB:

וְשָׁמַיִם בַּזֶּרֶת תִּכֵּן 12aB and staked out the heavens with a span,

With: 𝔐 (5) – 𝔊^{SQ} – 𝔖^{bcde} subordinate punctuation.

COLON 40:12aC:

וְכָ֥ל בַּשָּׁלִ֖שׁ עֲפַ֣ר הָאָ֑רֶץ 12aC and filled out a three–cup with the dust of the earth?

With: $\mathfrak{M}$ (2) – $\mathfrak{G}^{SQ}$ – $\mathfrak{S}^{acde}$ subordinate punctuation.

COLON 40:12bA:

וְשָׁקַ֤ל בַּפֶּ֙לֶס֙ הָרִ֔ים 12bA And weighed the mountains in scales

With: $\mathfrak{M}$ (5) – $\mathfrak{G}^{SQ}$ – $\mathfrak{S}^{e}$, $\mathfrak{S}^{ac}$ subordinate punctuation.

COLON 40:12bB:

וּגְבָע֖וֹת בְּמֹאזְנָֽיִם׃ 12bB and the hills in a balance?

With: $\mathfrak{M}$ (1) – $\mathfrak{G}^{SQ}$, major division marker in $\mathfrak{G}^{A}$ – $\mathfrak{S}^{abcde}$

COLON 40:13aA:

מִֽי־תִכֵּ֥ן אֶת־ר֖וּחַ יְהוָ֑ה 13aA Who staked out the spirit of the LORD

With: $\mathfrak{M}$ (2) – $\mathfrak{G}^{SQ}$ – $\mathfrak{S}^{abcde}$

COLON 40:13aB:

וְאִ֥ישׁ עֲצָת֖וֹ יוֹדִיעֶֽנּוּ׃ 13aB and which man made his counsel known to him?

With: $\mathfrak{M}$ (1) – $\mathfrak{G}^{SQ}$, colon in $\mathfrak{G}^{S}$ – $\mathfrak{S}^{abcde}$

Discussion: $\mathfrak{G}^{SQ}$ both have a dividing point after $\mathfrak{M}$ עצתו which is an adaptation to the longer Greek text and does not recommend itself for the Hebrew.

COLON 40:14aA:

אֶת־מִ֤י נוֹעָץ֙ וַיְבִינֵ֔הוּ 14aA Whom did he consult that he would have made him understand,

With: $\mathfrak{M}$ (5) – $\mathfrak{G}^{SQ}$ – $\mathfrak{S}^{abcde}$ all subordinate punctuation.

Colon parallelism: יעץ || בין.

COLON 40:14aB:

וַֽיְלַמְּדֵ֖הוּ בְּאֹ֣רַח מִשְׁפָּ֑ט 14aB and would have taught him the path of what is right,

With: $\mathfrak{M}$ (2) – $\mathfrak{G}^{SQ}$ – $\mathfrak{S}^{abcde}$ subordinate punctuation.

COLON 40:14aC:

{וַיְלַמְּדֵ֣הוּ דַ֔עַת} 14aC {and would have taught him knowledge,}

With: $\mathfrak{M}$ (5) – $\mathfrak{S}^{e}$, $\mathfrak{S}^{abcd}$ subordinate punctuation.
Colon parallelism: למד || דעת.
Discussion: We believe that this colon is a later addition. See below p. 45.

COLON 40:14aD:

וְדֶ֥רֶךְ תְּבוּנ֖וֹת יוֹדִיעֶֽנּוּ׃ 14aD and would have made known to him the way of deep understanding?

With: $\mathfrak{M}$ (1) – $\mathfrak{G}^{SAQ}$, major division marker in $\mathfrak{G}^{A}$, colon in $\mathfrak{G}^{S}$ – $\mathfrak{S}^{abcde}$
Colon parallelism: תבונה || ידע.

COLON 40:15aA:

הֵ֤ן גּוֹיִם֙ כְּמַ֣ר מִדְּלִ֔י 15aA Behold, the nations are like a drop from a bucket,

With: $\mathfrak{M}$ (5) – $\mathfrak{G}^{SQ}$ – $\mathfrak{S}^{abcde}$

COLON 40:15aB:

וּכְשַׁ֥חַק מֹאזְנַ֖יִם נֶחְשָׁ֑בוּ 15aB and are accounted as particles of dust on a balance.

With: $\mathfrak{M}$ (2) – $\mathfrak{G}^{SQ}$ – $\mathfrak{S}^{abcde}$

COLON 40:15bA:

הֵ֥ן אִיִּ֖ים כַּדַּ֥ק יִטּֽוֹל׃ 15bA Behold, he lifts up the islands like powder.

With: $\mathfrak{M}$ (1) – $\mathfrak{G}^{SQ}$ – $\mathfrak{S}^{abcde}$

COLON 40:16aA:

וּלְבָנ֕וֹן אֵ֥ין דֵּ֖י בָּעֵ֑ר 16aA And the Lebanon will not suffice for fuel,

With: $\mathfrak{M}$ (2) – $\mathfrak{G}^{SQ}$ – $\mathfrak{S}^{abde}$
Discussion: The Zaqeph Gadol (No. 6) on the first word of the colon has no parallel in any of the other witnesses. Like the Zaqeph Qaṭon (No. 5) in 16aB[4] as well as the Revia' (No. 7)[5] and Zarqa (No. 9)[6] in several similar cases, it has the function of marking a word in emphasized position, usually a so-called *casus pendens*, to indicate a slight pause in reading.[7]

[4] See further 44:17aA (?); 45:20bB; 47:7aA; 51:4bB; 54:14bB.

[5] See 41:13aA; 43:3aA, 24bA; 44:5bA, 7aB; 45:9aA, 12bA; 48:16bA; 49:6aA, 8bA, 23bA; 53:12bA.

[6] See 42:22aA; 50:2aB.

[7] For other cases of Zaqeph Gadol with the first word of a colon see 43:26aA;

COLON 40:16aB:

וְחַיָּתוֹ אֵין דֵּי עוֹלָה׃ 16aB and its beasts will not suffice for a burnt offering.

With: 𝔐 (1), major division markers, also in 1𝔔^{a} – 𝔊^{SQ} – 𝔖^{abcde}
Discussion: 𝔐 has a fairly strong accent with וחיתו (5) which is supported by 𝔊^{S}. However, there seems to be little reason to assume a colon consisting of only one word here. See our comment on the preceding colon.

COLON 40:17aA:

כָּל־הַגּוֹיִם כְּאַיִן נֶגְדּוֹ 17aA All nations are as nothing to him,

With: 𝔐 (2) – 𝔊^{SQ} – 𝔖^{abcd}, major division marker in 𝔖^{e} (rest of the verse is missing).
Discussion: 𝔖^{a} has a point after כל־הגוים but 𝔐's (8) hardly supports this.

COLON 40:17aB:

מֵאֶפֶס וָתֹהוּ נֶחְשְׁבוּ־לוֹ׃ 17aB they are accounted by him as less than non-existent and void.

With: 𝔐 (1) – 𝔊^{SBAQ}, major division markers in 𝔊^{SBA} – 𝔖^{abcde}, major division markers in 𝔖^{abde}
Colon parallelism: אפס || תהו.

COLON 40:18aA:

וְאֶל־מִי תְּדַמְּיוּן אֵל 18aA And to whom you would liken God?

With: 𝔐 (2) – 𝔊^{SQ} – 𝔖^{acde}

COLON 40:18aB:

וּמַה־דְּמוּת תַּעַרְכוּ לוֹ׃ 18aB And which likeness would you arrange for him?

With: 𝔐 (1) – 𝔊^{SQ} – 𝔖^{abcde}

COLON 40:19aA:

הַפֶּסֶל נָסַךְ חָרָשׁ 19aA An idol? A craftsman casts it,

With: 𝔐 (5) – 𝔊^{SQ} – 𝔖^{abcde} subordinate punctuation.

45:15aA; 47:4aA; 48:4aA, 8aB, 20bD; 49:3aB, 12aA; 52:11bB; 53:7bB.

COLON 40:19aB:

וְצֹרֵ֖ף בַּזָּהָ֣ב יְרַקְּעֶ֑נּוּ 19aB and the goldsmith overlays it with gold,

With: $\mathfrak{M}$ (2) – $\mathfrak{G}^{SQ}$ – $\mathfrak{S}^{abcde}$ subordinate punctuation.

COLON 40:19aC:

וּרְתֻקּ֥וֹת כֶּ֖סֶף צוֹרֵֽף׃ 19aC and with soldering of a goldsmith's silver.

With: $\mathfrak{M}$ (1) – $\mathfrak{G}^{SQ}$, major division marker in $\mathfrak{G}^{A}$
Discussion: In an attempt to offer a solution for the rather difficult Hebrew $\mathfrak{S}$ connected v. 19 with v. 20 and put a subordinate divider after v. 20 המסכן.

COLON 40:20aA:

הַֽמְסֻכָּ֣ן* תְּרוּמָ֔ה 20aA He who shapes the pedestal

With: $\mathfrak{M}$ (5) – $\mathfrak{S}^{abcde}$ subordinate punctuation.
Discussion: $\mathfrak{G}$ tries to solve the problems of $\mathfrak{M}$ in its own way.

COLON 40:20aB:

עֵ֥ץ לֹֽא־יִרְקַ֖ב יִבְחָ֑ר 20aB chooses wood that does not rot.

With: $\mathfrak{M}$ (2) – $\mathfrak{G}^{SQ}$ – $\mathfrak{S}^{abcde}$

COLON 40:20bA:

חָרָ֤שׁ חָכָם֙ יְבַקֶּשׁ־ל֔וֹ 20bA He seeks out a skilful craftsman

With: $\mathfrak{M}$ (5) – $\mathfrak{G}^{S}$ – $\mathfrak{S}^{abcde}$

COLON 40:20bB:

לְהָכִ֥ין פֶּ֖סֶל לֹ֥א יִמּֽוֹט׃ 20bB to set up an idol that will not topple.

With: $\mathfrak{M}$ (1), <ס> in the Aleppo Codex and the Codex Leningradensis (Petropolitanus) – $\mathfrak{G}^{SQ}$, major division marker in $\mathfrak{G}^{S}$ – $\mathfrak{S}^{abcde}$
Colon parallelism: כון || מוט.
Discussion: $\mathfrak{G}^{SQ}$ have an extra divider after פסל which the Masoretes gave a low accent (Ṭiphḥa, No. 8). None of the $\mathfrak{S}$ manuscripts supports this division.

COLON 40:21aA:

הֲל֤וֹא תֵֽדְעוּ֙ הֲל֣וֹא תִשְׁמָ֔עוּ 21aA Don't you know? Didn't you hear?

With: $\mathfrak{M}$ (5) – $\mathfrak{G}^{SQ}$ – $\mathfrak{S}^{abcde}$ all subordinate punctuation.

Colon parallelism: ידע || שמע; לא || לא.
Discussion: $\mathfrak{G}^{SQ}$ have an extra divider after תדעו where $\mathfrak{M}$ has a weak accent (Pashṭa, No. 10). It is not supported by $\mathfrak{S}$ and does not recommend itself.

COLON 40:21aB:

הֲל֛וֹא הֻגַּ֥ד מֵרֹ֖אשׁ לָכֶ֑ם 21aB Has it not been told to you from the beginning?

With: $\mathfrak{M}$ (2) – $\mathfrak{G}^{SQ}$ – $\mathfrak{S}^{abcde}$ subordinate punctuation.

COLON 40:21aC:

הֲלוֹא֙ הֲבִ֣ינֹתֶ֔ם מוֹסְד֖וֹת הָאָֽרֶץ׃ 21aC Don't you understand the foundations of the earth?

With: $\mathfrak{M}$ (1) – $\mathfrak{G}^{SQ}$ – $\mathfrak{S}^{ab}$, $\mathfrak{S}^{cde}$ subordinate punctuation.
Discussion: $\mathfrak{M}$ stands alone in attributing an extra divider to הבינתם. We decided to ignore it because both the sentence structure and the preceding cola starting with הלוא suggest that $\mathfrak{G}$ and $\mathfrak{S}$ have preserved the correct division here.

COLON 40:22aA:

הַיֹּשֵׁב֙ עַל־ח֣וּג הָאָ֔רֶץ 22aA It is he who is dwelling on the circle of the earth

With: $\mathfrak{M}$ (5) – $\mathfrak{G}^{SQ}$ – $\mathfrak{S}^{ab}$, subordinate punctuation $\mathfrak{S}^{cde}$

COLON 40:22aB:

וְיֹשְׁבֶ֖יהָ כַּחֲגָבִ֑ים 22aB and its dwellers are like grasshoppers.

With: $\mathfrak{M}$ (2) – $\mathfrak{G}^{SQ}$ – $\mathfrak{S}^{abcde}$
Discussion: $\mathfrak{G}^{SQ}$ have an otherwise unsupported divider after וישביה which receives accent 8 (Ṭiphḥa) in $\mathfrak{M}$.

COLON 40:22bA:

הַנּוֹטֶ֤ה כַדֹּק֙ שָׁמַ֔יִם 22bA It is he who stretches out the heavens like a membrane

With: $\mathfrak{M}$ (5) – $\mathfrak{G}^{SQ}$ – $\mathfrak{S}^{abce}$, $\mathfrak{S}^{d}$ subordinate punctuation.

COLON 40:22bB:

וַיִּמְתָּחֵ֥ם כָּאֹ֖הֶל לָשָֽׁבֶת׃ 22bB and spreads them like a tent to dwell in.

With: $\mathfrak{M}$ (1) – $\mathfrak{G}^{SQ}$, major division marker in $\mathfrak{G}^{A}$ – $\mathfrak{S}^{abcde}$

Colon 40:23aA:

D.ii.1 (Isa. 40:23)

הַנּוֹתֵ֥ן רוֹזְנִ֖ים לְאָ֑יִן 23aA It is he who is bringing princes to nothing,

With: $\mathfrak{M}$ (2) – $\mathfrak{G}^{SQ}$ – $\mathfrak{S}^{abcde}$

Colon 40:23aB:

שֹׁ֥פְטֵי אֶ֖רֶץ כַּתֹּ֥הוּ עָשָֽׂה׃ 23aB he makes the judges of the earth void.

With: $\mathfrak{M}$ (1) – $\mathfrak{G}^{SQ}$ – $\mathfrak{S}^{abcde}$

Colon 40:24aA:

אַ֣ף בַּל־נִטָּ֗עוּ אַ֚ף בַּל־זֹרָ֔עוּ 24aA Scarcely are they planted, scarcely are they sown,

With: $\mathfrak{M}$ (5) – $\mathfrak{G}^{SQ}$ – $\mathfrak{S}^{abcde}$
Colon parallelism: אף || אף; בל || בל; נטע || זרע.
Discussion: The Revia‘ (No. 7) with $\mathfrak{M}$ בל־נטעו finds support in $\mathfrak{G}^{S}$ only. We decided to ignore it because the next colon 24aB is about the same length as v. 24aA if the latter runs on to בל־זרעו.

Colon 40:24aB:

אַ֛ף בַּל־שֹׁרֵ֥שׁ בָּאָ֖רֶץ גִּזְעָ֑ם 24aB scarcely their stem has rooted in the earth,

With: $\mathfrak{M}$ (2) – $\mathfrak{G}^{SQ}$ – $\mathfrak{S}^{abcde}$

Colon 40:24bA:

וְגַם־נָשַׁ֤ף בָּהֶם֙ וַיִּבָ֔שׁוּ 24bA when he blows upon them, and they wither,

With: $\mathfrak{M}$ (5) – $\mathfrak{G}^{SQ}$ – $\mathfrak{S}^{abcde}$

Colon 40:24bB:

וּסְעָרָ֖ה כַּקַּ֥שׁ תִּשָּׂאֵֽם׃ 24bB and the storm carries them off like chaff.

With: $\mathfrak{M}$ (1), major division markers – $\mathfrak{G}^{SAQ}$, major division markers in all – $\mathfrak{S}^{abce}$ major division markers, $\mathfrak{S}^{d}$ point.

Colon 40:25aA:

וְאֶל־מִ֥י תְדַמְּי֖וּנִי וְאֶשְׁוֶ֑ה 25aA And to whom will you liken me, that I would be his equal?

With: $\mathfrak{M}$ (2)
Colon parallelism: דמה || שוה.
Discussion: The Ṭifḥa (No.8) with $\mathfrak{M}$ תדמיוני finds weak support in

$\mathfrak{G}^{Q}$. On the other hand, the Atnaḥ (No. 2) with $\mathfrak{M}$ ואשוה finds no support whatsoever in the ancient versions. Yet we believe $\mathfrak{M}$ deserves confidence, see our comment on v. 1aA above.

COLON 40:25aB:

יֹאמַ֖ר קָדֽוֹשׁ׃ 25aB says the Holy One.

With: $\mathfrak{M}$ (1) – $\mathfrak{G}^{SQ}$ – $\mathfrak{S}^{abcde}$

COLON 40:26aA:

שְׂאוּ־מָר֨וֹם עֵינֵיכֶ֜ם וּרְא֗וּ 26aA Lift up your eyes on high, and see:

With: $\mathfrak{M}$ (10) – $\mathfrak{G}^{S}$ – $\mathfrak{S}^{e}$
Colon parallelism: נשׂא עינים || ראה.
Discussion: $\mathfrak{G}^{Q}$ and $\mathfrak{S}^{abcde}$ (subordinate punctuation) contradict the conjunctive accent of $\mathfrak{M}$ with עיניכם. The rather weak accent $\mathfrak{M}$ has with וראו (No. 10) probably means it wanted to read on until אלה. But a division at this point is supported by $\mathfrak{G}^{S}$ and $\mathfrak{S}^{e}$. The well-attested colon parallelism speaks in favour of this division.

COLON 40:26aB:

מִי־בָ֣רָא אֵ֔לֶּה 26aB Who did create those over there?

With: $\mathfrak{M}$ (5) – $\mathfrak{G}^{SQ}$ – $\mathfrak{S}^{abcde}$

COLON 40:26aC:

הַמּוֹצִ֥יא בְמִסְפָּ֖ר צְבָאָ֑ם 26aC He who brings out their host in number!

With: $\mathfrak{M}$ (2) – $\mathfrak{G}^{SQ}$ – $\mathfrak{S}^{ae}$, $\mathfrak{S}^{bcd}$ subordinate punctuation.

COLON 40:26bA:

לְכֻלָּם֙ בְּשֵׁ֣ם יִקְרָ֔א 26bA All of them he calls by name;

With: $\mathfrak{M}$ (5) $\mathfrak{G}^{SQ}$; $\mathfrak{S}^{abcde}$

COLON 40:26bB:

מֵרֹ֣ב אוֹנִים֙ וְאַמִּ֣יץ כֹּ֔חַ 26bB because of him who is great in forces and mighty of strength,

With: $\mathfrak{M}$ (5) – $\mathfrak{G}^{Q}$
Colon parallelism: רב || אמיץ (unique); און || כח.
Discussion: Apparently tradition hesitates with regard to the correct division of the colon. $\mathfrak{G}^{SQ}$ and $\mathfrak{S}^{a}$ presuppose a division after אונים where $\mathfrak{M}$ has a rather weak accent 10 (Pashṭa). On the other hand,

𝔐's Zaqeph Qaṭon (No. 5) with כה is supported by 𝔊^{Q} only. Yet we prefer 𝔐 because it results in a more fluent syntax.

COLON 40:26bC:

אִישׁ לֹא נֶעְדָּר׃ 26bC not one of them is missing.

With: 𝔐 (1), major division markers – 𝔊^{SQ} – 𝔖^{abcde}, major division markers in 𝔖^{be}

COLON 40:27aA:

לָמָּה תֹאמַר יַעֲקֹב 27aA Why do you say, O Jacob,

With: 𝔐 (5) – 𝔊^{SQ} – 𝔖^{e}

COLON 40:27aB:

וּתְדַבֵּר יִשְׂרָאֵל 27aB and speak, O Israel:

With: 𝔐 (2) – 𝔊^{SQ} – 𝔖^{ace}, 𝔖^{bd} subordinate punctuation.

COLON 40:27bA:

נִסְתְּרָה דַרְכִּי מֵיְהוָה 27bA "My way is hidden from the LORD,

With: 𝔐 (5) – 𝔊^{SQ} – 𝔖^{acde} subordinate punctuation.

COLON 40:27bB:

וּמֵאֱלֹהַי מִשְׁפָּטִי יַעֲבוֹר׃ 27bB and my right is neglected by my God"?

With: 𝔐 (1) – 𝔊^{S} colon, 𝔊^{Q} point – 𝔖^{abcde}

COLON 40:28aA:

הֲלוֹא יָדַעְתָּ אִם־לֹא שָׁמַעְתָּ 28aA Don't you know? Or didn't you hear?

With: 𝔐 (7) – 𝔊^{SQ} – 𝔖^{abcde} subordinate punctuation.
Colon parallelism: הלוא || אם־לא; ידע || שמע.

COLON 40:28aB:

אֱלֹהֵי עוֹלָם ׀ יְהוָה 28aB The LORD is a God of eternity,

With: 𝔐 (10) – 𝔊^{S} – 𝔖^{e}, 𝔖^{abcd} subordinate punctuation.
Colon parallelism: יהוה || אלהים.
Discussion: 𝔐's Pashṭa (No. 10) seems to indicate that it preferred to read on to הארץ, a colon of six stressed units. It is a case of misjudging the elliptical nature of the next colon. With the ancient witnesses

cited we assume two cola of three stressed units each (so also BHS and many others).

COLON 40:28aC:

בּוֹרֵא֙ קְצ֣וֹת הָאָ֔רֶץ 28aC the Creator of the ends of the earth.

With: $\mathfrak{M}$ (5) – $\mathfrak{G}^{SQ}$ – $\mathfrak{S}^{abcde}$

COLON 40:28bA:

לֹ֥א יִיעַ֛ף וְלֹ֥א יִיגָ֖ע 28bA He does not become exhausted and does not weary,

With: $\mathfrak{M}$ (2) – $\mathfrak{G}^{SQ}$ – $\mathfrak{S}^{abcde}$
Colon parallelism: לא || לא; יעף || יגע.

COLON 40:28bB:

אֵ֥ין חֵ֖קֶר לִתְבוּנָתֽוֹ׃ 28bB it is impossible to trace his understanding.

With: $\mathfrak{M}$ (1) – $\mathfrak{G}^{SQ}$, major division marker in $\mathfrak{G}^{A}$ – $\mathfrak{S}^{abcde}$
Colon parallelism: חקר || בין.

COLON 40:29aA:

E.ii.1 (Isa. 40:29)
נֹתֵ֥ן לַיָּעֵ֖ף כֹּ֑חַ 29aA He is giving strength to the exhausted,

With: $\mathfrak{M}$ (2) – $\mathfrak{G}^{SQ}$ – $\mathfrak{S}^{abcde}$ subordinate punctuation.
Colon parallelism: Antithetical יעף || כח.

COLON 40:29aB:

וּלְאֵ֥ין אוֹנִ֖ים עָצְמָ֥ה יַרְבֶּֽה׃ 29aB and increases the vigour of him who has no force left.

With: $\mathfrak{M}$ (1) – $\mathfrak{G}^{SQ}$ – $\mathfrak{S}^{abcde}$
Colon parallelism: און || עצמה (unique).

COLON 40:30aA:

וְיִעֲפ֥וּ נְעָרִ֖ים וְיִגָ֑עוּ 30aA Yes, youths may become exhausted and and grow weary,

With: $\mathfrak{M}$ (2) – $\mathfrak{G}^{SQ}$ – $\mathfrak{S}^{abcde}$
Colon parallelism: יעף || יגע, see v. 28cA.
Discussion: $\mathfrak{G}^{Q}$ has a divider after נערים, the same point where $\mathfrak{G}^{S}$ has a major division marker. Both can only be interpreted as errors because $\mathfrak{G}^{Q}$ has a major division at the end of v. 30.

COLON 40:30aB:

וּבַחוּרִים כָּשׁוֹל יִכָּשֵׁלוּ׃ 30aB and young men may stagger terribly,

With: 𝔐 (1) – $\mathfrak{G}^{Q}$ has major divison markers – $\mathfrak{S}^{abcde}$

COLON 40:31aA:

וְקוֹיֵ יְהוָה יַחֲלִיפוּ כֹחַ 31aA but those waiting for the LORD will renew their strength,

With: 𝔐 (5) – $\mathfrak{G}^{SQ}$ – $\mathfrak{S}^{abde}$

COLON 40:31aB:

יַעֲלוּ אֵבֶר כַּנְּשָׁרִים 31aB they will grow new pinions, like eagles.

With: 𝔐 (2) – $\mathfrak{G}^{SQ}$ – $\mathfrak{S}^{abcde}$

COLON 40:31bA:

יָרוּצוּ וְלֹא יִיגָעוּ 31bA They will run and will not grow weary

With: 𝔐 (5) – $\mathfrak{G}^{SQ}$ – $\mathfrak{S}^{abcde}$

Colon parallelism: Antithetical רוץ || יגע (unique).

Discussion: Although $\mathfrak{G}^{S}$ has a divider after ירוצו this is insufficient reason to deviate from 𝔐.

COLON 40:31bB:

יֵלְכוּ וְלֹא יִיעָפוּ׃ 31bB they will walk and will not become exhausted.

With: 𝔐 (1) – major divison markers in $\mathfrak{G}^{SBAQ}$ – major division markers in $\mathfrak{S}^{abcde}$

Colon parallelism: Antithetical הלך || יעף (unique).

2.3 Isaiah 40 – Delimitation of Verse-lines

VERSE–LINE: 40:1a:

נַחֲמוּ נַחֲמוּ עַמִּי 1aA Comfort, comfort my people,
יֹאמַר אֱלֹהֵיכֶם׃ 1aB says your God.

𝔐 distinctive accents: 2 – 1.
Stresses: 3 + 2.
Verse-line parallelism: עמי || אלהיך.[1]

[1]Mostly in solemn covenantal formulae, e.g. Exod. 6:7; Lev. 26:12; Deut. 7:6; 29:12; Jer. 7:23; Ezek. 34:30; Hos. 2:25; Ps. 95:7; Ruth 1:16.

VERSE–LINE: 40:2a:

דַּבְּר֞וּ עַל־לֵ֤ב יְרוּשָׁלַ֙͏ִם֙	2aA	Speak to the heart of Jerusalem
וְקִרְא֣וּ אֵלֶ֔יהָ	2aB	and cry to her

𝔐 distinctive accents: 10 – 5.
Stresses: 3 + 2.
Verse-line parallelism: דבר || קרא; על || אל; grammatical parallelism.

VERSE–LINE: 40:2b:

כִּ֤י מָֽלְאָה֙ צְבָאָ֔הּ	2bA	that her forced labour is fulfilled,
כִּ֥י נִרְצָ֖ה עֲוֺנָ֑הּ	2bB	that her iniquity has been repaid,

𝔐 distinctive accents: 5 – 2.
Stresses: 3 + 3.
Verse-line parallelism: כי || כי; מלא || רצה; צבא || עון; ־ה || ־ה; grammatical parallelism.

VERSE–LINE: 40:2c:

כִּ֤י לָֽקְחָה֙ מִיַּ֣ד יְהוָ֔ה	2cA	that she has taken from the LORD's hand
כִּפְלַ֖יִם בְּכָל־חַטֹּאתֶֽיהָ׃	2cB	double for all her sins.

𝔐 distinctive accents: 5 – 1.
Stresses: 4 + 2.
Verse-line parallelism: None.

VERSE–LINE: 40:3a:

ק֣וֹל קוֹרֵ֔א בַּמִּדְבָּ֕ר	3aA	A voice of someone crying in the desert:
פַּנּ֖וּ דֶּ֣רֶךְ יְהוָ֑ה	3aB	Prepare the way of the LORD,

𝔐 distinctive accents: 6 – 2.[2]
Stresses: 3 + 3.
Verse-line parallelism: None.

VERSE–LINE: 40:3b:

יַשְּׁרוּ֙ בָּעֲרָבָ֔ה	3bA	make straight in the bare valley
מְסִלָּ֖ה לֵאלֹהֵֽינוּ׃	3bB	a highway for our God!

𝔐 distinctive accents: 5 – 1.
Stresses: 2 + 2.
Verse-line parallelism: None.

[2]For a similar sequence of accents see J. Kim, *The Structure of the Samson Cycle*, Kampen 1993, 265 (Judg. 16:20a).

VERSE–LINE: 40:4a:

כָּל־גֶּיא֙ יִנָּשֵׂ֔א	4aA	Every valley will be lifted up,
וְכָל־הַ֥ר וְגִבְעָ֖ה יִשְׁפָּ֑לוּ	4aB	and every mountain and hill will be made low,

𝔪 distinctive accents: 5 – 2.
Stresses: 2 + 3.
Verse-line parallelism: כל || כל; גיא || הר וגבעה; נשׂא || שׁפל.

VERSE–LINE: 40:4b:

וְהָיָ֤ה הֶֽעָקֹב֙ לְמִישׁ֔וֹר	4bA	and the rough terrain will become level,
וְהָרְכָסִ֖ים לְבִקְעָֽה׃	4bB	and the rocky places a plain.

𝔪 distinctive accents: 5 – 1.
Stresses: 3 + 2.
Verse-line parallelism: עקב || רכס; ל || ל; מישור || בקעה.
Discussion: The ellipsis of היה in v. 4bB connects this colon with v. 4bA.

VERSE–LINE: 40:5a:

וְנִגְלָ֖ה כְּב֣וֹד יְהוָ֑ה	5aA	And the glory of the LORD will be revealed.

𝔪 distinctive accent: 2, showing that we are dealing with a unicolon.
Stresses: 3.
Verse-line parallelism: None.

VERSE–LINE: 40:5b:

וְרָא֤וּ כָל־בָּשָׂר֙ יַחְדָּ֔ו	5bA	And all flesh will see it together,
כִּ֛י פִּ֥י יְהוָ֖ה דִּבֵּֽר׃	5bB	for the mouth of the LORD has spoken.

𝔪 distinctive accents: 5 – 1.
Stresses: 3 + 4.
Verse-line parallelism: None.

VERSE–LINE: 40:6a:

ק֚וֹל אֹמֵ֣ר קְרָ֔א	6aA	A voice of someone saying: Cry!
וְאָמַ֖ר מָ֣ה אֶקְרָ֑א	6aB	But it is said: "What should I cry?

𝔪 distinctive accents: 5 – 2.
Stresses: 3 + 3.
Verse-line parallelism: אמר || אמר; קרא || קרא.

VERSE–LINE: 40:6b:

כָּל־הַבָּשָׂר חָצִיר	6bA	All flesh is grass,
וְכָל־חַסְדּוֹ כְּצִיץ הַשָּׂדֶה׃	6bB	and all their loyalty is like a flower of the field.

𝔐 distinctive accents: 5 – 1.
Stresses: 2 + 3.
Verse-line parallelism: כל || כל; חציר || ציץ.

VERSE–LINE: 40:7a:

יָבֵשׁ חָצִיר נָבֵל צִיץ	7aA	The grass withers, the flower fades,
כִּי רוּחַ יְהוָה נָשְׁבָה בּוֹ	7aB	when the spirit of the LORD blows upon it ..."

𝔐 distinctive accents: 5 – 2.
Stresses: 4 + 5.
Verse-line parallelism: None.
Discussion: Despite the lack of parallelism the delimitation is not in doubt because the sentence runs on.

VERSE–LINE: 40:7b-8a:

אָכֵן חָצִיר הָעָם׃	7bA	Surely, the people is grass,
יָבֵשׁ חָצִיר נָבֵל צִיץ	8aB	the grass withers, the flower fades ...
וּדְבַר־אֱלֹהֵינוּ יָקוּם לְעוֹלָם׃	8aC	But the word of our God will stand to eternity!

𝔐 distinctive accents: 1 – 2 – 1.
Stresses: 3 + 4 + 3.
Verse-line parallelism: עם || אלהים;[3] יבש, נבל || קום.[4]
Discussion: The Masoretes took אכן חציר העם with v.7 as an explanatory addition. However, the external parallelism strongly suggests that חציר העם (v. 7bA) is an interpretation of כל־הבשׂר חציר (v. 6bA), whereas v.8a balances v.7a. So אכן חציר העם introduces the answer of the speaker of v. 8 and should be separated from v. 7. In 1Q[a] cola 7bA and 8aA were omitted and added later, thus also showing a tight connection between the two cola. There is no reason, therefore, to take 7bA as a gloss. The word אכן is characteristic of Second Isaiah.[5]

[3] One might also consider the possibility of a pair עם || דבר; the word of God and the people are often contrasted, e.g. Isa. 28:14; 51:16; Jer. 5:14; 6:19; 13:10; 23:22.
[4] Antithetical parallelism, the underlying metaphor being the fresh standing grainstalks (קמה) as compared to the dry grass.
[5] Isa. 45:15; 49:4; 53:4; cf. Barthélemy, 279-8.

VERSE–LINE: 40:9a:

עַ֣ל הַר־גָּבֹ֤הַ עֲלִי־לָךְ֙	9aA	Climb on a high mountain,
מְבַשֶּׂ֣רֶת צִיּ֔וֹן	9aB	O Zion, heraldess of good tidings!

𝔐 distinctive accents: 10 – 5.
Stresses: 3 + 2.
Verse-line parallelism: הר || ציון.

VERSE–LINE: 40:9b:

הָרִ֤ימִי בַכֹּ֙חַ֙ קוֹלֵ֔ךְ	9bA	Lift up your voice with strength,
מְבַשֶּׂ֖רֶת יְרוּשָׁלִָ֑ם	9bB	O Jerusalem, heraldess of good tidings!

𝔐 distinctive accents: 5 – 2.
Stresses: 3 + 2.
Verse-line parallelism: None.

VERSE–LINE: 40:9c:

הָרִ֙ימִי֙ אַל־תִּירָ֔אִי	9cA	Lift it up, do not fear!
אִמְרִי֙ לְעָרֵ֣י יְהוּדָ֔ה	9cB	Say to the cities of Judah,
הִנֵּ֖ה אֱלֹהֵיכֶֽם׃	9cC	Behold your God!

𝔐 distinctive accents: 5 – 5 – 1.
Stresses: 2 + 3 + 2.
Verse-line parallelism: יהודה || אלהים; רום || אמר (unique); grammatical parallelism.
Discussion: The accentual pattern 5–5–1 is fairly common.[6] See also the similar structure of the quadrocolon Isa. 48:20.

VERSE–LINE: 40:10a:

הִנֵּ֨ה אֲדֹנָ֤י יְהוִה֙ בְּחָזָ֣ק יָב֔וֹא	10aA	Behold, the Lord GOD will come as a mighty one,
וּזְרֹע֖וֹ מֹ֣שְׁלָה ל֑וֹ	10aB	and his arm will rule for him.

𝔐 distinctive accents: 5 – 2.
Stresses: 5 + 3.
Verse-line parallelism: חזק || זרוע.[7]

[6] See for Second Isaiah 40:26b; 42:24b; 44:17b, 24b; 45:13b; 47:9b.

[7] Deuteronomic phraseology used in connection with the Exodus. Cf. B.S. Childs, "Deuteronomic Formulae of the Exodus Tradition," in: B. Hartmann *et al.*, *Hebräische Wortforschung: Festschrift ... W. Baumgartner* (SVT, 16). Leiden 1967, 30-9; M. Weinfeld, *Deuteronomy and the Deuteronomic School*, Oxford 1972, 329.

VERSE–LINE: 40:10b:

הִנֵּה שְׂכָרוֹ אִתּוֹ 10bA Behold, his wages are with him,
וּפְעֻלָּתוֹ לְפָנָיו׃ 10bB and his recompense before him.

𝔐 distinctive accents: 5 – 1.
Stresses: 3 + 2.
Verse-line parallelism: שׂכר || פעלה;[8] ו־ || ו־|| ו־ || ו־.

VERSE–LINE: 40:11a:

כְּרֹעֶה עֶדְרוֹ יִרְעֶה 11aA Like a shepherd he will shepherd his flock,
בִּזְרֹעוֹ יְקַבֵּץ טְלָאִים 11aB in his arm he will gather the lambs,
וּבְחֵיקוֹ יִשָּׂא 11aC and in his lap he will take them up,

𝔐 distinctive accents: 5 – 5 –2.
Stresses: 3 + 3 + 2.
Verse-line parallelism: עדר || טלה (unique); רעה || קבץ; ב || ב; זרוע || חיק (unique); grammatical parallelism.
Discussion: 𝔐 opts for a tricolon with a unicolon. 𝔊 seems to skip ובחיקו ישׂא so that a tricolon remains. 𝔖 appears to read as a quadrocolon. In fact one might also consider the possibility of two bicola, with a more or less chiastic structure. We decided to follow 𝔐 in this doubtful case.

VERSE–LINE: 40:11b:

עָלוֹת יְנַהֵל׃ 11bA the nursing ewes he will lead gently.

𝔐 distinctive accents: 1.
Stresses: 2.
Verse-line parallelism: None (unicolon).

VERSE–LINE: 40:12a:

מִי־מָדַד בְּשָׁעֳלוֹ מַי* יָם* 12aA Who measured the waters of the sea in the hollow of his hand
וְשָׁמַיִם בַּזֶּרֶת תִּכֵּן 12aB and staked out the heavens with a span,
וְכָל בַּשָּׁלִשׁ עֲפַר הָאָרֶץ 12aC and filled out a three–cup with the dust of the earth?

𝔐 distinctive accents: [7] – 5 – 2.
Stresses: 3 + 3 + 4.
Verse-line parallelism: מדד || תכן || כול; ים || שׁמים || ארץ; ב || ב || ב; שׁעל || זרת|| שׁלשׁ (unique); grammatical parallelism.

[8]Quoted Isa. 62:11, see further Jer. 31:16; Prov. 11:18; Ruth 2:12.

VERSE–LINE: 40:12b:

וְשָׁקַ֤ל בַּפֶּ֙לֶס֙ הָרִ֔ים 12bA And weighed the mountains in scales
וּגְבָע֖וֹת בְּמֹאזְנָֽיִם׃ 12bB and the hills in a balance?

𝔐 distinctive accents: 5 – 1.
Stresses: 3 + 2.
Verse-line parallelism: ב || ב (common); פלס || מאזנים; הר || גבעה.

VERSE–LINE: 40:13a:

מִֽי־תִכֵּ֥ן אֶת־ר֖וּחַ יְהוָ֑ה 13aA Who staked out the spirit of the LORD
וְאִ֥ישׁ עֲצָת֖וֹ יוֹדִיעֶֽנּוּ׃ 13aB and which man made his counsel known to him?

𝔐 distinctive accents: 2 – 1.
Stresses: 3 + 3.
Verse-line parallelism: תכן || ידע; רוח || עצה.

VERSE–LINE: 40:14a:

אֶת־מִ֤י נוֹעָץ֙ וַיְבִינֵ֔הוּ 14aA Whom did he consult that he would have made him understand,
וַיְלַמְּדֵ֖הוּ בְּאֹ֣רַח מִשְׁפָּ֑ט 14aB and would have taught him the path of what is right,
{וַיְלַמְּדֵ֣הוּ דַ֔עַת} 14aC {and would have taught him knowledge,}
וְדֶ֥רֶךְ תְּבוּנ֖וֹת יוֹדִיעֶֽנּוּ׃ 14aD and would have made known to him the way of deep understanding?

𝔐 distinctive accents: 5 – 2 – [5] – 1.
Stresses: 3 + 3 + (2 +) 3.
Verse-line parallelism: יעץ || למד || ידע (unique); ־הו || ־הו; ארח || דרך; בין || תבונה; משפט || תבונה (unique).
Discussion: The Masoretes wanted to read this as two bicola. However, the very strong internal parallelism suggests a quadrocolon which has the additional advantage that the separating force of מִי is respected (see the analysis of the strophic structure). But in view of the shortness of 14aC as compared to the surrounding cola it is not unlikely that וַיְלַמְּדֵהוּ דַעַת was a mitigating gloss to וַיְלַמְּדֵהוּ בְּאֹרַח מִשְׁפָּט. It is missing in 𝔊. The combination of למד with דעת was a common one[9] and might easily have crept into the original tricolon.

VERSE–LINE: 40:15a:

הֵ֤ן גּוֹיִם֙ כְּמַ֣ר מִדְּלִ֔י 15aA Behold, the nations are like a drop from a bucket,

[9]Cf. Ps. 94:10; 119:66; Job 21:22; Prov. 30:3; Eccl. 12:9.

וּכְשַׁ֥חַק מֹאזְנַ֖יִם נֶחְשָׁ֑בוּ 15aB and are accounted as particles of dust on a balance.

𝔐 distinctive accents: 5 – 2.
Stresses: 4 + 3.
Verse-line parallelism: כ || כ; מר || שחק (unique); דלי || מאזנים (unique).

VERSE–LINE: 40:15b:

הֵ֥ן אִיִּ֖ים כַּדַּ֥ק יִטּֽוֹל׃ 15bA Behold, he lifts up the islands like powder.

𝔐 distinctive accent: 1.
Stresses: 4.
Verse-line parallelism: None.
Discussion: Although a tricolon with the accentual pattern 5 – 2 – 1 is certainly an option we prefer a bicolon with a unicolon because of the repeated הן and the deliberate change of subject (a passive construction with איים as the subject was possible).

VERSE–LINE: 40:16a:

וּלְבָנ֕וֹן אֵ֥ין דֵּ֖י בָּעֵ֑ר 16aA And the Lebanon will not suffice for fuel,
וְחַיָּת֔וֹ אֵ֥ין דֵּ֖י עוֹלָֽה׃ 16aB and its beasts will not suffice for a burnt offering.

𝔐 distinctive accents: 2 – 1.
Stresses: 4 + 4.
אין || אין; די || די; בער || עולה.

VERSE–LINE: 40:17a:

כָּל־הַגּוֹיִ֖ם כְּאַ֣יִן נֶגְדּ֑וֹ 17aA All nations are as nothing to him,
מֵאֶ֥פֶס וָתֹ֖הוּ נֶחְשְׁבוּ־לֽוֹ׃ 17aB they are accounted by him less than non-existent and void.

𝔐 distinctive accents: 2 – 1.
Stresses: 3 + 3.
Verse-line parallelism: אין || אפס; אין || תהו.

VERSE–LINE: 40:18a:

וְאֶל־מִ֖י תְּדַמְּי֣וּן אֵ֑ל 18aA And to whom you would liken God?
וּמַה־דְּמ֖וּת תַּ֥עַרְכוּ לֽוֹ׃ 18aB And which likeness would you arrange for him?

𝔐 distinctive accents: 2 – 1.
Stresses: 3 + 3.
Verse-line parallelism: מי || מה; דמה || דמות (unique); grammatical parallelism.

VERSE–LINE: 40:19a:

הַפֶּסֶל נָסַךְ חָרָשׁ 19aA An idol? A craftsman casts it,
וְצֹרֵף בַּזָּהָב יְרַקְּעֶנּוּ 19aB and the goldsmith overlays it with gold,
וּרְתֻקוֹת כֶּסֶף צוֹרֵף׃ 19aC and with soldering of a goldsmith's silver.

𝔐 distinctive accents: 5 – 2 – 1.
Stresses: 3 + 3 + 3.
Verse-line parallelism: נסך || רקע (unique); חרש || צרף; זהב || כסף.
Discussion: The ellipsis of רקע ב joins vv. 19aB and 19aC.

VERSE–LINE: 40:20a:

הַמְסֻכָּן* תְּרוּמָה 20aA He who shapes the pedestal
עֵץ לֹא־יִרְקַב יִבְחָר 20aB chooses wood that does not rot.

𝔐 distinctive accents: 5 – 2.
Stresses: 2 + 3.
Verse-line parallelism: None.

VERSE–LINE: 40:20b:

חָרָשׁ חָכָם יְבַקֶּשׁ־לוֹ 20bA He seeks out a skilful craftsman
לְהָכִין פֶּסֶל לֹא יִמּוֹט׃ 20bB to set up an idol that will not topple.

𝔐 distinctive accents: 5 – 1.
Stresses: 3 + 4.
Verse-line parallelism: None.

VERSE–LINE: 40:21a:

הֲלוֹא תֵדְעוּ הֲלוֹא תִשְׁמָעוּ 21aA Don't you know? Didn't you hear?
הֲלוֹא הֻגַּד מֵרֹאשׁ לָכֶם 21aB Has it not been told to you from the beginning?
הֲלוֹא הֲבִינֹתֶם מוֹסְדוֹת הָאָרֶץ׃ 21aC Don't you understand the foundations of the earth?

𝔐 distinctive accents: 5 – 2 – 1.
Stresses: 4 + 4 + 4.
Verse-line parallelism: הלוא || הלוא||הלוא || הלוא; ידע || נגד; שמע || בין; שמע || נגד.

VERSE–LINE: 40:22a:

הַיֹּשֵׁב עַל־חוּג הָאָרֶץ 22aA It is he who is dwelling on the circle of the earth
וְיֹשְׁבֶיהָ כַּחֲגָבִים 22aB and its dwellers are like grasshoppers.

𝔐 distinctive accents: 5 – 2.

Stresses: 3 + 2.
Verse-line parallelism: ישב || ישב.

VERSE–LINE: 40:22b:

הַנֹּוטֶה כַדֹּק שָׁמַיִם 22bA It is he who stretches out the heavens like a membrane
וַיִּמְתָּחֵם כָּאֹהֶל לָשָׁבֶת׃ 22bB and spreads them like a tent to dwell in.

𝔐 distinctive accents: 5– 1.
Stresses: 3 + 3.
Verse-line parallelism: נטה || מתח; כ || כ; דק || אהל (unique).

VERSE–LINE: 40:23a:

D.ii.1 (Isa. 40:23)
הַנֹּותֵן רֹוזְנִים לְאָיִן 23aA It is he who is bringing princes to nothing,
שֹׁפְטֵי אֶרֶץ כַּתֹּהוּ עָשָׂה׃ 23aB he makes the judges of the earth void.

𝔐 distinctive accents: 2 – 1.
Stresses: 3 + 4.
Verse-line parallelism: נתן || עשה; רזן || שפט; אין || תהו.

VERSE–LINE: 40:24a:

אַף בַּל־נִטָּעוּ אַף בַּל־זֹרָעוּ 24aA Scarcely are they planted, scarcely are they sown,
אַף בַּל־שֹׁרֵשׁ בָּאָרֶץ גִּזְעָם 24aB scarcely their stem has rooted in the earth,

𝔐 distinctive accents: 5 – 2.
Stresses: 4 + 4.
Verse-line parallelism: אף || אף; בל || בל; נטע || שרשׁ; זרע || שרשׁ.

VERSE–LINE: 40:24b:

וְגַם־נָשַׁף בָּהֶם וַיִּבָשׁוּ 24bA when he blows upon them, and they wither,
וּסְעָרָה כַּקַּשׁ תִּשָּׂאֵם׃ 24bB and the storm carries them off like chaff.

𝔐 distinctive accents: 5 – 1.
Stresses: 3 + 3.
Verse-line parallelism: נשף || סערה (unique).

VERSE–LINE: 40:25a:

וְאֶל־מִי תְדַמְּיוּנִי וְאֶשְׁוֶה 25aA And to whom will you liken me, that I would be his equal?
יֹאמַר קָדֹושׁ׃ 25aB says the Holy One.

𝔐 distinctive accents: 2 – 1.

Stresses: 3 + 2.
Verse-line parallelism: None.

VERSE–LINE: 40:26a:

שְׂאוּ־מָרוֹם עֵינֵיכֶם וּרְאוּ	26aA	Lift up your eyes on high, and see:
מִי־בָרָא אֵלֶּה	26aB	Who did create those over there?
הַמּוֹצִיא בְמִסְפָּר צְבָאָם	26aC	He who brings out their host in number!

𝔐 distinctive accents: 10 – 5 – 2.
Stresses: 3 + 2 + 3.
Verse-line parallelism: מרום || צבא.

VERSE–LINE: 40:26b:

לְכֻלָּם בְּשֵׁם יִקְרָא	26bA	All of them he calls by name;
מֵרֹב אוֹנִים וְאַמִּיץ כֹּחַ	26bB	because of him who is great in forces and mighty of strength,
אִישׁ לֹא נֶעְדָּר׃	26bC	not one of them is missing.

𝔐 distinctive accents: 5 – 5 – 1.
Stresses: 3 + 4 + 3.
Verse-line parallelism: None.

VERSE–LINE: 40:27a:

לָמָּה תֹאמַר יַעֲקֹב	27aA	Why do you say, O Jacob,
וּתְדַבֵּר יִשְׂרָאֵל	27aB	and speak, O Israel:

𝔐 distinctive accents: 5 – 2.
Stresses: 3 + 2.
Verse-line parallelism: אמר || דבר; יעקב || ישראל.
Discussion: The ellipsis of למה binds v. 27aB to v. 27aA.

VERSE–LINE: 40:27b:

נִסְתְּרָה דַרְכִּי מֵיְהוָה	27bA	"My way is hidden from the LORD,
וּמֵאֱלֹהַי מִשְׁפָּטִי יַעֲבוֹר׃	27bB	and my right is neglected by my God?"

𝔐 distinctive accents: 5 – 1.
Stresses: 3 + 3.
Verse-line parallelism: סתר || עבר; דרך || משפט; ־י || ־י; יהוה || אלהים.

VERSE–LINE: 40:28a:

הֲלוֹא יָדַעְתָּ אִם־לֹא שָׁמַעְתָּ	28aA	Don't you know? Or didn't you hear?
אֱלֹהֵי עוֹלָם ׀ יְהוָה	28aB	The LORD is a God of eternity,

בּוֹרֵא קְצוֹת הָאָרֶץ 28aC the Creator of the ends of the earth.

𝔐 distinctive accents: 7 – 10 – 5.
Stresses: 4 + 3 + 3.
Verse-line parallelism: יהוה || ברא.

Discussion: Obviously the Masoretes wanted to read a tricolon with the accentual sequence 7 – 5 – 2 which resulted in a very long second colon (six stressed units)[10] and left a meagre unicolon for the end of the verse.

VERSE–LINE: 40:28b:

לֹא יִיעַף וְלֹא יִיגָע 28bA He does not become exhausted and he does not grow weary,
אֵין חֵקֶר לִתְבוּנָתוֹ׃ 28bB it is impossible to trace his understanding.

𝔐 distinctive accents: 2 – 1.
Stresses: 4 + 3.
Verse-line parallelism: לא || אין.

VERSE–LINE: 40:29a:

E.ii.1 (Isa. 40:29)

נֹתֵן לַיָּעֵף כֹּחַ 29aA He is giving strength to the exhausted,
וּלְאֵין אוֹנִים עָצְמָה יַרְבֶּה׃ 29aB and increases the vigour of him who has no force left.

𝔐 distinctive accents: 2 – 1.
Stresses: 3 + 4.
Verse-line parallelism: נתן || רבה; ל || ל; יעף || אין אונים (unique); one might also note כח || און (cf. v. 26); כח || עצמה.

VERSE–LINE: 40:30a:

וְיִעֲפוּ נְעָרִים וְיִגָעוּ 30aA Yes, youths may become exhausted and grow weary,
וּבַחוּרִים כָּשׁוֹל יִכָּשֵׁלוּ׃ 30aB and young men may stagger terribly,

𝔐 distinctive accents: 2 – 1.
Stresses: 3 + 3.
Verse-line parallelism: יעף || כשל (unique); יגע || כשל (unique); בחור || נער;

VERSE–LINE: 40:31a:

וְקוֹיֵ יְהוָה יַחֲלִיפוּ כֹחַ 31aA but those waiting for the LORD will renew their strength,

[10] See our comment on p. 37.

יַעֲלוּ אֵבֶר כַּנְּשָׁרִים	31aB	they will grow new pinions, like eagles.

𝔐 distinctive accents: 5 – 2.
Stresses: 4 + 3.
Verse-line parallelism: חלף || יעל; grammatical parallelism.

VERSE–LINE: 40:31b:

יָרוּצוּ וְלֹא יִיגָעוּ	31bA	They will run and will not grow weary,
יֵלְכוּ וְלֹא יִיעָפוּ׃	31bB	they will walk and will not become exhausted.

𝔐 distinctive accents: 5 – 1.
Stresses: 3 + 3.
Verse-line parallelism: רוץ || הלך; לא || לא; יגע || יעף; grammatical parallelism.

2.4 Isaiah 40 – Delimitation of Strophes

STROPHE A.i.1 (Isa. 40:1–2a)

נַחֲמוּ נַחֲמוּ עַמִּי	1aA	Comfort, comfort my people,
יֹאמַר אֱלֹהֵיכֶם׃	1aB	says your God.
דַּבְּרוּ עַל־לֵב יְרוּשָׁלַםִ	2aA	Speak to the heart of Jerusalem
וְקִרְאוּ אֵלֶיהָ	2aB	and cry to her

≠ Masoretic verse.
Separation ↑: major division markers in the textual tradition; imperative(s); marker of direct speech.
Separation ↓: imperative(s).
Strophe parallelism: נחם || דבר על לב; עם || ירושלם; אמר || קרא.
Discussion: The Masoretes chose to connect v. 2a with the next two verse-lines because the sentence continues. However, as we shall demonstrate later,[1] it is not uncommon for sentences to ignore the boundary between strophes. This is one of the major reasons why it is impossible to base the analysis of Classical Hebrew poetry on syntax alone. The strong strophe parallelism between vv. 1 and 2a on the one hand, vv. 2b and 2c on the other, argues in favour of two distinct strophes.

STROPHE A.i.2 (Isa. 40:2b–c)

כִּי מָלְאָה צְבָאָהּ	2bA	that her forced labour is fulfilled,
כִּי נִרְצָה עֲוֺנָהּ	2bB	that her iniquity has been repaid,
כִּי לָקְחָה מִיַּד יְהוָה	2cA	that she has taken from the LORD's hand
כִּפְלַיִם בְּכָל־חַטֹּאתֶיהָ׃	2cB	double for all her sins.

[1]See p. 645, n. 32.

≠ Masoretic verse.
Separation ↑: deictic particle(s).
Separation ↓: major division markers in the textual tradition; deictic particle(s).
Strophe parallelism: כי || כי; מלא || לקח; ־ה || ־ה; עון || חטאת; grammatical parallelism.

STROPHE A.ii.1 (Isa. 40:3)

קוֹל קוֹרֵא בַּמִּדְבָּר	3aA	A voice of someone crying in the desert:
פַּנּוּ דֶּרֶךְ יְהוָה	3aB	Prepare the way of the LORD,
יַשְּׁרוּ בָּעֲרָבָה	3bA	make straight in the bare valley
מְסִלָּה לֵאלֹהֵינוּ׃	3bB	a highway for our God!

= Masoretic verse.
Separation ↑: major division markers in the textual tradition; imperative(s); marker of direct speech.
Separation ↓: imperative(s).
Strophe parallelism: ב || ב; מדבר || ערבה; פנה || ישר; דרך || מסלה; יהוה || אלהים; grammatical parallelism.

STROPHE A.ii.2 (Isa. 40:4)

כָּל־גֶּיא יִנָּשֵׂא	4aA	Every valley will be lifted up,
וְכָל־הַר וְגִבְעָה יִשְׁפָּלוּ	4aB	and every mountain and hill will be made low,
וְהָיָה הֶעָקֹב לְמִישׁוֹר	4bA	and the rough terrain will become level,
וְהָרְכָסִים לְבִקְעָה׃	4bB	and the rocky places a plain.

= Masoretic verse.
Separation ↑: repetitive verse-line parallelism; swapping (subject).
Separation ↓: repetitive verse-line parallelism.
Strophe parallelism: גיא || מישור (unique); הר || בקעה; הר || עקב; גבעה || מישור.

STROPHE A.ii.3 (Isa. 40:5)

וְנִגְלָה כְּבוֹד יְהוָה	5aA	And the glory of the LORD will be revealed.
וְרָאוּ כָל־בָּשָׂר יַחְדָּו	5bA	And all flesh will see it together,
כִּי פִּי יְהוָה דִּבֵּר׃	5bB	for the mouth of the LORD has spoken.

= Masoretic verse.
Separation ↑: None.
Separation ↓: major division markers in the textual tradition; deictic particle(s); marker of direct speech; swapping (subject).
Strophe parallelism: גלה || ראה; כבוד || בשׂר; יהוה || יהוה.

Discussion: We opted for a strophe consisting of a unicolon and a bicolon on the basis of 𝔐's Atnaḥ and the change of subject between v. 5a and v. 5b.

STROPHE A.iii.1 (Isa. 40:6)

קוֹל אֹמֵר קְרָא	6aA	A voice of someone saying: Cry!
וְאָמַר מָה אֶקְרָא	6aB	But it is said: "What should I cry?
כָּל־הַבָּשָׂר חָצִיר	6bA	All flesh is grass,
וְכָל־חַסְדּוֹ כְּצִיץ הַשָּׂדֶה׃	6bB	and all their loyalty is like a flower of the field.

= Masoretic verse.
Separation ↑: major division markers in the textual tradition; interrogative pronoun; imperative(s); markers of direct speech.
Separation ↓: major division marker in the textual tradition; repetitive verse-line parallelism.
Strophe parallelism: None.

STROPHE A.iii.2 (Isa. 40:7–8)

יָבֵשׁ חָצִיר נָבֵל צִיץ	7aA	The grass withers, the flower fades,
כִּי רוּחַ יְהוָה נָשְׁבָה בּוֹ	7aB	when the spirit of the LORD blows upon it ..."
אָכֵן חָצִיר הָעָם׃	7bA	Surely, the people is grass,
יָבֵשׁ חָצִיר נָבֵל צִיץ	8aB	the grass withers, the flower fades ...
וּדְבַר־אֱלֹהֵינוּ יָקוּם לְעוֹלָם׃	8aC	But the word of our God will stand to eternity!

≠ Masoretic verse.
Separation ↑: major division marker in the textual tradition; deictic particle(s); swapping (subject);
Separation ↓: major division markers in the textual tradition; deictic particle(s); repetitive verse-line parallelism;
Strophe parallelism: יבש || יבש; חציר || חציר; נבל || נבל; ציץ || ציץ; יהוה || אלהים.

Discussion: The strong parallelism between vv. 7 and 8 induced us to take the two Masoretic verses together. The idea that it is the same God who decided to punish Israel and to restore it now that it has paid for its inequity is a central theme in Second Isaiah.

STROPHE A.iv.1 (Isa. 40:9a–b)

עַל הַר־גָּבֹהַ עֲלִי־לָךְ	9aA	Climb on a high mountain,
מְבַשֶּׂרֶת צִיּוֹן	9aB	O Zion, heraldess of good tidings!
הָרִימִי בַכֹּחַ קוֹלֵךְ	9bA	Lift up your voice with strength,
מְבַשֶּׂרֶת יְרוּשָׁלִָם	9bB	O Jerusalem, heraldess of good tidings!

≠ Masoretic verse.
Separation ↑: major division markers in the textual tradition; imperative(s); vocative; swapping (adjunct).
Separation ↓: imperative(s); vocative; swapping (object).
Strophe parallelism: עלה || רום; ־ך || ־ך; בשׂר (verb) || בשׂר; ציון || ירושלם; grammatical parallelism.
Discussion: The Masoretes interpreted v. 9aA-9bB as a tricolon which was followed by another tricolon (our v. 9c). In our opinion the strong parallelistic structure of 9a-b argues against their decision to take 9aA–9aB as one colon.[2] Therefore we took v. 9c as one independent strophe (see below).

STROPHE A.iv.2 (Isa. 40:9c)

הָרִימִי אַל־תִּירָאִי	9cA	Lift it up, do not fear!
אִמְרִי לְעָרֵי יְהוּדָה	9cB	Say to the cities of Judah,
הִנֵּה אֱלֹהֵיכֶם׃	9cC	Behold your God!

≠ Masoretic verse.
Separation ↑: deictic particle(s); imperative(s); jussive(s);
Separation ↓: major division marker in the textual tradition; for the rest identical with the above.
Strophe parallelism: None (one verse-line).
Discussion: See our comment on the preceding strophe. In other cases strophes consisting of only one bicolon or tricolon were perfectly acceptable to the Masoretes.[3]

STROPHE A.v.1 (Isa. 40:10)

הִנֵּה אֲדֹנָי יְהוִה בְּחָזָק יָבוֹא	10aA	Behold, the Lord GOD will come as a mighty one,
וּזְרֹעוֹ מֹשְׁלָה לוֹ	10aB	and his arm will rule for him.
הִנֵּה שְׂכָרוֹ אִתּוֹ	10bA	Behold, his wages are with him,
וּפְעֻלָּתוֹ לְפָנָיו׃	10bB	and his recompense before him.

= Masoretic verse.
Separation ↑: major division marker in the textual tradition; deictic particle(s); swapping (subject); swapping (adjunct).
Separation ↓: deictic particle(s); repetitive verse-line parallelism.
Strophe parallelism: הנה || הנה; ־ו || ־ו.

---

[2]See our comment on p. 27.
[3]See our conclusions 645.

STROPHE A.v.2 (Isa. 40:11)

כְּרֹעֶה֙ עֶדְר֣וֹ יִרְעֶ֔ה	11aA	Like a shepherd he will shepherd his flock,
בִּזְרֹעוֹ֙ יְקַבֵּ֣ץ טְלָאִ֔ים	11aB	in his arm he will gather the lambs,
וּבְחֵיק֖וֹ יִשָּׂ֑א	11aC	and in his lap he will take them up,
עָל֖וֹת יְנַהֵֽל׃	11bA	the nursing ewes he will lead gently.

= Masoretic verse.
Separation ↑: swapping (object); swapping (adjunct).
Separation ↓: major division markers in the textual tradition; swapping (object).
Strophe parallelism: רעה || נהל; עול || טלה (unique); grammatical parallelism.

STROPHE B.i.1 (Isa. 40:12)

מִֽי־מָדַ֨ד בְּשָׁעֳלוֹ֙ מֵי* יָם*	12aA	Who measured the waters of the sea in the hollow of his hand
וְשָׁמַ֙יִם֙ בַּזֶּ֣רֶת תִּכֵּ֔ן	12aB	and staked out the heavens with a span,
וְכָ֥ל בַּשָּׁלִ֖שׁ עֲפַ֣ר הָאָ֑רֶץ	12aC	and filled out a three-cup with the dust of the earth?
וְשָׁקַ֤ל בַּפֶּ֙לֶס֙ הָרִ֔ים	12bA	And weighed the mountains in scales
וּגְבָע֖וֹת בְּמֹאזְנָֽיִם׃	12bB	and the hills in a balance?

= Masoretic verse.
Separation ↑: major division markers in the textual tradition; interrogative pronoun; repetitive verse-line parallelism; swapping (object); swapping (adjunct)
Separation ↓: major division marker in the textual tradition; repetitive verse-line parallelism; swapping (object); swapping (adjunct)
Strophe parallelism: מדד || שקל; ב || ב; שמים || ארץ || הר; various types of measures.

STROPHE B.i.2 (Isa. 40:13–14)

מִֽי־תִכֵּ֥ן אֶת־ר֖וּחַ יְהוָ֑ה	13aA	Who staked out the spirit of the LORD
וְאִ֥ישׁ עֲצָת֖וֹ יוֹדִיעֶֽנּוּ׃	13aB	and which man made his counsel known to him?
אֶת־מִ֤י נוֹעָץ֙ וַיְבִינֵ֔הוּ	14aA	Whom did he consult that he would have made him understand,
וַֽיְלַמְּדֵ֖הוּ בְּאֹ֣רַח מִשְׁפָּ֑ט	14aB	and would have taught him the path of what is right,
{וַיְלַמְּדֵ֣הוּ דַ֔עַת}	14aC	{and would have taught him knowledge,}
וְדֶ֥רֶךְ תְּבוּנ֖וֹת יוֹדִיעֶֽנּוּ׃	14aD	and would have made known to him the way of deep understanding?

≠ Masoretic verse.
Separation ↑: major division marker in the textual tradition; inter-

rogative pronoun; swapping (subject); swapping (object).
Separation ↓: major division markers in the textual tradition; interrogative pronoun; repetitive verse-line parallelism; swapping (object).
Strophe parallelism: מי || מי; עצה || יעץ; ידע || ידע; ־ו || ־ו; עצה || תבונה; grammatical parallelism.
Discussion: The very strong paralellistic ties between v. 13 and v. 14 argue in favour of combining the two verses into one strophe. This solution was not open to 𝔐 because it divided v. 14 into two bicola. This is not necessary if v. 14 is read as a tricolon or, if one prefers to maintain v. 14aC, a quadrocolon. The circumstance that $\mathfrak{G}^{A}$ has major division markers both after v. 12 and v. 14 suggests that it saw vv. 13–14 as a unit.

STROPHE B.ii.1 (Isa. 40:15)

הֵן גּוֹיִם֙ כְּמַר מִדְּלִי	15aA	Behold, the nations are like a drop from a bucket,
וּכְשַׁחַק מֹאזְנַיִם נֶחְשָׁבוּ	15aB	and are accounted as particles of dust on a balance.
הֵן אִיִּים כַּדַּק יִטּוֹל׃	15bA	Behold, he lifts up the islands like powder.

= Masoretic verse.
Separation ↑: major division markers in the textual tradition; deictic particle(s); repetitive verse-line parallelism; swapping (subject); swapping (adjunct).
Separation ↓: deictic particle(s); swapping (object; adjunct).
Strophe parallelism: הן || הן; גוי || אי; כ || כ; שחק || דק (unique).
Discussion: Although it would be possible to read this strophe as a tricolon, we prefer a bicolon plus a unicolon.[4]

STROPHE B.ii.2 (Isa. 40:16)

וּלְבָנוֹן אֵין דֵּי בָּעֵר	16aA	And the Lebanon will not suffice for fuel,
וְחַיָּתוֹ אֵין דֵּי עוֹלָה׃	16aB	and its beasts will not suffice for a burnt offering.

= Masoretic verse.
Separation ↑: repetitive verse-line parallelism. swapping (subject).
Separation ↓: major division markers in the textual tradition.
Strophe parallelism: None (one verse-line).

STROPHE B.ii.3 (Isa. 40:17)

כָּל־הַגּוֹיִם כְּאַיִן נֶגְדּוֹ	17aA	All nations are as nothing to him,

[4]See p. 46.

מֵאֶ֥פֶס וָתֹ֖הוּ נֶחְשְׁבוּ־לֽוֹ׃	17aB	they are accounted by him less than non-existent and void.

= Masoretic verse.
Separation ↑: major division markers in the textual tradition; swapping (adjunct).
Separation ↓: major division markers in the textual tradition.
Strophe parallelism: None (one verse-line).

STROPHE B.iii.1 (Isa. 40:18–19)

וְאֶל־מִ֖י תְּדַמְּי֣וּן אֵ֑ל	18aA	And to whom you would liken God?
וּמַה־דְּמ֖וּת תַּ֥עַרְכוּ לֽוֹ׃	18aB	And which likeness would you arrange for him?
הַפֶּ֙סֶל֙ נָסַ֣ךְ חָרָ֔שׁ	19aA	An idol? A craftsman casts it,
וְצֹרֵ֖ף בַּזָּהָ֣ב יְרַקְּעֶ֑נּוּ	19aB	and the goldsmith overlays it with gold,
וּרְתֻק֥וֹת כֶּ֖סֶף צוֹרֵֽף׃	19aC	and with soldering of a goldsmith's silver.

≠ Masoretic verse.
Separation ↑: major division markers in the textual tradition; interrogative pronouns.
Separation ↓: major division marker in the textual tradition; swapping (subject); swapping (object); swapping (adjunct).
Strophe parallelism: אל ‖ פסל.
Discussion: The parallelism between the two verses is rather weak, but from the viewpoint of content they supplement each other. The circumstance that at least 𝔊^{A} seems to have regarded vv. 18-19 as a unit emboldens us to deviate from 𝔐.

STROPHE B.iii.2 (Isa. 40:20)

הַֽמְסֻכָּ֣ן* תְּרוּמָ֔ה	20aA	He who shapes the pedestal
עֵ֥ץ לֹֽא־יִרְקַ֖ב יִבְחָ֑ר	20aB	chooses wood that does not rot.
חָרָ֤שׁ חָכָם֙ יְבַקֶּשׁ־ל֔וֹ	20bA	He seeks out a skilful craftsman
לְהָכִ֥ין פֶּ֖סֶל לֹ֥א יִמּֽוֹט׃	20bB	to set up an idol that will not topple.

= Masoretic verse.
Separation ↑: major division marker in the textual tradition; swapping (subject); swapping (object).
Separation ↓: major division markers in the textual tradition; swapping (object).
Strophe parallelism: סכן ‖ חרש (restored; unique); עץ ‖ פסל (unique).[5]

[5] Break-up of the phrase עץ פסל, cf. Isa. 45:20.

STROPHE B.iv.1 (Isa. 40:21)

הֲלוֹא תֵדְעוּ הֲלוֹא תִשְׁמָעוּ	21aA	Don't you know? Didn't you hear?
הֲלוֹא הֻגַּד מֵרֹאשׁ לָכֶם	21aB	Has it not been told to you from the beginning?
הֲלוֹא הֲבִינֹתֶם מוֹסְדוֹת הָאָרֶץ׃	21aC	Don't you understand the foundations of the earth?

= Masoretic verse.
Separation ↑: major division markers in the textual tradition; deictic particle(s); repetitive verse-line parallelism.
Separation ↓: major division marker in the textual tradition; for the rest identical with the above.
Strophe parallelism: None (one verse-line).
Discussion: One may hesitate between a bicolon plus a unicolon (like v. 15), or a tricolon. We prefer the latter option because of the strong verse-line parallelism.[6]

STROPHE B.iv.2 (Isa. 40:22)

הַיֹּשֵׁב עַל־חוּג הָאָרֶץ	22aA	It is he who is dwelling on the circle of the earth
וְיֹשְׁבֶיהָ כַּחֲגָבִים	22aB	and its dwellers are like grasshoppers.
הַנּוֹטֶה כַדֹּק שָׁמַיִם	22bA	It is he who stretches out the heavens like a membrane
וַיִּמְתָּחֵם כָּאֹהֶל לָשָׁבֶת׃	22bB	and spreads them like a tent to dwell in.

= Masoretic verse.
Separation ↑: major division marker in the textual tradition; repetitive verse-line parallelism.
Separation ↓: major division marker in the textual tradition; repetitive verse-line parallelism; swapping (adjunct).
Strophe parallelism: ישב ‖ ישב; כ ‖ כ; ארץ ‖ שמים; grammatical parallelism.

STROPHE B.v.1 (Isa. 40:23)

הַנּוֹתֵן רוֹזְנִים לְאָיִן	23aA	It is he who is bringing princes to nothing,
שֹׁפְטֵי אֶרֶץ כַּתֹּהוּ עָשָׂה׃	23aB	he makes the judges of the earth void.

= Masoretic verse.
Separation ↑: major division marker in the textual tradition; swapping (object); swapping (adjunct).
Separation ↓: None (one verse-line).
Strophe parallelism: None (one verse-line).

---

[6]See p. 47.

Discussion: There is hardly room for a different choice but to follow 𝔐. Strophes consisting of only one verse are by no means exceptional.[7]

STROPHE B.v.2 (Isa. 40:24)

אַף בַּל־נִטָּעוּ אַף בַּל־זֹרָעוּ	24aA	Scarcely are they planted, scarcely are they sown,
אַף בַּל־שֹׁרֵשׁ בָּאָרֶץ גִּזְעָם	24aB	scarcely their stem has rooted in the earth,
וְגַם־נָשַׁף בָּהֶם וַיִּבָשׁוּ	24bA	when he blows upon them, and they wither,
וּסְעָרָה כַּקַּשׁ תִּשָּׂאֵם׃	24bB	and the storm carries them off like chaff.

= Masoretic verse.
Separation ↑: deictic particle(s); repetitive verse-line parallelism; swapping (adjunct).
Separation ↓: major division markers in the textual tradition; deictic particle(s); swapping (subject); swapping (adjunct).
Strophe parallelism: אף || גם; ־ם || ־ם.
Discussion: Even though there is little parallelism between the two verses, the delimitation of the strophe is not in doubt because the sentence runs on through and the agricultural imagery forms a strong bond.

STROPHE C.i.1 (Isa. 40:25)

וְאֶל־מִי תְדַמְּיוּנִי וְאֶשְׁוֶה	25aA	And to whom will you liken me, that I would be his equal?
יֹאמַר קָדוֹשׁ׃	25aB	says the Holy One.

= Masoretic verse.
Separation ↑: major division markers in the textual tradition; interrogative pronoun; marker of direct speech; swapping (adjunct).
Separation ↓: None (one verse-line).
Strophe parallelism: None (one verse-line).
Discussion: See our remarks on v. 23.

STROPHE C.i.2 (Isa. 40:26)

שְׂאוּ־מָרוֹם עֵינֵיכֶם וּרְאוּ	26aA	Lift up your eyes on high, and see:
מִי־בָרָא אֵלֶּה	26aB	Who did create those over there?
הַמּוֹצִיא בְמִסְפָּר צְבָאָם	26aC	He who brings out their army in number!
לְכֻלָּם בְּשֵׁם יִקְרָא	26bA	All of them he calls by name;
מֵרֹב אוֹנִים וְאַמִּיץ כֹּחַ	26bB	because of him who is great in forces and mighty of strength,
אִישׁ לֹא נֶעְדָּר׃	26bC	not one of them is missing.

[7] See p. 645.

= Masoretic verse.
Separation ↑: demonstrative pronoun; interrogative pronoun; imperative(s); swapping (adjunct).
Separation ↓: major division markers in the textual tradition; swapping (subject); swapping (adjunct).
Strophe parallelism: ם־ || ם־; מספר || רב.

STROPHE C.ii.1 (Isa. 40:27)

לָ֤מָּה תֹאמַר֙ יַֽעֲקֹ֔ב	27aA	Why do you say, O Jacob,
וּתְדַבֵּ֖ר יִשְׂרָאֵ֑ל	27aB	and speak, O Israel:
נִסְתְּרָ֤ה דַרְכִּי֙ מֵֽיְהוָ֔ה	27bA	"My way is hidden from the LORD,
וּמֵאֱלֹהַ֖י מִשְׁפָּטִ֥י יַֽעֲבֽוֹר׃	27bB	and my right is neglected by my God?"

= Masoretic verse.
Separation ↑: major division markers in the textual tradition; interrogative pronoun; vocative; marker of direct speech.
Separation ↓: major division marker in the textual tradition; repetitive verse-line parallelism; swapping (subject); swapping (adjunct).
Strophe parallelism: יעקב || ישׂראל; יהוה || אלהים.

STROPHE C.ii.2 (Isa. 40:28)

הֲל֨וֹא יָדַ֜עְתָּ אִם־לֹ֣א שָׁמַ֗עְתָּ	28aA	Don't you know? Or didn't you hear?
אֱלֹהֵ֨י עוֹלָ֤ם ׀ יְהוָה֙	28aB	The LORD is a God of eternity,
בּוֹרֵא֙ קְצ֣וֹת הָאָ֔רֶץ	28aC	the Creator of the ends of the earth.
לֹ֥א יִיעַ֖ף וְלֹ֣א יִיגָ֑ע	28bA	He does not become exhausted and does not grow weary,
אֵ֥ין חֵ֖קֶר לִתְבוּנָתֽוֹ׃	28bB	it is impossible to trace his understanding.

= Masoretic verse.
Separation ↑: major division marker in the textual tradition; deictic particle(s); swapping (subject).
Separation ↓: major division marker in the textual tradition.
Strophe parallelism: הלוא || לא.
Discussion: Despite the lack of clear markers of separation downwards and the rather meagre strophe parallelism, the logical progression of thought renders the delimitation certain.

STROPHE C.iii.1 (Isa. 40:29)

נֹתֵ֥ן לַיָּעֵ֖ף כֹּ֑חַ	29aA	He is giving strength to the exhausted,
וּלְאֵ֥ין אוֹנִ֖ים עָצְמָ֥ה יַרְבֶּֽה׃	29aB	and increases the vigour of him who has no force left.

= Masoretic verse.

Separation ↑: major division marker in the textual tradition; repetitive verse-line parallelism; swapping (object); swapping (adjunct).
Separation ↓: None (one verse-line).
Strophe parallelism: None (one verse-line).
Discussion: One might consider the possibility to join v. 29 either to v. 28b or to v. 30. In both cases the parallelism would be a strong argument in favour of such a move. However, because the sentence runs on in v. 31, v. 30 must be regarded as a new beginning. Moreover, v. 28b speaks of the strength of God himself as the Creator, whereas v. 29 focuses on his gift of strength to the exhausted. Therefore it seems best to follow the lead of 𝔐 and keep v. 29 separate.

STROPHE C.iii.2 (Isa. 40:30)

וְיִעֲפוּ נְעָרִים וְיִגָעוּ	30aA	Yes, youths may become exhausted and grow weary,
וּבַחוּרִים כָּשׁוֹל יִכָּשֵׁלוּ׃	30aB	and young men may stagger terribly,

= Masoretic verse.
Separation ↑: paronomasia; swapping (subject).
Separation ↓: major division marker in the textual tradition.
Strophe parallelism: None (one verse-line).
Discussion: Again we encounter a strophe consisting of only one bicolon. The extra Petuḥa 𝔊^{S} has after נערים is obviously an error whereas its protuding line, Setuma and capital letter after תכשלו is supported by 𝔊^{Q}. See also our comment to v. 29.

STROPHE C.iii.3 (Isa. 40:31)

וְקוֹיֵ יְהוָה יַחֲלִיפוּ כֹחַ	31aA	but those waiting for the LORD will renew their strength,
יַעֲלוּ אֵבֶר כַּנְּשָׁרִים	31aB	they will grow new pinions, like eagles.
יָרוּצוּ וְלֹא יִיגָעוּ	31bA	They will run and will not grow weary,
יֵלְכוּ וְלֹא יִיעָפוּ׃	31bB	they will walk and will not become exhausted.

= Masoretic verse.
Separation ↑: major division markers in the textual tradition; swapping (subject).
Separation ↓: major division markers in the textual tradition; repetitive verse-line parallelism.
Strophe parallelism: קוה || רוץ (antithetical; unique); חלף כח || יגע and יעף (antithetical); grammatical parallelism.

2.5 Isaiah 40 – Delimitation of Canticles

CANTICLE A.i (40:1–2)

Separation ↑: major division markers in the textual tradition; thematic discontinuity as compared to chapter 39; change of subject.
Separation ↓: major division markers in the textual tradition.
Canticle parallelism: אלהים || יהוה (inclusion); לב || יד; ־ה || ־ה (f.s.) (concatenation).[1]
Strophes linked by on-running sentence (enjambment).
Thematic unity: yes. The second strophe describes why it is time comfort Jerusalem.

CANTICLE A.ii (40:3–5)

Separation ↑: major division markers in the textual tradition; thematic discontinuity.
Separation ↓: major division markers in the textual tradition.
Canticle parallelism: קול || פה (inclusion); קרא || דבר (inclusion); מדבר || הר; יהוה || יהוה (responsion and inclusion); ישר || מישור (root parallelism; responsion); כל || כל (inclusion).
Thematic unity: yes. A.ii.1 and A.ii.2 describe how a road must be prepared for the coming of the LORD. All apparent difficulties will disappear as soon as the work starts. A.ii.3 describes how the glory of the LORD will appear when the road is ready. The description as a whole ostensibly hints at the journey through the desert during the first Exodus.

CANTICLE A.iii (40:6–8)

Separation ↑: major division markers in the textual tradition; thematic discontinuity: a new speaker.
Separation ↓: major division markers in the textual tradition.
Canticle parallelism: קול || דבר(inclusion); חציר || חציר (unique; concatenation/responsion); ציץ || ציץ (unique; concatenation/responsion).
Strophes linked by on-running direct speech.
Thematic unity: yes.
Discussion: Because 𝔊[A] has major dividers after v. 5 and v. 8, the division markers after v. 6 which are not supported by any other witness may be interpreted as a delimiting the strophe.

[1] With regard to the strophic division see p. 51.

CANTICLE A.iv (40:9)

Separation ↑: major division markers in the textual tradition; thematic discontinuity; change of subject.
Separation ↓: major division markers in $\mathfrak{G}^{A}$.
Canticle parallelism: רום Hif. || רום Hif. (concatenation); ירושלם || יהודה (responsion); grammatical parallelism (imperatives).
Thematic unity: yes.
Discussion: For the reasons to divide this verse into two strophes see 2.4. The testimony for the separation downwards is weak. The major division markers in $\mathfrak{G}^{A}$ might just as well be regarded as nothing but strophe markers. However, because $\mathfrak{G}^{A}$ has a major division after v. 11, but not after v. 10, one might just as well cite its testimony in support of a canticle divider. Moreover, the change of subject in v. 10 as well as the strong bonds between v. 10 and v. 11 (see below) argue in favour of a division at this point.

CANTICLE A.v (40:10–11)

Separation ↑: major division markers in $\mathfrak{G}^{A}$; change of subject.
Separation ↓: major division markers in the textual tradition.
Canticle parallelism: זרוע || זרוע (responsion); משל || רעה (responsion).
Thematic unity: yes. The metaphors of v. 10b can only be understood on the basis of the metaphor of the shepherd in v. 11.[2]

CANTICLE B.i (40:12–14)

Separation ↑: major division markers in the textual tradition; thematic discontinuity; change of subject.
Separation ↓: major division markers in $\mathfrak{G}^{SA}$ (colon in $\mathfrak{G}^{S}$).
Canticle parallelism: מי || מי || מי (responsion/inclusion); תכן || תכן (responsion).
Thematic unity: yes. Both strophes describe the incomparable deity.
Discussion: With regard to $\mathfrak{G}^{A}$ after v. 12bB see our comment on A.iii. Again the division after v. 14 is rather weak, but the change of subject and the high level of coherence in the next canticle leave little room for a different caesura.

CANTICLE B.ii (40:15–17)

Separation ↑: major division markers in the textual tradition; thematic discontinuity – now the nations come into the picture; change of subject.

[2]See p. 19, n. 7.

Separation ↓: major division markers in the textual tradition.
Canticle parallelism: גוי || גוי (responsion/inclusion); כ || כ; אין אין (responsion); חשׁב || חשׁב (responsion/inclusion); חיה || גוי.
Thematic unity: yes. All strophes deal with the total insignificance of the nations. Perhaps one might wonder about the suitability of v. 16, but see below.
Discussion: In our opinion the Setuma (1Q^{a} Petuḥa) after v. 16 happened to land in the wrong place. The other ancient witnesses preserved the right tradition in placing their major dividers after v. 17. Verse 16 becomes understandable only if it is read in combination with v. 17 which explains the חיתו as כל־הגוים, making use of the standard parallelism between the two found in Ezekiel. If it is the will of God, all nations will become a huge sacrifice on the altar of the (then) densely forested Lebanon.

CANTICLE B.iii (40:18–20)

Separation ↑: major division markers in the textual tradition; thematic discontinuity; change of subject.
Separation ↓: major division markers in the textual tradition.
Canticle parallelism: חרשׁ || חרשׁ (unique; responsion); פסל || פסל (unique; responsion).
Thematic unity: yes. Both strophes deal with the futility of making idols.
Discussion: The independent testimony of two medieval codices and 𝔊^{S} strengthens the case for a canticle break at this point. With regard to the division markers in 𝔊^{A} after v. 19, they might be either an error, anticipating the break after v. 20, or might mark the delimitation of the strophe again (see our comment on A.iii).

CANTICLE B.iv (40:21–22)

Separation ↑: major division markers in the textual tradition; thematic discontinuity; change of subject.
Separation ↓: major division markers in 𝔊^{A}.
Canticle parallelism: ארץ || ארץ (concatenation); ארץ || שׁמים (responsion).
Thematic unity: yes. Both strophes describe God's work of creation in the beginning.
Discussion: Again the borderline between this canticle and the next is weakly attested. Because 𝔊^{A} also marks the end of v. 21 its division might well be a remnant of a strophe division. Moreover, the active participles of v. 22 are continued in v. 23 and this may have been a

reason for most ancient witnesses to omit major division markers after v.23. Yet vv. 23-24 contain a different theme, a conclusion based on the preceding canticle: because God is the almighty creator for whom those dwelling on earth are but tiny insects (B.iv), even mighty rulers on earth are nothing to him (B.v). That they are made into תהו (v. 23aB) indicates that he is contemplating new creative acts out of chaos (cf. Gen. 1:2). So there are definite links between the canticles, but they are on the higher level of the sub-canto rather than on the canticle level.

CANTICLE B.v (40:23–24)

Separation ↑: major division markers in $\mathfrak{G}^{A}$; some thematic discontinuity (see above).
Separation ↓: major division markers in the textual tradition.
Canticle parallelism: אין || קש (inclusion); ארץ || ארץ (see above).
Thematic unity: yes. Both strophes deal with the sorry fate of the rulers of the world. The suffixes of v. 24 connect this verse with the preceding.

CANTICLE C.i (40:25–26)

Separation ↑: major division markers in the textual tradition; thematic discontinuity; change of subject.
Separation ↓: major division markers in the textual tradition.
Canticle parallelism: מי || מי (responsion); קדוש || איש (antithetical; inclusion).
Thematic unity: yes. The argument for the incomparability of God derived from v. 26 can only be understood as such in the light of v. 25.

CANTICLE C.ii (40:27–28)

Separation ↑: major division markers in the textual tradition; change of subject.
Separation ↓: major division markers in $\mathfrak{G}^{A}$.
Canticle parallelism: אמר || ידע (responsion); דבר || שמע (responsion); אלהים || אלהים.
Thematic unity: yes. V. 28 provides an answer to v. 27. The two strophes are connected by the second person masculine singular.
Discussion: $\mathfrak{G}^{S}$ has a colon after v. 27 (no capital and no line projecting into the margin). If it may be regarded as a major division marker, it is probably a marking of a strophe end.

The borderline between this and the next canticle is attested by $\mathfrak{G}^{A}$ only. Moreover, the concatenation by means of the verb יעף (v. 28bA) and the adjective יעף (v. 29aA) as well as the lack of a change of subject in v. 29 might suggest that all these strophes belong to the same canticle. However, all canticles belonging to sub-canto C speak of the LORD's strength and therefore the argument is not conclusive. In our opinion v. 29 develops the idea that man may derive strength from the Almighty and in this sense makes a new start.

CANTICLE C.iii (40:29–31)

Separation ↑: major division markers in $\mathfrak{G}^{A}$; thematic discontinuity (focus on mankind, see above).
Separation ↓: major division markers in the textual tradition.
Canticle parallelism: יעף || יעף (unique; responsion/inclusion); כח || כח (responsion); יגע || יגע (inclusion); כשל || רוץ (responsion).
Strophes 2 and 3 linked by on-running sentence (enjambment).
Thematic unity: yes. All three strophes deal with the overcoming of the feeling of tiredness.
Discussion: See with regard to the delimitation of the upper limit of this canticle our discussion of the delimitation of the preceding canticle. The lower limit is attested abundantly by all ancient witnesses.

The major division markers found in and after v. 30 in $\mathfrak{G}^{S}$ and $\mathfrak{G}^{Q}$ are placed at such an illogical point that they cannot have been intended as periope . Probably they anticipated the major division after v. 31.

2.6 Isaiah 40 – Delimitation of Macrostructure

The overall structure of Isaiah 40 appears to be regular for the first two sub-canto's, but not for the last one.

SUB-CANTOS	CANTICLES	STROPHES
A	5	11 (2+3+2+2+2)
B	5	11 (2+3+2+2+2)
C	3	7 (2+2+3)

Distant parallelism connecting the canticles of **sub-canto A**:
עם (v. 1aA – A.i) || עם (v. 7bA – A.iii); אמר (v. 2aA – A.i) || אמר (v. 6aA, 6aB – A.iii) || אמר (v. 9cB – A.iv); אלהיכם (v. 1aB – A.i) || אלהינו (v. 3bB – A.ii) || אלהינו (v. 8aC – A.iii) אלהיכם (v. 9cC – A.iv); דבר (v. 2aA – A.i) || דבר (v. 5bB – A.ii) || דבר (noun; v. 8aC – A.iii); ירושלם (v. 2aA – A.i) || ירושלם (v. 9bB – A.iv); קרא (v. 2aB – A.i) || קרא (v.

3aA – A.ii) || קרא (v. 6aA, 6aB – A.iii); קול (v. 3aA – A.ii) || קול (v. 6aA – A.iii) – קול (v. 9bA – A.iv); all canticles but A.v start with an imperative.

Of course we might mention more here (כי, כל, הנה, בשר), but the above will suffice to make clear that the canticles A.i–A.v belong together and that reestablishment of spoken communication is the main theme of sub-canto A. A nice alternation of sub-themes may be observed between the canticles,

CANTICLE	THEME
A.i	Exhortation to shake off despair.
A.ii	Exhortation to make a start oneself (new Exodus) – God will appear.
A.iii	Exhortation to shake off despair.
A.iv	Exhortation to make a start oneself – God will appear.
A.v	God will lead his people like a flock (new Exodus).

Distant parallelism connecting the canticles of **sub-canto B**:
שמים (v. 12aB – A.i) || שמים (v. 22bA – B.iv); ארץ (v. 12aC – B.i) || ארץ (vv. 21aC, 22aA – B.iv) || ארץ (vv. 23aB, 24aB – B.v); ידע (vv. 13aB, 14aD – B.i) || ידע (v. 21aA – B.iv); בין (v. 14aA – B.i) || בין (v. 21aC – B.iv); provocative questions head B.i, B.iii, B.iv.

The main argument of sub-canto B seeks to rebut the objection of certain desperate Israelites that no one would be able to defeat the Babylonians and their allies. The coherence of the sub-canto can hardly be denied,

CANTICLE	THEME
B.i	Who can fathom the thoughts of the Creator to whom the mountains were dust?
B.ii	Also mighty nations are nothing but dust to him, raw material for a new creation.
B.iii	It is ridiculous to compare the incomparable Creator to anything made by man.
B.iv	The knowledge of the incomparable Creator should have convinced Israel of the insignificance of earthlings.
B.v	And therefore of his power to blow away mighty rulers like chaff.

Distant parallelism connecting the canticles of **sub-canto C**:
ברא (v. 26aB – C.i) || ברא (v. 28aC – C.ii); רב (v. 26bB – C.i) || רבה (v.

29aB – C.iii); אין (v. 26bB – C.i) || אין (v. 29aB – C.iii); כח (v. 26bB – C.i) || כח (v. 29aA – C.iii); יעף (v. 28bA – C.ii) || יעף (vv. 29aA, 30aA, 31bB – C.iii); יגע (v. 28bA – C.ii) || יגע (vv. 30aA, 31bA – C.iii); C.i and C.ii start with provocative questions.

How can the weary Israelites find the strength to make a new start themselves and go the road of a second Exodus? This is the question sub-canto C addresses. The parallelistic ties between the three canticles are strong enough to warrant the assumption that they belong together.

CANTICLE	THEME
C.i	The incomparable Creator is strong enough to lead out the heavenly armies.
C.ii	Because the Creator cannot grow tired, Israel need not despair nor become impatient.
C.iii	This God can give them the strength to embark upon their new Exodus.

As this overview of the sub-cantos shows, the last one comes back to certain themes of the first one. Yet the middle one is far from superfluous. It provides the main argument of the whole canto: with the incomparable Creator nothing is impossible. This is underscored by almost refrain-like repetitions (v. 14 || v. 21 || v. 28a; vv. 15, 17 || v. 23; v. 18 || v. 25). Nobody in heaven or earth can teach God what is the right way to follow (v. 14) and Israel has to learn this lesson (v. 27). But waiting for the LORD (v. 31aA) is by no means a state of apathic inactivity (contrast vv. 6-7a, 27b, 30). Israel itself has to make a new start in preparing the road for the LORD (v. 3), announcing the good news of his advent (v. 9) and finding new strength (vv. 9bA, 31a) – not in themselves, but in their God (v. 29). If they have the courage to make this new start, all difficulties on the road will disappear miraculously (vv. 4, 15-17, 23-24, 31b). In our opinion the macrostructure is coherent enough to defend the unity of the chapter (canto) in its present form. But obviously this merely serves to demonstrate that the final author or redactor produced a well-devised composition for which he may have made use of different materials he had at his disposal.

Chapter 3

The Structure of Isaiah 41

3.1 Isaiah 41: Text and Translation

פ <ס> – 1𝔔[a] – 𝔊[SBAQ] – 𝔖[abcde] ____________

A.i.1 (Isa. 41:1)

הַחֲרִישׁוּ אֵלַי אִיִּים	1aA	Be silent to me, islands,
וּלְאֻמִּים יַחֲלִיפוּ כֹחַ	1aB	and let the nations renew their strength,
יִגְּשׁוּ אָז יְדַבֵּרוּ	1bA	let them draw near, then let them speak up,
יַחְדָּו לַמִּשְׁפָּט נִקְרָבָה׃	1bB	let us go to court together.

{<פ>𝔊[AQ]}

A.i.2 (Isa. 41:2a–b)

מִי הֵעִיר מִמִּזְרָח צֶדֶק	2aA	Who wakes up justice from the east,
{𝔊[A]} *יִקְרָאֵהוּ לְרַגְלָיו	2aB	calls it to his feet?[1]
יִתֵּן לְפָנָיו גּוֹיִם	2bA	He puts nations before him,
וּמְלָכִים יֹרד*	2bB	and makes kings step down.[2]

A.i.3 (Isa. 41:2c–3)

יִתֵּן כֶּעָפָר חַרְבּוֹ	2cA	His sword makes like dust,
כְּקַשׁ נִדָּף קַשְׁתּוֹ׃	2cB	his bow (makes) like dispersed chaff.
יִרְדְּפֵם {𝔊[A]} יַעֲבוֹר שָׁלוֹם	3aA	He pursues them, passes on safely,
אֹרַח בְּרַגְלָיו לֹא יָבוֹא׃	3aB	does not go the road on foot.[3]

𝔊[S] – 𝔖[ae] ....

[1]We assume ellipsis of מי. With regard to the division into cola see p. 75. The expression לרגלו (plural, see 𝔊) should be understood as following in obedience, cf. Gen. 30:30; Hab. 3:5; Job 18:11. See also v. 25a below. It is God who commands justice to appear from the East, and obviously this is a reference to the rising sun, since times immemorial the god or symbol of justice because it exposes all sinister activities on earth. For the OT see Mal. 3:20 (tr. 4:2); Ps. 37:6. "Justice", a god in the Canaanite world, is subordinate to the Lord in the OT and has to obey his commands, cf. Ps. 85:14; J.C. de Moor, *The Rise of Yahwism*, Leuven [2]1997, 251. This is a proper introduction to the following lawsuit.

Of course, it is by no means excluded that this "sun of justice" is meant as a personification of Cyrus. Isa. 41:25 הַעִירוֹתִי מִצָּפוֹן וַיַּאת מִמִּזְרַח־שֶׁמֶשׁ יִקְרָא בִשְׁמִי even suggests that this is the intention of the prophet. See also Isa. 45:13 אָנֹכִי הַעִירֹתִהוּ בְצֶדֶק.

[2]The Hiphil jussive ירד rests on rabbinic exegesis (𝔗; bSanh., 108b; Gen. R., XLIII.3) and can not be defended by invoking the Qal in 45:1 (against Koole, 90). We suppose that a defective spelling, even attested by 1𝔔[a]'s partial emendation ירד = יוריד, caused a problem which already in Antiquity was solved in different ways.

[3]Meaning he was carried over difficult passages, as campaigning oriental rulers were.

A.ii.1 (Isa. 41:4)

מִי־פָעַל וְעָשָׂה	4aA	Who has worked and made (this)?
{$\mathfrak{G}^{SA}$} קֹרֵא הַדֹּרוֹת מֵרֹאשׁ	4aB	He who is calling the generations from the beginning!
אֲנִי יְהוָה רִאשׁוֹן	4bA	I, the LORD am the First,
וְאֶת־אַחֲרֹנִים אֲנִי־הוּא׃{<פ>}	4bB	and with the last ones I am the same One.

A.ii.2 (Isa. 41:5–6)

רָאוּ אִיִּים וְיִירָאוּ	5aA	The islands see (it) and fear,[4]
קְצוֹת הָאָרֶץ יֶחֱרָדוּ	5aB	the ends of the earth tremble,
קָרְבוּ וַיֶּאֱתָיוּן׃	5aC	they come near and approach.
אִישׁ אֶת־רֵעֵהוּ יַעְזֹרוּ	6aA	Each man helps his friend,
וּלְאָחִיו יֹאמַר חֲזָק׃	6aB	and speaks to his brother: "Be strong!"

{<ס>$\mathfrak{G}^{A}$}

A.ii.3 (Isa. 41:7)

וַיְחַזֵּק חָרָשׁ אֶת־צֹרֵף	7aA	The craftsman strengthens the goldsmith,
מַחֲלִיק פַּטִּישׁ אֶת־הוֹלֶם פָּעַם	7aB	the sheet metal worker the blacksmith,
אֹמֵר לַדֶּבֶק טוֹב הוּא	7bA	saying of the soldering: "It is good!",
וַיְחַזְּקֵהוּ בְמַסְמְרִים לֹא יִמּוֹט׃	7bB	and he strengthens it with nails so that it will not topple.

ס <פ> – $1\mathfrak{Q}^{a}$ – $\mathfrak{G}^{SBAQ}$ – ς^{d} ______________________________________

B.i.1 (Isa. 41:8)

וְאַתָּה יִשְׂרָאֵל עַבְדִּי	8aA	But you, O Israel, my servant,
יַעֲקֹב אֲשֶׁר בְּחַרְתִּיךָ	8aB	Jacob, whom I have chosen,
זֶרַע אַבְרָהָם אֹהֲבִי׃	8aC	seed of Abraham, my friend,

B.i.2 (Isa. 41:9)

אֲשֶׁר הֶחֱזַקְתִּיךָ מִקְצוֹת הָאָרֶץ	9aA	(you), whom I grasped from the ends of the earth,
וּמֵאֲצִילֶיהָ קְרָאתִיךָ	9aB	and whom I called from its farthest corners,
וָאֹמַר לְךָ עַבְדִּי־אַתָּה	9bA	you, to whom I said: You are my servant,
בְּחַרְתִּיךָ וְלֹא מְאַסְתִּיךָ׃	9bB	I have chosen you and have not rejected you,

B.i.3 (Isa. 41:10)

אַל־תִּירָא כִּי עִמְּךָ־אָנִי	10aA	Do not fear, for I am with you,
אַל־תִּשְׁתָּע כִּי־אֲנִי אֱלֹהֶיךָ	10aB	do not be afraid, for I am your God.
אִמַּצְתִּיךָ אַף־עֲזַרְתִּיךָ	10bA	I do strengthen you, and I do help you too,
אַף־תְּמַכְתִּיךָ בִּימִין צִדְקִי׃	10bB	I do hold you, with the right hand of my justice.

$\mathfrak{G}^{SAQ}$ . . . .

[4]The alternation of perfects, imperfects and inverted imperfects in Isa. 41:5-7 suggests a translation in the present tense which is also much more likely from the viewpoint of actuality. Compare also v. 5aC with v. 2aA. Cf. M.C.A. Korpel, J.C. de Moor, F. Sepmeijer, "Consistency with Regard to Tenses", see Abbreviations.

B.ii.1 (Isa. 41:11)

הֵן יֵבֹשׁוּ וְיִכָּלְמוּ	11aA	Behold, they will be ashamed and disgraced,
כֹּל הַנֶּחֱרִים בָּךְ	11aB	all who rage against you.
יִהְיוּ כְאַיִן וְיֹאבְדוּ	11bA	They will be as nothing and perish,
אַנְשֵׁי רִיבֶךָ׃	11bB	the men of your lawsuit.

B.ii.2 (Isa. 41:12)

תְּבַקְשֵׁם וְלֹא תִמְצָאֵם	12aA	You will search for them, but not find them,
אַנְשֵׁי מַצֻּתֶךָ	12aB	the men of your dispute.
יִהְיוּ כְאַיִן וּכְאֶפֶס	12bA	They will become as nothing and non-existent,
$\{\mathfrak{G}^{BA}\}$ אַנְשֵׁי מִלְחַמְתֶּךָ׃	12bB	the men of your warfare.

B.ii.3 (Isa. 41:13)

כִּי אֲנִי יְהוָה אֱלֹהֶיךָ	13aA	For I am the LORD your God,
מַחֲזִיק יְמִינֶךָ	13aB	who grasps your right hand,
הָאֹמֵר לְךָ אַל־תִּירָא	13bA	who says to you: Do not fear,
אֲנִי עֲזַרְתִּיךָ׃	13bB	it is I who helps you.

ס – $1\mathfrak{Q}^{a}$ – $\mathfrak{S}^{ac}$ . . . .

B.iii.1 (Isa. 41:14)

אַל־תִּירְאִי תּוֹלַעַת יַעֲקֹב	14aA	Do not fear, O worm Jacob,
רִמָּתֵי* יִשְׂרָאֵל	14aB	O maggot[5] Israel!
אֲנִי עֲזַרְתִּיךְ נְאֻם־יְהוָה	14bA	I am the one who helps you, declares the LORD,
$\{\mathfrak{G}^{SA}\mathfrak{S}^{b}\}$ וְגֹאֲלֵךְ קְדוֹשׁ יִשְׂרָאֵל׃	14bB	and your Redeemer is the Holy One of Israel.

B.iii.2 (Isa. 41:15)

הִנֵּה שַׂמְתִּיךְ לְמוֹרַג חָרוּץ חָדָשׁ	15aA	Behold, I make you into a sharp new threshing sledge,
בַּעַל פִּיפִיּוֹת	15aB	with many teeth.
תָּדוּשׁ הָרִים וְתָדֹק	15bA	You will thresh[6] mountains and crush (them),
וּגְבָעוֹת כַּמֹּץ תָּשִׂים׃	15bB	and hills you will make into chaff.

B.iii.3 (Isa. 41:16)

תִּזְרֵם וְרוּחַ תִּשָּׂאֵם	16aA	You will winnow them and the wind will take them up
$\{\mathfrak{G}^{SAQ}\}$ וּסְעָרָה תָּפִיץ אוֹתָם	16aB	and the gale will scatter them.

---

[5] $\mathfrak{M}$ defies the most ingenious solutions, e.g. Barthélemy, 287-8. Reading מֵתֵי "dead ones of" does not recommend itself either, despite the support of $\mathfrak{Q}^{a}$ מיתי, 1 MS^{Kenn}, α, θ and $\mathfrak{V}$. Many scholars emend מתי into רמת "maggot" (see Koole, 112). Because ב and ר resemble each other closely in the old Hebrew script, it is an attractive option to assume haplography and to interpret the י as a so-called paragogic *yod*, cf. Joüon, Muraoka §93l.

[6] Note the harsh transition from the feminine to the masculine singular – a common phenomenon in Second Isaiah.

וְאַתָּה֙ תָּגִ֣יל בַּֽיהוָ֔ה	16bA	And you will exult in the LORD,
בִּקְד֥וֹשׁ יִשְׂרָאֵ֖ל תִּתְהַלָּֽל׃	16bB	glory in the Holy One of Israel.

פ <ס> – 1$\mathfrak{Q}^{ab}$ – $\mathfrak{S}^{bde}$ ______________________

C.i.1 (Isa. 41:17)

הָעֲנִיִּ֨ים וְהָאֶבְיוֹנִ֜ים	17aA	The afflicted and poor
מְבַקְשִׁ֥ים מַ֙יִם֙ וָאַ֔יִן	17aB	are searching for water but there is none;
לְשׁוֹנָ֖ם בַּצָּמָ֣א נָשָׁ֑תָּה {$\mathfrak{G}^{SA}$}	17aC	their tongue is parched with thirst.
אֲנִ֤י יְהוָה֙ אֶעֱנֵ֔ם	17bA	I am the LORD, I will answer them,
אֱלֹהֵ֥י יִשְׂרָאֵ֖ל לֹ֥א אֶעֶזְבֵֽם׃	17bB	the God of Israel, I will not forsake them.

C.i.2 (Isa. 41:18)

אֶפְתַּ֤ח עַל־שְׁפָיִים֙ נְהָר֔וֹת	18aA	I will open rivers on the bare tracks,
וּבְת֥וֹךְ בְּקָע֖וֹת מַעְיָנ֑וֹת	18aB	and wells in the middle of the valleys.
אָשִׂ֤ים מִדְבָּר֙ לַאֲגַם־מַ֔יִם	18bA	I will make the desert a pool of water,
וְאֶ֥רֶץ צִיָּ֖ה לְמוֹצָ֥אֵי מָֽיִם׃	18bB	and the dry land springs of water.

C.i.3 (Isa. 41:19)

אֶתֵּ֤ן בַּמִּדְבָּר֙ אֶ֣רֶז שִׁטָּ֔ה	19aA	In the desert I will set cedars, acacias,
וַהֲדַ֖ס וְעֵ֣ץ שָׁ֑מֶן {<ס>}	19aB	and myrtles and pine-trees.
אָשִׂ֣ים בָּעֲרָבָ֗ה	19bA	In the bare valley I will put
בְּר֛וֹשׁ תִּדְהָ֥ר וּתְאַשּׁ֖וּר יַחְדָּֽו׃	19bB	junipers, ashes[7] and cypresses[8] together.

C.i.4 (Isa. 41:20)

לְמַ֨עַן יִרְא֤וּ וְיֵדְעוּ֙	20aA	That they may see and know,
וְיָשִׂ֣ימוּ וְיַשְׂכִּ֣ילוּ֙ יַחְדָּ֔ו	20aB	and may observe[9] and perceive together,
כִּ֥י יַד־יְהוָ֖ה עָ֣שְׂתָה זֹּ֑את	20bA	that the hand of the LORD has made this,
וּקְד֥וֹשׁ יִשְׂרָאֵ֖ל בְּרָאָֽהּ׃	20bB	and that the Holy One of Israel has created it.

פ <ס> – 1$\mathfrak{Q}^{ab}$ – $\mathfrak{G}^{SBAQ}$ – $\mathfrak{S}^{abe}$ ....

C.ii.1 (Isa. 41:21)

קָרְב֥וּ רִֽיבְכֶ֖ם	21aA	Bring near your case,
יֹאמַ֣ר יְהוָ֑ה	21aB	says the LORD,
הַגִּ֙ישׁוּ֙ עֲצֻמ֣וֹתֵיכֶ֔ם	21bA	bring closer your strong points,
יֹאמַ֖ר מֶ֥לֶךְ יַעֲקֹֽב׃ {$\mathfrak{G}^{A}$}	21bB	says the King of Jacob.

---

[7]Scholars differ on the determination of this tree. We follow J. Feliks, *Plant World of the Bible* (Hebr.), Ramat Gan 1968, 122-3.

[8]Feliks, *Plant World*, 84-5.

[9]Short for שׂים לב, Exod. 9:21; 1 Sam. 9:20; 2 Sam. 13:33, etc.

C.ii.2 (Isa. 41:22)

יַגִּישׁוּ וְיַגִּידוּ לָנוּ	22aA	Let them bring closer[10] and tell us
אֵת אֲשֶׁר תִּקְרֶינָה	22aB	what will happen.
הָרִאשֹׁנוֹת ׀ מָה הֵנָּה	22bA	The first things – what (do) they (mean)?[11]
הַגִּידוּ וְנָשִׂימָה לִבֵּנוּ וְנֵדְעָה אַחֲרִיתָן	22bB	Tell us, so that we may set our heart to it and know their outcome,
אוֹ הַבָּאוֹת הַשְׁמִיעֻנוּ׃	22bC	or cause us to hear the things to come.

C.ii.3 (Isa. 41:23)

הַגִּידוּ הָאֹתִיּוֹת לְאָחוֹר	23aA	Tell us the things to come in the future,
וְנֵדְעָה כִּי אֱלֹהִים אַתֶּם	23aB	that we may know that you are gods.
אַף־תֵּיטִיבוּ וְתָרֵעוּ	23bA	Do both something good and[12] something bad,
וְנִשְׁתָּעָה וְנִרָא* יַחְדָּו׃	23bB	that we will become afraid and will fear[13] together.

C.ii.4 (Isa. 41:24)

הֵן־אַתֶּם מֵאַיִן	24aA	Look, you are less than nothing,
וּפָעָלְכֶם מֵאָפַע	24aB	and your work is less than nought;[14]
תּוֹעֵבָה יִבְחַר בָּכֶם׃	24bA	an abomination is he who chooses you.

<פ> <ס> – $1\mathfrak{Q}^{a}$ – $\mathfrak{G}^{A}$ – $\mathfrak{S}^{ace}$ . . . .

C.iii.1 (Isa. 41:25)

הַעִירוֹתִי מִצָּפוֹן וַיַּאת	25aA	I wake up from the north him who is approaching,
מִמִּזְרַח־שֶׁמֶשׁ יִקְרָא בִשְׁמִי $\{\mathfrak{G}^{Q}\}$	25aB	from the east him who will call me[15] by name.

[10] The lively switch to a third person plural is normal and should not be corrected. Neither is there sufficient reason to read a Qal. Cf. Barthélemy, 290-1; De Waard, 158.

[11] See Gen. 21:29 מה הנה שבע כבשת האלה "What do those seven ewes mean?"

[12] As has been demonstrated by M.J. Mulder, "Filologische kanttekeningen bij Jes. 41:23b; 42:19b en 43:14b", in: *De Knecht: Studies rondom Deutero-Jesaja ... J.L. Koole*, Kampen 1978, 141-9 (141-2), the sequence אף ... ו must be understood as an emphatic copulative. Doing both good and bad is a demonstration of divine power; cf. Gen. 3:4; 2 Sam. 14:7; Jer. 10:5; Lam. 3:38, and De Moor, *ARTU*, 256, n. 216.

[13] Despite Barthélemy's learned defense of the Qere (Barthélemy, 292-3) the parallels Isa. 41:10 and Jer. 10:5 argue convincingly in favour of emending $\mathfrak{M}$ (with Koole, 132).

[14] We retain $\mathfrak{M}$, with Barthélemy, 293-5; Koole, 133.

[15] $\mathfrak{G}$, $1\mathfrak{Q}^{a}$ and $\mathfrak{T}$ all adopted different solutions for what they saw as problematical, namely that Cyrus would have invoked YHWH. This, however, was exactly what Second Isaiah expected, cf. Isa. 45:22-25. See also our comments on Isa. 41:2a above.

וְיָבֹא סְגָנִים כְּמוֹ־חֹמֶר	25bA	And when he comes,[16] governors (will become) as loam,
וּכְמוֹ יוֹצֵר יִרְמָס־טִיט׃ {$\mathfrak{G}^{A}$}	25bB	and as a potter he will tread the clay.

C.iii.2 (Isa. 41:26)

מִי־הִגִּיד מֵרֹאשׁ וְנֵדָעָה	26aA	Who told us from the beginning so that we might know,
וּמִלְּפָנִים וְנֹאמַר צַדִּיק	26aB	and beforehand, so that we might say: "He is right!"?
אַף אֵין־מַגִּיד	26bA	No, there was no one who was telling,
אַף אֵין מַשְׁמִיעַ	26bB	no, there was no one who let hear,
אַף אֵין־שֹׁמֵעַ אִמְרֵיכֶם׃ {ס<ס>$\mathfrak{G}^{SAQ}$}	26bC	no, there was no one who heard your words.

C.iii.3 (Isa. 41:27)

רִאשׁוֹן לְצִיּוֹן הִנֵּה הִנָּם	27aA	The First to Zion:[17] Look them over there!
וְלִירוּשָׁלִַם מְבַשֵּׂר אֶתֵּן׃	27aB	And to Jerusalem: I will give a herald of good tidings!

C.iii.4 (Isa. 41:28–29)

וְאֵרֶא וְאֵין אִישׁ	28aA	And when I look,[18] there is no man,[19]
וּמֵאֵלֶּה וְאֵין יוֹעֵץ	28aB	and with them, there is no counsellor,
וְאֶשְׁאָלֵם וְיָשִׁיבוּ דָבָר׃	28aC	that I could ask them and they would reply one word.
הֵן כֻּלָּם אָוֶן	29aA	Look, all of them are iniquity,[20]
אֶפֶס מַעֲשֵׂיהֶם	29aB	non-existent are their works
רוּחַ וָתֹהוּ נִסְכֵּיהֶם׃	29aC	wind and void their molten images.

פ <ס> – 1𝔔^{a} – $\mathfrak{G}^{SBAQ}$ – 𝔖^{abcde}

---

[16]Because ויאת reflects v. 23 האתיאות it is only natural to suppose that ויבא reflects v. 22 הבאות. So there is neither need to emend 𝔐 nor to assume an exceptional meaning for בוא here.

[17]Since ראשון apparently echoes מראש in v. 4aB (God), ראשון in v. 4bA, and in contrast to this, מראש v. 26aA (other gods), it is most likely that as in 44:6 and 48:12 it is a designation of God. Such a condensed way of introducing both addressee and sender of a message is fairly common in the ANE, cf. the Ugaritic letter KTU 2.15:1-2 as well as E. Ebeling, *Neubabylonische Briefe aus Uruk*, Berlin 1930, No. 194, 223, 246, 279, 293-295, 297, 338; E. Salonen, *Die Gruss- und Höflichkeitsformeln in babylonisch-assyrischen Briefen*, Helsinki 1967, 80. For a similar case see Isa. 47:4.

[18]A jussive before וְ may have conditional force, cf. König, *Syntax*, §193b.

[19]See our note on Isa. 50:2, p. 447, n. 1.

[20]1𝔔^{a} has אין, but the more difficult 𝔐 should be maintained. Cf. Barthélemy, 300-1; De Waard, 162-3.

3.2 Isaiah 41 – Delimitation of Cola

COLON 41:1aA:

הַחֲרִ֤ישׁוּ אֵלַי֙ אִיִּ֔ים 1aA Be silent to me, islands,

With: 𝔐 (5) – 𝔊^{SQ} – 𝔖^{abcde}

COLON 41:1aB:

וּלְאֻמִּ֖ים יַחֲלִ֣יפוּ כֹ֑חַ 1aB and let the nations renew their strength,

With: 𝔐 (2) – 𝔊^{SQ} – 𝔖^{abcde}

COLON 41:1bA:

יִגְּשׁוּ֙ אָ֣ז יְדַבֵּ֔רוּ 1bA let them draw near, then let them speak up,

With: 𝔐 (5) – 𝔊^{SQ} – 𝔖^{bcde}, 𝔖^{a} subordinate punctuation.
Colon parallelism: Possibly נגשׁ || דבר.

COLON 41:1bB:

יַחְדָּ֖ו לַמִּשְׁפָּ֥ט נִקְרָֽבָה׃ 1bB let us go to court together.

With: 𝔐 (1), major division markers in 1𝔔^{a} – 𝔊^{S}, major division markers in 𝔊^{AQ} – 𝔖^{abcde}

COLON 41:2aA:

מִ֤י הֵעִיר֙ מִמִּזְרָ֔ח צֶ֖דֶק 2aA Who wakes up justice from the east,

With: 𝔐 (8) – 𝔊^{SQ}
Discussion: 𝔐 has a major divider after מִמִּזְרָ֔ח (5) but is not supported by any of the ancient versions. Also 1𝔔^{a} which has ויקראהו (see also 𝔖) presupposes our division. 𝔖 has a major divider only after לרגלו which would result in a much too long colon. However, since ܙܕܩܘܬܐ which is the equivalent of צדק precedes ܡܢ ܡܕܢܚܐ "from the east", 𝔖 no doubt supports the colometry we have adopted as probably more original than that of 𝔐.[1] The Masoretic division seems to have been determined by rabbinic exegesis which applies the verse to Abraham (𝔗, Gen. R. XLIII.3, etc.).

COLON 41:2aB:

יִקְרָאֵ֖הוּ לְרַגְל֑וֹ* 2aB calls it to his feet?

With: 𝔐 (2) – 𝔊^{SQ}, major division marker in 𝔊^{A} – 𝔖^{abcde}

[1] The Mosul edition has a subordinate accent after ܡܢ ܡܕܢܚܐ.

COLON 41:2bA:

יִתֵּן לְפָנָיו גּוֹיִם 2bA He puts nations before him,

With: $\mathfrak{M}$ (10) – $\mathfrak{G}^{SQ}$ – $\mathfrak{S}^{abce}$, $\mathfrak{S}^{d}$ subordinate punctuation.
Discussion: Probably $\mathfrak{M}$ wanted to take 2bA and 2bB together as one colon, but the joint testimony of $\mathfrak{G}$ and $\mathfrak{S}$ argues against this option. The pair גוים || מלכים is distributed over two cola also in Isa. 45:1; 52:15; 60:3, 11; 62:2; Ps. 72:11; 102:16; 135:10.

COLON 41:2bB:

וּמְלָכִים יֹרְד* 2bB and makes kings step down.

With: $\mathfrak{M}$ (5) – $\mathfrak{G}^{SQ}$ – $\mathfrak{S}^{abcde}$

COLON 41:2cA:

יִתֵּן כֶּעָפָר חַרְבּוֹ 2cA His sword makes like dust,

With: $\mathfrak{M}$ (5) – $\mathfrak{G}^{SQ}$ – $\mathfrak{S}^{abcde}$

COLON 41:2cB:

כְּקַשׁ נִדָּף קַשְׁתּוֹ׃ 2cB his bow (makes) like dispersed chaff.

With: $\mathfrak{M}$ (1) – $\mathfrak{G}^{SQ}$ – $\mathfrak{S}^{abde}$

COLON 41:3aA:

יִרְדְּפֵם יַעֲבוֹר שָׁלוֹם 3aA He pursues them, passes on safely,

With: $\mathfrak{M}$ (2) – $\mathfrak{S}^{abcde}$[2]
Discussion: $\mathfrak{G}^{SQ}$ have a point after ירדפם, $\mathfrak{G}^{A}$ even a major division marker. Since $\mathfrak{G}^{SQ}$ also had dividing points after קשתו, it seems unlikely that they intended to make a break after only one word. $\mathfrak{S}$ does not support this. On the other hand, a divider is lacking in $\mathfrak{G}^{SQ}$ after שלום. In this case too $\mathfrak{S}$ supports $\mathfrak{M}$.

COLON 41:3aB:

אֹרַח בְּרַגְלָיו לֹא יָבוֹא׃ 3aB does not go the road on foot.

With: $\mathfrak{M}$ (1) – $\mathfrak{G}^{SQ}$, major division marker in $\mathfrak{G}^{S}$ – $\mathfrak{S}^{abcde}$, major division markers in $\mathfrak{S}^{a}$ and $\mathfrak{S}^{e}$.

COLON 41:4aA:

מִי־פָעַל וְעָשָׂה 4aA Who has worked and made (this)?

---

[2] In our opinion also $\mathfrak{S}^{c}$ has a single point.

With: 𝔐 (5) – 𝔊^{SBAQ} – 𝔖^{abcde}
Colon parallelism: פעל || עשׂה.

COLON 41:4aB:

קֹרֵא הַדֹּרוֹת מֵרֹאשׁ 4aB He who is calling the generations from the beginning!

With: 𝔐 (2) – 𝔊^{S}, major division markers in 𝔊^{S} and 𝔊^{A} – 𝔖^{abcde}

COLON 41:4bA:

אֲנִי יְהוָה רִאשׁוֹן 4bA I, the LORD am the first,

With: 𝔐 (5) – 𝔊^{SQ} – 𝔖^{abd}

COLON 41:4bB:

וְאֶת־אַחֲרֹנִים אֲנִי־הוּא׃ 4bB and with the last ones I am the same One.

With: 𝔐 (1) – 𝔊^{SQ}, indentation and § in 1𝔔^{a} – 𝔖^{abcde}

COLON 41:5aA:

רָאוּ אִיִּים וְיִירָאוּ 5aA The islands see (it) and fear,

With: 𝔐 (5) – 𝔊^{S}
Colon parallelism: ראה || ירא.
Discussion: Even though only 𝔊^{S} supports 𝔐 we prefer to follow their lead over the alternative offered by 𝔊^{Q} plus 𝔖^{abcde} which put the caesura after הארץ. 𝔖's colon is rather too long since it does not insert any other dividing point. But 𝔊^{Q} also puts in a dividing point after איים and this division looks like a serious possibility,

רָאוּ אִיִּים 5aA The islands see (it),
וְיִירָאוּ קְצוֹת הָאָרֶץ 5aB and the ends of the earth fear,
יֶחֱרָדוּ קָרְבוּ וַיֶּאֱתָיוּן׃ 5aC they tremble, come near and approach.

However, the presupposed colon parallelism between חרד and either קרב or אתה would be unique. It was perhaps for this reason that 𝔊 read יחדו for יחרדו.

COLON 41:5aB:

קְצוֹת הָאָרֶץ יֶחֱרָדוּ 5aB the ends of the earth tremble,

With: 𝔐 (2)
Discussion: 𝔊^{S} has a very long colon here and does not agree with 𝔊^{Q}; 𝔖 has a different colometry; we prefer 𝔐 even though it is not supported by the other witnesses (see our discussion of v. 5aA).

COLON 41:5aC:

קָרְבוּ וַיֶּאֱתָיוּן׃ 5aC they approach and come forward.

With: $\mathfrak{M}$ (1) – $\mathfrak{G}^{SQ}$ – $\mathfrak{S}^{acde}$
Colon parallelism: קרב || אתה (unique).

COLON 41:6aA:

אִישׁ אֶת־רֵעֵהוּ יַעְזֹרוּ 6aA Each man helps his friend,

With: $\mathfrak{M}$ (2) – $\mathfrak{G}^{SQ}$ – $\mathfrak{S}^{abcde}$

COLON 41:6aB:

וּלְאָחִיו יֹאמַר חֲזָק׃ 6aB and speaks to his brother: "Be strong!"

With: $\mathfrak{M}$ (1), major division marker in $1\mathfrak{Q}^{a}$ – $\mathfrak{G}^{A}$, major division marker – $\mathfrak{S}^{abcde}$
Discussion: The Setuma in $\mathfrak{G}^{A}$ is placed after βοηθῆσαι, but this has doubtlessly to do with $\mathfrak{G}$'s somewhat paraphrastic rendering which connects יאמר with v. 7. For the same reason $\mathfrak{G}^{S}$ and $\mathfrak{G}^{Q}$ have a point both here as well as after καὶ ἐρεῖ. All this should not be considered serious deviations from $\mathfrak{M}$ which is fully supported by $\mathfrak{S}$.

COLON 41:7aA:

וַיְחַזֵּק חָרָשׁ אֶת־צֹרֵף 7aA The craftsman strengthens the goldsmith,

With: $\mathfrak{M}$ (5) – $\mathfrak{S}^{e}$, $\mathfrak{S}^{abcd}$ subordinate punctuation.
Colon parallelism: חרשׁ || צרף.
Discussion: $\mathfrak{G}^{Q}$ and $\mathfrak{S}^{e}$ have a dividing point after חרשׁ, $\mathfrak{S}^{abcd}$ a subordinate divider, but this is a consequence of their free rendering which resulted in a longer text. $\mathfrak{S}$ supports $\mathfrak{M}$.

COLON 41:7aB:

מַחֲלִיק פַּטִּישׁ אֶת־הוֹלֶם פָּעַם 7aB the sheet metal worker the blacksmith,

With: $\mathfrak{M}$ (2) – $\mathfrak{G}^{SQ}$ – $\mathfrak{S}^{e}$, $\mathfrak{S}^{abcd}$ subordinate punctuation.
Colon parallelism: חלק Hiph. || הלם Qal (unique); פטישׁ || פעם (unique).

COLON 41:7bA:

אֹמֵר לַדֶּבֶק טוֹב הוּא 7bA saying of the soldering: "It is good!",

With: $\mathfrak{M}$ (5) – $\mathfrak{G}^{SQ}$ – $\mathfrak{S}^{acde}$, $\mathfrak{S}^{b}$ subordinate punctuation.

COLON 41:7bB:

וַיְחַזְּקֵהוּ בְמַסְמְרִים לֹא יִמּוֹט׃ 7bB and he strengthens it with nails so that it will not topple.

With: $\mathfrak{M}$ (1), major division markers – $\mathfrak{G}^{SBAQ}$, all with major division markers – $\mathfrak{S}^{abce}$, major division marker in $\mathfrak{S}^{d}$
Discussion: $\mathfrak{G}^{SQ}$ also have a point after במסמרים which is normal before καὶ and should not be regarded as a serious option for the Hebrew.

COLON 41:8aA:

וְאַתָּה֙ יִשְׂרָאֵל עַבְדִּי 8aA But you, O Israel, my servant,

With: $\mathfrak{M}$ (5) – $\mathfrak{S}^{cde}$, $\mathfrak{S}^{ab}$ subordinate punctuation.
Discussion: $\mathfrak{G}^{SQ}$ insert a point only after יעקב, in accordance with Greek idiom. $\mathfrak{S}$ supports $\mathfrak{M}$.

COLON 41:8aB:

יַעֲקֹב אֲשֶׁר בְּחַרְתִּיךָ 8aB Jacob, whom I have chosen,

With: $\mathfrak{M}$ (2) – $\mathfrak{G}^{SQ}$ – $\mathfrak{S}^{abcde}$ all subordinate punctuation.

COLON 41:8aC:

זֶרַע אַבְרָהָם אֹהֲבִי׃ 8aC seed of Abraham, my friend,

With: $\mathfrak{M}$ (1) – $\mathfrak{G}^{SQ}$ – $\mathfrak{S}^{e}$
Discussion: Most of the $\mathfrak{S}$ manuscripts we collated connect with v. 9 אשר החזקתיך which is not a plausible option.

COLON 41:9aA:

אֲשֶׁר הֶחֱזַקְתִּיךָ֙ מִקְצוֹת הָאָרֶץ 9aA (you), whom I grasped from the ends of the earth,

With: $\mathfrak{M}$ (5) – $\mathfrak{G}^{S}$, $\mathfrak{G}^{Q}$ other punctuation mark – $\mathfrak{S}^{e}$, $\mathfrak{S}^{b}$ subordinate punctuation.

COLON 41:9aB:

וּמֵאֲצִילֶיהָ קְרָאתִיךָ 9aB whom I called from its farthest corners,

With: $\mathfrak{M}$ (2) – $\mathfrak{G}^{SQ}$ – $\mathfrak{S}^{abcde}$

COLON 41:9bA:

וָאֹמַר לְךָ֙ עַבְדִּי־אַתָּה 9bA you, to whom I said: You are my servant,

With: $\mathfrak{M}$ (5) – $\mathfrak{G}^{SQ}$ – $\mathfrak{S}^{abcde}$

COLON 41:9bB:

בְּחַרְתִּ֫יךָ וְלֹ֫א מְאַסְתִּֽיךָ׃ 9bB I have chosen you and have not rejected you,

With: 𝔐 (1) – 𝔊^{SQ} – 𝔖^{abcde}
Colon parallelism: בחר || מאס.

COLON 41:10aA:

אַל־תִּירָא֙ כִּ֣י עִמְּךָ־אָ֔נִי 10aA Do not fear, for I am with you,

With: 𝔐 (5) – 𝔊^{SQ} – 𝔖^{abcde}
Discussion: The dividing points after אל־תירא in 𝔊^{SQ} and 𝔖^{d} should be regarded as subordinate punctuation, as in 𝔖^{a}.

COLON 41:10aB:

אַל־תִּשְׁתָּ֖ע כִּֽי־אֲנִ֣י אֱלֹהֶ֑יךָ 10aB do not be afraid, for I am your God.

With: 𝔐 (2) – 𝔖^{abcde}
Discussion: The dividing points after אל־תירא in 𝔊^{SQ} and 𝔖^{d} should be regarded as subordinate punctuation, as in 𝔖^{a}. 𝔊^{SQ} also agree in making אמצתיך a relative clause with אלהיך for which there is no proper justification. 𝔖 supports 𝔐.

COLON 41:10bA:

אִמַּצְתִּ֙יךָ֙ אַף־עֲזַרְתִּ֔יךָ 10bA I do strengthen you, and I do help you too,

With: 𝔐 (5) – 𝔊^{S} – 𝔖^{abcde}
Colon parallelism: אמץ || עזר (unique).

COLON 41:10bB:

אַף־תְּמַכְתִּ֖יךָ בִּימִ֥ין צִדְקִֽי׃ 10bB I do hold you, with the right hand of my justice.

With: 𝔐 (1) – 𝔊^{SAQ} major division markers (in 𝔊^{S} colon only) – 𝔖^{abcde}

COLON 41:11aA:

הֵ֤ן יֵבֹ֙שׁוּ֙ וְיִכָּ֣לְמ֔וּ 11aA Behold, they will be ashamed and disgraced,

With: 𝔐 (5) with (19)
Colon parallelism: בוש || כלם Niph.
Discussion: None of the ancient witnesses supports 𝔐. But this is obviously the consequence of the fact that the sentence runs on which made subdivision seem unnatural. However, a colon with six accented

units is rare and we prefer to stick to 𝔐's division[3] which results in a nice $A^1 - B^1 - A^2 - B^2$ parallelism. It should also be noted that the similar structure of v. 12 argues in favour of 𝔐.

COLON 41:11aB:

כָּל הַנֶּחֱרִים בָּךְ 11aB all who rage against you.

With: 𝔐 (2) – 𝔊^{SBAQ} – 𝔖^{abcde}

COLON 41:11bA:

יִהְיוּ כְאַיִן וְיֹאבְדוּ 11bA They will be as nothing and perish,

With: 𝔐 (8)
Colon parallelism: אבד || אין.
Discussion: 𝔊^{Q} and 𝔖^{bcd} have a point after כאין, 𝔖^{a} a subordinate punctuation mark. This colometry is unlikely in view of the parallel v. 12bA. 𝔊^{S} does not support it. See further at v. 11aA.

COLON 41:11bB:

אַנְשֵׁי רִיבֶךָ׃ 11bB the men of your lawsuit.

With: 𝔐 (1) – 𝔊^{SQ} – 𝔖^{abcde}

COLON 41:12aA:

תְּבַקְשֵׁם וְלֹא תִמְצָאֵם 12aA You will search for them, but not find them,

With: 𝔐 (5)
Colon parallelism: בקש || מצא.
Discussion: 𝔊^{SQ} have a point after תבקשם which is acceptable in Greek (two words), but hardly in Hebrew. It should be taken as indicating a subordinate punctuation. Again 𝔊 and 𝔖 skip 𝔐's dividing point because of the onrunning sentence. See further at v. 11aA.

COLON 41:12aB:

אַנְשֵׁי מַצֻּתֶךָ 12aB the men of your dispute.

With: 𝔐 (2) – 𝔊^{SQ} – 𝔖^{abcde}

---

[3] 𝔐 uses a combined accent here. Munaḥ–Zaqeph is a normal combination, cf. I. Yeivin, *Introduction to the Tiberian Masorah*, transl. E.J. Revell, [Atlanta] 1980, 183-4; J.D. Price, *The Syntax of Masoretic Accents in the Hebrew Bible*, Lewiston 1990, 125-7.

COLON 41:12bA:

יִהְי֥וּ כְאַ֛יִן וּכְאֶ֖פֶס 12bA They will become as nothing and non-existent,

With: 𝔐 (8)
Colon parallelism: אין || אפס.
Discussion: It is questionable whether 𝔐 wanted to divide at this point. If so, it stands alone again. See at v. 11aA.

COLON 41:12bB:

אַנְשֵׁ֖י מִלְחַמְתֶּֽךָ׃ 12bB the men of your warfare.

With: 𝔐 (1) – 𝔊^{SQ}, major division markers in 𝔊^{B} and 𝔊^{A} – 𝔖^{abcde}

COLON 41:13aA:

כִּ֗י אֲנִ֛י יְהוָ֥ה אֱלֹהֶ֖יךָ 13aA For I am the LORD your God,

With: 𝔐 (8) – 𝔖^{e}
Discussion: Probably 𝔐 wanted to read on until ימינך. Yet we believe that the common division ate this point (e.g. BHS) is right. See the identical and far better delimited colon in Isa. 43:3 and compare also 49:26.[4]

COLON 41:13aB:

מַחֲזִ֣יק יְמִינֶ֑ךָ 13aB who grasps your right hand,

With: 𝔐 (2) – 𝔊^{SQ} – 𝔖^{abcde}

COLON 41:13bA:

הָאֹמֵ֥ר לְךָ֛ אַל־תִּירָ֖א 13bA who says to you: Do not fear,

With: 𝔐 (8) – 𝔖^{abcde}
Discussion: 𝔖 clearly supports 𝔐.

COLON 41:13bB:

אֲנִ֥י עֲזַרְתִּֽיךָ׃ 13bB it is I who helps you.

With: 𝔐 (1) – 𝔖^{bde}, major division markers in 𝔖^{ac}
Discussion: 𝔊 is lacking at this point.

COLON 41:14aA:

אַל־תִּֽירְאִי֙ תּוֹלַ֣עַת יַעֲקֹ֔ב 14aA Do not fear, O worm Jacob,

With: 𝔐 (5) – 𝔊^{S} – 𝔖^{bce}

---

[4] For the Revia‘ with כי see our comment on p. 31.

COLON 41:14aB:

רִמַּתִי* יִשְׂרָאֵל 14aB O maggot Israel!

With: $\mathfrak{M}$ (2) – $\mathfrak{G}^{SQ}$ – $\mathfrak{S}^{abcde}$

COLON 41:14bA:

אֲנִי עֲזַרְתִּיךְ נְאֻם־יְהוָה 14bA I am the one who helps you, declares the LORD,

With: $\mathfrak{M}$ (5) – $\mathfrak{G}^{SQ}$ – $\mathfrak{S}^{bcde}$

COLON 41:14bB:

וְגֹאֲלֵךְ קְדוֹשׁ יִשְׂרָאֵל׃ 14bB and your Redeemer is the Holy One of Israel.

With: $\mathfrak{M}$ (1) – $\mathfrak{G}^{SQ}$, major division markers in $\mathfrak{G}^{SA}$ – $\mathfrak{S}^{abcde}$, major divison marker in $\mathfrak{S}^{b}$
Colon parallelism: גאל || קדוש ישׂראל.

COLON 41:15aA:

הִנֵּה שַׂמְתִּיךְ לְמוֹרַג חָרוּץ חָדָשׁ 15aA Behold, I make you into a sharp new threshing sledge,

With: $\mathfrak{M}$ (5) – $\mathfrak{G}^{Q}$
Discussion: The support for $\mathfrak{M}$'s division is weak ($\mathfrak{G}^{Q}$). But its Revia' (7) with שׂמתיך is reprensented in none of the other ancient traditions. Moreover, שׂים ל is never distributed over different cola. So we assume an extra long colon which is balanced by a short one, a not unusual phenomenon.[5] The other witnesses have a division only after פיפיות which results in an unacceptably long colon of seven feet.

COLON 41:15aB:

בַּעַל פִּיפִיּוֹת 15aB with many teeth.

With: $\mathfrak{M}$ (2) – $\mathfrak{G}^{SQ}$ – $\mathfrak{S}^{abcde}$

COLON 41:15bA:

תָּדוּשׁ הָרִים וְתָדֹק 15bA You will thresh mountains and crush (them),

With: $\mathfrak{M}$ (5) – $\mathfrak{S}^{abcde}$

---

[5]Cf. J.C. de Moor, "The Art of Versification in Ugarit and Israel", in: Y. Avishur, J. Blau (eds.), *Studies in Bible and the Ancient Near East Presented to S.E. Loewenstamm*, Jerusalem 1978, 138-9.

COLON 41:15bB:

וּגְבָעוֹת כַּמֹּץ תָּשִׂים׃ 15bB and hills you will make into chaff.

With: 𝔐 (1) – 𝔊^{Q} – 𝔖^{abcde}

COLON 41:16aA:

תִּזְרֵם וְרוּחַ תִּשָּׂאֵם 16aA You will winnow them and the wind will take them up

With: 𝔐 (5) – 𝔊^{SQ} – 𝔖^{abcde}
Discussion: 𝔊^{SQ} also have a point after תזרם; it should be regarded as a subordinate divider.

COLON 41:16aB:

וּסְעָרָה תָּפִיץ אוֹתָם 16aB and the gale will scatter them.

With: 𝔐 (2) – 𝔊^{SAQ}, major division markers in all three – 𝔖^{abcde}
Discussion: Because 𝔊 connects v. 16b with v. 17a, the major division markers in several 𝔊 manuscripts actually balance those which the other witnesses have after v. 16b.

COLON 41:16bA:

וְאַתָּה תָּגִיל בַּיהוָה 16bA And you will exult in the LORD,

With: 𝔐 (5) – 𝔖^{a}, 𝔖^{bcde} subordinate punctuation.
Discussion: The support of 𝔊 is lacking because it has a different division into verses at this point (see v. 16aB).

COLON 41:16bB:

בִּקְדוֹשׁ יִשְׂרָאֵל תִּתְהַלָּל׃ 16bB glory in the Holy One of Israel.

With: 𝔐 (1), major division markers – 𝔖^{bcde}, major division markers in 𝔖^{bde}, subordinate punctuation in 𝔖^{a}
Discussion: The support of 𝔊 is lacking because it has a different division into verses at this point (see v. 16aB).

COLON 41:17aA:

הָעֲנִיִּים וְהָאֶבְיוֹנִים 17aA The afflicted and poor

With: 𝔐 (13) – 𝔊^{SQ}
Colon parallelism: עני || אביון.
Discussion: Apparently 𝔐 did not want to indicate a break at this point and neither does 𝔖. Nevertheless we follow 𝔊^{SQ} because the considerable number of syllables makes a colon of five words ending

with ואין less likely. Both 𝔐 and 𝔖 would seem to have been led astray by the continuing phrase.

COLON 41:17aB:

מְבַקְשִׁים מַיִם וָאַיִן 17aB are searching for water but there is none;

With: 𝔐 (5) – 𝔊^{SQ} – 𝔖^{abcde}

COLON 41:17aC:

לְשׁוֹנָם בַּצָּמָא נָשָׁתָּה 17aC their tongue is parched with thirst.

With: 𝔐 (2) – 𝔊^{SQ}, major division markers in 𝔊^{SA} – 𝔖^{abcde}

COLON 41:17bA:

אֲנִי יְהוָה אֶעֱנֵם 17bA I am the LORD, I will answer them,

With: 𝔐 (5) – 𝔖^{abcde}
Discussion: 𝔊^{SQ} presuppose a different colometry,

אֲנִי יְהוָה 17bA I am the LORD,
אֶעֱנֵם אֱלֹהֵי יִשְׂרָאֵל 17bB I, the God of Israel, will answer them,
לֹא אֶעֶזְבֵם׃ 17bC I will not forsake them.

From the viewpoint of Hebrew syntax this is not an attractive option. 𝔖 supports 𝔐.

COLON 41:17bB:

אֱלֹהֵי יִשְׂרָאֵל לֹא אֶעֶזְבֵם׃ 17bB the God of Israel, I will not forsake them.

With: 𝔐 (1) – 𝔊^{SQ} – 𝔖^{abcd}

COLON 41:18aA:

אֶפְתַּח עַל־שְׁפָיִים נְהָרוֹת 18aA I will open rivers on the bare tracks,

With: 𝔐 (5) – 𝔊^{SQ} – 𝔖^{abcde} subordinate punctuation.

COLON 41:18aB:

וּבְתוֹךְ בְּקָעוֹת מַעְיָנוֹת 18aB and wells in the middle of the valleys.

With: 𝔐 (2) – 𝔊^{SQ} – 𝔖^{abcde}

COLON 41:18bA:

אָשִׂים מִדְבָּר לַאֲגַם־מַיִם 18bA I will make the desert a pool of water,

With: 𝔐 (5) – 𝔊^{SQ} – 𝔖^{abcde}

Colon parallelism: מדבר || מים.

COLON 41:18bB:

וְאֶרֶץ צִיָּה לְמוֹצָאֵי מָיִם׃ 18bB and the dry land springs of water.

With: 𝔐 (1) – $𝔊^{SQ}$ – $𝔖^{abcde}$
Colon parallelism: ציה || מים (unique).

COLON 41:19aA:

אֶתֵּן בַּמִּדְבָּר אֶרֶז שִׁטָּה 19aA In the desert I will set cedars, acacias,

With: 𝔐 (5) – $𝔊^{SQ}$ – $𝔖^{acde}$

COLON 41:19aB:

וַהֲדַס וְעֵץ שָׁמֶן 19aB and myrtles and pine-trees.

With: 𝔐 (2), major division marker in $1𝔔^{b}$– $𝔖^{abcde}$
Discussion: 𝔊 is lacking here.

COLON 41:19bA:

אָשִׂים בָּעֲרָבָה 19bA In the bare valley I will put

With: 𝔐 (7) – $𝔖^{e}$
Discussion: 𝔐 puts a caesura after בערבה (7) which is supported by $𝔖^{e}$. 𝔊 is lacking here. See the next colon.

COLON 41:19bB:

בְּרוֹשׁ תִּדְהָר וּתְאַשּׁוּר יַחְדָּו׃ 19bB junipers, maple-trees and cypresses together.

With: 𝔐 (1) – $𝔊^{SQ}$ – $𝔖^{abcde}$
Colon parallelism: ברוש || תדהר || תאשור.

COLON 41:20aA:

לְמַעַן יִרְאוּ וְיֵדְעוּ 20aA That they may see and know,

With: 𝔐 (7) – $𝔖^{b}$
Colon parallelism: ראה || ידע.
Discussion: Although 𝔐 is only weakly supported by $𝔖^{b}$, the well-attested colon parallelism argues in favour of its division.

COLON 41:20aB:

וְיָשִׂימוּ וְיַשְׂכִּילוּ יַחְדָּו 20aB and may observe and perceive together,

With: 𝔐 (5) – 𝔊^{SQ} – 𝔖^{abcde} all subordinate punctuation
Colon parallelism: At least grammatically.

COLON 41:20bA:

כִּי יַד־יְהוָה עָשְׂתָה זֹּאת 20bA that the hand of the LORD has made this,

With: 𝔐 (2) – 𝔊^{SQ} – 𝔖^{be}, 𝔖^{acd} subordinate punctuation.

COLON 41:20bB:

וּקְדוֹשׁ יִשְׂרָאֵל בְּרָאָהּ׃ 20bB and that the Holy One of Israel has created it.

With: 𝔐 (1), major division markers – 𝔊^{SBAQ}, all with major division markers – 𝔖^{abcde}, major division markers in 𝔖^{abe}

COLON 41:21aA:

קָרְבוּ רִיבְכֶם 21aA Bring near your case,

With: 𝔐 (8)
Discussion: Even though it is uncertain whether 𝔐 meant the accent as a colon divider, and even though none of our witnesses has a dividing accent here, we assume a break. See v. 21bA below as well as our remarks concerning 40:1aA (p. 23).[6]

COLON 41:21aB:

יֹאמַר יְהוָה 21aB says the LORD,

With: 𝔐 (2) – 𝔊^{SQ} – 𝔖^{abcde}

COLON 41:21bA:

הַגִּישׁוּ עֲצֻמוֹתֵיכֶם 21bA bring closer your strong points,

With: 𝔐 (5)
Discussion: Again 𝔐 stands alone in dividing at this point. See the preceding colon.

COLON 41:21bB:

יֹאמַר מֶלֶךְ יַעֲקֹב׃ 21bB says the King of Jacob.

With: 𝔐 (1) – 𝔊^{SQ}, major division marker in 𝔊^{A} – 𝔖^{abcde}

---

[6]Koole, 14, 45, 124, treats the passages involved in an inconsequent manner.

COLON 41:22aA:

יַגִּישׁוּ וְיַגִּידוּ לָנוּ 22aA Let them bring closer and tell us

With: 𝔐 (5) – $\mathfrak{G}^{S}$
Colon parallelism: נגשׁ Hiph. || נגד Hiph.
Discussion: Even though 𝔐 is only weakly supported, we accept its division. The colon parallelism argues in its favour. Again 𝔊 and 𝔖 have been led astray by the fact that the sentence runs on.

COLON 41:22aB:

אֵת אֲשֶׁר תִּקְרֶינָה 22aB what will happen.

With: 𝔐 (2) – $\mathfrak{G}^{SQ}$ – $\mathfrak{S}^{abcde}$

COLON 41:22bA:

הָרִאשֹׁנוֹת ׀ מָה הֵנָּה 22bA The first things – what (do) they (mean)?

With: 𝔐 (7).
Discussion: The point which $\mathfrak{G}^{S}$ and $\mathfrak{S}^{e}$ insert after הראשׁנות is a subordinate divider corresponding to 𝔐's Paseq. None of the ancient versions supports 𝔐 in putting a caesura after הנה. Yet we accept it because their alternative is to put a major divider after הגידו ($\mathfrak{G}^{SQ}$, $\mathfrak{S}^{abcde}$) which disturbs the nice colon parallelism in the next colon.

COLON 41:22bB:

הַגִּידוּ וְנָשִׂימָה לִבֵּנוּ וְנֵדְעָה אַחֲרִיתָן 22bB Tell us, so that we may set our heart to it and know their outcome,

With: 𝔐 (5) – $\mathfrak{G}^{S}$ – $\mathfrak{S}^{abcde}$
Colon parallelism: שׂים || נגד; שׂים לב || ידע.
Discussion: $\mathfrak{G}^{SQ}$ and $\mathfrak{S}^{e}$ have an extra point after לבנו which corresponds to 𝔐's Pashṭa (No. 10). The strong colon parallelism and the well-attested division after אחריתן argue in favour of 𝔐, despite its length. Cola of five stresses are not uncommon.[7]

COLON 41:22bC:

אוֹ הַבָּאוֹת הַשְׁמִיעֻנוּ׃ 22bC or cause us to hear the things to come.

With: 𝔐 (1) – $\mathfrak{G}^{SQ}$ – $\mathfrak{S}^{abcde}$
Colon parallelism: שׁמע || בוא.

---

[7]See p. 638-9.

COLON 41:23aA:

הַגִּידוּ הָאֹתִיּוֹת לְאָחוֹר 23aA Tell us the things to come in the future,

With: $\mathfrak{M}$ (5) – $\mathfrak{G}^{SQ}$ – $\mathfrak{S}^{abcde}$

COLON 41:23aB:

וְנֵדְעָה כִּי אֱלֹהִים אַתֶּם 23aB that we may know that you are gods.

With: $\mathfrak{M}$ (2) – $\mathfrak{G}^{SQ}$ – $\mathfrak{S}^{abcde}$

COLON 41:23bA:

אַף־תֵּיטִיבוּ וְתָרֵעוּ 23bA Do both something good and something bad,

With: $\mathfrak{M}$ (5) – $\mathfrak{G}^{Q}$ – $\mathfrak{S}^{abcde}$
Colon parallelism: יטב Hiph. || רעע Hiph.

COLON 41:23bB:

וְנִשְׁתָּעָה וְנִרָא* יַחְדָּו׃ 23bB that we will become afraid and will fear together.

With: $\mathfrak{M}$ (1) – $\mathfrak{G}^{SQ}$ – $\mathfrak{S}^{abcde}$
Colon parallelism: שׁתע || ירא.
Discussion: $\mathfrak{G}^{SQ}$ have a divider after ונשתעה which has the same force as $\mathfrak{M}$'s Ṭiphḥa.

COLON 41:24aA:

הֵן־אַתֶּם מֵאַיִן 24aA Look, you are less than nothing,

With: $\mathfrak{M}$ (5) – $\mathfrak{G}^{SQ}$ – $\mathfrak{S}^{abcd}$

COLON 41:24aB:

וּפָעָלְכֶם מֵאָפַע 24aB and your work is less than nought;

With: $\mathfrak{M}$ (2) – $\mathfrak{S}^{acd}$
Discussion: $\mathfrak{G}^{SQ}$ insert an extra point after ופעלכם which equals $\mathfrak{M}$'s Ṭiphḥa.

COLON 41:24bA:

תּוֹעֵבָה יִבְחַר בָּכֶם׃ 24bA an abomination is he who chooses you.

With: $\mathfrak{M}$ (1), major division markers – $\mathfrak{G}^{SAQ}$, major division marker in $\mathfrak{G}^{A}$ – $\mathfrak{S}^{abcde}$, major division markers in $\mathfrak{S}^{ace}$

COLON 41:25aA:

הַעִירוֹתִי מִצָּפוֹן וַיַּאת 25aA I wake up from the north him who is approaching,

With: 𝔐 (5)
Discussion: 𝔊 is lacking and 𝔖 has a subordinate punctuation after מצפון, but 𝔐 deserves confidence because ויאת expresses the obedience which is further explained in the next colon.

COLON 41:25aB:

מִמִּזְרַח־שֶׁמֶשׁ יִקְרָא בִשְׁמִי 25aB from the east him who will call me by name.

With: 𝔐 (2) – 𝔊^{SQ}, major division marker in 𝔊^{Q} – 𝔖^{abcde}
Discussion: 𝔊^{SQ} and 𝔖^{e} have an additional dividing point after שמש which should be regarded as a subordinate divider like 𝔐's Ṭiphḥa.

COLON 41:25bA:

וְיָבֹא סְגָנִים כְּמוֹ־חֹמֶר 25bA And when he comes, governors (will become) as loam,

With: 𝔐 (5) – 𝔊^{Q}
Discussion: Again 𝔊^{SQ} and this time 𝔖^{b} have an additional dividing point after סגנים. However, the renderings of 𝔊 and 𝔖 are rather free at this point.

COLON 41:25bB:

וּכְמוֹ יוֹצֵר יִרְמָס־טִיט׃ 25bB and as a potter he will tread the clay.

With: 𝔐 (1) – 𝔊^{AQ}, major division markers in 𝔊^{A} – 𝔖^{abcde}

COLON 41:26aA:

מִי־הִגִּיד מֵרֹאשׁ וְנֵדָעָה 26aA Who told (it) from the beginning so that we might know,

With: 𝔐 (5) – 𝔊^{Q}
Colon parallelism: נגד || ידע.
Discussion: 𝔊^{S} has a point after מראש and 𝔖^{abce} support this with subordinate punctuation. However, since both give a free rendering connecting ונדעה with ומלפנים, 𝔐's colometry is preferable.

COLON 41:26aB:

וּמִלְּפָנִים וְנֹאמַר צַדִּיק 26aB and beforehand, so that we might say: He is right!

With: $\mathfrak{M}$ (2) – $\mathfrak{G}^{SQ}$ – S^{abcde}
Discussion: $\mathfrak{G}^{SQ}$ have a point after מלפנים. This corresponds to the Ṭiphḥa of $\mathfrak{M}$.

COLON 41:26bA:

אַף אֵין־מַגִּיד 26bA No, there was no one who was telling,

With: $\mathfrak{M}$ (7) – $\mathfrak{G}^{SQ}$
Discussion: The identical structure of the three cola argues in favour of $\mathfrak{M}$ which is supported by $\mathfrak{G}$.

COLON 41:26bB:

אַף אֵין מַשְׁמִיעַ 26bB no, there was no one who let hear,

With: $\mathfrak{M}$ (5) – S^{abcde}
Discussion: $\mathfrak{G}$ is lacking at this point.

COLON 41:26bC:

אַף אֵין־שֹׁמֵעַ אִמְרֵיכֶם׃ 26bC no, there was no one who heard your words.

With: $\mathfrak{M}$ (1) – $\mathfrak{G}^{SAQ}$, major division markers in all of them – S^{abcde}

COLON 41:27aA:

רִאשׁוֹן לְצִיּוֹן הִנֵּה הִנָּם 27aA The First to Zion: Look them over there!

With: $\mathfrak{M}$ (2) – $\mathfrak{G}^{SBAQ}$ – S^{abcd}

COLON 41:27aB:

וְלִירוּשָׁלַםִ מְבַשֵּׂר אֶתֵּן׃ 27aB And to Jerusalem: I will give a herald of good tidings!

With: $\mathfrak{M}$ (1) – $\mathfrak{G}^{SQ}$ – S^{abcde}

COLON 41:28aA:

וְאֵרֶא וְאֵין אִישׁ 28aA And when I look, there is no man,

With: $\mathfrak{M}$ (5) – $\mathfrak{G}^{Q}$

COLON 41:28aB:

וּמֵאֵלֶּה וְאֵין יוֹעֵץ 28aB and with them, there is no counsellor,

With: $\mathfrak{M}$ (2) – $\mathfrak{G}^{SQ}$ – S^{c}, subordinate punctuation S^{ad}

COLON 41:28aC:

וְאֶשְׁאָלֵ֖ם וְיָשִׁ֥יבוּ דָבָֽר׃ 28aC that I could ask them and they would reply one word.

With: 𝔐 (1) – $\mathfrak{G}^{SQ}$ – $\mathfrak{S}^{abcde}$

COLON 41:29aA:

הֵ֣ן כֻּלָּ֔ם אָ֕וֶן 29aA Look, all of them are iniquity,

With: (𝔐 conjunctive accent) – $\mathfrak{S}^{abcde}$
Discussion: We prefer 𝔖 over 𝔐 which has a distinctive accent with כלם (5).[8] One would expect און ואפס and Isa. 29:20 supports 𝔖's division.

COLON 41:29aB:

אֶ֖פֶס מַעֲשֵׂיהֶ֑ם 29aB non-existent are their works

With: 𝔐 (2) – $\mathfrak{G}^{SQ}$ – $\mathfrak{S}^{abcde}$

COLON 41:29aC:

ר֥וּחַ וָתֹ֖הוּ נִסְכֵּיהֶֽם׃ 29aC wind and void their molten images.

With: 𝔐 (1), major division markers – $\mathfrak{G}^{SBAQ}$, all with major division markers – $\mathfrak{S}^{abcde}$, all with major division markers.

3.3 Isaiah 41 – Delimitation of Verse-lines

VERSE–LINE: 41:1a:

הַחֲרִ֤ישׁוּ אֵלַי֙ אִיִּ֔ים 1aA Be silent to me, islands,
וּלְאֻמִּ֖ים יַחֲלִ֣יפוּ כֹ֑חַ 1aB and let the nations renew their strength,

𝔐 distinctive accents: 5 – 2.
Stresses: 3 + 3.
Verse-line parallelism: אי || לאם.

VERSE–LINE: 41:1b:

יִגְּשׁוּ֙ אָ֣ז יְדַבֵּ֔רוּ 1bA let them draw near, then let them speak up,
יַחְדָּ֖ו לַמִּשְׁפָּ֥ט נִקְרָֽבָה׃ 1bB let us go to court together.

𝔐 distinctive accents: 5 – 1.
Stresses: 3 + 3.
Verse-line parallelism: נגש || קרב.

---

[8] 𝔊 is lacking here.

VERSE–LINE: 41:2a:

מִ֤י הֵעִיר֙ מִמִּזְרָ֔ח צֶ֖דֶק	2aA	Who wakes up justice from the East,
יִקְרָאֵ֣הוּ לְרַגְלָ֔יו*	2aB	calls it to his feet?

𝔐 distinctive accents: 8 – 2.
Stresses: 4 + 2.
Verse-line parallelism: עור ‖ קרא.

VERSE–LINE: 41:2b:

יִתֵּ֨ן לְפָנָ֤יו גּוֹיִם֙	2bA	He puts nations before him,
וּמְלָכִ֣ים יֹרְד*	2bB	and makes kings step down.

𝔐 distinctive accents: 10 – 5.
Stresses: 3 + 2.
Verse-line parallelism: גוי ‖ מלך; נתן לפניו ‖ ירד Hiph.

VERSE–LINE: 41:2c:

יִתֵּ֤ן כֶּֽעָפָר֙ חַרְבּ֔וֹ	2cA	His sword makes like dust,
כְּקַ֥שׁ נִדָּ֖ף קַשְׁתּֽוֹ׃	2cB	his bow (makes) like dispersed chaff.

𝔐 distinctive accents: 5 – 1.
Stresses: 3 + 3.
Verse-line parallelism: כ ‖ כ; עפר ‖ קש; חרב ‖ קשת; ־ו ‖ ־ו.

VERSE–LINE: 41:3a:

יִרְדְּפֵ֖ם יַעֲב֣וֹר שָׁל֑וֹם	3aA	He pursues them, passes on safely,
אֹ֚רַח בְּרַגְלָ֖יו לֹ֥א יָבֽוֹא׃	3aB	does not go the road on foot.

𝔐 distinctive accents: 2 – 1.
Stresses: 3 + 4.
Verse-line parallelism: רדף ‖ בוא; עבר ‖ בוא.

VERSE–LINE: 41:4a:

מִֽי־פָעַ֣ל וְעָשָׂ֔ה	4aA	Who has worked and made (this)?
קֹרֵ֥א הַדֹּר֖וֹת מֵרֹ֑אשׁ	4aB	He who is calling the generations from the beginning!

𝔐 distinctive accents: 5 – 2.
Stresses: 2 + 3.
Verse-line parallelism: None.

VERSE–LINE: 41:4b:

אֲנִ֤י יְהוָה֙ רִאשׁ֔וֹן	4bA	I, the LORD am the first,
וְאֶת־אַחֲרֹנִ֖ים אֲנִי־הֽוּא׃	4bB	and with the last ones I am the same.

𝔐 distinctive accents: 5 – 1.
Stresses: 3 + 2.
Verse-line parallelism: אני || אני; ראשון || אחרון; יהוה || הוא.

VERSE–LINE: 41:5a:

רָאוּ אִיִּים וְיִירָאוּ 5aA The islands see (it) and fear,
קְצוֹת הָאָרֶץ יֶחֱרָדוּ 5aB the ends of the earth tremble,
קָרְבוּ וַיֶּאֱתָיוּן׃ 5aC they come near and approach.

𝔐 distinctive accents: 5 – 2 – 1.
Stresses: 3 + 3 + 2.
Verse-line parallelism: אי || קצה הארץ; ירא || חרד.

VERSE–LINE: 41:6a:

אִישׁ אֶת־רֵעֵהוּ יַעְזֹרוּ 6aA Each man helps his friend,
וּלְאָחִיו יֹאמַר חֲזָק׃ 6aB and speaks to his brother: "Be strong!"

𝔐 distinctive accents: 2 – 1.
Stresses: 3 + 3.
Verse-line parallelism: רע || אח; עזר || חזק.

VERSE–LINE: 41:7a:

וַיְחַזֵּק חָרָשׁ אֶת־צֹרֵף 7aA The craftsman strengthens the goldsmith,
מַחֲלִיק פַּטִּישׁ אֶת־הוֹלֶם פָּעַם 7aB the sheet metal worker the blacksmith,

𝔐 distinctive accents: 5 – 2.
Stresses: 3 + 4.
Verse-line parallelism: חרש || צרף || מחליק פטיש || הולם פעם (unique); את || את.

VERSE–LINE: 41:7b:

אֹמֵר לַדֶּבֶק טוֹב הוּא 7bA saying of the soldering: "It is good!",
וַיְחַזְּקֵהוּ בְמַסְמְרִים לֹא יִמּוֹט׃ 7bB and he strengthens it with nails so that it will not topple.

𝔐 distinctive accents: 5 – 1.
Stresses: 4 + 4.
Verse-line parallelism: טוב || חזק.

VERSE–LINE: 41:8a:

וְאַתָּה יִשְׂרָאֵל עַבְדִּי 8aA But you, O Israel, my servant,
יַעֲקֹב אֲשֶׁר בְּחַרְתִּיךָ 8aB Jacob, whom I have chosen,
זֶרַע אַבְרָהָם אֹהֲבִי׃ 8aC seed of Abraham, my friend,

𝔐 distinctive accents: 5 – 2 – 1.
Stresses: 3 + 3 + 3.
Verse-line parallelism: ישׂראל || יעקב || אברהם (unique as poetic parallel); עבד || בחר; ־י || ־י; בחר || אהב; עבד || אהב.

VERSE–LINE: 41:9a:

אֲשֶׁר הֶחֱזַקְתִּיךָ מִקְצוֹת הָאָרֶץ	9aA	(you), whom I grasped from the ends of the earth,
וּמֵאֲצִילֶיהָ קְרָאתִיךָ	9aB	and whom I called from its farthest corners,

𝔐 distinctive accents: 5 – 2.
Stresses: 4 + 2.
Verse-line parallelism: חזק || קרא; ־ך || ־ך; מן || מן; קצה הארץ || אציל (unique); grammatical parallelism.

VERSE–LINE: 41:9b:

וָאֹמַר לְךָ עַבְדִּי־אַתָּה	9bA	you, to whom I said: You are my servant,
בְּחַרְתִּיךָ וְלֹא מְאַסְתִּיךָ׃	9bB	I have chosen you and have not rejected you,

𝔐 distinctive accents: 5 – 1.
Stresses: 3 + 3.
Verse-line parallelism: עבד || בחר; ־ך || ־ך.

VERSE–LINE: 41:10a:

אַל־תִּירָא כִּי עִמְּךָ־אָנִי	10aA	Do not fear, for I am with you,
אַל־תִּשְׁתָּע כִּי־אֲנִי אֱלֹהֶיךָ	10aB	do not be afraid, for I am your God.

𝔐 distinctive accents: 5 – 2.
Stresses: 3 + 3.
Verse-line parallelism: אל || אל; ירא || שׁתע (unique); כי || כי (common); אני || אני; ־ך || ־ך; grammatical parallelism.

VERSE–LINE: 41:10b:

אִמַּצְתִּיךָ אַף־עֲזַרְתִּיךָ	10bA	I do strengthen you, and I do help you too,
אַף־תְּמַכְתִּיךָ בִּימִין צִדְקִי׃	10bB	I do hold you, with the right hand of my justice.

𝔐 distinctive accents: 5 – 1.
Stresses: 2 + 3.
Verse-line parallelism: אמץ || עזר || תמכ (unique); ־ך || ־ך; אף || אף; grammatical parallelism.

VERSE–LINE: 41:11a:

הֵ֤ן יֵבֹ֙שׁוּ֙ וְיִכָּ֣לְמ֔וּ 11aA Behold, they will be ashamed and disgraced,
כֹּ֖ל הַנֶּחֱרִ֣ים בָּ֑ךְ 11aB all who rage against you.

𝔐 distinctive accents: 5 – 2.
Stresses: 3 + 3.
Verse-line parallelism: None.

VERSE–LINE: 41:11b:

יִהְי֧וּ כְאַ֛יִן וְיֹאבְד֖וּ 11bA They will be as nothing and perish,
אַנְשֵׁ֥י רִיבֶֽךָ׃ 11bB the men of your lawsuit.

𝔐 distinctive accents: 8 – 1.
Stresses: 3 + 2.
Verse-line parallelism: None.

VERSE–LINE: 41:12a:

תְּבַקְשֵׁם֙ וְלֹ֣א תִמְצָאֵ֔ם 12aA You will search for them, but not find them,
אַנְשֵׁ֖י מַצֻּתֶ֑ךָ 12aB the men of your dispute.

𝔐 distinctive accents: 5 – 2.
Stresses: 3 + 2.
Verse-line parallelism: None.

VERSE–LINE: 41:12b:

יִהְי֧וּ כְאַ֛יִן וּכְאֶ֖פֶס 12bA They will become as nothing and non-existent,
אַנְשֵׁ֥י מִלְחַמְתֶּֽךָ׃ 12bB the men of your warfare.

𝔐 distinctive accents: 8 – 1.
Stresses: 3 + 2.
Verse-line parallelism: None.

VERSE–LINE: 41:13a:

כִּ֗י אֲנִ֛י יְהוָ֥ה אֱלֹהֶ֖יךָ 13aA For I am the LORD your God,
מַחֲזִ֣יק יְמִינֶ֑ךָ 13aB who grasps your right hand,

𝔐 distinctive accents: 8 – 2.
Stresses: 4 + 2.
Verse-line parallelism: ךָ- || ךָ-.

VERSE–LINE: 41:13b:

הָאֹמֵ֥ר לְךָ֛ אַל־תִּירָ֖א 13bA who says to you: Do not fear,
אֲנִ֥י עֲזַרְתִּֽיךָ׃ 13bB it is I who helps you.

𝔐 distinctive accents: 8 – 1.
Stresses: 3 + 2.
Verse-line parallelism: ך־ || ך־.

VERSE–LINE: 41:14a:

אַל־תִּֽירְאִי֙ תּוֹלַ֣עַת יַעֲקֹ֔ב 14aA Do not fear, O worm Jacob,
רְמָתֵ֖י* יִשְׂרָאֵ֑ל 14aB O maggot Israel!

𝔐 distinctive accents: 5 – 2.
Stresses: 3 + 2.
Verse-line parallelism: תולעת || *רמה; יעקב || ישׂראל.
Discussion: The two cola are connected by ellipsis.

VERSE–LINE: 41:14b:

אֲנִ֤י עֲזַרְתִּיךְ֙ נְאֻם־יְהוָ֔ה 14bA I am the one who helps you, declares the LORD,
וְגֹאֲלֵ֖ךְ קְד֥וֹשׁ יִשְׂרָאֵֽל׃ 14bB and your Redeemer is the Holy One of Israel.

𝔐 distinctive accents: 5 – 1.
Stresses: 3 + 3.
Verse-line parallelism: עזר || גאל; ך־ (f.s.) || ך־ (f.s.); יהוה || קדוש ישׂראל; גאל || יהוה.

VERSE–LINE: 41:15a:

הִנֵּ֣ה שַׂמְתִּ֗יךְ לְמוֹרַג֙ חָר֣וּץ חָדָ֔שׁ 15aA Behold, I make you into a sharp new threshing sledge,
בַּ֖עַל פִּֽיפִיּ֑וֹת 15aB with many teeth.

𝔐 distinctive accents: 5 – 2.
Stresses: 5 + 2.
Verse-line parallelism: חרץ || בעל פיפיות (unique).

VERSE–LINE: 41:15b:

תָּד֤וּשׁ הָרִים֙ וְתָדֹ֔ק 15bA You will thresh mountains and crush (them),
וּגְבָע֖וֹת כַּמֹּ֥ץ תָּשִֽׂים׃ 15bB and hills you will make into chaff.

𝔐 distinctive accents: 5 – 1.
Stresses: 3 + 3.
Verse-line parallelism: הר || גבעה; דוש || דקק || שׂים כמץ (unique); grammatical parallelism.

VERSE–LINE: 41:16a:

תִּזְרֵם֙ וְר֣וּחַ תִּשָּׂאֵ֔ם	16aA	You will winnow them and the wind will take them up
וּסְעָרָ֖ה תָּפִ֣יץ אוֹתָ֑ם	16aB	and the gale will scatter them.

𝔐 distinctive accents: 5 – 2.
Stresses: 3 + 3.
Verse-line parallelism: רוח || סערה; נשׂא || פוץ; ־ם || ־ם; grammatical parallelism.

VERSE–LINE: 41:16b:

וְאַתָּה֙ תָּגִ֣יל בַּֽיהוָ֔ה	16bA	And you will exult in the LORD,
בִּקְד֥וֹשׁ יִשְׂרָאֵ֖ל תִּתְהַלָּֽל׃	16bB	glory in the Holy One of Israel.

𝔐 distinctive accents: 5 – 1.
Stresses: 3 + 3.
Verse-line parallelism: גיל || הלל; ב || ב; יהוה || קדוש ישׂראל; grammatical parallelism.

VERSE–LINE: 41:17a:

הָעֲנִיִּ֨ים וְהָאֶבְיוֹנִ֜ים	17aA	The afflicted and poor
מְבַקְשִׁ֥ים מַ֙יִם֙ וָאַ֔יִן	17aB	are searching for water but there is none;
לְשׁוֹנָ֖ם בַּצָּמָ֣א נָשָׁ֑תָּה	17aC	their tongue is parched with thirst.

𝔐 distinctive accents: 13 – 5 – 2.
Stresses: 2 + 3 + 3.
Verse-line parallelism: מים || צמא.

VERSE–LINE: 41:17b:

אֲנִ֤י יְהוָה֙ אֶעֱנֵ֔ם	17bA	I am the LORD, I will answer them,
אֱלֹהֵ֥י יִשְׂרָאֵ֖ל לֹ֥א אֶעֶזְבֵֽם׃	17bB	the God of Israel, I will not forsake them.

𝔐 distinctive accents: 5 – 1.
Stresses: 3 + 4.
Verse-line parallelism: יהוה || אלהי ישׂראל; ענה || לא עזב (unique); ־ם || ־ם (rhyme); grammatical parallelism.

VERSE–LINE: 41:18a:

אֶפְתַּ֤ח עַל־שְׁפָיִים֙ נְהָר֔וֹת	18aA	I will open rivers on the bare tracks,
וּבְת֥וֹךְ בְּקָע֖וֹת מַעְיָנ֑וֹת	18aB	and wells in the middle of the valleys.

𝔐 distinctive accents: 5 – 2.
Stresses: 3 + 3.

Verse-line parallelism: שׂפי || בקעה (unique); נהר || מעין; rhyme.
Discussion: The cola are connected by ellipsis.

VERSE–LINE: 41:18b:

אָשִׂ֤ים מִדְבָּר֙ לַאֲגַם־מַ֔יִם	18bA	I will make the desert a pool of water,
וְאֶ֥רֶץ צִיָּ֖ה לְמוֹצָ֥אֵי מָֽיִם׃	18bB	and the dry land springs of water.

𝔐 distinctive accents: 5 – 1.
Stresses: 3 + 4.
Verse-line parallelism: מדבר || ארץ ציה; ל || ל; אגם || מוצא; מים || מים.
Discussion: The cola are connected by ellipsis. This verse-line seems to be quoted in Ps. 107:35.

VERSE–LINE: 41:19a:

אֶתֵּ֣ן בַּמִּדְבָּ֗ר אֶ֚רֶז שִׁטָּ֔ה	19aA	In the desert I will set cedars, acacias,
וַהֲדַ֖ס וְעֵ֣ץ שָׁ֑מֶן	19aB	and myrtles and pine-trees.

𝔐 distinctive accents: 5 – 2.
Stresses: 4 + 3.
Verse-line parallelism: ארז || שׁטה || הדס || עץ שׁמן.

VERSE–LINE: 41:19b:

אָשִׂ֣ים בָּעֲרָבָ֗ה	19bA	In the bare valley I will put
בְּר֛וֹשׁ תִּדְהָ֥ר וּתְאַשּׁ֖וּר יַחְדָּֽו׃	19bB	junipers, ashes and cypresses together.

𝔐 distinctive accents: 7 – 1.
Stresses: 2 + 4.
Verse-line parallelism: None.
Discussion: Enjambment.

VERSE–LINE: 41:20a:

לְמַ֧עַן יִרְא֣וּ וְיֵדְע֗וּ	20aA	That they may see and know,
וְיָשִׂ֤ימוּ וְיַשְׂכִּ֙ילוּ֙ יַחְדָּ֔ו	20aB	and may observe and perceive together,

𝔐 distinctive accents: 7 – 5.
Stresses: 3 + 3.
Verse-line parallelism: ראה || שׂים; ראה || שׂכל; ידע || שׂכל; grammatical parallelism.

VERSE–LINE: 41:20b:

כִּ֥י יַד־יְהוָ֖ה עָ֣שְׂתָה זֹּ֑את	20bA	that the hand of LORD has made this,
וּקְד֥וֹשׁ יִשְׂרָאֵ֖ל בְּרָאָֽהּ׃	20bB	and that the Holy One of Israel has created it.

𝔪 distinctive accents: 2 – 1.
Stresses: 4 + 3.
Verse-line parallelism: יהוה || קדוש ישׂראל; עשׂה || ברא; זאת || ה־.

VERSE–LINE: 41:21a:

קָרְבוּ רִיבְכֶם	21aA	Bring near your case,
יֹאמַר יְהוָה	21aB	says the LORD,

𝔪 distinctive accents: 8 – 2.
Stresses: 2 + 2.
Verse-line parallelism: None.
Discussion: The verse-line parallelism is deliberately sacrificed to the strophe parallelism.[1]

VERSE–LINE: 41:21b:

הַגִּישׁוּ עֲצֻמוֹתֵיכֶם	21bA	bring closer your strong points,
יֹאמַר מֶלֶךְ יַעֲקֹב׃	21bB	says the King of Jacob.

𝔪 distinctive accents: 5 – 1.
Stresses: 2 + 3.
Verse-line parallelism: None.

VERSE–LINE: 41:22a:

יַגִּישׁוּ וְיַגִּידוּ לָנוּ	22aA	Let them bring closer and tell us
אֵת אֲשֶׁר תִּקְרֶינָה	22aB	what will happen.

𝔪 distinctive accents: 5 – 2.
Stresses: 3 + 3.
Verse-line parallelism: None.

Discussion: Bicolon, with the Masoretes.

VERSE–LINE: 41:22b:

הָרִאשֹׁנוֹת ׀ מָה הֵנָּה	22bA	The first things – what (do) they (mean)?
הַגִּידוּ וְנָשִׂימָה לִבֵּנוּ וְנֵדְעָה אַחֲרִיתָן	22bB	Tell us, so that we may set our heart to it and know their outcome,
אוֹ הַבָּאוֹת הַשְׁמִיעֻנוּ׃	22bC	or cause us to hear the things to come.

𝔪 distinctive accents: 7 – 5 – 1.
Stresses: 3 + 5 + 3.
Verse-line parallelism: ראשׁון || בוא; נגד || ידע || שׁמע; אחרית || בוא (unique); grammatical parallelism.

Discussion: Despite the long colon v. 22bB we follow 𝔪.[2]

[1]For an Ugaritic example of this device see KTU 1.6:I.62-65.
[2]See our remarks p. 88.

VERSE–LINE: 41:23a:

הַגִּידוּ הָאֹתִיּוֹת לְאָחוֹר	23aA	Tell us the things to come in the future,
וְנֵדְעָה כִּי אֱלֹהִים אַתֶּם	23aB	that we may know that you are gods.

𝔐 distinctive accents: 5 – 2.
Stresses: 3 + 4.
Verse-line parallelism: נגד || ידע.

VERSE–LINE: 41:23b:

אַף־תֵּיטִיבוּ וְתָרֵעוּ	23bA	Do both something good and something bad,
וְנִשְׁתָּעָה וְנִרָא* יַחְדָּו׃	23bB	that we will become afraid and will fear together.

𝔐 distinctive accents: 5 – 1.
Stresses: 2 + 3.
Verse-line parallelism: רעע || ירא.

VERSE–LINE: 41:24a:

הֵן־אַתֶּם מֵאַיִן	24aA	Look, you are less than nothing,
וּפָעָלְכֶם מֵאָפַע	24aB	and your work is less than nought;

𝔐 distinctive accents: 5 – 2.
Stresses: 2 + 2.
Verse-line parallelism: אתם || ־כם; מן || מן; אין || אפע.

VERSE–LINE: 41:24bA:

תּוֹעֵבָה יִבְחַר בָּכֶם׃	24bA	an abomination is he who chooses you.

𝔐 distinctive accent: 1.
Stresses: 3.
Verse-line parallelism: None (unicolon).

Discussion: It would be possible to read v. 24 as a tricolon, but we have opted for a bicolon plus unicolon because of the change of subject, the stronger parallelism between vv. 24aA and 24aB, and the different number of stresses (3 versus 2).

VERSE–LINE: 41:25a:

הַעִירוֹתִי מִצָּפוֹן וַיַּאת	25aA	I wake up from the north him who is approaching,
מִמִּזְרַח־שֶׁמֶשׁ יִקְרָא בִשְׁ	25aB	from the east him who will call me by name.

𝔐 distinctive accents: 5 – 2.
Stresses: 3 + 3.
Verse-line parallelism: עור || קרא; מן || מן; צפון || מזרח.

VERSE–LINE: 41:25b:

וְיָבֹ֣א סְגָנִים֙ כְּמוֹ־חֹ֔מֶר 25bA And when he comes, governors (will become) as loam,
וּכְמ֥וֹ יוֹצֵ֖ר יִרְמָס־טִֽיט׃ 25bB and as a potter he will tread the clay.

𝔐 distinctive accents: 5 – 1.
Stresses: 3 + 3.
Verse-line parallelism: בוא || רמס; כמו || כמו; חמר || טיט; grammatical parallelism.

VERSE–LINE: 41:26a:

מִֽי־הִגִּ֤יד מֵרֹאשׁ֙ וְנֵדָ֔עָה 26aA Who told us from the beginning so that we might know,
וּמִלְּפָנִ֖ים וְנֹאמַ֣ר צַדִּ֑יק 26aB and beforehand, so that we might say: "He is right!"?

𝔐 distinctive accents: 5 – 2.
Stresses: 3 + 3.
Verse-line parallelism: מן || מן; ראש || לפנים; ידע || אמר.
Discussion: The verse-lines are linked by ellipsis.

VERSE–LINE: 41:26bA:

אַ֣ף אֵין־מַגִּ֗יד 26bA No, there was no one who was telling,
אַ֚ף אֵ֣ין מַשְׁמִ֔יעַ 26bB no, there was no one who let hear,
אַ֥ף אֵין־שֹׁמֵ֖עַ אִמְרֵיכֶֽם׃ 26bC no, there was no one who heard your words.

𝔐 distinctive accents: 7 – 5 – 1.
Stresses: 2 + 3 + 3.
Verse-line parallelism: אף || אף || אף; אין || אין || אין; נגד || שמע Hiph. || שמע Qal; grammatical parallelism.

VERSE–LINE: 41:27a:

רִאשׁ֥וֹן לְצִיּ֖וֹן הִנֵּ֣ה הִנָּ֑ם 27aA The First to Zion: Look them over there!
וְלִירוּשָׁלִַ֖ם מְבַשֵּׂ֥ר אֶתֵּֽן׃ 27aB And to Jerusalem: I will give a herald of good tidings!

𝔐 distinctive accents: 2 – 1.
Stresses: 4 + 3.
Verse-line parallelism: ל || ל; ציון || ירושלם.

VERSE–LINE: 41:28a:

וְאֵ֙רֶא֙ וְאֵ֣ין אִ֔ישׁ 28aA And when I look, there is no man,
וּמֵאֵ֖לֶּה וְאֵ֣ין יוֹעֵ֑ץ 28aB and with them, there is no counsellor,

וְאֶשְׁאָלֵם וְיָשִׁיבוּ דָבָר׃	28aC	that I could ask them and they would reply one word.

𝔐 distinctive accents: 5 – 2 – 1.
Stresses: 3 + 3 + 3.
Verse-line parallelism: אין \|\| אין; איש \|\| יועץ; grammatical parallelism.

VERSE–LINE: 41:12b:

הֵן כֻּלָּם אָוֶן	29aA	Look, all of them are iniquity,
אֶפֶס מַעֲשֵׂיהֶם	29aB	non-existent are their works
רוּחַ וָתֹהוּ נִסְכֵּיהֶם׃	29aC	wind and void their molten images.

𝔐 distinctive accents: conjunctive accent – 2 – 1.
Stresses: 3 + 2 + 3.
Verse-line parallelism: און || אפס || רוח || תהו (unique); מעשׂה || נסך; ־הם || ־הם.

3.4 Isaiah 41 – Delimitation of Strophes

STROPHE A.i.1 (Isa. 41:1)

הַחֲרִישׁוּ אֵלַי אִיִּים	1aA	Be silent to me, islands,
וּלְאֻמִּים יַחֲלִיפוּ כֹחַ	1aB	and let the nations renew their strength,
יִגְּשׁוּ אָז יְדַבֵּרוּ	1bA	let them draw near, then let them speak up,
יַחְדָּו לַמִּשְׁפָּט נִקְרָבָה׃	1bB	let us go to court together.

= Masoretic verse.
Separation ↑: major division markers in the textual tradition; imperative(s); vocative; swapping (subject).
Separation ↓: major division markers in the textual tradition; deictic particle(s); jussive(s); cohortative(s); swapping (adjunct).
Strophe parallelism: חרש || דבר (antithetical); grammatical parallelism.

STROPHE A.i.2 (Isa. 41:2a–b)

מִי הֵעִיר מִמִּזְרָח צֶדֶק	2aA	Who wakes up justice from the east,
יִקְרָאֵהוּ לְרַגְלָיו*	2aB	calls it to his feet?
יִתֵּן לְפָנָיו גּוֹיִם	2bA	He puts nations before him,
וּמְלָכִים יֹרִד*	2bB	and makes kings step down.

≠ Masoretic verse.
Separation ↑: major division markers in the textual tradition; interrogative pronoun; swapping (adjunct).
Separation ↓: swapping (object).
Strophe parallelism: רגל || ירד.

Discussion: The division of the 𝔐 has everything to do with its exegesis of this difficult verse. See our remarks on the colometry pp. 75-6. Because both v. 2a and v. 2b describe the doing of obeisance the two should be read as one strophe.

STROPHE A.i.3 (Isa. 41:2c–3)

יִתֵּן כֶּעָפָר חַרְבּוֹ	2cA	His sword makes like dust,
כְּקַשׁ נִדָּף קַשְׁתּוֹ׃	2cB	his bow (makes) like dispersed chaff.
יִרְדְּפֵם יַעֲבוֹר שָׁלוֹם	3aA	He pursues them, passes on safely,
אֹרַח בְּרַגְלָיו לֹא יָבוֹא׃	3aB	does not go the road on foot.

≠ Masoretic verse.
Separation ↑: repetitive verse-line parallelism; swapping (subject); swapping (adjunct).
Separation ↓: major division markers in the textual tradition; swapping (object); swapping (adjunct).
Strophe parallelism: נדף ‖ רדף; חרב ‖ שלום (antithetical); grammatical parallelism.
Discussion: Because 𝔐's strophic division is of little value here (see the preceding strophe), we feel free to combine v. 2c and v. 3 which both describe the victorious passage of Cyrus.

STROPHE A.ii.1 (Isa. 41:4)

מִי־פָעַל וְעָשָׂה	4aA	Who has worked and made (this)?
קֹרֵא הַדֹּרוֹת מֵרֹאשׁ	4aB	He who is calling the generations from the beginning!
אֲנִי יְהוָה רִאשׁוֹן	4bA	I, the LORD am the First,
וְאֶת־אַחֲרֹנִים אֲנִי־הוּא׃	4bB	and with the last ones I am the same One.

= Masoretic verse.
Separation ↑: major division markers in the textual tradition; interrogative pronoun;
Separation ↓: major division markers in the textual tradition; independent pers. pronoun; swapping (adjunct).
Strophe parallelism: ראש ‖ ראשון.
Discussion: The major division markers after v. 4a in 𝔊[SA] are difficult to explain, especially those in 𝔊[S] which also has a division after v.3. Possibly they anticipate a tradition which is also attested by 1𝔔[a] – a major division after v. 4. In any case the circumstance that v. 4b contains the answer to v. 4a counsels against their division.

STROPHE A.ii.2 (Isa. 41:5–6)

רָא֤וּ אִיִּים֙ וְיִירָ֔אוּ	5aA	The islands see (it) and fear,
קְצ֥וֹת הָאָ֖רֶץ יֶחֱרָ֑דוּ	5aB	the ends of the earth tremble,
קָרְב֖וּ וַיֶּאֱתָיֽוּן׃	5aC	they come near and approach.
אִ֥ישׁ אֶת־רֵעֵ֖הוּ יַעְזֹ֑רוּ	6aA	Each man helps his friend,
וּלְאָחִ֖יו יֹאמַ֥ר חֲזָֽק׃	6aB	and speaks to his brother: "Be strong!"

≠ Masoretic verse.
Separation ↑: major division markers in the textual tradition; swapping (subject).
Separation ↓: major division markers in the textual tradition; imperative(s); marker of direct speech; swapping (subject); swapping (object); swapping (adjunct)
Strophe parallelism: אי ‖ איש; ירא ‖ עזר (antithetical); ירא ‖ חזק (antithetical; the same pair in v. 13); grammatical parallelism.
Discussion: The strophe parallelism and especially the contrast with vv. 10, 13 argue strongly in favour of joining vv. 5-6 into one strophe. An additional argument may be derived from the major dividers before v. 5 and after v. 6 (see p. 113).

STROPHE A.ii.3 (Isa. 41:7)

וַיְחַזֵּ֤ק חָרָשׁ֙ אֶת־צֹרֵ֔ף	7aA	The craftsman strengthens the goldsmith,
מַחֲלִ֥יק פַּטִּ֖ישׁ אֶת־ה֣וֹלֶם פָּ֑עַם	7aB	the sheet metal worker the blacksmith,
אֹמֵ֤ר לַדֶּ֙בֶק֙ ט֣וֹב ה֔וּא	7bA	saying of the soldering: "It is good!",
וַיְחַזְּקֵ֥הוּ בְמַסְמְרִ֖ים לֹ֥א יִמּֽוֹט׃	7bB	and he strengthens it with nails so that it will not topple.

= Masoretic verse.
Separation ↑: major division markers in the textual tradition; repetitive verse-line parallelism.
Separation ↓: major division markers in the textual tradition; demonstrative pronoun; marker of direct speech.
Strophe parallelism: חזק ‖ חזק; grammatical parallelism.

STROPHE B.i.1 (Isa. 41:8)

וְאַתָּה֙ יִשְׂרָאֵ֣ל עַבְדִּ֔י	8aA	But you, O Israel, my servant,
יַעֲקֹ֖ב אֲשֶׁ֣ר בְּחַרְתִּ֑יךָ	8aB	Jacob, whom I have chosen,
זֶ֖רַע אַבְרָהָ֥ם אֹהֲבִֽי׃	8aC	seed of Abraham, my friend,

= Masoretic verse.
Separation ↑: major division markers in the textual tradition; independent pers. pronoun; vocatives; repetitive verse-line parallelism.
Separation ↓: None (one verse-line).

Strophe parallelism: None (one verse-line).
Discussion: Despite the fact that the sentence runs on through vv. 9-10 we accept the division of 𝔐. See p. 640 for more examples of this phenomenon.

STROPHE B.i.2 (Isa. 41:9)

אֲשֶׁר הֶחֱזַקְתִּיךָ מִקְצוֹת הָאָרֶץ	9aA	(you), whom I grasped from the ends of the earth,
וּמֵאֲצִילֶיהָ קְרָאתִיךָ	9aB	and whom I called from its farthest corners,
וָאֹמַר לְךָ עַבְדִּי־אַתָּה	9bA	you, to whom I said: You are my servant,
בְּחַרְתִּיךָ וְלֹא מְאַסְתִּיךָ׃	9bB	I have chosen you and have not rejected you,

= Masoretic verse.
Separation ↑: repetitive verse-line parallelism; swapping (adjunct)
Separation ↓: independent pers. pronoun; marker of direct speech; repetitive verse-line parallelism.
Strophe parallelism: ־ךָ || ־ךָ || ־ךָ || ־ךָ (all m.s.); קרא || בחר; grammatical parallelism.

STROPHE B.i.3 (Isa. 41:10)

אַל־תִּירָא כִּי עִמְּךָ־אָנִי	10aA	Do not fear, for I am with you,
אַל־תִּשְׁתָּע כִּי־אֲנִי אֱלֹהֶיךָ	10aB	do not be afraid, for I am your God.
אִמַּצְתִּיךָ אַף־עֲזַרְתִּיךָ	10bA	I do strengthen you, and I do help you too,
אַף־תְּמַכְתִּיךָ בִּימִין צִדְקִי׃	10bB	I do hold you, with the right hand of my justice.

= Masoretic verse.
Separation ↑: deictic particle(s); independent pers. pronoun; jussive(s); repetitive verse-line parallelism; swapping (adjunct).
Separation ↓: major division markers in the textual tradition; deictic particle(s); repetitive verse-line parallelism.
Strophe parallelism: ירא || עזר; ־ךָ || ־ךָ || ־ךָ || ־ךָ (all m.s.); ירא || אמץ.

STROPHE B.ii.1 (Isa. 41:11)

הֵן יֵבֹשׁוּ וְיִכָּלְמוּ	11aA	Behold, they will be ashamed and disgraced,
כֹּל הַנֶּחֱרִים בָּךְ	11aB	all who rage against you.
יִהְיוּ כְאַיִן וְיֹאבְדוּ	11bA	They will be as nothing and perish,
אַנְשֵׁי רִיבֶךָ׃	11bB	the men of your lawsuit.

= Masoretic verse.
Separation ↑: major division markers in the textual tradition; deictic particle(s).
Separation ↓: None.

Strophe parallelism: בושׁ || אבד; חרה || ריב; ־ך || ־ך (m.s.); grammatical parallelism.

STROPHE B.ii.2 (Isa. 41:12)

תְּבַקְשֵׁם֙ וְלֹ֣א תִמְצָאֵ֔ם	12aA	You will search for them, but not find them,
אַנְשֵׁ֖י מַצֻּתֶ֑ךָ	12aB	the men of your dispute.
יִהְי֧וּ כְאַ֛יִן וּכְאֶ֖פֶס	12bA	They will become as nothing and non-existent,
אַנְשֵׁ֥י מִלְחַמְתֶּֽךָ׃	12bB	the men of your warfare.

= Masoretic verse.

Separation ↑: None, but note the redundant pronominal suffix.

Separation ↓: major division markers in the textual tradition.

Strophe parallelism: לא || אין; מצא || אין; אישׁ || אישׁ; מצות || מלחמה (unique); ־ך || ־ך (m.s.).

STROPHE B.ii.3 (Isa. 41:13)

כִּ֗י אֲנִ֛י יְהוָ֥ה אֱלֹהֶ֖יךָ	13aA	For I am the LORD your God,
מַחֲזִ֣יק יְמִינֶ֑ךָ	13aB	who grasps your right hand,
הָאֹמֵ֥ר לְךָ֛ אַל־תִּירָ֖א	13bA	who says to you: Do not fear,
אֲנִ֥י עֲזַרְתִּֽיךָ׃	13bB	it is I who helps you.

= Masoretic verse.

Separation ↑: major division markers in the textual tradition; deictic particle(s); independent pers. pronoun; repetitive verse-line parallelism.

Separation ↓: major division markers in the textual tradition; independent pers. pronoun; jussive(s); marker of direct speech; repetitive verse-line parallelism.

Strophe parallelism: אני || אני; חזק || עזר; חזק || ירא (antithetical); ־ך || ־ך || ־ך || ־ך(all m.s.).

STROPHE B.iii.1 (Isa. 41:14)

אַל־תִּֽירְאִי֙ תּוֹלַ֣עַת יַעֲקֹ֔ב	14aA	Do not fear, O worm Jacob,
רִמָּתִי* יִשְׂרָאֵ֑ל	14aB	O maggot Israel!
אֲנִ֤י עֲזַרְתִּיךְ֙ נְאֻם־יְהוָ֔ה	14bA	I am the one who helps you, declares the LORD,
וְגֹאֲלֵ֖ךְ קְד֥וֹשׁ יִשְׂרָאֵֽל׃	14bB	and your Redeemer is the Holy One of Israel.

= Masoretic verse.

Separation ↑: major division markers in the textual tradition; jussive(s); vocatives.

Separation ↓: major division markers in the textual tradition; independent pers. pronoun; marker of direct speech.
Strophe parallelism: ירא || עזר; יעקב || יהוה; ישׂראל || ישׂראל.

STROPHE B.iii.2 (Isa. 41:15)

הִנֵּה שַׂמְתִּיךְ לְמוֹרַג חָרוּץ חָדָשׁ	15aA	Behold, I make you into a sharp new threshing sledge,
בַּעַל פִּיפִיּוֹת	15aB	with many teeth.
תָּדוּשׁ הָרִים וְתָדֹק	15bA	You will thresh mountains and crush (them),
וּגְבָעוֹת כַּמֹּץ תָּשִׂים׃	15bB	and hills you will make into chaff.

= Masoretic verse.
Separation ↑: major division markers in the textual tradition; deictic particle(s).
Separation ↓: swapping (object); swapping (adjunct).
Strophe parallelism: שׂים || שׂים; both verse-lines use the threshing imagery.

STROPHE B.iii.3 (Isa. 41:16)

תִּזְרֵם וְרוּחַ תִּשָּׂאֵם	16aA	You will winnow them and the wind will take them up
וּסְעָרָה תָּפִיץ אוֹתָם	16aB	and the gale will scatter them.
וְאַתָּה תָּגִיל בַּיהוָה	16bA	And you will exult in the LORD,
בִּקְדוֹשׁ יִשְׂרָאֵל תִּתְהַלָּל׃	16bB	glory in the Holy One of Israel.

= Masoretic verse.
Separation ↑: repetitive verse-line parallelism; swapping (subject).
Separation ↓: major division markers in the textual tradition; independent pers. pronoun; swapping (adjunct).
Strophe parallelism: None.
Discussion: Because v. 16a sets forth the imagery of the grain harvest 𝔊^SAQ make a major incision after v. 16a, whereas several Hebrew and Syriac witnesses mark a major division after v. 16b. However, v. 16b does not tally with v. 17 and it is far more likely that this verse-line describes the equivalent of the joy of harvest time (cf. Isa. 9:3). So 𝔐's delimitation is to be preferred.

STROPHE C.i.1 (Isa. 41:17)

הָעֲנִיִּים וְהָאֶבְיוֹנִים	17aA	The afflicted and poor
מְבַקְשִׁים מַיִם וָאַיִן	17aB	are searching for water but there is none;
לְשׁוֹנָם בַּצָּמָא נָשָׁתָּה	17aC	their tongue is parched with thirst.
אֲנִי יְהוָה אֶעֱנֵם	17bA	I am the LORD, I will answer them,
אֱלֹהֵי יִשְׂרָאֵל לֹא אֶעֶזְבֵם׃	17bB	the God of Israel, I will not forsake them.

= Masoretic verse.
Separation ↑: major division markers in the textual tradition; swapping (subject); swapping (adjunct).
Separation ↓: independent pers. pronoun; repetitive verse-line parallelism.
Strophe parallelism: בקשׁ || עזב.
Discussion: $\mathfrak{G}^{SA}$ have a major division after v. 17a, possibly because from v. 17b the text continues in the first person. But the answering of the afflicted and poor is a well-known theme in the Psalms (see e.g. Ps. 86:1).

STROPHE C.i.2 (Isa. 41:18)

אֶפְתַּח עַל־שְׁפָיִים נְהָרוֹת	18aA	I will open rivers on the bare tracks,
וּבְתוֹךְ בְּקָעוֹת מַעְיָנוֹת	18aB	and wells in the middle of the valleys.
אָשִׂים מִדְבָּר לַאֲגַם־מַיִם	18bA	I will make the desert a pool of water,
וְאֶרֶץ צִיָּה לְמוֹצָאֵי מָיִם׃	18bB	and the dry land springs of water.

= Masoretic verse.
Separation ↑: swapping (adjunct).
Separation ↓: repetitive verse-line parallelism.
Strophe parallelism: שׁפי || מדבר; נהר || אגם; מעין || מוצא מים (unique); grammatical parallelism.

STROPHE C.i.3 (Isa. 41:19)

אֶתֵּן בַּמִּדְבָּר אֶרֶז שִׁטָּה	19aA	In the desert I will set cedars, acacias,
וַהֲדַס וְעֵץ שָׁמֶן	19aB	and myrtles and pine-trees.
אָשִׂים בָּעֲרָבָה	19bA	In the bare valley I will put
בְּרוֹשׁ תִּדְהָר וּתְאַשּׁוּר יַחְדָּו׃	19bB	junipers, ashes and cypresses together.

= Masoretic verse.
Separation ↑: swapping (adjunct).
Separation ↓: swapping (adjunct).
Strophe parallelism: נתן || שׂים; ב || ב; מדבר || ערבה; ארז || ברושׁ (the other pairs of trees are unique);
Discussion: The small space in $1\mathfrak{Q}^a$ is probably not a Setuma but a verse-line delimiter, as $1\mathfrak{Q}^a$ sometimes uses.[1]

STROPHE C.i.4 (Isa. 41:20)

לְמַעַן יִרְאוּ וְיֵדְעוּ	20aA	That they may see and know,
וְיָשִׂימוּ וְיַשְׂכִּילוּ יַחְדָּו	20aB	and may observe and perceive together,
כִּי יַד־יְהוָה עָשְׂתָה זֹּאת	20bA	that the hand of the LORD has made this,

[1] See pp. 643, 646-7.

וּקְד֥וֹשׁ יִשְׂרָאֵ֖ל בְּרָאָֽהּ׃	20bB	and that the Holy One of Israel has created it.

= Masoretic verse.
Separation ↑: deictic particle(s).
Separation ↓: major division markers in the textual tradition; deictic particle(s); demonstrative pronoun; swapping (subject).
Strophe parallelism: None.

STROPHE C.ii.1 (Isa. 41:21)

קָרְב֥וּ רִֽיבְכֶ֖ם	21aA	Bring near your case,
יֹאמַ֣ר יְהוָ֑ה	21aB	says the LORD,
הַגִּ֙ישׁוּ֙ עֲצֻמֽוֹתֵיכֶ֔ם	21bA	bring closer your strong points,
יֹאמַ֖ר מֶ֥לֶךְ יַעֲקֹֽב׃	21bB	says the King of Jacob.

= Masoretic verse.
Separation ↑: major division markers in the textual tradition; imperative(s); marker of direct speech.
Separation ↓: major division marker in the textual tradition; imperative(s); marker of direct speech.
Strophe parallelism: קרב \|\| נגש; ריב \|\| עצום (unique); ־כם \|\| ־כם; אמר \|\| אמר; יהוה \|\| יעקב; grammatical parallelism.

STROPHE C.ii.2 (Isa. 41:22)

יַגִּ֙ישׁוּ֙ וְיַגִּ֣ידוּ לָ֔נוּ	22aA	Let them bring closer and tell us
אֵ֖ת אֲשֶׁ֣ר תִּקְרֶ֑ינָה	22aB	what will happen.
הָרִאשֹׁנ֣וֹת ׀ מָ֣ה הֵ֗נָּה	22bA	The first things – what (do) they (mean)?[2]
הַגִּ֙ידוּ֙ וְנָשִׂ֣ימָה לִבֵּ֔נוּ וְנֵֽדְעָה֙ אַחֲרִיתָ֔ן	22bB	Tell us, so that we may set our heart to it and know their outcome,
א֥וֹ הַבָּא֖וֹת הַשְׁמִיעֻֽנוּ׃	22bC	or cause us to hear the things to come.

= Masoretic verse.
Separation ↑: major division marker in the textual tradition; jussive(s).
Separation ↓: independent pers. pronoun; interrogative pronoun; imperative(s); cohortative(s); swapping (subject); swapping (object).
Strophe parallelism: נגד \|\| נגד; ־נו \|\| ־נו; את אשר תקרינה \|\| הבאות (antithetical; unique); note that both are 3 f.p.

STROPHE C.ii.3 (Isa. 41:23)

הַגִּ֙ידוּ֙ הָאֹתִיּ֣וֹת לְאָח֔וֹר	23aA	Tell us the things to come in the future,
וְנֵ֣דְעָ֔ה כִּ֥י אֱלֹהִ֖ים אַתֶּ֑ם	23aB	that we may know that you are gods.

[2]See Gen. 21:29 מה הנה שבע כבשת האלה "What do those seven ewes mean?"

אַף־תֵּיטִיבוּ וְתָרֵעוּ	23bA	Do both something good and something bad,
וְנִשְׁתָּעָה וְנִרָא* יַחְדָּו׃	23bB	that we will become afraid and will fear together.

= Masoretic verse.
Separation ↑: deictic particle(s); independent pers. pronoun; imperative(s); cohortative(s).
Separation ↓: deictic particle(s); jussive(s); cohortative(s).
Strophe parallelism: Because doing both good and evil is proof of divine power[3] and fearing the deity is a common concept there is a strong semantic bond between the two verses even though no formal parallelism exists.

STROPHE C.ii.4 (Isa. 41:24)

הֵן־אַתֶּם מֵאַיִן	24aA	Look, you are less than nothing,
וּפָעָלְכֶם מֵאָפַע	24aB	and your work is less than nought;
תּוֹעֵבָה יִבְחַר בָּכֶם׃	24bA	an abomination is he who chooses you.

= Masoretic verse.
Separation ↑: deictic particle(s); independent pers. pronoun; repetitive verse-line parallelism.
Separation ↓: major division markers in the textual tradition;
Strophe parallelism: כם־ || כם־.

STROPHE C.iii.1 (Isa. 41:25)

הַעִירוֹתִי מִצָּפוֹן וַיַּאת	25aA	I wake up from the north him who is approaching,
מִמִּזְרַח־שֶׁמֶשׁ יִקְרָא בִשְׁמִי	25aB	from the east him who will call me by name.
וְיָבֹא סְגָנִים כְּמוֹ־חֹמֶר	25bA	And when he comes, governors (will become) as loam,
וּכְמוֹ יוֹצֵר יִרְמָס־טִיט׃	25bB	and as a potter he will tread the clay.

= Masoretic verse.
Separation ↑: major division markers in the textual tradition; repetitive verse-line parallelism; swapping (adjunct).
Separation ↓: major division marker in the textual tradition; repetitive verse-line parallelism; swapping (adjunct).
Strophe parallelism: בוא || אתה.
Discussion: The major division $\mathfrak{G}^{Q}$ has in the middle of v. 25 is obviously erroneous and should have been posited after v. 24. From that point until the end of v. 26 $\mathfrak{G}^{A}$ seems to mark the strophes again.

[3]See our remarks p. 73, n. 12.

STROPHE C.iii.2 (Isa. 41:26)

מִֽי־הִגִּ֤יד מֵרֹאשׁ֙ וְנֵדָ֔עָה	26aA	Who told us from the beginning so that we might know,
וּמִלְּפָנִ֖ים וְנֹאמַ֣ר צַדִּ֑יק	26aB	and beforehand, so that we might say: "He is right!"?
אַ֣ף אֵין־מַגִּ֗יד	26bA	No, there was no one who was telling,
אַ֚ף אֵ֣ין מַשְׁמִ֔יעַ	26bB	no, there was no one who let hear,
אַ֖ף אֵין־שֹׁמֵ֥עַ אִמְרֵיכֶֽם׃	26bC	no, there was no one who heard your words.

= Masoretic verse.
Separation ↑: major division marker in the textual tradition; interrogative pronoun; cohortative(s); marker of direct speech; repetitive verse-line parallelism.
Separation ↓: major division markers in the textual tradition; deictic particle(s); repetitive verse-line parallelism.
Strophe parallelism: נגד || נגד; אמר || אמר.

STROPHE C.iii.3 (Isa. 41:27)

רִאשׁ֥וֹן לְצִיּ֖וֹן הִנֵּ֣ה הִנָּ֑ם	27aA	The First to Zion: Look them over there!
וְלִירוּשָׁלִַ֖ם מְבַשֵּׂ֥ר אֶתֵּֽן׃	27aB	And to Jerusalem: I will give a herald of good tidings!

= Masoretic verse.
Separation ↑: major division markers in the textual tradition; deictic particle(s); marker of direct speech; swapping (object); swapping (adjunct).
Separation ↓: None (one verse-line).
Strophe parallelism: None (one verse-line).

STROPHE C.iii.4 (Isa. 41:28–29)

וְאֵ֙רֶא֙ וְאֵ֣ין אִ֔ישׁ	28aA	And when I look, there is no man,
וּמֵאֵ֖לֶּה וְאֵ֣ין יוֹעֵ֑ץ	28aB	and with them, there is no counsellor,
וְאֶשְׁאָלֵ֖ם וְיָשִׁ֥יבוּ דָבָֽר׃	28aC	that I could ask them and they would reply one word.
הֵ֣ן כֻּלָּ֔ם אָ֥וֶן	29aA	Look, all of them are iniquity,
אֶ֖פֶס מַעֲשֵׂיהֶ֑ם	29aB	non-existent are their works
ר֥וּחַ וָתֹ֖הוּ נִסְכֵּיהֶֽם׃	29aC	wind and void their molten images.

≠ Masoretic verse.
Separation ↑: demonstrative pronoun; repetitive verse-line parallelism.
Separation ↓: major division markers in the textual tradition; deictic particle(s); swapping (subject).
Strophe parallelism: ראה || הנה; אין || אפס.

Discussion: Admittedly it is somewhat uncertain whether vv. 28-29 represent one or two strophes. The parallelism between the two is rather weak. However, since both verses deal with the futility of the faith in images that are unable to speak (cf. Ps. 115:4-8; 135:15-18; Hab. 2:19), it seems a better option to combine the two than to treat them as independent strophes.

3.5 Isaiah 41 – Delimitation of Canticles

CANTICLE A.i (41:1–3)

Separation ↑: major division markers in the textual tradition; thematic discontinuity;[1] change of subject.
Separation ↓: major division markers in the textual tradition.
Canticle parallelism: לאם || גוי (inclusion); דבר || קרא (concatenation); משפט || צדק (concatenation); נתן || נתן (concatenation); רגל || רגל (inclusion).
Thematic unity: yes. As indicated by the canticle parallelism, all three strophes deal with God's lawsuit against the nations and their leaders.
Discussion: The suffix of ירדפם (3aA) links up with the nations and kings of v. 2b.

The major division markers found in 1Q^{a} and 𝔊^{AQ} after v. 1 may be regarded as remnants of an earlier strophe division because all three also have a major division after the preceding chapter. 𝔊^{A} ended the next strophe after v. 2aB which is unlikely.[2] The same manuscript marks the boundary after v. 3 proleptically.

CANTICLE A.ii (41:4–7)

Separation ↑: major division markers in the textual tradition; change of subject.
Separation ↓: major division markers in the textual tradition.
Canticle parallelism: In general terms, the work of God (v. 4a) is contrasted to the making of images (v. 7; inclusion); קרא || קרב (responsion); דור || אי (unique; responsion); חזק || חזק (concatenation/responsion).
Thematic unity: yes (see above for the first strophe).
Discussion: On the major dividers after v. 4aB see 3.4. Because 1Q^{a} and 𝔊^{A} also have dividers after v. 6 and v. 7, the dividers after vv. 4bB and 6aB may represent a remnant of an earlier strophic division.

[1]Even though יחליפו כח (1aB) clearly links Chapter 41 to Chapter 40 (31aA) the lawsuit and the veiled description of Cyrus are new.
[2]See our comments p. 104.

CANTICLE B.i (41:8–10)

Separation ↑: major division markers in the textual tradition; thematic discontinuity; change of subject.
Separation ↓: major division markers in the textual tradition.
Canticle parallelism: עבד || עבד (inclusion); בחר || בחר (ubique; inclusion); חזק || ירא (responsion) חזק || תמך (inclusion).
All three strophes linked by the continuing sentence (enjambment).
Thematic unity: yes.
Discussion: It would seem certain that the Greek tradition has preserved the correct canticle division here.

CANTICLE B.ii (41:11–13)

Separation ↑: major division markers in the textual tradition; change of subject.
Separation ↓: major division markers in the textual tradition.
Canticle parallelism: איש || איש (concatenation); כ || כ (responsion); אין || אין; ריב || מצות (unique; concatenation); ־ך || ־ך (in all strophes)
Thematic unity: yes.
Discussion: It seems that we have testimony here of two different traditions of canticle division. $\mathfrak{G}^{BA}$ have dividers after v. 12 and $\mathfrak{G}^{SA}$ plus $\mathfrak{S}^{b}$ after v. 14. The repeated אל תירא (13bA, 14aA) and אני עזרתיך (13bB, 14bA) might be cited in support of this division. On the other hand, these refrains might also serve to connect the canticles ii and iii of sub-canto B. The next major dividing point in $\mathfrak{G}^{SAQ}$ comes after v. 16aB and as a result these manuscripts have three coherent canticles of two strophes each. The problems start in v. 16b. $\mathfrak{G}^{SQ}$ ($\mathfrak{G}^{A}$ is lacking here) are forced to connect this verse-line with v. 17a which is clearly garbled in $\mathfrak{G}$: καὶ ἀγαλλιάσονται οἱ πτωχοὶ καὶ οἱ ἐνδεεῖς ζητήσουσιν γὰρ ὕδωρ καὶ οὐκ ἔσται "and the poor and the needy will exult, for they will seek water, and it is not there".[3] Though it is possible that their canticle division goes back on ancient (Hebrew?) tradition, it is hardly possible to accept the final one on this unreliable basis.

A different division has been preserved by $1\mathfrak{Q}^{a}$, $\mathfrak{M}$ and $\mathfrak{S}^{ac}$ (after v. 13). The refrain קדוש ישראל (14bB, 16bB) argues in its favour. Because the latter division is attested by both the Hebrew and Syriac tradition we opted for it.

[3]The interpunction in the two manuscripts shows that this is what they read.

CANTICLE B.iii (Isa. 41:14–16)

Separation ↑: major division markers in the textual tradition. change of subject.[4]
Separation ↓: major division markers in the textual tradition.
Canticle parallelism: תולעת || מורג (antithetical, unique; responsion); ירא || גיל (antithetical; inclusion); ךְ־ (f.s.) || ךְ־ (f.s.); קדוש ישראל || קדוש ישראל (responsion); דוש || זרה (unique; concatenation).
Thematic unity: yes. The antithetical parallelism between the soft worm of v. 14 and the sharp new threshing sledge of v. 15 connects the first two strophes, the threshing imagery connects strophes 2 and 3.
Discussion: The dividers in 𝔊^SAQ after v. 16aB mark the boundary after v. 16bB proleptically.

CANTICLE C.i (41:17–20)

Separation ↑: major division markers in the textual tradition; thematic discontinuity; change of subject.
Separation ↓: major division markers in the textual tradition.
Canticle parallelism: מים || מים (inclusion); אלהי ישראל || קדוש ישראל (responsion); שים || שים || שים (responsion/concatenation); מדבר || מדבר (concatenation).
Thematic unity: yes. The water in the dry land connects strophes 1–3. The first colon of strophe 4 would lack a subject if it were not the afflicted and poor mentioned in the first strophe. The miracles by which they will be saved are ascribed to the LORD by the responsions between vv. 17b and 20b.
Discussion: The major division markers in 𝔊^SA after v. 17aC and the small space (Setuma or verse-line delimiter?) in 1Q^a after v. 19aB are apparently erroneous. See with regard to 𝔊 our comment on B.ii.

CANTICLE C.ii (41:21–24)

Separation ↑: major division markers in the textual tradition; thematic discontinuity; change of subject.
Separation ↓: major division markers in the textual tradition.
Canticle parallelism: קרב || נגש (responsion); נגד || נגד (responsion); הראשנות || הבאות || האתיות (unique; responsion); ידע || ידע (both cohortatives); אחרית || אחור (unique); אתם || אתם; רעע || פעל.

[4]Note the change of gender: in v. 13 Israel is addressed in the 2nd person m.s., in v. 14-15a in the 2nd person f.s. which suddenly changes back to 2nd person m.s. from v. 15b onwards.

Thematic unity: yes. All four strophes are part of a polemic lawsuit meant to demonstrate the inability of other deities to do anything useful.
Discussion: The division markers in 𝔊[A] after v. 21 must be a remnant of strophe marking because the same manuscript also has major divison markers after v. 20.

CANTICLE C.iii (41:25–29)

Separation ↑: major division markers in the textual tradition; thematic discontinuity; change of subject.
Separation ↓: major division markers in the textual tradition.
Canticle parallelism: קרא בשם || ידע; נגד || בשׂר; ראשׁ || ראשׁון (as in 41:4!); אין || אין; שׁמע Hiph. || בשׂר; אמר (noun) || דבר (noun).
Thematic unity: The thematic unity between vv. 26-29 is not in doubt. All three strophes deal with the futility of the belief in powerless idols. This is even true of v. 27 because the scornful הנם must refer back to v. 26b. The relation between v. 25 and the other three strophes is not immediately apparent but becomes transparant if we compare C.ii, especially the parallelism between הראשׁנות (22bA) and מראשׁ (26aA): the verbs ויאת (25aA) and ויבא (25bA) are the explanation of הבאות (22bC) and האתיות (23aA).[5]
Discussion: 𝔊[Q] has a major divison after v. 25aB, but nothing after v. 24. This would seem to suggest that its division shifted to the wrong place. The dividers in 𝔊[A] after vv. 25 and 26 are probably remnants of an earlier strophe division. The somewhat better attested division after v. 26 is unlikely in view of the canticle parallelism we found. It is not attested in 𝔖.

3.6 Isaiah 41 – Delimitation of Macrostructure

The overall structure of Isaiah 41 appears to be fairly regular,

SUB-CANTOS	CANTICLES	STROPHES
A	2	6 (3+3)
B	3	6 (3+3+3)
C	3	12 (4+4+4)

Distant parallelism connecting the canticles of **sub-canto A**:
אי (v. 1aA – A.i) || אי (v. 5aA – A.ii); נגשׁ (v. 1bA – A.i) || קרב (v. 5aC

[5]With Beuken, 102.

– A.ii); מי (v. 2aA – A.i) || מי (v. 4aA – A.ii); קרא (v. 2aB – A.i) || קרא (v. 4aB – A.ii).

Cyrus is advancing as a whirlwind and the question who has instructed him to embark upon his victorious campaign is answered in the second canticle which contrasts the unlimited power of the Creator who is also the LORD of history with the futile reaction of the terrified nations trusting in their idols.

Distant parallelism connecting the canticles of **sub-canto B**: אתה (v. 8aA – B.i) || אתה (v. 16bA – B.iii); ישׂראל (v. 8aA – B.i) || ישׂראל (v. 14aB – B.iii) || ישׂראל (v. 16bB – B.iii); עבד (v. 8aA – B.i) || תולעת (v. 14aA – B.iii; unique, but in view of the strong distant parallelism and the other descriptions of the sorry state of the servant of the LORD, especially Isa. 53, intentional); יעקב (v.8aB – B.i) || יעקב (v. 14aA – B.iii); אמר (v. 9bA – B.ii) || אמר (v. 13bA – B.ii) || נאם (v. 14bA – B.iii); ירא (v. 10aA – B.i) || כלם (v. 11aA – B.ii) || ירא (v. 13bA – B.ii); ירא (v. 10aA – B.i) || גיל (v. 16bA – B.iii); עזר (v. 10bA – B.i) || עזר (v. 13bB – B.ii) || עזר (v. 14bA – B.iii); תמך (v. 10bB – B.i) || חזק (v. 13aB – B.ii); ימין (v. 10bB – B.i) || ימין (v. 13aB – B.ii); אבד (v. 11bA – B.ii) || פוץ (v. 16aB – B.iii).

In all three canticles Israel is addressed and all three contain promises of help for God's chosen people. B.ii and B.iii describe the destruction of Israel's opponents.

Distant parallelism connecting the canticles of **sub-canto C**: Whereas Jacob has a King (מלך, v. 21bB – C.i), the governors of the nations (סגן, v. 25bA – C.iii) will become as loam, so that the nations will have no counsellor left (מלך (v. 21bB – C.i) || יועץ (v. 28aB – C.iii). Furthermore אין (v. 17aB – C.i) || אין (v. 24aA – C.ii) || אין (v. 26bA-C, 28aA-B – C.iii); ידע (v. 20aA – C.i) || ידע (v. 22bB, 23aB – C.ii) || ידע (v. 26aA – C.iii); נגד (v. 22aA, 22bB, 23aA – C.ii) || נגד (vv. 26aA, 26bA – C.iii); שׁמע (v. 22bC – C.ii) || שׁמע (v. 26bB, bC – C.iii); בוא (v. 22bC – C.ii) || בוא (v. 25bA – C.iii); אתה (verb; v. 23aA – C.ii) || אתה (v. 25aA – C.iii).

In the last two canticles the issue is that the nations and their idols will be unable to tell what will happen in the future. Both the first and the last canticle contrast their failure with the way in which God lets Israel know the good news of its impending delivery.

For the canto as a whole, it is most significant that all three sub-cantos characterize the proceedings as a lawsuit (A: v. 1 – B: v. 11-12 – C: vv. 21-22). The inclusions between the first and the last sub-canto (A and C) are remarkable. Both emphasize that it is God who has spurred Cyrus on (A: v. 2 – C: v. 25), both describe his march as disastrous to the rulers of the nations (A: v. 2 – C: v. 25). In contrast to the idols from which some expect help (A: v. 7 C: v. 29), God will help Israel – this is the main theme of sub-canto B. The imagery of vv. 15-16 (B) would seem to indicate that Israel itself will play a role in Cyrus' demise of the nations (v. 2c – A).

Chapter 4

The Structure of Isaiah 42

4.1 Isaiah 42: Text and Translation

פ <ס> – $_1\mathfrak{Q}^{a}$ – $\mathfrak{G}^{SBAQ}$ – $\mathfrak{S}^{abcde}$ ______________________

A.i.1 (Isa. 42:1)

הֵן עַבְדִּי אֶתְמָךְ־בּוֹ	1aA	Behold, my servant whom I hold,[1]
בְּחִירִי רָצְתָה נַפְשִׁי	1aB	my chosen one, in whom my soul takes pleasure,
נָתַתִּי רוּחִי עָלָיו	1bA	I put my spirit on him,
מִשְׁפָּט לַגּוֹיִם יוֹצִיא׃	1bB	he will carry out justice for the nations.

A.i.2 (Isa. 42:2–3)

לֹא יִצְעַק וְלֹא יִשָּׂא	2aA	He will not shout or raise (his voice),[2]
וְלֹא־יַשְׁמִיעַ בַּחוּץ קוֹלוֹ׃	2aB	and he will not make his voice heard in the street.
קָנֶה רָצוּץ לֹא יִשְׁבּוֹר	3aA	A crushed reed he will not break,
וּפִשְׁתָּה כֵהָה לֹא יְכַבֶּנָּה	3aB	and a smouldering wick – he will not quench it.
לֶאֱמֶת יוֹצִיא מִשְׁפָּט׃	3aC	Truthfully he will bring forth justice.

A.i.3 (Isa. 42:4)

לֹא יִכְהֶה וְלֹא יֵרוֹץ*	4aA	He will not smoulder or be crushed,[3]
עַד־יָשִׂים בָּאָרֶץ מִשְׁפָּט	4aB	until he will put justice on earth,
וּלְתוֹרָתוֹ אִיִּים יְיַחֵילוּ׃	4aC	and the islands will await his teaching.

פ <ס> – $_1\mathfrak{Q}^{a}$ – $_4\mathfrak{Q}^{bh}$ – $\mathfrak{G}^{SBA}$ – $\mathfrak{S}^{abe}$ ....

A.ii.1 (Isa. 42:5)

כֹּה־אָמַר הָאֵל ׀ יְהוָה	5aA	Thus says God, the Lord,
בּוֹרֵא הַשָּׁמַיִם וְנוֹטֵיהֶם {$\mathfrak{G}^{A}$}	5aB	who created the heavens and stretched them out,

[1] It has often been argued that תמך should be rendered "to grasp (the hand)", hinting at royal investiture ceremonies of the ANE. See e.g. S.M. Paul, "Deutero-Isaiah and the Cuneiform Royal Inscriptions", *JAOS* 88 (1968), 180-6; M. Dijkstra, "De koninklijke Knecht: Voorstelling en investituur van de Knecht des Heren in Jesaja 42", in: H.H. Grosheide *et al.* (eds.), *De Knecht: Studies rondom Deutero-Jesaja aangeboden aan Prof. Dr. J.L. Koole*, Kampen 1978, 41-52. But since such a ceremony is unattested for ancient Israel and since Isa. 41:10 suggests a more neutral meaning, we prefer a non-committal translation.

[2] As in Isa. 42:11, the self-evident complement has been omitted.

[3] Although an intransitive Qal (so Koole, 153) is not entirely impossible, it is unlikely immediately after the transitive Qal in v. 3aA. With many others (probably also $\mathfrak{G}$) we vocalize as a Niphal, see for a judicious discussion A. Schoors, *The Preacher Sought to Find Pleasing Words*, Leuven 1992, 95.

	רֹקַע הָאָרֶץ וְצֶאֱצָאֶיהָ	5aC	who hammered out the earth and all that came forth from it,
	נֹתֵן נְשָׁמָה לָעָם עָלֶיהָ	5bA	who gives breath to the people on it,
{$\mathfrak{G}^{AQ}$}	וְרוּחַ לַהֹלְכִים בָּהּ׃	5bB	and spirit to those who walk on it,

A.ii.2 (Isa. 42:6)

	אֲנִי יְהוָה קְרָאתִיךָ בְצֶדֶק	6aA	I, the LORD, call[4] you justly
{$\mathfrak{G}^{A}$}	וְאַחְזֵק בְּיָדֶךָ וְאֶצָּרְךָ	6aB	and I will grasp your hand and will keep[5] you.
	וְאֶתֶּנְךָ לִבְרִית עָם	6bA	And I will make you a covenant of people,[6]
	לְאוֹר גּוֹיִם׃	6bB	a light for the nations,

A.ii.3 (Isa. 42:7)

	לִפְקֹחַ עֵינַיִם עִוְרוֹת	7aA	to open blind eyes,
	לְהוֹצִיא מִמַּסְגֵּר אַסִּיר	7bA	to bring prisoners from the dungeon,
{$\mathfrak{G}^{A}$}	מִבֵּית כֶּלֶא יֹשְׁבֵי חֹשֶׁךְ׃	7bB	from the house of confinement those who are sitting in darkness.

A.ii.4 (Isa. 42:8)

	אֲנִי יְהוָה הוּא שְׁמִי	8aA	I am the LORD, that is my name,
	וּכְבוֹדִי לְאַחֵר לֹא־אֶתֵּן	8bA	and my glory I will not give to another,
{$\mathfrak{G}^{S}$}	וּתְהִלָּתִי לַפְּסִילִים׃	8bB	nor my praise to graven images.

A.ii.5 (Isa. 42:9)

	הָרִאשֹׁנוֹת הִנֵּה־בָאוּ	9aA	The first things, look, they have come,
	וַחֲדָשׁוֹת אֲנִי מַגִּיד	9bA	and new things I am telling,
	בְּטֶרֶם תִּצְמַחְנָה אַשְׁמִיעַ אֶתְכֶם׃	9bB	before they sprout, I let you hear them.

פ <ס> – 1$\mathfrak{Q}^{a}$ – $\mathfrak{G}^{SBAQ}$ – $\mathfrak{S}^{abde}$

B.i.1 (Isa. 42:10)

	שִׁירוּ לַיהוָה שִׁיר חָדָשׁ	10aA	Sing for the LORD a new song,
	תְּהִלָּתוֹ מִקְצֵה הָאָרֶץ	10aB	his praise from the ends of the earth,
	יוֹרְדֵי הַיָּם וּמְלֹאוֹ	10bA	you who are sailing the sea and all that fills it,
{$\mathfrak{G}^{S}$}	אִיִּים וְיֹשְׁבֵיהֶם׃	10bB	you islands and those dwelling there!

[4] The tenses in this verse have long stymified translators. Cf., Barthélemy, 303-5. On the basis of our own research we propose an actual present, see M.C.A. Korpel, J.C. de Moor, F. Sepmeijer, "Consistency with Regard to Tenses".

[5] Despite impressive arguments to regard ואצרך as an exceptional form of the verb יצר (see Koole, 158-9) we keep to the derivation from נצר because the derivation of the parallel אצרך in Isa. 49:8 would seem to assured by נצורי in Isa. 49:6. Moreover, a deliberate antithesis is created, both here (v. 7) and there, between the captives of Israel and the Servant who has to lead them out.

[6] עם has to be understood as a collective here, cf. M.S. Smith, "*Berît 'Am / Berît'Ôlām*: A New Proposal for the Crux of Isa 42:6", *JBL* 100 (1981), 241-8, with bibliography.

B.i.2 (Isa. 42:11)

	יִשְׂא֤וּ מִדְבָּר֙ וְעָרָ֔יו	11aA	Let the desert and its towns raise (their voices)[7]
	חֲצֵרִ֖ים תֵּשֵׁ֣ב קֵדָ֑ר	11aB	the villages where Kedar lives,
	יָרֹ֨נּוּ֙ יֹ֣שְׁבֵי סֶ֔לַע	11bA	let the dwellers in the rocks rejoice,
	מֵרֹ֥אשׁ הָרִ֖ים יִצְוָֽחוּ׃	11bB	let them shout from the top of the mountains.

B.i.3 (Isa. 42:12)

	יָשִׂ֥ימוּ לַֽיהוָ֖ה כָּב֑וֹד	12aA	Let them give glory to the LORD,
	וּתְהִלָּת֖וֹ בָּאִיִּ֥ים יַגִּֽידוּ׃	12aB	and let them tell his praise on the islands.

1$\mathfrak{Q}^{a}$ (indentation, paragraphos) – $\mathfrak{G}^{SA}$ – $\mathfrak{S}^{d}$ . . . .

B.ii.1 (Isa. 42:13)

	יְהוָה֙ כַּגִּבּ֣וֹר יֵצֵ֔א	13aA	The LORD goes out like a hero,
	כְּאִ֥ישׁ מִלְחָמ֖וֹת יָעִ֣יר קִנְאָ֑ה	13aB	like a warrior he wakes up fury,
	יָרִ֙יעַ֙ אַף־יַצְרִ֔יחַ	13bA	he shouts, even yells,
	עַל־אֹיְבָ֖יו יִתְגַּבָּֽר׃	13bB	he shows himself a hero to his enemies.
{פ<ס>$\mathfrak{G}^{S}\mathfrak{S}^{abcde}$}			

B.ii.2 (Isa. 42:14)

	הֶחֱשֵׁ֙יתִי֙ מֵֽעוֹלָ֔ם	14aA	I have been quiet from eternity on.
{$\mathfrak{G}^{A}$}	אַחֲרִ֖ישׁ אֶתְאַפָּ֑ק	14aB	Shall I remain silent, restrain myself?[8]
	כַּיּוֹלֵדָ֣ה אֶפְעֶ֔ה	14bA	Like a woman in labour I will groan!
	אֶשֹּׁ֥ם וְאֶשְׁאַ֖ף יָֽחַד׃	14bB	I will gasp and pant together!

B.ii.3 (Isa. 42:15)

	אַחֲרִ֤יב הָרִים֙ וּגְבָע֔וֹת	15aA	I will lay waste mountains and hills
	וְכָל־עֶשְׂבָּ֖ם אוֹבִ֑ישׁ	15aB	and I will dry up all their vegetation.
	וְשַׂמְתִּ֤י נְהָרוֹת֙ לָֽאִיִּ֔ים	15bA	And I will make rivers into islands,
	וַאֲגַמִּ֖ים אוֹבִֽישׁ׃	15bB	and will dry up pools.

B.ii.4 (Isa. 42:16)

	וְהוֹלַכְתִּ֣י עִוְרִ֗ים בְּדֶ֙רֶךְ֙ לֹ֣א יָדָ֔עוּ	16aA	And I will let go blind ones on a way they do not know,
	בִּנְתִיב֥וֹת לֹֽא־יָדְע֖וּ אַדְרִיכֵ֑ם	16aB	on paths they do not know I will let you walk,
	אָשִׂים֩ מַחְשָׁ֨ךְ לִפְנֵיהֶ֜ם לָא֗וֹר	16bA	I will make the darkness for them into light,
{$\mathfrak{G}^{S}$}	וּמַעֲקַשִּׁים֙ לְמִישׁ֔וֹר	16bB	and the rough places (I will make) level.
{<ס>}	אֵ֚לֶּה הַדְּבָרִ֔ים עֲשִׂיתִ֖ם וְלֹ֥א עֲזַבְתִּֽים׃	16bC	These are the words which I will do and will not forsake.

---

[7] As in Isa. 42:2, the self-evident complement is omitted. See the verse-line parallelism in Isa. 52:8a. The problems in the ancient versions were created by this unusual construction, cf. De Waard, 163.

[8] Because of v. 13bA, we assume an unintroduced rhetorical question, cf. Joüon, Muraoka §161a.

III.B.ii.5 (Isa. 42:17)

נָסֹ֤גוּ אָחוֹר֙ {$\mathfrak{G}^{BA}$} יֵבֹ֣שׁוּ {$\mathfrak{G}^{S}$} בֹ֔שֶׁת	17aA	They move backwards, are deeply ashamed,
הַבֹּטְחִ֖ים בַּפָּ֑סֶל	17aB	those who trust in idols,[9]
הָאֹמְרִ֥ים לְמַסֵּכָ֖ה אַתֶּ֥ם אֱלֹהֵֽינוּ׃	17aC	those who say to molten images, 'You are our gods!'

ס <פ> – 1$\mathfrak{Q}^{a}$ – $\mathfrak{G}^{SA}$ – $\mathfrak{S}^{ae}$ ______________________________

C.i.1 (Isa. 42:18)

הַחֵרְשִׁ֖ים שְׁמָ֑עוּ	18aA	O deaf ones, hear!
וְהַעִוְרִ֖ים הַבִּ֥יטוּ לִרְאֽוֹת׃	18aB	And O blind ones, watch to see!

C.i.2 (Isa. 42:19)

מִ֤י עִוֵּר֙ כִּ֣י אִם־עַבְדִּ֔י	19aA	Who is blind but my servant?
וְחֵרֵ֖שׁ כְּמַלְאָכִ֣י אֶשְׁלָ֑ח	19aB	And deaf as my messenger whom I send?
מִ֤י עִוֵּר֙ כִּמְשֻׁלָּ֔ם	19bA	Who is blind as the one who had to do penance?[10]
וְעִוֵּ֖ר כְּעֶ֥בֶד יְהוָֽה׃	19bB	and as blind as the servant of the LORD?

C.i.3 (Isa. 42:20)

רָא֥וֹת* רַבּ֖וֹת וְלֹ֣א תִשְׁמֹ֑ר	20aA	There is much to see,[11] but you do not observe it,
פָּק֥וֹחַ אָזְנַ֖יִם וְלֹ֥א יִשְׁמָֽע׃	20aB	there is opening of the ears, but he does not hear.

<ס> – 1$\mathfrak{Q}^{a}$ – $\mathfrak{G}^{A}$ . . . .

C.ii.1 (Isa. 42:21)

יְהוָ֥ה חָפֵ֖ץ לְמַ֣עַן צִדְק֑וֹ	21aA	For the sake of his justice the LORD wants
יַגְדִּ֥יל תּוֹרָ֖ה וְיַאְדִּֽיר׃	21aB	to magnify his teaching and make it (even more) powerful.[12]

---

[9]Because אתם of the next colon excludes a singular, we assume a collective meaning of פסל and מסכה respectively.

[10]To be taken as a Pual of שׁלם, literally "the one who was a repayment", the one who had to pay for Israel's sins, compare Isa. 40:2; 53:5. Also Jer. 16:18 and Prov. 11:31 argue in favour of this translation. See further the passive participles in the description of the Servant in 42:22 בָּז֤וּז וְשָׁסוּי "spoiled and plundered"; 49:7 בזה "despised", מתעב "detested" (both emended); 53:3 וִיד֣וּעַ "acquainted (with illness)"; 53:4 מֻכֵּ֥ה אֱלֹהִ֖ים "smitten by God"; 53:5 מְחֹלָ֣ל "pierced"; 53:5 מְדֻכָּ֖א "crushed". See also 42:3 רָצוּץ֙ "crushed" with 42:4 *יָר֔וּץ "he will be crushed"; 48:12 מקראי "(Jacob) whom I have called" with 49:1 קראני "he called me"; 53:14aB *כֵּן־מָשְׁחָת (as emended by us).

[11]Inf.abs., with Qere. This is a rare form, cf. Joüon, Muraoka, §79p. It matches, however, with the parallel form פָּקוֹחַ. Either it is an archaic form in which the yod had been preserved or it is a simple writing error: a י for a ו. Although reading the Ketiv with several ancient witnesses is certainly justified (cf. Hulst, 149-50; Barthélemy, 307-9), we feel that the more difficult Qere has its advantages, among them the rhyme.

[12]With regard to our dealing with the tenses see above n. 4.

C.ii.2 (Isa. 42:22)

וְהוּא עַם־בָּזוּז וְשָׁסוּי	22aA	And he? A despoiled and plundered people!
הָפֵחַ בַּחוּרִים כֻּלָּם	22aB	There was ensnaring of them all in holes,[13]
וּבְבָתֵּי כְלָאִים הָחְבָּאוּ	22aC	and in houses of confinement they were hidden.
הָיוּ לָבַז וְאֵין מַצִּיל	22bA	They became spoil and there was none delivering,
מְשִׁסָּה וְאֵין־אֹמֵר הָשַׁב׃ {𝔊^{SA}𝔖^{a}}	22bB	plunder, and there was none saying: Give back!

C.ii.3 (Isa. 42:23)

מִי בָכֶם יַאֲזִין זֹאת	23aA	Who among you gives ear to this,
יַקְשִׁב וְיִשְׁמַע לְאָחוֹר׃ {𝔊^{S}}	23aB	listens and hears, for later times?

C.ii.4 (Isa. 42:24)

מִי־נָתַן לִמְשִׁסָּה* יַעֲקֹב	24aA	Who gave Jacob as plunder,[14]
וְיִשְׂרָאֵל לְבֹזְזִים {𝔊^{B}}	24aB	and Israel to despoilers?
הֲלוֹא יְהוָה	24aC	Was is not the LORD?[15]
זוּ חָטָאנוּ לוֹ	24bA	The One against whom we[16] have sinned?
וְלֹא־אָבוּ בִדְרָכָיו הָלוֹךְ	24bB	For they were not willing to walk in his ways,
וְלֹא שָׁמְעוּ בְּתוֹרָתוֹ׃	24bC	and did not listen to his teaching.

C.ii.5 (Isa. 42:25)

וַיִּשְׁפֹּךְ עָלָיו חֵמָה אַפּוֹ	25aA	So he poured out hot anger[17] on him,
וֶעֱזוּז מִלְחָמָה	25aB	and the violence of war.
וַתְּלַהֲטֵהוּ מִסָּבִיב וְלֹא יָדָע	25bA	And it set him on fire round about, but he knew not,
וַתִּבְעַר־בּוֹ וְלֹא־יָשִׂים עַל־לֵב׃	25bB	and it burned him, but he did not take it to heart.

פ <ס> – 1𝔔^{ab} – 4𝔔^{g} – 𝔊^{SBA} – 𝔖^{abcde}

---

[13] It is not necessary to change the vocalization for this rendering. Cf. Barthélemy, 309-10.

[14] We accept the Qere which we interpret as a *scriptio plena.*

[15] Many scholars remove this and the next colon as a later expansion which would not fit the context. See e.g. Merendino, 280; Spykerboer, 98. We fail to see the cogency of this argument. That the prophet would never answer his own questions is untrue. Cf. Isa. 41:4, 26.

[16] This kind of harsh transition should no longer be a reason to emend the text. Cf. Barthélemy, 310-1; De Waard, 165. Following Calvin, Koole, 196-7, aptly observes that the prophet on the one hand joins his people in a confession of guilt, on the other hand does not want to identify himself completely with those who had refused to obey God's commandments.

[17] It is not necessary to follow 1𝔔^{a} in emending the text into חמת. We assume hendiadys, cf. Waltke, O'Connor, §4.4.1b, p. 649, n.5.

4.2 Isaiah 42 – Delimitation of Cola

COLON 42:1aA:

הֵ֤ן עַבְדִּי֙ אֶתְמָךְ־בּ֔וֹ 1aA Behold, my servant whom I hold,

With: $\mathfrak{M}$ (5) – $\mathfrak{G}^{SQ}$ – $\mathfrak{S}^{abcde}$

Discussion: The dividing point which $\mathfrak{G}^{SQ}$ have after עבדי should be interpreted as a subordinate divider on a par with $\mathfrak{M}$'s Pashṭa (No. 10).

COLON 42:1aB:

בְּחִירִ֖י רָצְתָ֣ה נַפְשִׁ֑י 1aB my chosen one, in whom my soul takes pleasure,

With: $\mathfrak{M}$ (2) – $\mathfrak{G}^{SQ}$ – $\mathfrak{S}^{abcde}$

Discussion: Again $\mathfrak{G}^{SQ}$ use the point as a subordinate divider, this time after בחירי.

COLON 42:1bA:

נָתַ֤תִּי רוּחִי֙ עָלָ֔יו 1bA I put my spirit on him,

With: $\mathfrak{M}$ (5) – $\mathfrak{G}^{SQ}$ – $\mathfrak{S}^{abcde}$

COLON 42:1bB:

מִשְׁפָּ֖ט לַגּוֹיִ֥ם יוֹצִֽיא׃ 1bB he will carry out justice for the nations.

With: $\mathfrak{M}$ (1) – $\mathfrak{G}^{SQ}$ – $\mathfrak{S}^{abcde}$

COLON 42:2aA:

לֹ֥א יִצְעַ֖ק וְלֹ֣א יִשָּׂ֑א 2aA He will not shout or raise (his voice),

With: $\mathfrak{M}$ (2) – $\mathfrak{G}^{SQ}$ – $\mathfrak{S}^{abcd}$

Colon parallelism: צעק || נשׂא (unique).

COLON 42:2aB:

וְלֹֽא־יַשְׁמִ֥יעַ בַּח֖וּץ קוֹלֽוֹ׃ 2aB and he will not make his voice heard in the street.

With: $\mathfrak{M}$ (1) – $\mathfrak{G}^{SQ}$ – $\mathfrak{S}^{abcde}$

COLON 42:3aA:

קָנֶ֤ה רָצוּץ֙ לֹ֣א יִשְׁבּ֔וֹר 3aA A crushed reed he will not break,

With: $\mathfrak{M}$ (5) – $\mathfrak{G}^{SQ}$ – $\mathfrak{S}^{abcde}$

Colon parallelism: רצץ || שׁבר.

COLON 42:3aB:

וּפִשְׁתָּה כֵהָה לֹא יְכַבֶּנָּה 3aB and a smouldering wick – he will not quench it.

With: $\mathfrak{M}$ (2) – $\mathfrak{G}^{SQ}$ – $\mathfrak{S}^{abcde}$

COLON 42:3aC:

לֶאֱמֶת יוֹצִיא מִשְׁפָּט׃ 3aC Truthfully he will bring forth justice.

With: $\mathfrak{M}$ (1) – $\mathfrak{G}^{Q}$ – $\mathfrak{S}^{abcde}$
Discussion: $\mathfrak{G}^{S}$ has has a different colometry, connecting משפט with לק יכהה of v. 4. Apparently this is erroneous and the rest of the ancient witnesses supports $\mathfrak{M}$.

COLON 42:4aA:

לֹא יִכְהֶה וְלֹא יָרוּץ* 4aA He will not smoulder or be crushed,

With: $\mathfrak{M}$ (5) – $\mathfrak{G}^{SQ}$ – $\mathfrak{S}^{abcde}$

COLON 42:4aB:

עַד־יָשִׂים בָּאָרֶץ מִשְׁפָּט 4aB until he will put justice on earth,

With: $\mathfrak{M}$ (2) – $\mathfrak{G}^{SQ}$ – $\mathfrak{S}^{e}$, $\mathfrak{S}^{abcd}$ subordinate punctuation.

COLON 42:4aC:

וּלְתוֹרָתוֹ אִיִּים יְיַחֵילוּ׃ 4aC and the islands will await his teaching.

With: $\mathfrak{M}$ (1), major division markers – $\mathfrak{G}^{SBAQ}$, major division markers in $\mathfrak{G}^{SBA}$ – $\mathfrak{S}^{abcde}$, major division markers in $\mathfrak{S}^{abe}$

COLON 42:5aA:

כֹּה־אָמַר הָאֵל ׀ יְהוָה 5aA Thus says God, the LORD,

With: $\mathfrak{M}$ (7) – $\mathfrak{G}^{SQ}$ – $\mathfrak{S}^{a}$, $\mathfrak{S}^{bcde}$ subordinate punctuation.
Colon parallelism: אל || יהוה.

COLON 42:5aB:

בּוֹרֵא הַשָּׁמַיִם וְנוֹטֵיהֶם 5aB who created the heavens and stretched them out,

With: $\mathfrak{M}$ (5) – $\mathfrak{G}^{SAQ}$, major division marker in $\mathfrak{G}^{A}$– $\mathfrak{S}^{abcde}$ subordinate punctuation.
Colon parallelism: ברא || נטה.
Discussion: $\mathfrak{G}^{SQ}$ have a point after שמים which equals $\mathfrak{M}$'s Pashṭa.

COLON 42:5aC:

רֹקַע הָאָרֶץ וְצֶאֱצָאֶיהָ 5aC who hammered out the earth and all that came forth from it,

With: $\mathfrak{M}$ (2) – $\mathfrak{G}^{SQ}$ – $\mathfrak{S}^{acde}$, $\mathfrak{S}^{b}$ subordinate punctuation.

COLON 42:5bA:

נֹתֵן נְשָׁמָה לָעָם עָלֶיהָ 5bA who gives breath to the people on it,

With: $\mathfrak{M}$ (5) – $\mathfrak{G}^{SQ}$ – $\mathfrak{S}^{abcde}$

COLON 42:5bB:

וְרוּחַ לַהֹלְכִים בָּהּ׃ 5bB and spirit to those who walk on it,

With: $\mathfrak{M}$ (1) – $\mathfrak{G}^{SAQ}$, major division markers in $\mathfrak{G}^{A}$ and $\mathfrak{G}^{Q}$ – $\mathfrak{S}^{abcde}$

COLON 42:6aA:

אֲנִי יְהוָה קְרָאתִיךָ בְצֶדֶק 6aA I, the LORD, call you justly

With: $\mathfrak{M}$ (8) – $\mathfrak{G}^{SQ}$ – $\mathfrak{S}^{abcde}$

Discussion: The Masoretes wanted to read on to בידך, a colon of six stresses. The unanimous testimony of the other ancient witnesses emboldens us to deviate from them.

COLON 42:6aB:

וְאַחְזֵק בְּיָדֶךָ וְאֶצָּרְךָ 6aB and I will grasp your hand and will keep you.

With: $\mathfrak{M}$ (7) – $\mathfrak{G}^{AQ}$, major division marker in $\mathfrak{G}^{A}$ – $\mathfrak{S}^{abcd}$

Colon parallelism: חזק || נצר.

Discussion: $\mathfrak{M}$ has an Atnaḥ (2) with בידך and this is supported by $\mathfrak{G}^{Q}$ only. However, the latter has meant this dividing point apparently as a minor pause because it also has a point after ואצרך. So actually $\mathfrak{M}$ stands isolated. The colon parallelism is an additional argument against $\mathfrak{M}$ at this point.

COLON 42:6bA:

וְאֶתֶּנְךָ לִבְרִית עָם 6bA And I will make you a covenant of people,

With: $\mathfrak{M}$ (8) – $\mathfrak{G}^{SQ}$

Discussion: Both $\mathfrak{M}$ and $\mathfrak{S}$ read on until the end of the verse. However, Isa. 49:6, 51:4 and 60:3 favour the assumption that לאור גוים is a separate colon.

COLON 42:6bB:

לְא֥וֹר גּוֹיִֽם׃ 6bB a light for the nations,

With: 𝔐 (1) – 𝔊^{SQ} – 𝔖^{acde}, 𝔖^{b} subordinate punctuation.

COLON 42:7aA:

לִפְקֹ֖חַ עֵינַ֣יִם עִוְר֑וֹת 7aA to open blind eyes,

With: 𝔐 (2) – 𝔊^{SQ} – 𝔖^{bcde}

COLON 42:7bA:

לְהוֹצִ֤יא מִמַּסְגֵּר֙ אַסִּ֔יר 7bA to bring prisoners from the dungeon,

With: 𝔐 (5) – 𝔊^{SQ} – 𝔖^{abcde} all subordinate punctuation.

COLON 42:7bB:

מִבֵּ֥ית כֶּ֖לֶא יֹ֥שְׁבֵי חֹֽשֶׁךְ׃ 7bB from the house of confinement those who are sitting in darkness.

With: 𝔐 (1) – 𝔊^{AQ}, in 𝔊^{A} major division markers – 𝔖^{abcde}

COLON 42:8aA:

אֲנִ֥י יְהוָ֖ה ה֣וּא שְׁמִ֑י 8aA I am the LORD, that is my name,

With: 𝔐 (2) – 𝔊^{SQ} – 𝔖^{abcde}

Discussion: 𝔊^{SQ} have a divider after יהוה which should be regarded as the equivalent of 𝔐's Ṭiphḥa.

COLON 42:8bA:

וּכְבוֹדִי֙ לְאַחֵ֣ר לֹֽא־אֶתֵּ֔ן 8bA and my glory I will not give to another,

With: 𝔐 (5) – 𝔊^{SQ} – 𝔖^{abcde}

Colon parallelism: Absent, but note the chiastic structure of the verse.

COLON 42:8bB:

וּתְהִלָּתִ֖י לַפְּסִילִֽים׃ 8bB nor my praise to graven images.

With: 𝔐 (1) – 𝔊^{SQ}, major division markers in 𝔊^{S} – 𝔖^{abcde}

COLON 42:9aA:

הָרִאשֹׁנ֖וֹת הִנֵּה־בָ֑אוּ 9aA The first things, look, they have come,

With: 𝔐 (2) – 𝔊^{SQ} – 𝔖^{abcde}

Colon parallelism: ראשון || בוא.

COLON 42:9bA:

וַחֲדָשׁוֹת֙ אֲנִ֣י מַגִּ֔יד 9bA and new things I am telling,

With: $\mathfrak{M}$ (5) – $\mathfrak{G}^{SQ}$ – $\mathfrak{S}^{abcde}$

COLON 42:9bB:

בְּטֶ֥רֶם תִּצְמַ֖חְנָה אַשְׁמִ֥יעַ אֶתְכֶֽם׃ 9bB before they sprout, I let you hear them.

With: $\mathfrak{M}$ (1) – $\mathfrak{G}^{SBAQ}$, major division markers in all – $\mathfrak{S}^{abcde}$, major division markers in $\mathfrak{S}^{abde}$

COLON 42:10aA:

שִׁ֤ירוּ לַֽיהוָה֙ שִׁ֣יר חָדָ֔שׁ 10aA Sing for the LORD a new song,

With: $\mathfrak{M}$ (5) – $\mathfrak{G}^{SQ}$ – $\mathfrak{S}^{abce}$

COLON 42:10aB:

תְּהִלָּת֖וֹ מִקְצֵ֣ה הָאָ֑רֶץ 10aB his praise from the ends of the earth,

With: $\mathfrak{M}$ (2) – $\mathfrak{G}^{S}$ – $\mathfrak{S}^{abce}$

COLON 42:10bA:

יוֹרְדֵ֤י הַיָּם֙ וּמְלֹא֔וֹ 10bA you who are sailing the sea and all that fills it,

With: $\mathfrak{M}$ (5) – $\mathfrak{G}^{SQ}$ – $\mathfrak{S}^{abde}$, $\mathfrak{S}^{c}$ subordinate punctuation.

COLON 42:10bB:

אִיִּ֖ים וְיֹשְׁבֵיהֶֽם׃ 10bB you islands and those dwelling there!

With: $\mathfrak{M}$ (1) – $\mathfrak{G}^{SQ}$, paragraphos in $\mathfrak{G}^{S}$ – $\mathfrak{S}^{abcde}$

COLON 42:11aA:

יִשְׂא֤וּ מִדְבָּר֙ וְעָרָ֔יו 11aA Let the desert and its towns raise (their voices)

With: $\mathfrak{M}$ (5) – $\mathfrak{G}^{SQ}$ – $\mathfrak{S}^{acde}$
Colon parallelism: מדבר || עיר.
Discussion: $\mathfrak{G}^{SQ}$ also have a point after מדבר which should be regarded as a subordinate divider like $\mathfrak{M}$'s Pashṭa (No. 10).

COLON 42:11aB:

חֲצֵרִ֖ים תֵּשֵׁ֣ב קֵדָ֑ר 11aB the villages where Kedar lives,

With: $\mathfrak{M}$ (2) – $\mathfrak{G}^{SQ}$ – $\mathfrak{S}^{abcd}$, $\mathfrak{S}^{e}$ subordinate punctuation.

COLON 42:11bA:

יָרֹ֙נּוּ֙ יֹ֣שְׁבֵי סֶ֔לַע 11bA let the dwellers in the rocks rejoice,

With: 𝔐 (5) – 𝔊^{SQ} – 𝔖^{abcde}

COLON 42:11bB:

מֵרֹ֥אשׁ הָרִ֖ים יִצְוָֽחוּ׃ 11bB let them shout from the top of the mountains.

With: 𝔐 (1) – 𝔊^{SQ} – 𝔖^{abcde}

COLON 42:12aA:

יָשִׂ֥ימוּ לַֽיהוָ֖ה כָּב֑וֹד 12aA Let them give glory to the LORD,

With: 𝔐 (2) – 𝔊^{SQ} – 𝔖^{abcde}

COLON 42:12aB:

וּתְהִלָּת֖וֹ בָּאִיִּ֥ים יַגִּֽידוּ׃ 12aB and let them tell his praise on the islands.

With: 𝔐 (1), indentation in 1𝔔^{a} – 𝔊^{SAQ}, major division markers in 𝔊^{SA} – 𝔖^{abcde}, paragraphos in 𝔖^{d}

COLON 42:13aA:

יְהוָה֙ כַּגִּבּ֣וֹר יֵצֵ֔א 13aA The LORD goes out like a hero,

With: 𝔐 (5) – 𝔊^{SQ} – 𝔖^{abcde}

COLON 42:13aB:

כְּאִ֥ישׁ מִלְחָמ֖וֹת יָעִ֣יר קִנְאָ֑ה 13aB like a warrior he wakes up fury,

With: 𝔐 (2) – 𝔊^{SQ} – 𝔖^{abcde}
Discussion: Again 𝔊^{SQ} also have a dividing point where 𝔐 has a Ṭiphḥa (מלחמות).

COLON 42:13bA:

יָרִ֙יעַ֙ אַף־יַצְרִ֔יחַ 13bA he shouts, even yells,

With: 𝔐 (5).
Colon parallelism: רוע Hiph. || צרח Hiph. (unique).
Discussion: None of the ancient witnesses supports 𝔐 but this is clearly a consequence of their free renderings. 𝔊^{SQ} have a divider after איביו (𝔐 Ṭiphḥa).

Colon 42:13bB:

עַל־אֹיְבָיו יִתְגַּבָּר׃ 13bB he shows himself a hero to his enemies.

With: 𝔐 (1), major division markers in medieval manuscripts, but no major division marker attested in Qumran – 𝔊^{SQ}, major division marker in 𝔊^{S} – 𝔖^{abcde}, major division markers in all.

Colon 42:14aA:

הֶחֱשֵׁיתִי מֵעוֹלָם 14aA I have been quiet from eternity on.

With: 𝔐 (5).
Discussion: Both 𝔊^{S} and 𝔖 seem to connect מעולם with אחריש, leaving only one word as the first colon. In our opinion 𝔐 is preferable because of the contrast between past and present.

Colon 42:14aB:

אַחֲרִישׁ אֶתְאַפָּק 14aB Shall I remain silent, restrain myself?

With: 𝔐 (2) – 𝔊^{SAQ}, major division markers in 𝔊^{A} – 𝔖^{abcde} all subordinate punctuation.
Colon parallelism: חרש Hiph. || אפק Hitpa. (unique).

Colon 42:14bA:

כַּיּוֹלֵדָה אֶפְעֶה 14bA Like a woman in labour I will groan!

With: 𝔐 (5) – 𝔊^{SQ} – 𝔖^{abcde}

Colon 42:14bB:

אֶשֹּׁם וְאֶשְׁאַף יָחַד׃ 14bB I will gasp and pant at once!

With: 𝔐 (1) – 𝔊^{SQ}, colon in 𝔊^{S} – 𝔖^{abcde}
Colon parallelism: נשם || שאף (unique).

Colon 42:15aA:

אַחֲרִיב הָרִים וּגְבָעוֹת 15aA I will lay waste mountains and hills

With: 𝔐 (5) – 𝔖^{abce}
Colon parallelism: הר || גבעה.
Discussion: 𝔊 is lacking at this point.

Colon 42:15aB:

וְכָל־עֶשְׂבָּם אוֹבִישׁ 15aB and I will dry up all their vegetation.

With: 𝔐 (2) – 𝔖^{abcd}
Discussion: 𝔊 is lacking here.

COLON 42:15bA:

וְשַׂמְתִּ֤י נְהָרוֹת֙ לָֽאִיִּ֔ים 15bA And I will make rivers into islands,

With: 𝔐 (5) – 𝔊^{SQ} – 𝔖^{abce}

COLON 42:15bB:

וַאֲגַמִּ֖ים אוֹבִֽישׁ׃ 15bB and will dry up pools.

With: 𝔐 (1) – 𝔊^{SQ} – 𝔖^{abcde}

COLON 42:16aA:

וְהוֹלַכְתִּ֣י עִוְרִ֗ים בְּדֶ֙רֶךְ֙ לֹ֣א יָדָ֔עוּ 16aA And I will let go blind ones on a way they do not know,

With: 𝔐 (5) – 𝔊^{SQ} – 𝔖^{abcde}
Discussion: 𝔊 and 𝔖 do not recognize the Revi'a (7) with עורים although they accept such a divider in v. 16bA.

COLON 42:16aB:

בִּנְתִיב֥וֹת לֹא־יָדְע֖וּ אַדְרִיכֵ֑ם 16aB on paths they do not know I will let you walk,

With: 𝔐 (2) – 𝔊^{Q} – 𝔖^{abce}

COLON 42:16bA:

אָשִׂים֩ מַחְשָׁ֨ךְ לִפְנֵיהֶ֜ם לָא֗וֹר 16bA I will make the darkness for them into light,

With: 𝔐 (7) – 𝔊^{SQ} – 𝔖^{abcde}
Colon parallelism: Roots חשך || אור.

COLON 42:16bB:

וּמַֽעֲקַשִּׁים֙ לְמִישׁ֔וֹר 16bB and the rough places (I will make) level.

With: 𝔐 (5) – 𝔊^{SQ}, major division markers in 𝔊^{S} – 𝔖^{abde}, subordinate punctuation in 𝔖^{c}
Colon parallelism: Roots עקשׁ || ישר.

COLON 42:16bC:

אֵ֚לֶּה הַדְּבָרִ֔ים עֲשִׂיתִ֖ם וְלֹ֥א עֲזַבְתִּֽים׃ 16bC These are the words which I will do and will not forsake.

𝔐 (1), major division marker in 4Q^{g} – 𝔊^{SQ} – 𝔖^{abcde}
Colon parallelism: עשׂה || עזב.
Discussion: 𝔐 stands alone in making a major incision after הדברים (5). The rabbinic exposition of this verse in Exod. R. XIX.6 (see also Pes. R. XIV.11) required this rather peculiar scansion. We follow 𝔊^{SQ}. 𝔊^{SQ} have an extra dividing point after עשׂיתם which corresponds to the Ṭiphḥa (No.8) of 𝔐. The best attested division comes at the end of the verse. The resulting colon is rather long, but not unacceptably so, because also v. 16aA counts five stresses.

COLON 42:17aA:

נָסֹ֤גוּ אָחוֹר֙ יֵבֹ֣שׁוּ בֹ֔שֶׁת 17aA They move backwards, are deeply ashamed,

With: 𝔐 (5) – 𝔊^{SQ} – 𝔖^{bcde} subordinate punctuation.
Colon parallelism: סוג אחור || בושׁ; בושׁ || בשׁת.
Discussion: All manuscripts of the 𝔊 we consulted have major dividers after either אחור (𝔊^{SBA}, 𝔊^{S} a point only) and/or יבושׁו (𝔊^{S}). This can hardly be correct and is a good example of the confusion about the correct position of the major dividers in the Greek tradition.

COLON 42:17aB:

הַבֹּטְחִ֖ים בַּפָּ֑סֶל 17aB those who trust in idols,

With: 𝔐 (2) – 𝔊^{Q} – 𝔖^{a}, 𝔖^{bcde} subordinate punctuation.

COLON 42:17aC:

הָאֹמְרִ֥ים לְמַסֵּכָ֖ה אַתֶּ֥ם אֱלֹהֵֽינוּ׃ 17aC those who say to molten images, 'You are our gods!'

With: 𝔐 (1) – 𝔊^{SAQ}, major division markers in 𝔊^{SA} – 𝔖^{abce}, major division markers in 𝔖^{ae}, subordinate punctuation in 𝔖^{d}

COLON 42:18aA:

הַחֵרְשִׁ֖ים שְׁמָ֑עוּ 18aA O deaf ones, hear!

With: 𝔐 (2) – 𝔊^{SQ} – 𝔖^{abcde}

COLON 42:18aB:

וְהַעִוְרִ֖ים הַבִּ֥יטוּ לִרְאֽוֹת׃ 18aB And O blind ones, watch to see!

With: 𝔐 (1) – 𝔊^{SQ} – 𝔖^{abcde}
Colon parallelism: נבט Hiph. || ראה.

COLON 42:19aA:

מִ֤י עִוֵּר֙ כִּ֣י אִם־עַבְדִּ֔י 19aA Who is blind but my servant?

With: $\mathfrak{M}$ (5) – $\mathfrak{G}^{SQ}$ – $\mathfrak{S}^{abce}$ all subordinate punctuation.
Discussion: $\mathfrak{G}^{S}$ and $\mathfrak{G}^{Q}$ also have a point after עור[1] which corresponds to $\mathfrak{M}$'s Pashṭa.

COLON 42:19aB:

וְחֵרֵ֖שׁ כְּמַלְאָכִ֣י אֶשְׁלָ֑ח 19aB And deaf as my messenger whom I send?

With: $\mathfrak{M}$ (2) – $\mathfrak{G}^{SQ}$ – $\mathfrak{S}^{abcde}$
Discussion: $\mathfrak{G}^{S}$ and $\mathfrak{G}^{Q}$ also have a point after חרש which corresponds to $\mathfrak{M}$'s Ṭiphḥa.

COLON 42:19bA:

מִ֤י עִוֵּר֙ כִּמְשֻׁלָּ֔ם 19bA Who is blind as the one who had to do penance?

With: $\mathfrak{M}$ (5) – $\mathfrak{S}^{abcde}$ all subordinate punctuation.
Discussion: $\mathfrak{G}$ is lacking at this point.

COLON 42:19bB:

וְעִוֵּ֖ר כְּעֶ֥בֶד יְהוָֽה׃ 19bB and as blind as the servant of the LORD?

With: $\mathfrak{M}$ (1) – $\mathfrak{G}^{SQ}$ – $\mathfrak{S}^{abcde}$

COLON 42:20aA:

רָא֥וֹת* רַבּ֖וֹת וְלֹ֣א תִשְׁמֹ֑ר 20aA There is much to see, but you do not observe it,

With: $\mathfrak{M}$ (2) – $\mathfrak{G}^{SQ}$ – $\mathfrak{S}^{abcde}$
Colon parallelism: ראה || שמר.
Discussion: $\mathfrak{G}^{SQ}$ also have a point after רבות which should be seen as the equivalent of $\mathfrak{M}$'s Ṭiphḥa.

COLON 42:20aB:

פָּק֥וֹחַ אָזְנַ֖יִם וְלֹ֥א יִשְׁמָֽע׃ 20aB there is opening of the ears, but he does not hear.

With: $\mathfrak{M}$ (1), major division marker in 1$\mathfrak{Q}^{a}$ – $\mathfrak{G}^{SAQ}$, major division markers in $\mathfrak{G}^{A}$ – $\mathfrak{S}^{abcde}$
Colon parallelism: פקח אזן || שמע.
Discussion: $\mathfrak{G}^{SQ}$ also have a point after אזנים which should be seen as the equivalent of $\mathfrak{M}$'s Ṭiphḥa.

COLON 42:21aA:

יְהוָה חָפֵץ לְמַעַן צִדְקוֹ 21aA For the sake of his justice the LORD wants

With: $\mathfrak{M}$ (2) – $\mathfrak{G}^{SQ}$ – $\mathfrak{S}^{abcde}$ all subordinate punctuation.

COLON 42:21aB:

יַגְדִּיל תּוֹרָה וְיַאְדִּיר׃ 21aB to magnify his teaching and make it (even more) powerful.

With: $\mathfrak{M}$ (1) – $\mathfrak{G}^{S}$ – $\mathfrak{S}^{abcde}$
Colon parallelism: גדל Hiph. || אדר Hiph.
Discussion: Again the additional point $\mathfrak{G}^{SQ}$ have after תורה equals a Ṭiphḥa in $\mathfrak{M}$.

COLON 42:22aA:

וְהוּא עַם־בָּזוּז וְשָׁסוּי 22aA And he? A despoiled and plundered people!

With: $\mathfrak{M}$ (3) – $\mathfrak{G}^{SQ}$ – $\mathfrak{S}^{abcde}$
Colon parallelism: שסה || בזז.
Discussion: The Zarqa (No. 9) with והוא marks off the *casus pendens.*[1]

COLON 42:22aB:

הָפֵחַ בַּחוּרִים כֻּלָּם 22aB There was ensnaring of them all in holes,

With: $\mathfrak{M}$ (5) – $\mathfrak{G}^{SQ}$ – $\mathfrak{S}^{abcde}$

COLON 42:22aC:

וּבְבָתֵּי כְלָאִים הָחְבָּאוּ 22aC and in houses of confinement they were hidden.

With: $\mathfrak{M}$ (2) – $\mathfrak{G}^{SQ}$ – $\mathfrak{S}^{abcde}$

COLON 42:22bA:

הָיוּ לָבַז וְאֵין מַצִּיל 22bA They became spoil and there was none delivering,

With: $\mathfrak{M}$ (5) – $\mathfrak{G}^{Q}$ – $\mathfrak{S}^{bcde}$, $\mathfrak{S}^{a}$ subordinate punctuation.
Discussion: The additional point in $\mathfrak{G}^{SQ}$ after לבז corresponds to $\mathfrak{M}$'s Pashṭa.

COLON 42:22bB:

מְשִׁסָּה וְאֵין־אֹמֵר הָשַׁב׃ 22bB plunder, and there was none saying: Give back!

---

[1] See our comment on p. 31.

With: 𝔐 (1) – 𝔊^{SAQ}, major division markers in 𝔊^{SA} – 𝔖^{abcde}, major division marker in 𝔖^{a}
Discussion: Discussion: The additional point in 𝔊^{SQ} after משסה corresponds to 𝔐's Ṭiphḥa.

COLON 42:23aA:

מִי בָכֶם יַאֲזִין זֹאת 23aA Who among you gives ear to this,

With: 𝔐 (2) – 𝔊^{SQ} – 𝔖^{abcde} all subordinate punctuation.
Discussion: Again 𝔐's Ṭiphḥa with בכם corresponds to a point in 𝔊^{SQ}.

COLON 42:23aB:

יַקְשֵׁב וְיִשְׁמַע לְאָחוֹר׃ 23aB listens and hears, for later times?

With: 𝔐 (1) – 𝔊^{SQ}, major division markers in 𝔊^{S} – 𝔖^{abcde}
Colon parallelism: קשב || שמע.

COLON 42:24aA:

מִי־נָתַן לִמְשִׁסָּה* יַעֲקֹב 24aA Who gave Jacob as plunder,

With: 𝔐 (12) – 𝔊^{Q} – 𝔖^{e}
Discussion: It is not impossible that the Masoretes wanted to read v. 24a as a very long unicolon (7 stresses). The Tevir is hardly strong enough to warrant the assumption that they made an incision at this point and the Ṭiphḥa with לבוזים is a relatively minor accent. See v. 24aB. However, the twofold parallelism between v. 24aA and 24aB renders the poorly attested division after יעקב credible in our opinion.

COLON 42:24aB:

וְיִשְׂרָאֵל לְבֹזְזִים 24aB and Israel to despoilers?

With: 𝔐 (8) – 𝔊^{BSQ}, paragraphos in 𝔊^{B} – 𝔖^{abcde}
Discussion: Probably the Masoretes did not consider this a major division point.

COLON 42:24aC:

הֲלוֹא יְהוָה 24aC Was is not the LORD?

With: 𝔐 (2) – 𝔊^{S} – 𝔖^{abcde} all subordinate punctuation.

COLON 42:24bA:

זוּ חָטָאנוּ לוֹ 24bA The One against whom we have sinned?

With: $\mathfrak{M}$ (5) – $\mathfrak{G}^{SQ}$ – $\mathfrak{S}^{d}$, $\mathfrak{S}^{ce}$ subordinate punctuation.

COLON 42:24bB:

וְלֹא־אָבוּ בִדְרָכָיו הָלוֹךְ 24bB For they were not willing to walk in his ways,

With: $\mathfrak{M}$ (5) – $\mathfrak{G}^{SQ}$ – $\mathfrak{S}^{bce}$, $\mathfrak{S}^{a}$ subordinate punctuation.

COLON 42:24bC:

וְלֹא שָׁמְעוּ בְּתוֹרָתוֹ׃ 24bC and did not listen to his teaching.

With: $\mathfrak{M}$ (1) – $\mathfrak{G}^{SQ}$ – $\mathfrak{S}^{abcde}$

COLON 42:25aA:

וַיִּשְׁפֹּךְ עָלָיו חֵמָה אַפּוֹ 25aA So he poured out hot anger on him,

With: $\mathfrak{M}$ (5) – $\mathfrak{G}^{SQ}$ – $\mathfrak{S}^{a}$
Discussion: The Munaḥ (19) with חמה and the Zaqepf Qaṭon with אפו shows that the Masoretes had the same in mind as $1\mathfrak{Q}^{a}$, the construct chain חמת אפו although they may have regarded it grammatically as an apposition.[2] Because $\mathfrak{G}$ and $\mathfrak{S}^{a}$ support this, we accept this colometry.

COLON 42:25aB:

וֶעֱזוּז מִלְחָמָה 25aB and the violence of war.

With: $\mathfrak{M}$ (2) – $\mathfrak{G}^{SQ}$ – $\mathfrak{S}^{abcde}$

COLON 42:25bA:

וַתְּלַהֲטֵהוּ מִסָּבִיב וְלֹא יָדָע 25bA And it set him on fire round about, but he knew not,

With: $\mathfrak{M}$ (5) – $\mathfrak{G}^{SQ}$ – $\mathfrak{S}^{abcde}$
Discussion: $\mathfrak{G}^{SQ}$ and $\mathfrak{S}^{e}$ have an additional point after מסביב which corresponds to $\mathfrak{M}$'s Pashṭa.

COLON 42:25bB:

וַתִּבְעַר־בּוֹ וְלֹא־יָשִׂים עַל־לֵב׃ 25bB and it burned him, but he did not take it to heart.

With: $\mathfrak{M}$ (1), major division markers in $\mathfrak{M}$ and Qumran – $\mathfrak{G}^{SBAQ}$, major division markers in $\mathfrak{G}^{SBA}$ – $\mathfrak{S}^{abcde}$, major division markers in all manuscripts.

[2] Cf. König, *Syntax*, §285f.

4.3 Isaiah 42 – Delimitation of Verse-lines

VERSE–LINE: 42:1a:

הֵ֤ן עַבְדִּי֙ אֶתְמָךְ־בּ֔וֹ	1aA	Behold, my Servant whom I hold,
בְּחִירִ֖י רָצְתָ֣ה נַפְשִׁ֑י	1aB	my chosen one, in whom my soul takes pleasure,

𝔐 distinctive accents: 5 – 2.
Stresses: 3 + 3.
Verse-line parallelism: עבד || בחיר; ־י || ־י; rhyme.

VERSE–LINE: 42:1b:

נָתַ֤תִּי רוּחִי֙ עָלָ֔יו	1bA	I put my spirit on him,
מִשְׁפָּ֖ט לַגּוֹיִ֥ם יוֹצִֽיא׃	1bB	he will carry out justice for the nations.

𝔐 distinctive accents: 5 – 1.
Stresses: 3 + 3.
Verse-line parallelism: נתן || יצא Hiph.;[1] רוח || משפט.

VERSE–LINE: 42:2a:

לֹ֥א יִצְעַ֖ק וְלֹ֣א יִשָּׂ֑א	2aA	He will not shout or raise (his voice),
וְלֹא־יַשְׁמִ֥יעַ בַּח֖וּץ קוֹלֽוֹ׃	2aB	and he will not make his voice heard in the street.

𝔐 distinctive accents: 2 – 1.
Stresses: 4 + 3.
Verse-line parallelism: לא || לא; צעק || שמע קול (unique); נשא || שמע קול; grammatical parallelism.

VERSE–LINE: 42:3a:

קָנֶ֤ה רָצוּץ֙ לֹ֣א יִשְׁבּ֔וֹר	3aA	A crushed reed he will not break,
וּפִשְׁתָּ֥ה כֵהָ֖ה לֹ֣א יְכַבֶּ֑נָּה	3aB	and a smouldering wick – he will not quench it.
לֶאֱמֶ֖ת יוֹצִ֥יא מִשְׁפָּֽט׃	3aC	Truthfully he will bring forth justice.

𝔐 distinctive accents: 5 – 2 – 1.
Stresses: 4 + 4 + 3.
Verse-line parallelism: קנה || פשתה; לא || לא; שבר || כבה (unique); grammatical parallelism.

VERSE–LINE: 42:4a:

לֹ֤א יִכְהֶה֙ וְלֹ֣א יָר֔וּץ*	4aA	He will not smoulder or be crushed,

[1] The servant implements the work of the LORD, cf. v. 4aB.

עַד־יָשִׂים בָּאָרֶץ מִשְׁפָּט	4aB	until he will put justice on earth,
וּלְתוֹרָתוֹ אִיִּים יְיַחֵילוּ׃	4aC	and the islands will await his teaching.

𝔐 distinctive accents: 5 – 2 – 1.
Stresses: 4 + 3 + 3.
Verse-line parallelism: ארץ || אי; משפט || תורה; grammatical parallelism.

VERSE–LINE: 42:5a:

כֹּה־אָמַר הָאֵל ׀ יְהוָה	5aA	Thus says God, the LORD,
בּוֹרֵא הַשָּׁמַיִם וְנוֹטֵיהֶם	5aB	who created the heavens and stretched them out,
רֹקַע הָאָרֶץ וְצֶאֱצָאֶיהָ	5aC	who hammered out the earth and all that came forth from it,

𝔐 distinctive accents: 7 – 5 – 2.
Stresses: 3 + 3 + 3.
Verse-line parallelism: אל יהוה || ברא (participle); שמים || ארץ; ברא || רקע; נטה || רקע; grammatical parallelism.

VERSE–LINE: 42:5b:

נֹתֵן נְשָׁמָה לָעָם עָלֶיהָ	5bA	who gives breath to the people on it,
וְרוּחַ לַהֹלְכִים בָּהּ׃	5bB	and spirit to those who walk on it,

𝔐 distinctive accents: 5– 1.
Stresses: 4 + 3.
Verse-line parallelism: נשמה || רוח; ל || ל; על || ב; ה־ || ה־.
Discussion: The cola are connected by ellipsis.

VERSE–LINE: 42:6a:

אֲנִי יְהוָה קְרָאתִיךָ בְצֶדֶק	6aA	I, the LORD, call you justly
וְאַחְזֵק בְּיָדֶךָ וְאֶצָּרְךָ	6aB	and I will grasp your hand and will keep you.

𝔐 distinctive accents: 8 – 7.
Stresses: 4 + 3.
Verse-line parallelism: קרא || חזק; ךָ־ (m.s.) || ךָ־ (m.s.); ב || ב.
Discussion: We disregard the Masoretic division here.[2]

VERSE–LINE: 42:6b:

וְאֶתֶּנְךָ לִבְרִית עָם	6bA	And I will make you a covenant of people,
לְאוֹר גּוֹיִם׃	6bB	a light for the nations,

𝔐 distinctive accents: 8 – 1.
Stresses: 3 + 2.

[2]See p. 126.

Verse-line parallelism: ל || ל; ברית || אור (unique); עם || גוי.
Discussion: See our comment on p. 126.

VERSE–LINE: 42:7a:

לִפְקֹחַ עֵינַיִם עִוְרוֹת 7aA to open blind eyes,

𝔐 distinctive accents: 2.
Stresses: 3.
Verse-line parallelism: None (unicolon).
Discussion: The stronger parallelism between v. 7bA and 7bB seems to have induced the Masoretes to provide שמי with an Atnaḥ. Note the similar build of vv. 8 and 9.

VERSE–LINE: 42:7b:

לְהוֹצִיא מִמַּסְגֵּר אַסִּיר 7bA to bring prisoners from the dungeon,
מִבֵּית כֶּלֶא יֹשְׁבֵי חֹשֶׁךְ׃ 7bB from the house of confinement those who are sitting in darkness.

𝔐 distinctive accents: 5 – 1.
Stresses: 3 + 4.
Verse-line parallelism: מן || מן; מסגר || בית כלא (unique); אסיר || ישב חשך.
Discussion: The ellipsis constitutes a bond between the two cola.

VERSE–LINE: 42:8a:

אֲנִי יְהוָה הוּא שְׁמִי 8aA I am the LORD, that is my name,

𝔐 distinctive accents: 2.
Stresses: 4.
Verse-line parallelism: None (unicolon).
Discussion: Like vv. 7aA and 9aA.

VERSE–LINE: 42:8b:

וּכְבוֹדִי לְאַחֵר לֹא־אֶתֵּן 8bA and my glory I will not give to another,
וּתְהִלָּתִי לַפְּסִילִים׃ 8bB nor my praise to graven images.

𝔐 distinctive accents: 5 – 1.
Stresses: 3 + 2.
Verse-line parallelism: כבוד || תהלה; ־י || ־י; ל || ל; אחר || פסיל.
Discussion: Ellipsis connects the two cola.

VERSE–LINE: 42:9a:

הָרִאשֹׁנוֹת הִנֵּה־בָאוּ 9aA The first things, look, they have come,

𝔐 distinctive accents: 2.
Stresses: 2.
Verse-line parallelism: None (unicolon).
Discussion: See our comment on v. 7b.

VERSE–LINE: 42:9b:

וַחֲדָשׁוֹת אֲנִי מַגִּיד	9bA	and new things I am telling,
בְּטֶרֶם תִּצְמַחְנָה אַשְׁמִיעַ אֶתְכֶם׃	9bB	before they sprout, I let you hear them.

𝔐 distinctive accents: 5 – 1.
Stresses: 3 + 4.
Verse-line parallelism: חדש || צמח; נגד || שמע Hiph.

VERSE–LINE: 42:10a:

שִׁירוּ לַיהוָה שִׁיר חָדָשׁ	10aA	Sing for the LORD a new song,
תְּהִלָּתוֹ מִקְצֵה הָאָרֶץ	10aB	his praise from the ends of the earth,

𝔐 distinctive accents: 5 – 2.
Stresses: 4 + 3.
שיר || תהלה.
Discussion: The cola are connected by ellipsis.

VERSE–LINE: 42:10b:

יוֹרְדֵי הַיָּם וּמְלֹאוֹ	10bA	you who are sailing the sea and all that fills it,
אִיִּים וְיֹשְׁבֵיהֶם׃	10bB	you islands and those dwelling there!

𝔐 distinctive accents: 5 – 1.
Stresses: 3 + 2.
Verse-line parallelism: ירד || ישב; ים || אי; מלא || ישב.

VERSE–LINE: 42:11a:

יִשְׂאוּ מִדְבָּר וְעָרָיו	11aA	Let the desert and its towns raise (their voices)
חֲצֵרִים תֵּשֵׁב קֵדָר	11aB	the villages where Kedar lives,

𝔐 distinctive accents: 5 – 2.
Stresses: 3 + 3.
Verse-line parallelism: מדבר || קדר (unique); עיר || חצר.
Discussion: The cola are connected by ellipsis.

VERSE–LINE: 42:11b:

יָרֹנּוּ יֹשְׁבֵי סֶלַע	11bA	let the dwellers in the rocks rejoice,

מֵרֹ֥אשׁ הָרִ֖ים יִצְוָֽחוּ׃ 11bB let them shout from the top of the mountains.

𝔐 distinctive accents: 5 – 1.
Stresses: 3 + 3.
Verse-line parallelism: רנן || צוח; סלע || הר; grammatical parallelism.

VERSE–LINE: 42:12a:

יָשִׂ֥ימוּ לַיהוָ֖ה כָּב֑וֹד 12aA Let them give glory to the LORD,
וּתְהִלָּת֖וֹ בָּאִיִּ֥ים יַגִּֽידוּ׃ 12aB and let them tell his praise on the islands.

𝔐 distinctive accents: 2 – 1.
Stresses: 3 + 3.
Verse-line parallelism: שׂים || נגד; כבוד || תהלה; grammatical parallelism; rhyme.

VERSE–LINE: 42:13a:

יְהוָה֙ כַּגִּבּ֣וֹר יֵצֵ֔א 13aA The LORD goes out like a hero,
כְּאִ֥ישׁ מִלְחָמ֖וֹת יָעִ֣יר קִנְאָ֑ה 13aB like a warrior he wakes up fury,

𝔐 distinctive accents: 5 – 2.
Stresses: 3 + 4.
Verse-line parallelism: כ || כ; גבור || איש מלחמה; יצא || עור; grammatical parallelism.

VERSE–LINE: 42:13b:

יָרִ֙יעַ֙ אַף־יַצְרִ֔יחַ 13bA he shouts, even yells,
עַל־אֹיְבָ֖יו יִתְגַּבָּֽר׃ 13bB he shows himself a hero to his enemies.

𝔐 distinctive accents: 5 – 1.
Stresses: 2 + 2.
Verse-line parallelism: Grammatical parallelism.

VERSE–LINE: 42:14a:

הֶחֱשֵׁ֙יתִי֙ מֵעוֹלָ֔ם 14aA I have been quiet from eternity on.
אַחֲרִ֖ישׁ אֶתְאַפָּ֑ק 14aB Shall I remain silent, restrain myself?

𝔐 distinctive accents: 5 – 2.
Stresses: 2 + 2.
Verse-line parallelism: חשה || חרשׁ; חשה || אפק.

VERSE–LINE: 42:14b:

כַּיּוֹלֵדָ֣ה אֶפְעֶ֔ה 14bA Like a woman in labour I will groan!
אֶשֹּׁ֥ם וְאֶשְׁאַ֖ף יָֽחַד׃ 14bB I will gasp and pant together!

𝔐 distinctive accents: 5 – 1.
Stresses: 2 + 3.
Verse-line parallelism: פעה || נשם (unique); פעה || שׁאף (unique); grammatical parallelism.

VERSE–LINE: 42:15a:

אַחֲרִ֤יב הָרִים֙ וּגְבָע֔וֹת	15aA	I will lay waste mountains and hills
וְכָל־עֶשְׂבָּ֖ם אוֹבִ֑ישׁ	15aB	and I will dry up all their vegetation.

𝔐 distinctive accents: 5 – 2.
Stresses: 3 + 2.
Verse-line parallelism: חרב || יבשׁ; הר || עשׂב; grammatical parallelism.

VERSE–LINE: 42:15b:

וְשַׂמְתִּ֤י נְהָרוֹת֙ לָֽאִיִּ֔ים	15bA	And I will make rivers into islands,
וַאֲגַמִּ֖ים אוֹבִֽישׁ׃	15bB	and will dry up pools.

𝔐 distinctive accents: 5 – 1.
Stresses: 3 + 2.
Verse-line parallelism: נהר || אגם.

VERSE–LINE: 42:16a:

וְהוֹלַכְתִּ֣י עִוְרִ֗ים בְּדֶ֙רֶךְ֙ לֹ֣א יָדָ֔עוּ	16aA	And I will let go blind ones on a way they do not know,
בִּנְתִיב֥וֹת לֹֽא־יָדְע֖וּ אַדְרִיכֵ֑ם	16aB	on paths they do not know I will let you walk,

𝔐 distinctive accents: 5 – 2.
Stresses: 5 + 3.
Verse-line parallelism: הלך || דרך; ב || ב; דרך || נתיבה; לא || לא; ידע || ידע; grammatical parallelism.

VERSE–LINE: 42:16b:

אָשִׂ֨ים מַחְשָׁ֤ךְ לִפְנֵיהֶם֙ לָא֔וֹר	16bA	I will make the darkness for them into light,
וּמַֽעֲקַשִּׁים֙ לְמִישׁ֔וֹר	16bB	and the rough places (I will make) level.
אֵ֚לֶּה הַדְּבָרִ֔ים עֲשִׂיתִ֖ם וְלֹ֥א עֲזַבְתִּֽים׃	16bB	These are the words which I will do and will not forsake.

𝔐 distinctive accents: 7 – 5 – 1.
Stresses: 4 + 2 + 5.
Verse-line parallelism: שׂים || עשׂה; מחשך || מעקשׁ; ל || ל; מחשך || אור (antithetical); rhyme.
Discussion: The first two cola are linked by ellipsis.

Verse–line: 42:17a:

נָסֹ֤גוּ אָחוֹר֙ יֵבֹ֣שׁוּ בֹ֔שֶׁת 17aA They move backwards, are deeply ashamed,
הַבֹּטְחִ֖ים בַּפָּ֑סֶל 17aB those who trust in idols,
הָאֹמְרִ֥ים לְמַסֵּכָ֖ה אַתֶּ֥ם אֱלֹהֵֽינוּ׃ 17aC those who say to molten images, ‘You are our gods!’

𝔐 distinctive accents: 5 – 2 – 1.
Stresses: 4 + 2 + 4.
Verse-line parallelism: בוש || בטח; פסל || מסכה; פסל || אלהים; grammatical parallelism.

Verse–line: 42:18a:

הַחֵרְשִׁ֖ים שְׁמָ֑עוּ 18aA O deaf ones, hear!
וְהַעִוְרִ֖ים הַבִּ֥יטוּ לִרְא֫וֹת׃ 18aB And O blind ones, watch to see!

𝔐 distinctive accents: 2 – 1.
Stresses: 2 + 3.
Verse-line parallelism: חרש || עור; שמע || נבט; שמע || ראה; grammatical parallelism.

Verse–line: 42:19a:

מִ֤י עִוֵּר֙ כִּ֣י אִם־עַבְדִּ֔י 19aA Who is blind but my servant?
וְחֵרֵ֖שׁ כְּמַלְאָכִ֣י אֶשְׁלָ֑ח 19aB And deaf as my messenger whom I send?

𝔐 distinctive accents: 5 – 2.
Stresses: 4 + 3.
Verse-line parallelism: עור || חרש; עבד || מלאך; ־י || ־י.

Verse–line: 42:19b:

מִ֤י עִוֵּר֙ כִּמְשֻׁלָּ֔ם 19bA Who is blind as the one who had to do penance?
וְעִוֵּ֖ר כְּעֶ֥בֶד יְהוָֽה׃ 19bB and as blind as the servant of the Lord?

𝔐 distinctive accents: 5 – 1.
Stresses: 3 + 3.
Verse-line parallelism: עור || עור; כ || כ; משלם || עבד יהוה (unique).
Discussion: Ellipsis connects the cola.

Verse–line: 42:20a:

רָא֥וֹת* רַבּ֖וֹת וְלֹ֣א תִשְׁמֹ֑ר 20aA There is much to see, but you do not observe it,
פָּק֥וֹחַ אָזְנַ֖יִם וְלֹ֥א יִשְׁמָֽע׃ 20aB there is opening of the ears, but he does not hear.

𝔐 distinctive accents: 2 – 1.

Stresses: 4 + 4.
Verse-line parallelism: ראה || פקח; ראה || שמע; לא || לא; שמר || שמע.

VERSE–LINE: 42:21a:

יְהוָה חָפֵץ לְמַעַן צִדְקוֹ	21aA	For the sake of his justice the LORD wants
יַגְדִּיל תּוֹרָה וְיַאְדִּיר׃	21aB	to magnify his teaching and make it (even more) powerful.

𝔐 distinctive accents: 2 – 1.
Stresses: 4 + 3.
Verse-line parallelism: צדק || תורה.

Discussion: Division as a bicolon, with the Masoretes.

VERSE–LINE: 42:22a:

וְהוּא עַם־בָּזוּז וְשָׁסוּי	22aA	And he? A despoiled and plundered people!
הָפֵחַ בַּחוּרִים כֻּלָּם	22aB	There was ensnaring of them all in holes,
וּבְבָתֵּי כְלָאִים הָחְבָּאוּ	22aC	and in houses of confinement they were hidden.

𝔐 distinctive accents: 3 – 5 – 2.
Stresses: 3 + 3 + 3.
Verse-line parallelism: ב || ב; חור || בת כלא (unique).

Discussion: The threefold description of the dreadful experiences of the people, though not expressed in standard parallels, as well as the clear strophe parallelism between vv. 22a and 22b, argue for taking the three cola of v. 22a as a tricolon and not as a unicolon and a bicolon. The sequence of accents, though not descending, is not uncommon: "*Zaqef* cannot precede *segolta*, but usually follows it, marking divisions between it and *atnaḥ*".[3]

VERSE–LINE: 43:22b:

הָיוּ לָבַז וְאֵין מַצִּיל	22bA	They became spoil and there was none delivering,
מְשִׁסָּה וְאֵין־אֹמֵר הָשַׁב׃	22bB	plunder, and there was none saying: Give back!

𝔐 distinctive accents: 5 – 1.
Stresses: 4 + 3.
Verse-line parallelism: נצל || שוב Hiph. בז || משסה; אין || אין.
Discussion: Ellipsis connects the cola.

[3] I. Yeivin, *Introduction to the Tiberian Masorah*, transl. E.J. Revell (MasSt, 5), [Missoula] 1980, 188.

VERSE–LINE: 42:23a:

מִ֤י בָכֶם֙ יַאֲזִ֣ין זֹ֑את	23aA	Who among you gives ear to this,
יַקְשִׁ֥ב וְיִשְׁמַ֖ע לְאָחֽוֹר׃	23aB	listens and hears, for later times?

𝔐 distinctive accents: 2 – 1.
Stresses: 4 + 3.
Verse-line parallelism: אזן || קשב; אזן || שמע.
Discussion: Again ellipsis is a binding force.

VERSE–LINE: 42:24a:

מִֽי־נָתַ֨ן לִמְשׁוֹסָּ֧ה* יַעֲקֹ֛ב	24aA	Who gave Jacob as plunder,
וְיִשְׂרָאֵ֥ל לְבֹזְזִ֖ים	24aB	and Israel to despoilers?
הֲל֣וֹא יְהוָ֑ה	24aC	Was is not the LORD?

𝔐 distinctive accents: 12 – 8 – 2.
Stresses: 3 + 2 + 2.
Verse-line parallelism: ל || ל; משסה || בזז; יעקב || ישראל || יהוה.
Discussion: Vv. 24aA-B are connected by ellipsis. For מי and הלוא in one and the same verse-line see Mic. 1:5.

VERSE–LINE: 42:24b:

ז֚וּ חָטָ֣אנוּ ל֔וֹ	24bA	The One against whom we have sinned?
וְלֹֽא־אָב֤וּ בִדְרָכָיו֙ הָל֔וֹךְ	24bB	For they were not willing to walk in his ways,
וְלֹ֥א שָׁמְע֖וּ בְּתוֹרָתֽוֹ׃	24bC	and did not listen to his teaching.

𝔐 distinctive accents: 5 – 5 – 1.
Stresses: 3 + 3 + 3.
Verse-line parallelism: חטא || לא הלך || לא שמע; לא || לא; ב || ב; דרך || תורה; ו־ || ו־ || ו־. grammatical parallelism.

Discussion: The sequence of accents (5–5–1) generally indicates a tricolon. BHS and many exegetes combine הלוא יהוה and זה חטאנו לו into one verse-line, on the basis of the rhyme of הלוא || ולא. Furthermore, it is sometimes asserted that we are dealing with prose here. With regard to the division of the verse according to the BHS, one might refer to 45:21 where מי and הלוא introduce two different verse-lines. However, מי and הלוא may also occur in one verse-line (Mic. 1:5). The Masoretic division results in a tricolon which is balanced by the tricolon v. 24a.

VERSE–LINE: 42:25a:

וַיִּשְׁפֹּ֤ךְ עָלָיו֙ חֵמָ֣ה אַפּ֔וֹ	25aA	So he poured out hot anger on him,
וֶעֱז֖וּז מִלְחָמָ֑ה	25aB	and the violence of war.

𝔪 distinctive accents: 5 – 2.
Stresses: 4 + 2.
Verse-line parallelism: חמה || עזוז (unique); אף || מלחמה;
Discussion: Ellipsis connects the two cola.

VERSE–LINE: 42:25b:

וַתְּלַהֲטֵ֤הוּ מִסָּבִיב֙ וְלֹ֣א יָדָ֔ע	25bA	And it set him on fire round about, but he knew not,
וַתִּבְעַר־בּ֖וֹ וְלֹא־יָשִׂ֥ים עַל־לֵֽב׃	25bB	and it burned him, but he did not take it to heart.

𝔪 distinctive accents: 5 – 1.
Stresses: 4 + 3.
Verse-line parallelism: להט || בער; ־הו || ־ו; לא || לא; ידע || שים על לב; grammatical parallelism.

4.4 Isaiah 42 – Delimitation of Strophes

STROPHE A.i.1 (Isa. 42:1)

הֵ֤ן עַבְדִּי֙ אֶתְמָךְ־בּ֔וֹ	1aA	Behold, my servant whom I hold,
בְּחִירִ֖י רָצְתָ֣ה נַפְשִׁ֑י	1aB	my chosen one, in whom my soul takes pleasure,
נָתַ֤תִּי רוּחִי֙ עָלָ֔יו	1bA	I put my spirit on him,
מִשְׁפָּ֥ט לַגּוֹיִ֖ם יוֹצִֽיא׃	1bB	he will carry out justice for the nations.

= Masoretic verse.
Separation ↑: major division markers in the textual tradition; deictic particle(s); repetitive verse-line parallelism.
Separation ↓: swapping (object); swapping (adjunct).
Strophe parallelism: ־י || ־י; ־ו || ־ו; נפש || רוח.

STROPHE A.i.2 (Isa. 42:2–3)

לֹ֥א יִצְעַ֖ק וְלֹ֣א יִשָּׂ֑א	2aA	He will not shout or raise (his voice),
וְלֹא־יַשְׁמִ֥יעַ בַּח֖וּץ קוֹלֽוֹ׃	2aB	and he will not make his voice heard in the street.
קָנֶ֤ה רָצוּץ֙ לֹ֣א יִשְׁבּ֔וֹר	3aA	A crushed reed he will not break,
וּפִשְׁתָּ֥ה כֵהָ֖ה לֹ֣א יְכַבֶּ֑נָּה	3aB	and a smouldering wick – he will not quench it.
לֶאֱמֶ֖ת יוֹצִ֥יא מִשְׁפָּֽט׃	3aC	Truthfully he will bring forth justice.

≠ Masoretic verse.
Separation ↑: repetitive verse-line parallelism; swapping (adjunct).
Separation ↓: repetitive verse-line parallelism; swapping (object); swapping (adjunct).

Strophe parallelism: לא || לא || לא || לא; grammatical parallelism.
Discussion: Since every colon contains לא and describes the humble behaviour of the servant of the LORD we join the two verses.

STROPHE A.i.3 (Isa. 42:4)

לֹא יִכְהֶה וְלֹא יָרוּץ*	4aA	He will not smoulder or be crushed,
עַד־יָשִׂים בָּאָרֶץ מִשְׁפָּט	4aB	until he will put justice on earth,
וּלְתוֹרָתוֹ אִיִּים יְיַחֵילוּ׃	4aC	and the islands will await his teaching.

= Masoretic verse.
Separation ↑: swapping (adjunct).
Separation ↓: major division markers in the textual tradition.
Strophe parallelism: None (one verse-line).

STROPHE A.ii.1 (Isa. 42:5)

כֹּה־אָמַר הָאֵל ׀ יְהוָה	5aA	Thus says God, the LORD,
בּוֹרֵא הַשָּׁמַיִם וְנוֹטֵיהֶם	5aB	who created the heavens and stretched them out,
רֹקַע הָאָרֶץ וְצֶאֱצָאֶיהָ	5aC	who hammered out the earth and all that came forth from it,
נֹתֵן נְשָׁמָה לָעָם עָלֶיהָ	5bA	who gives breath to the people on it,
וְרוּחַ לַהֹלְכִים בָּהּ׃	5bB	and spirit to those who walk on it,

= Masoretic verse.
Separation ↑: major division markers in the textual tradition; deictic particle(s); marker of direct speech.
Separation ↓: major division markers in the textual tradition.
Strophe parallelism: grammatical parallelism.
Discussion: The verse-line 5b is connected with the preceding one by the participles and the suffixes 3 f.s.

STROPHE A.ii.2 (Isa. 42:6)

אֲנִי יְהוָה קְרָאתִיךָ בְצֶדֶק	6aA	I, the LORD, call you justly
וְאַחְזֵק בְּיָדֶךָ וְאֶצָּרְךָ	6aB	and I will grasp your hand and will keep hfill you.
וְאֶתֶּנְךָ לִבְרִית עָם	6bA	And I will make you a covenant of people,
לְאוֹר גּוֹיִם׃	6bB	a light for the nations,

= Masoretic verse.
Separation ↑: major division markers in the textual tradition; independent pers. pronoun; repetitive verse-line parallelism.
Separation ↓: repetitive verse-line parallelism.
Strophe parallelism: ךָ־ (m.s.) || ךָ־ (m.s.); grammatical parallelism.

Discussion: It might be that 𝔊^A started a new strophe with v. 6b. The resulting strophe parallelism between אור and עור would seem to support that division (see also v. 16). However, the very similar construction of Isa. 49:8-9 counsels against adopting this strophic division.

STROPHE A.ii.3 (Isa. 42:7)

לִפְקֹחַ עֵינַיִם עִוְרוֹת	7aA	to open blind eyes,
לְהוֹצִיא מִמַּסְגֵּר אַסִּיר	7bA	to bring prisoners from the dungeon,
מִבֵּית כֶּלֶא יֹשְׁבֵי חֹשֶׁךְ׃	7bB	from the house of confinement those who are sitting in darkness.

= Masoretic verse.
Separation ↑: None.
Separation ↓: major division markers in the textual tradition; repetitive verse-line parallelism; swapping (adjunct).
Strophe parallelism: ל || ל; עור || חשך; grammatical parallelism.

STROPHE A.ii.4 (Isa. 42:8)

אֲנִי יְהוָה הוּא שְׁמִי	8aA	I am the LORD, that is my name,
וּכְבוֹדִי לְאַחֵר לֹא־אֶתֵּן	8bA	and my glory I will not give to another,
וּתְהִלָּתִי לַפְּסִילִים׃	8bB	nor my praise to graven images.

= Masoretic verse.
Separation ↑: major division markers in the textual tradition; independent pers. pronouns.
Separation ↓: major division markers in the textual tradition; repetitive verse-line parallelism; swapping (object); swapping (adjunct).
Strophe parallelism: שם || כבוד; שם || תהלה; ־י || ־י.

STROPHE A.ii.5 (Isa. 42:9)

הָרִאשֹׁנוֹת הִנֵּה־בָאוּ	9aA	The first things, look, they have come,
וַחֲדָשׁוֹת אֲנִי מַגִּיד	9bA	and new things I am telling,
בְּטֶרֶם תִּצְמַחְנָה אַשְׁמִיעַ אֶתְכֶם׃	9bB	before they sprout, I let you hear them.

= Masoretic verse.
Separation ↑: major division markers in the textual tradition; deictic particle(s); swapping (subject).
Separation ↓: major division markers in the textual tradition; independent pers. pronoun; swapping (object).
Strophe parallelism: ראשון || חדש; בוא || צמח (unique).

STROPHE B.i.1 (Isa. 42:10)

שִׁירוּ לַיהוָה שִׁיר חָדָשׁ	10aA	Sing for the LORD a new song,
תְּהִלָּתוֹ מִקְצֵה הָאָרֶץ	10aB	his praise from the ends of the earth,
יוֹרְדֵי הַיָּם וּמְלֹאוֹ	10bA	you who are sailing the sea and all that fills it,
אִיִּים וְיֹשְׁבֵיהֶם׃	10bB	you islands and those dwelling there!

= Masoretic verse.

Separation ↑: major division markers in the textual tradition; imperative(s); swapping (adjunct)

Separation ↓: major division markers in the textual tradition; vocatives.

Strophe parallelism: קצה הארץ || אי; ארץ || ים.

Discussion: The sentence runs on through both verses.

STROPHE B.i.2 (Isa. 42:11)

יִשְׂאוּ מִדְבָּר וְעָרָיו	11aA	Let the desert and its towns raise (their voices)
חֲצֵרִים תֵּשֵׁב קֵדָר	11aB	the villages where Kedar lives,
יָרֹנּוּ יֹשְׁבֵי סֶלַע	11bA	let the dwellers in the rocks rejoice,
מֵרֹאשׁ הָרִים יִצְוָחוּ׃	11bB	let them shout from the top of the mountains.

= Masoretic verse.

Separation ↑: major division markers in the textual tradition; jussive(s).

Separation ↓: jussive(s); swapping (adjunct).

Strophe parallelism: נשא (קול) || רנן; מדבר || הר; ישב || ישב; grammatical parallelism.

STROPHE B.i.3 (Isa. 42:12)

יָשִׂימוּ לַיהוָה כָּבוֹד	12aA	Let them give glory to the LORD,
וּתְהִלָּתוֹ בָּאִיִּים יַגִּידוּ׃	12aB	and let them tell his praise on the islands.

= Masoretic verse.

Separation ↑: jussive(s); swapping (object); swapping (adjunct).

Separation ↓: major division markers in the textual tradition;

Strophe parallelism: None (one verse-line).

STROPHE B.ii.1 (Isa. 42:13)

יְהוָה כַּגִּבּוֹר יֵצֵא	13aA	The LORD goes out like a hero,
כְּאִישׁ מִלְחָמוֹת יָעִיר קִנְאָה	13aB	like a warrior he wakes up fury,
יָרִיעַ אַף־יַצְרִיחַ	13bA	he shouts, even yells,
עַל־אֹיְבָיו יִתְגַּבָּר׃	13bB	he shows himself a hero to his enemies.

= Masoretic verse.
Separation ↑: swapping (subject); swapping (adjunct).
Separation ↓: major division markers in the textual tradition; deictic particle(s); swapping (adjunct).
Strophe parallelism: גבור || גבר Hitpa. (unique); wordplay between יעיר and יריע; grammatical parallelism.

STROPHE B.ii.2 (Isa. 42:14)

הֶחֱשֵׁיתִי מֵעוֹלָם	14aA	I have been quiet from eternity on.
אַחֲרִישׁ אֶתְאַפָּק	14aB	Shall I remain silent, restrain myself?
כַּיּוֹלֵדָה אֶפְעֶה	14bA	Like a woman in labour I will groan!
אֶשֹּׁם וְאֶשְׁאַף יָחַד׃	14bB	I will gasp and pant together!

= Masoretic verse.
Separation ↑: major division markers in the textual tradition.
Separation ↓: swapping (adjunct).
Strophe parallelism: חשה || פעה (antithetical; unique); חרש || נשם (antithetical; unique); grammatical parallelism.

STROPHE B.ii.3 (Isa. 42:15)

אַחֲרִיב הָרִים וּגְבָעוֹת	15aA	I will lay waste mountains and hills
וְכָל־עֶשְׂבָּם אוֹבִישׁ	15aB	and I will dry up all their vegetation.
וְשַׂמְתִּי נְהָרוֹת לָאִיִּים	15bA	And I will make rivers into islands,
וַאֲגַמִּים אוֹבִישׁ׃	15bB	and will dry up pools.

= Masoretic verse.
Separation ↑: swapping (object).
Separation ↓: swapping (object).
Strophe parallelism: חרב || יבשׁ; יבשׁ || יבשׁ; הר || נהר; grammatical parallelism.

STROPHE B.ii.4 (Isa. 42:16)

וְהוֹלַכְתִּי עִוְרִים בְּדֶרֶךְ לֹא יָדָעוּ	16aA	And I will let go blind ones on a way they do not know,
בִּנְתִיבוֹת לֹא־יָדְעוּ אַדְרִיכֵם	16aB	on paths they do not know I will let you walk,
אָשִׂים מַחְשָׁךְ לִפְנֵיהֶם לָאוֹר	16bA	I will make the darkness for them into light,
וּמַעֲקַשִּׁים לְמִישׁוֹר	16bB	and the rough places I will make level.
אֵלֶּה הַדְּבָרִים עֲשִׂיתִם וְלֹא עֲזַבְתִּים׃	16bC	These are the words which I will do and will not forsake.

= Masoretic verse.
Separation ↑: repetitive verse-line parallelism; swapping (adjunct).

Separation ↓: major division marker in the textual tradition (4Q[g]); demonstrative pronoun; repetitive verse-line parallelism (ל || ל).
Strophe parallelism: עור || מחשך (unique); עור || אור (antithetical; unique); לא || לא; grammatical parallelism.

STROPHE III.B.ii.4 (Isa. 42:17)

נָסֹגוּ אָחוֹר יֵבֹשׁוּ בֹשֶׁת	17aA	They move backwards, are deeply ashamed,
הַבֹּטְחִים בַּפָּסֶל	17aB	those who trust in idols,
הָאֹמְרִים לְמַסֵּכָה אַתֶּם אֱלֹהֵינוּ׃	17aC	those who say to molten images, 'You are our gods!'

= Masoretic verse.
Separation ↑: major division marker in the textual tradition; independent pers. pronoun; paronomasia; marker of direct speech.
Separation ↓: major division markers in the textual tradition.
Strophe parallelism: None (one verse-line).

STROPHE C.i.1 (Isa. 42:18)

הַחֵרְשִׁים שְׁמָעוּ	18aA	O deaf ones, hear!
וְהַעִוְרִים הַבִּיטוּ לִרְאוֹת׃	18aB	And O blind ones, watch to see!

= Masoretic verse.
Separation ↑: major division markers in the textual tradition; imperative(s); vocatives.
Separation ↓: None (one verse-line).
Strophe parallelism: None (one verse-line).

STROPHE C.i.2 (Isa. 42:19)

מִי עִוֵּר כִּי אִם־עַבְדִּי	19aA	Who is blind but my servant?
וְחֵרֵשׁ כְּמַלְאָכִי אֶשְׁלָח	19aB	And deaf as my messenger whom I send?
מִי עִוֵּר כִּמְשֻׁלָּם	19bA	Who is blind as the one who had to do penance?
וְעִוֵּר כְּעֶבֶד יְהוָה׃	19bB	and as blind as the servant of the LORD?

= Masoretic verse.
Separation ↑: deictic particle(s); interrogative pronoun; repetitive verse-line parallelism.
Separation ↓: interrogative pronoun; repetitive verse-line parallelism.
Strophe parallelism: מי || מי; עור || עור; עבד || עבד; כ || כ.

STROPHE C.i.3 (Isa. 42:20)

רָאוֹת* רַבּוֹת וְלֹא תִשְׁמֹר	20aA	There is much to see, but you do not observe it,
פָּקוֹחַ אָזְנַיִם וְלֹא יִשְׁמָע׃	20aB	there is opening of the ears, but he does not hear.

= Masoretic verse.

Separation ↑: repetitive verse-line parallelism.
Separation ↓: major division markers in the textual tradition.
Strophe parallelism: None (one verse-line).

STROPHE C.ii.1 (Isa. 42:21)

יְהוָ֥ה חָפֵ֖ץ לְמַ֣עַן צִדְק֑וֹ	21aA	For the sake of his justice the LORD wants
יַגְדִּ֥יל תּוֹרָ֖ה וְיַאְדִּֽיר׃	21aB	to magnify his teaching and make it (even more) powerful.

= Masoretic verse.
Separation ↑: major division markers in the textual tradition; swapping (subject).
Separation ↓: None (one verse-line).
Strophe parallelism: None (one verse-line).

STROPHE C.ii.2 (Isa. 42:22)

וְהוּא֙ עַם־בָּז֣וּז וְשָׁס֔וּי	22aA	And he? A despoiled and plundered people!
הָפֵ֤חַ בַּֽחוּרִים֙ כֻּלָּ֔ם	22aB	There was ensnaring of them all in holes,
וּבְבָתֵּ֥י כְלָאִ֖ים הָחְבָּ֑אוּ	22aC	and in houses of confinement they were hidden.
הָי֤וּ לָבַז֙ וְאֵ֣ין מַצִּ֔יל	22bA	They became spoil and there was none delivering,
מְשִׁסָּ֖ה וְאֵין־אֹמֵ֥ר הָשַֽׁב׃	22bB	plunder, and there was none saying: Give back!

= Masoretic verse.
Separation ↑: independent pers. pronoun; swapping (subject); swapping (adjunct).
Separation ↓: major division markers in the textual tradition; imperative(s); marker of direct speech; repetitive verse-line parallelism.
Strophe parallelism: בזז || בז; בזז || משסה; שסה || משסה (unique).

STROPHE C.ii.3 (Isa. 42:23)

מִ֥י בָכֶ֖ם יַאֲזִ֣ין זֹ֑את	23aA	Who among you gives ear to this,
יַקְשִׁ֥ב וְיִשְׁמַ֖ע לְאָחֽוֹר׃	23aB	listens and hears, for later times?

= Masoretic verse.
Separation ↑: major division markers in the textual tradition; demonstrative pronoun; interrogative pronoun.
Separation ↓: major division markers in the textual tradition.
Strophe parallelism: None (one verse-line).

STROPHE C.ii.4 (Isa. 42:24)

מִֽי־נָתַ֨ן לִמְשׁוֹסָּ֤ה* יַעֲקֹב	24aA	Who gave Jacob as plunder,

וְיִשְׂרָאֵל לְבֹזְזִים	24aB	and Israel to despoilers?
הֲלוֹא יְהוָה	24aC	Was is not the LORD?
זוּ חָטָאנוּ לוֹ	24bA	The One against whom we have sinned?
וְלֹא־אָבוּ בִדְרָכָיו הָלוֹךְ	24bB	For they were not willing to walk in his ways,
וְלֹא שָׁמְעוּ בְּתוֹרָתוֹ׃	24bC	and did not listen to his teaching.

= Masoretic verse.

Separation ↑: major division markers in the textual tradition; interrogative pronoun; swapping (adjunct).

Separation ↓: swapping (adjunct).

Strophe parallelism: הלוא || לא.

Discussion: Despite the rather weak strophe parallelism the connection between the two verse-lines is not in doubt because the second gives the reason for the first and v. 24b cannot be understood without reference to v. 24a.

STROPHE C.ii.5 (Isa. 42:25)

וַיִּשְׁפֹּךְ עָלָיו חֵמָה אַפּוֹ	25aA	So he poured out hot anger on him,
וֶעֱזוּז מִלְחָמָה	25aB	and the violence of war.
וַתְּלַהֲטֵהוּ מִסָּבִיב וְלֹא יָדָע	25bA	And it set him on fire round about, but he knew not,
וַתִּבְעַר־בּוֹ וְלֹא־יָשִׂים עַל־לֵב׃	25bB	and it burned him, but he did not take it to heart.

= Masoretic verse.

Separation ↑: swapping (adjunct).

Separation ↓: major division markers in the textual tradition; repetitive verse-line parallelism.

Strophe parallelism: חמה || בער.

4.5 Isaiah 42 – Delimitation of Canticles

CANTICLE A.i (42:1–4)

Separation ↑: major division markers in the textual tradition; thematic discontinuity; change of subject.

Separation ↓: major division markers in the textual tradition.

Canticle parallelism: משפט || משפט || משפט (threefold responsion); גוי || אי (responsion); יצא Hiph. || יצא Hiph. (responsion); רצץ || רצץ (concatenation); כהה || כהה (concatenation).

Thematic unity: yes. The second and third strophes can be understood only in the light of the first one. All canticles emphasize the chosen servant's role in bringing justice to the world, but in a humble way, not by putting too much strain on people already suffering enough. The servant himself is a fellow-sufferer who will not, however, forsake his mission.

CANTICLE A.ii (42:5–9)

Separation ↑: major division markers in the textual tradition; change of subject.
Separation ↓: major division markers in the textual tradition.
Canticle parallelism: אמר || נגד (inclusion); אמר || שׁמע Hiph. (inclusion); צאצא || צמח (inclusion; unique); נתן || נתן || נתן (responsion/inclusion); עם || עם (responsion); אני || אני || אני (responsion/inclusion). Strophes ii.2 and ii.3 linked by an on-running sentence (enjambment).
Thematic unity: yes. The argument that the almighty Creator should be able to implement something totally new provides a link between beginning and end of this canticle (inclusion). This is the basis for the firm belief that the mission of the servant will succeed. God will do this, however, only because of his own honour and to spite those who put trust in idols. It is important to note that the servant is addressed first in the 2nd person m.s., but finally in the 2nd person m.p. (v. 9bB). Apparently he is a collective body.
Discussion: The isolated Petuḥa in $\mathfrak{G}^A$ after v. 5aB is obviously an error. No capital is used. $\mathfrak{G}^A$ and $\mathfrak{G}^S$ seem to have preserved traces of a strophic division again ($\mathfrak{G}^A$ after v. 5bB [supported by $\mathfrak{G}^Q$], v. 6aB[1], v. 7bB, and $\mathfrak{G}^S$ after v. 8bB, v. 9bB and v. 10bB.

CANTICLE B.i (42:10–12)

Separation ↑: major division markers in the textual tradition; thematic discontinuity; change of subject.
Separation ↓: major division markers in the textual tradition.
Canticle parallelism: שׁיר || רנן (inclusion); יהוה || יהוה (inclusion); תהלה || תהלה (unique; inclusion); מן || מן (inclusion); ארץ || הר (inclusion); אי || אי (responsion); ישׁב || ישׁב (responsion); imperatives and jussives.
Thematic unity: yes. All three strophes contain adhortations to praise the LORD.
Discussion: On the break in $\mathfrak{G}^S$ after v. 10bB see our comment on canticle A.ii. The division between v. 12 and v. 13 is not attested as abundantly as those after vv. 4, 9, 13, 17 and 25. But the spread over three different lines of tradition would seem sufficient, although the markings in $\mathfrak{G}^S$ and $\mathfrak{S}^d$ are marginal paragraphoi only. Yet we believe the division after v. 13 to rest on an erroneous tradition which

[1]See p. 147-8.

was probably caused by the fact that v. 13 speaks of God in the third person, but vv. 14-17 in the first person. However, such abrupt transitions are by no means unusual in Second Isaiah and v. 14 fits much better to v. 13 than to vv. 10-12.

CANTICLE B.ii (42:13–17)

Separation ↑: major division markers in the textual tradition; thematic discontinuity; change of subject.
Separation ↓: major division markers in the textual tradition.
Canticle parallelism: יהוה || אלהים (inclusion; in this case antithetical); רוע || חשה (antithetical; unique); צרח || חרש (antithetical; unique); רוע || פעה (unique).

Thematic unity: yes. At first sight it may appear that at least vv. 15-16 are unconnected to the rest of the canticle. However, in both these strophes the reversal of normal conditions is invoked to highlight the universal power of God.[2] The enemies (v. 13) appear to be those who trust in idols (v. 17) who will certainly be confounded because God is able to put them to shame.[3]

Discussion: With regard to the dividers after v. 13 see our discussion of canticle B.i. $\mathfrak{G}^{A}$ with its divider in the middle of v. 14 seems to limp after the others who divide after v. 13, just as the Setuma or Petuḥa in $4\mathfrak{Q}^{g}$ after v. 16 seems to anticipate the division after v. 17. $\mathfrak{G}^{SBA}$ all indicate the major division after v. 17 proleptically and in the first two cases redundantly in the middle of v. 17aA.

CANTICLE C.i (42:18–20)

Separation ↑: major division markers in the textual tradition.
Separation ↓: major division markers in the textual tradition.
Canticle parallelism: חרש || חרש (unique; responsion); שמע || שמע (inclusion); עור || עור (responsion/inclusion); ראה || ראה (inclusion).

Thematic unity: yes. All three strophes speak of blindness and deafness. It is important that again the servant seems to be identified more or less with the plural of the first strophe.

Discussion: The major division between vv. 20 and 21 is weakly attested, but not controversial.

---

[2]See our note p. 73, n. 12.

[3]It is typical of enemies to retreat (Jer. 46:5; Ps. 9:3; 35:4; 56:9; 70:3; 129:5) as opposed to heroes (2 Sam. 1:22).

CANTICLE C.ii (42:21–25)

Separation ↑: major division markers in the textual tradition; thematic discontinuity; change of subject.
Separation ↓: major division markers in the textual tradition.
Canticle parallelism: תורה || תורה (inclusion); בזז || בזז (responsion); משסה || משסה (inclusion); שמע || ידע (responsion).
Thematic unity: yes. All three strophes try to explain why it was inevitable for the LORD to punish his people.
Discussion: The dividers after v. 22 and v. 23 might go back to the occasional strophic division in certain ancient manuscripts. The clearly erroneous paragraphos which $\mathfrak{G}^{B}$ has in the middle of v. 24 might derive from the same division.

4.6 Isaiah 42 – Delimitation of Macrostructure

The overall structure of Isaiah 42 appears to be completely regular,

SUB-CANTOS	CANTICLES	STROPHES
A	2	8 (3+5)
B	2	8 (3+5)
C	2	8 (3+5)

Distant parallelism connecting the canticles of **sub-canto A**:
תמך (v. 1aA – A.i) || חזק (v. 6aB – A.ii); נתן רוח (v. 1bA – A.i) || נתן רוח/נשמה (v. 5bA-B – A.ii); גוי (v. 1bB – A.i) || גוי (v. 6bB – A.ii); יצא Hiph. (v. 1bB, 3aC – A.1) || יצא Hiph. (v. 7bA – A.ii).

Both canticles describe the mission of the servant of the LORD. In both he has a message for the nations and is promised the continuous support of his Sender. In both he is supposed to bring relief to the weary and oppressed. Bringing about justice seems to be bringing prisoners out from the dungeon. Again the courage to withstand the pressures of the moment and to trust not in images but in the God of Israel is founded in the latter's power as the Creator of the whole cosmos.

Distant parallelism connecting the canticles of **sub-canto B**:
אי (vv. 10bB, 12aB – B. i) || אי (v. 15bA – B.ii); רנן (v. 11bA – B.i) || רוע (v. 13bA – B.ii); הר (v. 11bB – B.i) || הר (v. 15aA – B.ii).

Distant parallelism connecting the canticles of **sub-canto C**:
שמע (vv. 18aA, 20aB – C.i) || שמע (vv. 23aB, 24bC – C.ii); שמר (v. 20aA – C.i) || תורה (vv. 21aB, 24bC – C.ii).[1]

Both canticles address the difficult question why the LORD had rejected his chosen servant. Both point to Israel's sins and stubbornness the inevitable consequence had been that penance had to be done.

Many scholars are of the opinion that the chapter is a pastiche of different redactional pieces. The so-called Servant Song (42:1-4), the 'Naherwartungsschicht' (42:5-9, 10-13, 18-23) and the passages denouncing the idols (42:8bB, 17) are all considered later additions to a small Deutero-Isaianic kernel which might perhaps be found in 42:14-16. This is not the place to discuss the arguments put forward in favour of such views. What we do want to point out, however, is the following. If one wants to maintain the supposition of various redactional layers one has to pay due attention to the fact that the regular structure we found presupposes utmost care for the composition as a whole on the part of the final redactor. Failure to recognize this will result in failure to do justice to his literary artistry and his theological intentions.

An analysis of the content of the whole canto confirms its careful composition. The connections between the first and the last sub-canto are particularly clear (inclusion). The servant of the LORD appears in both and is described as a collective personality who is himself suffering from God's punishment. He is among the crushed, the despoiled and emprisoned, the blind and deaf ones of Israel. Yet he is admonished to fulfil his liberating mission and to obey his LORD. Only in as far as he does so, he is not identical to Israel as a whole. One might say, therefore, that the servants of the LORD are those Israelites who are obediently fulfilling their divinely inspired mission.

Even sub-canto B, containing the song of praise which is often seen as a particularly odd insertion, appears to be carefully embedded in its context. Actually it appears to be the LORD himself who is leading out the blind prisoners (v. 16). This is in line with Second Isaiah's theology that the servant is but an instrument in the hand of God, be it not a will-less object. The new things God is telling (v. 9) prompt a new song of praise (v. 10). His praise and his glory (vv. 8, 10, 12) are sung by the inhabitants of Kedar which to Second Isaiah may have been Edom (cf. Isa. 21:16-17). Because Edom had betrayed Israel when the Babylonians captured Judah they may have been included

[1] In our opinion v. 24bC warrants the opinion that this is a deliberate break-up of the common expression שמר תורה.

in the "enemies" (v. 13) whose mountains will be laid waste (v. 15). In other words, to the final author of Ch. 42 their praise may have been enforced. The whole world, even Israel's former enemies, must recognize the LORD's sovereignty. Only in as far as they do so, they are included in the message of salvation.

Again, we do not deny the possibility of a complicated redactional process lying before the final shape of this canto. But we believe it to be wrong to pay attention to the supposed fragments only. The final product has its own beauty and any probing into its literary history should take into account that fragmenting this well-balanced composition puts a heavy burden of proof on the investigator.

Chapter 5

The Structure of Isaiah 43

5.1 Isaiah 43: Text and Translation

פ <ס> – $1\mathfrak{Q}^{ab}$ – $4\mathfrak{Q}^{g}$ – $\mathfrak{G}^{SBA}$ – $\mathfrak{S}^{abcde}$ ________________________

A.i.1 (Isa. 43:1)

וְעַתָּה כֹּה־אָמַר יְהוָה	1aA	But now, thus says the LORD,
בֹּרַאֲךָ יַעֲקֹב וְיֹצֶרְךָ יִשְׂרָאֵל	1aB	who created you, O Jacob, and who formed you, O Israel,
אַל־תִּירָא כִּי גְאַלְתִּיךָ	1bA	Do not fear, for I redeem you,
קָרָאתִי בְשִׁמְךָ לִי־אָתָּה׃	1bB	I call you by your name, you are mine!

A.i.2 (Isa. 43:2)

כִּי־תַעֲבֹר בַּמַּיִם אִתְּךָ־אָנִי {$\mathfrak{G}^{A}$}	2aA	When you pass through the waters , I am with you,
וּבַנְּהָרוֹת לֹא יִשְׁטְפוּךָ	2aB	and through the rivers – they will not overwhelm you.
כִּי־תֵלֵךְ בְּמוֹ־אֵשׁ לֹא תִכָּוֶה	2bA	When you walk through fire, you will not be scorched,
וְלֶהָבָה לֹא תִבְעַר־בָּךְ׃	2bB	and no flame will burn you.

<פ> – $1\mathfrak{Q}^{a}$ . . . .

A.ii.1 (Isa. 43:3)

כִּי אֲנִי יְהוָה אֱלֹהֶיךָ	3aA	For I am the LORD, your God,
קְדוֹשׁ יִשְׂרָאֵל מוֹשִׁיעֶךָ {$\mathfrak{G}^{SA}$}	3aB	the Holy One of Israel, your saviour.
נָתַתִּי כָפְרְךָ מִצְרַיִם	3bA	I give Egypt as your ransom,
כּוּשׁ וּסְבָא תַּחְתֶּיךָ׃ {$\mathfrak{G}^{A}$}	3bB	Cush and Sheba in exchange for you.

A.ii.2 (Isa. 43:4)

מֵאֲשֶׁר יָקַרְתָּ בְעֵינַי נִכְבַּדְתָּ	4aA	Since you are precious in my eyes, honoured,
וַאֲנִי אֲהַבְתִּיךָ	4aB	and (since) I love you,
וְאֶתֵּן אָדָם תַּחְתֶּיךָ	4bA	I will give people in exchange for you,
וּלְאֻמִּים תַּחַת נַפְשֶׁךָ׃	4bB	and nations in exchange for your life.

. . . .

A.iii.1 (Isa. 43:5)

אַל־תִּירָא כִּי אִתְּךָ־אָנִי	5aA	Do not fear, for I am with you.
מִמִּזְרָח אָבִיא זַרְעֶךָ	5bA	From the east I will bring your seed,
וּמִמַּעֲרָב אֲקַבְּצֶךָּ׃ {$\mathfrak{G}^{A}$}	5bB	and from the west I will gather you.

A.iii.2 (Isa. 43:6)

אֹמַר לַצָּפוֹן תֵּנִי	6aA	I will say to the north, 'Give up!'
וּלְתֵימָן אַל־תִּכְלָאִי	6aB	And to the south, 'Do not withhold!'

הָבִ֤יאִי בָנַי֙ מֵֽרָח֔וֹק	6bA	'Bring my sons from afar,
{<ס>} וּבְנוֹתַ֖י מִקְצֵ֥ה הָאָֽרֶץ׃	6bB	and my daughters from the end of the earth,

A.iii.3 (Isa. 43:7)

כֹּ֚ל הַנִּקְרָ֣א בִשְׁמִ֔י	7aA	everyone who is called by my name,
וְלִכְבוֹדִ֖י בְּרָאתִ֑יו	7aB	and whom I created for my glory,
יְצַרְתִּ֖יו אַף־עֲשִׂיתִֽיו׃	7aC	whom I formed, also made.'

{<ס>$\mathfrak{G}^{A}$}

A.iii.4 (Isa. 43:8)

הוֹצִ֛יא עַם־עִוֵּ֖ר וְעֵינַ֣יִם יֵ֑שׁ	8aA	Let him bring out[1] the people who are blind, yet have eyes,
וְחֵרְשִׁ֖ים וְאׇזְנַ֥יִם לָֽמוֹ׃	8aB	and those who are deaf, yet have ears!

<ס> – 1$\mathfrak{Q}^{a}$ – $\mathfrak{G}^{S}$ ______

B.i.1 (Isa. 43:9a–b)

כׇּֽל־הַגּוֹיִ֞ם נִקְבְּצ֣וּ יַחְדָּ֗ו	9aA	Let all the nations gather together,
וְיֵאָֽסְפוּ֙ לְאֻמִּ֔ים	9aB	and let the peoples assemble!
מִ֤י בָהֶם֙ יַגִּ֣יד זוּ אֹתֶה*	9bA	Who among them will tell what is coming?[2]
{$\mathfrak{G}^{A}$} וְרִאשֹׁנ֖וֹת יַשְׁמִיעֻ֑נוּ	9bB	Let them make us hear first things!

B.i.2 (Isa. 43:9c–10a)

יִתְּנ֤וּ עֵדֵיהֶם֙ וְיִצְדָּ֔קוּ	9cA	Let them give their witnesses so that they may be justified,
{$\mathfrak{G}^{SA}$} וְיִשְׁמְע֖וּ וְיֹאמְר֥וּ אֱמֶֽת׃	9cB	so that one may hear and say: "It is true!"
אַתֶּ֤ם עֵדַי֙ נְאֻם־יְהוָ֔ה	10aA	You are my witnesses, declares the LORD,
וְעַבְדִּ֖י אֲשֶׁ֣ר בָּחָ֑רְתִּי	10aB	and (you are)[3] my Servant, whom I have chosen.

[1]The difficulty of this form was already felt in Antiquity (1$\mathfrak{Q}^{b}$ and $\mathfrak{G}$ read a 1st. pers. sing., 1$\mathfrak{Q}^{a}$ a plural imperative). The interpretation as a perfect is attested by $\mathfrak{C}$. On the basis of הביא in Jer. 17:18 one might assume an exceptional form of the 2nd pers. masc. imperative. But it is much better to suppose it is simply a 3rd pers. sing. precative perfect. Such a perfect occurs in the very next verse, as is generally recognized. Cf. König, *Syntax*, §173; J.C.L. Gibson, *Davidson's Introductory Hebrew Grammar: Syntax*, Edinburgh [4]1994, §60c. The subject can only be the one who is called by the name of the LORD (v. 7), the part of Israel aware of its vocation which is designated as the Servant, cf. Isa. 42:7.

[2]In Isa. 41:22-23 הראשנות ... הגידו and הגידו האתיות form an external parallel pair. This raises the question whether זאת in our verse could be a defective spelling of זו אֹתֶה "that what is coming". The spelling of זאת as זואת in 1$\mathfrak{Q}^{a}$ lends some support to this emendation. For relative זו in Second Isaiah cf. Isa. 42:24; 43:21.

[3]The classic view that ועבדי introduces a second subject next to אתם (e.g. Koole, 221, with earlier literature) is difficult to reconcile with Isa. 41:8-9; 42:1-9; 44:1-2; 49:7; 55:4 where the collective body of Israel is called the chosen servant and witness. See also 43:20! For the same reason there is no need to emend וְעַבְדִּי into וְעַבְדַי.

B.i.3 (Isa. 43:10b–c)

לְמַעַן תֵּדְעוּ וְתַאֲמִינוּ לִי וְתָבִינוּ	10bA	So that you may know and believe me and will understand,
כִּי־אֲנִי הוּא	10bB	that I am the same One.
לְפָנַי לֹא־נוֹצַר אֵל	10cA	Before me no god was formed,
וְאַחֲרַי לֹא יִהְיֶה׃	10cB	nor will there be one after me.

ס <פ> – $1\mathfrak{Q}^{a}$ – $\mathfrak{S}^{a}$ . . . .

B.ii.1 (Isa. 43:11)

אָנֹכִי אָנֹכִי יְהוָה	11aA	I, I am the LORD,
וְאֵין מִבַּלְעָדַי מוֹשִׁיעַ׃	11aB	and apart from me there is no saviour.

B.ii.2 (Isa. 43:12)

אָנֹכִי הִגַּדְתִּי וְהוֹשַׁעְתִּי וְהִשְׁמַעְתִּי	12aA	It is I who told and saved and made heard,
וְאֵין בָּכֶם זָר {$\mathfrak{G}^{SA}$}	12aB	and not a stranger who was among you.
וְאַתֶּם עֵדַי נְאֻם־יְהוָה	12bA	And you are my witnesses, declares the LORD,
וַאֲנִי־אֵל׃	12bB	that I am God.

B.ii.3 (Isa. 43:13)

גַּם־מִיּוֹם אֲנִי הוּא	13aA	Also from today on[4] I am the same One,
וְאֵין מִיָּדִי מַצִּיל	13aB	and no one delivers from my hand;
אֶפְעַל וּמִי יְשִׁיבֶנָּה׃	13bA	I work, and who can reverse it?

ס <פ> – $1\mathfrak{Q}^{a}$– $\mathfrak{G}^{SA}$ – $\mathfrak{S}^{bcde}$ ________________________________

C.i.1 (Isa. 43:14)

כֹּה־אָמַר יְהוָה	14aA	Thus says the LORD,
גֹּאַלְכֶם קְדוֹשׁ יִשְׂרָאֵל	14aB	your Redeemer, the Holy One of Israel:
לְמַעַנְכֶם שִׁלַּחְתִּי בָבֶלָה {$\mathfrak{G}^{Q}$}	14bA	For your sake I send (messengers)[5] to Babylon,
וְהוֹרַדְתִּי בָרִיחִים כֻּלָּם	14bB	and I make them all descend as fugitives (?),[6]
וְכַשְׂדִּים בָּאֳנִיּוֹת רִנָּתָם׃	14bC	yes, the Chaldaeans in their eulogized[7] ships.

{<פ/ס>$\mathfrak{G}^{Q}$}

---

[4]מיום has perplexed ancient and modern exegetes alike (see Barthélemy, 314-6). In view of Ezek. 48:35 "from today, henceforth" is the most likely rendering. One should take into account that the preceding גם refers back to v. 12 which invoked the past in support of the testimony of v. 12bB: as in the past, God will be a saviour now and in the future.

[5]The text is deliberately opaque at this point by omitting the object. Perhaps Cyrus is meant here, as most modern exegetes believe. But it is more likely that the rather common omission of 'messengers' with the verb שלח has to be assumed here too. Cf. *HALAT*, 1401, 2.a.β for the Qal. It is rather at the disturbing news of Cyrus' advent which is announced by their couriers that the Babylonians decide to flee.

[6]Both ancient and modern translators are guessing at this point (see *HALAT*, 1144; Barthélemy, 316-8; De Waard, 167-8). We follow the prevailing opinion.

[7]Although רנה could just as well denote moaning, a contrast seems to be called

C.i.2 (Isa. 43:15)

אֲנִי יְהוָה קְדוֹשְׁכֶם	15aA	I am the LORD, your Holy One,
בּוֹרֵא יִשְׂרָאֵל מַלְכְּכֶם׃	15aB	Creator of Israel, your King.

ס <פ> – $1\mathfrak{Q}^{a}$ – $\mathfrak{G}^{SA}$ – $\mathfrak{S}^{abcde}$ . . . .

C.ii.1 (Isa. 43:16–17a)

כֹּה אָמַר יְהוָה	16aA	Thus says the LORD,
הַנּוֹתֵן בַּיָּם דָּרֶךְ	16aB	who makes[8] a way through the sea,
וּבְמַיִם עַזִּים נְתִיבָה׃	16aC	and a path through mighty waters,
הַמּוֹצִיא רֶכֶב־וָסוּס	17aA	who leads out chariots[9] and horses,
חַיִל וְעִזּוּז	17aB	armies and mighty forces:

C.ii.2 (Isa. 43:17b)

יַחְדָּו יִשְׁכְּבוּ בַּל־יָקוּמוּ	17bA	Together they lie down, do not rise (again),
דָּעֲכוּ כַּפִּשְׁתָּה כָבוּ׃	17bB	they are extinguished, quenched like a wick.

<ס> – $\mathfrak{G}^{SAQ}$ . . . .

C.iii.1 (Isa. 43:18)

אַל־תִּזְכְּרוּ רִאשֹׁנוֹת	18aA	Do not try to remember the first things,
וְקַדְמֹנִיּוֹת אַל־תִּתְבֹּנָנוּ׃	18aB	and do not try to understand things of old.

C.iii.2 (Isa. 43:19)

הִנְנִי עֹשֶׂה חֲדָשָׁה	19aA	Behold, I am about to make a new thing,
עַתָּה תִצְמָח	19aB	now it will sprout.
הֲלוֹא תֵדָעוּהָ {$\mathfrak{G}^{A}$}	19aC	Don't you know?
אַף אָשִׂים בַּמִּדְבָּר דֶּרֶךְ	19bA	Yes, I make a way in the desert,
בִּישִׁמוֹן נְתִיבוֹת*׃	19bB	paths[10] in the wilderness.

C.iii.3 (Isa. 43:20)

תְּכַבְּדֵנִי חַיַּת הַשָּׂדֶה	20aA	The wild beasts of the field will honour me,
תַּנִּים וּבְנוֹת יַעֲנָה	20aB	jackals and ostriches,
כִּי־נָתַתִּי בַמִּדְבָּר מַיִם	20bA	for I give water in the desert,

---

for here. Cf. NIV: "in the ships in which they took pride"; M.J. Mulder, "Filologische kanttekeningen bij Jes. 41:23b; 42:19b en 43:14b", in: *De Knecht: Studies rondom Deutero-Jesaja ... J.L. Koole*, Kampen 1978, 141-9 (147).

[8] Translators and exegetes are divided over the tense to choose here. Obviously the prophet is referring to the events of the Exodus but is he only recalling the past or is he actualizing? We have chosen the latter option for two reasons: 1. המוציא רכב־וסוס is hard to reconcile with the canonical descriptions of the Exodus. 2. The alternation between imperfects and perfects in v. 17b suggests a translation in the present tense, cf. M.C.A. Korpel, J.C. de Moor, F. Sepmeijer, "Consistency with Regard to Tenses", see Abbreviations.

[9] We assume collectives.

[10] With $1\mathfrak{Q}^{a}$. The same parallelism is found in 43:16. Probably the similar phrasing of v. 20bB caused $\mathfrak{M}$'s error. Cf. Barthélemy, 318-9; De Waard, 168-9; Oswalt, 151, n. 43.

נְהָרוֹת בִּישִׁמֹן	20bB	rivers in the wilderness,
{ס} :לְהַשְׁקוֹת עַמִּי בְחִירִי	20bC	to give drink to my people, my chosen one.

C.iii.4 (Isa. 43:21)

עַם־זוּ יָצַרְתִּי לִי	21aA	The people whom I have formed for myself
:תְּהִלָּתִי* יְסַפֵּרוּ	21aB	will tell my praiseworthy deeds.[11]

ס <פ> – $_1\mathfrak{Q}^{a}$– $\mathfrak{G}^{SBA}$ – $\mathfrak{S}^{abce}$ ____________________________________

D.i.1 (Isa. 43:22)

וְלֹא־אֹתִי קָרָאתָ יַעֲקֹב	22aA	Yet you did not call upon me, O Jacob,
:כִּי־יָגַעְתָּ בִּי יִשְׂרָאֵל	22aB	that you would have wearied yourselves for me,[12] O Israel!

D.i.2 (Isa. 43:23)

לֹא־הֵבֵיאתָ לִּי שֵׂה עֹלֹתֶיךָ	23aA	You did not bring me the rams[13] of your burnt offerings,
וּזְבָחֶיךָ לֹא כִבַּדְתָּנִי	23aB	and with your sacrifices you did not honour me.
לֹא הֶעֱבַדְתִּיךָ בְּמִנְחָה	23bA	I have not made you serve with oblations,
:וְלֹא הוֹגַעְתִּיךָ בִּלְבוֹנָה	23bB	and I have not wearied you with incense.

D.i.3 (Isa. 43:24)

לֹא־קָנִיתָ לִּי בַכֶּסֶף קָנֶה	24aA	You did not buy me cane with silver,
וְחֵלֶב זְבָחֶיךָ לֹא הִרְוִיתָנִי	24aB	and the fat of your sacrifices you did not lavish on me.
אַךְ הֶעֱבַדְתַּנִי בְּחַטֹּאותֶיךָ	24bA	No, you made me serve by your sins,
:הוֹגַעְתַּנִי בַּעֲוֹנֹתֶיךָ	24bB	and made me weary with your iniquities.

ס – $_1\mathfrak{Q}^{a}$– $\mathfrak{G}^{SAQ}$ . . . .

D.ii.1 (Isa. 43:25–26)

אָנֹכִי אָנֹכִי הוּא	25aA	I, I am he,
מֹחֶה פְשָׁעֶיךָ לְמַעֲנִי	25aB	who wipes out your transgressions for my own sake,
{<ס>} :וְחַטֹּאתֶיךָ לֹא אֶזְכֹּר	25aC	and do not remember[14] your sins.
הַזְכִּירֵנִי נִשָּׁפְטָה יָחַד	26aA	Help me to remember, let us argue our case together!
:סַפֵּר אַתָּה לְמַעַן תִּצְדָּק	26aB	You tell (us), that you may be justified ...

{<ס>$\mathfrak{G}^{A}$}

D.ii.2 (Isa. 43:27)

אָבִיךָ הָרִאשׁוֹן חָטָא	27aA	Your first father sinned,

[11] With $\mathfrak{G}$ and $\mathfrak{C}$ we read a plural because v. 21aB reflects Exod. 15:11 just as v. 21aA reflects Exod. 15:16.

[12] יגע + ב means "to weary oneself for" (Isa. 62:8) or "to weary oneself by" (Isa. 57:10; Ps. 69:4), with Koole, 248.

[13] Parallel to וזבחיך we assume a collective meaning.

[14] The addition of עוד ($\mathfrak{Q}^{a}$ and 1 medieval ms) is unlikely on textcritical grounds (see Barthélemy, 319-20).

וּמְלִיצֶיךָ פָּשְׁעוּ בִי׃	27aB	and your spokesmen transgressed against me.

D.ii.3 (Isa. 43:28)

וַאֲחַלֵּל שָׂרֵי קֹדֶשׁ	28aA	So I had to defile the chiefs of the sanctuary,
וְאֶתְּנָה* לַחֵרֶם יַעֲקֹב	28bA	and had[15] to devote Jacob to the ban,
וְיִשְׂרָאֵל לְגִדּוּפִים׃	28bB	and Israel to insults.

ס <פ> – 1𝔔^{a} – 𝔊^{SA} – 𝔖^{abe} ______________________________

5.2 Isaiah 43 – Delimitation of Cola

COLON 43:1aA:

וְעַתָּה כֹּה־אָמַר יְהוָה	1aA	But now, thus says the LORD,

With: 𝔐 (10) – 𝔊^{SQ} – 𝔖^{cde}, 𝔖^{b} subordinate punctuation.
Discussion: It is likely that 𝔐 wanted the colon to end after יעקב (provided with a Zaqeph Qaṭon). Since such long cola are not unusual, this is a serious alternative. Since in other cases only the name of יהוה,[1] sometimes adorned with only one epithet at the most,[2] follows the 'Botenformel', we chose to follow the ancient witnesses cited. This has the additional advantage of a more balanced colometry.

COLON 43:1aB:

בֹּרַאֲךָ יַעֲקֹב וְיֹצֶרְךָ יִשְׂרָאֵל	1aB	who created you, O Jacob, and who formed you, O Israel,

With: 𝔐 (2) – 𝔊^{SQ} – 𝔖^{abcde}
Colon parallelism: ברא || יצר; יעקב || ישׂראל.
Discussion: 𝔐 stands alone in assuming a caesura after יעקב (5). Because this results in a rather unbalanced verse (see our comment on the previous colon), we believe that the other witnesses deserve confidence.

COLON 43:1bA:

אַל־תִּירָא כִּי גְאַלְתִּיךָ	1bA	Do not fear, for I redeem you,

With: 𝔐 (5) – 𝔊^{SQ} – 𝔖^{cde}, 𝔖^{ab} subordinate punctuation.

---

[15]𝔐 interpreted the imperfects as referring to the future (cf. 𝔗), doubtlessly because of the cohortative ואתנה. With the other ancient versions we assume it is a consecutive imperfect. Cf. GK §107b, n. 2.

[1]43:16; 44:2; 45:1, 11, 14; 49:7, 8, 25; 50:1; 52:3.

[2]42:5; 44:6, 24; 45:18; 48:17; 49:22; 51:22; 52:4. See also our more detailed comments on p. 268.

COLON 43:1bB:

קְרָאתִי בְשִׁמְךָ לִי־אָתָּה׃ 1bB I call you by your name, you are mine!

With: $\mathfrak{M}$ (1) – $\mathfrak{G}^{SQ}$ – $\mathfrak{S}^{abcde}$
Colon parallelism: ־ך || אתה.
Discussion: The extra point after בשמך in $\mathfrak{G}^{SQ}$ corresponds to the Masoretic Ṭiphḥa.

COLON 43:2aA:

כִּי־תַעֲבֹר בַּמַּיִם אִתְּךָ־אָנִי 2aA When you pass through the waters , I am with you,

With: $\mathfrak{M}$ (5) – $\mathfrak{G}^{SAQ}$, major division marker in $\mathfrak{G}^{A}$ – $\mathfrak{S}^{abcde}$

COLON 43:2aB:

וּבַנְּהָרוֹת לֹא יִשְׁטְפוּךָ 2aB and through the rivers – they will not overwhelm you.

With: $\mathfrak{M}$ (2) – $\mathfrak{G}^{SQ}$ – $\mathfrak{S}^{abcde}$

COLON 43:2bA:

כִּי־תֵלֵךְ בְּמוֹ־אֵשׁ לֹא תִכָּוֶה 2bA When you walk through fire, you will not be scorched,

With: $\mathfrak{M}$ (5) – $\mathfrak{G}^{SQ}$ – $\mathfrak{S}^{abcde}$
Discussion: $\mathfrak{G}^{SQ}$ also have a point after במו־אש; it should be regarded as the equivalent of $\mathfrak{M}$'s Pashṭa.

COLON 43:2bB:

וְלֶהָבָה לֹא תִבְעַר־בָּךְ׃ 2bB and no flame will burn you.

With: $\mathfrak{M}$ (1), major division marker in 1$\mathfrak{Q}^{a}$ – $\mathfrak{G}^{SQ}$ – $\mathfrak{S}^{abcde}$

COLON 43:3aA:

כִּי אֲנִי יְהוָה אֱלֹהֶיךָ 3aA For I am the LORD, your God,

With: $\mathfrak{M}$ (5) – $\mathfrak{G}^{SQ}$ – $\mathfrak{S}^{bcde}$ subordinate punctuation.
Colon parallelism: יהוה || אלהים.
Discussion: For the Revia' (No. 7) with כי see our comment on p. 31.

COLON 43:3aB:

קְדוֹשׁ יִשְׂרָאֵל מוֹשִׁיעֶךָ 3aB the Holy One of Israel, your saviour.

With: $\mathfrak{M}$ (2) – $\mathfrak{G}^{SAQ}$, major division markers in $\mathfrak{G}^{S}$ and $\mathfrak{G}^{A}$ – $\mathfrak{S}^{abcde}$

COLON 43:3bA:

נָתַ֤תִּי כָפְרְךָ֙ מִצְרַ֔יִם 3bA I give Egypt as your ransom,

With: 𝔐 (5) – 𝔖^{abcde} all subordinate punctuation.
Discussion: Despite the weak support for 𝔐 we accept its divison. 𝔊 takes כוש with v. 3bA which is not in accordance with Hebrew idiom.

COLON 43:3bB:

כּ֥וּשׁ וּסְבָ֖א תַּחְתֶּֽיךָ׃ 3bB Cush and Sheba in exchange for you.

With: 𝔐 (1) – 𝔊^{SQ}, major division markers in 𝔊^{A} – 𝔖^{abcde}

COLON 43:4aA:

מֵאֲשֶׁ֨ר יָקַ֧רְתָּ בְעֵינַ֛י נִכְבַּ֖דְתָּ 4aA Since you are precious in my eyes, honoured,

With: 𝔐 (8) – 𝔊^{SQ} – 𝔖^{abcde}
Colon parallelism: כבד יקר Niph. (unique).
Discussion: The unanimous testimony of tradition contradicts 𝔐's Ṭiphḥa which was hardly intended as a major divider. The resulting extremely long colon (6 stressed words) argues against this division. 𝔊^{SQ} have an extra point after בעיני which reflects 𝔐's Tevir (12).

COLON 43:4aB:

וַאֲנִ֣י אֲהַבְתִּ֑יךָ 4aB and (since) I love you,

With: 𝔐 (2) – 𝔊^{SQ} – 𝔖^{abcd}

COLON 43:4bA:

וְאֶתֵּ֤ן אָדָם֙ תַּחְתֶּ֔יךָ 4bA I will give people in exchange for you,

With: 𝔐 (5) – 𝔊^{SQ} – 𝔖^{acde} all subordinate punctuation.

COLON 43:4bB:

וּלְאֻמִּ֖ים תַּ֥חַת נַפְשֶֽׁךָ׃ 4bB and nations in exchange for your life.

With: 𝔐 (1) – 𝔊^{SQ} – 𝔖^{abcde}

COLON 43:5aA:

אַל־תִּירָ֖א כִּ֣י אִתְּךָ־אָ֑נִי 5aA Do not fear, for I am with you.

With: 𝔐 (2) – 𝔊^{SQ} – 𝔖^{abcde}

COLON 43:5bA:

מִמִּזְרָח֙ אָבִ֣יא זַרְעֶ֔ךָ 5bA From the east I will bring your offspring,

With: $\mathfrak{M}$ (5) – $\mathfrak{G}^{SQ}$ – $\mathfrak{S}^{abcde}$

COLON 43:5bB:

וּמִמַּעֲרָ֖ב אֲקַבְּצֶֽךָּ׃ 5bB and from the west I will gather you.

With: $\mathfrak{M}$ (1) – $\mathfrak{G}^{SAQ}$, major division marker in $\mathfrak{G}^{A}$ – $\mathfrak{S}^{abcde}$

COLON 43:6aA:

אֹמַ֤ר לַצָּפוֹן֙ תֵּ֔נִי 6aA I will say to the north, 'Give up!'

With: $\mathfrak{M}$ (5) – $\mathfrak{G}^{SQ}$ – $\mathfrak{S}^{abcde}$

COLON 43:6aB:

וּלְתֵימָ֖ן אַל־תִּכְלָ֑אִי 6aB And to the south, 'Do not withhold!'

With: $\mathfrak{M}$ (2) – $\mathfrak{G}^{SQ}$ – $\mathfrak{S}^{abcde}$

COLON 43:6bA:

הָבִ֤יאִי בָנַי֙ מֵרָח֔וֹק 6bA 'Bring my sons from afar,

With: $\mathfrak{M}$ (5) – $\mathfrak{G}^{SQ}$ – $\mathfrak{S}^{abcde}$ all subordinate punctuation.

COLON 43:6bB:

וּבְנוֹתַ֖י מִקְצֵ֥ה הָאָֽרֶץ׃ 6bB and my daughters from the end of the earth,

With: $\mathfrak{M}$ (1) – $\mathfrak{G}^{SQ}$ – $\mathfrak{S}^{abcde}$

COLON 43:7aA:

כֹּ֚ל הַנִּקְרָ֣א בִשְׁמִ֔י 7aA everyone who is called by my name,

With: $\mathfrak{M}$ (5) – $\mathfrak{G}^{SQ}$ – $\mathfrak{S}^{abcd}$ all subordinate punctuation.

COLON 43:7aB:

וְלִכְבוֹדִ֖י בְּרָאתִ֑יו 7aB and whom I created for my glory,

With: $\mathfrak{M}$ (2) – $\mathfrak{G}^{SQ}$ – $\mathfrak{S}^{e}$

COLON 43:7aC:

יְצַרְתִּ֖יו אַף־עֲשִׂיתִֽיו׃ 7aC whom I formed, also made.

With: $\mathfrak{M}$ (1) – $\mathfrak{G}^{SAQ}$, major division markers in $\mathfrak{G}^{A}$ – $\mathfrak{S}^{abcde}$
Colon parallelism: יצר || עשה; rhyme ־תיו || ־תיו.

COLON 43:8aA:

הוֹצִיא עַם־עִוֵּר וְעֵינַיִם יֵשׁ 8aA Let him bring out the people who are blind, yet have eyes,

With: 𝔐 (2) – 𝔊^{SQ} – 𝔖^{a}
Discussion: Although almost all ancient witnesses have a caesura after עם־עור (𝔊^{SQ}, 𝔖^{bcde}) we believe that the Masoretes were right in providing this word with a Ṭiphḥa, because the same witnesses appear to be inconsequent in recognizing v. 8aB as a complete colon.

COLON 43:8aB:

וְחֵרְשִׁים וְאָזְנַיִם לָמוֹ׃ 8aB and those who are deaf, yet have ears!

With: 𝔐 (1), major division marker in in 1𝔔^{a} – 𝔊^{SQ}, paragraphos in 𝔊^{S} – 𝔖^{abcde}

COLON 43:9aA:

כָּל־הַגּוֹיִם נִקְבְּצוּ יַחְדָּו 9aA Let all the nations gather together,

With: 𝔐 (7) – 𝔊^{SQ} – 𝔖^{abcde}
Colon parallelism: כל || יחדו/יחד.

COLON 43:9aB:

וְיֵאָסְפוּ לְאֻמִּים 9aB and let the nations assemble!

With: 𝔐 (5) – 𝔖^{abcde}

COLON 43:9bA:

מִי בָהֶם יַגִּיד זוּ אֹתֶה* 9bA Who among them will tell what is coming?

With: 𝔐 (5) – 𝔊^{SQ} – 𝔖^{abcde} all subordinate punctuation.
Discussion: 𝔊^{S} and 𝔊^{Q} have an extra point after בהם which corresponds to 𝔐's Pashṭa.

COLON 43:9bB:

וְרִאשֹׁנוֹת יַשְׁמִיעֻנוּ 9bB Let them make us hear first things!

With: 𝔐 (2) – 𝔊^{SQ}, major division marker in 𝔊^{A} – 𝔖^{abcde}
Discussion: Discussion: 𝔊^{S} and 𝔊^{Q} have an extra point after וראשנות which corresponds to 𝔐's Ṭiphḥa.

COLON 43:9cA:

יִתְּנוּ עֵדֵיהֶם וְיִצְדָּקוּ 9cA Let them give their witnesses so that they may be justified,

With: $\mathfrak{M}$ (5) – $\mathfrak{G}^{Q}$ – $\mathfrak{S}^{abcde}$
Discussion: $\mathfrak{G}^{S}$ and $\mathfrak{G}^{Q}$ have an extra point after דיהם which corresponds to $\mathfrak{M}$'s Pashṭa again.

COLON 43:9cB:

וְיִשְׁמְעוּ וְיֹאמְרוּ אֱמֶת׃ 9cB so that one may hear and say: "It is true!"

With: $\mathfrak{M}$ (1) – $\mathfrak{G}^{SQ}$, major division markers in $\mathfrak{G}^{S}$ and $\mathfrak{G}^{A}$
Discussion: $\mathfrak{S}^{abcde}$ have an extra point after ויאמרו, a common phenomenon with the introduction of direct speech. $\mathfrak{G}^{S}$ and $\mathfrak{G}^{Q}$ support $\mathfrak{M}$ which has a conjunctive accent here. Moreover, $\mathfrak{S}$ connects אמת with the following verse which is clearly erroneous because the other nations can hardly say, "Truly, you are *my* witnesses".

COLON 43:10aA:

אַתֶּם עֵדַי נְאֻם־יְהוָה 10aA You are my witnesses, declares the LORD,

With: $\mathfrak{M}$ (5) – $\mathfrak{G}^{SQ}$
Discussion: $\mathfrak{G}^{S}$ and $\mathfrak{G}^{Q}$ have an extra dividing point after די where $\mathfrak{M}$ has a Pashṭa again. $\mathfrak{S}$ lacks a major divider after יהוה, probably because the phrase runs on.

COLON 43:10aB:

וְעַבְדִּי אֲשֶׁר בָּחָרְתִּי 10aB and (you are) my Servant, whom I have chosen.

With: $\mathfrak{M}$ (2) – $\mathfrak{G}^{SQ}$ – $\mathfrak{S}^{abcde}$
Colon parallelism: עבד || בחר.

COLON 43:10bA:

לְמַעַן תֵּדְעוּ וְתַאֲמִינוּ לִי וְתָבִינוּ 10bA So that you may know and believe me and will understand,

With: $\mathfrak{M}$ (10) – $\mathfrak{G}^{SQ}$
Colon parallelism: Although the combination of the three verbs ידע, אמן Hiph. and בין is unique, the pairs ידע || בין and אמן Hiph. || בין are attested.
Discussion: The decision how to divide is difficult, because $\mathfrak{S}^{abcde}$ have a dividing point after לי (where $\mathfrak{M}$ has a conjunctive accent) whereas $\mathfrak{G}^{S}$ and $\mathfrak{G}^{Q}$ support $\mathfrak{M}$'s Pashṭa which, though being a rather weak

accent itself, is the only acceptable point to make an incision because a verse of seven accented units is implausible. The colon parallelism argues in favour of this choice.

COLON 43:10bB:

כִּֽי־אֲנִ֣י ה֔וּא 10bB that I am the same One.

With: 𝔐 (5) – 𝔊^{SQ} – 𝔖^{abcde}

COLON 43:10cA:

לְפָנַי֙ לֹא־נ֣וֹצַר אֵ֔ל 10cA Before me no god was formed,

With: 𝔐 (5) – 𝔊^{Q} – 𝔖^{abcde}

COLON 43:10cB:

וְאַחֲרַ֖י לֹ֥א יִהְיֶֽה׃ 10cB nor will there be one after me.

With: 𝔐 (1), plus ס <פ>, פ in 1𝔔^{a} – 𝔊^{Q} – 𝔖^{abcde}, major division marker in 𝔖^{a}

COLON 43:11aA:

אָנֹכִ֥י אָנֹכִ֖י יְהוָ֑ה 11aA I, I am the LORD,

With: 𝔐 (2) – 𝔊^{Q} – 𝔖^{e}
Colon parallelism: אנכי || אנכי.
Discussion: The support for 𝔐 is weak, but sufficient.

COLON 43:11aB:

וְאֵ֥ין מִבַּלְעָדַ֖י מוֹשִֽׁיעַ׃ 11aB and apart from me there is no saviour.

With: 𝔐 (1) – 𝔊^{SQ} – 𝔖^{abcde}

COLON 43:12aA:

אָנֹכִ֞י הִגַּ֤דְתִּי וְהוֹשַׁ֙עְתִּי֙ וְהִשְׁמַ֔עְתִּי 12aA It is I who told and saved and made heard,

With: 𝔐 (5) – 𝔊^{S} – 𝔖^{abcde}
Colon parallelism: נגד Hiph. || ישׁע Hiph. || שׁמע Hiph. Note also the fourfold rhyme.
Discussion: 𝔊^{S} and 𝔊^{Q} have an extra dividing point after והושעתי (𝔐 Pashṭa).

COLON 43:12aB:

וְאֵין בָּכֶם זָר 12aB and not a stranger who was among you.

With: 𝔐 (2) – 𝔊[SQ], major division markers in 𝔊[S] (colon only) and 𝔊[A] – 𝔖[abcde]

COLON 43:12bA:

וְאַתֶּם עֵדַי נְאֻם־יְהוָה 12bA And you are my witnesses, declares the LORD,

With: 𝔐 (8) – 𝔊[Q] – 𝔖[e]
Discussion: Perhaps the Masoretes did not want to make a major break at this point. However, the formula נאם יהוה is always at the end of a colon. Therefore 𝔊[Q] and 𝔖[e] probably preserve an authentic tradition.

COLON 43:12bB:

וַאֲנִי־אֵל׃ 12bB that I am God.

With: 𝔐 (1) – 𝔖[abcde]
Discussion: 𝔊 shortens and possibly wanted to connect with the next verse (cf. RSV).

COLON 43:13aA:

גַּם־מִיּוֹם אֲנִי הוּא 13aA Also from today on I am the same One,

With: 𝔐 (5) – 𝔊[SQ] – 𝔖[abcde]

COLON 43:13aB:

וְאֵין מִיָּדִי מַצִּיל 13aB and no one delivers from my hand;

With: 𝔐 (2) – 𝔊[SQ] – 𝔖[abcde]

COLON 43:13bA:

אֶפְעַל וּמִי יְשִׁיבֶנָּה׃ 13bA I work, and who can reverse it?

With: 𝔐 (1), plus ס <פ>, פ in 1𝔔[a] – 𝔊[SAQ], major division markers in 𝔊[S] and 𝔊[A] – 𝔖[abcde], major division markers in 𝔖[bcde]
Discussion: 𝔊[S] and 𝔊[Q] have an extra divider, corresponding to 𝔐's Ṭiphḥa, after אפעל.

COLON 43:14aA:

כֹּה־אָמַר יְהוָה 14aA Thus says the LORD,

With: $\mathfrak{M}$ (12) – $\mathfrak{G}^{Q}$ – $\mathfrak{S}^{e}$, $\mathfrak{S}^{ab}$ subordinate punctuation.
Discussion: Again the Masoretes seem to have preferred a much longer colon ending with ישׂראל (Atnaḥ). See our treatment of 43:1aA.

COLON 43:14aB:

גֹּאַלְכֶם קְדוֹשׁ יִשְׂרָאֵל 14aB your Redeemer, the Holy One of Israel:

With: $\mathfrak{M}$ (2) – $\mathfrak{G}^{SQ}$ – $\mathfrak{S}^{abcde}$
Colon parallelism: גאל || קדוש ישׂראל.

COLON 43:14bA:

לְמַעַנְכֶם שִׁלַּחְתִּי בָבֶלָה 14bA For your sake I send (messengers) to Babylon,

With: $\mathfrak{M}$ (7) – $\mathfrak{G}^{SQ}$, major division marker in $\mathfrak{G}^{Q}$ – $\mathfrak{S}^{de}$, $\mathfrak{S}^{ab}$ subordinate punctuation.

COLON 43:14bB:

וְהוֹרַדְתִּי בָרִיחִים כֻּלָּם 14bB and I make them all descend as fugitives (?),

With: $\mathfrak{M}$ (5) – $\mathfrak{G}^{SQ}$ – $\mathfrak{S}^{abcde}$ all subordinate punctuation.

COLON 43:14bC:

וְכַשְׂדִּים בָּאֳנִיּוֹת רִנָּתָם׃ 14bC yes, the Chaldaeans in their eulogized ships.

With: $\mathfrak{M}$ (1) – $\mathfrak{G}^{SQ}$, major division markers in $\mathfrak{G}^{Q}$ – $\mathfrak{S}^{abcde}$

COLON 43:15aA:

אֲנִי יְהוָה קְדוֹשְׁכֶם 15aA I am the LORD, your Holy One,

With: $\mathfrak{M}$ (2) – $\mathfrak{G}^{SQ}$ – $\mathfrak{S}^{bcde}$, $\mathfrak{S}^{a}$ subordinate punctuation.
Colon parallelism: יהוה || קדשׁכם.

COLON 43:15aB:

בּוֹרֵא יִשְׂרָאֵל מַלְכְּכֶם׃ 15aB Creator of Israel, your King.

With: $\mathfrak{M}$ (1), plus ס, indentation and paragraphos in $1\mathfrak{Q}^{a}$ – $\mathfrak{G}^{SQ}$, major division markers in $\mathfrak{G}^{SA}$ – $\mathfrak{S}^{abcde}$

COLON 43:16aA:

כֹּה אָמַר יְהוָה 16aA Thus says the LORD

With: 𝔐 (5) – 𝔊^{Q} – 𝔖^{bcde} all subordinate punctuation.

COLON 43:16aB:

הַנּוֹתֵן בַּיָּם דָּרֶךְ 16aB who makes a way through the sea,

With: 𝔐 (2) – 𝔊^{SQ} – 𝔖^{abcde} all subordinate punctuation.

COLON 43:16aC:

וּבְמַיִם עַזִּים נְתִיבָה׃ 16aC and a path through mighty waters,

With: 𝔐 (1) – 𝔊^{SQ} – 𝔖^{abcde}

COLON 43:17aA:

הַמּוֹצִיא רֶכֶב־וָסוּס 17aA who leads out chariots and horses,

With: 𝔐 (8) – 𝔊^{SQ}
Colon parallelism: רכב || סוס.
Discussion: It is questionable whether the Masoretes wanted to divide at this point. Yet we accept 𝔊, even though it is not seconded by 𝔖. It seems clear to us that v. 17a must be connected with v.16,[3] so it is 𝔐's erroneous strophic division which resulted in a different colometry. Second Isaiah is fond of such pairs.[4] For a similar case involving two such pairs see our comment on 51:19b.[5]

COLON 43:17aB:

חַיִל וְעִזּוּז 17aB armies and mighty forces:

With: 𝔐 (2) – 𝔊^{SQ} – 𝔖^{abcde}
Colon parallelism: חיל || עזוז (unique).
Discussion: None of the ancient witnesses supports the modern proposal (e.g. in BHS) to transpose the dividing accent.

COLON 43:17bA:

יַחְדָּו יִשְׁכְּבוּ בַּל־יָקוּמוּ 17bA Together they lie down, do not rise (again),

With: 𝔐 (5) – 𝔊^{SQ} – 𝔖^{cde}

---

[3]See p. 192-3.

[4]Cf. Isa. 41:17aA; 43:20aB; 44:14aB; 46:1aB; 47:9aC; 47:10aC; 50:6bB; 51:3cA, 3cB; 51:11bA, 11bB; 55:1bC.

[5]See p. 504.

Colon parallelism: שכב || קום (antithetical).
Discussion: 𝔊[SQ] have an extra dividing point after ישכבו (𝔐 Pashṭa).

COLON 43:17bB:

דָּעֲכוּ כַּפִּשְׁתָּה כָבוּ׃ 17bB they are extinguished, quenched like a wick.

With: 𝔐 (1) – 𝔊[SAQ], major division markers in all three – 𝔖[abcde]
Colon parallelism: דעך || כבה (unique).
Discussion: 𝔊[SQ] have an extra dividing point after ישכבו (𝔐 Ṭiphḥa).

COLON 43:18aA:

אַל־תִּזְכְּרוּ רִאשֹׁנוֹת 18aA Do not try to remember the first things,

With: 𝔐 (2) – 𝔖[abcde]
Discussion: Probably 𝔊 divided after וקדמניות (𝔊[S] has a point), but this is unlikely.

COLON 43:18aB:

וְקַדְמֹנִיּוֹת אַל־תִּתְבֹּנָנוּ׃ 18aB and do not try to understand things of old.

With: 𝔐 (1) – 𝔊[SQ] – 𝔖[abcde]

COLON 43:19aA:

הִנְנִי עֹשֶׂה חֲדָשָׁה 19aA Behold, I am about to make a new thing,

With: 𝔐 (10) – 𝔊[SQ] – 𝔖[abcde]
Discussion: The Pashṭa of 𝔐 was probably not meant as a major divider, but the unanimous testimony of the ancient versions supports our decision. Possibly the Masoretes wanted a divider only after תצמח because in jBer., 11b, and bBer. 13a, the verse is quoted up to that word.

COLON 43:19aB:

עַתָּה תִצְמָח 19aB now it will sprout.

With: 𝔐 (5) – 𝔊[SQ]
Discussion: 𝔖 takes the cola 19aB and 19aC together.

COLON 43:19aC:

הֲלוֹא תֵדָעוּהָ 19aC Don't you know?

With: 𝔐 (2) – 𝔊[SAQ], major division markers in 𝔊[A] – 𝔖[abcde]

COLON 43:19bA:

אַ֣ף אָשִׂ֤ים בַּמִּדְבָּר֙ דֶּ֔רֶךְ 19bA Yes, I will make a way in the desert,

With: 𝔐 (5) – 𝔊^{SQ} – 𝔖^{abcde} all subordinate punctuation.

COLON 43:19bB:

בִּֽישִׁמֹ֖ון נְתִיבֹֽות*׃ 19bB paths in the wilderness.

With: 𝔐 (1) – 𝔊^{SQ} – 𝔖^{abcde}

COLON 43:20aA:

תְּֽכַבְּדֵ֙נִי֙ חַיַּ֣ת הַשָּׂדֶ֔ה 20aA The wild beasts of the field will honour me,

With: 𝔐 (5) – 𝔊^{SQ} – 𝔖^{abcde}

COLON 43:20aB:

תַּנִּ֖ים וּבְנֹ֣ות יַעֲנָ֑ה 20aB jackals and ostriches,

With: 𝔐 (2) – 𝔊^{SQ} – 𝔖^{abcde}
Colon parallelism: תן || יענה.

COLON 43:20bA:

כִּֽי־נָתַ֨תִּי בַמִּדְבָּ֜ר מַ֗יִם 20bA for I give water in the desert,

With: 𝔐 (7) – 𝔊^{SQ} – 𝔖^{acde} all subordinate punctuation.
Colon parallelism: מדבר || מים (antithetical).

COLON 43:20bB:

נְהָרֹות֙ בִּֽישִׁמֹ֔ן 20bB rivers in the wilderness,

With: 𝔐 (5) – 𝔊^{SQ} – 𝔖^{abcde}
Colon parallelism: נהר || ישימון (antithetical).

COLON 43:20bC:

לְהַשְׁקֹ֖ות עַמִּ֥י בְחִירִֽי׃ 20bC to give drink to my people, my chosen one.

With: 𝔐 (1), ס in Codex Reuchlinianus – 𝔊^{SQ} – 𝔖^{abcde}

COLON 43:21aA:

עַם־זוּ֙ יָצַ֣רְתִּי לִ֔י 21aA The people whom I have formed for myself

With: 𝔐 (5) – 𝔊^{SQ}
Discussion: It is certainly remarkable that in this short strophe (one

verse-line) no Atnaḥ has been employed. 𝔖 avoids a break in the continuing sentence. But 𝔐 is supported bij 𝔊.

COLON 43:21aB:

תְּהִלָּתִי* יְסַפֵּרוּ׃ 21aB will tell my praiseworthy deeds.

With: 𝔐 (1), plus ס (other MSS פ), indentation in 1𝔔^{a} – 𝔊^{SBAQ}, major division markers in 𝔊^{SBA} – 𝔖^{abcde}, major division markers in 𝔖^{abce}

COLON 43:22aA:

וְלֹא־אֹתִי קָרָאתָ יַעֲקֹב 22aA Yet you did not call upon me, O Jacob,

With: 𝔐 (2) – 𝔊^{SQ} – 𝔖^{ae} subordinate punctuation.
Discussion: 𝔊^{SQ} support 𝔐 against 𝔖.

COLON 43:22aB:

כִּי־יָגַעְתָּ בִּי יִשְׂרָאֵל׃ 22aB that you would have wearied yourselves for me, O Israel!

With: 𝔐 (1) – 𝔊^{SQ} – 𝔖^{abcde}

COLON 43:23aA:

לֹא־הֵבֵיאתָ לִּי שֵׂה עֹלֹתֶיךָ 23aA You did not bring me the rams of your burnt offerings,

With: 𝔐 (5) – 𝔊^{SQ} – 𝔖^{abcde}

COLON 43:23aB:

וּזְבָחֶיךָ לֹא כִבַּדְתָּנִי 23aB and with your sacrifices you did not honour me.

With: 𝔐 (2) – 𝔊^{Q} – 𝔖^{abde}, 𝔖^{c} subordinate punctuation.

COLON 43:23bA:

לֹא הֶעֱבַדְתִּיךָ בְּמִנְחָה 23bA I have not made you serve with oblations,

With: 𝔐 (5) – 𝔖^{abcde}
Discussion: 𝔊 is lacking here.

COLON 43:23bB:

וְלֹא הוֹגַעְתִּיךָ בִּלְבוֹנָה׃ 23bB and I have not wearied you with incense.

With: 𝔐 (1) – 𝔊^{SQ} – 𝔖^{abcde}

COLON 43:24aA:

לֹֽא־קָנִ֨יתָ לִּ֤י בַכֶּ֨סֶף֙ קָנֶ֔ה 24aA You did not buy me cane with silver,

With: 𝔐 (5) – 𝔊^{SQ} – 𝔖^{abcde}

COLON 43:24aB:

וְחֵ֥לֶב זְבָחֶ֖יךָ לֹ֣א הִרְוִיתָ֑נִי 24aB and the fat of your sacrifices you did not lavish on me.

With: 𝔐 (2) – 𝔊^{SQ} – 𝔖^{abcde}

COLON 43:24bA:

אַ֗ךְ הֶעֱבַדְתַּ֨נִי֙ בְּחַטֹּאותֶ֔יךָ 24bA No, you made me serve by your sins,

With: 𝔐 (5) – 𝔖^{acde} subordinate punctuation.
Discussion: Even though none of the ancient versions lends sufficient support to 𝔐 we accept the latter's division. For the Revia' with אך see our comment on p. 31.

COLON 43:24bB:

הוֹגַעְתַּ֖נִי בַּעֲוֺנֹתֶֽיךָ׃ 24bB and made me weary with your iniquities.

With: 𝔐 (1), major division markers, also in 1Q^{a} – 𝔊^{SAQ}, major division markers in all three – 𝔖^{abcde}

COLON 43:25aA:

אָנֹכִ֨י אָנֹכִ֥י ה֛וּא 25aA I, I am he,

With: 𝔐 (12)
Colon parallelism: אנכי || אנכי (see v. 11aA above).
Discussion: Since none of our ancient witnesses contains any divider before למעני and 𝔐's Tevir can hardly be seen as sufficient reason to make an incision after הוא, we were strongly inclined to accept the extremely long colon of six stressed units. Additional arguments in favour of this decision might be the similar construction in Isa. 51:12, where the participle מנחמכם belongs to the colon, and Deut. 32:39 where an equally long colon of six stressed units is likely according to P. Sanders.[6]

However, both in Deut. 32:39 and the very similar 1 Chron. 28:10 𝔐 has a Revia' with עתה which opens the possibility – a possibility recognized by Sanders – to read Deut. 32:39b as a tricolon. Moreover,

[6]See P. Sanders, *The Provenance of Deuteronomy 32* (OTS, 37), Leiden: Brill, 1996, 237-9.

Isa. 43:11aA (same chapter) and the rhythmical balance of Isa. 43:25 (3 + 3 + 3 stresses) argue in favour of dividing the verse-line after הוא (𝔐 Tevir, No. 12).

Many commentators propose to join למעני with the rest of the verse, despite the problem this creates with the rendering of the following copula. Nothing in the tradition supports this modern view.

COLON 43:25aB:

מֹחֶה פְשָׁעֶיךָ לְמַעֲנִי 25aB who wipes out your transgressions for my own sake,

With: 𝔐 (2) – 𝔊^{SQ} – 𝔖^{abcde}
Discussion: See our comments on the preceding colon.

COLON 43:25aC

וְחַטֹּאתֶיךָ לֹא אֶזְכֹּר׃ 25aC and do not remember your sins.

With: 𝔐 (1), major division marker in 1𝔔^{a} and possibly in 1𝔔^{b} – 𝔊^{Q}, 𝔊^{S} colon – 𝔖^{abcde}

COLON 43:26aA:

הַזְכִּירֵנִי נִשָּׁפְטָה יָחַד 26aA Help me to remember, let us argue our case together!

With: 𝔐 (2) – 𝔊^{SQ}, colon in 𝔊^{S} – 𝔖^{abcde}
Discussion: For the Zaqeph Gadol (No. 6) with הזכירני see p. 31.

COLON 43:26aB:

סַפֵּר אַתָּה לְמַעַן תִּצְדָּק׃ 26aB You tell (us), that you may be justified ...

With: 𝔐 (1), Setuma in 1𝔔^{a} – 𝔊^{SAQ}, major division markers in 𝔊^{A} – 𝔖^{abcde}
Discussion: 𝔊^{S} and 𝔊^{Q} have an extra point after אתה which corresponds to 𝔐's Ṭiphḥa.

COLON 43:27aA:

אָבִיךָ הָרִאשׁוֹן חָטָא 27aA Your first father sinned,

With: 𝔐 (2) – 𝔊^{SQ} – 𝔖^{abcde}

COLON 43:27aB:

וּמְלִיצֶיךָ פָּשְׁעוּ בִי׃ 27aB and your spokesmen transgressed against me.

With: 𝔐 (1) – 𝔊^{SQ} – 𝔖^{abcde}

COLON 43:28aA:

וַאֲחַלֵּל שָׂרֵי קֹדֶשׁ 28aA So I had to defile the chiefs of the sanctuary,

With: $\mathfrak{M}$ (2) – $\mathfrak{G}^{SQ}$ – $\mathfrak{S}^{abcde}$

COLON 43:28bA:

וְאֶתְּנָה* לַחֵרֶם יַעֲקֹב 28bA and had to devote Jacob to the ban,

With: $\mathfrak{M}$ (5) – $\mathfrak{G}^{S}$ – $\mathfrak{S}^{e}$
Discussion: The supporting evidence for $\mathfrak{M}$'s division is weak, but sufficient.

COLON 43:28bB:

וְיִשְׂרָאֵל לְגִדּוּפִים׃ 28bB and Israel to insults.

With: $\mathfrak{M}$ (1), Petuḥa in 1$\mathfrak{Q}^{a}$ – $\mathfrak{G}^{SAQ}$, major division markers in $\mathfrak{G}^{S}$ and $\mathfrak{G}^{A}$ – $\mathfrak{S}^{abcde}$, major division markers in $\mathfrak{S}^{abe}$

5.3 Isaiah 43 – Delimitation of Verse-lines

VERSE–LINE: 43:1a:

וְעַתָּה כֹּה־אָמַר יְהוָה 1aA But now, thus says the LORD,
בֹּרַאֲךָ יַעֲקֹב וְיֹצֶרְךָ יִשְׂרָאֵל 1aB who created you, O Jacob, and who formed you, O Israel,

$\mathfrak{M}$ distinctive accents: 10 – 2.
Stresses: 3 + 4.
Verse-line parallelism: יהוה || יעקב || ישׂראל.
Discussion: The Masoretes preferred to read on until יעקב. See our comment pp. 164, 268.

VERSE–LINE: 43:1b:

אַל־תִּירָא כִּי גְאַלְתִּיךָ 1bA Do not fear, for I redeem you,
קָרָאתִי בְשִׁמְךָ לִי־אָתָּה׃ 1bB I call you by your name, you are mine!

$\mathfrak{M}$ distinctive accents: 5 – 1.
Stresses: 3 + 3.
Verse-line parallelism: ־ך || ־ך; ־ך || אתה; גאל || קרא בשם; grammatical parallelism.

VERSE–LINE: 43:2a:

כִּֽי־תַעֲבֹ֤ר בַּמַּ֙יִם֙ אִתְּךָ־אָ֔נִי 2aA When you pass through the waters , I am with you,
וּבַנְּהָר֖וֹת לֹ֣א יִשְׁטְפ֑וּךָ 2aB and through the rivers – they will not overwhelm you.

𝔐 distinctive accents: 5 – 2.
Stresses: 3 + 3.
Verse-line parallelism: עבר || שטף; ב || ב; מים || נהר; ־ך || ־ך (see v. 1b above).
Discussion: The cola are connected by ellipsis.

VERSE–LINE: 43:2b:

כִּֽי־תֵלֵ֤ךְ בְּמוֹ־אֵשׁ֙ לֹ֣א תִכָּוֶ֔ה 2bA When you walk through fire, you will not be scorched,
וְלֶהָבָ֖ה לֹ֥א תִבְעַר־בָּֽךְ׃ 2bB and no flame will burn you.

𝔐 distinctive accents: 5 – 1.
Stresses: 4 + 3.
Verse-line parallelism: במו || ב; אש || להבה; לא || לא; כוה || בער (unique).

VERSE–LINE: 43:3a:

כִּ֗י אֲנִי֙ יְהוָ֣ה אֱלֹהֶ֔יךָ 3aA For I am the LORD, your God,
קְד֥וֹשׁ יִשְׂרָאֵ֖ל מוֹשִׁיעֶ֑ךָ 3aB the Holy One of Israel, your saviour.

𝔐 distinctive accents: 5 – 2.
Stresses: 4 + 3.
Verse-line parallelism: יהוה אלהים || קדוש ישראל; יהוה || מושיע; ־ך || ־ך.
Discussion: Ellipsis connects the cola.

VERSE–LINE: 43:3b:

נָתַ֤תִּי כָפְרְךָ֙ מִצְרַ֔יִם 3bA I give Egypt as your ransom,
כּ֥וּשׁ וּסְבָ֖א תַּחְתֶּֽיךָ׃ 3bB Cush and Sheba in exchange for you.

𝔐 distinctive accents: 5 – 1.
Stresses: 3 + 3.
Verse-line parallelism: כפר || תחת; ־ך || ־ך; מצרים || כוש || סבא.
Discussion: Again the cola are connected by ellipsis.

VERSE–LINE: 43:4a:

מֵאֲשֶׁ֨ר יָקַ֧רְתָּ בְעֵינַ֛י נִכְבַּ֖דְתָּ 4aA Since you are precious in my eyes, honoured,
וַאֲנִ֣י אֲהַבְתִּ֑יךָ 4aB and (since) I love you,

𝔐 distinctive accents: 8 – 2.
Stresses: 4 + 2.

Verse-line parallelism: יקר בעינים || אהב (unique); כבד || אהב (unique).
Discussion: 𝔐 reads on until the Atnaḥ, a unicolon of six stresses which we do not accept (see p. 166).

VERSE–LINE: 43:4b:

וְאֶתֵּ֤ן אָדָם֙ תַּחְתֶּ֔יךָ	4bA	I will give people in exchange for you,
וּלְאֻמִּ֖ים תַּ֥חַת נַפְשֶֽׁךָ׃	4bB	and nations in exchange for your life.

𝔐 distinctive accents: 5 – 1.
Stresses: 3 + 3.
Verse-line parallelism: אדם || לאמ; תחת || תחת; ־ך || ־ך.
Discussion: The cola are connected by ellipsis.

VERSE–LINE: 43:5a:

אַל־תִּירָ֖א כִּ֣י אִתְּךָ־אָ֑נִי	5aA	Do not fear, for I am with you.

𝔐 distinctive accents: 2.
Stresses: 3.
Verse-line parallelism: None (unicolon).

VERSE–LINE: 43:5b:

מִמִּזְרָח֙ אָבִ֣יא זַרְעֶ֔ךָ	5bA	From the east I will bring your offspring,
וּמִֽמַּעֲרָ֖ב אֲקַבְּצֶֽךָּ׃	5bB	and from the west I will gather you.

𝔐 distinctive accents: 5 – 1.
Stresses: 3 + 2.
Verse-line parallelism: מן || מן; מזרח || מערב; בוא || קבץ; ־ך || ־ך; grammatical parallelism.

VERSE–LINE: 43:6a:

אֹמַ֤ר לַצָּפוֹן֙ תֵּ֔נִי	6aA	I will say to the north, 'Give up!'
וּלְתֵימָ֖ן אַל־תִּכְלָ֑אִי	6aB	And to the south, 'Do not withhold!'

𝔐 distinctive accents: 5 – 2.
Stresses: 3 + 2.
Verse-line parallelism: ל || ל; צפון || תימן; נתן || כלא (antithetical, unique); grammatical parallelism; rhyme.
Discussion: Ellipsis is a binding force again.

VERSE–LINE: 43:6b:

הָבִ֤יאִי בָנַי֙ מֵֽרָח֔וֹק	6bA	'Bring my sons from afar,
וּבְנוֹתַ֖י מִקְצֵ֥ה הָאָֽרֶץ׃	6bB	and my daughters from the end of the earth,

𝔐 distinctive accents: 5 – 1.
Stresses: 3 + 3.
Verse-line parallelism: בן || בת; מן || מן; רחוק || קצה הארץ; rhyme.
Discussion: Ellipsis connects the two cola.

VERSE–LINE: 43:7a:

כֹּל הַנִּקְרָא בִשְׁמִי	7aA	everyone who is called by my name,
וְלִכְבוֹדִי בְּרָאתִיו	7aB	and whom I created for my glory,
יְצַרְתִּיו אַף־עֲשִׂיתִיו׃	7aC	whom I formed, also made.'

𝔐 distinctive accents: 5 – 2 – 1.
Stresses: 3 + 2 + 2.
Verse-line parallelism: שם || כבוד; ־י || ־י; ברא || יצר; ברא || עשה; ־ו || ־ו; grammatical parallelism; rhyme.
Discussion: Ellipsis of כל connects the last two cola to the first colon.

VERSE–LINE: 43:8a:

הוֹצִיא* עַם־עִוֵּר וְעֵינַיִם יֵשׁ	8aA	Let him bring out the people who are blind, yet have eyes,
וְחֵרְשִׁים וְאָזְנַיִם לָמוֹ׃	8aB	and those who are deaf, yet have ears!

𝔐 distinctive accents: 2 – 1.
Stresses: 4 + 3.
Verse-line parallelism: עור || חרש; עין || אזן.

VERSE–LINE: 43:9a:

כָּל־הַגּוֹיִם נִקְבְּצוּ יַחְדָּו	9aA	Let all the nations gather together,
וְיֵאָסְפוּ לְאֻמִּים	9aB	and let the peoples assemble!

𝔐 distinctive accents: 7 – 5.
Stresses: 3 + 2.
Verse-line parallelism: גוי || לאם; קבץ || אסף; rhyme.
Discussion: The Masoretes wanted to read on until ישמיענו, a quadrocolon with the accentual pattern 7 – 5 – 5 – 2, followed by a bicolon. In our opinion it is much more likely that the two verses containing the עדים (vv. 9c, 10a) should be combined. See p. 193.

VERSE–LINE: 43:9b:

מִי בָהֶם יַגִּיד זוֹ אַתָּה*	9bA	Who among them will tell what is coming?
וְרִאשֹׁנוֹת יַשְׁמִיעֻנוּ	9bB	Let them make us hear first things!

𝔐 distinctive accents: 5 – 2.
Stresses: 5 + 2.

Verse-line parallelism: נגד || שמע Hiph.; אתה || ראשון (unique, but see our comment on the translation).
Discussion: Ellipsis of מי בהם connects the second colon to the first. Again the Masoretes opted for a quadrocolon (accentual pattern: 10 – 5 – 5 – 1) or a tricolon with an extremely long first colon (7 stressed units; see p. 638-9).

Verse–line: 43:9c:

יִתְּנ֤וּ עֵדֵיהֶם֙ וְיִצְדָּ֔קוּ	9cA	Let them give their witnesses so that they may be justified,
וְיִשְׁמְע֖וּ וְיֹאמְר֥וּ אֱמֶֽת׃	9cB	so that one may hear and say: "It is true!"

𝔐 distinctive accents: 5 – 1.
Stresses: 3 + 3.
Verse-line parallelism: עד || שמע; צדק || אמת; grammatical parallelism; rhyme.

Verse–line: 43:10a:

אַתֶּ֤ם עֵדַי֙ נְאֻם־יְהוָ֔ה	10aA	You are my witnesses, declares the Lord,
וְעַבְדִּ֖י אֲשֶׁ֣ר בָּחָ֑רְתִּי	10aB	and (you are) my Servant, whom I have chosen.

𝔐 distinctive accents: 5 – 2.
Stresses: 3 + 3.
Verse-line parallelism: עד || עבד; -י || -י.
Discussion: Ungrammatical ellipsis connects the cola.

Verse–line: 43:10b:

לְמַ֣עַן תֵּ֠דְעוּ וְתַאֲמִ֨ינוּ לִ֤י וְתָבִ֙ינוּ֙	10bA	So that you may know and believe me and will understand,
כִּֽי־אֲנִ֣י ה֔וּא	10bB	that I am he.

𝔐 distinctive accents: 10 – 5.
Stresses: 5 + 2.
Verse-line parallelism: -י || אני.

Verse–line: 43:10c:

לְפָנַי֙ לֹא־נ֣וֹצַר אֵ֔ל	10cA	Before me no god was formed,
וְאַחֲרַ֖י לֹ֥א יִהְיֶֽה׃	10cB	nor will there be one after me.

𝔐 distinctive accents: 5 – 1.
Stresses: 3 + 3.
Verse-line parallelism: לפנים || אחרי; -י || -י; לא || לא.

VERSE–LINE: 43:11a:

אָנֹכִ֥י אָנֹכִ֖י יְהוָ֑ה	11aA	I, I am the LORD,
וְאֵ֥ין מִבַּלְעָדַ֖י מוֹשִֽׁיעַ׃	11aB	and apart from me there is no saviour.

𝔐 distinctive accents: 2 – 1.
Stresses: 3 + 3.
Verse-line parallelism: אנכי || ־י. יהוה || מושיע.

VERSE–LINE: 43:12a:

אָנֹכִ֞י הִגַּ֤דְתִּי וְהוֹשַׁ֙עְתִּי֙ וְהִשְׁמַ֔עְתִּי	12aA	It is I who tells and saves and causes to hear,
וְאֵ֥ין בָּכֶ֖ם זָ֑ר	12aB	and there is no stranger among you.

𝔐 distinctive accents: 5 – 2.
Stresses: 4 + 3.
Verse-line parallelism: None, but obviously communication with a stranger may be difficult if not impossible.

VERSE–LINE: 43:12b:

וְאַתֶּ֥ם עֵדַ֛י נְאֻם־יְהוָ֖ה	12bA	And you are my witnesses, declares the LORD,
וַאֲנִי־אֵֽל׃	12bB	and I am God.

𝔐 distinctive accents: 8 – 1.
Stresses: 3 + 1.
Verse-line parallelism: אתם || אני (antithetical); יהוה || אל.

VERSE–LINE: 43:13a:

גַּם־מִיּוֹם֙ אֲנִ֣י ה֔וּא	13aA	Also from the day I am he,
וְאֵ֥ין מִיָּדִ֖י מַצִּ֑יל	13aB	and there is no one delivering from my hand;

𝔐 distinctive accents: 5 – 2.
Stresses: 3 + 3.
Verse-line parallelism: אני || ־י; מן || מן.

VERSE–LINE: 43:13b:

אֶפְעַ֖ל וּמִ֥י יְשִׁיבֶֽנָּה׃	13bA	I work, and who can reverse it?

𝔐 distinctive accent: 1.
Stresses: 3.
Verse-line parallelism: None (unicolon).
Discussion: Although it is possible to read the v. 13 as a tricolon (accents 5 – 2 – 1) we prefer a bicolon plus a unicolon because the ואין–cola v. 11aB and 12aB are also ending bicola.

VERSE–LINE: 43:14a:

כֹּה־אָמַר יְהוָה	14aA	Thus says the LORD,
גֹּאַלְכֶם קְדוֹשׁ יִשְׂרָאֵל	14aB	your Redeemer, the Holy One of Israel:

𝔐 distinctive accents: 12 – 2.
Stresses: 2 + 3.
Verse-line parallelism: יהוה || גאל; יהוה || קדוש ישראל;
Discussion: See on our decision to regard the Tevir (No. 12) as a colon divider p. 172.

VERSE–LINE: 43:14b:

לְמַעַנְכֶם שִׁלַּחְתִּי בָבֶלָה	14bA	For your sake I send (messengers) to Babylon,
וְהוֹרַדְתִּי בָרִיחִים כֻּלָּם	14bB	and I make them all descend as fugitives (?),
וְכַשְׂדִּים בָּאֳנִיּוֹת רִנָּתָם׃	14bC	yes, the Chaldaeans in their eulogized ships.

𝔐 distinctive accents: 7 – 5 – 1.
Stresses: 3 + 3 + 3.
Verse-line parallelism: ב || ב; בבל || כשדים; ־ם || ־ם; grammatical parallelism; rhyme.
Discussion: Ellipsis connects the cola 14bB and 14bC.

VERSE–LINE: 43:15a:

אֲנִי יְהוָה קְדוֹשְׁכֶם	15aA	I am the LORD, your Holy One,
בּוֹרֵא יִשְׂרָאֵל מַלְכְּכֶם׃	15aB	Creator of Israel, your King.

𝔐 distinctive accents: 2 – 1.
Stresses: 3 + 3.
Verse-line parallelism: יהוה || מלך (chiastically); יהוה || ברא; יהוה || מלך; ־כם || ־כם.
Discussion: The ellipsis of אני יהוה in the second colon is a binding force.

VERSE–LINE: 43:16a:

כֹּה אָמַר יְהוָה	16aA	Thus says the LORD,
הַנּוֹתֵן בַּיָּם דָּרֶךְ	16aB	who makes a way through the sea,
וּבְמַיִם עַזִּים נְתִיבָה׃	16aC	and a path through mighty waters,

𝔐 distinctive accents: 5 – 2 – 1.
Stresses: 3 + 3 + 3.
Verse-line parallelism: ב || ב; ים || מים; דרך || נתיבה.
Discussion: Ellipsis of הנותן forms a connection between 16aB and 16aC.

VERSE–LINE: 43:17a:

הַמּוֹצִיא רֶכֶב־וָסוּס 17aA who leads out chariots and horses,
חַיִל וְעִזּוּז 17aB armies and mighty forces:

𝔐 distinctive accents: 8 – 2.
Stresses: 2 + 2.
Verse-line parallelism: רכב || סוס || חיל.
Discussion: Ellipsis of המוציא (see p. 173, on the colometry).

VERSE–LINE: 43:17b:

יַחְדָּו יִשְׁכְּבוּ בַּל־יָקוּמוּ 17bA Together they lie down, do not rise (again),
דָּעֲכוּ כַּפִּשְׁתָּה כָבוּ׃ 17bB they are extinguished, quenched like a wick.

𝔐 distinctive accents: 5 – 1.
Stresses: 3 + 3.
Verse-line parallelism: שׁכב, בל קום || דעך, כבה; rhyme.

VERSE–LINE: 43:18a:

אַל־תִּזְכְּרוּ רִאשֹׁנוֹת 18aA Do not try to remember the first things,
וְקַדְמֹנִיּוֹת אַל־תִּתְבֹּנָנוּ׃ 18aB and do not try to understand things of old.

𝔐 distinctive accents: 2 – 1.
Stresses: 2 + 2.
Verse-line parallelism: אל || אל; זכר || בין; ראשון || קדמוני; grammatical parallelism.

VERSE–LINE: 43:19a:

הִנְנִי עֹשֶׂה חֲדָשָׁה 19aA Behold, I am about to make a new thing,
עַתָּה תִצְמָח 19aB now it will sprout.
הֲלוֹא תֵדָעוּהָ 19aC Don't you know?

𝔐 distinctive accents: 10 – 5 – 2.
Stresses: 3 + 2 + 2.
Verse-line parallelism: חדשׁ || צמח;

VERSE–LINE: 43:19b:

אַף אָשִׂים בַּמִּדְבָּר דֶּרֶךְ 19bA Yes, I make a way in the desert,
בִּישִׁמֹון נְתִיבוֹת*׃ 19bB paths in the wilderness.

𝔐 distinctive accents: 5 – 1.
Stresses: 4 + 2.
Verse-line parallelism: ב || ב; מדבר || ישׁמון; דרך || נתיבה.
Discussion: Again ellipsis is a connecting force.

VERSE–LINE: 43:20a:

תְּכַבְּדֵ֙נִי֙ חַיַּ֣ת הַשָּׂדֶ֔ה 20aA The wild beasts of the field will honour me,
תַּנִּ֖ים וּבְנ֣וֹת יַעֲנָ֑ה 20aB jackals and ostriches,

𝔐 distinctive accents: 5 – 2.
Stresses: 3 + 3.
Verse-line parallelism: חיה || תן (unique); חיה || יענה (unique).
Discussion: Ellipsis.

VERSE–LINE: 43:20b:

כִּֽי־נָתַ֨תִּי בַמִּדְבָּ֜ר מַ֗יִם 20bA for I give water in the desert,
נְהָרוֹת֙ בִּישִׁימֹ֔ן 20bB rivers in the wilderness,
לְהַשְׁק֖וֹת עַמִּ֥י בְחִירִֽי׃ 20bC to give drink to my people, my chosen one.

𝔐 distinctive accents: 7 – 5 – 1.
Stresses: 3 + 2 + 3.
Verse-line parallelism: ב || ב; מדבר || ישמון; מים || נהר; נתן מים || שקה Hiph.
Discussion: Again ellipsis is used as a binding device.

VERSE–LINE: 43:21a:

עַם־ז֙וּ֙ יָצַ֣רְתִּי לִ֔י 21aA The people whom I have formed for myself
תְּהִלָּתִ֖י* יְסַפֵּֽרוּ׃ 21aB will tell my praiseworthy deeds.

𝔐 distinctive accents: 5 – 1.
Stresses: 3 + 2.
Verse-line parallelism: י־ || י־.
Discussion: The parallelism is so weak that one may regard this verse-line as an example of enjambment.

VERSE–LINE: 43:22a:

וְלֹא־אֹתִ֥י קָרָ֖אתָ יַעֲקֹ֑ב 22aA Yet you did not call upon me, O Jacob,
כִּֽי־יָגַ֥עְתָּ בִּ֖י יִשְׂרָאֵֽל׃ 22aB that you would have wearied yourselves for me, O Israel!

𝔐 distinctive accents: 2 – 1.
Stresses: 3 + 3.
Verse-line parallelism: י־ || י־; קרא || יגע; יעקב || ישׂראל.

VERSE–LINE: 43:23a:

לֹא־הֵבֵ֤יאתָ לִּי֙ שֵׂ֣ה עֹלֹתֶ֔יךָ 23aA You did not bring me the rams of your burnt offerings,
וּזְבָחֶ֖יךָ לֹ֣א כִבַּדְתָּ֑נִי 23aB and with your sacrifices you did not honour me.

𝔐 distinctive accents: 5 – 2.
Stresses: 4 + 3.
Verse-line parallelism: לא || לא; בוא || כבד; ־י || ־י; עולה || זבח; ־ך || ־ך.

VERSE–LINE: 43:23b:

לֹא הֶעֱבַדְתִּיךָ בְּמִנְחָה 23bA I have not made you serve with oblations,
וְלֹא הוֹגַעְתִּיךָ בִּלְבוֹנָה׃ 23bB and I have not wearied you with incense.

𝔐 distinctive accents: 5 – 1.
Stresses: 3 + 3.
Verse-line parallelism: לא || לא; עבד || יגע; ב || ב; מנחה || לבונה; grammatical parallelism; rhyme.

VERSE–LINE: 43:24a:

לֹא־קָנִיתָ לִּי בַכֶּסֶף קָנֶה 24aA You did not buy me cane with silver,
וְחֵלֶב זְבָחֶיךָ לֹא הִרְוִיתָנִי 24aB and the fat of your sacrifices you did not lavish on me.

𝔐 distinctive accents: 5 – 2.
Stresses: 4 + 4.
Verse-line parallelism: לא || לא; קנה || רוה (unique); ־י || ־ני; קנה || חלב (unique); קנה || זבח; grammatical parallelism.

VERSE–LINE: 43:24b:

אַךְ הֶעֱבַדְתַּנִי בְּחַטֹּאותֶיךָ 24bA No, you made me serve by your sins,
הוֹגַעְתַּנִי בַּעֲוֺנֹתֶיךָ׃ 24bB and made me weary with your iniquities.

𝔐 distinctive accents: 5 – 1.
Stresses: 3 + 2.
Verse-line parallelism: עבד || יגע; ־ני || ־ני; ב || ב; חטאת || עון; ־ך || ־ך; grammatical parallelism; rhyme.

VERSE–LINE: 43:25a:

אָנֹכִי אָנֹכִי הוּא 25aA I, I am he,
מֹחֶה פְשָׁעֶיךָ לְמַעֲנִי 25aB who wipes out your transgressions for my own sake,
וְחַטֹּאתֶיךָ לֹא אֶזְכֹּר׃ 25aC and do not remember your sins.

𝔐 distinctive accents: 12 – 2 – 1.
Stresses: 3 + 3 + 3.
Verse-line parallelism: אנכי || ־י; מחה || זכר (antithetical); פשע || חטאת; ־ך || ־ך.
Discussion: 𝔐 presupposes a first colon of six stresses which we rejected after due deliberation (p. 177-8, 639).

VERSE–LINE: 43:26a:

הַזְכִּירֵ֕נִי נִשָּׁפְטָ֖ה יָ֑חַד 26aA Help me to remember, let us argue our case together!
סַפֵּ֥ר אַתָּ֖ה לְמַ֥עַן תִּצְדָּֽק׃ 26aB You tell (us), that you may be justified ...

𝔐 distinctive accents: 2 – 1.
Stresses: 3 + 4.
Verse-line parallelism: זכר || ספר; שׁפט || צדק.

VERSE–LINE: 43:27a:

אָבִ֥יךָ הָרִאשׁ֖וֹן חָטָ֑א 27aA Your first father sinned,
וּמְלִיצֶ֖יךָ פָּ֥שְׁעוּ בִֽי׃ 27aB and your spokesmen transgressed against me.

𝔐 distinctive accents: 2 – 1.
Stresses: 3 + 3.
Verse-line parallelism: אב || מליץ (unique); ־ךָ || ־ךָ; חטא || פשׁע.
Discussion: We follow the Masoretic accents because of the stronger bonds between v. 28bA and bB. See below.

VERSE–LINE: 43:28a:

וַאֲחַלֵּ֖ל שָׂ֣רֵי קֹ֑דֶשׁ 28aA So I had to defile the chiefs of the sanctuary,

𝔐 distinctive accents: 2.
Stresses: 3.
Verse-line parallelism: None (unicolon).

VERSE–LINE: 43:28b:

וְאֶתְּנָ֤ה* לַחֵ֙רֶם֙ יַעֲקֹ֔ב 28bA and had to devote Jacob to the ban,
וְיִשְׂרָאֵ֖ל לְגִדּוּפִֽים׃ 28bB and Israel to insults.

𝔐 distinctive accents: 5 – 1.
Stresses: 3 + 2.
Verse-line parallelism: יעקב || ישׂראל; ל || ל; חרם || גדוף (unique).
Discussion: Ellipsis forms an extra bond between 28bA and 28bB.

5.4 Isaiah 43 – Delimitation of Strophes

STROPHE A.i.1 (Isa. 43:1)

וְעַתָּה כֹּה־אָמַר יְהוָה	1aA	But now, thus says the LORD,
בֹּרַאֲךָ יַעֲקֹב וְיֹצֶרְךָ יִשְׂרָאֵל	1aB	who created you, O Jacob, and who formed you, O Israel,
אַל־תִּירָא כִּי גְאַלְתִּיךָ	1bA	Do not fear, for I redeem you,
קָרָאתִי בְשִׁמְךָ לִי־אָתָּה׃	1bB	I call you by your name, you are mine!

= Masoretic verse.
Separation ↑: major division markers in the textual tradition; deictic particle(s); vocatives; marker of direct speech.
Separation ↓: deictic particle(s); independent pers. pronoun; jussive(s); repetitive verse-line parallelism; swapping (adjunct).
Strophe parallelism: ךָ־ (m.s.) || ךָ־ (m.s.); ברא || גאל.
Discussion: The verse-lines must be connected because the sentence runs on.

STROPHE A.i.2 (Isa. 43:2)

כִּי־תַעֲבֹר בַּמַּיִם אִתְּךָ־אָנִי	2aA	When you pass through the waters , I am with you,
וּבַנְּהָרוֹת לֹא יִשְׁטְפוּךָ	2aB	and through the rivers – they will not overwhelm you.
כִּי־תֵלֵךְ בְּמוֹ־אֵשׁ לֹא תִכָּוֶה	2bA	When you walk through fire, you will not be scorched,
וְלֶהָבָה לֹא תִבְעַר־בָּךְ׃	2bB	and no flame will burn you.

= Masoretic verse.
Separation ↑: deictic particle(s); independent pers. pronoun; repetitive verse-line parallelism; swapping (adjunct).
Separation ↓: major division markers in the textual tradition; deictic particle(s); repetitive verse-line parallelism.
Strophe parallelism: כי || כי; עבר || הלך; ךָ־ (m.s.) || ךָ־ (m.s.); ב || במו; מים || אש (antithetical); wordplay between תעבר and תבער; grammatical parallelism.

STROPHE A.ii.1 (Isa. 43:3)

כִּי אֲנִי יְהוָה אֱלֹהֶיךָ	3aA	For I am the LORD, your God,
קְדוֹשׁ יִשְׂרָאֵל מוֹשִׁיעֶךָ	3aB	the Holy One of Israel, your saviour.
נָתַתִּי כָפְרְךָ מִצְרַיִם	3bA	I give Egypt as your ransom,
כּוּשׁ וּסְבָא תַּחְתֶּיךָ׃	3bB	Cush and Sheba in exchange for you.

= Masoretic verse.
Separation ↑: major division markers in the textual tradition; deictic

particle(s); independent pers. pronoun; repetitive verse-line parallelism.
Separation ↓: major division markers in the textual tradition; repetitive verse-line parallelism; swapping (adjunct).
Strophe parallelism: ךָ־ (m.s.) || ךָ־ (m.s.); ישׂראל || מצרים.
Discussion: Apparently 𝔊^{SA} presuppose a different strophic division, but their solution has little in favour of it. See p. 200.

STROPHE A.ii.2 (Isa. 43:4)

מֵאֲשֶׁ֨ר יָקַ֧רְתָּ בְעֵינַ֛י נִכְבַּ֖דְתָּ	4aA	Since you are precious in my eyes, honoured,
וַאֲנִ֣י אֲהַבְתִּ֑יךָ	4aB	and (since) I love you,
וְאֶתֵּ֤ן אָדָם֙ תַּחְתֶּ֔יךָ	4bA	I will give people in exchange for you,
וּלְאֻמִּ֖ים תַּ֥חַת נַפְשֶֽׁךָ׃	4bB	and nations in exchange for your life.

= Masoretic verse.
Separation ↑: major division markers in the textual tradition; independent pers. pronoun.
Separation ↓: repetitive verse-line parallelism.
Strophe parallelism: ךָ־ (m.s.) || ךָ־ (m.s.).
Discussion: The continuing sentence connects the verse-lines (enjambment).

STROPHE A.iii.1 (Isa. 43:5)

אַל־תִּירָ֖א כִּ֣י אִתְּךָ־אָ֑נִי	5aA	Do not fear, for I am with you.
מִמִּזְרָח֙ אָבִ֣יא זַרְעֶ֔ךָ	5bA	From the east I will bring your seed,
וּמִמַּעֲרָ֖ב אֲקַבְּצֶֽךָּ׃	5bB	and from the west I will gather you.

= Masoretic verse.
Separation ↑: deictic particle(s); independent pers. pronoun; jussive(s).
Separation ↓: major division markers in the textual tradition; repetitive verse-line parallelism; swapping (adjunct).
Strophe parallelism: ךָ־ (m.s.) || ךָ־ (m.s.); grammatical parallelism.

STROPHE A.iii.2 (Isa. 43:6)

אֹמַ֤ר לַצָּפוֹן֙ תֵּ֔נִי	6aA	I will say to the north, 'Give up!'
וּלְתֵימָ֖ן אַל־תִּכְלָ֑אִי	6aB	And to the south, 'Do not withhold!'
הָבִ֤יאִי בָנַי֙ מֵֽרָח֔וֹק	6bA	'Bring my sons from afar,
וּבְנוֹתַ֖י מִקְצֵ֥ה הָאָֽרֶץ׃	6bB	and my daughters from the end of the earth,

= Masoretic verse.
Separation ↑: major division markers in the textual tradition; imperative(s); jussive(s); marker of direct speech; swapping (adjunct).

Separation ↓: major division marker in the textual tradition; imperative(s); repetitive verse-line parallelism.
Strophe parallelism: צפון || רחוק; כלא || בוא Hiph. (antithetical); grammatical parallelism.

STROPHE A.iii.3 (Isa. 43:7)

כֹּל הַנִּקְרָא בִשְׁמִי	7aA	everyone who is called by my name,
וְלִכְבוֹדִי בְּרָאתִיו	7aB	and whom I created for my glory,
יְצַרְתִּיו אַף־עֲשִׂיתִיו׃	7aC	whom I formed, also made.'

= Masoretic verse.
Separation ↑: major division marker in the textual tradition; deictic particle(s); repetitive verse-line parallelism; swapping (adjunct).
Separation ↓: major division markers in the textual tradition.
Strophe parallelism: None (one verse).

STROPHE A.iii.4 (Isa. 43:8)

הוֹצִיא עַם־עִוֵּר וְעֵינַיִם יֵשׁ	8aA	Let him bring out the people who are blind, yet have eyes,
וְחֵרְשִׁים וְאָזְנַיִם לָמוֹ׃	8aB	and those who are deaf, yet have ears!

= Masoretic verse.
Separation ↑: major division markers in the textual tradition; precative perfect.
Separation ↓: major division markers in the textual tradition.
Strophe parallelism: None (one verse-line).

STROPHE B.i.1 (Isa. 43:9a–b)

כָּל־הַגּוֹיִם נִקְבְּצוּ יַחְדָּו	9aA	Let all the nations gather together,
וְיֵאָסְפוּ לְאֻמִּים	9aB	and let the peoples assemble!
מִי בָהֶם יַגִּיד זו אֹתֶה*	9bA	Who among them will tell what is coming?
וְרִאשֹׁנוֹת יַשְׁמִיעֻנוּ	9bB	Let them make us hear first things!

≠ Masoretic verse.
Separation ↑: major division markers in the textual tradition; precative perfect; jussive(s); swapping (subject).
Separation ↓: major division markers in the textual tradition; interrogative pronoun; swapping (object).
Strophe parallelism: None.
Discussion: Despite the lack of strophe parallelism the connection between the two verses is guaranteed by בהם. The Masoretes wanted to read v. 9 as a quadrocolon (see p. 183). In our opinion it is much more likely that the two verses containing the עדים (vv. 9c, 10a) should be combined. 𝔊[A] lends some support to this view.

STROPHE B.i.2 (Isa. 43:9c–10a)

יִתְּנוּ עֵדֵיהֶם וְיִצְדָּקוּ	9cA	Let them give their witnesses so that they may be justified,
וְיִשְׁמְעוּ וְיֹאמְרוּ אֱמֶת׃	9cB	so that one may hear and say: "It is true!"
אַתֶּם עֵדַי נְאֻם־יְהוָה	10aA	You are my witnesses, declares the LORD,
וְעַבְדִּי אֲשֶׁר בָּחָרְתִּי	10aB	and (you are) my Servant, whom I have chosen.

≠ Masoretic verse.
Separation ↑: major division markers in the textual tradition; jussive(s); marker of direct speech.
Separation ↓: independent pers. pronoun; marker of direct speech.
Strophe parallelism: עד (noun) || עד (noun); אמר || נאם.
Discussion: Whereas 𝔊^SA seem to have taken v. 9c as an independent strophe, the Masoretes decided to take it with v. 9a-b, creating a rather odd balance between the verse-lines (see our comment on the preceding strophe). In our opinion the parallelism between the two verse-lines vv. 9c and 10a justifies our joining them into one strophe. Moreover, the Masoretic division creates the illogical situation that the Israelites are supposed to start believing in their God on the basis of their own testimony. It is much more satisfying to see this recognition as the outcome of a lawsuit in which they compare the testimony of the nations with their own words. This is achieved by combining vv. 9c and 10a.

It seems likely that the למען at the beginning of v. 10bA prompted the Masoretes to take v. 10a with the rest of what is now v. 10. However, sentences running on through more than one strophe are not unusual.[1]

STROPHE B.i.3 (Isa. 43:10b–c)

לְמַעַן תֵּדְעוּ וְתַאֲמִינוּ לִי וְתָבִינוּ	10bA	So that you may know and believe me and will understand,
כִּי־אֲנִי הוּא	10bB	that I am the same One.
לְפָנַי לֹא־נוֹצַר אֵל	10cA	Before me no god was formed,
וְאַחֲרַי לֹא יִהְיֶה׃	10cB	nor will there be one after me.

≠ Masoretic verse.
Separation ↑: deictic particle(s); independent pers. pronouns.
Separation ↓: major division markers in the textual tradition; repetitive verse-line parallelism; swapping (adjunct).
Strophe parallelism: אני || י־.
Discussion: See our comment on the preceding strophe.

[1] See below pp. 654-5.

STROPHE B.ii.1 (Isa. 43:11)

אָנֹכִי אָנֹכִי יְהוָה	11aA	I, I am the LORD,
וְאֵין מִבַּלְעָדַי מוֹשִׁיעַ׃	11aB	and apart from me there is no saviour.

= Masoretic verse.
Separation ↑: major division markers in the textual tradition; independent pers. pronouns; swapping (adjunct).
Separation ↓: None (one verse-line).
Strophe parallelism: None (one verse-line).
Discussion: One would be inclined to connect this verse with v. 10b-c, were it not for the major division markers separating them. Moreover, the canticle B.ii appears to be an elaboration of the preceding one. So we are dealing with concatenation of canticles here. The אנכי instead of אני creates a distinction.

STROPHE B.ii.2 (Isa. 43:12)

אָנֹכִי הִגַּדְתִּי וְהוֹשַׁעְתִּי וְהִשְׁמַעְתִּי	12aA	It is I who told and saved and made heard,
וְאֵין בָּכֶם זָר	12aB	and not a stranger who was among you.
וְאַתֶּם עֵדַי נְאֻם־יְהוָה	12bA	And you are my witnesses, declares the LORD,
וַאֲנִי־אֵל׃	12bB	that I am God.

= Masoretic verse.
Separation ↑: independent pers. pronoun.
Separation ↓: independent pers. pronouns; marker of direct speech.
Strophe parallelism: אנכי || אתם; אנכי || אני; נגד || עד (noun).
Discussion: 𝔊[SA] seem to presuppose a different colometry which joined v. 11 to v. 12. From the viewpoint of parallelism this was an attractive option. However, the attested strophe parallelism renders 𝔐's division at least as attractive.

STROPHE B.ii.3 (Isa. 43:13)

גַּם־מִיּוֹם אֲנִי הוּא	13aA	Also from today on I am the same One,
וְאֵין מִיָּדִי מַצִּיל	13aB	and no one delivers from my hand;
אֶפְעַל וּמִי יְשִׁיבֶנָּה׃	13bA	I work, and who can reverse it?

= Masoretic verse.
Separation ↑: deictic particle(s); independent pers. pronouns; repetitive verse-line parallelism; swapping (adjunct).
Separation ↓: major division markers in the textual tradition; interrogative pronoun.
Strophe parallelism: נצל || שׁוב Hiph.

STROPHE C.i.1 (Isa. 43:14)

כֹּה־אָמַר יְהוָה	14aA	Thus says the LORD,
גֹּאַלְכֶם קְדוֹשׁ יִשְׂרָאֵל	14aB	your Redeemer, the Holy One of Israel:
לְמַעַנְכֶם שִׁלַּחְתִּי בָבֶלָה	14bA	For your sake I send (messengers) to Babylon,
וְהוֹרַדְתִּי בָרִיחִים כֻּלָּם	14bB	and I make them all descend as fugitives (?),
וְכַשְׂדִּים בָּאֳנִיּוֹת רִנָּתָם׃	14bC	yes, the Chaldaeans in their eulogized ships.

= Masoretic verse.
Separation ↑: major division markers in the textual tradition; deictic particle(s); marker of direct speech.
Separation ↓: major division markers in the textual tradition; swapping (adjunct).
Strophe parallelism: ־כם ‖ ־כם; ישראל ‖ בבל.
Discussion: The introduction of the direct speech cannot be separated from its content. 𝔊[Q] has a major division marker after בבלה but probably it is merely lagging behind the other witnesses which have a major division after v. 13. See further p. 201.

STROPHE C.i.2 (Isa. 43:15)

אֲנִי יְהוָה קְדוֹשְׁכֶם	15aA	I am the LORD, your Holy One,
בּוֹרֵא יִשְׂרָאֵל מַלְכְּכֶם׃	15aB	Creator of Israel, your King.

= Masoretic verse.
Separation ↑: major division markers in the textual tradition; independent pers. pronoun; repetitive verse-line parallelism.
Separation ↓: major division markers in the textual tradition.
Strophe parallelism: None (one verse-line).

STROPHE C.ii.1 (Isa. 43:16–17a)

כֹּה אָמַר יְהוָה	16aA	Thus says the LORD,
הַנּוֹתֵן בַּיָּם דָּרֶךְ	16aB	who makes a way through the sea,
וּבְמַיִם עַזִּים נְתִיבָה׃	16aC	and a path through mighty waters,
הַמּוֹצִיא רֶכֶב־וָסוּס	17aA	who leads out chariots and horses,
חַיִל וְעִזּוּז	17aB	armies and mighty forces:

≠ Masoretic verse.
Separation ↑: major division markers in the textual tradition; deictic particle(s); marker of direct speech; swapping (adjunct).
Separation ↓: repetitive verse-line parallelism (ו in pairs).
Strophe parallelism: עז ‖ עזוז (unique); grammatical parallelism.
Discussion: The Masoretes took v. 17 as a tricolon or as a unicolon followed by a bicolon. It is no valid objection that the sentence runs

on through two strophes in that case, because this is a fairly common phenomenon. However, the association of a path through the waters, horses and chariots obviously hints at the Exodus. Just as God had saved his people on that occasion, so he will do now. The pairing of הנותן and המוציא is more natural therefore and v. 17b describes the result with regard to Israel's enemies in a separate strophe.

STROPHE C.ii.2 (Isa. 43:17b)

יַחְדָּו יִשְׁכְּבוּ בַּל־יָקוּמוּ	17bA	Together they lie down, do not rise (again),
דָּעֲכוּ כַּפִּשְׁתָּה כָבוּ׃	17bB	they are extinguished, quenched like a wick.

≠ Masoretic verse.
Separation ↑: swapping (adjunct).
Separation ↓: major division markers in the textual tradition.
Strophe parallelism: None (one verse-line).
Discussion: See our comments on the preceding strophe.

STROPHE C.iii.1 (Isa. 43:18)

אַל־תִּזְכְּרוּ רִאשֹׁנוֹת	18aA	Do not try to remember the first things,
וְקַדְמֹנִיּוֹת אַל־תִּתְבֹּנָנוּ׃	18aB	and do not try to understand things of old.

= Masoretic verse.
Separation ↑: major division markers in the textual tradition; jussive(s); swapping (object).
Separation ↓: None (one verse-line).
Strophe parallelism: None (one verse-line).

STROPHE C.iii.2 (Isa. 43:19)

הִנְנִי עֹשֶׂה חֲדָשָׁה	19aA	Behold, I am about to make a new thing,
עַתָּה תִצְמָח	19aB	now it will sprout.
הֲלוֹא תֵדָעוּהָ	19aC	Don't you know?
אַף אָשִׂים בַּמִּדְבָּר דֶּרֶךְ	19bA	Yes, I make a way in the desert,
בִּישִׁמוֹן נְתִיבוֹת*׃	19bB	paths in the wilderness.

= Masoretic verse.
Separation ↑: deictic particle(s).
Separation ↓: deictic particle(s); swapping (adjunct).
Strophe parallelism: עשה || שים.

STROPHE C.iii.3 (Isa. 43:20)

תְּכַבְּדֵנִי חַיַּת הַשָּׂדֶה	20aA	The wild beasts of the field will honour me,
תַּנִּים וּבְנוֹת יַעֲנָה	20aB	jackals and ostriches,

כִּֽי־נָתַתִּי בַמִּדְבָּר מַיִם	20bA	for I give water in the desert,
נְהָרוֹת בִּישִׁימֹן	20bB	rivers in the wilderness,
לְהַשְׁקוֹת עַמִּי בְחִירִֽי׃	20bC	to give drink to my people, my chosen one.

= Masoretic verse.
Separation ↑: None.
Separation ↓: major division marker in the textual tradition; deictic particle(s); repetitive verse-line parallelism; swapping (adjunct).
Strophe parallelism: שׂדה || מדבר.
Discussion: The association of jackals and ostriches with the desert is well known.[2] This forms a link between the two verse-lines.

STROPHE C.iii.4 (Isa. 43:21)

עַם־זוּ יָצַרְתִּי לִי	21aA	The people whom I have formed for myself
תְּהִלָּתִי* יְסַפֵּֽרוּ׃	21aB	will tell my praiseworthy deeds.

= Masoretic verse.
Separation ↑: major division marker in the textual tradition; repetitive verse-line parallelism; swapping (subject); swapping (object).
Separation ↓: major division markers in the textual tradition.
Strophe parallelism: None (one verse-line).

STROPHE D.i.1 (Isa. 43:22)

וְלֹא־אֹתִי קָרָאתָ יַעֲקֹב	22aA	Yet you did not call upon me, O Jacob,
כִּֽי־יָגַעְתָּ בִּי יִשְׂרָאֵֽל׃	22aB	that you would have wearied yourselves for me, O Israel!

= Masoretic verse.
Separation ↑: major division markers in the textual tradition; deictic particle(s); vocatives; repetitive verse-line parallelism; swapping (object).
Separation ↓: None (one verse-line).
Strophe parallelism: None (one verse-line).

STROPHE D.i.2 (Isa. 43:23)

לֹֽא־הֵבֵיאתָ לִּי שֵׂה עֹלֹתֶיךָ	23aA	You did not bring me the rams of your burnt offerings,
וּזְבָחֶיךָ לֹא כִבַּדְתָּנִי	23aB	and with your sacrifices you did not honour me.
לֹא הֶעֱבַדְתִּיךָ בְּמִנְחָה	23bA	I have not made you serve with oblations,
וְלֹא הוֹגַעְתִּיךָ בִּלְבוֹנָֽה׃	23bB	and I have not wearied you with incense.

= Masoretic verse.

[2]See e.g. Mal. 1:3; Lam. 4:3.

Separation ↑: repetitive verse-line parallelism; swapping (object); swapping (adjunct).
Separation ↓: repetitive verse-line parallelism.
Strophe parallelism: לא || לא; עולה || מנחה; זבח (noun) || לבנה (unique); grammatical parallelism.

STROPHE D.i.3 (Isa. 43:24)

לֹא־קָנִיתָ לִּי בַכֶּסֶף קָנֶה	24aA	You did not buy me cane with silver,
וְחֵלֶב זְבָחֶיךָ לֹא הִרְוִיתָנִי	24aB	and the fat of your sacrifices you did not lavish on me.
אַךְ הֶעֱבַדְתַּנִי בְּחַטֹּאותֶיךָ	24bA	No, you made me serve by your sins,
הוֹגַעְתַּנִי בַּעֲוֹנֹתֶיךָ׃	24bB	and made me weary with your iniquities.

= Masoretic verse.
Separation ↑: repetitive verse-line parallelism; swapping (object); swapping (adjunct).
Separation ↓: major division markers in the textual tradition; deictic particle(s); repetitive verse-line parallelism.
Strophe parallelism: ב || ב; ־ך (m.s.) || ־ך (m.s.); ־ני || ־ני; grammatical parallelism.

STROPHE D.ii.1 (Isa. 43:25–26)

אָנֹכִי אָנֹכִי הוּא	25aA	I, I am he,
מֹחֶה פְשָׁעֶיךָ לְמַעֲנִי	25aB	who wipes out your transgressions for my own sake,
וְחַטֹּאתֶיךָ לֹא אֶזְכֹּר׃	25aC	and do not remember your sins.
הַזְכִּירֵנִי נִשָּׁפְטָה יָחַד	26aA	Help me to remember, let us argue our case together!
סַפֵּר אַתָּה לְמַעַן תִּצְדָּק׃	26aB	You tell (us), that you may be justified ...

≠ Masoretic verse.
Separation ↑: major division markers in the textual tradition; independent pers. pronouns; swapping (object).
Separation ↓: major division markers in the textual tradition; independent pers. pronoun; imperative(s); cohortative(s).
Strophe parallelism: אנכי || אתה; למען || למען; זכר Qal || זכר Hiph.
Discussion: 1Q[a] and 1Q[b] have a narrow space at the end of v. 25 which might be interpreted as a narrow Setuma. This would confirm the Masoretic strophic division. However, 1Q[a] and 𝔊[A] also indicate a division after v. 26 and in our opinion the parallelism justifies the reading of the two verse-lines as one strophe.

STROPHE D.ii.2 (Isa. 43:27)

אָבִ֥יךָ הָרִאשׁ֖וֹן חָטָ֑א	27aA	Your first father sinned,
וּמְלִיצֶ֖יךָ פָּ֥שְׁעוּ בִֽי׃	27aB	and your spokesmen transgressed against me.

= Masoretic verse.
Separation ↑: major division markers in the textual tradition; swapping (subject).
Separation ↓: None (one verse-line).
Strophe parallelism: None (one verse-line).

STROPHE D.ii.3 (Isa. 43:28)

וַאֲחַלֵּ֖ל שָׂ֣רֵי קֹ֑דֶשׁ	28aA	So I had to defile the chiefs of the sanctuary,
וְאֶתְּנָ֤ה* לַחֵ֙רֶם֙ יַֽעֲקֹ֔ב	28bA	and had to devote Jacob to the ban,
וְיִשְׂרָאֵ֖ל לְגִדּוּפִֽים׃	28bB	and Israel to insults.

= Masoretic verse.
Separation ↑: None.
Separation ↓: swapping (adjunct).
Strophe parallelism: חלל || נתן לחרם (unique).

5.5 Isaiah 43 – Delimitation of Canticles

CANTICLE A.i (43:1–2)

Separation ↑: major division markers in the textual tradition; thematic discontinuity;[1] change of subject.
Separation ↓: major division marker in the textual tradition.
Canticle parallelism: ךָ־ (m.s.) || ךָ־ (m.s.) || ךָ־ (m.s.) || ךָ־ (m.s.) (responsion/ concatenation/inclusion); כי || כי (concatenation/inclusion); אני || אתה (concatenation).
Thematic unity: yes. In both strophes Israel is addressed with a message of salvation.
Discussion: Only 1Q[a] has preserved a Petuḥa after v. 2. However, 𝔊[SA] have major dividers after v. 3aB which may be interpreted as indicating the same borderline.[2]

[1] Again there is a link between this and the preceding chapter (the burning, בער (42:25bB – 43:2bB). However, this is a superficial link since Israel does not notice the burning in 42:25 whereas 43:2 presupposes the hurt of it. Note that in 42:25 Israel is described in the 3rd person, but is addressed in the 2nd person in 43:1-2.

[2] See p. 646-8.

CANTICLE A.ii (43:3–4)

Separation ↑: major division marker in the textual tradition; thematic discontinuity; change of subject.
Separation ↓: See below.
Canticle parallelism: אני || אני (responsion); ך־ || ך־ || ך־ || ך־ (responsion/concatenation/inclusion); תחת || תחת (responsion).
Thematic unity: yes. In both strophes God gives other nations in exchange for Israel.
Discussion: This is one of the very rare cases where we are assuming a canticle division even though none of the ancient witnesses supports it. Superficially it may look as if the theme of vv. 3-4 is continued in vv. 5-8. However, in the latter the element of exchange is missing. Moreover, the refrain-like repetition of אל תירא (vv. 1bA, 5aA) and אתך־אני (vv. 2aA, 5aA) would seem to indicate a new beginning.

CANTICLE A.iii (43:5-8)

Separation ↑: thematic discontinuity (see above); change of subject.
Separation ↓: major division markers in the textual tradition.
Canticle parallelism: מן || מן (responsion); מזרח, מערב || צפון || תימן || רחוק (concatenation/responsion); בוא Hiph. || בוא Hiph. (responsion); בוא Hiph. || יצא Hiph. (responsion); זרע || בן, בת (inclusion).
Strophes A.iii.2 and A.iii.3 are linked by a continuing sentence (enjambment).
Thematic unity: yes. All strophes speak of the return of the exiles.
Discussion: See for the upper limit of this canticle our discussion of A.ii. 1Q[a] has a small Setuma at the end of v. 7 which corresponds to major division markings in 𝔊[A]. Like the Setuma in the Parma Bible after v. 6, these markings indicate the end of strophes. It would be possible to defend the same with regard to the larger Setuma in 1Q[a] after v. 8, were it not for the paragraphos in 𝔊[S] and the thematic change in vv. 9-10. It must indicate a canticle division.

CANTICLE B.i (43:9–10)

Separation ↑: major division markers in the textual tradition; thematic discontinuity; change of subject.
Separation ↓: major division markers in the textual tradition.
Canticle parallelism: שמע || שמע (concatenation).
Strophes 1 and 2 are connected by the suffix ־הם and the jussives in v. 9cA. Strophes 2 and 3 are linked by an on-running sentence (enjambment).

Thematic unity: yes. The three strophes describe an invitation to start a lawsuit and announce its expected result.
Discussion: For the strophic divisions in $\mathfrak{G}^{A}$ and $\mathfrak{G}^{SA}$ see our comments on p. 193.

CANTICLE B.ii (43:11–13)

Separation ↑: major division markers in the textual tradition.
Separation ↓: major division markers in the textual tradition.
Canticle parallelism: אנכי || אנכי (responsion); אנכי || אני (responsion); אין || אין || אין (responsion); ישׁע || ישׁע (concatenation); ישׁע || נצל (responsion); אני || אני (concatenation).
Thematic unity: yes. The self-praise and the personal pronouns of the 1st person singular form a strong bond between the three strophes.
Discussion: From a thematic point of view the delimitation between canticles B.i and B.ii may seem somewhat doubtful. But the division between the two is firmly established in four different lines of tradition.

The major dividers in $\mathfrak{G}^{A}$ and the colon in $\mathfrak{G}^{S}$ after v. 12aB point to a slightly different strophic division which does not effect the structure of the canticle. See p. 194.

CANTICLE C.i (43:14–15)

Separation ↑: major division markers in the textual tradition; thematic discontinuity.
Separation ↓: major division markers in the textual tradition.
Canticle parallelism: יהוה || יהוה (responsion); גאל || ברא (responsion); קדושׁ || קדושׁ (responsion); ישׂראל || ישׂראל (responsion).
Thematic unity: yes. Beginning and end describe the ultimate power of Israel's divine King which lends credibility to the prophecy in between.
Discussion: The division marker (capital) after v. 14bA in $\mathfrak{G}^{Q}$ may be a case of belated marking because this manuscript is missing among the witnesses attesting the division after v. 13. The dividers after v. 14 in $4\mathfrak{Q}^{g}$ and $\mathfrak{G}^{Q}$ mark the end of a strophe.

CANTICLE C.ii (43:16–17)

Separation ↑: major division markers in the textual tradition.
Separation ↓: major division markers in the textual tradition.
Canticle parallelism: None.
Strophes linked by on-running sentence (enjambment).
Thematic unity: yes. As with the Exodus, the Israelites will pass safely through the waters, whereas the chariotry of the Babylonians will drown ("quenched like a wick").

Discussion: It is remarkable that the space in the Parma Bible is confirmed by three of our Greek witnesses.

CANTICLE C.iii (43:18–21)

Separation ↑: major division markers in the textual tradition; thematic discontinuity; change of subject.
Separation ↓: major division markers in the textual tradition.
Canticle parallelism: ראשון || חדש (concatenation); בין || ידע (concatenation); מדבר || מדבר (responsion); ישימון || ישימון (unique; responsion); כבד Pi. || ספר תהלה (unique;[3] responsion); עם (noun) || עם (noun) (concatenation).
Thematic unity: yes. The miracles during Israel's journey through the desert will be renewed.
Discussion: 𝔊[A] ends v. 19 one verse-line earlier than 𝔐. This is less likely because as a result the next strophe becomes exceptionally long (three verse-lines). The Setuma after v. 20 in the Codex Reuchlin probably ends the strophe because the same manuscript also has a Setuma after v. 21.

CANTICLE D.i (43:22–24)

Separation ↑: major division markers in the textual tradition; thematic discontinuity; change of subject.
Separation ↓: major division markers in the textual tradition.
Canticle parallelism: לא || לא || לא || לא (responsion/inclusion); יגע || יגע || יגע (responsion); זבח (noun) || זבח (noun) (unique; responsion); עבד (verb) || עבד (verb) (responsion).
Thematic unity: yes. All three strophes denounce the inadequacy of Israel's service of the LORD.

CANTICLE D.ii (43:25–28)

Separation ↑: major division markers in the textual tradition; change of subject.
Separation ↓: major division markers in the textual tradition.
Canticle parallelism: פשע (noun) || פשע (verb); חטאת || חטא (verb); אב || יעקב (inclusion).
Thematic unity: yes. Justification of Israel's punishment.
Discussion: With regard to the strophic division of vv. 25-26 see p. 198.

[3]But cf. Ps. 22:24.

5.6 Isaiah 43 – Delimitation of Macrostructure

The overall structure of Isaiah 43 appears to be completely symmetric,

SUB-CANTOS	CANTICLES	STROPHES
A	3	8 (2+2+4)
B	2	6 (3+3)
C	3	8 (2+2+4)
D	2	6 (3+3)

Distant parallelism connecting the canticles of **sub-canto A**:
ברא (v. 1aB – A.i) || ברא (v. 7aB – A.iii); יצר (v. 1aB – A.i) || יצר (v. 7aC – A. iii); אל (v. 1bA – A.i) || אל (v. 5aA – A. iii); ירא (v. 1bA – A.i) || ירא (v. 5aA – A.iii); גאל (v. 1bA – A.i) || ישע (v. 3aB – A.ii); קרא בשם (v. 1bB – A.i) || קרא בשם (v. 7aA – A.iii).

All three canticles describe Israel's position as the LORD's special property. He created this people for himself and will bring them back safely from their exile wherever they may be and whoever will have to suffer in their place.[1]

Distant parallelism connecting the canticles of **sub-canto B**:
נגד (v. 9bA – B.i) || נגד (v. 12aA – B.ii); שמע Hiph. (v. 9bB – B.i) || שמע Hiph. (v. 12aA – B.ii); אתם (v. 10aA – B.i) || אתם (v. 12bA – B.ii); עד (noun) (vv. 9cA, 10aA – B.i) || עד (noun) (v. 12bA – B.ii); אני הוא (v. 10bB – B.i) || אני הוא (v. 13aA – B.ii) (unique); יצר (v. 10cB – B.i) || פעל (v. 13bA – B.ii).

The two canticles describe a fictitious lawsuit in which Israel has to testify that since its God is the only one from the days of creation on, nobody will be able to withstand him.

Distant parallelism connecting the canticles of **sub-canto C**:
כה אמר יהוה (v. 14aA – C.i) || כה אמר יהוה (v. 16aA – C.ii); רנה (v. 14bC – C.i) || תהלה (v. 21aB – C.iii; antithetical); ברא (v. 15aB – C.i) || יצר (v. 21aA – C.iii); ים (v. 16aB – C.ii) || מדבר (v. 19bA – C.iii); דרך (v. 16aB – C.ii) || דרך (v. 19bA – C.iii); נתיבה (v. 16aC – C.ii) || נתיבה (v. 19bB – C.iii); מים (v. 16aC – C.ii) || מים (v. 20bA – C.iii).

Since the chariots of the Babylonians seem to be equated with those of the Egyptians during the Exodus (vv. 16-17) it seems likely that their descending into their ships will be of no avail: they will drown (v. 14) whereas God will prepare the way for Israel, both through water and desert (vv. 16, 19-20).

[1]It seems that Persia's campaign against Egypt was impendent or had taken place, cf. v. 3b.

Distant parallelism connecting the canticles of **sub-canto D**:
חטאת (v. 24bA – D.i) || חטאת (v. 25aC – D.ii); עון (v. 24bB – D.i) || פשׁע (v. 25aB – D.ii).

Like sub-canto B, the final sub-canto describes a lawsuit. This time the outcome is that Israel's punishment had been deserved. Since it were the שׂרי קדשׁ (v. 28aA) who were responsible for the correct presentation of sacrifices, the neglect of the cult described in vv. 23-24a is an accusation addressed to them in the first place.

In all four sub-cantos the common theme is the delivery of Israel from the nations which oppress them. The reason why is the LORD's election of his own people, not any special merit of the Israelites themselves, on the contrary. The faith in his ability to deliver them is based on his power as the Creator as well as his miraculous help during the Exodus. There is a certain corrsepondence between sub-cantos A and C on the one hand (see especially vv. 2 and 16), B and D on the other (see especially vv. 9c, 26aB).

Chapter 6

The Structure of Isaiah 44

6.1 Isaiah 44: Text and Translation

ס<פ> – $1\mathfrak{Q}^{a}$ – $\mathfrak{G}^{S\Lambda}$ – $\mathfrak{S}^{abe}$

A.i.1 (Isa. 44:1)

וְעַתָּה שְׁמַע יַעֲקֹב עַבְדִּי	1aA	But now, hear, O Jacob, my servant,
וְיִשְׂרָאֵל בָּחַרְתִּי בוֹ׃	1aB	and Israel, whom I have chosen!

{<פ/ס>$\mathfrak{G}^{S}$}

A.i.2 (Isa. 44:2)

כֹּה־אָמַר יְהוָה עֹשֶׂךָ	2aA	Thus says the LORD who made you,
וְיֹצֶרְךָ מִבֶּטֶן יַעְזְרֶךָּ {<ס>}	2aB	yes, he who formed you from the womb, who helps you:
אַל־תִּירָא עַבְדִּי יַעֲקֹב	2bA	Do not fear, my servant Jacob,
וִישֻׁרוּן בָּחַרְתִּי בוֹ׃	2bB	and Jeshurun, whom I have chosen!

A.i.3 (Isa. 44:3)

כִּי אֶצָּק־מַיִם עַל־צָמֵא	3aA	For I shall pour out water on the thirsty (soil),
וְנֹזְלִים עַל־יַבָּשָׁה	3aB	and streams on the dry (ground).
אֶצֹּק רוּחִי עַל־זַרְעֶךָ	3bA	I will pour out my spirit on your seed,
וּבִרְכָתִי עַל־צֶאֱצָאֶיךָ׃	3bB	and my blessing on what comes forth for you.

A.i.4 (Isa. 44:4)

וְצָמְחוּ בְּבֵין חָצִיר	4aA	And they will sprout amidst[1] the grass,
כַּעֲרָבִים עַל־יִבְלֵי־מָיִם׃	4aB	like willows[2] by watercourses.

A.i.5 (Isa. 44:5)

זֶה יֹאמַר לַיהוָה אָנִי	5aA	One person shall say, 'I am the LORD's!'
וְזֶה יִקְרָא בְשֵׁם־יַעֲקֹב	5aB	and another will call himself[3] by the name of Jacob;

[1]Most modern authors agree in accepting $\mathfrak{M}$, cf. Koole, 265-6; Barthélemy, 322-4; De Waard, 170-1; Oswalt, 163. Differently e.g. Schoors, 79, n.1.

[2]With J. Feliks, *Plant World of the Bible* (Hebr.), Ramat Gan 1976, 113-5; M. Zohary, *Plants of the Bible*, Cambridge 1982, 131.

[3]In view of the active יאמר and יכתב we regard it as unlikely that יקרא and יכנה should be revocalized as passives. We assume that the Qal and Piel forms could acquire a reflexive meaning, like נשא Qal in Ps. 89:10 (also attested in Akkadian and Ugaritic), פתח Qal in Isa. 45:8, גוח Qal in Job 38:8; 40:23, לבש Qal in 2 Sam. 13:18; Est. 6:8, נשל Qal in Deut. 19:5; 28:40, and, in our opinion, מאס Qal in Job 42:6 ("I despise myself").

וְזֶה יִכְתֹּב יָדוֹ לַיהוָה	5bA	yet another will write on[4] his hand, 'The LORD's!'
וּבְשֵׁם יִשְׂרָאֵל יְכַנֶּה׃	5bB	and with the name of Israel he will surname himself.

פ <ס> – 1$\mathfrak{Q}^{a}$– $\mathfrak{G}^{SBA}$ – $\mathfrak{S}^{abcde}$ ....

A.ii.1 (Isa. 44:6)

כֹּה־אָמַר יְהוָה מֶלֶךְ־יִשְׂרָאֵל	6aA	Thus says the LORD, the King of Israel,
וְגֹאֲלוֹ יְהוָה צְבָאוֹת	6aB	and his Redeemer, the LORD of hosts:
אֲנִי רִאשׁוֹן וַאֲנִי אַחֲרוֹן	6bA	I am the First, and I am the Last,
וּמִבַּלְעָדַי אֵין אֱלֹהִים׃ {$\mathfrak{G}^{A}$}	6bB	apart from me there is no God.

A.ii.2 (Isa. 44:7)

וּמִי־כָמוֹנִי	7aA	And who is like me?
יִקְרָא {$\mathfrak{G}^{Q}$} וְיַגִּידֶהָ וְיַעְרְכֶהָ לִי	7aB	Let him call out, tell it and lay it out for me,
מִשּׂוּמִי עַם־עוֹלָם	7aC	from the moment I established[5] the people of eternity.
וְאֹתִיּוֹת וַאֲשֶׁר תָּבֹאנָה יַגִּידוּ לָנוּ*׃ {$\mathfrak{G}^{SA}$}	7bA	Also the things to come and what will happen – let them tell us![6]

A.ii.3 (Isa. 44:8)

אַל־תִּפְחֲדוּ וְאַל־תִּרְהוּ	8aA	Do not quiver and do not be afraid!
הֲלֹא מֵאָז הִשְׁמַעְתִּיךָ וְהִגַּדְתִּי {$\mathfrak{G}^{SA}$}	8aB	Have I not made you hear (it) from then on, and have I not told you?
וְאַתֶּם עֵדָי {$\mathfrak{G}^{Q}$}	8aC	Yes, you[7] are my witnesses!

---

[4]Although it is possible to assume haplography of the ב an adverbial accusative is perfectly acceptable. Under the Neo-Babylonian empire the owner's name was often written in the slave's hand, cf. I. Mendelsohn, *Slavery in the Ancient Near East*, New York 1949, 42-4; *CAD* Š 2, 225a, 231b. It is remarkable that in many cases the Babylonian texts do not use a preposition, but an accusative (*rittašu*). So the Israelite's decision to write the LORD's name on his hand was an act of defiance in response to vv.1-2.

[5]Cf. Barthélemy, 326-8. The expression "the people of eternity" designates either the long dead (Ezek. 26:20) as a reference to primordial times, or the people of Israel (2 Sam. 7:24, cf. 7:10; also v. 8aB).

[6]With $\mathfrak{T}$ and Isa. 41:22 we assume an accidental transformation of נו into מו, a scribal error which is found more often. Cf. R. Weiss, *Leshonenu* 26 (1962), 97-103; *JBL* (82) 1963), 188-94. Because of the change of number in יגידו a change of direction is not impossible, however. The speaker might be designating the imaginary audience by the third person plural למו.

[7]Note the harsh transition from singular to plural which is characteristic of Second Isaiah and is a consequence of his viewing the 'servant' Israel (cf. vv. 1, 5) as a corporate personality. For the servant(s) as a witness(es), see our note on 43:10, p. 160, n. 3.

$\{\mathfrak{G}^{B}\}$ הֲיֵשׁ אֱלוֹהַּ מִבַּלְעָדַי 8bA Is there a God apart from me?
וְאֵין צוּר בַּל־יָדָעְתִּי׃ 8bB 'No, there is no Rock; I know of none.'[8]

<O> – $1\mathfrak{Q}^{a}$ ____

B.i.1 (Isa. 44:9)

יֹצְרֵי־פֶסֶל כֻּלָּם תֹּהוּ 9aA Those who form idols – all of them are void,
$\{\mathfrak{G}^{S}\}$ וַחֲמוּדֵיהֶם בַּל־יוֹעִילוּ 9aB their cherished ones do not profit.
וְעֵדֵיהֶם הֵמָּה 9bA Yet they[9] are their witnesses,
בַּל־יִרְאוּ וּבַל־יֵדְעוּ 9bB (though) they do not see and they do not know,
לְמַעַן יֵבֹשׁוּ׃ 9bC so that they will be put to shame.

B.i.2 (Isa. 44:10)

מִי־יָצַר אֵל וּפֶסֶל נָסָךְ 10aA Who forms a god and casts an idol
לְבִלְתִּי הוֹעִיל׃ 10aB which does not profit?

B.i.3 (Isa. 44:11)

הֵן כָּל־חֲבֵרָיו יֵבֹשׁוּ 11aA Behold, all its[10] friends will be put to shame,
$\{\mathfrak{G}^{SA}\}$ וְחֵרְשִׁים* הֵמָּה מֵאָדָם 11aB for they are more deaf[11] than a human being!
יִתְקַבְּצוּ כֻלָּם יַעֲמֹדוּ 11bA Let them all[12] gather, stand there,
יִפְחֲדוּ יֵבֹשׁוּ יָחַד׃ 11bB let them quiver, altogether be put to shame.

<O> – $1\mathfrak{Q}^{a}$ ....

B.ii.1 (Isa. 44:12a)

חָרַשׁ בַּרְזֶל מַעֲצָד 12aA The craftsman of the iron of the adze[13] –

---

[8] We assume unintroduced direct speech of the servant Israel, cf. our note on p. 17, n. 2.

[9] The *puncta extraordinaria* express unfounded doubt with regard to the correctness of the text. In our opinion the emphatic המה refers back to the חמודים of v. 9aB, i.e. the idols. Compare vv. 9aB and 10aB, as well as המה in v. 11aB.

[10] The suffix refers back to the object of v. 10, the idol (cf. Hos. 4:17, with Delitzsch, 452; Koole, 284; Oswalt, 177, and others).

[11] The Masoretic vocalization points to the noun חרש I: 'craftsmen', with $\mathfrak{T}$ and $\mathfrak{V}$. But $\mathfrak{G}$ and $\mathfrak{S}$ seem to presuppose a derivation from חרש II, 'deaf'. Also NAB translates 'deaf'. We prefer this solution because one expects a reason for the shame, as in v. 9bB. The המה of v. 11aB corresponds to the המה of v. 9bA. The idols are even more deaf than their makers. The harsh transition between singular and plural is hardly surprising with Second Isaiah. See n. 7 above.

[12] Here the makers are meant again, as the distant parallelism (inclusion) with כלם in v. 9aA shows. See also כל־חבריו in v. 11aA.

[13] For recent evaluations of the textual problems see Koole, 285-6; Barthélemy, 329-30; De Waard, 172-3; Oswalt, 177-8. We prefer to accept $\mathfrak{M}$, taking the three words as a construct chain. The author wanted to bring home the irrationality of the idol maker's behaviour. The same smith who forged an ordinary implement like a מעצד is the maker of a 'god'. Compare the reasoning in vv. 12c, 13, 14-15, 16-17, 19.

וּפָעַל בַּפֶּחָם	12aB	he also works (it)[14] in the coalfire,
וּבַמַּקָּבוֹת יִצְּרֵהוּ	12aC	and forms it with hammers.

B.ii.2 (Isa. 44:12b)

וַיִּפְעָלֵהוּ בִּזְרוֹעַ כֹּחוֹ	12bA	And (while) he works[15] it with his strong arm,
גַּם־רָעֵב וְאֵין כֹּחַ	12bB	he also becomes hungry, so there is no strength anymore,
לֹא־שָׁתָה מַיִם {𝔊^{A}} וַיִּיעָף׃	12bC	he has drunk no water, so he grows weary.[16]

<ס> – 1𝔔^{a} ....

B.iii.1 (Isa. 44:13a–b)

חָרַשׁ עֵצִים נָטָה קָו	13aA	The woodworker stretches a line tight,
יְתָאֲרֵהוּ בַשֶּׂרֶד {𝔊^{S}}	13bA	he outlines it with a stylus,[17]
יַעֲשֵׂהוּ בַּמַּקְצֻעוֹת	13bB	he makes it with chisels,[18]
וּבַמְּחוּגָה יְתָאֳרֵהוּ	13bC	and with a pair of compasses he outlines it.

B.iii.2 (Isa. 44:13c)

וַיַּעֲשֵׂהוּ כְּתַבְנִית אִישׁ	13cA	Thus he makes it (into something) like a shapely[19] man,
כְּתִפְאֶרֶת אָדָם לָשֶׁבֶת בָּיִת׃	13cB	like a glorious human being, to dwell in a house.

....

B.iv.1 (Isa. 44:14)

לִכְרָת־לוֹ אֲרָזִים	14aA	To cut for himself cedars
וַיִּקַּח תִּרְזָה וְאַלּוֹן	14aB	he takes a stone pine[20] or an oak,
וַיְאַמֶּץ־לוֹ בַּעֲצֵי־יָעַר	14aC	and makes it for himself the strongest[21] among the trees in the forest,
נָטַע אֹרֶן	14bA	he plants a laurel,[22]
וְגֶשֶׁם יְגַדֵּל׃	14bB	and showers make (it) grow.

[14] We assume a proleptic double-duty suffix with יצרהו (cf. ויפעלהו in v. 12bB), a fairly common phenomenon in Ugaritic and ancient Hebrew. This suffix of יצרהו obviously refers back to v. 10aA מי יצר אל, cf. חבריו in v. 11aA.

[15] For the interpretation of the inverted imperfect after a perfect and a normal imperfect as an actual present see M.C.A. Korpel, J.C. de Moor, F. Sepmeijer, "Consistency with Regard to Tenses", see Abbreviations.

[16] See the preceding note.

[17] Cf. *HALAT*, 1262.

[18] Cf. *HALAT*, 594.

[19] In Babylonian the noun *tabnītu* means 'beautiful shape' (Von Soden, *AHw*, 1299). It is not improbable that in the Babylonian exile it was understood that way. The idealization of beauty in Babylonian sculpture was well-known of course. In any case this balances תפארת nicely.

[20] Cf. Feliks, *Plant World of the Bible* (Hebr.), 90-1; Zohary, *Plants of the Bible*, 113.

[21] Arboriculture in Antiquity is attested in Ugarit, cf. J.C. de Moor, "Frustula Ugaritica", *JNES* 24 (1965), 355-64 (362).

[22] Cf. Feliks, *Plant World of the Bible* (Hebr.), 92-3; Zohary, *Plants of the Bible*, 120; *HAHAT*, 101.

B.iv.2 (Isa. 44:15)

וְהָיָה לְאָדָם לְבָעֵר	15aA	And it will serve a human being for fuel,
וַיִּקַּח מֵהֶם וַיָּחָם	15aB	so he takes[23] of it and warms himself,
אַף־יַשִּׂיק וְאָפָה לָחֶם	15aC	also he kindles it to bake bread.
אַף־יִפְעַל־אֵל וַיִּשְׁתָּחוּ	15bA	Also he works (it) into a god and bows down,
עָשָׂהוּ פֶסֶל וַיִּסְגָּד־לָמוֹ׃	15bB	he makes an idol and worships it.

𝔊[A] . . . .

B.v.1 (Isa. 44:16)

חֶצְיוֹ שָׂרַף בְּמוֹ־אֵשׁ	16aA	Half of it he burns in the fire,
עַל־חֶצְיוֹ בָּשָׂר יֹאכֵל	16aB	and over half of it meat which[24] he wants to eat
יִצְלֶה צָלִי וְיִשְׂבָּע	16aC	he roasts as a roast and becomes satisfied.
אַף־יָחֹם וְיֹאמַר הֶאָח	16bA	Also he warms himself and says: "Ah!
חַמּוֹתִי רָאִיתִי אוּר׃	16bB	I become warm, I see the glow!"

B.v.2 (Isa. 44:17)

וּשְׁאֵרִיתוֹ	17aA	And the rest of it –
לְאֵל עָשָׂה לְפִסְלוֹ	17aB	he makes into a god! Into his idol!
יִסְגָּד־לוֹ* וְיִשְׁתַּחוּ וְיִתְפַּלֵּל אֵלָיו	17bA	He worships it,[25] and bows down and prays to it,
וְיֹאמַר הַצִּילֵנִי	17bB	and says "Deliver me!
כִּי אֵלִי אָתָּה׃	17bC	For you are my god!"

<פ> <ס> – 1Q[a] – 𝔊[SA] . . . .

B.vi.1 (Isa. 44:18–19a)

לֹא יָדְעוּ וְלֹא יָבִינוּ	18aA	They do not know and they do not understand,
כִּי טַח מֵרְאוֹת עֵינֵיהֶם	18aB	for smeared[26] are their eyes so they cannot see,
מֵהַשְׂכִּיל לִבֹּתָם׃	18aC	their hearts so they cannot perceive.
וְלֹא־יָשִׁיב אֶל־לִבּוֹ	19aA	And no one reconsiders it in his heart,
וְלֹא דַעַת וְלֹא־תְבוּנָה	19aB	and there is no knowledge and no understanding,

B.vi.2 (Isa. 44:19b–c)

לֵאמֹר חֶצְיוֹ שָׂרַפְתִּי בְמוֹ־אֵשׁ	19bA	to say "Half of it I burn in the fire,
וְאַף אָפִיתִי עַל־גֶּחָלָיו לֶחֶם	19bB	and also I bake bread over its coals,
אֶצְלֶה בָשָׂר וְאֹכֵל	19bC	I grill meat and eat (it) –
וְיִתְרוֹ לְתוֹעֵבָה אֶעֱשֶׂה	19cA	should I make the rest into an abomination,
לְבוּל עֵץ אֶסְגּוֹד׃	19cB	and should I worship a block of wood?"

---

[23] See note 15.

[24] We take יאכל as an asyndetic relative phrase.

[25] With the Qere.

[26] Root טחח, cf. Koole, 294; *HAHAT*, 422; Oswalt, 183, n. 60.

B.vi.3 (Isa. 44:20)

רֹעֶה אֵפֶר	20aA	The one who heeds[27] ashes –
לֵב הוּתַל הִטָּהוּ	20aB	(his) deluded[28] heart leads him astray.
וְלֹא־יַצִּיל אֶת־נַפְשׁוֹ	20bA	So he will not deliver his soul,
וְלֹא יֹאמַר הֲלוֹא שֶׁקֶר בִּימִינִי׃	20bB	and will not say, “Is it not a lie (I have) in my right hand?”

ס <פ> – $1\mathfrak{Q}^{a}$ – $\mathfrak{G}^{SBA}$ – $\mathfrak{S}^{abe}$ ————————————

C.i.1 (Isa. 44:21)

זְכָר־אֵלֶּה יַעֲקֹב	21aA	Remember these things, O Jacob,
וְיִשְׂרָאֵל כִּי עַבְדִּי־אָתָּה	21aB	and Israel, for you are my servant!
יְצַרְתִּיךָ עֶבֶד־לִי אַתָּה	21bA	I formed you, you are a servant for me,
יִשְׂרָאֵל לֹא תִנָּשֵׁנִי׃	21bB	O Israel, you will be not forgotten[29] by me!

C.i.2 (Isa. 44:22)

מָחִיתִי כָעָב פְּשָׁעֶיךָ	22aA	I sweep away your transgressions like a cloud,
וְכֶעָנָן חַטֹּאותֶיךָ	22aB	and like a shroud your sins.
שׁוּבָה אֵלַי כִּי גְאַלְתִּיךָ׃	22bA	Return to me, for I redeem you.

{<פ>$1\mathfrak{Q}^{a}\mathfrak{G}^{SBA}\mathfrak{S}^{a}$}

C.i.3 (Isa. 44:23)

רָנּוּ שָׁמַיִם כִּי־עָשָׂה יְהוָה	23aA	Rejoice, O heavens, for the LORD makes[30] (it),
הָרִיעוּ תַּחְתִּיּוֹת אָרֶץ	23aB	shout, O lower parts of the earth!
פִּצְחוּ הָרִים רִנָּה	23aC	Break forth, O mountains into rejoicing,
יַעַר וְכָל־עֵץ בּוֹ	23aD	O forest and every tree in it!
כִּי־גָאַל יְהוָה יַעֲקֹב	23bA	For the LORD redeems Jacob,
וּבְיִשְׂרָאֵל יִתְפָּאָר׃	23bB	and in Israel he glorifies himself.

פ <ס> – $1\mathfrak{Q}^{a}$ – $4\mathfrak{Q}^{bc}$ – $\mathfrak{G}^{SBAQ}$ – $\mathfrak{S}^{ae}$ . . . .

C.ii.1 (Isa. 44:24)

כֹּה־אָמַר יְהוָה גֹּאֲלֶךָ	24aA	Thus says the LORD, your Redeemer,
וְיֹצֶרְךָ מִבָּטֶן {$\mathfrak{G}^{A}$}	24aB	and he who formed you from the womb,
אָנֹכִי יְהוָה עֹשֶׂה כֹּל	24bA	I am the LORD, he who made everything,
נֹטֶה שָׁמַיִם לְבַדִּי	24bB	who stretched out heaven alone,
רֹקַע הָאָרֶץ{$\mathfrak{G}^{S}$}מִי* אִתִּי׃	24bC	who hammered out the earth – who[31] was with me?

---

[27] The one who treats wood which may become ashes respectfully. Compare Hos. 12:2 רעה רוח ‘to heed wind’; Prov. 15:14 רעה אולת ‘to heed folly’. Similarly Oswalt, 184 (“He feeds on ashes”). The parallelism with Isa. 44:28 (responsion) counsels against the option to assume a derivation from רעה II ‘to have dealings with’.

[28] We assume an asyndetical relative clause.

[29] Cf. Barthélemy, 331-2; De Waard, 173-4; Oswalt, 186, n. 72.

[30] We opt for a concordant translation because of the intentional contrast with עשה in vv. 13bA, 13cA, 15bB, 17aB, 19cA, on the one hand, and the parallelism with יצר in v. 21bA, 24aB, as well as עשה in v. 24bA, on the other.

C.ii.2 (Isa. 44:25)

מֵפֵר֙ אֹת֣וֹת בַּדִּ֔ים	25aA	who breaks the signs of fabulists,[32]
{$\mathfrak{G}^{A}$} וְקֹסְמִ֖ים יְהוֹלֵ֑ל	25aB	and ridicules diviners,
מֵשִׁ֧יב חֲכָמִ֛ים אָח֖וֹר	25bA	who makes wise men turn backwards,
וְדַעְתָּ֥ם יְשַׂכֵּֽל׃	25bB	and makes their knowledge foolish,

C.ii.3 (Isa. 44:26)

מֵקִים֙ דְּבַ֣ר עַבְדּ֔וֹ	26aA	who confirms the word of his servant,[33]
{$\mathfrak{G}^{A}$} וַעֲצַ֥ת מַלְאָכָ֖יו יַשְׁלִ֑ים	26aB	and fulfills the counsel of his messengers,
{$\mathfrak{G}^{Q}$} הָאֹמֵ֣ר לִירוּשָׁלַ֩ם תּוּשָׁ֗ב	26bA	who says to Jerusalem, "Be inhabited!",[34]
וּלְעָרֵ֤י יְהוּדָה֙ תִּבָּנֶ֔ינָה	26bB	and to the cities of Judah: "Let them be rebuilt!" –
{$\mathfrak{G}^{A}$} וְחָרְבוֹתֶ֖יהָ אֲקוֹמֵֽם׃	26bC	yes, her ruins I will raise up again! –

C.ii.4 (Isa. 44:27)

{$\mathfrak{G}^{Q}$} הָאֹמֵ֥ר לַצּוּלָ֖ה חֳרָ֑בִי	27aA	who says to the deep: "Become dry!
{$\mathfrak{G}^{A}$} וְנַהֲרֹתַ֖יִךְ אוֹבִֽישׁ׃	27aB	Yes, your rivers I will make dry!",

C.ii.5 (Isa. 44:28)

{$\mathfrak{G}^{Q}$} הָאֹמֵ֤ר לְכ֙וֹרֶשׁ֙ רֹעִ֔י	28aA	who says to Cyrus: "My shepherd,
{$\mathfrak{G}^{A}$} וְכָל־חֶפְצִ֖י יַשְׁלִ֑ם	28aB	who will fulfill all I want,
וְלֵאמֹ֤ר לִירוּשָׁלַ֙ם֙ תִּבָּנֶ֔ה	28bA	namely, by saying to Jerusalem: "Let it be rebuilt!",
וְהֵיכָ֖ל תִּוָּסֵֽד׃	28bB	and to[35] the temple: "Let it be founded!"[36]

ס <פ> – $_{1}\mathfrak{Q}^{ab}$ – $\mathfrak{G}^{SBAQ}$ – $\mathfrak{S}^{be}$

---

[31] We read מִי אִתִּי, with the Ketiv, $1\mathfrak{Q}^{a}$, $\mathfrak{G}$, and $\mathfrak{V}$. The Qere reading is מֵאִתִּי, which is supported by $\mathfrak{C}$ and $\mathfrak{S}$. However, the מִי–questions in Isa. 40:12-14 argue in favour of the Ketiv. Cf. Barthélemy, 332-3; Oswalt, 189, n. 78.

[32] In apparent contrast with לבדי (v. 24bB) the oracle priests are designated with a name which had acquired a derogatory meaning in the language of pious Israelites, but was derived from a root the Canaanites formerly used in a positive sense for the improvising singers of their tales. Cf. J.C. de Moor, *The Seasonal Pattern in the Ugaritic Myth of Baʿlu* (AOAT, 16), Neukirchen-Vluyn 1971, 75-6; G. del Olmo Lete, J. Sanmartín, *Diccionario de la lengua ugarítica*, vol. 1, Barcelona 1996, 104.

[33] $\mathfrak{M}$ should be accepted as the most difficult reading.

[34] The jussive Hophal form has been taken as a passive of the Hiphil with the meaning of 'to be inhabited'. Cf. Koole, 313.

[35] The ל of לירושלם functions as a double-duty preposition, cf. König, *Syntax*, §319l.

[36] Adaptation of gender: the preceding feminine תבנה determined the gender of this jussive with a normally masculine subject.

6.2 Isaiah 44 – Delimitation of Cola

COLON 44:1aA:

וְעַתָּה שְׁמַע יַעֲקֹב עַבְדִּי 1aA But now, hear, O Jacob, my servant,

With: $\mathfrak{M}$ (2) – $\mathfrak{G}^{SQ}$
Discussion: $\mathfrak{S}$ lacks a division at this point.

COLON 44:1aB:

וְיִשְׂרָאֵל בָּחַרְתִּי בוֹ׃ 1aB and Israel, whom I have chosen!

With: $\mathfrak{M}$ (1) – $\mathfrak{G}^{SQ}$, major division markers in $\mathfrak{G}^{S}$ – $\mathfrak{S}^{abcde}$

COLON 44:2aA:

כֹּה־אָמַר יְהוָה עֹשֶׂךָ 2aA Thus says the LORD who made you,

With: $\mathfrak{M}$ (12) – $\mathfrak{G}^{S}$ – $\mathfrak{S}^{a}$ subordinate punctuation.
Discussion: The 'Botenformel' created problems for the Masoretes who treated it in widely diverging ways. In this case they wanted to divide after מבטן which has the support of $\mathfrak{G}^{SQ}$, but leaves only one word for the next colon. Since $\mathfrak{G}^{S}$ also has a point after עשך which is in accordance with general usage in Second Isaiah,[1] we decided to assume a caesura at this point. $\mathfrak{S}$ is divided over the point where subordinate punctuation should be inserted, but $\mathfrak{S}^{a}$ supports our choice.

COLON 44:2aB:

וְיֹצֶרְךָ מִבֶּטֶן יַעְזְרֶךָּ 2aB yes, he who formed you from the womb, who helps you:

With: $\mathfrak{M}$ (2) – $\mathfrak{G}^{SQ}$ – $\mathfrak{S}^{abcde}$

COLON 44:2bA:

אַל־תִּירָא עַבְדִּי יַעֲקֹב 2bA Do not fear, my servant Jacob,

With: $\mathfrak{M}$ (5) – $\mathfrak{G}^{SQ}$ – $\mathfrak{S}^{a}$

COLON 44:2bB:

וִישֻׁרוּן בָּחַרְתִּי בוֹ׃ 2bB and Jeshurun, whom I have chosen!

With: $\mathfrak{M}$ (1) – $\mathfrak{G}^{SQ}$ – $\mathfrak{S}^{abcde}$

[1]See our remarks p. 164, 268.

COLON 44:3aA:

כִּ֤י אֶצָּק־מַ֙יִם֙ עַל־צָמֵ֔א 3aA For I shall pour out water on the thirsty (soil),

With: $\mathfrak{M}$ (5) – $\mathfrak{G}^{Q}$ – $\mathfrak{S}^{ace}$ subordinate punctuation.
Colon parallelism: מים || צמא (antithetical).

COLON 44:3aB:

וְנֹזְלִ֖ים עַל־יַבָּשָׁ֑ה 3aB and streams on the dry (ground).

With: $\mathfrak{M}$ (2) – $\mathfrak{G}^{SQ}$ – $\mathfrak{S}^{abcde}$
Colon parallelism: נזל || יבשה (antithetical, unique).

COLON 44:3bA:

אֶצֹּ֤ק רוּחִי֙ עַל־זַרְעֶ֔ךָ 3bA I will pour out my spirit on your seed,

With: $\mathfrak{M}$ (5) – $\mathfrak{G}^{SQ}$ – $\mathfrak{S}^{de}$, $\mathfrak{S}^{a}$ subordinate punctuation.

COLON 44:3bB:

וּבִרְכָתִ֖י עַל־צֶאֱצָאֶֽיךָ׃ 3bB and my blessing on what comes forth for you.

With: $\mathfrak{M}$ (1) – $\mathfrak{G}^{S}$ – $\mathfrak{S}^{abcde}$

COLON 44:4aA:

וְצָמְח֖וּ בְּבֵ֣ין חָצִ֑יר 4aA And they will sprout amidst the grass,

With: $\mathfrak{M}$ (2) – $\mathfrak{G}^{Q}$ – $\mathfrak{S}^{be}$, $\mathfrak{S}^{acd}$ subordinate punctuation.

COLON 44:4aB:

כַּעֲרָבִ֖ים עַל־יִבְלֵי־מָֽיִם׃ 4aB like willows by watercourses.

With: $\mathfrak{M}$ (1) – $\mathfrak{G}^{SQ}$ – $\mathfrak{S}^{abcde}$

COLON 44:5aA:

זֶ֤ה יֹאמַר֙ לַֽיהוָ֣ה אָ֔נִי 5aA One person shall say, 'I am the LORD's!'

With: $\mathfrak{M}$ (5) – $\mathfrak{G}^{SQ}$ – $\mathfrak{S}^{abcde}$
Discussion: $\mathfrak{G}^{S}$ and $\mathfrak{S}^{e}$ have a point after יאמר ($\mathfrak{M}$ Pashṭa) which is obviously intended as a minor break introducing the direct oration.

COLON 44:5aB:

וְזֶ֖ה יִקְרָ֣א בְּשֵׁם־יַעֲקֹ֑ב 5aB and another will call himself by the name of Jacob;

With: $\mathfrak{M}$ (2) – $\mathfrak{G}^{SQ}$ – $\mathfrak{S}^{abcde}$

COLON 44:5bA:

וְזֶה יִכְתֹּב יָדוֹ לַיהוָה 5bA yet another will write on his hand, 'The LORD's!'

With: 𝔐 (5) – 𝔊^{SQ} – 𝔖^{abcde} all subordinate punctuation.
Discussion: For the Revia' (No. 7) with וזה see our comment on p. 31.

COLON 44:5bB:

וּבְשֵׁם יִשְׂרָאֵל יְכַנֶּה׃ 5bB and with the name of Israel he will surname himself.

With: 𝔐 (1) major division markers, also in 1𝔔^{a}– 𝔊^{SBA} all three with major division markers – 𝔖^{abcde} all with major division markers.

COLON 44:6aA:

כֹּה־אָמַר יְהוָה מֶלֶךְ־יִשְׂרָאֵל 6aA Thus says the LORD, the King of Israel,

With: 𝔐 (12).
Colon parallelism: יהוה || מלך.
Discussion: BHS and many translations and commentators assume a major break after ישראל, but none of our ancient witnesses supports this.[2] 𝔐 seems to have read on until צבאות, a colon of six stressed units. As in other occurrences of the 'Botenformel', we believe 𝔐's division to be erroneous, even though in this case none of our other witnesses supports our view. We have based our colometry on similar cases, like 44:2, 24, where the second colon is also introduced by ו, and the almost identical 43:14.

COLON 44:6aB:

וְגֹאֲלוֹ יְהוָה צְבָאוֹת 6aB and his Redeemer, the LORD of hosts:

With: 𝔐 (2) – 𝔊^{SQ} – 𝔖^{abcde}

COLON 44:6bA:

אֲנִי רִאשׁוֹן וַאֲנִי אַחֲרוֹן 6bA I am the First, and I am the Last,

With: 𝔐 (5) – 𝔊^{SQ} – 𝔖^{abcde}
Colon parallelism: אני || אני; ראשון || אחרון.

---

[2]They all divide after וגאלו. Even though the resulting length of the colon and the a-symmetrical rhythm are within the bounds of the acceptable, it would be the only case of two epithets following the 'Botenformel'.

COLON 44:6bB:

וּמִבַּלְעָדַי אֵין אֱלֹהִים׃ 6bB apart from me there is no God.

With: $\mathfrak{M}$ (1) – $\mathfrak{G}^{SAQ}$, major division markers in $\mathfrak{G}^{A}$ – $\mathfrak{S}^{acde}$

COLON 44:7aA:

וּמִי־כָמוֹנִי 7aA And who is like me?

With: $\mathfrak{G}^{SQ}$ – $\mathfrak{S}^{abcde}$
Discussion: $\mathfrak{M}$ has a conjunctive accent here (Munaḥ) and a Revia‘ with יקרא which finds partial support in $\mathfrak{G}^{Q}$ – partial, because like all other witnesses, $\mathfrak{G}^{Q}$ also has a point after כמוני.

COLON 44:7aB:

יִקְרָא וְיַגִּידֶהָ וְיַעְרְכֶהָ לִי 7aB Let him call out, tell it and lay it out for me,

With: $\mathfrak{M}$ (5) – $\mathfrak{G}^{S}$ – $\mathfrak{S}^{abcde}$
Colon parallelism: קרא || נגד, and נגד || ערך; ה־ || ה־.
Discussion: $\mathfrak{M}$ stands almost alone in assuming a break after יקרא (see our comment on v. 7aA as well as on p. 31).

COLON 44:7aC:

מִשּׂוּמִי עַם־עוֹלָם 7aC from the moment I established the people of eternity.

With: $\mathfrak{M}$ (2) – $\mathfrak{G}^{SQ}$ – $\mathfrak{S}^{acde}$, $\mathfrak{S}^{b}$ subordinate punctuation.
Colon parallelism: None.

COLON 44:7bA:

וְאֹתִיּוֹת וַאֲשֶׁר תָּבֹאנָה יַגִּידוּ לָמוֹ*׃ 7bA Also the things to come and what will happen – let them tell us!

With: $\mathfrak{M}$ (1) – $\mathfrak{G}^{SQ}$ – $\mathfrak{S}^{abcde}$
Colon parallelism: אתה || בוא.
Discussion: None of the ancient versions supports a division after תבאנה. The colon parallelism argues against taking ואתיות with the preceding colon.

COLON 44:8aA:

אַל־תִּפְחֲדוּ וְאַל־תִּרְהוּ 8aA Do not quiver and do not be afraid!

With: $\mathfrak{M}$ (5) – $\mathfrak{G}^{SQ}$ – $\mathfrak{S}^{abcde}$
Colon parallelism: אל || אל; פחד || רהה (unique).

COLON 44:8aB:

הֲלֹ֥א מֵאָ֛ז הִשְׁמַעְתִּ֥יךָ וְהִגַּ֖דְתִּי 8aB Have I not made you hear (it) from then on,
and have I not told you?

With: 𝔐 (8) – 𝔊^{SAQ}, major division markers in 𝔊^{SA} – 𝔖^{acde} all subordinate punctuation.
Colon parallelism: שמע || נגד.
Discussion: Only 𝔊^{S} and 𝔖^{e} have an extra point after השמעתיך where 𝔐 has a conjunctive accent. Possibly the Masoretes wanted to read on until עדי.

COLON 44:8aC:

וְאַתֶּ֣ם עֵדָ֑י 8aC Yes, you are my witnesses!

With: 𝔐 (2) – 𝔊^{SQ}, major division marker in 𝔊^{Q} – 𝔖^{bde}

COLON 44:8bA:

הֲיֵ֤שׁ אֱל֙וֹהַּ֙ מִבַּלְעָדַ֔י 8bA Is there a God apart from me?

With: 𝔐 (5) – 𝔊^{SBQ}, major division markers in 𝔊^{B} – 𝔖^{b}, subordinate punctuation in 𝔖^{acde}

COLON 44:8bB:

וְאֵ֥ין צ֖וּר בַּל־יָדָֽעְתִּי׃ 8bB 'No, there is no Rock; I know of none.'

With: 𝔐 (1), major division marker in 1Q^{a} – 𝔊^{SQ} – 𝔖^{abde}
Colon parallelism: אין || בל.

COLON 44:9aA:

יֹֽצְרֵי־פֶ֤סֶל כֻּלָּם֙ תֹּ֔הוּ 9aA Those who form idols – all of them are void,

With: 𝔐 (5) – 𝔊^{Q} – 𝔖^{abcd}

COLON 44:9aB:

וַחֲמוּדֵיהֶ֖ם בַּל־יוֹעִ֑ילוּ 9aB their cherished ones do not profit,

With: 𝔐 (2) – 𝔊^{SQ}, major division marker in 𝔊^{S} – 𝔖^{abcde}
Discussion: 𝔊^{S} and 𝔊^{Q} have an extra point, corresponding to 𝔐's Ṭiphḥa, after וחמודים. 𝔖 does not support this.

COLON 44:9bA:

וְעֵדֵיהֶ֣ם הֵ֗מָּה 9bA Yet they are their witnesses,

With: 𝔐 (7) – 𝔖^{be}

Discussion: Because 𝔊 is lacking at this point, the support 𝔖[be] lend to 𝔐's Revia' is important. Contrary to the currently prevailing opinion, we believe the witnesses to be the idols who do not see and know nothing (cf. Ps. 115:4-7; 135:15-18; see also our emendation for v. 11aB) and therefore will be useless as witnesses. As a result their worshippers will be shamed (vv. 9bC, 11bB). They themselves are just as blind and ignorant as their idols (v. 18a).

COLON 44:9bB:

בַּל־יִרְאוּ וּבַל־יֵדְעוּ 9bB (though) they do not see and they do not know,

With: 𝔐 (8) – 𝔖[abcde]
Colon parallelism: בל || בל; ראה || ידע.
Discussion: 𝔊 is lacking here, but the testimony of 𝔖 is strong enough to assume a break at this point, against 𝔐.

COLON 44:9bC:

לְמַעַן יֵבֹשׁוּ׃ 9bC so that they will be put to shame.

With: 𝔐 (1).
Discussion: Neither 𝔊 nor 𝔖 has a divider at the end of this verse. 𝔖 follows 𝔊 in taking מי as a relative pronoun because in this way it becomes clearer that the worshippers are the subject of יבשו. 𝔗 and 𝔙 support 𝔐 and we accept this tradition because a relative function of מי is unlikely.

COLON 44:10aA:

מִי־יָצַר אֵל וּפֶסֶל נָסָךְ 10aA Who forms a god and casts an idol

With: 𝔐 (2).
Colon parallelism: אל || פסל; יצר || נסך (unique).
Discussion: 𝔊[SQ] have a dividing point and 𝔖 subordinate punctuation after אל which is a consequence of their decision to take the last word of v. 9 with v. 10 (see above).

COLON 44:10aB:

לְבִלְתִּי הוֹעִיל׃ 10aB which does not profit?

With: 𝔐 (1) – 𝔊[SQ] – 𝔖[acde]

COLON 44:11aA:

הֵן כָּל־חֲבֵרָיו יֵבֹשׁוּ 11aA Behold, all its friends will be put to shame,

With: 𝔐 (5) – 𝔊[SQ]
Discussion: 𝔖 is lacking here.

COLON 44:11aB:

וְחָרָשִׁים* הֵמָּה מֵאָדָם 11aB for they are more deaf then a human being!

With: 𝔐 (2) – $\mathfrak{G}^{SAQ}$, major division markers in $\mathfrak{G}^{SA}$ – $\mathfrak{s}^{abcde}$

COLON 44:11bA:

יִתְקַבְּצוּ כֻלָּם֙ יַעֲמֹ֔דוּ 11bA Let them all gather, stand there,

With: 𝔐 (5) – $\mathfrak{G}^{SQ}$ – $\mathfrak{s}^{abcde}$
Colon parallelism: קבץ Hitpa. || עמד (unique).

COLON 44:11bB:

יִפְחֲדוּ יֵבֹשׁוּ יָחַד׃ 11bB let them quiver, altogether be put to shame.

With: 𝔐 (1), Setuma in 1𝔔^{a} – $\mathfrak{G}^{SQ}$ – $\mathfrak{s}^{abcde}$
Colon parallelism: פחד || בוש (unique).

COLON 44:12aA:

חָרַשׁ בַּרְזֶל מַעֲצָ֔ד 12aA The craftsman of the iron of the adze –

With: 𝔐 (5) – $\mathfrak{G}^{SQ}$ – $\mathfrak{s}^{abcde}$ all subordinate punctuation.

COLON 44:12aB:

וּפָעַל֙ בַּפֶּחָ֔ם 12aB he also works (it) in the coalfire,

With: 𝔐 (5) – $\mathfrak{G}^{Q}$ – $\mathfrak{s}^{abe}$

COLON 44:12aC:

וּבַמַּקָּבוֹת יִצְּרֵהוּ 12aC and forms it with hammers,

With: 𝔐 (2) – $\mathfrak{G}^{SQ}$ – $\mathfrak{s}^{abcde}$

COLON 44:12bA:

וַיִּפְעָלֵהוּ֙ בִּזְר֣וֹעַ כֹּח֔וֹ 12bA And (while) he works it with his strong arm.

With: 𝔐 (5) – $\mathfrak{G}^{SQ}$ – $\mathfrak{s}^{abcde}$

COLON 44:12bB:

גַּם־רָעֵב֙ וְאֵ֣ין כֹּ֔חַ 12bB he also becomes hungry, so there is no strength anymore,

With: 𝔐 (5) – $\mathfrak{G}^{S}$ – $\mathfrak{s}^{abcde}$

COLON 44:12bC:

לֹא־שָׁתָה מַיִם 12bC he has drunk no water, so he grows weary.

With: 𝔐 (1), Setuma in 1Q^{a} – S^{abcd}, S^{e} subordinate punctuation.
Discussion: 𝔊^{S} and 𝔊^{Q} put a point after מים where 𝔐 has a Ṭiphḥa. 𝔊^{A} even has major dividing marks at this point. But since 𝔊 simply omits וייעף this is not a substantial difference with S which supports the Masoretic tradition.

COLON 44:13aA:

חָרַשׁ עֵצִים נָטָה קָו 13aA The woodworker stretches a line tight,

With: 𝔐 (3) – 𝔊^{SQ} – S^{abcde}

COLON 44:13bA:

יְתָאֲרֵהוּ בַשֶּׂרֶד 13bA and he outlines it with a stylus,

With: 𝔐 (5) – 𝔊^{Q}, major division marker in 𝔊^{S} but the rest of v. 13b is lacking.
Discussion: V. 13b is lacking in S.

COLON 44:13bB:

יַעֲשֵׂהוּ בַּמַּקְצֻעוֹת 13bB he makes it with chisels,

With: 𝔐 (5)
Discussion: 𝔊 and S are both lacking at this point.

COLON 44:13bC:

וּבַמְּחוּגָה יְתָאֳרֵהוּ 13bC and with a pair of compasses he outlines it.

With: 𝔐 (2)
Discussion: 𝔊 and S are both lacking at this point.

COLON 44:13cA:

וַיַּעֲשֵׂהוּ כְּתַבְנִית אִישׁ 13cA Thus he makes it (into something) like a shapely man,

With: 𝔐 (5) – 𝔊^{SQ} – S^{be}, S^{ac} subordinate punctuation.

COLON 44:13cB:

כְּתִפְאֶרֶת אָדָם לָשֶׁבֶת בָּיִת׃ 13cB like a glorious human being, to dwell in a house.

With: 𝔐 (1) – 𝔊^{Q} – S^{e}

Discussion: The support for 𝔐's division is rather weak, but sufficient in view of the difficulty of the text.

COLON 44:14aA:

לִכְרָת־לוֹ אֲרָזִים 14aA To cut for himself cedars

With: 𝔐 (5).
Discussion: 𝔊 and 𝔖 are both lacking.

COLON 44:14aB:

וַיִּקַּח תִּרְזָה וְאַלּוֹן 14aB he takes a stone pine or an oak,

With: 𝔐 (5).
Discussion: 𝔊 and 𝔖 are both lacking.

COLON 44:14aC:

וַיְאַמֶּץ־לוֹ בַּעֲצֵי־יָעַר 14aC and makes it for himself the strongest among the trees in the forest,

With: 𝔐 (2) – 𝔊^{SQ} – 𝔖^{abcde}, all subordinate punctuation.

COLON 44:14bA:

נָטַע אֹרֶן 14bA he plants a laurel,

With: 𝔐 (8) – 𝔊^{SQ}
Discussion: 𝔐 and 𝔖 probably wanted to read a unicolon. But the deliberate change of subject contrasting the busy work of the arborist with the God-given rain which he is unable to manipulate clearly supports 𝔊.

COLON 44:14bB:

וְגֶשֶׁם יְגַדֵּל׃ 14bB and showers make (it) grow.

With: 𝔐 (1) – 𝔊^{SQ} – 𝔖^{e}
Discussion: As in other cases, 𝔖^{e} is the only manuscript which supports 𝔐. The other 𝔖 manuscripts have no divider at the end of the verse.

COLON 44:15aA:

וְהָיָה לְאָדָם לְבָעֵר 15aA And it will serve a human being for fuel,

With: 𝔐 (5) – 𝔊^{SQ} – 𝔖^{abcde}

COLON 44:15aB:

וַיִּקַּח מֵהֶם֙ וַיָּחָם 15aB so he takes of it and warms himself,

With: $\mathfrak{M}$ (5) – $\mathfrak{G}^{SQ}$

COLON 44:15aC:

אַף־יַשִּׂ֥יק וְאָ֣פָה לָ֑חֶם 15aC also he kindles it to bake bread.

With: $\mathfrak{M}$ (2) – $\mathfrak{G}^{SQ}$ – $\mathfrak{S}^{abcde}$

COLON 44:15bA:

אַף־יִפְעַל־אֵל֙ וַיִּשְׁתָּ֔חוּ 15bA Also he works (it) into a god and bows down,

With: $\mathfrak{M}$ (5) – $\mathfrak{G}^{SQ}$ – $\mathfrak{S}^{abcde}$

COLON 44:15bB:

עָשָׂ֥הוּ פֶ֖סֶל וַיִּסְגָּד־לָֽמוֹ׃ 15bB he makes an idol and worships it.

With: $\mathfrak{M}$ (1) – $\mathfrak{G}$ absent, but major division markers in $\mathfrak{G}^{A}$ – $\mathfrak{S}^{abcde}$

COLON 44:16aA:

חֶצְיוֹ֙ שָׂרַ֣ף בְּמוֹ־אֵ֔שׁ 16aA Half of it he burns in the fire,

With: $\mathfrak{M}$ (5) – $\mathfrak{G}^{SQ}$ – $\mathfrak{S}^{abcde}$, all subordinate punctuation.

COLON 44:16aB:

עַל־חֶצְיוֹ֙ בָּשָׂ֣ר יֹאכֵ֔ל 16aB and over half of it meat which he wants to eat

With: $\mathfrak{M}$ (5) – $\mathfrak{G}^{SQ}$ – $\mathfrak{S}^{abcde}$

COLON 44:16aC:

יִצְלֶ֥ה צָלִ֖י וְיִשְׂבָּ֑ע 16aC he roasts as a roast and becomes satisfied.

With: $\mathfrak{M}$ (2) – $\mathfrak{G}^{SQ}$ – $\mathfrak{S}^{acde}$ subordinate punctuation.

COLON 44:16bA:

אַף־יָחֹם֙ וְיֹאמַ֣ר הֶאָ֔ח 16bA Also he warms himself and says: "Ah!

With: $\mathfrak{M}$ (5) – $\mathfrak{G}^{S}$ – $\mathfrak{S}^{bcde}$, $\mathfrak{S}^{a}$ subordinate punctuation.
Discussion: $\mathfrak{S}^{abcde}$ and perhaps $\mathfrak{G}^{S}$ have an extra point after אף־יחם where $\mathfrak{M}$ has a Pashṭa. Probably this was caused by the introduction of direct speech that follows.

COLON 44:16bB:

חַמּוֹתִי רָאִיתִי אוּר׃ 16bB I become warm, I see the glow!"

With: 𝔐 (1) – 𝔊^{SQ} – 𝔖^{abcde}

COLON 44:17aA:

וּשְׁאֵרִיתוֹ 17aA And the rest of it –

With: 𝔐 (5).
Discussion: None of the ancient witnesses supports 𝔐. Yet we believe it to be right. The syntactical order Object – Prepositional Adjunct – Verb – Prepositional Adjunct indicates a small dramatic pause after the first word. Cola of only one stressed unit are rare, but not impossible.[3] However, it is also possible to interpret the Zaqeph Qaṭon on the analogy of other similar cases involving a *casus pendens*,[4] so that a bicolon instead of a tricolon would be the result.

COLON 44:17aB:

לְאֵל עָשָׂה לְפִסְלוֹ 17aB he makes into a god! Into his idol!

With: 𝔐 (2) – 𝔊^{SQ} – 𝔖^{bce}, 𝔖^{d} subordinate punctuation.
Colon parallelism: אל (god) || פסל (see v. 10aA above).

COLON 44:17bA:

יִסְגָּד־לוֹ* וְיִשְׁתַּחוּ וְיִתְפַּלֵּל אֵלָיו 17bA He worships it, and bows down and prays to it,

With: 𝔐 (5) – 𝔖^{abcde}
Colon parallelism: סגד || שחה; פלל || שחה.
Discussion: 𝔊^{S} and 𝔖^{be} have an extra point after יסגד־לו where 𝔐 has a conjunctive accent. Both 𝔊^{S} and 𝔊^{Q} have another dividing point after ויאמר which is not supported by 𝔐 and 𝔖. In our opinion the colon parallelism argues in favour of 𝔐 and the majority of 𝔖-manuscripts. It is noteworthy that not one of the ancient witnesses supports the colometry adopted in most modern editions and translations which are apparently based on biased opinions about metrical regularity.

---

[3]Cf. M.C.A. Korpel, J.C. de Moor, "Fundamentals of Ugaritic and Hebrew Poetry", in: W. van der Meer, J.C. de Moor (eds.), *The Structural Analysis of Biblical and Canaanite Poetry*, Sheffield 1988, 1-61 (7-9); J.C. de Moor, "Micah 1: A Structural Approach", *ibid.*, 172-85 (178, n. 13); M.C.A. Korpel, "The Poetic Structure of the Priestly Blessing", *JSOT* 45 (1989), 3-13. See also p. 638.

[4]See our comment on p. 31.

COLON 44:17bB:

וַיֹּאמַר֙ הַצִּילֵ֔נִי 17bB and says "Deliver me!

With: $\mathfrak{M}$ (5) – $\mathfrak{G}^{SQ}$ – S^{abcde}

COLON 44:17bC:

כִּ֥י אֵלִ֖י אָֽתָּה׃ 17bC For you are my god!"

With: $\mathfrak{M}$ (1), Setuma in $1\mathfrak{Q}^{a}$, BH^{2}, Petuḥa in Biblia Rabbinica – $\mathfrak{G}^{SAQ}$, major division markers in $\mathfrak{G}^{S}$ and $\mathfrak{G}^{Q}$ – S^{abcde}

COLON 44:18aA:

לֹ֥א יָדְע֖וּ וְלֹ֣א יָבִ֑ינוּ 18aA They do not know and they do not understand,

With: $\mathfrak{M}$ (2) – $\mathfrak{G}^{SQ}$ – S^{acde}, S^{b} subordinate punctuation.
Colon parallelism: ידע || בין.

COLON 44:18aB:

כִּ֣י טַ֤ח מֵֽרְאוֹת֙ עֵֽינֵיהֶ֔ם 18aB for smeared are their eyes so they cannot see,

With: $\mathfrak{M}$ (5) – $\mathfrak{G}^{SQ}$ – S^{e}
Discussion: Support for $\mathfrak{M}$ is weak, but sufficient.

COLON 44:18aC:

מֵהַשְׂכִּ֖יל לִבֹּתָֽם׃ 18aC their hearts so they cannot perceive.

With: $\mathfrak{M}$ (1) – $\mathfrak{G}^{SQ}$ – S^{abcde}

COLON 44:19aA:

וְלֹֽא־יָשִׁ֣יב אֶל־לִבּ֗וֹ 19aA And no one reconsiders it in his heart,

With: $\mathfrak{M}$ (7) – $\mathfrak{G}^{SQ}$ – S^{abcde}

COLON 44:19aB:

וְלֹ֨א דַ֤עַת וְלֹֽא־תְבוּנָה֙ 19aB and there is no knowledge and no understanding,

With: $\mathfrak{M}$ (9) – $\mathfrak{G}^{SQ}$ – S^{e}
Colon parallelism: דעת || תבונה; לא || לא.
Discussion: $\mathfrak{G}^{S}$ and $\mathfrak{G}^{Q}$ have an extra point after דעת which is not supported by S. The same manuscripts plus S^{e} have an extra point after ולא־תבונה which contradicts $\mathfrak{M}$'s division (Segolta [3] with לאמר). Because it is typical of Second Isaiah's style to place לאמר at the

beginning of a colon[5] we choose to follow these ancient witnesses in contrast to 𝔐.

COLON 44:19bA:

לֵאמֹר חֶצְיוֹ שָׂרַפְתִּי בְמוֹ־אֵשׁ 19bA to say "Half of it I burn in the fire,

With: 𝔐 (7) – 𝔊^{SQ} – 𝔖^{e}, 𝔖^{abcd} subordinate punctuation.
Discussion: Although לאמר has been provided by a Segolta (No. 3) this is hardly meant to be a major divider here. See our comment on the preceding colon.

COLON 44:19bB:

וְאַף אָפִיתִי עַל־גֶּחָלָיו לֶחֶם 19bB and also I bake bread over its coals,

With: 𝔐 (5) – 𝔊^{SQ} – 𝔖^{abcde} all subordinate punctuation.

COLON 44:19bC:

אֶצְלֶה בָשָׂר וְאֹכֵל 19bC I grill meat and eat (it) –

With: 𝔐 (2) – 𝔊^{SQ} – 𝔖^{ace}, 𝔖^{bd} subordinate punctuation.
Colon parallelism: צלה || אכל.

COLON 44:19cA:

וְיִתְרוֹ לְתוֹעֵבָה אֶעֱשֶׂה 19cA should I make the rest into an abomination,

With: 𝔐 (2) – 𝔊^{SQ}
Discussion: It is remarkable that none of the 𝔖 manuscripts has a dividing point here.

COLON 44:19cB:

לְבוּל עֵץ אֶסְגּוֹד׃ 19cB and should I worship a block of wood?"

With: 𝔐 (1) – 𝔊^{SQ} – 𝔖^{abcde}

COLON 44:20aA:

רֹעֶה אֵפֶר 20aA The one who heeds ashes –

With: 𝔐 (5).
Discussion: Even though none of the ancient versions supports 𝔐 we accept its division because the rather difficult syntax forced the ancient translators to adopt free renderings. This is also the reason why 𝔊^{Q} and 𝔖^{bcde} have a dividing point after לב (𝔐 conjunctive accent).

[5] Isa. 44:28; 49:9; 51:16.

COLON 44:20aB:

לֵב הוּתַל הִטָּהוּ 20aB (his) deluded heart leads him astray.

With: 𝔐 (2) – $𝔊^{S}$ – $𝔖^{a}$
Colon parallelism: תלל Hoph. || נטה Hiph. (unique).
Discussion: 𝔐 has the support of our most ancient witnesses.

COLON 44:20bA:

וְלֹא־יַצִּיל אֶת־נַפְשׁוֹ 20bA So he will not deliver his soul,

With: 𝔐 (10) – $𝔊^{SQ}$ – $𝔖^{abcde}$
Discussion: Obviously 𝔐 did not intend the Pashṭa (10) as a major divider. 𝔐 wanted to divide after יאמר. However, all ancient versions agree in taking ולא יאמר as the beginning of the next colon. This would seem the preferable solution because the imperfect of אמר is very often at the head of a new colon.[6]

COLON 44:20bB:

וְלֹא יֹאמַר הֲלוֹא שֶׁקֶר בִּימִינִי׃ 20bB and will not say, "Is it not a lie (I have) in my right hand?"

With: 𝔐 (1), major division markers, Petuḥa in $1𝔔^{a}$ – $𝔊^{SBAQ}$, major division markers in $𝔊^{SBA}$ – $𝔖^{abcde}$, major division markers in $𝔖^{abe}$

COLON 44:21aA:

זְכָר־אֵלֶּה יַעֲקֹב 21aA Remember these things, O Jacob,

With: 𝔐 (5) – $𝔖^{abcde}$ all subordinate punctuation.
Discussion: The support for 𝔐 is weak, but a different colometry is hard to imagine.

COLON 44:21aB:

וְיִשְׂרָאֵל כִּי עַבְדִּי־אָתָּה 21aB and Israel, for you are my servant!

With: 𝔐 (2) – $𝔊^{SQ}$ – $𝔖^{abcde}$

COLON 44:21bA:

יְצַרְתִּיךָ עֶבֶד־לִי אַתָּה 21bA I formed you, you are a servant for me,

With: 𝔐 (5) – $𝔖^{abe}$
Colon parallelism: ךָ־ || אתה.

[6]Isa. 40:1, 25; 41:21 (twice); 44:5, 17; 45:9; 48:5, 7; 49:20.

Discussion: Even though 𝔖 shortens the colon a little, it seems to support 𝔐. $\mathfrak{G}^{S}$ and $\mathfrak{G}^{Q}$ take אתה with the next colon which destroys the nice strophe parallelism between v. 21aB and v. 21bA.

COLON 44:21bB:

יִשְׂרָאֵל לֹא תִנָּשֵׁנִי׃ 21bB O Israel, you will be not forgotten by me!

With: 𝔐 (1) – $\mathfrak{G}^{S}$ – $\mathfrak{S}^{abcde}$

COLON 44:22aA:

מָחִיתִי כָעָב פְּשָׁעֶיךָ 22aA I sweep away your transgressions like a cloud,

With: 𝔐 (5) – $\mathfrak{G}^{SQ}$ – $\mathfrak{S}^{abcde}$

COLON 44:22aB:

וְכֶעָנָן חַטֹּאותֶיךָ 22aB and like a shroud your sins.

With: 𝔐 (2) – $\mathfrak{G}^{SQ}$ – $\mathfrak{S}^{abcde}$

COLON 44:22bA:

שׁוּבָה אֵלַי כִּי גְאַלְתִּיךָ׃ 22bA Return to me, for I redeem you.

With: 𝔐 (1) – $\mathfrak{G}^{SBAQ}$, major division markers in $\mathfrak{G}^{SBA}$ – $\mathfrak{S}^{abcde}$, major division marker in $\mathfrak{S}^{a}$

COLON 44:23aA:

רָנּוּ שָׁמַיִם כִּי־עָשָׂה יְהוָה 23aA Rejoice, O heavens, for the LORD makes (it),

With: 𝔐 (7) – $\mathfrak{G}^{SQ}$ – $\mathfrak{S}^{abcde}$
Discussion: $\mathfrak{G}^{SQ}$ have an extra point after שמים before ὅτι, as is normal in Greek.

COLON 44:23aB:

הָרִיעוּ תַּחְתִּיּוֹת אָרֶץ 23aB shout, O lower parts of the earth!

With: 𝔐 (5) – $\mathfrak{G}^{SQ}$ – $\mathfrak{S}^{abcde}$

COLON 44:23aC:

פִּצְחוּ הָרִים רִנָּה 23aC Break forth, O mountains into rejoicing,

With: 𝔐 (5) – $\mathfrak{G}^{SQ}$ – $\mathfrak{S}^{abcde}$

COLON 44:23aD:

יַ֖עַר וְכָל־עֵ֣ץ בּ֑וֹ 23aD O forest and every tree in it!

With: $\mathfrak{M}$ (2) – $\mathfrak{G}^{SQ}$ – $\mathfrak{S}^{abcde}$
Colon parallelism: יער || עץ.

COLON 44:23bA:

כִּֽי־גָאַ֤ל יְהוָה֙ יַֽעֲקֹ֔ב 23bA For the LORD redeems Jacob,

With: $\mathfrak{M}$ (5) – $\mathfrak{G}^{SQ}$ – $\mathfrak{S}^{e}$

COLON 44:23bB:

וּבְיִשְׂרָאֵ֖ל יִתְפָּאָֽר׃ 23bB and in Israel he glorifies himself.

With: $\mathfrak{M}$ (1), major division markers, also in 1$\mathfrak{Q}^{a}$ and 4$\mathfrak{Q}^{bc}$ – $\mathfrak{G}^{SBAQ}$, major division markers in all of them – $\mathfrak{S}^{abcde}$, major division markers in $\mathfrak{S}^{ae}$

COLON 44:24aA:

כֹּֽה־אָמַ֤ר יְהוָה֙ גֹּֽאֲלֶ֔ךָ 24aA Thus says the LORD, your Redeemer,

With: $\mathfrak{M}$ (5) – $\mathfrak{G}^{SQ}$
Colon parallelism: יהוה || גאל.
Discussion: Despite the fact that $\mathfrak{S}$ does not support $\mathfrak{M}$ we decided to accept the latter's colometry.[7]

COLON 44:24aB:

וְיֹצֶרְךָ֖ מִבָּ֑טֶן 24aB and he who formed you from the womb,

With: $\mathfrak{M}$ (2) – $\mathfrak{G}^{SAQ}$, major division markers in $\mathfrak{G}^{A}$ – $\mathfrak{S}^{abcde}$

COLON 44:24bA:

אָנֹכִ֤י יְהוָה֙ עֹ֣שֶׂה כֹּ֔ל 24bA I am the LORD, he who made everything,

With: $\mathfrak{M}$ (5) – $\mathfrak{G}^{SQ}$ – $\mathfrak{S}^{abcde}$

COLON 44:24bB:

נֹטֶ֤ה שָׁמַ֙יִם֙ לְבַדִּ֔י 24bB who stretched out heaven alone,

With: $\mathfrak{M}$ (5) – $\mathfrak{G}^{SQ}$ – $\mathfrak{S}^{abcde}$

[7] See our comments on pp. 164, 268.

COLON 44:24bC:

רֹקַ֥ע הָאָ֖רֶץ מִ֥י* אִתִּֽי׃ 24bC who hammered out the earth – who was with me?

With: $\mathfrak{M}$ (1) – $\mathfrak{S}^{abcde}$
Discussion: $\mathfrak{G}$ ends the verse after הארץ and connects מי אתי with the next. This division is less likely because all the following verses start with a participle.

COLON 44:25aA:

מֵפֵר֙ אֹת֣וֹת בַּדִּ֔ים 25aA who breaks the signs of fabulists,

With: $\mathfrak{M}$ (5) – $\mathfrak{G}^{SQ}$ – $\mathfrak{S}^{acde}$ all subordinate punctuation.

COLON 44:25aB:

וְקֹסְמִ֖ים יְהוֹלֵ֑ל 25aB and ridicules diviners,

With: $\mathfrak{M}$ (2) – $\mathfrak{G}^{SAQ}$, major division markers in $\mathfrak{G}^{A}$ – $\mathfrak{S}^{abcde}$

COLON 44:25bA:

מֵשִׁ֧יב חֲכָמִ֛ים אָח֖וֹר 25bA who makes wise men turn backwards,

With: $\mathfrak{M}$ (8) – $\mathfrak{G}^{SQ}$ – $\mathfrak{S}^{a}$, $\mathfrak{S}^{bcde}$ subordinate punctuation.

COLON 44:25bB:

וְדַעְתָּ֥ם יְשַׂכֵּֽל׃ 25bB and makes their knowledge foolish,

With: $\mathfrak{M}$ (1) – $\mathfrak{G}^{SQ}$ – $\mathfrak{S}^{abcde}$

COLON 44:26aA:

מֵקִים֙ דְּבַ֣ר עַבְדּ֔וֹ 26aA who confirms the word of his servant,

With: $\mathfrak{M}$ (5) – $\mathfrak{G}^{SQ}$ – $\mathfrak{S}^{bcde}$, $\mathfrak{S}^{a}$ subordinate punctuation.

COLON 44:26aB:

וַעֲצַ֥ת מַלְאָכָ֖יו יַשְׁלִ֑ים 26aB and fulfills the counsel of his messengers,

With: $\mathfrak{M}$ (2) – $\mathfrak{G}^{SAQ}$, major division markers in $\mathfrak{G}^{A}$ – $\mathfrak{S}^{abcde}$

COLON 44:26bA:

הָאֹמֵ֨ר לִירוּשָׁלַ֜͏ִם תּוּשָׁ֗ב 26bA who says to Jerusalem, "Be inhabited!",

With: $\mathfrak{M}$ (7) – $\mathfrak{G}^{SQ}$, major division mark in $\mathfrak{G}^{Q}$ – $\mathfrak{S}^{bd}$, $\mathfrak{S}^{ace}$ subordinate punctuation.

COLON 44:26bB:

וּלְעָרֵי יְהוּדָה תִּבָּנֶינָה 26bB and to the cities of Judah: "Let them be rebuilt!" –

With: 𝔐 (5) – $\mathfrak{G}^{SQ}$ – $\mathfrak{S}^{abcde}$

COLON 44:26bC:

וְחָרְבוֹתֶיהָ אֲקוֹמֵם׃ 26bC yes, her ruins I will raise up again! –

With: 𝔐 (1) – $\mathfrak{G}^{SAQ}$, major division markers in $\mathfrak{G}^{A}$ – $\mathfrak{S}^{abcde}$

COLON 44:27aA:

הָאֹמֵר לַצּוּלָה חֳרָבִי 27aA who says to the deep: "Become dry!

With: 𝔐 (2) – $\mathfrak{G}^{SQ}$, major division mark in $\mathfrak{G}^{Q}$ – $\mathfrak{S}^{bce}$, $\mathfrak{S}^{a}$ subordinate punctuation.

COLON 44:27aB:

וְנַהֲרֹתַיִךְ אוֹבִישׁ׃ 27aB Yes, your rivers I will make dry!",

With: 𝔐 (1) – $\mathfrak{G}^{SAQ}$, major division markers in $\mathfrak{G}^{A}$ – $\mathfrak{S}^{abcde}$

COLON 44:28aA:

הָאֹמֵר לְכוֹרֶשׁ רֹעִי 28aA who says to Cyrus: "My shepherd,

With: 𝔐 (5) – $\mathfrak{G}^{SQ}$, major division marker in $\mathfrak{G}^{Q}$ – $\mathfrak{S}^{bcde}$, $\mathfrak{S}^{a}$ subordinate punctuation.

COLON 44:28aB:

וְכָל־חֶפְצִי יַשְׁלִם 28aB who will fulfill all I want,

With: 𝔐 (2) – $\mathfrak{G}^{SAQ}$, major division markers in $\mathfrak{G}^{A}$ – $\mathfrak{S}^{abcde}$

COLON 44:28bA:

וְלֵאמֹר לִירוּשָׁלַםִ תִּבָּנֶה 28bA namely, by saying to Jerusalem: "Let it be rebuilt!",

With: 𝔐 (5) – $\mathfrak{G}^{SQ}$ – $\mathfrak{S}^{abce}$ subordinate punctuation.

COLON 44:28bB:

וְהֵיכָל תִּוָּסֵד׃ 28bB and to the temple: "Let it be founded!"

With: 𝔐 (1), major division markers, also in 1$\mathfrak{Q}^{a}$ and 1$\mathfrak{Q}^{b}$ – $\mathfrak{G}^{SBAQ}$, all with major division markers – $\mathfrak{S}^{abcde}$, major division markers in $\mathfrak{S}^{be}$

6.3 Isaiah 44 – Delimitation of Verse-lines

Verse–line: 44:1a:

וְעַתָּ֥ה שְׁמַ֖ע יַעֲקֹ֣ב עַבְדִּ֑י	1aA	But now, hear, O Jacob, my servant,
וְיִשְׂרָאֵ֖ל בָּחַ֥רְתִּי בֽוֹ׃	1aB	and Israel, whom I have chosen!

𝔐 distinctive accents: 2 – 1.
Stresses: 4 + 3.
Verse-line parallelism: יעקב || ישׂראל; עבד || בחר.
Discussion: The cola are connected by ellipsis.

Verse–line: 44:2a:

כֹּֽה־אָמַ֨ר יְהוָ֥ה עֹשֶׂ֛ךָ	2aA	Thus says the Lord who made you,
וְיֹצֶרְךָ֥ מִבֶּ֖טֶן יַעְזְרֶ֑ךָּ	2aB	yes, he who formed you from the womb, who helps you:

𝔐 distinctive accents: 12 – 2.
Stresses: 3 + 3.
Verse-line parallelism: עשׂה || יצר; ־ך || ־ך. rhyme.
Discussion: In addition to the parallelism the ellipsis forms a bond between the cola. See with regard to the delimitation of cola p. 212.

Verse–line: 44:2b:

אַל־תִּירָא֙ עַבְדִּ֣י יַעֲקֹ֔ב	2bA	Do not fear, my servant Jacob,
וִישֻׁר֖וּן בָּחַ֥רְתִּי בֽוֹ׃	2bB	and Jeshurun, whom I have chosen!

𝔐 distinctive accents: 5 – 1.
Stresses: 3 + 3.
Verse-line parallelism: עבד || בחר; יעקב || ישׁרון (unique).
Discussion: Ellipsis.

Verse–line: 44:3a:

כִּ֤י אֶצָּק־מַ֙יִם֙ עַל־צָמֵ֔א	3aA	For I shall pour out water on the thirsty (soil),
וְנֹזְלִ֖ים עַל־יַבָּשָׁ֑ה	3aB	and streams on the dry (ground).

𝔐 distinctive accents: 5 – 2.
Stresses: 3 + 2.
Verse-line parallelism: מים || נזל; על || על; צמא || יבשׁה (unique).
Discussion: Ellipsis connects the cola.

Verse–line: 44:3b:

אֶצֹּ֤ק רוּחִי֙ עַל־זַרְעֶ֔ךָ	3bA	I will pour out my spirit on your seed,

וּבִרְכָתִ֖י עַל־צֶאֱצָאֶֽיךָ׃	3bB	and my blessing on what comes forth for you.

𝔐 distinctive accents: 5 – 1.
Stresses: 3 + 2.
Verse-line parallelism: רוח || ברכה (unique); זרע || צאצא; ־ך || ־ך; rhyme.
Discussion: Ellipsis.

VERSE–LINE: 44:4a:

וְצָמְח֖וּ בְּבֵ֣ין חָצִ֑יר	4aA	And they will sprout amidst the grass,
כַּעֲרָבִ֖ים עַל־יִבְלֵי־מָֽיִם׃	4aB	like willows by watercourses.

𝔐 distinctive accents: 2 – 1.
Stresses: 3 + 2.
Verse-line parallelism: None.
Discussion: The sentence runs on through the two cola.

VERSE–LINE: 44:5a:

זֶ֤ה יֹאמַר֙ לַיהוָ֣ה אָ֔נִי	5aA	One person shall say, 'I am the LORD's!'
וְזֶ֖ה יִקְרָ֣א בְשֵׁם־יַעֲקֹ֑ב	5aB	and another will call himself by the name of Jacob;

𝔐 distinctive accents: 5 – 2.
Stresses: 4 + 3.
Verse-line parallelism: זה || זה; אמר || קרא; יהוה || יעקב; grammatical parallelism.

VERSE–LINE: 44:5b:

וְזֶ֗ה יִכְתֹּ֤ב יָדוֹ֙ לַֽיהוָ֔ה	5bA	yet another will write on his hand, 'The LORD's!'
וּבְשֵׁ֥ם יִשְׂרָאֵ֖ל יְכַנֶּֽה׃	5bB	and with the name of Israel he will surname himself.

𝔐 distinctive accents: 5 – 1.
Stresses: 4 + 3.
Verse-line parallelism: כתב || כנה (unique); יהוה || ישׂראל; grammatical parallelism.

VERSE–LINE: 44:6a:

כֹּה־אָמַ֨ר יְהוָ֧ה מֶלֶךְ־יִשְׂרָאֵ֛ל	6aA	Thus says the LORD, the King of Israel,
וְגֹאֲל֖וֹ יְהוָ֣ה צְבָא֑וֹת	6aB	and his Redeemer, the LORD of hosts:

𝔐 distinctive accents: 12 – 2.
Stresses: 3 + 3.
Verse-line parallelism: יהוה || יהוה צבאות; מלך || גאל.
Discussion: Ellipsis.

VERSE–LINE: 44:6b:

אֲנִ֤י רִאשׁוֹן֙ וַאֲנִ֣י אַחֲר֔וֹן	6bA	I am the First, and I am the Last,
וּמִבַּלְעָדַ֖י אֵ֥ין אֱלֹהִֽים׃	6bB	apart from me there is no God.

𝔐 distinctive accents: 5 – 1.
Stresses: 4 + 3.
Verse-line parallelism: אני || ־י.

VERSE–LINE: 44:7a:

וּמִֽי־כָמ֣וֹנִי	7aA	And who is like me?
יִקְרָ֞א וְיַגִּידֶ֤הָ וְיַעְרְכֶ֙הָ֙ לִ֔י	7aB	Let him call out, tell it and lay it out for me,
מִשּׂוּמִ֖י עַם־עוֹלָ֑ם	7aC	from the moment I established the people of eternity.

𝔐 distinctive accents: conjunctive – 5 – 1.
Stresses: 1 + 3 + 2.
Verse-line parallelism: ־ני || ־י; rhyme.
Discussion: With regard to the colometry see p. 215. There is no clear verse-line parallelism apart from the rhyme of the two suffixes 1 c.sg., but this is compensated for by the strophe parallelism between verses 7a and 7b.

VERSE–LINE: 44:7b:

וְאֹתִיּ֛וֹת וַאֲשֶׁ֥ר תָּבֹ֖אנָה יַגִּ֥ידוּ לָֽנוּ*׃	7bA	Also the things to come and what will happen – let them tell us!

𝔐 distinctive accent: 1.
Stresses: 5.
Verse-line parallelism: None (unicolon).
Discussion: The ancient witnesses regard this as a unicolon. Note, however, the strophe parallelism between verse-lines 7a and 7b.

VERSE–LINE: 44:8a:

אַֽל־תִּפְחֲדוּ֙ וְאַל־תִּרְה֔וּ	8aA	Do not quiver and do not be afraid!
הֲלֹ֥א מֵאָ֛ז הִשְׁמַעְתִּ֖יךָ וְהִגַּ֑דְתִּי	8aB	Have I not made you hear (it) from then on, and have I not told you?
וְאַתֶּ֣ם עֵדָ֑י	8aC	Yes, you are my witnesses!

𝔐 distinctive accents: 5 – 8 – 2.
Stresses: 2 + 4 + 2.
Verse-line parallelism: אל || לא; שמע || עד.
Discussion: Probably the Masoretes wanted to read this verse-line as a bicolon ending with עדי. The rhythmical balance would be 2 + 6.

However, in our discussion of the delimitation of cola[1] we argue for a tricolon with a more regular rhythmical balance (2 + 4 + 2), which corresponds closely to that of the tricolon of v. 7a.

VERSE–LINE: 44:8b:

הֲיֵשׁ אֱלוֹהַ מִבַּלְעָדַי	8bA	Is there a God apart from me?
וְאֵין צוּר בַּל־יָדָעְתִּי׃	8bB	'No, there is no Rock; I know of none.'

𝔐 distinctive accents: 5 – 1.
Stresses: 3 + 3.
Verse-line parallelism: יש || אין (antithetical); אלוה || צור; wordplay between מבלעדי and בל־ידעתי.

VERSE–LINE: 44:9a:

יֹצְרֵי־פֶסֶל כֻּלָּם תֹּהוּ	9aA	Those who form idols – all of them are void,
וַחֲמוּדֵיהֶם בַּל־יוֹעִילוּ	9aB	their cherished ones do not profit.

𝔐 distinctive accents: 5 – 2.
Stresses: 3 + 2.
Verse-line parallelism: תהו || בל יעל; rhyme.

VERSE–LINE: 44:9b:

וְעֵדֵיהֶם הֵמָּה	9bA	Yet they are their witnesses,
בַּל־יִרְאוּ וּבַל־יֵדְעוּ	9bB	(though) they do not see and they do not know,
לְמַעַן יֵבֹשׁוּ׃	9bC	so that they will be put to shame.

𝔐 distinctive accents: 7 – 8 – 1.
Stresses: 2 + 2 + 2.
Verse-line parallelism: עד || ידע; grammatical parallelism; rhyme.
Discussion: The Masoretes had some problems in dividing this verse-line into smaller cola. They took it as a bicolon. With the support of 𝔖 we assume a break after ידעו, so that it becomes a tricolon.[2] In Ps. 119:80 למען לא אבוש also is a colon in its own right.

VERSE–LINE: 44:10a:

מִי־יָצַר אֵל וּפֶסֶל נָסָךְ	10aA	Who forms a god and casts an idol
לְבִלְתִּי הוֹעִיל׃	10aB	which does not profit?

𝔐 distinctive accents: 2 – 1.
Stresses: 4 + 2.
Verse-line parallelism: None.

[1]See p. 216.
[2]See p. 216-7.

Discussion: With the Masoretes. Also in Jer. 7:8 לבלתי הועיל is a colon in its own right following an Atnaḥ (No. 2).

VERSE–LINE: 44:11a:

הֵן כָּל־חֲבֵרָיו יֵבֹשׁוּ	11aA	Behold, all its friends will be put to shame,
וְחָרָשִׁים* הֵמָּה מֵאָדָם	11aB	for they are more deaf than a human being!

𝔐 distinctive accents: 5 – 2.
Stresses: 3 + 3.
Verse-line parallelism: None: 'synthetical' parallelism.
Discussion: As with v. 7, the strophe parallelism compensates for the lack of verse-line parallelism.

VERSE–LINE: 44:11b:

יִתְקַבְּצוּ כֻלָּם יַעֲמֹדוּ	11bA	Let them all gather, stand there,
יִפְחֲדוּ יֵבֹשׁוּ יָחַד׃	11bB	let them quiver, altogether be put to shame.

𝔐 distinctive accents: 5 – 1.
Stresses: 3 + 3.
Verse-line parallelism: כלם || יחד; grammatical parallelism.

VERSE–LINE: 44:12a:

חָרַשׁ בַּרְזֶל מַעֲצָד	12aA	The craftsman of the iron of the adze –
וּפָעַל בַּפֶּחָם	12aB	he also works (it) in the coalfire,
וּבַמַּקָּבוֹת יִצְּרֵהוּ	12aC	and forms it with hammers.

𝔐 distinctive accents: 5 – 5 – 2.
Stresses: 3 + 2 + 2.
Verse-line parallelism: חרש || פעל prl יצר; מעצד || מקבת (unique); ב || ב.
Discussion: The sequence of accents 5 – 5 – 2 generally indicates a tricolon.[3]

VERSE–LINE: 44:12b:

וַיִּפְעָלֵהוּ בִּזְרוֹעַ כֹּחוֹ	12bA	And (while) he works it with his strong arm.
גַּם־רָעֵב וְאֵין כֹּחַ	12bB	he also becomes hungry, so there is no strength anymore,
לֹא־שָׁתָה מַיִם וַיִּיעָף׃	12bC	he has drunk no water, so he grows weary.

[3]See also Isa. 44:14a, 15a, 16a; 54:16a; cf. Josh. 23:2 with W.T. Koopmans, "The poetic Prose of Joshua 23," in: Van der Meer, De Moor (eds.) , *Structural Analysis*, 90; Judg. 15:16, with Kim, *Samson Cycle*, 289; Judg. 16:10, 11, with Idem, 334; Judg. 16:19, with Idem, 347; Judg. 16:25, with Idem, 360; Joel 2:16, 17, 25, with Van der Meer, *Oude woorden*, 75; Jonah 1:8, with R. De Hoop, "The Book of Jonah as Poetry," in: Van der Meer, de Moor, *Structural Analysis*, 166.

𝔐 distinctive accents: 5 – 5 – 1.
Stresses: 3 + 3 + 3.
Verse-line parallelism: כח || כח; רעב || לא שתה; כח || יעף (antithetical).

VERSE–LINE: 44:13a:

חָרַשׁ עֵצִים נָטָה קָו 13aA The woodworker stretches a line tight,

𝔐 distinctive accents: 3.
Stresses: 4.
Verse-line parallelism: None (unicolon).
Discussion: The Masoretes opted for a quadrocolon.[4] But this is hardly correct. The grammatical parallelism in the following three cola (three times an imperfect, against a perfect in the first colon), the repetition of the suffix 3 m.sg., lacking in the first colon, and the threefold repetition of the preposition ב, again lacking in the first colon – all this argues decisively in favour of a unicolon (v. 13a) followed by a tricolon (v. 13b).

VERSE–LINE: 44:13b:

יְתָאֲרֵהוּ בַשֶּׂרֶד 13bA he outlines it with a stylus,
יַעֲשֵׂהוּ בַּמַּקְצֻעוֹת 13bB he makes it with chisels,
וּבַמְּחוּגָה יְתָאֳרֵהוּ 13bC and with a pair of compasses he outlines it.

𝔐 distinctive accents: 5 – 5 – 2.
Stresses: 2 + 2 + 2.
Verse-line parallelism: תאר || עשה|| תאר (unique); ב || ב || ב; ־הו || ־הו || ־הו; שׂרד || מקצועה || מחוגה (unique).
Discussion: See our comment on v. 12a.

VERSE–LINE: 44:13c:

וַיַּעֲשֵׂהוּ כְּתַבְנִית אִישׁ 13cA Thus he makes it (into something) like a shapely man,
כְּתִפְאֶרֶת אָדָם לָשֶׁבֶת בָּיִת׃ 13cB like a glorious human being, to dwell in a house.

𝔐 distinctive accents: 5 – 1.
Stresses: 3 + 4.
Verse-line parallelism: כ || כ; תבנית || תפארת; איש || אדם.

VERSE–LINE: 44:14a:

לִכְרָת־לוֹ אֲרָזִים 14aA To cut for himself cedars

[4]Compare I. Yeivin, *Introduction to the Masorah*, trans. E.J. Revell (MasSt, 5), [Missoula] 1980, 188, for the Segolta in v. 13aA.

וַיִּקַּח תִּרְזָה וְאַלּוֹן 14aB he takes a stone pine or an oak,
וַיְאַמֶּץ־לוֹ בַּעֲצֵי־יָעַר 14aC and makes it for himself the strongest among the trees in the forest,

𝔐 distinctive accents: 5 – 5 – 2.
Stresses: 2 + 3 + 2.
Verse-line parallelism: ארז || תרזה || אלון || עץ; ל || ל; ־ו || ־י.
Discussion: With the Masoretes. See our comment on v. 12a.

VERSE–LINE: 44:14b:

נָטַע אֹרֶן 14bA he plants a laurel,
וְגֶשֶׁם יְגַדֵּל׃ 14bB and showers make (it) grow.

𝔐 distinctive accents: 8 – 1.
Stresses: 2 + 2.
Verse-line parallelism: נטע || גדל.
Discussion: This bicolon is based on our delimititation of cola. See p. 220. The Masoretes preferred a unicolon.

VERSE–LINE: 44:15a:

וְהָיָה לְאָדָם לְבָעֵר 15aA And it will serve a human being for fuel,
וַיִּקַּח מֵהֶם וַיָּחָם 15aB so he takes of it and warms himself,
אַף־יַשִּׂיק וְאָפָה לָחֶם 15aC also he kindles it to bake bread.

𝔐 distinctive accents: 5 – 5 – 2.
Stresses: 3 + 3 + 3.
Verse-line parallelism: בער || חמם || נשק.
Discussion: With the Masoretes. See our comment on v. 12a.

VERSE–LINE: 44:15b:

אַף־יִפְעַל־אֵל וַיִּשְׁתָּחוּ 15bA Also he works (it) into a god and bows down,
עָשָׂהוּ פֶסֶל וַיִּסְגָּד־לָמוֹ׃ 15bB he makes an idol and worships it.

𝔐 distinctive accents: 5 – 1.
Stresses: 2 + 3.
Verse-line parallelism: פעל || עשׂה; אל || פסל; שׁחה || סגד.

VERSE–LINE: 44:16a:

חֶצְיוֹ שָׂרַף בְּמוֹ־אֵשׁ 16aA Half of it he burns in the fire,
עַל־חֶצְיוֹ בָּשָׂר יֹאכֵל 16aB and over half of it meat which he wants to eat
יִצְלֶה צָלִי וְיִשְׂבָּע 16aC he roasts as a roast and becomes satisfied.

𝔐 distinctive accents: 5 – 5 – 2.

Stresses: 3 + 3 + 3.
Verse-line parallelism: חצי || חצי; ־ו || ־ו; שׂרף || צלה; אכל || צלה; אכל || שׂבע; grammatical parallelism.
Discussion: With the Masoretes. See our comment on v. 12a.

VERSE–LINE: 44:16b:

אַף־יָחֹם וְיֹאמַר הֶאָח	16bA	Also he warms himself and says: "Ah!
חַמּוֹתִי רָאִיתִי אוּר׃	16bB	I become warm, I see the glow!"

𝔐 distinctive accents: 5 – 1.
Stresses: 3 + 3.
Verse-line parallelism: חמם || חמם.

VERSE–LINE: 44:17a:

וּשְׁאֵרִיתוֹ	17aA	And the rest of it –
לְאֵל עָשָׂה לְפִסְלוֹ	17aB	he makes into a god! Into his idol!

𝔐 distinctive accents: 5 – 2.
Stresses: 1 + 3.
Verse-line parallelism: ־ו || ־ו; rhyme.
Discussion: See our delimitation of the cola, p. 222.

VERSE–LINE: 44:17b:

יִסְגָּד־לוֹ* וְיִשְׁתַּחוּ וְיִתְפַּלֵּל אֵלָיו	17bA	He worships it, and bows down and prays to it,
וְיֹאמַר הַצִּילֵנִי	17bB	and says "Deliver me!
כִּי אֵלִי אָתָּה׃	17bC	For you are my god!"

𝔐 distinctive accents: 5 – 5 – 1.
Stresses: 4 + 2 + 3.
Verse-line parallelism: ־ני || ־י; פלל || אמר; grammatical parallelism.

VERSE–LINE: 44:18a:

לֹא יָדְעוּ וְלֹא יָבִינוּ	18aA	They do not know and they do not understand,
כִּי טַח מֵרְאוֹת עֵינֵיהֶם	18aB	for smeared are their eyes so they cannot see,
מֵהַשְׂכִּיל לִבֹּתָם׃	18aC	their hearts so they cannot perceive.

𝔐 distinctive accents: 2 – 5 – 1.
Stresses: 4 + 4 + 2.
Verse-line parallelism: ידע || בין || ראה || שׂכל; לא || לא || מן || מן (unique); לב || עין.

Discussion: The Masoretes took the first colon as a single one, a kind of heading. However, the parallelism in verse-line 19a between twice לא followed by the roots ידע and בין in one colon, and לב in the previous colon seems to presuppose verse-line 18a to be a tricolon and not a unicolon followed by a bicolon. The parallelism in v. 18a forms a chiasm with the repeated parallelism in v. 19a. See also the parallelism between ידע and ראה and בין and שׂכל, mentioned above.

VERSE–LINE: 44:19a:

וְלֹא־יָשִׁיב אֶל־לִבּוֹ 19aA And no one reconsiders it in his heart,
וְלֹא דַעַת וְלֹא־תְבוּנָה 19aB and there is no knowledge and no understanding,

𝔐 distinctive accents: 7 – 9.
Stresses: 2 + 3.
Verse-line parallelism: לב || ידע || בין (compare v. 18a); לא || לא || לא.
Discussion: 𝔐 seems to have been led astray by the continuing sentence v. 19a-b. The delimitation of cola determines our choice here. See pp. 223-4 as well as p. 249.

VERSE–LINE: 44:19b:

לֵאמֹר חֶצְיוֹ שָׂרַפְתִּי בְמוֹ־אֵשׁ 19bA to say "Half of it I burn in the fire,
וְאַף אָפִיתִי עַל־גֶּחָלָיו לֶחֶם 19bB and also I bake bread over its coals,
אֶצְלֶה בָשָׂר וְאֹכֵל 19bC I grill meat and eat (it) –

𝔐 distinctive accents: 7 – 5 – 2.
Stresses: 4 + 4 + 3.
Verse-line parallelism: שׂרף || אפה || צלה (unique, but for שׂרף || צלה, see v. 16a above); אשׁ || גחלת; ־ו || ־ו; במו || על; grammatical parallelism.

VERSE–LINE: 44:19c:

וְיִתְרוֹ לְתוֹעֵבָה אֶעֱשֶׂה 19cA should I make the rest into an abomination,
לְבוּל עֵץ אֶסְגּוֹד׃ 19cB and should I worship a block of wood?"

𝔐 distinctive accents: 5 – 1.
Stresses: 3 + 3.
Verse-line parallelism: ל || ל; תועבה || בול עץ (unique); grammatical parallelism.

VERSE–LINE: 44:20a:

רֹעֶה אֵפֶר 20aA The one who heeds ashes –
לֵב הוּתַל הִטָּהוּ 20aB (his) deluded heart leads him astray.

𝔐 distinctive accents: 5 – 2.
Stresses: 2 + 3.
None.
Discussion: With the Masoretes.

VERSE–LINE: 44:20b:

וְלֹֽא־יַצִּיל אֶת־נַפְשׁוֹ 20bA So he will not deliver his soul,
וְלֹא יֹאמַר הֲלוֹא שֶׁקֶר בִּימִינִֽי׃ 20bB and will not say, "Is it not a lie (I have) in my right hand?"

𝔐 distinctive accents: 10 – 1.
Stresses: 2 + 5.
Verse-line parallelism: לא || לא || הלוא; grammatical parallelism.
Discussion: 𝔐's Maqqeph between ולא and יציל was the logical consquence of the decision to divide the verse after יאמר.

VERSE–LINE: 44:21a:

זְכָר־אֵלֶּה יַֽעֲקֹב 21aA Remember these things, O Jacob,
וְיִשְׂרָאֵל כִּי עַבְדִּי־אָתָּה 21aB and Israel, for you are my servant!

𝔐 distinctive accents: 5 – 2.
Stresses: 2 + 3.
Verse-line parallelism: יעקב || ישׂראל.
Discussion: The ellipsis forms a bond between the cola.

VERSE–LINE: 44:21b:

יְצַרְתִּיךָ עֶֽבֶד־לִי אַתָּה 21bA I formed you, you are a servant for me,
יִשְׂרָאֵל לֹא תִנָּשֵֽׁנִי׃ 21bB O Israel, you will be not forgotten by me!

𝔐 distinctive accents: 5 – 1.
Stresses: 3 + 3.
Verse-line parallelism: ־י || ־ני.

VERSE–LINE: 44:22a:

מָחִיתִי כָעָב פְּשָׁעֶיךָ 22aA I sweep away your transgressions like a cloud,
וְכֶעָנָן חַטֹּאותֶיךָ 22aB and like a shroud your sins.

𝔐 distinctive accents: 5 – 2.
Stresses: 3 + 2.
Verse-line parallelism: כ || כ; עב || ענן; פשע || חטאת; ־ך || ־ך; rhyme.
Discussion: Ellipsis.

VERSE–LINE: 44:22b:

שׁוּבָה אֵלַי כִּי גְאַלְתִּיךָ׃ 22bA Return to me, for I redeem you.

𝔐 distinctive accents: 1.
Stresses: 4.
Verse-line parallelism: None (unicolon).
Discussion: The strong parallelism in v. 22a necessitates the assumption of a unicolon here, with 𝔐. Furthermore, the grammatical chiasm between vv. 21 and 22 is in favour of a unicolon. Verse-lines 21a and 22b directly address Israel and Jacob by means of imperatives whereas verse-lines 21b and 22a describe the LORD's acts.

VERSE–LINE: 44:23a:

רָנּוּ שָׁמַיִם כִּי־עָשָׂה יְהוָה 23aA Rejoice, O heavens, for the LORD makes (it),
הָרִיעוּ תַּחְתִּיּוֹת אָרֶץ 23aB shout, O lower parts of the earth!
פִּצְחוּ הָרִים רִנָּה 23aC Break forth, O mountains into rejoicing,
יַעַר וְכָל־עֵץ בּוֹ 23aD O forest and every tree in it!

𝔐 distinctive accents: 7 – 5 – 5 – 2.
Stresses: 4 + 3 + 3 + 3.
Verse-line parallelism: רנן || רוע || פצח רנה; שמים || תחתיות ארץ || הר || יער וכל־עץ (unique); שמים || ארץ || הר; הרים || יער; הר || עץ; grammatical parallelism.
Discussion: With the Masoretes. The strong parallelism indicates that v. 23a is a quadrocolon and not a composition of two bicola. The sequence of accents (7 – 5 – 5 – 2) is also attested elsewhere.[5]

VERSE–LINE: 44:23b:

כִּי־גָאַל יְהוָה יַעֲקֹב 23bA For the LORD redeems Jacob,
וּבְיִשְׂרָאֵל יִתְפָּאָר׃ 23bB and in Israel he glorifies himself.

𝔐 distinctive accents: 5 – 1.
Stresses: 3 + 2.
Verse-line parallelism: גאל || פאר; יעקב || ישׂראל.

VERSE–LINE: 44:24a:

כֹּה־אָמַר יְהוָה גֹּאֲלֶךָ 24aA Thus says the LORD, your Redeemer,
וְיֹצֶרְךָ מִבָּטֶן 24aB and he who formed you from the womb,

[5] Isa. 47:10a; 49:5a, 21b, and see Gen. 16:2, 3, with L. Roersma, in: Watson, De Moor, *Verse in Ancient Near Eastern Prose*, 220; Judg. 15:6a-b, with Kim, *Samson Cycle*, 274; Jonah 1:7, with De Hoop, in Van der Meer, De Moor, *Structural Analysis*, 74.

𝔐 distinctive accents: 5 – 2.
Stresses: 3 + 2.
Verse-line parallelism: ךָ־ || ךָ־.

VERSE–LINE: 44:24b:

אָנֹכִי יְהוָה עֹשֶׂה כֹּל 24bA I am the LORD, he who made everything,
נֹטֶה שָׁמַיִם לְבַדִּי 24bB who stretched out heaven alone,
רֹקַע הָאָרֶץ מִי* אִתִּי׃ 24bC who hammered out the earth – who was with me?

𝔐 distinctive accents: 5 – 5 – 1.
Stresses: 4 + 3 + 4.
Verse-line parallelism: עשׂה || נטה || רקע; לבדי || מי אתי; אנכי || ־י || ־י; שׁמים || ארץ; grammatical parallelism; rhyme.
Discussion: Ellipsis of אנכי connects the cola.

VERSE–LINE: 44:25a:

מֵפֵר אֹתוֹת בַּדִּים 25aA who breaks the signs of fabulists,
וְקֹסְמִים יְהוֹלֵל 25aB and ridicules diviners,

𝔐 distinctive accents: 5 – 2.
Stresses: 3 + 2.
Verse-line parallelism: פרר || הלל (unique); בד || קסם; rhyme.

VERSE–LINE: 44:25b:

מֵשִׁיב חֲכָמִים אָחוֹר 25bA who makes wise men turn backwards,
וְדַעְתָּם יְשַׂכֵּל׃ 25bB and makes their knowledge foolish,

𝔐 distinctive accents: 8 – 1.
Stresses: 3 + 2.
Verse-line parallelism: חכם || דעת; חכם || סכל (antithetical).

VERSE–LINE: 44:26a:

מֵקִים דְּבַר עַבְדּוֹ 26aA who confirms the word of his servant,
וַעֲצַת מַלְאָכָיו יַשְׁלִים 26aB and fulfills the counsel of his messengers,

𝔐 distinctive accents: 5 – 2.
Stresses: 3 + 3.
Verse-line parallelism: קום || שׁלם; דבר || עצה; עבד || מלאך; ־ו || ־ו.

VERSE–LINE: 44:26b:

הָאֹמֵר לִירוּשָׁלַ͏ִם תּוּשָׁב 26bA who says to Jerusalem, "Be inhabited!",
וּלְעָרֵי יְהוּדָה תִּבָּנֶינָה 26bB and to the cities of Judah: "Let them be rebuilt!" –
וְחָרְבוֹתֶיהָ אֲקוֹמֵם׃ 26bC yes, her ruins I will raise up again! –

𝔐 distinctive accents: 7 – 5 – 1.
Stresses: 3 + 3 + 2.
Verse-line parallelism: ל || ל; ירושלם || יהודה; ישב || בנה || קום.

VERSE–LINE: 44:27a:

הָאֹמֵ֥ר לַצּוּלָ֖ה חֳרָ֑בִי	27aA	who says to the deep: "Become dry!
וְנַהֲרֹתַ֖יִךְ אוֹבִֽישׁ׃	27aB	Yes, your rivers I will make dry!",

𝔐 distinctive accents: 2 – 1.
Stresses: 3 + 2.
Verse-line parallelism: צולה || נהר; חרב || יבש.

VERSE–LINE: 44:28a:

הָאֹמֵ֤ר לְכ֙וֹרֶשׁ֙ רֹעִ֔י	28aA	who says to Cyrus: "My shepherd,
וְכָל־חֶפְצִ֖י יַשְׁלִ֑ם	28aB	who will fulfill all I want,

𝔐 distinctive accents: 5 – 2.
Stresses: 3 + 2.
Verse-line parallelism: ִי- || ִי-.

VERSE–LINE: 44:28b:

וְלֵאמֹ֤ר לִירוּשָׁלִַ֙ם֙ תִּבָּנֶ֔ה	28bA	namely, by saying to Jerusalem: "Let it be rebuilt!",
וְהֵיכָ֖ל תִּוָּסֵֽד׃	28bB	and to the temple: "Let it be founded!"

𝔐 distinctive accents: 5 – 1.
Stresses: 3 + 2.
Verse-line parallelism: ירושלם || היכל; בנה || יסד; grammatical parallelism.

6.4 Isaiah 44 – Delimitation of Strophes

STROPHE A.i.1 (Isa. 44:1)

וְעַתָּה שְׁמַע יַעֲקֹב עַבְדִּי	1aA	But now, hear, O Jacob, my servant,
וְיִשְׂרָאֵל בָּחַרְתִּי בוֹ׃	1aB	and Israel, whom I have chosen!

= Masoretic verse.
Separation ↑: major division markers in the textual tradition; deictic particle(s); imperative(s); vocatives.
Separation ↓: major division markers in the textual tradition.
Strophe parallelism: None (one verse-line).

STROPHE A.i.2 (Isa. 44:2)

כֹּה־אָמַר יְהוָה עֹשֶׂךָ	2aA	Thus says the LORD who made you,
וְיֹצֶרְךָ מִבֶּטֶן יַעְזְרֶךָּ	2aB	yes, he who formed you from the womb, who helps you:
אַל־תִּירָא עַבְדִּי יַעֲקֹב	2bA	Do not fear, my servant Jacob,
וִישֻׁרוּן בָּחַרְתִּי בוֹ׃	2bB	and Jeshurun, whom I have chosen!

= Masoretic verse.
Separation ↑: major division markers in the textual tradition; deictic particle(s); marker of direct speech; repetitive verse-line parallelism.
Separation ↓: jussive(s); vocatives.
Strophe parallelism: יהוה || יעקב.
Discussion: Even though the parallelism is weak, the delimitation is not in doubt. Just as lack of parallelism on the level of the verse-line may be compensated for by strophe parallelism, so lack of strophe parallelism may be balanced by canticle parallelism (cf. v. 1).

The small Setuma in 1Q^{a} must be regarded as a marker of the beginning of the divine speech, not as an alternative strophic division. 1Q^{a} also supports the break after v. 1.

STROPHE A.i.3 (Isa. 44:3)

כִּי אֶצָּק־מַיִם עַל־צָמֵא	3aA	For I shall pour out water on the thirsty (soil),
וְנֹזְלִים עַל־יַבָּשָׁה	3aB	and streams on the dry (ground).
אֶצֹּק רוּחִי עַל־זַרְעֶךָ	3bA	I will pour out my spirit on your seed,
וּבִרְכָתִי עַל־צֶאֱצָאֶיךָ׃	3bB	and my blessing on what comes forth for you.

= Masoretic verse.
Separation ↑: deictic particle(s); repetitive verse-line parallelism.
Separation ↓: repetitive verse-line parallelism.

Strophe parallelism: יצק || יצק (unique); על || על || על || על; מים || רוח (unique); grammatical parallelism.

STROPHE A.i.4 (Isa. 44:4)

וְצָמְחוּ בְּבֵין חָצִיר	4aA	And they will sprout amidst the grass,
כַּעֲרָבִים עַל־יִבְלֵי־מָיִם׃	4aB	like willows by watercourses.

= Masoretic verse.
Separation ↑: None.
Separation ↓: None (one verse-line).
Strophe parallelism: None (one verse-line).
Discussion: The strophe is weakly delimited, but the Masoretic division need not be doubted. Again canticle parallelism compensates for the lack of parallelism on the level of the strophe. See vv. 2 and 3.

STROPHE A.i.5 (Isa. 44:5)

זֶה יֹאמַר לַיהוָה אָנִי	5aA	One person shall say, 'I am the LORD's!'
וְזֶה יִקְרָא בְשֵׁם־יַעֲקֹב	5aB	and another will call himself by the name of Jacob;
וְזֶה יִכְתֹּב יָדוֹ לַיהוָה	5bA	yet another will write on his hand, 'The LORD's!'
וּבְשֵׁם יִשְׂרָאֵל יְכַנֶּה׃	5bB	and with the name of Israel he will surname himself.

= Masoretic verse.
Separation ↑: demonstrative pronouns; independent pers. pronoun; marker of direct speech; swapping (adjunct).
Separation ↓: major division markers in the textual tradition; demonstrative pronoun; swapping (adjunct).
Strophe parallelism: זה || זה || זה; קרא בשם || כנה; יעקב || ישׂראל; ב || ב; שׁם || שׁם.

STROPHE A.ii.1 (Isa. 44:6)

כֹּה־אָמַר יְהוָה מֶלֶךְ־יִשְׂרָאֵל	6aA	Thus says the LORD, the King of Israel,
וְגֹאֲלוֹ יְהוָה צְבָאוֹת	6aB	and his Redeemer, the LORD of hosts:
אֲנִי רִאשׁוֹן וַאֲנִי אַחֲרוֹן	6bA	I am the First, and I am the Last,
וּמִבַּלְעָדַי אֵין אֱלֹהִים׃	6bB	apart from me there is no God.

= Masoretic verse.
Separation ↑: major division markers in the textual tradition; deictic particle(s); marker of direct speech; repetitive verse-line parallelism.
Separation ↓: major division markers in the textual tradition; independent pers. pronouns; swapping (adjunct).
Strophe parallelism: יהוה || אלהים.

STROPHE A.ii.2 (Isa. 44:7)

וּמִי־כָמוֹנִי	7aA	And who is like me?
יִקְרָא וְיַגִּידֶהָ וְיַעְרְכֶהָ לִי	7aB	Let him call out, tell it and lay it out for me,
מִשּׂוּמִי עַם־עוֹלָם	7aC	from the moment I established the people of eternity.
וְאֹתִיּוֹת וַאֲשֶׁר תָּבֹאנָה יַגִּידוּ לָנוּ*׃	7bA	Also the things to come and what will happen – let them tell us!

= Masoretic verse.
Separation ↑: major division markers in the textual tradition; interrogative pronoun; jussive(s).
Separation ↓: major division markers in the textual tradition; jussive(s); swapping (object).
Strophe parallelism: נגד || נגד; ל || ל; עולם || אתה (unique).
Discussion: The break 𝔊^{Q} indicates in the middle of v. 7aB is obviously a strophic division lagging behind 𝔊^{A} which has it after v. 6bB.

STROPHE A.ii.3 (Isa. 44:8)

אַל־תִּפְחֲדוּ וְאַל־תִּרְהוּ	8aA	Do not quiver and do not be afraid!
הֲלֹא מֵאָז הִשְׁמַעְתִּיךְ וְהִגַּדְתִּי	8aB	Have I not made you hear (it) from then on, and have I not told you?
וְאַתֶּם עֵדָי	8aC	Yes, you are my witnesses!
הֲיֵשׁ אֱלוֹהַּ מִבַּלְעָדַי	8bA	Is there a God apart from me?
וְאֵין צוּר בַּל־יָדָעְתִּי׃	8bB	'No, there is no Rock; I know of none.'

= Masoretic verse.
Separation ↑: major division markers in the textual tradition; deictic particle(s); independent pers. pronoun; jussive(s); swapping (adjunct).
Separation ↓: major division marker in the textual tradition.
Strophe parallelism: אל (neg.) || בל; הלא || ־ה; grammatical parallelism.
Discussion: The Greek witnesses all have major dividers at highly unlikely places in v. 8. Therefore we assume them to anticipate the major division marker 1𝔔^{a} has after v. 8.

STROPHE B.i.1 (Isa. 44:9)

יֹצְרֵי־פֶסֶל כֻּלָּם תֹּהוּ	9aA	Those who form idols – all of them are void,
וַחֲמוּדֵיהֶם בַּל־יוֹעִילוּ	9aB	their cherished ones do not profit.
וְעֵדֵיהֶם הֵמָּה	9bA	Yet they are their witnesses,
בַּל־יִרְאוּ וּבַל־יֵדְעוּ	9bB	(though) they do not see and they do not know,
לְמַעַן יֵבֹשׁוּ׃	9bC	so that they will be put to shame.

= Masoretic verse.

Separation ↑: major division marker in the textual tradition; swapping (subject).
Separation ↓: independent pers. pronoun.
Strophe parallelism: הם־ || ־הם; בל || בל; grammatical parallelism.
Discussion: The paragraphos in $\mathfrak{G}^{S}$ after v. 9aB may have been intended to mark the boundary between vv. 8 and 9.

STROPHE B.i.2 (Isa. 44:10)

מִֽי־יָצַ֥ר אֵ֛ל וּפֶ֥סֶל נָסָ֖ךְ	10aA	Who forms a god and casts an idol
לְבִלְתִּ֥י הוֹעִֽיל׃	10aB	which does not profit?

= Masoretic verse.
Separation ↑: interrogative pronoun.
Separation ↓: None (one verse-line).
Strophe parallelism: None (one verse-line).

STROPHE B.i.3 (Isa. 44:11)

הֵ֤ן כָּל־חֲבֵרָיו֙ יֵבֹ֔שׁוּ	11aA	Behold, all its friends will be put to shame,
וְחָרָשִׁ֥ים* הֵ֖מָּה מֵאָדָ֑ם	11aB	for they are more deaf than a human being!
יִֽתְקַבְּצ֤וּ כֻלָּם֙ יַעֲמֹ֔דוּ	11bA	Let them all gather, stand there,
יִפְחֲד֥וּ יֵבֹ֖שׁוּ יָֽחַד׃	11bB	let them quiver, altogether be put to shame.

= Masoretic verse.
Separation ↑: deictic particle(s); independent pers. pronoun; swapping (subject).
Separation ↓: major division marker in the textual tradition; jussive(s).
Strophe parallelism: כל || כל; בוש || בוש; grammatical parallelism.
Discussion: The division markers after מאדם in $\mathfrak{G}^{SA}$ are unlikely from the viewpoint of the parallelism between vv. 11a and 11b. Probably they anticipate the same break as is indicated in 1Q[a] after v. 11.

STROPHE B.ii.1 (Isa. 44:12a)

חָרַ֤שׁ בַּרְזֶל֙ מַעֲצָ֔ד	12aA	The craftsman of the iron of the adze –
וּפָעַל֙ בַּפֶּחָ֔ם	12aB	he also works (it) in the coalfire,
וּבַמַּקָּב֖וֹת יִצְּרֵ֑הוּ	12aC	and forms it with hammers.

≠ Masoretic verse.
Separation ↑: major division marker in the textual tradition; swapping (subject); swapping (adjunct).
Separation ↓: None (one verse-line).
Strophe parallelism: None (one verse-line).

Discussion: $\mathfrak{M}$ read v. 12 as one strophe with two tricola. In v. 13 $\mathfrak{M}$ may have preferred a quadrocolon plus bicolon.[1] However, in both cases the first verse-line describes the work of the craftsman in a neutral or even positive way, whereas the second gives the account an ironic twist. Moreover, a quadrocolon as the first verse-line of v. 13 is hardly acceptable[2] and v. 13c describes the result of the woodworker's effort, not the production process itself. If, then, v. 13 must be divided into two strophes, we deem it best to assume the same for v. 12.

STROPHE B.ii.2 (Isa. 44:12b)

וַיִּפְעָלֵהוּ בִּזְרוֹעַ כֹּחוֹ	12bA	And (while) he works it with his strong arm,
גַּם־רָעֵב וְאֵין כֹּחַ	12bB	he also becomes hungry, so there is no strength anymore,
לֹא־שָׁתָה מַיִם וַיִּיעָף׃	12bC	he has drunk no water, so he grows weary.

≠ Masoretic verse.
Separation ↑: deictic particle(s).
Separation ↓: major division marker in the textual tradition.
Strophe parallelism: None (one verse-line).
Discussion: See our comment on v. 12a. The major division marking in $\mathfrak{G}^A$ after מים obviously anticipates the break $1\mathfrak{Q}^a$ has after v. 12.

STROPHE B.iii.1 (Isa. 44:13a–b)

חָרַשׁ עֵצִים נָטָה קָו	13aA	The woodworker stretches a line tight,
יְתָאֲרֵהוּ בַשֶּׂרֶד	13bA	he outlines it with a stylus,
יַעֲשֵׂהוּ בַּמַּקְצֻעוֹת	13bB	he makes it with chisels,
וּבַמְּחוּגָה יְתָאֳרֵהוּ	13bC	and with a pair of compasses he outlines it.

≠ Masoretic verse.
Separation ↑: major division marker in the textual tradition; swapping (subject).
Separation ↓: repetitive verse-line parallelism; swapping (adjunct).
Strophe parallelism: קו ‖ שרד, etc. (carpenter's instruments).
Discussion: See our comment on v. 12a.

STROPHE B.iii.2 (Isa. 44:13c)

וַיַּעֲשֵׂהוּ כְּתַבְנִית אִישׁ	13cA	Thus he makes it (into something) like a shapely man,
כְּתִפְאֶרֶת אָדָם לָשֶׁבֶת בָּיִת׃	13cB	like a glorious human being, to dwell in a house.

[1] Compare I. Yeivin, *Introduction to the Masorah*, trans. E.J. Revell (MasSt, 5), [Missoula] 1980, 188, for the Segolta in v. 13aA.
[2] See p. 235.

≠ Masoretic verse.
Separation ↑: repetitive verse-line parallelism.
Separation ↓: None (one verse-line).
Strophe parallelism: None (one verse-line).
Discussion: See our comment on v. 12a. The Petuḥa in $\mathfrak{G}^{S}$ lags behind the division point after v. 12 indicated by $1\mathfrak{Q}^{a}$.

STROPHE B.iv.1 (Isa. 44:14)

לִכְרָת־לוֹ אֲרָזִים	14aA	To cut for himself cedars
וַיִּקַּח תִּרְזָה וְאַלּוֹן	14aB	he takes a stone pine or an oak,
וַיְאַמֶּץ־לוֹ בַּעֲצֵי־יָעַר	14aC	and makes it for himself the strongest among the trees in the forest,
נָטַע אֹרֶן	14bA	he plants a laurel,
וְגֶשֶׁם יְגַדֵּל׃	14bB	and showers make (it) grow.

= Masoretic verse.
Separation ↑: swapping (adjunct).
Separation ↓: swapping (subject).
Strophe parallelism: כרת ‖ נטע (antithetical; unique); תרזה, etc. ‖ ארן (unique); אמץ ‖ גדל (unique).

STROPHE B.iv.2 (Isa. 44:15)

וְהָיָה לְאָדָם לְבָעֵר	15aA	And it will serve a human being for fuel,
וַיִּקַּח מֵהֶם וַיָּחָם	15aB	so he takes of it and warms himself,
אַף־יַשִּׂיק וְאָפָה לָחֶם	15aC	also he kindles it to bake bread.
אַף־יִפְעַל־אֵל וַיִּשְׁתָּחוּ	15bA	Also he works (it) into a god and bows down,
עָשָׂהוּ פֶסֶל וַיִּסְגָּד־לָמוֹ׃	15bB	he makes an idol and worships it.

= Masoretic verse.
Separation ↑: deictic particle(s).
Separation ↓: major division markers in the textual tradition; deictic particle(s).
Strophe parallelism: אדם ‖ אל (antithetical); אף ‖ אף; grammatical parallelism.

STROPHE B.v.1 (Isa. 44:16)

חֶצְיוֹ שָׂרַף בְּמוֹ־אֵשׁ	16aA	Half of it he burns in the fire,
עַל־חֶצְיוֹ בָּשָׂר יֹאכֵל	16aB	and over half of it meat which he wants to eat
יִצְלֶה צָלִי וְיִשְׂבָּע	16aC	he roasts as a roast and becomes satisfied.
אַף־יָחֹם וְיֹאמַר הֶאָח	16bA	Also he warms himself and says: “Ah!
חַמּוֹתִי רָאִיתִי אוּר׃	16bB	I become warm, I see the glow!”

= Masoretic verse.
Separation ↑: major division markers in the textual tradition; repetitive verse-line parallelism; swapping (object); swapping (adjunct).
Separation ↓: deictic particle(s); marker of direct speech.
Strophe parallelism: שׂרף || חמם; אשׁ || אור.

STROPHE B.v.2 (Isa. 44:17)

וּשְׁאֵרִיתוֹ	17aA	And the rest of it –
לְאֵל עָשָׂה לְפִסְלוֹ	17aB	he makes into a god! Into his idol!
יִסְגָּד־לוֹ* וְיִשְׁתַּחוּ וְיִתְפַּלֵּל אֵלָיו	17bA	He worships it, and bows down and prays to it,
וְיֹאמַר הַצִּילֵנִי	17bB	and says "Deliver me!
כִּי אֵלִי אָתָּה׃	17bC	For you are my god!"

= Masoretic verse.
Separation ↑: swapping (object); swapping (adjunct).
Separation ↓: major division markers in the textual tradition; deictic particle(s); independent pers. pronoun; imperative(s); marker of direct speech.
Strophe parallelism: אל (noun) || אל (noun).

STROPHE B.vi.1 (Isa. 44:18–19a)

לֹא יָדְעוּ וְלֹא יָבִינוּ	18aA	They do not know and they do not understand,
כִּי טַח מֵרְאוֹת עֵינֵיהֶם	18aB	for smeared are their eyes so they cannot see,
מֵהַשְׂכִּיל לִבֹּתָם׃	18aC	their hearts so they cannot perceive.
וְלֹא־יָשִׁיב אֶל־לִבּוֹ	19aA	And no one reconsiders it in his heart,
וְלֹא דַעַת וְלֹא־תְבוּנָה	19aB	and there is no knowledge and no understanding,

≠ Masoretic verse.
Separation ↑: major division markers in the textual tradition; deictic particle(s); repetitive verse-line parallelism; swapping (adjunct).
Separation ↓: repetitive verse-line parallelism.
Strophe parallelism: לא || לא; ידע || דעת; בין || תבונה; לב || לב.
Discussion: 𝔐's v. 19 is definitely too long, probably because they did not want to separate לאמר from v. 19a.[3] In view of the very strong parallelism between v. 18 and v. 19a on the one hand, and vv. 19b-c on the other, we choose to combine the two into one strophe.

[3]See our comment pp. 223-4.

STROPHE B.vi.2 (Isa. 44:19b–c)

לֵאמֹר חֶצְיוֹ שָׂרַפְתִּי בְמוֹ־אֵשׁ	19bA	to say "Half of it I burn in the fire,
וְאַף אָפִיתִי עַל־גֶּחָלָיו לֶחֶם	19bB	and also I bake bread over its coals,
אֶצְלֶה בָשָׂר וְאֹכֵל	19bC	I grill meat and eat (it) –
וְיִתְרוֹ לְתוֹעֵבָה אֶעֱשֶׂה	19cA	should I make the rest into an abomination,
לְבוּל עֵץ אֶסְגּוֹד׃	19cB	and should I worship a block of wood?"

≠ Masoretic verse.
Separation ↑: deictic particle(s); marker of direct speech; swapping (object); swapping (adjunct).
Separation ↓: swapping (object); swapping (adjunct).
Strophe parallelism: חצי || יתר; grammatical parallelism. Obviously גחלת and בול עץ are associated.
Discussion: The two verse-lines are connected by direct speech and content.

STROPHE B.vi.3 (Isa. 44:20)

רֹעֶה אֵפֶר	20aA	The one who heeds ashes –
לֵב הוּתַל הִטָּהוּ	20aB	(his) deluded heart leads him astray.
וְלֹא־יַצִּיל אֶת־נַפְשׁוֹ	20bA	So he will not deliver his soul,
וְלֹא יֹאמַר הֲלוֹא שֶׁקֶר בִּימִינִי׃	20bB	and will not say, "Is it not a lie (I have) in my right hand?"

= Masoretic verse.
Separation ↑: swapping (subject).
Separation ↓: major division markers in the textual tradition; deictic particle(s); repetitive verse-line parallelism.
Strophe parallelism: לב || נפש.

STROPHE C.i.1 (Isa. 44:21)

זְכָר־אֵלֶּה יַעֲקֹב	21aA	Remember these things, O Jacob,
וְיִשְׂרָאֵל כִּי עַבְדִּי־אָתָּה	21aB	and Israel, for you are my servant!
יְצַרְתִּיךָ עֶבֶד־לִי אַתָּה	21bA	I formed you, you are a servant for me,
יִשְׂרָאֵל לֹא תִנָּשֵׁנִי׃	21bB	O Israel, you will be not forgotten by me!

= Masoretic verse.
Separation ↑: major division markers in the textual tradition; deictic particle(s); demonstrative pronouns; imperative(s); vocative.
Separation ↓: independent pers. pronoun; vocative; swapping (subject).
Strophe parallelism: ישראל || ישראל; ־י || ־י; אתה || אתה.

STROPHE C.i.2 (Isa. 44:22)

מָחִיתִי כָעָב פְּשָׁעֶיךָ	22aA	I sweep away your transgressions like a cloud,
וְכֶעָנָן חַטֹּאותֶיךָ	22aB	and like a shroud your sins.
שׁוּבָה אֵלַי כִּי גְאַלְתִּיךָ׃	22bA	Return to me, for I redeem you.

= Masoretic verse.
Separation ↑: repetitive verse-line parallelism; swapping (adjunct).
Separation ↓: major division markers in the textual tradition; deictic particle(s); imperative(s);
Strophe parallelism: מחה פשע || גאל (unique); grammatical parallelism.

STROPHE C.i.3 (Isa. 44:23)

רָנּוּ שָׁמַיִם כִּי־עָשָׂה יְהוָה	23aA	Rejoice, O heavens, for the LORD makes (it),
הָרִיעוּ תַּחְתִּיּוֹת אָרֶץ	23aB	shout, O lower parts of the earth!
פִּצְחוּ הָרִים רִנָּה	23aC	Break forth, O mountains into rejoicing,
יַעַר וְכָל־עֵץ בּוֹ	23aD	O forest and every tree in it!
כִּי־גָאַל יְהוָה יַעֲקֹב	23bA	For the LORD redeems Jacob,
וּבְיִשְׂרָאֵל יִתְפָּאָר׃	23bB	and in Israel he glorifies himself.

= Masoretic verse.
Separation ↑: major division markers in the textual tradition; deictic particle(s); imperative(s); vocatives.
Separation ↓: major division markers in the textual tradition; deictic particle(s); swapping (adjunct).
Strophe parallelism: עשה || גאל; יהוה || יהוה.

STROPHE C.ii.1 (Isa. 44:24)

כֹּה־אָמַר יְהוָה גֹּאֲלֶךָ	24aA	Thus says the LORD, your Redeemer,
וְיֹצֶרְךָ מִבָּטֶן	24aB	and he who formed you from the womb,
אָנֹכִי יְהוָה עֹשֶׂה כֹּל	24bA	I am the LORD, he who made everything,
נֹטֶה שָׁמַיִם לְבַדִּי	24bB	who stretched out heaven alone,
רֹקַע הָאָרֶץ מִי* אִתִּי׃	24bC	who hammered out the earth – who was with me?

= Masoretic verse.
Separation ↑: major division markers in the textual tradition; deictic particle(s); marker of direct speech; repetitive verse-line parallelism.
Separation ↓: independent pers. pronoun; interrogative pronoun; repetitive verse-line parallelism; swapping (subject).
Strophe parallelism: יהוה || יהוה; גאל || עשה; יצר || עשה; grammatical parallelism.
Discussion: $\mathfrak{G}^{A}$ seems to favour a different strophic division: 24a – 24b+25a – 25b+26a – 26b – 27 – 28a – 28b. Because in this man-

ner האמר in v. 26bA, 27aA and 28aA always heads a strophe, it is worthwhile to consider this possibility seriously.

The parallelism in vv. 25b-26a would create a nice contrast which, however, is left intact if one regards it as canticle parallelism. With 𝔊^{A}'s strophic division the parallelism in vv. 24b-25a becomes awkward and v. 28b is left dangling. The strong parallelism in vv. 24 and 25 argues in favour of 𝔐's strophic division. The circumstance that 𝔊^{Q} has secondary paragraphoi only after vv. 26bA, 27aA and 28aA would seem to point to ad-hoc inventions of both 𝔊^{A} and a marginal editor of 𝔊^{Q} meant to highlight the repetition of האמר, be it that the scribes chose different ways to do so.

Because 𝔊 connects the last word of v. 24 with v. 25 (which is impossible from the viewpoint of the Hebrew) the break indicated by 𝔊^{S} may be regarded as indicating the end of the strophe.

STROPHE C.ii.2 (Isa. 44:25)

מֵפֵר אֹתוֹת בַּדִּים	25aA	who breaks the signs of fabulists,
וְקֹסְמִים יְהוֹלֵל	25aB	and ridicules diviners,
מֵשִׁיב חֲכָמִים אָחוֹר	25bA	who makes wise men turn backwards,
וְדַעְתָּם יְשַׂכֵּל׃	25bB	and makes their knowledge foolish,

= Masoretic verse.
Separation ↑: swapping (object).
Separation ↓: swapping (object).
Strophe parallelism: פרר ‖ שוב; קסם ‖ חכם (unique); הלל ‖ חכם (unique); grammatical parallelism.
Discussion: With regard to 𝔊^{A} see our comment on v. 24.

STROPHE C.ii.3 (Isa. 44:26)

מֵקִים דְּבַר עַבְדּוֹ	26aA	who confirms the word of his servant,
וַעֲצַת מַלְאָכָיו יַשְׁלִים	26aB	and fulfills the counsel of his messengers,
הָאֹמֵר לִירוּשָׁלִַם תּוּשָׁב	26bA	who says to Jerusalem, "Be inhabited!",
וּלְעָרֵי יְהוּדָה תִּבָּנֶינָה	26bB	and to the cities of Judah: "Let them be rebuilt!" –
וְחָרְבוֹתֶיהָ אֲקוֹמֵם׃	26bC	yes, her ruins I will raise up again! –

= Masoretic verse.
Separation ↑: swapping (object).
Separation ↓: major division markers in the textual tradition; jussive(s); marker of direct speech; swapping (object).
Strophe parallelism: דבר ‖ אמר; קום ‖ קום; grammatical parallelism.
Discussion: With regard to the division markers in 𝔊^{A} and 𝔊^{Q} see our comment on v. 24.

STROPHE C.ii.4 (Isa. 44:27)

הָאֹמֵר לַצּוּלָה חֳרָבִי	27aA	who says to the deep: “Become dry!
וְנַהֲרֹתַיִךְ אוֹבִישׁ׃	27aB	Yes, your rivers I will make dry!”,

= Masoretic verse.
Separation ↑: major division markers in the textual tradition; imperative(s); marker of direct speech; swapping (object).
Separation ↓: major division markers in the textual tradition.
Strophe parallelism: None (one verse-line).
Discussion: With regard to the division markers in 𝔊^A and 𝔊^Q see our comment on v. 24.

STROPHE C.ii.5 (Isa. 44:28)

הָאֹמֵר לְכוֹרֶשׁ רֹעִי	28aA	who says to Cyrus: “My shepherd,
וְכָל־חֶפְצִי יַשְׁלִם	28aB	who will fulfill all I want,
וְלֵאמֹר לִירוּשָׁלַםִ תִּבָּנֶה	28bA	namely, by saying to Jerusalem: “Let it be rebuilt!”,
וְהֵיכָל תִּוָּסֵד׃	28bB	and to the temple: “Let it be founded!”

= Masoretic verse.
Separation ↑: major division markers in the textual tradition; jussive(s); marker of direct speech.
Separation ↓: major division markers in the textual tradition; jussive(s); marker of direct speech; swapping (adjunct).
Strophe parallelism: אמר || אמר; ל || ל.
Discussion: With regard to the division markers in 𝔊^A and 𝔊^Q after רעי and ישלם respectively, see our comment on v. 24.

6.5 Isaiah 44 – Delimitation of Canticles

CANTICLE A.i (44:1–5)

Separation ↑: major division markers in the textual tradition; thematic discontinuity; change of subject.
Separation ↓: major division markers in the textual tradition.
Canticle parallelism: ישראל || ישרון (responsion); ישראל || ישראל (inclusion); יעקב || יעקב (inclusion/responsion); עבד || עבד (inclusion), obviously completed by v. 5;[1] בחר || בחר; יהוה || יהוה (responsion/inclusion); מים || מים (responsion).
Thematic unity: yes. All strophes describe the restoration of Israel, especially the restoration of the young generation which will accept its destination as servants of the LORD.

[1] See our note 4 on p. 206.

Discussion: The major dividers some of our witnesses have after v. 1 mark the end of the opening strophe. On the marker 1Q^{a} has after v. 2aB see p. 243.

CANTICLE A.ii (44:6–8)

Separation ↑: major division markers in the textual tradition; thematic discontinuity; change of subject.
Separation ↓: major division markers in the textual tradition.
Canticle parallelism: ראשון || עולם (responsion); מבלעדי || מבלעדי (responsion); אין || יש (responsion); אלהים || אלוה (responsion); נגד || נגד (responsion/concatenation); מן || מן (responsion); עולם || אז (responsion).
Thematic unity: yes. All three strophes deal with the incomparability of God. Having been told about this from the beginnning, Israel has to speak up as his witness against those who believe in other deities.
Discussion: $\mathfrak{G}^{A}$ indicates the end of strophes A.ii.1 and A.ii.2. With regard to the major division markings some of the Greek witness have in the middle of A.ii.2 and A.ii.3, see our remarks on the strophic division.

The lower limit of this canticle is attested in 1Q^{a} alone. However, we had reason to suspect that the Greek witnesses knew this borderline too.[2] With v. 9 a long diatribe against the making of idols begins, so the delimitation of this canticle is not in doubt.

CANTICLE B.i (44:9–11)

Separation ↑: major division marker(s) in the textual tradition; thematic discontinuity; change of subject.
Separation ↓: major division marker(s) in the textual tradition.
Canticle parallelism: יצר || יצר (responsion); פסל || פסל (responsion; unique); כל || כל (responsion/inclusion); בל || בלתי (unique); יעל || יעל (responsion); המה || המה (responsion); בוש || בוש (inclusion/responsion).
Thematic unity: yes. All three strophes try to demonstrate the uselessness of idols.
Discussion: Only 1Q^{a} has preserved the lower delimitation of this canticle. However, it seems likely that $\mathfrak{G}^{SA}$ are anticipating the same demarcation line. The strong canticle parallelism would seem sufficient confirmation of the unity of the piece.

[2]See p. 245-6.

CANTICLE B.ii (44:12a–b)

Separation ↑: major division marker(s) in the textual tradition; change of subject.
Separation ↓: major division marker(s) in the textual tradition.
Canticle parallelism: פעל || פעל (responsion; unique); ב || ב.
Thematic unity: yes. Description of the work of the idol's smith.
Discussion: See with regard to the decision to distribute v. 12 over two strophes p. 246-7. Upper and lower delimitation of this small canticle have been preserved in 1𝔔^{a} and – be it anticipating – in 𝔊^{A}. Also 𝔊^{S} may have known this borderline, but indicated it belatedly.[3]

CANTICLE B.iii (44:13a–c)

Separation ↑: major division marker(s) in the textual tradition; thematic discontinuity; change of subject.
Separation ↓: None.
Canticle parallelism: עשׂה || עשׂה (concatenation); ־הו || ־הו (concatenation).
Thematic unity: yes. Description of the idol's woodworker.
Discussion: Because vv. 14-20 continue to harp on the futility of the woodworker's occupation, it is understandable that the tradition has preserved no transition marker after v. 13. From the viewpoint of the macrostructure of the subcanto and canto it is dispensable.[4] However, v. 14 starts all over again with the planting of trees by the woodworker, whereas v. 13 has already described the final phase of his shaping the idol. Therefore we assume a low-level break here, exceptionally without the support of ancient witnesses.

CANTICLE B.iv (44:14–15)

Separation ↑: thematic discontinuity (planting of trees).
Separation ↓: major division markers in the textual tradition.
Canticle parallelism: לקח || לקח (responsion).
Thematic unity: yes. Both strophes express wonder about the excessive human care and intensive human use of wood that is at the same time the material for the idol which is worshipped as if it were divine. The remark that trees do not grow by human intervention but by rain (v. 14bB) hints at the One who is the giver of rain and who would never approve of the woodworker's behaviour according to the author of these lines.
Discussion: The lower delimitation of this canticle is marked in 𝔊^{A}.

---

[3] See p. 248.
[4] See below pp. 257-9.

CANTICLE B.v (44:16–17)

Separation ↑: major division markers in the textual tradition.
Separation ↓: major division markers in the textual tradition.
Canticle parallelism: חצי || שׁארית (responsion; unique); אמר || אמר.
Thematic unity: yes. Further mockery of the use of wood for an image of a god.

CANTICLE B.vi (44:18–20)

Separation ↑: major division markers in the textual tradition; change of subject.
Separation ↓: major division markers in the textual tradition.
Canticle parallelism: לב || לב (responsion/inclusion); לא || לא (responsion); אמר || אמר.
Strophes B.vi.1 and B.vi.2 are linked by an on-running sentence (enjambment).
Thematic unity: yes. Further arguments against the reasoning of the worshippers of idols.

CANTICLE C.i (44:21–23)

Separation ↑: major division markers in the textual tradition; thematic discontinuity; change of subject.
Separation ↓: major division markers in the textual tradition.
Canticle parallelism: זכר || מחה (cf. 43:25); יעקב || יעקב (inclusion); ישׂראל || ישׂראל (inclusion/responsion); יצר || עשׂה (inclusion); גאל || גאל (responsion).
Thematic unity: yes. See the discussion below.
Discussion: Many ancient witnesses assume a break after v. 22 and many a modern scholar might be inclined to assume that this is tangible proof of the late insertion of this hymn at this point. However, the redemption of Jacob/Israel described in vv. vv. 21-22 seems to be the very reason for this sudden rejoicing. The references to all parts of creation in the overloaded quadrocolon v. 23a seem to tie in with Second Isaiah's argument that with the almighty Creator anything is possible and render it almost certain that the standard pair יצר (v. 21bA) || עשׂה (v. 23aA) has not been chosen accidentally. Actually it clearly refers back to the same pair at the beginning of this chapter – 44:2 where the creation of the servant Jacob is also cited as a source of hope (עשׂך, יצרך מבטן). And it is taken up explicitly at the beginning of the next canticle, C.ii.1 (v.24 – גאלך || יצרך מבטן, again addressed to the servant of the LORD). Here too the creation of heaven and earth

is adduced as a sure sign that God will be able to keep his promises to his servant (v. 24b, see als v. 27).

For all these reasons we believe that *if* v. 23 was inserted at a later time it was done in an extremely clever way. As we have seen in the case of 42:10-12,[5] and will see in the case of 49:13; 52:9; 54:1, it is often not as easy as it seems to excise these sudden adhortations to rejoice from their context. The circumstance that the tradition sometimes sets these hymns apart (see especially 49:13 as a case comparable to 44:23) is insufficient reason, in our opinion, to do so in a modern structural analysis.

CANTICLE C.ii (44:24–28)

Separation ↑: major division markers in the textual tradition; change of subject.
Separation ↓: major division markers in the textual tradition.
Canticle parallelism: אמר || אמר (5 times, vv. 24aA, 26bA, 27aA, 28aA, 28bA; inclusion/responsion), see also v. 26aA דבר עבדו; דעת || עצה (concatenation); שלם Hiph. || שלם Hiph. (unique; responsion); ירושלם || ירושלם (responsion); בנה || בנה (responsion).
All five strophes are linked by an on-running sentence (enjambment).
Thematic unity: yes. He who laid the foundations of the earth promises his servant Israel to keep his word in ordering Cyrus to rebuild Jerusalem and its temple.
Discussion: For 𝔊^{AQ} in vv. 25-28aB, see our comments on the strophic division.

6.6 Isaiah 44 – Delimitation of Macrostructure

The overall structure of Isaiah 44 appears to be completely symmetric,

SUB-CANTOS	CANTICLES	STROPHES
A	2	7 (5+3)
B	6	6 (3+2+2+2+2+3)
C	2	7 (3+5)

If one prefers to join B.iii and B.iv because no delimitation is attested[1] this does not disturb the symmetry seriously:

[5]See pp. 154-8.
[1]See above, p. 255.

SUB-CANTOS	CANTICLES	STROPHES
A	2	7 (5+3)
B	5	5 (3+2+4+2+3)
C	2	7 (3+5)

Distant parallelism connecting the canticles of **sub-canto A**:
שמע (v. 1aA – A.i) || שמע (v. 8aB – A.ii); ישׂראל (vv. 1aB, 5bB – A.i) || ישׂראל (v. 6aA – A.ii); יהוה (vv. 5aA, 5bA – A.i) || יהוה (vv. 6aA, 6aB – A.ii);[2] עזר (v. 2aB – A.i) || גאל (v. 6aB – A.ii); אל־תירא (v. 2bA – A.i) || אל־תפחדו ואל־תרהו (v. 8aA – A.ii); קרא (v. 5aB – A.i) || קרא (v. 7aB – A.ii).

Distant parallelism connecting the canticles of **sub-canto B**:
יצר (vv. 9aA, 10aA – B.i) || יצר (v. 12aC – B.ii); פסל (vv. 9aA, 10aA – B.i) || פסל (v. 15bB – B.iv) || פסל (v. 17aB – B.v); בל יראו (v. 9bB – B.i) || טח מראות עיניהם (v. 18aB – B.vi); בל־ידעו (v. 9bB – B.i) || לא ידעו (v. 18aA – B.vi); פעל (vv. 12aB, 12bA – B.ii) || פעל (v. 15bA – B.iv); עשׂה (vv. 13bB, 13cA – B.iii) || עשׂה (v. 15bB – B.iv) || עשׂה (v. 17aB – B.v) || עשׂה (v. 19cA – B.vi), etcetera. The interrelatedness of the canticles constituting this sub-canto is evident enough.

Distant parallelism connecting the canticles of **sub-canto C**:
עבדי (v. 21aB – C.i) || עבדו (v. 26aA – C.ii); יצר (v. 21bA – C.i) || יצר (v. 24aB – C.ii); גאל (vv. 22bA, 23bA – C.i) || גאל (v. 24aA – C.ii); שמים (v. 23aA – C.i) || שמים (v. 24bB – C.ii); עשׂה (v. 23aA – C.i) || עשׂה (v. 24bA – C.ii); ארץ (v. 23aB – C.i) || ארץ (v. 24bC – C.ii).

In its present form the canto exhibits a lot of coherence. As in other cases, beginning and end link up with each other. Both A and C address Israel as the servant of the LORD. Both find the certainty of its delivery in the fact that it is the Creator, also Jacob's Creator, who is promising his people help. Both beginning and end speak of Israel's impendent redemption.

Often the middle sub-canto (B) is seen as a 'Fremdkörper', but the very regular structure renders it difficult to simply omit it. Moreover, the use of the same verbs יצר and עשׂה which are used in A and C apparently creates a deliberate contrast between the work of God and the work of the idol makers, as was the case in Ch. 40. The ignorance of the idols and their makers (vv. 9, 18- 20) is matched by that of the diviners (v. 25). The inability of the idols to deliver their worshippers

[2]Mostly we do not cite such very common parallels. But here we make an exception because they concatenate the two canticles and explain the use of the unique title מלך ישׂראל: the Israelites are his servants, not of the Babylonians.

(vv. 17, 20 – B) stands in stark contrast to Israel's salvation by its Redeemer (vv. 6, 23 – A and C). Also it is not so easy to separate sub-canto A.ii from B.i: v. 8aC ואתם עדי seems to balance v. 9bA ועדיהם המה, v. 8aA אל־תפחדו seems to be contrasted with v. 11bB יפחדו, v. 9bB בל ידעו seems to echo v. 8bB בל־ידעו. Because the latter theme is also taken up in B.vi (vv. 18-19, 20), one might perhaps consider the possibility to regard the long elaboration of the argument in B.ii-v as secondary. In that case the remaining structure would still be symmetrical:

SUB-CANTOS	CANTICLES	STROPHES
A	2	7 (5+3)
B	2	2 (3+3)
C	2	7 (3+5)

However, if one removes B.ii-v, he is forced to assume that vv. 15 (B.iv), 16-17 (B.v) are a later elaboration of vv. 19-20 which might be an additional reason to omit sub-canto B entirely. We do not pronounce judgment on these complicated matters,[3] realizing that scholars are deeply divided over the redactional history of Second Isaiah. However, we do want to point out that even if one recognizes various layers in the chapter the structural regularity of the canto in its final form warrants the minimum assumption that a very skilful final redactor has been at work whose composition deserves to be also read as a complete whole, whatever its previous stages may have been.

[3] We merely note that Spykerboer, 113-26 and Holter, 127-212, see 44:9-20 as a sophisticated piece of literature.

Chapter 7

The Structure of Isaiah 45–46

7.1 Isaiah 45–46: Text and Translation

ס <פ> – 1Q^{ab} – 𝔊^{SBAQ} – 𝔖^{be} ________________________________

I.A.i.1 (Isa. 45:1a)

כֹּה־אָמַר יְהוָה	1aA	Thus says the LORD
לִמְשִׁיחוֹ לְכוֹרֶשׁ אֲשֶׁר־הֶחֱזַקְתִּי בִימִינוֹ	1aB	to his[1] anointed one, to Cyrus, whose right hand I have grasped,

I.A.i.2 (Isa. 45:1b)

לְרַד־לְפָנָיו גּוֹיִם	1bA	To subdue[2] nations before him,
וּמָתְנֵי מְלָכִים אֲפַתֵּחַ	1bB	yes, I will ungird the loins of kings,
לִפְתֹּחַ לְפָנָיו דְּלָתַיִם	1cA	to open doors before him,
וּשְׁעָרִים לֹא יִסָּגֵרוּ׃	1cB	yes, the gates will not be shut.

𝔊^{A} ....

I.A.ii.1 (Isa. 45:2)

אֲנִי לְפָנֶיךָ אֵלֵךְ	2aA	I will go before you,
וַהֲרוּרִים* אוֹשֶׁר*	2aB	and mountains[3] I will make straight,[4]
דַּלְתוֹת נְחוּשָׁה אֲשַׁבֵּר	2bA	doors of bronze I will shatter,
וּבְרִיחֵי בַרְזֶל אֲגַדֵּעַ׃	2bB	and bars of iron I will smash.

I.A.ii.2 (Isa. 45:3)

וְנָתַתִּי לְךָ אוֹצְרוֹת חֹשֶׁךְ	3aA	And I will give you the treasures of darkness
וּמַטְמֻנֵי מִסְתָּרִים	3aB	and hidden hoards in secret places,
לְמַעַן תֵּדַע כִּי־אֲנִי יְהוָה	3bA	that you may know that I am the LORD
הַקּוֹרֵא בְשִׁמְךָ אֱלֹהֵי יִשְׂרָאֵל׃	3bB	who calls you by your name, the God of Israel.

I.A.ii.3 (Isa. 45:4)

לְמַעַן עַבְדִּי יַעֲקֹב	4aA	For the sake of my servant Jacob,
וְיִשְׂרָאֵל בְּחִירִי	4aB	and Israel, my chosen one,

---

[1] 𝔊 and 𝔙 harmonize in rendering "*my* anointed one". Such harsh transitions belong to Second Isaiah's style.

[2] Cf. Joüon, Muraoka, §82l.

[3] With 1Q^{b}, compare also 1Q^{a}𝔊.

[4] With the Ketiv we read an imperfect Hiphil.

וָאֶקְרָ֤א לְךָ֙ בִּשְׁמֶ֔ךָ	4bA	I call you[5] by your name,
אֲכַנְּךָ֖ {$\mathfrak{G}^{Q}$} וְלֹ֥א יְדַעְתָּֽנִי׃	4bB	I surname you, although you do not know me.

<ס> – $1\mathfrak{Q}^{ab}$ ________________________________

I.B.i.1 (Isa. 45:5)

אֲנִ֤י יְהוָה֙ וְאֵ֣ין ע֔וֹד	5aA	I am the LORD and there is no other,
זוּלָתִ֖י אֵ֣ין אֱלֹהִ֑ים	5aB	besides me there is no god.
אֲאַזֶּרְךָ֖ וְלֹ֥א יְדַעְתָּֽנִי׃	5bA	I will gird you, although you do not know me,

I.B.i.2 (Isa. 45:6)

לְמַ֣עַן יֵדְע֗וּ מִמִּזְרַח־שֶׁ֙מֶשׁ֙ וּמִמַּ֣עֲרָבָ֔ה	6aA	so that they may know from the east to the west,
כִּי־אֶ֖פֶס בִּלְעָדָ֑י {$\mathfrak{G}^{S}$}	6aB	that nothing exists apart from me –
אֲנִ֥י יְהוָ֖ה וְאֵ֥ין עֽוֹד׃	6aC	I am the LORD and there is no other,

I.B.i.3 (Isa. 45:7)

יוֹצֵ֥ר אוֹר֙ וּבוֹרֵ֣א חֹ֔שֶׁךְ	7aA	he who forms light and creates darkness,
עֹשֶׂ֥ה שָׁל֖וֹם וּב֣וֹרֵא רָ֑ע	7aB	who makes peace and creates evil –
אֲנִ֥י יְהוָ֖ה עֹשֶׂ֥ה כָל־אֵֽלֶּה׃	7aC	I am the LORD who makes all these things.

ס <פ> – $1\mathfrak{Q}^{ab}$ – $\mathfrak{G}^{SBAQ}$ – $\mathfrak{S}^{abe}$ ....

I.B.ii.1 (Isa. 45:8)

הַרְעִ֤יפוּ שָׁמַ֙יִם֙ מִמַּ֔עַל	8aA	Drip, O heavens, from above,
וּשְׁחָקִ֖ים יִזְּלוּ־צֶ֑דֶק	8aB	and let the clouds pour down justice;
תִּפְתַּח־אֶ֣רֶץ וְיִפְרַח*־יֶ֗שַׁע	8bA	let the earth open up[6] and let salvation blossom –[7]
וּצְדָקָ֤ה תַצְמִ֙יחַ֙ יַ֔חַד {$\mathfrak{G}^{SQ}$}	8bB	and let justice make sprout communion,[8]
אֲנִ֥י יְהוָ֖ה בְּרָאתִֽיו׃	8bC	I am the LORD, I create it.

ס <פ> – $1\mathfrak{Q}^{a}$ – $\mathfrak{S}^{bde}$ ________________________________

I.C.i.1 (Isa. 45:9)

ה֗וֹי רָ֚ב אֶת־יֹ֣צְר֔וֹ	9aA	Woe to him who quarrels with the one who formed him,
חֶ֖רֶשׂ{$\mathfrak{G}^{AQ}$}אֶת־חַרְשֵׂ֣י אֲדָמָ֑ה {$\mathfrak{G}^{B}$}	9aB	a pot among the pots[9] of earth.

---

[5]For the interpretation of the inverted imperfect next to a normal imperfect (אכנך) and a perfect (ידעתני) as an actual present see M.C.A. Korpel, J.C. de Moor, F. Sepmeijer, "Consistency with Regard to Tenses", see Abbreviations.

[6]For the reflexive meaning of פתח Qal see our note with Isa. 44:5aB (above p. 205, n. 3).

[7]With $1\mathfrak{Q}^{a}$. Cf. Barthélemy, 336-7; Oswalt, 199, n. 13; contrast Beuken, 238-9; Koole, 331. The parallelism between the roots פתח and פרח in Song 7:13 lends support to the emendation.

[8]We take יחד as a noun here, because this accords better with the Hiphil of the verb צמח.

[9]Most modern commentators prefer the reading of $\mathfrak{M}$, cf. Young, 203; Koole,

הֲיֹאמַר חֹמֶר לְיֹצְרוֹ מַה־תַּעֲשֶׂה	9bA	Does the clay say to him who forms it, "What do you make?"
{ס} וּפָעָלְךָ אֵין־יָדַיִם לוֹ׃	9bB	or (does) your work which (itself) has no hands[10] (say this)?

I.C.i.2 (Isa. 45:10)

הוֹי אֹמֵר לְאָב מַה־תּוֹלִיד	10aA	Woe to him who says to a father, "What do you beget?"
וּלְאִשָּׁה מַה־תְּחִילִין׃	10aB	or to a wife, "What do you bring to birth?"

ס <פ> – 1𝔔[a] – 𝔊[SBA] – 𝔖[abe] . . . .

I.C.ii.1 (Isa. 45:11)

כֹּה־אָמַר יְהוָה	11aA	Thus says the LORD,
{𝔖[ad]} קְדוֹשׁ יִשְׂרָאֵל וְיֹצְרוֹ	11aB	the Holy One of Israel and the one who formed it,
הָאֹתִיּוֹת שְׁאָלוּנִי עַל־בָּנַי	11bA	The things to come? Interrogate[11] me concerning my children,[12]
{𝔊[SAQ]} וְעַל־פֹּעַל יָדַי תְּצַוֻּנִי׃	11bB	command me[13] with regard the work of my hands.

I.C.ii.2 (Isa. 45:12)

אָנֹכִי עָשִׂיתִי אֶרֶץ	12aA	It is I who made the earth,
וְאָדָם עָלֶיהָ בָרָאתִי	12aB	and created man upon it,
אֲנִי יָדַי נָטוּ שָׁמַיִם	12bA	I – my hands stretched out the heavens,
וְכָל־צְבָאָם צִוֵּיתִי׃	12bB	and all their host I command.

336-7; Barthélemy, 338-9; De Waard, 175-6; Oswalt, 206-7, n. 31. For חרש "earthenware, pot" see Jer. 19:1; Prov. 26:23. The imagery is a loose elaboration of Isa. 29:16 which itself picks up a traditional ancient oriental theme, as the Hurrian parable of the coppersmith proves, cf. E. Neu, *Das hurritische Epos der Freilassung*, vol. 1, Wiesbaden 1996, 80-3. Possibly the metaphor was chosen to identify the protesting party as the youth of Israel, cf. Lam. 4:2.

[10] We assume ellipsis of היאמר and מה־תעשה. Multiple ellipsis was by no means rare, cf. J.C. de Moor, "Syntax Peculiar to Ugaritic Poetry", in: J.C. de Moor, W.G.E. Watson (eds.), *Verse in Ancient Near Eastern Prose* (AOAT, 42), Neukirchen-Vluyn 1993, 191-205 (202-204). Furthermore, we take אין־ידים לו as an asyndetic relative clause, cf. Jer. 5:21; Ps. 72:12.

[11] Concerning the textual problems see e.g. Barthélemy, 341-2; De Waard, 176-7. We see no reason at all to deviate from 𝔐. Many translations read v. 11b as questions (e.g. RSV, NIV, JPS) but the imperative next to the jussive renders this solution unattractive. In our opinion the commands have to be understood as a challenging imitation of a trial (ריב, cf. v. 9aA), just like the imperatives in Isa. 41:1, 21-23, etc. The issue during these mock trials was time and again who would be able to predict the future, cf. Isa. 41:23; 44:7.

[12] 𝔊 has a plus here: "and concerning my daughters". Exactly because v. 13 foretells the return of the exiles we suspect that this plus is an adaptation to Isa. 43:6 and 49:22 where the same is predicted.

[13] The heavy irony should not be masked by a mitigating translation which obscures the contrast with v. 12, especially 12bB.

I.C.ii.3 (Isa. 45:13)

אָנֹכִי֙ הַעִירֹתִ֣הוּ בְצֶ֔דֶק	13aA	It is I who woke him up in justice,
וְכָל־דְּרָכָ֖יו אֲיַשֵּׁ֑ר	13aB	yes, all his ways I will make straight.
הֽוּא־יִבְנֶ֤ה עִירִי֙ וְגָלוּתִ֣י יְשַׁלֵּ֔חַ	13bA	It is he who will rebuild my city and will send my exiles home,
לֹ֤א בִמְחִיר֙ וְלֹ֣א בְשֹׁ֔חַד	13bB	not for a price and not for presents,
אָמַ֖ר יְהוָ֥ה צְבָאֽוֹת׃	13bC	says the LORD of hosts.

פ <ס> – 1Qa – 𝔊SBAQ – Sabce ________________________________

II.A.i.1 (Isa. 45:14a–b)

כֹּ֣ה ׀ אָמַ֣ר יְהוָ֗ה	14aA	Thus says the LORD,
יְגִ֨יעַ מִצְרַ֥יִם	14aB	The resources of Egypt
וּֽסְחַר־כּוּשׁ֮ וּסְבָאִים֒	14aC	and the merchandise of Cush and the Sabeans,
אַנְשֵׁ֣י מִדָּ֗ה עָלַ֤יִךְ יַעֲבֹ֙רוּ֙	14bA	tall men[14] will pass over to you[15]
וְלָ֣ךְ יִהְי֔וּ אַחֲרַ֣יִךְ יֵלֵ֔כוּ	14bB	and will be yours, they will go behind you,
בַּזִּקִּ֖ים יַעֲבֹ֑רוּ	14bC	in chains they will pass;

II.A.i.2 (Isa. 45:14c–d)

וְאֵלַ֤יִךְ יִשְׁתַּחֲוּוּ֙	14cA	and they will bow down for you,
אֵלַ֣יִךְ יִתְפַּלָּ֔לוּ	14cB	and they will pray to you:
אַ֣ךְ בָּ֥ךְ אֵ֛ל	14dA	"Only in you is God
וְאֵ֥ין ע֖וֹד אֶ֥פֶס אֱלֹהִֽים׃	14dB	and there does not exist any other god."

II.A.i.3 (Isa. 45:15)

אָכֵ֕ן אַתָּ֖ה אֵ֣ל מִסְתַּתֵּ֑ר	15aA	However,[16] you are a God hiding himself,
אֱלֹהֵ֥י יִשְׂרָאֵ֖ל מוֹשִֽׁיעַ׃	15aB	O Saviour God of Israel!

II.A.i.4 (Isa. 45:16)

בּ֥וֹשׁוּ וְגַֽם־נִכְלְמ֖וּ כֻּלָּ֑ם	16aA	They are ashamed and disgraced, all of them;
יַחְדָּו֙ הָלְכ֣וּ בַכְּלִמָּ֔ה	16aB	altogether they go in disgrace,
חָרָשֵׁ֖י צִירִֽים׃	16aC	the craftsmen with their drawings.

ס – <ס> – 1Qa – 𝔊SBAQ – Sabcde . . . .

[14] For the colometry see 276-8. The tall men are depicted as enslaved enemies who have to carry their own tribute. Cf. Num. 13:22; 2 Sam. 21:20; 1 Chron. 11:23; 20:6, as well as Ps. 68:30-32; 72:10. For עבר על in the sense of "passing before a master for inspection" see Gen. 32:22; Exod. 30:13-14; 2 Sam. 15:18; 24:20.

[15] Cf. 2 Sam. 24:20. The suffixes prove that it is Zion who is addressed here, without being introduced at all. This is not uncommon in prophetic literature, see e.g. Jer. 13:20; Mic. 1:14, 16; 2:10.

[16] For this nuance of the particle see e.g. *HALAT*, 46, אכן I, 2; *HAHAT*, 55, אכן 2; *DCH*, vol. 1, 248, אכן 2; in Second Isaiah also 49:4; 53:4.

II.A.ii.1 (Isa. 45:17)

יִשְׂרָאֵל֙ נוֹשַׁע בַּיהוָה	17aA	But[17] Israel is saved by the LORD,
תְּשׁוּעַת עוֹלָמִים	17aB	a salvation of ages.
לֹא־תֵבֹשׁוּ וְלֹא־תִכָּלְמוּ	17bA	They will not be ashamed and and not be disgraced
עַד־עוֹלְמֵי עַד׃	17bB	to ages everlasting.

פ <ס> – $1\mathfrak{Q}^{a}$ – $\mathfrak{G}^{SB}$ – $\mathfrak{S}^{b}$ ______________________________

II.B.i.1 (Isa. 45:18)

כִּי כֹה אָמַר־יְהוָה בּוֹרֵא הַשָּׁמַיִם	18aA	For thus says the LORD, who created the heavens,
הוּא הָאֱלֹהִים יֹצֵר הָאָרֶץ	18aB	he (who) is God, who formed the earth,
וְעֹשָׂהּ֙ הוּא כוֹנְנָהּ	18aC	and the One who made it, he (who) established it –
לֹא־תֹהוּ בְרָאָהּ	18bA	not as a void he created it,
לָשֶׁבֶת יְצָרָהּ {$\mathfrak{G}^{A}\mathfrak{S}^{ab}$}	18bB	to be inhabited he formed it –
אֲנִי יְהוָה וְאֵין עוֹד׃	18bC	I am the LORD and there is no other.

II.B.i.2 (Isa. 45:19)

לֹא בַסֵּתֶר דִּבַּרְתִּי	19aA	I did not speak in secret,
בִּמְקוֹם֙ אֶרֶץ חֹשֶׁךְ	19aB	in a place of the land of darkness,
לֹא אָמַרְתִּי לְזֶרַע יַעֲקֹב תֹּהוּ בַקְּשׁוּנִי	19aC	I have not said to the seed of Jacob: "Seek me in the void!"
אֲנִי יְהוָה֙ דֹּבֵר צֶדֶק	19bA	I am the LORD, who speaks what is just,
מַגִּיד מֵישָׁרִים׃	19bB	who tells what is straight.

$\mathfrak{G}^{SA}$ – $\mathfrak{S}^{b}$ . . . .

II.B.ii.1 (Isa. 45:20)

הִקָּבְצוּ וָבֹאוּ	20aA	Assemble and come,
הִתְנַגְּשׁוּ יַחְדָּו	20aB	draw near together,
פְּלִיטֵי הַגּוֹיִם	20aC	survivors of the nations.
לֹא יָדְעוּ הַנֹּשְׂאִים֙ אֶת־עֵץ פִּסְלָם	20bA	They do not know, those who are carrying the wood of their idols,
וּמִתְפַּלְלִים אֶל־אֵל לֹא יוֹשִׁיעַ׃	20bB	who pray to a god that does not save.

II.B.ii.2 (Isa. 45:21a–b)

הַגִּידוּ וְהַגִּישׁוּ	21aA	Tell and bring near,
אַף יִוָּעֲצוּ יַחְדָּו	21aB	yes, let them take counsel together:
מִי הִשְׁמִיעַ זֹאת מִקֶּדֶם	21bA	Who has made this heard from olden times,
מֵאָז הִגִּידָהּ {$\mathfrak{G}^{SQ}$}	21bB	has told it since then?

II.B.ii.3 (Isa. 45:21c–d)

הֲלוֹא אֲנִי יְהוָה֙	21cA	Was it not I, the LORD?
וְאֵין־עוֹד אֱלֹהִים֙ מִבַּלְעָדַי	21cB	And there is no God apart from me,

[17] The emphasized position of the subject justifies the assumption of a contrast.

אֵֽל־צַדִּ֣יק וּמוֹשִׁ֔יעַ	21dA	a just God and Saviour,
אַ֖יִן זוּלָתִֽי׃	21dB	there is none besides me.

$\mathfrak{G}^{SB}$ ———————————————————————

II.C.i.1 (Isa. 45:22)

פְּנוּ־אֵלַ֥י וְהִוָּשְׁע֖וּ	22aA	Turn unto me and be saved,
כָּל־אַפְסֵי־אָ֑רֶץ	22aB	all you ends of the earth,
כִּ֥י אֲנִי־אֵ֖ל וְאֵ֥ין עֽוֹד׃	22bA	for I am God and there is no other.

II.C.i.2 (Isa. 45:23)

בִּ֣י נִשְׁבַּ֔עְתִּי{$\mathfrak{G}^{A}$}	23aA	I swear[18] by myself,
יָצָ֨א מִפִּ֧י צְדָקָ֛ה	23aB	justice goes forth from my mouth,
דָּבָ֖ר וְלֹ֣א יָשׁ֑וּב	23aC	a word which shall not return:
כִּי־לִי֙ תִּכְרַ֣ע כָּל־בֶּ֔רֶךְ	23bA	Unto me every knee shall bow,
תִּשָּׁבַ֖ע כָּל־לָשֽׁוֹן׃	23bB	every tongue shall swear.

II.C.i.3 (Isa. 45:24–25)

אַ֧ךְ בַּיהוָ֛ה לִ֥י אָמַ֖ר צְדָק֣וֹת	24aA	"Only in the LORD", they say to me, "is full justice,
וָעֹ֑ז עָדָ֤יו יָבוֹא֙	24aB	and strength comes to him,
וְיֵבֹ֔שׁוּ כֹּ֖ל הַנֶּחֱרִ֥ים בּֽוֹ׃	24aC	but all who are raging against him shall be put to shame.
בַּיהוָ֛ה {$\mathfrak{G}^{A}$} יִצְדְּק֥וּ וְיִֽתְהַלְל֖וּ	25aA	In the Lord will be justified and will glory
כָּל־זֶ֥רַע יִשְׂרָאֵֽל׃	25aB	all the seed of Israel."

<פ> – $1\mathfrak{Q}^{a}$ – $4\mathfrak{Q}^{b}$ – $\mathfrak{G}^{SBA}$ . . . .

II.C.ii.1 (Isa. 46:1)

כָּרַ֥ע בֵּל֙ קֹרֵ֣ס נְב֔וֹ	1aA	Bel bows, Nebo cringes,
הָיוּ֙ עֲצַבֵּיהֶ֔ם לַחַיָּ֖ה וְלַבְּהֵמָ֑ה	1aB	their grievous images are for the beasts and the cattle,
נְשֻׂאֹֽתֵיכֶם֙ עֲמוּס֔וֹת	1bA	the objects you wanted to be carried become a burden,
מַשָּׂ֖א לַעֲיֵפָֽה׃	1bB	a load to a weary animal.[19]

II.C.ii.2 (Isa. 46:2)

קָֽרְס֤וּ כָֽרְעוּ֙ יַחְדָּ֔ו	2aA	They cringe, they bow together,
לֹ֥א יָכְל֖וּ מַלֵּ֣ט מַשָּׂ֑א	2aB	they are unable to save the load,
וְנַפְשָׁ֖ם בַּשְּׁבִ֥י הָלָֽכָה׃	2bA	and they themselves go into captivity.

ס <פ> – $1\mathfrak{Q}^{a}$ – $4\mathfrak{Q}^{b}$ – $\mathfrak{G}^{SBAQ}$ – ς^{abcde} ———————————————

III.A.i.1 (Isa. 46:3)

שִׁמְע֤וּ אֵלַי֙ בֵּ֣ית יַעֲקֹ֔ב	3aA	Listen to me, O house of Jacob,
וְכָל־שְׁאֵרִ֖ית בֵּ֣ית יִשְׂרָאֵ֑ל	3aB	and all the remnant of the house of Israel,

[18] See for the actual present above n. 5.

[19] The feminine singular refers back to the בהמה of v. 1aB. The prophet mocks at the religious processions of the Babylonians.

הַעֲמֻסִים מִנִּי־בֶטֶן	3bA	you who were a burden from the womb,
הַנְּשֻׂאִים מִנִּי־רָחַם׃	3bB	who were carried since your birth.

III.A.i.2 (Isa. 46:4)

וְעַד־זִקְנָה אֲנִי הוּא	4aA	Even unto (your) old age I am the same One,
וְעַד־שֵׂיבָה אֲנִי אֶסְבֹּל	4aB	and unto (your) greyness I will continue to bear (you);
אֲנִי עָשִׂיתִי וַאֲנִי אֶשָּׂא	4bA	I have made (you) and I will continue to carry,
וַאֲנִי אֶסְבֹּל וַאֲמַלֵּט׃	4bB	will continue to bear and will continue to save (you).

ס <פ> – 1$\mathfrak{Q}^{a}$ – $\mathfrak{G}^{SA}$ – $\mathfrak{S}^{abe}$ ....

III.A.ii.1 (Isa. 46:5)

לְמִי תְדַמְּיוּנִי וְתַשְׁווּ	5aA	And to whom will you liken me and make me equal,
{$\mathfrak{G}^{Q}$} וְתַמְשִׁלוּנִי וְנִדְמֶה׃	5aB	and compare me that we may be alike?

III.A.ii.2 (Isa. 46:6)

הַזָּלִים זָהָב מִכִּיס	6aA	Those who pour out[20] gold from the purse,
וְכֶסֶף בַּקָּנֶה יִשְׁקֹלוּ	6aB	and weigh out silver on the scales,
יִשְׂכְּרוּ צוֹרֵף וְיַעֲשֵׂהוּ אֵל	6bA	hire a goldsmith and he makes a god of it;
יִסְגְּדוּ אַף־יִשְׁתַּחֲווּ׃	6bB	then they worship, even bow down!

III.A.ii.3 (Isa. 46:7)

יִשָּׂאֻהוּ עַל־כָּתֵף יִסְבְּלֻהוּ	7aA	They lift him up, they bear him on the shoulder,
וְיַנִּיחֻהוּ תַחְתָּיו וְיַעֲמֹד	7aB	they put him down and (there) he stands;
מִמְּקוֹמוֹ לֹא יָמִישׁ	7aC	he will not move from his place.
אַף־יִצְעַק אֵלָיו וְלֹא יַעֲנֶה	7bA	Even when one cries out to him, he does not answer;
מִצָּרָתוֹ לֹא יוֹשִׁיעֶנּוּ׃	7bB	from his anguish he does not save him.

ס – 1$\mathfrak{Q}^{a}$ – – $\mathfrak{G}^{SAQ}$ – $\mathfrak{S}^{abce}$ ________________________________

III.B.i.1 (Isa. 46:8–9)

זִכְרוּ־זֹאת וְהִתְאֹשָׁשׁוּ	8aA	Remember this and behave like men,[21]
הָשִׁיבוּ פוֹשְׁעִים עַל־לֵב׃	8aB	bring it back to your hearts, O transgressors.
זִכְרוּ רִאשֹׁנוֹת מֵעוֹלָם	9aA	Remember the first things, from eternity on,
כִּי אָנֹכִי אֵל וְאֵין עוֹד	9aB	that I am God, and there is no other,
אֱלֹהִים וְאֶפֶס כָּמוֹנִי׃	9aC	a God – and none like me exists! –

[20] Cf. *HAHAT*, 297; Oswalt, 227, n. 8.

[21] We follow Qimchi and others who regard this as a denominative verb derived from איש; see H. Leene, "Isaiah 46:8 – Summons to be Human?", *JSOT* 30 (1984), 111-21; Koole, 382-3; for other proposals *HAHAT*, 113; Oswalt, 232, n. 25. In our opinion the meaning is determined by the parallel אבירי לב in v. 12aA. As in Ps. 76:6, this is an ironic description of pseudo-heroes.

III.B.i.2 (Isa. 46:10)

מַגִּיד מֵרֵאשִׁית אַחֲרִית	10aA	who tells the outcome from the beginning[22]
וּמִקֶּדֶם אֲשֶׁר לֹא־נַעֲשׂוּ	10aB	and from olden times that which had not yet been made,
אֹמֵר {𝔊^{A}} עֲצָתִי תָקוּם	10bA	who says, "My counsel shall stand,
וְכָל־חֶפְצִי אֶעֱשֶׂה׃	10bB	and everything I want I will make!",

III.B.i.3 (Isa. 46:11)

קֹרֵא מִמִּזְרָח עַיִט	11aA	who calls the Vulture[23] from the east,
מֵאֶרֶץ מֶרְחָק אִישׁ עֲצָתוֹ	11aB	from a land far away the man of his[24] counsel.
אַף־דִּבַּרְתִּי אַף־אֲבִיאֶנָּה	11bA	As I have spoken (it), so I will bring it about,
יָצַרְתִּי אַף־אֶעֱשֶׂנָּה׃	11bB	(as) I have formed (it),[25] so I will make it.

ס <פ> – 1𝔔^{a} – 4𝔔^{b} – 𝔊^{SBAQ} – 𝔖^{abcde} ....

III.B.ii.1 (Isa. 46:12)

שִׁמְעוּ אֵלַי אַבִּירֵי לֵב	12aA	Listen to me, you mighty of heart,[26]
הָרְחוֹקִים מִצְּדָקָה׃	12aB	you who are far from justice.

III.B.ii.2 (Isa. 46:13)

קֵרַבְתִּי צִדְקָתִי לֹא תִרְחָק	13aA	I bring near my justice, it is not far off;
וּתְשׁוּעָתִי לֹא תְאַחֵר	13aB	and my salvation, it will not tarry;
וְנָתַתִּי בְצִיּוֹן תְּשׁוּעָה	13bA	yes, I give in Zion my salvation,
לְיִשְׂרָאֵל תִּפְאַרְתִּי׃	13bB	to Israel my glory.

ס <פ> – 1𝔔^{a} – 𝔊^{SBA} – 𝔖^{abe} ______________________________

---

[22] In our opinion this statement betrays that the author knew some kind of history of Israel starting with Genesis. Of course there are many other indications pointing in the same direction.

[23] This is probably a designation of Cyrus, cf. כל־חפצי 44:28 (Cyrus) – כל־חפצי, עצתי 46:10, ואיש עצתו 46:11. The epithet may have been derived from the Persian emblem, cf. H.B. Tristram, *The Natural History of the Bible*, London [4]1875, 174; A. Parmelee, *All the Birds of the Bible*, New York1959, 146; *HALAT*, 772.

The Ugaritic word *'ṭ* is *not* a bird, but the name of a species of fish, cf. J.C. de Moor, "Fishes in KTU 4.427:23-29", *UF* 28 (1996), 155-7.

[24] With 1𝔔^{a} and the Ketiv.

[25] For יצר describing a mental process in God, cf. J.C. de Moor, "The Duality in God and Man: Gen. 1:26-27 as P's Interpretation of the Yahwistic Creation Account", in: J.C. de Moor (ed.), *Intertextuality in Ugarit and Israel* (OTS, 40), Leiden 1998, 112-25 (125).

[26] See note 21 above.

7.2 Isaiah 45–46 – Delimitation of Cola

COLON 45:1aA:

כֹּה־אָמַר יְהוָה֒ 1aA Thus says the LORD

With: 𝔐 (9) – 𝔊^{S} – 𝔖^{d}, 𝔖^{ace} subordinate punctuation, 𝔖^{b} subordinate punctuation after למשיחו.

Discussion: Probably the Masoretes wanted to read on until בימינו which resulted in a very long verse with six stressed units. This happens more often after the 'Botenformel' which the Masoretes appear to have treated rather inconsistently.[1] Where the formula כה אמר יהוה ל occurs the Masoretes sometimes decided to place a major dividing accent with יהוה,[2] sometimes with the prepositional adjunct.[3] In this case the decision is complicated by the fact that 𝔖^{b} divides after למשיחו (cf. BHS) whereas 𝔊^{S} and 𝔊^{Q} (also) have a point after לכורש (cf. RSV). The presence of a dividing point in two different ancient witnesses emboldens us to put the caesura after יהוה. It seems quite likely that in this particular case the choice of the Masoretes was influenced by the rabbinic exegesis of this text in bMeg., 12a.[4]

COLON 45:1aB:

לִמְשִׁיחוֹ֒ לְכ֣וֹרֶשׁ אֲשֶׁר־הֶחֱזַ֣קְתִּי בִֽימִינ֗וֹ 1aB to his anointed one, to Cyrus, whose right hand I have grasped,

With: 𝔐 (7) – 𝔊^{Q} – 𝔖^{abcde}

Discussion: 𝔊^{S} and 𝔊^{Q} have an extra dividing point after לכורש which is not supported by 𝔐 and 𝔖.

COLON 45:1bA:

לְרַד־לְפָנָיו֙ גּוֹיִ֔ם 1bA to subdue nations before him,

With: 𝔐 (5) – 𝔊^{SQ} – 𝔖^{e}

COLON 45:1bB:

וּמָתְנֵ֥י מְלָכִ֖ים אֲפַתֵּ֑חַ 1bB yes, I will ungird the loins of kings,

With: 𝔐 (2) – 𝔊^{SQ}

Discussion: 𝔖 presupposes the following colometry,

[1]See our notes at pp. 164, 268.

[2]Isa. 56:4; Jer. 4:3.

[3]Jer. 14:10; Amos 5:4.

[4]Cf. M.B. Cohen, "Masoretic Accents as a Biblical Commentary", *JANES* 4 (1972), 2-11.

לְרַד־לְפָנָיו גּוֹיִם וּמָתְנֵי מְלָכִים 1bA to subdue nations and the loins of kings before him,

אֲפַתֵּחַ לִפְתֹּחַ לְפָנָיו דְּלָתַיִם 1bB yes, I will surely open doors before him.

This division does not recommend itself because of the strange combination of רדד with מתנים.

COLON 45:1cA:

לִפְתֹּחַ לְפָנָיו דְּלָתַיִם 1cA to open doors before him,

With: 𝔐 (5) – $\mathfrak{G}^{SQ}$ – $\mathfrak{S}^{abcde}$

COLON 45:1cB:

וּשְׁעָרִים לֹא יִסָּגֵרוּ׃ 1cB yes, the gates will not be shut.

With: 𝔐 (1) – $\mathfrak{G}^{SAQ}$, major division markers in $\mathfrak{G}^{A}$ – $\mathfrak{S}^{abc}$, $\mathfrak{S}^{de}$ subordinate punctuation.

COLON 45:2aA:

אֲנִי לְפָנֶיךָ אֵלֵךְ 2aA I will go before you,

With: 𝔐 (5) – $\mathfrak{G}^{Q}$ – $\mathfrak{S}^{ab}$

COLON 45:2aB:

וַהֲרוּרִים* אוֹשֵׁר* 2aB and mountains I will make straight,

With: 𝔐 (2) – $\mathfrak{G}^{SQ}$ – $\mathfrak{S}^{abcde}$

COLON 45:2bA:

דַּלְתוֹת נְחוּשָׁה אֲשַׁבֵּר 2bA doors of bronze I will shatter,

With: 𝔐 (5) – $\mathfrak{G}^{SQ}$ – $\mathfrak{S}^{abcde}$

COLON 45:2bB:

וּבְרִיחֵי בַרְזֶל אֲגַדֵּעַ׃ 2bB and bars of iron I will smash.

With: 𝔐 (1) – $\mathfrak{G}^{S}$ – $\mathfrak{S}^{abcde}$

COLON 45:3aA:

וְנָתַתִּי לְךָ אוֹצְרוֹת חֹשֶׁךְ 3aA And I will give you the treasures of darkness

With: 𝔐 (5) – $\mathfrak{G}^{S}$

Discussion: Only $\mathfrak{G}^{S}$ supports 𝔐, no doubt because the translators did not recognize the ellipsis.

COLON 45:3aB:

וּמַטְמֻנֵ֖י מִסְתָּרִ֑ים 3aB and hidden hoards in secret places,

With: $\mathfrak{M}$ (2) – $\mathfrak{G}^{SQ}$ – $\mathfrak{S}^{abcde}$

COLON 45:3bA:

לְמַ֣עַן תֵּדַ֗ע כִּֽי־אֲנִ֧י יְהוָ֛ה 3bA that you may know that I am the LORD

With: $\mathfrak{M}$ (12) – $\mathfrak{G}^{S}$

Discussion: The Masoretes intended the Revi'a (7) with תדע as a major divider here. In the other four places where the formula occurs $\mathfrak{M}$ has a Zaqeph Qaṭon (5).[5] However, none of the ancient versions has a dividing point after תדע. $\mathfrak{G}^{SQ}$ and $\mathfrak{S}^{cde}$ divide after בשמך which would result in a very long colon, although $\mathfrak{G}^{S}$ also has a dividing point after יהוה ($\mathfrak{M}$ Tevir, No. 12). From the viewpoint of colometric balance we regard this as the best option. Moreover, the characteristic verse-line parallelism between קרא בשם and ידע argues in favour of this delimitation.[6]

COLON 45:3bB:

הַקּוֹרֵ֥א בְשִׁמְךָ֖ אֱלֹהֵ֥י יִשְׂרָאֵֽל׃ 3bB who calls you by your name, the God of Israel.

With: $\mathfrak{M}$ (1) – $\mathfrak{G}^{SQ}$ – $\mathfrak{S}^{abcde}$

COLON 45:4aA:

לְמַ֙עַן֙ עַבְדִּ֣י יַעֲקֹ֔ב 4aA For the sake of my servant Jacob,

With: $\mathfrak{M}$ (5) – $\mathfrak{G}^{SQ}$ – $\mathfrak{S}^{e}$

COLON 45:4aB:

וְיִשְׂרָאֵ֖ל בְּחִירִ֑י 4aB and Israel, my chosen one,

With: $\mathfrak{M}$ (2) – $\mathfrak{G}^{SQ}$ – $\mathfrak{S}^{abcde}$

COLON 45:4bA:

וָאֶקְרָ֤א לְךָ֙ בִּשְׁמֶ֔ךָ 4bA I call you by your name,

With: $\mathfrak{M}$ (5) – $\mathfrak{G}^{S}$

Discussion: Part of the tradition (also) divides after אכנך ($\mathfrak{G}^{S}$ [but see above], $\mathfrak{G}^{Q}$ which even has a capital letter indicating a major break, and $\mathfrak{S}^{b}$). Yet we are convinced that $\mathfrak{M}$ is preferable here (cf. Isa. 44:5).

---

[5] Exod. 8:6, 18; 9:29; Deut. 29:5; Jer. 44:29.

[6] See p. 293.

COLON 45:4bB:

אֲכַנְּךָ וְלֹא יְדַעְתָּנִי׃ 4bB I surname you, although you do not know me.

With: 𝔐 (1), small spaces (Setumot) in several manuscripts, among them 1𝔔^{a} and 1𝔔^{b} – 𝔊^{SQ} – 𝔖^{abcde}

COLON 45:5aA:

אֲנִי יְהוָה וְאֵין עוֹד 5aA I am the LORD and there is no other,

With: 𝔐 (5) – 𝔖^{abcde}
Discussion: 𝔊 is lacking at this point.

COLON 45:5aB:

זוּלָתִי אֵין אֱלֹהִים 5aB besides me there is no god.

With: 𝔐 (2) – 𝔊^{SQ} – 𝔖^{abcde}

COLON 45:5bA:

אֲאַזֶּרְךָ וְלֹא יְדַעְתָּנִי׃ 5bA I will gird you, although you do not know me,

With: 𝔐 (1) – 𝔊^{SQ} – 𝔖^{abcde}

COLON 45:6aA:

לְמַעַן יֵדְעוּ מִמִּזְרַח־שֶׁמֶשׁ וּמִמַּעֲרָבָה 6aA so that they may know from the east to the west,

With: 𝔐 (5) – 𝔊^{S} – 𝔖^{abcde} all subordinate punctuation.
Colon parallelism: מזרח || מערב.
Discussion: None of the ancient witnesses has a dividing point after ידעו where 𝔐 has a Revia‘ (7). Also the support for 𝔐's Zaqeph Qaṭon with וממערבה is rather weak which is no doubt due to the fact that the sentence runs on.

COLON 45:6aB:

כִּי־אֶפֶס בִּלְעָדָי 6aB that nothing exists apart from me –

With: 𝔐 (2) – 𝔊^{SQ}, paragraphos in 𝔊^{S} – 𝔖^{abcde}

COLON 45:6aC:

אֲנִי יְהוָה וְאֵין עוֹד׃ 6aC I am the LORD and there is no other,

With: 𝔐 (1) – 𝔊^{SQ} – 𝔖^{abcde}
Discussion: 𝔊^{S} and 𝔊^{Q} have an extra point for 𝔐's Ṭiphḥa.

COLON 45:7aA:

יוֹצֵ֥ר אוֹר֙ וּבוֹרֵ֣א חֹ֔שֶׁךְ 7aA he who forms light and creates darkness,

With: 𝔐 (5) – 𝔊^{SQ} – 𝔖^{abcde}
Colon parallelism: יצר || ברא; אור || חשך.
Discussion: 𝔊^{S} and 𝔊^{Q} have an extra point after אור (Pashṭa in 𝔐).

COLON 45:7aB:

עֹ֥שֶׂה שָׁל֖וֹם וּב֣וֹרֵא רָ֑ע 7aB who makes peace and creates evil –

With: 𝔐 (2) – 𝔊^{SQ} – 𝔖^{abcde}
Colon parallelism: עשה || ברא; שלום || רע.
Discussion: 𝔊^{S} and 𝔖^{e} have an extra point after שלום which corresponds to 𝔐's Ṭiphḥa.

COLON 45:7aC:

אֲנִ֥י יְהוָ֖ה עֹשֶׂ֥ה כָל־אֵֽלֶּה׃ 7aC I am the LORD who makes all these things.

With: 𝔐 (1), major division markers, also in 1𝔔^{a} – 𝔊^{SBAQ}, all with major division markers – 𝔖^{abcde}, major division markers in 𝔖^{abe}
Discussion: 𝔊^{SQ} insert an extra point after יהוה (𝔐 Ṭiphḥa).

COLON 45:8aA:

הַרְעִ֤יפוּ שָׁמַ֙יִם֙ מִמַּ֔עַל 8aA Drip, O heavens, from above,

With: 𝔐 (5) – 𝔊^{SQ} – 𝔖^{abcde}
Colon parallelism: שמים || מעל.

COLON 45:8aB:

וּשְׁחָקִ֖ים יִזְּלוּ־צֶ֑דֶק 8aB and let the clouds pour down justice;

With: 𝔐 (2) – 𝔊^{SQ} – 𝔖^{abcde}

COLON 45:8bA:

תִּפְתַּח־אֶ֣רֶץ וְיִפְרוּ*־יֶ֗שַׁע 8bA let the earth open up and let salvation blossom,

With: 𝔐 (7) – 𝔊^{SQ} – 𝔖^{abcde}
Colon parallelism: See our remark p. 261, n. 7.

COLON 45:8bB:

וּצְדָקָ֛ה תַצְמִ֥יחַ יַ֖חַד 8bB and let justice make sprout communion,

With: 𝔐 (5) – 𝔊[SQ], colon in 𝔊[S], major other division markers in 𝔊[Q] – 𝔖[abcde]

Discussion: Apparently 𝔊[SQ] connected v. 8bC with v. 9. This is an unlikely division because usually הוי is at the beginning of a verse.

COLON 45:8bC:

אֲנִי יְהוָה בְּרָאתִיו׃ 8bC I am the LORD, I create it.

With: 𝔐 (1) – 𝔊[SQ] – 𝔖[abcde], major division markers in 𝔖[bde]

COLON 45:9aA:

הוֹי רָב אֶת־יֹצְרוֹ 9aA Woe to him who quarrels with the one who formed him,

With: 𝔐 (5) – 𝔊[Q] – 𝔖[b], 𝔖[cde] subordinate punctuation.
Discussion: For 𝔐's Revia' (No. 7) with הוי see our comment on p. 31.

COLON 45:9aB:

חֶרֶשׂ אֶת־חַרְשֵׂי אֲדָמָה 9aB a pot among the pots of earth.

With: 𝔐 (2) – 𝔊[SBQ], paragraphos in 𝔊[B] – 𝔖[abcde]
Discussion: 𝔊[A] and 𝔊[Q] seem to have taken חרשׂ with the preceding colon and have major dividers at this point. 𝔊's paraphrasis enabled them to do so, but it is incompatible with the Hebrew.

COLON 45:9bA:

הֲיֹאמַר חֹמֶר לְיֹצְרוֹ מַה־תַּעֲשֶׂה 9bA Does the clay say to him who forms it, "What do you make?"

With: 𝔐 (5) – 𝔊[SQ] – 𝔖[abcde] all subordinate punctuation.
Colon parallelism: יצר || עשׂה.
Discussion: 𝔊[SQ] and 𝔖[e] have a point after ליצרו which is merely a pause before the direct speech (𝔐 Pashṭa).

COLON 45:9bB:

וּפָעָלְךָ אֵין־יָדַיִם לוֹ׃ 9bB or (does) your work which (itself) has no hands (say this)?

With: 𝔐 (1), Setuma in many manuscripts – 𝔊[SQ] – 𝔖[a], all others subordinate punctuation.

COLON 45:10aA:

הוֹי אֹמֵר לְאָב מַה־תּוֹלִיד 10aA Woe to him who says to a father, "What do you beget?"

With: 𝔐 (2) – $\mathfrak{G}^{SQ}$ – S^{abcde}

COLON 45:10aB:

וּלְאִשָּׁה מַה־תְּחִילִין׃ 10aB or to a wife, "What do you bring to birth?"

With: 𝔐 (1), major division markers, also in $1\mathfrak{Q}^{a}$ – $\mathfrak{G}^{SBAQ}$, major division markers in all except $\mathfrak{G}^{Q}$ – S^{abcde}, major division markers in S^{abe}

COLON 45:11aA:

כֹּה־אָמַר יְהוָה 11aA Thus says the LORD,

With: 𝔐 (12).
Discussion: 𝔐 supported by S wanted to read up to and including ויצרו, a very long colon. $\mathfrak{G}^{SQ}$ made a break after ישראל. The so-called 'Botenformel' has been treated inconsistently by the Masoretes and the ancient versions.[7] In v. 14aA which also heads a canticle both 𝔐 and the ancient versions insert a divider directly after the tetragrammaton (see below). It is for this reason that we decided to insert a ceasura here too, despite the lack of any ancient confirmation.

COLON 45:11aB:

קְדוֹשׁ יִשְׂרָאֵל וְיֹצְרוֹ 11aB the Holy One of Israel and the one who formed it,

With: 𝔐 (2) – S^{abcde}
Discussion: See our comments on v. 11aA. After this colon, S has an extra colon (ܡܪܝܐ ܚܝܠܬܢܐ ܫܡܗ "the LORD of hosts is his name") which was probably borrowed from texts like Isa. 51:15 and 54:5. After this colon, S^{ad} have major divison markers, but this must be an error, or was perhaps meant as an asterisk to mark the plus, because the direct speech has yet to start at this point.

COLON 45:11bA:

הָאֹתִיּוֹת שְׁאָלוּנִי עַל־בָּנַי 11bA The things to come? Interrogate me concerning my children

With: 𝔐 (12) – $\mathfrak{G}^{SQ}$ – S^{abde}, S^{c} subordinate punctuation.
Discussion: The ancient witnesses disagree with regard to the delimitation of this colon. $\mathfrak{G}^{S}$ and $\mathfrak{G}^{Q}$ have a first divider after האתיות which they connect with ויצרו which reflects a free paraphrasis rather than a different 'Vorlage'. 𝔐 has no support whatsoever for its Zaqeph Qaṭon

[7] See our note to 43:1, p. 164. See also above, on v. 1.

with שאלוני. However, all other ancient witnesses have a divider after על־בני which we accept because the two resulting cola are nicely balanced.

COLON 45:11bB:

וְעַל־פֹּעַל יָדַי תְּצַוֻּנִי׃ 11bB command me with regard the work of my hands.

With: $\mathfrak{M}$ (1) – $\mathfrak{G}^{SAQ}$, all with major division markers – $\mathfrak{S}^{abcde}$

COLON 45:12aA:

אָנֹכִי עָשִׂיתִי אֶרֶץ 12aA It is I who made the earth,

With: $\mathfrak{M}$ (5) – $\mathfrak{G}^{SQ}$

COLON 45:12aB:

וְאָדָם עָלֶיהָ בָרָאתִי 12aB and created man upon it,

With: $\mathfrak{M}$ (2) – $\mathfrak{G}^{SQ}$ – $\mathfrak{S}^{abcde}$

COLON 45:12bA:

אֲנִי יָדַי נָטוּ שָׁמַיִם 12bA I – my hands stretched out the heavens,

With: $\mathfrak{M}$ (5) – $\mathfrak{G}^{SQ}$ – $\mathfrak{S}^{abcde}$
Discussion: For the Revia‘ (No. 7) with אני see our comment on p. 31.

COLON 45:12bB:

וְכָל־צְבָאָם צִוֵּיתִי׃ 12bB and all their host I command.

With: $\mathfrak{M}$ (1) – $\mathfrak{G}^{SQ}$ – $\mathfrak{S}^{abcde}$

COLON 45:13aA:

אָנֹכִי הַעִירֹתִהוּ בְצֶדֶק 13aA It is I who wake him up in justice,

With: $\mathfrak{M}$ (5) – $\mathfrak{G}^{SQ}$ – $\mathfrak{S}^{abe}$, $\mathfrak{S}^{cd}$ subordinate punctuation.

COLON 45:13aB:

וְכָל־דְּרָכָיו אֲיַשֵּׁר 13aB yes, all his ways I will make straight.

With: $\mathfrak{M}$ (2) – $\mathfrak{G}^{SQ}$ – $\mathfrak{S}^{abcde}$

COLON 45:13bA:

הוּא־יִבְנֶה עִירִי וְגָלוּתִי יְשַׁלֵּחַ 13bA It is he who will rebuild my city and will send my exiles home,

With: $\mathfrak{M}$ (5) – $\mathfrak{G}^{SQ}$ – $\mathfrak{S}^{abcde}$
Discussion: $\mathfrak{G}^{S}$ and $\mathfrak{G}^{Q}$ have an extra point after עירי ($\mathfrak{M}$ Pashṭa).

Colon 45:13bB:

לֹא בִמְחִיר וְלֹא בְשֹׁחַד 13bB not for a price and not for presents,

With: $\mathfrak{M}$ (5) – $\mathfrak{G}^{SQ}$
Discussion: Even though only $\mathfrak{G}$ has the same division as $\mathfrak{M}$ we believe they deserve confidence.[8]

Colon 45:13bC:

אָמַר יְהוָה צְבָאוֹת׃ 13bC says the Lord of hosts.

With: $\mathfrak{M}$ (1) – $\mathfrak{G}^{SBAQ}$, all with major division markers – $\mathfrak{S}^{abcde}$, $\mathfrak{S}^{abce}$ with major division markers.

Colon 45:14aA:

כֹּה ׀ אָמַר יְהוָה 14aA Thus says the Lord,

With: $\mathfrak{M}$ (7) – $\mathfrak{G}^{SQ}$ – $\mathfrak{S}^{abcde}$

Colon 45:14aB:

יְגִיעַ מִצְרַיִם 14aB The resources of Egypt

With: $\mathfrak{G}^{SQ}$ – $\mathfrak{S}^{acde}$ subordinate punctuation.
Discussion: The Masoretes read a conjunctive accent here (Merekha). Probably they intended to take everything up to מדה as one long colon (6 stressed units). However, none of the ancient witnesses has a break after מדה. Isa. 43:3b argues in favour of taking מצרים in one colon and the combination כוש וסבא in the next one which is what all other ancient witnesses support here too (see below).

Colon 45:14aC:

וּסְחַר־כּוּשׁ וּסְבָאִים 14aC and the merchandise of Cush and the Sabeans,

With: $\mathfrak{M}$ (9) – $\mathfrak{G}^{SQ}$ – $\mathfrak{S}^{abcde}$
Discussion: See the preceding colon. $\mathfrak{M}$'s low level distinctive accent indicates that the Masoretes did not regard it as a major divider.

Colon 45:14bA:

אַנְשֵׁי מִדָּה עָלַיִךְ יַעֲבֹרוּ 14bA tall men will pass over to you

[8]See also our comments on p. 23.

With: $\mathfrak{M}$ (10) – $\mathfrak{G}^{SQ}$ – $\mathfrak{S}^{abcde}$
Discussion: See above. Again $\mathfrak{G}$ and $\mathfrak{S}$ presuppose a different and in our opinion better division.

COLON 45:14bB:

וְלָךְ יִהְיוּ אַחֲרַיִךְ יֵלֵכוּ 14bB and will be yours, they will go behind you,

With: $\mathfrak{M}$ (5) – $\mathfrak{G}^{SQ}$ – $\mathfrak{S}^{abcde}$
Discussion: $\mathfrak{G}^{SQ}$ and $\mathfrak{S}^{a}$ support $\mathfrak{M}$'s divider with יהיו. The resulting quadrocolon is a real option, but we prefer to follow the more solidly attestated divider with ילכו, so that the tricola 14a and 14b balance each other.

COLON 45:14bC:

בַּזִּקִּים יַעֲבֹרוּ 14bC in chains they will pass;

With: $\mathfrak{M}$ (2) – $\mathfrak{G}^{SQ}$ – $\mathfrak{S}^{ade}$

COLON 45:14cA:

וְאֵלַיִךְ יִשְׁתַּחֲווּ 14cA and they will bow down for you,

With: $\mathfrak{M}$ (10) – $\mathfrak{G}^{SQ}$ – $\mathfrak{S}^{abe}$
Discussion: Although it is possible to interpret the pair שחה || פלל as colon parallelism,[9] we follow the ancient versions in assuming a bicolon (compare the distribution of imperfects in v. 14bB-C).

COLON 45:14cB:

אֵלַיִךְ יִתְפַּלָּלוּ 14cB and they will pray to you:

With: $\mathfrak{M}$ (5) – $\mathfrak{G}^{SQ}$ – $\mathfrak{S}^{abcde}$

COLON 45:14dA:

אַךְ בָּךְ אֵל 14dA "Only in you is God

With: $\mathfrak{M}$ (12) – $\mathfrak{G}^{SQ}$
Discussion: The Masoretes wanted to read on until the end of the verse, a colon of six stressed units. However, in the next verse they distribute אל || אלהים over two cola (so also in Isa. 45:21; 46:9) which renders the division in $\mathfrak{G}^{SQ}$ more likely.

[9] As in Isa. 44:17bA, see p. 237.

Colon 45:14dB:

וְאֵ֥ין ע֛וֹד אֶ֖פֶס אֱלֹהִֽים׃ 14dB and there does not exist any other god.

With: 𝔐 (1) – 𝔊^{SQ} – 𝔖^{abcde}

Colon 45:15aA:

אָכֵ֕ן אַתָּ֖ה אֵ֣ל מִסְתַּתֵּ֑ר 15aA However, you are a God hiding himself,

With: 𝔐 (2) – 𝔊^{SQ}
Discussion: 𝔖 was misguided by the continuing sentence. For the Zaqeph Gadol with אכן see p. 31.

Colon 45:15aB:

אֱלֹהֵ֥י יִשְׂרָאֵ֖ל מוֹשִֽׁיעַ׃ 15aB O Saviour God of Israel!

With: 𝔐 (1) – 𝔊^{SQ} – 𝔖^{abcde}

Colon 45:16aA:

בּ֥וֹשׁוּ וְגַֽם־נִכְלְמ֖וּ כֻּלָּ֑ם 16aA They are ashamed and disgraced, all of them;

With: 𝔐 (2) – 𝔊^{Q}
Colon parallelism: בוש || כלם.
Discussion: 𝔖 takes יחדו with the first colon.

Colon 45:16aB:

יַחְדָּו֙ הָלְכ֣וּ בַכְּלִמָּ֔ה 16aB altogether they go in disgrace,

With: 𝔐 (5) – 𝔊^{SQ}
Discussion: 𝔖 combines the remainder of v. 16 because the sentence runs on.

Colon 45:16aC:

חָרָשֵׁ֖י צִירִֽים׃ 16aC the craftsmen with their drawings.

With: 𝔐 (1), Seder; Setuma in 1𝔔^{a} – 𝔊^{SQ}, major division markers in all – 𝔖^{abce}, 𝔖^{d} subordinate puntuation.

Colon 45:17aA:

יִשְׂרָאֵל֙ נוֹשַׁ֣ע בַּֽיהוָ֔ה 17aA But Israel is saved by the Lord,

With: 𝔐 (5) – 𝔊^{Q} – 𝔖^{e}
Discussion: The support for 𝔐 is weak, probably because the sentence runs on.

COLON 45:17aB:

תְּשׁוּעַת עוֹלָמִים 17aB a salvation of ages.

With: $\mathfrak{M}$ (2) – $\mathfrak{G}^{SQ}$ – $\mathfrak{S}^{abcde}$

COLON 45:17bA:

לֹא־תֵבֹשׁוּ וְלֹא־תִכָּלְמוּ 17bA They will not be ashamed and and not be disgraced

With: $\mathfrak{M}$ (8) – $\mathfrak{G}^{Q}$
Colon parallelism: בוש || כלם.
Discussion: $\mathfrak{M}$ and most other witnesses read on until the end of the verse. We accept $\mathfrak{G}^{Q}$'s division because it results in a better balance between v. 17a and v. 17b.

COLON 45:17bB:

עַד־עוֹלְמֵי עַד׃ 17bB to ages everlasting."

With: $\mathfrak{M}$ (1), major dividers in many manuscripts, also 1$\mathfrak{Q}^{a}$ – $\mathfrak{G}^{SBQ}$, major division markers in $\mathfrak{G}^{SB}$ – $\mathfrak{S}^{abcde}$, major division markers in $\mathfrak{S}^{b}$

COLON 45:18aA:

כִּי כֹה אָמַר־יְהוָה בּוֹרֵא הַשָּׁמַיִם 18aA For thus says the LORD, who created the heavens,

With: $\mathfrak{M}$ (13) – $\mathfrak{G}^{SQ}$
Discussion: Apparently $\mathfrak{M}$ wanted to read on to האלהים (Revia', unsupported by the other witnesses), a colon of no less than seven stressed units. In our opinion it is better to follow $\mathfrak{G}^{S}$ and $\mathfrak{G}^{Q}$ so that we have a case here of a 'Botenformel' enlarged with an epithet.[10] See also the next colon.

COLON 45:18aB:

הוּא הָאֱלֹהִים יֹצֵר הָאָרֶץ 18aB He (who) is God, who formed the earth,

With: – $\mathfrak{G}^{SQ}$ – $\mathfrak{S}^{abcde}$ all subordinate punctuation.
Discussion: $\mathfrak{M}$ has a conjunctive accent here which is obviously a consequence of its Revia' with האלהים (see our comment on the preceding colon). The division of $\mathfrak{G}$ and $\mathfrak{S}$, however, results in a nice verse-line parallelism: יהוה || אלהים, ברא || יצר || עשה, and שמים || ארץ.[11]

---

[10] See our comment p. 164.
[11] All these are standard parallels. See the Index of Parallel Words.

COLON 45:18aC:

וְעֹשָׂהּ֙ ה֣וּא כֽוֹנְנָ֔הּ 18aC and the One who made it, He is the One who established it –

With: 𝔐 (5) – 𝔊^{SQ} – 𝔖^{abcde}
Colon parallelism: עשׂה || כון.
Discussion: 𝔊^{SQ} and 𝔖^{e} have an extra point after ועשׂה (𝔐 Pashṭa), but the suffixes 3rd fem. sg. as well as the colon parallelism argue in favour of the colometry proposed.

COLON 45:18bA:

לֹא־תֹ֥הוּ בְרָאָ֖הּ 18bA not as a void he created it,

With: 𝔐 (8) – 𝔊^{SQ} – 𝔖^{abcde}

COLON 45:18bB:

לָשֶׁ֣בֶת יְצָרָ֑הּ 18bB to be inhabited he formed it –

With: 𝔐 (2) – 𝔊^{SAQ}, major division markers in 𝔊^{A} – 𝔖^{abcde}, major division markers in 𝔖^{ab}

COLON 45:18bC:

אֲנִ֥י יְהוָ֖ה וְאֵ֥ין עֽוֹד׃ 18bC I am the LORD and there is no other.

With: 𝔐 (1) – 𝔊^{SQ} – 𝔖^{abcde}

COLON 45:19aA:

לֹ֨א בַסֵּ֜תֶר דִּבַּ֗רְתִּי 19aA I did not speak in secret,

With: 𝔐 (7) – 𝔊^{SQ} – 𝔖^{e}

COLON 45:19aB:

בִּמְקוֹם֙ אֶ֣רֶץ חֹ֔שֶׁךְ 19aB in a place of the land of darkness,

With: 𝔐 (5) – 𝔊^{SQ} – 𝔖^{abcde}

COLON 45:19aC:

לֹ֤א אָמַ֙רְתִּי֙ לְזֶ֣רַע יַעֲקֹ֔ב תֹּ֖הוּ בַקְּשׁ֑וּנִי 19aC I have not said to the seed of Jacob: "Seek me in the void!"

With: 𝔐 (2) – 𝔊^{SQ} – 𝔖^{abcde}
Discussion: in 𝔊^{S} and 𝔊^{Q} an extra point after יעקב corresponds to 𝔐's Ṭiphḥa.

Colon 45:19bA:

אֲנִ֣י יְהוָ֗ה דֹּבֵ֥ר צֶ֙דֶק 19bA I am the Lord, who speaks what is just,

With: 𝔐 (5) – $\mathfrak{G}^{SQ}$ – $\mathfrak{S}^{ae}$ subordinate punctuation.

Colon 45:19bB:

מַגִּ֖יד מֵישָׁרִֽים׃ 19bB who tells what is straight.

With: 𝔐 (1) – $\mathfrak{G}^{SAQ}$, major division markers in $\mathfrak{G}^{SA}$ – $\mathfrak{S}^{abcde}$, major division marker in $\mathfrak{S}^{b}$

Colon 45:20aA:

הִקָּבְצ֥וּ וָבֹ֛אוּ 20aA Assemble and come,

With: 𝔐 (12) – $\mathfrak{G}^{SQ}$
Colon parallelism: בוא || קבץ.
Discussion: The colometric analysis of v. 20 is far from simple. 𝔐 probably intended a colon of six stresses running on through הגוים. However, there are clear indications that the first two imperatives should be taken as a pair. The colon parallelism does not include נגש which is never found in poetical parallelism with בוא *and* קבץ. So this argues against joining the three imperatives. Moreover, in the next verse (Isa. 45:21aA) the second imperative is provided with a Zaqeph Qaṭon, in Isa. 45:22 the vocative follows immediately after the pair, in Isa. 46:8 the second imperative is provided with an Atnaḥ, and in Isa. 48:14 the second imperative has a Zaqeph Qaṭon again. All this suggests that $\mathfrak{G}^{SQ}$ preserve the right colometry here.

Colon 45:20aB:

הִֽתְנַגְּשׁ֥וּ יַחְדָּ֖ו 20aB draw near together,

With: 𝔐 (8) – $\mathfrak{G}^{Q}$ – $\mathfrak{S}^{b}$, $\mathfrak{S}^{acde}$ subordinate punctuation.

Colon 45:20aC:

פְּלִיטֵ֣י הַגּוֹיִ֑ם 20aC survivors of the nations.

With: 𝔐 (2) – $\mathfrak{G}^{SQ}$ – $\mathfrak{S}^{abcde}$

Colon 45:20bA:

לֹ֣א יָדְע֗וּ הַנֹּֽשְׂאִים֙ אֶת־עֵ֣ץ פִּסְלָ֔ם 20bA They do not know, those who are carrying the wood of their idols,

With: 𝔐 (5) – $\mathfrak{G}^{S}$ – $\mathfrak{S}^{abcde}$ all subordinate punctuation.
Discussion: 𝔐's Revia‘ with ידעו is without support.

COLON 45:20bB:

וּמִתְפַּלְלִ֔ים אֶל־אֵ֖ל לֹ֥א יוֹשִֽׁיעַ׃ 20bB who pray to a god that does not save.

With: 𝔐 (1) – 𝔊^SQ – 𝔖^bcd, 𝔖^ae subordinate punctuation.
Discussion: 𝔊^S and 𝔊^Q have an extra point after אל־אל which corresponds to the Tiphḥa (8) of 𝔐. The latter's Zaqeph Qaṭon with ומתפללים is unsupported by the other ancient witnesses. See p. 31.

COLON 45:21aA:

הַגִּ֣ידוּ וְהַגִּ֔ישׁוּ 21aA Tell and bring near,

With: 𝔐 (5) – 𝔊^SQ
Colon parallelism: נגד || נגשׁ.
Discussion: The colon parallelism supports this division.

COLON 45:21aB:

אַ֥ף יִֽוָּעֲצ֖וּ יַחְדָּ֑ו 21aB yes, let them take counsel together:

With: 𝔐 (2) – 𝔊^S – 𝔖^abcde

COLON 45:21bA:

מִ֣י הִשְׁמִיעַ֩ זֹ֨את מִקֶּ֜דֶם 21bA Who has made this heard from olden times,

With: 𝔐 (13) – 𝔊^S – 𝔖^abcde
Discussion: Again 𝔐 seems to adopt an extra long colon (six stresses) ending only with הגידה.

COLON 45:21bB:

מֵאָ֣ז הִגִּידָ֗הּ 21bB has told it since then?

With: 𝔐 (7) – 𝔊^SQ, colon in 𝔊^S capital in 𝔊^Q
Discussion: In 𝔖 this colon is absent.

COLON 45:21cA:

הֲל֨וֹא אֲנִ֤י יְהוָה֙ 21cA Was it not I, the LORD?

With: 𝔐 (10) – 𝔊^SQ – 𝔖^ad, 𝔖^bce subordinate punctuation.

COLON 45:21cB:

וְאֵֽין־ע֤וֹד אֱלֹהִים֙ מִבַּלְעָדַ֔י 21cB And there is no God apart from me,

With: 𝔐 (5) – 𝔊^SQ – 𝔖^abcde

Colon 45:21dA:

אֵל־צַדִּיק וּמוֹשִׁיעַ 21dA a just and a saving God,

With: $\mathfrak{M}$ (5) – $\mathfrak{G}^{Q}$ – $\mathfrak{S}^{abe}$ subordinate punctuation.
Colon parallelism: צדיק || ישע (root).
Discussion: The colon parallelism favours the division.

Colon 45:21dB:

אַיִן זוּלָתִי׃ 21dB there is none besides me.

With: $\mathfrak{M}$ (1) – $\mathfrak{G}^{SBQ}$, major division markers in $\mathfrak{G}^{SB}$ – $\mathfrak{S}^{abcde}$

Colon 45:22aA:

פְּנוּ־אֵלַי וְהִוָּשְׁעוּ 22aA Turn unto me and be saved,

With: $\mathfrak{M}$ (8) – $\mathfrak{G}^{SQ}$
Colon parallelism: פנה || ישע (root).
Discussion: Both $\mathfrak{M}$ and $\mathfrak{S}$ assumed a longer colon ending with כל־אפסי־ארץ. The colon parallelism and $\mathfrak{G}$ argue against this. See also our comment on v. 20aA.

Colon 45:22aB:

כָּל־אַפְסֵי־אָרֶץ 22aB all you ends of the earth,

With: $\mathfrak{M}$ (2) – $\mathfrak{G}^{SQ}$ – $\mathfrak{S}^{abcde}$

Colon 45:22bA:

כִּי אֲנִי־אֵל וְאֵין עוֹד׃ 22bA for I am God and there is no other.

With: $\mathfrak{M}$ (1) – $\mathfrak{G}^{SQ}$ – $\mathfrak{S}^{abcde}$
Discussion: $\mathfrak{G}^{SQ}$ have an extra point after אל ($\mathfrak{M}$ Ṭiphḥa).

Colon 45:23aA:

בִּי נִשְׁבַּעְתִּי 23aA I swear by myself,

With: $\mathfrak{M}$ (5) – $\mathfrak{G}^{SAQ}$, major division markers in $\mathfrak{G}^{A}$ – $\mathfrak{S}^{be}$, $\mathfrak{S}^{acd}$ subordinate punctuation.

Colon 45:23aB:

יָצָא מִפִּי צְדָקָה 23aB justice goes forth from my mouth,

With: $\mathfrak{M}$ (12) – $\mathfrak{G}^{SQ}$
Discussion: $\mathfrak{M}$ and $\mathfrak{S}$ read on until ישוב, apparently because they did not recognize the ellipsis, as was often the case.

COLON 45:23aC:

דָּבָר וְלֹא יָשׁוּב 23aC a word which shall not return:

With: 𝔐 (2) – 𝔊^{SQ} – 𝔖^{bcde}

COLON 45:23bA:

כִּי־לִי תִּכְרַע כָּל־בֶּרֶךְ 23bA Unto me every knee shall bow,

With: 𝔐 (5) – 𝔊^{SQ} – 𝔖^{ab}, 𝔖^{cde} subordinate punctuation.

COLON 45:23bB:

תִּשָּׁבַע כָּל־לָשׁוֹן׃ 23bB every tongue shall swear.

With: 𝔐 (1) – 𝔖^{abcde}
Discussion: 𝔊 connects with v. 24 in a free rendering.

COLON 45:24aA:

אַךְ בַּיהוָה לִי אָמַר צְדָקוֹת 24aA "Only in the LORD", they say to me, "is full justice,

With: – 𝔖^{abcde}
Discussion: 𝔐's colometry for v. 24 is shared by none of the other witnesses. 𝔊^{Q} and 𝔖^{e} have a point after אמר (𝔐 Ṭiphḥa). We follow 𝔖's mainstream.

COLON 45:24aB:

וָעֹז עָדָיו יָבוֹא 24aB and strength comes to him,

With: – 𝔊^{SQ} – 𝔖^{abcde}
𝔐 has a conjunctive accent. See our remark on v. 24aA.

COLON 45:24aC:

וְיֵבֹשׁוּ כֹּל הַנֶּחֱרִים בּוֹ׃ 24aC but all who are raging against him shall be put to shame.

With: 𝔐 (1) – 𝔖^{abcde}

COLON 45:25aA:

בַּיהוָה יִצְדְּקוּ וְיִתְהַלְלוּ 25aA In the Lord will be justified and will glory

With: 𝔐 (8) – 𝔊^{Q} – 𝔖^{b}

COLON 45:25aB:

כָּל־זֶרַע יִשְׂרָאֵל׃ 25aB all the seed of Israel."

With: 𝔐 (1), Setuma in 1Q[a] and 4Q[b] – $\mathfrak{G}^{SBAQ}$, major division markers in $\mathfrak{G}^{SBA}$ – $\mathfrak{S}^{abde}$, $\mathfrak{S}^{c}$ subordinate punctuation.

Colon 46:1aA:

כָּרַ֥ע בֵּל֙ קֹרֵ֣ס נְב֔וֹ 1aA Bel bows, Nebo cringes,

With: 𝔐 (5) – $\mathfrak{G}^{SQ}$ – $\mathfrak{S}^{abcde}$
Colon parallelism: בל || נבו (unique); כרע || קרס.
Discussion: $\mathfrak{G}^{SQ}$ have an extra dividing point after בל (𝔐 Pashṭa).

Colon 46:1aB:

הָיוּ֙ עֲצַבֵּיהֶ֔ם לַחַיָּ֖ה וְלַבְּהֵמָ֑ה 1aB their grievous images are for the beasts and the cattle,

With: 𝔐 (2) – $\mathfrak{G}^{SQ}$ – $\mathfrak{S}^{abcde}$
Colon parallelism: חיה || בהמה.
Discussion: 𝔐's Zaqeph Qaṭon (5) has only the weak support of subordinate punctuation in 𝔖.

Colon 46:1bA:

נְשֻׂאֹתֵיכֶ֣ם עֲמוּס֔וֹת 1bA the objects you wanted to be carried become a burden,

With: 𝔐 (5) – $\mathfrak{G}^{SQ}$
Colon parallelism: נשא || עמס.
Discussion: 𝔖 is lacking at this point.

Colon 46:1bB:

מַשָּׂ֖א לַעֲיֵפָֽה׃ 1bB a load to a weary animal.

With: 𝔐 (1) – $\mathfrak{G}^{Q}$ – $\mathfrak{S}^{abcde}$

Colon 46:2aA:

קָרְס֨וּ כָרְע֜וּ יַחְדָּ֗ו 2aA They cringe, they bow together,

With: 𝔐 (5) – $\mathfrak{G}^{SQ}$ – $\mathfrak{S}^{abcde}$
Colon parallelism: קרס || כרע.

Colon 46:2aB:

לֹ֥א יָכְל֖וּ מַלֵּ֣ט מַשָּׂ֑א 2aB they are unable to save the load,

With: 𝔐 (2) – $\mathfrak{G}^{SQ}$ – $\mathfrak{S}^{abcde}$

COLON 46:2bA:

וְנַפְשָׁם בַּשְּׁבִי הָלָכָה׃ 2bA and they themselves go into captivity.

With: 𝔐 (1), major division markers, also in 1𝔔^{a} and 4𝔔^{b} – 𝔊^{SBAQ}, major division markers in all – 𝔖^{abcde}, major division markers in all.

COLON 46:3aA:

שִׁמְעוּ אֵלַי בֵּית יַעֲקֹב 3aA Listen to me, O house of Jacob,

With: 𝔐 (5) – 𝔊^{SQ} – 𝔖^{ace} subordinate punctuation.

COLON 46:3aB:

וְכָל־שְׁאֵרִית בֵּית יִשְׂרָאֵל 3aB and all the remnant of the house of Israel,

With: 𝔐 (2) – 𝔊^{Q} – 𝔖^{acde}, 𝔖^{b} subordinate punctuation.

COLON 46:3bA:

הָעֲמֻסִים מִנִּי־בֶטֶן 3bA you who were a burden from the womb,

With: 𝔐 (5) – 𝔊^{Q} – 𝔖^{d} apparently misplaced point after הנשאים, 𝔖^{e} subordinate punctuation.
Discussion: Although the support for 𝔐 is weak, we accepts its colometric division.

COLON 46:3bB:

הַנְּשֻׂאִים מִנִּי־רָחַם׃ 3bB who were carried since your birth.

With: 𝔐 (1) – 𝔊^{Q} – 𝔖^{abcde}

COLON 46:4aA:

וְעַד־זִקְנָה אֲנִי הוּא 4aA Even unto (your) old age I am the same One,

With: 𝔐 (5) – 𝔊^{SQ} – 𝔖^{bde}

COLON 46:4aB:

וְעַד־שֵׂיבָה אֲנִי אֶסְבֹּל 4aB and unto (your) greyness I will bear (you);

With: 𝔐 (2) – 𝔊^{SQ} – 𝔖^{abcde}

COLON 46:4bA:

אֲנִי עָשִׂיתִי וַאֲנִי אֶשָּׂא 4bA I have made (you) and I will continue to carry,

With: 𝔐 (5) – 𝔊^{SQ} – 𝔖^{abcde}

Discussion: 𝔊[S] and 𝔊[Q] have an extra point after עשׂיתי which corresponds to Pashṭa (10) in 𝔐.

COLON 46:4bB:

וַאֲנִ֥י אֶסְבֹּ֖ל וַאֲמַלֵּֽט׃ 4bB will continue to bear and will continue to save (you).

With: 𝔐 (1), major division markers, also in 1Q[a] – 𝔊[SAQ], major division markers in 𝔊[SA] – 𝔖[abcde], major divsion markers in 𝔖[abe]
Discussion: 𝔐's Ṭiphḥa (8) is represented by a dividing point after אסבל in 𝔊[SQ].

COLON 46:5aA:

לְמִ֥י תְדַמְּי֖וּנִי וְתַשְׁו֑וּ 5aA And to whom will you liken me and make me equal,

With: 𝔐 (2).
Colon parallelism: דמה || שוה.
Discussion: 𝔊 shortens the colon and possibly reads the next word differently. 𝔖 condenses 𝔐 in a different way. In view of Isa. 40:18, 25, there is hardly room for doubting the correctness of 𝔐's division.

COLON 46:5aB:

וְתַמְשְׁל֖וּנִי וְנִדְמֶֽה׃ 5aB and compare me that we may be alike?

With: 𝔐 (1) – 𝔊[SQ], paragraphos in 𝔊[Q] – 𝔖[abcde]
Colon parallelism: משל || דמה (unique).
Discussion: Although 𝔖 shortens the colon, it may be assumed to have read a divider here.

COLON 46:6aA:

הַזָּלִ֤ים זָהָב֙ מִכִּ֔יס 6aA Those who pour out gold from the purse,

With: 𝔐 (5) – 𝔊[SQ] – 𝔖[ace], 𝔖[bd] subordinate punctuation.

COLON 46:6aB:

וְכֶ֖סֶף בַּקָּנֶ֣ה יִשְׁקֹ֑לוּ 6aB and weigh out silver on the scales,

With: 𝔐 (2) – 𝔊[SQ] – 𝔖[a], 𝔖[bcde] subordinate punctuation.

COLON 46:6bA:

יִשְׂכְּר֤וּ צוֹרֵף֙ וְיַעֲשֵׂ֣הוּ אֵ֔ל 6bA hire a goldsmith and he makes a god of it;

With: 𝔐 (5) – 𝔊[SQ] – 𝔖[abcd]
Discussion: 𝔊[SQ] have an extra point after צורף (𝔐 Pashṭa).

Colon 46:6bB:

יִסְגְּדוּ אַף־יִשְׁתַּחֲווּ׃ 6bB then they worship, even bow down!

With: $\mathfrak{M}$ (1) – $\mathfrak{G}^{SQ}$ – $\mathfrak{S}^{abcde}$
Colon parallelism: סגד || שחה.

Colon 46:7aA:

יִשָּׂאֻהוּ עַל־כָּתֵף יִסְבְּלֻהוּ 7aA They lift him up, they bear him on the shoulder,

With: $\mathfrak{M}$ (13) – $\mathfrak{G}^{SQ}$ – $\mathfrak{S}^{e}$
Colon parallelism: נשׂא || סבל.
Discussion: $\mathfrak{M}$ has an extra long colon running on to ויעמד (6 stresses). $\mathfrak{G}^{S}$ and $\mathfrak{S}^{be}$ have a point after על־כתף, $\mathfrak{G}^{SQ}$ have another point after ויניחהו, and finally $\mathfrak{S}^{abcde}$ have a point after תחתיו. The witnesses cited above support the colometry we prefer because it seems more logical to start a new colon with ו and because the colon parallelism favours two distinct pairs.

Colon 46:7aB:

וְיַנִּיחֻהוּ תַחְתָּיו וְיַעֲמֹד 7aB they put him down and (there) he stands;

With: $\mathfrak{M}$ (5) – $\mathfrak{G}^{Q}$
Colon parallelism: נוח Hiph. || עמד (unique).
Discussion: $\mathfrak{S}$ is lacking.

Colon 46:7aC:

מִמְּקוֹמוֹ לֹא יָמִישׁ 7aC he will not move from his place.

With: $\mathfrak{M}$ (2) – $\mathfrak{G}^{SQ}$ – $\mathfrak{S}^{abcde}$

Colon 46:7bA:

אַף־יִצְעַק אֵלָיו וְלֹא יַעֲנֶה 7bA Even when one cries out to him, he does not answer;

With: $\mathfrak{M}$ (5).
Colon parallelism: צעק || ענה.
Discussion: $\mathfrak{G}^{SQ}$ and $\mathfrak{S}^{ace}$ have an extra point after אליו ($\mathfrak{M}$ Pashṭa). This is a serious option which would make v. 7b a tricolon. However, the attested colon parallelism speaks in favour of $\mathfrak{M}$.

Colon 46:7bB:

מִצָּרָתוֹ לֹא יוֹשִׁיעֶנּוּ׃ 7bB from his anguish he does not save him.

With: 𝔐 (1), major division markers, also in 1Q^{a} – 𝔊^{SAQ}, major division markers in all three – 𝔖^{abcde}, major division markers in 𝔖^{abce}

COLON 46:8aA:

זִכְרוּ־זֹאת וְהִתְאֹשָׁשׁוּ 8aA Remember this and behave like men,

With: 𝔐 (2) – 𝔊^{SQ} – 𝔖^{abcde}

COLON 46:8aB:

הָשִׁיבוּ פוֹשְׁעִים עַל־לֵב׃ 8aB bring it back to your hearts, O transgressors.

With: 𝔐 (1) – 𝔊^{Q} – 𝔖^{abcde}
Discussion: 𝔊^{SQ} have an extra point after the vocative פושעים (𝔐 Ṭiphḥa).

COLON 46:9aA:

זִכְרוּ רִאשֹׁנוֹת מֵעוֹלָם 9aA Remember the first things, from eternity on,

With: 𝔐 (2) – 𝔊^{SQ} – 𝔖^{abcde}
Colon parallelism: ראשון || עולם.

COLON 46:9aB:

כִּי אָנֹכִי אֵל וְאֵין עוֹד 9aB that I am God, and there is no other,

With: 𝔐 (5).
Discussion: 𝔊^{S} and 𝔊^{Q} have an extra divider after אל which corresponds to the Pashṭa in 𝔐. None of the other ancient witnesses supports 𝔐 which is understandable because on the one hand texts like Isa. 45:5aA, 6bA, 18bC suggest that אין־עוד is at the end of the colon, whereas on the other texts like Isa. 45:14dB and 45:21cB open the possibility to take אלהים with this colon. The latter option was chosen by 𝔖 (𝔊 is lacking). The nice verse-line parallelism made us opt for the Masoretic division.[12]

COLON 46:9aC:

אֱלֹהִים וְאֶפֶס כָּמוֹנִי׃ 9aC a God – and none like me exists! –

With: 𝔐 (1) – 𝔊^{SQ} – 𝔖^{be}, but 𝔖^{acd}, recognizing the unfinished sentence, subordinate punctuation.

---

12 See p. 307.

COLON 46:10aA:

מַגִּ֤יד מֵֽרֵאשִׁית֙ אַחֲרִ֔ית 10aA who tells the outcome from the beginning

With: $\mathfrak{M}$ (5) – $\mathfrak{G}^{S}$ – $\mathfrak{S}^{abcde}$
Colon parallelism: ראשית || אחרית.

COLON 46:10aB:

וּמִקֶּ֖דֶם אֲשֶׁ֣ר לֹא־נַעֲשׂ֑וּ 10aB and from olden times that which had not yet been made,

With: $\mathfrak{M}$ (2) – $\mathfrak{G}^{SQ}$ – $\mathfrak{S}^{e}$

COLON 46:10bA:

אֹמֵר֙ עֲצָתִ֣י תָק֔וּם 10bA who says, "My counsel shall stand,

With: $\mathfrak{M}$ (5) – $\mathfrak{G}^{SQ}$ – $\mathfrak{S}^{abcd}$
Discussion: $\mathfrak{S}^{abcde}$ introduce the direct speech with a point and $\mathfrak{G}^{A}$ even inserts a capital letter and a protruding line here. Yet these markers should be regarded as the equivalent of $\mathfrak{M}$'s Pashṭa.

COLON 46:10bB:

וְכָל־חֶפְצִ֖י אֶעֱשֶֽׂה׃ 10bB and everything I want I will make!",

With: $\mathfrak{M}$ (1) – $\mathfrak{G}^{SQ}$ – $\mathfrak{S}^{bcde}$

COLON 46:11aA:

קֹרֵ֤א מִמִּזְרָח֙ עַ֔יִט 11aA who calls the Vulture from the east,

With: $\mathfrak{M}$ (5) – $\mathfrak{G}^{SQ}$ – $\mathfrak{S}^{e}$, $\mathfrak{S}^{abcd}$ subordinate punctuation.

COLON 46:11aB:

מֵאֶ֥רֶץ מֶרְחָ֖ק אִ֣ישׁ עֲצָתִ֑ו 11aB from a land far away the man of his counsel.

With: $\mathfrak{M}$ (2) – $\mathfrak{G}^{Q}$ – $\mathfrak{S}^{bce}$, $\mathfrak{S}^{d}$ subordinate punctuation.
Discussion: Again $\mathfrak{G}^{SQ}$ have an extra point where $\mathfrak{M}$ has a Ṭiphḥa (מרחק).

COLON 46:11bA:

אַף־דִּבַּ֙רְתִּי֙ אַף־אֲבִיאֶ֔נָּה 11bA As I have spoken (it), so I will bring it about,

With: $\mathfrak{M}$ (5) – $\mathfrak{G}^{Q}$ – $\mathfrak{S}^{bcd}$, $\mathfrak{S}^{a}$ subordinate punctuation.
Colon parallelism: דבר || בוא Hiph.

COLON 46:11bB:

יָצַרְתִּי אַף־אֶעֱשֶׂנָּה׃ 11bB (as) I have formed (it), so I will make it.

With: 𝔐 (1), major division markers, also in 1𝔔^{a} and 4𝔔^{bc} – 𝔊^{SBAQ}, all with major division markers – 𝔖^{abcde}, all with major division markers. Colon parallelism: יצר || עשׂה.

COLON 46:12aA:

שִׁמְעוּ אֵלַי אַבִּירֵי לֵב 12aA Listen to me, you mighty of heart,

With: 𝔐 (2) – 𝔊^{SQ} – 𝔖^{de}

COLON 46:12aB:

הָרְחוֹקִים מִצְּדָקָה׃ 12aB you who are far from justice.

With: 𝔐 (1) – 𝔊^{SQ} – 𝔖^{be}, 𝔖^{acd} subordinate punctuation because of the introduction of direct speech.

COLON 46:13aA:

קֵרַבְתִּי צִדְקָתִי לֹא תִרְחָק 13aA I bring near my justice, it is not far off;

With: 𝔐 (5) – 𝔖^{abde}
Discussion: 𝔊 is lacking.

COLON 46:13aB:

וּתְשׁוּעָתִי לֹא תְאַחֵר 13aB and my salvation, it will not tarry;

With: 𝔐 (2) – 𝔊^{SQ} – 𝔖^{abcde}
Discussion: 𝔊^{S} and 𝔊^{Q} presuppose an extra divider after ותשועתי (𝔐 Ṭiphḥa).

COLON 46:13bA:

וְנָתַתִּי בְצִיּוֹן תְּשׁוּעָה 13bA yes, I give in Zion my salvation,

With: 𝔐 (5) – 𝔖^{e}, 𝔖^{abc} subordinate punctuation.
Discussion: 𝔐 is only weakly supported, obviously because the ellipsis in v. 13bB went unnoticed.

COLON 46:13bB:

לְיִשְׂרָאֵל תִּפְאַרְתִּי׃ 13bB to Israel my glory.

With: 𝔐 (2), major division markers, also in 1𝔔^{a} – 𝔊^{SBAQ}, major division markers in 𝔊^{SBA} – 𝔖^{abde}, 𝔖^{c} subordinate punctuation, major division markers in 𝔖^{abe}

7.3 Isaiah 45–46 – Delimitation of Verse-lines

VERSE–LINE: 45:1a:

כֹּה־אָמַר יְהוָה	1aA	Thus says the LORD
לִמְשִׁיחוֹ לְכוֹרֶשׁ אֲשֶׁר־הֶחֱזַקְתִּי בִימִינוֹ	1aB	to his anointed one, to Cyrus, whose right hand I have grasped,

𝔐 distinctive accents: 9 – 7.
Stresses: 2 + 4.
Verse-line parallelism: None.
Discussion: The 'Botenformel' often caused problems with regard to the delimitation of cola and verses because the verse-line starting with the 'Botenformel' is a sentence running on over two or more cola, without clear parallelism. The delimitation of verse-line 1a is based on our delimitation of cola.[1]

VERSE–LINE: 45:1b:

לְרַד־לְפָנָיו גּוֹיִם	1bA	To subdue nations before him,
וּמָתְנֵי מְלָכִים אֲפַתֵּחַ	1bB	yes, I will ungird the loins of kings,

𝔐 distinctive accents: 5 – 2.
Stresses: 2 + 3.
Verse-line parallelism: גוי || מלך; פנים || מתנים; rhyme.
Discussion: As in other cases, the verse-line parallelism is weak, but is compensated for on the level of the strophe.

VERSE–LINE: 45:1c:

לִפְתֹּחַ לְפָנָיו דְּלָתַיִם	1cA	to open doors before him,
וּשְׁעָרִים לֹא יִסָּגֵרוּ׃	1cB	yes, the gates will not be shut.

𝔐 distinctive accents: 5 – 1.
Stresses: 3 + 3.
Verse-line parallelism: פתח || סגר (antithetical); דלת || שׁער.

VERSE–LINE: 45:2a:

אֲנִי לְפָנֶיךָ אֵלֵךְ	2aA	I will go before you,
וַהֲרוּרִים* אוֹשֵׁר*	2aB	and mountains I will make straight,

𝔐 distinctive accents: 5 – 2.
Stresses: 3 + 2.

[1]See our comment on p. 268.

Verse-line parallelism: הלך לפנים || ישר (unique); grammatical parallelism.

VERSE–LINE: 45:2b:

דַּלְתוֹת נְחוּשָׁה אֲשַׁבֵּר	2bA	doors of bronze I will shatter,
וּבְרִיחֵי בַרְזֶל אֲגַדֵּעַ׃	2bB	and bars of iron I will smash.

𝔐 distinctive accents: 5 – 1.
Stresses: 3 + 3.
Verse-line parallelism: דלת || בריח; נחושה || ברזל; שבר || גדע; grammatical parallelism.

VERSE–LINE: 45:3a:

וְנָתַתִּי לְךָ אוֹצְרוֹת חֹשֶׁךְ	3aA	And I will give you the treasures of darkness
וּמַטְמֻנֵי מִסְתָּרִים	3aB	and hidden hoards in secret places,

𝔐 distinctive accents: 5 – 2.
Stresses: 4 + 2.
Verse-line parallelism: אוצר || מטמון; חשך || מסתר.
Discussion: The cola are connected by ellipsis.

VERSE–LINE: 45:3b:

לְמַעַן תֵּדַע כִּי־אֲנִי יְהוָה	3bA	that you may know that I am the LORD
הַקּוֹרֵא בְשִׁמְךָ אֱלֹהֵי יִשְׂרָאֵל׃	3bB	who calls you by your name, the God of Israel.

𝔐 distinctive accents: 12 – 1.
Stresses: 4 + 4.
Verse-line parallelism: יהוה || אלהי ישראל; קרא בשם || ידע.

VERSE–LINE: 45:4a:

לְמַעַן עַבְדִּי יַעֲקֹב	4aA	For the sake of my servant Jacob,
וְיִשְׂרָאֵל בְּחִירִי	4aB	and Israel, my chosen one,

𝔐 distinctive accents: 5 – 2.
Stresses: 3 + 2.
Verse-line parallelism: יעקב || ישראל; עבד || בחיר; ־י || ־י; rhyme.
Discussion: Ellipsis of למען connects the cola.

VERSE–LINE: 45:4b:

וָאֶקְרָא לְךָ בִּשְׁמֶךָ	4bA	I call you by your name,
אֲכַנְּךָ וְלֹא יְדַעְתָּנִי׃	4bB	I surname you, although you do not know me.

𝔐 distinctive accents: 5 – 1.
Stresses: 3 + 3.
Verse-line parallelism: ־ך || ־ך; קרא בשם || ידע; קרא בשם || כנה; rhyme.

VERSE–LINE: 45:5a:

אֲנִ֤י יְהוָה֙ וְאֵ֣ין ע֔וֹד 5aA I am the LORD and there is no other,
זוּלָתִ֖י אֵ֣ין אֱלֹהִ֑ים 5aB besides me there is no god.

𝔐 distinctive accents: 5 – 2.
Stresses: 4 + 3.
Verse-line parallelism: אני || ־י; אין || אין; יהוה || אלהים; rhyme.

VERSE–LINE: 45:5b:

אֲאַזֶּרְךָ֖ וְלֹ֥א יְדַעְתָּֽנִי׃ 5bA I will gird you, although you do not know me,

𝔐 distinctive accents: 1.
Stresses: 3.
Verse-line parallelism: None (unicolon).
Discussion: The parallelism between the first two cola of v. 5 argues in favour of a bicolon and a unicolon. Furthermore, v. 5b corresponds to v. 4b which the Masoretes separated from the preceding bicolon by the Athaḥ, as is the case here.

VERSE–LINE: 45:6a

לְמַ֣עַן יֵדְע֗וּ מִמִּזְרַח־שֶׁ֙מֶשׁ֙ וּמִמַּ֣עֲרָבָ֔הּ 6aA so that they may know from the east to the west,
כִּי־אֶ֖פֶס בִּלְעָדָ֑י 6aB that nothing exists apart from me –
אֲנִ֥י יְהוָ֖ה וְאֵ֥ין עֽוֹד׃ 6aC I am the LORD and there is no other,

𝔐 distinctive accents: 5 – 2 – 1.
Stresses: 4 + 2 + 4.
Verse-line parallelism: ־י || אני (see v. 5a above).
Discussion: Because the sentence is running on over three cola there is only weak parallelism in this verse. In most other cases the expression אני יהוה is part of the first colon of a verse-line which might argue in favour of a bicolon followed by a unicolon.[2] However, the expression אני יהוה may also occur at the end of a verse-line,[3] and in Isa. 49:26 it even occurs in the second colon of a tricolon. We prefer a tricolon here because v. 6aB corresponds to v. 5aB, proving that v. 6aB belongs to the same verse-line as v. 6aC, just as v. 5aB belongs to the same

[2] Cf. Isa. 41:4, 13, 17; 42:6, 8; 43:3, 15; 45:3, 5, 19, 21; 49:23.
[3] Cf. Isa. 45:7, 18, see also Lev. 26:25; Num. 3:13, 45; 10:10; Ezek. 5:15, 17; 6:14, etc.

verse-line as v. 5aA. Moreover, the clear parallelism in the next verse-line (v. 7) where the same refrain is ending the verse-line supports the view that v. 6 is a tricolon too. See also the tricolon v. 8b.

VERSE-LINE: 45:7a:

יוֹצֵר אוֹר וּבוֹרֵא חֹשֶׁךְ	7aA	he who forms light and creates darkness,
עֹשֶׂה שָׁלוֹם וּבוֹרֵא רָע	7aB	who makes peace and creates evil –
אֲנִי יְהוָה עֹשֶׂה כָל־אֵלֶּה׃	7aC	I am the LORD who makes all these things.

𝔐 distinctive accents: 5 – 2 – 1.
Stresses: 4 + 4 + 4.
Verse-line parallelism: יצר || עשה || עשה; יצר || ברא; אור || שלום; ברא || ברא; ברא || עשה; חשך || רע.
Discussion: See our discussion of v. 6.

VERSE-LINE: 45:8a:

הַרְעִיפוּ שָׁמַיִם מִמַּעַל	8aA	Drip, O heavens, from above,
וּשְׁחָקִים יִזְּלוּ־צֶדֶק	8aB	and let the clouds pour down justice;

𝔐 distinctive accents: 5 – 2.
Stresses: 3 + 2.
Verse-line parallelism: שמים || שחקים; רעף || נזל.

VERSE-LINE: 45:8b:

תִּפְתַּח־אֶרֶץ וְיִפְרַח*־יֶשַׁע	8bA	let the earth open up and let salvation blossom –
וּצְדָקָה תַצְמִיחַ יַחַד	8bB	and let justice make sprout communion,
אֲנִי יְהוָה בְּרָאתִיו׃	8bC	I am the LORD, I create it.

𝔐 distinctive accents: 7 – 5 – 1.
Stresses: 2 + 3 + 3.
Verse-line parallelism: פרח || צמח; ישע || צדקה.
Discussion: Compare the tricola vv. 6 and 7.

VERSE-LINE: 45:9a:

הוֹי רָב אֶת־יֹצְרוֹ	9aA	Woe to him who quarrels with the one who formed him,
חֶרֶשׂ אֶת־חַרְשֵׂי אֲדָמָה	9aB	a pot among the pots of earth.

𝔐 distinctive accents: 5 – 2.
Stresses: 3 + 3.
Verse-line parallelism: את || את; roots יצר || חרשׂ.

VERSE–LINE: 45:9b:

הֲיֹאמַר חֹמֶר לְיֹצְרוֹ מַה־תַּעֲשֶׂה 9bA Does the clay say to him who forms it, "What do you make?"
וּפָעָלְךָ אֵין־יָדַיִם לוֹ׃ 9bB or (does) your work which (itself) has no hands (say this)?

𝔐 distinctive accents: 5 – 1.
Stresses: 4 + 3.
Verse-line parallelism: חמר || פעל (unique); יצר || פעל. עשה || פעל; ־ו || ־ו; rhyme.
Discussion: Multiple ellipsis connects the two cola.[4]

VERSE–LINE: 45:10a:

הוֹי אֹמֵר לְאָב מַה־תּוֹלִיד 10aA Woe to him who says to a father, "What do you beget?"
וּלְאִשָּׁה מַה־תְּחִילִין׃ 10aB or to a wife, "What do you bring to birth?"

𝔐 distinctive accents: 2 – 1.
Stresses: 4 + 2.
Verse-line parallelism: ל || ל; אב || אשה; מה || מה; ילד || חיל.
Discussion: The cola are connected by ellipsis.

VERSE–LINE: 45:11a:

כֹּה־אָמַר יְהוָה 11aA Thus says the LORD,
קְדוֹשׁ יִשְׂרָאֵל וְיֹצְרוֹ 11aB the Holy One of Israel and the one who formed it,

𝔐 distinctive accents: 12 – 2.
Stresses: 2 + 3.
Verse-line parallelism: יהוה || קדוש ישראל.

VERSE–LINE: 45:11b:

הָאֹתִיּוֹת שְׁאָלוּנִי עַל־בָּנַי 11bA The things to come? Interrogate me concerning my children,
וְעַל־פֹּעַל יָדַי תְּצַוֻּנִי׃ 11bB command me with regard the work of my hands.

𝔐 distinctive accents: 12 – 1.
Stresses: 3 + 3.
Verse-line parallelism: שאל || צוה (unique); על || על; בן || פעל יד; ־ני || ־ני; ־י || ־י; rhyme.

[4]See our comments p. 262, n. 10.

VERSE–LINE: 45:12a:

אָנֹכִי֙ עָשִׂ֣יתִי אֶ֔רֶץ 12aA It is I who made the earth,
וְאָדָ֖ם עָלֶ֣יהָ בָרָ֑אתִי 12aB and created man upon it,

𝔐 distinctive accents: 5 – 2.
Stresses: 3 + 3.
Verse-line parallelism: עשׂה || ברא; ארץ || אדם; grammatical parallelism; rhyme.

VERSE–LINE: 45:12b:

אֲנִ֗י יָדַי֙ נָט֣וּ שָׁמַ֔יִם 12bA I – my hands stretched out the heavens,
וְכָל־צְבָאָ֖ם צִוֵּֽיתִי׃ 12bB and all their host I command.

𝔐 distinctive accents: 5 – 1.
Stresses: 4 + 2.
Verse-line parallelism: נטה || צוה; שׁמים || צבא; rhyme.

VERSE–LINE: 45:13a:

אָנֹכִי֙ הַעִירֹתִ֣הוּ בְצֶ֔דֶק 13aA It is I who woke him up in justice,
וְכָל־דְּרָכָ֖יו אֲיַשֵּׁ֑ר 13aB yes, all his ways I will make straight.

𝔐 distinctive accents: 5 – 2.
Stresses: 3 + 2.
Verse-line parallelism: צדק || ישׁר; ־הו || ־יו.

VERSE–LINE: 45:13b:

הֽוּא־יִבְנֶ֤ה עִירִי֙ וְגָלוּתִ֣י יְשַׁלֵּ֔חַ 13bA It is he who will rebuild my city and will send my exiles home,
לֹ֤א בִמְחִיר֙ וְלֹ֣א בְשֹׁ֔חַד 13bB not for a price and not for presents,
אָמַ֖ר יְהוָ֥ה צְבָאֽוֹת׃ 13bC says the LORD of hosts.

𝔐 distinctive accents: 5 – 5 – 1.
Stresses: 4 + 4 + 3.
Verse-line parallelism: None.
Discussion: With the Masoretes. The sequence of accents (5 – 5 – 1) is attested elsewhere, also in Second Isaiah. The cola are connected by the continuing sentence (enjambment).

VERSE–LINE: 45:14a:

כֹּ֣ה ׀ אָמַ֣ר יְהוָ֗ה 14aA Thus says the LORD,
יְגִ֨יעַ מִצְרַ֜יִם 14aB The resources of Egypt
וּֽסְחַר־כּ֣וּשׁ וּסְבָאִ֗ים 14aC and the merchandise of Cush and the Sabeans,

𝔐 distinctive accents: 7 – conjunctive accent – 9.
Stresses: 3 + 2 + 2.
Verse-line parallelism: יגיע || סחר; מצרים|| כוש || סבאים.
Discussion: See with regard to the delimitation of the cola p. 276. The established parallelism between the gentilics warrants the assumption of a tricolon.

VERSE–LINE: 45:14b:

אַנְשֵׁי מִדָּה עָלַיִךְ יַעֲבֹרוּ	14bA	tall men will pass over to you
וְלָךְ יִהְיוּ אַחֲרַיִךְ יֵלֵכוּ	14bB	and will be yours, they will go behind you,
בַּזִּקִּים יַעֲבֹרוּ	14bC	in chains they will pass;

𝔐 distinctive accents: 10 – 5 – 2.
Stresses: 4 + 4 + 2.
Verse-line parallelism: עבר || הלך || עבר; ־ךְ || ־ךְ; grammatical parallelism; rhyme.
Discussion: 𝔐's problematic colometry has been earlier discussed on p. 277. In view of the strong parallelism and consistent imagery of slavery the delimitation of the verse-line as a tricolon is beyond doubt. Because the rest of the Masoretic verse concerns the religious consequences of the submission of Egypt and its allies, it is best to regard it as an independent strophe.

VERSE–LINE: 45:14c:

וְאֵלַיִךְ יִשְׁתַּחֲווּ	14cA	and they will bow down for you,
אֵלַיִךְ יִתְפַּלָּלוּ	14cB	and they will pray to you:

𝔐 distinctive accents: 10 – 5.
Stresses: 2 + 2.
Verse-line parallelism: אל || אל; ־ךְ || ־ךְ; שחה || פלל; grammatical parallelism; rhyme.
Discussion: See our comment on v. 14b as well as p. 277 on the colometry.

VERSE–LINE: 45:14d:

אַךְ בָּךְ אֵל	14dA	"Only in you is God
וְאֵין עוֹד אֶפֶס אֱלֹהִים׃	14dB	and there does not exist any other god."

𝔐 distinctive accents: 12 – 1.
Stresses: 3 + 4.
Verse-line parallelism: אל || אלהים; אין || אפס.
Discussion: See p. 277-8 on the colometry.

VERSE–LINE: 45:15a:

אָכֵן אַתָּה אֵל מִסְתַּתֵּר	15aA	However, you are a God hiding himself,
אֱלֹהֵי יִשְׂרָאֵל מוֹשִׁיעַ׃	15aB	O Saviour God of Israel!

𝔐 distinctive accents: 2 – 1.
Stresses: 4 + 3.
Verse-line parallelism: אל || אלהי ישׂראל; roots סתר || ישׁע; grammatical parallelism.

VERSE–LINE: 45:16a:

בּוֹשׁוּ וְגַם־נִכְלְמוּ כֻּלָּם	16aA	They are ashamed and disgraced, all of them,

𝔐 distinctive accent: 2.
Stresses: 3.
Verse-line parallelism: None (unicolon).
Discussion: Our decision to read v. 16 as a unicolon followed by a bicolon is based mainly on 𝔐's Atnaḥ (No. 2) which cannot be followed by a Zaqeph Qaṭon (No. 5) in the same verse-line. However, the pair כלם || כלמה and the attested verse-line parallelism between יחד and כלם in 44:11b render a tricolon an attractive option.

VERSE–LINE: 45:16b:

יַחְדָּו הָלְכוּ בַכְּלִמָּה	16bA	altogether they go in disgrace,
חָרָשֵׁי צִירִים׃	16bB	the craftsmen with their drawings.

𝔐 distinctive accents: 5 – 1.
Stresses: 3 + 2.
Verse-line parallelism: None.
Discussion: No parallelism, but the cola are connected because the sentence runs on (enjambment). See our comment on v. 16a.

VERSE–LINE: 45:17a:

יִשְׂרָאֵל נוֹשַׁע בַּיהוָה	17aA	But Israel is saved by the LORD,
תְּשׁוּעַת עוֹלָמִים	17aB	a salvation of ages.

𝔐 distinctive accents: 5 – 2.
Stresses: 3 + 2.
Verse-line parallelism: Roots ישׁע || ישׁע.

VERSE–LINE: 45:17b:

לֹא־תֵבֹשׁוּ וְלֹא־תִכָּלְמוּ	17bA	They will not be ashamed and and not be disgraced
עַד־עוֹלְמֵי עַד׃	17bB	to ages everlasting."

𝔐 distinctive accents: 8 – 1.
Stresses: 2 + 2.
Verse-line parallelism: None.
Discussion: No parallelism because the sentence runs on (enjambment).

VERSE–LINE: 45:18a:

כִּ֣י כֹ֣ה אָֽמַר־יְהוָ֡ה בּוֹרֵ֨א הַשָּׁמַ֜יִם	18aA	For thus says the LORD, who created the heavens,
ה֣וּא הָאֱלֹהִ֗ים יֹצֵ֨ר הָאָ֤רֶץ	18aB	he (who) is God, who formed the earth,
וְעֹשָׂהּ֙ ה֣וּא כֽוֹנְנָ֔הּ	18aC	and the One who made it, he (who) established it –

𝔐 distinctive accents: 13 – conjunctive accent – 5.
Stresses: 5 + 4 + 3.
Verse-line parallelism: יהוה || אלהים; ברא || יצר prl עשׂה; שמים || ארץ; הוא || הוא; יצר || כון;
Discussion: Judging from the use of the Revia' (No. 7) with האלהים, the Zaqeph Qaṭon (No. 5) with כוננה and the Atnaḥ (No. 2) with יצרה, the Masoretes wanted to read on to יצרה, taking the verse-line 18a as a tricolon consisting of three exceptionally long cola, followed by a unicolon. Probably the sudden switch from the third person to the first in v.18bC motivated their choice. Such unexpected switches, however, are common with Second Isaiah. Our delimitation of verse-line 18a as a tricolon with shorter cola is based on the delimitation of cola which is supported by several ancient versions (see p. 279-80). It is supported by the parallelism indicated above.

VERSE–LINE: 45:18b:

לֹא־תֹ֥הוּ בְרָאָ֖הּ	18bA	not as a void he created it,
לָשֶׁ֣בֶת יְצָרָ֑הּ	18bB	to be inhabited he formed it –
אֲנִ֥י יְהוָ֖ה וְאֵ֥ין עֽוֹד׃	18bC	I am the LORD and there is no other.

𝔐 distinctive accents: 8 – 2 – 1.
Stresses: 2 + 2 + 4.
Verse-line parallelism: תהו || ישׁב (antithetical; unique); ברא || יצר; ־ה || ־ה; ברא || יהוה; grammatical parallelism; rhyme.
Discussion: The expression אני יהוה was treated in different ways by the Masoretes. See our comment on v. 6b above.

VERSE–LINE: 45:19a:

לֹ֨א בַסֵּ֜תֶר דִּבַּ֗רְתִּי	19aA	I did not speak in secret,
בִּמְקוֹם֙ אֶ֣רֶץ חֹ֔שֶׁךְ	19aB	in a place of the land of darkness,

לֹא אָמַרְתִּי לְזֶרַע יַעֲקֹב תֹּהוּ בַקְּשׁוּנִי 19aC I have not said to the seed of Jacob: "Seek me in the void!"

𝔐 distinctive accents: 7 – 5 – 2.
Stresses: 3 + 3 + 6.
Verse-line parallelism: לא || לא; ב || ב; סתר || חשך; דבר || אמר; חשך || תהו; grammatical parallelism.
Discussion: The cola vv. 19aA and 19aB are joined by ellipsis.

VERSE–LINE: 45:19b:

אֲנִי יְהוָה דֹּבֵר צֶדֶק 19bA I am the LORD, who speaks what is just,
מַגִּיד מֵישָׁרִים׃ 19bB who tells what is straight.

𝔐 distinctive accents: 5 – 1.
Stresses: 4 + 2.
Verse-line parallelism: דבר || נגד; צדק || מישרים; grammatical parallelism.
Discussion: Again ellipsis forms a bond between the cola.

VERSE–LINE: 45:20a:

הִקָּבְצוּ וָבֹאוּ 20aA Assemble and come,
הִתְנַגְּשׁוּ יַחְדָּו 20aB draw near together,
פְּלִיטֵי הַגּוֹיִם 20aC survivors of the nations.

𝔐 distinctive accents: 12 – 8 – 2.
Stresses: 2 + 2 + 2.
Verse-line parallelism: קבץ || יחד; בוא || נגש; grammatical parallelism; rhyme.
Discussion: 𝔐 wanted to read this as one colon with six stresses. With the support of 𝔊[SQ] we decided to adopt a different colometry.[5]

VERSE–LINE: 45:20b:

לֹא יָדְעוּ הַנֹּשְׂאִים אֶת־עֵץ פִּסְלָם 20bA They do not know, those who are carrying the wood of their idols,
וּמִתְפַּלְלִים אֶל־אֵל לֹא יוֹשִׁיעַ׃ 20bB who pray to a god that does not save.

𝔐 distinctive accents: 5 – 1.
Stresses: 5 + 4.
Verse-line parallelism: לא || לא; פסל || אל; grammatical parallelism; rhyme.
Discussion: Ellipsis of לא ידעו in v. 20bB connects the cola.

[5]See p. 281.

VERSE–LINE: 45:21a:

הַגִּ֥ידוּ וְהַגִּ֖ישׁוּ	21aA	Tell and bring near,
אַ֥ף יִוָּעֲצ֖וּ יַחְדָּ֑ו	21aB	yes, let them take counsel together:

𝔐 distinctive accents: 5 – 2.
Stresses: 2 + 3.
Verse-line parallelism: נגד || יעץ; rhyme.

VERSE–LINE: 45:21b:

מִ֣י הִשְׁמִ֣יעַ זֹ֠את מִקֶּ֜דֶם	21bA	Who has made this heard from olden times,
מֵאָ֣ז הִגִּידָ֗הּ	21bB	has told it since then?

𝔐 distinctive accents: 13 – 7.
Stresses: 4 + 2.
Verse-line parallelism: שמע || נגד; זאת || ־ה; מן || מן; קדם || אז; grammatical parallelism.
Discussion: See p. 282 on the colometry.

VERSE–LINE: 45:21c:

הֲל֨וֹא אֲנִ֤י יְהוָה֙	21cA	Was it not I, the LORD?
וְאֵֽין־ע֤וֹד אֱלֹהִים֙ מִבַּלְעָדַ֔י	21cB	And there is no God apart from me,

𝔐 distinctive accents: 10 – 5.
Stresses: 3 + 3.
Verse-line parallelism: אני || ־י; יהוה || אל;
Discussion: See our comment on v. 6a above.

VERSE–LINE: 45:21d:

אֵֽל־צַדִּ֣יק וּמוֹשִׁ֔יעַ	21dA	a just God and Saviour,
אַ֖יִן זוּלָתִֽי׃	21dB	there is none besides me.

𝔐 distinctive accents: 5 – 1.
Stresses: 2 + 2.
Verse-line parallelism: None.
Discussion: Because the sentence is running on there is no parallelism (enjambment).

VERSE–LINE: 45:22a:

פְּנוּ־אֵלַ֥י וְהִוָּשְׁע֖וּ	22aA	Turn unto me and be saved,
כָּל־אַפְסֵי־אָ֑רֶץ	22aB	all you ends of the earth,

𝔐 distinctive accents: 8 – 2.
Stresses: 2 + 1.

Verse-line parallelism: None.
Discussion: See for the colometry p. 283. No parallelism because the sentence runs on (enjambment).

VERSE–LINE: 45:22b:

כִּי אֲנִי־אֵל וְאֵין עוֹד׃	22bA	for I am God and there is no other.

𝔐 distinctive accents: 1.
Stresses: 4.
Verse-line parallelism: None (unicolon).
Discussion: We follow 𝔐 in assuming a bicolon followed by a unicolon. In view of the immediately preceding אל ... מושיע (v. 21dA) a tricolon is a good alternative.

VERSE–LINE: 45:23a:

בִּי נִשְׁבַּעְתִּי	23aA	I swear by myself,
יָצָא מִפִּי צְדָקָה	23aB	justice goes forth from my mouth,
דָּבָר וְלֹא יָשׁוּב	23aC	a word which shall not return:

𝔐 distinctive accents: 5 – 12 – 2.
Stresses: 2 + 3 + 3.
Verse-line parallelism: ־י || ־י; פה || דבר; שבע || יצא מפה || דבר; יצא || שׁוב; rhyme.
Discussion: See for the colometry p. 283-4. The parallelism indicated above as well as the ellipsis in v. 23aC justify the assumption of a tricolon.

VERSE–LINE: 45:23b:

כִּי־לִי תִּכְרַע כָּל־בֶּרֶךְ	23bA	Unto me every knee shall bow,
תִּשָּׁבַע כָּל־לָשׁוֹן׃	23bB	every tongue shall swear.

𝔐 distinctive accents: 5 – 1.
Stresses: 3 + 2.
Verse-line parallelism: כרע || שׁבע (unique); כל || כל; ברך || לשׁון; grammatical parallelism.
Discussion: The ellipsis of לי (or: בי) in v. 23bB connects the cola.

VERSE–LINE: 45:24a:

אַךְ בַּיהוָה לִי אָמַר צְדָקוֹת	24aA	"Only in the LORD", they say to me, "is full justice,
וָעֹז עָדָיו יָבוֹא	24aB	and strength comes to him,
וְיֵבֹשׁוּ כֹּל הַנֶּחֱרִים בּוֹ׃	24aC	but all who are raging against him shall be put to shame.

𝔐 distinctive accents: conjunctive accent – conjunctive accent – 1.
Stresses: 5 + 3 + 4.
Verse-line parallelism: ב || ב; צדקה || עז (unique); ־ו || ־ו;
Discussion: See p. 284 for the colometry. The strophe parallelism between ביהוה לי אמר צדקות (24aA) and ביהוה יצדקו (25aA) as well as between כל הנצרים בו (24aC) and כל־זרע ישׂראל (25aB) strongly suggests to regard v. 24 as a tricolon balancing v. 25.

VERSE–LINE: 45:25a:

בַּיהוָ֛ה יִצְדְּק֥וּ וְיִֽתְהַלְל֖וּ	25aA	In the Lord will be justified and will glory
כָּל־זֶ֥רַע יִשְׂרָאֵֽל׃	25aB	all the seed of Israel."

𝔐 distinctive accents: 8 – 1.
Stresses: 3 + 2.
Verse-line parallelism: יהוה || ישׂראל.
Discussion: Because the sentence runs on there is no clear parallelism (enjambment). This is one of the rare occasions that an Atnaḥ is missing in a Masoretic verse.

VERSE–LINE: 46:1a:

כָּרַ֥ע בֵּל֙ קֹרֵ֣ס נְב֔וֹ	1aA	Bel bows, Nebo cringes,
הָיוּ֙ עֲצַבֵּיהֶ֔ם לַחַיָּ֖ה וְלַבְּהֵמָ֑ה	1aB	their grievous images are for the beasts and the cattle,

𝔐 distinctive accents: 5 – 2.
Stresses: 4 + 4.
Verse-line parallelism: נבו ,בל || עצב.

VERSE–LINE: 46:1b:

נְשֻׂאֹתֵיכֶם֙ עֲמוּס֔וֹת	1bA	the objects you wanted to be carried become a burden,
מַשָּׂ֖א לַעֲיֵפָֽה׃	1bB	a load to a weary animal.

𝔐 distinctive accents: 5 – 1.
Stresses: 2 + 2.
Verse-line parallelism: נשׂא || משׂא; עמס || משׂא.

VERSE–LINE: 46:2a:

קָרְס֤וּ כָֽרְעוּ֙ יַחְדָּ֔ו	2aA	They cringe, they bow together,
לֹ֥א יָכְל֖וּ מַלֵּ֣ט מַשָּׂ֑א	2aB	they are unable to save the load,

𝔐 distinctive accents: 5 – 2.
Stresses: 3 + 4.
Verse-line parallelism: grammatical parallelism; rhyme.

Discussion: Verse 2 might be either a single verse-line, consisting of three cola (tricolon), or two verse-lines (bicolon + unicolon). The grammatical parallelism and rhyme (assonance and alliteration) in the first two cola (twice a perfect 3 m.p.) and the change of subject in the third colon favour the latter which was also the option chosen by the Masoretes.

VERSE–LINE: 46:2b:

וְנַפְשָׁם בַּשְּׁבִי הָלָכָה׃ 2bA and they themselves go into captivity.

𝔐 distinctive accents: 1.
Stresses: 3.
Verse-line parallelism: None (unicolon).
Discussion: See our discussion of v. 2a.

VERSE–LINE: 46:3a:

שִׁמְעוּ אֵלַי בֵּית יַעֲקֹב 3aA Listen to me, O house of Jacob,
וְכָל־שְׁאֵרִית בֵּית יִשְׂרָאֵל 3aB and all the remnant of the house of Israel,

𝔐 distinctive accents: 5 – 2.
Stresses: 4 + 3.
Verse-line parallelism: בית יעקב || בית ישׂראל.
Discussion: The cola are connected by ellipsis.

VERSE–LINE: 46:3b:

הָעֲמֻסִים מִנִּי־בֶטֶן 3bA you who were a burden from the womb,
הַנְּשֻׂאִים מִנִּי־רָחַם׃ 3bB who were carried since your birth.

𝔐 distinctive accents: 5 – 1.
Stresses: 2 + 2.
Verse-line parallelism: עמס || נשׂא; מן || מן; בטן || רחם; rhyme.

VERSE–LINE: 46:4a:

וְעַד־זִקְנָה אֲנִי הוּא 4aA Even unto (your) old age I am the same One,
וְעַד־שֵׂיבָה אֲנִי אֶסְבֹּל 4aB and unto (your) greyness I will continue to bear (you);

𝔐 distinctive accents: 5 – 2.
Stresses: 3 + 3.
Verse-line parallelism: עד || עד; זקן || שׂיבה; אני || אני; rhyme.

VERSE–LINE: 46:4b:

אֲנִ֤י עָשִׂ֙יתִי֙ וַאֲנִ֣י אֶשָּׂ֔א	4bA	I have made (you) and I will continue to carry,
וַאֲנִ֥י אֶסְבֹּ֖ל וַאֲמַלֵּֽט׃	4bB	will continue to bear and will continue to save (you).

𝔐 distinctive accents: 5 – 1.
Stresses: 4 + 3.
Verse-line parallelism: אני || אני; נשׂא || סבל; grammatical parallelism; rhyme.

VERSE–LINE: 46:5a:

לְמִ֥י תְדַמְּי֖וּנִי וְתַשְׁו֑וּ	5aA	And to whom will you liken me and make me equal,
וְתַמְשִׁל֖וּנִי וְנִדְמֶֽה׃	5aB	and compare me that we may be alike?

𝔐 distinctive accents: 2 – 1.
Stresses: 3 + 2.
Verse-line parallelism: דמה || דמה; ־ני || ־ני; שוה || משל (unique); grammatical parallelism; rhyme.

VERSE–LINE: 46:6a:

הַזָּלִ֤ים זָהָב֙ מִכִּ֔יס	6aA	Those who pour out gold from the purse,
וְכֶ֖סֶף בַּקָּנֶ֣ה יִשְׁקֹ֑לוּ	6aB	and weigh out silver on the scales,

𝔐 distinctive accents: 5 – 2.
Stresses: 3 + 3.
Verse-line parallelism: זול || שקל (unique); זהב || כסף.

VERSE–LINE: 46:6b:

יִשְׂכְּר֤וּ צוֹרֵף֙ וְיַעֲשֵׂ֣הוּ אֵ֔ל	6bA	hire a goldsmith and he makes a god of it;
יִסְגְּד֖וּ אַף־יִשְׁתַּחֲוֽוּ׃	6bB	then they worship, even bow down!

𝔐 distinctive accents: 5 – 1.
Stresses: 4 + 2.
Verse-line parallelism: grammatical parallelism.
Discussion: In this case the colon parallelism compensates for the weakness of the verse-line parallelism.

VERSE–LINE: 46:7a:

יִ֠שָּׂאֻהוּ עַל־כָּתֵ֨ף יִסְבְּלֻ֜הוּ	7aA	They lift him up, they bear him on the shoulder,
וְיַנִּיחֻ֤הוּ תַחְתָּיו֙ וְיַעֲמֹ֔ד	7aB	they put him down and (there) he stands;
מִמְּקוֹמ֖וֹ לֹ֣א יָמִ֑ישׁ	7aC	he will not move from his place.

𝔐 distinctive accents: 13 – 5 – 2.
Stresses: 3 + 3 + 3.
Verse-line parallelism: על || תחת; עמד || מוש (antithetical); ־הו || ־הו; ־הו || ־ו || ־ו.

VERSE–LINE: 46:7b:

אַף־יִצְעַק אֵלָיו וְלֹא יַעֲנֶה	7bA	Even when one cries out to him, he does not answer;
מִצָּרָתוֹ לֹא יוֹשִׁיעֶנּוּ׃	7bB	from his anguish he does not save him.

𝔐 distinctive accents: 5 – 1.
Stresses: 4 + 3.
Verse-line parallelism: צעק || צרה; ענה || ישע; לא || לא; grammatical parallelism.

VERSE–LINE: 46:8a:

זִכְרוּ־זֹאת וְהִתְאֹשָׁשׁוּ	8aA	Remember this and behave like men,
הָשִׁיבוּ פוֹשְׁעִים עַל־לֵב׃	8aB	bring it back to your hearts, O transgressors.

𝔐 distinctive accents: 2 – 1.
Stresses: 2 + 3.
Verse-line parallelism: זכר || שוב על לב; grammatical parallelism; rhyme.

VERSE–LINE: 46:9a:

זִכְרוּ רִאשֹׁנוֹת מֵעוֹלָם	9aA	Remember the first things, from eternity on,
כִּי אָנֹכִי אֵל וְאֵין עוֹד	9aB	that I am God, and there is no other,
אֱלֹהִים וְאֶפֶס כָּמוֹנִי׃	9aC	a God – and none like me exists! –

𝔐 distinctive accents: 2 – 5 – 1.
Stresses: 3 + 5 + 3.
Verse-line parallelism: אנכי || ־ני; ראשון || אל (unique); rhyme.
Discussion: The Masoretes divided v. 9 into a unicolon plus a bicolon. Probably they dit not connect כי with the verb זכר but took it as the beginning of a new, concluding line. The expression זכר ...כי, however, always belongs to one verse-line.[6]

VERSE–LINE: 46:10a:

מַגִּיד מֵרֵאשִׁית אַחֲרִית	10aA	who tells the outcome from the beginning
וּמִקֶּדֶם אֲשֶׁר לֹא־נַעֲשׂוּ	10aB	and from olden times that which had not yet been made,

𝔐 distinctive accents: 5 – 2.

[6]Cf. Ps. 25:6; 42:5; 78:35, 39; Job 7:7; 36:24.

Stresses: 3 + 3.
Verse-line parallelism: מן || מן; ראשית || קדם.
Discussion: The ellipsis of מגיד connects v. 10aB with v. 10aA.

VERSE–LINE: 46:10b:

אֹמֵר֙ עֲצָתִ֣י תָק֔וּם	10bA	who says, “My counsel shall stand,
וְכָל־חֶפְצִ֖י אֶעֱשֶֽׂה׃	10bB	and everything I want I will make!”,

𝔐 distinctive accents: 5 – 1.
Stresses: 3 + 2.
Verse-line parallelism: עצה || חפץ (unique); ־י || ־י; קום || עשׂה; rhyme.

VERSE–LINE: 46:11a:

קֹרֵ֤א מִמִּזְרָח֙ עַ֔יִט	11aA	who calls the Vulture from the east,
מֵאֶ֥רֶץ מֶרְחָ֖ק אִ֣ישׁ עֲצָת֑וֹ	11aB	from a land far away the man of his counsel.

𝔐 distinctive accents: 5 – 2.
Stresses: 3 + 4.
Verse-line parallelism: מן || מן; מזרח || ארץ מרחוק (unique); עיט || איש עצתו (unique).
Discussion: Ellipsis connects the cola.

VERSE–LINE: 46:11b:

אַף־דִּבַּ֙רְתִּי֙ אַף־אֲבִיאֶ֔נָּה	11bA	As I have spoken (it), so I will bring it about,
יָצַ֖רְתִּי אַף־אֶעֱשֶֽׂנָּה׃	11bB	(as) I have formed (it), so I will make it.

𝔐 distinctive accents: 5 – 2.
Stresses: 2 + 2.
Verse-line parallelism: אף || אף; דבר || יצר (unique); בוא || עשׂה; ־נה || ־נה; grammatical parallelism; rhyme.

VERSE–LINE: 46:12a:

שִׁמְע֥וּ אֵלַ֖י אַבִּ֣ירֵי לֵ֑ב	12aA	Listen to me, you mighty of heart,
הָרְחוֹקִ֖ים מִצְּדָקָֽה׃	12aB	you who are far from justice.

𝔐 distinctive accents: 2 – 1.
Stresses: 4 + 2.
Verse-line parallelism: None, but the complementarity of the two cola is obvious. Note the proximity of לב and צדקה in Ps. 36:11; 40:11.
Discussion: Again we encounter a case where the canticle parallelism compensates for a rather weak verse-line parallelism (cf. v. 13).

VERSE–LINE: 46:13a:

קֵרַ֤בְתִּי צִדְקָתִי֙ לֹ֣א תִרְחָ֔ק 13aA I bring near my justice, it is not far off;
וּתְשׁוּעָתִ֖י לֹ֣א תְאַחֵ֑ר 13aB and my salvation, it will not tarry;

𝔐 distinctive accents: 5 – 2.
Stresses: 4 + 3.
Verse-line parallelism: צדקה || תשועה; ־י || ־י; לא || לא; רחק || אחר; grammatical parallelism; rhyme.

VERSE–LINE: 46:13b:

וְנָתַתִּ֤י בְצִיּוֹן֙ תְּשׁוּעָ֔ה 13bA yes, I give in Zion my salvation,
לְיִשְׂרָאֵ֖ל תִּפְאַרְתִּֽי׃ 13bB to Israel my glory.

𝔐 distinctive accents: 5 – 1.
Stresses: 3 + 2.
Verse-line parallelism: ב || ל; ציון || ישׂראל; תשׁועה || תפארת (unique); rhyme.
Discussion: The cola are connected by ellipsis.

7.4 Isaiah 45–46 – Delimitation of Strophes

STROPHE I.A.i.1 (Isa. 45:1a)

כֹּֽה־אָמַ֣ר יְהוָה֮ 1aA Thus says the LORD
לִמְשִׁיחוֹ֮ לְכ֣וֹרֶשׁ אֲשֶׁר־הֶחֱזַ֣קְתִּי בִֽימִינוֹ֒ 1aB to his anointed one, to Cyrus, whose right hand I have grasped,

≠ Masoretic verse.
Separation ↑: major division markers in the textual tradition; deictic particle(s); marker of direct speech.
Separation ↓:
Strophe parallelism: None (one verse-line).
Discussion: Because the Masoretic accents and the strophe parallelism make it clear that vv. 1b and 1c belong together, v. 1a must be a separate strophe introducing the canticle.

STROPHE I.A.i.2 (Isa. 45:1b–c)

לְרַד־לְפָנָיו֙ גּוֹיִ֔ם 1bA To subdue nations before him,
וּמָתְנֵ֥י מְלָכִ֖ים אֲפַתֵּ֑חַ 1bB yes, I will ungird the loins of kings,
לִפְתֹּ֤חַ לְפָנָיו֙ דְּלָתַ֔יִם 1cA to open doors before him,
וּשְׁעָרִ֖ים לֹ֥א יִסָּגֵֽרוּ׃ 1cB yes, the gates will not be shut.

≠ Masoretic verse.
Separation ↑: swapping (object).

Separation ↓: major division marker in the textual tradition; swapping (subject).
Strophe parallelism: ל || ל; פנים || פנים; פתח || פתח; grammatical parallelism.

STROPHE I.A.ii.1 (Isa. 45:2)

אֲנִי לְפָנֶיךָ אֵלֵךְ	2aA	I will go before you,
וַהֲרוּרִים* אוֹשִׁר*	2aB	and mountains I will make straight,
דַּלְתוֹת נְחוּשָׁה אֲשַׁבֵּר	2bA	doors of bronze I will shatter,
וּבְרִיחֵי בַרְזֶל אֲגַדֵּעַ׃	2bB	and bars of iron I will smash.

= Masoretic verse.
Separation ↑: major division marker in the textual tradition; independent pers. pronoun; swapping (object); swapping (adjunct).
Separation ↓: swapping (object).
Strophe parallelism: grammatical parallelism.

STROPHE I.A.ii.2 (Isa. 45:3)

וְנָתַתִּי לְךָ אוֹצְרוֹת חֹשֶׁךְ	3aA	And I will give you the treasures of darkness
וּמַטְמֻנֵי מִסְתָּרִים	3aB	and hidden hoards in secret places,
לְמַעַן תֵּדַע כִּי־אֲנִי יְהוָה	3bA	that you may know that I am the LORD
הַקּוֹרֵא בְשִׁמְךָ אֱלֹהֵי יִשְׂרָאֵל׃	3bB	who calls you by your name, the God of Israel.

= Masoretic verse.
Separation ↑: swapping (adjunct).
Separation ↓: deictic particle(s); independent pers. pronoun.
Strophe parallelism: ־ךָ || ־ךָ.
Discussion: Both the marking of strophic separation and parallelistic bond between the verse-lines are weak, but since the sentence continues in v. 3b (enjambment) the unity of the strophe need not be doubted.

STROPHE I.A.ii.3 (Isa. 45:4)

לְמַעַן עַבְדִּי יַעֲקֹב	4aA	For the sake of my servant Jacob,
וְיִשְׂרָאֵל בְּחִירִי	4aB	and Israel, my chosen one,
וָאֶקְרָא לְךָ בִּשְׁמֶךָ	4bA	I call you by your name,
אֲכַנְּךָ וְלֹא יְדַעְתָּנִי׃	4bB	I surname you, although you do not know me.

= Masoretic verse.
Separation ↑: repetitive verse-line parallelism; swapping (adjunct).
Separation ↓: major division markers in the textual tradition; repetitive verse-line parallelism.

Strophe parallelism: roots בחר || קרא.

STROPHE I.B.i.1 (Isa. 45:5)

אֲנִ֤י יְהוָה֙ וְאֵ֣ין ע֔וֹד	5aA	I am the LORD and there is no other,
זוּלָתִ֖י אֵ֣ין אֱלֹהִ֑ים	5aB	besides me there is no god.
אֲאַזֶּרְךָ֖ וְלֹ֥א יְדַעְתָּֽנִי׃	5bA	I will gird you, although you do not know me,

= Masoretic verse.
Separation ↑: major division markers in the textual tradition; independent pers. pronoun; swapping (adjunct).
Separation ↓: None.
Strophe parallelism: ־י || ־ני; אין || לא.

STROPHE I.B.i.2 (Isa. 45:6)

לְמַ֣עַן יֵדְע֗וּ מִמִּזְרַח־שֶׁ֙מֶשׁ֙ וּמִמַּ֣עֲרָבָ֔הּ	6aA	so that they may know from the east to the west,
כִּי־אֶ֖פֶס בִּלְעָדָ֑י	6aB	that nothing exists apart from me –
אֲנִ֥י יְהוָ֖ה וְאֵ֥ין עֽוֹד׃	6aC	I am the LORD and there is no other,

= Masoretic verse.
Separation ↑: deictic particle(s); independent pers. pronoun.
Separation ↓: None (one verse-line).
Strophe parallelism: None (one verse-line).

STROPHE I.B.i.3 (Isa. 45:7)

יוֹצֵ֥ר אוֹר֙ וּבוֹרֵ֣א חֹ֔שֶׁךְ	7aA	he who forms light and creates darkness,
עֹשֶׂ֥ה שָׁל֖וֹם וּב֣וֹרֵא רָ֑ע	7aB	who makes peace and creates evil –
אֲנִ֥י יְהוָ֖ה עֹשֶׂ֥ה כָל־אֵֽלֶּה׃	7aC	I am the LORD who makes all these things.

= Masoretic verse.
Separation ↑: demonstrative pronoun; independent pers. pronoun; repetitive verse-line parallelism.
Separation ↓: major division markers in the textual tradition.
Strophe parallelism: None (one verse-line).

STROPHE I.B.ii.1 (Isa. 45:8)

הַרְעִ֤יפוּ שָׁמַ֙יִם֙ מִמַּ֔עַל	8aA	Drip, O heavens, from above,
וּשְׁחָקִ֖ים יִזְּלוּ־צֶ֑דֶק	8aB	and let the clouds pour down justice;
תִּפְתַּח־אֶ֣רֶץ וְיִפְרַח*־יֶ֗שַׁע	8bA	let the earth open up and let salvation blossom –
וּצְדָקָ֤ה תַצְמִ֙יחַ֙ יַ֔חַד	8bB	and let justice make sprout communion,
אֲנִ֥י יְהוָ֖ה בְּרָאתִֽיו׃	8bC	I am the LORD, I create it.

= Masoretic verse.
Separation ↑: major division markers in the textual tradition; imperative(s); jussive(s); vocative; swapping (subject).
Separation ↓: major division markers in the textual tradition; independent pers. pronoun; jussive(s); swapping (subject).
Strophe parallelism: שמים || ארץ; צדק || ישע.

STROPHE I.C.i.1 (Isa. 45:9)

הֹוי רָב אֶת־יֹצְרֹו	9aA	Woe to him who quarrels with the one who formed him,
חֶרֶשׂ אֶת־חַרְשֵׂי אֲדָמָה	9aB	a pot among the pots of earth.
הֲיֹאמַר חֹמֶר לְיֹצְרֹו מַה־תַּעֲשֶׂה	9bA	Does the clay say to him who forms it, "What do you make?"
וּפָעָלְךָ אֵין־יָדַיִם לֹו׃	9bB	or (does) your work which (itself) has no hands (say this)?

= Masoretic verse.
Separation ↑: major division markers in the textual tradition; deictic particle(s); repetitive verse-line parallelism.
Separation ↓: major division markers in the textual tradition; interrogative pronoun; marker of direct speech.
Strophe parallelism: יצר || יצר; יצר || פעל; חרש || חמר (unique).

STROPHE I.C.i.2 (Isa. 45:10)

הֹוי אֹמֵר לְאָב מַה־תֹּולִיד	10aA	Woe to him who says to a father, "What do you beget?"
וּלְאִשָּׁה מַה־תְּחִילִין׃	10aB	or to a wife, "What do you bring to birth?"

= Masoretic verse.
Separation ↑: major division markers in the textual tradition; deictic particle(s); interrogative pronouns; marker of direct speech; repetitive verse-line parallelism.
Separation ↓: major division markers in the textual tradition.
Strophe parallelism: None (one verse-line).

STROPHE I.C.ii.1 (Isa. 45:11)

כֹּה־אָמַר יְהוָה	11aA	Thus says the LORD,
קְדֹושׁ יִשְׂרָאֵל וְיֹצְרֹו	11aB	the Holy One of Israel and the one who formed it,
הָאֹתִיֹּות שְׁאָלוּנִי עַל־בָּנַי	11bA	The things to come? Interrogate me concerning my children,
וְעַל־פֹּעַל יָדַי תְּצַוֻּנִי׃	11bB	command me with regard the work of my hands.

= Masoretic verse.

Separation ↑: major division markers in the textual tradition; deictic particle(s); marker of direct speech.
Separation ↓: major division markers in the textual tradition; imperative(s); jussive(s); repetitive verse-line parallelism; swapping (object); swapping (adjunct).
Strophe parallelism: ישׂראל || בני (in this form unique); יצר || פעל.

STROPHE I.C.ii.2 (Isa. 45:12)

אָנֹכִי עָשִׂיתִי אֶרֶץ	12aA	It is I who made the earth,
וְאָדָם עָלֶיהָ בָרָאתִי	12aB	and created man upon it,
אֲנִי יָדַי נָטוּ שָׁמַיִם	12bA	I – my hands stretched out the heavens,
וְכָל־צְבָאָם צִוֵּיתִי׃	12bB	and all their host I command.

= Masoretic verse.
Separation ↑: major division markers in the textual tradition; independent pers. pronoun; swapping (subject); swapping (object); swapping (adjunct).
Separation ↓: independent pers. pronoun; swapping (subject); swapping (object).
Strophe parallelism: אנכי || אני; עשׂה || נטה; עשׂה || צוה; ארץ || שׁמים; ברא || צוה; grammatical parallelism.

STROPHE I.C.ii.3 (Isa. 45:13)

אָנֹכִי הַעִירֹתִהוּ בְצֶדֶק	13aA	It is I who woke him up in justice,
וְכָל־דְּרָכָיו אֲיַשֵּׁר	13aB	yes, all his ways I will make straight.
הוּא־יִבְנֶה עִירִי וְגָלוּתִי יְשַׁלֵּחַ	13bA	It is he who will rebuild my city and will send my exiles home,
לֹא בִמְחִיר וְלֹא בְשֹׁחַד	13bB	not for a price and not for presents,
אָמַר יְהוָה צְבָאוֹת׃	13bC	says the LORD of hosts.

= Masoretic verse.
Separation ↑: independent pers. pronoun; swapping (object).
Separation ↓: major division markers in the textual tradition; independent pers. pronoun; marker of direct speech; swapping (object).
Strophe parallelism: צדק || שׁחד (antithetical; unique); דרך || עיר.

STROPHE II.A.i.1 (Isa. 45:14a–b)

כֹּה ׀ אָמַר יְהוָה	14aA	Thus says the LORD,
יְגִיעַ מִצְרַיִם	14aB	The resources of Egypt
וּסְחַר־כּוּשׁ וּסְבָאִים	14aC	and the merchandise of Cush and the Sabeans,
אַנְשֵׁי מִדָּה עָלַיִךְ יַעֲבֹרוּ	14bA	tall men will pass over to you
וְלָךְ יִהְיוּ אַחֲרַיִךְ יֵלֵכוּ	14bB	and will be yours, they will go behind you,
בַּזִּקִּים יַעֲבֹרוּ	14bC	in chains they will pass;

= Masoretic verse.
Separation ↑: major division markers in the textual tradition; deictic particle(s); marker of direct speech; swapping (subject).
Separation ↓: repetitive verse-line parallelism; swapping (subject); swapping (adjunct).
Strophe parallelism: None.
Discussion: The verse-lines are connected by enjambment.

STROPHE II.A.i.2 (Isa. 45:14c–d)

וְאֵלַיִךְ יִשְׁתַּחֲווּ	14cA	and they will bow down for you,
אֵלַיִךְ יִתְפַּלָּלוּ	14cB	and they will pray to you:
אַךְ בָּךְ אֵל	14dA	“Only in you is God
וְאֵין עוֹד אֶפֶס אֱלֹהִים׃	14dB	and there does not exist any other god.”

= Masoretic verse.
Separation ↑: repetitive verse-line parallelism; swapping (adjunct).
Separation ↓: deictic particle(s); swapping (adjunct).
Strophe parallelism: ךְ- (f.s.) || ךְ- (f.s.).

STROPHE II.A.i.3 (Isa. 45:15)

אָכֵן אַתָּה אֵל מִסְתַּתֵּר	15aA	However, you are a God hiding himself,
אֱלֹהֵי יִשְׂרָאֵל מוֹשִׁיעַ׃	15aB	O Saviour God of Israel!

= Masoretic verse.
Separation ↑: deictic particle(s); independent pers. pronoun; swapping (subject).
Separation ↓: None (one verse-line).
Strophe parallelism: None (one verse-line).

STROPHE II.A.i.4 (Isa. 45:16)

בּוֹשׁוּ וְגַם־נִכְלְמוּ כֻּלָּם	16aA	They are ashamed and disgraced, all of them;
יַחְדָּו הָלְכוּ בַכְּלִמָּה	16aB	altogether they go in disgrace,
חָרָשֵׁי צִירִים׃	16aC	the craftsmen with their drawings.

= Masoretic verse.
Separation ↑: deictic particle(s).
Separation ↓: major division markers in the textual tradition; swapping (adjunct).
Strophe parallelism: בוש || כלם; כלם || הלך בכלמה (unique); grammatical parallelism.

STROPHE II.A.ii.1 (Isa. 45:17)

יִשְׂרָאֵל נוֹשַׁע בַּיהוָה	17aA	But Israel is saved by the LORD,
תְּשׁוּעַת עוֹלָמִים	17aB	a salvation of ages.
לֹא־תֵבֹשׁוּ וְלֹא־תִכָּלְמוּ	17bA	They will not be ashamed and and not be disgraced
עַד־עוֹלְמֵי עַד׃	17bB	to ages everlasting.

= Masoretic verse.
Separation ↑: major division markers in the textual tradition; swapping (subject).
Separation ↓: major division markers in the textual tradition.
Strophe parallelism: עולם || עולם.

STROPHE II.B.i.1 (Isa. 45:18)

כִּי כֹה אָמַר־יְהוָה בּוֹרֵא הַשָּׁמַיִם	18aA	For thus says the LORD, who created the heavens,
הוּא הָאֱלֹהִים יֹצֵר הָאָרֶץ	18aB	he (who) is God, who formed the earth,
וְעֹשָׂהּ הוּא כוֹנְנָהּ	18aC	and the One who made it, he (who) established it –
לֹא־תֹהוּ בְרָאָהּ	18bA	not as a void he created it,
לָשֶׁבֶת יְצָרָהּ	18bB	to be inhabited he formed it –
אֲנִי יְהוָה וְאֵין עוֹד׃	18bC	I am the LORD and there is no other.

= Masoretic verse.
Separation ↑: major division markers in the textual tradition; deictic particle(s); independent pers. pronouns; marker of direct speech; repetitive verse-line parallelism; swapping (subject).
Separation ↓: independent pers. pronoun; swapping (adjunct).
Strophe parallelism: ברא || ברא; יצר || יצר; יהוה || יהוה.
Discussion: $\mathfrak{G}^{A}$ and $\mathfrak{S}^{ab}$ presuppose a major break after יצרה. Because $\mathfrak{G}^{A}$ and $\mathfrak{S}^{b}$ also have a major division after v. 19, we must assume that these witnesses regarded v. 18bC as the beginning of the next strophe. The formula אני יהוה may occur both in the first verse-line of a strophe[1] and in the last one.[2] However, the consequence of transposing v. 18bC would be either a quadrocolon as v. 19a, or a strophe of three verse-lines with a tricolon in the middle. Neither of these solutions is attractive and so we prefer $\mathfrak{M}$'s division. Probably these witnesses wanted to mark the beginning of the direct speech after the convoluted introduction.

[1]Isa. 41:13; 42:6, 8; 45:5, 21c.
[2]Isa. 41:4, 17; 43:15; 45:6, 7, 8, 19; 49:23, 26.

STROPHE II.B.i.2 (Isa. 45:19)

לֹא בַסֵּתֶר דִּבַּרְתִּי	19aA	I did not speak in secret,
בִּמְקוֹם אֶרֶץ חֹשֶׁךְ	19aB	in a place of the land of darkness,
לֹא אָמַרְתִּי לְזֶרַע יַעֲקֹב תֹּהוּ בַקְּשׁוּנִי	19aC	I have not said to the seed of Jacob: "Seek me in the void!"
אֲנִי יְהוָה דֹּבֵר צֶדֶק	19bA	I am the LORD, who speaks what is just,
מַגִּיד מֵישָׁרִים׃	19bB	who tells what is straight.

= Masoretic verse.
Separation ↑: imperative(s); marker of direct speech; repetitive verse-line parallelism; swapping (adjunct).
Separation ↓: major division markers in the textual tradition; independent pers. pronoun.
Strophe parallelism: דבר Piel ‖ דבר Qal (unique in poetry); תהו ‖ צדק (antithetical).

STROPHE II.B.ii.1 (Isa. 45:20)

הִקָּבְצוּ וָבֹאוּ	20aA	Assemble and come,
הִתְנַגְּשׁוּ יַחְדָּו	20aB	draw near together,
פְּלִיטֵי הַגּוֹיִם	20aC	survivors of the nations.
לֹא יָדְעוּ הַנֹּשְׂאִים אֶת־עֵץ פִּסְלָם	20bA	They do not know, those who are carrying the wood of their idols,
וּמִתְפַּלְלִים אֶל־אֵל לֹא יוֹשִׁיעַ׃	20bB	who pray to a god that does not save.

= Masoretic verse.
Separation ↑: major division markers in the textual tradition; imperative(s); vocative.
Separation ↓: repetitive verse-line parallelism.
Strophe parallelism: פליט ‖ ישע.

STROPHE II.B.ii.2 (Isa. 45:21a–b)

הַגִּידוּ וְהַגִּישׁוּ	21aA	Tell and bring near,
אַף יִוָּעֲצוּ יַחְדָּו	21aB	yes, let them take counsel together:
מִי הִשְׁמִיעַ זֹאת מִקֶּדֶם	21bA	Who has made this heard from olden times,
מֵאָז הִגִּידָהּ	21bB	has told it since then?

≠ Masoretic verse.
Separation ↑: deictic particle(s); imperative(s); jussive(s).
Separation ↓: major division markers in the textual tradition; demonstrative pronoun; interrogative pronoun; repetitive verse-line parallelism; swapping (adjunct).
Strophe parallelism: נגד ‖ שמע; נגד ‖ נגד.
Discussion: The strophe parallelism as well as the major division

markers in $\mathfrak{G}^{SQ}$ indicate that v. 21a-b and v. 21c-d are independent strophes, thus confirming our analysis on the levels of cola and verse-lines.

STROPHE II.B.ii.3 (Isa. 45:21c–d)

הֲלוֹא אֲנִי יְהוָה	21cA	Was it not I, the LORD?
וְאֵין־עוֹד אֱלֹהִים מִבַּלְעָדַי	21cB	And there is no God apart from me,
אֵל־צַדִּיק וּמוֹשִׁיעַ	21dA	a just God and Saviour,
אַיִן זוּלָתִי׃	21dB	there is none besides me.

≠ Masoretic verse.
Separation ↑: major division markers in the textual tradition; deictic particle(s); independent pers. pronoun.
Separation ↓: major division markers in the textual tradition.
Strophe parallelism: יהוה || אל; אין || אין; אלהים || אל; בלעדי || זולת.
Discussion: See our comment on v. 21a-b.

STROPHE II.C.i.1 (Isa. 45:22)

פְּנוּ־אֵלַי וְהִוָּשְׁעוּ	22aA	Turn unto me and be saved,
כָּל־אַפְסֵי־אָרֶץ	22aB	all you ends of the earth,
כִּי אֲנִי־אֵל וְאֵין עוֹד׃	22bA	for I am God and there is no other.

= Masoretic verse.
Separation ↑: major division markers in the textual tradition; imperative(s); vocative.
Separation ↓: deictic particle(s); independent pers. pronoun.
Strophe parallelism: None.

STROPHE II.C.i.2 (Isa. 45:23)

בִּי נִשְׁבַּעְתִּי	23aA	I swear by myself,
יָצָא מִפִּי צְדָקָה	23aB	justice goes forth from my mouth,
דָּבָר וְלֹא יָשׁוּב	23aC	a word which shall not return:
כִּי־לִי תִּכְרַע כָּל־בֶּרֶךְ	23bA	Unto me every knee shall bow,
תִּשָּׁבַע כָּל־לָשׁוֹן׃	23bB	every tongue shall swear.

= Masoretic verse.
Separation ↑: swapping (adjunct).
Separation ↓: deictic particle(s); jussive(s); repetitive verse-line parallelism; swapping (adjunct).
Strophe parallelism: שבע || שבע; ־י || ־י.

STROPHE II.C.i.3 (Isa. 45:24–25)

אַךְ בַּיהוָה לִי אָמַר צְדָקוֹת	24aA	"Only in the LORD", they say to me, "is full justice,
וָעֹז עָדָיו יָבוֹא	24aB	and strength comes to him,
וְיֵבֹשׁוּ כֹּל הַנֶּחֱרִים בּוֹ׃	24aC	but all who are raging against him shall be put to shame.
בַּיהוָה יִצְדְּקוּ וְיִתְהַלְלוּ	25aA	In the Lord will be justified and will glory
כָּל־זֶרַע יִשְׂרָאֵל׃	25aB	all the seed of Israel."

≠ Masoretic verse.
Separation ↑: deictic particle(s); marker of direct speech; repetitive verse-line parallelism; swapping (subject); swapping (adjunct).
Separation ↓: major division markers in the textual tradition; swapping (adjunct).
Strophe parallelism: ב ‖ ב; יהוה ‖ יהוה; צדקה ‖ צדק Qal (unique); כל ‖ כל.

STROPHE II.C.ii.1 (Isa. 46:1)

כָּרַע בֵּל קֹרֵס נְבוֹ	1aA	Bel bows, Nebo cringes,
הָיוּ עֲצַבֵּיהֶם לַחַיָּה וְלַבְּהֵמָה	1aB	their grievous images are for the beasts and the cattle,
נְשֻׂאֹתֵיכֶם עֲמוּסוֹת	1bA	the objects you wanted to be carried become a burden,
מַשָּׂא לַעֲיֵפָה׃	1bB	a load to a weary animal.

= Masoretic verse.
Separation ↑: major division markers in the textual tradition.
Separation ↓: None.
Strophe parallelism: עצב ‖ נשואה (unique); בהמה ‖ עיפה (unique).

STROPHE II.C.ii.2 (Isa. 46:2)

קָרְסוּ כָרְעוּ יַחְדָּו	2aA	They cringe, they bow together,
לֹא יָכְלוּ מַלֵּט מַשָּׂא	2aB	they are unable to save the load,
וְנַפְשָׁם בַּשְּׁבִי הָלָכָה׃	2bA	and they themselves go into captivity.

= Masoretic verse.
Separation ↑: None.
Separation ↓: major division markers in the textual tradition; swapping (subject); swapping (adjunct).
Strophe parallelism: None.
Discussion: The lack of parallelism on the level of the strophe is compensated by the strong canticle parallelism.

STROPHE III.A.i.1 (Isa. 46:3)

שִׁמְעוּ אֵלַי בֵּית יַעֲקֹב	3aA	Listen to me, O house of Jacob,
וְכָל־שְׁאֵרִית בֵּית יִשְׂרָאֵל	3aB	and all the remnant of the house of Israel,
הַעֲמֻסִים מִנִּי־בֶטֶן	3bA	you who were a burden from the womb,
הַנְּשֻׂאִים מִנִּי־רָחַם׃	3bB	who were carried since your birth.

= Masoretic verse.
Separation ↑: major division markers in the textual tradition; imperative(s); vocatives; repetitive verse-line parallelism.
Separation ↓: repetitive verse-line parallelism.
Strophe parallelism: None.
Discussion: Canticle parallelism compensates for the lack of strophe parallelism.

STROPHE III.A.i.2 (Isa. 46:4)

וְעַד־זִקְנָה אֲנִי הוּא	4aA	Even unto (your) old age I am the same One,
וְעַד־שֵׂיבָה אֲנִי אֶסְבֹּל	4aB	and unto (your) greyness I will continue to bear (you);
אֲנִי עָשִׂיתִי וַאֲנִי אֶשָּׂא	4bA	I have made (you) and I will continue to carry,
וַאֲנִי אֶסְבֹּל וַאֲמַלֵּט׃	4bB	will continue to bear and will continue to save (you).

= Masoretic verse.
Separation ↑: independent pers. pronouns; repetitive verse-line parallelism; swapping (adjunct).
Separation ↓: major division markers in the textual tradition; independent pers. pronouns; repetitive verse-line parallelism.
Strophe parallelism: אני || אני; סבל || סבל (unique); grammatical parallelism.

STROPHE III.A.ii.1 (Isa. 46:5)

לְמִי תְדַמְּיוּנִי וְתַשְׁווּ	5aA	And to whom will you liken me and make me equal,
וְתַמְשִׁלוּנִי וְנִדְמֶה׃	5aB	and compare me that we may be alike?

= Masoretic verse.
Separation ↑: major division markers in the textual tradition; interrogative pronoun; swapping (adjunct).
Separation ↓: major division marker in the textual tradition.
Strophe parallelism: None (one verse-line).

STROPHE III.A.ii.2 (Isa. 46:6)

הַזָּלִ֤ים זָהָב֙ מִכִּ֔יס	6aA	Those who pour out gold from the purse,
וְכֶ֖סֶף בַּקָּנֶ֣ה יִשְׁקֹ֑לוּ	6aB	and weigh out silver on the scales,
יִשְׂכְּר֤וּ צוֹרֵף֙ וְיַעֲשֵׂ֣הוּ אֵ֔ל	6bA	hire a goldsmith and he makes a god of it;
יִסְגְּד֖וּ אַף־יִשְׁתַּחֲוֽוּ׃	6bB	then they worship, even bow down!

= Masoretic verse.
Separation ↑: major division marker in the textual tradition; swapping (subject); swapping (object); swapping (adjunct).
Separation ↓: deictic particle(s).
Strophe parallelism: grammatical parallelism.

STROPHE III.A.ii.3 (Isa. 46:7)

יִ֠שָּׂאֻהוּ עַל־כָּתֵ֨ף יִסְבְּלֻ֜הוּ	7aA	They lift him up, they bear him on the shoulder,
וְיַנִּיחֻ֤הוּ תַחְתָּיו֙ וְיַעֲמֹ֔ד	7aB	they put him down and (there) he stands;
מִמְּקוֹמ֖וֹ לֹ֣א יָמִ֑ישׁ	7aC	he will not move from his place.
אַף־יִצְעַ֤ק אֵלָיו֙ וְלֹ֣א יַעֲנֶ֔ה	7bA	Even when one cries out to him, he does not answer;
מִצָּרָת֖וֹ לֹ֥א יוֹשִׁיעֶֽנּוּ׃	7bB	from his anguish he does not save him.

= Masoretic verse.
Separation ↑: swapping (adjunct).
Separation ↓: major division markers in the textual tradition; deictic particle(s); swapping (adjunct).
Strophe parallelism: לא \|\| לא; grammatical parallelism.

STROPHE III.B.i.1 (Isa. 46:8–9)

זִכְרוּ־זֹ֖את וְהִתְאֹשָׁ֑שׁוּ	8aA	Remember this and behave like men,
הָשִׁ֥יבוּ פוֹשְׁעִ֖ים עַל־לֵֽב׃	8aB	bring it back to your hearts, O transgressors.
זִכְר֥וּ רִאשֹׁנ֖וֹת מֵעוֹלָ֑ם	9aA	Remember the first things, from eternity on,
כִּ֣י אָנֹכִ֤י אֵל֙ וְאֵ֣ין ע֔וֹד	9aB	that I am God, and there is no other,
אֱלֹהִ֖ים וְאֶ֥פֶס כָּמֽוֹנִי׃	9aC	a God – and none like me exists! –

≠ Masoretic verse.
Separation ↑: major division markers in the textual tradition; demonstrative pronoun; imperative(s); vocative;
Separation ↓: deictic particle(s); independent pers. pronoun; imperative(s); vocative.
Strophe parallelism: זכר \|\| זכר.

STROPHE III.B.i.2 (Isa. 46:10)

מַגִּ֤יד מֵֽרֵאשִׁית֙ אַחֲרִ֔ית	10aA	who tells the outcome from the beginning
וּמִקֶּ֖דֶם אֲשֶׁ֣ר לֹא־נַעֲשׂ֑וּ	10aB	and from olden times that which had not yet been made,
אֹמֵר֙ עֲצָתִ֣י תָק֔וּם	10bA	who says, "My counsel shall stand,
וְכָל־חֶפְצִ֖י אֶעֱשֶֽׂה׃	10bB	and everything I want I will make!",

= Masoretic verse.
Separation ↑: repetitive verse-line parallelism; swapping (adjunct).
Separation ↓: marker of direct speech; swapping (subject); swapping (object).
Strophe parallelism: נגד ‖ אמר; עשׂה ‖ עשׂה; grammatical parallelism.

STROPHE III.B.i.3 (Isa. 46:11)

קֹרֵ֤א מִמִּזְרָח֙ עַ֔יִט	11aA	who calls the Vulture from the east,
מֵאֶ֥רֶץ מֶרְחָ֖ק אִ֣ישׁ עֲצָת֑וֹ	11aB	from a land far away the man of his counsel.
אַף־דִּבַּ֙רְתִּי֙ אַף־אֲבִיאֶ֔נָּה	11bA	As I have spoken (it), so I will bring it about,
יָצַ֖רְתִּי אַף־אֶעֱשֶֽׂנָּה׃	11bB	(as) I have formed (it), so I will make it.

= Masoretic verse.
Separation ↑: repetitive verse-line parallelism; swapping (adjunct).
Separation ↓: major division markers in the textual tradition; deictic particle(s); repetitive verse-line parallelism.
Strophe parallelism: קרא ‖ דבר.

STROPHE III.B.ii.1 (Isa. 46:12)

שִׁמְע֥וּ אֵלַ֖י אַבִּ֣ירֵי לֵ֑ב	12aA	Listen to me, you mighty of heart,
הָרְחוֹקִ֖ים מִצְּדָקָֽה׃	12aB	you who are far from justice.

= Masoretic verse.
Separation ↑: major division markers in the textual tradition; imperative(s); vocatives.
Separation ↓: None (one verse-line).
Strophe parallelism: None (one verse-line).

STROPHE III.B.ii.2 (Isa. 46:13)

קֵרַ֤בְתִּי צִדְקָתִי֙ לֹ֣א תִרְחָ֔ק	13aA	I bring near my justice, it is not far off;
וּתְשׁוּעָתִ֖י לֹ֣א תְאַחֵ֑ר	13aB	and my salvation, it will not tarry;
וְנָתַתִּ֤י בְצִיּוֹן֙ תְּשׁוּעָ֔ה	13bA	yes, I give in Zion my salvation,
לְיִשְׂרָאֵ֖ל תִּפְאַרְתִּֽי׃	13bB	to Israel my glory.

= Masoretic verse.
Separation ↑: repetitive verse-line parallelism; swapping (subject).

Separation ↓: major division markers in the textual tradition; swapping (adjunct).
Strophe parallelism: צדקה || תפארת; צדקה || תשועה; תשועה || תשועה; י־ || י־; grammatical parallelism.

7.5 Isaiah 45–46 – Delimitation of Canticles

CANTICLE I.A.i (45:1)

Separation ↑: major division markers in the textual tradition.
Separation ↓: major division markers in the textual tradition.
Canticle parallelism: ימין || פנה (concatenation/responsion).
The strophes are linked by an on-running sentence (enjambment).
Thematic unity: yes. The two strophes together describe the election of Cyrus for his mission.
Discussion: The delimitation of this canticle may seem somewhat uncertain. Ch. 44 ends with Cyrus so one might be tempted to connect the two chapters. However, the upper limit is attested in so many witnesses that it can hardly be ignored. Also כה־אמר יהוה suggests a new start. The lower delimitation is very uncertain however. Only $\mathfrak{G}^{A}$ indicates a major break here. Nevertheless we accept its testimony because v. 1a and v. 1b-c speak about Cyrus in the 3rd person, whereas in vv. 2-5 he is addressed directly.

CANTICLE I.A.ii (45:2–4)

Separation ↑: major division markers in the textual tradition.
Separation ↓: major division markers in the textual tradition.
Canticle parallelism: ך־ (m.s.) || ך־ (m.s.) in all strophes; אני || אני (inclusion); למען || למען (concatenation); ידע || ידע (responsion); קרא בשם || קרא בשם; ישראל || ישראל.
Thematic unity: yes. The first two strophes promise Cyrus support and success, the last two (3b and 4) give the reasons why. All three strophes address Cyrus in the second person.
Discussion: See our discussion of I.A.i for the upper delimitation. Although the lower delimitation is attested in Qumran only it is practically certain that $\mathfrak{G}^{Q}$ supports this delimitation in a proleptic way.

CANTICLE I.B.i (45:5–7)

Separation ↑: major division markers in the textual tradition; thematic discontinuity (the unicity of the LORD becomes the major theme).
Separation ↓: major division markers in the textual tradition.

Canticle parallelism: אני || אני || אני (double inclusion); יהוה || יהוה || יהוה (double inclusion); אין || אין (responsion); עוד || עוד (inclusion); זולת || בלעדי (responsion); ידע || ידע (concatenation); שמש || אור (responsion). The strophes are linked by an on-running sentence (enjambment).
Thematic unity: yes. All strophes emphasize the uniqueness and absolute power of the LORD who created the universe.
Discussion: Of course one might point to the second person singular in v. 5bA to advocate a connection with the preceding verses. And the refrain-like אני יהוה might be invoked to defend a connection with v. 8 (cf. 8bC). However, the testimony of the ancient witnesses argues against both proposals. Moreover, the change of subject suggests a new beginning in v. 8aA. The thematic unity of vv. 5-7 as well as the fact that the sentence runs on through all three strophes favour our delimitation.

𝔊[S] has a paragraphos with v. 6 but no other indication of a major break. Probably it was added later on rather carelessly and was intended to mark the break after v. 7.

CANTICLE I.B.ii.1 (45:8)

Separation ↑: major division markers in the textual tradition; change of subject.
Separation ↓: major division markers in the textual tradition.
Canticle parallelism: None (one strophe).
Thematic unity: yes. The strophe invites the whole cosmos to join in the praise of the LORD.
Discussion: Many modern commentators regard the hymn as a separate unit which was inserted later on. It is remarkable that apparently it was still recognized as a separate unit in Antiquity. See further our comments below, p. 328-30 (macro).

At first sight it may appear that the division between vv. 7 and 8 is more firmly established in the tradition than that between vv. 8 and 9. However, since it is likely that the division markers which 𝔊[SQ] place after v. 8bB may be interpreted as proleptic markers whereas the division markers 𝔊[BAQ] have in v. 9 are clearly lagging behind, actually almost the same group of witnesses may be assumed to have had a major division after v. 8.

CANTICLE I.C.i (45:9–10)

Separation ↑: major division markers in the textual tradition; thematic discontinuity; change of subject.
Separation ↓: major division markers in the textual tradition.

Canticle parallelism: הוי || הוי (responsion); יצר || אב (responsion/concatenation); מה || מה (concatenation); אמר || אמר (concatenation).
Thematic unity: yes. Both strophes seek to demonstrate the impossibility of challenging the Creator by adducing a simile.
Discussion: The Hebrew tradition hesitates between a major break after v. 9 or after v. 10. As a result many manuscripts, including $1\mathfrak{Q}^{a}$ and $\mathfrak{M}$, have a break after both verses. From the viewpoint of thematic unity the break after v. 10 has to be preferred. The latter option also has the support of several Greek and Syriac manuscripts, whereas the former has not. It is true that v. 11 picks up the theme again, but nevertheless there are more arguments to join that verse with vv. 12-13 (see below). The unity of vv. 9-10 is also indicated by the combination of the similes of potter and father in v. 11.

CANTICLE I.C.ii.1 (45:11–13)

Separation ↑: major division markers in the textual tradition; change of subject.
Separation ↓: major division markers in the textual tradition.
Canticle parallelism: אמר || אמר (inclusion); קדוש ישראל || יהוה צבאות (inclusion); יצר || עשׂה (responsion); יצר || ברא (responsion); י־ || י־ (responsion); יד || יד (responsion); צוה || צוה (responsion; unique in poetry); אנכי || אנכי; כל || כל (concatenation); צבא || צבא (responsion).
Thematic unity: yes. The canticle draws the conclusion from the preceding one: the power of the almighty Creator to fulfil his promise of restoration should not be challenged by his children.
Discussion: $\mathfrak{S}$ has a plus at the end of v. 11aB ("the Lord of hosts is his name")[1] and after that $\mathfrak{S}^{ad}$ indicate a major break which, however, is hardly appropriate after the introduction of the direct speech. None of the other witnesses supports it.

Since $\mathfrak{G}^{SA}$ support the break after v. 10, the division markers in $\mathfrak{G}^{SA}$ after v. 11 must be regarded as a remnant of a strophic division. Only $\mathfrak{G}^{Q}$ may have connected v. 11 with the preceding which is correct from the viewpoint of content, but is not in line with the argument as a whole (see above: Thematic unity).

CANTICLE II.A.i (45:14–16)

Separation ↑: major division markers in the textual tradition; thematic discontinuity.
Separation ↓: major division markers in the textual tradition.

---

[1] On the plus in $\mathfrak{G}$, see p. 262, n. 12.

Canticle parallelism: יהוה || אל || אל (inclusion/responsion); מצרים || ישׂראל (responsion); הלך || הלך (responsion); ךְ־ (f.s.) || ךְ־ (f.s.) (concatenation/responsion); עבר || שׂחה (concatenation).
Thematic unity: yes. All four strophes deal with the disgrace of foreign nations who will subject themselves to Israel because they have been convinced that their own idols will not help them so that they have to convert themselves to the LORD who cannot be depicted by craftsmen.

CANTICLE II.A.ii.1 (45:17)

Separation ↑: major division markers in the textual tradition.
Separation ↓: major division markers in the textual tradition.
Canticle parallelism: None (one strophe).
Thematic unity: yes. V. 17b cannot be understood without v. 17a and the strophe parallelism עולמים || עולמים underscores the unity.
Discussion: We believe the upper delimitation of this strophe to have accidentally moved to the position where it is now according to the ancient witnesses. We will argue this point of view when discussing the macrostructure of the chapter.

CANTICLE II.B.i (45:18–19)

Separation ↑: major division markers in the textual tradition; thematic discontinuity; change of subject.
Separation ↓: major division markers in the textual tradition.
Canticle parallelism: אמר || דבר (responsion/inclusion); אמר || אמר (responsion); יהוה || יהוה (inclusion); ארץ || ארץ (responsion); תהו || תהו (concatenation).
Thematic unity: yes. Both strophes emphasize that the God of Israel has revealed himself not in chaos, but through his reliable word in the created world.
Discussion: The lower delimitation is weakly attested in the ancient witnesses. Yet we trust them because they belong to different traditions. Moreover, the change of subject and theme indicates that with v. 20 a new canticle starts.

𝔊^{A} and 𝔖^{ab} have an extra caesura after v. 18bB. We have discussed this earlier.[2]

CANTICLE II.B.ii (45:20–21)

Separation ↑: major division markers in the textual tradition; thematic discontinuity; change of subject.

[2]See p. 315.

Separation ↓: major division markers in the textual tradition.
Canticle parallelism: נגשׁ || נגשׁ (responsion); יחדו || יחדו (unique; responsion); ידע || נגד (concatenation); פסל || אלהים; אל (noun) || אל (noun) (responsion); ישׁע || ישׁע (responsion).
Thematic unity: yes. All three strophes challenge the nations in a lawsuit the inevitable outcome of which will be that they have to recognize the unicity of the God of Israel.
Discussion: The division markers in 𝔊^SQ,[3] after v. 21b find no support in any of the other witnesses. Because 𝔊^S also has a full-fledged division marking after v. 21 these dividers may be remnants of a strophe division.[4]

The division between II.B.ii and II.C.i is attested in 𝔊^SB only. Indeed there is much which argues in favour of connecting the following verses to the same structural unit: the imperatives in vv. 20a and 22aA; the verb ישׁע (vv. 20bB, 21dA, 22aA); the addressees (vv. 20aC, 22aB); אני יהוה (v. 21cA) || אני־אל (v. 22bA); אין זולתי (v. 21dB) || אין עוד (v. 22bA); צדיק (v. 21dA) || צדקה (vv. 23aB, 24aA), צדק (v. 25aA). However, as this survey shows, the links are confined mainly to v. 22 and could therefore be regarded as a concatenation between the two sub-cantos. Similar links can be observed elsewhere in the chapter: I.A (v. 4bB) "you" – I.B (v. 5bA) "you"; I.B (v. 8bC) ברא – I.C (v. 9aA) יצר; I.C (v. 13bB) מחיר – II.A (v. 14aB) יגיע,[5] and I.C (v. 13bC) אמר יהוה || II.A (v. 14aA) אמר יהוה. So this type of evidence is not always conclusive, especially not when so many elements mentioned are also found elswhere in the chapter. Moreover, v. 23bA לי תכרע כל־ברך clearly prepares the stage for 46:1 כרע בל קרס נבו and 46:2 קרסו כרעו יחדו. Because this is a unique[6] and very specific link, we regard it as more likely that vv. 22-25 should be connected with 46:1-2. Therefore, all taken together, we venture to accept the caesura found in 𝔊^SB. The divider in 𝔊^A after v. 23aA may be a belated marking of the same break.

CANTICLE II.C.i (45:22–25)

Separation ↑: major division markers in the textual tradition; change of subject.
Separation ↓: major division markers in the textual tradition.
Canticle parallelism: כל־אפסי־ארץ || כל־ברך (unique; inclusion); צדקה || צדקה (responsion); צדקה || צדק (verb; inclusion); כל || כל (concatenation).

---

[3]In 𝔊^S a colon only.
[4]See pp. 316-7.
[5]See Isa. 55:1-2.
[6]The verb כרע does not occur elswhere in Isa. 40–55.

Thematic unity: yes. All nations have to recognize the LORD's justice and power.
Discussion: See our discussion of the previous canticle. The major division markers in 𝔊[A] after ביהוה can be interpreted only as redundant anticipation of the major division after v. 25 which is also attested by the same manuscript.

CANTICLE II.C.ii (46:1–2)

Separation ↑: major division markers in the textual tradition; change of subject.
Separation ↓: major division markers in the textual tradition.
Canticle parallelism: קרס ‖ קרס (unique; responsion); כרע ‖ כרע (responsion); משׂא ‖ משׂא (concatenation).
Thematic unity: yes. The two strophes describe the Babylonian gods doing hommage (to the LORD, cf. 45:23) and their inability to escape from captivity.

CANTICLE III.A.i (46:3–4)

Separation ↑: major division markers in the textual tradition; thematic discontinuity; change of subject.
Separation ↓: major division markers in the textual tradition.
Canticle parallelism: מני־בטן ‖ עד־זקנה (antithetical, unique; concatenation); נשׂא ‖ נשׂא (responsion); מני־רחם ‖ עד־שׂיבה (antithetical, unique; concatenation).
Thematic unity: yes. Both strophes describe how Israel has been a burden the LORD has had to carry from the very beginning of Israel's existence.[7]

CANTICLE III.A.ii (46:5–7)

Separation ↑: major division markers in the textual tradition; thematic discontinuity.
Separation ↓: major division markers in the textual tradition.
Canticle parallelism: אף ‖ אף (responsion).
Thematic unity: yes. The first strophe states the incomparability of God, the other two give an ironic description of the irrational behaviour of those who believe in idols.
Discussion: Despite the very low level of canticle parallelism the unity of the canticle cannot be doubted.

[7] This might be a veiled reference to Ps. 68:20 (see also Hos. 11:3) and a reaction to Jer. 23:23, see also Jer. 23:36, 38.

CANTICLE III.B.i (46:8–11)

Separation ↑: major division markers in the textual tradition; thematic discontinuity;
Separation ↓: major division markers in the textual tradition.
Canticle parallelism: ראשון || ראשית (concatenation); מן || מן (concatenation); עולם || קדם (concatenation); עשׂה || עשׂה (inclusion/responsion); אמר || קרא (concatenation); אמר || דבר (inclusion); עצה || עצה (unique; concatenation).
The strophes are linked by an on-running sentence (enjambment).
Thematic unity: yes. History should convince the unfaithful Israelites (and, in our opinion, all worshippers of idols, vv. 5–7) that God always does whatever he wants and that therefore Cyrus must be seen as the instrument in his hand to achieve his objectives.

CANTICLE III.B.ii (46:12–13)

Separation ↑: major division markers in the textual tradition; thematic discontinuity; change of subject.
Separation ↓: major division markers in the textual tradition.
Canticle parallelism: צדקה || צדקה (concatenation); רחוק || רחק (unique; concatenation).
Thematic unity: yes. Both strophes speak of God's justice which is far removed from that of the unfaithful worshippers of idols, both Israelites and foreigeners in our opinion (see v. 8), but not far from (faithful) Zion.

7.6 Isaiah 45–46 – Delimitation of Macrostructure

We have taken the chapters 45 and 46 together because both deal with the purpose of the mission of king Cyrus. We point specifically to the correspondence between 45:3bB הקורא בשמך (see also v. 4bA) and 46:11 קרא ממזרח עיט. The phrase אנכי העירתהו בצדק (45:13) links up with קרבתי צדקתי (46:13) as a description of his advent (cf. 46:11). This in turn should be connected with the other texts in this piece dealing with the LORD's justice: 45:8, 19, 21, 23-25; 46:12. And these in turn are so intimately connected with the ongoing lawsuit and its typical argumentative style that it becomes very difficult to view the two chapters as separate units. Finally, the obvious link between לי תכרע כל־ברך (45:23) and כרע בל קרס נבו (46:1), קרסו כרעו יחדו (46:2) renders the joining of the two chapters an attractive working hypothesis.

The overall structure of Isaiah 45–46 appears to be more complicated than that of the preceding cantos because the composition[1] itself consists of three cantos.

CANTOS	SUB-CANTOS	CANTICLES	STROPHES
I	A	2	5 (2+3)
	B	2	4 (3+1)
	C	2	5 (2+3)
II	A	2	5 (4+1)
	B	2	5 (2+3)
	C	2	5 (3+2)
III	A	2	5 (2+3)
	B	2	5 (3+2)

It should be emphasized once again that the high degree of regularity in this composition on the level of strophes and canticles is not an artefact. The structure we established rests almost exclusively on evidence culled from ancient manuscripts. As we have admitted in the introduction,[2] the division into larger units such as sub-cantos and cantos is a far more hazardous operation because here no ancient witnesses are available.

Nevertheless even the division into strophes and canticles can never be taken over automatically and uncritically from the available witnesses, because the scribes had only a fuzzy idea of the function of the division markers they found in the manuscripts they copied.

[1]One might call such a superstructure a 'cantata'.

[2]See p. 16.

Many small errors were the result, as we have seen. In the case of Isa. 45–46 it seems clear now that the person responsible for the final editing of this composition aimed at a nice alternation of canticles counting 2+3 and 3+2 strophes respectively. This raises the question whether sub-canto II.A (45:14–17) in its present form (4+1 strophes) is what he intended.

If we take a closer look at the passage involved, it appears that the two strophes vv. 14a-b and 14c-d are closely connected thematically, but have fewer ties with the next three strophes (vv. 15, 16, 17). The parallelism connecting the latter is very strong: the hiddenness of God (v. 15aA) contrasts with the drawings of the craftsmen (v. 16aC); the phrase אלהי ישׂראל מושׁיע (v. 15aB) clearly balances ישׂראל נושׁע ביהוה (v. 17aA); the shame and disgrace of the worshippers of idols (v. 16) is contrasted with the lack of shame and disgrace in Israel (v. 17b). All this emboldens us to suggest that somehow the well-attested division between vv. 16 and 17 has got in the wrong place[3] and was originally positioned between vv. 14 and 15, in line with the alternation between 2+3 and 3+2 strophes per canticle. If this hypothesis is correct, the error must have occurred quite early.

The other irregularity occurs in sub-canto I.B (45:5-8). Instead of the expected 3+2 pattern we find a pattern 3+1 here. Many scholars regard 45:8 as a later hymnical addition, but more recent authors regard it as an authentic Deutero-Isaianic text.[4] As we have seen in the case of 44:23, such hymnical strophes were isolated by the tradents more often, despite the fact that they are firmly embedded in the context.[5] If this is true here too, it seems likely that at an early date (before ca. 200 BCE) a strophe has dropped from canticle I.B.ii.

The structure of the **canto I** (45:1-13) is more or less concentric. It starts with Cyrus (45:1-5) and ends with him (45:13). God will make his campaigns run smoothly (45:2, 13). His mission will serve a twofold purpose: to save Israel (45:4, 13) and to make all nations recognize the universal power of the Creator (45:6). This recognition is also required of Israel itself which seems to doubt the power of its Creator (45:9-12).[6]

---

[3]We have already discussed quite a number of similar cases in the earlier chapters and will continue to do so below. See our general conclusions in this respect, pp. 646-8.

[4]E.g. Beuken, 238; Melugin, 125; Koole, 329-30; Hermisson, 3; Van Oorschot, 84-7; Grimm, Dittert, 256.

[5]See pp. 256-7.

[6]As noted before (p. 262, n. 9), this might be a reaction to bitter complaints among the youth of Israel.

Canto II (45:14-46:2) too exhibits a more or less concentric structure. It starts with the subjection of the idol serving nations to the people of Israel which itself will be saved (II.A, 45:14-17). The canto ends with the subjection of the nations and their idols to the God of Israel (II.C, 45:22-46:2). The middle part (II.B, 45:18-21) is a justification of God who has revealed himself to Israel from the beginning not as a God who loves chaos (תהו) but an inhabited world. It seems as if this too is a reaction to certain complaints. After all, the prophets had announced that it was God who would turn the land into תהו.[7]

Canto III (46:3-13) consists of only two sub-cantos which both state that God will continue to save Israel despite its unfaithfulness. There is no reason to suppose that this canto is incomplete. The refrain-like vv. 3 and 12 identify the "mighty of heart" as the "house of Jacob" (inclusion).

As there is a certain concatenation of canticles in this chapter,[8] so the cantos are to some extent linked. The "not for a price and not for presents" at the end of canto I (45:13bB) links up with the tribute brought by Egypt and Cush at the beginning of canto II (45:14a). The images of the Babylonian gods become a burden to their worshippers at the end of canto II (46:1-2), just as Israel has been and will remain a burden to God according to the beginning of canto III (46:3-4). As we shall see later on, this way of linking cantos appears to be a macrostructural device.[9]

Distant parallelism connecting the canticles of **sub-canto I.A**: משיח (45:1aB – I.A.i) || עבד (45:4aA – I.A.ii); דלת (45:1cA – I.A.i) || דלת (45:2bA – I.A.ii); שער (45:1cB – I.A.i) || בריח (45:2bB – I.A.ii).

Distant parallelism connecting the canticles of **sub-canto I.B**: אני (45:5aA, 6aC, 7aC – I.B.i) || אני (45:8bC – I.B.ii); יהוה (45:5aA, 6aC, 7aC – I.B.i) || יהוה (45:8bC – I.B.ii); אור (45:7aA – I.B.i) || שמים (45:8aA – I.B.ii); ברא (45:7aA, 7aB – I.B.i) || ברא (45:8bC – I.B.ii); שלום (45:7aB – I.B.i) || ישע (45:8bA – I.B.ii).

Distant parallelism connecting the canticles of **sub-canto I.C**: יצר (45:9aA, 9bA – I.C.i) || יצר (45:11aB – 1.C.ii); אדמה (45:9aB – I.C.i) || אדם (45:12aB – I.C.ii); פעל (45:9bB – I.C.i) || פעל (45:11bB – I.C.ii); יד (45:9bB – I.C.i) || יד (45:11bB – I.C.ii); אב (45:10aA – I.C.i), אשה (45:10aB – I.C.i) || בן (45:11bA – I.C.ii).

---

[7] Isa. 24:10; 34:11; Jer. 4:13; also Isa. 5:6 as emended by several scholars.
[8] See pp. 322-8.
[9] See pp. 663-4.

Distant parallelism connecting the canticles of **sub-canto II.A**: See our discussion above.
Distant parallelism connecting the canticles of **sub-canto II.B**: אלהים (45:18aB – I.B.i) || אלהים (45:21cB – I.B.ii); אני יהוה (45:19bA – II.B.i) || אני יהוה (45:21cA – II.B.ii); אין עוד (45:18bC – II.B.i), אין עוד (45:21cB – II.B.ii) || אין זולתי (45:21dB – II.B.ii); נגד (45:19bB – II.B.i) || נגד (45:21aA, 21bB – II.B.ii).

Distant parallelism connecting the canticles of **sub-canto II.C**: ישע (45:22aA – II.C.i) || מלט (46:2aA – II.C.ii); כרע (45:23bA – II.C.ii) || כרע (46:1aA, 2aA – II.C.ii).

Distant parallelism connecting the canticles of **sub-canto III.A**: נשׂא (46:3bB, 4bA – III.A.i) || נשׂא (46:7aA – III.A.ii); סבל (46:4aB – III.A.i) || סבל (46:7aA – III.A.ii); עשׂה (46:4bA – III.A.i) || עשׂה (46:6bA – III.A.ii), apparently antithetically, as in other cases; מלט (46:4bB – III.A.i) || ישע (46:7bB – III.A.ii).

Distant parallelism connecting the canticles of **sub-canto III.B**: פשע (46:8aB – III.B.i) || אביר לב (46:12aA – III.B.ii); מרחק (46:11aB – III.B.i) || רחוק (46:12aB – III.B.ii), רחק (46:13aA – III.B.ii).

Our macrostructural analysis has resulted in recovering a well-composed unit, even though we had reason to suppose that it has suffered minor damage even before the 2nd century BCE. Of course this high level of sophistication of the composition need not mean that Isa. 45–46 has been a unit from the start. But its regularity is certainly a factor which should be taken into account in future investigations.

Chapter 8

The Structure of Isaiah 47

8.1 Isaiah 47: Text and Translation

ס <פ> – 1Qa – 𝔊SBA – 𝔖abcde ______________________

A.i.1 (Isa. 47:1)

רְדִ֣י ׀ וּשְׁבִ֣י עַל־עָפָ֗ר בְּתוּלַת֙ בַּת־בָּבֶ֔ל {𝔊Q}	1aA	Come down, sit in the dust, O virgin daughter of Babel,
שְׁבִי־לָאָ֥רֶץ אֵין־כִּסֵּ֖א בַּת־כַּשְׂדִּ֑ים	1aB	sit on the ground, no throne, O daughter of the Chaldeans!
כִּ֣י לֹ֤א תוֹסִ֙יפִי֙ יִקְרְאוּ־לָ֔ךְ	1bA	For never again you will be called
רַכָּ֖ה וַעֲנֻגָּֽה׃	1bB	tender and delicate.[1]

A.i.2 (Isa. 47:2)

קְחִ֥י רֵחַ֖יִם וְטַ֣חֲנִי קָ֑מַח	2aA	Take millstones and grind flour,
גַּלִּ֨י צַמָּתֵ֧ךְ חֶשְׂפִּי־שֹׁ֛בֶל	2bA	remove your veil, strip off your dangling jewelry,[2]
גַּלִּי־שׁ֖וֹק עִבְרִ֥י נְהָרֽוֹת׃	2bB	uncover your thighs, pass through rivers.

A.i.3 (Isa. 47:3a)

תִּגָּל֙ עֶרְוָתֵ֔ךְ	3aA	Let your nakedness be uncovered,
גַּ֥ם תֵּרָאֶ֖ה חֶרְפָּתֵ֑ךְ	3aB	also your humiliation be seen.

A.i.4 (Isa. 47:3b)

נָקָ֣ם אֶקָּ֔ח {𝔊A}	3bA	I will take vengeance,
וְלֹ֥א אֶפְגַּ֖ע אָדָֽם׃	3bB	I will spare nobody.[3]

ס <פ> – 1Qa – 𝔖abe . . . .

---

[1]With Zorell, 612, and many others; because a positive quality is required (see the parallel v. 5bB and Deut. 28:56), the translation "verwöhnt, verzärtelt" (spoilt, pampered) (so *HALAT*, 805) is less likely.

[2]The technical terms for צמה and שבל are rare. The meaning of the first is fairly certain, cf. *HALAT*, 967-8. The second is a *hapax legomenon* which 1Qa simplifies in reading שוליך on the analogy of Jer. 13:26. We connect it with Mari Akkadian *šubulu* (*CAD* Š 3, 190) and interpret this as the type of jewelry oriental women use(d) to wear on their forehead. For other proposals see *HALAT*, 1296; Franke, 113-4.

[3]Alternatively: "I will nobody allow to intercede", cf. Barthélemy, 348-9; De Waard, 178-9. If so, the phrase may be contrasted with the servant of the LORD's intercession for Israel, Isa. 53:12cB, p. 550, n. 22.

A.ii.1 (Isa. 47:4)

גֹּאֲלֵנוּ יְהוָה צְבָאוֹת שְׁמוֹ	4aA	Our Redeemer, LORD of hosts is his name,
{<ס>𝔊^{SA}} קְדוֹשׁ יִשְׂרָאֵל׃	4aB	the Holy One of Israel:[4]

A.ii.2 (Isa. 47:5)

שְׁבִי דוּמָם וּבֹאִי בַחֹשֶׁךְ בַּת־כַּשְׂדִּים	5aA	Sit down in silence and go into darkness, daughter of the Chaldeans,
כִּי לֹא תוֹסִיפִי יִקְרְאוּ־לָךְ	5bA	for never again you will be called:
{𝔊^{A}} גְּבֶרֶת מַמְלָכוֹת׃	5bB	mistress of kingdoms.

A.ii.3 (Isa. 47:6)

קָצַפְתִּי עַל־עַמִּי	6aA	I have been angry with my people,
חִלַּלְתִּי נַחֲלָתִי	6aB	I have defiled my heritage,
וָאֶתְּנֵם בְּיָדֵךְ	6aC	and I gave them into your hand.
לֹא־שַׂמְתְּ לָהֶם רַחֲמִים	6bA	(But) you showed them no mercy,
עַל־זָקֵן הִכְבַּדְתְּ עֻלֵּךְ מְאֹד׃	6bB	even[5] upon old men you made your yoke very heavy.

A.ii.4 (Isa. 47:7)

וַתֹּאמְרִי לְעוֹלָם אֶהְיֶה גְבָרֶת {𝔊^{A}}	7aA	But you said, "I will be mistress for ever",
עַד לֹא־שַׂמְתְּ אֵלֶּה עַל־לִבֵּךְ	7bA	when you still[6] had not taken these things to heart,
לֹא זָכַרְתְּ אַחֲרִיתָהּ׃	7bB	still did not realize[7] its outcome.

ס <פ> – 1𝔔^{a} – 𝔊^{S} – 𝔖^{a} ___________________________

B.i.1 (Isa. 47:8)

וְעַתָּה שִׁמְעִי־זֹאת עֲדִינָה הַיּוֹשֶׁבֶת לָבֶטַח	8aA	And now, hear this, you who are living in luxury,[8] who are sitting securely,
הָאֹמְרָה בִּלְבָבָהּ	8aB	who say in your heart,
אֲנִי וְאַפְסִי עוֹד	8aC	"I am, and no other than me[9] exists.

---

[4] We assume introduction of direct speech without the verb אמר, as in Isa. 41:27aA; see p. 74, n. 17. ותאמרי forms an antithetical inclusion with this introduction of the LORD's words.

[5] The emphasized position of על־זקן justifies this rendering.

[6] Many modern commentaries and translations connect עד with the following colon. None of the ancient witnesses supports this and the resulting expression is pleonastic after לעולם. The expression עד לא followed by a perfect is also attested in Prov. 8:26. It can only mean "when he still had not done ...", "before he had done ...".

[7] Cf. W. Schottroff, *"Gedenken" im Alten Orient und im Alten Testament*, Neukirchen 1964, 141, 174; *HAHAT*, 301, זכר Qal 8.

[8] Not 'wanton' or 'voluptuous', cf. *HALAT*, 748.

[9] Many scholars, e.g. Koole, 403; Oswalt, 244, n. 18, take the י as a so-called *yod-compaginis*. But in view of the identical form in v. 10bB and in Zeph. 2:15 we regard this as unlikely. We agree with the analysis of Joüon, Muraoka, §160n.

לֹ֤א אֵשֵׁב֙ אַלְמָנָ֔ה	8bA	I shall not sit like a widow,
וְלֹ֥א אֵדַ֖ע שְׁכֽוֹל׃ {$\mathfrak{G}^{S}$}	8bB	and I shall not know[10] bereavement".

B.i.2 (Isa. 47:9)

וְתָבֹאנָה֩ לָּ֨ךְ שְׁתֵּי־אֵ֥לֶּה רֶ֛גַע	9aA	But they will come to you, these two, suddenly,
בְּי֥וֹם אֶחָ֖ד	9aB	in one day:
שְׁכ֣וֹל וְאַלְמֹ֑ן	9aC	bereavement and widowhood;
כְּתֻמָּם֙ בָּ֣אוּ עָלַ֔יִךְ	9bA	in full measure they will come upon you,
בְּרֹ֣ב כְּשָׁפַ֔יִךְ	9bB	despite the multitude of your sorceries
בְּעָצְמַ֥ת חֲבָרַ֖יִךְ מְאֹֽד׃	9bC	and the exceptional power of your spells.

B.i.3 (Isa. 47:10)

וַתִּבְטְחִ֣י בְרָעָתֵ֗ךְ {$\mathfrak{G}^{A}$}	10aA	Yes, you felt secure in your evil,
אָמַ֙רְתְּ֙ אֵ֣ין רֹאָ֔נִי	10aB	you said: "No one sees me!"
חָכְמָתֵ֥ךְ וְדַעְתֵּ֖ךְ הִ֣יא שׁוֹבְבָ֑תֶךְ	10aC	Your wisdom and your knowledge led you astray.
וַתֹּאמְרִ֣י בְלִבֵּ֔ךְ	10bA	And you said in your heart:
אֲנִ֖י וְאַפְסִ֥י עֽוֹד׃	10bB	"I am, and and no other than me exists".

B.i.4 (Isa. 47:11)

וּבָ֨א עָלַ֜יִךְ רָעָ֗ה	11aA	But an evil comes upon you
לֹ֤א תֵֽדְעִי֙ שַׁחְרָ֔הּ	11aB	which you will not be able to charm away.[11]
וְתִפֹּ֤ל עָלַ֙יִךְ֙ הֹוָ֔ה	11aC	And a disaster will fall upon you
לֹ֥א תוּכְלִ֖י כַּפְּרָ֑הּ {<פ>}	11aD	for which you will not be able to atone,
וְתָבֹ֨א עָלַ֧יִךְ פִּתְאֹ֛ם שֹׁאָ֖ה	11bA	and devastation will come upon you suddenly
לֹ֥א תֵדָֽעִי׃	11bB	which you will not (yet) know.

$\mathfrak{G}^{SA}$ ....

B.ii.1 (Isa. 47:12–13a)

עִמְדִי־נָ֤א בַחֲבָרַ֙יִךְ֙	12aA	Stand fast in your spells,
וּבְרֹ֣ב כְּשָׁפַ֔יִךְ	12aB	and in the multitude of your sorceries,
בַּאֲשֶׁ֥ר יָגַ֖עַתְּ מִנְּעוּרָ֑יִךְ	12aC	with which you have wearied yourself from your youth.
אוּלַ֛י תּוּכְלִ֥י הוֹעִ֖יל	12bA	If only[12] you could find profit,
אוּלַ֥י תַּעֲרֽוֹצִי׃	12bB	if only you could inspire terror –
נִלְאֵ֖ית בְּרֹ֣ב עֲצָתָ֑יִךְ {$\mathfrak{G}^{SA}$}	13aC	you tire yourself out with the multitude of your counsel.

---

[10] $1\mathfrak{Q}^{a}$ אראה is inferior, see E.Y. Kutscher, *The Language and Linguistic Background of the Isaiah Scroll*, Leiden 1974, 284. Possibly the scribe wanted to contrast the fate of lady Babylon with that of the Servant, Isa. 53:10.

[11] With Oswalt, 245, n. 26; *HALAT*, 1359-60, and others.

[12] The normal meanings "perhaps" or "if" do not fit here.

B.ii.2 (Isa. 47:13b–c)

יַעַמְדוּ־נָא וְיוֹשִׁיעֻךְ הֹבְרֵי* שָׁמַיִם	13bA	Let them stand fast and save you, those who bow to[13] heaven,
הַחֹזִים בַּכּוֹכָבִים	13bB	who observe the stars,
מוֹדִיעִם לֶחֳדָשִׁים	13cA	who let (you) know month by month
מֵאֲשֶׁר יָבֹאוּ עָלָיִךְ׃ {𝔊^B}	13cB	some of the things that[14] will come to you.

B.ii.3 (Isa. 47:14)

הִנֵּה הָיוּ כְקַשׁ אֵשׁ שְׂרָפָתַם	14aA	Behold, they are like chaff, a fire burns them up.
לֹא־יַצִּילוּ אֶת־נַפְשָׁם מִיַּד לֶהָבָה	14aB	they cannot deliver themselves from the power of the flame.
אֵין־גַּחֶלֶת לַחְמָם	14bA	No coal to warm[15] oneself,
אוּר לָשֶׁבֶת נֶגְדּוֹ׃	14bB	no glow to sit by!

B.ii.4 (Isa. 47:15)

כֵּן הָיוּ־לָךְ {𝔊^A} אֲשֶׁר יָגָעַתְּ	15aA	Such to you are those (for)[16] whom you have wearied yourself,
סֹחֲרַיִךְ מִנְּעוּרַיִךְ	15aB	who have trafficked with you from your youth.
אִישׁ לְעֶבְרוֹ תָּעוּ	15bA	They go astray, each in his own direction,
אֵין מוֹשִׁיעֵךְ׃	15bB	none will be your saviour.

ס <פ> – 1𝔔^a – 𝔊^SBAQ – 𝔖^abe ______________________________

[13]We follow the Qere. 1𝔔^a has חוברי which is apparently an adaptation to vv. 9bC, 12aA. On the basis of Ugaritic *hbr* most modern Hebraists assume the meaning 'to worship' (so e.g. *HAHAT*, 266; *DCH*, 487 as a second option), but the Ugaritic verb means 'to bow down to'. In our opinion the writer wryly notes the absurdity of bowing not to the ground, but to the astral bodies.

[14]The assumption of a dittography is unsatisfactory because the error would have created a more difficult text. The ancient versions are not to be trusted in a case like this. They experienced the same difficulty as modern translators. We take מן in a partitive sense which makes the statement ironic again: the main events elude the astrologers.

[15]Neither emendation nor a rendering 'their bread' is necessary here. Job 30:4 proves that this type of infinitive of חמם was acceptable.

[16]Because it is difficult to see how the ב might have gone lost after באשר in v. 12, we maintain 𝔐 and assume ellipsis of ל after the preceding לך.

8.2 Isaiah 47 – Delimitation of Cola

COLON 47:1aA:

רְדִ֣י ׀ וּשְׁבִ֣י עַל־עָפָ֗ר בְּתוּלַת֙ בַּת־בָּבֶ֔ל 1aA Come down, sit in the dust, O virgin daughter of Babel,

With: $\mathfrak{M}$ (5) – $\mathfrak{G}^{SQ}$, major division markers in $\mathfrak{G}^{Q}$ – $\mathfrak{S}^{abcde}$
Colon parallelism: ירד || ישב; בתולה || בת.
Discussion: It is fairly certain that the Masoretes considered the Revia' with על־עפר as a colon delimiter because the pattern 7 – 5 – 2 is common with tricola. $\mathfrak{M}$ has the support of $\mathfrak{G}^{SQ}$. However, since $\mathfrak{S}$ does not support a division at this point and because neither $\mathfrak{M}$ nor $\mathfrak{G}$ has a divider at the corresponding point in the next colon, we decided to skip it. Cola of five accented units are rare, but not exceptional.[1] For a long colon of comparable structure see below, v. 5aA.

COLON 47:1aB:

שְׁבִי־לָאָ֥רֶץ אֵין־כִּסֵּ֖א בַּת־כַּשְׂדִּ֑ים 1aB sit on the ground, no throne, O daughter of the Chaldeans!

With: $\mathfrak{M}$ (2) – $\mathfrak{G}^{SQ}$ – $\mathfrak{S}^{be}$, $\mathfrak{S}^{acd}$ subordinate punctuation.
Colon parallelism: ארץ || כסא (antithetical).

COLON 47:1bA:

כִּ֣י לֹ֤א תוֹסִ֙יפִי֙ יִקְרְאוּ־לָ֔ךְ 1bA For never again you will be called

With: $\mathfrak{M}$ (5).
Discussion: None of the ancient witnesses supports $\mathfrak{M}$ here. However, the reason for this is obviously that they were led astray by the fact that the sentence runs on. Compare v. 5bA.

COLON 47:1bB:

רַכָּ֖ה וַעֲנֻגָּֽה׃ 1bB tender and delicate.

With: $\mathfrak{M}$ (1) – $\mathfrak{G}^{SQ}$ – $\mathfrak{S}^{abcde}$
Colon parallelism: רך || ענג.

COLON 47:2aA:

קְחִ֥י רֵחַ֖יִם וְטַ֣חֲנִי קָ֑מַח 2aA Take millstones and grind flour,

With: $\mathfrak{M}$ (2) – $\mathfrak{G}^{SQ}$ – $\mathfrak{S}^{abcde}$

[1] See below p. 639.

COLON 47:2bA:

גַּלִּי צַמָּתֵךְ חֶשְׂפִּי־שֹׁבֶל 2bA remove your veil, strip off your dangling jewelry,

With: $\mathfrak{M}$ (12) – $\mathfrak{G}^{SQ}$ – $\mathfrak{S}^{abcde}$
Colon parallelism: גלה || חשף; צמה || שבל (unique).
Discussion: It seems likely that $\mathfrak{M}$ wanted to read on until נהרות, a colon of six stressed feet. The other witnesses do not support this and the colon parallelism argues in their favour.
$\mathfrak{G}^{SQ}$ and $\mathfrak{S}^{e}$ have an extra point after צמתך ($\mathfrak{M}$ conjunctive accent) which would make v. 2b a tricolon. The rhythmical balance, however, would be disturbed.
In $\mathfrak{G}^{A}$ vv. 2bA and 2bBα have been written colometrically:

ἀποκάλυψαι τὸ κατακάλυμμά σου
ἀνακάλυψαι τὰς πολιάς
ἀνάσυραι τὰς κνήμας

This is rather a monk's risqué joke than a colometry resting on authentic tradition.

COLON 47:2bB:

גַּלִּי־שׁוֹק עִבְרִי נְהָרוֹת׃ 2bB uncover your thighs, pass through rivers.

With: $\mathfrak{M}$ (1) – $\mathfrak{G}^{SQ}$ – $\mathfrak{S}^{abcde}$
Discussion: $\mathfrak{G}^{SQ}$ have an additional dividing point after שוק ($\mathfrak{M}$ Ṭiphḥa).

COLON 47:3aA:

תִּגָּל עֶרְוָתֵךְ 3aA Let your nakedness be uncovered,

With: $\mathfrak{M}$ (5) – $\mathfrak{G}^{SQ}$ – $\mathfrak{S}^{e}$

COLON 47:3aB:

גַּם תֵּרָאֶה חֶרְפָּתֵךְ 3aB also your humiliation be seen.

With: $\mathfrak{M}$ (2) – $\mathfrak{G}^{SQ}$ – $\mathfrak{S}^{abcde}$

COLON 47:3bA:

נָקָם אֶקָּח 3bA I will take vengeance,

With: $\mathfrak{M}$ (5) – $\mathfrak{G}^{SAQ}$, major division markers in $\mathfrak{G}^{A}$ – $\mathfrak{S}^{e}$

COLON 47:3bB:

וְלֹא אֶפְגַּע אָדָם׃ 3bB I will spare nobody.

With: 𝔐 (1), major division markers, also in 1Q^{a} – 𝔊^{SQ} – 𝔖^{abcde}, major division markers in 𝔖^{abe}

COLON 47:4aA:

גֹּאֲלֵ֕נוּ יְהוָ֥ה צְבָא֖וֹת שְׁמ֑וֹ 4aA Our Redeemer, LORD of hosts is his name,

With: 𝔐 (2) – 𝔖^{be}
Discussion: The ancient versions hesitate between putting a point here or after צבאות. The latter option was chosen by 𝔊^{Q} and 𝔖^{ac}. It cannot be doubted, however, that שמו must be at the end of the colon.[2] For the Zaqeph Gadol (No. 6) with גאלנו see p. 31.

COLON 47:4aB:

קְד֥וֹשׁ יִשְׂרָאֵֽל׃ 4aB the Holy One of Israel:

With: 𝔐 (1), Setuma in 1Q^{a} – 𝔊^{SAQ}, major division markers in 𝔊^{SA} – 𝔖^{abcde}

COLON 47:5aA:

שְׁבִ֥י דוּמָ֛ם וּבֹ֥אִי בַחֹ֖שֶׁךְ 5aA Sit down in silence and go into darkness,
בַּת־כַּשְׂדִּ֑ים daughter of the Chaldeans,

With: 𝔐 (2) – 𝔊^{SQ} – 𝔖^{ab}, 𝔖^{ce} subordinate punctuation.
Colon parallelism: ישב || בוא; דומם || חשך.
Discussion: 𝔊^{SQ} and 𝔖^{e} have an additional point after דומם where 𝔐 has a Tevir (No.12). For a similar long colon see v. 1aA.

COLON 47:5bA:

כִּ֣י לֹ֤א תוֹסִ֙יפִי֙ יִקְרְאוּ־לָ֔ךְ 5bA for never again you will be called:

With: 𝔐 (5).
Discussion: Again 𝔐 stands alone in dividing after יקראו־לך. No doubt this should be ascribed to the fact that the sentence runs on. Compare v. 1bA.

COLON 47:5bB:

גְּבֶ֖רֶת מַמְלָכֽוֹת׃ 5bB mistress of kingdoms.

With: 𝔐 (1) – 𝔊^{AQ}, major division markers in 𝔊^{A} – 𝔖^{abcde}

---

[2] See Isa. 48:2; 51:15; 54:11.

COLON 47:6aA:

קָצַפְתִּי עַל־עַמִּי 6aA I have been angry with my people,

With: $\mathfrak{M}$ (7) – $\mathfrak{G}^{SQ}$
Discussion: Because the sequence of accents 7–5–2 is fairly common to delimit a tricolon in $\mathfrak{M}$, we decided to follow $\mathfrak{G}$ even though it is not supported by $\mathfrak{S}$.

COLON 47:6aB:

חִלַּלְתִּי נַחֲלָתִי 6aB I have defiled my heritage,

With: $\mathfrak{M}$ (5) – $\mathfrak{G}^{SQ}$ – $\mathfrak{S}^{abcde}$

COLON 47:6aC:

וָאֶתְּנֵם בְּיָדֵךְ 6aC and I gave them into your hand.

With: $\mathfrak{M}$ (2) – $\mathfrak{G}^{SQ}$ – $\mathfrak{S}^{be}$, $\mathfrak{S}^{acd}$ subordinate punctuation.

COLON 47:6bA:

לֹא־שַׂמְתְּ לָהֶם רַחֲמִים 6bA (But) you showed them no mercy,

With: $\mathfrak{M}$ (5) – $\mathfrak{G}^{Q}$ – $\mathfrak{S}^{abcde}$

COLON 47:6bB:

עַל־זָקֵן הִכְבַּדְתְּ עֻלֵּךְ מְאֹד׃ 6bB even upon old men you made your yoke very heavy.

With: $\mathfrak{M}$ (1) – $\mathfrak{G}^{SQ}$ – $\mathfrak{S}^{abcde}$

COLON 47:7aA:

וַתֹּאמְרִי לְעוֹלָם אֶהְיֶה גְבָרֶת 7aA But you said, “I will be mistress for ever”,

With: $\mathfrak{M}$ (2) – $\mathfrak{G}^{SAQ}$, major division markers in $\mathfrak{G}^{A}$ – $\mathfrak{S}^{abcde}$
Discussion: $\mathfrak{M}$'s Zaqeph Qaṭon (No.5) with ותאמרי finds no support in the ancient versions. See p. 31.

COLON 47:7bA:

עַד לֹא־שַׂמְתְּ אֵלֶּה עַל־לִבֵּךְ 7bA when you still had not taken these things to heart,

With: $\mathfrak{M}$ (5) – $\mathfrak{G}^{SQ}$ – $\mathfrak{S}^{e}$

COLON 47:7bB:

לֹא זָכַרְתְּ אַחֲרִיתָהּ׃ 7bB still did not realize its outcome.

With: $\mathfrak{M}$ (1), major division markers, also in $1\mathfrak{Q}^{a}$ – $\mathfrak{G}^{SQ}$, major division markers in $\mathfrak{G}^{S}$ – $\mathfrak{S}^{abcde}$, major division marker in $\mathfrak{S}^{a}$

COLON 47:8aA:

וְעַתָּה שִׁמְעִי־זֹאת עֲדִינָה הַיּוֹשֶׁבֶת לָבֶטַח 8aA And now, hear this, you who are living in luxury, who are sitting securely,

With: $\mathfrak{M}$ (5) – $\mathfrak{G}^{S}$ – $\mathfrak{S}^{abcde}$ all subordinate punctuation.
Colon parallelism: עדין || ישב לבטח (unique).
Discussion: The colometry of $\mathfrak{M}$ is shared by few other witnesses which is no doubt to be explained by the presence of another dividing point after עדינה in $\mathfrak{G}^{SQ}$, with subordinate punctuation in $\mathfrak{S}^{abde}$. $\mathfrak{M}$ did not want to divide here (Pashṭa, No. 10) which we believe to be an acceptable point of view. Should one judge differently, this makes the verse a quadrocolon.

COLON 47:8aB:

הָאֹמְרָה בִּלְבָבָהּ 8aB who say in your heart,

With: $\mathfrak{M}$ (5) – $\mathfrak{G}^{Q}$ – $\mathfrak{S}^{e}$

COLON 47:8aC:

אֲנִי וְאַפְסִי עוֹד 8aC "I am, and no other than me exists.

With: $\mathfrak{M}$ (2) – $\mathfrak{G}^{SQ}$ – $\mathfrak{S}^{abcde}$

COLON 47:8bA:

לֹא אֵשֵׁב אַלְמָנָה 8bA I shall not sit like a widow,

With: $\mathfrak{M}$ (5) – $\mathfrak{G}^{Q}$ – $\mathfrak{S}^{e}$

COLON 47:8bB:

וְלֹא אֵדַע שְׁכוֹל׃ 8bB and I shall not know bereavement".

With: $\mathfrak{M}$ (1) – $\mathfrak{G}^{SQ}$, paragraphos in $\mathfrak{G}^{S}$ – $\mathfrak{S}^{abcde}$

COLON 47:9aA:

וְתָבֹאנָה לָּךְ שְׁתֵּי־אֵלֶּה רֶגַע 9aA But they will come to you, these two, suddenly,

With: $\mathfrak{M}$ (12) – $\mathfrak{G}^{S}$
Discussion: $\mathfrak{M}$ has an extremely long colon here: up to ואלמן (8 stresses), obviously due to the fact that the sentence runs on, as is often the

case. The division of $\mathfrak{G}^{S}$ is corroborated by the verse-line parallelism between רגע and יום in Job 21:13.

COLON 47:9aB:

בְּי֣וֹם אֶחָ֑ד 9aB in one day:

With: $\mathfrak{M}$ (8) – $\mathfrak{G}^{SQ}$ – $\mathfrak{S}^{abcde}$
Discussion: The unanimous testimony of the ancient witnesses contradicts $\mathfrak{M}$'s Ṭiphḥa (No. 8).

COLON 47:9aC:

שְׁכ֣וֹל וְאַלְמֹ֔ן 9aC bereavement and widowhood;

With: $\mathfrak{M}$ (2) – $\mathfrak{G}^{Q}$
Colon parallelism: שכול || אלמון.
Discussion: The support for $\mathfrak{M}$ is weak, but the colon parallelism argues in its favour.

COLON 47:9bA:

כְּתֻמָּם֙ בָּ֣אוּ עָלַ֔יִךְ 9bA in full measure they will come upon you,

With: $\mathfrak{M}$ (5) – $\mathfrak{G}^{S}$ – $\mathfrak{S}^{abcde}$

COLON 47:9bB:

בְּרֹ֣ב כְּשָׁפַ֔יִךְ 9bB despite the multitude of your sorceries

With: $\mathfrak{M}$ (5) – $\mathfrak{G}^{S}$

COLON 47:9bC:

בְּעָצְמַ֥ת חֲבָרַ֖יִךְ מְאֹֽד׃ 9bC and the exceptional power of your spells.

With: $\mathfrak{M}$ (1) – $\mathfrak{G}^{S}$ – $\mathfrak{S}^{abcde}$

COLON 47:10aA:

וַתִּבְטְחִ֤י בְרָעָתֵךְ֙ 10aA Yes, you felt secure in your evil,

With: $\mathfrak{M}$ (7) – $\mathfrak{G}^{SAQ}$, major division markers in $\mathfrak{G}^{A}$ – $\mathfrak{S}^{c}$

COLON 47:10aB:

אָמַ֕רְתְּ אֵ֣ין רֹאָ֑נִי 10aB you said: "No one sees me!"

With: $\mathfrak{M}$ (5) – $\mathfrak{G}^{SQ}$ – $\mathfrak{S}^{abce}$
Discussion: $\mathfrak{G}^{SQ}$ have an extra point after אמרת, as usual after the introduction of direct oration ($\mathfrak{M}$ Pashṭa, No. 10).

COLON 47:10aC:

חָכְמָתֵךְ וְדַעְתֵּךְ הִיא שׁוֹבְבָתֶךְ 10aC Your wisdom and your knowledge led you astray.

With: 𝔐 (2) – 𝔊^{SQ} – 𝔖^{abce}
Colon parallelism: חכמה || דעת.

COLON 47:10bA:

וַתֹּאמְרִי בְלִבֵּךְ 10bA And you said in your heart:

With: 𝔐 (5) – 𝔊^{SQ} – 𝔖^{b}

COLON 47:10bB:

אֲנִי וְאַפְסִי עוֹד׃ 10bB "I am, and and no other than me exists".

With: 𝔐 (1) – 𝔊^{SQ} – 𝔖^{abcde}
Discussion: 𝔊^{Q} and 𝔖^{e} mark the natural pause after אני (the Masoretes opted for Ṭiphḥa, No. 8).

COLON 47:11aA:

וּבָא עָלַיִךְ רָעָה 11aA But an evil comes upon you

With: 𝔐 (7) – 𝔊^{SQ} – 𝔖^{e}

COLON 47:11aB:

לֹא תֵדְעִי שַׁחְרָהּ 11aB which you will not be able to charm away.

With: 𝔐 (5) – 𝔖^{abcde}
Discussion: Both 𝔊 and 𝔖 give a paraphrasis because they did not understand שׁחרה anymore. 𝔖 may be interpreted as supporting 𝔐.

COLON 47:11aC:

וְתִפֹּל עָלַיִךְ הֹוָה 11aC And a disaster will fall upon you

With: 𝔐 (5) – 𝔊^{SQ}

COLON 47:11aD:

לֹא תוּכְלִי כַּפְּרָהּ 11aD for which you will not be able to atone,

With: 𝔐 (2), Petuḥa in 1𝔔^{b} – 𝔊^{SQ} – 𝔖^{bcde}

COLON 47:11bA:

וְתָבֹא עָלַיִךְ פִּתְאֹם שֹׁאָה 11bA and devastation will come upon you suddenly

With: $\mathfrak{M}$ (8) – $\mathfrak{G}^{SQ}$ – $\mathfrak{S}^{e}$
Discussion: Probably the Masoretes wanted to read on to the end of the verse, thus creating a colon of six stressed units. In our opinion it is more likely that we have a bicolon here with 4 + 2 stresses, a fairly common phenomenon.[3]

COLON 47:11bB:

לֹא תֵדְעִי׃ 11bB which you will not (yet) know.

With: $\mathfrak{M}$ (1) – $\mathfrak{G}^{SAQ}$, major division markers in $\mathfrak{G}^{SA}$ – $\mathfrak{S}^{abcde}$

COLON 47:12aA:

עִמְדִי־נָא בַחֲבָרַיִךְ 12aA Stand fast in your spells,

With: $\mathfrak{M}$ (10) – $\mathfrak{G}^{SQ}$
Discussion: $\mathfrak{M}$ reads on until כשפיך. Despite the fact that it is supported by $\mathfrak{S}$ we assume that a tricolon is meant because of the close corresponcence with v. 9b which also $\mathfrak{M}$ interpreted as a tricolon. The rhyme between the three cola supports this decision.

COLON 47:12aB:

וּבְרֹב כְּשָׁפַיִךְ 12aB and in the multitude of your sorceries,

With: $\mathfrak{M}$ (5) – $\mathfrak{G}^{SQ}$ – $\mathfrak{S}^{abcde}$ all subordinate punctuation.

COLON 47:12aC:

בַּאֲשֶׁר יָגַעַתְּ מִנְּעוּרָיִךְ 12aC with which you have wearied yourself from your youth.

With: $\mathfrak{M}$ (2) – $\mathfrak{G}^{SQ}$ – $\mathfrak{S}^{abcde}$

COLON 47:12bA:

אוּלַי תּוּכְלִי הוֹעִיל 12bA If only you could find profit,

With: $\mathfrak{M}$ (8) – $\mathfrak{G}^{SQ}$ – $\mathfrak{S}^{abcde}$
Discussion: $\mathfrak{M}$ wanted to read on to the end of the verse.

COLON 47:12bB:

אוּלַי תַּעֲרוֹצִי׃ 12bB if only you could inspire terror –

With: $\mathfrak{M}$ (1) – $\mathfrak{S}^{abcde}$
Discussion: $\mathfrak{G}$ is lacking.

---

[3] In Second Isaiah for example 40:2c; 41:2a, 9a, 13a; 42:16b, 25a; 43:4a, etc., see also 47:9aA-B, 13bA-B, etc. Cf. J.C. de Moor, "The Art of Versification in Ugarit and Israel", in: *Studies in Bible and the Ancient Near East Presented to Samuel E. Loewenstamm*, Jerusalem 1978, 119-139 (138-9).

COLON 47:13aA:

נִלְאֵית בְּרֹב עֲצָתָיִךְ 13aC you tire yourself out with the multitude of your counsel.

With: $\mathfrak{M}$ (2) – $\mathfrak{G}^{SAQ}$, major division markers in $\mathfrak{G}^{SQ}$ – $\mathfrak{S}^{abcde}$

COLON 47:13bA:

יַעַמְדוּ־נָא וְיוֹשִׁיעֻךְ הֹבְרֵי* שָׁמַיִם 13bA Let them stand fast and save you, those who bow to heaven,

With: $\mathfrak{M}$ (7) – $\mathfrak{G}^{SQ}$ – $\mathfrak{S}^{abcde}$ all subordinate punctuation.
Colon parallelism: עמד || ישע.

COLON 47:13bB:

הַחֹזִים בַּכּוֹכָבִים 13bB who observe the stars,

With: $\mathfrak{M}$ (5) – $\mathfrak{G}^{S}$ – $\mathfrak{S}^{abcde}$ subordinate punctuation.

COLON 47:13cA:

מוֹדִיעִם לֶחֳדָשִׁים 13cA who let (you) know month by month

With: $\mathfrak{M}$ (5) – $\mathfrak{S}^{e}$
Discussion: $\mathfrak{G}$ is lacking.

COLON 47:13cB:

מֵאֲשֶׁר יָבֹאוּ עָלָיִךְ׃ 13cB some of the things that will come to you.

With: $\mathfrak{M}$ (1) – $\mathfrak{G}^{SQ}$, paragraphos in $\mathfrak{G}^{B}$ – $\mathfrak{S}^{abcde}$

COLON 47:14aA:

הִנֵּה הָיוּ כְקַשׁ אֵשׁ שְׂרָפָתַם 14aA Behold, they are like chaff, a fire burns them up.

With: $\mathfrak{M}$ (5) – $\mathfrak{G}^{SQ}$ – $\mathfrak{S}^{abcde}$

COLON 47:14aB:

לֹא־יַצִּילוּ אֶת־נַפְשָׁם מִיַּד לֶהָבָה 14aB they cannot deliver themselves from the power of the flame.

With: $\mathfrak{M}$ (2) – $\mathfrak{G}^{SQ}$ – $\mathfrak{S}^{bcde}$

COLON 47:14bA:

אֵין־גַּחֶלֶת לַחְמָם 14bA No coal to warm oneself,

With: $\mathfrak{M}$ (5) – $\mathfrak{S}^{abcde}$
Discussion: $\mathfrak{G}$ is lacking.

COLON 47:14bB:

אֽוֹר לָשֶׁ֥בֶת נֶגְדּֽוֹ׃ 14bB no glow to sit by!

With: 𝔐 (1) – 𝔊^{SQ} – 𝔖^{abcde}

COLON 47:15aA:

כֵּ֤ן הָֽיוּ־לָ֖ךְ אֲשֶׁ֣ר יָגָ֑עַתְּ 15aA Such to you are those (for) whom you have wearied yourself,

With: 𝔐 (2).
Discussion: 𝔊^{SQ} have a point after היו־לך, and 𝔊^{A} even two major division markers. The point in the other two manuscripts corresponds to 𝔐's Ṭiphḥa and was not intended as a principal divider. 𝔖 has no interpunction after היו־לך.
Because 𝔊 and 𝔖 give different paraphrases of the verse this is one of the rare cases where neither of them supports 𝔐.

COLON 47:15aB:

סֹחֲרַ֖יִךְ מִנְּעוּרַ֑יִךְ 15aB who have trafficked with you from your youth.

With: 𝔐 (7) – 𝔊^{S} – 𝔖^{abcde}

COLON 47:15bA:

אִ֤ישׁ לְעֶבְרוֹ֙ תָּע֔וּ 15bA They go astray, each in his own direction,

With: 𝔐 (5) – 𝔊^{SQ} – 𝔖^{ce} subordinate punctuation.

COLON 47:15bB:

אֵ֥ין מוֹשִׁיעֵֽךְ׃ 15bB none will be your saviour.

With: 𝔐 (1), major division markers, also in 1𝔔^{a} – 𝔊^{SBAQ}, all with major division markers – 𝔖^{abcde}, major division markers in 𝔖^{abe}

8.3 Isaiah 47 – Delimitation of Verse-lines

VERSE–LINE: 47:1a:

רְדִ֣י ׀ וּשְׁבִ֣י עַל־עָפָ֗ר בְּתוּלַת֙ בַּת־בָּבֶ֔ל 1aA Come down, sit in the dust, O virgin daughter of Babel,
שְׁבִי־לָאָ֥רֶץ אֵין־כִּסֵּ֖א בַּת־כַּשְׂדִּ֑ים 1aB sit on the ground, no throne, O daughter of the Chaldeans!

𝔐 distinctive accents: 5 – 2.
Stresses: 5 + 3.
Verse-line parallelism: ישב || ישב; על || ל; עפר || ארץ; בת || בת; בבל || כשדים; grammatical parallelism.

VERSE–LINE: 47:1b:

כִּי לֹא תוֹסִיפִי יִקְרְאוּ־לָךְ 1bA For never again you will be called
רַכָּה וַעֲנֻגָּה׃ 1bB tender and delicate.

𝔐 distinctive accents: 5 – 1.
Stresses: 4 + 2.
Verse-line parallelism: None.
Discussion: No parallelism because the sentence is running on (enjambment).

VERSE–LINE: 47:2a:

קְחִי רֵחַיִם וְטַחֲנִי קָמַח 2aA Take millstones and grind flour,

𝔐 distinctive accents: 2.
Stresses: 4.
Verse-line parallelism: None (unicolon).

VERSE–LINE: 47:2b:

גַּלִּי צַמָּתֵךְ חֶשְׂפִּי־שֹׁבֶל 2bA remove your veil, strip off your dangling jewelry,
גַּלִּי־שׁוֹק עִבְרִי נְהָרוֹת׃ 2bB uncover your thighs, pass through rivers.

𝔐 distinctive accents: 12 – 1.
Stresses: 3 + 3.
Verse-line parallelism: גלה || גלה; חשף || גלה; grammatical parallelism; rhyme.

VERSE–LINE: 47:3a:

תִּגָּל עֶרְוָתֵךְ 3aA Let your nakedness be uncovered,
גַּם תֵּרָאֶה חֶרְפָּתֵךְ 3aB also your humiliation be seen.

𝔐 distinctive accents: 5 – 2.
Stresses: 2 + 3.
Verse-line parallelism: גלה || ראה Niphal; ערוה || חרפה; ־ך (f.s.) || ־ך (f.s.); grammatical parallelism; rhyme.

VERSE–LINE: 47:3b:

נָקָם אֶקָּח 3bA I will take vengeance,
וְלֹא אֶפְגַּע אָדָם׃ 3bB I will spare nobody.

𝔐 distinctive accents: 5 – 1.
Stresses: 2 + 3.
Verse-line parallelism: grammatical parallelism; rhyme.

VERSE–LINE: 47:4a:

גֹּאֲלֵנוּ יְהוָה צְבָאוֹת שְׁמוֹ 4aA Our Redeemer, the LORD of hosts is his name,
קְדוֹשׁ יִשְׂרָאֵל׃ 4aB the Holy One of Israel:

𝔐 distinctive accents: 2 – 1.
Stresses: 4 + 2.
Verse-line parallelism: גאל || קדוש ישראל; יהוה צבאות || קדוש ישראל.

VERSE–LINE: 47:5a:

שְׁבִי דוּמָם וּבֹאִי בַחֹשֶׁךְ בַּת־כַּשְׂדִּים 5aA Sit down in silence and go into darkness, daughter of the Chaldeans,

𝔐 distinctive accents: 2.
Stresses: 5.
Verse-line parallelism: None (unicolon).

VERSE–LINE: 47:5b:

כִּי לֹא תוֹסִיפִי יִקְרְאוּ־לָךְ 5bA for never again you will be called:
גְּבֶרֶת מַמְלָכוֹת׃ 5bB mistress of kingdoms.

𝔐 distinctive accents: 5 – 1.
Stresses: 4 + 2.
Verse-line parallelism: None.
No parallelism because the sentence is running on.

VERSE–LINE: 47:6a:

קָצַפְתִּי עַל־עַמִּי 6aA I have been angry with my people,
חִלַּלְתִּי נַחֲלָתִי 6aB I have defiled my heritage,
וָאֶתְּנֵם בְּיָדֵךְ 6aC and I gave them into your hand.

𝔐 distinctive accents: 7 – 5 – 2.
Stresses: 2 + 2 + 2.
Verse-line parallelism: קצף || חלל; עם || נחלה; ־י || ־י; grammatical parallelism; rhyme.

VERSE–LINE: 47:6b:

לֹא־שַׂמְתְּ לָהֶם רַחֲמִים 6bA (But) you showed them no mercy,
עַל־זָקֵן הִכְבַּדְתְּ עֻלֵּךְ מְאֹד׃ 6bB even upon old men you made your yoke very heavy.

𝔐 distinctive accents: 5 – 1.
Stresses: 3 + 4.
Verse-line parallelism: None, although v. 6bB gives an illustration of what is said in v. 6bA.

VERSE–LINE: 47:7a:

וַתֹּ֣אמְרִ֔י לְעוֹלָ֖ם אֶהְיֶ֣ה גְבָ֑רֶת	7aA	But you said, "I will be mistress for ever",

𝔐 distinctive accents: 2.
Stresses: 4.
Verse-line parallelism: None (unicolon).

VERSE–LINE: 47:7b:

עַ֚ד לֹא־שַׂ֣מְתְּ אֵ֙לֶּה֙ עַל־לִבֵּ֔ךְ	7bA	when you still had not taken these things to heart,
לֹ֥א זָכַ֖רְתְּ אַחֲרִיתָֽהּ׃	7bB	still did not realize its outcome.

𝔐 distinctive accents: 5 – 1.
Stresses: 4 + 3.
Verse-line parallelism: לא || לא; שים על־לב || זכר; grammatical parallelism.
Discussion: Ellipsis of עד in v. 7bB connects the verse-lines.

VERSE–LINE: 47:8a:

וְעַתָּ֞ה שִׁמְעִי־זֹ֤את עֲדִינָה֙ הַיּוֹשֶׁ֣בֶת לָבֶ֔טַח	8aA	And now, hear this, you who are living in luxury, who are sitting securely,
הָאֹֽמְרָה֙ בִּלְבָבָ֔הּ	8aB	who say in your heart,
אֲנִ֖י וְאַפְסִ֣י ע֑וֹד	8aC	"I am, and no other than me exists.

𝔐 distinctive accents: 5 – 5 – 2.
Stresses: 5 + 2 + 3.
Verse-line parallelism: None. Discussion: No parallelism, but ellipsis in v. 8aB and direct speech in v. 8aC connects the verse-lines.

VERSE–LINE: 47:8b:

לֹ֤א אֵשֵׁב֙ אַלְמָנָ֔ה	8bA	I shall not sit like a widow,
וְלֹ֥א אֵדַ֖ע שְׁכֽוֹל׃	8bB	and I shall not know bereavement".

𝔐 distinctive accents: 5 – 1.
Stresses: 3 + 3.
Verse-line parallelism: לא || לא; אלמנה || שכול; grammatical parallelism.

VERSE–LINE: 47:9a:

וְתָבֹאנָה֩ לָּ֨ךְ שְׁתֵּי־אֵ֥לֶּה רֶ֛גַע	9aA	But they will come to you, these two, suddenly,
בְּי֥וֹם אֶחָ֖ד	9aB	in one day:
שְׁכ֣וֹל וְאַלְמֹ֑ן	9aC	bereavement and widowhood;

𝔐 distinctive accents: 12 – 8 – 2.

Stresses: 4 + 2 + 2.
Verse-line parallelism: רגע || יום.

VERSE–LINE: 47:9b:

כְּתֻמָּם בָּאוּ עָלַיִךְ	9bA	in full measure they will come upon you,
בְּרֹב כְּשָׁפַיִךְ	9bB	despite the multitude of your sorceries
בְּעָצְמַת חֲבָרַיִךְ מְאֹד׃	9bC	and the exceptional power of your spells.

𝔐 distinctive accents: 5 – 5 – 1.
Stresses: 3 + 2 + 3.
Verse-line parallelism: ךְ- (f.s.) || ךְ- (f.s.) || ךְ- (f.s.); תם || רב || מאד (unique); כשפים || חבר (cf. v. 12).
Discussion: For the sequence of accents (5 – 5 – 1) cf. pp. 43, 641.

VERSE–LINE: 47:10a:

וַתִּבְטְחִי בְרָעָתֵךְ	10aA	Yes, you felt secure in your evil,
אָמַרְתְּ אֵין רֹאָנִי	10aB	you said: "No one sees me!"
חָכְמָתֵךְ וְדַעְתֵּךְ הִיא שׁוֹבְבָתֶךְ	10aC	Your wisdom and your knowledge led you astray.

𝔐 distinctive accents: 7 – 5 – 2.
Stresses: 2 + 3 + 4.
Verse-line parallelism: ךְ- (f.s.) || ךְ- (f.s.) || ךְ- (f.s.); בטח || שׁוב Polel (unique).

VERSE–LINE: 47:10b:

וַתֹּאמְרִי בְלִבֵּךְ	10bA	And you said in your heart:
אֲנִי וְאַפְסִי עוֹד׃	10bB	"I am, and and no other than me exists".

𝔐 distinctive accents: 5 – 1.
Stresses: 2 + 3.
Verse-line parallelism: None.
Discussion: With the Masoretes. Because the sentence runs on, there is no parallelism.

VERSE–LINE: 47:11a:

וּבָא עָלַיִךְ רָעָה	11aA	But an evil comes upon you
לֹא תֵדְעִי שַׁחְרָהּ	11aB	which you will not be able to charm away.
וְתִפֹּל עָלַיִךְ הֹוָה	11aC	And a disaster will fall upon you
לֹא תוּכְלִי כַּפְּרָהּ	11aD	for which you will not be able to atone,

𝔐 distinctive accents: 7 – 5 – 5 – 2.
Stresses: 3 + 3 + 3 + 3.

Verse-line parallelism: בוא || נפל; על || על; ־ך (f.s.) || ־ך (f.s.); רעה || הוה; לא || לא; ידע || יכל; grammatical parallelism; rhyme.
Discussion: With the Masoretes, who took the four cola as one verse-line. The sequence of accents (7 – 5 – 5 – 2) is not uncommon in quadrocola.[1] The rhythmical balance of the cola (3 + 3 + 3 + 3) and the rhyme are in favour of the Masoretes' view and render two bicola less likely.

VERSE–LINE: 47:11b:

וְתָבֹא עָלַיִךְ פִּתְאֹם שֹׁאָה	11bA	and devastation will come upon you suddenly
לֹא תֵדָעִי׃	11bB	which you will not (yet) know.

𝔐 distinctive accents: 8 – 1.
Stresses: 4 + 2.
Verse-line parallelism: None.
Discussion: Because the sentence is continuing there is no verse-line parallelism.

VERSE–LINE: 47:12a:

עִמְדִי־נָא בַחֲבָרַיִךְ	12aA	Stand fast in your spells,
וּבְרֹב כְּשָׁפַיִךְ	12aB	and in the multitude of your sorceries,
בַּאֲשֶׁר יָגַעַתְּ מִנְּעוּרָיִךְ	12aC	with which you have wearied yourself from your youth.

𝔐 distinctive accents: 10 – 5 – 2.
Stresses: 2 + 2 + 3.
Verse-line parallelism: ב || ב; ־ך (f.s.) || ־ך (f.s.) || ־ך (f.s.); חבר || כשפים.
Discussion: The cola are connected by ellipsis.

VERSE–LINE: 47:12b–13a:

אוּלַי תּוּכְלִי הוֹעִיל	12bA	If only you could find profit,
אוּלַי תַּעֲרוֹצִי׃	12bB	if only you could inspire terror –
נִלְאֵית בְּרֹב עֲצָתָיִךְ	13aC	you tire yourself out with the multitude of your counsel.

𝔐 distinctive accents: 8 – 1 – 2 (wrong division).
Stresses: 3 + 2 + 3.
Verse-line parallelism: אולי || אולי (unique); יכל || לאה; grammatical parallelism; rhyme.
Discussion: In our opinion 𝔐's division is wrong at this point. The phrase ברב כשפיך (12aB) renders it attractive to balance it with ברב

[1] See our comments on p. 240, 641.

עצתיך in strophe parallelism.[2] The attested parallelism between יכל and לאה may be interpreted as verse-line parallelism. Finally, 𝔊^SA have major division markers after v. 13aC which suggests that they ended the strophe there (the same two manuscripts have dividers after v. 11).

The reason why the Masoretes chose to take v. 13aC with v. 13b may be that they knew this to be the form in which the verse was cited in Num. R. XX.7. The parallelism between the roots חזה and ידע in Num. 24:16 (Balaam) which corresponds to the pair חזים || מודעים in Isa. 47:13 may have suggested the application of the latter to Balaam.

VERSE–LINE: 47:13b:

יַעַמְדוּ־נָא וְיוֹשִׁיעֻךְ הֹבְרֵי* שָׁמַיִם	13bA	Let them stand fast and save you, those who bow to heaven,
הַחֹזִים בַּכּוֹכָבִים	13bB	who observe the stars,

𝔐 distinctive accents: 7 – 5.
Stresses: 4 + 2.
Verse-line parallelism: הבר || חזה (unique); כוכבים || שמים; grammatical parallelism.
Discussion: Ellipsis joins the cola.

VERSE–LINE: 47:13c:

מוֹדִיעִם לֶחֳדָשִׁים	13cA	who let (you) know month by month
מֵאֲשֶׁר יָבֹאוּ עָלָיִךְ:	13cB	some of the things that will come to you.

𝔐 distinctive accents: 5 – 1.
Stresses: 2 + 3.
None.
Discussion: No parallelism because the sentence is running on.

VERSE–LINE: 47:14a:

הִנֵּה הָיוּ כְקַשׁ אֵשׁ שְׂרָפָתַם	14aA	Behold, they are like chaff, a fire burns them up.
לֹא־יַצִּילוּ אֶת־נַפְשָׁם מִיַּד לֶהָבָה	14aB	they cannot deliver themselves from the power of the flame.

𝔐 distinctive accents: 5 – 2.
Stresses: 5 + 4.
Verse-line parallelism: אש || להבה; ־ם || ־ם.

[2]See further p. 358.

VERSE–LINE: 47:14b:

אֵין־גַּחֶלֶת לַחְמָם	14bA	No coal to warm oneself,
אוּר לָשֶׁבֶת נֶגְדּוֹ׃	14bB	no glow to sit by!

𝔐 distinctive accents: 5 – 1.
Stresses: 2 + 3.
Verse-line parallelism: גחלת ‖ אור (unique).
Discussion: The cola are connected by ellipsis.

VERSE–LINE: 47:15a:

כֵּן הָיוּ־לָךְ אֲשֶׁר יָגָעַתְּ	15aA	Such to you are those (for) whom you have wearied yourself,
סֹחֲרַיִךְ מִנְּעוּרַיִךְ	15aB	who have trafficked with you from your youth.

𝔐 distinctive accents: 2 – 7.
Stresses: 3 + 2.
Verse-line parallelism: ךְ־ (f.s.) ‖ ךְ־ (f.s.); יגע ‖ סחר.
Discussion: The Masoretes wanted to read v. 15 as a unicolon followed by a tricolon. In our opinion היו requires an immediately following subject. Moreover, the nouns יגיע and סחר occur in verse-line paralelism in Isa. 45:14. So we decided to opt for two bicola.

VERSE–LINE: 47:15b:

אִישׁ לְעֶבְרוֹ תָּעוּ	15bA	They go astray, each in his own direction,
אֵין מוֹשִׁיעֵךְ׃	15bB	none will be your saviour.

𝔐 distinctive accents: 5 – 1.
Stresses: 3 + 2.
Verse-line parallelism: None.

8.4 Isaiah 47 – Delimitation of Strophes

STROPHE A.i.1 (Isa. 47:1)

רְדִי ׀ וּשְׁבִי עַל־עָפָר בְּתוּלַת בַּת־בָּבֶל	1aA	Come down, sit in the dust, O virgin daughter of Babel,
שְׁבִי־לָאָרֶץ אֵין־כִּסֵּא בַּת־כַּשְׂדִּים	1aB	sit on the ground, no throne, O daughter of the Chaldeans!
כִּי לֹא תוֹסִיפִי יִקְרְאוּ־לָךְ	1bA	For never again you will be called
רַכָּה וַעֲנֻגָּה׃	1bB	tender and delicate.

= Masoretic verse.
Separation ↑: major division markers in the textual tradition; imperative(s); vocatives; repetitive verse-line parallelism.

Separation ↓: deictic particle(s).
Strophe parallelism: None.
Discussion: For the rather long first colon see p. 337. Despite the lack of strophe parallelism the delimitation is not in doubt because royalty was renowned for its delicate built, not being subjected to manual labour.[1] Compare the next strophe by way of contrast.

STROPHE A.i.2 (Isa. 47:2)

קְחִ֥י רֵחַ֖יִם וְטַ֣חֲנִי קָ֑מַח	2aA	Take millstones and grind flour,
גַּלִּ֨י צַמָּתֵ֜ךְ חֶשְׂפִּי־שֹׁ֧בֶל	2bA	remove your veil, strip off your dangling jewelry,
גַּלִּי־שׁ֖וֹק עִבְרִ֥י נְהָרֽוֹת׃	2bB	uncover your thighs, pass through rivers.

= Masoretic verse.
Separation ↑: imperative(s).
Separation ↓: imperative(s).
Strophe parallelism: grammatical parallelism. Discussion: This strophe is a good example of the importance of grammatical parallelism. There is no clear-cut semantic parallelism between the two verse-lines, but the six imperatives f.s. compensate for this lack.

STROPHE A.i.3 (Isa. 47:3a)

תִּגָּל֙ עֶרְוָתֵ֔ךְ	3aA	Let your nakedness be uncovered,
גַּ֥ם תֵּרָאֶ֖ה חֶרְפָּתֵ֑ךְ	3aB	also your humiliation be seen.

≠ Masoretic verse.
Separation ↑: deictic particle(s); jussive(s); repetitive verse-line parallelism.
Separation ↓: None (one verse-line).
Strophe parallelism: None (one verse-line).
Discussion: See below on v. 3b.

STROPHE A.i.4 (Isa. 47:3b)

נָקָ֣ם אֶקָּ֔ח	3bA	I will take vengeance,
וְלֹ֥א אֶפְגַּ֖ע אָדָֽם׃	3bB	I will spare nobody.

≠ Masoretic verse.
Separation ↑: swapping (object).
Separation ↓: major division markers in the textual tradition.
Strophe parallelism: None (one verse-line).
Discussion: 𝔐 took vv. 3a and 3b together as one strophe. Important

[1]See v. 5bB! Cf. R. Castellino, *Two Šulgi Hymns*, Roma 1972, 48-9, line 168.

as this testimony is, we believe that there are good reasons to adopt a different division here. The total lack of parallelism between vv. 3a and 3b, though in itself not conclusive, renders a separation of the two verse-lines a serious alternative. The change of subject is noticeable. The different object which breaks away from the metaphorical language of the three preceding strophes would seem to clinch the matter in favour of two strophes. As we have seen many times by now, strophes of only one verse-line are by no means a rarity. See also the next strophe.

STROPHE A.ii.1 (Isa. 47:4)

גֹּאֲלֵנוּ יְהוָה צְבָאוֹת שְׁמוֹ	4aA	Our Redeemer, LORD of hosts is his name,
קְדוֹשׁ יִשְׂרָאֵל׃	4aB	the Holy One of Israel:

= Masoretic verse.
Separation ↑: major division markers in the textual tradition.
Separation ↓: major division markers in the textual tradition.
Strophe parallelism: None (one verse-line).
Discussion: This strophe of only one verse-line is delimited by major division markers in the tradition. $1\mathfrak{Q}^{a}$ has both of them.

STROPHE A.ii.2 (Isa. 47:5)

שְׁבִי דוּמָם וּבֹאִי בַחֹשֶׁךְ בַּת־כַּשְׂדִּים	5aA	Sit down in silence and go into darkness, daughter of the Chaldeans,
כִּי לֹא תוֹסִיפִי יִקְרְאוּ־לָךְ	5bA	for never again you will be called:
גְּבֶרֶת מַמְלָכוֹת׃	5bB	mistress of kingdoms.

= Masoretic verse.
Separation ↑: major division markers in the textual tradition; imperative(s); vocative.
Separation ↓: major division markers in the textual tradition; deictic particle(s).
Strophe parallelism: כשדים || ממלכות.

STROPHE A.ii.3 (Isa. 47:6)

קָצַפְתִּי עַל־עַמִּי	6aA	I have been angry with my people,
חִלַּלְתִּי נַחֲלָתִי	6aB	I have defiled my heritage,
וָאֶתְּנֵם בְּיָדֵךְ	6aC	and I gave them into your hand.
לֹא־שַׂמְתְּ לָהֶם רַחֲמִים	6bA	(But) you showed them no mercy,
עַל־זָקֵן הִכְבַּדְתְּ עֻלֵּךְ מְאֹד׃	6bB	even upon old men you made your yoke very heavy.

= Masoretic verse.

Separation ↑: major division markers in the textual tradition; repetitive verse-line parallelism.
Separation ↓: swapping (adjunct).
Strophe parallelism: קצף || רחמים (antithetical); עם || זקן.

STROPHE A.ii.4 (Isa. 47:7)

וַתֹּאמְרִ֔י לְעוֹלָ֖ם אֶהְיֶ֣ה גְבָ֑רֶת	7aA	But you said, "I will be mistress for ever",
עַ֠ד לֹא־שַׂ֤מְתְּ אֵ֙לֶּה֙ עַל־לִבֵּ֔ךְ	7bA	when you still had not taken these things to heart,
לֹ֥א זָכַ֖רְתְּ אַחֲרִיתָֽהּ׃	7bB	still did not realize its outcome.

= Masoretic verse.
Separation ↑: marker of direct speech; swapping (adjunct).
Separation ↓: major division markers in the textual tradition; demonstrative pronoun.
Strophe parallelism: None.
Discussion: The sentence continues in the second verse-line.

STROPHE B.i.1 (Isa. 47:8)

וְעַתָּ֞ה שִׁמְעִי־זֹ֤את עֲדִינָה֙ הַיּוֹשֶׁ֣בֶת לָבֶ֔טַח	8aA	And now, hear this, you who are living in luxury, who are sitting securely,
הָאֹֽמְרָה֙ בִּלְבָבָ֔הּ	8aB	who say in your heart,
אֲנִ֖י וְאַפְסִ֣י ע֑וֹד	8aC	"I am, and no other than me exists.
לֹ֤א אֵשֵׁב֙ אַלְמָנָ֔ה	8bA	I shall not sit like a widow,
וְלֹ֥א אֵדַ֖ע שְׁכֽוֹל׃	8bB	and I shall not know bereavement".

= Masoretic verse.
Separation ↑: major division markers in the textual tradition; deictic particle(s); demonstrative pronoun; independent pers. pronoun; imperative(s); vocative; marker of direct speech.
Separation ↓: major division markers in the textual tradition; repetitive verse-line parallelism.
Strophe parallelism: ישב || ישב.

STROPHE B.i.2 (Isa. 47:9)

וְתָבֹאנָה֩ לָּ֨ךְ שְׁתֵּי־אֵ֥לֶּה רֶ֛גַע	9aA	But they will come to you, these two, suddenly,
בְּי֥וֹם אֶחָ֖ד	9aB	in one day:
שְׁכ֣וֹל וְאַלְמֹ֑ן	9aC	bereavement and widowhood;
כְּתֻמָּם֙ בָּ֣אוּ עָלַ֔יִךְ	9bA	in full measure they will come upon you,
בְּרֹ֣ב כְּשָׁפַ֔יִךְ	9b	despite the multitude of your sorceries
בְּעָצְמַ֥ת חֲבָרַ֖יִךְ מְאֹֽד׃	9bC	and the exceptional power of your spells.

= Masoretic verse.
Separation ↑: demonstrative pronoun; swapping (adjunct).
Separation ↓: repetitive verse-line parallelism; swapping (adjunct).
Strophe parallelism: בוא || בוא; ךְ־ (f.s.) || ךְ־ (f.s.).

STROPHE B.i.3 (Isa. 47:10)

וַתִּבְטְחִי בְרָעָתֵךְ	10aA	Yes, you felt secure in your evil,
אָמַרְתְּ אֵין רֹאָנִי	10aB	you said: "No one sees me!"
חָכְמָתֵךְ וְדַעְתֵּךְ הִיא שׁוֹבְבָתֶךְ	10aC	Your wisdom and your knowledge led you astray.
וַתֹּאמְרִי בְלִבֵּךְ	10bA	And you said in your heart:
אֲנִי וְאַפְסִי עוֹד׃	10bB	"I am, and and no other than me exists".

= Masoretic verse.
Separation ↑: independent pers. pronoun; marker of direct speech; repetitive verse-line parallelism.
Separation ↓: independent pers. pronoun; marker of direct speech.
Strophe parallelism: ב || ב; ךְ־ (f.s.) || ךְ־ (f.s.); grammatical parallelism.

STROPHE B.i.4 (Isa. 47:11)

וּבָא עָלַיִךְ רָעָה	11aA	But an evil comes upon you
לֹא תֵדְעִי שַׁחְרָהּ	11aB	which you will not be able to charm away.
וְתִפֹּל עָלַיִךְ הֹוָה	11aC	And a disaster will fall upon you
לֹא תוּכְלִי כַּפְּרָהּ	11aD	for which you will not be able to atone,
וְתָבֹא עָלַיִךְ פִּתְאֹם שֹׁאָה	11bA	and devastation will come upon you suddenly
לֹא תֵדָעִי׃	11bB	which you will not (yet) know.

= Masoretic verse.
Separation ↑: repetitive verse-line parallelism; swapping (adjunct).
Separation ↓: major division markers in the textual tradition; swapping (adjunct).
Strophe parallelism: בוא || בוא; על || על; ךְ־ (f.s.) || ךְ־ (f.s.); הוה || שׁואה (unique); לא || לא; ידע || ידע.

STROPHE B.ii.1 (Isa. 47:12–13a)

עִמְדִי־נָא בַחֲבָרַיִךְ	12aA	Stand fast in your spells,
וּבְרֹב כְּשָׁפַיִךְ	12aB	and in the multitude of your sorceries,
בַּאֲשֶׁר יָגַעַתְּ מִנְּעוּרָיִךְ	12aC	with which you have wearied yourself from your youth.
אוּלַי תּוּכְלִי הוֹעִיל	12bA	If only you could find profit,
אוּלַי תַּעֲרוֹצִי׃	12bB	if only you could inspire terror –
נִלְאֵית בְּרֹב עֲצָתָיִךְ	13aC	you tire yourself out with the multitude of your counsel.

≠ Masoretic verse.

Separation ↑: major division markers in the textual tradition; imperative(s); repetitive verse-line parallelism.
Separation ↓: major division markers in the textual tradition; repetitive verse-line parallelism.
Strophe parallelism: ב || ב; רב (noun) || רב (noun); יגע || לאה (unique); ־ך (f.s.) || ־ך (f.s.); grammatical parallelism.
Discussion: The strophe parallelism suggests that v. 13aC should be joined with v. 12.[2] 𝔊^{SA} have major division markers after v. 13aC which suggests that they ended the strophe there (the same two manuscripts have dividers after v. 11).

STROPHE B.ii.2 (Isa. 47:13b–c)

יַעַמְדוּ־נָא וְיוֹשִׁיעֻךְ הֹבְרֵי* שָׁמַיִם	13bA	Let them stand fast and save you, those who bow to heaven,
הַחֹזִים בַּכּוֹכָבִים	13bB	who observe the stars,
מוֹדִיעִם לֶחֳדָשִׁים	13cA	who let you know month by month
מֵאֲשֶׁר יָבֹאוּ עָלָיִךְ׃	13cB	some of the things that will come to you.

≠ Masoretic verse.
Separation ↑: major division markers in the textual tradition; jussive(s).
Separation ↓: major division markers in the textual tradition.
Strophe parallelism: חזה || ידע;[3] grammatical parallelism.

STROPHE B.ii.3 (Isa. 47:14)

הִנֵּה הָיוּ כְקַשׁ אֵשׁ שְׂרָפָתַם	14aA	Behold, they are like chaff, a fire burns them up.
לֹא־יַצִּילוּ אֶת־נַפְשָׁם מִיַּד לֶהָבָה	14aB	they cannot deliver themselves from the power of the flame.
אֵין־גַּחֶלֶת לַחְמָם	14bA	No coal to warm oneself,
אוּר לָשֶׁבֶת נֶגְדּוֹ׃	14bB	no glow to sit by!

= Masoretic verse.
Separation ↑: major division markers in the textual tradition; deictic particle(s); repetitive verse-line parallelism.
Separation ↓: repetitive verse-line parallelism.
Strophe parallelism: אשׁ || גחלת; אשׁ || אור; שׂרף || חמם.

STROPHE B.ii.4 (Isa. 47:15)

כֵּן הָיוּ־לָךְ אֲשֶׁר יָגָעַתְּ	15aA	Such to you are those (for) whom you have wearied yourself,

[2]See also our comments pp. 351-2.
[3]See our remarks p. 352.

סֹחֲרַיִךְ מִנְּעוּרַיִךְ	15aB	who have trafficked with you from your youth.
אִישׁ לְעֶבְרוֹ תָּעוּ	15bA	They go astray, each in his own direction,
אֵין מוֹשִׁיעֵךְ׃	15bB	none will be your saviour.

= Masoretic verse.
Separation ↑: deictic particle(s); repetitive verse-line parallelism.
Separation ↓: major division markers in the textual tradition; swapping (subject); swapping (adjunct).
Strophe parallelism: ךְ־ (f.s.) || ךְ־ (f.s.); grammatical parallelism.

8.5 Isaiah 47 – Delimitation of Canticles

CANTICLE A.i (47:1–3)

Separation ↑: major division markers in the textual tradition; thematic discontinuity; change of subject.
Separation ↓: major division markers in the textual tradition.
Canticle parallelism: לקח || לקח; גלה Piel || גלה Piel (concatenation); grammatical parallelism: the imperatives and jussives connect the first three strophes (responsion/concatenation).
Thematic unity: yes. The first three strophes describe the humiliation of Babel in metaphors, the fourth explains.
Discussion: The major division markers $\mathfrak{G}^{Q}$ has after בת־בבל in 47:1 are a typical example of markers lagging behind the actual division point after 46:13 which has been marked correctly in $\mathfrak{G}^{SBA}$.

The major division markers in $\mathfrak{G}^{A}$ in v. 3 after אקח indicate the borderline between vv. 3 and 4 proleptically.

CANTICLE A.ii (47:4–7)

Separation ↑: major division markers in the textual tradition; change of subject.
Separation ↓: major division markers in the textual tradition.
Canticle parallelism: לא || לא || לא (responsion); גבירה || גבירה (inclusion); ישׂראל || עם (responsion); שׂים || שׂים (responsion).
Thematic unity: yes. The first strophe introduces the speaker, in the next three strophes lady Babel is addressed and her former fame and behaviour criticized.
Discussion: The delimiters after v. 4 might be lagging behind the division between vv. 3 and 4 in other witnesses ($\mathfrak{G}^{SA}$) or might indicate the beginning of the direct speech ($_{1}\mathfrak{Q}^{a}$).

$\mathfrak{G}^{A}$ delimits the strophe after v. 5 and indicates the division between vv. 7 and 8 proleptically.

CANTICLE B.i (47:8–11)

Separation ↑: major division markers in the textual tradition.
Separation ↓: major division markers in the textual tradition.
Canticle parallelism: בטח || בטח (responsion); אמר || אמר (responsion /inclusion); ב || ב (responsion); לבב || לב (inclusion); אני || אני (inclusion); עוד || עוד (inclusion); אלמנה || אלמן (concatenation); שׁכול || שׁכול (concatenation); בוא || בוא (responsion/inclusion); רגע || פתאם (inclusion); רעה || רעה (responsion); דעת || ידע (responsion/inclusion).
Thematic unity: yes. The falsity of Babel's self-confidence.
Discussion: The paragraphos in $\mathfrak{G}^{S}$ after v. 8 was probably intended to mark the major division after v. 7. The markers $\mathfrak{G}^{A}$ has after ברעתך in v. 10 can only be explained as a belated delimitation of the preceding strophe. The Petuḥa 1$\mathfrak{Q}^{b}$ has after כפרה in v. 11 proleptically indicates the same delimitation which $\mathfrak{G}^{SA}$ mark properly after v. 11.

CANTICLE B.ii (47:12–15)

Separation ↑: major division markers in the textual tradition.
Separation ↓: major division markers in the textual tradition.
Canticle parallelism: עמד || עמד (responsion); נא־ || נא־ (responsion); ך־ || ך־ (responsion/inclusion); יגע || יגע (responsion); מן || מן (responsion); נעורים || נעורים (responsion); ישׁע || נצל (responsion); ישׁע || ישׁע (inclusion); היה || היה (responsion).
Thematic unity: yes. Babel's sorcerers and astrologers will fail to help her.
Discussion: Several Greek manuscripts appear to have marked the end of strophes.

8.6 Isaiah 47 – Delimitation of Macrostructure

The structure of Isaiah 47 appears to be completely regular:

SUB-CANTOS	CANTICLES	STROPHES
A	2	8 (4+4)
B	2	8 (4+4)

The unity of the canto is generally recognized and is confirmed by the distant parallelism connecting the canticles of the two sub-cantos.

Sub-canto A:
שׁבי (v. 1aA – A.i) || שׁבי (v. 5aA – A.ii); בת־כשׂדים (v. 1aB – A.i) || בת־כשׂדים (v. 5aA – A.ii); כי לא תוסיפי יקראו־לך (v. 1bA – A.i) || כי לא תוסיפי יקראו־לך (v. 5bA – A.ii).

Sub-canto B:
ישׁב (v. 8aA – B.i) || ישׁב (v. 14bB – B.ii); בוא (vv. 9aA, 9bA, 11aA, 11bA – B.i) || בוא (v. 13cB – B.ii); ברב כשׁפיך (v. 9bB – B.i) || ברב כשׁפיך, ברב עצתיך (vv. 12aB, 13aC – B.ii).

Again we observe a certain correspondence between the beginning and end of the canto. The sitting in the dust (v.1) stands in stark contrast with the sitting by a cosy fire (v. 14). The suggestion of improper contacts with lovers in v. 15 corresponds to their flattering words of v. 1b as well as the forced stripping in vv. 2-3. That no man (אדם) will be spared (v. 3) is balanced by the statement that every man (אישׁ) will flee for his life (v. 15).[1]

[1]For the pair אדם || אישׁ see the Index.

Chapter 9

The Structure of Isaiah 48

9.1 Isaiah 48: Text and Translation

ס <פ> – 1𝔔^{a} – 𝔊^{SBAQ} – 𝔖^{abe} ________________________________

A.i.1 (Isa. 48:1)

שִׁמְעוּ־זֹאת בֵּית־יַעֲקֹב	1aA	Listen to this, O house of Jacob,
הַנִּקְרָאִים בְּשֵׁם יִשְׂרָאֵל	1aB	who are called by the name of Israel,
וּמִמְּעֵי* יְהוּדָה יָצָאוּ	1aC	who have come forth from the loins[1] of Judah;
הַנִּשְׁבָּעִים ׀ בְּשֵׁם יְהוָה	1bA	who swear by the name of the LORD,
וּבֵאלֹהֵי יִשְׂרָאֵל יַזְכִּירוּ	1bB	and invoke the God of Israel,
{ס} לֹא בֶאֱמֶת וְלֹא בִצְדָקָה׃	1bC	– (but) not in truth and not in justice,

A.i.2 (Isa. 48:2)

כִּי־מֵעִיר הַקֹּדֶשׁ נִקְרָאוּ	2aA	although[2] they call[3] themselves after the holy city,
{𝔊^{Q}} וְעַל־אֱלֹהֵי יִשְׂרָאֵל נִסְמָכוּ	2aB	and rely on the God of Israel,
יְהוָה צְבָאוֹת שְׁמוֹ׃	2aC	LORD of hosts is his name.

ס <פ> – 1𝔔^{a} – 𝔊^{A} ....

[1]Rashi's interpretation of מים as "semen" was based on 𝔗 but cannot be sustained because his appeal to Num. 24:7 is unacceptable (the word simply means 'water' there), despite the acclaim of Barthélemy, 352; De Waard, 180, and others. In view of the context, the proposal to understand the expression as a reference to the natural sources of the land of Judah (so e.g. Koole, 418) is unattractive. A reduplicated form of מן (Franke, 171) is unlikely when no suffix follows.

The conjectural reading ממעי יהודה, favoured by many scholars, finds strong support in v. 19aB וצאצאי מעיך and restores the problematic text to a well-known expression (Gen. 15:4). Also the description the Servant Israel in Isa. 49:1 may be cited in support of this emendation. Therefore we accept it despite the fact that 𝔐 offers the most difficult reading which is supported by most ancient versions. After all, letters did drop out occasionally. Cf. F. Delitzsch, *Die Lese- und Schreibfehler in Alten Testament*, Berlin 1920, §§89-90; J. Kennedy, *An Aid to the Textual Amendment of the Old Testament*, Edinburgh 1928, 131-8.

[2]For the concessive function of כי see e.g. Th.C. Vriezen, "Einige Notizen zur Übersetzung des Bindewortes 'כי'", in: *Von Ugarit nach Qumran* (BZAW, 77), Berlin 1958, 266-73; *HALAT*, 449; A. Aejmelaeus, "Function and Interpretation of כי in Biblical Hebrew", *JBL* 105 (1986), 193-209.

[3]Most modern translations opt for the present tense here, and with good reason (note the imperfect יזכירו in v. 1bB). Cf. M.C.A. Korpel, J.C. de Moor, F. Sepmeijer, "Consistency with Regard to Tenses", see Abbreviations.

A.ii.1 (Isa. 48:3)

הָרִאשֹׁנוֹת מֵאָז הִגַּדְתִּי	3aA	The first things I have told from old,[4]
וּמִפִּי יָצְאוּ וְאַשְׁמִיעֵם	3aB	they went forth[5] from my mouth and I made them heard,
$\{\mathfrak{G}^{SA}\}$ פִּתְאֹם עָשִׂיתִי וַתָּבֹאנָה׃	3bA	suddenly I acted and they came (to pass).

A.ii.2 (Isa. 48:4)

מִדַּעְתִּי כִּי קָשֶׁה אָתָּה	4aA	Because I know that you are obstinate,
וְגִיד בַּרְזֶל עָרְפֶּךָ	4aB	and your neck is an iron sinew
וּמִצְחֲךָ נְחוּשָׁה׃	4aC	and your forehead bronze,

A.ii.3 (Isa. 48:5)

וָאַגִּיד לְךָ מֵאָז	5aA	I told (them) to you from of old,
$\{\mathfrak{G}^{AQ}\}$ בְּטֶרֶם תָּבוֹא הִשְׁמַעְתִּיךָ	5aB	before it came, I made you hear it,
פֶּן־תֹּאמַר עָצְבִּי עָשָׂם	5bA	lest you should say, "My grievous image[6] did it,
וּפִסְלִי וְנִסְכִּי צִוָּם׃	5bB	my idol or[7] my molten image commanded it".

$\mathfrak{G}^{S}$ ....

A.iii.1 (Isa. 48:6)

$\{\mathfrak{G}^{Q}\}$ שָׁמַעְתָּ חֲזֵה כֻּלָּהּ	6aA	You have heard (all this), (now) observe it all,
וְאַתֶּם הֲלוֹא תַגִּידוּ	6aB	And you[8] – would you not tell (now)?
הִשְׁמַעְתִּיךָ חֲדָשׁוֹת מֵעַתָּה	6bA	From now on I make you hear new things
וּנְצֻרוֹת וְלֹא יְדַעְתָּם׃	6bB	and well-kept things which you do not know.

A.iii.2 (Isa. 48:7)

עַתָּה נִבְרְאוּ וְלֹא מֵאָז	7aA	They are created now, not in olden times,[9]
וְלִפְנֵי־יוֹם וְלֹא שְׁמַעְתָּם	7aB	and before today, no, you did not hear of them,[10]
$\{\mathfrak{G}^{A}\}$ פֶּן־תֹּאמַר הִנֵּה יְדַעְתִּין׃	7bA	lest you should say, "Behold, I knew them!"

A.iii.3 (Isa. 48:8)

גַּם לֹא־שָׁמַעְתָּ גַּם לֹא יָדַעְתָּ	8aA	No, you did not listen, no, you would not know,

---

[4] Lit. "from then on", i.e. from the moment they were there.

[5] On the disagreement between the feminine subject and the masculine verbal predicate and the suffix see Brockelmann, HS, §124.

[6] A translation should not obliterate the derogatory and therefore illogical nature of the term used. Here it has been vocalized in an irregular manner, probably in conformity with the vowels of the word בשת 'shame' which underlines the prophet's critique.

[7] Because the verbal predicate is in the singular.

[8] Note the switch from singular to plural, and back, in v. 5. This in accordance with Second Isaiah's view of Israel as a corporate personality.

[9] See note 4.

[10] Koole, 427, solves the problems satisfactorily.

גַּם מֵאָז לֹא־פִתְּחָה אָזְנֶךָ	8aB	no, from of old your ear has not been opened.
כִּי יָדַעְתִּי בָּגוֹד תִּבְגּוֹד	8bA	For I know that you are very treacherous,
וּפֹשֵׁעַ מִבֶּטֶן קֹרָא לָךְ׃	8bB	and that you are called a transgressor from birth.[11]

. . . .

A.iv.1 (Isa. 48:9)

לְמַעַן שְׁמִי אַאֲרִיךְ אַפִּי	9aA	For my name's sake I defer my anger,
וּתְהִלָּתִי אֶחֱטָם־לָךְ	9aB	and (for the sake of)[12] my praise I restrain myself with regard to you,
{<ס>$\mathfrak{G}^{SQ}$} לְבִלְתִּי הַכְרִיתֶךָ׃	9bA	so as not to cut you off.[13]

A.iv.2 (Isa. 48:10)

הִנֵּה צְרַפְתִּיךָ וְלֹא בְכָסֶף	10aA	Behold, I have refined you, but not like[14] silver,
בְּחַרְתִּיךָ בְּכוּר עֹנִי׃	10aB	I have chosen[15] you in the furnace of affliction.

A.iv.3 (Isa. 48:11)

לְמַעֲנִי לְמַעֲנִי אֶעֱשֶׂה	11aA	For my sake, for my sake only, I will do (this).
כִּי אֵיךְ אֵיחָל*	11aB	How could I[16] suffer profanation?
וּכְבוֹדִי לְאַחֵר לֹא־אֶתֵּן׃	11bA	No, I will not give my glory to any other.

ס <פ> – $1\mathfrak{Q}^{a}$ – $4\mathfrak{Q}^{d}$ – $\mathfrak{G}^{SBAQ}$ – $\mathfrak{S}^{abcde}$ ________________________________

B.i.1 (Isa. 48:12)

שְׁמַע אֵלַי יַעֲקֹב	12aA	Listen to me, O Jacob,
וְיִשְׂרָאֵל מְקֹרָאִי	12aB	and Israel, whom I have called.
אֲנִי־הוּא אֲנִי רִאשׁוֹן	12bA	I am the same, I am the First,
אַף אֲנִי אַחֲרוֹן׃	12bB	I am also the Last.

B.i.2 (Isa. 48:13)

אַף־יָדִי יָסְדָה אֶרֶץ	13aA	Also it was my hand which laid the foundation of the earth,
{$\mathfrak{G}^{A}$} וִימִינִי טִפְּחָה שָׁמָיִם	13aB	and my right hand which spread out the heavens.
קֹרֵא אֲנִי אֲלֵיהֶם	13bA	When I call to them,
{$\mathfrak{G}^{A}$} יַעַמְדוּ יַחְדָּו׃	13bB	they stand up together.

---

[11] An allusion to Gen. 27:36 and Hos. 12:3? This is what v. 12aB suggests.

[12] We assume ellipsis.

[13] For the infinitive after לבלתי see Isa. 44:10.

[14] The ב has to be taken here as *beth essentiae*, cf. Koole, 431; Barthélemy, 353; Franke, 200-1; Oswalt, 265, n. 34.

[15] There is no need to emend the text, because the writer himself has partially suspended his metaphorical speech in the preceding colon.

[16] Three manuscripts from Qumran read איחל ($1\mathfrak{Q}^{a}$ and $4\mathfrak{Q}^{c,d}$). The first person singular is supported by $\mathfrak{V}$ and $\mathfrak{S}$. Therefore $\mathfrak{M}$ as well as the renderings of $\mathfrak{T}$ and $\mathfrak{G}$ must be regarded as attempts to avoid blasphemy. With Barthélemy, 354-5; De Waard, 180-1.

B.i.3 (Isa. 48:14a)

הִקָּבְצוּ כֻלְּכֶם וּשְׁמָעוּ	14aA	Assemble, all of you and listen!
מִי בָהֶם הִגִּיד אֶת־אֵלֶּה	14aB	Who among them[17] was able to tell these things?

$\mathfrak{G}^{SA}$ . . . .

B.ii.1 (Isa. 48:14b)

יְהוָה אֲהֵבוֹ יַעֲשֶׂה חֶפְצוֹ בְּבָבֶל	14bA	'The-LORD-loves-him'[18] will do his will in Babylon,
וּזְרֹעוֹ כַּשְׂדִּים׃	14bB	and his arm among[19] the Chaldeans.

B.ii.2 (Isa. 48:15)

אֲנִי אֲנִי דִּבַּרְתִּי אַף־קְרָאתִיו	15aA	I, it was I who spoke, also called him,
{$\mathfrak{G}^{S}$} הֲבִיאֹתִיו וְהִצְלִיחַ דַּרְכּוֹ׃	15aB	brought him, and made his way successful.

B.ii.3 (Isa. 48:16)

{$\mathfrak{G}^{A}$} קִרְבוּ אֵלַי שִׁמְעוּ־זֹאת	16aA	Draw near to me and listen to this:
לֹא מֵרֹאשׁ בַּסֵּתֶר דִּבַּרְתִּי	16aB	from the beginning I have not spoken in secret,
מֵעֵת הֱיוֹתָהּ שָׁם אָנִי	16aC	from the time it came to be, I was there.
וְעַתָּה אֲדֹנָי יְהוִה שְׁלָחַנִי	16bA	And now the Lord GOD has sent me,
וְרוּחוֹ׃	16bB	and (has sent)[20] his spirit.

פ <ס> – $1\mathfrak{Q}^{a}$ – $4\mathfrak{Q}^{d}$ – $\mathfrak{G}^{SA}$ – $\mathfrak{S}^{abe}$ . . . .

B.iii.1 (Isa. 48:17)

כֹּה־אָמַר יְהוָה גֹּאַלְךָ	17aA	Thus says the LORD, your Redeemer,
קְדוֹשׁ יִשְׂרָאֵל	17aB	the Holy One of Israel:
אֲנִי יְהוָה אֱלֹהֶיךָ	17bA	I am the LORD your God,
מְלַמֶּדְךָ לְהוֹעִיל	17bB	who teaches you to profit,
מַדְרִיכֲךָ בְּדֶרֶךְ תֵּלֵךְ׃	17bC	who lets you go on the way you should walk.

B.iii.2 (Isa. 48:18)

לוּא הִקְשַׁבְתָּ לְמִצְוֹתָי	18aA	O that you had listened to my commandments!
וַיְהִי כַנָּהָר שְׁלוֹמֶךָ	18bA	Then your peace would have been like a river,
וְצִדְקָתְךָ כְּגַלֵּי הַיָּם׃	18bB	and your justice like the waves of the sea,

---

[17] Obviously the idols, in contrast to v. 5 (see also 43:9; 45:21); cf. Young, 256; Koole, 438; Barthélemy, 355-6; De Waard, 181-2; Oswalt, 273, n. 54; 276.

[18] With many others we assume this to be an alias for Cyrus (cf. Isa. 44:28), coined after 2 Sam. 12:24.

[19] We assume ellipsis of the preposition ב.

[20] In our opinion ellipsis of the verbal predicate is the only viable option from the viewpoint of poetic structure. רוח is the object of שלח in Judg. 9:23 and Ps. 104:30. In the latter instance the spirit is send to perform a creative act, as in Isa. 40:13. This fits the present context too (cf. v. 16a) and obviously refers to the work of the spirit in the servant (Isa. 42:1) as the personification of faithful Israel (Isa. 44:3).

B.iii.3 (Isa. 48:19)

וַיְהִי כַחוֹל זַרְעֶךָ	19aA	and your seed would have been like the sand,
וְצֶאֱצָאֵי מֵעֶיךָ כִּמְעֹתָיו	19aB	and the offspring of your bowels like its grains
לֹא־יִכָּרֵת	19bA	Never would be cut off
וְלֹא־יִשָּׁמֵד שְׁמוֹ מִלְּפָנָי׃	19bB	nor be destroyed its name from before me.

<ס> – $1\mathfrak{Q}^{a}$ indentation – $4\mathfrak{Q}^{d}$ – $\mathfrak{G}^{SQ}$ – $\mathcal{S}^{be}$ ....

B.iv.1 (Isa. 48:20)

צְאוּ מִבָּבֶל	20aA	Go forth from Babylon!
{$\mathfrak{G}^{A}$} בִּרְחוּ מִכַּשְׂדִּים	20aB	Flee from the Chaldaeans!
בְּקוֹל רִנָּה הַגִּידוּ	20bA	Tell this with a rejoicing voice,
הַשְׁמִיעוּ זֹאת	20bB	make this be heard,
הוֹצִיאוּהָ עַד־קְצֵה הָאָרֶץ	20bC	let it go forth to the end of the earth,
אִמְרוּ גָּאַל יְהוָה עַבְדּוֹ יַעֲקֹב׃	20bD	say: "The LORD redeems[21] his servant Jacob!"

B.iv.2 (Isa. 48:21)

וְלֹא צָמְאוּ	21aA	And they do not thirst
בָּחֳרָבוֹת הוֹלִיכָם	21aB	in the wilderness where he makes them walk,
מַיִם מִצּוּר הִזִּיל לָמוֹ	21aC	he makes water flow for them from the rock.
וַיִּבְקַע־צוּר	21bA	He cleaves the rock
{$\mathfrak{G}^{A}$} וַיָּזֻבוּ מָיִם׃	21bB	and water gushes forth.

B.iv.3 (Isa. 48:22)

אֵין שָׁלוֹם	22aA	There is no peace,
אָמַר יְהוָה לָרְשָׁעִים׃	22aB	– says the LORD – for the wicked![22]

ס <פ> – $1\mathfrak{Q}^{a}$ – $1\mathfrak{Q}^{b}$ – $4\mathfrak{Q}^{d}$ – $\mathfrak{G}^{SBAQ}$ – $\mathcal{S}^{abcde}$ ______________________________

[21] In this and the following verses the incompatibility of the Hebrew and English modes of expressing tense becomes painfully clear. In view of the context it is fairly certain that the ancient author wanted to express past, present and future at the same time. Cf. note 3 (Korpel, De Moor, Sepmeijer).

[22] The extra colon in $\mathfrak{G}$ was borrowed from Exod. 17:6.

9.2 Isaiah 48 – Delimitation of Cola

COLON 48:1aA:

שִׁמְעוּ־זֹאת בֵּית־יַעֲקֹב 1aA Listen to this, O house of Jacob,

With: $\mathfrak{M}$ (7) – $\mathfrak{G}^{SQ}$ – $\mathfrak{S}^{abcde}$ all subordinate punctuation.

COLON 48:1aB:

הַנִּקְרָאִים בְּשֵׁם יִשְׂרָאֵל 1aB who are called by the name of Israel,

With: $\mathfrak{M}$ (5) – $\mathfrak{G}^{SQ}$ – $\mathfrak{S}^{abc}$, $\mathfrak{S}^{de}$ subordinate punctuation.

COLON 48:1aC:

וּמִמְּעֵי* יְהוּדָה יָצָאוּ 1aC who have come forth from the loins of Judah;

With: $\mathfrak{M}$ (2) – $\mathfrak{G}^{SQ}$ – $\mathfrak{S}^{abcde}$

COLON 48:1bA:

הַנִּשְׁבָּעִים ׀ בְּשֵׁם יְהוָה 1bA who swear by the name of the LORD,

With: $\mathfrak{M}$ (7) – $\mathfrak{S}^{abcde}$ all subordinate punctuation.
Discussion: $\mathfrak{G}^{SQ}$ read on until ישׂראל which is very unlikely in view of the parallelism.

COLON 48:1bB:

וּבֵאלֹהֵי יִשְׂרָאֵל יַזְכִּירוּ 1bB and invoke the God of Israel,

With: $\mathfrak{M}$ (5) – $\mathfrak{S}^{abcde}$
Discussion: Because of their wrong division of the preceding colon $\mathfrak{G}^{SQ}$ were forced to take יזכירו with the next colon.

COLON 48:1bC:

לֹא בֶאֱמֶת וְלֹא בִצְדָקָה׃ 1bC – (but) not in truth and not in justice,

With: $\mathfrak{M}$ (1), Seder – $\mathfrak{G}^{SQ}$ – $\mathfrak{S}^{abcde}$
Colon parallelism: לא || לא; ב || ב; אמת || צדקה.
Discussion: $\mathfrak{G}^{S}$ and $\mathfrak{G}^{Q}$ have an extra divider after באמת which corresponds to $\mathfrak{M}$'s Ṭiphḥa (No. 8).

COLON 48:2aA:

כִּי־מֵעִיר הַקֹּדֶשׁ נִקְרָאוּ 2aA although they call themselves after the holy city,

With: 𝔐 (5) – $\mathfrak{G}^{S}$ – S^{bcde}, S^{a} subordinate punctuation.

COLON 48:2aB:

וְעַל־אֱלֹהֵי יִשְׂרָאֵל נִסְמָכוּ 2aB and rely on the God of Israel,

With: 𝔐 (2) – $\mathfrak{G}^{SQ}$, major divison marker in $\mathfrak{G}^{Q}$ – S^{abcde}

COLON 48:2aC:

יְהוָה צְבָאוֹת שְׁמוֹ׃ 2aC LORD of hosts is his name.

With: 𝔐 (1), major division markers, also in 1𝔔^{a} – $\mathfrak{G}^{SAQ}$, major division markers in $\mathfrak{G}^{A}$ – S^{abcde}

COLON 48:3aA:

הָרִאשֹׁנוֹת מֵאָז הִגַּדְתִּי 3aA The first things I have told from old,

With: 𝔐 (5) – $\mathfrak{G}^{SQ}$ – S^{acde}

COLON 48:3aB:

וּמִפִּי יָצְאוּ וְאַשְׁמִיעֵם 3aB they went forth from my mouth and I made them heard,

With: 𝔐 (2) – $\mathfrak{G}^{SQ}$ – S^{abcde}
Colon parallelism: יצא מפה || שמע.
Discussion: $\mathfrak{G}^{SQ}$ and S^{be} have an extra point after יצאו (𝔐 Ṭiphḥa) which is unlikely because it creates a disturbance of the rhythmical balance (3 + 3 + 3 stresses).

COLON 48:3bA:

פִּתְאֹם עָשִׂיתִי וַתָּבֹאנָה׃ 3bA suddenly I acted and they came (to pass).

With: 𝔐 (1) – $\mathfrak{G}^{SAQ}$, major division markers in $\mathfrak{G}^{SA}$ – S^{abcde}
Colon parallelism: Possibly עשה || בוא.

COLON 48:4aA:

מִדַּעְתִּי כִּי קָשֶׁה אָתָּה 4aA Because I know that you are obstinate,

With: 𝔐 (2) – $\mathfrak{G}^{SQ}$ – S^{abcde}
Discussion: For the Zaqeph Gadol (No. 6) with מדעתי see our comment on p. 31.

COLON 48:4aB:

וְגִיד בַּרְזֶל עָרְפֶּךָ 4aB and your neck is an iron sinew

With: 𝔐 (5) – $\mathfrak{G}^{SQ}$ – S^{abcde}

COLON 48:4aC:

וּמִצְחֲךָ נְחוּשָׁה׃ 4aC and your forehead bronze,

With: $\mathfrak{M}$ (1) – $\mathfrak{G}^{SQ}$ – $\mathfrak{S}^{abcde}$

COLON 48:5aA:

וָאַגִּיד לְךָ מֵאָז 5aA I told (them) to you from of old,

With: $\mathfrak{M}$ (5) – $\mathfrak{G}^{SQ}$ – $\mathfrak{S}^{bd}$, $\mathfrak{S}^{ace}$ subordinate punctuation.

COLON 48:5aB:

בְּטֶרֶם תָּבוֹא הִשְׁמַעְתִּיךָ 5aB before it came, I made you hear it,

With: $\mathfrak{M}$ (2) – $\mathfrak{G}^{SAQ}$, major division markers in $\mathfrak{G}^{A}$ and $\mathfrak{G}^{Q}$ – $\mathfrak{S}^{abcde}$
Colon parallelism: בוא || שמע.

COLON 48:5bA:

פֶּן־תֹּאמַר עָצְבִּי עָשָׂם 5bA lest you should say, “My grievous image did it,

With: $\mathfrak{M}$ (5) – $\mathfrak{G}^{SQ}$ – $\mathfrak{S}^{abcde}$ all subordinate punctuation.

COLON 48:5bB:

וּפִסְלִי וְנִסְכִּי צִוָּם׃ 5bB my idol or my molten image commanded it”.

With: $\mathfrak{M}$ (1) – $\mathfrak{G}^{SQ}$, major division markers in $\mathfrak{G}^{S}$ – $\mathfrak{S}^{abcde}$
Colon parallelism: פסל || נסך.

COLON 48:6aA:

שָׁמַעְתָּ חֲזֵה כֻּלָּהּ 6aA You have heard (all this), (now) observe it all,

With: $\mathfrak{M}$ (5) – $\mathfrak{G}^{SQ}$, paragraphos in $\mathfrak{G}^{Q}$ – $\mathfrak{S}^{abcde}$
Colon parallelism: שמע || חזה.

COLON 48:6aB:

וְאַתֶּם הֲלוֹא תַגִּידוּ 6aB And you – would you not tell (now)?

With: $\mathfrak{M}$ (2) – $\mathfrak{G}^{SQ}$ – $\mathfrak{S}^{abcde}$

COLON 48:6bA:

הִשְׁמַעְתִּיךָ חֲדָשׁוֹת מֵעַתָּה 6bA From now on I make you hear new things

With: $\mathfrak{M}$ (5) – $\mathfrak{G}^{SQ}$

COLON 48:6bB:

וּנְצֻר֖וֹת וְלֹ֥א יְדַעְתָּֽם׃ 6bB and well-kept things which you do not know.

With: 𝔐 (1) – 𝔊^{S} – 𝔖^{abcde}
Discussion: 𝔊^{SQ} and 𝔖^{d} have an extra point after ונצרות where 𝔐 has a Ṭiphḥa.

COLON 48:7aA:

עַתָּ֤ה נִבְרְאוּ֙ וְלֹ֣א מֵאָ֔ז 7aA They are created now, not in olden times,

With: 𝔐 (5) – 𝔊^{S} – 𝔖^{abcde}
Colon parallelism: אז || עתה.

COLON 48:7aB:

וְלִפְנֵי־י֖וֹם וְלֹ֣א שְׁמַעְתָּ֑ם 7aB and before today, no, you did not hear of them,

With: 𝔐 (2) – 𝔊^{S} – 𝔖^{abcde}

COLON 48:7bA:

פֶּן־תֹּאמַ֖ר הִנֵּ֥ה יְדַעְתִּֽין׃ 7bA lest you should say, “Behold, I knew them!”

With: 𝔐 (1) – 𝔊^{SAQ}, major division markers in 𝔊^{A} – 𝔖^{abcde}

COLON 48:8aA:

גַּ֣ם לֹֽא־שָׁמַ֗עְתָּ גַּ֚ם לֹ֣א יָדַ֔עְתָּ 8aA No, you did not listen, no, you would not know,

With: 𝔐 (5) – 𝔊^{SQ} – 𝔖^{abcde}
Colon parallelism: גם || גם; שמע || ידע.
Discussion: None of the other ancient witnesses supports 𝔐's Revia‘ (No. 7) with לא־שמעת.

COLON 48:8aB:

גַּ֕ם מֵאָ֖ז לֹא־פִתְּחָ֣ה אָזְנֶ֑ךָ 8aB no, from of old your ear has not been opened.

With: 𝔐 (2) – 𝔊^{SQ} – 𝔖^{abcde}
Discussion: For the Zaqeph Gadol (No. 6) with גם[2] see p. 31.

COLON 48:8bA:

כִּ֤י יָדַ֙עְתִּי֙ בָּג֣וֹד תִּבְגּ֔וֹד 8bA For I know that you are very treacherous,

With: 𝔐 (5) – 𝔊^{SQ} – 𝔖^{abcde}

COLON 48:8bB:

וּפֹשֵׁעַ מִבֶּטֶן קֹרָא לָךְ׃ 8bB and that you are called a transgressor from birth.

With: 𝔐 (1) – 𝔊^{SQ} – 𝔖^{abcde}

COLON 48:9aA:

לְמַעַן שְׁמִי אַאֲרִיךְ אַפִּי 9aA For my name's sake I defer my anger,

With: 𝔐 (5) – 𝔊^{SQ} – 𝔖^{abcde}

Discussion: 𝔊^{SQ} and 𝔖^{e} have an extra point after שְׁמִי (𝔐 has a Pashṭa, No. 10).

COLON 48:9aB:

וּתְהִלָּתִי אֶחֱטָם־לָךְ 9aB and (for the sake of) my praise I restrain myself with regard to you,

With: 𝔐 (2) – 𝔊^{SQ} – 𝔖^{ace} subordinate punctuation.

COLON 48:9bA:

לְבִלְתִּי הַכְרִיתֶךָ׃ 9bA so as not to cut you off.

With: 𝔐 (1), Setuma in 1𝔔^{a} – 𝔊^{SQ}, paragraphos in 𝔊^{S}, major division markers in 𝔊^{Q} – 𝔖^{bce}, subordinate punctuation in 𝔖^{ad}

COLON 48:10aA:

הִנֵּה צְרַפְתִּיךָ וְלֹא בְכָסֶף 10aA Behold, I have refined you, but not like silver,

With: 𝔐 (2) – 𝔊^{SQ} – 𝔖^{abcde}

COLON 48:10aB:

בְּחַרְתִּיךָ בְּכוּר עֹנִי׃ 10aB I have chosen you in the furnace of affliction.

With: 𝔐 (1) – 𝔊^{SQ} – 𝔖^{abcde}

COLON 48:11aA:

לְמַעֲנִי לְמַעֲנִי אֶעֱשֶׂה 11aA For my sake, for my sake only, I will do (this).

With: 𝔐 (8) – 𝔊^{SQ}

Colon parallelism: למען || למען.

Discussion: Even though neither 𝔐 nor 𝔖 supports this colometry, we believe 𝔊^{SQ} to have preserved the correct division. The surrounding cola all count three stresses.

COLON 48:11aB:

כִּי אֵיךְ אֵיחָל* 11aB How could I suffer profanation?

With: $\mathfrak{M}$ (2) – $\mathfrak{G}^{SQ}$ – $\mathfrak{S}^{abcde}$

COLON 48:11bA:

וּכְבוֹדִי לְאַחֵר לֹא־אֶתֵּן׃ 11bA No, I will not give my glory to any other.

With: $\mathfrak{M}$ (1), major division markers, also in $1\mathfrak{Q}^{a}$ and $4\mathfrak{Q}^{d}$ – $\mathfrak{G}^{SBAQ}$, major division markers in all of them – $\mathfrak{S}^{abcde}$, all with major divison markers.

COLON 48:12aA:

שְׁמַע אֵלַי יַעֲקֹב 12aA Listen to me, O Jacob,

With: $\mathfrak{M}$ (5) – $\mathfrak{G}^{Q}$ – $\mathfrak{S}^{abcde}$ subordinate punctuation mark.

COLON 48:12aB:

וְיִשְׂרָאֵל מְקֹרָאִי 12aB and Israel, whom I have called.

With: $\mathfrak{M}$ (2) – $\mathfrak{G}^{SQ}$ – $\mathfrak{S}^{abcde}$

COLON 48:12bA:

אֲנִי־הוּא אֲנִי רִאשׁוֹן 12bA I am the same, I am the First,

With: $\mathfrak{M}$ (5) – $\mathfrak{G}^{SQ}$
Colon parallelism: אני || אני.

COLON 48:12bB:

אַף אֲנִי אַחֲרוֹן׃ 12bB I am also the Last.

With: $\mathfrak{M}$ (1) – $\mathfrak{G}^{SQ}$ – $\mathfrak{S}^{abcde}$

COLON 48:13aA:

אַף־יָדִי יָסְדָה אֶרֶץ 13aA Also it was my hand which laid the foundation of the earth,

With: $\mathfrak{M}$ (5) – $\mathfrak{G}^{SQ}$ – $\mathfrak{S}^{abcde}$

COLON 48:13aB:

וִימִינִי טִפְּחָה שָׁמָיִם 13aB and my right hand which spread out the heavens.

With: $\mathfrak{M}$ (2) – $\mathfrak{G}^{SAQ}$, major division marker in $\mathfrak{G}^{A}$ – $\mathfrak{S}^{abcde}$

COLON 48:13bA:

קֹרֵא אֲנִי אֲלֵיהֶם 13bA When I call to them,

With: $\mathfrak{M}$ (8) – $\mathfrak{G}^{SQ}$ – $\mathfrak{S}^{a}$
Discussion: The support from $\mathfrak{S}$ is weak because the sentence runs on.

COLON 48:13bB:

יַעַמְדוּ יַחְדָּו׃ 13bB they stand up together.

With: $\mathfrak{M}$ (1) – $\mathfrak{G}^{SAQ}$, major division markers in $\mathfrak{G}^{A}$ – $\mathfrak{S}^{abcde}$

COLON 48:14aA:

הִקָּבְצוּ כֻלְּכֶם וּשֲׁמָעוּ 14aA Assemble, all of you and listen!

With: $\mathfrak{M}$ (5) – $\mathfrak{G}^{SQ}$ – $\mathfrak{S}^{abcde}$
Colon parallelism: קבץ || שמע (unique).

COLON 48:14aB:

מִי בָהֶם הִגִּיד אֶת־אֵלֶּה 14aB Who among them was able to tell these things?

With: $\mathfrak{M}$ (2) – $\mathfrak{G}^{SAQ}$, major division markers in $\mathfrak{G}^{S}$ and $\mathfrak{G}^{A}$ – $\mathfrak{S}^{abcde}$

COLON 48:14bA:

יְהוָה אֲהֵבוֹ יַעֲשֶׂה חֶפְצוֹ בְּבָבֶל 14bA 'The-LORD-loves-him' will do his will in Babylon,

With: $\mathfrak{M}$ (5) – $\mathfrak{G}^{SQ}$ – $\mathfrak{S}^{e}$
Discussion: Only $\mathfrak{G}^{S}$ supports $\mathfrak{M}$'s Zaqeph Qaṭon with אהבו.

COLON 48:14bB:

וּזְרֹעוֹ כַּשְׂדִּים׃ 14bB and his arm among the Chaldeans.

With: $\mathfrak{M}$ (1) – $\mathfrak{G}^{SQ}$ – $\mathfrak{S}^{abcde}$

COLON 48:15aA:

אֲנִי אֲנִי דִּבַּרְתִּי אַף־קְרָאתִיו 15aA I, it was I who spoke, also called him,

With: $\mathfrak{M}$ (2) – $\mathfrak{G}^{SQ}$ – $\mathfrak{S}^{abcde}$
Colon parallelism: אני || אני; דבר || קרא.

COLON 48:15aB:

הֲבִיאֹתִיו וְהִצְלִיחַ דַּרְכּוֹ׃ 15aB brought him, and made his way successful.

With: $\mathfrak{M}$ (1) – $\mathfrak{G}^{SQ}$ – $\mathfrak{S}^{abcde}$

COLON 48:16aA:

קִרְבוּ אֵלַי שִׁמְעוּ־זֹאת 16aA Draw near to me and listen to this:

With: $\mathfrak{M}$ (7) – $\mathfrak{G}^{SA}$, major division markers in $\mathfrak{G}^{A}$ – $\mathfrak{S}^{abcd}$
Colon parallelism: קרב || שמע.

COLON 48:16aB:

לֹא מֵרֹאשׁ בַּסֵּתֶר דִּבַּרְתִּי 16aB from the beginning I have not spoken in secret,

With: $\mathfrak{M}$ (5) – $\mathfrak{G}^{SQ}$ – $\mathfrak{S}^{abcde}$

COLON 48:16aC:

מֵעֵת הֱיוֹתָהּ שָׁם אָנִי 16aC from the time it came to be, I was there.

With: $\mathfrak{M}$ (2) – $\mathfrak{G}^{SQ}$ – $\mathfrak{S}^{abcde}$

COLON 48:16bA:

וְעַתָּה אֲדֹנָי יְהוִה שְׁלָחַנִי 16bA And now the Lord GOD has sent me,

With: $\mathfrak{M}$ (8) – $\mathfrak{G}^{SQ}$
Colon parallelism: אדני || יהוה.
Discussion: $\mathfrak{M}$ and $\mathfrak{S}$ read on to the end of the verse. Since cola of only one word are attested,[1] and since it is unlikely that the prophet wanted to put himself on a par with the spirit of the LORD we accept $\mathfrak{G}$'s division. For the Revia‘ (No. 7) with ועתה see p. 31.

COLON 48:16bB:

וְרוּחוֹ׃ 16bB and (has sent) his spirit.

With: $\mathfrak{M}$ (1), major division markers, also in 1$\mathfrak{Q}^{a}$ and 4$\mathfrak{Q}^{d}$ – $\mathfrak{G}^{SAQ}$, major division markers in $\mathfrak{G}^{SA}$ – $\mathfrak{S}^{abcde}$, major division markers in $\mathfrak{S}^{abe}$

COLON 48:17aA:

כֹּה־אָמַר יְהוָה גֹּאַלְךָ 17aA Thus says the LORD, your Redeemer,

With: $\mathfrak{M}$ (8) – $\mathfrak{G}^{SQ}$
Colon parallelism: יהוה || גאל.
Discussion: $\mathfrak{M}$ and $\mathfrak{S}$ read on to ישׂראל, but $\mathfrak{G}$'s division is more likely in view of the inconsistencies in the treatment of the ‘Botenformel’.[2]

[1] A famous example being Num. 6:24-25. See our note on p. 222.
[2] See our remarks pp. 164, 268.

COLON 48:17aB:

קְד֣וֹשׁ יִשְׂרָאֵ֑ל 17aB the Holy One of Israel:

With: 𝔐 (2) – 𝔊^SQ – 𝔖^abcde

COLON 48:17bA:

אֲנִ֨י יְהוָ֤ה אֱלֹהֶ֙יךָ֙ 17bA I am the LORD your God,

With: 𝔐 (10) – 𝔊^SQ
Colon parallelism: יהוה || אלהים.
Discussion: 𝔐 and 𝔖 read on until להועיל. In our opinion a more satisfactory balance is achieved if מלמדך and מדריכך both head a new colon.

COLON 48:17bB:

מְלַמֶּדְךָ֣ לְהוֹעִ֔יל 17bB who teaches you to profit,

With: 𝔐 (5) – 𝔖^abcde
Discussion: 𝔊 reads on to תלך; see our comment on the preceding colon.

COLON 48:17bC:

מַדְרִֽיכְךָ֖ בְּדֶ֥רֶךְ תֵּלֵֽךְ׃ 17bC who lets you go on the way you should walk.

With: 𝔐 (1) – 𝔊^SQ – 𝔖^abcde
Colon parallelism: דרך || הלך.

COLON 48:18aA:

ל֥וּא הִקְשַׁ֖בְתָּ לְמִצְוֺתָ֑י 18aA O that you had listened to my commandments!

With: 𝔐 (2) – 𝔊^SQ – 𝔖^abcde

COLON 48:18bA:

וַיְהִ֤י כַנָּהָר֙ שְׁלוֹמֶ֔ךָ 18bA Then your peace would have been like a river,

With: 𝔐 (5) – 𝔊^SQ – 𝔖^bcde

COLON 48:18bB:

וְצִדְקָתְךָ֖ כְּגַלֵּ֥י הַיָּֽם׃ 18bB and your justice like the waves of the sea,

With: 𝔐 (1) – 𝔊^SQ – 𝔖^abcde

COLON 48:19aA:

וַיְהִ֤י כַחוֹל֙ זַרְעֶ֔ךָ 19aA and your seed would have been like the sand,

With: 𝔐 (5) – 𝔊^{SQ} – S^{abcde}

COLON 48:19aB:

וְצֶאֱצָאֵ֥י מֵעֶ֖יךָ כִּמְעֹתָ֑יו 19aB and the offspring of your bowels like its grains

With: 𝔐 (2) – 𝔊^{Q} – S^{abcde}
Discussion: 𝔊^{SQ} have an extra point corresponding to 𝔐's Ṭiphḥa (No. 8) after כמעתיו.

COLON 48:19bA:

לֹֽא־יִכָּרֵ֧ת 19bA Never would be cut off

With: – 𝔊^{SQ} – S^{de}, S^{a} subordinate punctuation.
Discussion: 𝔐 has a conjunctive accent here, but the witnesses for a divider after יכרת are fairly strong. On cola with only one stressed unit, see v. 16bA above. The pair כרת || שמד always occurs in verse-line parallelism.[3]

COLON 48:19bB:

וְלֹֽא־יִשָּׁמֵ֛ד שְׁמ֖וֹ מִלְּפָנָֽי׃ 19bB nor be destroyed its name from before me.

With: 𝔐 (1), major division markers in 1Q^{a} and 4Q^{d} – 𝔊^{SQ}, major division markers in both – S^{abcde}, major division markers in S^{be}

COLON 48:20aA:

צְא֣וּ מִבָּבֶ֗ל 20aA Go forth from Babylon!

With: 𝔐 (9) – S^{bde}, S^{a} subordinate punctuation.
Discussion: 𝔐 and 𝔊 take v. 20aA and 20aB as one colon. In the only other poetical passage where the pair יצא || ברח occurs it is a case of verse-line parallelism (Job 14:2). In our opinion S deserves confidence here.

COLON 48:20aB:

בִּרְח֣וּ מִכַּשְׂדִּ֔ים 20aB Flee from the Chaldaeans!

With: 𝔐 (3) – 𝔊^{SAQ}, major division markers in 𝔊^{A} – S^{abcde}

[3] Cf. Lev. 26:30; 1 Sam. 24:21; Isa. 10:17; Ezek. 25:7; Ps. 37:38.

COLON 48:20bA:

בְּקוֹל רִנָּה הַגִּידוּ 20bA Tell this with a rejoicing voice,

With: – $\mathfrak{G}^{SQ}$ – $\mathfrak{S}^{abcde}$

Discussion: None of our ancient witnesses confirms $\mathfrak{M}$'s Revia' with רנה.

COLON 48:20bB:

הַשְׁמִיעוּ זֹאת 20bB make this be heard,

With: $\mathfrak{M}$ (5) – $\mathfrak{G}^{SQ}$ – $\mathfrak{S}^{ae}$ subordinate punctuation.

COLON 48:20bC:

הוֹצִיאוּהָ עַד־קְצֵה הָאָרֶץ 20bC let it go forth to the end of the earth,

With: $\mathfrak{M}$ (2) – $\mathfrak{G}^{Q}$ – $\mathfrak{S}^{abcde}$

COLON 48:20bD:

אִמְרוּ גָּאַל יְהוָה עַבְדּוֹ יַעֲקֹב׃ 20bD say: "The LORD redeems his servant Jacob!"

With: $\mathfrak{M}$ (1) – $\mathfrak{G}^{SBAQ}$ – $\mathfrak{S}^{abcde}$

Discussion: $\mathfrak{M}$'s Zaqeph Gadol (No. 6) with אמרו is a minor dividing accent.[4] None of the ancient witnesses has a dividing point here. See our comment on p. 31. The Masoretes dealt inconsistently with such cases; cf. the conjunctive accent with אמרו in Jer. 50:2.

COLON 48:21aA:

וְלֹא צָמְאוּ 21aA And they do not thirst

With: $\mathfrak{M}$ (7) – $\mathfrak{G}^{SQ}$

Discussion: $\mathfrak{S}$ is lacking here.

COLON 48:21aB:

בָּחֳרָבוֹת הוֹלִיכָם 21aB in the wilderness where he makes them walk,

With: $\mathfrak{M}$ (5) – $\mathfrak{G}^{Q}$ – $\mathfrak{S}^{abcde}$

COLON 48:21aC:

מַיִם מִצּוּר הִזִּיל לָמוֹ 21aC he makes water flow for them from the rock

With: $\mathfrak{M}$ (2) – $\mathfrak{G}^{SQ}$ – $\mathfrak{S}^{abcde}$

---

[4] Similar cases are Jer. 4:5; 31:10; 46:14.

COLON 48:21bA:

וַיִּבְקַע־צוּר 21bA He cleaves the rock

With: 𝔐 (5) – 𝔊[SQ]

COLON 48:21bB:

וַיָּזֻבוּ מָיִם׃ 21bB and water gushes forth.

With: 𝔐 (1) – 𝔊[SAQ], major division marker in 𝔊[A]

COLON 48:22aA:

אֵין שָׁלוֹם 22aA There is no peace,

With: 𝔐 (5) – 𝔊[Q]
Discussion: The support for 𝔐 is weak because the sentence runs on which made division seem unnecessary.

COLON 48:22aB:

אָמַר יְהוָה לָרְשָׁעִים׃ 22aB – says the LORD – for the wicked!

With: 𝔐 (1), major division markers, also in 1𝔔[a], 4𝔔[b,d] – 𝔊[SBAQ], major division markers in all – 𝔖[abcde], major division markers in all.

9.3 Isaiah 48 – Delimitation of Verse-lines

VERSE–LINE: 48:1a:

שִׁמְעוּ־זֹאת בֵּית־יַעֲקֹב	1aA	Listen to this, O house of Jacob,
הַנִּקְרָאִים בְּשֵׁם יִשְׂרָאֵל	1aB	who are called by the name of Israel,
וּמִמְּעֵי* יְהוּדָה יָצָאוּ	1aC	who have come forth from the loins of Judah;

𝔐 distinctive accents: 7 – 5 – 2.
Stresses: 2 + 3 + 3.
Verse-line parallelism: שמע || קרא; יעקב || ישׂראל || יהודה.
Discussion: The second colon is connected with the first by ellipsis.

VERSE–LINE: 48:1b:

הַנִּשְׁבָּעִים ׀ בְּשֵׁם יְהוָה	1bA	who swear by the name of the LORD,
וּבֵאלֹהֵי יִשְׂרָאֵל יַזְכִּירוּ	1bB	and invoke the God of Israel,
לֹא בֶאֱמֶת וְלֹא בִצְדָקָה׃	1bC	– (but) not in truth and not in justice,

𝔐 distinctive accents: 7 – 5 – 1.
Stresses: 3 + 3 + 4.
Verse-line parallelism: שבע || זכר; ב || ב || ב || ב; שם יהוה || אלהי ישׂראל.
Discussion: Ellipsis in the third colon.

VERSE–LINE: 48:2a:

כִּֽי־מֵעִ֤יר הַקֹּ֙דֶשׁ֙ נִקְרָ֔אוּ	2aA	although they call themselves after the holy city,
וְעַל־אֱלֹהֵ֥י יִשְׂרָאֵ֖ל נִסְמָ֑כוּ	2aB	and rely on the God of Israel,
יְהוָ֥ה צְבָא֖וֹת שְׁמֽוֹ׃	2aC	the LORD of hosts is his name.

𝔐 distinctive accents: 5 – 2 – 1.
Stresses: 3 + 3 + 3.
Verse-line parallelism: אלהי ישׂראל || יהוה צבאות; grammatical parallelism.

Discussion: On the basis of the Masoretic accents the verse might be divided into a bicolon followed by a unicolon. The major division marker in 𝔊^{Q} cannot be regarded as favouring such a division because it clearly anticipates the division after v. 2 which is attested in several other manuscripts. A tricolon is in accordance with the comparable verse-line 51:15 where a tricolon cannot be doubted.[1]

VERSE–LINE: 48:3a:

הָרִאשֹׁנוֹת֙ מֵאָ֣ז הִגַּ֔דְתִּי	3aA	The first things I have told from old,
וּמִפִּ֥י יָצְא֖וּ וְאַשְׁמִיעֵ֑ם	3aB	they went forth from my mouth and I made them heard,

𝔐 distinctive accents: 5 – 2.
Stresses: 3 + 3.
Verse-line parallelism: מן || מן; נגד || שׁמע Hiph.

VERSE–LINE: 48:3b:

פִּתְאֹ֥ם עָשִׂ֖יתִי וַתָּבֹֽאנָה׃	3bA	suddenly I acted and they came (to pass).

𝔐 distinctive accents: 1.
Stresses: 3.
Verse-line parallelism: None (unicolon).
Discussion: Because the sequence of accents 5 – 2 – 1 is often used in strophes consisting of only one verse-line, one might consider this as an alternative. We opted for a bicolon and a unicolon because of the parallelism. However, if Second Isaiah was acquainted with the concept of creation by word alone (Gen. 1),[2] this argument looses its cogency.

---

[1]See p. 518.
[2]See in this connection our remark p. 267, n.22.

VERSE–LINE: 48:4a:

מִדַּעְתִּי כִּי קָשֶׁה אָתָּה 4aA Because I know that you are obstinate,
וְגִיד בַּרְזֶל עָרְפֶּךָ 4aB and your neck is an iron sinew
וּמִצְחֲךָ נְחוּשָׁה׃ 4aC and your forehead bronze,

𝔐 distinctive accents: 2 – 5 – 1.
Stresses: 4 + 3 + 2.
Verse-line parallelism: ערף || קשה; ערף || מצח; ־ך || ־ך; ברזל || נחושה.
Discussion: The Masoretes divided v. 4 into a unicolon plus a bicolon. Because קשה and ערף always occur together, the first two cola cannot be separated. Moreover, vv. 4aB and 4aC are connected with v. 4aA by ellipsis of מדעתי כי. For these reasons a tricolon is to be preferred.

VERSE–LINE: 48:5a:

וָאַגִּיד לְךָ מֵאָז 5aA I told (them) to you from of old,
בְּטֶרֶם תָּבוֹא הִשְׁמַעְתִּיךָ 5aB before it came, I made you hear it,

𝔐 distinctive accents: 5 – 2.
Stresses: 3 + 3.
Verse-line parallelism: נגד || שמע Hiph.; ־ך || ־ך; מאז || בטרם (unique).

VERSE–LINE: 48:5b:

פֶּן־תֹּאמַר עָצְבִּי עָשָׂם 5bA lest you should say, "My grievous image did it,
וּפִסְלִי וְנִסְכִּי צִוָּם׃ 5bB my idol or my molten image commanded it".

𝔐 distinctive accents: 5 – 1.
Stresses: 3 + 3.
Verse-line parallelism: עצב || פסל; עצב || נסך; ־י || ־י; עשה || צוה; ־ם || ־ם; grammatical parallelism.

VERSE–LINE: 48:6a:

שָׁמַעְתָּ חֲזֵה כֻּלָּהּ 6aA You have heard (all this), (now) observe it all,
וְאַתֶּם הֲלוֹא תַגִּידוּ 6aB And you – would you not tell (now)?

𝔐 distinctive accents: 5 – 2.
Stresses: 3 + 3.
Verse-line parallelism: שמע || נגד.

VERSE–LINE: 48:6b:

הִשְׁמַעְתִּיךָ חֲדָשׁוֹת מֵעַתָּה 6bA From now on I make you hear new things
וּנְצֻרוֹת וְלֹא יְדַעְתָּם׃ 6bB and well-kept things which you do not know.

𝔐 distinctive accents: 5 – 1.
Stresses: 3 + 3.
Verse-line parallelism: שׁמע || ידע; חדשׁ || נצר (unique).
Discussion: Ellipsis connects the two cola.

VERSE–LINE: 48:7a:

עַתָּה נִבְרְאוּ וְלֹא מֵאָז	7aA	They are created now, not in olden times,
וְלִפְנֵי־יוֹם וְלֹא שְׁמַעְתָּם	7aB	and before today, no, you did not hear of them,

𝔐 distinctive accents: 5 – 2.
Stresses: 4 + 3.
Verse-line parallelism: עתה || יום; לא || לא.

VERSE–LINE: 48:7b:

פֶּן־תֹּאמַר הִנֵּה יְדַעְתִּין׃	7bA	lest you should say, "Behold, I knew them!"

𝔐 distinctive accents: 1.
Stresses: 3.
Verse-line parallelism: None (unicolon).
Discussion: Although a tricolon could be read here, on the basis of the Masoretic accents (5 – 2 – 1), the similarity with v. 5 shows that the Masoretes meant v. 7 to be taken as a bicolon followed by a unicolon.

VERSE–LINE: 48:8a:

גַּם לֹא־שָׁמַעְתָּ גַּם לֹא יָדַעְתָּ	8aA	No, you did not listen, no, you would not know,
גַּם מֵאָז לֹא־פִתְּחָה אָזְנֶךָ	8aB	no, from of old your ear has not been opened.

𝔐 distinctive accents: 5 – 2.
Stresses: 5 + 4.
Verse-line parallelism: שׁמע || פתח און; גם || גם.

VERSE–LINE: 48:8b:

כִּי יָדַעְתִּי בָּגוֹד תִּבְגּוֹד	8bA	For I know that you are very treacherous,
וּפֹשֵׁעַ מִבֶּטֶן קֹרָא לָךְ׃	8bB	and that you are called a transgressor from birth.

𝔐 distinctive accents: 5 – 2.
Stresses: 4 + 4.
Verse-line parallelism: בגד || פשׁע (unique).

VERSE–LINE: 48:9a:

לְמַ֤עַן שְׁמִי֙ אַאֲרִ֣יךְ אַפִּ֔י	9aA	For my name's sake I defer my anger,
וּתְהִלָּתִ֖י אֶחֱטָם־לָ֑ךְ	9aB	and (for the sake of) my praise I restrain myself with regard to you,

𝔪 distinctive accents: 5 – 2.
Stresses: 4 + 2.
Verse-line parallelism: שׁם || תהלה; ־י || ־י; ארך || חטם (unique); grammatical parallelism; rhyme.
Discussion: We assume ellipsis of למען. Although one might consider the possibility of a tricolon, the parallelism between vv. 9a and 9b argues in favour of a bicolon plus a tricolon.

VERSE–LINE: 48:9b:

לְבִלְתִּ֖י הַכְרִיתֶֽךְ׃	9bA	so as not to cut you off.

𝔪 distinctive accents: 1.
Stresses: 2.
Verse-line parallelism: None (unicolon).

VERSE–LINE: 48:10a:

הִנֵּ֥ה צְרַפְתִּ֖יךְ וְלֹ֣א בְכָ֑סֶף	10aA	Behold, I have refined you, but not like silver,
בְּחַרְתִּ֖יךְ בְּכ֥וּר עֹֽנִי׃	10aB	I have chosen you in the furnace of affliction.

𝔪 distinctive accents: 2 – 1.
Stresses: 4 + 3.
Verse-line parallelism: צרף || בחר (unique); ־ךְ (m.s.) || ־ךְ (m.s.); ב || ב; grammatical parallelism; rhyme.

VERSE–LINE: 48:11a:

לְמַעֲנִ֧י לְמַעֲנִ֛י אֶעֱשֶׂ֖ה	11aA	For my sake, for my sake only, I will do (this).
כִּ֣י אֵ֣יךְ אֵיחָ֑ל*	11aB	How could I suffer profanation?

𝔪 distinctive accents: 8 – 2.
Stresses: 3 + 3.
Verse-line parallelism: עשׂה || חלל.
Discussion: The similar built of v. 9 as well as the verse-line parallelism argue in favour of a bicolon plus a unicolon.

VERSE–LINE: 48:11b:

וּכְבוֹדִ֖י לְאַחֵ֥ר לֹא־אֶתֵּֽן׃	11bA	No, I will not give my glory to any other.

𝔪 distinctive accents: 1.
Stresses: 3.
Verse-line parallelism: None (unicolon).

VERSE–LINE: 48:12a:

שְׁמַע אֵלַי יַעֲקֹב 12aA Listen to me, O Jacob,
וְיִשְׂרָאֵל מְקֹרָאִי 12aB and Israel, whom I have called.

𝔐 distinctive accents: 5 – 2.
Stresses: 3 + 2.
Verse-line parallelism: שמע || קרא; יעקב || ישׂראל; ־י || ־י.
Discussion: The cola are connected by ellipsis.

VERSE–LINE: 48:12b:

אֲנִי־הוּא אֲנִי רִאשׁוֹן 12bA I am the same, I am the First,
אַף אֲנִי אַחֲרוֹן׃ 12bB I am also the Last.

𝔐 distinctive accents: 5 – 1.
Stresses: 3 + 3.
Verse-line parallelism: אני || אני; ראשׁון || אחרון; grammatical parallelism; rhyme.

VERSE–LINE: 48:13a:

אַף־יָדִי יָסְדָה אֶרֶץ 13aA Also it was my hand which laid the foundation of the earth,
וִימִינִי טִפְּחָה שָׁמָיִם 13aB and my right hand which spread out the heavens.

𝔐 distinctive accents: 5 – 2.
Stresses: 3 + 3.
Verse-line parallelism: יד || ימין; ־י || ־י; יסד || טפח (unique); ארץ || שׁמים; grammatical parallelism; rhyme.

VERSE–LINE: 48:13b:

קֹרֵא אֲנִי אֲלֵיהֶם 13bA When I call to them,
יַעַמְדוּ יַחְדָּו׃ 13bB they stand up together.

𝔐 distinctive accents: 8 – 1.
Stresses: 3 + 2.
Verse-line parallelism: None.

Discussion: Because the sentence is running on there is no parallelism.

VERSE–LINE: 48:14a:

הִקָּבְצוּ כֻלְּכֶם וּשֲׁמָעוּ 14aA Assemble, all of you and listen!
מִי בָהֶם הִגִּיד אֶת־אֵלֶּה 14aB Who among them was able to tell these things?

𝔐 distinctive accents: 5 – 2.

Stresses: 3 + 4.
Verse-line parallelism: שמע || נגד.

VERSE–LINE: 48:14b:

יְהוָה אֲהֵבוֹ יַעֲשֶׂה חֶפְצוֹ בְּבָבֶל	14bA	'The-LORD-loves-him' will do his will in Babylon,
וּזְרֹעוֹ כַּשְׂדִּים׃	14bB	and his arm among the Chaldeans.

𝔐 distinctive accents: 5 – 1.
Stresses: 5 + 2.
Verse-line parallelism: ־ו || ־ו; בבל || כשדים.
Discussion: Ellipsis forms a bond between the cola.

VERSE–LINE: 48:15a:

אֲנִי אֲנִי דִּבַּרְתִּי אַף־קְרָאתִיו	15aA	I, it was I who spoke, also called him,
הֲבִיאֹתִיו וְהִצְלִיחַ דַּרְכּוֹ׃	15aB	brought him, and made his way successful.

𝔐 distinctive accents: 2 – 1.
Stresses: 4 + 3.
Verse-line parallelism: דבר || בוא Hiph.; קרא || בוא; ־ו || ־ו; grammatical parallelism.

VERSE–LINE: 48:16a:

קִרְבוּ אֵלַי שִׁמְעוּ־זֹאת	16aA	Draw near to me and listen to this:
לֹא מֵרֹאשׁ בַּסֵּתֶר דִּבַּרְתִּי	16aB	from the beginning I have not spoken in secret,
מֵעֵת הֱיוֹתָהּ שָׁם אָנִי	16aC	from the time it came to be, I was there.

𝔐 distinctive accents: 7 – 5 – 2.
Stresses: 3 + 4 + 4.
Verse-line parallelism: שמע || דבר; מן || מן; ראש || עת (unique).

VERSE–LINE: 48:16b:

וְעַתָּה אֲדֹנָי יְהוִה שְׁלָחַנִי	16bA	And now the LORD God has sent me,
וְרוּחוֹ׃	16bB	and (has sent) his spirit.

𝔐 distinctive accents: 8 – 1.
Stresses: 4 + 1.
Verse-line parallelism: None (ellipsis).
Discussion: With regard to the delimitation of cola see p. 374. The cola are connected by ellipsis.[3]

---

[3]See p. 365, n. 20.

VERSE–LINE: 48:17a:

כֹּה־אָמַר יְהוָה גֹּאַלְךָ 17aA Thus says the LORD, your Redeemer,
קְדוֹשׁ יִשְׂרָאֵל 17aB the Holy One of Israel:

𝔐 distinctive accents: 8 – 2.
Stresses: 3 + 2.
Verse-line parallelism: יהוה || קדוש ישׂראל; גאל || קדוש ישׂראל.

VERSE–LINE: 48:17b:

אֲנִי יְהוָה אֱלֹהֶיךָ 17bA I am the LORD your God,
מְלַמֶּדְךָ לְהוֹעִיל 17bB who teaches you to profit,
מַדְרִיכֲךָ בְּדֶרֶךְ תֵּלֵךְ׃ 17bC who lets you go on the way you should walk.

𝔐 distinctive accents: 10 – 5 – 1.
Stresses: 3 + 2 + 3.
Verse-line parallelism: ךָ־ (m.s.) || ךָ־ (m.s.) || ךָ־ (m.s.); למד || דרך Hiph.; grammatical parallelism; rhyme.
Discussion: Ellipsis connects the last two cola with the first one.

VERSE–LINE: 48:18a:

לוּא הִקְשַׁבְתָּ לְמִצְוֺתָי 18aA O that you had listened to my commandments!

𝔐 distinctive accents: 2.
Stresses: 3.
Verse-line parallelism: None (unicolon).
Discussion: The parallelism in vv. 18bA-B favours 𝔐's division.

VERSE–LINE: 48:18b:

וַיְהִי כַנָּהָר שְׁלוֹמֶךָ 18bA Then your peace would have been like a river,
וְצִדְקָתְךָ כְּגַלֵּי הַיָּם׃ 18bB and your justice like the waves of the sea,

𝔐 distinctive accents: 5 – 1.
Stresses: 3 + 3.
Verse-line parallelism: כ || כ; נהר || גל; נהר || ים; שׁלום || צדקה; ךָ־ (m.s.) || ךָ־ (m.s.); rhyme.

VERSE–LINE: 48:19a:

וַיְהִי כַחוֹל זַרְעֶךָ 19aA and your seed would have been like the sand,
וְצֶאֱצָאֵי מֵעֶיךָ כִּמְעֹתָיו 19aB and the offspring of your bowels like its grains

𝔐 distinctive accents: 5 – 2.

Stresses: 3 + 3.
Verse-line parallelism: כ || כ; חול || מעה (unique); זרע || צאצא; ךָ־ (m.s.) || ךָ־ (m.s.); rhyme.
Discussion: Again ellipsis forms an extra link between the cola.

VERSE–LINE: 48:19b:

לֹא־יִכָּרֵת	19bA	Never would be cut off
וְלֹא־יִשָּׁמֵד שְׁמוֹ מִלְּפָנָי׃	19bB	nor be destroyed its name from before me.

𝔐 distinctive accents: conjunctive accent – 1.
Stresses: 1 + 3.
Verse-line parallelism: לא || לא; כרת || שׁמד; grammatical parallelism; rhyme.

Discussion: For the colometry see p. 376. Actually this is a case of ellipsis in the first colon of a bicolon.[4]

VERSE–LINE: 48:20a:

צְאוּ מִבָּבֶל	20aA	Go forth from Babylon!
בִּרְחוּ מִכַּשְׂדִּים	20aB	Flee from the Chaldaeans!

𝔐 distinctive accents: 9 – 3.
Stresses: 2 + 2.
Verse-line parallelism: יצא || ברח; מן || מן; בבל || כשׂדים; grammatical parallelism; rhyme.

VERSE–LINE: 48:20b:

בְּקוֹל רִנָּה הַגִּידוּ	20bA	Tell this with a rejoicing voice,
הַשְׁמִיעוּ זֹאת	20bB	make this be heard,
הוֹצִיאוּהָ עַד־קְצֵה הָאָרֶץ	20bC	let it go forth to the end of the earth,
אִמְרוּ גָּאַל יְהוָה עַבְדּוֹ יַעֲקֹב׃	20bD	say: "The LORD redeems his servant Jacob!"

𝔐 distinctive accents: conjunctive accent – 5 – 2 – 1.
Stresses: 3 + 2 + 3 + 5.
Verse-line parallelism: נגד || שׁמע Hiph. || יצא Hiph. || אמר; זאת || ה־; grammatical parallelism.

Discussion: The delimitation of the verse is based on our delimitation of cola (see pp. 376-7). The series of imperatives in parallelism

[4]For some Ugaritic examples of this phenomenon see J.C. de Moor, "Syntax Peculiar to Ugaritic Poetry", in: J.C. de Moor, W.G.E. Watson (eds.), *Verse in Ancient Near Eastern Prose* (AOAT, 42), Neukirchen 1993, 191-205 (201).

strongly suggests a quadrocolon. Furthermore, Jer. 4:5 offers a similar pattern.

VERSE–LINE: 48:21a:

וְלֹא צָמְאוּ	21aA	And they do not thirst
בָּחֳרָבוֹת הוֹלִיכָם	21aB	in the wilderness where he makes them walk,
מַיִם מִצּוּר הִזִּיל לָמוֹ	21aC	he makes water flow for them from the rock.

𝔐 distinctive accents: 7 – 5 – 2.
Stresses: 2 + 2 + 4.
Verse-line parallelism: צמא || מים; ־ם || ־מו; grammatical parallelism.
Discussion: Possibly 𝔐 took v. 21aA-B as one colon (see the colometrical analysis), but the accentual pattern 7 – 5 – 2 is common with tricola.

VERSE–LINE: 48:21b:

וַיִּבְקַע־צוּר	21bA	He cleaves the rock
וַיָּזֻבוּ מָיִם׃	21bB	and water gushes forth.

𝔐 distinctive accents: 5 – 1.
Stresses: 1 + 2.
Verse-line parallelism: צור || מים.[5]

VERSE–LINE: 48:22a:

אֵין שָׁלוֹם	22aA	There is no peace,
אָמַר יְהוָה לָרְשָׁעִים׃	22aB	– says the LORD – for the wicked!

𝔐 distinctive accents: 5 – 1.
Stresses: 2 + 3.
Verse-line parallelism: שלום || רשע (antithetical).

[5] Although the words are not semantically related they have become a well-known word-pair in the Old Testament. See the colon parallelism in Ps. 78:20; 105:41; 114:8, and compare Ps. 78:15-16. Cf. Exod. 17:6; Num 20:8, 10, 11; Deut. 8:15; Neh. 9:15.

9.4 Isaiah 48 – Delimitation of Strophes

STROPHE A.i.1 (Isa. 48:1)

שִׁמְעוּ־זֹאת בֵּית־יַעֲקֹב	1aA	Listen to this, O house of Jacob,
הַנִּקְרָאִים בְּשֵׁם יִשְׂרָאֵל	1aB	who are called by the name of Israel,
וּמִמְּעֵי* יְהוּדָה יָצָאוּ	1aC	who have come forth from the loins of Judah;
הַנִּשְׁבָּעִים ׀ בְּשֵׁם יְהוָה	1bA	who swear by the name of the LORD,
וּבֵאלֹהֵי יִשְׂרָאֵל יַזְכִּירוּ	1bB	and invoke the God of Israel,
לֹא בֶאֱמֶת וְלֹא בִצְדָקָה׃	1bC	– (but) not in truth and not in justice,

= Masoretic verse.
Separation ↑: major division markers in the textual tradition; demonstrative pronoun; imperative(s); vocative; swapping (adjunct).
Separation ↓: swapping (adjunct).
Strophe parallelism: ב || ב; שם || שם; ישראל || יהוה; קרא בשם || זכר; grammatical parallelism.

STROPHE A.i.2 (Isa. 48:2)

כִּי־מֵעִיר הַקֹּדֶשׁ נִקְרָאוּ	2aA	although they call themselves after the holy city,
וְעַל־אֱלֹהֵי יִשְׂרָאֵל נִסְמָכוּ	2aB	and rely on the God of Israel,
יְהוָה צְבָאוֹת שְׁמוֹ׃	2aC	LORD of hosts is his name.

= Masoretic verse.
Separation ↑: deictic particle(s); swapping (adjunct).
Separation ↓: major division markers in the textual tradition.
Strophe parallelism: None (one verse-line).

STROPHE A.ii.1 (Isa. 48:3)

הָרִאשֹׁנוֹת מֵאָז הִגַּדְתִּי	3aA	The first things I have told from old,
וּמִפִּי יָצְאוּ וְאַשְׁמִיעֵם	3aB	they went forth from my mouth and I made them heard,
פִּתְאֹם עָשִׂיתִי וַתָּבֹאנָה׃	3bA	suddenly I acted and they came (to pass).

= Masoretic verse.
Separation ↑: major division markers in the textual tradition; swapping (object); swapping (adjunct).
Separation ↓: major division markers in the textual tradition; swapping (adjunct).
Strophe parallelism: ראשון || בוא; יצא מפה || עשה; grammatical parallelism.
Discussion: The necessity to keep these verse-lines together follows also from a comparison with 42:9; 44:7.

STROPHE A.ii.2 (Isa. 48:4)

מִדַּעְתִּי כִּי קָשֶׁה אָתָּה	4aA	Because I know that you are obstinate,
וְגִיד בַּרְזֶל עָרְפֶּךָ	4aB	and your neck is an iron sinew
וּמִצְחֲךָ נְחוּשָׁה׃	4aC	and your forehead bronze,

= Masoretic verse.
Separation ↑: major division markers in the textual tradition; deictic particle(s); repetitive verse-line parallelism; swapping (subject).
Separation ↓: None (one verse-line).
Strophe parallelism: None (one verse-line).

STROPHE A.ii.3 (Isa. 48:5)

וָאַגִּיד לְךָ מֵאָז	5aA	I told (them) to you from of old,
בְּטֶרֶם תָּבוֹא הִשְׁמַעְתִּיךָ	5aB	before it came, I made you hear it,
פֶּן־תֹּאמַר עָצְבִּי עָשָׂם	5bA	lest you should say, “My grievous image did it,
וּפִסְלִי וְנִסְכִּי צִוָּם׃	5bB	my idol or my molten image commanded it”.

= Masoretic verse.
Separation ↑: repetitive verse-line parallelism; swapping (adjunct).
Separation ↓: major division markers in the textual tradition; deictic particle(s); marker of direct speech; repetitive verse-line parallelism; swapping (subject).
Strophe parallelism: נגד || אמר.

STROPHE A.iii.1 (Isa. 48:6)

שָׁמַעְתָּ חֲזֵה כֻּלָּהּ	6aA	You have heard (all this), (now) observe it all,
וְאַתֶּם הֲלוֹא תַגִּידוּ	6aB	And you – would you not tell (now)?
הִשְׁמַעְתִּיךָ חֲדָשׁוֹת מֵעַתָּה	6bA	From now on I make you hear new things
וּנְצֻרוֹת וְלֹא יְדַעְתָּם׃	6bB	and well-kept things which you do not know.

= Masoretic verse.
Separation ↑: major division markers in the textual tradition; deictic particle(s); independent pers. pronoun; imperative(s); swapping (subject).
Separation ↓: None.
Strophe parallelism: שמע || שמע; הלוא || לא; נגד || ידע.

STROPHE A.iii.2 (Isa. 48:7)

עַתָּה נִבְרְאוּ וְלֹא מֵאָז	7aA	They are created now, not in olden times,
וְלִפְנֵי־יוֹם וְלֹא שְׁמַעְתָּם	7aB	and before today, no, you did not hear of them,
פֶּן־תֹּאמַר הִנֵּה יְדַעְתִּין׃	7bA	lest you should say, “Behold, I knew them!”

= Masoretic verse.

Separation ↑: deictic particle(s); repetitive verse-line parallelism.
Separation ↓: major division markers in the textual tradition; deictic particle(s); marker of direct speech.
Strophe parallelism: שׁמע || ידע.

STROPHE A.iii.3 (Isa. 48:8)

גַּם לֹא־שָׁמַעְתָּ גַּם לֹא יָדַעְתָּ	8aA	No, you did not listen, no, you would not know,
גַּם מֵאָז לֹא־פִתְּחָה אָזְנֶךָ	8aB	no, from of old your ear has not been opened.
כִּי יָדַעְתִּי בָּגוֹד תִּבְגּוֹד	8bA	For I know that you are very treacherous,
וּפֹשֵׁעַ מִבֶּטֶן קֹרָא לָךְ׃	8bB	and that you are called a transgressor from birth.

= Masoretic verse.
Separation ↑: major division markers in the textual tradition; deictic particle(s); repetitive verse-line parallelism.
Separation ↓: deictic particle(s); paronomasia; swapping (object); swapping (adjunct).
Strophe parallelism: שׁמע || קרא; ידע || ידע; ־ךָ (m.s.) || ־ךָ (m.s.).

STROPHE A.iv.1 (Isa. 48:9)

לְמַעַן שְׁמִי אַאֲרִיךְ אַפִּי	9aA	For my name's sake I defer my anger,
וּתְהִלָּתִי אֶחֱטָם־לָךְ	9aB	and (for the sake of) my praise I restrain myself with regard to you,
לְבִלְתִּי הַכְרִיתֶךָ׃	9bA	so as not to cut you off.

= Masoretic verse.
Separation ↑: repetitive verse-line parallelism; swapping (adjunct).
Separation ↓: major division markers in the textual tradition.
Strophe parallelism: ל || ל; ־ךָ (m.s.) || ־ךָ (m.s.).

STROPHE A.iv.2 (Isa. 48:10)

הִנֵּה צְרַפְתִּיךָ וְלֹא בְכָסֶף	10aA	Behold, I have refined you, but not like silver,
בְּחַרְתִּיךָ בְּכוּר עֹנִי׃	10aB	I have chosen you in the furnace of affliction.

= Masoretic verse.
Separation ↑: major division markers in the textual tradition; deictic particle(s); repetitive verse-line parallelism.
Separation ↓: None (one verse-line).
Strophe parallelism: None (one verse-line).

STROPHE A.iv.3 (Isa. 48:11)

לְמַעֲנִי לְמַעֲנִי אֶעֱשֶׂה	11aA	For my sake, for my sake only, I will do (this).

כִּי אֵיךְ אֵיחָל*	11aB	How could I suffer profanation?
וּכְבוֹדִי לְאַחֵר לֹא־אֶתֵּן׃	11bA	No, I will not give my glory to any other.

= Masoretic verse.
Separation ↑: deictic particle(s); paronomasia.
Separation ↓: major division markers in the textual tradition; swapping (object); swapping (adjunct).
Strophe parallelism: ל || ל; ־י || ־י; עשה || נתן; grammatical parallelism.

STROPHE B.i.1 (Isa. 48:12)

שְׁמַע אֵלַי יַעֲקֹב	12aA	Listen to me, O Jacob,
וְיִשְׂרָאֵל מְקֹרָאִי	12aB	and Israel, whom I have called.
אֲנִי־הוּא אֲנִי רִאשׁוֹן	12bA	I am the same, I am the First,
אַף אֲנִי אַחֲרוֹן׃	12bB	I am also the Last.

= Masoretic verse.
Separation ↑: major division markers in the textual tradition; imperative(s); vocatives; repetitive verse-line parallelism.
Separation ↓: deictic particle(s); independent pers. pronouns; repetitive verse-line parallelism.
Strophe parallelism: None.

STROPHE B.i.2 (Isa. 48:13)

אַף־יָדִי יָסְדָה אֶרֶץ	13aA	Also it was my hand which laid the foundation of the earth,
וִימִינִי טִפְּחָה שָׁמָיִם	13aB	and my right hand which spread out the heavens.
קֹרֵא אֲנִי אֲלֵיהֶם	13bA	When I call to them,
יַעַמְדוּ יַחְדָּו׃	13bB	they stand up together.

= Masoretic verse.
Separation ↑: deictic particle(s); swapping (subject).
Separation ↓: major division markers in the textual tradition; independent pers. pronoun.
Strophe parallelism: None.

STROPHE B.i.3 (Isa. 48:14a)

הִקָּבְצוּ כֻלְּכֶם וּשְׁמָעוּ	14aA	Assemble, all of you and listen!
מִי בָהֶם הִגִּיד אֶת־אֵלֶּה	14aB	Who among them was able to tell these things?

= Masoretic verse.
Separation ↑: major division markers in the textual tradition; demonstrative pronoun; interrogative pronoun; imperative(s); vocative.

Separation ↓: major division markers in the textual tradition.
Strophe parallelism: None (one verse-line).

STROPHE B.ii.1 (Isa. 48:14b)

יְהוָה אֲהֵבוֹ יַעֲשֶׂה חֶפְצוֹ בְּבָבֶל	14bA	'The-LORD-loves-him' will do his will in Babylon,
וּזְרֹעוֹ כַּשְׂדִּים׃	14bB	and his arm among the Chaldeans.

= Masoretic verse.
Separation ↑: major division markers in the textual tradition; swapping (subject).
Separation ↓: None (one verse-line).
Strophe parallelism: None (one verse-line).

STROPHE B.ii.2 (Isa. 48:15)

אֲנִי אֲנִי דִּבַּרְתִּי אַף־קְרָאתִיו	15aA	I, it was I who spoke, also called him,
הֲבִיאֹתִיו וְהִצְלִיחַ דַּרְכּוֹ׃	15aB	brought him, and made his way successful.

= Masoretic verse.
Separation ↑: deictic particle(s); independent pers. pronoun; repetitive verse-line parallelism.
Separation ↓: major division markers in the textual tradition.
Strophe parallelism: None (one verse-line).

STROPHE B.ii.3 (Isa. 48:16)

קִרְבוּ אֵלַי שִׁמְעוּ־זֹאת	16aA	Draw near to me and listen to this:
לֹא מֵרֹאשׁ בַּסֵּתֶר דִּבַּרְתִּי	16aB	from the beginning I have not spoken in secret,
מֵעֵת הֱיוֹתָהּ שָׁם אָנִי	16aC	from the time it came to be, I was there.
וְעַתָּה אֲדֹנָי יְהוִה שְׁלָחַנִי	16bA	And now the Lord GOD has sent me,
וְרוּחוֹ׃	16bB	and (has sent) his spirit.

= Masoretic verse.
Separation ↑: major division markers in the textual tradition; demonstrative pronoun; independent pers. pronoun; imperative(s); swapping (adjunct).
Separation ↓: major division markers in the textual tradition; deictic particle(s); swapping (subject).
Strophe parallelism: דבר || שלח; עת || עתה (unique).

STROPHE B.iii.1 (Isa. 48:17)

כֹּה־אָמַר יְהוָה גֹּאַלְךָ	17aA	Thus says the LORD, your Redeemer,
קְדוֹשׁ יִשְׂרָאֵל	17aB	the Holy One of Israel:

אֲנִי יְהוָה אֱלֹהֶיךָ	17bA	I am the LORD your God,
מְלַמֶּדְךָ לְהוֹעִיל	17bB	who teaches you to profit,

= Masoretic verse.
Separation ↑: major division markers in the textual tradition; deictic particle(s); marker of direct speech.
Separation ↓: independent pers. pronoun; repetitive verse-line parallelism.
Strophe parallelism: ךָ־ (m.s.) || ךָ־ (m.s.); יהוה || יהוה.

STROPHE B.iii.2 (Isa. 48:18)

לוּא הִקְשַׁבְתָּ לְמִצְוֹתָי	18aA	O that you had listened to my commandments!
וַיְהִי כַנָּהָר שְׁלוֹמֶךָ	18bA	Then your peace would have been like a river,
וְצִדְקָתְךָ כְּגַלֵּי הַיָּם׃	18bB	and your justice like the waves of the sea,

= Masoretic verse.
Separation ↑: deictic particle(s); precative perfect; repetitive verse-line parallelism; swapping (adjunct).
Separation ↓: repetitive verse-line parallelism; swapping (adjunct).
Strophe parallelism: מצוה || צדקה.

STROPHE B.iii.3 (Isa. 48:19)

וַיְהִי כַחוֹל זַרְעֶךָ	19aA	and your seed would have been like the sand,
וְצֶאֱצָאֵי מֵעֶיךָ כִּמְעֹתָיו	19aB	and the offspring of your bowels like its grains
לֹא־יִכָּרֵת	19bA	Never would be cut off
וְלֹא־יִשָּׁמֵד שְׁמוֹ מִלְּפָנָי׃	19bB	nor be destroyed your name from before me.

= Masoretic verse.
Separation ↑: repetitive verse-line parallelism; swapping (adjunct).
Separation ↓: major division markers in the textual tradition; repetitive verse-line parallelism.
Strophe parallelism: זרע || שם.

STROPHE B.iv.1 (Isa. 48:20)

צְאוּ מִבָּבֶל	20aA	Go forth from Babylon!
בִּרְחוּ מִכַּשְׂדִּים	20aB	Flee from the Chaldaeans!
בְּקוֹל רִנָּה הַגִּידוּ	20bA	Tell this with a rejoicing voice,
הַשְׁמִיעוּ זֹאת	20bB	make this be heard,
הוֹצִיאוּהָ עַד־קְצֵה הָאָרֶץ	20bC	let it go forth to the end of the earth,
אִמְרוּ גָּאַל יְהוָה עַבְדּוֹ יַעֲקֹב׃	20bD	say: "The LORD redeems his servant Jacob!"

= Masoretic verse.

Separation ↑: major division markers in the textual tradition; imperative(s); repetitive verse-line parallelism.
Separation ↓: demonstrative pronoun; imperative(s); marker of direct speech; swapping (adjunct).
Strophe parallelism: יצא || יצא; grammatical parallelism.

STROPHE B.iv.2 (Isa. 48:21)

וְלֹא צָמְאוּ	21aA	And they do not thirst
בָּחֳרָבוֹת הוֹלִיכָם	21aB	in the wilderness where he makes them walk,
מַיִם מִצּוּר הִזִּיל לָמוֹ	21aC	he makes water flow for them from the rock
וַיִּבְקַע־צוּר	21bA	He cleaves the rock
וַיָּזֻבוּ מָיִם׃	21bB	and water gushes forth.

= Masoretic verse.
Separation ↑: swapping (object); swapping (adjunct).
Separation ↓: major division markers in the textual tradition; repetitive verse-line parallelism.
Strophe parallelism: מים || מים; צור || צור.

STROPHE B.iv.3 (Isa. 48:22)

אֵין שָׁלוֹם	22aA	There is no peace,
אָמַר יְהוָה לָרְשָׁעִים׃	22aB	– says the LORD – for the wicked!

= Masoretic verse.
Separation ↑: major division markers in the textual tradition.
Separation ↓: major division markers in the textual tradition; marker of direct speech.
Strophe parallelism: None.

9.5 Isaiah 48 – Delimitation of Canticles

CANTICLE A.i (48:1–2)

Separation ↑: major division markers in the textual tradition; thematic discontinuity; change of subject.
Separation ↓: major division markers in the textual tradition.
Canticle parallelism: קרא || קרא (responsion); שם || שם (inclusion /responsion); אלהי ישראל || אלהי ישראל (concatenation); יהוה || יהוה (concatenation).
The strophes are linked by an on-running sentence (enjambment).
Thematic unity: yes. In both strophes Israel is accused of insincerity.
Discussion: The Seder mark which all Tiberian Masoretic manuscripts

put after v. 1 was probably intended to mark the beginning of the canto because it now stands in the middle of a sentence. The Petuḥa in 𝔊^Q after v. 2aB indicates the well-attested break after v. 2aC in a proleptic way.

CANTICLE A.ii (48:3–5)

Separation ↑: major division markers in the textual tradition; thematic discontinuity; change of subject.
Separation ↓: major division markers in the textual tradition.
Canticle parallelism: מן || מן (responsion); אז || אז (responsion); נגד || נגד (responsion); שמע || שמע (responsion); עשׂה || עשׂה (responsion); בוא || בוא (inclusion).
The strophes 2 and 3 are linked by an on-running sentence (enjambment).
Thematic unity: yes. All three strophes emphasize that God made his plans known to Israel because he knew how obstinate they were. There is a certain irony in the way the middle strophe describes them as made of metal, as if they were similar to their idols.
Discussion: We interpret the division markers in 𝔊^SA after v. 3bA as markers of the end of the strophe. The markers in 𝔊^AQ after v. 5aB can only be explained as anticipating the same division 𝔊^S has after v. 5bB. 𝔊^Q also marks this incision belatedly (and redundantly) after v. 6aA. In both cases 𝔊^Q does not indicate the break *prima manu*, but by a paragraphos in the margin.

CANTICLE A.iii (48:6–8)

Separation ↑: major division markers in the textual tradition.
Separation ↓: None.
Canticle parallelism: שמע || שמע || שמע (responsion/concatenation); נגד || אמר (inclusion); מן || מן || מן (concatenation/responsion/inclusion); עתה || עתה || אז || אז (concatenation/inclusion); לא || לא || לא (concatenation/responsion); ידע || ידע || ידע (responsion).
Thematic unity: yes. All three strophes denounce Israel's failure to listen and learn, both in past and present.
Discussion: This is one of the very rare occasions where we assume a canticle end without having any support from tradition. The very strong canticle parallelism between vv. 6-8 on the one hand, and vv. 9-11 on the other, emboldens us to assume that the major division markers which are found in 1Q^a and 𝔊^SQ after v. 9 have shifted place accidentally.

CANTICLE A.iv (48:9–11)

Separation ↑: None.
Separation ↓: major division markers in the textual tradition.
Canticle parallelism: למען || למען (responsion); ־י || ־י (responsion /inclusion); שׁם || כבוד (inclusion); תהלה || כבוד (inclusion); ־ך (m.s.) || ־ך (m.s.) (responsion/concatenation).
Thematic unity: yes. All three strophes explain why God did not destroy sinful Israel but chose to chasten it by affliction.
Discussion: With regard to the upper delimitation of this canticle, see our comment on the previous one.

CANTICLE B. i (48:12–14)

Separation ↑: major division markers in the textual tradition.
Separation ↓: major division markers in the textual tradition.
Canticle parallelism: שׁמע || שׁמע (inclusion); קרא || קרא (inclusion); אני || אני (responsion); אף || אף (concatenation); עמד || קבץ (concatenation).
Thematic unity: yes. The Creator of the universe is able to summon all powers in heaven and on earth to testify for him whereas the idols have nothing to tell.
Discussion: With no less than three major division markers $\mathfrak{G}^A$ seems uncertain about the point where to insert them. It seems to us that the division after v. 14 which is also attested in $\mathfrak{G}^S$ must be preferred.

CANTICLE B.ii (48:14–16)

Separation ↑: major division markers in the textual tradition; thematic discontinuity; change of subject.
Separation ↓: major division markers in the textual tradition.
Canticle parallelism: יהוה || יהוה (inclusion); עשׂה || בוא (responsion); אני || אני (responsion); דבר || דבר (responsion).
Thematic unity: partially. The connection between vv. 14-15 is clear enough: Cyrus' mission is the will of God. But a link with v. 16 is not immediately apparent, unless it was the prophet's intention to say that it was his personal mission to announce the arrival of Cyrus as a new act of God in history.
Discussion: The same problematic transition between vv. 15 and 16 may have been a reason for $\mathfrak{G}^S$ to assume a break at this point. $\mathfrak{G}^A$ is lagging behind with a break after זאת. Nearly all ancient witnesses agree with regard to the break after v. 16.

CANTICLE B.iii (48:17–19)

Separation ↑: major division markers in the textual tradition; thematic discontinuity; change of subject.
Separation ↓: major division markers in the textual tradition.
Canticle parallelism: ־ך || ־ך || ־ך (responsion/inclusion/concatenation); ־י || ־ני (inclusion); ים || חול (concatenation).
The strophes 2 and 3 are linked by an on-running sentence (enjambment).
Thematic unity: yes. It would have been of great profit if Israel would have listened to the teaching of the LORD.
Discussion: The lower boundary is abundantly attested. $\mathfrak{G}^{A}$ is apparently lagging behind with its marking after v. 20aB.

CANTICLE B.iv (48:20–22)

Separation ↑: major division markers in the textual tradition; thematic discontinuity; change of subject.
Separation ↓: major division markers in the textual tradition.
Canticle parallelism: אמר || אמר (responsion); יהוה || יהוה (responsion).
Thematic unity: partial. Although parallelism is lacking between vv. 20 and 21, the theme uniting the two strophes is obviously the new Exodus, this time from Babel. In our opinion also v. 22 is not a strange appendix, although it may seem that at first sight. We will deal with this problem when discussing the macrostructure of Ch. 48.
Discussion: For the division markers in $\mathfrak{G}^{A}$ after v. 20aB see our discussion of the previous canticle. $\mathfrak{G}^{A}$'s Setuma after v. 21b is an indication that it too felt the need to isolate this seemingly strange verse.

9.6 Isaiah 48 – Delimitation of Macrostructure

The overall structure of Isaiah 48 appears to be fairly regular,

SUB-CANTOS	CANTICLES	STROPHES
A	4	11 (2+3+3+3)
B	4	12 (3+3+3+3)

The division into two sub-cantos was made already in Antiquity: no demarcation line in Ch. 48 is attested so well as that between vv. 11 and 12. The almost identical opening lines suggested this dichotomy: "Listen to this, O house of Jacob / who are called by the name of Israel" (48:1aA-B), "Listen to me, O Jacob, / and Israel, whom I have called" (48:12aA-B). Also other keywords like קרא (1aB, 2aA, 8bB,

12aB, 13bA, 15aA), נגד (3aA, 5aA, 6aB, 14aB, 20bA)), שמע (1aA, 3aB, 5aB, 6aA, 6bA, 7aB, 8aA, 12aA, 14aA, 16aA, 20bB), צדקה (1bC, 18bB) and כרת (9bA, 19bA) connect the two sub-cantos.

Sub-canto A mainly contains accusations addressed to Israel, explaining why it had to be punished and why God did not destroy his people totally. Sub-canto B describes how God will use Cyrus to redeem his people – if they listen to the words of the LORD's messenger and keep his commandments.

Other distant parallelism connecting the canticles of **sub-canto A**: שם יהוה (v. 1aB – A.i), יהוה צבאות שמו (v. 2aC – A.i) || למען שמי (v. 9aA – A.iv); ראשונות (v. 3aA – A.ii) || חדשות (v. 6bA); מאז (v. 3aA, 5aA – A.ii) || מאז (v. 7aA, 8aB – A.iii); ידע (v. 4aA – A.ii) || ידע (vv. 6bB, 7bA, 8aA – A.iii). ברזל, נחושה (vv. 4aB, 4aC – A.ii) || כסף (v. 10aA – A.iv).

Other distant parallelism connecting the canticles of **sub-canto B**: יעקב (v. 12aA – B.i) || יעקב (v. 20bD – B.iv); ישראל (v. 12aB – B.i) || ישראל (v.17aB – B.iii); יד (v. 13aA – B.i) || זרוע (v. 14bB – B.ii); בבל, כשדים (v. 14bA-B – B.ii) || בבל, כשדים (v. 20aA-B – B.iv); דרך (v. 15aB – B.ii) || דרך (v. 17bC – B.iii); גאל (v. 17aA – B.iii) || גאל (v. 20bD – B.iv); שלום (v. 18bA – B.iii) || שלום (v. 22aB – B.iv); נהר (v. 18bA – B.iii) || מים (v. 21aC – B.iv).

Isa. 48:22 is often seen as one of the latest additions to the book, an attempt to restrict the message of peace (v. 18) to pious Jews which would also be traceable in Isa. 57:21 and 66:24.[1] In our opinion the latter text has little to do with the former two passages. If we look at Isa. 57:21, it would seem fairly certain that it is taken from Second Isaiah. The replacement of יהוה by אלהי and especially fact that Isa. 57:19-20 practically invited to insert a reference to Isa. 48:22 argue in favour of the priority of the latter.

It should not be glossed over that the peace promised in v. 18 is conditional and retrospective. Therefore v. 22 can hardly be seen as a reduction of what was stated in v. 18. In fact, the whole chapter deals with the problem that Israel refused to listen to the LORD's warnings in the past and should not make the same mistake now with regard to Second Isaiah's message of salvation. Apparently there were Israelites who did not believe him – as we have seen, Second Isaiah addresses this group again and again. The obvious allusion to the incident at

[1]So lately again U. Berges, *Das Buch Jesaja: Komposition und Endgestalt*, Freiburg 1998, 39, 276, 320, 333. Among recent scholars who maintain the authenticity of 48:22 are Melugin, 142; Beuken, 304 (with reservations); Koole, 456; Knight, 124; Franke, 240; Oswalt, 280.

Meribah in 48:21 (cf. Exod. 17:1-7; Num. 20:1-13) renders a warning about Israel's rebellion in 48:22 not so anomalous as it may seem at first. Several times we have observed by now that Second Isaiah loves to return to his point of departure at the end of a canto. In this case the canto starts with an accusation of Israel for its unfaithfulness which is further described as stiffening the neck (48:4), terminology used to describe the rebellion at Meribah (cf. Ps. 95:8; Neh. 9:15-16) which was seen as exemplary of Israel's later sins. Therefore it is not unthinkable that 48:22 links up with the beginning of the canto. From the viewpoint of structure it is strange that the first canticle counts only two strophes, whereas all others have three. Perhaps a further strophe (A.i.3) describing Israel's sins in greater detail in the manner of Jer. 6-8 or Mic. 3, denouncing its false reliance on peace for the holy city, may have been omitted later on because it was deemed too offensive. If that were the case, a reminder at the end of the canto would not be inappropriate.

Chapter 10

The Structure of Isaiah 49

10.1 Isaiah 49: Text and Translation

ס<פ> – 1𝔔^{ab} – 4𝔔^{d} – 𝔊^{SBAQ} – 𝔖^{abcde} ______________________

A.i.1 (Isa. 49:1)

שִׁמְעוּ אִיִּים אֵלַי	1aA	Listen to me, you islands,
וְהַקְשִׁיבוּ לְאֻמִּים מֵרָחוֹק	1aB	and pay attention, you nations from afar:
יְהוָה מִבֶּטֶן קְרָאָנִי	1bA	The LORD called me from the womb,
מִמְּעֵי אִמִּי הִזְכִּיר שְׁמִי׃	1bB	from the loins of my mother He mentioned my name.

A.i.2 (Isa. 49:2)

וַיָּשֶׂם פִּי כְּחֶרֶב חַדָּה	2aA	And he made my mouth like a sharpened sword,
בְּצֵל יָדוֹ הֶחְבִּיאָנִי	2aB	in the shadow of his hand he hid me.
וַיְשִׂימֵנִי לְחֵץ בָּרוּר	2bA	He made me into a polished arrow,
בְּאַשְׁפָּתוֹ הִסְתִּירָנִי׃	2bB	in his quiver he concealed me.

A.i.3 (Isa. 49:3)

וַיֹּאמֶר לִי עַבְדִּי־אָתָּה	3aA	And he said to me, You are my servant,
יִשְׂרָאֵל אֲשֶׁר־בְּךָ אֶתְפָּאָר׃	3aB	Israel, in whom I will glorify myself.

{<פ>𝔊^{A}}

A.i.4 (Isa. 49:4)

וַאֲנִי אָמַרְתִּי לְרִיק יָגַעְתִּי	4aA	But I said, For nothing I wearied myself,
לְתֹהוּ וְהֶבֶל כֹּחִי כִלֵּיתִי	4aB	for voidness and vanity I have spent my strength.
אָכֵן מִשְׁפָּטִי אֶת־יְהוָה	4bA	Yet my right is with the LORD,
וּפְעֻלָּתִי אֶת־אֱלֹהָי׃	4bB	and my recompense with my God.

<ס> – 1𝔔^{a} – 𝔊^{SA} – 𝔖^{abe} ....

A.ii.1 (Isa. 49:5)

וְעַתָּה ׀ אָמַר יְהוָה	5aA	But now, the LORD says –
יֹצְרִי מִבֶּטֶן לְעֶבֶד לוֹ	5aB	he who formed me from the womb to be his servant,
לְשׁוֹבֵב יַעֲקֹב אֵלָיו	5aC	to make Jacob return to him,
{𝔖^{b}} וְיִשְׂרָאֵל לוֹ* יֵאָסֵף	5aD	and Israel that must be gathered to him[1]
וְאֶכָּבֵד בְּעֵינֵי יְהוָה	5bA	– for I am honoured in the LORD's eyes,
וֵאלֹהַי הָיָה עֻזִּי׃	5bB	and my God is[2] my strength –

[1]With 1𝔔^{a}, the Qere and some ancient versions.

[2]For the frequent alternation of the normal imperfect with perfect and/or in-

A.ii.2 (Isa. 49:6)

וַיֹּאמֶר נָקֵל מִהְיוֹתְךָ לִי עֶבֶד	6aA	now he says, It is too little that you should be a servant for me,
לְהָקִים אֶת־שִׁבְטֵי יַעֲקֹב	6aB	to restore the tribes of Jacob,
וּנְצוּרֵי* יִשְׂרָאֵל לְהָשִׁיב {$\mathfrak{G}^{A}$}	6aC	and to bring back the well-kept[3] of Israel.
וּנְתַתִּיךָ לְאוֹר גּוֹיִם	6bA	I will also make you a light to the nations,
לִהְיוֹת יְשׁוּעָתִי עַד־קְצֵה הָאָרֶץ׃	6bB	to be my salvation to the ends of the earth.

ס <פ> – $_1\mathfrak{Q}^{ab}$ – $_4\mathfrak{Q}^{d}$ – $\mathfrak{G}^{SBA}$ – $\mathfrak{S}^{bcde}$ ______________________________

B.i.1 (Isa. 49:7a–b)

כֹּה אָמַר־יְהוָה	7aA	Thus says the LORD,
גֹּאֵל יִשְׂרָאֵל קְדוֹשׁוֹ	7aB	the Redeemer of Israel, his Holy One,
לִבְזֶה*־נֶפֶשׁ לִמְתָעֵב* גּוֹי לְעֶבֶד מֹשְׁלִים	7bA	to the one whose life was despised,[4] whose nation was detested,[5] to the servant of rulers,

B.i.2 (Isa. 49:7c–d)

מְלָכִים יִרְאוּ וָקָמוּ	7cA	Kings will see (it) and rise up,
שָׂרִים וְיִשְׁתַּחֲווּ	7cB	princes and they will bow down,
לְמַעַן יְהוָה אֲשֶׁר נֶאֱמָן	7dA	for the sake of the LORD who is faithful,
קְדֹשׁ יִשְׂרָאֵל וַיִּבְחָרֶךָּ׃	7dB	the Holy One of Israel who has chosen you.

<פ> <ס> – $_1\mathfrak{Q}^{ab}$ – $_4\mathfrak{Q}^{d}$ – $\mathfrak{G}^{SBA}$ – $\mathfrak{S}^{b}$ ....

B.ii.1 (Isa. 49:8)

כֹּה ׀ אָמַר יְהוָה	8aA	Thus says the LORD,
בְּעֵת רָצוֹן עֲנִיתִיךָ	8aB	In the time of favour I answer you,
וּבְיוֹם יְשׁוּעָה עֲזַרְתִּיךָ	8aC	and on the day of salvation I help you.[6]
וְאֶצָּרְךָ וְאֶתֶּנְךָ לִבְרִית עָם	8bA	Yes, I will keep you and make you into a covenant of people,

---

verted imperfect as a way to describe the actual present, see M.C.A. Korpel, J.C. de Moor, F. Sepmeijer, "Consistency with Regard to Tenses", see Abbreviations.

[3] With the Qere we read a passive participle. Cf. Isa. 42:6; 48:6; 49:8.

[4] It is most likely that the original vocalization was that of an Aramaizing passive participle Peal which already $_1\mathfrak{Q}^{a}$ and $_4\mathfrak{Q}^{d}$ normalized in reading לבזוי. Almost all ancient versions read a passive participle here which in view of Isa. 53:3 is only natural. $\mathfrak{M}$ stands alone. Cf. Barthélemy, 358-60.

The meaning of נפש must be the same as in Isa. 53:10-12: 'life' (p. 548, n. 16). Obviously the function of the genitive is epexegetical in this and the following case, "despised as to life", "detested as a nation", cf. Waltke, O'Connor, § 9.5.3c.

[5] With many others and all ancient versions we read a participle Pual. For גוי as a designation of the nation of Israel see R.E. Clements, *ThWAT*, Bd. 1, 965-73.

[6] We have chosen the actualizing present for this allusion to Ps. 69:14. However, a rendering in the past tense referring to God's salvatory acts in history is certainly not excluded.

לְהָקִים אֶרֶץ	8bB	to restore the earth,[7]
לְהַנְחִיל נְחָלוֹת שֹׁמֵמוֹת׃	8bC	to make (them) inherit the desolate heritages again,

B.ii.2 (Isa. 49:9)

לֵאמֹר לַאֲסוּרִים֙ צֵאוּ	9aA	to say to the prisoners: Go out!
לַאֲשֶׁר בַּחֹשֶׁךְ הִגָּלוּ	9aB	and to those in darknesss: Appear!
עַל־דְּרָכִים יִרְעוּ	9bA	Along the ways they will pasture,
וּבְכָל־שְׁפָיִים מַרְעִיתָם׃	9bB	yes, on all bare tracks will be their pasturage.

B.ii.3 (Isa. 49:10)

לֹא יִרְעָבוּ וְלֹא יִצְמָאוּ	10aA	They will neither hunger nor thirst,
וְלֹא־יַכֵּם שָׁרָב וָשָׁמֶשׁ	10aB	nor will scorching heat or sun smite them.
כִּי־מְרַחֲמָם יְנַהֲגֵם	10bA	For he who has mercy upon them will guide them,
וְעַל־מַבּוּעֵי מַיִם יְנַהֲלֵם׃	10bB	and by springs of water he will lead them gently.

B.ii.4 (Isa. 49:11–12)

וְשַׂמְתִּי כָל־הָרַי לַדָּרֶךְ	11aA	And I will make all my mountains into a way,
וּמְסִלֹּתַי יְרֻמוּן׃ {𝔊^{A}}	11aB	and my highways will be raised up.
הִנֵּה־אֵלֶּה מֵרָחוֹק יָבֹאוּ	12aA	Behold, these are coming from afar,
וְהִנֵּה־אֵלֶּה֙ מִצָּפוֹן וּמִיָּם	12aB	and behold, these from the north and from the west,
וְאֵלֶּה מֵאֶרֶץ סִינִים׃	12aC	and these from the land of the Syanites.

<ס> – 1𝔔^{ab} – 𝔊^{SBAQ} ....

B.iii.1 (Isa. 49:13)

רָנּוּ שָׁמַיִם֙ וְגִילִי אָרֶץ	13aA	Rejoice, O heavens and exult, O earth,
יִפְצְחוּ הָרִים רִנָּה	13aB	let the mountains break forth into rejoicing,
כִּי־נִחַם יְהוָה֙ עַמּוֹ	13bA	for the LORD comforts[8] his people,
וַעֲנִיָּו יְרַחֵם׃	13bB	and has mercy upon his afflicted ones.

ס <פ> – 1𝔔^{ab} – 4𝔔^{d} – 𝔊^{SBAQ} – 𝔖^{abce} ________________________________

[7]Many translations render 'land' here, apparently because of the next colon. This is an undue reduction of v. 6 "I will also make you a light to the nations, to be my salvation to the ends of the earth". Moreover, this rendering overlooks the fact that Isa. 49:8 is a partial quotation of Isa. 42:6, "I will keep you, and I will make you a covenant of people, a light for the nations". This obvious parallel forces us to assume that the verse is in harmony with Second Isaiah's universalism. Not only Israel (v. 6aB), but *all* nations will have to return to their former properties. Cf. Deut. 32:8-9. The enormous scope of the Servant's task is equalled by the statement in Isa. 51:16 "and to lay the foundation of the earth".

[8]See note 2 above.

C.i.1 (Isa. 49:14)

וַתֹּ֥אמֶר צִיּ֖וֹן עֲזָבַ֣נִי יְהוָ֑ה	14aA	But Zion said, “The LORD has forsaken me,
{𝔊^{S}} וַאדֹנָ֖י שְׁכֵחָֽנִי׃	14aB	and the LORD[9] has forgotten me”.

C.i.2 (Isa. 49:15)

הֲתִשְׁכַּ֤ח אִשָּׁה֙ עוּלָ֔הּ	15aA	Can a woman forget her suckling,
מֵרַחֵ֖ם בֶּן־בִּטְנָ֑הּ	15aB	and have no mercy for the child of her womb?
גַּם־אֵ֣לֶּה תִשְׁכַּ֔חְנָה	15bA	Even if these were to forget,
וְאָנֹכִ֖י לֹ֥א אֶשְׁכָּחֵֽךְ׃	15bB	I will not forget you!

𝔊^{SAQ} ....

C.ii.1 (Isa. 49:16–17)

הֵ֥ן עַל־כַּפַּ֖יִם חַקֹּתִ֑יךְ	16aA	Behold, I have you imprinted on (my) handpalms,[10]
חוֹמֹתַ֥יִךְ נֶגְדִּ֖י תָּמִֽיד׃	16aB	your walls are always before me.
מִֽהֲר֖וּ בֹּנָ֑יִךְ* מֵהוֹרְסַ֣יִךְ*	17aA	Your builders[11] are faster than your wreckers,[12]
{𝔊^{SQ}} וּמַחֲרִבַ֖יִךְ מִמֵּ֥ךְ יֵצֵֽאוּ׃	17aB	and your destroyers go forth from you.

C.ii.2 (Isa. 49:18)

שְׂאִֽי־סָבִ֤יב עֵינַ֙יִךְ֙ וּרְאִ֔י	18aA	Lift up your eyes round about and see:
{𝔊^{SA}} כֻּלָּ֖ם נִקְבְּצ֣וּ בָֽאוּ־לָ֑ךְ	18aB	All of them are assembled, they come to you.
חַי־אָ֣נִי נְאֻם־יְהוָ֗ה	18bA	As I live, declares the LORD,
כִּ֤י כֻלָּם֙ כַּעֲדִ֣י תִלְבָּ֔שִׁי	18bB	you will wear all of them as an ornament,
וּֽתְקַשְּׁרִ֖ים כַּכַּלָּֽה׃	18bC	and you will bind them on like a bride.

𝔊^{A} – ϛ^{e} ....

---

[9]A rendering “my Lord” as a designation of her husband is unlikely because we should expect אֲדֹנִי then (cf. Gen. 18:12). 𝔐 is confirmed by 1𝔔^{a}, 𝔊 and 𝔗.

[10]Neither an architectural sketch nor a tattooed name explains the wording of the Hebrew in a satisfactory way. A different solution may be proposed here. In Babylonian the word for a drawing engraved in clay or stone is *uṣurtu*. But the same word may denote the lines in a hand (Von Soden, *AHw*, 1440). The protective hands of God have rested for so long on Jerusalem (compare the similar imagery in Ps. 80:17; 139:5) that its outlines stand imprinted in his palms for ever.

[11]With a host of ancient witnesses and most modern scholars we emend 𝔐, cf. Schoors, 105; Barthélemy, 364-7; De Waard, 184-5; Oswalt, 301, n. 57. Apparently 𝔐 was influenced by vv. 15, 21-22, 25, as well as 54:12-13. Since the children of Zion are at the same time her builders, Koole, 58, may be right in assuming a certain *double entendre*.

[12]For this emendation which is partially supported by 1𝔔^{a} see Barthélemy.

C.iii.1 (Isa. 49:19)

כִּי חָרְבֹתַיִךְ וְשֹׁמְמֹתַיִךְ וְאֶרֶץ הֲרִסֻתֵיךְ	19aA	Surely, your ruins, your desolated places and your wrecked land –[13]
כִּי עַתָּה תֵּצְרִי מִיּוֹשֵׁב	19bA	(but) surely, now you will be too narrow for the inhabitants,
וְרָחֲקוּ מְבַלְּעָיִךְ׃ {𝔊^{AQ}}	19bB	and those who devoured you will be far away.

C.iii.2 (Isa. 49:20)

עוֹד יֹאמְרוּ בְאָזְנַיִךְ	20aA	Again they will say it in your ears,
בְּנֵי שִׁכֻּלָיִךְ	20aB	the children of your bereavement:
צַר־לִי הַמָּקוֹם	20bA	"The place is too narrow for me!
גְּשָׁה־לִּי וְאֵשֵׁבָה׃	20bB	Move up for me that I may dwell too!"

C.iii.3 (Isa. 49:21)

וְאָמַרְתְּ בִּלְבָבֵךְ	21aA	And you will say in your heart:
מִי יָלַד־לִי אֶת־אֵלֶּה	21aB	"Who begot[14] these for me?
וַאֲנִי שְׁכוּלָה וְגַלְמוּדָה	21aC	For I myself was bereaved and barren,
גֹּלָה ׀ וְסוּרָה	21bA	an exiled and displaced person –
וְאֵלֶּה מִי גִדֵּל	21bB	so who brought these up?
הֵן אֲנִי נִשְׁאַרְתִּי לְבַדִּי	21bC	Behold, I was left alone,
אֵלֶּה אֵיפֹה הֵם׃	21bD	these then – whence are they?

פ <ס> – 1Q^{a} – 𝔊^{SBAQ} – S^{abe} ________________________

D.i.1 (Isa. 49:22)

כֹּה־אָמַר אֲדֹנָי יְהוִה	22aA	Thus says the Lord GOD:
הִנֵּה אֶשָּׂא אֶל־גּוֹיִם יָדִי	22aB	Behold, I will lift up my hand to the nations,
וְאֶל־עַמִּים אָרִים נִסִּי	22aC	and to the peoples I will raise my banner,
וְהֵבִיאוּ בָנַיִךְ בְּחֹצֶן	22bA	and they will bring your sons in their arms,
וּבְנֹתַיִךְ עַל־כָּתֵף תִּנָּשֶׂאנָה׃	22bB	and your daughters will be carried on their shoulders.

D.i.2 (Isa. 49:23a–b)

וְהָיוּ מְלָכִים אֹמְנַיִךְ	23aA	Kings will be your nursing fathers,
וְשָׂרוֹתֵיהֶם מֵינִיקֹתַיִךְ	23aB	and their princesses your nurses.
אַפַּיִם אֶרֶץ יִשְׁתַּחֲווּ לָךְ	23bA	Noses to the ground they will bow down for you,
וַעֲפַר רַגְלַיִךְ יְלַחֵכוּ	23bB	and lick the dust of your feet.

[13] We see no compelling reason for emending the text in an arbitrary way. The prophet anticipates Zion's objections.

[14] Because of the masculine verbs ילד and גדל we do not follow the majority in translating "Who bore these for me?". Cf. Deut. 32:18; Ps. 2:7. The metaphor at the background is God as Zion's husband who gave her new children miraculously and cared for them in her absence. The OT could just as well say that God 'bore' these children and so the imagery is deliberately opaque. Cf. M.C.A. Korpel, *A Rift in the Clouds: Ugaritic and Israelite Descriptions of the Divine*, Münster 1990, 247-51.

D.i.3 (Isa. 49:23c)

וְיָדַעַתְּ כִּי־אֲנִי יְהוָה	23cA	And you will know that I am the LORD:
אֲשֶׁר לֹא־יֵבֹשׁוּ קֹוָי׃	23cB	those waiting for me will not be put to shame.

ס <פ> – 1Q[a] – 𝔊[SAQ] – 𝔖[e] . . . .

D.ii.1(Isa. 49:24)

הֲיֻקַּח מִגִּבּוֹר מַלְקוֹחַ	24aA	"Can spoil be taken away from a hero?
וְאִם־שְׁבִי צַדִּיק יִמָּלֵט׃ {<ס>𝔊[BAQ]}	24aB	Or captives escape from their legal owner?"[15]

D.ii.2 (Isa. 49:25)

כִּי־כֹה אָמַר יְהוָה	25aA	Yet thus says the LORD,
גַּם־שְׁבִי גִבּוֹר יֻקָּח	25aB	Even the captives of a hero will be taken away,
וּמַלְקוֹחַ עָרִיץ יִמָּלֵט {<ס>𝔊[Q]}	25aC	and the spoil of the tyrant will escape.
וְאֶת־יְרִיבֵךְ אָנֹכִי אָרִיב	25bA	I myself will contend with him who contends with you,
וְאֶת־בָּנַיִךְ אָנֹכִי אוֹשִׁיעַ׃ {ס̊}	25bB	and your children I myself will save.

D.ii.3 (Isa. 49:26)

וְהַאֲכַלְתִּי אֶת־מוֹנַיִךְ אֶת־בְּשָׂרָם	26aA	And I will make your oppressors eat their own flesh,
וְכֶעָסִיס דָּמָם יִשְׁכָּרוּן	26aB	and they will become drunk with their own blood, as with new wine.
וְיָדְעוּ כָל־בָּשָׂר	26bA	And all flesh will know,
כִּי אֲנִי יְהוָה מוֹשִׁיעֵךְ	26bB	that I am the LORD, your Saviour,
וְגֹאֲלֵךְ אֲבִיר יַעֲקֹב׃	26bC	and your Redeemer, the Mighty One of Jacob.

ס <פ> – 1Q[a] – 𝔊[SBAQ] – 𝔖[abce] ___________________________________

---

[15] Literally: "the captive of a just man". We find it hard to accept 1Q[a]'s reading עריץ because it is an obvious harmonization with v. 25 (Van der Kooij, 315; Koole, 72). 𝔐 which offers the most difficult text is corroborated by α, θ, σ and 𝔗. Just as Babylonian *kittu* equals Hebrew צדק (Korpel, *A Rift in the Clouds*, 286-9), we believe that Hebrew צדיק occasionally equals Babylonian *kīnu* in the sense of 'legitimate' (cf. *CAD* K, 392). According to ancient Oriental law captives became the legal property of the victor. Their escape was prevented by strong, internationally enforced measures.

We assume that v. 24 is a final utterance of disbelief on the part of Zion. For unintroduced direct speech see our remarks on p. 17, n.2.

10.2 Isaiah 49 – Delimitation of Cola

COLON 49:1aA:

שִׁמְע֤וּ אִיִּים֙ אֵלַ֔י 1aA Listen to me, you islands,

With: $\mathfrak{M}$ (5) – $\mathfrak{G}^{SQ}$
Discussion: Despite the lack of support from $\mathfrak{S}$ we accept $\mathfrak{M}$'s colometry on the analogy of Isa. 46:3, 12; 48:12; 51:1, 7.

COLON 49:1aB:

וְהַקְשִׁ֥יבוּ לְאֻמִּ֖ים מֵרָח֑וֹק 1aB and pay attention, you nations from afar:

With: $\mathfrak{M}$ (2) – $\mathfrak{G}^{Q}$
Discussion: $\mathfrak{G}^{SQ}$ and $\mathfrak{S}^{bc}$ put a dividing point after לאמים. Apparently they take מרחוק in a temporal sense which is unlikely in the light of other passages in Second Isaiah.[1] Strangely enough $\mathfrak{G}^{Q}$ also has a point after διὰ χρόνου πολλοῦ.

COLON 49:1bA:

יְהוָה֙ מִבֶּ֣טֶן קְרָאָ֔נִי 1bA The LORD called me from the womb,

With: $\mathfrak{M}$ (5) – $\mathfrak{S}^{abcde}$
Discussion: $\mathfrak{G}^{SQ}$ have a point after יהוה corresponding to $\mathfrak{M}$'s Pashṭa (No. 10). However, $\mathfrak{G}$ has a plus here (λέγει).

COLON 49:1bB:

מִמְּעֵ֥י אִמִּ֖י הִזְכִּ֥יר שְׁמִֽי׃ 1bB from the loins of my mother He mentioned my name.

With: $\mathfrak{M}$ (1) – $\mathfrak{G}^{SQ}$ – $\mathfrak{S}^{abcde}$
Colon parallelism: ִי־ || ִי־.

COLON 49:2aA:

וַיָּ֤שֶׂם פִּי֙ כְּחֶ֣רֶב חַדָּ֔ה 2aA And he made my mouth like a sharpened sword,

With: $\mathfrak{M}$ (5) – $\mathfrak{G}^{SQ}$ – $\mathfrak{S}^{ab}$, $\mathfrak{S}^{cde}$ subordinate punctuation.

COLON 49:2aB:

בְּצֵ֥ל יָד֖וֹ הֶחְבִּיאָ֑נִי 2aB in the shadow of his hand he hid me.

With: $\mathfrak{M}$ (2) – $\mathfrak{G}^{Q}$ – $\mathfrak{S}^{abcde}$

---

[1] Isa. 43:6; 49:12.

COLON 49:2bA:

וַיְשִׂימֵנִי לְחֵץ בָּרוּר 2bA He made me into a polished arrow,

With: 𝔐 (5) – 𝔊^{SQ} – 𝔖^{abe}, 𝔖^{cd} subordinate punctuation.

COLON 49:2bB:

בְּאַשְׁפָּתוֹ הִסְתִּירָנִי׃ 2bB in his quiver he concealed me.

With: 𝔐 (1) – 𝔊^{SQ} – 𝔖^{abcde}

COLON 49:3aA:

וַיֹּאמֶר לִי עַבְדִּי־אָתָּה 3aA And he said to me, You are my servant,

With: 𝔐 (2) – 𝔊^{Q} – 𝔖^{acde}

COLON 49:3aB:

יִשְׂרָאֵל אֲשֶׁר־בְּךָ אֶתְפָּאָר׃ 3aB Israel, in whom I will glorify myself.

With: 𝔐 (1), major division markers in 1Q^{a} – 𝔊^{SAQ}, major division markers in 𝔊^{A} – 𝔖^{abcde}
Discussion: For the Zaqeph Gadol (No. 6) with ישׂראל see our comment on p. 31.

COLON 49:4aA:

וַאֲנִי אָמַרְתִּי לְרִיק יָגַעְתִּי 4aA But I said, For nothing I wearied myself,

With: 𝔐 (5) – 𝔊^{Q} – 𝔖^{abcde} all subordinate punctuation.
Colon parallelism: Grammatical parallelism.
Discussion: As is customary before direct speech, 𝔊^{SQ} have an extra point after אמרתי which corresponds to the Pashṭa of 𝔐.

COLON 49:4aB:

לְתֹהוּ וְהֶבֶל כֹּחִי כִלֵּיתִי 4aB for voidness and vanity I have spent my strength.

With: 𝔐 (2) – 𝔊^{SQ} – 𝔖^{abcde}
Colon parallelism: תהו || הבל (unique).

COLON 49:4bA:

אָכֵן מִשְׁפָּטִי אֶת־יְהוָה 4bA Yet my right is with the LORD,

With: 𝔐 (5) – 𝔊^{SQ} – 𝔖^{e}, 𝔖^{cd} subordinate punctuation.

COLON 49:4bB:

וּפְעֻלָּתִי אֶת־אֱלֹהָי׃ 4bB and my recompense with my God.

With: 𝔐 (1), Setuma in 1Q^{a} – 𝔊^{SAQ}, major division markers in 𝔊^{SQ} – 𝔖^{abcde}, major division markers in 𝔖^{abe}

COLON 49:5aA:

וְעַתָּה ׀ אָמַר יְהוָה 5aA But now, the LORD says –

With: 𝔐 (7) – 𝔖^{abcde} all subordinate punctuation.
Discussion: See our discussion on p. 164.

COLON 49:5aB:

יֹצְרִי מִבֶּטֶן לְעֶבֶד לוֹ 5aB he who formed me from the womb to be his servant,

With: 𝔐 (5) – 𝔊^{SQ} – 𝔖^{be}, 𝔖^{acd} subordinate punctuation.

COLON 49:5aC:

לְשׁוֹבֵב יַעֲקֹב אֵלָיו 5aC to make Jacob return to him,

With: 𝔐 (5) – 𝔖^{be}
Discussion: The support for 𝔐 is weak, but sufficient.

COLON 49:5aD:

וְיִשְׂרָאֵל לֹו* יֵאָסֵף 5aD and Israel that must be gathered to him

With: 𝔐 (2) – 𝔊^{S} – 𝔖^{abcde}, major division marker in 𝔖^{b}

COLON 49:5bA:

וְאֶכָּבֵד בְּעֵינֵי יְהוָה 5bA – for I am honoured in the LORD's eyes,

With: 𝔐 (5) – 𝔊^{SQ} – 𝔖^{acde}

COLON 49:5bB:

וֵאלֹהַי הָיָה עֻזִּי׃ 5bB and my God is my strength –

With: 𝔐 (1) – 𝔊^{SQ} – 𝔖^{abcde}
Colon parallelism: ־י || ־י.

COLON 49:6aA:

וַיֹּאמֶר נָקֵל מִהְיוֹתְךָ לִי עֶבֶד 6aA now he says, It is too little that you should be a servant for me,

With: $\mathfrak{M}$ (5) – $\mathfrak{G}^{SQ}$ – $\mathfrak{S}^{acde}$ subordinate punctuation.
Discussion: $\mathfrak{S}^{bce}$ have an extra point to introduce the direct oration ($\mathfrak{M}$ Revia‘, No. 7). In our opinion this is insufficient reason to assume a quadrocolon with a first colon of only one word. See our comment on p. 31.

COLON 49:6aB:

לְהָקִים֙ אֶת־שִׁבְטֵ֣י יַעֲקֹ֔ב 6aB to restore the tribes of Jacob,

With: $\mathfrak{M}$ (5) – $\mathfrak{G}^{Q}$ – $\mathfrak{S}^{acde}$ subordinate punctuation.

COLON 49:6aC:

וּנְצוּרֵ֥י* יִשְׂרָאֵ֖ל לְהָשִׁ֑יב 6aC and to bring back the well-kept of Israel.

With: $\mathfrak{M}$ (2) – $\mathfrak{G}^{SAQ}$, major division markers in $\mathfrak{G}^{A}$ – $\mathfrak{S}^{abcde}$ all subordinate punctuation.

COLON 49:6bA:

וּנְתַתִּ֙יךָ֙ לְא֣וֹר גּוֹיִ֔ם 6bA I will also make you a light to the nations,

With: $\mathfrak{M}$ (5) – $\mathfrak{G}^{SQ}$ – $\mathfrak{S}^{de}$, $\mathfrak{S}^{abc}$ subordinate punctuation.

COLON 49:6bB:

לִהְי֥וֹת יְשׁוּעָתִ֖י עַד־קְצֵ֥ה הָאָֽרֶץ׃ 6bB to be my salvation to the ends of the earth.

With: $\mathfrak{M}$ (1), major division markers, also in $1\mathfrak{Q}^{a}$, $1\mathfrak{Q}^{b}$ and $4\mathfrak{Q}^{d}$ – $\mathfrak{G}^{SAQ}$, major division markers in $\mathfrak{G}^{SBA}$ – $\mathfrak{S}^{abcde}$, major division markers in $\mathfrak{S}^{bcde}$
Discussion: $\mathfrak{G}^{Q}$ and $\mathfrak{S}^{a}$ have an extra point after ישועתי where $\mathfrak{M}$ has a Ṭiphḥa (No. 8).

COLON 49:7aA:

כֹּ֣ה אָֽמַר־יְהוָ֡ה 7aA Thus says the LORD,

With: None of the witnesses.
Discussion: Neither the Masoretes nor the ancient versions divide at this point. However, time and again the ‘Botenformel’ creates this kind of problems and so we decided to accept the customary modern division on the analogy of other similar cases.[2] See also below on vv. 8aA, 22aA, 25aA.

[2]See our comment on p. 164.

COLON 49:7aB:

גֹּאֵל יִשְׂרָאֵל קְדוֹשׁוֹ 7aB the Redeemer of Israel, his Holy One,

With: 𝔐 (7) – 𝔖^{abcde}
Colon parallelism: גאל || קדוש ישׂראל.

COLON 49:7bA:

לִבְזֹה*־נֶפֶשׁ לִמְתָעֵב* גּוֹי לְעֶבֶד מֹשְׁלִים 7bA to the one whose life was despised, whose nation was detested, to the servant of rulers,

With: 𝔐 (5) – 𝔊^{SQ} – 𝔖^{b}, 𝔖^{acde} subordinate punctuation.
Colon parallelism: ל || ל || ל; בזה || תעב (unique); גוי || משׁל.
Discussion: 𝔊^{Q} and 𝔖^{b} have an extra point after לבזה־נפשׁ (𝔐 Geresh, No. 13), adding the addressee to v. 7aB. None of the ancient witnesses supports a division after גוי, as is customary in modern editions (e.g. BHS). Since a verse of 5 cola is within the bounds of the acceptable, we see no reason to deviate from the tradition.

COLON 49:7cA:

מְלָכִים יִרְאוּ וָקָמוּ 7cA Kings will see (it) and rise up,

With: 𝔐 (5) – 𝔊^{Q} – 𝔖^{abcde}
Colon parallelism: ראה || קום.

COLON 49:7cB:

שָׂרִים וְיִשְׁתַּחֲווּ 7cB princes and they will bow down,

With: 𝔐 (2) – 𝔊^{Q} – 𝔖^{abcde}

COLON 49:7dA:

לְמַעַן יְהוָה אֲשֶׁר נֶאֱמָן 7dA for the sake of the LORD who is faithful,

With: 𝔐 (5) – 𝔖^{acd}
Discussion: 𝔊^{SQ} and 𝔖^{e} have an extra point after יהוה where 𝔐 has a Pashṭa (No. 10). 𝔊 takes אשׁר נאמן קדשׁ ישׂראל as one colon which results in a very unlikely verse.

COLON 49:7dB:

קְדֹשׁ יִשְׂרָאֵל וַיִּבְחָרֶךָּ׃ 7dB the Holy One of Israel who has chosen you.

With: 𝔐 (1), major division markers in 1𝔔^{a}, 1𝔔^{b} and 4𝔔^{d} – 𝔊^{SBAQ}, major division markers in all but 𝔊^{Q} – 𝔖^{abcde}, major division markers in 𝔖^{b}
Discussion: With regard to 𝔊, see the preceding colon.

COLON 49:8aA:

כֹּה ׀ אָמַר יְהוָה 8aA Thus says the LORD,

With: $\mathfrak{M}$ (7) – $\mathfrak{G}^{SQ}$ – $\mathfrak{S}^{abcde}$

Discussion: It is important that in this case all ancient witnesses agree in putting a caesura after the 'Botenformel'. See our comment on p. 164.

COLON 49:8aB:

בְּעֵת רָצוֹן עֲנִיתִיךָ 8aB In the time of favour I answer you,

With: $\mathfrak{M}$ (5) – $\mathfrak{G}^{SQ}$ – $\mathfrak{S}^{abcde}$

COLON 49:8aC:

וּבְיוֹם יְשׁוּעָה עֲזַרְתִּיךָ 8aC and on the day of salvation I help you.

With: $\mathfrak{M}$ (2) – $\mathfrak{G}^{Q}$ – $\mathfrak{S}^{abcde}$

COLON 49:8bA:

וְאֶצָּרְךָ וְאֶתֶּנְךָ לִבְרִית עָם 8bA Yes, I will keep you and make you into a covenant of people,

With: $\mathfrak{M}$ (5) – $\mathfrak{G}^{SQ}$

Discussion: $\mathfrak{S}$ does not have a divider here because it adds ܘܢܘܗܪܐ ܠܥܡ̈ܡܐ "and to a light for the nations". See v. 6. For the Revia' (No. 7) with ואצרך see our comment on p. 31.

COLON 49:8bB:

לְהָקִים אֶרֶץ 8bB to restore the earth,

With: $\mathfrak{M}$ (5) – $\mathfrak{G}^{Q}$ – $\mathfrak{S}^{a}$ subordinate punctuation.

Discussion: Apparently part of the tradition joined v. 8bB and 8bC.

COLON 49:8bC:

לְהַנְחִיל נְחָלוֹת שֹׁמֵמוֹת׃ 8bC to make (them) inherit the desolate heritages again,

With: $\mathfrak{M}$ (1) – $\mathfrak{G}^{SQ}$ – $\mathfrak{S}^{abcde}$

COLON 49:9aA:

לֵאמֹר לַאֲסוּרִים צֵאוּ 9aA to say to the prisoners: Go out!

With: $\mathfrak{M}$ (5) – $\mathfrak{G}^{Q}$ – $\mathfrak{S}^{abcde}$

COLON 49:9aB:

לַאֲשֶׁר בַּחֹשֶׁךְ הִגָּלוּ 9aB and to those in darknesss: Appear!

With: $\mathfrak{M}$ (2) – $\mathfrak{G}^{SQ}$ – $\mathfrak{S}^{abcde}$

COLON 49:9bA:

עַל־דְּרָכִים יִרְעוּ 9bA Along the ways they will pasture,

With: $\mathfrak{M}$ (5) – $\mathfrak{G}^{SQ}$ – $\mathfrak{S}^{abcde}$

COLON 49:9bB:

וּבְכָל־שְׁפָיִים מַרְעִיתָם׃ 9bB yes, on all bare tracks will be their pasturage.

With: $\mathfrak{M}$ (1) – $\mathfrak{G}^{SQ}$ – $\mathfrak{S}^{abcde}$
Colon parallelism: שפי || מרעית (antithetical; unique).

COLON 49:10aA:

לֹא יִרְעָבוּ וְלֹא יִצְמָאוּ 10aA They will neither hunger nor thirst,

With: $\mathfrak{M}$ (5) – $\mathfrak{G}^{SQ}$ – $\mathfrak{S}^{abcde}$
Colon parallelism: לא || לא; רעב || צמא.

COLON 49:10aB:

וְלֹא־יַכֵּם שָׁרָב וָשָׁמֶשׁ 10aB nor will scorching heat or sun smite them.

With: $\mathfrak{M}$ (2) – $\mathfrak{G}^{SQ}$ – $\mathfrak{S}^{abcd}$
Colon parallelism: שרב || שמש (unique).

COLON 49:10bA:

כִּי־מְרַחֲמָם יְנַהֲגֵם 10bA For he who has mercy upon them will guide them,

With: $\mathfrak{M}$ (5) – $\mathfrak{G}^{SQ}$ – $\mathfrak{S}^{b}$, $\mathfrak{S}^{acde}$ subordinate punctuation.

COLON 49:10bB:

וְעַל־מַבּוּעֵי מַיִם יְנַהֲלֵם׃ 10bB and by springs of water he will lead them gently.

With: $\mathfrak{M}$ (1) – $\mathfrak{G}^{Q}$ – $\mathfrak{S}^{abcde}$

COLON 49:11aA:

וְשַׂמְתִּי כָל־הָרַי לַדָּרֶךְ 11aA And I will make all my mountains into a way,

With: $\mathfrak{M}$ (2) – $\mathfrak{G}^{SQ}$ – $\mathfrak{S}^{abcde}$

COLON 49:11aB:

וּמְסִלֹּתַ֖י יְרֻמֽוּן׃ 11aB and my highways will be raised up.

With: $\mathfrak{M}$ (1) – $\mathfrak{G}^{AQ}$, major division markers in $\mathfrak{G}^{A}$ – $\mathfrak{S}^{abcde}$

COLON 49:12aA:

הִנֵּה־אֵ֕לֶּה מֵרָח֖וֹק יָבֹ֑אוּ 12aA Behold, these are coming from afar,

With: $\mathfrak{M}$ (2) – $\mathfrak{G}^{Q}$ – $\mathfrak{S}^{abce}$ subordinate punctuation.
Discussion: For the Zaqeph Gadol (No. 6) with אלה see our comment on p. 31.

COLON 49:12aB:

וְהִנֵּה־אֵ֙לֶּה֙ מִצָּפ֣וֹן וּמִיָּ֔ם 12aB and behold, these from the north and from the west,

With: $\mathfrak{M}$ (5) – $\mathfrak{G}^{SQ}$ – $\mathfrak{S}^{e}$
Colon parallelism: צפון || ים.[3]
Discussion: $\mathfrak{G}^{Q}$ and $\mathfrak{S}^{abcde}$ have a point after מצפון but this is a result of inserting an extra אלה before מים.

COLON 49:12aC:

וְאֵ֖לֶּה מֵאֶ֥רֶץ סִינִֽים׃ 12aC and these from the land of the Syanites.

With: $\mathfrak{M}$ (1), major division markers in 1$\mathfrak{Q}^{a}$ and 1$\mathfrak{Q}^{b}$ – $\mathfrak{G}^{SBAQ}$, all with major division markers – $\mathfrak{S}^{abcde}$

COLON 49:13aA:

רָנּ֤וּ שָׁמַ֙יִם֙ וְגִ֣ילִי אָ֔רֶץ 13aA Rejoice, O heavens and exult, O earth,

With: $\mathfrak{M}$ (5) – $\mathfrak{G}^{SQ}$ – $\mathfrak{S}^{abcde}$
Colon parallelism: רנן || גיל; שמים || ארץ.
Discussion: $\mathfrak{G}^{SQ}$ and $\mathfrak{S}^{e}$ have an extra point after שמים ($\mathfrak{M}$ Pashṭa, No. 10).

COLON 49:13aB:

יִפְצְח֥וּ הָרִ֖ים רִנָּ֑ה 13aB let the mountains break forth into rejoicing,

With: $\mathfrak{M}$ (2) – $\mathfrak{G}^{SQ}$ – $\mathfrak{S}^{acde}$

COLON 49:13bA:

כִּֽי־נִחַ֤ם יְהוָה֙ עַמּ֔וֹ 13bA for the LORD comforts his people,

With: $\mathfrak{M}$ (5) – $\mathfrak{G}^{SQ}$ – $\mathfrak{S}^{abce}$ subordinate punctuation.

---

[3] As in Ps. 107:3; verse-line parallelism in Amos 8:12.

Colon 49:13bB:

וַעֲנִיָּו יְרַחֵם׃ 13bB and has mercy upon his afflicted ones.

With: $\mathfrak{M}$ (1), major division markers, also in 1$\mathfrak{Q}^{a}$, 1$\mathfrak{Q}^{b}$ and 4$\mathfrak{Q}$d – $\mathfrak{G}^{SBAQ}$, all with major division markers – $\mathfrak{S}^{abcde}$, $\mathfrak{S}^{abce}$ with major division markers.

Colon 49:14aA:

וַתֹּאמֶר צִיּוֹן עֲזָבַנִי יְהוָה 14aA But Zion said, "The Lord has forsaken me,

With: $\mathfrak{M}$ (2) – $\mathfrak{G}^{SQ}$ – $\mathfrak{S}^{e}$

Colon parallelism: ציון || יהוה.

Discussion: $\mathfrak{G}^{S}$ and $\mathfrak{S}^{acde}$ have an extra point after ציון ($\mathfrak{M}$ Ṭiphḥa, No. 8) to introduce the direct oration, as is more often the case.

Colon 49:14aB:

וַאדֹנָי שְׁכֵחָנִי׃ 14aB and the Lord has forgotten me".

With: $\mathfrak{M}$ (1) – $\mathfrak{G}^{SQ}$, major division markers in $\mathfrak{G}^{S}$ – $\mathfrak{S}^{abcde}$

Colon 49:15aA:

הֲתִשְׁכַּח אִשָּׁה עוּלָהּ 15aA Can a woman forget her suckling,

With: $\mathfrak{M}$ (5) – $\mathfrak{G}^{Q}$ – $\mathfrak{S}^{abcde}$ all subordinate punctuation.

Colon parallelism: אשה || בן.

Colon 49:15aB:

מֵרַחֵם בֶּן־בִּטְנָהּ 15aB and have no mercy for the child of her womb?

With: $\mathfrak{M}$ (2) – $\mathfrak{G}^{SQ}$ – $\mathfrak{S}^{abcde}$ subordinate punctuation.

Colon 49:15bA:

גַּם־אֵלֶּה תִשְׁכַּחְנָה 15bA Even if these were to forget,

With: $\mathfrak{M}$ (5) – $\mathfrak{G}^{Q}$

Discussion: Despite the rather weak support we accept $\mathfrak{M}$'s colometry.

Colon 49:15bB:

וְאָנֹכִי לֹא אֶשְׁכָּחֵךְ׃ 15bB I will not forget you!

With: $\mathfrak{M}$ (1) – $\mathfrak{G}^{SAQ}$, major division markers in $\mathfrak{G}^{A}$, paragraphoi in $\mathfrak{G}^{S}$ and $\mathfrak{G}^{Q}$ – $\mathfrak{S}^{abcde}$

COLON 49:16aA:

הֵן עַל־כַּפַּיִם חַקֹּתִיךְ 16aA Behold, I have you imprinted on (my) handpalms,

With: 𝔐 (2) – $\mathfrak{G}^{SQ}$ – $\mathfrak{S}^{abcde}$

COLON 49:16aB:

חוֹמֹתַיִךְ נֶגְדִּי תָּמִיד׃ 16aB your walls are always before Me.

With: 𝔐 (1) – $\mathfrak{G}^{Q}$ – $\mathfrak{S}^{abcde}$

COLON 49:17aA:

מִהֲרוּ *בֹּנַיִךְ* מֵהוֹרְסַיִךְ* 17aA Your builders are faster than your wreckers,

With: – $\mathfrak{G}^{SQ}$ – $\mathfrak{S}^{e}$
Colon parallelism: בנה || הרס (antithetical).
Discussion: $\mathfrak{G}^{S}$ and $\mathfrak{S}^{d}$ have a point after בניך, but this hardly corresponds to 𝔐's Atnaḥ because 𝔐 presupposes a different interpretation of the verse which also resulted in the conjunctive accent with מהרסיך. The colon parallelism favours the choice of the witnesses cited.

COLON 49:17aB:

וּמַחֲרִבַיִךְ מִמֵּךְ יֵצֵאוּ׃ 17aB and your destroyers go forth from you.

With: 𝔐 (1) – $\mathfrak{G}^{SQ}$, both also have a paragraphos – $\mathfrak{S}^{abcde}$

COLON 49:18aA:

שְׂאִי־סָבִיב עֵינַיִךְ וּרְאִי 18aA Lift up your eyes round about and see:

With: 𝔐 (5)
Colon parallelism: נשׂא עינים || ראה.
Discussion: Though none of the other witnesses supports 𝔐 we accept the latter's colometry. because it is in accordance with the attested colon parallelism.

COLON 49:18aB:

כֻּלָּם נִקְבְּצוּ בָאוּ־לָךְ 18aB All of them are assembled, they come to you.

With: 𝔐 (2) – $\mathfrak{G}^{SAQ}$, major division markers in $\mathfrak{G}^{SA}$ – $\mathfrak{S}^{abcde}$
Colon parallelism: קבץ || בוא.
Discussion: $\mathfrak{G}^{SQ}$ divide after כלם; $\mathfrak{S}$ does not support this.

COLON 49:18bA:

חַי־אָנִי נְאֻם־יְהוָה 18bA As I live, declares the LORD,

With: $\mathfrak{M}$ (7) – $\mathfrak{G}^{SQ}$ – $\mathfrak{S}^{abcde}$ subordinate punctuation.

COLON 49:18bB:

כִּי כֻלָּם כָּעֲדִי תִלְבָּשִׁי 18bB you will wear all of them as an ornament,

With: $\mathfrak{M}$ (5) – $\mathfrak{G}^{Q}$ – $\mathfrak{S}^{abcde}$

COLON 49:18bC:

וּתְקַשְּׁרִים כַּכַּלָּה׃ 18bC and you will bind them on like a bride.

With: $\mathfrak{M}$ (1) – $\mathfrak{G}^{SAQ}$, major division markers in $\mathfrak{G}^{A}$ – $\mathfrak{S}^{abcde}$, major division marker in $\mathfrak{S}^{e}$

COLON 49:19aA:

כִּי חָרְבֹתַיִךְ וְשֹׁמְמֹתַיִךְ וְאֶרֶץ הֲרִסֻתֵךְ 19aA Surely, your ruins, your desolated places and your wrecked land –

With: $\mathfrak{M}$ (2) – $\mathfrak{S}^{abcde}$ all subordinate punctuation.
Colon parallelism: Roots חרב || שמם || הרס.
Discussion: None of our witnesses agrees with $\mathfrak{M}$'s Zaqeph Qaṭon (No. 5) with ושממתיך. Although the support for the Atnaḥ is also far from impressive, we believe that it is the best option because the threefold colon parallelism is attested.

COLON 49:19bA:

כִּי עַתָּה תֵּצְרִי מִיּוֹשֵׁב 19bA (but) surely, now you will be too narrow for the inhabitants,

With: $\mathfrak{M}$ (5) – $\mathfrak{G}^{SQ}$ – $\mathfrak{S}^{abcde}$

COLON 49:19bB:

וְרָחֲקוּ מְבַלְּעָיִךְ׃ 19bB and those who devoured you will be far away.

With: $\mathfrak{M}$ (1) – $\mathfrak{G}^{SAQ}$, major division markers in $\mathfrak{G}^{AQ}$ – $\mathfrak{S}^{abd}$, $\mathfrak{S}^{ce}$ subordinate punctuation.

COLON 49:20aA:

עוֹד יֹאמְרוּ בְאָזְנַיִךְ 20aA Again they will say it in your ears,

With: $\mathfrak{M}$ (5)

Discussion: None of the other ancient witnesses has the same colometry. Apparently this was caused by the fact that the sentence runs on. However, the fixed expression אמר באזנים always ends a colon[4] and so the Masoretes were right.

COLON 49:20aB:

בְּנֵי שִׁכֻּלָיִךְ 20aB the children of your bereavement:

With: $\mathfrak{M}$ (2) – $\mathfrak{G}^{SQ}$ – $\mathfrak{S}^{abcd}$ subordinate punctuation.

COLON 49:20bA:

צַר־לִי הַמָּקוֹם 20bA "The place is too narrow for me!

With: $\mathfrak{M}$ (8) – $\mathfrak{G}^{Q}$ – $\mathfrak{S}^{bcde}$, $\mathfrak{S}^{a}$ subordinate punctuation.

COLON 49:20bB:

גְּשָׁה־לִּי וְאֵשֵׁבָה׃ 20bB Move up for me that I may dwell too!"

With: $\mathfrak{M}$ (1) – $\mathfrak{G}^{Q}$ – $\mathfrak{S}^{abcde}$

COLON 49:21aA:

וְאָמַרְתְּ בִּלְבָבֵךְ 21aA And you will say in your heart:

With: $\mathfrak{M}$ (7) – $\mathfrak{G}^{Q}$ – $\mathfrak{S}^{a}$, $\mathfrak{S}^{bce}$ subordinate punctuation.

COLON 49:21aB:

מִי יָלַד־לִי אֶת־אֵלֶּה 21aB "Who begot these for me?

With: $\mathfrak{M}$ (5) – $\mathfrak{G}^{Q}$ – $\mathfrak{S}^{abcde}$ subordinate punctuation.

COLON 49:21aC:

וַאֲנִי שְׁכוּלָה וְגַלְמוּדָה 21aC For I myself was bereaved and barren,

With: $\mathfrak{M}$ (2) – $\mathfrak{G}^{SQ}$ – $\mathfrak{S}^{acde}$, $\mathfrak{S}^{b}$ subordinate punctuation.
Colon parallelism: שכולה || גלמודה (unique).

COLON 49:21bA:

גֹּלָה ׀ וְסוּרָה 21bA an exiled and displaced person,

With: $\mathfrak{M}$ (7) – $\mathfrak{S}^{abcde}$
Colon parallelism: גלה || סור.
Discussion: $\mathfrak{G}$ is absent at this point.

[4] Judg. 17:2; Ezek. 9:5; Job 33:8.

COLON 49:21bB:

וְאֵלֶּה מִי גִדֵּל 21bB so who brought these up?

With: 𝔐 (5) – 𝔊^{SQ} – 𝔖^{abcde}

COLON 49:21bC:

הֵן אֲנִי נִשְׁאַרְתִּי לְבַדִּי 21bC Behold, I was left alone,

With: 𝔐 (5) – 𝔊^{Q} – 𝔖^{abcde}

COLON 49:21bD:

אֵלֶּה אֵיפֹה הֵם׃ 21bD these then – whence are they?

With: 𝔐 (1), major division markers, also in 1Q^{a} – 𝔊^{SBAQ}, major division markers in all – 𝔖^{abcde}, major division markers in 𝔖^{abe}

COLON 49:22aA:

כֹּה־אָמַר אֲדֹנָי יְהוִה 22aA Thus says the Lord GOD:

With: 𝔐 (7) – 𝔊^{SQ} – 𝔖^{abcde}

Discussion: Again all witnesses agree with regard to the delimitation of the 'Botenformel'.

COLON 49:22aB:

הִנֵּה אֶשָּׂא אֶל־גּוֹיִם יָדִי 22aB Behold, I will lift up my hand to the nations,

With: 𝔐 (5) – 𝔊^{Q} – 𝔖^{abd}, 𝔖^{ce} subordinate punctuation.

COLON 49:22aC:

וְאֶל־עַמִּים אָרִים נִסִּי 22aC and to the peoples I will raise my banner,

With: 𝔐 (2) – 𝔊^{SQ} – 𝔖^{abcde}

COLON 49:22bA:

וְהֵבִיאוּ בָנַיִךְ בְּחֹצֶן 22bA and they will bring your sons in their arms,

With: 𝔐 (5) – 𝔊^{Q} – 𝔖^{abcde}

COLON 49:22bB:

וּבְנֹתַיִךְ עַל־כָּתֵף תִּנָּשֶׂאנָה׃ 22bB and your daughters will be carried on their shoulders.

With: 𝔐 (1) – 𝔊^{SQ} – 𝔖^{abcde}

COLON 49:23aA:

וְהָיוּ מְלָכִים אֹמְנַיִךְ 23aA Kings will be your nursing fathers,

With: 𝔐 (7) – 𝔊^{SQ} – 𝔖^{abcde} subordinate punctuation.

COLON 49:23aB:

וְשָׂרוֹתֵיהֶם מֵינִיקֹתַיִךְ 23aB and their princesses your nurses.

With: 𝔐 (5) – 𝔊^{SQ} – 𝔖^{abcde}

COLON 49:23bA:

אַפַּיִם אֶרֶץ יִשְׁתַּחֲווּ לָךְ 23bA Noses to the ground they will bow down for you,

With: 𝔐 (5) – 𝔊^{SQ} – 𝔖^{abcd}
Discussion: For the Revia‘ (No. 7) with אפים see our comment, p. 31.

COLON 49:23bB:

וַעֲפַר רַגְלַיִךְ יְלַחֵכוּ 23bB and lick the dust of your feet.

With: 𝔐 (2) – 𝔊^{SQ} – 𝔖^{abcde}

COLON 49:23cA:

וְיָדַעַתְּ כִּי־אֲנִי יְהוָה 23cA And you will know that I am the LORD:

With: 𝔐 (5) – 𝔊^{Q} – 𝔖^{bcd} subordinate punctuation.

COLON 49:23cB:

אֲשֶׁר לֹא־יֵבֹשׁוּ קֹוָי׃ 23cB those waiting for me will not be put to shame.

With: 𝔐 (1), major division markers, also in 1𝔔^{a} – 𝔊^{SAQ}, all three with major division markers – 𝔖^{bcde}, major division marker in 𝔖^{e}. Subordinate punctuation in 𝔖^{a}

COLON 49:24aA:

הֲיֻקַּח מִגִּבּוֹר מַלְקוֹחַ 24aA “Can spoil be taken away from a hero?

With: 𝔐 (2) – 𝔊^{SQ} – 𝔖^{abcde} subordinate punctuation.

COLON 49:24aB:

וְאִם־שְׁבִי צַדִּיק יִמָּלֵט׃ 24aB Or captives escape from their legal owner?”

With: 𝔐 (1), Setuma in 1𝔔^{a} – 𝔊^{SBAQ}, major division markers in 𝔊^{BAQ} – 𝔖^{abcde}

COLON 49:25aA:

כִּי־כֹ֣ה ׀ אָמַ֣ר יְהוָ֗ה 25aA Yet thus says the LORD,

With: $\mathfrak{M}$ (7) – $\mathfrak{G}^{S}$ – $\mathfrak{S}^{abcde}$

COLON 49:25aB:

גַּם־שְׁבִ֤י גִבּוֹר֙ יֻקָּ֔ח 25aB Even the captives of a hero will be taken away,

With: $\mathfrak{M}$ (5) – $\mathfrak{S}^{abcde}$
Discussion: $\mathfrak{G}$ erroneously divides after ומלקוח.

COLON 49:25aC:

וּמַלְק֥וֹחַ עָרִ֖יץ יִמָּלֵ֑ט 25aC and the spoil of the tyrant will escape.

With: $\mathfrak{M}$ (2), Setuma in $1\mathfrak{Q}^{a}$ – $\mathfrak{G}^{SQ}$, major division markers in $\mathfrak{G}^{Q}$

COLON 49:25bA:

וְאֶת־יְרִיבֵךְ֙ אָנֹכִ֣י אָרִ֔יב 25bA I myself will contend with him who contends with you,

With: $\mathfrak{M}$ (5) – $\mathfrak{G}^{SQ}$ – $\mathfrak{S}^{abcde}$
Colon parallelism: Roots ריב || ריב.

COLON 49:25bB:

וְאֶת־בָּנַ֖יִךְ אָנֹכִ֥י אוֹשִֽׁיעַ׃ 25bB and your children I myself will save.

With: $\mathfrak{M}$ (1), Seder – $\mathfrak{G}^{SQ}$ – $\mathfrak{S}^{abcde}$

COLON 49:26aA:

וְהַאֲכַלְתִּ֤י אֶת־מוֹנַ֙יִךְ֙ אֶת־בְּשָׂרָ֔ם 26aA And I will make your oppressors eat their own flesh,

With: $\mathfrak{M}$ (5) – $\mathfrak{G}^{Q}$ – $\mathfrak{S}^{abcde}$ all subordinate punctuation.
Colon parallelism: את (nota acc.) || את (nota acc.).

COLON 49:26aB:

וְכֶעָסִ֖יס דָּמָ֣ם יִשְׁכָּר֑וּן 26aB and they will become drunk with their own blood, as with new wine.

With: $\mathfrak{M}$ (2) – $\mathfrak{G}^{Q}$ – $\mathfrak{S}^{abcde}$
Discussion: $\mathfrak{G}^{S}$ and $\mathfrak{G}^{Q}$ erroneously divide after דמם.

COLON 49:26bA:

וְיָדְעוּ כָל־בָּשָׂר 26bA And all flesh will know,

With: $\mathfrak{M}$ (7) – $\mathfrak{G}^{Q}$ – $\mathfrak{S}^{acd}$ subordinate punctuation.

COLON 49:26bB:

כִּי אֲנִי יְהוָה מוֹשִׁיעֵךְ 26bB that I am the LORD, your Saviour,

With: $\mathfrak{M}$ (5) – $\mathfrak{G}^{SQ}$ – $\mathfrak{S}^{abcde}$
Colon parallelism: יהוה || מושיע.

COLON 49:26bC:

וְגֹאֲלֵךְ אֲבִיר יַעֲקֹב׃ 26bC and your Redeemer, the Mighty One of Jacob.

With: $\mathfrak{M}$ (1), major division markers, also in 1$\mathfrak{Q}^{a}$ – $\mathfrak{G}^{SBAQ}$, all with major division markers – $\mathfrak{S}^{abcde}$, major division markers in $\mathfrak{S}^{abce}$
Colon parallelism: גאל || אביר.

10.3 Isaiah 49 – Delimitation of Verse-lines

VERSE–LINE: 49:1a:

שִׁמְעוּ אִיִּים אֵלַי 1aA Listen to me, you islands,
וְהַקְשִׁיבוּ לְאֻמִּים מֵרָחוֹק 1aB and pay attention, you nations from afar:

$\mathfrak{M}$ distinctive accents: 5 – 2.
Stresses: 3 + 3.
Verse-line parallelism: שמע || קשב; אי || לאם; grammatical parallelism.

VERSE–LINE: 49:1b:

יְהוָה מִבֶּטֶן קְרָאָנִי 1bA The LORD called me from the womb,
מִמְּעֵי אִמִּי הִזְכִּיר שְׁמִי׃ 1bB from the loins of my mother He mentioned my name.

$\mathfrak{M}$ distinctive accents: 5 – 1.
Stresses: 3 + 4.
Verse-line parallelism: מן || מן; בטן || מעים; קרא || זכר שם; ־ני || ־י; rhyme.

VERSE–LINE: 49:2a:

וַיָּשֶׂם פִּי כְּחֶרֶב חַדָּה 2aA And he made my mouth like a sharpened sword,
בְּצֵל יָדוֹ הֶחְבִּיאָנִי 2aB in the shadow of his hand he hid me.

$\mathfrak{M}$ distinctive accents: 5 – 2.
Stresses: 4 + 3.
Verse-line parallelism: פה || יד; ־י || ־ני.

VERSE–LINE: 49:2b:

וַיְשִׂימֵנִי לְחֵץ בָּרוּר	2bA	He made me into a polished arrow,
בְּאַשְׁפָּתוֹ הִסְתִּירָנִי׃	2bB	in his quiver he concealed me.

𝔐 distinctive accents: 5 – 1.
Stresses: 3 + 2.
Verse-line parallelism: ־ני || ־ני; חץ || אשפה.

VERSE–LINE: 49:3a:

וַיֹּאמֶר לִי עַבְדִּי־אָתָּה	3aA	And he said to me, You are my servant,
יִשְׂרָאֵל אֲשֶׁר־בְּךָ אֶתְפָּאָר׃	3aB	Israel, in whom I will glorify myself.

𝔐 distinctive accents: 2 – 1.
Stresses: 3 + 3.
Verse-line parallelism: אתה || ־ך.
Discussion: The cola are also connected by ellipsis.

VERSE–LINE: 49:4a:

וַאֲנִי אָמַרְתִּי לְרִיק יָגַעְתִּי	4aA	But I said, For nothing I exhausted myself,
לְתֹהוּ וְהֶבֶל כֹּחִי כִלֵּיתִי	4aB	for voidness and vanity I have spent my strength.

𝔐 distinctive accents: 5 – 2.
Stresses: 4 + 4.
Verse-line parallelism: ל || ל; ריק || תהו (unique); ריק || הבל; יגע || כלה; grammatical parallelism; rhyme.

VERSE–LINE: 49:4b:

אָכֵן מִשְׁפָּטִי אֶת־יְהוָה	4bA	Yet my right is with the LORD,
וּפְעֻלָּתִי אֶת־אֱלֹהָי׃	4bB	and my recompense with my God.

𝔐 distinctive accents: 5 – 1.
Stresses: 3 + 2.
Verse-line parallelism: משפט || פעלה; ־י || ־י; את || את; יהוה || אלהים; grammatical parallelism; rhyme.

VERSE–LINE: 49:5a:

וְעַתָּה ׀ אָמַר יְהוָה	5aA	But now, the LORD says –
יֹצְרִי מִבֶּטֶן לְעֶבֶד לוֹ	5aB	he who formed me from the womb to be his servant,
לְשׁוֹבֵב יַעֲקֹב אֵלָיו	5aC	to make Jacob return to him,
וְיִשְׂרָאֵל לוֹ* יֵאָסֵף	5aD	and Israel that must be gathered to him

𝔐 distinctive accents: 7 – 5 – 5 – 2.

Stresses: 3 + 4 + 3 + 3.
Verse-line parallelism: יהוה || יעקב || ישׂראל; ל || ל || ל; ־ו || ־ו || ־ו; שׁוב || אסף. Discussion: With the Masoretes we read this verse-line as a quadrocolon. The similar structure of v. 6a supports this view. The sequence of accents is attested elsewhere.[1] The continuing sentence and the ellipsis in v. 5aD are also connecting forces.

VERSE–LINE: 49:5b:

וְאֶכָּבֵד בְּעֵינֵי יְהוָה 5bA – for I am honoured in the LORD's eyes,
וֵאלֹהַי הָיָה עֻזִּי׃ 5bB and my God is my strength –

𝔐 distinctive accents: 5 – 1.
Stresses: 3 + 3.
Verse-line parallelism: כבד || עז; יהוה || אלהים.

VERSE–LINE: 49:6a:

וַיֹּאמֶר נָקֵל מִהְיוֹתְךָ לִי עֶבֶד 6aA now he says, It is too little that you should be a servant for me,
לְהָקִים אֶת־שִׁבְטֵי יַעֲקֹב 6aB to restore the tribes of Jacob,
וּנְצוּרֵי* יִשְׂרָאֵל לְהָשִׁיב 6aC and to bring back the well-kept of Israel.

𝔐 distinctive accents: 5 – 5 – 2.
Stresses: 5 + 3 + 3.
Verse-line parallelism: ל || ל || ל; קום || נצר; קום || שׁוב; יעקב || ישׂראל.

VERSE–LINE: 49:6b:

וּנְתַתִּיךָ לְאוֹר גּוֹיִם 6bA I will also make you a light to the nations,
לִהְיוֹת יְשׁוּעָתִי עַד־קְצֵה הָאָרֶץ׃ 6bB to be my salvation to the ends of the earth.

𝔐 distinctive accents: 5 – 1.
Stresses: 3 + 4.
Verse-line parallelism: ל || ל; אור || ישׁועה; גוי || קצה הארץ; grammatical parallelism.
Discussion: Ellipsis connects the strophes.

VERSE–LINE: 49:7a:

כֹּה אָמַר־יְהוָה 7aA Thus says the LORD,
גֹּאֵל יִשְׂרָאֵל קְדוֹשׁוֹ 7aB the Redeemer of Israel, his Holy One,

𝔐 distinctive accents: conjunctive accent – 7.
Stresses: 2 + 3.

[1]See our comment on p. 240.

Verse-line parallelism: יהוה || גאל; יהוה || קדושׁ ישׂראל.
Discussion: This verse-line is based on our delimitation of cola.

VERSE–LINE: 49:7b:

לִבְזֹה*־נֶ֫פֶשׁ לִמְתָ֫עֵב* גּוֹי֙ לְעֶ֣בֶד מֹשְׁלִ֔ים	7bA	to the one whose life was despised, whose nation was detested, to the servant of rulers,

𝔐 distinctive accents: 5.
Stresses: 5.
Verse-line parallelism: None (unicolon).
Discussion: We accept the extra long colon.[2]

VERSE–LINE: 49:7c:

מְלָכִים֙ יִרְא֣וּ וָקָ֔מוּ	7cA	Kings will see (it) and rise up,
שָׂרִ֖ים וְיִֽשְׁתַּחֲוּ֑וּ	7cB	princes and they will bow down,

𝔐 distinctive accents: 5 – 2.
Stresses: 3 + 2.
Verse-line parallelism: מלך || שׂר; ראה || קום || שחה Hitpa.
Discussion: The cola are also connected by ellipsis.

VERSE–LINE: 49:7d:

לְמַ֤עַן יְהוָה֙ אֲשֶׁ֣ר נֶאֱמָ֔ן	7dA	for the sake of the LORD who is faithful,
קְדֹ֥שׁ יִשְׂרָאֵ֖ל וַֽיִּבְחָרֶֽךָּ׃	7dB	the Holy One of Israel who has chosen you.

𝔐 distinctive accents: 5 – 1.
Stresses: 4 + 3.
Verse-line parallelism: יהוה || קדושׁ ישׂראל.
Discussion: Again ellipsis forms a bond between the cola.

VERSE–LINE: 49:8a:

כֹּ֣ה ׀ אָמַ֣ר יְהוָ֗ה	8aA	Thus says the LORD,
בְּעֵ֤ת רָצוֹן֙ עֲנִיתִ֔יךָ	8aB	In the time of favour I answer you,
וּבְי֥וֹם יְשׁוּעָ֖ה עֲזַרְתִּ֑יךָ	8aC	and on the day of salvation I help you.

𝔐 distinctive accents: 7 – 5 – 2.
Stresses: 3 + 3 + 3.
Verse-line parallelism: ב || ב; עת || יום; רצון || ישׁועה; ענה || עזר; ־ךָ || ־ךָ;
grammatical parallelism; rhyme.

[2]Cf. pp. 410, 639.

Verse–line: 49:8b:

וְאֶצָּרְךָ וְאֶתֶּנְךָ לִבְרִית עָם 8bA Yes, I will keep you and make you into a covenant of people,
לְהָקִים אֶרֶץ 8bB to restore the earth,
לְהַנְחִיל נְחָלוֹת שֹׁמֵמוֹת׃ 8bC to make (them) inherit the desolate heritages again,

𝔐 distinctive accents: 5 – 5 –1.
Stresses: 4 + 2 + 3.
Verse-line parallelism: נצר || קום Hiph.; ל || ל || ל; עם || נחלה; grammatical parallelism.
Discussion: Enjambment connects the three cola.

Verse–line: 49:9a:

לֵאמֹר לַאֲסוּרִים צֵאוּ 9aA to say to the prisoners: Go out!
לַאֲשֶׁר בַּחֹשֶׁךְ הִגָּלוּ 9aB and to those in darknesss: Appear!

𝔐 distinctive accents: 5 – 2.
Stresses: 3 + 3.
Verse-line parallelism: ל || ל (see v. 4a above); אסר || אשר בחשך; יצא || גלה; grammatical parallelism; rhyme.
Discussion: Ellipsis connects the cola.

Verse–line: 49:9b:

עַל־דְּרָכִים יִרְעוּ 9bA Along the ways they will pasture,
וּבְכָל־שְׁפָיִים מַרְעִיתָם׃ 9bB yes, on all bare tracks will be their pasturage.

𝔐 distinctive accents: 5 – 1.
Stresses: 2 + 2.
Verse-line parallelism: דרך || שפי; רעה || מרעית; rhyme.
Discussion: Ellipsis connects the cola.

Verse–line: 49:10a:

לֹא יִרְעָבוּ וְלֹא יִצְמָאוּ 10aA They will neither hunger nor thirst,
וְלֹא־יַכֵּם שָׁרָב וָשָׁמֶשׁ 10aB nor will scorching heat or sun smite them.

𝔐 distinctive accents: 5 – 2.
Stresses: 4 + 3.
Verse-line parallelism: לא || לא.
Discussion: Although there is no clear parallelism apart from the repetition of the negation, the semantic relationship between the two cola is obvious.

VERSE–LINE: 49:10b:

כִּי־מְרַחֲמָם יְנַהֲגֵם 10bA For he who has mercy upon them will guide them,
וְעַל־מַבּוּעֵי מַיִם יְנַהֲלֵם׃ 10bB and by springs of water he will lead them gently.

𝔐 distinctive accents: 5 – 1.
Stresses: 2 + 3.
Verse-line parallelism: נהג || נהל (unique); ־ם || ־ם; grammatical parallelism; rhyme.

VERSE–LINE: 49:11a:

וְשַׂמְתִּי כָל־הָרַי לַדָּרֶךְ 11aA And I will make all my mountains into a way,
וּמְסִלֹּתַי יְרֻמוּן׃ 11aB and my highways will be raised up.

𝔐 distinctive accents: 2 – 1.
Stresses: 3 + 2.
Verse-line parallelism: ־י || ־י; דרך || מסלה.

VERSE–LINE: 49:12a:

הִנֵּה־אֵלֶּה מֵרָחוֹק יָבֹאוּ 12aA Behold, these are coming from afar,
וְהִנֵּה־אֵלֶּה מִצָּפוֹן וּמִיָּם 12aB and behold, these from the north and from the west,
וְאֵלֶּה מֵאֶרֶץ סִינִים׃ 12aC and these from the land of the Syanites.

𝔐 distinctive accents: 2 – 5 – 1.
Stresses: 3 + 3 + 3.
Verse-line parallelism: הנה || הנה; אלה || אלה || אלה; מן || מן || מן; רחוק || צפון || ים || ארץ סינים; rhyme.
Discussion: The ellipsis of יבאו binds vv. 12aB-C to v. 12aA.

VERSE–LINE: 49:13a:

רָנּוּ שָׁמַיִם וְגִילִי אָרֶץ 13aA Rejoice, O heavens and exult, O earth,
יִפְצְחוּ הָרִים רִנָּה 13aB let the mountains break forth into rejoicing,

𝔐 distinctive accents: 5 – 2.
Stresses: 4 + 3.
Verse-line parallelism: רנן || פצח רנה; שמים || ארץ || הר; גיל || פצח רנה.

VERSE–LINE: 49:13b:

כִּי־נִחַם יְהוָה עַמּוֹ 13bA for the LORD comforts his people,
וַעֲנִיָּו יְרַחֵם׃ 13bB and has mercy upon his afflicted ones.

𝔐 distinctive accents: 5 – 1.

Stresses: 3 + 2.
Verse-line parallelism: נחם Pi. || רחם; עם || עני; ־ו || ־ו.

VERSE–LINE: 49:14a:

וַתֹּאמֶר צִיּוֹן עֲזָבַנִי יְהוָה	14aA	But Zion said, "The LORD has forsaken me,
וַאדֹנָי שְׁכֵחָנִי׃	14aB	and the Lord has forgotten me".

𝔐 distinctive accents: 2 – 1.
Stresses: 4 + 2.
Verse-line parallelism: עזב || שכח; ־ני || ־ני; יהוה || אדני; grammatical parallelism; rhyme.

VERSE–LINE: 49:15a:

הֲתִשְׁכַּח אִשָּׁה עוּלָהּ	15aA	Can a woman forget her suckling,
מֵרַחֵם בֶּן־בִּטְנָהּ	15aB	and have no mercy for the child of her womb?

𝔐 distinctive accents: 5 – 2.
Stresses: 3 + 2.
Verse-line parallelism: שכח || רחם (antithetical); עול || בטן (unique); ־ה || ־ה; rhyme.
Discussion: The cola are linked by ellipsis.

VERSE–LINE: 49:15b:

גַּם־אֵלֶּה תִשְׁכַּחְנָה	15bA	Even if these were to forget,
וְאָנֹכִי לֹא אֶשְׁכָּחֵךְ׃	15bB	I will not forget you!

𝔐 distinctive accents: 5 – 1.
Stresses: 2 + 3.
Verse-line parallelism: שכח || שכח. rhyme.

VERSE–LINE: 49:16a:

הֵן עַל־כַּפַּיִם חַקֹּתִיךְ	16aA	Behold, I have you imprinted on (my) handpalms,
חוֹמֹתַיִךְ נֶגְדִּי תָּמִיד׃	16aB	your walls are always before me.

𝔐 distinctive accents: 2 – 1.
Stresses: 3 + 3.
Verse-line parallelism: ־ך (f.s.) || ־ך (f.s.).

VERSE–LINE: 49:17a:

מִהֲרוּ בֹּנַיִךְ* מֵהוֹרְסַיִךְ*	17aA	Your builders are faster than your wreckers,
וּמַחֲרִבַיִךְ מִמֵּךְ יֵצֵאוּ׃	17aB	and your destroyers go forth from you.

𝔐 distinctive accents: conjunctive accent – 1.
Stresses: 3 + 3.
Verse-line parallelism: בנה || חרב (antithetical); הרס || חרב; ךְ־ (f.s.) || ךְ־ (f.s.); יצא || מהר; rhyme.
Discussion: In our discussion of the delimitation of cola we proposed to deviate from 𝔐.[3] The equal number of stresses (3 + 3) in the resulting verse-line, also in the surrounding verse-lines, favours this decision.

VERSE–LINE: 49:18a:

שְׂאִי־סָבִיב עֵינַיִךְ וּרְאִי	18aA	Lift up your eyes round about and see:
כֻּלָּם נִקְבְּצוּ בָאוּ־לָךְ	18aB	All of them are assembled, they come to you.

𝔐 distinctive accents: 5 – 2.
Stresses: 3 + 3.
Verse-line parallelism: ךְ־ (f.s.) || ךְ־ (f.s.).

VERSE–LINE: 49:18b:

חַי־אָנִי נְאֻם־יְהוָה	18bA	As I live, declares the LORD,
כִּי כֻלָּם כָּעֲדִי תִלְבָּשִׁי	18bB	you will wear all of them as an ornament,
וּתְקַשְּׁרִים כַּכַּלָּה׃	18bC	and you will bind them on like a bride.

𝔐 distinctive accents: 7 – 5 – 1.
Stresses: 2 + 4 + 2.
Verse-line parallelism: כ || כ; לבש || קשׁר (unique); grammatical parallelism.

VERSE–LINE: 49:19a:

כִּי חָרְבֹתַיִךְ וְשֹׁמְמֹתַיִךְ וְאֶרֶץ הֲרִסֻתֵךְ	19aA	Surely, your ruins, your desolated places and your wrecked land –

𝔐 distinctive accents: 2.
Stresses: 5.
Verse-line parallelism: None (unicolon).

VERSE–LINE: 49:19b:

כִּי עַתָּה תֵּצְרִי מִיּוֹשֵׁב	19bA	(but) surely, now you will be too narrow for the inhabitants,
וְרָחֲקוּ מְבַלְּעָיִךְ׃	19bB	and those who devoured you will be far away.

𝔐 distinctive accents: 5 – 1.
Stresses: 4 + 2.
Verse-line parallelism: None.

[3] See p. 415.

Discussion: Although there is no parallelism the accents make it clear that the two cola were supposed to be read as one verse-line. But on a higher level a certain paralellism with v. 17 is undeniable.

VERSE–LINE: 49:20a:

עוֹד יֹאמְרוּ בְאָזְנַיִךְ	20aA	Again they will say it in your ears,
בְּנֵי שִׁכֻּלָיִךְ	20aB	the children of your bereavement:

𝔐 distinctive accents: 5 – 2.
Stresses: 3 + 2.
Verse-line parallelism: ךְ־ (f.s.) ‖ ךְ־ (f.s.); rhyme.
Discussion: The sentence runs on, causing the lack of clear parallels.

VERSE–LINE: 49:20b:

צַר־לִי הַמָּקוֹם	20bA	"The place is too narrow for me!
גְּשָׁה־לִּי וְאֵשֵׁבָה׃	20bB	Move up for me that I may dwell too!"

𝔐 distinctive accents: 8 – 1.
Stresses: 2 + 2.
Verse-line parallelism: ל ‖ ל; י־ ‖ י־; מקום ‖ ישב; rhyme.

VERSE–LINE: 49:21a:

וְאָמַרְתְּ בִּלְבָבֵךְ	21aA	And you will say in your heart:
מִי יָלַד־לִי אֶת־אֵלֶּה	21aB	"Who begot these for me?
וַאֲנִי שְׁכוּלָה וְגַלְמוּדָה	21aC	For I myself was bereaved and barren,

𝔐 distinctive accents: 7 – 5 – 2.
Stresses: 2 + 3 + 3.
Verse-line parallelism: ילד ‖ שכולה (antithetical); ילד ‖ גלמוד (antithetical); י־ ‖ אני.

VERSE–LINE: 49:21b:

גֹּלָה ׀ וְסוּרָה	21bA	an exiled and displaced person –
וְאֵלֶּה מִי גִדֵּל	21bB	so who brought these up?
הֵן אֲנִי נִשְׁאַרְתִּי לְבַדִּי	21bC	Behold, I was left alone,
אֵלֶּה אֵיפֹה הֵם׃	21bD	these then – whence are they?

𝔐 distinctive accents: 7 – 5 – 5 – 2.
Stresses: 2 + 3 + 4 + 3.
Verse-line parallelism: סור ‖ לבד; אלה ‖ אלה; מי ‖ איפה.
Discussion: With the Masoretes.[4]

[4] For the sequence of accents see on p. 240.

VERSE–LINE: 49:22a:

כֹּה־אָמַר אֲדֹנָי יְהוִה 22aA Thus says the LORD God:
הִנֵּה אֶשָּׂא אֶל־גּוֹיִם יָדִי 22aB Behold, I will lift up my hand to the nations,
וְאֶל־עַמִּים אָרִים נִסִּי 22aC and to the peoples I will raise my banner,

𝔐 distinctive accents: 7 – 5 – 2.
Stresses: 3 + 4 + 3.
Verse-line parallelism: נשׂא || רום; אל || אל; גוים || עמים; יד || נס; ־י || ־י; grammatical parallelism; rhyme.

VERSE–LINE: 49:22b:

וְהֵבִיאוּ בָנַיִךְ בְּחֹצֶן 22bA and they will bring your sons in their arms,
וּבְנֹתַיִךְ עַל־כָּתֵף תִּנָּשֶׂאנָה׃ 22bB and your daughters will be carried on their shoulders.

𝔐 distinctive accents: 5 – 1.
Stresses: 3 + 3.
Verse-line parallelism: בוא Hiph. || נשׂא; בן || בת; ־ך (f.s.) || ־ך (f.s.); על || ב; חצן || כתף; rhyme.

VERSE–LINE: 49:23a:

וְהָיוּ מְלָכִים אֹמְנַיִךְ 23aA Kings will be your nursing fathers,
וְשָׂרוֹתֵיהֶם מֵינִיקֹתַיִךְ 23aB and their princesses your nurses.

𝔐 distinctive accents: 7 – 5.
Stresses: 3 + 2.
Verse-line parallelism: מלך || שׂרה; אמן || ינק; ־ך (f.s.) || ־ך (f.s.); rhyme.

Discussion: Ungrammatical ellipsis connects the cola.

VERSE–LINE: 49:23b:

אַפַּיִם אֶרֶץ יִשְׁתַּחֲווּ לָךְ 23bA Noses to the ground they will bow down for you,
וַעֲפַר רַגְלַיִךְ יְלַחֵכוּ 23bB and lick the dust of your feet.

𝔐 distinctive accents: 5 – 2.
Stresses: 4 + 3.
Verse-line parallelism: ארץ || עפר; שׁחה || לחך (unique); ־ך (f.s.) || ־ך (f.s.); grammatical parallelism.
Discussion: The accents show that the Masoretes were inclined to take the first four cola of v. 23 as one verse-line. Apparently they did so because of the repetition of the suffix 2 f.s. at the end of each colon. However, the strong parallelism in both halves leaves no doubt that we have to read two bicola here instead of a quadrocolon.

VERSE–LINE: 49:23c:

וְיָדַעַתְּ כִּי־אֲנִי יְהוָה	23cA	And you will know that I am the LORD:
אֲשֶׁר לֹא־יֵבֹשׁוּ קֹוָי׃	23cB	those waiting for me will not be put to shame.

𝔐 distinctive accents: 5 – 1.
Stresses: 3 + 3.
Verse-line parallelism: אני || י״.
Discussion: Because the sentence runs on, clear parallels are missing here. See, however, the same connection between knowing יהוה and the assurance not to be put to shame in Joel 2:27, and compare the opposite utterance in Isa. 44:9.

VERSE–LINE: 49:24a:

הֲיֻקַּח מִגִּבּוֹר מַלְקוֹחַ	24aA	"Can spoil be taken away from a hero?
וְאִם־שְׁבִי צַדִּיק יִמָּלֵט׃	24aB	Or captives escape from their legal owner?"

𝔐 distinctive accents: 2 – 1.
Stresses: 3 + 3.
Verse-line parallelism: לקח || מלט (antithetical); גבור || צדיק (unique); מלקוח || שבי; grammatical parallelism.

VERSE–LINE: 49:25a:

כִּי־כֹה ׀ אָמַר יְהוָה	25aA	Yet thus says the LORD,
גַּם־שְׁבִי גִבּוֹר יֻקָּח	25aB	Even the captives of a hero will be taken away,
וּמַלְקוֹחַ עָרִיץ יִמָּלֵט	25aC	and the spoil of the tyrant will escape.

𝔐 distinctive accents: 7 – 5 – 2.
Stresses: 3 + 3 + 3.
Verse-line parallelism: שבי || מלקוח; גבור || עריץ; לקח || מלט; grammatical parallelism.

VERSE–LINE: 49:25b:

וְאֶת־יְרִיבֵךְ אָנֹכִי אָרִיב	25bA	I myself will contend with him who contends with you,
וְאֶת־בָּנַיִךְ אָנֹכִי אוֹשִׁיעַ׃	25bB	and your children I myself will save.

𝔐 distinctive accents: 5 – 1.
Stresses: 3 + 3.
Verse-line parallelism: את || את; ־ך (f.s.) || ־ך (f.s.); אנכי || אנכי; ריב || ישע; grammatical parallelism.

VERSE–LINE: 49:26a:

וְהַאֲכַלְתִּי אֶת־מוֹנַיִךְ אֶת־בְּשָׂרָם	26aA	And I will make your oppressors eat their own flesh,
וְכֶעָסִיס דָּמָם יִשְׁכָּרוּן	26aB	and they will become drunk with their own blood, as with new wine.

𝔐 distinctive accents: 5 – 2.
Stresses: 3 + 3.
Verse-line parallelism: אכל || שׁכר; בשׂר || דם; ־ם || ־ם; rhyme.

VERSE–LINE: 49:26b:

וְיָדְעוּ כָל־בָּשָׂר	26bA	And all flesh will know,
כִּי אֲנִי יְהוָה מוֹשִׁיעֵךְ	26bB	that I am the LORD, your Saviour,
וְגֹאֲלֵךְ אֲבִיר יַעֲקֹב׃	26bC	and your Redeemer, the Mighty One of Jacob.

𝔐 distinctive accents: 7 – 5 – 1.
Stresses: 2 + 4 + 3.
Verse-line parallelism: יהוה || גאל; ישׁע || אביר; ־ךְ (f.s.) || ־ךְ (f.s.); ישׁע || גאל; rhyme.
Discussion: Ellipsis of אני forms an extra bond.

10.4 Isaiah 49 – Delimitation of Strophes

STROPHE A.i.1 (Isa. 49:1)

שִׁמְעוּ אִיִּים אֵלַי	1aA	Listen to me, you islands,
וְהַקְשִׁיבוּ לְאֻמִּים מֵרָחוֹק	1aB	and pay attention, you nations from afar:
יְהוָה מִבֶּטֶן קְרָאָנִי	1bA	The LORD called me from the womb,
מִמְּעֵי אִמִּי הִזְכִּיר שְׁמִי׃	1bB	from the loins of my mother He mentioned my name.

= Masoretic verse.
Separation ↑: major division markers in the textual tradition; imperative(s); vocatives.
Separation ↓: swapping (subject); swapping (adjunct).
Strophe parallelism: שׁמע || קרא; מן || מן.

STROPHE A.i.2 (Isa. 49:2)

וַיָּשֶׂם פִּי כְּחֶרֶב חַדָּה	2aA	And he made my mouth like a sharpened sword,
בְּצֵל יָדוֹ הֶחְבִּיאָנִי	2aB	in the shadow of his hand he hid me.
וַיְשִׂימֵנִי לְחֵץ בָּרוּר	2bA	He made me into a polished arrow,
בְּאַשְׁפָּתוֹ הִסְתִּירָנִי׃	2bB	in his quiver he concealed me.

= Masoretic verse.

Separation ↑: swapping (adjunct).
Separation ↓: repetitive verse-line parallelism; swapping (adjunct).
Strophe parallelism: שׂים || שׂים; חרב || חץ; חד || ברור (unique); ב || ב; חבא || סתר; ־ני || ־ני; grammatical parallelism.

STROPHE A.i.3 (Isa. 49:3)

וַיֹּאמֶר לִי עַבְדִּי־אָתָּה	3aA	And he said to me, You are my servant,
יִשְׂרָאֵל אֲשֶׁר־בְּךָ אֶתְפָּאָר׃	3aB	Israel, in whom I will glorify myself.

= Masoretic verse.
Separation ↑: swapping (subject); swapping (adjunct).
Separation ↓: major division markers in the textual tradition.
Strophe parallelism: None (one verse-line).

STROPHE A.i.4 (Isa. 49:4)

וַאֲנִי אָמַרְתִּי לְרִיק יָגַעְתִּי	4aA	But I said, For nothing I wearied myself,
לְתֹהוּ וְהֶבֶל כֹּחִי כִלֵּיתִי	4aB	for voidness and vanity I have spent my strength.
אָכֵן מִשְׁפָּטִי אֶת־יְהוָה	4bA	Yet my right is with the LORD,
וּפְעֻלָּתִי אֶת־אֱלֹהָי׃	4bB	and my recompense with my God.

= Masoretic verse.
Separation ↑: major division markers in the textual tradition; independent pers. pronoun; marker of direct speech; swapping (object); swapping (adjunct).
Separation ↓: major division markers in the textual tradition; deictic particle(s); repetitive verse-line parallelism.
Strophe parallelism: ריק || פעולה (antithetical; unique).

STROPHE A.ii.1 (Isa. 49:5)

וְעַתָּה ׀ אָמַר יְהוָה	5aA	But now, the LORD says –
יֹצְרִי מִבֶּטֶן לְעֶבֶד לוֹ	5aB	he who formed me from the womb to be his servant,
לְשׁוֹבֵב יַעֲקֹב אֵלָיו	5aC	to make Jacob return to him,
וְיִשְׂרָאֵל לוֹ* יֵאָסֵף	5aD	and Israel that must be gathered to him
וְאֶכָּבֵד בְּעֵינֵי יְהוָה	5bA	– for I am honoured in the LORD's eyes,
וֵאלֹהַי הָיָה עֻזִּי׃	5bB	and my God is my strength –

= Masoretic verse.
Separation ↑: major division markers in the textual tradition; deictic particle(s); marker of direct speech; swapping (adjunct).
Separation ↓: swapping (subject).
Strophe parallelism: עבד || כבד (antithetical; unique).[1]

[1] But see 1 Sam. 22:14 (David), perhaps a deliberate allusion. Cf. Isa. 55:3-5.

STROPHE A.ii.2 (Isa. 49:6)

וַיֹּאמֶר נָקֵל מִהְיוֹתְךָ לִי עֶבֶד	6aA	now he says, It is too little that you should be a servant for me,
לְהָקִים אֶת־שִׁבְטֵי יַעֲקֹב	6aB	to restore the tribes of Jacob,
וּנְצוּרֵי* יִשְׂרָאֵל לְהָשִׁיב	6aC	and to bring back the well-kept of Israel.
וּנְתַתִּיךָ לְאוֹר גּוֹיִם	6bA	I will also make you a light to the nations,
לִהְיוֹת יְשׁוּעָתִי עַד־קְצֵה הָאָרֶץ׃	6bB	to be my salvation to the ends of the earth.

= Masoretic verse.
Separation ↑: marker of direct speech; repetitive verse-line parallelism; swapping (object).
Separation ↓: major division markers in the textual tradition; repetitive verse-line parallelism.
Strophe parallelism: היה ‖ היה; ל ‖ ל; קום Hiph. ‖ ישועה; grammatical parallelism.

STROPHE B.i.1 (Isa. 49:7a–b)

כֹּה אָמַר־יְהוָה	7aA	Thus says the LORD,
גֹּאֵל יִשְׂרָאֵל קְדוֹשׁוֹ	7aB	the Redeemer of Israel, his Holy One,
לִבְזֵה*־נֶפֶשׁ לִמְתָעֵב* גּוֹי לְעֶבֶד מֹשְׁלִים	7bA	to the one whose life was despised, whose nation was detested, to the servant of rulers,

≠ Masoretic verse.
Separation ↑: deictic particle(s); marker of direct speech.
Separation ↓: repetitive verse-line parallelism.
Strophe parallelism: None (enjambment).
Discussion: In 𝔐 v. 7 is only one very long strophe, probably because the sentence runs on. In our opinion it is necessary to distribute v. 7 over two strophes, with the colometrical support of the ancient witnesses and the concentric canticle parallelism.[2]

STROPHE B.i.2 (Isa. 49:7c–d)

מְלָכִים יִרְאוּ וָקָמוּ	7cA	Kings will see (it) and rise up,
שָׂרִים וְיִשְׁתַּחֲווּ	7cB	princes and they will bow down,
לְמַעַן יְהוָה אֲשֶׁר נֶאֱמָן	7dA	for the sake of the LORD who is faithful,
קְדֹשׁ יִשְׂרָאֵל וַיִּבְחָרֶךָּ׃	7dB	the Holy One of Israel who has chosen you.

≠ Masoretic verse.
Separation ↑: swapping (subject)
Separation ↓: major division markers in the textual tradition;

[2] See pp. 409-10, 423-4.

Strophe parallelism: None, but the canticle parallelism compensates for the lack of strophe parallelism.
Discussion: See our comment on the previous strophe.

STROPHE B.ii.1 (Isa. 49:8)

כֹּה ׀ אָמַר יְהֹוָה	8aA	Thus says the LORD,
בְּעֵת רָצוֹן עֲנִיתִיךָ	8aB	In the time of favour I answer you,
וּבְיוֹם יְשׁוּעָה עֲזַרְתִּיךָ	8aC	and on the day of salvation I help you.
וְאֶצָּרְךָ וְאֶתֶּנְךָ לִבְרִית עָם	8bA	Yes, I will keep you and make you into a covenant of people,
לְהָקִים אֶרֶץ	8bB	to restore the earth,
לְהַנְחִיל נְחָלוֹת שֹׁמֵמוֹת׃	8bC	to make (them) inherit the desolate heritages again,

= Masoretic verse.
Separation ↑: major division markers in the textual tradition; deictic particle(s); marker of direct speech; repetitive verse-line parallelism; swapping (adjunct).
Separation ↓: repetitive verse-line parallelism.
Strophe parallelism: קום Hiph. || ישועה;

STROPHE B.ii.2 (Isa. 49:9)

לֵאמֹר לַאֲסוּרִים צֵאוּ	9aA	to say to the prisoners: Go out!
לַאֲשֶׁר בַּחֹשֶׁךְ הִגָּלוּ	9aB	and to those in darknesss: Appear!
עַל־דְּרָכִים יִרְעוּ	9bA	Along the ways they will pasture,
וּבְכָל־שְׁפָיִים מַרְעִיתָם׃	9bB	yes, on all bare tracks will be their pasturage.

= Masoretic verse.
Separation ↑: imperative(s); repetitive verse-line parallelism.
Separation ↓: swapping (adjunct).
Strophe parallelism: יצא || רעה; ב || ב.

STROPHE B.ii.3 (Isa. 49:10)

לֹא יִרְעָבוּ וְלֹא יִצְמָאוּ	10aA	They will neither hunger nor thirst,
וְלֹא־יַכֵּם שָׁרָב וָשָׁמֶשׁ	10aB	nor will scorching heat or sun smite them.
כִּי־מְרַחֲמָם יְנַהֲגֵם	10bA	For he who has mercy upon them will guide them,
וְעַל־מַבּוּעֵי מַיִם יְנַהֲלֵם׃	10bB	and by springs of water he will lead them gently.

= Masoretic verse.
Separation ↑: repetitive verse-line parallelism.
Separation ↓: deictic particle(s); swapping (subject); swapping (adjunct).
Strophe parallelism: צמא || מים; נכה || רחם (antithetical); ־הם || ־הם.

STROPHE B.ii.4 (Isa. 49:11–12)

וְשַׂמְתִּי כָל־הָרַי לַדָּרֶךְ	11aA	And I will make all my mountains into a way,
וּמְסִלֹּתַי יְרֻמוּן׃	11aB	and my highways will be raised up.
הִנֵּה־אֵלֶּה מֵרָחוֹק יָבֹאוּ	12aA	Behold, these are coming from afar,
וְהִנֵּה־אֵלֶּה מִצָּפוֹן וּמִיָּם	12aB	and behold, these from the north and from the west,
וְאֵלֶּה מֵאֶרֶץ סִינִים׃	12aC	and these from the land of the Syanites.

≠ Masoretic verse.
Separation ↑: swapping (subject).
Separation ↓: major division markers in the textual tradition; deictic particle(s); demonstrative pronouns; repetitive verse-line parallelism; swapping (adjunct).
Strophe parallelism: None, but the association of דרך and the verb בוא constitutes a strong link between the two verse-lines.
Discussion: For the reason just mentioned we believe that the two verses may be combined into one strophe. In Isa. 42:16 too, the going on the road and the flattening of mountains are described in one strophe.

STROPHE B.iii.1 (Isa. 49:13)

רָנּוּ שָׁמַיִם וְגִילִי אָרֶץ	13aA	Rejoice, O heavens and exult, O earth,
יִפְצְחוּ הָרִים רִנָּה	13aB	let the mountains break forth into rejoicing,
כִּי־נִחַם יְהוָה עַמּוֹ	13bA	for the LORD comforts his people,
וַעֲנִיָּו יְרַחֵם׃	13bB	and has mercy upon his afflicted ones.

= Masoretic verse.
Separation ↑: major division markers in the textual tradition; imperative(s); jussive(s); vocatives.
Separation ↓: major division markers in the textual tradition; deictic particle(s); swapping (object).
Strophe parallelism: רנן || נחם.

STROPHE C.i.1 (Isa. 49:14)

וַתֹּאמֶר צִיּוֹן עֲזָבַנִי יְהוָה	14aA	But Zion said, "The LORD has forsaken me,
וַאדֹנָי שְׁכֵחָנִי׃	14aB	and the LORD has forgotten me".

= Masoretic verse.
Separation ↑: major division markers in the textual tradition; marker of direct speech; swapping (subject).
Separation ↓: major division markers in the textual tradition.
Strophe parallelism: None (one verse-line).

STROPHE C.i.2 (Isa. 49:15)

הֲתִשְׁכַּח אִשָּׁה֙ עוּלָהּ	15aA	Can a woman forget her suckling,
מֵרַחֵם בֶּן־בִּטְנָהּ	15aB	and have no mercy for the child of her womb?
גַּם־אֵלֶּה תִשְׁכַּחְנָה	15bA	Even if these were to forget,
וְאָנֹכִי לֹא אֶשְׁכָּחֵךְ׃	15bB	I will not forget you!

= Masoretic verse.
Separation ↑: major division markers in the textual tradition.
Separation ↓: major division markers in the textual tradition; deictic particle(s); demonstrative pronoun; independent pers. pronoun; repetitive verse-line parallelism; swapping (subject).
Strophe parallelism: שׁכח || שׁכח.

STROPHE C.ii.1 (Isa. 49:16–17)

הֵן עַל־כַּפַּיִם חַקֹּתִיךְ	16aA	Behold, I have you imprinted on (my) handpalms,
חוֹמֹתַיִךְ נֶגְדִּי תָּמִיד׃	16aB	your walls are always before me.
מַהֲרוּ בֹּנַיִךְ* מֵהוֹרְסַיִךְ*	17aA	Your builders are faster than your wreckers,
וּמַחֲרִבַיִךְ מִמֵּךְ יֵצֵאוּ׃	17aB	and your destroyers go forth from you.

≠ Masoretic verse.
Separation ↑: major division markers in the textual tradition; deictic particle(s); repetitive verse-line parallelism; swapping (adjunct).
Separation ↓: major division markers in the textual tradition; repetitive verse-line parallelism; swapping (subject); swapping (adjunct).
Strophe parallelism: ־ךְ || ־יִךְ || ־יִךְ || ־יִךְ.
Discussion: The persistent use of the suffix ־יִךְ and the imagery of God having the outlines of Zion imprinted in his hand in combination with onrushing builders argues in favour of taking vv. 16-17 together as one strophe, against the Masoretic tradition which vocalized v. 17a differently and therefore could not consider this possibility.

STROPHE C.ii.2 (Isa. 49:18)

שְׂאִי־סָבִיב עֵינַיִךְ֙ וּרְאִי	18aA	Lift up your eyes round about and see:
כֻּלָּם נִקְבְּצוּ בָאוּ־לָךְ	18aB	All of them are assembled, they come to you.
חַי־אָנִי נְאֻם־יְהוָה	18bA	As I live, declares the LORD,
כִּי כֻלָּם֙ כַּעֲדִי תִלְבָּשִׁי	18bB	you will wear all of them as an ornament,
וּתְקַשְּׁרִים כַּכַּלָּה׃	18bC	and you will bind them on like a bride.

= Masoretic verse.
Separation ↑: major division markers in the textual tradition; imperative(s); swapping (subject); swapping (adjunct).

Separation ↓: major division markers in the textual tradition; deictic particle(s); independent pers. pronoun; swapping (object); swapping (adjunct).
Strophe parallelism: None.
Discussion: Although parallelism is lacking, the imagery connects the two verses: the young builders themselves will be an ornament to Zion (cf. Isa. 54:12-13).

STROPHE C.iii.1 (Isa. 49:19)

כִּי חָרְבֹתַיִךְ וְשֹׁמְמֹתַיִךְ וְאֶרֶץ הֲרִסֻתֵךְ	19aA	Surely, your ruins, your desolated places and your wrecked land –
כִּי עַתָּה תֵּצְרִי מִיּוֹשֵׁב	19bA	(but) surely, now you will be too narrow for the inhabitants,
וְרָחֲקוּ מְבַלְּעָיִךְ׃	19bB	and those who devoured you will be far away.

= Masoretic verse.
Separation ↑: major division markers in the textual tradition; deictic particle(s); repetitive verse-line parallelism.
Separation ↓: major division markers in the textual tradition; deictic particle(s).
Strophe parallelism: חרבה || ישב; הריסות || בלע; ־יך (f.s.) || ־יך (f.s.).

STROPHE C.iii.2 (Isa. 49:20)

עוֹד יֹאמְרוּ בְאָזְנַיִךְ	20aA	Again they will say it in your ears,
בְּנֵי שִׁכֻּלָיִךְ	20aB	the children of your bereavement:
צַר־לִי הַמָּקוֹם	20bA	"The place is too narrow for me!
גְּשָׁה־לִּי וְאֵשֵׁבָה׃	20bB	Move up for me that I may dwell too!"

= Masoretic verse.
Separation ↑: major division markers in the textual tradition; marker of direct speech; repetitive verse-line parallelism; swapping (adjunct).
Separation ↓: imperative(s); jussive(s); repetitive verse-line parallelism.
Strophe parallelism: None.
Discussion: Despite the lack of strophe parallelism the delimitation of the strophe is not in doubt. Direct speech and the evocation of the image of numerous offspring connect the two bicola.

STROPHE C.iii.3 (Isa. 49:21)

וְאָמַרְתְּ בִּלְבָבֵךְ	21aA	And you will say in your heart:
מִי יָלַד־לִי אֶת־אֵלֶּה	21aB	"Who begot these for me?
וַאֲנִי שְׁכוּלָה וְגַלְמוּדָה	21aC	For I myself was bereaved and barren,

גֹּלָ֣ה ׀ וְסוּרָ֗ה	21bA	an exiled and displaced person –
וְאֵ֙לֶּה֙ מִ֣י גִדֵּ֔ל	21bB	so who brought these up?
הֵ֤ן אֲנִי֙ נִשְׁאַ֣רְתִּי לְבַדִּ֔י	21bC	Behold, I was left alone,
אֵ֖לֶּה אֵיפֹ֥ה הֵֽם׃	21bD	these then – whence are they?

= Masoretic verse.
Separation ↑: independent pers. pronoun; interrogative pronoun; marker of direct speech; swapping (adjunct).
Separation ↓: major division markers in the textual tradition; deictic particle(s); demonstrative pronoun; independent pers. pronoun; interrogative pronoun.
Strophe parallelism: מי || מי; ילד || גדל; ל || ל; ־י || ־י; אלה || אלה; אני || אני.

STROPHE D.i.1 (Isa. 49:22)

כֹּֽה־אָמַ֞ר אֲדֹנָ֣י יְהוִ֗ה	22aA	Thus says the Lord GOD:
הִנֵּ֨ה אֶשָּׂ֤א אֶל־גּוֹיִם֙ יָדִ֔י	22aB	Behold, I will lift up my hand to the nations,
וְאֶל־עַמִּ֖ים אָרִ֣ים נִסִּ֑י	22aC	and to the peoples I will raise my banner,
וְהֵבִ֤יאוּ בָנַ֙יִךְ֙ בְּחֹ֔צֶן	22bA	and they will bring your sons in their arms,
וּבְנֹתַ֖יִךְ עַל־כָּתֵ֥ף תִּנָּשֶֽׂאנָה׃	22bB	and your daughters will be carried on their shoulders.

= Masoretic verse.
Separation ↑: major division markers in the textual tradition; deictic particle(s); marker of direct speech; repetitive verse-line parallelism; swapping (adjunct).
Separation ↓: repetitive verse-line parallelism; swapping (object); swapping (adjunct).
Strophe parallelism: גוים || בנים.

STROPHE D.i.2 (Isa. 49:23a–b)

וְהָי֨וּ מְלָכִ֜ים אֹמְנַ֗יִךְ	23aA	Kings will be your nursing fathers,
וְשָׂרֽוֹתֵיהֶם֙ מֵינִ֣יקֹתַ֔יִךְ	23aB	and their princesses your nurses.
אַפַּ֗יִם אֶ֚רֶץ יִשְׁתַּ֣חֲווּ לָ֔ךְ	23bA	Noses to the ground they will bow down for you,
וַעֲפַ֥ר רַגְלַ֖יִךְ יְלַחֵ֑כוּ	23bB	and lick the dust of your feet.

≠ Masoretic verse.
Separation ↑: repetitive verse-line parallelism.
Separation ↓: repetitive verse-line parallelism; swapping (object); swapping (adjunct).
Strophe parallelism: ־יך (f.s.) || ־יך (f.s.) ־יך (f.s.) || ־יך (f.s.); in a general sense there is parallelism between v. 23a and v. 23b because nursing was often a slave's task.

Discussion: The Masoretes constructed v. 23 as a quadrocolon plus a bicolon. In favour of this solution one might cite v. 26bA where the phrase כי . . . וידעו heads the second half of a bicolon. However, there are many cases where the phrase "and you/they will know" is standing at the head of a verse.[3] So this is at least an option. The semantic dichotomy in two bicola v. 23a and v. 23b[4] on the one hand and the fourfold repetition of ־יך on the other made us decide to take vv. 23a-b as a separate strophe.

STROPHE D.i.3 (Isa. 49:23c)

וְיָדַ֙עַתְּ֙ כִּֽי־אֲנִ֣י יְהוָ֔ה	23cA	And you will know that I am the LORD:
אֲשֶׁ֥ר לֹֽא־יֵבֹ֖שׁוּ קֹוָֽי׃	23cB	those waiting for me will not be put to shame.

≠ Masoretic verse.
Separation ↑: deictic particle(s); independent pers. pronoun.
Separation ↓: major division markers in the textual tradition.
Strophe parallelism: None (one verse-line).
Discussion: See our comment on the previous strophe.

STROPHE D.ii.1(Isa. 49:24)

הֲיֻקַּ֥ח מִגִּבּ֖וֹר מַלְק֑וֹחַ	24aA	"Can spoil be taken away from a hero?
וְאִם־שְׁבִ֥י צַדִּ֖יק יִמָּלֵֽט׃	24aB	Or captives escape from their legal owner?"

= Masoretic verse.
Separation ↑: major division markers in the textual tradition; swapping (adjunct).
Separation ↓: major division markers in the textual tradition;
Strophe parallelism: None (one verse-line).

STROPHE D.ii.2 (Isa. 49:25)

כִּי־כֹ֣ה ׀ אָמַ֣ר יְהוָ֗ה	25aA	Yet thus says the LORD,
גַּם־שְׁבִ֤י גִבּוֹר֙ יֻקָּ֔ח	25aB	Even the captives of a hero will be taken away,
וּמַלְק֥וֹחַ עָרִ֖יץ יִמָּלֵ֑ט	25aC	and the spoil of the tyrant will escape.
וְאֶת־יְרִיבֵךְ֙ אָנֹכִ֣י אָרִ֔יב	25bA	I myself will contend with him who contends with you,
וְאֶת־בָּנַ֖יִךְ אָנֹכִ֥י אוֹשִֽׁיעַ׃	25bB	and your children I myself will save.

= Masoretic verse.

[3]Ex. 7:5; 14:18; 29:46; Ezek. 6:10, 13; 11:12; 12:15; 17:24; 20:24, 44; 21:10; 30:8; 34:30; 35:12; 37:13, 28; 39:22, 23, 28; Joel 2:27; 4:17; Mal. 2:4; Job 5:24, 25.
[4]See our comments on p. 430.

Separation ↑: major division markers in the textual tradition; deictic particle(s); marker of direct speech; swapping (subject).
Separation ↓: independent pers. pronoun; swapping (object).
Strophe parallelism: מלט || ישׁע (unique).

STROPHE D.ii.3 (Isa. 49:26)

וְהַאֲכַלְתִּי אֶת־מוֹנַיִךְ אֶת־בְּשָׂרָם	26aA	And I will make your oppressors eat their own flesh,
וְכֶעָסִיס דָּמָם יִשְׁכָּרוּן	26aB	and they will become drunk with their own blood, as with new wine.
וְיָדְעוּ כָל־בָּשָׂר	26bA	And all flesh will know,
כִּי אֲנִי יְהוָה מוֹשִׁיעֵךְ	26bB	that I am the LORD, your Saviour,
וְגֹאֲלֵךְ אֲבִיר יַעֲקֹב׃	26bC	and your Redeemer, the Mighty One of Jacob.

= Masoretic verse.
Separation ↑: swapping (object); swapping (adjunct).
Separation ↓: major division markers in the textual tradition; deictic particle(s); independent pers. pronoun; repetitive verse-line parallelism.
Strophe parallelism: בשׂר || בשׂר; דם || בשׂר.

10.5 Isaiah 49 – Delimitation of Canticles

CANTICLE A.i (49:1–4)

Separation ↑: major division markers in the textual tradition; thematic discontinuity; change of subject.
Separation ↓: major division markers in the textual tradition.
Canticle parallelism: י־ || י־ || י־ || י־; אמר || אמר (responsion); עבד || פעלה (inclusion).
Thematic unity: yes. All strophes deal with the call of the servant.
Discussion: The major division markers in $1Q^a$ and $\mathfrak{G}^A$ after v. 3 are simply marking the end of v. 3, possibly to indicate the change of speaker. Both manuscripts also have the well-attested break after v. 4.

CANTICLE A.ii (49:5–6)

Separation ↑: major division markers in the textual tradition; change of subject.
Separation ↓: major division markers in the textual tradition.
Canticle parallelism: אמר || אמר (responsion); עבד || עבד (responsion); ל || ל (responsion); שׁוב || שׁוב (responsion); יעקב || יעקב, ישׂראל (responsion); היה || היה (concatenation); עז || ישׁועה (responsion); י־ || י־ (responsion).

Thematic unity: The strophes are linked by an on-running sentence (enjambment).
Discussion: The stray diamond in $\mathfrak{S}^b$ after v. 5aD must be an error, or perhaps an attempt to mark the point where the main clause is picked up again. The same manuscript has the well-attested incisions after vv. 4 and 6. $\mathfrak{G}^A$ indicates the latter break also proleptically and redundantly after v. 6aC.

CANTICLE B.i (49:7a-d)

Separation ↑: major division markers in the textual tradition.
Separation ↓: major division markers in the textual tradition.
Canticle parallelism: יהוה || יהוה (inclusion); ישׂראל || ישׂראל (inclusion); קדוש || קדוש (inclusion; a typical example of the break-up of a stereotyped phrase); משל || מלך (concatenation).
The strophes are linked by an on-running sentence (enjambment).
Thematic unity: yes. The servant will be exalted over kings and princes because of the Holy One of Israel.

CANTICLE B.ii (49:8–12)

Separation ↑: major division markers in the textual tradition.
Separation ↓: major division markers in the textual tradition.
Canticle parallelism: אמר || אמר (responsion); נתן || שים (inclusion); ארץ || ארץ (responsion); דרך || דרך (inclusion); רעה || נהג (responsion); רעה || נהל (responsion).
Thematic unity: yes. New Exodus and miracles underway.
Discussion: Again $\mathfrak{G}^A$ indicates the break after v. 12 in a proleptic and redundant way after v. 11aB.

CANTICLE B.iii (49:13)

Separation ↑: major division markers in the textual tradition; change of subject.
Separation ↓: major division markers in the textual tradition.
Canticle parallelism: None (one strophe).
Thematic unity: yes. A hymn and its reason.
Discussion: See our discussion of the macrostructure below.

CANTICLE C.i (49:14–15)

Separation ↑: major division markers in the textual tradition; thematic discontinuity; change of subject.
Separation ↓: major division markers in the textual tradition.

Canticle parallelism: שׁכח || שׁכח (concatenation/inclusion)
Thematic unity: yes. A complaint of Zion and its analogy.
Discussion: 𝔊[S] seems to mark the end of the first strophe.

CANTICLE C.ii (49:16–18)

Separation ↑: major division markers in the textual tradition.
Separation ↓: major division markers in the textual tradition.
Canticle parallelism: ־יך (f.s.) || ־יך (f.s.) (responsion/concatenation); מהר || בוא (concatenation).
Thematic unity: yes. The children of Zion will come back to her to rebuild her beautifully.
Discussion: We decided to make an incision after v. 18bC because this breaking point seems to be attested in two different traditions although 𝔖[e] is difficult to read at this point. Also the parallelism between תצרי in v. 19bA and צר לי in v. 20bA on the one hand and שׁכיך in v. 20aB and שׁכולה in v. 21aC on the other favours the decision to keep these strophes together. Of course there is a certain correspondence between the two canticles belonging to the same sub-canto (e.g. v. 17aB || v. 19bB).

𝔊[SQ] both have a paragraphos at the end of the first strophe. But since they also they have one after v. 15 it may be an error. The much more prominent major division markers which are found in 𝔊[SA] after v. 18aB anticipate the break after v. 18, in the case of 𝔊[A] redundantly because it also marks the latter.

CANTICLE C.iii (49:19–21)

Separation ↑: major division markers in the textual tradition.
Separation ↓: major division markers in the textual tradition.
Canticle parallelism: צרר || צר (responsion); ישׁב || ישׁב (responsion); אמר || אמר (responsion); ב || ב (responsion); אזן || לבב (responsion); שׁכלים || שׁכולה (responsion).
Thematic unity: yes. The disbelief of Zion that her destroyed city will ever be inhabited again by numerous offspring.
Discussion: See our discussion of the previous canticle. 𝔊[AQ] mark the end of v. 19.

CANTICLE D.i (49:22–23c)

Separation ↑: major division markers in the textual tradition; change of subject.
Separation ↓: major division markers in the textual tradition.

Canticle parallelism: יהוה || יהוה (inclusion); גוי || מלך (responsion); בן || אמן (concatenation); בת || ינק (concatenation);
Thematic unity: yes. The LORD will summon the nations to bring Zion's children back and serve them so that Zion will have to acknowledge that it is worthwhile to wait for his salvatory acts.

CANTICLE D.ii (49:24–26)

Separation ↑: major division markers in the textual tradition; change of subject.
Separation ↓: major division markers in the textual tradition.
Canticle parallelism: לקח || לקח (concatenation); גבור || גבור (concatenation); גבור || אביר (inclusion; unique) מלקוח || מלקוח (concatenation; unique); שבי || שבי (concatenation); מלט || מלט (concatenation); יהוה || יהוה (inclusion); אנכי || אני (responsion); ישע || ישע (responsion).
Thematic unity: yes. A final objection of Zion is countered: captives will be taken from their legal owners because the LORD is more powerful than Zion's oppressors.
Discussion: Since $1\mathfrak{Q}^{a}$ and $\mathfrak{G}^{AQ}$ are also among the witnesses for the caesura after v. 23, the major division markers they have after v. 24 are hardly more than markers of the end of the first strophe which were deemed necessary to separate the question from the answer.

The major division markers in $1\mathfrak{Q}^{a}$ and $\mathfrak{G}^{Q}$ after v. 25aC might testify to a different strophical division, keeping the verse-lines in the first person singular separated form v. 25a. From the viewpoint of poetical structure a strophe of three verse-lines is not likely and so $\mathfrak{M}$'s division must be preferred.

As is more often the case, $\mathfrak{M}$'s Seder mark is placed one strophe too early.

10.6 Isaiah 49 – Delimitation of Macrostructure

The overall structure of Isaiah 49 appears to be fairly symmetric,

SUB-CANTOS	CANTICLES	STROPHES
A	2	6 (4+2)
B	3	7 (2+4+1)
C	3	7 (2+2+3)
D	2	6 (3+3)

One might defend that the chapter should be divided into two canto's. The first one would cover our sub-cantos A–B (vv. 1-13) and would deal with the servant of the LORD and his initial doubt (v. 4a). The second canto would cover our sub-cantos C–D (vv. 14-26) which deal with Zion's doubt about the possibility of restoration. Such a further division would not disturb the symmetry of the chapter in its present form.

However, the message of hope expressed in the second half of the chapter is actually the same as that of the first half. The restoration of Israel will take place (vv. 5aC-D, 6aB-C, 8-12, 13b || vv.17-18, 19-21, 22b, 23c, 25, 26bC), despite the foreign nations that still oppress them (vv. 7, 9a, 12, 17, 21b, 22-23, 25-26), but whose kings will become Israel's servants (vv. 7 and 23). If both the servant of the LORD and Zion are seen as corporate personalities, representing their people, the difference between the two halves of the chapter becomes more or less theoretical. The two personages are not identical though. They may share the same hope, but the servant is not merely a child of Zion's 'womb' (vv. 1bA, 15aB), but one of those who await the salvatory acts of the LORD, knowing that the LORD will use them to implement his plans (vv. 2, 4b, 5a, 6, 8, 9, 23c – cf. 40:31), even though they too sometimes have difficulty to shake off despair (v. 4a).

Just as the prophet distinguishes between believers and non-believers in his own people, so he does with regard to the foreign nations. If the nations listen to his message (v. 1a) and humbly fulfil their task in respect to Israel and its God (v. 7c-d, 17, 19bB, 22-23) they will be included in the universal salvation (vv. 6b, 8b). But if the nations choose to remain tyrants and oppressors, God will punish them mercilessly (vv. 24-26). In this sense the beginning and end of the chapter link up with each other.

Distant parallelism connecting the canticles of the four sub-cantos:

Sub-canto A:
לאם (v. 1aA – A.i) || גוי (v. 6bA – A.ii [inclusion]); עבדי (v. 3aA – A.i) || לי עבד (6aA – A.ii); כחי (v. 4aB – A.i) || עזי (v. 5bB – A.ii); משפטי (v. 4bA – A.i) || ישועתי (v. 6bB – A.ii).

Sub-canto B:
כה אמר־יהוה (v. 7aA – B.i) || כה אמר יהוה (v. 8aA – B.ii); גאל (v. 7aB – B.i) || נחם (v. 13bA – B.iii); עם (v. 8bA – B.ii) || עם (v. 13bA – B.iii); ארץ (v. 8bB – B.ii) || ארץ (v. 13aA – B.iii); אסר (v. 9aA – B.ii) || עני (v. 13bB); הר (v. 11aA – B.ii) || הר (v. 13aB – B.iii).

Sub-canto C:
עזב (v. 14aA – C.i) || שׁאר לבד (v. 21bC – C.iii) (unique); בן (v. 15aB – C.i) || בנה (v. 17aA – C.ii, by allusion) || בן (v. 20aB – C.iii); הרס (v. 17aA – C.ii) || הריסות (v. 19aA – C.iii; unique); הרס (v. 17aA – C.ii)

|| בלע (v. 19bB); חרב (verb; v. 17aB – C.ii) || חרבה (v. 19aA – C.iii; unique).

Sub-canto D:
כה אמר אדני יהוה (v. 22aA – D.i) || כי־כה אמר יהוה (v. 25aA – D.ii); בניך (v. 22bA – D.i) || בניך (v. 25bB – D.ii); וידעת כי־אני יהוה (v. 23cA – D.i) || וידעו כל־בשׂר כי אני יהוה (v. 26bA – D.ii).

As we have seen, the structure of this canto in its final form is more or less symmetrical. It seems an easy solution to assume that B.iii, with only one strophe, is a later addition, as has been argued by many scholars, be it on different grounds.[1] However, as has been shown above, B.iii is firmly embedded in its sub-canto. The same was true in other, similar, cases.[2] If B.iii is removed, the whole symmetry is destroyed and one is almost obliged to accept further purging to restore some kind of order comparable to what the final editor has achieved here. However, it is extremely difficult to say what would be redundant in C.iii then. And so we believe that it would testify to good scholarship to start from the assumption that the easiest solution is not always the best.

---

[1]Lately Melugin, 83; Van Oorschot, 160-2; Berges, 359.
[2]See p. 256-7.

Chapter 11

The Structure of Isaiah 50:1–51:8

11.1 Isaiah 50:1–51:8: Text and Translation

ס<פ> – $1\mathfrak{Q}^{a}$ – $\mathfrak{G}^{SBAQ}$ – $\mathfrak{S}^{abce}$ ________________

A.i.1 (Isa. 50:1a-b)

כֹּה ׀ אָמַר יְהוָה	1aA	Thus says the LORD,
אֵי זֶה סֵפֶר כְּרִיתוּת אִמְּכֶם	1aB	Where is the writ of divorce of your mother,
אֲשֶׁר שִׁלַּחְתִּיהָ	1aC	by which I sent her away?
אוֹ מִי מִנּוֹשַׁי	1bA	Or to which of my creditors was it
אֲשֶׁר־מָכַרְתִּי אֶתְכֶם לוֹ	1bB	that I did sell you?

{<ס>}

A.i.2 (Isa. 50:1c)

הֵן בַּעֲוֺנֹתֵיכֶם נִמְכַּרְתֶּם	1cA	Behold, because of your iniquities you were sold,
וּבְפִשְׁעֵיכֶם שֻׁלְּחָה אִמְּכֶם׃	1cB	and because of your transgressions your mother was sent away.

{<ס>}

A.i.3 (Isa. 50:2a)

מַדּוּעַ בָּאתִי וְאֵין אִישׁ	2aA	Why was there no man[1] when I came?
קָרָאתִי וְאֵין עוֹנֶה	2aB	(Why) did no one answer when I called?

<ס> – $1\mathfrak{Q}^{a}$ – $\mathfrak{G}^{S}$ . . . .

A.ii.1 (Isa. 50:2b)

הֲקָצוֹר קָצְרָה יָדִי מִפְּדוּת	2bA	Is my hand far too short to redeem?
וְאִם־אֵין־בִּי כֹחַ לְהַצִּיל	2bB	Or is there no strength to deliver with me?

{<ס>$\mathfrak{G}^{A}$}

A.ii.2 (Isa. 50:2c–d)

הֵן בְּגַעֲרָתִי אַחֲרִיב יָם	2cA	Behold, by my rebuke I can dry up the sea,
אָשִׂים נְהָרוֹת מִדְבָּר	2cB	make rivers into a desert.
תִּבְאַשׁ דְּגָתָם מֵאֵין מַיִם	2dA	Their fish will stink for lack of water,
וְתָמֹת בַּצָּמָא׃ {<ס>}	2dB	and will die of thirst.

A.ii.3 (Isa. 50:3)

אַלְבִּישׁ שָׁמַיִם קַדְרוּת	3aA	I can clothe the heavens in blackness,
וְשַׂק אָשִׂים כְּסוּתָם׃	3aB	and make sackcloth their covering.

ס <פ> – $1\mathfrak{Q}^{a}$ – $\mathfrak{G}^{SBA}$ – $\mathfrak{S}^{abcde}$ ________________

[1] Isa. 66:4 shows that one should translate this noun literally here. No other 'lover' had been able to replace the God of Israel. This is traditional imagery (Hos. 1-2). The 'man' who had 'bought' her presumably left her soon after.

B.i.1 (Isa. 50:4)

אֲדֹנָי יְהוִה נָתַן לִי לְשׁוֹן לִמּוּדִים	4aA	The Lord GOD gives[2] me a tongue of disciples
לָדַעַת לָעוּת אֶת־יָעֵף דָּבָר	4aB	to know how to make witnesses[3] those too tired for words.
יָעִיר ׀ בַּבֹּקֶר בַּבֹּקֶר	4bA	Morning by morning he wakens,
יָעִיר לִי אֹזֶן	4bB	he wakens my ear
{<ס>} לִשְׁמֹעַ כַּלִּמּוּדִים׃	4bC	to hear like disciples do.

B.i.2 (Isa. 50:5)

{$\mathfrak{G}^{AQ}$} אֲדֹנָי יְהוִה פָּתַח־לִי אֹזֶן	5aA	The Lord GOD opens my ear,
וְאָנֹכִי לֹא מָרִיתִי	5aB	and I do not resist,
אָחוֹר לֹא נְסוּגֹתִי׃	5aC	I do not move backwards.

<ס> – 1$\mathfrak{Q}^{a}$ . . . .

B.ii.1 (Isa. 50:6)

גֵּוִי נָתַתִּי לְמַכִּים	6aA	My back I give to those who smite,
{$\mathfrak{G}^{A}$} וּלְחָיַי לְמֹרְטִים	6aB	and my cheeks to those who pull out my beard.
פָּנַי לֹא הִסְתַּרְתִּי	6bA	My face I do not hide,
{<ס>} מִכְּלִמּוֹת וָרֹק׃	6bB	from disgrace and spitting.

B.ii.2 (Isa. 50:7–8a)

וַאדֹנָי יְהוִה יַעֲזָר־לִי	7aA	Since[4] the Lord GOD helps me,
עַל־כֵּן לֹא נִכְלָמְתִּי	7aB	therefore I am not disgraced,
עַל־כֵּן שַׂמְתִּי פָנַי כַּחַלָּמִישׁ	7bA	therefore I set my face like flint,
{<ס>} וָאֵדַע כִּי־לֹא אֵבוֹשׁ׃	7bB	since I know that I will not be put to shame –
קָרוֹב מַצְדִּיקִי	8aC	he who justifies me is near.

$\mathfrak{G}^{SB}$ – $\mathfrak{S}^{abe}$ . . . .

---

[2]In our opinion the alternation of tenses in vv. 4-10 is best explained as an expression of the actual present. Cf. M.C.A. Korpel, J.C. de Moor, F. Sepmeijer, "Consistency with Regard to Tenses", see Abbreviations.

[3]We propose to derive the highly problematic לעות from the well-known verb עוד 'to testify', or with the accusative 'to take as a witness' (Isa. 8:2; Jer. 32:10, 25, 44). The Qal occurs as equivalent of the Hiphil in Lam. 2:13 and it is not uncommon for the Qal to have the same meaning as the causative stem. Cf. M.C.A. Korpel, "Avian Spirits in Ugarit and in Ezekiel 13", in: N. Wyatt *et al.* (eds.), *Ugarit, Religion and Culture* (UBL, 12), Münster 1996, 99-113 (101, n. 9, with further bibliography). With regard to the form, we take it as a feminine infinitive construct of the type *qtult* (compare לדעת): **'ūdt* > **'ūtt* (assimilation) > *'ūt* (normal reduction of duplication at the end of words).

In Second Isaiah it is the task of faithful Israel to bear witness of the LORD (43:10 [the servant, and with ידע!]; 43:12; 44:8; 55:4). The supposed combination לדעת לעות resembles the combination of derivatives of the same roots in Ps. 119:79, 125, 152. Finally, the strophe parallelism between לעות and לשמע strongly favours this derivation (see the Index).

[4]For the causal meaning of ו see *HAHAT*, 289; *DCH*, vol. 2, 597. Note the chiastic structure: ו – על־כן – על־כן – ו.

B.iii.1 (Isa. 50:8b)

מִי־יָרִיב אִתִּי נַעַמְדָה יָּחַד	8bA	Who will go into court with me? Let us stand up together!
מִי־בַעַל מִשְׁפָּטִי יִגַּשׁ אֵלָי׃ {<ס>𝔊[A]}	8bB	Who will be the opponent in my case? Let him draw near to me!

B.iii.2 (Isa. 50:9)

הֵן אֲדֹנָי יְהוִה יַעֲזָר־לִי	9aA	Behold, the Lord GOD helps me;
מִי־הוּא יַרְשִׁיעֵנִי {<ס>}	9aB	who will pronounce me guilty?
הֵן כֻּלָּם כַּבֶּגֶד יִבְלוּ	9bA	Behold, all of them will wear out like a garment,
עָשׁ יֹאכְלֵם׃	9bB	the moth will eat them up.

<ס> – 1Q[a] – 𝔊[SA] ....

B.iv.1 (Isa. 50:10a)

מִי בָכֶם יְרֵא יְהוָה	10aA	Who among you is fearing the LORD?
שֹׁמֵעַ בְּקוֹל עַבְדּוֹ	10aB	Is listening to the voice of his servant?

B.iv.2 (Isa. 50:10b–c)

אֲשֶׁר ׀ הָלַךְ חֲשֵׁכִים	10bA	Let he who walks in darkness,
וְאֵין נֹגַהּ לוֹ	10bB	and has no light,
יִבְטַח בְּשֵׁם יְהוָה	10cA	trust[5] in the name of the LORD,
וְיִשָּׁעֵן בֵּאלֹהָיו׃	10cB	and rely upon his God.

<ס> – 1Q[a] – 𝔊[SA] – 𝔖[b] ....

B.v.1 (Isa. 50:11a–b)

הֵן כֻּלְּכֶם קֹדְחֵי אֵשׁ	11aA	Behold, all of you who are kindling fire,
מְאַזְּרֵי זִיקוֹת	11aB	who are surrounding yourselves with torches,[6]
לְכוּ ׀ בְּאוּר אֶשְׁכֶם	11bA	walk into the blaze[7] of your fire,
וּבְזִיקוֹת בִּעַרְתֶּם	11bB	and into the torches which you burn.

B.v.2 (Isa. 50:11c)

מִיָּדִי הָיְתָה־זֹּאת לָכֶם	11cA	From my hand this comes over you,
לְמַעֲצֵבָה תִּשְׁכָּבוּן׃	11cB	you will lie down in a place of torment.

פ <ס> – 1Q[ab] – 𝔊[SBAQ] – 𝔖[bcde] ____

[5]Like many modern translators and commentators, 𝔊 and 𝔙 recognized the jussive.

[6]The noun is related to Akkadian *zīqtu* 'torch', cf. *HALAT*, 257; *HAHAT*, 299. As a consequence, the verb אזר "to gird" has a metaphorical meaning. For older interpretations, see Barthélemy, 371-3.

[7]𝔊, 𝔖 and 𝔙 have read אור "light". ℭ supports 𝔐. Isa. 43:2 argues in favour of a rendering "walk into/through the blaze of your fire" rather than the all too bleak "walk in/by the light of your fire" (RSV, NIV, NJB, JPS).

C.i.1 (Isa. 51:1)

שִׁמְעוּ אֵלַי רֹדְפֵי צֶדֶק	1aA	Listen to me, you who pursue justice,
מְבַקְשֵׁי יְהוָה	1aB	you who seek the LORD!
הַבִּיטוּ אֶל־צוּר חֻצַּבְתֶּם	1bA	Look to the rock from which you were hewn,
{$\mathfrak{G}^{A}$} וְאֶל־מַקֶּבֶת בּוֹר נֻקַּרְתֶּם׃	1bB	and to the quarry from which you were dug.

C.i.2 (Isa. 51:2)

הַבִּיטוּ אֶל־אַבְרָהָם אֲבִיכֶם	2aA	Look to Abraham, your father
וְאֶל־שָׂרָה תְּחוֹלֶלְכֶם	2aB	and to Sarah who was in labour for you.
כִּי־אֶחָד קְרָאתִיו	2bA	For he was only one when I called him,
וַאֲבָרְכֵהוּ וְאַרְבֵּהוּ׃	2bB	but I blessed him and made him many.

ס – $\mathfrak{G}^{A}$ . . . .

C.ii.1 (Isa. 51:3a–b)

כִּי־נִחַם יְהוָה צִיּוֹן	3aA	When the LORD has comforted Zion,
נִחַם כָּל־חָרְבֹתֶיהָ	3aB	has comforted all her ruins,
וַיָּשֶׂם מִדְבָּרָהּ כְּעֵדֶן	3bA	and has made her desert like Eden,
וְעַרְבָתָהּ כְּגַן־יְהוָה	3bB	and her bare valley like the garden of the LORD,

C.ii.2 (Isa. 51:3c)

שָׂשׂוֹן וְשִׂמְחָה יִמָּצֵא בָהּ	3cA	gladness and joy will be found in her,
תּוֹדָה וְקוֹל זִמְרָה׃	3cB	thanksgiving and the voice of singing.[8]

ס <פ> – $1\mathfrak{Q}^{ab}$ – $\mathfrak{G}^{SBAQ}$ – $\mathfrak{S}^{ad}$ . . . .

C.iii.1 (Isa. 51:4)

הַקְשִׁיבוּ אֵלַי עַמִּי	4aA	Listen to me, my people,[9]
וּלְאוּמִּי אֵלַי הַאֲזִינוּ	4aB	and give ear to me, my nation,
כִּי תוֹרָה מֵאִתִּי תֵצֵא	4bA	for teaching will go out from me,
וּמִשְׁפָּטִי לְאוֹר עַמִּים אַרְגִּיעַ׃	4bB	and I will let my judgment flare out[10] as a light to the peoples.

C.iii.2 (Isa. 51:5)

קָרוֹב צִדְקִי יָצָא יִשְׁעִי	5aA	Near is my justice, my salvation goes out,
{$\mathfrak{G}^{AQ}$} וּזְרֹעַי עַמִּים יִשְׁפֹּטוּ	5aB	and my arms will judge the peoples,
אֵלַי אִיִּים יְקַוּוּ	5bA	the islands wait for me,
וְאֶל־זְרֹעִי יְיַחֵלוּן׃	5bB	and are awaiting my arm.

$\mathfrak{G}^{SAQ}$ . . . .

---

[8]The extra colon in $1\mathfrak{Q}^{a}$ was added on the analogy of Isa. 35:10 and 51:11.

[9]Cf. Barthélemy, 374; De Waard, 188-9.

[10]Translation somewhat uncertain. Cf. Oswalt, 331, n. 13.

C.iv.1 (Isa. 51:6a)

שְׂאוּ לַשָּׁמַיִם עֵינֵיכֶם	6aA	Lift up your eyes to the heavens,
וְהַבִּיטוּ אֶל־הָאָרֶץ מִתַּחַת	6aB	and look at the earth beneath.[11]

C.iv.2 (Isa. 51:6b–c)

כִּי־שָׁמַיִם כֶּעָשָׁן נִמְלָחוּ	6bA	For the heavens vanish[12] like smoke,
וְהָאָרֶץ כַּבֶּגֶד תִּבְלֶה	6bB	and the earth wears out like a garment,
וְיֹשְׁבֶיהָ כְּמוֹ־כֵן יְמוּתוּן	6bC	and its inhabitants die like gnats,
וִישׁוּעָתִי לְעוֹלָם תִּהְיֶה	6cA	but my salvation will be to eternity,
וְצִדְקָתִי לֹא תֵחָת׃	6cB	and my justice will not be shattered.

ס <פ> – $_1\mathfrak{Q}^{ab}$ – $\mathfrak{G}^{SBAQ}$ – $\mathfrak{S}^{be}$ . . . .

C.v.1 (Isa. 51:7)

שִׁמְעוּ אֵלַי יֹדְעֵי צֶדֶק	7aA	Listen to me, you who know justice,
עַם תּוֹרָתִי בְלִבָּם	7aB	you people, in whose heart is my teaching.
אַל־תִּירְאוּ חֶרְפַּת אֱנוֹשׁ	7bA	Do not fear humiliation by human beings,
וּמִגִּדֻּפֹתָם אַל־תֵּחָתּוּ׃	7bB	and do not be shattered because of their insults.[13]

C.v.2 (Isa. 51:8)

כִּי כַבֶּגֶד יֹאכְלֵם עָשׁ	8aA	For the moth will eat them like garment,
וְכַצֶּמֶר יֹאכְלֵם סָס	8aB	yes, like wool the larva[14] of the moth will eat them,
וְצִדְקָתִי לְעוֹלָם תִּהְיֶה	8bA	but my justice will be to eternity,
וִישׁוּעָתִי לְדוֹר דּוֹרִים׃	8bB	and my salvation from generation to generation.

ס<פ> – $_1\mathfrak{Q}^{ab}$ – $_4\mathfrak{Q}^{c}$ – $\mathfrak{G}^{SBAQ}$ – $\mathfrak{S}^{abde}$ ________________________________

[11]The extra colon in $_1\mathfrak{Q}^{a}$ was taken from Isa. 40:26.

[12]Both the cognates (*HALAT*, 556 [but *not* Ugaritic *mlḥ*!]) and similar expressions in other ancient oriental texts (De Moor, *ARTU*, 184, n. 10) suggest this meaning for מלח Niphal.

[13]Oswalt, 332, n. 19, proposes to read ממגדפתם (with $\mathfrak{Q}^{a,b}$), but see Isa. 43:28 and Ezek. 5:15.

[14]Since it is the larva rather than the moth itself that eats the wool. However, also in Antiquity the two seem to have been identified. Cf. Isa. 50:9 and J.P. Brown, "The Literary Contexts of the Common Hebrew-Greek Vocabulary", *JSS* 13 (1968), 163-91; *HALAT*, 718-9; *CAD* (S), 196-7.

11.2 Isaiah 50:1–51:8 – Delimitation of Cola

Colon 50:1aA:

כֹּ֚ה ׀ אָמַ֣ר יְהוָ֗ה 1aA Thus says the Lord,

With: 𝔐 (7) – 𝔖^{abcde}

Colon 50:1aB:

אֵ֣י זֶ֩ה סֵ֨פֶר כְּרִית֤וּת אִמְּכֶם֙ 1aB Where is the writ of divorce of your mother,

With: 𝔐 (10) – 𝔊^{Q}

Discussion: 𝔐 read on to שלחתיה, a colon of seven stresses. We opt for a shorter colon, even though only 𝔊^{Q} supports our view unequivocally. However, since 𝔖 shortens the verse a little, it may be interpreted as actually supporting 𝔐's division.

Colon 50:1aC:

אֲשֶׁ֣ר שִׁלַּחְתִּ֔יהָ 1aC by which I sent her away?

With: 𝔐 (5) – 𝔊^{SQ} – 𝔖^{abcde}

Colon 50:1bA:

א֚וֹ מִ֣י מִנּוֹשַׁ֔י 1bA Or to which of my creditors was it

With: 𝔐 (5).

Discussion: Even though none of the other ancient witnesses supports it, we believe the division of 𝔐 to be right. Apparently the circumstance that the sentence runs on confused them.

Colon 50:1bB:

אֲשֶׁר־מָכַ֥רְתִּי אֶתְכֶ֖ם ל֑וֹ 1bB that I did sell you?

With: 𝔐 (2) – 𝔊^{SQ} – 𝔖^{abcde}

Colon 50:1cA:

הֵ֤ן בַּעֲוֺנֹֽתֵיכֶם֙ נִמְכַּרְתֶּ֔ם 1cA Behold, because of your iniquities you were sold,

With: 𝔐 (5) – 𝔊^{SQ} – 𝔖^{abe}

Colon 50:1cB:

וּבְפִשְׁעֵיכֶ֖ם שֻׁלְּחָ֥ה אִמְּכֶֽם׃ 1cB and because of your transgressions your mother was sent away.

With: 𝔐 (1) – 𝔊^{SQ} – 𝔖^{abcde}

COLON 50:2aA:

מַדּ֫וּעַ בָּ֫אתִי וְאֵ֣ין אִ֔ישׁ 2aA Why was there no man when I came?

With: $\mathfrak{M}$ (7) – $\mathfrak{G}^{SQ}$ – $\mathfrak{S}^{abcde}$

COLON 50:2aB:

קָרָ֫אתִי֙ וְאֵ֣ין עוֹנֶ֔ה 2aB (Why) did no one answer when I called?

With: $\mathfrak{M}$ (3), Setuma in 1$\mathfrak{Q}^{a}$ – $\mathfrak{G}^{SQ}$, major division markers in $\mathfrak{G}^{S}$ – $\mathfrak{S}^{abcde}$

Colon parallelism: קרא || ענה.

Discussion: For the Zarqa (No. 9) with קראתי see p. 31.

COLON 50:2bA:

הֲקָצ֨וֹר קָצְרָ֤ה יָדִי֙ מִפְּד֔וּת 2bA Is my hand far too short to redeem?

With: $\mathfrak{M}$ (5) – $\mathfrak{G}^{SQ}$ – $\mathfrak{S}^{abcde}$ all subordinate punctuation.

COLON 50:2bB:

וְאִם־אֵֽין־בִּ֥י כֹ֖חַ לְהַצִּ֑יל 2bB Or is there no strength to deliver with me?

With: $\mathfrak{M}$ (2), Setuma in 1$\mathfrak{Q}^{a}$ – $\mathfrak{G}^{SAQ}$, major division markers in $\mathfrak{G}^{A}$ – $\mathfrak{S}^{abcde}$

COLON 50:2cA:

הֵ֣ן בְּגַעֲרָתִ֞י אַחֲרִ֣יב יָ֗ם 2cA Behold, by my rebuke I can dry up the sea,

With: $\mathfrak{M}$ (7) – $\mathfrak{G}^{SQ}$ – $\mathfrak{S}^{abcde}$

Colon parallelism: ים || חרב (antithetical).

COLON 50:2cB:

אָשִׂ֤ים נְהָרוֹת֙ מִדְבָּ֔ר 2cB make rivers into a desert.

With: $\mathfrak{M}$ (5) – $\mathfrak{G}^{SQ}$ – $\mathfrak{S}^{abcde}$

Colon parallelism: נהר || מדבר (antithetical).

COLON 50:2dA:

תִּבְאַ֤שׁ דְּגָתָם֙ מֵאֵ֣ין מַ֔יִם 2dA Their fish will stink for lack of water,

With: $\mathfrak{M}$ (5) – $\mathfrak{G}^{Q}$

Discussion: We follow $\mathfrak{M}$'s division even though it is only weakly supported. Because the prophet is hinting at the story of the first plague (Exod. 7:18, 21) the imperfects תבאש and ותמת may be a assumed to stand in verse-line parallelism.

COLON 50:2dB:

וְתָמֹ֖ת בַּצָּמָֽא׃ 2dB and will die of thirst.

With: $\mathfrak{M}$ (1) – $\mathfrak{G}^{SQ}$ – $\mathfrak{S}^{abcde}$

COLON 50:3aA:

אַלְבִּ֥ישׁ שָׁמַ֖יִם קַדְר֑וּת 3aA I can clothe the heavens in blackness,

With: $\mathfrak{M}$ (2) – $\mathfrak{G}^{Q}$ – $\mathfrak{S}^{abcde}$ all subordinate punctuation.

COLON 50:3aB:

וְשַׂ֖ק אָשִׂ֥ים כְּסוּתָֽם׃ 3aB and make sackcloth their covering.

With: $\mathfrak{M}$ (1), major division markers, also in 1$\mathfrak{Q}^{a}$ – $\mathfrak{G}^{SBAQ}$, major division markers in $\mathfrak{G}^{SBA}$ – $\mathfrak{S}^{abcde}$, major division markers in all.

COLON 50:4aA:

אֲדֹנָ֣י יְהֹוִ֗ה נָ֤תַן לִי֙ לְשׁ֣וֹן לִמּוּדִ֔ים 4aA The Lord GOD gives me a tongue of disciples

With: $\mathfrak{M}$ (5) – $\mathfrak{G}^{SQ}$ – $\mathfrak{S}^{b}$, $\mathfrak{S}^{acde}$ subordinate punctuation.
Colon parallelism: אדני || יהוה.
Discussion: With six stressed units, the colon is rather long. However, the testimony supporting $\mathfrak{M}$ is strong and a short unit like לי might be taken together with the preceding word as one accented combination.

COLON 50:4aB:

לָדַ֛עַת לָע֥וּת אֶת־יָעֵ֖ף דָּבָ֑ר 4aB to know how to make witnesses those too tired for words.

With: $\mathfrak{M}$ (2) – $\mathfrak{G}^{SQ}$ – $\mathfrak{S}^{abcde}$
Colon parallelism: ל || ל.

COLON 50:4bA:

יָעִ֣יר ׀ בַּבֹּ֣קֶר בַּבֹּ֗קֶר 4bA Morning by morning he wakens,

With: $\mathfrak{M}$ (7) – $\mathfrak{G}^{Q}$
Colon parallelism: בבקר || בבקר.
Discussion: $\mathfrak{S}$ divides after the first בבקר, but the attested colon parallelism favours $\mathfrak{M}$ which is supported by $\mathfrak{G}^{Q}$.

COLON 50:4bB:

יָעִ֥יר לִי֙ אֹ֔זֶן 4bB he wakens my ear

With: $\mathfrak{M}$ (5).

Discussion: None of the ancient witnesses supports 𝔐, but this is no doubt a consequence of the fact that the sentence spills over into the next colon.

COLON 50:4bC:

לִשְׁמֹעַ כַּלִּמּוּדִים׃ 4bC to hear like disciples do.

With: 𝔐 (1), Setuma in 1𝔔^{a} – 𝔖^{abcde}
Discussion: 𝔊 takes כלמודים with v. 5, but 𝔖 supports 𝔐.

COLON 50:5aA:

אֲדֹנָי יְהוִה פָּתַח־לִי אֹזֶן 5aA The Lord GOD opens my ear,

With: 𝔐 (5) – 𝔊^{SAQ}, major division markers in 𝔊^{AQ} – 𝔖^{bcde}, 𝔖^{a} subordinate punctuation.
Colon parallelism: אדני || יהוה.

COLON 50:5aB:

וְאָנֹכִי לֹא מָרִיתִי 5aB and I do not resist,

With: 𝔐 (2) – 𝔖^{abcde}

COLON 50:5aC:

אָחוֹר לֹא נְסוּגֹתִי׃ 5aC I do not move backwards.

With: 𝔐 (1) – 𝔊^{SQ} – 𝔖^{abcde}

COLON 50:6aA:

גֵּוִי נָתַתִּי לְמַכִּים 6aA My back I give to those who smite,

With: 𝔐 (5) – 𝔊^{SQ}

COLON 50:6aB:

וּלְחָיַי לְמֹרְטִים 6aB and my cheeks to those who pull out my beard.

With: 𝔐 (2) – 𝔊^{SAQ}, major division markers in 𝔊^{A} – 𝔖^{abcde}

COLON 50:6bA:

פָּנַי לֹא הִסְתַּרְתִּי 6bA My face I do not hide,

With: 𝔐 (5) – 𝔊^{Q}
Discussion: Again most ancient witnesses were led astray by the continuing sentence. Only 𝔊^{Q} supports 𝔐.

COLON 50:6bB:

מִכְּלִמּ֖וֹת וָרֹֽק׃ 6bB from disgrace and spitting.

With: $\mathfrak{M}$ (1) – $\mathfrak{G}^{SQ}$ – $\mathfrak{S}^{abcde}$
Colon parallelism: כלמה || רקק (unique).

COLON 50:7aA:

וַאדֹנָ֤י יְהוִה֙ יַֽעֲזָר־לִ֔י 7aA Since the Lord GOD helps me,

With: $\mathfrak{M}$ (5) – $\mathfrak{G}^{SQ}$ – $\mathfrak{S}^{abcde}$
Colon parallelism: אדני || יהוה.

COLON 50:7aB:

עַל־כֵּ֖ן לֹ֣א נִכְלָ֑מְתִּי 7aB therefore I am not disgraced,

With: $\mathfrak{M}$ (2) – $\mathfrak{G}^{Q}$ – $\mathfrak{S}^{abcde}$

COLON 50:7bA:

עַל־כֵּ֞ן שַׂ֤מְתִּי פָנַי֙ כַּֽחַלָּמִ֔ישׁ 7bA therefore I set my face like flint,

With: $\mathfrak{M}$ (5) – $\mathfrak{G}^{SQ}$ – $\mathfrak{S}^{abcde}$

COLON 50:7bB:

וָאֵדַ֖ע כִּי־לֹ֥א אֵבֽוֹשׁ׃ 7bB since I know that I will not be put to shame –

With: $\mathfrak{M}$ (1) – $\mathfrak{G}^{SQ}$ – $\mathfrak{S}^{b}$, $\mathfrak{S}^{acde}$ subordinate punctuation.
Discussion: The subordinate punctuation of $\mathfrak{S}$ is important to the dilimitation of the verse. Because $1\mathfrak{Q}^{a}$ indicates the beginning of verses in this pericope, it is certain that it presupposes the same tradition as $\mathfrak{M}$.

COLON 50:8aA:

קָרוֹב֙ מַצְדִּיקִ֔י 8aC he who justifies me is near.

With: $\mathfrak{M}$ (5) – $\mathfrak{G}^{SBQ}$, major division markers in $\mathfrak{G}^{BQ}$ – $\mathfrak{S}^{abcde}$, major division markers in $\mathfrak{S}^{abe}$

COLON 50:8bA:

מִֽי־יָרִ֥יב אִתִּ֖י נַ֣עַמְדָה יָּ֑חַד 8bA Who will go into court with me? Let us stand up together!

With: $\mathfrak{M}$ (2) – $\mathfrak{G}^{SQ}$ – $\mathfrak{S}^{abcde}$
Discussion: $\mathfrak{G}^{SQ}$ have an extra point after אתי ($\mathfrak{M}$ Ṭiphḥa).

Colon 50:8bB:

מִֽי־בַ֥עַל מִשְׁפָּטִ֖י יִגַּ֥שׁ אֵלָֽי׃ 8bB Who will be the opponent in my case? Let him draw near to me!

With: 𝔐 (1), probably a Setuma in 1Q^{a} – 𝔊^{SAQ}, major division markers in 𝔊^{A} – 𝔖^{abcde}
Discussion: Again 𝔊^{SQ} have an extra point where 𝔐 has a Ṭiphḥa (משפטי).

Colon 50:9aA:

הֵ֣ן אֲדֹנָ֤י יְהוִה֙ יַֽעֲזָר־לִ֔י 9aA Behold, the Lord God helps me;

With: 𝔐 (5) – 𝔊^{SQ} – 𝔖^{a} subordinate punctuation.
Colon parallelism: אדני || יהוה.

Colon 50:9aB:

מִי־ה֖וּא יַרְשִׁיעֵ֑נִי 9aB who will pronounce me guilty?

With: 𝔐 (2) – 𝔊^{SQ} – 𝔖^{abcde}

Colon 50:9bA:

הֵ֤ן כֻּלָּם֙ כַּבֶּ֣גֶד יִבְל֔וּ 9bA Behold, all of them will wear out like a garment,

With: 𝔐 (5) – 𝔊^{SQ} – 𝔖^{abcde}

Colon 50:9bB:

עָ֖שׁ יֹאכְלֵֽם׃ 9bB the moth will eat them up.

With: 𝔐 (1), Setuma in 1Q^{a} – 𝔊^{SAQ}, major division markers in 𝔊^{SA} – 𝔖^{abcde}

Colon 50:10aA:

מִ֤י בָכֶם֙ יְרֵ֣א יְהוָ֔ה 10aA Who among you is fearing the Lord?

With: 𝔐 (5) – 𝔊^{SQ} – 𝔖^{b}, 𝔖^{acde} subordinate punctuation.

Colon 50:10aB:

שֹׁמֵ֖עַ בְּק֣וֹל עַבְדּ֑וֹ 10aB Is listening to the voice of his servant?

With: 𝔐 (2) – 𝔊^{SQ} – 𝔖^{abcde}

Colon 50:10bA:

אֲשֶׁר ׀ הָלַךְ חֲשֵׁכִים 10bA Let he who walks in darkness,

With: 𝔐 (7) – 𝔊[S]
Discussion: It is questionable whether Masoretes intended the Revia' as a colon divider here. Probably they wanted to read v. 10 as one strophe, consisting of a bicolon and a tricolon with the accentual pattern 5–5–2. This division presupposes rabbinic exegesis which relates אשר with the participles of v. 10a, applying them to various pious men.[1] 𝔖 too read on until לו. Though the resulting colon of six stressed units is not unacceptably long, we believe 𝔊[S] to have preserved the correct colometry in line with the fact that 𝔊 recognized the jussives in v. 10b-c, making it a strophe in its own right.

Colon 50:10bB:

וְאֵין נֹגַהּ לוֹ 10bB and has no light,

With: 𝔐 (5) – 𝔊[SQ] – 𝔖[e], 𝔖[abcd] subordinate punctuation.

Colon 50:10cA:

יִבְטַח בְּשֵׁם יְהוָה 10cA trust in the name of the Lord,

With: 𝔐 (5) – 𝔊[SQ] – 𝔖[e], 𝔖[a] subordinate punctuation.

Colon 50:10cB:

וְיִשָּׁעֵן בֵּאלֹהָיו׃ 10cB and rely upon his God.

With: 𝔐 (1), Setuma in 1Q[a] because there was sufficient space to add הנה to this line if the scribe had wanted this – 𝔊[SAQ], major division markers in 𝔊[SA] – 𝔖[abcde], major division marker in 𝔖[b]

Colon 50:11aA:

הֵן כֻּלְּכֶם קֹדְחֵי אֵשׁ 11aA Behold, all of you who are kindling fire,

With: 𝔐 (8) – 𝔊[SQ] – 𝔖[abcde]
Discussion: The unanimous testimony of the Greek and Syriac witnesses makes 𝔐's Ṭiphḥa a principal divider here, even though it is doubtful whether the Masoretes intended it as such.

Colon 50:11aB:

מְאַזְּרֵי זִיקוֹת 11aB who are surrounding yourselves with torches,

With: 𝔐 (2) – 𝔊[SQ] – 𝔖[abcde]

---

[1]So 𝔗; bBer., 6b; Gen. R., LX.1; Midr. Ps. XXXI.1; LXX.4.

COLON 50:11bA:

לְכוּ ׀ בְּאוּר אֶשְׁכֶם 11bA walk into the blaze of your fire,

With: 𝔐 (7) – 𝔊^{SQ} – 𝔖^{de}

COLON 50:11bB:

וּבְזִיקוֹת בִּעַרְתֶּם 11bB and into the torches which you burn.

With: 𝔐 (5) – 𝔊^{Q} – 𝔖^{abcde}

COLON 50:11cA:

מִיָּדִי הָיְתָה־זֹּאת לָכֶם 11cA From my hand this comes over you,

With: 𝔐 (5) – 𝔊^{SQ} – 𝔖^{e}, 𝔖^{a} subordinate punctuation.

COLON 50:11cB:

לְמַעֲצֵבָה תִּשְׁכָּבוּן׃ 11cB you will lie down in a place of torment.

With: 𝔐 (1), major division markers, also in 1𝔔^{a} and 1𝔔^{b} – 𝔊^{SBAQ}, major division markers in all – 𝔖^{abcde}, major division markers in 𝔖^{bcde}

COLON 51:1aA:

שִׁמְעוּ אֵלַי רֹדְפֵי צֶדֶק 1aA Listen to me, you who pursue justice,

With: 𝔐 (8) – 𝔊^{SQ} – 𝔖^{ade} subordinate punctuation
Discussion: The ellipsis in the second colon induced 𝔐 and 𝔖 to read on until יהוה.

COLON 51:1aB:

מְבַקְשֵׁי יְהוָה 1aB you who seek the LORD!

With: 𝔐 (2) – 𝔊^{SQ} – 𝔖^{abcde}

COLON 51:1bA:

הַבִּיטוּ אֶל־צוּר חֻצַּבְתֶּם 1bA Look to the rock from which you were hewn,

With: 𝔐 (5) – 𝔊^{SQ} – 𝔖^{abcde} all subordinate punctuation.

COLON 51:1bB:

וְאֶל־מַקֶּבֶת בּוֹר נֻקַּרְתֶּם׃ 1bB and to the quarry from which you were dug.

With: 𝔐 (1) – 𝔊^{SAQ}, major division markers in 𝔊^{A} – 𝔖^{abcde}
Discussion: 𝔊^{SQ} have an extra point after בור which equals 𝔐's Ṭiphḥa (No. 8).

COLON 51:2aA:

הַבִּיטוּ אֶל־אַבְרָהָם אֲבִיכֶם 2aA Look to Abraham, your father

With: 𝔐 (5) – 𝔊^{SQ} – 𝔖^{be}, 𝔖^{ac} subordinate punctuation.

COLON 51:2aB:

וְאֶל־שָׂרָה תְּחוֹלֶלְכֶם 2aB and to Sarah who was in labour for you.

With: 𝔐 (2) – 𝔊^{SQ} – 𝔖^{abcd}

COLON 51:2bA:

כִּי־אֶחָד קְרָאתִיו 2bA For he was only one when I called him,

With: 𝔐 (5) – 𝔊^{SQ}

Discussion: 𝔊^{S} and 𝔖^{d} have an extra point after כי־אחד where 𝔐 has a conjunctive accent. Moreover, 𝔖 does not support 𝔐 here because it slightly facilitates the text.

COLON 51:2bB:

וַאֲבָרְכֵהוּ וְאַרְבֵּהוּ׃ 2bB but I blessed him and made him many.

With: 𝔐 (1), Setuma – 𝔊^{SAQ}, major division markers in 𝔊^{A} – 𝔖^{abcde}

Colon parallelism: ברך || רבה Hiphil.

Discussion: 𝔊^{SQ} have an extra point after ואברכהו (𝔐 Ṭiphḥa).

COLON 51:3aA:

כִּי־נִחַם יְהוָה צִיּוֹן 3aA When the LORD has comforted Zion,

With: 𝔐 (7) – 𝔊^{SQ} – 𝔖^{cde}, 𝔖^{ab} subordinate punctuation.

Colon parallelism: יהוה || ציון.

COLON 51:3aB:

נִחַם כָּל־חָרְבֹתֶיהָ 3aB has comforted all her ruins,

With: 𝔐 (5) – 𝔊^{SQ} – 𝔖^{abcde}

COLON 51:3bA:

וַיָּשֶׂם מִדְבָּרָהּ כְּעֵדֶן 3bA and has made her desert like Eden,

With: 𝔐 (5) – 𝔖^{abcde}

Colon parallelism: מדבר || עדן (antithetical).

Discussion: 𝔊 is lacking here.

COLON 51:3bB:

וְעַרְבָתָהּ כְּגַן־יְהוָה 3bB and her bare valley like the garden of the LORD,

With: 𝔐 (2) – 𝔊^{SQ} – 𝔖^{abcde}

COLON 51:3cA:

שָׂשׂוֹן וְשִׂמְחָה יִמָּצֵא בָהּ 3cA gladness and joy will be found in her,

With: 𝔐 (5) – 𝔊^{SQ} – 𝔖^{abcde}
Colon parallelism: Roots ששׂון || שׂמחה.

COLON 51:3cB:

תּוֹדָה וְקוֹל זִמְרָה׃ 3cB thanksgiving and the voice of singing.

With: 𝔐 (1), major division markers, also in 1𝔔^{a} and 1𝔔^{b} – 𝔊^{SBAQ}, major division markers in all – 𝔖^{abcde}, major division markers in 𝔖^{ad}
Colon parallelism: Roots ידה Hiphil || זמר.

COLON 51:4aA:

הַקְשִׁיבוּ אֵלַי עַמִּי 4aA Listen to me, my people,

With: 𝔐 (5) – 𝔊^{Q}
Discussion: Despite the weak attestation we accept 𝔐's division.

COLON 51:4aB:

וּלְאוּמִּי אֵלַי הַאֲזִינוּ 4aB and give ear to me, my nation,

With: 𝔐 (2) – 𝔊^{SQ} – 𝔖^{b}, 𝔖^{acde} subordinate punctuation.

COLON 51:4bA:

כִּי תוֹרָה מֵאִתִּי תֵצֵא 4bA for teaching will go out from me,

With: 𝔐 (5) – 𝔊^{SQ} – 𝔖^{abcde}

COLON 51:4bB:

וּמִשְׁפָּטִי לְאוֹר עַמִּים אַרְגִּיעַ׃ 4bB and I will let my judgment flare out as a light to the peoples.

With: 𝔐 (1) – 𝔊^{Q} (but see below) – 𝔖^{abcde} (but see below).
Discussion: The Zaqeph Qaṭon (No. 5) with ומשפטי is found in all Tiberian manuscripts and so it is no mistake. However, no other witness supports 𝔐 in this respect. The second of the two Zaqephs fol-

lowing each other immediately is the weaker one.[2]

𝔊 connects ארגיע with v. 5 and 𝔖 skips it. So the point 𝔊^{S} and all 𝔖-mss have after עמים may be interpreted as actually supporting 𝔐.

COLON 51:5aA:

קָר֤וֹב צִדְקִי֙ יָצָ֣א יִשְׁעִ֔י 5aA Near is my justice, my salvation goes out,

With: 𝔐 (5) – 𝔊^{SQ} – 𝔖^{abcde}

Colon parallelism: Roots צדק || ישע; י־ || י־.

Discussion: 𝔊^{SQ} have an extra point after צדקי where 𝔐 has a Pashṭa (No. 10). It is not supported by 𝔖.

COLON 51:5aB:

וּזְרֹעַ֖י עַמִּ֣ים יִשְׁפֹּ֑טוּ 5aB and my arms will judge the peoples,

With: 𝔐 (2) – 𝔊^{SAQ}, major division markers in 𝔊^{A} and 𝔊^{Q} – 𝔖^{abcde}

COLON 51:5bA:

אֵלַי֙ אִיִּ֣ים יְקַוּ֔וּ 5bA the islands wait for me,

With: 𝔐 (5) – 𝔊^{SQ} – 𝔖^{ab} subordinate punctuation.

COLON 51:5bB:

וְאֶל־זְרֹעִ֖י יְיַחֵלֽוּן׃ 5bB and are awaiting my arm.

With: 𝔐 (1) – 𝔊^{SAQ}, all with major division markers – 𝔖^{abcde}

COLON 51:6aA:

שְׂא֨וּ לַשָּׁמַ֜יִם עֵֽינֵיכֶ֗ם 6aA Lift up your eyes to the heavens,

With: 𝔐 (13) – 𝔊^{SQ} – 𝔖^{abcde} all subordinate punctuation.

Discussion: Apparently 𝔐 read two cola of six stressed units each, resulting in a convoluted tricolon with the accentual pattern 7–5–2:

שׂאו לשמים עיניכם והביטו אל־הארץ מתחת
כי־שמים כעשן נמלחו והארץ כבגד תבלה
וישביה כמו־כן ימותון

In our opinion such a totally unbalanced structure is improbable. Therefore the unanimous testimony of the other ancient witnesses which divide after עיניכם, מתחת, נמלחו, תבלה and ימותון is precious evidence of a definitely more reasonable colometry.

[2]Compare p. 587, and see also our comment on p.31.

Colon 51:6aB:

וְהַבִּיטוּ אֶל־הָאָרֶץ מִתַּחַת 6aB and look at the earth beneath.

With: 𝔐 (7) – 𝔊^{SQ} – 𝔖^{abcde}
Discussion: See our comments on v. 6aA.

Colon 51:6bA:

כִּי־שָׁמַיִם כֶּעָשָׁן נִמְלָחוּ 6bA For the heavens vanish like smoke,

With: 𝔐 (10) – 𝔊^{SQ} – 𝔖^{abcde}
Discussion: See our comment on v. 6aA.

Colon 51:6bB:

וְהָאָרֶץ כַּבֶּגֶד תִּבְלֶה 6bB and the earth wears out like a garment,

With: 𝔐 (5) – 𝔊^{SQ} – 𝔖^{abcde}

Colon 51:6bC:

וְיֹשְׁבֶיהָ כְּמוֹ־כֵן יְמוּתוּן 6bC and its inhabitants die like gnats,

With: 𝔐 (2) – 𝔊^{SQ} – 𝔖^{abcde}
Discussion: See our comment on v. 6aA.

Colon 51:6cA:

וִישׁוּעָתִי לְעוֹלָם תִּהְיֶה 6cA but my salvation will be to eternity,

With: 𝔐 (5) – 𝔊^{SQ} – 𝔖^{b}, 𝔖^{acde} subordinate punctuation.

Colon 51:6cB:

וְצִדְקָתִי לֹא תֵחָת׃ 6cB and my justice will not be shattered.

With: 𝔐 (1), major division markers, also in 1𝔔^{a} and 1𝔔^{b} – 𝔊^{SBAQ}, all with major division markers – 𝔖^{abcde}, major division markers in 𝔖^{be}

Colon 51:7aA:

שִׁמְעוּ אֵלַי יֹדְעֵי צֶדֶק 7aA Listen to me, you who know justice,

With: 𝔐 (5) – 𝔊^{SQ} – 𝔖^{abcde} all subordinate punctuation.

Colon 51:7aB:

עַם תּוֹרָתִי בְלִבָּם 7aB you people, in whose heart is my teaching.

With: 𝔐 (2) – 𝔊^{SQ} – 𝔖^{abcde}

COLON 51:7bA:

אַל־תִּֽירְאוּ֙ חֶרְפַּ֣ת אֱנ֔וֹשׁ	7bA	Do not fear humiliation by human beings,

With: 𝔐 (5) – 𝔊^{SQ} – 𝔖^{abcde}

COLON 51:7bB:

וּמִגִּדֻּפֹתָ֖ם אַל־תֵּחָֽתּוּ׃	7bB	and do not be shattered because of their insults.

With: 𝔐 (1) – 𝔊^{SQ} – 𝔖^{abcde}

COLON 51:8aA:

כִּ֤י כַבֶּ֙גֶד֙ יֹאכְלֵ֣ם עָ֔שׁ	8aA	For the moth will eat them like garment,

With: 𝔐 (5) – 𝔊^{SQ} – 𝔖^{b}

COLON 51:8aB:

וְכַצֶּ֖מֶר יֹאכְלֵ֣ם סָ֑ס	8aB	yes, like wool the larva of the moth will eat them,

With: 𝔐 (2) – 𝔊^{SQ} – 𝔖^{abcde}

COLON 51:8bA:

וְצִדְקָתִי֙ לְעוֹלָ֣ם תִּֽהְיֶ֔ה	8bA	but my justice will be to eternity,

With: 𝔐 (5) – 𝔊^{SQ} – 𝔖^{b}, 𝔖^{acde} subordinate punctuation.

COLON 51:8bB:

וִישׁוּעָתִ֖י לְד֥וֹר דּוֹרִֽים׃	8bB	and my salvation from generation to generation.

With: 𝔐 (1), major division markers, also in 1Q^{a}, 1Q^{b} and 4Q^{c} – 𝔊^{SBAQ}, major division markers in all – 𝔖^{abcde}, major division markers in 𝔖^{abde}

11.3 Isaiah 50:1–51:8 – Delimitation of Verse-lines

VERSE–LINE: 50:1a:

כֹּ֣ה ׀ אָמַ֣ר יְהוָ֗ה	1aA	Thus says the LORD,
אֵ֣י זֶ֠ה סֵ֣פֶר כְּרִית֤וּת אִמְּכֶם֙	1aB	Where is the writ of divorce of your mother,
אֲשֶׁ֣ר שִׁלַּחְתִּ֔יהָ	1aC	by which I sent her away?

𝔐 distinctive accents: 7 – 10 – 5.
Stresses: 3 + 5 + 2.
Verse-line parallelism: כריתות || שלח.

Discussion: 𝔐 has divided this verse-line in only two cola, the first one

of which runs on to שלחתיה (enjambment). In that case the pattern of accents would be normal: 7 – 5. As defended above, we opt for splitting up the first colon into two shorter cola, which causes the abnormal sequence of accents (7 – 10 – 2).
Because the sentence is running on over three cola clear, semantical parallelism is weak.

VERSE–LINE: 50:1b:

אוֹ מִי מִנּוֹשַׁי	1bA	Or to which of my creditors was it
אֲשֶׁר־מָכַרְתִּי אֶתְכֶם לוֹ	1bB	that I did sell you?

𝔐 distinctive accents: 5 – 2.
Stresses: 3 + 3.
Verse-line parallelism: נשה || מכר.
Discussion: The sentence runs on, causing a lack of clear parallels. The semantical relationship between the two cola cannot be doubted however.

VERSE–LINE: 50:1c:

הֵן בַּעֲוֹנֹתֵיכֶם נִמְכַּרְתֶּם	1cA	Behold, because of your iniquities you were sold,
וּבְפִשְׁעֵיכֶם שֻׁלְּחָה אִמְּכֶם׃	1cB	and because of your transgressions your mother was sent away.

𝔐 distinctive accents: 5 – 1.
Stresses: 3 + 3.
Verse-line parallelism: ב || ב; עון || פשע; ־כם || ־כם; מכר || שלח; grammatical parallelism; rhyme.

VERSE–LINE: 50:2a:

מַדּוּעַ בָּאתִי וְאֵין אִישׁ	2aA	Why was there no man when I came?
קָרָאתִי וְאֵין עוֹנֶה	2aB	(Why) did no one answer when I called?

𝔐 distinctive accents: 7 – 3.
Stresses: 4 + 3.
Verse-line parallelism: בוא || קרא; אין || אין; grammatical parallelism; rhyme.
Discussion: The cola are connected by ellipsis.

VERSE–LINE: 50:2b:

הֲקָצוֹר קָצְרָה יָדִי מִפְּדוּת	2bA	Is my hand far too short to redeem?
וְאִם־אֵין־בִּי כֹחַ לְהַצִּיל	2bB	Or is there no strength to deliver with me?

𝔐 distinctive accents: 5 – 2.
Stresses: 4 + 3.
Verse-line parallelism: יד || כח; ־י || ־י; פדה || נצל; rhyme.

VERSE–LINE: 50:2c:

הֵ֣ן בְּגַעֲרָתִ֞י אַחֲרִ֣יב יָ֗ם	2cA	Behold, by my rebuke I can dry up the sea,
אָשִׂ֤ים נְהָרוֹת֙ מִדְבָּ֔ר	2cB	make rivers into a desert.

𝔐 distinctive accents: 5 – 2.
Stresses: 4 + 3.
Verse-line parallelism: חרב || מדבר; ים || נהר; ים || מדבר (antithetical); grammatical parallelism.
Discussion: Ellipsis is a connecting force.

VERSE–LINE: 50:2d:

תִּבְאַ֤שׁ דְּגָתָם֙ מֵאֵ֣ין מַ֔יִם	2dA	Their fish will stink for lack of water,
וְתָמֹ֖ת בַּצָּמָֽא׃	2dB	and will die of thirst.

𝔐 distinctive accents: 5 – 1.
Stresses: 4 + 2.
Verse-line parallelism: באש || מות; מים || צמא (antithetical).

VERSE–LINE: 50:3a:

אַלְבִּ֥ישׁ שָׁמַ֖יִם קַדְר֑וּת	3aA	I will clothe the heavens in blackness,
וְשַׂ֖ק אָשִׂ֥ים כְּסוּתָֽם׃	3aB	and make sackcloth their covering.

𝔐 distinctive accents: 2 – 1.
Stresses: 3 + 3.
Verse-line parallelism: לבש || כסה; קדרות || כסות (unique); grammatical parallelism.

VERSE–LINE: 50:4a:

אֲדֹנָ֣י יְהוִ֗ה נָ֤תַן לִי֙ לְשׁ֣וֹן לִמּוּדִ֔ים	4aA	The Lord GOD gives me a tongue of disciples
לָדַ֛עַת לָע֥וּת אֶת־יָעֵ֖ף דָּבָ֑ר	4aB	to know how to make witnesses those too tired for words.

𝔐 distinctive accents: 5 – 2.
Stresses: 6 + 4.
Verse-line parallelism: ל || ל; לשון || דבר; למוד || ידע.

VERSE–LINE: 50:4b:

יָעִ֣יר ׀ בַּבֹּ֣קֶר בַּבֹּ֗קֶר	4bA	Morning by morning he wakens,
יָעִ֥יר לִי֙ אֹ֔זֶן	4bB	he wakens my ear
לִשְׁמֹ֖עַ כַּלִּמּוּדִֽים׃	4bC	to hear like disciples do.

𝔐 distinctive accents: 7 – 5 – 1.
Stresses: 3 + 3 + 2.

Verse-line parallelism: עור || עור; אזן (noun) || שמע; grammatical parallelism.
Discussion: Ellipsis connects vv. 4bA-B.

VERSE–LINE: 50:5a:

אֲדֹנָי יְהוִה פָּתַח־לִי אֹזֶן	5aA	The Lord GOD opens my ear,
וְאָנֹכִי לֹא מָרִיתִי	5aB	and I do not resist,
אָחוֹר לֹא נְסוּגֹתִי׃	5aC	I do not move backwards.

𝔐 distinctive accents: 5 – 2 – 1.
Stresses: 4 + 3 + 3.
Verse-line parallelism: ־י || אנכי; פתח אזן || מרה (לא);[1] לא || לא; מרה || סוג; grammatical parallelism; rhyme.

VERSE–LINE: 50:6a:

גֵּוִי נָתַתִּי לְמַכִּים	6aA	My back I give to those who smite,
וּלְחָיַי לְמֹרְטִים	6aB	and my cheeks to those who pull out my beard.

𝔐 distinctive accents: 5 – 2.
Stresses: 3 + 2.
Verse-line parallelism: גו || לחי (unique); ־י || ־י; ל || ל; נכה || מרט; rhyme.
Discussion: The cola are connected by ellipsis.

VERSE–LINE: 50:6b:

פָּנַי לֹא הִסְתַּרְתִּי	6bA	My face I do not hide,
מִכְּלִמּוֹת וָרֹק׃	6bB	from disgrace and spitting.

𝔐 distinctive accents: 5 – 1.
Stresses: 3 + 2.
Verse-line parallelism: None.
Discussion: Because the sentence is running on there is no poetic parallelism.

VERSE–LINE: 50:7a:

וַאדֹנָי יְהוִה יַעֲזָר־לִי	7aA	Since the Lord GOD helps me,
עַל־כֵּן לֹא נִכְלָמְתִּי	7aB	therefore I am not disgraced,

𝔐 distinctive accents: 5 – 2.
Stresses: 3 + 3.
Verse-line parallelism: None.

[1] The two expressions are probably related. At least the similar word–pair שמע || מרה (לא) seems to be common, cf. Exod. 23:21; Deut. 1:43; 9:23; 21:18, 20; Josh. 1:18; 1 Sam. 12:14,15; Ezek. 20:8. Compare also Lam. 1:18.

Discussion: Again the sentence runs on, causing the lack of clear parallels. However, the second colon describes the logical result of the first. Moreover, the chiastic structure of the strophe compensates for the lack of parallelism on the level of the verse-lines.

VERSE–LINE: 50:7b-8a:

עַל־כֵּן שַׂמְתִּי פָנַי כַּחַלָּמִישׁ	7bA	therefore I set my face like flint,
וָאֵדַע כִּי־לֹא אֵבוֹשׁ׃	7bB	since I know that I will not be put to shame –
קָרוֹב מַצְדִּיקִי	8aC	he who justifies me is near.

𝔐 distinctive accents: 5 – 1 – 5.
Stresses: 4 + 3 + 2.
Verse-line parallelism: ־י ‖ ־י; בוש ‖ צדק (antithetical).
Discussion: Our delimitation rests on the ancient witnesses (major division markers in 𝔊[BQ] and in 𝔖[abe]) who differ in their delimitation of verses from 𝔐 and 1𝔔[a] that start a new verse-line with v. 8a (1𝔔[a] indicates the end of verses/strophes by narrow spaces in this pericope). Probably the Hebrew witnesses took our v. 8aC as the beginning of a new verse-line because of the supposed parallelism between צדק ‖ ריב, although it is not particularly well-attested.[2] They overlooked, however, the parallel structure of vv. 7a and 7b-8a. Colon 7aA corresponds to 8aC, just as 7aB to 7bB, whereas 7bA forms a plus which links strophes B.ii.1 and B.ii.2 (פנים). The resulting parallelism between the roots עזר and צדק has a parallel in Isa. 41:10b.

VERSE–LINE: 50:8b:

מִי־יָרִיב אִתִּי נַעַמְדָה יָּחַד	8bA	Who will go into court with me? Let us stand up together!
מִי־בַעַל מִשְׁפָּטִי יִגַּשׁ אֵלָי׃	8bB	Who will be the opponent in my case? Let him draw near to me!

𝔐 distinctive accents: 2 – 1.
Stresses: 4 + 4.
Verse-line parallelism: מי ‖ מי; ריב ‖ משפט; ־י ‖ ־י; עמד ‖ נגש.

VERSE–LINE: 50:9a:

הֵן אֲדֹנָי יְהוִה יַעֲזָר־לִי	9aA	Behold, the Lord GOD helps me;
מִי־הוּא יַרְשִׁיעֵנִי	9aB	who will pronounce me guilty?

𝔐 distinctive accents: 5 – 2.
Stresses: 4 + 2.

[2] Verse-line parallelism in Jer. 12:1; colon parallelism in Prov. 18:17. Collocation in Deut. 25:1; 2 Sam. 15:4; Jer. 11:20; 20:12.

Verse-line parallelism: None, but help against the רשע was expected from God (Ps. 37:40) and king (2 Chron. 19:2).

VERSE–LINE: 50:9b:

הֵן כֻּלָּם כַּבֶּגֶד יִבְלוּ	9bA	Behold, all of them will wear out like a garment,
עָשׁ יֹאכְלֵם׃	9bB	the moth will eat them up.

𝔐 distinctive accents: 5 – 1.
Stresses: 4 + 2.
Verse-line parallelism: ־ם || ־ם; בלה || אכל.

VERSE–LINE: 50:10a:

מִי בָכֶם יְרֵא יְהוָה	10aA	Who among you is fearing the LORD?
שֹׁמֵעַ בְּקוֹל עַבְדּוֹ	10aB	Is listening to the voice of his Servant?

𝔐 distinctive accents: 5 – 2.
Stresses: 4 + 3.
Verse-line parallelism: ירא || שמע; יהוה || עבדו; grammatical parallelism.

VERSE–LINE: 50:10b:

אֲשֶׁר ׀ הָלַךְ חֲשֵׁכִים	10bA	Let he who walks in darkness,
וְאֵין נֹגַהּ לוֹ	10bB	and has no light,

𝔐 distinctive accents: 7 – 5.
Stresses: 3 + 3.
Verse-line parallelism: חשכה || נגה (antithetical).

VERSE–LINE: 50:10c:

יִבְטַח בְּשֵׁם יְהוָה	10cA	trust in the name of the LORD,
וְיִשָּׁעֵן בֵּאלֹהָיו׃	10cB	and rely upon his God.

𝔐 distinctive accents: 5 – 1.
Stresses: 3 + 2.
Verse-line parallelism: בטח || שען; ב || ב; שם יהוה || אלהים; grammatical parallelism.

VERSE–LINE: 50:11a:

הֵן כֻּלְּכֶם קֹדְחֵי אֵשׁ	11aA	Behold, all of you who are kindling fire,
מְאַזְּרֵי זִיקוֹת	11aB	who are surrounding yourselves with torches,

𝔐 distinctive accents: 8 – 2.
Stresses: 4 + 2.
Verse-line parallelism: אש || זיקות (unique).

VERSE–LINE: 50:11b:

לְכ֣וּ ׀ בְּא֣וּר אֶשְׁכֶ֗ם 11bA walk into the blaze of your fire,
וּבְזִיקוֹת֙ בִּעַרְתֶּ֔ם 11bB and into the torches which you burn.

𝔐 distinctive accents: 7 – 5.
Stresses: 3 + 2.
Verse-line parallelism: ב || ב; אור || זיקות (unique); אש || בער.
Discussion: 𝔐 reads v. 11 as a bicolon followed by a tricolon. The parallelism rather strongly suggests three bicola.

VERSE–LINE: 50:11c:

מִיָּדִי֙ הָֽיְתָה־זֹּ֣את לָכֶ֔ם 11cA From my hand this comes over you,
לְמַעֲצֵבָ֖ה תִּשְׁכָּבֽוּן׃ 11cB you will lie down in a place of torment.

𝔐 distinctive accents: 5 – 1.
Stresses: 3 + 2.
Verse-line parallelism: ל || ל.

VERSE–LINE: 51:1a:

שִׁמְע֥וּ אֵלַ֛י רֹ֥דְפֵי צֶ֖דֶק 1aA Listen to me, you who pursue justice,
מְבַקְשֵׁ֣י יְהוָ֑ה 1aB you who seek the LORD!

𝔐 distinctive accents: 8 – 2.
Stresses: 4 + 2.
Verse-line parallelism: רדף || בקשׁ; צדק || יהוה; grammatical parallelism.
Discussion: Ellipsis connects the cola.

VERSE–LINE: 51:1b:

הַבִּ֙יטוּ֙ אֶל־צ֣וּר חֻצַּבְתֶּ֔ם 1bA Look to the rock from which you were hewn,
וְאֶל־מַקֶּ֥בֶת בּ֖וֹר נֻקַּרְתֶּֽם׃ 1bB and to the quarry from which you were dug.

𝔐 distinctive accents: 5 – 1.
Stresses: 3 + 3.
Verse-line parallelism: אל (prep.) || אל (prep.); צור || מקבת בור; חצב || נקר (unique); grammatical parallelism; rhyme.
Discussion: The cola are bound together by ellipsis.

VERSE–LINE: 51:2a:

הַבִּ֙יטוּ֙ אֶל־אַבְרָהָ֣ם אֲבִיכֶ֔ם 2aA Look to Abraham, your father
וְאֶל־שָׂרָ֖ה תְּחוֹלֶלְכֶ֑ם 2aB and to Sarah who was in labour for you.

𝔐 distinctive accents: 5 – 2.
Stresses: 3 + 2.

Verse-line parallelism: אל (prep.) || אל (prep.); אברהם || שׂרה; אב || חיל (unique); ־כם || ־כם; grammatical parallelism.
Discussion: Again ellipsis forms a binding force between the cola.

VERSE–LINE: 51:2b:

כִּי־אֶחָד קְרָאתִיו	2bA	For he was only one when I called him,
וַאֲבָרְכֵהוּ וְאַרְבֵּהוּ׃	2bB	but I blessed him and made him many.

𝔐 distinctive accents: 5 – 1.
Stresses: 2 + 2.
Verse-line parallelism: קרא || ברך; ־ו || ־הו || ־הו; rhyme.

VERSE–LINE: 51:3a:

כִּי־נִחַם יְהוָה צִיּוֹן	3aA	When the LORD has comforted Zion,
נִחַם כָּל־חָרְבֹתֶיהָ	3aB	has comforted all her ruins,

𝔐 distinctive accents: 7 – 5.
Stresses: 3 + 2.
Verse-line parallelism: נחם || נחם; grammatical parallelism.
Discussion: The Masoretes took verse-lines 3a and 3b together as one verse-line and 1Q[a] seems to support this. No doubt the on-running sentence motivated their choice. However, the strong parallelism in vv. 3a-b on the one hand, and v. 3c on the other, as well as the change of subject in v. 3c, suggest three bicola rather than a quadrocolon plus bicolon. Sentences running on through several verse-lines, or even strophes, are not uncommon.[3]

The cola of the verse-lines vv. 3a, 3b and 3c are connected by different kinds of ellipsis, as one would expect if they constitute three different verse-lines.

VERSE–LINE: 51:3b:

וַיָּשֶׂם מִדְבָּרָהּ כְּעֵדֶן	3bA	and has made her desert like Eden,
וְעַרְבָתָהּ כְּגַן־יְהוָה	3bB	and her bare valley like the garden of the LORD,

𝔐 distinctive accents: 5 – 2.
Stresses: 3 + 2.
Verse-line parallelism: מדבר || ערבה; ־ה || ־ה; כ || כ; עדן || גן־יהוה; rhyme.
Discussion: See our comment on v. 3a.

[3]See pp. 640, n. 23; 645.

VERSE–LINE: 51:3c:

שָׂשׂוֹן וְשִׂמְחָה יִמָּצֵא בָהּ	3cA	gladness and joy will be found in her,
תּוֹדָה וְקוֹל זִמְרָה׃	3cB	thanksgiving and the voice of singing.

𝔐 distinctive accents: 5 – 1.
Stresses: 4 + 3.
Verse-line parallelism: שׂשׂון || תודה; שׂמחה || זמרה; rhyme.
Discussion: See our comment on v. 3a.

VERSE–LINE: 51:4a:

הַקְשִׁיבוּ אֵלַי עַמִּי	4aA	Listen to me, my people,
וּלְאוּמִּי אֵלַי הַאֲזִינוּ	4aB	and give ear to me, my nation,

𝔐 distinctive accents: 5 – 2.
Stresses: 3 + 3.
Verse-line parallelism: קשב || אזן; אל (prep.) || אל (prep.); ִי־ || ִי־ (twice); עם || לאם; grammatical parallelism; rhyme.

VERSE–LINE: 51:4b:

כִּי תוֹרָה מֵאִתִּי תֵצֵא	4bA	for teaching will go out from me,
וּמִשְׁפָּטִי לְאוֹר עַמִּים אַרְגִּיעַ׃	4bB	and I will let my judgment flare out as a light to the peoples.

𝔐 distinctive accents: 5 – 1.
Stresses: 4 + 4.
Verse-line parallelism: תורה || משפט; תורה || אור; ִי־ || ִי־; rhyme.

VERSE–LINE: 51:5a:

קָרוֹב צִדְקִי יָצָא יִשְׁעִי	5aA	Near is my justice, my salvation goes out,
וּזְרֹעַי עַמִּים יִשְׁפֹּטוּ	5aB	and my arms will judge the peoples,

𝔐 distinctive accents: 5 – 2.
Stresses: 4 + 3.
Verse-line parallelism: צדק || שפט; ישע || זרוע; ִי־ || ִי־ || ַי־.

VERSE–LINE: 51:5b:

אֵלַי אִיִּים יְקַוּוּ	5bA	the islands wait for me,
וְאֶל־זְרֹעִי יְיַחֵלוּן׃	5bB	and are awaiting my arm.

𝔐 distinctive accents: 5 – 1.
Stresses: 3 + 2.
Verse-line parallelism: אל (prep.) || אל (prep.); ַי־ || ִי־; קוה || יחל; grammatical parallelism.

VERSE–LINE: 51:6a:

שְׂאוּ לַשָּׁמַיִם עֵינֵיכֶם	6aA	Lift up your eyes to the heavens,
וְהַבִּיטוּ אֶל־הָאָרֶץ מִתַּחַת	6aB	and look at the earth beneath.

𝔐 distinctive accents: 13 – 7.
Stresses: 3 + 3.
Verse-line parallelism: נשׂא עינים || נבט (unique); ל || אל; שׁמים || ארץ; grammatical parallelism.
Discussion: In addition to our comments on the colometry of 50:6[4] it may be remarked that the parallelism in vv. 6aA-B, 6bA-B and 6cA-B is so strong that a division of the six cola into three verse-lines can hardly be doubted. Every one of these verse-lines consists of two cola with 3 + 3 stresses.

VERSE–LINE: 51:6b:

כִּי־שָׁמַיִם כֶּעָשָׁן נִמְלָחוּ	6bA	For the heavens vanish like smoke,
וְהָאָרֶץ כַּבֶּגֶד תִּבְלֶה	6bB	and the earth wears out like a garment,
וְיֹשְׁבֶיהָ כְּמוֹ־כֵן יְמוּתוּן	6bC	and its inhabitants die like gnats,

𝔐 distinctive accents: 10 – 5 – 2.
Stresses: 3 + 3 + 3.
Verse-line parallelism: שׁמים || ארץ || ישׁביה; כ || כ || כ; מלח || בלה || מות; עשׁן || בגד || כן (unique).
Discussion: See our comments on v. 6a.

VERSE–LINE: 51:6c:

וִישׁוּעָתִי לְעוֹלָם תִּהְיֶה	6cA	but my salvation will be to eternity,
וְצִדְקָתִי לֹא תֵחָת׃	6cB	and my justice will not be shattered.

𝔐 distinctive accents: 5 – 1.
Stresses: 3 + 3.
Verse-line parallelism: ישׁועה || צדקה; ־י || ־י; היה לעולם || לא חתת; grammatical parallelism; rhyme.
Discussion: See our comments on v. 6a.

VERSE–LINE: 51:7a:

שִׁמְעוּ אֵלַי יֹדְעֵי צֶדֶק	7aA	Listen to me, you who know justice,
עַם תּוֹרָתִי בְלִבָּם	7aB	you people, in whose heart is my teaching.

𝔐 distinctive accents: 5 – 2.
Stresses: 4 + 3.

---
[4] See pp. 455-6.

Verse-line parallelism: ־י || ־י; ידע || לב; צדק || תורה.
Discussion: Ellipsis forms a bond between the cola.

VERSE–LINE: 51:7b:

אַל־תִּֽירְאוּ֙ חֶרְפַּ֣ת אֱנ֔וֹשׁ	7bA	Do not fear humiliation by human beings,
וּמִגִּדֻּפֹתָ֖ם אַל־תֵּחָֽתּוּ׃	7bB	and do not be shattered because of their insults.

𝔐 distinctive accents: 5 – 1.
Stresses: 3 + 2.
Verse-line parallelism: אל (not) || אל (not); ירא || חתת; חרפה || גדוף; grammatical parallelism; rhyme.

VERSE–LINE: 51:8a:

כִּ֤י כַבֶּ֙גֶד֙ יֹאכְלֵ֣ם עָ֔שׁ	8aA	For the moth will eat them like garment,
וְכַצֶּ֖מֶר יֹאכְלֵ֣ם סָ֑ס	8aB	yes, like wool the larva of the moth will eat them,

𝔐 distinctive accents: 5 – 2.
Stresses: 4 + 3.
Verse-line parallelism: כ || כ; בגד || צמר; אכל || אכל; עשׁ || סס (unique); grammatical parallelism; rhyme.

VERSE–LINE: 51:8b:

וְצִדְקָתִי֙ לְעוֹלָ֣ם תִּהְיֶ֔ה	8bA	but my justice will be to eternity,
וִישׁוּעָתִ֖י לְד֥וֹר דּוֹרִֽים׃	8bB	and my salvation from generation to generation.

𝔐 distinctive accents: 5 – 1.
Stresses: 3 + 3.
Verse-line parallelism: צדקה || ישׁועה; ־י || ־י; ל || ל; עולם || דור דורים; rhyme.
Discussion: The cola are linked by ellipsis.

11.4 Isaiah 50:1–51:8 – Delimitation of Strophes

STROPHE A.i.1 (Isa. 50:1a-b)

כֹּה ׀ אָמַר יְהוָה	1aA	Thus says the LORD,
אֵי זֶה סֵפֶר כְּרִיתוּת אִמְּכֶם	1aB	Where is the writ of divorce of your mother,
אֲשֶׁר שִׁלַּחְתִּיהָ	1aC	by which I sent her away?
אוֹ מִי מִנּוֹשַׁי	1bA	Or to which of my creditors was it
אֲשֶׁר־מָכַרְתִּי אֶתְכֶם לוֹ	1bB	that I did sell you?

≠ Masoretic verse.
Separation ↑: major division markers in the textual tradition; deictic particle(s); demonstrative pronoun; marker of direct speech.
Separation ↓: division marker in the textual tradition; interrogative pronoun; swapping (adjunct).
Strophe parallelism: ־כם || ־כם; שלח || מכר;[1] grammatical parallelism.
Discussion: Since it is impossible to maintain the Masoretic colometry of this verse,[2] it has to be distributed over two strophes. The most natural way to achieve this is to keep the two questions together and to start a new strophe with the explanatory verse-line 1c. It is noteworthy that 1Q[a] has a somewhat wider space after לו which might well be interpreted as a small Setuma indicating the end of a strophe. Similar Setumot occur throughout this part of the manuscript, sometimes alternating with even smaller spaces (but wider than those between words) which obviously indicate the end of verse-lines.

STROPHE A.i.2 (Isa. 50:1c)

הֵן בַּעֲוֹנֹתֵיכֶם נִמְכַּרְתֶּם	1cA	Behold, because of your iniquities you were sold,
וּבְפִשְׁעֵיכֶם שֻׁלְּחָה אִמְּכֶם׃	1cB	and because of your transgressions your mother was sent away.

≠ Masoretic verse.
Separation ↑: deictic particle(s); repetitive verse-line parallelism; swapping (adjunct).
Separation ↓: None (one verse-line).
Strophe parallelism: None (one verse-line).
Discussion: 1Q[a] has a small Setuma indicating the end of the strophe here.

[1] It might well be that Second Isaiah reacts here to Jer. 3:8.
[2] See pp. 452, 464-5.

STROPHE A.i.3 (Isa. 50:2a)

מַדּוּעַ בָּאתִי וְאֵין אִישׁ	2aA	Why was there no man when I came?
קָרָאתִי וְאֵין עוֹנֶה	2aB	(Why) did no one answer when I called?

≠ Masoretic verse.
Separation ↑: repetitive verse-line parallelism.
Separation ↓: major division markers in the textual tradition.
Strophe parallelism: None (one verse-line).
Discussion: 𝔐 joins vv. 2a and 2b into one strophe. From the viewpoint of content this is illogical. 2a clearly sets forth the imagery of husband and wife (v. 1) and 2b forms the introduction of the polemic in vv. 2-3 which is based in all three strophes on the Exodus tradition.[3] The circumstance that two different traditions have major division markers between the two halves of v. 2 emboldens us to assume two single line strophes.

STROPHE A.ii.1 (Isa. 50:2b)

הֲקָצוֹר קָצְרָה יָדִי מִפְּדוּת	2bA	Is my hand far too short to redeem?
וְאִם־אֵין־בִּי כֹחַ לְהַצִּיל	2bB	Or is there no strength to deliver with me?

≠ Masoretic verse.
Separation ↑: major division markers in the textual tradition; paronomasia; swapping (adjunct).
Separation ↓: major division markers in the textual tradition.
Strophe parallelism: None (one verse-line).
Discussion: See our comments on v. 2a. In this case the fairly small Setuma in 1𝔔[a] is supported by 𝔊[A].

STROPHE A.ii.2 (Isa. 50:2c–d)

הֵן בְּגַעֲרָתִי אַחֲרִיב יָם	2cA	Behold, by my rebuke I can dry up the sea,
אָשִׂים נְהָרוֹת מִדְבָּר	2cB	make rivers into a desert.
תִּבְאַשׁ דְּגָתָם מֵאֵין מַיִם	2dA	Their fish will stink for lack of water,
וְתָמֹת בַּצָּמָא׃	2dB	and will die of thirst.

≠ Masoretic verse.
Separation ↑: major division markers in the textual tradition; deictic particle(s); swapping (adjunct).
Separation ↓: division marker in the textual tradition.
Strophe parallelism: ב ‖ ב; ים ‖ מים; מדבר ‖ צמא.
Discussion: See our remarks on v. 2a. Again 1𝔔[a] marks the end of the strophe by a small Setuma.

---

[3]See p. 488.

STROPHE A.ii.3 (Isa. 50:3)

אַלְבִּישׁ שָׁמַיִם קַדְרוּת	3aA	I can clothe the heavens in blackness,
וְשַׂק אָשִׂים כְּסוּתָם׃	3aB	and make sackcloth their covering.

= Masoretic verse.
Separation ↑: division marker in the textual tradition; swapping (object).
Separation ↓: major division markers in the textual tradition.
Strophe parallelism: None (one verse-line).

STROPHE B.i.1 (Isa. 50:4)

אֲדֹנָי יְהוִה נָתַן לִי לְשׁוֹן לִמּוּדִים	4aA	The Lord GOD gives me a tongue of disciples
לָדַעַת לָעוּת אֶת־יָעֵף דָּבָר	4aB	to know how to make witnesses those too tired for words.
יָעִיר ׀ בַּבֹּקֶר בַּבֹּקֶר	4bA	Morning by morning he wakens,
יָעִיר לִי אֹזֶן	4bB	he wakens my ear
לִשְׁמֹעַ כַּלִּמּוּדִים׃	4bC	to hear like disciples do.

= Masoretic verse.
Separation ↑: major division markers in the textual tradition; swapping (subject); swapping (adjunct).
Separation ↓: division marker in the textual tradition; repetitive verse-line parallelism; swapping (adjunct).
Strophe parallelism: לשון || אזן (unique); למוד || למוד (unique); ל || ל; עוד || שמע; יעף || עור (antithetical; unique).
Discussion: Again 1Q[a] marks the end of the strophe with a small Setuma. It is possible that the major division markers in 𝔊[AQ] after אזן are indicating the same strophe division, but are lagging behind somewhat.

STROPHE B.i.2 (Isa. 50:5)

אֲדֹנָי יְהוִה פָּתַח־לִי אֹזֶן	5aA	The Lord GOD opens my ear,
וְאָנֹכִי לֹא מָרִיתִי	5aB	and I do not resist,
אָחוֹר לֹא נְסוּגֹתִי׃	5aC	I do not move backwards.

= Masoretic verse.
Separation ↑: division marker in the textual tradition; independent pers. pronoun; repetitive verse-line parallelism; swapping (subject); swapping (adjunct).
Separation ↓: division marker in the textual tradition.
Strophe parallelism: None (one verse-line).

Discussion: Again 1𝔔^a has the small Setuma which it uses to mark the end of a strophe. This time, however, we interpret it as the end of a canticle.[4]

STROPHE B.ii.1 (Isa. 50:6)

גֵּוִי נָתַתִּי לְמַכִּים	6aA	My back I give to those who smite,
וּלְחָיַי לְמֹרְטִים	6aB	and my cheeks to those who pull out my beard.
פָּנַי לֹא הִסְתַּרְתִּי	6bA	My face I do not hide,
מִכְּלִמּוֹת וָרֹק׃	6bB	from disgrace and spitting.

= Masoretic verse.
Separation ↑: division marker in the textual tradition; repetitive verse-line parallelism; swapping (object).
Separation ↓: division marker in the textual tradition; swapping (object).
Strophe parallelism: גו || פנים (unique); לחי || פנים (unique); grammatical parallelism.
Discussion: Again 1𝔔^a has a small Setuma at the end of the verse.

STROPHE B.ii.2 (Isa. 50:7–8a)

וַאדֹנָי יְהוִה יַעֲזָר־לִי	7aA	Since the Lord GOD helps me,
עַל־כֵּן לֹא נִכְלָמְתִּי	7aB	therefore I am not disgraced,
עַל־כֵּן שַׂמְתִּי פָנַי כַּחַלָּמִישׁ	7bA	therefore I set my face like flint,
וָאֵדַע כִּי־לֹא אֵבוֹשׁ׃	7bB	since I know that I will not be put to shame –
קָרוֹב מַצְדִּיקִי	8aC	he who justifies me is near.

≠ Masoretic verse.
Separation ↑: division marker in the textual tradition; deictic particle(s); swapping (subject).
Separation ↓: major division markers in the textual tradition; deictic particle(s).
Strophe parallelism: עזר || צדק Hiphil (unique); על־כן || על־כן; לא || לא; כלם || בוש.
Discussion: 1𝔔^a has a small Setuma after אבוש, confirming 𝔐's division. However, we feel that the combined testimony of 𝔊 and 𝔖 deserves our preference.[5]

[4]See p. 485 below.
[5]See p. 486.

STROPHE B.iii.1 (Isa. 50:8b)

מִֽי־יָרִ֥יב אִתִּ֖י נַ֣עַמְדָה יָּ֑חַד	8bA	Who will go into court with me? Let us stand up together!
מִֽי־בַ֥עַל מִשְׁפָּטִ֖י יִגַּ֥שׁ אֵלָֽי׃	8bB	Who will be the opponent in my case? Let him draw near to me!

≠ Masoretic verse.
Separation ↑: major division markers in the textual tradition; interrogative pronoun; cohortative(s).
Separation ↓: major division markers in the textual tradition.
Strophe parallelism: None (one verse-line).
Discussion: Again the small Setuma in 1QIsa[a] is supported by 𝔊[A].

STROPHE B.iii.2 (Isa. 50:9)

הֵ֣ן אֲדֹנָ֤י יְהוִה֙ יַֽעֲזָר־לִ֔י	9aA	Behold, the Lord GOD helps me;
מִי־ה֖וּא יַרְשִׁיעֵ֑נִי	9aB	who will pronounce me guilty?
הֵ֤ן כֻּלָּם֙ כַּבֶּ֣גֶד יִבְל֔וּ	9bA	Behold, all of them will wear out like a garment,
עָ֖שׁ יֹאכְלֵֽם׃	9bB	the moth will eat them up.

= Masoretic verse.
Separation ↑: major division markers in the textual tradition; deictic particle(s); independent pers. pronoun; interrogative pronoun; swapping (subject);
Separation ↓: major division markers in the textual tradition; deictic particle(s); swapping (subject); swapping (adjunct).
Strophe parallelism: הן || הן.
Discussion: 1QIsa[a] has a small Setuma after v. 9aB, but this is an unlikely division point because of the attested strophe parallelism between הן and הן.

STROPHE B.iv.1 (Isa. 50:10a)

מִ֤י בָכֶם֙ יְרֵ֣א יְהוָ֔ה	10aA	Who among you is fearing the LORD?
שֹׁמֵ֖עַ בְּק֣וֹל עַבְדּ֑וֹ	10aB	Is listening to the voice of his servant?

≠ Masoretic verse.
Separation ↑: major division markers in the textual tradition; interrogative pronoun; swapping (adjunct).
Separation ↓: None (one verse-line).
Strophe parallelism: None (one verse-line).
Discussion: 𝔐 has a bicolon plus a quadrocolon as one strophe. 1QIsa[a] seems to support this, because it does not have a small Setuma after עבדו. In our opinion two strophes are more likely. Just as in vv. 8b-9 the two rhetorical questions in a bicolon are followed by a strophe

consisting of two bicola. The problem arose from the fact that the Hebrew witnesses did not recognize the jussives anymore and therefore took אשר to refer to the preceding verse-line.[6]

STROPHE B.iv.2 (Isa. 50:10b–c)

אֲשֶׁר ׀ הָלַךְ חֲשֵׁכִים	10bA	Let he who walks in darkness,
וְאֵין נֹגַהּ לוֹ	10bB	and has no light,
יִבְטַח בְּשֵׁם יְהוָה	10cA	trust in the name of the LORD,
וְיִשָּׁעֵן בֵּאלֹהָיו׃	10cB	and rely upon his God.

≠ Masoretic verse.
Separation ↑: swapping (subject).
Separation ↓: major division markers in the textual tradition; jussive(s); repetitive verse-line parallelism.
Strophe parallelism: נגה || יהוה.
Discussion: Though there is no strophe parallelism, the unity of the strophe is guaranteed by the sentence that runs on through both bicola.

STROPHE B.v.1 (Isa. 50:11a–b)

הֵן כֻּלְּכֶם קֹדְחֵי אֵשׁ	11aA	Behold, all of you who are kindling fire,
מְאַזְּרֵי זִיקוֹת	11aB	who are surrounding yourselves with torches,
לְכוּ ׀ בְּאוּר אֶשְׁכֶם	11bA	walk into the blaze of your fire,
וּבְזִיקוֹת בִּעַרְתֶּם	11bB	and into the torches which you burn.

≠ Masoretic verse.
Separation ↑: major division markers in the textual tradition; deictic particle(s).
Separation ↓: imperative(s); repetitive verse-line parallelism.
Strophe parallelism: קדח || בער (unique); אש || אש; זיקה || זיקה (unique).
Discussion: 𝔐 presupposes a bicolon followed by a quadrocolon. Because of the parallelism we have opted for three bicola.[7] Because the sentence runs on through vv. 11a-b and because the parallelism is much more stronger between these two bicola than between vv. 11b-c, we prefer the former combination.

STROPHE B.v.2 (Isa. 50:11c)

מִיָּדִי הָיְתָה־זֹּאת לָכֶם	11cA	From my hand this comes over you,
לְמַעֲצֵבָה תִּשְׁכָּבוּן׃	11cB	you will lie down in a place of torment.

≠ Masoretic verse.

---

[6]See our comment p. 449, n. 5.
[7]See p. 470.

Separation ↑: demonstrative pronoun; repetitive verse-line parallelism; swapping (adjunct).
Separation ↓: major division markers in the textual tradition.
Strophe parallelism: None (one verse-line).
Discussion: See our comment on the previous strophe.

STROPHE C.i.1 (Isa. 51:1)

שִׁמְעוּ אֵלַי רֹדְפֵי צֶדֶק	1aA	Listen to me, you who pursue justice,
מְבַקְשֵׁי יְהוָה	1aB	you who seek the LORD!
הַבִּיטוּ אֶל־צוּר חֻצַּבְתֶּם	1bA	Look to the rock from which you were hewn,
וְאֶל־מַקֶּבֶת בּוֹר נֻקַּרְתֶּם׃	1bB	and to the quarry from which you were dug.

= Masoretic verse.
Separation ↑: major division markers in the textual tradition; imperative(s); vocatives.
Separation ↓: major division markers in the textual tradition; imperative(s); repetitive verse-line parallelism.
Strophe parallelism: שמע || נבט; אל (prep.) || אל (prep.); grammatical parallelism.

STROPHE C.i.2 (Isa. 51:2)

הַבִּיטוּ אֶל־אַבְרָהָם אֲבִיכֶם	2aA	Look to Abraham, your father
וְאֶל־שָׂרָה תְּחוֹלֶלְכֶם	2aB	and to Sarah who was in labour for you.
כִּי־אֶחָד קְרָאתִיו	2bA	For he was only one when I called him,
וַאֲבָרְכֵהוּ וְאַרְבֵּהוּ׃	2bB	but I blessed him and made him many.

= Masoretic verse.
Separation ↑: major division markers in the textual tradition; imperative(s); repetitive verse-line parallelism.
Separation ↓: major division markers in the textual tradition; deictic particle(s); swapping (adjunct).
Strophe parallelism: None.
Discussion: Despite the lack of strophe parallelism the delimitation is not in doubt. The markers of separation are sufficient to establish the boundaries. Moreover, the two verse-lines are obviously connected by the patriarchal blessing. See especially Gen. 22:17 which suggests that the rather peculiar choice of the verb חול was motivated by the desire to create a wordplay with the noun חול 'sand'.

STROPHE C.ii.1 (Isa. 51:3a–b)

כִּי־נִחַם יְהוָה צִיּוֹן	3aA	When the LORD has comforted Zion,
נִחַם כָּל־חָרְבֹתֶיהָ	3aB	has comforted all her ruins,

וַיָּ֤שֶׂם מִדְבָּרָהּ֙ כְּעֵ֔דֶן	3bA	and has made her desert like Eden,
וְעַרְבָתָ֖הּ כְּגַן־יְהוָ֑ה	3bB	and her bare valley like the garden of the LORD,

≠ Masoretic verse.
Separation ↑: major division markers in the textual tradition; deictic particle(s); repetitive verse-line parallelism.
Separation ↓: repetitive verse-line parallelism.
Strophe parallelism: עדן || ציון; מדבר || חרבה; יהוה || יהוה (unique).[8]
Discussion: The Masoretes opted for a quadrocolon with a bicolon in v. 3. We have given our arguments for assuming three bicola.[9] The strong parallelism between vv. 3a and 3b justifies the conclusion that they should be joined into one strophe.

STROPHE C.ii.2 (Isa. 51:3c)

שָׂשׂ֤וֹן וְשִׂמְחָה֙ יִמָּ֣צֵא בָ֔הּ	3cA	gladness and joy will be found in her,
תּוֹדָ֖ה וְק֥וֹל זִמְרָֽה׃	3cB	thanksgiving and the voice of singing.

≠ Masoretic verse.
Separation ↑: swapping (subject)
Separation ↓: major division markers in the textual tradition.
Strophe parallelism: None (one verse-line).
Discussion: See our comments on the previous strophe.

STROPHE C.iii.1 (Isa. 51:4)

הַקְשִׁ֤יבוּ אֵלַי֙ עַמִּ֔י	4aA	Listen to me, my people,
וּלְאוּמִּ֖י אֵלַ֣י הַאֲזִ֑ינוּ	4aB	and give ear to me, my nation,
כִּ֤י תוֹרָה֙ מֵאִתִּ֣י תֵצֵ֔א	4bA	for teaching will go out from me,
וּמִשְׁפָּטִ֕י לְא֥וֹר עַמִּ֖ים אַרְגִּֽיעַ׃	4bB	and I will let my judgment flare out as a light to the peoples.

= Masoretic verse.
Separation ↑: major division markers in the textual tradition; imperative(s); vocatives; swapping (adjunct).
Separation ↓: deictic particle(s); swapping (subject); swapping (object); swapping (adjunct).
Strophe parallelism: עם || לאם.[10]

---

[8] Cf. Ezek. 36:35, although it is difficult to say which of the two came first. D. Block, *The Book of Ezekiel: Chapters 25–48* (NICOT), Grand Rapids 1998, 343, is inclined to accept Ezek. 36:16-38 as Ezekielian.

[9] See p. 471-2.

[10] See also the collocation of אזן Hiph. and/or קשב Hiph. with תורה or משפט in Isa. 1:10; Jer. 6:19; Hos. 5:1; Ps. 78:1.

STROPHE C.iii.2 (Isa. 51:5)

קָרוֹב צִדְקִי יָצָא יִשְׁעִי	5aA	Near is my justice, my salvation goes out,
וּזְרֹעַי עַמִּים יִשְׁפֹּטוּ	5aB	and my arms will judge the peoples,
אֵלַי אִיִּים יְקַוּוּ	5bA	the islands wait for me,
וְאֶל־זְרֹעִי יְיַחֵלוּן׃	5bB	and are awaiting my arm.

= Masoretic verse.
Separation ↑: swapping (subject); swapping (object).
Separation ↓: major division markers in the textual tradition; [11] swapping (subject); swapping (adjunct).
Strophe parallelism: זרוע || זרוע; ־י || ־י; עם || אי.

STROPHE C.iv.1 (Isa. 51:6a)

שְׂאוּ לַשָּׁמַיִם עֵינֵיכֶם	6aA	Lift up your eyes to the heavens,
וְהַבִּיטוּ אֶל־הָאָרֶץ מִתַּחַת	6aB	and look at the earth beneath.

≠ Masoretic verse.
Separation ↑: major division markers in the textual tradition; imperative(s); swapping (adjunct).
Separation ↓: None (one verse-line).
Strophe parallelism: None (one verse-line).
Discussion: The division in $\mathfrak{M}$ is unacceptable.[12] Since the coherence between vv. 6b-c is much greater than that between the introductory v. 6a and v, 6b, we decided to join vv. 6b-c into one strophe.

STROPHE C.iv.2 (Isa. 51:6b–c)

כִּי־שָׁמַיִם כֶּעָשָׁן נִמְלָחוּ	6bA	For the heavens vanish like smoke,
וְהָאָרֶץ כַּבֶּגֶד תִּבְלֶה	6bB	and the earth wears out like a garment,
וְיֹשְׁבֶיהָ כְּמוֹ־כֵן יְמוּתוּן	6bC	and its inhabitants die like gnats,
וִישׁוּעָתִי לְעוֹלָם תִּהְיֶה	6cA	but my salvation will be to eternity,
וְצִדְקָתִי לֹא תֵחָת׃	6cB	and my justice will not be shattered.

≠ Masoretic verse.
Separation ↑: deictic particle(s); swapping (subject); swapping (adjunct).
Separation ↓: major division markers in the textual tradition; swapping (subject); swapping (adjunct).
Strophe parallelism: None.
Discussion: See our comment on the previous strophe. Though formal

[11] $\mathfrak{G}^{SAQ}$. In 1$\mathfrak{Q}^{a}$ there is a hyphen-like mark after ייחלון, as if a corrector noted the omission of a Setuma at this point.
[12] See our comments pp. 462, 473.

parallelism is lacking, the semantic antithesis between vv. 6b and 6c is obvious enough. The same phenomenon may be observed in the next two strophes.

STROPHE C.v.1 (Isa. 51:7)

שִׁמְעוּ אֵלַי יֹדְעֵי צֶדֶק	7aA	Listen to me, you who know justice,
עַם תּוֹרָתִי בְלִבָּם	7aB	you people, in whose heart is my teaching.
אַל־תִּירְאוּ חֶרְפַּת אֱנוֹשׁ	7bA	Do not fear humiliation by human beings,
וּמִגִּדֻּפֹתָם אַל־תֵּחָתּוּ׃	7bB	and do not be shattered because of their insults.

= Masoretic verse.
Separation ↑: major division markers in the textual tradition; imperative(s); vocatives.
Separation ↓: jussive(s); swapping (adjunct).
Strophe parallelism: None.
Discussion: Again the contrast between divine justice and human insults provides a sufficient basis for accepting 𝔐.

STROPHE C.v.2 (Isa. 51:8)

כִּי כַבֶּגֶד יֹאכְלֵם עָשׁ	8aA	For the moth will eat them like garment,
וְכַצֶּמֶר יֹאכְלֵם סָס	8aB	yes, like wool the larva of the moth will eat them,
וְצִדְקָתִי לְעוֹלָם תִּהְיֶה	8bA	but my justice will be to eternity,
וִישׁוּעָתִי לְדוֹר דּוֹרִים׃	8bB	and my salvation from generation to generation.

= Masoretic verse.
Separation ↑: deictic particle(s); swapping (adjunct).
Separation ↓: major division markers in the textual tradition; swapping (subject); swapping (adjunct).
Strophe parallelism: None.
Discussion: Again no formal parallelism, but an obvious contrast between perishability and permanence, as in the preceeding two strophes.

11.5 Isaiah 50:1–51:8 – Delimitation of Canticles

CANTICLE A.i (50:1–2a)

Separation ↑: major division markers in the textual tradition; thematic discontinuity.
Separation ↓: major division markers in the textual tradition.
Canticle parallelism: אמר || קרא (inclusion); אם (noun) || אם (noun)

(responsion); ־כם || ־כם (responsion/concatenation); שׁלח || שׁלח (responsion); מכר || מכר (concatenation); אם || אישׁ (concatenation).
Thematic unity: yes. All three strophes deal with the separation between God and his 'wife' Zion.
Discussion: The thematic unity of A.i on the one hand and A.ii on the other argues strongly in favour of the ancient witnesses who separate v. 2a from v. 2b. It is difficult to see why the Masoretes opted for joining the two verse-lines, but the reason might well be that they found the verse in *this* form in Cant. R., I.57.

CANTICLE A.ii (50:2b–3)

Separation ↑: major division markers in the textual tradition; thematic discontinuity.
Separation ↓: major division markers in the textual tradition.
Canticle parallelism: ים || שׁמים (responsion).
Thematic unity: yes. The first strophe poses a rhetorical question about God's ability to deliver. The next two strophes answer that question by referring to the plagues of Egypt.[1]
Discussion: The rather small Setuma in 1Q[a] may be a marker of the end of the strophe since 1Q[a] also has a Setuma after other strophes in this part of the manuscript.[2] 𝔊[A] may be interpreted as a belated marking of the boundary after v. 2aB.

CANTICLE B.i (50:4–5)

Separation ↑: major division markers in the textual tradition; thematic discontinuity; change of subject.
Separation ↓: division marker in the textual tradition (small Setuma in 1Q[a]).
Canticle parallelism: אדני יהוה || אדני יהוה (responsion); אזן || אזן (concatenation); שׁמע || מרה (antithetical; concatenation).
Thematic unity: yes. Description of the prophet's obedient fulfilment of his vocation.
Discussion: Although 1Q[a] has only a small Setuma after v. 5aC, the markings in 𝔊[AQ] after v. 5aA may be interpreted as proleptic indicators of the same borderline.

CANTICLE B.ii (50:6–8a)

Separation ↑: division marker in the textual tradition.
Separation ↓: major division markers in the textual tradition.

[1] See our remarks p. 488.
[2] See pp. 475-9.

Canticle parallelism: פנים || פנים (responsion); כלמה || כלם (concatenation).
Thematic unity: yes. Both strophes describe why the prophet was able to bear insults from his opponents.
Discussion: $\mathfrak{G}^{A}$'s division markers after v. 6aB may represent a belated and redundant confirmation of the previous boundary, as happens more often in this manuscript.

CANTICLE B.iii (50:8b-9)

Separation ↑: major division markers in the textual tradition; thematic discontinuity; change of subject.
Separation ↓: major division markers in the textual tradition.
Canticle parallelism: ריב || עזר (concatenation); יי || יי (concatenation).
Thematic unity: yes. The first strophe invites to enter into court, the second describes the expected outcome of the case.
Discussion: 1$\mathfrak{Q}^{a}$ and $\mathfrak{G}^{A}$ mark the end of the first strophe.

CANTICLE B.iv (50:10a–c)

Separation ↑: major division markers in the textual tradition; thematic discontinuity; change of subject.
Separation ↓: major division markers in the textual tradition.
Canticle parallelism: ירא || בטח (inclusion); יהוה || יהוה (inclusion).
Thematic unity: yes. An invitation to follow the example of the servant of the LORD and put one's trust in God.

CANTICLE B.v (50:11a–c)

Separation ↑: major division markers in the textual tradition; change of subject.
Separation ↓: major division markers in the textual tradition.
Canticle parallelism: no formal parallelism, but v. 11c describes the pain inflicted by the fire described in the previous strophe.
Thematic unity: yes. Those who rely on their own light in the darkness – apparently torches kindled during nightly religious rituals – will be punished.

CANTICLE C.i (51:1–2)

Separation ↑: major division markers in the textual tradition; thematic discontinuity; change of subject.
Separation ↓: major division markers in the textual tradition.
Canticle parallelism: נבט || נבט (concatenation).

Thematic unity: yes. V. 2 explains the metaphors used in v. 1.
Discussion: 𝔊^A marks the end of the first strophe.

CANTICLE C.ii (51:3a–c)

Separation ↑: major division markers in the textual tradition; thematic discontinuity; change of subject.
Separation ↓: major division markers in the textual tradition.
Canticle parallelism: נחם || שׂשׂון (inclusion); נחם || שׂמחה (inclusion).
The strophes are linked by an on-running sentence (enjambment).
Thematic unity: yes. When the LORD restores Zion it will be a reason for great joy.

CANTICLE C.iii (51:4–5)

Separation ↑: major division markers in the textual tradition; thematic discontinuity; change of subject.
Separation ↓: major division markers in the textual tradition.
Canticle parallelism: אל (prep.) || אל (prep.) (inclusion); י־ || י־ (inclusion/responsion); עם || עם (responsion/concatenation); לאם || אי (inclusion); תורה || ישׁע (unique, but see C.v); משׁפט || צדק (concatenation).
Thematic unity: yes. Both Israel and the nations have to await God's just verdict.
Discussion: 𝔊^Q has a paragraphos which may have been positioned a little early. As is more often the case, 𝔊^A seems to anticipate the boundary after v. 5 prematurely and redundantly after v. 5aB.

CANTICLE C.iv (51:6a–c)

Separation ↑: major division markers in the textual tradition; change of subject.
Separation ↓: major division markers in the textual tradition.
Canticle parallelism: שׁמים || שׁמים (concatenation); ארץ || ארץ (concatenation).
Thematic unity: yes. The seemingly immovable heaven and earth will perish if God decides so.

CANTICLE C.v (51:7–8)

Separation ↑: major division markers in the textual tradition.
Separation ↓: major division markers in the textual tradition.
Canticle parallelism: צדק || צדקה (inclusion); תורה || ישׁועה (inclusion; cf. C.iii).
Thematic unity: yes. In contrast to insults by human beings God's salvatory justice will remain for ever.

11.6 Isaiah 50:1–51:8 – Delimitation of Macrostructure

The reasons we have for taking this pericope as a canto are the relatively clear delimitation of the next canto as well as the coherence of the canto itself. The point of departure of the latter is that the children of Zion reproach God for having sold them to the foreign nations and doubt whether he is able to undo this now (sub-canto A). Sub-canto B states that it is better to endure God's chastiment, like the servant (prophet) himself, than to be rebel to him. Just as God was able to give Abraham and Sarah numerous offspring, so he will be able to comfort Zion – his salvatory justice is for all generations.

The overall structure of Isaiah 50:1–51:8 appears to be fairly regular,

SUB-CANTOS	CANTICLES	STROPHES
A	2	6 (3+3)
B	5	10 (2+2+2+2+2)
C	5	10 (2+2+2+2+2)

Perhaps the different structure of the first sub-canto might give rise to the supposition that it cannot belong to the same unit as the next two sub-cantos. It might be a stray fragment. Or it might be connected with the previous chapter. However, such hypotheses would rob the canto of its main argument which is that the Almighty who smote Egypt with plagues[1] and made the sea dry to let Israel pass through safely[2] is able to redeem his people again, despite the doubt expressed by some (cf. 50:2b). This is the gist of the servant's message of encouragement (50:4). Just as God is able to clothe the heavens in rags (50:3; 51:6), so his opponents will be worn out like a garment (50:9; 51:6, 8). In view of this strong coherence it would be folly to sacrifice 50:1-3 to a presumably higher degree of regularity.

Distant parallelism connecting the canticles of **sub-canto A**:
מכר (50:1bB, 1cA – A.i) || פדות (50:2bA – A.ii).

Distant parallelism connecting the canticles of **sub-canto B**:
אדני יהוה (50:4aA, 5aA – B.i) || אדני יהוה (50:7aA – B.ii) || אדני יהוה (50:9aA – B.iii) || יהוה, אלהים (50:10cA-B) (inclusion/responsion); עזר (50:7aA – B.ii) || עזר (50:9aA – B.iii); ל (50:7aA – B.ii) || ל (50:9aA

[1]Compare 50:2b with Exod. 8:23; 50:2d with Exod. 7:18, 21; 50:3 with Exod. 10:15, 21, 22; 14:20; 50:2bB and 51:5 with Exod. 6:6 and 15:6.

[2]Compare 50:2c with Ps. 106:9.

– B.iii); י־ (50:7aA – B.ii) || י־ (50:9aA – B.iii); צדק Hiph. (50:8aC – B.ii) || רשׁע Hiph. (50:9aB – B.iii).

Distant parallelism connecting the canticles of **sub-canto C**: שׁמע (51:1aA – C.i) || קשׁב (51:4aA – C.iii) || שׁמע (51:7aA – C.v); אל (prep.) (51:1aA – C.i) || אל (prep.) (51:4aA – C.iii) || אל (51:7aA – C.v); י־ (51:1aA – C.i) || י־ (51:4aA – C.iii) || י־ (51:7aA – C.v); צדק (51:1aA – C.i) || צדק (51:5aA – C.iii) || צדקה (51:6cB – C.iv) || צדקה (51:8bA – C.v); ישׁע (51:5aA – C.iii) || ישׁועה (51:6cA – C.iv) || ישׁועה (51:8bB – C.v); כ (51:6bB – C.iv) || כ (51:8aA – B.v); בגד (51:6bB – C.iv) || בגד (51:8aA – B.v); בלה (51:6bB – C.iv) || אכל (51:8aA, 8aB – C.v); ל (51:6cA – C.iv) || ל (51:8bA – C.v); עולם (51:6cA – C.iv) || עולם (51:8bA – C.v); היה (51:6cA – C.iv) || היה (51:8bA – C.v).

It may appear that the servant part (B) has little to do with the part addressing the righteous of Israel (C). However, subtle hints indicate that it is the prophet himself who, as the archetypal servant of the LORD, is speaking here. Of course it is the LORD who is teaching (51:4bA, 7aB) and it is he who will pronounce judgment over the nations (51:5aB). But it is his servant who has to implement these tasks[3] and it is therefore an obvious hint at 42:6 and 49:6 when 50:4bB speaks of לאור עמים. Just as the servant is able to suffer insults because he awaits justification by the LORD (50:6-7, cf. Ch. 53), so he admonishes those craving for justice (51:1, 7a) to bear humiliation and insults obediently because God's eternal justice is bound to materialize for them (51:7b, cf. 6c and 8b).

[3] See with regard to משׁפט also Isa. 42:1, 3, 4.

Chapter 12

The Structure of Isaiah 51:9–52:12

12.1 Isaiah 51:9–52:12: Text and Translation

ס<פ> – 1𝔔^{ab} – 4𝔔^{c} – 𝔊^{SBAQ} – 𝔖^{abde} ________________

A.i.1 (Isa. 51:9a–b)

עוּרִי עוּרִי לִבְשִׁי־עֹז זְרוֹעַ יְהוָה {𝔊^{Q}}	9aA	Wake up, wake up, clothe yourself with strength, O arm of the LORD.
עוּרִי כִּימֵי קֶדֶם	9bA	Wake up, as in the days of old,
{𝔊^{Q}} דֹּרוֹת עוֹלָמִים	9bB	of the generations of primordial times!

A.i.2 (Isa. 51:9c)

הֲלוֹא אַתְּ־הִיא הַמַּחְצֶבֶת רַהַב	9cA	Was is not you who hewed[1] Rahab,
מְחוֹלֶלֶת תַּנִּין׃	9cB	who pierced the Tannin?[2]

A.i.3 (Isa. 51:10)

הֲלוֹא אַתְּ־הִיא הַמַּחֲרֶבֶת יָם	10aA	Was it not you who dried up the sea,
מֵי תְּהוֹם רַבָּה	10aB	the waters of the great flood?
הַשָּׂמָה מַעֲמַקֵּי־יָם	10bA	Who made the depths of the sea
{<ס>} דֶּרֶךְ לַעֲבֹר גְּאוּלִים׃	10bB	a way for the passing over of the redeemed ones?

A.i.4 (Isa. 51:11)

וּפְדוּיֵי יְהוָה יְשׁוּבוּן	11aA	So the ransomed of the LORD will return,
וּבָאוּ צִיּוֹן בְּרִנָּה	11aB	and come to Zion with rejoicing,
וְשִׂמְחַת עוֹלָם עַל־רֹאשָׁם	11aC	and eternal joy will be on their heads,
שָׂשׂוֹן וְשִׂמְחָה יַשִּׂיגוּן	11bA	gladness and joy will overtake (them),
נָסוּ יָגוֹן וַאֲנָחָה׃	11bB	torment and sighing flee away.[3]

ס <פ> – 1𝔔^{a} – 4𝔔^{c} – 𝔊^{SBA} – 𝔖^{bcde} ....

A.ii.1 (Isa. 51:12)

אָנֹכִי אָנֹכִי הוּא מְנַחֶמְכֶם	12aA	I, I am he – the one who comforts you.

---

[1] 1𝔔^{a} has המוחצת, obviously harmonizing with Job 26:12. Although the Ugaritic texts use the verb *mḫṣ* in connection with the defeat of the Sea (KTU 1.4:II.24; 1.6:V.2 = *mḫš* in 1.3:III.38), this alone is no reason to follow 1𝔔^{a}.

[2] Oswalt, 339, translates "the twisting monster", without proper justification.

[3] For the rendering as an actual present, see M.C.A. Korpel, J.C. de Moor, F. Sepmeijer, "Consistency with Regard to Tenses", see Abbreviations.

מִֽי־אַ֤תְּ וַתִּֽירְאִי֙ מֵאֱנ֣וֹשׁ יָמ֔וּת	12bA	Who are you[4] that you fear man who dies,
וּמִבֶּן־אָדָ֖ם חָצִ֥יר יִנָּתֵֽן׃	12bB	and the son of man – grass given away?[5]

A.ii.2 (Isa. 51:13a)

וַתִּשְׁכַּ֞ח יְהוָ֣ה עֹשֶׂ֗ךָ	13aA	But you forget the LORD, who made you,[6]
נוֹטֶ֣ה שָׁמַ֘יִם֮ וְיֹסֵ֣ד אָ֒רֶץ֒	13aB	who stretched out the heavens and laid the foundation of the earth.

A.ii.3 (Isa. 51:13b-c)

וַתְּפַחֵ֨ד תָּמִ֜יד כָּל־הַיּ֗וֹם	13bA	And you quiver continually all the day
{𝔊^SQ} מִפְּנֵי֙ חֲמַ֣ת הַמֵּצִ֔יק	13bB	because of the fury of the oppressor
כַּאֲשֶׁ֥ר כּוֹנֵ֖ן לְהַשְׁחִ֑ית	13bC	when he aims[7] to annihilate.
וְאַיֵּ֖ה חֲמַ֥ת הַמֵּצִֽיק׃	13cA	But where is the fury of the oppressor?

A.ii.4 (Isa. 51:14)

מִהַ֥ר צֹעֶ֖ה לְהִפָּתֵ֑חַ	14aA	Soon the cellarman[8] will be released;
וְלֹא־יָמ֣וּת לַשַּׁ֔חַת	14bA	he will not die in the Pit of Annihilation,[9]
וְלֹ֥א יֶחְסַ֖ר לַחְמֽוֹ׃	14bB	neither will his bread be lacking.

<פ> – 1𝔔^a – 𝔊^AQ – 𝔖^b ....

A.iii.1 (Isa. 51:15)

וְאָנֹכִי֙ יְהוָ֣ה אֱלֹהֶ֔יךָ	15aA	For I am the LORD, your God,
רֹגַ֣ע הַיָּ֔ם וַיֶּהֱמ֖וּ גַּלָּ֑יו	15aB	who stirs up[10] the sea so that its waves roar
{𝔊^A} יְהוָ֥ה צְבָא֖וֹת שְׁמֽוֹ׃	15aC	– LORD of hosts is his name.

A.iii.2 (Isa. 51:16)

וָאָשִׂ֤ם דְּבָרַי֙ בְּפִ֔יךָ	16aA	And I put[11] my words in your mouth,
וּבְצֵ֥ל יָדִ֖י כִּסִּיתִ֑יךָ	16aB	and cover you with the shadow of my hand,[12]

---

[4] On the harsh transition from 2nd masc. pl. to 2nd fem. sg., see M.C.A. Korpel, "The Female Servant of the LORD in Isaiah 54", in: B. Becking, M. Dijkstra (eds.), *On Reading Prophetic Texts*, Leiden 1996, 153-67 (163-4).

[5] One might render "who is made into grass", but we prefer to make ינתן asyndetically dependent on חציר. The unmentioned indirect object is death, cf. Ezek. 31:14.

[6] Harsh transition to masculine singular, see note 4 above.

[7] Like an archer, cf. Oswalt, 344, n. 58.

[8] We interpret צעה after Jer. 48:12 and understand it as a deliberately ambiguous term: the prisoner who will become a cellarer. This establishes the strophe parallelism with v. 14bB and links up with Isa. 55:1-2.

[9] We adopt this wordy rendering to highlight the parallel with v. 13bC.

[10] 𝔗 and 𝔖 harmonize with Isa. 17:13; 50:2. The verb must have a meaning similar to גרש in Isa. 57:20. Cf. Job 26:12.

[11] See n. 3 above.

[12] Cf. Isa. 49:2, also with פה. This proves that it is the servant who is addressed here as the representative of his people (note the plural in v. 12aA). See also 50:4.

{$\mathfrak{S}^{b}$} לִנְטֹעַ שָׁמַיִם וְלִיסֹד אָרֶץ	16bA	to plant[13] the heavens and and to found the earth,
וְלֵאמֹר לְצִיּוֹן עַמִּי־אָתָּה׃	16bB	and to say to Zion, "You are my people!"

ס <פ> – 1$\mathfrak{Q}^{a}$ – $\mathfrak{G}^{SAQ}$ – $\mathfrak{S}^{abce}$ ________________________________

B.i.1 (Isa. 51:17a)

הִתְעוֹרְרִי הִתְעוֹרְרִי קוּמִי יְרוּשָׁלִַם	17aA	Wake yourself, wake yourself, stand up, O Jerusalem,

B.i.2 (Isa. 51:17b–c)

אֲשֶׁר שָׁתִית מִיַּד יְהוָה	17bA	you who have drunk from the hand of the LORD
אֶת־כּוֹס חֲמָתוֹ	17bB	the cup of his fury,
אֶת־קֻבַּעַת כּוֹס הַתַּרְעֵלָה	17cA	the beaker, the cup of reeling,
שָׁתִית מָצִית׃	17cB	you had to drink, to drain.

B.i.3 (Isa. 51:18)

אֵין־מְנַהֵל לָהּ	18aA	There was no one leading her
מִכָּל־בָּנִים יָלָדָה	18aB	of all the sons[14] she bore,
וְאֵין מַחֲזִיק בְּיָדָהּ	18bA	and there was no one grasping her hand
מִכָּל־בָּנִים גִּדֵּלָה׃	18bB	of all the sons she brought up.

$\mathfrak{G}^{Q}$ ....

B.ii.1 (Isa. 51:19)

שְׁתַּיִם הֵנָּה קֹרְאֹתַיִךְ	19aA	These two things have happened to you –
{$\mathfrak{G}^{A}$} מִי יָנוּד לָךְ	19aB	who will condole you? –
הַשֹּׁד וְהַשֶּׁבֶר	19bA	destruction and breakdown
וְהָרָעָב וְהַחֶרֶב	19bB	famine and sword –
מִי אֲנַחֲמֵךְ׃	19bC	by whom can I comfort you?[15]

B.ii.2 (Isa. 51:20)

בָּנַיִךְ עֻלְּפוּ שָׁכְבוּ	20aA	Your sons have fainted; they lie down

---

[13]Many translations, starting with $\mathfrak{G}$, try to avoid a literal rendering of the infinitives. In our opinion this happens for theological reasons far removed from the theology of the prophet himself.

[14]The rendering "children" (NJB) is impossible because of the masculine participles and because it was a son's task to escort his drunken parents home. Cf. KTU 1.17:I.30 par.; 1.114:18-19. Moreover, v. 20 excludes the possibility in a definitive way (עלפו, שכבו, המלאים).

[15]The first person singular is surprising and was changed into a 3rd pers. sg. masc. by 1$\mathfrak{Q}^{a}$, $\mathfrak{G}$, $\mathfrak{S}$, σ and $\mathfrak{V}$ which is an obvious harmonization, yet is followed by numerous modern translations and commentators. It seems likely that Second Isaiah is quoting Nah. 3:7 here, cf. K. Spronk, *Nahum* (HCOT), Kampen 1997, 125. Therefore the medieval commentators may be right in assuming that מאין אבקש מנחמים לך is compressed here into מי אנחמך "by whom can I comfort you?". Cf. Barthélemy, 376; De Waard, 189-90.

בְּרֹאשׁ כָּל־חוּצוֹת	20aB	at the head of every street,[16]
כְּתוֹא מִכְמָר	20aC	like an antelope[17] caught in a net.
הַמְלֵאִים חֲמַת־יְהוָה	20bA	They are filled with the fury of the LORD,
גַּעֲרַת אֱלֹהָיִךְ׃	20bB	the rebuke of your God.

<ס> – 1$\mathfrak{Q}^{a}$ – $\mathfrak{G}^{SBA}$ – $\mathfrak{S}^{abce}$ . . . .

B.iii.1 (Isa. 51:21–22a)

לָכֵן שִׁמְעִי־נָא זֹאת עֲנִיָּה	21aA	Therefore hear now this, O afflicted one,
{ס<פ>$\mathfrak{G}^{S}$} וּשְׁכֻרַת וְלֹא מִיָּיִן׃	21aB	and drunken one,[18] though not with wine:
כֹּה־אָמַר אֲדֹנַיִךְ יְהוָה	22aA	Thus says your Lord GOD
וֵאלֹהַיִךְ יָרִיב עַמּוֹ	22aB	and your God who goes into court for his people:

B.iii.2 (Isa. 51:22b–c)

הִנֵּה לָקַחְתִּי מִיָּדֵךְ	22bA	Behold, I take from your hand
אֶת־כּוֹס הַתַּרְעֵלָה	22bB	the cup of reeling,
אֶת־קֻבַּעַת כּוֹס חֲמָתִי	22cA	the beaker, the cup of my fury –
לֹא־תוֹסִיפִי לִשְׁתּוֹתָהּ עוֹד׃	22cB	you will not have to drink it again.

{$\mathfrak{G}^{A}$}

B.iii.3 (Isa. 51:23)

וְשַׂמְתִּיהָ בְּיַד־מוֹגַיִךְ	23aA	And I will put it into the hand of those who torment you,
אֲשֶׁר־אָמְרוּ לְנַפְשֵׁךְ	23aB	who say to you,
שְׁחִי וְנַעֲבֹרָה	23aC	"Bow down, that we may pass over",
וַתָּשִׂימִי כָאָרֶץ גֵּוֵךְ	23bA	and you had to make your back like the ground
וְכַחוּץ לַעֹבְרִים׃	23bB	and like a street for those who pass over.

ס <פ> – 1$\mathfrak{Q}^{a}$ – $\mathfrak{G}^{SAQ}$ – $\mathfrak{S}^{abcde}$ ________________________________

C.i.1 (Isa. 52:1a–b)

עוּרִי עוּרִי לִבְשִׁי עֻזֵּךְ צִיּוֹן	1aA	Wake up, wake up, clothe yourself with your strength, o Zion
לִבְשִׁי ׀ בִּגְדֵי תִפְאַרְתֵּךְ	1bA	clothe yourself with your glorious garments,
יְרוּשָׁלַםִ עִיר הַקֹּדֶשׁ	1bB	O, Jerusalem, holy city:

---

[16]All ancient witnesses have this colon which from the viewpoint of structure is unproblematic. The circumstance that it seems to reflect Lam. 2:19 (and some other texts) becomes understandable as soon as it is realized that it was one of Second Isaiah's main theological objectives to refute the type of theology to which the Book of Lamentations testifies.

[17]The identification is somewhat uncertain. Cf. *HALAT*, 1542-3. Egyptian and Mesopotamian iconography shows that the animal was mercilessly hunted.

[18]The construct state reflects the writer's intention to start an expression like שכרת יין which on second thoughts he corrects in the middle. Cf. Joel 1:8 חֲגֻרַת־שַׂק.

C.i.2 (Isa. 52:1c)

כִּ֣י לֹ֥א יוֹסִ֛יף יָבֹא־בָ֥ךְ ע֖וֹד	1cA	for there shall no more come into you
{<פ/ס>𝔊^A} עָרֵ֥ל וְטָמֵֽא׃	1cB	the uncircumcised and the unclean.

C.i.3 (Isa. 52:2)

הִתְנַעֲרִ֧י מֵעָפָ֛ר	2aA	Shake yourself free from the dust,
ק֥וּמִי שְּׁבִ֖י יְרוּשָׁלִָ֑ם	2aB	stand up, take your seat,[19] O Jerusalem!
הִֽתְפַּתְּחוּ מוֹסְרֵ֣י צַוָּארֵ֔ךְ*	2bA	The chains on your neck are released,[20]
{ס𝔊^AQ} שְׁבִיָּ֖ה בַּת־צִיּֽוֹן׃	2bB	O captive, daughter of Zion!

C.i.4 (Isa. 52:3)

כִּי־כֹה֙ אָמַ֣ר יְהוָ֔ה	3aA	For thus says the LORD:
חִנָּ֖ם נִמְכַּרְתֶּ֑ם	3aB	For nothing you were sold
וְלֹ֥א בְכֶ֖סֶף תִּגָּאֵֽלוּ׃	3aC	and without silver you will be redeemed.

<ס> – 𝔊^SBA – 𝔖^b ....

C.ii.1 (Isa. 52:4)

כִּ֣י כֹ֤ה אָמַר֙ אֲדֹנָ֣י יְהוִ֔ה	4aA	For thus says the Lord GOD:
מִצְרַ֛יִם יָרַד־עַמִּ֥י בָרִאשֹׁנָ֖ה לָג֣וּר שָׁ֑ם	4aB	At first my people went down to Egypt to sojourn there,
וְאַשּׁ֖וּר בְּאֶ֥פֶס עֲשָׁקֽוֹ׃	4aC	and Assyria oppressed them for nothing.[21]

C.ii.2 (Isa. 52:5)

{𝔊^SBQ} וְעַתָּ֤ה מִי לִ֨י־פֹה֙ נְאֻם־יְהוָ֔ה	5aA	But now, what[22] do I have here? declares the LORD,
כִּֽי־לֻקַּ֥ח עַמִּ֖י חִנָּ֑ם	5aB	that my people has been taken away for nothing?

---

[19]Since in v. 1 Zion and Jerusalem are also paired, it may seem more likely that שבי parallels שביה in v. 2bB. However, the unanimous testimony of the ancient witnesses (note especially 1Q^a ושבי) cautions against emending the text of v. 2aB. Moreover, v. 2aA has two imperatives too, so a second imperative in v. 2aB creates a better balance. A similar wordplay between the verb ישב and the noun שבי occurs in Jer. 20:6. Finally it should be noted that the imperative of ישב creates a nice contrast with Isa. 47:1.

[20]Although it is tempting to follow the Qere, making Zion responsible for taking part in her own liberation – an idea very important to Second Isaiah, illustrated by v. 2a – the Ketiv must be regarded as the more difficult reading which in the end we prefer, with e.g. Barthélemy, 379-80; De Waard, 192.

[21]In Second Isaiah אפס means "nonity, non-existence". So a rendering "in the end" is not very likely. No other text can be cited in corroboration of the presumed temporal meaning of אפס. The best interpretation takes the ב as a *beth pretii*, as in v. 3aC. See the judicious treatment by Koole, 179-80.

[22]The Ketiv is the more difficult reading which for that reason is preferable. Both Ugaritic and Hebrew מי may sometimes be rendered "what?". Cf. J.C. de Moor, *The Seasonal Pattern in the Ugaritic Myth of Ba'lu* (AOAT, 16), Neukirchen 1971, 194; GK §137a.

מֹשְׁלָיו* יְהֵילִ֙ילוּ֙ {$\mathfrak{G}^{SA}$}נְאֻם־יְהוָ֔ה	5bA	Those who rule it[23] ululate,[24] declares the LORD,
וְתָמִ֥יד כָּל־הַיּ֖וֹם שְׁמִ֥י מִנֹּאָֽץ׃ {<ס>$\mathfrak{G}^{BQ}$}	5bB	and all day long my name is reviled.

C.ii.3 (Isa. 52:6)

לָכֵ֛ן יֵדַ֥ע עַמִּ֖י שְׁמִ֑י	6aA	Therefore my people will know my name,
לָכֵן֙ בַּיּ֣וֹם הַה֔וּא	6bA	therefore,[25] on that day,
כִּֽי־אֲנִי־ה֥וּא{$\mathfrak{G}^{S}$}הַֽמְדַבֵּ֖ר הִנֵּֽנִי׃	6bB	when[26] I am going to speak: Here I am!

<פ> <ס> – ס̄ – 1$\mathfrak{Q}^{a}$ – $\mathfrak{G}^{A}$ – S^{abcde} ....

C.iii.1 (Isa. 52:7)

מַה־נָּאו֨וּ עַל־הֶהָרִ֜ים	7aA	How beautiful on the mountains
רַגְלֵ֣י מְבַשֵּׂ֗ר מַשְׁמִ֧יעַ שָׁל֛וֹם	7aB	are the feet of the herald who announces peace,
מְבַשֵּׂ֥ר ט֖וֹב מַשְׁמִ֣יעַ יְשׁוּעָ֑ה	7aC	the herald of good tidings who announces salvation,
אֹמֵ֥ר לְצִיּ֖וֹן מָלַ֥ךְ אֱלֹהָֽיִךְ׃ {<ס>$\mathfrak{G}^{S}$}	7bA	who says to Zion, "Your God is king!"

C.iii.2 (Isa. 52:8)

ק֥וֹל צֹפַ֛יִךְ נָ֥שְׂאוּ {$\mathfrak{G}^{S}$} ק֖וֹל	8aA	The voices of[27] your watchmen! They raise their voices,
יַחְדָּ֣ו יְרַנֵּ֑נוּ	8aB	they rejoice together,
כִּ֣י עַ֤יִן בְּעַ֙יִן֙ יִרְא֔וּ	8bA	for with their own eyes they see with delight[28]
בְּשׁ֥וּב יְהוָ֖ה צִיּֽוֹן׃{<ס>$\mathfrak{G}^{SAQ}$}	8bB	how the LORD returns to Zion.[29]

C.iii.3 (Isa. 52:9)

פִּצְח֤וּ רַנְּנוּ֙ יַחְדָּ֔ו	9aA	Break forth, rejoice together
חָרְב֖וֹת יְרוּשָׁלִָ֑ם	9aB	you ruins of Jerusalem!

---

[23]The Ketiv is merely a defective spelling. Because of v. 5bB only foreign rulers can have been meant here and this brings to mind Isa. 49:7 where Israel is called an עבד משלים "servant of rulers" who has to suffer insult.

[24]In our opinion there is no need for emendation. Onomatopoeic ילל could well have had both a positive and a negative meaning, depending on the context, as is the case with רנן.

[25]Some ancient witnesses omit the second לכן for stylistic reasons, but see Isa. 30:18.

[26]One has to assume either ellipsis of ידע or take כי in a temporal sense which is certainly admissable (see e.g. Isa. 40:7aB; 51:3aA).

[27]Exactly the repetition of קול counsels against taking the first קול in the sense of an adhortation to hear. See our remarks on Isa. 40:3, p. 17, n. 2.

[28]If verbs of seeing are constructed with ב, always some emotional extra is present, like gloating, rejoicing or pity.

[29]1$\mathfrak{Q}^{a}$ adds ברחמים "with compassion" which was probably derived from Zech. 1:16. Cf. Barthélemy, 382-3.

כִּֽי־נִחַם יְהוָה֙ עַמּ֔וֹ	9bA	For the LORD comforts[30] his people,
{$\mathfrak{G}^{S}$} גָּאַ֖ל יְרוּשָׁלִָֽם׃	9bB	he redeems Jerusalem.

C.iii.4 (Isa. 52:10)

חָשַׂ֤ף יְהוָה֙ אֶת־זְר֣וֹעַ קָדְשׁ֔וֹ	10aA	The LORD bares his holy arm
לְעֵינֵ֖י כָּל־הַגּוֹיִ֑ם	10aB	before the eyes of all the nations;
וְרָאוּ֙ כָּל־אַפְסֵי־אָ֔רֶץ	10bA	and all the ends of the earth will see
אֵ֖ת יְשׁוּעַ֥ת אֱלֹהֵֽינוּ׃	10bB	the salvation of our God.

ס – $1\mathfrak{Q}^{ab}$ – $4\mathfrak{Q}^{c}$ – $\mathfrak{G}^{SAQ}$ – $\mathfrak{S}^{b}$ . . . .

C.iv.1 (Isa. 52:11)

ס֤וּרוּ ס֙וּרוּ֙ צְא֣וּ מִשָּׁ֔ם	11aA	Depart, depart, go out from there!
טָמֵ֖א אַל־תִּגָּ֑עוּ	11aB	Do not touch the unclean!
צְא֣וּ מִתּוֹכָ֔הּ	11bA	Go out from the midst of her!
הִבָּ֕רוּ נֹשְׂאֵ֖י כְּלֵ֥י יְהוָֽה׃	11bB	Keep yourselves pure, you who carry the vessels of the LORD.[31]

C.iv.2 (Isa. 52:12)

כִּ֣י לֹ֤א בְחִפָּזוֹן֙ תֵּצֵ֔אוּ	12aA	For you will not go out in haste,
וּבִמְנוּסָ֖ה לֹ֣א תֵלֵכ֑וּן	12aB	and you will not go in flight,
כִּֽי־הֹלֵ֤ךְ לִפְנֵיכֶם֙ יְהוָ֔ה	12bA	for the LORD will go before you,
וּמְאַסִּפְכֶ֖ם אֱלֹהֵ֥י יִשְׂרָאֵֽל׃	12bB	and the God of Israel will be your rearguard.

ס <פ> – $1\mathfrak{Q}^{a}$ – $4\mathfrak{Q}^{c}$ – $\mathfrak{G}^{SBAQ}$ – $\mathfrak{S}^{abcde}$ ________________________________

[30] See our note on Isa. 49:13, p. 402.

[31] The priests and Levites are meant, in apparent contrast to Lam. 4:15 (note the use of the verb נצה). There was a strong expectation that the holy vessels would turn up in the treasuries of the Babylonians which Cyrus would open (Isa. 45:3) and that Persian king would give them back to the exiles (Ezra 1:7; see also Jer. 27:16; 28:3, 6). Because v. 12 draws an obvious parallel with the Exodus again, the author may have thought of the כלי כסף וכלי זהב which the Egyptians had to give the Israelites when the people of God left the country (Exod. 11:2; 12:35-36).

12.2 Isaiah 51:9–52:12 – Delimitation of Cola

COLON 51:9aA:

עוּרִ֨י עוּרִ֤י לִבְשִׁי־עֹז֙ זְר֣וֹעַ יְהוָ֔ה 9aA Wake up, wake up, clothe yourself with strength, O arm of the LORD.

With: 𝔐 (5) – 𝔊^{SQ}, major division marker in 𝔊^{Q} – 𝔖^{abcd}
Colon parallelism: The roots עור || עור.
Discussion: 𝔊^{S}, 𝔊^{Q} and 𝔖^{b} have an extra point after the second עורי, but in 𝔊 this is caused by the insertion of Ιερουσαλημ. It is possible to divide after לבשי־עז where 𝔐 has a Pashṭa (No. 10) and 𝔊^{Q} as well as 𝔖^{e} have a point. But the division after יהוה is better attested[1] and the resulting colon of five stressed units is certainly not without parallel.

COLON 51:9bA:

עוּרִי֙ כִּ֣ימֵי קֶ֔דֶם 9bA Wake up, as in the days of old,

With: 𝔐 (5) – 𝔊^{SQ} – 𝔖^{acde}

COLON 51:9bB:

דֹּר֖וֹת עוֹלָמִ֑ים 9bB of the generations of primordial times!

With: 𝔐 (2) – 𝔊^{SQ}, major division markers in 𝔊^{Q} – 𝔖^{abcde}

COLON 51:9cA:

הֲל֥וֹא אַתְּ־הִ֛יא הַמַּחְצֶ֥בֶת רַ֖הַב 9cA Was is not you who hewed Rahab,

With: 𝔐 (8) – 𝔖^{be} subordinate punctuation.
Discussion: The Masoretes wanted to read on to the end of the verse, a colon of six feet. Even though our division finds no support in the ancient witnesses (𝔊 is unfortunately lacking at this point) we believe that the strong parallelism המחצבת || מחוללת and רהב || תנין favours a bicolon.

COLON 51:9cB:

מְחוֹלֶ֥לֶת תַּנִּֽין׃ 9cB who pierced the Tannin?

With: 𝔐 (1) – 𝔖^{abcde}
Discussion: 𝔊 is lacking.

[1]𝔊^{Q} even seems to indicate the end of the verse-lines in this strophe.

COLON 51:10aA:

הֲל֤וֹא אַתְּ־הִיא֙ הַמַּחֲרֶ֣בֶת יָ֔ם 10aA Was it not you who dried up the sea,

With: 𝔐 (5) – 𝔊[SQ] – 𝔖[abcde] all subordinate punctuation.

COLON 51:10aB:

מֵ֖י תְּה֣וֹם רַבָּ֑ה 10aB the waters of the great flood?

With: 𝔐 (2) – 𝔊[SQ] – 𝔖[acde]

COLON 51:10bA:

הַשָּׂמָה֙ מַעֲמַקֵּי־יָ֔ם 10bA Who made the depths of the sea

With: 𝔐 (5) – 𝔊[S]
Discussion: Even though 𝔐 is supported by 𝔊[S] only, it has the best papers. As in many other instances, the enjambment caused confusion. But see with regard to 𝔖 our comment on the next colon.

COLON 51:10bB:

דֶּ֖רֶךְ לַעֲבֹ֥ר גְּאוּלִֽים׃ 10bB a way for the passing over of the redeemed ones?

With: 𝔐 (1), major division markers in some editions, also 1Q[a]
Discussion: 𝔖[acd] have a dividing point after דרך (𝔐 Ṭiphḥa) which may seem a serious alternative for the division after ים. However, one suspects that this choice was necessitated by 𝔖's totally different colometry for the sequal which presupposes for the Hebrew,

השמה מעמקי־ים דרך
לעבר גאולים ופדויי יהוה
ישובון ובאו ציון ברנה

However, whereas the verbs גאל and פדה do occur in verse-line parallelism,[2] they are never attested in colon parallelism. The redactional preparation of Second Isaiah in Isa. 35 has apparently divided Isa. 51:10-11 in a way very similar to 𝔐 (Isa. 35:8-10). Also the Setuma in 1Q[a] presupposes the same division. Possibly 𝔖's reading was inspired by 𝔊 which, however, stopped at ופדויי, taking it as a word in the absolute state.

[2] Jer. 31:11; Hos. 13:14; Ps. 69:19.

Colon 51:11aA:

וּפְדוּיֵ֨י יְהוָ֜ה יְשׁוּב֗וּן 11aA So the ransomed of the Lord will return,

With: 𝔐 (7) – 𝔊^{SQ}
Discussion: With regard to 𝔖 see the preceding colon.

Colon 51:11aB:

וּבָ֤אוּ צִיּוֹן֙ בְּרִנָּ֔ה 11aB and come to Zion with rejoicing,

With: 𝔐 (5) – 𝔊^{SQ} – 𝔖^{abcde}

Colon 51:11aC:

וְשִׂמְחַ֥ת עוֹלָ֖ם עַל־רֹאשָׁ֑ם 11aC and eternal joy will be on their heads,

With: 𝔐 (2) – 𝔊^{Q} – 𝔖^{abce}
Discussion: 𝔊^{SQ} have an extra point after עולם which equals 𝔐's Ṭiphḥa.

Colon 51:11bA:

שָׂשׂ֤וֹן וְשִׂמְחָה֙ יַשִּׂיג֔וּן 11bA gladness and joy will overtake (them),

With: 𝔐 (5) – 𝔖^{ab}, 𝔖^{cde} subordinate punctuation.
Colon parallelism: ששׂון || שׂמחה.
Discussion: 𝔊 is lacking here.

Colon 51:11bB:

נָ֖סוּ יָג֥וֹן וַאֲנָחָֽה׃ 11bB torment and sighing flee away.

With: 𝔐 (1), major division markers, also in 1𝔔^{a} – 𝔊^{SBAQ}, major division markers in 𝔊^{SBA} – 𝔖^{abcde}, major division markers in 𝔖^{bcde}
Colon parallelism: יגון || אנחה.

Colon 51:12aA:

אָנֹכִ֧י אָנֹכִ֛י ה֖וּא מְנַחֶמְכֶ֑ם 12aA I, I am he – the one who comforts you.

With: 𝔐 (2) – 𝔊^{SQ} – 𝔖^{abcde} (but see below).
Colon parallelism: אנכי || אנכי.
Discussion: 𝔖 has a plus after this colon ("says the Lord"), but may be considered to support 𝔐. Despite the bicolon Isa. 43:25a, it is unlikely that מנחמכם constitutes a colon of one word.

Colon 51:12bA:

מִי־אַ֣תְּ וַתִּֽירְאִי֙ מֵאֱנ֣וֹשׁ יָמ֔וּת 12bA Who are you that you fear man who dies,

With: 𝔐 (5) – 𝔊^{S} – 𝔖^{acd}

Colon 51:12bB:

וּמִבֶּן־אָדָם חָצִיר יִנָּתֵן׃ 12bB and the son of man – grass given away?

With: 𝔐 (1) – 𝔊^{SQ} – 𝔖^{bde}, 𝔖^{ac} subordinate punctuation.
Discussion: 𝔊^{SQ} have an extra point after אדם where 𝔐 has a Ṭiphḥa.

Colon 51:13aA:

וַתִּשְׁכַּח יְהוָה עֹשֶׂךָ 13aA But you forget the Lord, who made you,

With: 𝔐 (7) – 𝔊^{SQ} (𝔊^{S} colon) – 𝔖^{b}, the other manuscripts subordinate punctuation.

Colon 51:13aB:

נוֹטֶה שָׁמַיִם וְיֹסֵד אָרֶץ 13aB who stretched out the heavens and laid the foundation of the earth.

With: 𝔐 (3) – 𝔊^{SQ} – 𝔖^{abcde}
Colon parallelism: נטה || יסד; שמים || ארץ.
Discussion: 𝔊^{SQ} have an extra point after שמים (𝔐 Zarqa, No. 9).

Colon 51:13bA:

וַתְּפַחֵד תָּמִיד כָּל־הַיּוֹם 13bA And you quiver continually all the day

With: 𝔐 (7) – 𝔊^{Q} – 𝔖^{e}, 𝔖^{b} subordinate punctuation.
Colon parallelism: תמיד || כל־היום.
Discussion: Though the caesura is poorly attested, the attested colon parallelism speaks in its favour.

Colon 51:13bB:

מִפְּנֵי חֲמַת הַמֵּצִיק 13bB because of the fury of the oppressor

With: 𝔐 (5) – 𝔊^{SQ}, major division marks in both – 𝔖^{abcde} all subordinate punctuation.

Colon 51:13bC:

כַּאֲשֶׁר כּוֹנֵן לְהַשְׁחִית 13bC when he aims to annihilate.

With: 𝔐 (2) – 𝔊^{SQ} – 𝔖^{abcde}

Colon 51:13cA:

וְאַיֵּה חֲמַת הַמֵּצִיק׃ 13cA But where is the fury of the oppressor?

With: 𝔐 (1) – 𝔊^{SQ} – 𝔖^{e}, all other manuscripts subordinate punctuation.

Discussion: 𝔖 tried to solve the problems with v. 14 by making its first colon a relative clause.

Colon 51:14aA:

מִהַר צֹעֶה לְהִפָּתֵחַ 14aA Soon the cellarman will be released;

With: 𝔐 (2) – 𝔖^{abcde}
Discussion: 𝔊 condenses v. 14 into a short free paraphrasis which does not allow for any comparison with 𝔐.

Colon 51:14bA:

וְלֹא־יָמוּת לַשַּׁחַת 14bA he will not die in the Pit of Annihilation,

With: 𝔐 (5) – 𝔖^{abcde}
Discussion: With regard to 𝔊 see v. 14aA.

Colon 51:14bB:

וְלֹא יֶחְסַר לַחְמוֹ׃ 14bB neither will his bread be lacking.

With: 𝔐 (1), Petuḥa in 1𝔔^{a} – 𝔊^{SAQ}, major division marks in 𝔊^{AQ} – 𝔖^{abcde}, major division mark in 𝔖^{b}

Colon 51:15aA:

וְאָנֹכִי יְהוָה אֱלֹהֶיךָ 15aA For I am the Lord, your God,

With: 𝔐 (5) – 𝔊^{Q} – 𝔖^{a}, 𝔖^{bcde} subordinate punctuation.
Colon parallelism: יהוה || אלהים.

Colon 51:15aB:

רֹגַע הַיָּם וַיֶּהֱמוּ גַּלָּיו 15aB who stirs up the sea so that its waves roar –

With: 𝔐 (2)
Colon parallelism: ים || גל.
Discussion: 𝔐 has a Zaqeph Qaṭon (No. 5) with הים which is supported by 𝔊^{SQ}, but not by 𝔖. However, in Jer. 31:35 the same two cola are quoted, and there 𝔐 has only a Pashṭa (No. 10) with הים, so the Masoretes took the phrase as one colon.

Colon 51:15aC:

יְהוָה צְבָאוֹת שְׁמוֹ׃ 15aC Lord of hosts is his name.

With: 𝔐 (1) – 𝔊^{SAQ}, major division markers in 𝔊^{A} – 𝔖^{abcd}, 𝔖^{e} lacking.

COLON 51:16aA:

וָאָשִׂ֤ים דְּבָרַי֙ בְּפִ֔יךָ 16aA And I put my words in your mouth,

With: $\mathfrak{M}$ (5) – $\mathfrak{G}^{SQ}$ – $\mathfrak{S}^{e}$, $\mathfrak{S}^{abcd}$ subordinate punctuation.

COLON 51:16aB:

וּבְצֵ֥ל יָדִ֖י כִּסִּיתִ֑יךָ 16aB and cover you with the shadow of my hand,

With: $\mathfrak{M}$ (2) – $\mathfrak{G}^{SQ}$ – $\mathfrak{S}^{abcde}$

COLON 51:16bA:

לִנְטֹ֤עַ שָׁמַ֙יִם֙ וְלִיסֹ֣ד אָ֔רֶץ 16bA to plant the heavens and and to found the earth,

With: $\mathfrak{M}$ (5) – $\mathfrak{G}^{SQ}$ – $\mathfrak{S}^{bcde}$, major division markers in $\mathfrak{S}^{b}$
Colon parallelism: נטע || יסד; שמים || ארץ.

COLON 51:16bB:

וְלֵאמֹ֥ר לְצִיּ֖וֹן עַמִּי־אָֽתָּה׃ 16bB and to say to Zion, "You are my people!"

With: $\mathfrak{M}$ (1), major division markers, also in 1Q[a] – $\mathfrak{G}^{SAQ}$, major division markers in all three – $\mathfrak{S}^{abcde}$, major division markers in all but $\mathfrak{S}^{d}$

COLON 51:17aA:

הִתְעוֹרְרִ֣י הִתְעוֹרְרִ֗י ק֚וּמִי יְר֣וּשָׁלִַ֔ם 17aA Wake yourself, wake yourself, stand up, O Jerusalem,

With: $\mathfrak{M}$ (5) – $\mathfrak{G}^{SQ}$ – $\mathfrak{S}^{a}$, $\mathfrak{S}^{bcde}$ subordinate punctuation.
Colon parallelism: עור || עור; עור || קום.
Discussion: The division is very difficult here. Whereas $\mathfrak{M}$ has a conjunctive accent with the second עורי in v. 9aA and a weak divider (Tevir, No. 12) in 52:1aA, it has a Revia' (No. 7) here which is supported by $\mathfrak{G}^{SQ}$. So it is possible to read v. 17aA as a bicolon.[3] However, $\mathfrak{S}$ does not support a bicolon[4] and the similarity with 51:9 and 52:1 suggests that the three imperatives followed by a vocative belong to the same colon. Because קום does occur in parallelism with עור it is admissable to assume colon parallelism.

COLON 51:17bA:

אֲשֶׁ֥ר שָׁתִ֛ית מִיַּ֥ד יְהוָ֖ה 17bA you who have drunk from the hand of the LORD

With: $\mathfrak{M}$ (8).

---

[3] For similar cases see our comments on 45:20aA, p. 281.

[4] Even though $\mathfrak{S}^{a}$ does have a subordinate punctuation mark.

Discussion: 𝔐's extremely long colon of six stressed units stands under the suspicion of having been caused by the fact that the sentence runs on, and the ancient witnesses support 𝔐 in this respect. Yet we believe it is admissable to deviate from the unanimous verdict of tradition here (with BHS and most modern commentators). In the almost identical v. 22b-c the evidence for two bicola is much stronger.

COLON 51:17bB:

אֶת־כּ֖וֹס חֲמָת֑וֹ 17bB the cup of his fury,

With: 𝔐 (2) – 𝔊^{SQ} – 𝔖^{abcde}

COLON 51:17cA:

אֶת־קֻבַּ֜עַת כּ֧וֹס הַתַּרְעֵלָ֛ה 17cA the beaker, the cup of reeling,

With: 𝔐 (12).
Colon parallelism: קבעת || כוס (as in v. 22cA).
Discussion: See our comment on v. 17bA.

COLON 51:17cB:

שָׁתִ֥ית מָצִֽית׃ 17cB you had to drink, to drain.

With: 𝔐 (1) – 𝔊^{SQ} – 𝔖^{abcde}
Colon parallelism: שתה || מצה.

COLON 51:18aA:

אֵין־מְנַהֵ֣ל לָ֔הּ 18aA There was no one leading her

With: 𝔐 (5)
Discussion: None of the other ancient witnesses has a caesura here, apparently because the verse spills over into the next colon (enjambment). But the strophe parallelism מכל־בנים ילדה || מכל־בנים גדלה clearly favours 𝔐.

COLON 51:18aB:

מִכָּל־בָּנִ֖ים יָלָ֑דָה 18aB of all the sons she bore,

With: 𝔐 (2) – 𝔊^{SQ} – 𝔖^{bcd}, 𝔖^{ae} subordinate punctuation.
Discussion: Two isolated witnesses have an illogical dividing point after מכל (𝔊^{Q} and 𝔖^{e}).

COLON 51:18bA:

וְאֵ֤ין מַחֲזִיק֙ בְּיָדָ֔הּ 18bA and there was no one grasping her hand

With: $\mathfrak{M}$ (5) – $\mathfrak{G}^{SQ}$
Discussion: $\mathfrak{S}$ was led astray by the onrunning sentence.

COLON 51:18bB:

מִכָּל־בָּנִים גִּדֵּלָה׃ 18bB of all the sons she brought up.

With: $\mathfrak{M}$ (1) – $\mathfrak{G}^{SQ}$, paragraphos in $\mathfrak{G}^{Q}$ – $\mathfrak{S}^{abcd}$, $\mathfrak{S}^{e}$ subordinate punctuation.
Discussion: $\mathfrak{G}^{SQ}$ have an extra point after בנים ($\mathfrak{M}$ Ṭiphḥa).

COLON 51:19aA:

שְׁתַּיִם הֵנָּה קֹרְאֹתַיִךְ 19aA These two things have happened to you –

With: $\mathfrak{M}$ (5) – $\mathfrak{G}^{SQ}$ – $\mathfrak{S}^{e}$, but $\mathfrak{S}^{a}$ subordinate punctuation.

COLON 51:19aB:

מִי יָנוּד לָךְ 19aB who will condole you? –

With: $\mathfrak{M}$ (2) – $\mathfrak{G}^{SAQ}$, major division markers in $\mathfrak{G}^{A}$ – $\mathfrak{S}^{abcde}$

COLON 51:19bA:

הַשֹּׁד וְהַשֶּׁבֶר 19bA destruction and breakdown

With: $\mathfrak{M}$ (12) – $\mathfrak{G}^{SQ}$
Colon parallelism: שׁד || שׁבר.
Discussion: Apparently $\mathfrak{M}$ wanted to read on until אנחמך, a colon of six stressed units. Because שׁד || שׁבר and רעב || חרב are fixed pairs[5] which are not combined anywhere else, we believe that the Greek tradition has preserved the correct colometry in this case.

COLON 51:19bB:

וְהָרָעָב וְהַחֶרֶב 19bB famine and sword –

With: $\mathfrak{M}$ (8) – $\mathfrak{G}^{SQ}$
Colon parallelism: רעב || חרב.
Discussion: See v. 19bA.

COLON 51:19bC:

מִי אֲנַחֲמֵךְ׃ 19bC by whom can I comfort you?

With: $\mathfrak{M}$ (1) – $\mathfrak{G}^{SQ}$ – $\mathfrak{S}^{abcde}$

[5]Second Isaiah is fond of such pairs, cf. Isa. 41:17aA; 43:20aB; 44:14aB; 46:1aB; 47:9aC; 47:10aC; 50:6bB; 51:3cA, 3cB; 51:11bA, 11bB; 52:1cB; 55:1bC. For a very similar case involving two such pairs see 43:17a.

COLON 51:20aA:

בָּנַיִךְ עֻלְּפוּ שָׁכְבוּ 20aA Your sons have fainted; they lie down

With: 𝔐 (12) – S^{cd}
Colon parallelism: עלף || שׁכב (unique).
Discussion: $\mathfrak{G}^{SQ}$ divide after עלפו where 𝔐 has a conjunctive accent. 𝔐 seems to prefer to read on until מכמר, or perhaps חוצות which was provided with a Ṭiphḥa (No. 8). This is one of the rare occasions where part of the S-tradition has a solution different from both. We accept this division which agrees with that of BHS and many others. The ancient witnesses were deluded once again by the onrunning sentence (enjambment or 'synthetic' parallelism).

COLON 51:20aB:

בְּרֹאשׁ כָּל־חוּצוֹת 20aB at the head of every street,

With: 𝔐 (8) – $\mathfrak{G}^{S}$ – S^{b}, S^{acde} subordinate punctuation.
Discussion: Even though the incision is poorly attested we accept it because the expression בראשׁ כל־חוצות is always at the end of a colon.[6]

COLON 51:20aC:

כְּתוֹא מִכְמָר 20aC like an antelope caught in a net.

With: 𝔐 (2) – $\mathfrak{G}^{SQ}$ – S^{abcde}

COLON 51:20bA:

הַמְלֵאִים חֲמַת־יְהוָה 20bA They are filled with the fury of the LORD,

With: 𝔐 (8) – $\mathfrak{G}^{Q}$ – S^{e}
Discussion: It is questionable whether 𝔐 is really supported by the witnesses cited. However, since the only other attestation of the pair חמה || גערה occurs in verse-line parallelism,[7] we accept a break at this point, with BHS and many others.

COLON 51:20bB:

גַּעֲרַת אֱלֹהָיִךְ׃ 20bB the rebuke of your God.

With: 𝔐 (1), Setuma in 1$\mathfrak{Q}^{a}$ – $\mathfrak{G}^{SBAQ}$, major division markers in $\mathfrak{G}^{SBA}$ – S^{abcde}, major divison markers in all but S^{d}

[6]Nah. 3:10; Lam. 2:19; 4:1.
[7]Isa. 66:15.

COLON 51:21aA:

לָכֵן שִׁמְעִי־נָא זֹאת עֲנִיָּה 21aA Therefore hear now this, O afflicted one,

With: 𝔐 (2) – 𝔊^{S} – 𝔖^{e}, 𝔖^{abcd} subordinate punctuation.

COLON 51:21aB:

וּשְׁכֻרַת וְלֹא מִיָּיִן׃ 21aB and drunken one, though not with wine:

With: 𝔐 (1), major division markers, also in 1𝔔^{a} – 𝔊^{SQ}, major divison markers in 𝔊^{S} – 𝔖^{abcde}

COLON 51:22aA:

כֹּה־אָמַר אֲדֹנַיִךְ יְהוָה 22aA Thus says your Lord GOD

With: 𝔐 (7) – 𝔊^{SQ} – 𝔖^{abcde}
Colon parallelism: אדני || יהוה.

COLON 51:22aB:

וֵאלֹהַיִךְ יָרִיב עַמּוֹ 22aB and your God who goes into court for his people:

With: 𝔐 (5) – 𝔊^{SQ} – 𝔖^{abcde}

COLON 51:22bA:

הִנֵּה לָקַחְתִּי מִיָּדֵךְ 22bA Behold, I take from your hand

With: 𝔐 (8) – 𝔊^{Q} – 𝔖^{a}
Discussion: The division is weakly attested because most were deluded by the fact that the sentence runs on. However, v. 17 argues in favour of a caesura at this point.

COLON 51:22bB:

אֶת־כּוֹס הַתַּרְעֵלָה 22bB the cup of reeling,

With: 𝔐 (2) – 𝔊^{SQ} – 𝔖^{cde}, 𝔖^{b} subordinate punctuation.

COLON 51:22cA:

אֶת־קֻבַּעַת כּוֹס חֲמָתִי 22cA the beaker, the cup of my fury –

With: 𝔐 (5) – 𝔊^{SQ}
Colon parallelism: כוס || קבעת.

COLON 51:22cB:

לֹא־תוֹסִיפִי לִשְׁתּוֹתָהּ עוֹד׃ 22cB you will not have to drink it again.

With: $\mathfrak{M}$ (1) – $\mathfrak{G}^{SAQ}$, major division markers in $\mathfrak{G}^{A}$ – $\mathfrak{S}^{acde}$

COLON 51:23aA:

וְשַׂמְתִּיהָ בְּיַד־מוֹגַיִךְ 23aA And I will put it into the hand of those who torment you,

With: $\mathfrak{M}$ (5) – $\mathfrak{G}^{SQ}$ – $\mathfrak{S}^{bcde}$, $\mathfrak{S}^{a}$ subordinate punctuation.

COLON 51:23aB:

אֲשֶׁר־אָמְרוּ לְנַפְשֵׁךְ 23aB who say to you,

With: $\mathfrak{M}$ (8) – $\mathfrak{G}^{Q}$ – $\mathfrak{S}^{e}$

Discussion: If one chooses to follow $\mathfrak{M}$, $\mathfrak{G}^{S}$ and $\mathfrak{S}$, the verse becomes a bicolon. However, the rhythmical balance makes a tricolon a more attractive option.

COLON 51:23aC:

שְׁחִי וְנַעֲבֹרָה 23aC "Bow down, that we may pass over",

With: $\mathfrak{M}$ (2) – $\mathfrak{G}^{SQ}$ – $\mathfrak{S}^{abcde}$

COLON 51:23bA:

וַתָּשִׂימִי כָאָרֶץ גֵּוֵךְ 23bA and you had to make your back like the ground

With: $\mathfrak{M}$ (5) – $\mathfrak{G}^{Q}$ – $\mathfrak{S}^{b}$, $\mathfrak{S}^{acde}$ subordinate punctuation.

COLON 51:23bB:

וְכַחוּץ לַעֹבְרִים׃ 23bB and like a street for those who pass over.

With: $\mathfrak{M}$ (1), major division markers, also in $1\mathfrak{Q}^{a}$ – $\mathfrak{G}^{SAQ}$, major division markers in all three – $\mathfrak{S}^{abcde}$, all with major division markers.

COLON 52:1aA:

עוּרִי עוּרִי לִבְשִׁי עֻזֵּךְ צִיּוֹן 1aA Wake up, wake up, clothe yourself with your strength, o Zion

With: $\mathfrak{M}$ (2) – $\mathfrak{G}^{Q}$ – $\mathfrak{S}^{abcde}$ all subordinate punctuation.

Colon parallelism: עור || עור.

Discussion: $\mathfrak{G}^{SQ}$ have a dividing point after the second עורי ($\mathfrak{M}$ Tevir, No. 12) but on the analogy of 51:9 and 51:17aA we decided to read the verse as a unicolon.

COLON 52:1bA:

לִבְשִׁי ׀ בִּגְדֵי תִפְאַרְתֵּךְ 1bA clothe yourself with your glorious garments,

With: 𝔐 (7) – 𝔖^{e}
Discussion: Even though only one Syriac manuscript has a dividing point, we assume a caesura here, like BHS and most modern commentators. The other witnesses were led astray by the enjambment.

COLON 52:1bB:

יְרוּשָׁלַםִ עִיר הַקֹּדֶשׁ 1bB O, Jerusalem, holy city:

With: 𝔐 (5) – 𝔊^{SQ} – 𝔖^{abcde}
Discussion: 𝔊^{SQ} have an extra point after ירושלם (𝔐 Pashṭa, No.10).

COLON 52:1cA:

כִּי לֹא יוֹסִיף יָבֹא־בָךְ עוֹד 1cA for there shall no more come into you

With: 𝔐 (8).
Discussion: Mostly this verse is regarded as a late prose insertion, breathing the same 'particularistic' atmosphere as texts like Ezek. 44:7, 9; Zech. 8:3; Neh. 11:1; 2 Chron. 23:19; 36:14. However, the expression כי לא יסף occurs also in Isa. 47:1, 5, and a pair like ערל וטמא is in line with Second Isaiah's style.[8] This prompts the question whether the prosaic character of the verse-line may not be attributed to enjambment. Even though none of our ancient witnesses has a caesura before וטמא – even 𝔐's Ṭiphḥa can hardly have been meant as such – this is not a decisive argument, because the ancient scribes often had difficulty in recognizing enjambment. We assume a break after עוד because 51:22 and 54:4 strongly suggest that this adverb is at the end of a colon.
With regard to the concept itself, it need not contradict Second Isaiah's universalism. He may have required circumcision of foreigners in accordance with older law (Gen. 17:12, 27; Exod. 12:48; Josh. 8:33) and the purity of Jerusalem and the cultic personnel preoccupied him very much (Isa. 43:28; 47:6; 48:2; 52:11).

COLON 52:1cB:

עָרֵל וְטָמֵא׃ 1cB the uncircumcised and the unclean.

With: 𝔐 (1), Setuma in 1𝔔^{a}, Petuḥa in Codex Reuchlin – 𝔊^{AQ}, major division markers in 𝔊^{A} – 𝔖^{abcde}
Colon parallelism: ערל || טמא (unique).

[8]See our note on Isa. 51:19bA above.

COLON 52:2aA:

הִתְנַעֲרִ֧י מֵעָפָ֛ר 2aA Shake yourself free from the dust,

With: 𝔐 (12) – 𝔊^{SQ}
Discussion: Neither 𝔐 nor the ancient versions wanted to make a break here, although 𝔊^{SQ} might be interpreted in that way. However, since v. 2aA is preparatory to v. 2aB the colometry chosen is defensible.

COLON 52:2aB:

ק֥וּמִי שְּׁבִ֖י יְרוּשָׁלִָ֑ם 2aB stand up, take your seat, O Jerusalem!

With: 𝔐 (2) – 𝔊^{SQ} – 𝔖^{cd}, 𝔖^{abe} subordinate punctuation.
Colon parallelism: קום || ישב.

COLON 52:2bA:

הִתְפַּתְּחוּ מוֹסְרֵ֣י צַוָּארֵ֔ךְ* 2bA The chains on your neck are released,

With: 𝔐 (5) – 𝔊^{SQ}
Discussion: 𝔖 was confused by the enjambment.

COLON 52:2bB:

שְׁבִיָּ֖ה בַּת־צִיּֽוֹן׃ 2bB O captive, daughter of Zion!

With: 𝔐 (1), Setuma in many manuscripts, among them 1Q^{a} – 𝔊^{SAQ}, major division markers in 𝔊^{AQ} – 𝔖^{abcde}

COLON 52:3aA:

כִּי־כֹה֙ אָמַ֣ר יְהוָ֔ה 3aA For thus says the LORD:

With: 𝔐 (5) – 𝔊^{S} – 𝔖^{abcde}

COLON 52:3aB:

חִנָּ֖ם נִמְכַּרְתֶּ֑ם 3aB For nothing you were sold

With: 𝔐 (2) – 𝔊^{SQ} – 𝔖^{a} subordinate punctuation.

COLON 52:3aC:

וְלֹ֥א בְכֶ֖סֶף תִּגָּאֵֽלוּ׃ 3aC and without silver you will be redeemed.

With: 𝔐 (1), Setuma in some medieval manuscripts – 𝔊^{SBAQ}, major division markers in 𝔊^{SBA} – 𝔖^{abcde}, major division marker in 𝔖^{b}

COLON 52:4aA:

כִּ֣י כֹ֤ה אָמַר֙ אֲדֹנָ֣י יְהוִ֔ה 4aA For thus says the Lord GOD:

With: $\mathfrak{M}$ (5) – $\mathfrak{G}^{SQ}$ – $\mathfrak{S}^{abcde}$
Colon parallelism: אדני || יהוה.

COLON 52:4aB:

מִצְרַ֛יִם יָֽרַד־עַמִּ֥י בָרִאשֹׁנָ֖ה לָג֣וּר שָׁ֑ם 4aB At first my people went down to Egypt to sojourn there,

With: $\mathfrak{M}$ (2) – $\mathfrak{G}^{SQ}$ – $\mathfrak{S}^{abcde}$
Discussion: Although a colon of five stressed units is rather long and enjambment may be assumed, we see no compelling reason to ignore the unanimous verdict of the ancient witnesses.

COLON 52:4aC:

וְאַשּׁ֖וּר בְּאֶ֥פֶס עֲשָׁקֽוֹ׃ 4aC and Assyria oppressed them for nothing.

With: $\mathfrak{M}$ (1) – $\mathfrak{G}^{SQ}$ – $\mathfrak{S}^{abcde}$

COLON 52:5aA:

וְעַתָּ֤ה מִי־לִי־פֹה֙ נְאֻם־יְהוָ֔ה 5aA But now, what do I have here? declares the LORD,

With: $\mathfrak{M}$ (5) – $\mathfrak{G}^{SQ}$ – $\mathfrak{S}^{abcde}$ all subordinate punctuation.
Discussion: $\mathfrak{G}^{SBQ}$ have an unlikely major division after מי לי־פה.

COLON 52:5aB:

כִּֽי־לֻקַּ֥ח עַמִּ֖י חִנָּ֑ם 5aB that my people has been taken away for nothing?

With: $\mathfrak{M}$ (2) – $\mathfrak{G}^{S}$ – $\mathfrak{S}^{abce}$, $\mathfrak{S}^{d}$ absent.

COLON 52:5bA:

מֹשְׁלָ֤יו* יְהֵילִ֙ילוּ֙ נְאֻם־יְהוָ֔ה 5bA Those who rule it ululate, declares the LORD,

With: $\mathfrak{M}$ (5) – $\mathfrak{G}^{SQ}$ – $\mathfrak{S}^{abce}$, $\mathfrak{S}^{d}$ absent.

COLON 52:5bB:

וְתָמִ֥יד כָּל־הַיּ֖וֹם שְׁמִ֥י מִנֹּאָֽץ׃ 5bB and all day long my name is reviled.

With: $\mathfrak{M}$ (1) – $\mathfrak{G}^{SBQ}$, major division markers in $\mathfrak{G}^{BQ}$, but in $\mathfrak{G}^{B}$ not *prima manu* – $\mathfrak{S}^{abcde}$
Colon parallelism: תמיד || כל־היום.

Colon 52:6aA:

לָכֵן יֵדַע עַמִּי שְׁמִי 6aA Therefore my people will know my name,

With: 𝔐 (2) – 𝔊^{S}
Colon parallelism: י־ || י־.
Discussion: 𝔖 condenses the verse a little.

Colon 52:6bA:

לָכֵן בַּיּוֹם הַהוּא 6bA therefore, on that day,

With: 𝔐 (5) – 𝔊^{SQ} – 𝔖^{abcde}

Colon 52:6bB:

כִּי־אֲנִי־הוּא הַֽמְדַבֵּר הִנֵּֽנִי׃ 6bB when I am going to speak: Here I am!

With: 𝔐 (1), major division markers in the Parma Bible and in 1Q^{a} – 𝔊^{AQ}, major division markers in 𝔊^{A} – 𝔖^{abcde}, major division markers in all.
Colon parallelism: אני || ־ני.
Discussion: 𝔊^{SQ} have a divider after כי־אני־הוא, 𝔊^{S} even with major division markers which apparently proleptically indicate the major break at the end of the verse. 𝔊's rendering which connects the rest of the verse with the next verse, is impossible from the viewpoint of the Hebrew text.

Colon 52:7aA:

מַה־נָּאווּ עַל־הֶהָרִים 7aA How beautiful on the mountains

With: 𝔐 (13) – 𝔊^{SQ}
Discussion: Once again a sentence running on through several cola created division problems. Apparently 𝔐 wanted to stop only after the first מבשׂר (Revia‘, No. 7).[9] But none of the other ancient witnesses supports this and the next colon becomes intolerably long (6 feet). A much nicer parallelism results if we follow the division presented by 𝔊^{SQ}. See further below.

Colon 52:7aB:

רַגְלֵי מְבַשֵּׂר מַשְׁמִיעַ שָׁלוֹם 7aB are the feet of the herald who announces peace,

With: 𝔐 (12) – 𝔊^{SQ} – 𝔖^{cde} subordinate punctuation.

[9] Apparently following their division in Nah. 2:1 which Second Isaiah is quoting here, cf. K. Spronk, *Nahum* (HCOT), Kampen 1997, 79-80.

Colon parallelism: בשׂר || שׁמע Hiphil.[10]
Discussion: On 𝔐 see our note on v. 7aA. We follow the other witnesses because a much better parallellistic balance on the level of the verse-line is the result: מבשׂר || מבשׂר; משׁמיע || משׁמיע; שׁלום || ישׁועה (unique); טוב || שׁלום.

COLON 52:7aC:

מְבַשֵּׂ֥ר ט֖וֹב מַשְׁמִ֣יעַ יְשׁוּעָ֑ה 7aC the herald of good tidings who announces salvation,

With: 𝔐 (2) – $\mathfrak{S}^{abcde}$
Colon parallelism: בשׂר || שׁמע Hiphil; טוב || ישׁועה (unique).
Discussion: 𝔐 has a Ṭiphḥa (No. 8) with טוב and $\mathfrak{G}^{SQ}$ as well as $\mathfrak{S}^{ae}$ support a divider at this point. However, for the reasons mentioned at v. 7aB not too much weight should be accorded to this testimony. Only 𝔖 supports 𝔐's Atnaḥ. $\mathfrak{G}^{S}$ and $\mathfrak{G}^{Q}$ differ. The first has a point after Σιων, the second after λέγων.

COLON 52:7bA:

אֹמֵ֥ר לְצִיּ֖וֹן מָלַ֥ךְ אֱלֹהָֽיִךְ׃ 7bA who says to Zion, "Your God is king!"

With: 𝔐 (1) – $\mathfrak{G}^{SQ}$, paragraphos in $\mathfrak{G}^{S}$ – $\mathfrak{S}^{abcde}$
Colon parallelism: ציון || אלהים.

COLON 52:8aA:

ק֥וֹל צֹפַ֛יִךְ נָ֥שְׂאוּ ק֖וֹל 8aA The voices of your watchmen! They raise their voices,

With: 𝔐 (8) – $\mathfrak{S}^{be}$
Colon parallelism: קול || קול.
Discussion: $\mathfrak{G}^{SQ}$ divide after נשׂאו, $\mathfrak{G}^{S}$ even has a major division marker here. However, because נשׂא קול is a very common expression, one cannot separate the second קול from its verb. Also the Masoretes took נשׂא and קול together, as it appears from the conjunctive accent with נשׂאו.

COLON 52:8aB:

יַחְדָּ֣ו יְרַנֵּ֑נוּ 8aB they rejoice together,

With: 𝔐 (2) – $\mathfrak{G}^{SQ}$ – $\mathfrak{S}^{abcde}$

[10]As in Nah. 2:1, see the preceding footnote.

COLON 52:8bA:

כִּ֣י עַ֤יִן בְּעַ֙יִן֙ יִרְא֔וּ 8bA for with their own eyes they see with delight

With: $\mathfrak{M}$ (5) – $\mathfrak{G}^{SQ}$ – $\mathfrak{S}^{e}$
Colon parallelism: עין || עין.

COLON 52:8bB:

בְּשׁ֥וּב יְהוָ֖ה צִיּֽוֹן׃ 8bB how the LORD returns to Zion.

With: $\mathfrak{M}$ (1) – $\mathfrak{G}^{SAQ}$, all with major division markers – $\mathfrak{S}^{abce}$
Colon parallelism: יהוה || ציון.

COLON 52:9aA:

פִּצְח֤וּ רַנְּנוּ֙ יַחְדָּ֔ו 9aA Break forth, rejoice together

With: $\mathfrak{M}$ (5) – $\mathfrak{S}^{e}$, $\mathfrak{S}^{a}$ subordinate punctuation.
Colon parallelism: פצח || רנן.
Discussion: $\mathfrak{M}$ is only weakly supported, but this has no doubt to do with the enjambment. The colon parallelism supports $\mathfrak{M}$'s division.

COLON 52:9aB:

חָרְב֖וֹת יְרוּשָׁלִָ֑ם 9aB you ruins of Jerusalem!

With: $\mathfrak{M}$ (2) – $\mathfrak{G}^{SQ}$ – $\mathfrak{S}^{acde}$, $\mathfrak{S}^{b}$ subordinate punctuation.

COLON 52:9bA:

כִּֽי־נִחַ֤ם יְהוָה֙ עַמּ֔וֹ 9bA For the LORD comforts his people,

With: $\mathfrak{M}$ (5) – $\mathfrak{G}^{SQ}$ – $\mathfrak{S}^{e}$

COLON 52:9bB:

גָּאַ֖ל יְרוּשָׁלִָֽם׃ 9bB he redeems Jerusalem.

With: $\mathfrak{M}$ (1) – $\mathfrak{G}^{SQ}$, major division markers in $\mathfrak{G}^{S}$ – $\mathfrak{S}^{abcde}$

COLON 52:10aA:

חָשַׂ֤ף יְהוָה֙ אֶת־זְר֣וֹעַ קָדְשׁ֔וֹ 10aA The LORD bares his holy arm

With: $\mathfrak{M}$ (5) – $\mathfrak{G}^{Q}$ – $\mathfrak{S}^{a}$
Discussion: Again the enjambment explains the rather weak support for $\mathfrak{M}$.

COLON 52:10aB:

לְעֵינֵ֖י כָּל־הַגּוֹיִ֑ם 10aB before the eyes of all the nations;

With: $\mathfrak{M}$ (2) – $\mathfrak{G}^{SQ}$ – $\mathfrak{S}^{abcde}$

COLON 52:10bA:

וְרָא֙וּ כָּל־אַפְסֵי־אָ֔רֶץ 10bA and all the ends of the earth will see

With: $\mathfrak{M}$ (5) – $\mathfrak{G}^{Q}$
Discussion: See our note on the preceding colon.

COLON 52:10bB:

אֵ֖ת יְשׁוּעַ֥ת אֱלֹהֵֽינוּ׃ 10bB the salvation of our God.

With: $\mathfrak{M}$ (1), major division markers, also in 1$\mathfrak{Q}^{a}$, 1$\mathfrak{Q}^{b}$, 4$\mathfrak{Q}^{c}$ – $\mathfrak{G}^{SAQ}$, all with major division markers – $\mathfrak{S}^{abcde}$, major division marker in $\mathfrak{S}^{b}$

COLON 52:11aA:

ס֤וּרוּ ס֙וּרוּ֙ צְא֣וּ מִשָּׁ֔ם 11aA Depart, depart, go out from there!

With: $\mathfrak{M}$ (5) – $\mathfrak{G}^{SQ}$ – $\mathfrak{S}^{abcde}$
Colon parallelism: סור || סור; סור || יצא (unique).
Discussion: $\mathfrak{G}^{Q}$ and $\mathfrak{S}^{e}$ have an extra point after סורו^{2} where $\mathfrak{M}$ has a Pashṭa (No. 10). But triplets of imperatives are characteristic of this canto, cf. 51:9, 17; 52:1.

COLON 52:11aB:

טָמֵ֖א אַל־תִּגָּ֑עוּ 11aB Do not touch the unclean!

With: $\mathfrak{M}$ (2) – $\mathfrak{G}^{SQ}$ – $\mathfrak{S}^{abcde}$

COLON 52:11bA:

צְא֣וּ מִתּוֹכָ֔הּ 11bA Go out from the midst of her!

With: $\mathfrak{M}$ (5) – $\mathfrak{G}^{Q}$ – $\mathfrak{S}^{ae}$ subordinate punctuation.

COLON 52:11bB:

הִבָּ֕רוּ נֹשְׂאֵ֖י כְּלֵ֥י יְהוָֽה׃ 11bB Keep yourselves pure, you who carry the vessels of the LORD.

With: $\mathfrak{M}$ (1) – $\mathfrak{G}^{SQ}$ – $\mathfrak{S}^{abcde}$
Discussion: $\mathfrak{G}^{SQ}$ have an extra point after הברו corresponding to $\mathfrak{M}$'s Zaqeph Magnum (No. 6). Nevertheless this should not be regarded as a major divider.[11]

COLON 52:12aA:

כִּ֣י לֹ֤א בְחִפָּזוֹן֙ תֵּצֵ֔אוּ 12aA For you will not go out in haste,

---

[11] See our comment on p. 31.

With: 𝔐 (5) – 𝔊^{SQ} – 𝔖^{ae}, 𝔖^{cd} subordinate punctuation.

COLON 52:12aB:

וּבִמְנוּסָה לֹא תֵלֵכוּן 12aB and you will not go in flight,

With: 𝔐 (2) – 𝔊^{SQ} – 𝔖^{abcde}

COLON 52:12bA:

כִּי־הֹלֵךְ לִפְנֵיכֶם יְהוָה 12bA for the LORD will go before you,

With: 𝔐 (5) – 𝔊^{SQ} – 𝔖^{a}, 𝔖^{bcde} subordinate punctuation.

COLON 52:12bB:

וּמְאַסִּפְכֶם אֱלֹהֵי יִשְׂרָאֵל׃ 12bB and the God of Israel will be your rearguard.

With: 𝔐 (1), major division markers, also in 1𝔔^{a} and 4𝔔^{c} – 𝔊^{SBAQ}, major division markers in all – 𝔖^{abcde}, all with major division markers.

12.3 Isaiah 51:9–52:12 – Delimitation of Verse-lines

VERSE–LINE: 51:9a:

עוּרִי עוּרִי לִבְשִׁי־עֹז זְרוֹעַ יְהוָה 9aA Wake up, wake up, clothe yourself with strength, O arm of the LORD.

𝔐 accents: 5.
Stresses: 5.
Verse-line parallelism: None (unicolon).
Discussion: The delimitation of this verse depends on the colometry.[1]

VERSE–LINE: 51:9b:

עוּרִי כִּימֵי קֶדֶם 9bA Wake up, as in the days of old,
דֹּרוֹת עוֹלָמִים 9bB of the generations of primordial times!

𝔐 accents: 5 – 2.
Stresses: 3 + 2.
Verse-line parallelism: קדם || עולם.
Discussion: The cola are connected by ellipsis as well.

VERSE–LINE: 51:9c:

הֲלוֹא אַתְּ־הִיא הַמַּחְצֶבֶת רַהַב 9cA Was is not you who hewed Rahab,
מְחוֹלֶלֶת תַּנִּין׃ 9cB who pierced the Tannin?

𝔐 accents: 8 – 1.
Stresses: 4 + 2.

---

[1]See p. 497.

Verse-line parallelism: חצב || חלל (unique); רהב || תנין (unique); grammatical parallelism; rhyme.
Discussion: Ellipsis links the two cola.

VERSE–LINE: 51:10a:

הֲלֹ֤וא אַתְּ־הִיא֙ הַמַּחֲרֶ֣בֶת יָ֔ם	10aA	Was it not you who dried up the sea,
מֵ֖י תְּה֣וֹם רַבָּ֑ה	10aB	the waters of the great flood?

𝔐 accents: 5 – 2.
Stresses: 4 + 3.
Verse-line parallelism: ים || מים; ים || תהום.
Discussion: Again ellipsis is connecting the cola.

VERSE–LINE: 51:10b:

הַשָּׂ֙מָה֙ מַֽעֲמַקֵּי־יָ֔ם	10bA	Who made the depths of the sea
דֶּ֖רֶךְ לַעֲבֹ֥ר גְּאוּלִֽים׃	10bB	a way for the passing over of the redeemed ones?

𝔐 accents: 5 – 1.
Stresses: 2 + 3.
Verse-line parallelism: None.
Discussion: Because the sentence is running on clear parallelism is lacking.

VERSE–LINE: 51:11a:

וּפְדוּיֵ֙י יְהוָ֜ה יְשׁוּב֗וּן	11aA	So the ransomed of the LORD will return,
וּבָ֤אוּ צִיּוֹן֙ בְּרִנָּ֔ה	11aB	and come to Zion with rejoicing,
וְשִׂמְחַ֥ת עוֹלָ֖ם עַל־רֹאשָׁ֑ם	11aC	and eternal joy will be on their heads,

𝔐 distinctive accents: 7 – 5 – 2.
Stresses: 3 + 3 + 3.
Verse-line parallelism: יהוה || ציון; שוב || בוא; רנה || שמחה.

VERSE–LINE: 51:11b:

שָׂשׂ֤וֹן וְשִׂמְחָה֙ יַשִּׂיג֔וּן	11bA	gladness and joy they will overtake (them),
נָ֖סוּ יָג֥וֹן וַאֲנָחָֽה׃	11bB	torment and sighing flee away.

𝔐 distinctive accents: 5 – 1.
Stresses: 3 + 3.
Verse-line parallelism: ששון || יגון (antithetical); שמחה || יגון (antithetical).

VERSE–LINE: 51:12a:

אָנֹכִ֧י אָנֹכִ֛י ה֖וּא מְנַחֶמְכֶ֑ם 12aA I, I am he – the one who comforts you.

𝔐 distinctive accents: 2.
Stresses: 4.
Verse-line parallelism: None (unicolon).
Discussion: We accept 𝔐's division because the parallelism is connecting vv. 12bA-B is stronger than that connecting vv. 12aA and 12bA.

VERSE–LINE: 51:12b:

מִֽי־אַ֤תְּ וַתִּֽירְאִי֙ מֵאֱנ֣וֹשׁ יָמ֔וּת 12bA Who are you that you fear man who dies,
וּמִבֶּן־אָדָ֖ם חָצִ֥יר יִנָּתֵֽן׃ 12bB and the son of man – grass given away?

𝔐 distinctive accents: 5 – 1.
Stresses: 4 + 3.
Verse-line parallelism: מן || מן; אנוש || בן־אדם.
Discussion: Ellipsis forms an extra bond.

VERSE–LINE: 51:13a:

וַתִּשְׁכַּ֞ח יְהוָ֣ה עֹשֶׂ֗ךָ 13aA But you forget the LORD, who made you,
נוֹטֶ֤ה שָׁמַ֙יִם֙ וְיֹסֵ֣ד אָ֔רֶץ 13aB who stretched out the heavens and laid the foundation of the earth.

𝔐 distinctive accents: 7 – 3.
Stresses: 3 + 4.
Verse-line parallelism: עשה || נטה; עשה || יסד.
Discussion: Ellipsis connects the cola.

VERSE–LINE: 51:13b:

וַתְּפַחֵ֨ד תָּמִ֜יד כָּל־הַיּ֗וֹם 13bA And you quiver continually all the day
מִפְּנֵי֙ חֲמַ֣ת הַמֵּצִ֔יק 13bB because of the fury of the oppressor
כַּאֲשֶׁ֥ר כּוֹנֵ֖ן לְהַשְׁחִ֑ית 13bC when he aims to annihilate.

𝔐 distinctive accents: 7 – 5 – 2.
Stresses: 3 + 3 + 3.
Verse-line parallelism: חמה || שחת.
Discussion: We accept the delimitation of 𝔐 because it is supported by $\mathfrak{S}^{abcde}$, all with subordinate punctuation.[2]

---

[2]With regard to the division markers in $\mathfrak{G}^{SQ}$ after v. 13bB see our comment on p. 539.

VERSE–LINE: 51:13c:

וְאַיֵּ֖ה חֲמַ֥ת הַמֵּצִֽיק׃ 13cA But where is the fury of the oppressor?

𝔐 distinctive accents: 1.
Stresses: 3.
Verse-line parallelism: None (unicolon).

VERSE–LINE: 51:14a:

מִהַ֥ר צֹעֶ֖ה לְהִפָּתֵ֑חַ 14aA Soon the cellarman will be released;

𝔐 distinctive accents: 2.
Stresses: 3.
Verse-line parallelism: None (unicolon).
Discussion: 𝔐's delimitation is acceptable because v. 14bA-B are linked by ולא.

VERSE–LINE: 51:14b:

וְלֹא־יָמ֣וּת לַשַּׁ֔חַת 14bA he will not die in the Pit of Annihilation,
וְלֹ֥א יֶחְסַ֖ר לַחְמֽוֹ׃ 14bB neither will his bread be lacking.

𝔐 distinctive accents: 5 – 1.
Stresses: 2 + 3.
Verse-line parallelism: לא || לא; מות || חסר לחם; grammatical parallelism.

VERSE–LINE: 51:15a:

וְאָנֹכִי֙ יְהוָ֣ה אֱלֹהֶ֔יךָ 15aA For I am the LORD, your God,
רֹגַ֣ע הַיָּ֔ם וַיֶּהֱמ֖וּ גַּלָּ֑יו 15aB who stirs up the sea so that its waves roar
יְהוָ֥ה צְבָא֖וֹת שְׁמֽוֹ׃ 15aC – the LORD of hosts is his name.

𝔐 distinctive accents: 5 – 2 – 1.
Stresses: 3 + 4 + 3.
Verse-line parallelism: יהוה אלהים || יהוה צבאות.
Discussion: Cola b and c are also quoted in Jer. 31:35, showing that the third colon cannot be separated from the preceding one.[3] Because of the sequence of accents this means that the Masoretic verse 15 must be taken as a tricolon and not as a bicolon followed by a unicolon (so BHS).

VERSE–LINE: 51:16a:

וָאָשִׂ֤ים דְּבָרַי֙ בְּפִ֔יךָ 16aA And I put my words in your mouth,
וּבְצֵ֥ל יָדִ֖י כִּסִּיתִ֑יךָ 16aB and cover you with the shadow of my hand,

[3]See p. 501.

𝔐 distinctive accents: 5 – 2.
Stresses: 3 + 3.
Verse-line parallelism: ־י || ־י; פה || יד; ־ך (m.s.) || ־ך (m.s.); rhyme.

VERSE–LINE: 51:16b:

לִנְטֹעַ שָׁמַיִם֙ וְלִיסֹד אָרֶץ 16bA to plant the heavens and to found the earth,
וְלֵאמֹר לְצִיּוֹן עַמִּי־אָתָּה׃ 16bB and to say to Zion, "You are my people!"

𝔐 distinctive accents: 5 – 1.
Stresses: 4 + 3.
Verse-line parallelism: ל || ל || ל; grammatical parallelism.

VERSE–LINE: 51:17a:

הִתְעוֹרְרִי הִתְעוֹרְרִי קוּמִי יְרוּשָׁלִַם 17aA Wake yourself, wake yourself, stand up, O Jerusalem,

𝔐 distinctive accents: 5.
Stresses: 4.
Verse-line parallelism: None (unicolon).
Discussion: The delimitation of Masoretic v. 17 is based on our delimitiation of cola.[4]

VERSE–LINE: 51:17b:

אֲשֶׁר שָׁתִית מִיַּד יְהוָה 17bA you who have drunk from the hand of the LORD
אֶת־כּוֹס חֲמָתוֹ 17bB the cup of his fury,

𝔐 distinctive accents: 8 – 2.
Stresses: 4 + 2.
Verse-line parallelism: שתה || כוס.
Discussion: See our comment on verse-line 17a. The sentence runs on, weakening the parallelism. The nice chiasmus and the semantical parallelism on the level of the strophe (vv. 17b and 17c) compensates for this.

VERSE–LINE: 51:17c:

אֶת־קֻבַּעַת כּוֹס הַתַּרְעֵלָה 17cA the beaker, the cup of reeling,
שָׁתִית מָצִית׃ 17cB you had to drink, to drain.

𝔐 distinctive accents: 12 – 1.
Stresses: 3 + 2.
Verse-line parallelism: כוס || שתה; קבעת || שתה.

[4] See pp. 502-3.

VERSE–LINE: 51:18:

אֵין־מְנַהֵל לָהּ	18aA	There was no one leading her
מִכָּל־בָּנִים יָלָדָה	18aB	of all the sons she bore,

𝔐 distinctive accents: 5 – 2.
Stresses: 2 + 2.
Verse-line parallelism: rhyme.
Discussion: Because the sentence is running on there is no poetic parallelism. Again this is compensated by strong parallelism on the higher level of the strophe, just as was the case in v.17.

VERSE–LINE: 51:18b:

וְאֵין מַחֲזִיק בְּיָדָהּ	18bA	and there was no one grasping her hand
מִכָּל־בָּנִים גִּדֵּלָה׃	18bB	of all the sons she brought up.

𝔐 distinctive accents: 5 – 1.
Stresses: 3 + 2.
Verse-line parallelism: rhyme.
Discussion: See our comment on v. 18a.

VERSE–LINE: 51:19a:

שְׁתַּיִם הֵנָּה קֹרְאֹתַיִךְ	19aA	These two things have happened to you –
מִי יָנוּד לָךְ	19aB	who will condole you? –

𝔐 distinctive accents: 5 – 2.
Stresses: 3 + 3.
Verse-line parallelism: ךְ- (f.s.) ‖ ךְ- (f.s.).
Discussion: The second colon reacts on the first which results in the absence of word-pairs. The strophe parallelism compensates for this lack. See also our comments on the preceding verse-lines.

VERSE–LINE: 51:19b:

הַשֹּׁד וְהַשֶּׁבֶר	19bA	destruction and breakdown
וְהָרָעָב וְהַחֶרֶב	19bB	famine and sword –
מִי אֲנַחֲמֵךְ׃	19bC	by whom can I comfort you?

𝔐 distinctive accents: 12 – 8 – 1.
Stresses: 2 + 2 + 2.
Verse-line parallelism: שׁד ‖ נחם.
Discussion: See our comment on the preceding verse-line.

VERSE–LINE: 51:20a:

בָּנַ֜יִךְ עֻלְּפ֨וּ שָׁכְב֛וּ 20aA Your sons have fainted; they lie down
בְּרֹ֥אשׁ כָּל־חוּצ֖וֹת 20aB at the head of every street,
כְּת֣וֹא מִכְמָ֑ר 20aC like an antelope caught in a net.

𝔐 distinctive accents: 12 – 8 – 2.
Stresses: 3 + 2 + 2.
Verse-line parallelism: None.
Discussion: The sentence spills over from the first into the second and third colon which causes the lack of clear parallels.

VERSE–LINE: 51:20b:

הַֽמְלֵאִ֥ים חֲמַת־יְהוָ֖ה 20bA They are filled with the fury of the LORD,
גַּעֲרַ֥ת אֱלֹהָֽיִךְ׃ 20bB the rebuke of your God.

𝔐 distinctive accents: 8 – 1.
Stresses: 2 + 2.
Verse-line parallelism: חמה || גערה; יהוה || אלהים.
Discussion: Ellipsis connects the cola.

VERSE–LINE: 51:21a:

לָכֵ֛ן שִׁמְעִי־נָ֥א זֹ֖את עֲנִיָּ֑ה 21aA Therefore hear now this, O afflicted one,
וּשְׁכֻרַ֖ת וְלֹ֥א מִיָּֽיִן׃ 21aB and drunken one, though not with wine:

𝔐 distinctive accents: 2 – 1.
Stresses: 4 + 3.
Verse-line parallelism: None.
Discussion: The sentence runs on over two cola. Only the vocatives relate them to each other. Apparently עני || שכרה was meant as a parallelism but the word-pair is not attested elsewhere in the OT.

VERSE–LINE: 51:22a:

כֹּֽה־אָמַ֞ר אֲדֹנַ֣יִךְ יְהוָ֗ה 22aA Thus says your Lord GOD
וֵאלֹהַ֙יִךְ֙ יָרִ֣יב עַמּ֔וֹ 22aB and your God who goes into court for his people:

𝔐 distinctive accents: 7 – 5.
Stresses: 3 + 3.
Verse-line parallelism: ךְ־ (f.s.) || ךְ־ (f.s.); יהוה || אלהים.

VERSE–LINE: 51:22b:

הִנֵּ֥ה לָקַ֛חְתִּי מִיָּדֵ֖ךְ 22bA Behold, I take from your hand
אֶת־כּ֣וֹס הַתַּרְעֵלָ֑ה 22bB the cup of reeling,

𝔐 distinctive accents: 8 – 2.
Stresses: 3 + 2.
Verse-line parallelism: None.
Discussion: Because the sentence is running on there is no poetic parallelism. See also our comment on v. 17.

VERSE–LINE: 51:22c:

אֶת־קֻבַּעַת כּוֹס חֲמָתִי 22cA the beaker, the cup of my fury –
לֹא־תוֹסִיפִי לִשְׁתּוֹתָהּ עוֹד׃ 22cB you will not have to drink it again.

𝔐 distinctive accents: 5 – 1.
Stresses: 3 + 3.
Verse-line parallelism: קבעת || שתה; כוס || שתה.
Discussion: The sentence runs on, which causes the lack of clear parallels (only 'synthetical parallelism').

VERSE–LINE: 51:23a:

וְשַׂמְתִּיהָ בְּיַד־מוֹגַיִךְ 23aA And I will put it into the hand of those who torment you,
אֲשֶׁר־אָמְרוּ לְנַפְשֵׁךְ 23aB who say to you,
שְׁחִי וְנַעֲבֹרָה 23aC "Bow down, that we may pass over",

𝔐 distinctive accents: 5 – 8 – 2.
Stresses: 2 + 2 + 2.
Verse-line parallelism: יד || נפש; ־ךְ (ms.) || ־ךְ (m.s.).
Discussion: See our discussion on the delimitation of the cola of this verse.[5]

VERSE–LINE: 51:23b:

וַתָּשִׂימִי כָאָרֶץ גֵּוֵךְ 23bA and you had to make your back like the ground
וְכַחוּץ לַעֹבְרִים׃ 23bB and like a street for those who pass over.

𝔐 distinctive accents: 5 – 1.
Stresses: 3 + 2.
Verse-line parallelism: כ || כ; ארץ || חוץ.

VERSE–LINE: 52:1a:

עוּרִי עוּרִי לִבְשִׁי עֻזֵּךְ צִיּוֹן 1aA Wake up, wake up, clothe yourself with your strength, o Zion

𝔐 distinctive accents: 2.
Stresses: 5.
Verse-line parallelism: None (unicolon).

[5] Above p. 507.

VERSE–LINE: 52:1b:

לִבְשִׁ֣י ׀ בִּגְדֵ֣י תִפְאַרְתֵּ֗ךְ	1bA	clothe yourself with your glorious garments,
יְרוּשָׁלַ֙͏ִם֙ עִ֣יר הַקֹּ֔דֶשׁ	1bB	O, Jerusalem, holy city:

𝔐 distinctive accents: 7 – 5.
Stresses: 3 + 3.
Verse-line parallelism: קדש || תפארת.

VERSE–LINE: 52:1c:

כִּ֣י לֹ֥א יוֹסִ֛יף יָבֹא־בָ֥ךְ ע֖וֹד	1cA	for there shall no more come into you
עָרֵ֥ל וְטָמֵֽא׃	1cB	the uncircumcised and the unclean.

𝔐 distinctive accents: 8 – 1.
Stresses: 5 + 2.
Verse-line parallelism: None.
Discussion: The enjambment in this verse-line is the reason for the lack of parallelism.

VERSE–LINE: 52:2a:

הִתְנַעֲרִ֧י מֵעָפָ֛ר	2aA	Shake yourself free from the dust,
ק֥וּמִי שְּׁבִ֖י יְרוּשָׁלָ֑͏ִם	2aB	stand up, take your seat, O Jerusalem!

𝔐 distinctive accents: 12 – 2.
Stresses: 2 + 3.
Verse-line parallelism: None.[6]
Discussion: The sentence is running on over two cola, so there is no formal parallelism. But the imagery vividly describes the rising of a mourning woman from the ground to occupy her throne again.

VERSE–LINE: 52:2b:

הִתְפַּתְּחוּ֙ מוֹסְרֵ֣י צַוָּארֵ֔ךְ*	2bA	The chains on your neck are released,
שְׁבִיָּ֖ה בַּת־צִיּֽוֹן׃	2bB	O captive, daughter of Zion!

𝔐 distinctive accents: 5 – 1.
Stresses: 3 + 2.
Verse-line parallelism: מוסר || שביה.

VERSE–LINE: 52:3a:

כִּי־כֹ֞ה אָמַ֣ר יְהוָ֔ה	3aA	For thus says the LORD:
חִנָּ֖ם נִמְכַּרְתֶּ֑ם	3aB	For nothing you were sold

[6] See, however, the collocation of קום, עפר and ישב in a comparable context in 1 Sam. 2:8, and of עפר and ישב in Isa. 47:1; Lam. 2:10.

וְלֹ֥א בְכֶ֖סֶף תִּגָּאֵֽלוּ׃ 3aC and without silver you will be redeemed.

𝔐 distinctive accents: 5 – 2 – 1.
Stresses: 3 + 2 + 3.
Verse-line parallelism: חנם || כסף (antithetical); מכר || גאל.

VERSE–LINE: 52:4a:

כִּ֣י כֹ֤ה אָמַר֙ אֲדֹנָ֣י יְהוִ֔ה 4aA For thus says the Lord GOD:
מִצְרַ֛יִם יָֽרַד־עַמִּ֥י בָרִאשֹׁנָ֖ה לָג֣וּר שָׁ֑ם 4aB At first my people went down to Egypt to sojourn there,
וְאַשּׁ֖וּר בְּאֶ֥פֶס עֲשָׁקֽוֹ׃ 4aC and Assyria oppressed them for nothing.

𝔐 distinctive accents: 5 – 2 – 1.
Stresses: 5 + 5 + 3.
Verse-line parallelism: מצרים || אשור.

VERSE–LINE: 52:5a:

וְעַתָּ֤ה מִי לִי־פֹה֙ נְאֻם־יְהוָ֔ה 5aA But now, what do I have here? declares the LORD,
כִּֽי־לֻקַּ֥ח עַמִּ֖י חִנָּ֑ם 5aB that my people has been taken away for nothing?

𝔐 distinctive accents: 5 – 2.
Stresses: 4 + 3.
Verse-line parallelism: None.
Discussion: The sentence runs on (enjambment). As a result, word-pairs are missing.

VERSE–LINE: 52:5b:

מֹשְׁלָ֤יו* יְהֵילִ֨ילוּ֙ נְאֻם־יְהוָ֔ה 5bA Those who rule it ululate, declares the LORD,
וְתָמִ֥יד כָּל־הַיּ֖וֹם שְׁמִ֥י מִנֹּאָֽץ׃ 5bB and all day long my name is reviled.

𝔐 distinctive accents: 5 – 1.
Stresses: 3 + 4.
Verse-line parallelism: ילל || נאץ שם (unique).

VERSE–LINE: 52:6a:

לָכֵ֛ן יֵדַ֥ע עַמִּ֖י שְׁמִ֑י 6aA Therefore my people will know my name,

𝔐 distinctive accents: 2.
Stresses: 4.
Verse-line parallelism: None (unicolon).
Discussion: We follow the Masoretes in assuming a unicolon plus a bicolon in v.6 (הוא || הוא).

VERSE–LINE: 52:6b:

לָכֵן֙ בַּיּ֣וֹם הַה֔וּא	6bA	therefore, on that day,
כִּֽי־אֲנִי־ה֥וּא הַֽמְדַבֵּ֖ר הִנֵּֽנִי׃	6bB	when I am going to speak: Here I am!

𝔐 distinctive accents: 5 – 1.
Stresses: 3 + 3.
Verse-line parallelism: הוא || הוא.
Discussion: Again the sentence is running on through the two cola of a verse-line, causing the absence of clear parallelism.

VERSE–LINE: 52:7a:

מַה־נָּאו֨וּ עַל־הֶהָרִ֜ים	7aA	How beautiful on the mountains
רַגְלֵ֣י מְבַשֵּׂ֗ר מַשְׁמִ֥יעַ שָׁל֛וֹם	7aB	are the feet of the herald who announces peace,
מְבַשֵּׂ֥ר ט֖וֹב מַשְׁמִ֣יעַ יְשׁוּעָ֑ה	7aC	the herald of good tidings who announces salvation,

𝔐 distinctive accents: 13 – 12 – 2.
Stresses: 2 + 4 + 4.
Verse-line parallelism: בשׂר (verb) || בשׂר (verb); שׁמע || שׁמע; שׁלום || טוב; שׁלום || ישׁועה; grammatical parallelism; rhyme.

VERSE–LINE: 52:7b:

אֹמֵ֥ר לְצִיּ֖וֹן מָלַ֥ךְ אֱלֹהָֽיִךְ׃	7bA	who says to Zion, "Your God is king!"

𝔐 distinctive accents: 1.
Stresses: 4.
Verse-line parallelism: None (unicolon).
Discussion: With 𝔐. Technically a quadrocolon would have been possible by taking vv. 7a and 7b as one verse-line.

VERSE–LINE: 52:8a:

ק֥וֹל צֹפַ֛יִךְ נָ֥שְׂאוּ ק֖וֹל	8aA	The voices of your watchmen! They raise their voices,
יַחְדָּ֣ו יְרַנֵּ֑נוּ	8aB	they rejoice together,

𝔐 distinctive accents: 8 – 2.
Stresses: 4 + 2.
Verse-line parallelism: נשׂא קול || רנן.

VERSE–LINE: 52:8b:

כִּ֣י עַ֤יִן בְּעַ֙יִן֙ יִרְא֔וּ	8bA	for with their own eyes they see with delight
בְּשׁ֥וּב יְהוָ֖ה צִיּֽוֹן׃	8bB	how the LORD returns to Zion.

𝔐 distinctive accents: 5 – 1.
Stresses: 4 + 3.
Verse-line parallelism: None.
Discussion: Enjambment: the sentence spills over into the next colon which causes lack of parallelism. Parallelism, however, in this canticle (Isa. 52:7-10) frequently is observed on the level of the colon, the strophe, and all the more on the level of the canticle. See the delimitation of cola above and the delimitation of strophes and canticles below.

VERSE–LINE: 52:9a:

פִּצְח֤וּ רַנְּנוּ֙ יַחְדָּ֔ו 9aA Break forth, rejoice together
חָרְב֖וֹת יְרוּשָׁלִָ֑ם 9aB you ruins of Jerusalem!

𝔐 distinctive accents: 5 – 2.
Stresses: 3 + 2.
Verse-line parallelism: None.
Discussion: See our comment on v. 8b.

VERSE–LINE: 52:9b:

כִּֽי־נִחַ֤ם יְהוָה֙ עַמּ֔וֹ 9bA For the LORD comforts his people,
גָּאַ֖ל יְרוּשָׁלִָֽם׃ 9bB he redeems Jerusalem.

𝔐 distinctive accents: 5 – 1.
Stresses: 3 + 2.
Verse-line parallelism: נחם || גאל; עם || ירושלם; grammatical parallelism.

VERSE–LINE: 52:10a:

חָשַׂ֤ף יְהוָה֙ אֶת־זְר֣וֹעַ קָדְשׁ֔וֹ 10aA The LORD bares his holy arm
לְעֵינֵ֖י כָּל־הַגּוֹיִ֑ם 10aB before the eyes of all the nations;

𝔐 distinctive accents: 5 – 2.
Stresses: 4 + 2.
Verse-line parallelism: זרוע || עין. None.
Discussion: The parallelism is weak because the sentence runs on. See our comment on v. 8b.

VERSE–LINE: 52:10b:

וְרָאוּ֙ כָּל־אַפְסֵי־אָ֔רֶץ 10bA and all the ends of the earth will see
אֵ֖ת יְשׁוּעַ֥ת אֱלֹהֵֽינוּ׃ 10bB the salvation of our God.

𝔐 distinctive accents: 5 – 1.
Stresses: 2 + 3.
Verse-line parallelism: None.

Discussion: Enjambment. See our comment on the preceding verse-line.

VERSE–LINE: 52:11a:

סוּרוּ סוּרוּ צְאוּ מִשָּׁם	11aA	Depart, depart, go out from there!
טָמֵא אַל־תִּגָּעוּ	11aB	Do not touch the unclean!

𝔐 distinctive accents: 5 – 2.
Stresses: 4 + 2.
Verse-line parallelism: סור || טמא;[7] סור || אל נגע.[8]

VERSE–LINE: 52:11b:

צְאוּ מִתּוֹכָהּ	11bA	Go out from the midst of her!
הִבָּרוּ נֹשְׂאֵי כְּלֵי יְהוָה׃	11bB	Keep yourselves pure, you who carry the vessels of the LORD.

𝔐 distinctive accents: 5 – 1.
Stresses: 2 + 4.
Verse-line parallelism: grammatical parallelism.
Discussion: Enjambment – because the sentence runs on through the two cola of the verse-line there is no parallelism. Parallelism, however, is observed on the level of the strophe. See the delimitation of strophes below.

VERSE–LINE: 52:12a:

כִּי לֹא בְחִפָּזוֹן תֵּצֵאוּ	12aA	For you will not go out in haste,
וּבִמְנוּסָה לֹא תֵלֵכוּן	12aB	and you will not go in flight,

𝔐 distinctive accents: 5 – 2.
Stresses: 4 + 3.
Verse-line parallelism: לא || לא; ב || ב; roots חפז || נוס; יצא || הלך; grammatical parallelism.

VERSE–LINE: 52:12b:

כִּי־הֹלֵךְ לִפְנֵיכֶם יְהוָה	12bA	for the LORD will go before you,
וּמְאַסִּפְכֶם אֱלֹהֵי יִשְׂרָאֵל׃	12bB	and the God of Israel will be your rearguard.

𝔐 distinctive accents: 5 – 1.
Stresses: 3 + 3.
Verse-line parallelism: יהוה || אלהי ישראל; הלך לפנים || אסף Pi.; ־כם || ־כם; rhyme.

[7] Almost certainly an allusion to Lam. 4:15.
[8] As in Lam. 4:15, see the preceding note.

12.4 Isaiah 51:9–52:12 – Delimitation of Strophes

STROPHE A.i.1 (Isa. 51:9a–b)

עוּרִי עוּרִי לִבְשִׁי־עֹז זְרוֹעַ יְהוָה	9aA	Wake up, wake up, clothe yourself with strength, O arm of the LORD.
עוּרִי כִּימֵי קֶדֶם	9bA	Wake up, as in the days of old,
דֹּרוֹת עוֹלָמִים	9bB	of the generations of primordial times!

≠ Masoretic verse.
Separation ↑: major division markers in the textual tradition; imperative(s); vocative; repetitive verse-line parallelism.
Separation ↓: imperative(s).
Strophe parallelism: עור || עור; grammatical parallelism.
Discussion: Although it would be possible to follow the Masoretes in reading 51:9 as a tricolon followed by a bicolon, the strong parallelism between vv. 9a and 9b – which is not set forth in v. 9c – suggests a division into two strophes. This separation is supported by the major division markers in 𝔊^{Q} after v. 9bB. This manuscript is among the host of manuscripts which testifies to the separation between 51:8 and 51:9. Whereas its division mark[1] after v. 9aA may be interpreted as a redundant marker lagging behind the major division line, this solution is not possible for the second marking after v. 9bB.[2] It must represent a genuine old marker of the end of a strophe.

STROPHE A.i.2 (Isa. 51:9c)

הֲלוֹא אַתְּ־הִיא הַמַּחְצֶבֶת רַהַב	9cA	Was is not you who hewed Rahab,
מְחוֹלֶלֶת תַּנִּין׃	9cB	who pierced the Tannin?

≠ Masoretic verse.
Separation ↑: major division markers in the textual tradition; deictic particle(s); independent pers. pronouns.
Separation ↓: None (one verse-line).
Strophe parallelism: None (one verse-line).
Discussion: See our discussion of the previous strophe.

STROPHE A.i.3 (Isa. 51:10)

הֲלוֹא אַתְּ־הִיא הַמַּחֲרֶבֶת יָם	10aA	Was it not you who dried up the sea,
מֵי תְּהוֹם רַבָּה	10aB	the waters of the great flood?
הַשָּׂמָה מַעֲמַקֵּי־יָם	10bA	Who made the depths of the sea

[1] A capital letter only.
[2] A point, Petuḥa, protruding line, capital and paragraphos.

דֶּרֶךְ לַעֲבֹר גְּאוּלִים׃	10bB	a way for the passing over of the redeemed ones?

= Masoretic verse.
Separation ↑: deictic particle(s); independent pers. pronouns.
Separation ↓: None.
Strophe parallelism: ים || ים; grammatical parallelism.
Discussion: We do not take into account the Setuma in 1Q[a] because it is merely left open for an erasure.

STROPHE A.i.4 (Isa. 51:11)

וּפְדוּיֵי יְהוָה יְשׁוּבוּן	11aA	So the ransomed of the LORD will return,
וּבָאוּ צִיּוֹן בְּרִנָּה	11aB	and come to Zion with rejoicing,
וְשִׂמְחַת עוֹלָם עַל־רֹאשָׁם	11aC	and eternal joy will be on their heads,
שָׂשׂוֹן וְשִׂמְחָה יַשִּׂיגוּן	11bA	gladness and joy will overtake (them),
נָסוּ יָגוֹן וַאֲנָחָה׃	11bB	torment and sighing flee away.

= Masoretic verse.
Separation ↑: swapping (subject).
Separation ↓: major division markers in the textual tradition; swapping (subject).
Strophe parallelism: רנה || ששון; שמחה || שמחה; grammatical parallelism.

STROPHE A.ii.1 (Isa. 51:12)

אָנֹכִי אָנֹכִי הוּא מְנַחֶמְכֶם	12aA	I, I am he – the one who comforts you.
מִי־אַתְּ וַתִּירְאִי מֵאֱנוֹשׁ יָמוּת	12bA	Who are you that you fear man who dies,
וּמִבֶּן־אָדָם חָצִיר יִנָּתֵן׃	12bB	and the son of man – grass given away?

= Masoretic verse.
Separation ↑: major division markers in the textual tradition; independent pers. pronouns.
Separation ↓: independent pers. pronoun; interrogative pronoun; repetitive verse-line parallelism; swapping (subject).
Strophe parallelism: נחם || ירא (antithetical).

STROPHE A.ii.2 (Isa. 51:13a)

וַתִּשְׁכַּח יְהוָה עֹשֶׂךָ	13aA	But you forget the LORD, who made you,
נוֹטֶה שָׁמַיִם וְיֹסֵד אָרֶץ	13aB	who stretched out the heavens and laid the foundation of the earth.

≠ Masoretic verse.
Separation ↑: None.
Separation ↓: None (one verse-line).
Strophe parallelism: None (one verse-line).

Discussion: The delimitation of this strophe is very problematic because no markers of separation are present. 𝔐 takes 51:13a with 13b-c, but this results in an overloaded verse. The harsh transition from the second person feminine to the second person masculine renders it impossible to join v. 13a with the preceding verse. The major division markers in $\mathfrak{G}^{SQ}$ after v. 13bB do not help either. They are placed in such an improbable place that the only conclusion can be that they moved there accidentally from the end of the verse by homoioteleuton (twice המציק). The parallelism between vv. 13bB and 13cA suggests that these at least should be taken together as one strophe. Thus we isolate v. 13a as a separate strophe by way of elimination only.

STROPHE A.ii.3 (Isa. 51:13b-c)

וַתְּפַחֵד תָּמִיד כָּל־הַיּוֹם	13bA	And you quiver continually all the day
מִפְּנֵי חֲמַת הַמֵּצִיק	13bB	because of the fury of the oppressor
כַּאֲשֶׁר כּוֹנֵן לְהַשְׁחִית	13bC	when he aims to annihilate.
וְאַיֵּה חֲמַת הַמֵּצִיק׃	13cA	But where is the fury of the oppressor?

≠ Masoretic verse.
Separation ↑: None (but see the discussion).
Separation ↓: None.
Strophe parallelism: חמה || חמה; צוק || צוק (unique); grammatical parallelism.
Discussion: Again the absence of markers of separation is noticeable (see our comments on the previous strophe). Yet the binding force of the strophe parallelism is strong enough to defend the unity of the strophe. Moreover, the colon parallelism תמיד || כל־היום lends a certain emphasis to the opening verse of the strophe, be it in an unusual way.

STROPHE A.ii.4 (Isa. 51:14)

מִהַר צֹעֶה לְהִפָּתֵחַ	14aA	Soon the cellarman will be released;
וְלֹא־יָמוּת לַשַּׁחַת	14bA	he will not die in the Pit of Annihilation,
וְלֹא יֶחְסַר לַחְמוֹ׃	14bB	neither will his bread be lacking.

= Masoretic verse.
Separation ↑: None.
Separation ↓: major division markers in the textual tradition; repetitive verse-line parallelism.
Strophe parallelism: צעה || שחת (unique); ל || ל.
Discussion: Although a tricolon is an option, we follow 𝔐.

STROPHE A.iii.1 (Isa. 51:15)

וְאָנֹכִי֙ יְהוָ֣ה אֱלֹהֶ֔יךָ	15aA	For I am the LORD, your God,
רֹגַ֣ע הַיָּ֔ם וַיֶּהֱמ֖וּ גַּלָּ֑יו	15aB	who stirs up the sea so that its waves roar
יְהוָ֥ה צְבָא֖וֹת שְׁמֽוֹ׃	15aC	– LORD of hosts is his name.

= Masoretic verse.
Separation ↑: major division markers in the textual tradition; independent pers. pronoun;
Separation ↓: major division markers in the textual tradition.
Strophe parallelism: None (one verse-line).

STROPHE A.iii.2 (Isa. 51:16)

וָאָשִׂ֤ים דְּבָרַי֙ בְּפִ֔יךָ	16aA	And I put my words in your mouth,
וּבְצֵ֥ל יָדִ֖י כִּסִּיתִ֑יךָ	16aB	and cover you with the shadow of my hand,
לִנְטֹ֤עַ שָׁמַ֙יִם֙ וְלִיסֹ֣ד אָ֔רֶץ	16bA	to plant the heavens and and to found the earth,
וְלֵאמֹ֥ר לְצִיּ֖וֹן עַמִּי־אָֽתָּה׃	16bB	and to say to Zion, "You are my people!"

= Masoretic verse.
Separation ↑: major division markers in the textual tradition; repetitive verse-line parallelism; swapping (adjunct).
Separation ↓: major division markers in the textual tradition; independent pers. pronoun; marker of direct speech; repetitive verse-line parallelism.
Strophe parallelism: שׂים || נטע; דבר || אמר

STROPHE B.i.1 (Isa. 51:17a)

הִתְעוֹרְרִ֣י הִתְעוֹרְרִ֗י ק֚וּמִי יְר֣וּשָׁלַ֔ם	17aA	Wake yourself, wake yourself, stand up, O Jerusalem,

≠ Masoretic verse.
Separation ↑: major division markers in the textual tradition; imperative(s); vocative.
Separation ↓: None (one verse-line).
Strophe parallelism: None (one verse-line).
Discussion: 𝔐's colometry is problematic and we decided to deviate from it.[3] The parallelism in vv. 17b-c is strong enough to make it a strophe. It is no valid objection that the sentence runs on through two strophes.[4] We believe that also in v. 22 the introductory verse-line and the two bicola should be separated.

---

[3] See pp. 502-3.
[4] See pp. 654-5.

STROPHE B.i.2 (Isa. 51:17b–c)

אֲשֶׁ֥ר שָׁתִ֛ית מִיַּ֥ד יְהוָ֖ה	17bA	you who have drunk from the hand of the LORD
אֶת־כּ֣וֹס חֲמָת֑וֹ	17bB	the cup of his fury,
אֶת־קֻבַּ֜עַת כּ֤וֹס הַתַּרְעֵלָה֙	17cA	the beaker, the cup of reeling,
שָׁתִ֖ית מָצִֽית׃	17cB	you had to drink, to drain.

≠ Masoretic verse.
Separation ↑: swapping (adjunct).
Separation ↓: swapping (object).
Strophe parallelism: שתה || שתה; את (nota acc.) || את (nota acc.); כוס || כוס.
Discussion: See our comment on the previous strophe.

STROPHE B.i.3 (Isa. 51:18)

אֵין־מְנַהֵל֙ לָ֔הּ	18aA	There was no one leading her
מִכָּל־בָּנִ֖ים יָלָ֑דָה	18aB	of all the sons she bore,
וְאֵ֤ין מַחֲזִיק֙ בְּיָדָ֔הּ	18bA	and there was no one grasping her hand
מִכָּל־בָּנִ֖ים גִּדֵּֽלָה׃	18bB	of all the sons she brought up.

= Masoretic verse.
Separation ↑: None.
Separation ↓: major division marker in the textual tradition.
Strophe parallelism: אין || אין; ־ה || ־ה; מן || מן; כל || כל; ילד || גדל. grammatical parallelism.
Discussion: The strophe parallelism compensates for the lack of verse-line parallelism.

STROPHE B.ii.1 (Isa. 51:19)

שְׁתַּ֤יִם הֵ֙נָּה֙ קֹרְאֹתַ֔יִךְ	19aA	These two things have happened to you –
מִ֖י יָנ֣וּד לָ֑ךְ	19aB	who will condole you? –
הַשֹּׁ֧ד וְהַשֶּׁ֛בֶר	19bA	destruction and breakdown
וְהָרָעָ֥ב וְהַחֶ֖רֶב	19bB	famine and sword –
מִ֥י אֲנַחֲמֵֽךְ׃	19bC	by whom can I comfort you?

= Masoretic verse.
Separation ↑: major division marker in the textual tradition; independent pers. pronoun; interrogative pronoun; swapping (subject);
Separation ↓: interrogative pronoun.
Strophe parallelism: מי || מי; נוד || נחם; ־ךְ (f.s.) || ־ךְ (f.s.).
Discussion: Again strophe parallelism compensates for the lack of verse-line parallelism.

STROPHE B.ii.2 (Isa. 51:20)

בָּנַיִךְ עֻלְּפוּ שָׁכְבוּ	20aA	Your sons have fainted; they lie down
בְּרֹאשׁ כָּל־חוּצוֹת	20aB	at the head of every street,
כְּתוֹא מִכְמָר	20aC	like an antelope caught in a net.
הַמְלֵאִים חֲמַת־יְהוָה	20bA	They are filled with the fury of the LORD,
גַּעֲרַת אֱלֹהָיִךְ׃	20bB	the rebuke of your God.

= Masoretic verse.
Separation ↑: swapping (subject).
Separation ↓: major division markers in the textual tradition.
Strophe parallelism: None.
Discussion: Despite the lack of parallelism the delimition of the strophe is not in doubt because the sentence continues through the two verse-lines. Moreover, the underlying imagery in both verse-lines is that of youngsters lying unconscious as if they have had too much wine.

STROPHE B.iii.1 (Isa. 51:21–22a)

לָכֵן שִׁמְעִי־נָא זֹאת עֲנִיָּה	21aA	Therefore hear now this, O afflicted one,
וּשְׁכֻרַת וְלֹא מִיָּיִן׃	21aB	and drunken one, though not with wine:
כֹּה־אָמַר אֲדֹנַיִךְ יְהוָה	22aA	Thus says your Lord GOD
וֵאלֹהַיִךְ יָרִיב עַמּוֹ	22aB	and your God who goes into court for his people:

≠ Masoretic verse.
Separation ↑: major division markers in the textual tradition; deictic particle(s); demonstrative pronoun; imperative(s); vocative.
Separation ↓: deictic particle(s); marker of direct speech; repetitive verse-line parallelism.
Strophe parallelism: שמע || אמר.
Discussion: The Masoretes, Codex Reuchlin and 𝔊[S] seem to have taken v. 21 as an independent strophe. However, since vv. 22b-c obviously belong together (see also v. 17), we are convinced that v. 22a should be connected with v. 21. The imperative of שמע followed by a vocative and the formula כה אמר יהוה occurs fairly often in one and the same strophe, e.g. Jer. 19:3; 42:15; Ezek. 6:3; 36:4; 25:3. 1𝔔[a] furnishes an explanation for the erroneous division of the witnesses mentioned: it has a small Setuma which the ancients sometimes used to mark the end of verses or strophes. And which obviously caused a lot of confusion.

STROPHE B.iii.2 (Isa. 51:22b–c)

הִנֵּה לָקַחְתִּי מִיָּדֵךְ	22bA	Behold, I take from your hand
אֶת־כּוֹס הַתַּרְעֵלָה	22bB	the cup of reeling,
אֶת־קֻבַּעַת כּוֹס חֲמָתִי	22cA	the beaker, the cup of my fury –
לֹא־תוֹסִיפִי לִשְׁתּוֹתָהּ עוֹד׃	22cB	you will not have to drink it again.

≠ Masoretic verse.
Separation ↑: deictic particle(s);
Separation ↓: major division markers in the textual tradition; swapping (object).
Strophe parallelism: את (nota acc.) || את (nota acc.); כוס || קבעת.
Discussion: See our discussion of the previous strophe as well as v. 17.

STROPHE B.iii.3 (Isa. 51:23)

וְשַׂמְתִּיהָ בְּיַד־מוֹגַיִךְ	23aA	And I will put it into the hand of those who torment you,
אֲשֶׁר־אָמְרוּ לְנַפְשֵׁךְ	23aB	who say to you,
שְׁחִי וְנַעֲבֹרָה	23aC	"Bow down, that we may pass over",
וַתָּשִׂימִי כָאָרֶץ גֵּוֵךְ	23bA	and you had to make your back like the ground
וְכַחוּץ לַעֹבְרִים׃	23bB	and like a street for those who pass over.

= Masoretic verse.
Separation ↑: major division markers in the textual tradition; imperative(s); cohortative(s); marker of direct speech; repetitive verse-line parallelism.
Separation ↓: major division markers in the textual tradition; repetitive verse-line parallelism; swapping (adjunct).
Strophe parallelism: שׂים || שׂים; עבר || עבר.

STROPHE C.i.1 (Isa. 52:1a–b)

עוּרִי עוּרִי לִבְשִׁי עֻזֵּךְ צִיּוֹן	1aA	Wake up, wake up, clothe yourself with your strength, o Zion
לִבְשִׁי ׀ בִּגְדֵי תִפְאַרְתֵּךְ	1bA	clothe yourself with your glorious garments,
יְרוּשָׁלַםִ עִיר הַקֹּדֶשׁ	1bB	O, Jerusalem, holy city:

≠ Masoretic verse.
Separation ↑: major division markers in the textual tradition; imperative(s); vocative;
Separation ↓: imperative(s); vocative.
Strophe parallelism: לבשׁ || לבשׁ; עז || תפארת; ־ךְ (f.s.) || ־ךְ (f.s.); ציון || ירושלם; grammatical parallelism.
Discussion: The major dividers in 1𝔔^{a}, the Codex Reuchlin and $\mathfrak{G}^{A}$ seem to support 𝔐's delimitation of v. 1. Nevertheless we feel confi-

dent in separating 52:1c from 52:1a-b because the parallelism between these verse-lines is so strong, whereas v. 1c introduces a new element. Moreover, the analogy with 51:9 argues in favour of this delimitation (51:17 is less similar: there the next verse-line does not have an imperative).

STROPHE C.i.2 (Isa. 52:1c)

כִּי לֹא יוֹסִיף יָבֹא־בָךְ עוֹד	1cA	for there shall no more come into you
עָרֵל וְטָמֵא׃	1cB	the uncircumcised and the unclean.

≠ Masoretic verse.
Separation ↑: deictic particle(s).
Separation ↓: major division markers in the textual tradition.
Strophe parallelism: None (one verse-line).
Discussion: See our discussion of the previous strophe.

STROPHE C.i.3 (Isa. 52:2)

הִתְנַעֲרִי מֵעָפָר	2aA	Shake yourself free from the dust,
קוּמִי שְׁבִי יְרוּשָׁלִָם	2aB	stand up, take your seat, O Jerusalem!
הִתְפַּתְּחוּ מוֹסְרֵי צַוָּארֵךְ*	2bA	The chains on your neck are released,
שְׁבִיָּה בַּת־צִיּוֹן׃	2bB	O captive, daughter of Zion!

= Masoretic verse.
Separation ↑: major division markers in the textual tradition; imperative(s); vocative.
Separation ↓: major division markers in the textual tradition; vocative.
Strophe parallelism: ירושלם || ציון.

STROPHE C.i.4 (Isa. 52:3)

כִּי־כֹה אָמַר יְהוָה	3aA	For thus says the LORD:
חִנָּם נִמְכַּרְתֶּם	3aB	For nothing you were sold
וְלֹא בְכֶסֶף תִּגָּאֵלוּ׃	3aC	and without silver you will be redeemed.

= Masoretic verse.
Separation ↑: major division markers in the textual tradition; deictic particle(s); marker of direct speech; swapping (adjunct).
Separation ↓: major division markers in the textual tradition.
Strophe parallelism: None (one verse-line).

STROPHE C.ii.1 (Isa. 52:4)

כִּי כֹה אָמַר אֲדֹנָי יְהוִה	4aA	For thus says the Lord GOD:

מִצְרַיִם יָרַד־עַמִּי בָרִאשֹׁנָה לָגוּר שָׁם	4aB	At first my people went down to Egypt to sojourn there,
וְאַשּׁוּר בְּאֶפֶס עֲשָׁקוֹ׃	4aC	and Assyria oppressed them for nothing.

= Masoretic verse.
Separation ↑: major division markers in the textual tradition; deictic particle(s); marker of direct speech; swapping (subject); swapping (adjunct).
Separation ↓: None (one verse-line).
Strophe parallelism: None (one verse-line).

STROPHE C.ii.2 (Isa. 52:5)

וְעַתָּה מִי לִי־פֹה נְאֻם־יְהוָה	5aA	But now, what do I have here? declares the LORD,
כִּי־לֻקַּח עַמִּי חִנָּם	5aB	that my people has been taken away for nothing?
מֹשְׁלָיו* יְהֵילִילוּ נְאֻם־יְהוָה	5bA	Those who rule it ululate, declares the LORD,
וְתָמִיד כָּל־הַיּוֹם שְׁמִי מִנֹּאָץ׃	5bB	and all day long my name is reviled.

= Masoretic verse.
Separation ↑: deictic particle(s); interrogative pronoun; marker of direct speech.
Separation ↓: major division markers in the textual tradition; marker of direct speech; swapping (subject); swapping (adjunct).
Strophe parallelism: נאם || נאם; ־י || ־י.

STROPHE C.ii.3 (Isa. 52:6)

לָכֵן יֵדַע עַמִּי שְׁמִי	6aA	Therefore my people will know my name,
לָכֵן בַּיּוֹם הַהוּא	6bA	therefore, on that day,
כִּי־אֲנִי־הוּא הַמְדַבֵּר הִנֵּנִי׃	6bB	when I am going to speak: Here I am!

= Masoretic verse.
Separation ↑: major division markers in the textual tradition; deictic particle(s)
Separation ↓: major division markers in the textual tradition; deictic particle(s); independent pers. pronouns
Strophe parallelism: לכן || לכן; ־י || אני.

STROPHE C.iii.1 (Isa. 52:7)

מַה־נָּאווּ עַל־הֶהָרִים	7aA	How beautiful on the mountains
רַגְלֵי מְבַשֵּׂר מַשְׁמִיעַ שָׁלוֹם	7aB	are the feet of the herald who announces peace,
מְבַשֵּׂר טוֹב מַשְׁמִיעַ יְשׁוּעָה	7aC	the herald of good tidings who announces salvation,

אֹמֵ֥ר לְצִיּ֖וֹן מָלַ֥ךְ אֱלֹהָֽיִךְ׃	7bA	who says to Zion, "Your God is king!"

= Masoretic verse.
Separation ↑: major division markers in the textual tradition; deictic particle(s); repetitive verse-line parallelism; swapping (adjunct).
Separation ↓: major division markers in the textual tradition; marker of direct speech.
Strophe parallelism: הר || ציון.

STROPHE C.iii.2 (Isa. 52:8)

ק֥וֹל צֹפַ֛יִךְ נָ֥שְׂאוּ ק֖וֹל	8aA	The voices of your watchmen! They raise their voices,
יַחְדָּ֣ו יְרַנֵּ֑נוּ	8aB	they rejoice together,
כִּ֣י עַ֤יִן בְּעַ֙יִן֙ יִרְא֔וּ	8bA	for with their own eyes they see with delight
בְּשׁ֥וּב יְהוָ֖ה צִיּֽוֹן׃	8bB	how the LORD returns to Zion.

= Masoretic verse.
Separation ↑: major division markers in the textual tradition; swapping (object); swapping (adjunct).
Separation ↓: major division markers in the textual tradition; deictic particle(s); swapping (adjunct).
Strophe parallelism: צפה || ראה (unique); grammatical parallelism.

STROPHE C.iii.3 (Isa. 52:9)

פִּצְח֤וּ רַנְּנוּ֙ יַחְדָּ֔ו	9aA	Break forth, rejoice together
חָרְב֖וֹת יְרוּשָׁלִָ֑ם	9aB	you ruins of Jerusalem!
כִּֽי־נִחַ֤ם יְהוָה֙ עַמּ֔וֹ	9bA	For the LORD comforts his people,
גָּאַ֖ל יְרוּשָׁלִָֽם׃	9bB	he redeems Jerusalem.

= Masoretic verse.
Separation ↑: major division markers in the textual tradition; imperative(s); vocative.
Separation ↓: major division markers in the textual tradition; deictic particle(s).
Strophe parallelism: ירושלם || ירושלם.

STROPHE C.iii.4 (Isa. 52:10)

חָשַׂ֤ף יְהוָה֙ אֶת־זְר֣וֹעַ קָדְשׁ֔וֹ	10aA	The LORD bares his holy arm
לְעֵינֵ֖י כָּל־הַגּוֹיִ֑ם	10aB	before the eyes of all the nations;
וְרָאוּ֙ כָּל־אַפְסֵי־אָ֔רֶץ	10bA	and all the ends of the earth will see
אֵ֖ת יְשׁוּעַ֥ת אֱלֹהֵֽינוּ׃	10bB	the salvation of our God.

= Masoretic verse.
Separation ↑: major division markers in the textual tradition.

Separation ↓: major division markers in the textual tradition.
Strophe parallelism: יהוה || אלהים; עין || ראה; כל || כל; גוים || אפסי־ארץ.

STROPHE C.iv.1 (Isa. 52:11)

סוּרוּ סוּרוּ צְאוּ מִשָּׁם	11aA	Depart, depart, go out from there!
טָמֵא אַל־תִּגָּעוּ	11aB	Do not touch the unclean!
צְאוּ מִתּוֹכָהּ	11bA	Go out from the midst of her!
הִבָּרוּ נֹשְׂאֵי כְּלֵי יְהוָה׃	11bB	Keep yourselves pure, you who carry the vessels of the LORD.

= Masoretic verse.
Separation ↑: major division markers in the textual tradition; imperative(s); swapping (object).
Separation ↓: imperative(s); vocative.
Strophe parallelism: יצא || יצא; מן || מן; טמא || ברר (unique); grammatical parallelism.

STROPHE C.iv.2 (Isa. 52:12)

כִּי לֹא בְחִפָּזוֹן תֵּצֵאוּ	12aA	For you will not go out in haste,
וּבִמְנוּסָה לֹא תֵלֵכוּן	12aB	and you will not go in flight,
כִּי־הֹלֵךְ לִפְנֵיכֶם יְהוָה	12bA	for the LORD will go before you,
וּמְאַסִּפְכֶם אֱלֹהֵי יִשְׂרָאֵל׃	12bB	and the God of Israel will be your rearguard.

= Masoretic verse.
Separation ↑: deictic particle(s); swapping (adjunct).
Separation ↓: major division markers in the textual tradition; deictic particle(s); swapping (adjunct).
Strophe parallelism: הלך || הלך.

12.5 Isaiah 51:9–52:12 – Delimitation of Canticles

CANTICLE A.i (51:9–11)

Separation ↑: major division markers in the textual tradition; change of subject.
Separation ↓: major division markers in the textual tradition.
Canticle parallelism: יהוה || יהוה (responsion); עולם || עולם (inclusion); הלוא || הלוא (concatenation); את (f.s.) || את (f.s.) (concatenation); היא || היא (responsion); רהב || ים (concatenation/responsion); תנין || תהום (concatenation); גאל || פדה (concatenation); עבר || בוא (concatenation); grammatical parallelism between the participles.
Thematic unity: yes. The LORD's victory over the sea and his wondrous acts at the Sea of Reeds are a guarantee that the exiles will return to Zion.

Discussion: Because $\mathfrak{G}^{Q}$ is among the witnesses attesting the major break after 51:8, the capital letters it has with the third ἐξεγείρου and with οὐ may be regarded as redundant extra markers of that division. The Setuma in $1\mathfrak{Q}^{a}$ after v. 10bB is nothing but an erasure.

CANTICLE A.ii (51:12–14)

Separation ↑: major division markers in the textual tradition; change of subject.
Separation ↓: major division markers in the textual tradition.
Canticle parallelism: ירא || פחד (inclusion); מות || מות (inclusion); שחת (verb) || שחת (noun) (unique; responsion).
Thematic unity: yes. Why are the oppressed fearing their oppressors? Their God being the almighty Creator they should trust that he will not let them die in the dungeon.
Discussion: The paragraphos in $\mathfrak{G}^{S}$ and the capital letter in $\mathfrak{G}^{Q}$ after the first המציק / τοῦ θλίβοντός σε is an interesting case of an erroneously placed major division mark. Originally it must have been positioned after the *second* המציק (v. 13cA) to mark the end of the strophe (homoioteleuton).

CANTICLE A.iii (51:15–16)

Separation ↑: major division markers in the textual tradition; thematic discontinuity; change of subject.
Separation ↓: major division markers in the textual tradition.
Canticle parallelism: אלהיך || עמי־אתה (inclusion);[1] ־ך (m.s.) || ־ך (m.s.) (responsion); ים || שמים (inclusion).
Thematic unity: yes. Just as the Creator is Lord over the sea, so he can realize his plans by the words of his servant.
Discussion: $\mathfrak{G}^{A}$ marks the end of v. 15. $\mathfrak{S}^{b}$ indicates the break after v. 16 proleptically and redundantly after v. 16bA. Because this happens rarely in manuscripts of $\mathfrak{S}$ it is probably an error.

CANTICLE B.i (51:17–18)

Separation ↑: major division markers in the textual tradition; change of subject.
Separation ↓: major division markers in the textual tradition.
Canticle parallelism: יד || יד (inclusion).
Thematic unity: yes. Although the canticle parallelism is weak in a formal sense, the ancient Oriental custom that children had to lead

[1] Allusion to the covenantal formula, see p. 39, n.1.

their drunken parents home[2] forms a strong bond between the two strophes.
Discussion: The paragraphos after v. 18 in 𝔊[Q] finds some support in the major division markers 𝔊[A] inserts belatedly after 51:19aB. In our opinion it is warranted to take this break as a canticle boundary because vv. 19-20 switch to the second person again and describe Zion's loss of her children.

CANTICLE B.ii (51:19-20)

Separation ↑: major division marker in the textual tradition; change of subject.
Separation ↓: major division markers in the textual tradition.
Canticle parallelism: ךְ־ (f.s.) || ךְ־ (f.s.).
Thematic unity: yes. The first strophe prepares Zion for the terrible news of the death of her children which is described in a euphemistic way in the second strophe. Apparently the prophet refers to other passages describing the loss of children as the main שׁבר Zion had to suffer.[3]
Discussion: See our discussion of the previous canticle for 𝔊[A] after v. 19aB.

CANTICLE (B.iii 51:21–23)

Separation ↑: major division markers in the textual tradition.
Separation ↓: major division markers in the textual tradition.
Canticle parallelism: שׁמע, אמר || אמר (responsion/inclusion); ךְ־ (f.s.) || ךְ־ (f.s.) || ךְ־ (f.s.) || ךְ־ (f.s.); לקח || שׂים (responsion); יד || יד (reponsion).
Thematic unity: yes. The beaker of the LORD's fury is passed on from lady Zion to lady Babylon.
Discussion: With regard to the dividers after v. 21aB see our discussion of the delimitation of strophes.[4] 𝔊[A] marks the end of strophe B.iii.2 (after v. 22cB).

CANTICLE C.i (52:1–3)

Separation ↑: major division markers in the textual tradition; change of subject.
Separation ↓: major division markers in the textual tradition.
Canticle parallelism: עור || קום (responsion); ציון || ציון (inclusion); ירושלם || ירושלם (inclusion); קדשׁ || טמא (antithetical; concatenation);

[2]On this filial duty, cf. De Moor, *ARTU*, 228, n.31.
[3]Jer. 10:18-20; 14:16-17; Lam. 2:11-12; 4:10.
[4]See p. 533.

פתח Hitpa. || גאל Niph. (unique; responsion).
Thematic unity: yes. Zion is encouraged to shake off the signs of her uncleanliness and slavery, because she will be redeemed without ransom being paid.
Discussion: 1QIsa[a], Codex Reuchlin and 𝔊[A] mark the end of v. 1, whereas 𝔐, the Codex Reuchlin, 1QIsa[a], 𝔊[AQ] have division markers after v.2. The latter is probably an error because the Codex Reuchlin, 𝔊[SBA] and 𝔖[b] all have major division markers after v. 3. Because some of these witnesses have a double marking, the two traditions more or less exclude each other. In this rare case it is easy to see how the error came into being. 𝔐 and its supporters rest on a tradition which inserted the break at the wrong כי כה אמר, at v. 3aA instead of v. 4aA. It is true that vv. 4-5 elaborate the theme of Zion being 'bought' for free, but vv. 1-3 concern Zion's redemption from slavery and therefore should not be separated.

CANTICLE C.ii (52:4–6)

Separation ↑: major division markers in the textual tradition.
Separation ↓: major division markers in the textual tradition.
Canticle parallelism: אמר || נאם (responsion/inclusion); אמר || דבר (inclusion); בראשנה || עתה (antithetical; concatenation) עם || עם || עם (responsion); יי || יי || יי (responsion).
Thematic unity: yes. All three strophes speak of the injustice done to the people of God by foreign nations. As in the past, God will deliver them now that the Babylonians oppress them.
Discussion: Some of the Greek manuscripts put a caesura before נאם. Since 𝔊[BQ] also mark the end of the strophe, as 1QIsa[a] does with a small Setuma, the markers in 𝔊[SBQ] in v. 5aA are probably a remnant of a strophe divider after v. 4 whereas the markers in 𝔊[SA] in v. 5bA proleptically indicate the strophe end after v. 5bB.

The major division marks 𝔊[S] has in the middle of v. 6bB – a highly improbable point – obviously indicate the major break after v. 6 proleptically.

CANTICLE C.iii (52:7–10)

Separation ↑: major division markers in the textual tradition; thematic discontinuity; change of subject.
Separation ↓: major division markers in the textual tradition.
Canticle parallelism: ישועה || ישועה (inclusion); ציון || ציון (responsion) || ירושלם (responsion/concatenation); אלהים || אלהים (responsion); יחדו || יחדו (unique; responsion); רנן || רנן (unique; responsion); עין || עין

(inclusion); ראה || ראה (responsion); עם || גוי (concatenation).
Thematic unity: yes. The LORD's glorious return to Zion.
Discussion: 1Q[a] has a small Setuma after v. 7 which corresponds to a paragraphos in 𝔊[S]. The same Greek manuscript belatedly indicates this strophe end by a protruding line starting at an improbable point in the middle of v. 8aA.

𝔊[SAQ] indicate the end of the strophe C.iii.2 (v. 8) and again this corresponds to a small Setuma in 1Q[a]. 𝔊[S] marks the end of strophe C.iii.3 (v. 9), but here a small Setuma is lacking in 1Q[a].

CANTICLE C.iv (52:11–12)

Separation ↑: major division markers in the textual tradition; thematic discontinuity; change of subject.
Separation ↓: major division markers in the textual tradition.
Canticle parallelism: יצא || יצא (responsion/concatenation); יהוה || יהוה (responsion).
Thematic unity: yes. Both strophes refer to a second Exodus.

12.6 Isaiah 51:9–52:12 – Delimitation of Macrostructure

The coherence of the canto cannot be doubted. The imperatives עורי (51:9), התעוררי (51:17) and עורי (52:1) create an obvious structural framework which was already recognized in Antiquity. Beginning and end deal with the theme of a joyful return to Zion. The first and third sub-cantos derive the faith in the possibility of this return from God's unlimited power as the Creator and his wondrous acts in connection with the First Exodus (51:9-11, 15; 52:4, 11-12). As in 40:10-11, God himself will lead back his people (51:11; 52:8).[1] The strong 'arm' of God which had played such a prominent role in the First Exodus is invoked again (51:9; 52:10; cf. 40:10-11). However, Jerusalem herself too has to become active in shaking off her chains and restoring her own strength (51:17; 52:1, 2; cf. 52:7-9 and 40:9). 'Zion' has to be understood here as a designation of those who accept the words of the LORD as his faithful servants – only then Zion will be God's people (51:16). One of the central themes of Second Isaiah's message reappears here. As soon as people realize that they themselves have to get involved in God's salvatory acts, nothing is impossible for them, not

[1] In our opinion this is one of many indications that Second Isaiah was viewing the restoration of Zion from the viewpoint of the Babylonian exiles. For him, God was in Babylonia, not in Jerusalem.

even the founding of heaven and earth (51:16). They will be ransomed by their God (51:10-11; 52:3, 9), but they themselves have to wake up from their stupor.

The middle part (subcanto B) describes this stuporous state in vivid metaphors, recognizing that it had been unavoidable for the LORD to punish lady Jerusalem, but at the same time emphasizing that it is now the turn of her oppressors to be punished for their licentious behaviour (51:22-23). The opening verse of this sub-canto renders it impossible to detach it from the rest of the canto. The closing lines confirm this: the best way to take revenge for the enemy's passing over Zion's body (51:23) is to pass over the road through the 'sea' again (51:10), to leave the oppressor's country (52:11-12), a new 'Passover'.

In spite of this apparently coherent composition, the canto's structure appears to be rather irregular,

SUB-CANTOS	CANTICLES	STROPHES
A	3	10 (4+4+2)
B	3	8 (3+2+3)
C	4	13 (4+3+4+2)

It is tempting to regard C.ii (52:4-6) as a later expansion. If these verses are omitted, the structure becomes totally symmetric,

SUB-CANTOS	CANTICLES	STROPHES
A	3	10 (4+4+2)
B	3	8 (3+2+3)
C	3	10 (4+4+2)

Many scholars view 52:3-6 as a later addition in prose[2] but our findings seem to confirm the analysis of others who isolate vv. 4-6 only.[3] It looks suspiciously as if the terse phrase חנם נמכרתם (v. 3aB) provoked further explanation (vv. 4aC, 5aB). However, we shall not pursue this matter any further in a book primarily dealing with the structural analysis of Second Isaiah – a phase preceding literary and redactional criticism. In any case it would seem clear that the major division

[2]E.g. Whybray, 165; Melugin, 162-3; Van Oorschot, 134-5; Grimm, Dittert, 390.

[3]So e.g. O.H. Steck, *Bereitete Heimkehr: Jesaja 35 als redaktionelle Brücke zwischen dem Ersten und dem Zweiten Jesaja* (SBS, 121), Stuttgart 1985, 80.

markers which the tradition has preserved after 52:3 should not be neglected in future discussions of this matter.

Distant parallelism connecting the canticles of the three sub-cantos:

Sub-canto A:
ים || ים (51:10aA, 10bA – A.i) || ים (51:15aB – A.iii); ציון (51:11aB – A.i) || ציון (51:16bB – A.iii); אנחה (51:11bB – A.i) || נחם (51:12aA – A.ii); נוטה שמים ויסד ארץ (51:13aB – A.ii) || לנטע שמים וליסד ארץ (51:16bA – A.iii).

Sub-canto B:
קום (51:17aA – B.i) || שחה (51:23a – B.iii) (antithetical; unique); שתה (51:17bA, 17cB – B.i) || שתה (51:22cB – B.iii); יד (51:17bA, 18bA – B.i) || יד (51:22bA, 23aA – B.iii); כוס חמה (51:17bB – B.i) || כוס חמה (51:22 – B.iii);[4] את־קבעת כוס התרעלה (51:17cA – B.i) || את־כוס התרעלה את־קבעת (51:22bB-cA – B.iii); בן (51:18aB, 18bB – B.i) || בן (51:20aA – B.ii).

Sub-canto C:
טמא (52:1cB – C.i) || טמא (52:11aB – C.iv); ציון (52:1aA, 2bB – C. i) || ציון (52:7bA, 8bB – C.iii); ירושלם (52:1bB, 2aB – C.i) || ירושלם (52:9aB, 9bB – C.iii); חנם (52:3aB – C.i) || חנם (52:5aB – C.ii); גאל (52:3aC – C.i) || גאל (52:9bB – C.iii); עם (noun) (52:4aB, 5aB, 6aA – C.ii) || עם (noun) (52: 9bA – C.iii).

[4]See also Isa. 51:20bA and Jer. 25:15.

Chapter 13

The Structure of Isaiah 52:13–53:12

13.1 Isaiah 52:13–53:12: Text and Translation

ס <פ> – 1𝔔^{a} – 4𝔔^{c} – 𝔊^{SBAQ} – 𝔖^{abcde} ______________________

A.i.1 (Isa. 52:13)

הִנֵּה יַשְׂכִּיל עַבְדִּי	13aA	Behold, my servant will be successful,[1]
יָרוּם וְנִשָּׂא וְגָבַהּ מְאֹד׃	13aB	he shall be exalted and lifted up, and shall be very high.

A.i.2 (Isa. 52:14)

כַּאֲשֶׁר שָׁמְמוּ עָלֶיךָ רַבִּים	14aA	As many were left desolated for you[2]
כֵּן־מָשְׁחַת* מֵאִישׁ מַרְאֵהוּ	14aB	– his appearance was so marred,[3] beyond human semblance,
וְתֹאֲרוֹ מִבְּנֵי אָדָם׃	14aC	and his looks[4] beyond those of sons of men –

A.i.3 (Isa. 52:15)

כֵּן יַזֶּה גּוֹיִם רַבִּים	15aA	so shall he make many nations jump up;[5]
{𝔊^{A}} עָלָיו יִקְפְּצוּ מְלָכִים פִּיהֶם	15aB	kings shall shut their mouths because of him.
כִּי אֲשֶׁר לֹא־סֻפַּר לָהֶם רָאוּ	15bA	For that which was never told them they see
וַאֲשֶׁר לֹא־שָׁמְעוּ הִתְבּוֹנָנוּ׃	15bB	and that which they had never heard they understand.

<ס> <פ> – 1𝔔^{a} – 4𝔔^{c} – 𝔊^{SBAQ} ______________________

[1]Neither the emendation ישׂראל nor the translation "will have understanding" (cf. Isa. 41:20; 44:18; Jer. 3:15; Dan. 12:3, etc.) recommends itself here. We follow 𝔗. See also Isa. 49:4 and 53:10.

[2]There is insufficient reason to emend to עליו. 𝔗 and 𝔖 try to remove the harsh transition which is, however, perfectly normal in North West Semitic poetry, see e.g. GK §144p; M.C.A. Korpel, "Exegesis in the Work of Ilimilku of Ugarit", in: J.C. de Moor (ed.), *Intertextuality in Ugarit and Israel* (OTS, 40), Leiden 1998, 86-111 (99).

[3]We resolve the age-old crux in vocalizing as a Hophal participle. The verb שׁחת Hiphil is often used to describe the destruction of human beings, even the anointed of the LORD (2 Sam. 1:14). The servant is often described with rare passive participles which were not always recognized by the Masoretes, see p. 122, n. 10.

[4]Cf. *HALAT*, 1545.

[5]Cf. Oswalt, 374, n.56; for other proposals see H.-J. Hermisson, "Das vierte Gottesknechtlied", in: B. Janowski, P. Stuhlmacher, *Der leidende Gottesknecht: Jesaja 53 und seine Wirkungsgeschichte*, Tübingen 1996, 1-25 (6, n. 13).

B.i.1 (Isa. 53:1)

מִי הֶאֱמִין לִשְׁמֻעָתֵנוּ	1aA	Who believes what we have heard?
וּזְרוֹעַ יְהוָה עַל־מִי נִגְלָתָה׃	1aB	And to whom has the arm of the LORD been revealed?

B.i.2 (Isa. 53:2)

וַיַּעַל כַּיּוֹנֵק לְפָנָיו	2aA	For he grew up before him[6] like a fresh shoot,
וְכַשֹּׁרֶשׁ מֵאֶרֶץ צִיָּה	2aB	and like a root out of dry ground.
לֹא־תֹאַר לוֹ וְלֹא הָדָר	2bA	He had no (good) looks and no splendour,
וְנִרְאֵהוּ וְלֹא־מַרְאֶה וְנֶחְמְדֵהוּ׃	2bB	that we should look at him, and no (fine) appearance that we should desire him.

B.i.3 (Isa. 53:3)

{$\mathfrak{G}^{AQ}$} נִבְזֶה וַחֲדַל אִישִׁים	3aA	He was despised and rejected by men;
אִישׁ מַכְאֹבוֹת וִידוּעַ חֹלִי	3aB	a man of sorrows, and acquainted with illness;
וּכְמַסְתֵּר פָּנִים מִמֶּנּוּ	3bA	and as one who causes people to hide their faces from him
נִבְזֶה וְלֹא חֲשַׁבְנֻהוּ׃	3bB	he was despised, and we thought nothing of him.

$\mathfrak{G}^{S}$ – $\mathfrak{S}^{e}$ ....

B.ii.1 (Isa. 53:4)

אָכֵן חֳלָיֵנוּ הוּא נָשָׂא	4aA	Yet it was he who has borne our illnesses,
וּמַכְאֹבֵינוּ סְבָלָם	4aB	and carried our sorrows;
וַאֲנַחְנוּ חֲשַׁבְנֻהוּ נָגוּעַ	4bA	but we thought of him as stricken,
מֻכֵּה אֱלֹהִים וּמְעֻנֶּה׃	4bB	smitten by God, and afflicted.

B.ii.2 (Isa. 53:5)

וְהוּא מְחֹלָל מִפְּשָׁעֵנוּ	5aA	But he was the one pierced because of our transgressions,
מְדֻכָּא מֵעֲוֹנֹתֵינוּ	5aB	crushed because of our iniquities;
מוּסַר שְׁלוֹמֵנוּ עָלָיו	5bA	upon him was the chastisement that brings us peace,[7]
וּבַחֲבֻרָתוֹ נִרְפָּא־לָנוּ׃	5bB	and with his wounds we are healed.

B.ii.3 (Isa. 53:6)

{$\mathfrak{G}^{S}$} כֻּלָּנוּ כַּצֹּאן תָּעִינוּ	6aA	All of us went astray, like sheep,
{<ס>} אִישׁ לְדַרְכּוֹ פָּנִינוּ	6aB	we have turned every one to his own way.

[6]There is no need to emend the text. The suffix refers back to the LORD, mentioned in v. 1. The children would not have been destroyed מלפניו if their fathers had not transgressed (Isa. 48:19). Koole, *Jesaja II*, vol. 2, 225, points to the prophetic self-consciousness of the prophet standing before the LORD, 1 Kgs 17:1, like a servant before his king, Gen. 41:46; 1 Sam. 16:21, etc.

[7]See our note on Isa. 42:19b, p. 122, n.10.

וַיהוָה הִפְגִּיעַ בּוֹ	6bA	Yet the LORD inflicted on him
אֵת עֲוֹן כֻּלָּנוּ׃	6bB	the iniquity of us all.

$\mathfrak{G}^{Q}$ ....

B.iii.1 (Isa. 53:7)

נִגַּשׂ וְהוּא נַעֲנֶה	7aA	It was exacted,[8] and he was the one afflicted,
{$\mathfrak{G}^{SA}$} וְלֹא יִפְתַּח־פִּיו	7aB	yet he opened not his mouth.
כַּשֶּׂה לַטֶּבַח יוּבָל	7bA	Like a young ram he was led to the slaughter,
וּכְרָחֵל לִפְנֵי גֹזְזֶיהָ נֶאֱלָמָה	7bB	and like an ewe that is dumb before its shearers –
וְלֹא יִפְתַּח פִּיו׃	7bC	and he opened not his mouth.

B.iii.2 (Isa. 53:8)

מֵעֹצֶר וּמִמִּשְׁפָּט לֻקָּח	8aA	Without restraint and without arbitration[9] he was taken away,
וְאֶת־דּוֹרוֹ מִי יְשׂוֹחֵחַ	8aB	and as for his generation,[10] who cared?
כִּי נִגְזַר מֵאֶרֶץ חַיִּים	8bA	For it[11] was cut off out of the land of the living,
{<פ>$\mathfrak{G}^{A}$} מִפֶּשַׁע עַמִּי נֶגַע לָמוֹ׃	8bB	because of the transgression of my people the blow was on them.[12]

B.iii.3 (Isa. 53:9-10a)

וַיִּתֵּן אֶת־רְשָׁעִים קִבְרוֹ	9aA	And they[13] made his grave with the wicked
וְאֶת־עָשִׁיר בְּמֹתָיו	9aB	and with the rich[14] in his death.

[8]See on this translation K. Vitringa, *Uitlegging over het boek der profeetsyen van Jezaias*, dl. 5, Leiden 1741, 902-3; Koole, 239. The antecedent is עון, v. 6bB. This translation is the only one which accounts for the emphatic והוא. See for the problematic way one has to explain it otherwise, Hermisson, "Das vierte Gottes-knechtlied", 7, n. 23.

[9]The difficult עצר probably denotes a restraining force (cf. Prov. 30:16; Ps 107:39). This balances nicely with שׂיח Pol. in the parallel colon. See also v. 7bA.

[10]Any translation of דורו involves exegesis. Mostly we have translated this noun by "generation" (Isa. 41:4; 51:8-9) and it seems advisable not to depart from that rendering; so also KJV, RSV, Segond, cf. L.G. Rignell, "Isa. LII 13 – LIII 12", *VT* 3 (1953), 87-93 (88). Keeping on the safe side we take it that the *nota accusativi* makes דורו an object. So דורו designates the younger generation that is neglected by the older 'we'. This interpretation opens the possibility to understand למו in v. 8bB as a normal plural, with $\mathfrak{T}$, α, σ, θ. It is not correct, we believe, to invoke the testimony of $\mathfrak{V}$ and $\mathfrak{S}$ here (so Oswalt, 390, n. 16), because the singular – which is possible, but rare – obviously fitted the Christian exegesis.

[11]The antecedent is דורו.

[12]See the preceding footnotes. It is incorrect to state that עמי excludes a collective interpretation (so Hermisson, "Das vierte Gottesknechtslied", 8, n. 30). It happens more often that the prophet differentiates subtly between himself and the sinners who nevertheless remain 'his' people. Cf. p. 123, n. 16.

[13]It is not necessary to read ויתנו. See Waltke, O'Connor, §4.4.2.

[14]There is no need to emend $\mathfrak{M}$. Next to רשעים, עשיר must be a collective body. Because they are said to have sinned they seem to belong to the group of unfaithful

עַל לֹא־חָמָס עָשָׂה	9bA	Although he had done no violence,
{$\mathfrak{G}^{S}$} וְלֹא מִרְמָה בְּפִיו׃	9bB	and there was no deceit in his mouth,
וַיהוָה חָפֵץ דַּכְּאוֹ הֶחֱלִי	10aC	yet the LORD wanted to crush him, he made him ill.[15]

$1\mathfrak{Q}^{a}$ indentation – $\mathfrak{G}^{A}$ ___________________

C.i.1 (Isa. 53:10b–c)

אִם־תָּשִׂים אָשָׁם נַפְשׁוֹ	10bA	If you make his life[16] a guilt offering,
{$\mathfrak{G}^{S}$} יִרְאֶה זֶרַע יַאֲרִיךְ יָמִים	10cA	he will see offspring, will prolong (his) days,
וְחֵפֶץ יְהוָה בְּיָדוֹ יִצְלָח׃	10cB	and what the LORD wants will succeed by his hand.

Israelites who confess their sins in vv. 5, 6, 8, 11, 12. See also Isa. 48:22; 55:7. The Murashu archives prove that some Israelites became very rich in Babylonia, be it that they had to conform, to some extent at least, to Babylonian religious practice (theophoric naming for example). The attested verse-line parallelism between the roots רשע and עשר confirms that no emendation is required here, cf. Jer. 5:26-27 (also noted by W.L. Holladay, *Jeremiah*, vol. 1, Philadelphia 1986, 198); Mic. 6:11-12.

[15] $1\mathfrak{Q}^{a}$ ויחללהו is an obvious adaptation to v. 5 which should not be followed.

[16] The restoration of the major division point between v. 10a and v. 10b, further argued below pp. 564-5, removes some of the age-old problems in connection with the translation and interpretation of this colon. It has always been unlikely that תשים would be a rare case of a 3rd person masculine *tqtl*-imperfect, despite the fact that such forms have been discovered in Ugaritic (so H.J. van Dijk, "Does Third Masculine Singular TAQTUL Exist in Hebrew?", *VT* 19 (1969), 440-7 (442-3), and others). Or that the feminine נפש would be the subject of the verb (so Koole, 258). Because of נפשו in v. 12 it is certain that it must be the object and that it means 'life' (see for this meaning *HALAT*, 673). This is also the most satisfactory translation for נפשו in v. 11. It would be irrational to defend different meanings for נפשו in three consecutive verses.

As a result, only the 2nd person masculine is a viable option for תשים. This has often been rejected because of the harsh transition from 3rd to 2nd person masculine. However, such sudden transitions are common in Second Isaiah. They often mark the beginning of a new strophe and the dividers we found in $1\mathfrak{Q}^{a}$ and $\mathfrak{G}^{A}$ argue in favour of a new start at this point. Elsewhere in Second Isaiah שים with double accusative and God as the subject means "make X Y, change X (1st acc.) into Y (2nd acc.)" (Isa. 50:2; 51:10) and it is in this manner that 2 Cor. 5:21 renders the phrase: τὸν μὴ γνόντα ἁμαρτίαν ὑπὲρ ἡμῶν ἁμαρτίαν ἐποίησεν (cf. Lev. 5:17; $\mathfrak{G}$ often translates the Hebrew אשם by ἁμαρτία).

Therefore we are of the opinion that the prophet asks God to accept the sorry life of the servant as the guilt-offering required because of Israels sins (see v. 7). The canticle parallelism with v. 12 shows that Second Isaiah gives a new interpretation of the law here: the sins (חטא) of the Israelites made an enormous אשם necessary (cf. Lev. 5:5-7, 15, 17-18; 19:22), but God might be willing to accept the suffering and even death of Israel's innocent youth instead. By this act of grace God will allow them to live on, as the following cola clearly express. Only the interpretation of the servant as a corporate personality can account for both his death (vv. 8b, 9a) and his future prosperous life (52:13, 15; 53:10c, 12a).

C.i.2 (Isa. 53:11)

מֵעֲמַל נַפְשׁוֹ יִרְאֶה	11aA	After the distress of his life he will see,[17]
יִשְׂבָּע בְּדַעְתּוֹ	11aB	and will be satisfied by his knowledge.
יַצְדִּיק {צַדִּיק} עַבְדִּי לָרַבִּים	11bA	My servant {a righteous one}[18] will justify[19] many,
{<ס>$\mathfrak{G}^S$} וַעֲוֺנֹתָם הוּא יִסְבֹּל׃	11bB	and it is he who will[20] carry their iniquities.

C.i.3 (Isa. 53:12)

לָכֵן אֲחַלֶּק־לוֹ בָרַבִּים	12aA	Therefore I will give him a share with[21] the many,
וְאֶת־עֲצוּמִים יְחַלֵּק שָׁלָל	12aB	and with mighty ones he will share the spoil,
תַּחַת אֲשֶׁר הֶעֱרָה לַמָּוֶת נַפְשׁוֹ	12bA	because he exposed his life to death,
וְאֶת־פֹּשְׁעִים נִמְנָה	12bB	and was counted among the transgressors,

---

[17] The addition of אור in 𝔊 and several Qumran scrolls is of an exegetical nature and should not be followed, even though it still has supporters (e.g. Oswalt, 399, n. 43). Although the addition might be an expression of the conviction that the exaltation of the servant will take place in the hereafter (cf. Job 33:28-30 and K. Spronk, *Beatific Afterlife in Ancient Israel and in the Ancient Near East* (AOAT, 219), Neukirchen 1986, 19-20), we prefer a different explanation. The pair ראה || ידע or דעת is common in Second Isaiah (see the Index) and this provides a solid basis for interpreting the text without having recourse to emendation: the servant will gain insight (|| knowledge). The ancient interpreters (correctly) connected this with the spiritual blindness of the servant described in 42:18-20 and consequently they felt that they should clarify the difficult text of 53:11 by adding the word אור from 42:16.

[18] We regard this as a dittography or explanatory gloss. With A. Gelston, "Some Notes on Second Isaiah", *VT* 21 (1971), 517-27, and many others.

[19] The rendering "he will show himself to be righteous" (e.g. Beuken, 192) is not commendable for the following reasons: 1. The servant *is* righteous (v. 9b). 2. This rendering does not balance v. 11bB. 3. The only other instance of צדק Hiphil in Second Isaiah means "to justify, put in the right" (Isa. 50:8, with ℭ and F.V. Reiterer, *Gerechtigkeit als Heil*, Graz 1976, 111-4). In itself this need not imply vicariousness, but v. 5b and v. 12b do suggest it was meant as such and it was interpreted in this manner by the apostle Paul, Rom. 5:15, 19; 1 Cor. 15:3; 2 Cor. 5:14-15, 21; cf. O. Hofius, "Das vierte Gottesknechtlied in den Briefen des Neuen Testaments", in: B. Janowski, P. Stuhlmacher (eds.), *Der leidende Gottesknecht: Jesaja 53 und seine Wirkungsgeschichte*, Tübingen 1996, 107-27 (122-3). It is questionable, however, whether Paul's exegesis may be called "innovative", as Hofius states in line with many others. Cf. J.W. van Henten, *The Maccabean Martyrs as Saviours of the Jewish People: A Study of 2 an 4 Maccabees*, Leiden 1997, 160-3; J.C. de Moor, "The Targumic Background of Mark 12,1-12: The Parable of the Wicked Tenants", *JSJ* 29 (1998), 63-80.

[20] Both the preceding cola and the perfect סבלם in v.4 suggest a future tense here.

[21] Hardly anything else. The parallel חלק את must be explained after Prov. 16:9. See also את פשעים in v. 12b and the distant parallel את־רשעים || את־עשיר in v. 9.

וְהוּא חֵטְא־רַבִּים נָשָׂא 12bC and it was he who has borne the sins of many,

וְלַפֹּשְׁעִים יַפְגִּיעַ׃ 12bD and will continue to intercede for transgressors.[22]

ס <פ> – 1𝔔^{ab} – 4𝔔^{bd} – 𝔊^{SBAQ} – 𝔖^{abcde} ________________

13.2 Isaiah 52:13–53:12 – Delimitation of Cola

COLON 52:13aA:

הִנֵּה יַשְׂכִּיל עַבְדִּי 13aA Behold, my servant will be successful,

With: 𝔐 (2) – 𝔊^{SQ} – 𝔖^{d}

Discussion: The majority of 𝔖 manuscripts we collated have a point after ירום which is a serious option because derivatives of the roots שׂכל and רום occur in verse-line parallelism in Job 17:4. So the verbs might stand in colon parallelism here, balancing the pair נשׂא || גבה. Moreover, two nice pairs of grammatical parallelism would come into existence, twice a *yqtl* balanced by twice a *wqtl*. And finally it has to be observed that in Zech. 9:4 and Ps. 7:15 too the first colon after הנה has a *yqtl* and the second colon starts with *wqtl*.

Nevertheless we believe that the isolated 𝔖^{d} which supports 𝔐, 𝔊^{SQ} and ℭ has preserved the correct colometry. See our comment on the next colon.

COLON 52:13aB:

יָרוּם וְנִשָּׂא וְגָבַהּ מְאֹד׃ 13aB he shall be exalted and lifted up, and shall be very high.

With: 𝔐 (1) – 𝔊^{SQ} – 𝔖^{abcde}

Colon parallelism: רום || נשׂא; נשׂא || גבה.

Discussion: The semantically very strong and well-attested colon parallelism argues in favour of this colometry. Threefold colon parallelism is not uncommon.[1] The three verbs describing the servant's future exaltation in this colon are used in apparent contrast to the three verbs describing his sorry fate in 53:4bB.

---

[22] We assume that פגע Hiphil with ב (v. 6) has a different meaning from פגע with ל which we interpret after Isa. 59:16; Jer. 15:11; 36:25; Job 36:32. Thus the imperfect יפגיע parallels יצדיק in v. 11bA. For the durative future translation of the imperfect see our rendering of Isa. 46:4.

[1] See M.C.A. Korpel, J.C. de Moor, "Fundamentals of Ugaritic and Hebrew Poetry", in: W. van der Meer, J.C. de Moor, *The Structural Analysis of Biblical and Canaanite Poetry* (JSOT.S, 74), Sheffield 1988, 6-7.

COLON 52:14aA:

כַּאֲשֶׁר שָׁמְמוּ עָלֶיךָ רַבִּים 14aA As many were left desolated because of you

With: $\mathfrak{M}$ (5) – $\mathfrak{G}^{SQ}$ – S^{abcde}

COLON 52:14aB:

כֵּן־מָשְׁחַת* מֵאִישׁ מַרְאֵהוּ 14aB – his appearance was so marred, beyond human semblance,

With: $\mathfrak{M}$ (2) – $\mathfrak{G}^{SQ}$ – S^{abcde}

COLON 52:14aC:

וְתֹאֲרוֹ מִבְּנֵי אָדָם׃ 14aC and his looks beyond that of sons of men –

With: $\mathfrak{M}$ (1) – $\mathfrak{G}^{SQ}$ – S^{abcde}

COLON 52:15aA:

כֵּן יַזֶּה גּוֹיִם רַבִּים 15aA so shall he make many nations jump up;

With: $\mathfrak{M}$ (5) – $\mathfrak{G}^{SQ}$ – S^{abcd}, S^{e} subordinate punctuation.

COLON 52:15aB:

עָלָיו יִקְפְּצוּ מְלָכִים פִּיהֶם 15aB kings shall shut their mouths because of him.

With: $\mathfrak{M}$ (2) – $\mathfrak{G}^{SQ}$, major division marker in $\mathfrak{G}^{A}$ – S^{abcde}

COLON 52:15bA:

כִּי אֲשֶׁר לֹא־סֻפַּר לָהֶם רָאוּ 15bA For that which was never told them they see

With: $\mathfrak{M}$ (5) – $\mathfrak{G}^{SQ}$ – S^{abcde}

Colon parallelism: Roots ספר || ראה.

COLON 52:15bB:

וַאֲשֶׁר לֹא־שָׁמְעוּ הִתְבּוֹנָנוּ׃ 15bB and that which they had never heard they understand.

With: $\mathfrak{M}$ (1), major division markers in Qumran and in some Masoretic manuscripts – $\mathfrak{G}^{SBAQ}$ (major division markers in all manuscripts) – S^{abcde}

Colon parallelism: שמע || בין.

COLON 53:1aA:

מִי הֶאֱמִין לִשְׁמֻעָתֵנוּ 1aA Who believes what we have heard?

With: $\mathfrak{M}$ (2) – $\mathfrak{G}^{SQ}$ – $\mathfrak{S}^{abcde}$
Colon parallelism: אמן || שמע, referring to the disbelief in the message of the prophet and his followers.[2]

COLON 53:1aB:

וּזְרוֹעַ יְהוָה עַל־מִי נִגְלָתָה׃ 1aA And to whom has the arm of the LORD been revealed?

With: $\mathfrak{M}$ (1) – $\mathfrak{G}^{SQ}$ – $\mathfrak{S}^{abcde}$

COLON 53:2aA:

וַיַּעַל כַּיּוֹנֵק לְפָנָיו 2aA For he grew up before him like a fresh shoot,

With: $\mathfrak{M}$ (7) – $\mathfrak{G}^{Q}$ – $\mathfrak{S}^{abcd}$, $\mathfrak{S}^{e}$ subordinated punctuation.

COLON 53:2aB:

וְכַשֹּׁרֶשׁ מֵאֶרֶץ צִיָּה 2aB and like a root out of dry ground.

With: $\mathfrak{M}$ (5) – $\mathfrak{G}^{SQ}$ – $\mathfrak{S}^{abcde}$

COLON 53:2bA:

לֹא־תֹאַר לוֹ וְלֹא הָדָר 2bA He had no (good) looks, and no splendour,

With: $\mathfrak{M}$ (2) – $\mathfrak{G}^{SQ}$ – $\mathfrak{S}^{abcde}$
Colon parallelism: תאר || הדר (unique).

COLON 53:2bB:

וְנִרְאֵהוּ וְלֹא־מַרְאֶה וְנֶחְמְדֵהוּ׃ 2bB that we should look at him, and no (fine) appearance that we should desire him.

With: $\mathfrak{M}$ (1) – $\mathfrak{G}^{SQ}$ – $\mathfrak{S}^{abcde}$
Colon parallelism: Grammatical colon parallelism; rhyme.
Discussion: $\mathfrak{G}^{SQ}$ also have a dividing point after ונראהו where $\mathfrak{M}$ has a conjunctive accent. $\mathfrak{S}$ does not support $\mathfrak{G}^{SQ}$. Possibly the Greek interpunctors were misled by the enjambment. But since similar ultra-short cola follow in v. 3, it is more likely that they wanted to add extra dramatic emphasis to these verses.

COLON 53:3aA:

נִבְזֶה וַחֲדַל אִישִׁים 3aA He was despised and rejected by men;

With: $\mathfrak{M}$ (5); $\mathfrak{G}^{SAQ}$, major division markers in $\mathfrak{G}^{AQ}$ – $\mathfrak{S}^{abcde}$

[2] One of the subtle references to the fact that the prophet sees himself in the role of a second Moses, cf. Exod. 4:1, 8-9, 31; 19:9.

Colon parallelism: בזה || חדל אישים (unique).
Discussion: 𝔊^{SQ} have an extra dividing point after נבזה which is weakly supported by 𝔐 (Pashṭa, No. 10) and contradicted by 𝔖.

COLON 53:3aB:

אִ֣ישׁ מַכְאֹב֖וֹת וִיד֣וּעַ חֹ֑לִי 3aB a man of sorrows, and acquainted with illness;

With: 𝔐 (2) – 𝔊^{SQ} – 𝔖^{abcde}
Colon parallelism: מכאב || חלי.
Discussion: 𝔊^{SQ} also have a point after מכאבות (𝔐 Ṭiphḥa, No. 8) but this is not supported by 𝔖 and the colon parallelism argues in favour of 𝔐.

COLON 53:3bA:

וּכְמַסְתֵּ֤ר פָּנִים֙ מִמֶּ֔נּוּ 3bA and as one who causes people to hide their faces from him

With: 𝔐 (5) – 𝔊^{SQ} – 𝔖^{a}, 𝔖^{bcde} subordinate punctuation.

COLON 53:3bB:

נִבְזֶ֖ה וְלֹ֥א חֲשַׁבְנֻֽהוּ׃ 3bB he was despised, and we thought nothing of him.

With: 𝔐 (1); 𝔊^{SQ}, 𝔊^{S} major division marker (only a paragraphos, probably by a second hand) – 𝔖^{abcde}, 𝔖^{e} with a major division marker.
Colon parallelism: בזה || לא חשב (unique).

COLON 53:4aA:

אָכֵ֤ן חֳלָיֵ֙נוּ֙ ה֣וּא נָשָׂ֔א 4aA Yet it was he who has borne our illnesses,

With: 𝔐 (5) – 𝔊^{SQ} – 𝔖^{bcde}, 𝔖^{a} subordinate punctuation.

COLON 53:4aB:

וּמַכְאֹבֵ֖ינוּ סְבָלָ֑ם 4aB and carried our sorrows;

With: 𝔐 (2) – 𝔊^{SQ} – 𝔖^{abcde}

COLON 53:4bA:

וַאֲנַ֣חְנוּ חֲשַׁבְנֻ֔הוּ נָג֛וּעַ 4bA but we thought of him as stricken,

With: 𝔐 (12) – 𝔊^{S} – 𝔖^{abcde}
Discussion: 𝔐 stands alone in dividing after חשבנו (Zaqeph Qaṭon, No. 5). Apparently the Masoretes wanted to keep the three passive participles together.

COLON 53:4bB:

מֻכֵּ֥ה אֱלֹהִ֖ים וּמְעֻנֶּֽה׃ 4bB smitten by God, and afflicted.

With: $\mathfrak{M}$ (1) – $\mathfrak{G}^{SQ}$ – $\mathfrak{S}^{abcde}$
Colon parallelism: roots נכה || ענה.

COLON 53:5aA:

וְהוּא֙ מְחֹלָ֣ל מִפְּשָׁעֵ֔נוּ 5aA But he was the one pierced because of our transgressions,

With: $\mathfrak{M}$ (5) – $\mathfrak{G}^{SQ}$ – $\mathfrak{S}^{a}$, $\mathfrak{S}^{bcd}$ subordinate punctuation.

COLON 53:5aB:

מְדֻכָּ֖א מֵעֲוֺנֹתֵ֑ינוּ 5aB crushed because of our iniquities;

With: $\mathfrak{M}$ (2) – $\mathfrak{G}^{SQ}$ – $\mathfrak{S}^{abde}$, $\mathfrak{S}^{c}$ subordinate punctuation.

COLON 53:5bA:

מוּסַ֤ר שְׁלוֹמֵ֙נוּ֙ עָלָ֔יו 5bA upon him was the chastisement that brings us peace,

With: $\mathfrak{M}$ (5) – $\mathfrak{G}^{SQ}$ – $\mathfrak{S}^{abcde}$

COLON 53:5bB:

וּבַחֲבֻרָת֖וֹ נִרְפָּא־לָֽנוּ׃ 5bB and with his wounds we are healed.

With: $\mathfrak{M}$ (1) – $\mathfrak{G}^{SQ}$ – $\mathfrak{S}^{abcd}$, $\mathfrak{S}^{e}$ subordinate punctuation.

COLON 53:6aA:

כֻּלָּ֙נוּ֙ כַּצֹּ֣אן תָּעִ֔ינוּ 6aA All of us went astray, like sheep,

With: $\mathfrak{M}$ (5) – $\mathfrak{G}^{SQ}$, major division marker in $\mathfrak{G}^{S}$ – $\mathfrak{S}^{abcd}$

COLON 53:6aB:

אִ֥ישׁ לְדַרְכּ֖וֹ פָּנִ֑ינוּ 6aB we have turned every one to his own way.

With: $\mathfrak{M}$ (2), major division marker in $1\mathfrak{Q}^{a}$ – $\mathfrak{G}^{SQ}$ – $\mathfrak{S}^{abcde}$

COLON 53:6bA:

וַֽיהוָה֙ הִפְגִּ֣יעַ בּ֔וֹ 6bA Yet the LORD inflicted on him

With: $\mathfrak{M}$ (5) – $\mathfrak{G}^{Q}$
Discussion: The weak attestation of the colon division should be ascribed to the continuing sentence.

COLON 53:6bB:

אֶת עֲוֺן כֻּלָּנוּ׃ 6bB the iniquity of us all.

With: $\mathfrak{M}$ (1) – $\mathfrak{G}^{SQ}$, major dividing mark in $\mathfrak{G}^{Q}$ – $\mathfrak{S}^{abcde}$

COLON 53:7aA:

נִגַּשׂ וְהוּא נַעֲנֶה 7aA It was exacted, and he was the one afflicted,

With: $\mathfrak{M}$ (9) – $\mathfrak{G}^{SQ}$
Discussion: Despite the fact that $\mathfrak{M}$ and $\mathfrak{S}$ do not seem to support this division we believe that the repetitive parallelism between v. 7aB and 7bC – which is undoubtedly a colon in its own right – justifies the assumption that also v. 7aA is a separate colon, as $\mathfrak{G}^{SQ}$ have understood it to be.

COLON 53:7aB:

וְלֹא יִפְתַּח־פִּיו 7aB yet he opened not his mouth;

With: $\mathfrak{M}$ (3) – $\mathfrak{G}^{SAQ}$, major dividing marks in $\mathfrak{G}^{SA}$ – $\mathfrak{S}^{abcde}$

COLON 53:7bA:

כַּשֶּׂה לַטֶּבַח יוּבָל 7bA Like a young ram he was led to the slaughter,

With: $\mathfrak{M}$ (5) – $\mathfrak{G}^{SQ}$ – $\mathfrak{S}^{abcde}$

COLON 53:7bB:

וּכְרָחֵל לִפְנֵי גֹזְזֶיהָ נֶאֱלָמָה 7bB and like an ewe that is dumb before its shearers –

With: $\mathfrak{M}$ (2) – $\mathfrak{G}^{SQ}$ – $\mathfrak{S}^{b}$
Discussion: For the Zaqeph Gadol (No. 6) with וכרחל see p. 31.

COLON 53:7bC:

וְלֹא יִפְתַּח פִּיו׃ 7bC and he opened not his mouth.

With: $\mathfrak{M}$ (1) – $\mathfrak{G}^{SQ}$ – $\mathfrak{S}^{abcde}$

COLON 53:8aA:

מֵעֹצֶר וּמִמִּשְׁפָּט לֻקָּח 8aA Without restraint and without arbitration he was taken away,

With: $\mathfrak{M}$ (5) – $\mathfrak{G}^{SQ}$ – $\mathfrak{S}^{abcde}$
Discussion: $\mathfrak{G}^{Q}$ and $\mathfrak{S}^{e}$ have an extra point after מעצר where $\mathfrak{M}$ has a conjunctive accent (No. 20). Nothing in the text recommends this division.

COLON 53:8aB:

וְאֶת־דּוֹרוֹ מִי יְשׂוֹחֵחַ 8aB and as for his generation, who cared?

With: $\mathfrak{M}$ (2) – $\mathfrak{G}^{SQ}$ – $\mathfrak{S}^{abcde}$

COLON 53:8bA:

כִּי נִגְזַר מֵאֶרֶץ חַיִּים 8bA For it was cut off out of the land of the living,

With: $\mathfrak{M}$ (5) – $\mathfrak{G}^{SQ}$ – $\mathfrak{S}^{b}$, $\mathfrak{S}^{acde}$ subordinate punctuation.

COLON 53:8bB:

מִפֶּשַׁע עַמִּי נֶגַע לָמוֹ׃ 8bB because of the transgression of my people the blow was on them.

With: $\mathfrak{M}$ (1), major division markers in $1\mathfrak{Q}^{a}$ – $\mathfrak{G}^{SQ}$, major division marker in $\mathfrak{G}^{A}$ – $\mathfrak{S}^{abcde}$

COLON 53:9aA:

וַיִּתֵּן אֶת־רְשָׁעִים קִבְרוֹ 9aA And they made his grave with the wicked

With: $\mathfrak{M}$ (5) – $\mathfrak{G}^{SQ}$

Discussion: $\mathfrak{S}$ does not support $\mathfrak{M}$ and $\mathfrak{G}$.

COLON 53:9aB:

וְאֶת־עָשִׁיר בְּמֹתָיו 9aB and with the rich in his death.

With: $\mathfrak{M}$ (2) – $\mathfrak{G}^{SQ}$ – $\mathfrak{S}^{abcde}$

COLON 53:9bA:

עַל לֹא־חָמָס עָשָׂה 9bA Although he had done no violence,

With: $\mathfrak{M}$ (5) – $\mathfrak{G}^{SQ}$

Discussion: $\mathfrak{S}$ does not support $\mathfrak{M}$ and $\mathfrak{G}$.

COLON 53:9bB:

וְלֹא מִרְמָה בְּפִיו׃ 9bB and there was no deceit in his mouth,

With: $\mathfrak{M}$ (1) – $\mathfrak{G}^{SQ}$, major division marker in $\mathfrak{G}^{S}$ – $\mathfrak{S}^{abcde}$

COLON 53:10aC:

וַיהוָה חָפֵץ דַּכְּאוֹ הֶחֱלִי 10aC yet the LORD wanted to crush him, he made him ill.

With: $\mathfrak{M}$ (5), major division marker in $1\mathfrak{Q}^{a}$ – $\mathfrak{G}^{SAQ}$, major division marker in $\mathfrak{G}^{A}$ – $\mathfrak{S}^{abcde}$

Colon parallelism: דכא || חלה (unique, but see vv. 3, 5).

COLON 53:10bA:

אִם־תָּשִׂים אָשָׁם נַפְשׁוֹ 10bA If you make his life a guilt offering,

With: 𝔐 (5) – $\mathfrak{S}^{abcde}$
Discussion: $\mathfrak{G}^{SQ}$ divide after אשם which is unlikely because נפש is feminine which does not go well with the masculine יראה when the feminine subject precedes the verbal predicate.

COLON 53:10cA:

יִרְאֶה זֶרַע יַאֲרִיךְ יָמִים 10cA he will see offspring, will prolong (his) days,

With: 𝔐 (2); $\mathfrak{G}^{SQ}$, major division marker in $\mathfrak{G}^{S}$ – $\mathfrak{S}^{abcde}$
Colon parallelism: ראה זרע || ארך ימים.

COLON 53:10cB:

וְחֵפֶץ יְהוָה בְּיָדוֹ יִצְלָח׃ 10cB and what the LORD wants will succeed by his hand.

With: 𝔐 (1) – $\mathfrak{G}^{Q}$ – $\mathfrak{S}^{abcde}$

COLON 53:11aA:

מֵעֲמַל נַפְשׁוֹ יִרְאֶה 11aA After the distress of his life he will see,

With: $\mathfrak{G}^{SQ}$ – $\mathfrak{S}^{acde}$
Discussion: $\mathfrak{G}^{SQ}$ have a dividing point after נפשו. 𝔐 and 𝔖 do not support this. 𝔐 has a conjunctive accent (No. 19) with יראה and divides only after ישבע. Apparently the Masoretes understood the two verbs as a *hendiaduoin*.[3] However, the pair ראה || שבע is attested in verseline parallelism[4] and this would seem to confirm the division of the other ancient witnesses. The same division is found in BHS and most modern commentaries.

COLON 53:11aB:

יִשְׂבָּע בְּדַעְתּוֹ 11aB and will be satisfied by his knowledge.

With: 𝔐 (7) – $\mathfrak{G}^{SQ}$
Discussion: 𝔖 does not support this division. See our comment on the preceding colon.

---

[3] This division is also found in Tanna de R. Eliyahu Rabba, 25:2.
[4] Jer. 44:17; Ps. 91:16.

COLON 53:11bA:

יַצְדִּיק {צַדִּיק} עַבְדִּי לָרַבִּים 11bA My servant {a righteous one} will justify many,

With: $\mathfrak{M}$ (2) – $\mathfrak{G}^{SQ}$ – $\mathfrak{S}^{abcde}$
Colon parallelism: None.[5]
Discussion: Even though an impressive number of ancient witnesses has a divider after צדיק ($\mathfrak{G}^{S}$, $\mathfrak{S}^{abcde}$), the very paraphrastic nature of their renderings counsels against accepting their division. Moreover, $\mathfrak{M}$ (Tevir, No. 12) and $\mathfrak{G}^{Q}$ do not support it, whereas all agree with regard to the end of the verse.

COLON 53:11bB:

וַעֲוֺנֹתָם הוּא יִסְבֹּל׃ 11bB and it is he who will bear their iniquities.

With: $\mathfrak{M}$ (1), major division marker in $1\mathfrak{Q}^{a}$ – $\mathfrak{G}^{SQ}$, major division marker in $\mathfrak{G}^{S}$ – $\mathfrak{S}^{abcde}$
Colon parallelism: None.
Discussion: $\mathfrak{G}^{Q}$ and $\mathfrak{S}^{a}$ have an extra dividing point after ועונתם which is not supported by the other witnesses. Probably it equals the Ṭiphḥa (No. 8) of $\mathfrak{M}$ which serves to mark off the *casus pendens*.

COLON 53:12aA:

לָכֵן אֲחַלֶּק־לוֹ בָרַבִּים 12aA Therefore I will give him a share with the many,

With: $\mathfrak{M}$ (7) – $\mathfrak{G}^{SQ}$ – $\mathfrak{S}^{a}$, $\mathfrak{S}^{bcde}$ subordinate punctuation.

COLON 53:12aB:

וְאֶת־עֲצוּמִים יְחַלֵּק שָׁלָל 12aB and with mighty ones he will share the spoil,

With: $\mathfrak{M}$ (3) – $\mathfrak{G}^{SQ}$ – $\mathfrak{S}^{abcde}$

COLON 53:12bA:

תַּחַת אֲשֶׁר הֶעֱרָה לַמָּוֶת נַפְשׁוֹ 12bA because he exposed his life to death,

With: $\mathfrak{M}$ (5) – $\mathfrak{G}^{SQ}$ – $\mathfrak{S}^{abcde}$ all subordinate punctuation.
Discussion: For the Revia‘ (No. 7) with תחת see p. 31.

COLON 53:12bB:

וְאֶת־פֹּשְׁעִים נִמְנָה 12bB and was counted among the transgressors.

[5] We regard צדיק as a dittography or gloss.

With: 𝔐 (2) – 𝔊^{SQ} – 𝔖^{acde}, 𝔖^{b} subordinate punctuation.

COLON 53:12bC:

וְהוּא חֵטְא־רַבִּים נָשָׂא 12bC Yes, it was he who has borne the sins of many,

With: 𝔐 (5) – 𝔊^{SQ} – 𝔖^{abcd} all subordinate punctuation.

COLON 53:12bD:

וְלַפֹּשְׁעִים יַפְגִּיעַ׃ 12bD and for transgressors he will intercede.

With: 𝔐 (1), major division markers in 1𝔔^{a}, 1𝔔^{b} and 4𝔔^{bd} – 𝔊^{SBAQ}, major division markers in all – 𝔖^{abcde}, major division markers in all.

13.3 Isaiah 52:13–53:12 – Delimitation of Verse-lines

VERSE–LINE: 52:13a:

הִנֵּה יַשְׂכִּיל עַבְדִּי 13aA Behold, my servant will be successful,
יָרוּם וְנִשָּׂא וְגָבַהּ מְאֹד׃ 13aB he shall be exalted and lifted up, and shall be very high.

𝔐 distinctive accents: 2 – 1.
Stresses: 3 + 4.
Verse-line parallelism: שׂכל || רום; שׂכל || נשׂא (unique); שׂכל || גבה (unique); grammatical parallelism.

VERSE–LINE: 52:14a:

כַּאֲשֶׁר שָׁמְמוּ עָלֶיךָ רַבִּים 14aA As many were left desolated for you
כֵּן־מִשְׁחַת* מֵאִישׁ מַרְאֵהוּ 14aB – his appearance was so marred, beyond human semblance,
וְתֹאֲרוֹ מִבְּנֵי אָדָם׃ 14aC and his looks beyond those of sons of men –

𝔐 distinctive accents: 5 – 2 – 1.
Stresses: 4 + 3 + 3.
Verse-line parallelism: כאשר || כן; roots שמם || שחת; מן || מן; איש || בן אדם; מראה || תאר; ־הו || ־ו.

VERSE–LINE: 52:15a:

כֵּן יַזֶּה גּוֹיִם רַבִּים 15aA so shall he make many nations jump up;
עָלָיו יִקְפְּצוּ מְלָכִים פִּיהֶם 15aB kings shall shut their mouths because of him.

𝔐 distinctive accents: 5 – 2.
Stresses: 4 + 4.
Verse-line parallelism: גוי || מלך.

VERSE–LINE: 52:15b:

כִּי אֲשֶׁר לֹא־סֻפַּר לָהֶם רָאוּ	15bA	For that which was never told them they see
וַאֲשֶׁר לֹא־שָׁמְעוּ הִתְבּוֹנָנוּ׃	15bB	and that which they had never heard they understand.

𝔐 distinctive accents: 5 – 1.
Stresses: 5 + 3.
Verse-line parallelism: אשר || אשר; לא || לא; ספר || שׁמע; ראה || בין; grammatical parallelism; rhyme.

VERSE–LINE: 53:1a:

מִי הֶאֱמִין לִשְׁמֻעָתֵנוּ	1aA	Who believes what we have heard?
וּזְרוֹעַ יְהוָה עַל־מִי נִגְלָתָה׃	1aB	And to whom has the arm of the LORD been revealed?

𝔐 distinctive accents: 2 – 1.
Stresses: 3 + 4.
Verse-line parallelism: מי || מי; roots שׁמע || גלה.

VERSE–LINE: 53:2a:

וַיַּעַל כַּיּוֹנֵק לְפָנָיו	2aA	For he grew up before him like a fresh shoot,
וְכַשֹּׁרֶשׁ מֵאֶרֶץ צִיָּה	2aB	and like a root out of dry ground.

𝔐 distinctive accents: 7 – 5.
Stresses: 3 + 3.
Verse-line parallelism: כ || כ; יונק || שׁרשׁ.
Discussion: According to the Masoretes v. 2 consists of a tricolon and a unicolon. The strong parallelism in v. 2a on the one hand, and in v. 2b on the other,[1] makes it more natural to divide v. 2 into two bicola. Ellipsis connects the cola. Apparently the Masoretes wanted to keep the cola with the 3rd person masc. sg. together and considered the change to the 1st person common plur. as a sign of the transition to a second verse-line.

VERSE–LINE: 53:2b:

לֹא־תֹאַר לוֹ וְלֹא הָדָר	2bA	He had no (good) looks and no splendour,
וְנִרְאֵהוּ וְלֹא־מַרְאֶה וְנֶחְמְדֵהוּ׃	2bB	that we should look at him, and no (fine) appearance that we should desire him.

𝔐 distinctive accents: 2 – 1.
Stresses: 4 + 3.

[1] Especially the parallelism between תאר || מראה in v. 2b which hardly can be distributed over two verse-lines because the two words always – except for Isa. 53:2b – occur in colon parallelism (see Index of Parallel Words).

Verse-line parallelism: לא || לא; ־ו || ־הו || ־הו; תאר || מראה; roots הדר || חמד.
Discussion: For v. 2b as a bicolon see our comment on v. 2a.

VERSE–LINE: 53:3a:

נִבְזֶה֙ וַחֲדַ֣ל אִישִׁ֔ים	3aA	He was despised and rejected by men;
אִ֥ישׁ מַכְאֹב֖וֹת וִיד֣וּעַ חֹ֑לִי	3aB	a man of sorrows, and acquainted with illness;

𝔐 distinctive accents: 5 – 2.
Stresses: 3 + 4.
Verse-line parallelism: איש || איש.

VERSE–LINE: 53:3b:

וּכְמַסְתֵּ֤ר פָּנִים֙ מִמֶּ֔נּוּ	3bA	and as one who causes people to hide their faces from him
נִבְזֶ֖ה וְלֹ֥א חֲשַׁבְנֻֽהוּ׃	3bB	he was despised, and we thought nothing of him.

𝔐 distinctive accents: 5 – 1.
Stresses: 3 + 3.
Verse-line parallelism: סתר פנים || בזה; ־ו || ־הו.

VERSE–LINE: 53:4a:

אָכֵ֤ן חֳלָיֵ֙נוּ֙ ה֣וּא נָשָׂ֔א	4aA	Yet it was he who has borne our illnesses,
וּמַכְאֹבֵ֖ינוּ סְבָלָ֑ם	4aB	and carried our sorrows;

𝔐 distinctive accents: 5 – 2.
Stresses: 4 + 2.
Verse-line parallelism: חלי || מכאוב; ־נו || ־נו; נשא || סבל; rhyme.

VERSE–LINE: 53:4b:

וַאֲנַ֣חְנוּ חֲשַׁבְנֻ֔הוּ נָג֛וּעַ	4bA	but we thought of him as stricken,
מֻכֵּ֥ה אֱלֹהִ֖ים וּמְעֻנֶּֽה׃	4bB	smitten by God, and afflicted.

𝔐 distinctive accents: 12 – 1.
Stresses: 3 + 3.
Verse-line parallelism: נגע || נכה (unique); נגע || ענה (unique).
Discussion: Ellipsis connects the cola.

VERSE–LINE: 53:5a:

וְהוּא֙ מְחֹלָ֣ל מִפְּשָׁעֵ֔נוּ	5aA	But he was the one pierced because of our transgressions,
מְדֻכָּ֖א מֵעֲוֺנֹתֵ֑ינוּ	5aB	crushed because of our iniquities;

𝔐 distinctive accents: 5 – 2.
Stresses: 3 + 2.
Verse-line parallelism: roots חלל || דכא; מן || מן; פשע || עון; ־נו || ־נו; rhyme.
Discussion: The cola are connected by ellipsis.

VERSE–LINE: 53:5b:

מוּסַ֤ר שְׁלוֹמֵ֙נוּ֙ עָלָ֔יו	5bA	upon him was the chastisement that brings us peace,
וּבַחֲבֻרָת֖וֹ נִרְפָּא־לָֽנוּ׃	5bB	and with his wounds we are healed.

𝔐 distinctive accents: 5 – 1.
Stresses: 3 + 2.
Verse-line parallelism: מוסר || חבורה (unique); שלום || רפא; ־נו || ־נו; על || ב; ־ו || ־ו.

VERSE–LINE: 53:6a:

כֻּלָּ֙נוּ֙ כַּצֹּ֣אן תָּעִ֔ינוּ	6aA	All of us went astray, like sheep,
אִ֥ישׁ לְדַרְכּ֖וֹ פָּנִ֑ינוּ	6aB	we have turned every one to his own way.

𝔐 distinctive accents: 5 – 2.
Stresses: 3 + 3.
Verse-line parallelism: כל || איש; תעה || פנה לדרכו; grammatical parallelism; rhyme.

VERSE–LINE: 53:6b:

וַֽיהוָה֙ הִפְגִּ֣יעַ בּ֔וֹ	6bA	Yet the LORD inflicted on him
אֵ֖ת עֲוֺ֥ן כֻּלָּֽנוּ׃	6bB	the iniquity of us all.

𝔐 distinctive accents: 5 – 1.
Stresses: 3 + 3.
Verse-line parallelism: None.
Discussion: No parallelism, because the sentence runs on (enjambment).

VERSE–LINE: 53:7a:

נִגַּ֨שׂ וְה֣וּא נַעֲנֶ֔ה	7aA	It was exacted, and he was the one afflicted,
וְלֹ֣א יִפְתַּח־פִּ֗יו	7aB	yet he opened not his mouth.

𝔐 distinctive accents: 9 – 3.
Stresses: 3 + 2.
Verse-line parallelism: None.
Discussion: The enjambment in this verse-line is the reason for the lack

of parallelism. 𝔐 wanted to read a tricolon, or even a quadrocolon,[2] followed by a very short unicolon. This is highly unlikely because of the repetitive ולא יפתח פיו.

VERSE–LINE: 53:7b:

כַּשֶּׂה֙ לַטֶּ֣בַח יוּבָ֔ל	7bA	Like a young ram he was led to the slaughter,
וּכְרָחֵ֕ל לִפְנֵ֥י גֹזְזֶ֖יהָ נֶאֱלָ֑מָה	7bB	and like an ewe that is dumb before its shearers –
וְלֹ֥א יִפְתַּ֖ח פִּֽיו׃	7bC	and he opened not his mouth.

𝔐 distinctive accents: 5 – 2 – 1.
Stresses: 3 + 4 + 3.
Verse-line parallelism: כ || כ; שה || רחל (unique); ל || ל; טבח || גזז; אלם || פתח פה (antithetical).

VERSE–LINE: 53:8a:

מֵעֹ֤צֶר וּמִמִּשְׁפָּט֙ לֻקָּ֔ח	8aA	Without restraint and without arbitration he was taken away,
וְאֶת־דּוֹר֖וֹ מִ֣י יְשׂוֹחֵ֑חַ	8aB	and as for his generation, who cared?

𝔐 distinctive accents: 5 – 2.
Stresses: 3 + 3.
Verse-line parallelism: עצר || שיח (unique).[3]

VERSE–LINE: 53:8b:

כִּ֤י נִגְזַר֙ מֵאֶ֣רֶץ חַיִּ֔ים	8bA	It was cut off out of the land of the living,
מִפֶּ֥שַׁע עַמִּ֖י נֶ֥גַע לָֽמוֹ׃	8bB	because of the transgression of my people the blow was on them.

𝔐 distinctive accents: 5 – 1.
Stresses: 4 + 4.
Verse-line parallelism: גזר || נגע; מן || מן.

VERSE–LINE: 53:9a:

וַיִּתֵּ֤ן אֶת־רְשָׁעִים֙ קִבְר֔וֹ	9aA	And they made his grave with the wicked
וְאֶת־עָשִׁ֖יר בְּמֹתָ֑יו	9aB	and with the rich in his death.

𝔐 distinctive accents: 5 – 2.
Stresses: 3 + 2.

---

[2]For the Segolta (No. 3) see our remarks pp. 144, 235, on 42:22a and 44:13a.
[3]See our comments p. 547, n. 10. In our opinion this verse-line describes the passivity of the older generation when their youngsters were picked up and led away to be slaughtered without proper trial. They do not try to restrain the oppressors nor do they really care.

Verse-line parallelism: את || את; רשע || עשיר; roots קבר || מות; ־ו || ־ו.

VERSE–LINE: 53:9bA–10aC:

עַל לֹא־חָמָס עָשָׂה	9bA	Although he had done no violence,
וְלֹא מִרְמָה בְּפִיו׃	9bB	and there was no deceit in his mouth,
וַיהוָה חָפֵץ דַּכְּאוֹ הֶחֱלִי	10aC	yet the LORD wanted to crush him, he made him ill.

𝔐 distinctive accents: 5 – 1 – 5.
Stresses: 3 + 3 + 4.
Verse-line parallelism: לא || לא; roots חמס || רמה; חמס || דכא (unique); חמס || חלי; roots רמה || חלה.
Discussion: We take this verse-line as a tricolon by adding the first colon of v. 10. Although it would be possible to interpret the major division markers in 1Q^{a} and 𝔊^{A} as lagging behind the division indicated by 𝔊^{S} after v. 9, three arguments speak in favour of a reversal of this argument:

1. The division after 10a is indicated in two different traditions, so it is more likely that 𝔊^{S} is anticipating the same division point as 1Q^{a} and 𝔊^{A}.

2. The resulting verse-line parallelism between חמס and חלי in Jer. 6:7, as well as the strophe parallelism between the roots דכא and מות in Ps. 143:3. See also the comparable strophe parallelism in Mic. 6:12-13.

3. The great difficulty of reconciling v. 10a with v. 10c if they belong to the same strophe.

The restoration of the division between the first and the second colon of v. 10 results in a more logic meaning of the first colon. It then contrasts with 9b. Although the servant had done no evil, the LORD nevertheless wanted to crush him. This balances v. 9a much better: just as the servant was undeservedly buried with the wicked, so God has slain him undeservedly with a mortal illness.

The new division makes the colon describing the negative will of the LORD with regard to the servant the last colon of the canticle, which is in line with the preceding canticle which also ends with a statement about the LORD's seemingly unjust treatment of his servant.

What then moved the Masoretes to take v. 10a with the next verse-lines? The answer is relatively simple: they had to comply with authoritative rabbinical teaching. Because in bBer., 5a, these cola had been grouped together, the Masoretes had to follow suit.

"Raba, in the name of R. Sahorah, in the name of R. Huna, says: If the Holy One, blessed be He, is pleased with a man, he crushes him with painful sufferings. For it is said: *And the Lord was pleased with [him, hence] he crushed him by disease.* Now, you might think that this is so even if he did not accept them with love. Therefore it is said: *To see if his soul would offer itself in restitution.* Even as the trespass-offering must be brought by consent, so also the sufferings must be endured with consent. And if he did accept them, what is his reward? *He will see his seed, prolong his days.* And more than that, *his knowledge [of the Torah] will endure with him* (v. 11) . For it is said: *The purpose of the Lord will prosper in his hand.*" (Soncino translation)

VERSE–LINE: 53:10b:

אם־תשים אשם נפשו 10bA If you make the guilt offering his life,

𝔐 distinctive accents: 5.
Stresses: 3.
Verse-line parallelism: None (unicolon).
Discussion: The change of subject (2nd p. masc.)[4] coincides with the beginning of new canticle. See our comments on the previous verse-line. Because in vv. 10cA and 10cB the servant is the subject again, we assume that these cola belong together (see below) which makes 10bA a unicolon.

VERSE–LINE: 53:10c:

יראה זרע יאריך ימים 10cA he will see offspring, will prolong (his) days,
וחפץ יהוה בידו יצלח׃ 10cB and what the LORD wants will succeed by his hand.

𝔐 distinctive accents: 2 – 1.
Stresses: 4 + 4.
Verse-line parallelism: ראה זרע || צלח;[5] ארך ימים || צלח.

[4]See p. 548.
[5]Unique, but see the comparable, opposite judgement upon king Jehoiachin of whom it is said that he will *not* succeed, and that he will be childless (although he has sons), because his offspring will not succeed to sit on the throne of David and rule in Judah (Jer. 22:30).

VERSE–LINE: 53:11a:

מֵעֲמַ֤ל נַפְשׁוֹ֙ יִרְאֶ֔ה	11aA	After the distress of his life he will see,
יִשְׂבָּ֑ע בְּדַעְתּ֗וֹ	11aB	and will be satisfied by his knowledge.

𝔐 distinctive accents: conjunctive accent – 7.
Stresses: 3 + 2.
Verse-line parallelism: ראה || שׂבע; grammatical parallelism.
Discussion: The delimitation of this verse, with sequence of accents deviating from 𝔐, is based on our delimitation of cola.

VERSE–LINE: 53:11b:

יַצְדִּ֥יק {צַדִּ֛יק} עַבְדִּ֖י לָֽרַבִּ֑ים	11bA	My servant {a righteous one} will justify many,
וַעֲוֺנֹתָ֖ם ה֥וּא יִסְבֹּֽל׃	11bB	and it is he who will carry their iniquities.

𝔐 distinctive accents: 2 – 1.
Stresses: 3 (4) + 3.
Verse-line parallelism: צדק || סבל עון;[6] grammatical parallelism.

VERSE–LINE: 53:12a:

לָכֵ֞ן אֲחַלֶּק־ל֣וֹ בָרַבִּ֗ים	12aA	Therefore I will give him a share with the many,
וְאֶת־עֲצוּמִים֮ יְחַלֵּ֣ק שָׁלָל֒	12aB	and with mighty ones he will share the spoil,

𝔐 distinctive accents: 7 – 3.
Stresses: 3 + 3.
Verse-line parallelism: חלק || חלק; רב || עצום.
Discussion: 𝔐 joins v. 12a and v. 12b, a quadrocolon.[7] In our opinion the parallelism renders a combination of v. 12bA-B with v. 12bC-D more plausible.

VERSE–LINE: 53:12b:

תַּ֗חַת אֲשֶׁ֨ר הֶעֱרָ֤ה לַמָּ֙וֶת֙ נַפְשׁ֔וֹ	12bA	because he exposed his life to death,
וְאֶת־פֹּשְׁעִ֖ים נִמְנָ֑ה	12bB	and was counted among the transgressors.
וְהוּא֙ חֵטְא־רַבִּ֣ים נָשָׂ֔א	12bC	and it was he who has borne the sins of many,
וְלַפֹּשְׁעִ֖ים יַפְגִּֽיעַ׃	12bD	and will continue to intercede for transgressors.

𝔐 distinctive accents: 5 – 2 – 5 – 1.
Stresses: 5 + 2 + 3 + 2.

---

[6]Unique. For the expression סבל עון cf. Lam. 5:7 where the younger generation complains that they have to bear the iniquities of their fathers.

[7]With regard to the position of the Segolta (No. 3) see our remarks pp. 144, 235, on 42:22a and 44:13a.

Verse-line parallelism: ערה || נשׂא; מות || פשׁע; פשׁע || חטא || פשׁע; נשׂא || פגע.
Discussion: As stated above, 𝔐 has a quadrocolon at the beginning of this strophe. We decided to take the cola starting with תחת אשׁר together as a quadrocolon for the following reasons:

1. All three cola starting with ו seem to be dependent on תחת אשׁר.
2. The strong parallelism between the four cola (see above).
3. Whoever mixes with bad company risks his life (פגע, נפשׁ, Judg. 18:25).
4. $\mathfrak{S}^{b}$ has a point after v. 12aB, but subordinate punctuation after all following cola, indicating that it at least regarded these cola as a unit.

13.4 Isaiah 52:13–53:12 – Delimitation of Strophes

STROPHE A.i.1 (Isa. 52:13)

הִנֵּה יַשְׂכִּיל עַבְדִּי	13aA	Behold, my servant will be successful,
יָרוּם וְנִשָּׂא וְגָבַהּ מְאֹד׃	13aB	he shall be exalted and lifted up, and shall be very high.

= Masoretic verse.
Separation ↑: major division markers in the textual tradition; deictic particle(s)
Separation ↓: None (one verse-line).
Strophe parallelism: None (one verse-line).

STROPHE A.i.2 (Isa. 52:14)

כַּאֲשֶׁר שָׁמְמוּ עָלֶיךָ רַבִּים	14aA	As many were left desolated for you
כֵּן־מִשְׁחַת* מֵאִישׁ מַרְאֵהוּ	14aB	– his appearance was so marred, beyond human semblance,
וְתֹאֲרוֹ מִבְּנֵי אָדָם׃	14aC	and his looks beyond those of sons of men –

= Masoretic verse.
Separation ↑: deictic particle(s); repetitive verse-line paralllelism; swapping (adjunct).
Separation ↓: None (one verse-line).
Strophe parallelism: None (one verse-line).
Discussion: The change of subject marks the beginning of a new strophe. Despite the continuing sentence and the repeated כן it is not possible to join vv. 14 and 15. This would create a strophe of three verse-lines with markers of separation in the middle.

STROPHE A.i.3 (Isa. 52:15)

כֵּן יַזֶּה גּוֹיִם רַבִּים	15aA	so shall he make many nations jump up;
עָלָיו יִקְפְּצוּ מְלָכִים פִּיהֶם	15aB	kings shall shut their mouths because of him.
כִּי אֲשֶׁר לֹא־סֻפַּר לָהֶם רָאוּ	15bA	For that which was never told them they see
וַאֲשֶׁר לֹא־שָׁמְעוּ הִתְבּוֹנָנוּ׃	15bB	and that which they had never heard they understand.

= Masoretic verse.
Separation ↑: deictic particle(s); swapping (adjunct).
Separation ↓: major division markers in the textual tradition; deictic particle(s); repetitive verse-line paralllelism; swapping (object).
Strophe parallelism: קפץ פה || ספר (unique; antithetical).
Discussion: The second verse-line is dependent on the first.

STROPHE B.i.1 (Isa. 53:1)

מִי הֶאֱמִין לִשְׁמֻעָתֵנוּ	1aA	Who believes what we have heard?
וּזְרוֹעַ יְהוָה עַל־מִי נִגְלָתָה׃	1aB	And to whom has the arm of the LORD been revealed?

= Masoretic verse.
Separation ↑: major division markers in the textual tradition; interrogative pronouns; swapping (subject); swapping (adjunct).
Separation ↓: None (one verse-line).
Strophe parallelism: None (one verse-line).

STROPHE B.i.2 (Isa. 53:2)

וַיַּעַל כַּיּוֹנֵק לְפָנָיו	2aA	For he grew up before him like a fresh shoot,
וְכַשֹּׁרֶשׁ מֵאֶרֶץ צִיָּה	2aB	and like a root out of dry ground.
לֹא־תֹאַר לוֹ וְלֹא הָדָר	2bA	He had no (good) looks and no splendour,
וְנִרְאֵהוּ וְלֹא־מַרְאֶה וְנֶחְמְדֵהוּ׃	2bB	that we should look at him, and no (fine) appearance that we should desire him.

= Masoretic verse.
Separation ↑: repetitive verse-line paralllelism.
Separation ↓: repetitive verse-line paralllelism.
Strophe parallelism: None.
Discussion: Despite the lack of verse-line parallelism and the rather meagre markers of separation upwards and downwards, the delimitation of the strophe can hardly be in doubt. The word הדר describes royal splendour,[1] תאר brings to mind the beauty of young David (1 Sam. 16:18), as does מראה (1 Sam. 17:42). Therefore שרש too may have been chosen deliberately. In the Ugaritic legend of Aqhatu *šrš* is the designation of Dani'ilu's son and heir and a similar terminology

[1] G. Warmuth, *ThWAT*, Bd. 2, 360-1.

is used for the Davidic sprout in the rather late text Isa. 11:10. The downfall of the Davidic dynasty may perhaps be acknowledged here, but of course it may also be the author's intention to describe the lost beauty of Zion's youth in general (cf. Lam. 4:1-4; contrast Isa. 54:12-13).

STROPHE B.i.3 (Isa. 53:3)

נִבְזֶה וַחֲדַל אִישִׁים	3aA	He was despised and rejected by men;
אִישׁ מַכְאֹבוֹת וִידוּעַ חֹלִי	3aB	a man of sorrows, and acquainted with illness;
וּכְמַסְתֵּר פָּנִים מִמֶּנּוּ	3bA	and as one who causes people to hide their faces from him
נִבְזֶה וְלֹא חֲשַׁבְנֻהוּ׃	3bB	he was despised, and we thought nothing of him.

= Masoretic verse.
Separation ↑: None.
Separation ↓: major division markers in the textual tradition; swapping (adjunct).
Strophe parallelism: בזה || בזה; grammatical parallelism.

STROPHE B.ii.1 (Isa. 53:4)

אָכֵן חֳלָיֵנוּ הוּא נָשָׂא	4aA	Yet it was he who has borne our illnesses,
וּמַכְאֹבֵינוּ סְבָלָם	4aB	and carried our sorrows;
וַאֲנַחְנוּ חֲשַׁבְנֻהוּ נָגוּעַ	4bA	but we thought of him as stricken,
מֻכֵּה אֱלֹהִים וּמְעֻנֶּה׃	4bB	smitten by God, and afflicted.

= Masoretic verse.
Separation ↑: major division markers in the textual tradition; deictic particle(s); independent pers. pronoun; swapping (subject); swapping (object).
Separation ↓: independent pers. pronoun; swapping (subject); swapping (object).
Strophe parallelism: חלי || נכה; מכאב || נגע.

STROPHE B.ii.2 (Isa. 53:5)

וְהוּא מְחֹלָל מִפְּשָׁעֵנוּ	5aA	But he was the one pierced because of our transgressions,
מְדֻכָּא מֵעֲוֹנֹתֵינוּ	5aB	crushed because of our iniquities;
מוּסַר שְׁלוֹמֵנוּ עָלָיו	5bA	upon him was the chastisement that brings us peace,
וּבַחֲבֻרָתוֹ נִרְפָּא־לָנוּ׃	5bB	and with his wounds we are healed.

= Masoretic verse.
Separation ↑: independent pers. pronoun; swapping (subject).

Separation ↓: swapping (adjunct).
Strophe parallelism: ־נו || ־נו || ־נו || ־נו. Only weak parallelism, but the relation between the two verse-lines is obvious enough.

STROPHE B.ii.3 (Isa. 53:6)

כֻּלָּנוּ כַּצֹּאן תָּעִינוּ	6aA	All of us went astray, like sheep,
אִישׁ לְדַרְכּוֹ פָּנִינוּ	6aB	we have turned every one to his own way.
וַיהוָה הִפְגִּיעַ בּוֹ	6bA	Yet the LORD inflicted on him
אֵת עֲוֺן כֻּלָּנוּ׃	6bB	the iniquity of us all.

= Masoretic verse.
Separation ↑: swapping (subject); swapping (adjunct).
Separation ↓: major division markers in the textual tradition; swapping (subject).
Strophe parallelism: כל || כל; ־נו || ־נו.

STROPHE B.iii.1 (Isa. 53:7)

נִגַּשׂ וְהוּא נַעֲנֶה	7aA	It was exacted, and he was the one afflicted,
וְלֹא יִפְתַּח־פִּיו	7aB	yet he opened not his mouth.
כַּשֶּׂה לַטֶּבַח יוּבָל	7bA	Like a young ram he was led to the slaughter,
וּכְרָחֵל לִפְנֵי גֹזְזֶיהָ נֶאֱלָמָה	7bB	and like an ewe that is dumb before its shearers –
וְלֹא יִפְתַּח פִּיו׃	7bC	and he opened not his mouth.

= Masoretic verse.
Separation ↑: major division markers in the textual tradition; independent pers. pronoun.
Separation ↓: repetitive verse-line paralllelism; swapping (adjunct).
Strophe parallelism: לא || לא; פתח || פתח; פה || פה.

STROPHE B.iii.2 (Isa. 53:8)

מֵעֹצֶר וּמִמִּשְׁפָּט לֻקָּח	8aA	Without restraint and without arbitration he was taken away,
וְאֶת־דּוֹרוֹ מִי יְשׂוֹחֵחַ	8aB	and as for his generation, who cared?
כִּי נִגְזַר מֵאֶרֶץ חַיִּים	8bA	For it was cut off out of the land of the living,
מִפֶּשַׁע עַמִּי נֶגַע לָמוֹ׃	8bB	because of the transgression of my people the blow was on them.

= Masoretic verse.
Separation ↑: interrogative pronoun; swapping (object); swapping (adjunct).
Separation ↓: major division markers in the textual tradition; deictic particle(s); swapping (adjunct).
Strophe parallelism: מן || מן; דור || עם.

STROPHE B.iii.3 (Isa. 53:9-10a)

וַיִּתֵּ֤ן אֶת־רְשָׁעִים֙ קִבְר֔וֹ	9aA	And they made his grave with the wicked
וְאֶת־עָשִׁ֖יר בְּמֹתָ֑יו	9aB	and with the rich in his death.
עַ֚ל לֹא־חָמָ֣ס עָשָׂ֔ה	9bA	Although he had done no violence,
וְלֹ֥א מִרְמָ֖ה בְּפִֽיו׃	9bB	and there was no deceit in his mouth,
וַיהוָ֞ה חָפֵ֤ץ דַּכְּאוֹ֙ הֶֽחֱלִ֔י	10aC	yet the LORD wanted to crush him, he made him ill.

≠ Masoretic verse.
Separation ↑: major division markers in the textual tradition; repetitive verse-line paralllelism; swapping (adjunct).
Separation ↓: major division markers in the textual tradition; repetitive verse-line paralllelism; swapping (subject); swapping (object).
Strophe parallelism: רשע || חמס; עשיר || מרמה; מות || דכא; מות || חלה.
Discussion: We have given our reasons for connecting v. 10aC earlier.[2]

STROPHE C.i.1 (Isa. 53:10b–c)

אִם־תָּשִׂ֤ים אָשָׁם֙ נַפְשׁ֔וֹ	10bA	If you make his life a guilt offering,
יִרְאֶ֥ה זֶ֖רַע יַאֲרִ֣יךְ יָמִ֑ים	10cA	he will see offspring, will prolong (his) days,
וְחֵ֥פֶץ יְהוָ֖ה בְּיָד֥וֹ יִצְלָֽח׃	10cB	and what the LORD wants will succeed by his hand.

≠ Masoretic verse.
Separation ↑: major division markers in the textual tradition; deictic particle(s).
Separation ↓: swapping (subject); swapping (adjunct).
Strophe parallelism: נפש || יד; ־ו || ־ו.

STROPHE C.i.2 (Isa. 53:11)

מֵעֲמַ֤ל נַפְשׁוֹ֙ יִרְאֶ֔ה	11aA	After the distress of his life he will see,
יִשְׂבָּ֖ע בְּדַעְתּ֑וֹ	11aB	and will be satisfied by his knowledge.
יַצְדִּ֥יק {צַדִּ֛יק} עַבְדִּ֖י לָֽרַבִּ֑ים	11bA	My servant {a righteous one} will justify many,
וַעֲוֺנֹתָ֖ם ה֥וּא יִסְבֹּֽל׃	11bB	and it is he who will carry their iniquities.

= Masoretic verse.
Separation ↑: swapping (adjunct).
Separation ↓: major division markers in the textual tradition; independent pers. pronoun; swapping (object).
Strophe parallelism: grammatical parallelism.

[2] See pp. 564-5.

STROPHE C.i.3 (Isa. 53:12)

לָכֵ֞ן אֲחַלֶּק־ל֣וֹ בָרַבִּ֗ים	12aA	Therefore I will give him a share with the many,
וְאֶת־עֲצוּמִים֮ יְחַלֵּ֣ק שָׁלָל֒	12aB	and with mighty ones he will share the spoil,
תַּ֗חַת אֲשֶׁ֨ר הֶעֱרָ֤ה לַמָּ֨וֶת֙ נַפְשׁ֔וֹ	12bA	because he exposed his life to death,
וְאֶת־פֹּשְׁעִ֖ים נִמְנָ֑ה	12bB	and was counted among the transgressors,
וְהוּא֙ חֵטְא־רַבִּ֣ים נָשָׂ֔א	12bC	and it was he who has borne the sins of many,
וְלַפֹּשְׁעִ֖ים יַפְגִּֽיעַ׃	12bD	and will continue to intercede for transgressors.

= Masoretic verse.
Separation ↑: major division markers in the textual tradition; deictic particle(s); repetitive verse-line paralllelism; swapping (adjunct).
Separation ↓: major division markers in the textual tradition; independent pers. pronoun; swapping (subject); swapping (adjunct).
Strophe parallelism: רבים || רבים; את || את; עצום || פשע; grammatical parallelism.

13.5 Isaiah 52:13–53:12 – Delimitation of Canticles

CANTICLE A.i (52:13–15)
Separation ↑: major division markers in the textual tradition; thematic discontinuity; change of subject.
Separation ↓: major division markers in the textual tradition.
Canticle parallelism: על || על (responsion); רבים || רבים (responsion); כן || כן (responsion); אדם || גוי (concatenation).
The second and third strophes are linked by an on-running sentence (enjambment).
Thematic unity: yes. The first and third strophes describe the servant's future exaltation, as compared to his suffering in the past.
Discussion: The markers of a major division point $\mathfrak{G}^{A}$ has after v. 15aB might be interpreted as an indication that the scribe wanted to start a new strophe with v. 15b. In that case it probably joined v. 15a with v. 14 which from the viewpoint of content is understandable. However, enjambment of strophes is by no means rare[1] and the Masoretic division has the advantage that it does not separate the plurals of v. 15b from their antecedents.

CANTICLE B.i (53:1–3)

Separation ↑: major division markers in the textual tradition; change of subject.

[1]See pp. 654-5.

Separation ↓: major division markers in the textual tradition.
Canticle parallelism: לא || לא (responsion).
Thematic unity: yes. All three strophes describe the astonishment and horror of a group designated as 'we' when they are confronted with the suffering of the servant who was probably still a young man (כיונק).
Discussion: Despite the lack of standard parallelistic pairs the unity of the canticle cannot be doubted. The dividers $\mathfrak{G}^{AQ}$ have at the end of v. 3aA can only be interpreted as anticipating the same division that is indicated after v. 3bB in $\mathfrak{G}^{S}$ and $\mathfrak{S}^{e}$.

CANTICLE B.ii (53:4–6)

Separation ↑: major division markers in the textual tradition.
Separation ↓: major division markers in the textual tradition.
Canticle parallelism: חלי || עון (responsion/inclusion); חלי || רפא (inclusion); ־נו || ־נו || ־נו ((responsion/inclusion); הוא || הוא (responsion); חלל || נכה (concatenation); אלהים || יהוה (responsion); ענה || דכא (concatenation).
Thematic unity: yes. In all three strophes the 'we' deplore how the servant had to suffer for their illnesses/sins. In all three this suffering is seen as a chastiment inflicted by God. The middle strophe explains this as vicarious suffering which brings peace/healing for the 'we'.
Discussion: At first sight it may seem that the delimitation of this canticle rests on tenuous evidence, especially with regard to the lower boundary. However, the major division marker (colon) $\mathfrak{G}^{S}$ has after תעינו and the Setuma in 1Q^{a} after פנינו can be seen as proleptic markers of the division at the end of v. 6 which has been preserved in $\mathfrak{G}^{Q}$. In a similar way, the unlikely division markers after v. 7aB in $\mathfrak{G}^{SA}$ may be interpreted as lagging behind the same division line. If this is true the boundary between vv. 6 and 7 is attested by four witnesses.

CANTICLE B.iii (53:7–10aC)

Separation ↑: major division markers in the textual tradition.
Separation ↓: major division markers in the textual tradition.
Canticle parallelism: ענה || חלה (inclusion); פה || פה (inclusion/responsion); יבל || לקח (concatenation); חיים || מות (concatenation); פשע || רשע (concatenation);
Thematic unity: yes. Further description of the servant's suffering, revealing that he was seen as a representative of the younger generation as a whole.
Discussion: Now that the indentation in 1Q^{a} after v. 8 has got the

support of $\mathfrak{G}^A$ it becomes more likely that the former represents a real division marking.[2] However, because both witnesses also attest the boundary between vv. 9 and 10, we suppose that in this case they simply preserve a trace of an earlier strophe division.

The lower boundary of canticle B.iii is marked in $1\mathfrak{Q}^a$ and $\mathfrak{G}^A$ but $\mathfrak{G}^S$ seems to indicate the same division both anticipating (after v. 9bB) and lagging behind (after v. 10cA).

CANTICLE C.i (53:10bA–12)

Separation ↑: major division markers in the textual tradition; thematic discontinuity; change of subject.
Separation ↓: major division markers in the textual tradition.
Canticle parallelism: אשם || חטא (inclusion); נפש || נפש || נפש (responsion/inclusion); ־ו || ־ו || ־ו (responsion/inclusion); רבים || רבים (concatenation/responsion); עון || חטא (responsion); הוא || הוא (responsion); סבל || נשא (responsion).
Thematic unity: yes. God will accept the vicarious suffering of the innocent youth of Israel by way of guilt offering and will reward them with a prosperous life.
Discussion: The division markers in $\mathfrak{G}^S$ after v. 10cA have been discussed above. We interpret the markers in $1\mathfrak{Q}^a$ and $\mathfrak{G}^S$ after v. 11 as a remnant of strophic division because both are also among the host of witnesses indicating a major break after v. 12.

13.6 Isaiah 52:13–53:12 – Delimitation of Macrostructure

Difficult as the canto may be to interpret, its macrostructural built is relatively straightforward and symmetric:

SUB-CANTOS	CANTICLES	STROPHES
A	1	3 (3)
B	3	9 (3+3+3)
C	1	3 (3)

The unity of the canto is generally recognized and is confirmed by distant parallelism. We decided to assume two sub-cantos, each consisting of only one canticle (A and C) and describing the exaltation

[2] For different views of this problem see Oesch, T 25*, n. 30.

of the servant, as the frame around the main sub-canto B. As in other cases, beginning and end of the canto link up with each other:

Links between the sub-cantos A and C:
שׂכל (52:13aA) || צלח (53: 10cB); עבדי (52:13aA) || עבדי (53:11bA); נשׂא (52:13aB) || נשׂא (53:12bC); רבים (52:14aA, 15aA) || רבים (53:11bA, 12aA); *מלכים (52:15aB) || עצומים (53:12aB).

The middle sub-canto describing the suffering of the servant of the LORD is linked with the other two sub-cantos by concatenation: שׂמע || שׂמע (52:15bB – 53:1aA) and יהוה חפץ (53:10aC) || חפץ יהוה (53:10cB).

The distant parallelism connecting the canticles of **sub-canto B** is clear enough but we mention a few particularly cogent cases:
זרוע (53:1aB) || יד (53:10cB);[1] חלי (53:3aB – B.i) || חלינו (53:4aA – B.ii) || החלי (53:10aC – B.iii); חשׁבנו (53:3bB – B.i) || חשׁבנו (53:4bA – B.ii); נגע (53:4aA – B.ii) || נגע (53:8bB – B.iii); ענה (53:4bB – B.ii) || ענה (53:7aA – B.iii); פשׁע (53:5aA – B.ii) || פשׁע (53:8bB – B.iii); דכא (53:5aB – B.ii) || דכא (53:10aC – B.iii).

In this study we try to keep exegesis to a minimum. Yet we want to add a few remarks of an exegetical nature here. We believe that the joining of v. 10aC to v. 9 which was based on the testimony of ancient witnesses provides an important new clue for the interpretation of these theologically important verses. The macrostructural links between v. 10aC and vv. 3aB, 4aA, 5aB confirm that this colon belongs to sub-canto C. Our analysis also supports the interpretation of the servant as a corporate personality, the embodiment of faithful Israel and especially its innocent youth which had to bear the chastiment for the sins of the fathers. Second Isaiah may have seen himself as one of these young people, a suffering young prophet like Jeremiah,[2] whom he seems to quote in Isa. 53:7-8 (cf. Jer. 11:19).[3] The resignation the servant of Isa. 53 shows in bearing his lot has obvious parallels in Isa. 42:2 and 50:6-7.

---

[1] The latter answers the question of 53:1b: the hand of the servant will implement what the arm of the LORD does. This is a fundamental issue for Second Isaiah.

[2] Cf. Jer. 1:6.

[3] The authenticity of Jer. 11:19 is practically beyond doubt, cf. W. McKane, *Jeremiah* (ICC), vol. 1, Edinburgh 1986, 255.

Chapter 14

The Structure of Isaiah 54

14.1 Isaiah 54: Text and Translation

ס <פ> – 1𝔔^{ab} – 4𝔔^{bd} – 𝔊^{SBAQ} – 𝔖^{abcde} ______________________

i.1 (Isa. 54:1)

רָנִּי עֲקָרָה לֹא יָלָדָה	1aA	Rejoice, O barren one,[1] who did not bear!
פִּצְחִי רִנָּה וְצַהֲלִי לֹא־חָלָה	1aB	Break forth into rejoicing and radiate,[2] you who did not bring to birth!
כִּי־רַבִּים בְּנֵי־שׁוֹמֵמָה	1bA	For the children of the desolate one[3] will be more
מִבְּנֵי בְעוּלָה	1bB	than the children of the one who has a husband,
אָמַר יְהוָה׃ {<ס>}	1bC	says the LORD.

i.2 (Isa. 54:2)

הַרְחִיבִי ׀ מְקוֹם אָהֳלֵךְ	2aA	Enlarge the place of your tent,
וִירִיעוֹת מִשְׁכְּנוֹתַיִךְ יַטּוּ אַל־תַּחְשֹׂכִי	2aB	and let them stretch out the cloth of your dwellings – do not hold back!
הַאֲרִיכִי מֵיתָרַיִךְ	2bA	Lengthen your cords,
וִיתֵדֹתַיִךְ חַזֵּקִי׃	2bB	and strengthen your tent pegs!

i.3 (Isa. 54:3)

כִּי־יָמִין וּשְׂמֹאול תִּפְרֹצִי {𝔊^{Q}}	3aA	For you will spread out to the right and to the left,[4]
וְזַרְעֵךְ גּוֹיִם יִירָשׁ	3bA	and your seed[5] will dispossess[6] the nations
וְעָרִים נְשַׁמּוֹת יוֹשִׁיבוּ׃	3bB	and will settle in the desolate cities.

𝔊^{SA} ....

[1]An allusion to Sarah (cf. Gen. 11:30), as was noted by J. van der Merwe, *Pentateuchtradisies in die prediking van Deuterojesaja*, Groningen 1955, 115. Compare Isa. 51:2.

[2]We take the verb in the same meaning as Ugaritic *ṣhl* "to radiate" (said of the brow, in a context very similar to ours, KTU 1.17:II.9). See also Ps. 104:15.

[3]Note the external parallelism between 1bA and 3bB. The first meaning will be 'lonely woman' here, as in 2 Sam. 13:20, but because of v. 3 we translate 'desolate woman'. Second Isaiah is neutralizing the oracles of doom of First Isaiah here, cf. Isa. 1:7; 6:11.

[4]The editors of BHS have taken vv. 2b and 3a as one verse-line. There is little to recommend this. The Masoretes read v. 3 as a unicolon plus bicolon. The imperatives and jussives of the preceding verses are not continued. Verse 3 explains v. 2 and introduces a new thought, alluding to the blessing of Jacob in Gen. 28:14.

[5]In the OT 'seed' can refer to the offspring of women. Cf. Ruth 4:11-12. Here, the offspring of the matriarch Zion and the 'servant' Jacob is meant, cf. Isa. 53:10.

[6]The explicit use of the root ירשׁ again reminds us of the promise to the patriarchs, cf. Gen. 15:7, see also Van der Merwe, *Pentateuchtradisies*, 240.

ii.1 (Isa. 54:4)

אַל־תִּירְאִי כִּי־לֹא תֵבוֹשִׁי	4aA	Do not fear, for you will not be put to shame,
וְאַל־תִּכָּלְמִי כִּי לֹא תַחְפִּירִי	4aB	and do not feel disgraced, for you will not become embarrassed.
כִּי בֹשֶׁת עֲלוּמַיִךְ תִּשְׁכָּחִי	4bA	For the shame of your youth[7] you will forget,
וְחֶרְפַּת אַלְמְנוּתַיִךְ לֹא תִזְכְּרִי־עוֹד׃	4bB	and the humiliation of your widowhood[8] you will remember no more.

ii.2 (Isa. 54:5)

כִּי בֹעֲלַיִךְ עֹשַׂיִךְ	5aA	For your husband is your Maker,[9]
יְהוָה צְבָאוֹת שְׁמוֹ	5aB	LORD of Hosts is his name;
וְגֹאֲלֵךְ קְדוֹשׁ יִשְׂרָאֵל	5bA	and your Redeemer is the Holy One of Israel,
אֱלֹהֵי כָל־הָאָרֶץ יִקָּרֵא׃	5bB	God of all the earth he is called.

<ס> – $_1\mathfrak{Q}^{b}$ – $\mathfrak{G}^{BA}$ . . . .

iii.1 (Isa. 54:6)

כִּי־כְאִשָּׁה עֲזוּבָה וַעֲצוּבַת רוּחַ	6aA	For like a forsaken wife, tormented in spirit,
קְרָאָךְ יְהוָה	6aB	the LORD did call you;
וְאֵשֶׁת נְעוּרִים כִּי תִמָּאֵס	6bA	but a wife of youth – how[10] can she be rejected?
אָמַר אֱלֹהָיִךְ׃ {$\mathfrak{G}^{S}$}	6bB	says your God.

iii.2 (Isa. 54:7-8)

בְּרֶגַע קָטֹן עֲזַבְתִּיךְ	7aA	For a brief moment I have forsaken you,
וּבְרַחֲמִים גְּדֹלִים אֲקַבְּצֵךְ׃	7aB	but with great mercy I will gather you.
בְּשֶׁצֶף קֶצֶף הִסְתַּרְתִּי פָנַי רֶגַע מִמֵּךְ	8aA	In a surge of anger I hid my face from you for a moment,
וּבְחֶסֶד עוֹלָם רִחַמְתִּיךְ	8aB	but with eternal loyalty I have mercy upon you,
אָמַר גֹּאֲלֵךְ יְהוָה׃	8aC	says your Redeemer, the LORD.

ס – $_4\mathfrak{Q}^{d}$ – $\mathfrak{S}^{de}$ . . . .

iv.1 (Isa. 54:9)

כִּימֵי* נֹחַ זֹאת לִי	9aA	As in the days of Noah[11] is this to me,

[7]Schoors, 82, proposed "bondage", but Ugaritic does not support his argument – *ġlmt* means "young woman".

[8]Second Isaiah reacts to the laments of his days here, which explains the imagery. Cf. Jer. 31:19; 51:5; Lam. 1:1.

[9]Plurals of majesty because similar forms occur elsewhere, cf. Waltke, O'Connor, §7.4.3d; Joüon, Muraoka, §136e.

[10]With Qimchi and most modern commentators we take כי as the introduction of a rhetorical question. Cf. Lam. 5:22 and Koole, 291.

[11]With $_1\mathfrak{Q}^{a}$, the Cairo Codex and the ancient versions (with the notable exception of $\mathfrak{G}$). See also Matth. 24:37. After כ other prepositions may drop out (Joüon, Muraoka, §133h).

אֲשֶׁר נִשְׁבַּעְתִּי מֵעֲבֹר מֵי־נֹחַ עוֹד עַל־הָאָרֶץ	9aB	when I swore that the waters of Noah would never again cover the earth.
כֵּן נִשְׁבַּעְתִּי מִקְּצֹף עָלַיִךְ	9bA	So now I swear that I will no longer be angry with you,
וּמִגְּעָר־בָּךְ׃	9bB	or will rebuke you.

iv.2 (Isa. 54:10)

כִּי הֶהָרִים יָמוּשׁוּ	10aA	Though the mountains may move,
וְהַגְּבָעוֹת תְּמוּטֶנָה	10aB	and the hills may topple,
וְחַסְדִּי מֵאִתֵּךְ לֹא־יָמוּשׁ	10bA	my loyalty will not move away from you,
וּבְרִית שְׁלוֹמִי לֹא תָמוּט {𝔊^{A}}	10bB	and the covenant of my peace will not topple,
אָמַר מְרַחֲמֵךְ יְהוָה׃	10bC	says the LORD who has mercy upon you.

ס <פ> – 1𝔔^{a} – 4𝔔^{cd} – 𝔖^{bce} . . . .

v.1 (Isa. 54:11)

עֲנִיָּה סֹעֲרָה לֹא נֻחָמָה {𝔊^{SB}}	11aA	O afflicted one, storm-tossed, not comforted –
הִנֵּה אָנֹכִי מַרְבִּיץ בַּפּוּךְ אֲבָנַיִךְ	11bA	behold, I will set your stones in antimony,[12]
וִיסַדְתִּיךְ בַּסַּפִּירִים׃ {𝔊^{A}}	11bB	and lay your foundations in lapis lazuli.

v.2 (Isa. 54:12–14a)

וְשַׂמְתִּי כַּדְכֹד שִׁמְשֹׁתַיִךְ	12aA	And I will make your battlements of red jasper,[13]
וּשְׁעָרַיִךְ לְאַבְנֵי אֶקְדָּח	12aB	and your gates of flintstones,[14]
וְכָל־גְּבוּלֵךְ לְאַבְנֵי־חֵפֶץ׃	12aC	and your whole borderline of precious stones.
וְכָל־בָּנַיִךְ לִמּוּדֵי יְהוָה {𝔊^{Q}}	13aA	And all your children[15] will be disciples of the LORD,
וְרַב שְׁלוֹם בָּנָיִךְ׃	13aB	and great will be the peace of your children
בִּצְדָקָה תִּכּוֹנָנִי	14aC	– in justice you will be established.[16]

𝔊^{SA} . . . .

[12]As seen by Koole, 302-3, and others, the metaphors of Zion as a beautiful woman and as a city are mixed here.

[13]Most ancient versions have "jasper". The Semitic cognates (Cf. *HALAT*, 439) argue in favour of the common red variety of this stone. Nothing justifies the guess "rubin".

[14]The addition of לאבני renders it likely that אקדח is a type of stone of which different varieties existed. The cognates point to flintstones.

[15]There is no need to emend the text after 1𝔔^{a}. Cf. Barthélemy, 408-9. The parallel pair בנים || בנים is common and occurs even in Second Isaiah, cf. Isa. 51:18; 54:1.

[16]With most modern commentators we take the first colon of v. 14 with the previous verse. To their arguments we may now add the following: a) 𝔊^{SA} have major division markers after this colon. b) The responsion between יסר (v. 11bB) and כון Polel (v. 14aC) is also attested as verse-line parallelism in Ps. 24:2; Prov. 3:19.

vi.1 (Isa. 54:14b)

רַחֲקִי מֵעֹשֶׁק כִּי־לֹא תִירָאִי	14bA	Stay far away from oppression, for you need not fear,
וּמִמְּחִתָּה כִּי לֹא־תִקְרַב אֵלָיִךְ׃ {<ס>}	14bB	and from terror, for it shall not come near to you.

vi.2 (Isa. 54:15)

הֵן גּוֹר יָגוּר אֶפֶס מֵאוֹתִי	15aA	Behold, do they attack you,[17] it will not be my doing.
מִי־גָר אִתָּךְ עָלַיִךְ יִפּוֹל׃	15aB	Whoever attacks you, will fall over you.

<ס> – 1Q[a] – 𝔊[SA] . . . .

vii.1 (Isa. 54:16)

הֵן אָנֹכִי בָּרָאתִי חָרָשׁ	16aA	Behold, it is I who created the craftsman,
נֹפֵחַ בְּאֵשׁ פֶּחָם	16aB	who blows the fire of coals
וּמוֹצִיא כְלִי לְמַעֲשֵׂהוּ	16aC	and produces the weapon for its purpose.
וְאָנֹכִי בָּרָאתִי מַשְׁחִית לְחַבֵּל׃	16bA	And it is I who created the destroyer to work havoc.

vii.2 (Isa. 54:17a)

כָּל־כְּלִי יוּצַר עָלַיִךְ לֹא יִצְלָח	17aA	No weapon formed against you, will have success,
וְכָל־לָשׁוֹן תָּקוּם־אִתָּךְ לַמִּשְׁפָּט תַּרְשִׁיעִי {<ס>𝔊[SAQ]}	17aB	and every tongue rising against you in court you will prove guilty.

vii.3 (Isa. 54:17b)

זֹאת נַחֲלַת עַבְדֵי יְהוָה	17bA	This is the heritage of the servants of the LORD,
וְצִדְקָתָם מֵאִתִּי נְאֻם־יְהוָה׃	17bB	and their justice from me declares the LORD.

ס – 1Q[a] – 𝔊[SBAQ] – 𝔖[abcde] ____

[17] Cf. *HAHAT*, 208; *DCH*, vol. 2, 336.

14.2 Isaiah 54 – Delimitation of Cola

COLON 54:1aA:

רָנִּי עֲקָרָה לֹא יָלָדָה 1aA Rejoice, O barren one, who did not bear!

With: $\mathfrak{M}$ (2) – $\mathfrak{G}^{SQ}$ – $\mathfrak{S}^{abcde}$
Colon parallelism: עקרה || ילד(antithetical).

COLON 54:1aB:

פִּצְחִי רִנָּה וְצַהֲלִי לֹא־חָלָה 1aB Break forth into rejoicing and radiate, you who did not bring to birth!

With: $\mathfrak{M}$ (5) – $\mathfrak{G}^{SQ}$ – $\mathfrak{S}^{abcde}$
Colon parallelism: פצח רנה || צהל (unique).

COLON 54:1bA:

כִּי־רַבִּים בְּנֵי־שׁוֹמֵמָה 1bA For the children of the desolate one will be more

With: $\mathfrak{M}$ (12) – $\mathfrak{G}^{SQ}$ – $\mathfrak{S}^{e}$
Discussion: Apparently $\mathfrak{M}$ wanted to read on until the end of the verse because the sentence continues (enjambment). But the witnesses cited justify our choice.

COLON 54:1bB:

מִבְּנֵי בְעוּלָה 1bB than the children of the one who has a husband,

With: $\mathfrak{M}$ (8) – $\mathfrak{G}^{SQ}$ – $\mathfrak{S}^{bcd}$
Discussion: See our note on the preceding colon.

COLON 54:1bC:

אָמַר יְהוָה׃ 1bC says the LORD.

With: $\mathfrak{M}$ (1), possibly a Setuma in 1$\mathfrak{Q}^{a}$ – $\mathfrak{G}^{SQ}$ – $\mathfrak{S}^{ae}$, $\mathfrak{S}^{cd}$ subordinate punctuation.
Discussion: Both BHK and BHS join אמר יהוה to מבני בעולה to form one colon. However, if אמר יהוה is at the end of a verse, cases like 45:13; 48:22; 54:6,8,10 prove that אמר יהוה must be regarded as an independent colon. The ancient witnesses confirm this.

COLON 54:2aA:

הַרְחִיבִי ׀ מְקוֹם אָהֳלֵךְ 2aA Enlarge the place of your tent,

With: $\mathfrak{M}$ (7) – $\mathfrak{G}^{SQ}$ – $\mathfrak{S}^{abcde}$

COLON 54:2aB:

וִירִיעוֹת מִשְׁכְּנוֹתַיִךְ יַטּוּ אַל־תַּחְשֹׂכִי 2aB and let them stretch out the cloth of your dwellings – do not hold back!

With: $\mathfrak{M}$ (2) – $\mathfrak{G}^{SQ}$ – $\mathfrak{S}^{abcde}$

COLON 54:2bA:

הַאֲרִיכִי מֵיתָרַיִךְ 2bA Lengthen your cords,

With: $\mathfrak{M}$ (5) – $\mathfrak{G}^{SQ}$

COLON 54:2bB:

וִיתֵדֹתַיִךְ חַזֵּקִי׃ 2bB and strengthen your tent pegs!

With: $\mathfrak{M}$ (1) – $\mathfrak{G}^{SQ}$ – $\mathfrak{S}^{abcde}$

COLON 54:3aA:

כִּי־יָמִין וּשְׂמֹאול תִּפְרֹצִי 3aA For you will spread out to the right and to the left,

With: $\mathfrak{M}$ (2) – $\mathfrak{G}^{SQ}$, paragraphos in $\mathfrak{G}^{Q}$ – $\mathfrak{S}^{abcde}$
Colon parallelism: ימין || שׂמאל.
Discussion: $\mathfrak{G}^{SQ}$ have an extra point after כי־ימין where $\mathfrak{M}$ has a conjunctive accent. $\mathfrak{S}$ supports $\mathfrak{M}$. BHK and BHS print v. 2b and v. 3a as if they belong to one and the same verse. The ancient witnesses argue against this decision.

COLON 54:3bA:

וְזַרְעֵךְ גּוֹיִם יִירָשׁ 3bA and your seed will dispossess the nations

With: $\mathfrak{M}$ (5) – $\mathfrak{G}^{SQ}$ – $\mathfrak{S}^{abcde}$

COLON 54:3bB:

וְעָרִים נְשַׁמּוֹת יוֹשִׁיבוּ׃ 3bB and will settle in the desolate cities.

With: $\mathfrak{M}$ (1) – $\mathfrak{G}^{SAQ}$, major division markers in $\mathfrak{G}^{SA}$ – $\mathfrak{S}^{abcde}$

COLON 54:4aA:

אַל־תִּירְאִי כִּי־לֹא תֵבוֹשִׁי 4aA Do not fear, for you will not be put to shame,

With: $\mathfrak{M}$ (5) – $\mathfrak{G}^{SQ}$ – $\mathfrak{S}^{abcde}$
Colon parallelism: אל || לא.

Colon 54:4aB:

וְאַל־תִּכָּלְמִי כִּי לֹא תַחְפִּירִי 4aB and do not feel disgraced, for you will not become embarrassed.

With: $\mathfrak{M}$ (2) – $\mathfrak{G}^{SQ}$ – $\mathfrak{S}^{abcde}$
Colon parallelism: אל || לא; כלם || חפר.

Colon 54:4bA:

כִּי בֹשֶׁת עֲלוּמַיִךְ תִּשְׁכָּחִי 4bA For the shame of your youth you will forget,

With: $\mathfrak{M}$ (5) – $\mathfrak{G}^{SQ}$ – $\mathfrak{S}^{acde}$

Colon 54:4bB:

וְחֶרְפַּת אַלְמְנוּתַיִךְ לֹא תִזְכְּרִי־עוֹד׃ 4bB and the humiliation of your widowhood you will remember no more.

With: $\mathfrak{M}$ (1) – $\mathfrak{G}^{SQ}$ – $\mathfrak{S}^{abcde}$

Colon 54:5aA:

כִּי בֹעֲלַיִךְ עֹשַׂיִךְ 5aA For your husband is your Maker,

With: $\mathfrak{M}$ (5) – $\mathfrak{G}^{SQ}$ – $\mathfrak{S}^{abcde}$
Colon parallelism: ־ךְ || ־ךְ.

Colon 54:5aB:

יְהוָה צְבָאוֹת שְׁמוֹ 5aB Lord of Hosts is his name;

With: $\mathfrak{M}$ (2) – $\mathfrak{G}^{SQ}$ – $\mathfrak{S}^{abce}$

Colon 54:5bA:

וְגֹאֲלֵךְ קְדוֹשׁ יִשְׂרָאֵל 5bA and your Redeemer is the Holy One of Israel,

With: $\mathfrak{M}$ (5) – $\mathfrak{G}^{SQ}$ – $\mathfrak{S}^{abcde}$
Colon parallelism: גאל || קדוש ישראל.

Colon 54:5bB:

אֱלֹהֵי כָל־הָאָרֶץ יִקָּרֵא׃ 5bB God of all the earth he is called.

With: $\mathfrak{M}$ (1), Setuma in 1$\mathfrak{Q}^{b}$ – $\mathfrak{G}^{SBAQ}$, major division markers in $\mathfrak{G}^{BA}$ – $\mathfrak{S}^{abcde}$

Colon 54:6aA:

כִּי־כְאִשָּׁה עֲזוּבָה וַעֲצוּבַת רוּחַ 6aA For like a forsaken wife, tormented in spirit,

With: $\mathfrak{M}$ (8)
Colon parallelism: עזב || עצב (unique).
Discussion: Again the circumstance that the sentence runs on confused the ancients, both in vv. 6a and 6b which would both count 6 stressed units. Only $\mathfrak{G}^{S}$ has a point after עזובה, but in our opinion it is prefereable to divide after רוח which results in a nice parallelism between קראך יהוה and אמר אלהיך. See also our arguments with v. 6bB.

COLON 54:6aB:

קְרָאָ֣ךְ יְהוָ֑ה 6aB the LORD did call you;

With: $\mathfrak{M}$ (2) – $\mathfrak{G}^{SQ}$ – $\mathfrak{S}^{abcde}$

COLON 54:6bA:

וְאֵ֧שֶׁת נְעוּרִ֛ים כִּ֥י תִמָּאֵ֖ס 6bA but a wife of youth – how can she be rejected?

With: $\mathfrak{M}$ (8) – $\mathfrak{G}^{SQ}$

COLON 54:6bB:

אָמַ֥ר אֱלֹהָֽיִךְ׃ 6bB says your God.

With: $\mathfrak{M}$ (1) – $\mathfrak{G}^{SQ}$, paragraphos in $\mathfrak{G}^{S}$ – $\mathfrak{S}^{abcde}$
Discussion: As we argued before, the Masoretes wanted to join v. 6bA and v. 6bB. However, Isa. 54:1bC, 8aC and 10bC, all in the same chapter, argue in favour of treating v. 6bB as an independent colon, a decision supported by $\mathfrak{G}^{S}$ and $\mathfrak{G}^{Q}$ (see our comment on v. 6bA).

COLON 54:7aA:

בְּרֶ֥גַע קָטֹ֖ן עֲזַבְתִּ֑יךְ 7aA For a brief moment I have forsaken you,

With: $\mathfrak{M}$ (2) – $\mathfrak{G}^{SQ}$ – $\mathfrak{S}^{abce}$ subordinate punctuation.

COLON 54:7aB:

וּבְרַחֲמִ֥ים גְּדֹלִ֖ים אֲקַבְּצֵֽךְ׃ 7aB but with great mercy I will gather you.

With: $\mathfrak{M}$ (1) – $\mathfrak{G}^{SQ}$ – $\mathfrak{S}^{abcde}$

COLON 54:8aA:

בְּשֶׁ֣צֶף קֶ֗צֶף הִסְתַּ֨רְתִּי פָנַ֥י רֶ֙גַע֙ מִמֵּ֔ךְ 8aA In a surge of anger I hid my face from you for a moment,

With: $\mathfrak{M}$ (5) – $\mathfrak{G}^{SQ}$ – $\mathfrak{S}^{abce}$ subordinate punctuation.
Discussion: We suspect that this very long colon (6 feet) has to be

divided after קצף ($\mathfrak{M}$ Revia‘, No. 7) or הסתרתי ($\mathfrak{M}$ conjunctive accent, but $\mathfrak{G}^{S}$ and $\mathfrak{S}^{d}$ have a point here). On the other hand, however, the division after ממך has stronger support and since v. 8aA in this form balances the much shorter v. 8aB, we accept $\mathfrak{M}$.

COLON 54:8aB:

וּבְחֶסֶד עוֹלָם רִחַמְתִּיךְ 8aB but with eternal loyalty I have mercy upon you,

With: $\mathfrak{M}$ (2) – $\mathfrak{G}^{SQ}$ – $\mathfrak{S}^{cde}$ subordinate punctuation.

COLON 54:8aC:

אָמַר גֹּאֲלֵךְ יְהוָה׃ 8aC says your Redeemer, the LORD.

With: $\mathfrak{M}$ (1), Setuma in many manuscripts, among them 4$\mathfrak{Q}^{d}$ – $\mathfrak{G}^{SQ}$ – $\mathfrak{S}^{abcde}$, major division markers in $\mathfrak{S}^{de}$

COLON 54:9aA:

כִּימֵי* נֹחַ זֹאת לִי 9aA As in the days of Noah is this to me,

With: $\mathfrak{M}$ (5) – $\mathfrak{G}^{SQ}$ – $\mathfrak{S}^{a}$, $\mathfrak{S}^{bcde}$ subordinate punctuation.
Discussion: $\mathfrak{G}^{SQ}$ have an extra point after נח ($\mathfrak{M}$ Pashṭa, No. 10).

COLON 54:9aB:

אֲשֶׁר נִשְׁבַּעְתִּי מֵעֲבֹר מֵי־נֹחַ עוֹד עַל־הָאָרֶץ 9aB when I swore that the waters of Noah would never again cover the earth.

With: $\mathfrak{M}$ (2) – $\mathfrak{S}^{abcde}$
Discussion: Again the colon creates the impression of being overloaded with six feet. One might consider a division after נשבעתי ($\mathfrak{M}$ Revia‘, No. 7), but no other ancient witness supports this. $\mathfrak{G}^{S}$ and $\mathfrak{G}^{Q}$ have a point after מי־נח which would be a serious alternative if $\mathfrak{G}$ did not give a rather free rendering here. All in all it seems best to follow $\mathfrak{M}$ and $\mathfrak{S}$ in dividing after על־הארץ.

COLON 54:9bA:

כֵּן נִשְׁבַּעְתִּי מִקְּצֹף עָלַיִךְ 9bA So now I swear that I will no longer be angry with you,

With: $\mathfrak{M}$ (8) – $\mathfrak{G}^{Q}$ – $\mathfrak{S}^{e}$
Discussion: $\mathfrak{M}$ and most other ancient witnesses wanted to read on until the end of the verse. We accept, however, the division of the witnesses cited because it results in a nice verse-line parallelism.

COLON 54:9bB:

וּמִגְּעָר־בָּךְ׃ 9bB or will rebuke you.

With: $\mathfrak{M}$ (1) – $\mathfrak{S}^{abcde}$
Discussion: $\mathfrak{G}$ connects with v. 10 in a free rendering.

COLON 54:10aA:

כִּי הֶהָרִים יָמוּשׁוּ 10aA Though the mountains may move,

With: $\mathfrak{M}$ (5) – $\mathfrak{G}^{SQ}$ – $\mathfrak{S}^{abcde}$

COLON 54:10aB:

וְהַגְּבָעוֹת תְּמוּטֶנָה 10aB and the hills may topple,

With: $\mathfrak{M}$ (2) – $\mathfrak{G}^{SQ}$ – $\mathfrak{S}^{abcde}$
Discussion: This verse is a good illustration that the ancients had no difficulty with a sentence running on through several verses if the parallelism was obvious enough.

COLON 54:10bA:

וְחַסְדִּי מֵאִתֵּךְ לֹא־יָמוּשׁ 10bA my loyalty will not move away from you,

With: $\mathfrak{M}$ (7) – $\mathfrak{G}^{SQ}$ – $\mathfrak{S}^{abcde}$

COLON 54:10bB:

וּבְרִית שְׁלוֹמִי לֹא תָמוּט 10bB and the covenant of my peace will not topple,

With: $\mathfrak{M}$ (5) – $\mathfrak{G}^{SAQ}$, major division markers in $\mathfrak{G}^{A}$ – $\mathfrak{S}^{be}$, $\mathfrak{S}^{ad}$ subordinate punctuation.
Discussion: $\mathfrak{G}^{SQ}$ have an extra divider after שלומי ($\mathfrak{M}$ Pashṭa, No. 10).

COLON 54:10bC:

אָמַר מְרַחֲמֵךְ יְהוָה׃ 10bC says the LORD who has mercy upon you.

With: $\mathfrak{M}$ (1), major division markers, also in 1$\mathfrak{Q}^{a}$ and 4$\mathfrak{Q}^{cd}$ – $\mathfrak{G}^{SQ}$ – $\mathfrak{S}^{abcde}$, major division markers in $\mathfrak{S}^{bce}$

COLON 54:11aA:

עֲנִיָּה סֹעֲרָה לֹא נֻחָמָה 11aA O afflicted one, storm-tossed, not comforted –

With: $\mathfrak{M}$ (2) – $\mathfrak{G}^{SBQ}$, major division markers in $\mathfrak{G}^{SB}$ – $\mathfrak{S}^{cde}$, $\mathfrak{S}^{a}$ subordinate punctuation.
Colon parallelism: סער || נחם (antithetical; unique).

Discussion: $\mathfrak{G}^{SQ}$ have an extra point after סערה ($\mathfrak{M}$ Ṭiphḥa, No. 8).

COLON 54:11bA:

הִנֵּ֨ה אָנֹכִ֜י מַרְבִּ֤יץ בַּפּוּךְ֙ אֲבָנַ֔יִךְ 11bA behold, I will set your stones in antimony,

With: $\mathfrak{M}$ (5) – $\mathfrak{G}^{SQ}$ – $\mathfrak{S}^{abcde}$

COLON 54:11bB:

וִיסַדְתִּ֖יךְ בַּסַּפִּירִֽים׃ 11bB and lay your foundations in lapis lazuli.

With: $\mathfrak{M}$ (1) – $\mathfrak{G}^{SAQ}$, major division markers in $\mathfrak{G}^{A}$ – $\mathfrak{S}^{abcde}$

COLON 54:12aA:

וְשַׂמְתִּ֤י כַּדְכֹד֙ שִׁמְשֹׁתַ֔יִךְ 12aA And I will make your battlements of red jasper,

With: $\mathfrak{M}$ (5) – $\mathfrak{G}^{SQ}$ – $\mathfrak{S}^{abcde}$

COLON 54:12aB:

וּשְׁעָרַ֖יִךְ לְאַבְנֵ֣י אֶקְדָּ֑ח 12aB and your gates of flintstones,

With: $\mathfrak{M}$ (2) – $\mathfrak{G}^{SQ}$ – $\mathfrak{S}^{abcde}$

COLON 54:12aC:

וְכָל־גְּבוּלֵ֖ךְ לְאַבְנֵי־חֵֽפֶץ׃ 12aC and your whole borderline of precious stones.

With: $\mathfrak{M}$ (1) – $\mathfrak{G}^{SQ}$ – $\mathfrak{S}^{abcde}$

COLON 54:13aA:

וְכָל־בָּנַ֖יִךְ לִמּוּדֵ֣י יְהוָ֑ה 13aA And all your children will be disciples of the LORD,

With: $\mathfrak{M}$ (2) – $\mathfrak{G}^{SQ}$, paragraphos in $\mathfrak{G}^{Q}$ – $\mathfrak{S}^{abcde}$

COLON 54:13aB:

וְרַ֖ב שְׁל֥וֹם בָּנָֽיִךְ׃ 13aB and great will be the peace of your children

With: $\mathfrak{M}$ (1) – $\mathfrak{G}^{SQ}$ – $\mathfrak{S}^{abd}$, $\mathfrak{S}^{ce}$ subordinate punctuation.

COLON 54:14aC:

בִּצְדָקָ֖ה תִּכּוֹנָ֑נִי 14aC – in justice you will be established.

With: $\mathfrak{M}$ (2) – $\mathfrak{G}^{SAQ}$, major division markers in $\mathfrak{G}^{SA}$ – $\mathfrak{S}^{abcde}$

COLON 54:14bA:

רַחֲקִי מֵעֹשֶׁק כִּי־לֹא תִירָאִי 14bA Stay far away from oppression, for you need not fear,

With: $\mathfrak{M}$ (5) – $\mathfrak{G}^{SQ}$ – $\mathfrak{S}^{abcde}$

COLON 54:14bB:

וּמִמְּחִתָּה כִּי לֹא־תִקְרַב אֵלָיִךְ׃ 14bB and from terror, for it shall not come near to you.

With: $\mathfrak{M}$ (1), Setuma in $1\mathfrak{Q}^{a}$ – $\mathfrak{G}^{SQ}$ – $\mathfrak{S}^{abcde}$
Discussion: None of the other ancient witnesses supports $\mathfrak{M}$'s Zaqeph with וממחתה and it is obviously the weaker of the two.[1]

COLON 54:15aA:

הֵן גּוֹר יָגוּר אֶפֶס מֵאוֹתִי 15aA Behold, do they attack you, it will not be my doing.

With: $\mathfrak{M}$ (2) – $\mathfrak{G}^{SQ}$ – $\mathfrak{S}^{abcde}$

COLON 54:15aB:

מִי־גָר אִתָּךְ עָלַיִךְ יִפּוֹל׃ 15aB Whoever attacks you, will fall over you.

With: $\mathfrak{M}$ (1), Setuma in $1\mathfrak{Q}^{a}$– $\mathfrak{G}^{SAQ}$, major division markers in $\mathfrak{G}^{SA}$ – $\mathfrak{S}^{abcde}$

COLON 54:16aA:

הֵן אָנֹכִי בָּרָאתִי חָרָשׁ 16aA Behold, it is I who created the craftsman,

With: $\mathfrak{M}$ (5) – $\mathfrak{S}^{e}$
Discussion: $\mathfrak{G}$ has a free paraphrasis resulting in a dividing point after בראתי which is not supported by any other witness ($\mathfrak{M}$ conjunctive accent). Only one manuscript in the Peshiṭta tradition has preserved the divider which corresponds to $\mathfrak{M}$'s Zaqeph Qaṭon which is no doubt correct.

COLON 54:16aB:

נֹפֵחַ בְּאֵשׁ פֶּחָם 16aB who blows the fire of coals

With: $\mathfrak{M}$ (5) – $\mathfrak{G}^{SQ}$ – $\mathfrak{S}^{abcde}$ all subordinate punctuation.

---

[1] See also pp. 461-2, on 51:4bB.

COLON 54:16aC:

וּמוֹצִ֥יא כְלִ֖י לְמַעֲשֵׂ֑הוּ 16aC and produces the weapon for its purpose.

With: $\mathfrak{M}$ (2) – $\mathfrak{G}^{SQ}$ – $\mathfrak{S}^{abcde}$

COLON 54:16bA:

וְאָנֹכִ֛י בָּרָ֥אתִי מַשְׁחִ֖ית לְחַבֵּֽל׃ 16bA And it is I who created the destroyer to work havoc.

With: $\mathfrak{M}$ (1) – $\mathfrak{S}^{abcde}$

Discussion: $\mathfrak{G}^{SQ}$ have an extra point after בראתי[2] ($\mathfrak{M}$ conjunctive accent). Their paraphrastic rendering made it impossible to honour a division at this point.

COLON 54:17aA:

כָּל־כְּלִ֞י יוּצַ֤ר עָלַ֙יִךְ֙ לֹ֣א יִצְלָ֔ח 17aA No weapon formed against you, will have success,

With: $\mathfrak{M}$ (5) – $\mathfrak{G}^{SQ}$ – $\mathfrak{S}^{abcde}$

COLON 54:17aB:

וְכָל־לָשׁ֛וֹן תָּֽקוּם־אִתָּ֥ךְ לַמִּשְׁפָּ֖ט תַּרְשִׁ֑יעִי 17aB and every tongue rising against you in court you will prove guilty.

With: $\mathfrak{M}$ (2); although 1$\mathfrak{Q}^{a}$ has a shortened text, it clearly indicates a Petuḥa here – $\mathfrak{G}^{SQ}$; $\mathfrak{G}^{SAQ}$ all indicate a major break here, despite some expansion – $\mathfrak{S}^{abcde}$

Discussion: $\mathfrak{G}^{SQ}$ have an extra point after למשפט where $\mathfrak{M}$ has a Ṭiphḥa (No. 8). The remaining תרשיעי can hardly be regarded as an independent colon of one word.

COLON 54:17bA:

זֹ֗את נַֽחֲלַת֙ עַבְדֵ֣י יְהוָ֔ה 17bA This is the heritage of the servants of the LORD,

With: $\mathfrak{G}^{SQ}$ – $\mathfrak{S}^{a}$, $\mathfrak{S}^{bcde}$ all subordinate punctuation.

Discussion: $\mathfrak{M}^{2}$ has a conjunctive accent (Dargah, No.23) here which is obviously wrong. The Snaith Bible,[3] has a Geresh (No. 13, disjunctive). The ancient witnesses prove this to be the superior reading.

---

[2]Not only the Codex Leningradensis (Petropolitanus), but also the Cairo and Aleppo codices.

[3]ספר תורה נביאים וכתובים מדויק היטיב על פי המסורה, ed. N.H. Snaith, London 1958, 693.

COLON 54:17bB:

וְצִדְקָתָ֛ם מֵאִתִּ֖י נְאֻם־יְהוָֽה׃ 17bB and their justice from me, declares the LORD.

With: 𝔐 (1), with major division markers, also in 1𝔔[a] – 𝔊[SBAQ], major division markers in all – 𝔖[abcde], major division markers in all.

14.3 Isaiah 54 – Delimitation of Verse-lines

VERSE–LINE: 54:1a:

רָנִּ֥י עֲקָרָ֖ה לֹ֣א יָלָ֑דָה 1aA Rejoice, O barren one, who did not bear!
פִּצְחִ֨י רִנָּ֧ה וְצַהֲלִ֛י לֹא־חָ֖לָה 1aB Break forth into rejoicing and radiate,
you who did not bring to birth!

𝔐 distinctive accents: 2 – 5.
Stresses: 4 + 4.
Verse-line parallelism: רנן || פצח רנה; רנן || צהל; לא || לא; ילד || חיל; grammatical parallelism; rhyme.
Discussion: On the basis of 44:23 and 49:13 (and even 52:9) it is much more likely that רנן and פצח רנה stand in verse-line parallelism. See also the verse-line parallelism between צהל and רנן in Isa. 24:14; Jer. 31:17. So we deviate from 𝔐 here. The reason why the Masoretes may have decided to treat v. 1aA as an independent colon might be that only this colon is cited in bBer., 10a.

VERSE–LINE: 54:1b:

כִּֽי־רַבִּ֧ים בְּנֵֽי־שׁוֹמֵמָ֛ה 1bA For the children of the desolate one will be more
מִבְּנֵ֥י בְעוּלָ֖ה 1bB than the children of the one who has a husband,
אָמַ֥ר יְהוָֽה׃ 1bC says the LORD.

𝔐 distinctive accents: 12 – 8 – 1.
Stresses: 2 + 2 + 2.
Verse-line parallelism: בן || בן; שמם || בעל (antithetical, unique).

VERSE–LINE: 54:2a:

הַרְחִ֣יבִי ׀ מְק֣וֹם אָהֳלֵ֗ךְ 2aA Enlarge the place of your tent,
וִירִיע֧וֹת מִשְׁכְּנוֹתַ֛יִךְ יַטּ֖וּ אַל־תַּחְשֹׂ֑כִי 2aB and let them stretch out the cloth of your dwellings – do not hold back!

𝔐 distinctive accents: 7 – 2.
Stresses: 3 + 4.
Verse-line parallelism: roots רחב || נטה; מקום || משכן; אהל || משכן; ־ך (f.s.) || ־ך (f.s.).

VERSE–LINE: 54:2b:

הַאֲרִיכִי מֵיתָרַיִךְ	2bA	Lengthen your cords,
וִיתֵדֹתַיִךְ חַזֵּקִי׃	2bB	and strengthen your tent pegs!

𝔐 distinctive accents: 5 – 1.
Stresses: 2 + 2.
Verse-line parallelism: ארך || חזק; מיתר || יתד; ךְ־ (f.s.) || ךְ־ (f.s.); grammatical parallelism; rhyme.

VERSE–LINE: 54:3a:

כִּי־יָמִין וּשְׂמֹאול תִּפְרֹצִי	3aA	For you will spread out to the right and to the left,

𝔐 distinctive accents: 2.
Stresses: 3.
Verse-line parallelism: None (unicolon).

VERSE–LINE: 54:3b:

וְזַרְעֵךְ גּוֹיִם יִירָשׁ	3bA	and your seed will dispossess the nations
וְעָרִים נְשַׁמּוֹת יוֹשִׁיבוּ׃	3bB	and will settle in the desolate cities.

𝔐 distinctive accents: 5 – 1.
Stresses: 3 + 3.
Verse-line parallelism: גוי || עיר; ירש || ישב.

VERSE–LINE: 54:4a:

אַל־תִּירְאִי כִּי־לֹא תֵבוֹשִׁי	4aA	Do not fear, for you will not be put to shame,
וְאַל־תִּכָּלְמִי כִּי לֹא תַחְפִּירִי	4aB	and do not feel disgraced, for you will not become embarrassed.

𝔐 distinctive accents: 5 – 2.
Stresses: 3 + 4.
Verse-line parallelism: אל (not) || אל (not); ירא || כלם (unique); כי || כי; לא || לא; בוש || חפר; בוש || כלם; grammatical parallelism; rhyme.

VERSE–LINE: 54:4b:

כִּי בֹשֶׁת עֲלוּמַיִךְ תִּשְׁכָּחִי	4bA	For the shame of your youth you will forget,
וְחֶרְפַּת אַלְמְנוּתַיִךְ לֹא תִזְכְּרִי־עוֹד׃	4bB	and the humiliation of your widowhood you will remember no more.

𝔐 distinctive accents: 5 – 1.
Stresses: 4 + 4.
Verse-line parallelism: בשת || הרפה; עלומים || אלמנות; שכח || זכר (antithetical); grammatical parallelism; rhyme.

VERSE–LINE: 54:5a:

כִּי בֹעֲלַיִךְ עֹשַׂיִךְ 5aA For your husband is your Maker,
יְהוָה צְבָאוֹת שְׁמוֹ 5aB LORD of Hosts is his name;

𝔐 distinctive accents: 5 – 2.
Stresses: 3 + 3.
Verse-line parallelism: בעל || יהוה (אדון). In our opinion this text strongly suggests that the tetragrammaton was pronounced as אדני much earlier than the 𝔊 and Qumran.[1] Compare also Isa. 26:13 יְהוָה אֱלֹהֵינוּ בְּעָלוּנוּ אֲדֹנִים זוּלָתֶךָ לְבַד־בְּךָ נַזְכִּיר שְׁמֶךָ.
Discussion: Note that the lack of clear parallelism on the level of the verse is compensated by colon parallelism and strophe parallelism.

VERSE–LINE: 54:5b:

וְגֹאֲלֵךְ קְדוֹשׁ יִשְׂרָאֵל 5bA and your Redeemer is the Holy One of Israel,
אֱלֹהֵי כָל־הָאָרֶץ יִקָּרֵא׃ 5bB God of all the earth he is called.

𝔐 distinctive accents: 5 – 1.
Stresses: 3 + 3.
Verse-line parallelism: גאל || אלהים; קדוש ישׂראל || אלהים; ישׂראל || כל־הארץ.

VERSE–LINE: 54:6a:

כִּי־כְאִשָּׁה עֲזוּבָה וַעֲצוּבַת רוּחַ 6aA For like a forsaken wife, tormented in spirit,
קְרָאָךְ יְהוָה 6aB the LORD did call you;

𝔐 distinctive accents: 8 – 2.
Stresses: 4 + 2.
Verse-line parallelism: None.
Discussion: Because the sentence runs on through the two cola of the verse-line there is no verse-line parallelism. There is, however, compensating parallelism on the level of the strophe (see the delimitation of strophes).

VERSE–LINE: 54:6b:

וְאֵשֶׁת נְעוּרִים כִּי תִמָּאֵס 6bA but a wife of youth – how can she be rejected?
אָמַר אֱלֹהָיִךְ׃ 6bB says your God.

𝔐 distinctive accents: 8 – 1.
Stresses: 4 + 2.
Verse-line parallelism: None.

[1]For the very early date of the controversy between Baal and YHWH over the title 'lord' see J.C. de Moor, *The Rise of Yahwism: The Roots of Israelite Monotheism*, Leuven [2]1997, 437 s.v. 'lord'.

Discussion: The sentence runs on through the two cola of the verse-line. See our comment on v. 6a.

VERSE–LINE: 54:7a:

בְּרֶ֥גַע קָטֹ֖ן עֲזַבְתִּ֑יךְ	7aA	For a brief moment I have forsaken you,
וּבְרַחֲמִ֥ים גְּדֹלִ֖ים אֲקַבְּצֵֽךְ׃	7aB	but with great mercy I will gather you.

𝔐 distinctive accents: 2 – 1.
Stresses: 3 + 3.
Verse-line parallelism: קטן || גדל (antithetical); עזב || קבץ (antithetical); ךְ- (f.s.) || ךְ- (f.s.).

VERSE–LINE: 54:8a:

בְּשֶׁ֣צֶף קֶ֗צֶף הִסְתַּ֨רְתִּי פָנַ֥י רֶ֙גַע֙ מִמֵּ֔ךְ	8aA	In a surge of anger I hid my face from you for a moment,
וּבְחֶ֥סֶד עוֹלָ֖ם רִֽחַמְתִּ֑יךְ	8aB	but with eternal loyalty I have mercy upon you,
אָמַ֥ר גֹּאֲלֵ֖ךְ יְהוָֽה׃	8aC	says your Redeemer, the LORD.

𝔐 distinctive accents: 5 – 2 – 1.
Stresses: 6 + 3 + 3.
Verse-line parallelism: ב || ב; שצף קצף || חסד עולם (antithetical, unique); סתר פנים || רחם (antithetical, unique); רגע || עולם (antithetical, unique); ךְ- (f.s.) || ךְ- (f.s.) || ךְ-; grammatical parallelism; rhyme.
Discussion: The repetition of ב and ךְ- and the similar structure of vv. 8aA-B suggests that the antithetical words have to be taken as parallel pairs. Again strophe parallelism compensates for the rather weak verse-line parallelism (see delimitation of strophes).

VERSE–LINE: 54:9a:

כִּימֵ֥י* נֹ֙חַ֙ זֹ֣את לִ֔י	9aA	As in the days of Noah is this to me,
אֲשֶׁ֣ר נִשְׁבַּ֗עְתִּי מֵעֲבֹ֛ר מֵי־נֹ֥חַ ע֖וֹד עַל־הָאָ֑רֶץ	9aB	when I swore that the waters of Noah would never again cover the earth.

𝔐 distinctive accents: 5 – 2.
Stresses: 4 + 6.
Verse-line parallelism: נח || נח.

VERSE–LINE: 54:9b:

כֵּ֥ן נִשְׁבַּ֛עְתִּי מִקְּצֹ֥ף עָלַ֖יִךְ	9bA	So now I swear that I will no longer be angry with you,
וּמִגְּעָר־בָּֽךְ׃	9bB	or will rebuke you.

𝔐 distinctive accents: 8 – 1.
Stresses: 4 + 1.

Verse-line parallelism: מן || מן; קצף || גער (unique); על || ב; ־ך (f.s.) || ־ך (f.s.); grammatical parallelism.
Discussion: The diverging pattern of stressed units is rare, but is also attested in Isa. 48:16b. The cola are connected by ellipsis.

VERSE–LINE: 54:10a:

כִּ֤י הֶֽהָרִים֙ יָמ֔וּשׁוּ 10aA Though the mountains may move,
וְהַגְּבָע֖וֹת תְּמוּטֶ֑נָה 10aB and the hills may topple,

𝔐 distinctive accents: 5 – 2.
Stresses: 3 + 2.
Verse-line parallelism: הר || גבעה; מוש || מוט.
Discussion: Ellipsis connects the cola of this verse-line.

VERSE–LINE: 54:10b:

וְחַסְדִּ֞י מֵאִתֵּ֣ךְ לֹֽא־יָמ֗וּשׁ 10bA my loyalty will not move away from you,
וּבְרִ֤ית שְׁלוֹמִי֙ לֹ֣א תָמ֔וּט 10bB and the covenant of my peace will not topple,
אָמַ֥ר מְרַחֲמֵ֖ךְ יְהוָֽה׃ 10bC says the LORD who has mercy upon you.

𝔐 distinctive accents: 7 – 5 – 1.
Stresses: 3 + 4 + 3.
Verse-line parallelism: חסד || שלום || רחם; חסד || ברית; חסד || שלום; חסד || רחם; ־י || ־י; ־ך (f.s.) || ־ך (f.s.); לא || לא; מוש || מוט.

VERSE–LINE: 54:11a:

עֲנִיָּ֥ה סֹעֲרָ֖ה לֹ֣א נֻחָ֑מָה 11aA O afflicted one, storm-tossed, not comforted –

𝔐 distinctive accents: 2.
Stresses: 4.
Verse-line parallelism: None (unicolon).

VERSE–LINE: 54:11b:

הִנֵּ֨ה אָנֹכִ֜י מַרְבִּ֤יץ בַּפּוּךְ֙ אֲבָנַ֔יִךְ 11bA behold, I will set your stones in antimony,
וִיסַדְתִּ֖יךְ בַּסַּפִּירִֽים׃ 11bB and lay your foundations in lapis lazuli.

𝔐 distinctive accents: 5 – 1.
Stresses: 5 + 2.
Verse-line parallelism: רבץ || יסד (unique); ב || ב; פוך || ספיר (unique); ־ך (f.s.) || ־ך (f.s.).

VERSE–LINE: 54:12a:

וְשַׂמְתִּי כַּדְכֹד שִׁמְשֹׁתַיִךְ	12aA	And I will make your battlements of red jasper,
וּשְׁעָרַיִךְ לְאַבְנֵי אֶקְדָּח	12aB	and your gates of flintstones,
וְכָל־גְּבוּלֵךְ לְאַבְנֵי־חֵפֶץ׃	12aC	and your whole borderline of precious stones.

𝔐 distinctive accents: 5 – 2 – 1.
Stresses: 3 + 3 + 2.
Verse-line parallelism: כדכד || אקדח || חפץ; שמש || שער || גבול; ־ך (f.s.) || ־ך (f.s.) || ־ך (f.s.); ל || ל || ל; אבן || אבן; rhyme.
Discussion: Ellipsis connects the cola.

VERSE–LINE: 54:13a-14a:

וְכָל־בָּנַיִךְ לִמּוּדֵי יְהוָה	13aA	And all your children will be disciples of the LORD,
וְרַב שְׁלוֹם בָּנָיִךְ׃	13aB	and great will be the peace of your children
בִּצְדָקָה תִּכּוֹנָנִי	14aC	– in justice you will be established.

𝔐 distinctive accents: 2 – 1 – 2.
Stresses: 3 + 3 + 2.
Verse-line parallelism: בן || בן; ־ך (f.s.) || ־ך (f.s.); שלום || צדקה; rhyme.
Discussion: For this division see our comment on p. 578, n. 16.

VERSE–LINE: 54:14b:

רַחֲקִי מֵעֹשֶׁק כִּי־לֹא תִירָאִי	14bA	Stay far away from oppression, for you need not fear,
וּמִמְּחִתָּה כִּי לֹא־תִקְרַב אֵלָיִךְ׃	14bB	and from terror, for it shall not come near to you.

𝔐 distinctive accents: 5 – 1.
Stresses: 4 + 4.
Verse-line parallelism: מן || מן; עשק || מחתה (unique); כי || כי; לא || לא.
Discussion: The cola are connected by ellipsis.

VERSE–LINE: 54:15a:

הֵן גּוֹר יָגוּר אֶפֶס מֵאוֹתִי	15aA	Behold, do they attack you, it will not be my doing.
מִי־גָר אִתָּךְ עָלַיִךְ יִפּוֹל׃	15aB	Whoever attacks you, will fall over you.

𝔐 distinctive accents: 2 – 1.
Stresses: 5 + 4.
Verse-line parallelism: גור || גור; את || את.

VERSE–LINE: 54:16a:

הֵן אָנֹכִי בָּרָאתִי חָרָשׁ	16aA	Behold, it is I who created the craftsman,
נֹפֵחַ בְּאֵשׁ פֶּחָם	16aB	who blows the fire of coals
וּמוֹצִיא כְלִי לְמַעֲשֵׂהוּ	16aC	and produces the weapon for its purpose.

𝔐 distinctive accents: 5 – 5 – 2.
Stresses: 4 + 3 + 3.
Verse-line parallelism: roots ברא || עשׂה; חרשׁ || מעשׂה.
Discussion: The enjambment in this verse-line is the reason for the lack of explicit parallels.

VERSE–LINE: 54:16b:

וְאָנֹכִי בָּרָאתִי מַשְׁחִית לְחַבֵּל׃	16bA	And it is I who created the destroyer to work havoc.

𝔐 distinctive accents: 1.
Stresses: 4.
Verse-line parallelism: None (unicolon).

VERSE–LINE: 54:17a:

כָּל־כְּלִי יוּצַר עָלַיִךְ לֹא יִצְלָח	17aA	No weapon formed against you, will have success,
וְכָל־לָשׁוֹן תָּקוּם־אִתָּךְ לַמִּשְׁפָּט תַּרְשִׁיעִי	17aB	and every tongue rising against you in court you will prove guilty.

𝔐 distinctive accents: 5 – 2.
Stresses: 5 + 4.
Verse-line parallelism: כל || כל; כלי || לשׁון (unique); על || את; ךְ־ (f.s.) || ךְ־ (f.s.); צלח || רשׁע (antithetical).

VERSE–LINE: 54:17b:

זֹאת נַחֲלַת עַבְדֵי יְהוָה	17bA	This is the heritage of the servants of the LORD,
וְצִדְקָתָם מֵאִתִּי נְאֻם־יְהוָה׃	17bB	and their justice from me declares the LORD.

𝔐 distinctive accents: conjunctive accent – 1.
Stresses: 4 + 3.
Verse-line parallelism: נחלה || צדקה (unique); יהוה || יהוה.
Discussion: The ellipsis of זאת in v. 17bB forms an additional bond.

14.4 Isaiah 54 – Delimitation of Strophes

STROPHE i.1 (Isa. 54:1)

רָנִּי עֲקָרָה לֹא יָלָדָה	1aA	Rejoice, O barren one, who did not bear!
פִּצְחִי רִנָּה וְצַהֲלִי לֹא־חָלָה	1aB	Break forth into rejoicing and radiate, you who did not bring to birth!
כִּי־רַבִּים בְּנֵי־שׁוֹמֵמָה	1bA	For the children of the desolate one will be more
מִבְּנֵי בְעוּלָה	1bB	than the children of the one who has a husband,
אָמַר יְהוָה׃	1bC	says the LORD.

= Masoretic verse.
Separation ↑: major division markers in the textual tradition; imperative(s); vocatives; repetitive verse-line parallelism.
Separation ↓: major division marker in the textual tradition; deictic particle(s); marker of direct speech; repetitive verse-line parallelism.
Strophe parallelism: עקר || שׁמם.

STROPHE i.2 (Isa. 54:2)

הַרְחִיבִי ׀ מְקוֹם אָהֳלֵךְ	2aA	Enlarge the place of your tent,
וִירִיעוֹת מִשְׁכְּנוֹתַיִךְ יַטּוּ אַל־תַּחְשֹׂכִי	2aB	and let them stretch out the cloth of your dwellings – do not hold back!
הַאֲרִיכִי מֵיתָרַיִךְ	2bA	Lengthen your cords,
וִיתֵדֹתַיִךְ חַזֵּקִי׃	2bB	and strengthen your tent pegs!

= Masoretic verse.
Separation ↑: major division marker in the textual tradition; imperative(s); jussive(s); repetitive verse-line parallelism; swapping (object).
Separation ↓: imperative(s); repetitive verse-line parallelism; swapping (object).
Strophe parallelism: רחב || ארך; יריעה || מיתר; ־ךְ (f.s.) || ־ךְ (f.s.); grammatical parallelism.

STROPHE i.3 (Isa. 54:3)

כִּי־יָמִין וּשְׂמֹאול תִּפְרֹצִי	3aA	For you will spread out to the right and to the left,
וְזַרְעֵךְ גּוֹיִם יִירָשׁ	3bA	and your seed will dispossess the nations
וְעָרִים נְשַׁמּוֹת יוֹשִׁיבוּ׃	3bB	and will settle in the desolate cities.

= Masoretic verse.
Separation ↑: deictic particle(s); swapping (adjunct).
Separation ↓: major division markers in the textual tradition; swapping (subject); swapping (object).

Strophe parallelism: None, but the allusion to Gen. 28:14 connects the two verse-lines.

STROPHE ii.1 (Isa. 54:4)

אַל־תִּירְאִי כִּי־לֹא תֵבוֹשִׁי	4aA	Do not fear, for you will not be put to shame,
וְאַל־תִּכָּלְמִי כִּי לֹא תַחְפִּירִי	4aB	and do not feel disgraced, for you will not become embarrassed.
כִּי בֹשֶׁת עֲלוּמַיִךְ תִּשְׁכָּחִי	4bA	For the shame of your youth you will forget,
וְחֶרְפַּת אַלְמְנוּתַיִךְ לֹא תִזְכְּרִי־עוֹד׃	4bB	and the humiliation of your widowhood you will remember no more.

= Masoretic verse.
Separation ↑: major division markers in the textual tradition; deictic particle(s); jussive(s).
Separation ↓: deictic particle(s); swapping (object).
Strophe parallelism: בוש || בשת; חפר || חרפה (unique); grammatical parallelism.

STROPHE ii.2 (Isa. 54:5)

כִּי בֹעֲלַיִךְ עֹשַׂיִךְ	5aA	For your husband is your Maker,
יְהוָה צְבָאוֹת שְׁמוֹ	5aB	LORD of Hosts is his name;
וְגֹאֲלֵךְ קְדוֹשׁ יִשְׂרָאֵל	5bA	and your Redeemer is the Holy One of Israel,
אֱלֹהֵי כָל־הָאָרֶץ יִקָּרֵא׃	5bB	God of all the earth he is called.

= Masoretic verse.
Separation ↑: deictic particle(s); swapping (subject).
Separation ↓: major division markers in the textual tradition; swapping (subject).
Strophe parallelism: עשה || גאל; ךְ־ (f.s.) || ךְ־ (f.s.); יהוה || אלהים; קרא || שם.

STROPHE iii.1 (Isa. 54:6)

כִּי־כְאִשָּׁה עֲזוּבָה וַעֲצוּבַת רוּחַ	6aA	For like a forsaken wife, tormented in spirit,
קְרָאָךְ יְהוָה	6aB	the LORD did call you;
וְאֵשֶׁת נְעוּרִים כִּי תִמָּאֵס	6bA	but a wife of youth – how can she be rejected?
אָמַר אֱלֹהָיִךְ׃	6bB	says your God.

= Masoretic verse.
Separation ↑: major division markers in the textual tradition; swapping (adjunct).
Separation ↓: major division marker in the textual tradition; deictic particle(s); marker of direct speech; swapping (subject).
Strophe parallelism: אשה || אשה; עזב || נעורים (antithetical); קרא || אמר; יהוה || אלהים; ךְ־ (f.s.) || ךְ־ (f.s.).

STROPHE iii.2 (Isa. 54:7–8)

בְּרֶגַע קָטֹן עֲזַבְתִּיךְ	7aA	For a brief moment I have forsaken you,
וּבְרַחֲמִים גְּדֹלִים אֲקַבְּצֵךְ׃	7aB	but with great mercy I will gather you.
בְּשֶׁצֶף קֶצֶף הִסְתַּרְתִּי פָנַי רֶגַע מִמֵּךְ	8aA	In a surge of anger I hid my face from you for a moment,
וּבְחֶסֶד עוֹלָם רִחַמְתִּיךְ	8aB	but with eternal loyalty I have mercy upon you,
אָמַר גֹּאֲלֵךְ יְהוָה׃	8aC	says your Redeemer, the LORD.

≠ Masoretic verse.
Separation ↑: major division marker in the textual tradition; repetitive verse-line parallelism; swapping (adjunct).
Separation ↓: repetitive verse-line parallelism; swapping (adjunct).
Strophe parallelism: רגע || רגע (unique); ךְ־ (f.s.) || ךְ־ (f.s.); ב || ב; שׁצף || רגע (unique); עזב || סתר פנים; רחמים || קצף (antithetical); חסד || רחמים; רחמים || רחם; קבץ || רחם; grammatical parallelism.
Discussion: The very strong parallelistic bond argues against 𝔐's distribution over two verses.

STROPHE iv.1 (Isa. 54:9)

כִּימֵי* נֹחַ זֹאת לִי	9aA	As in the days of Noah is this to me,
אֲשֶׁר נִשְׁבַּעְתִּי מֵעֲבֹר מֵי־נֹחַ עוֹד עַל־הָאָרֶץ	9aB	when I swore that the waters of Noah would never again cover the earth.
כֵּן נִשְׁבַּעְתִּי מִקְּצֹף עָלַיִךְ	9bA	So now I swear that I will no longer be angry with you,
וּמִגְּעָר־בָּךְ׃	9bB	or will rebuke you.

= Masoretic verse.
Separation ↑: major division markers in the textual tradition; demonstrative pronoun; repetitive verse-line parallelism; swapping (adjunct).
Separation ↓: deictic particle(s); repetitive verse-line parallelism.
Strophe parallelism: כ || כן; שׁבע || שׁבע; grammatical parallelism.

STROPHE iv.2 (Isa. 54:10)

כִּי הֶהָרִים יָמוּשׁוּ	10aA	Though the mountains may move,
וְהַגְּבָעוֹת תְּמוּטֶנָה	10aB	and the hills may topple,
וְחַסְדִּי מֵאִתֵּךְ לֹא־יָמוּשׁ	10bA	my loyalty will not move away from you,
וּבְרִית שְׁלוֹמִי לֹא תָמוּט	10bB	and the covenant of my peace will not topple,
אָמַר מְרַחֲמֵךְ יְהוָה׃	10bC	says the LORD who has mercy upon you.

= Masoretic verse.
Separation ↑: deictic particle(s); swapping (subject).
Separation ↓: major division markers in the textual tradition; marker

of direct speech; repetitive verse-line parallelism; swapping (subject); swapping (adjunct).
Strophe parallelism: מוּשׁ || מוּשׁ (unique); מוט || מוט (unique).

STROPHE v.1 (Isa. 54:11)

עֲנִיָּה סֹעֲרָה לֹא נֻחָמָה	11aA	O afflicted one, storm-tossed, not comforted –
הִנֵּה אָנֹכִי מַרְבִּיץ בַּפּוּךְ אֲבָנַיִךְ	11bA	behold, I will set your stones in antimony,
וִיסַדְתִּיךְ בַּסַּפִּירִים׃	11bB	and lay your foundations in lapis lazuli.

= Masoretic verse.
Separation ↑: major division markers in the textual tradition; vocatives.
Separation ↓: major division markers in the textual tradition; deictic particle(s); independent pers. pronoun; repetitive verse-line parallelism; swapping (adjunct).
Strophe parallelism: None.
Discussion: Despite the lack of parallelism the delimitation of the strophe is beyond doubt. In addition to the markers of separation enumerated above it may be observed that v. 11a requires v. 11b to be comprehensible.

STROPHE v.2 (Isa. 54:12–14a)

וְשַׂמְתִּי כַּדְכֹד שִׁמְשֹׁתַיִךְ	12aA	And I will make your battlements of red jasper,
וּשְׁעָרַיִךְ לְאַבְנֵי אֶקְדָּח	12aB	and your gates of flintstones,
וְכָל־גְּבוּלֵךְ לְאַבְנֵי־חֵפֶץ׃	12aC	and your whole borderline of precious stones.
וְכָל־בָּנַיִךְ לִמּוּדֵי יְהוָה	13aA	And all your children will be disciples of the LORD,
וְרַב שְׁלוֹם בָּנָיִךְ׃	13aB	and great will be the peace of your children
בִּצְדָקָה תִּכּוֹנָנִי	14aC	– in justice you will be established.

≠ Masoretic verse.
Separation ↑: major division markers in the textual tradition; repetitive verse-line parallelism; swapping (adjunct).
Separation ↓: major division markers in the textual tradition; repetitive verse-line parallelism; swapping (adjunct).
Strophe parallelism: שׂים || כון Polel; אך (f.s.) || ־ך (f.s.); כל || כל.
Discussion: The Masoretes took vv. 12 and 13 as separate strophes, probably because v. 13 was quoted many times in rabbinic literature,[1] but v. 12 was not.[2] It is far more likely, however, that the precious

[1] E.g. bBer., 64a; bYeb., 122b; bNaz., 66b; bKar., 28b; Gen. R., XCV.3.
[2] Disregarding a few quotations in Pesiqta Rabbati.

stones of v. 12 were seen as complementary to the children of v. 13, just like Zion's attire and her children were combined in one strophe in Isa. 49:18. The parallelism confirms this. It is therefore not impossible that also the assonance between אבנים and בנים was intentional.[3] Like most commentators, we take v. 14aC with v. 13, with the support of $\mathfrak{G}^{AS}$.[4] This opens the possibility that the precious 'stones' of the new Zion were intended in a metaphorical way. See also v. 17 as well as our remarks concerning the macrostructure of Ch. 54.

STROPHE vi.1 (Isa. 54:14b)

רַחֲקִי מֵעֹשֶׁק כִּי־לֹא תִירָאִי	14bA	Stay far away from oppression, for you need not fear,
וּמִמְּחִתָּה כִּי לֹא־תִקְרַב אֵלָיִךְ׃	14bB	and from terror, for it shall not come near to you.

≠ Masoretic verse.
Separation ↑: major division markers in the textual tradition; imperative(s); repetitive verse-line parallelism.
Separation ↓: major division marker in the textual tradition.
Strophe parallelism: None (one verse-line).
Discussion: With regard to v. 14a, see our discussion of the previous strophe.

STROPHE vi.2 (Isa. 54:15)

הֵן גּוֹר יָגוּר אֶפֶס מֵאוֹתִי	15aA	Behold, do they attack you, it will not be my doing.
מִי־גָר אִתָּךְ עָלַיִךְ יִפּוֹל׃	15aB	Whoever attacks you, will fall over you.

= Masoretic verse.
Separation ↑: major division marker in the textual tradition; deictic particle(s); interrogative pronoun; paronomasia; swapping (adjunct).
Separation ↓: major division markers in the textual tradition.
Strophe parallelism: None (one verse-line).

STROPHE vii.1 (Isa. 54:16)

הֵן אָנֹכִי בָּרָאתִי חָרָשׁ	16aA	Behold, it is I who created the craftsman,
נֹפֵחַ בְּאֵשׁ פֶּחָם	16aB	who blows the fire of coals
וּמוֹצִיא כְלִי לְמַעֲשֵׂהוּ	16aC	and produces the weapon for its purpose.
וְאָנֹכִי בָּרָאתִי מַשְׁחִית לְחַבֵּל׃	16bA	And it is I who created the destroyer to work havoc.

= Masoretic verse.

[3]Later on this wordplay became very important, cf. K. Snodgrass, *The Parable of the Wicked Tenants*, Tübingen 1983, 63-5, 113-8.
[4]See p. 578, n. 16.

Separation ↑: major division markers in the textual tradition; deictic particle(s); independent pers. pronoun.
Separation ↓: independent pers. pronoun.
Strophe parallelism: אנכי || אנכי; ברא || ברא; ל || ל; grammatical parallelism.

STROPHE vii.2 (Isa. 54:17a)

כָּל־כְּלִ֞י יוּצַ֤ר עָלַ֙יִךְ֙ לֹ֣א יִצְלָ֔ח	17aA	No weapon formed against you, will have success,
וְכָל־לָשׁ֛וֹן תָּֽקוּם־אִתָּ֥ךְ לַמִּשְׁפָּ֖ט תַּרְשִׁ֑יעִי	17aB	and every tongue rising against you in court you will prove guilty.

≠ Masoretic verse.
Separation ↑: repetitive verse-line parallelism; swapping (subject).
Separation ↓: major division markers in the textual tradition.
None (one verse-line).
Discussion: Although there does exist a parallelistic link with v. 17b (משפט || צדקה; את || את), the sudden transition from a second person feminine to a third person plural seems to indicate a break. 1Q[a] and $\mathfrak{G}^{SAQ}$ all have major division markers at this point[5] which would seem to indicate a strophe end, because all these witnesses also have a major break after v. 17.

STROPHE vii.3 (Isa. 54:17b)

זֹ֡את נַחֲלַת֩ עַבְדֵ֨י יְהוָ֜ה	17bA	This is the heritage of the servants of the LORD,
וְצִדְקָתָ֛ם מֵאִתִּ֖י נְאֻם־יְהוָֽה׃	17bB	and their justice from me, declares the LORD.

≠ Masoretic verse.
Separation ↑: major division markers in the textual tradition; demonstrative pronoun; marker of direct speech; repetitive verse-line parallelism.
Separation ↓: major division markers in the textual tradition.
Strophe parallelism: None (one verse-line).

[5] 1Q after a minus, $\mathfrak{G}^{SAQ}$ after a plus.

14.5 Isaiah 54 – Delimitation of Canticles

CANTICLE i (54:1–3)

Separation ↑: major division markers in the textual tradition; thematic discontinuity; change of subject.
Separation ↓: major division markers in the textual tradition.
Canticle parallelism: בן || זרע (responsion); שמם || שמם (responsion); רחב || פרץ (unique; responsion); ך־ (f.s.) || ך־ (f.s.) (inclusion).
Thematic unity: yes. All three strophes promise Zion numerous offspring and the territory to accommodate them.
Discussion: 1Q^a marks the end of v.1. The paragraphos in 𝔊^Q after תפרצי apparently marks the break after v. 3 proleptically.

CANTICLE ii (54:4–5)

Separation ↑: major division markers in the textual tradition; change of subject.
Separation ↓: major division markers in the textual tradition.
Canticle parallelism: כי || כי (responsion/concatenation); ך־ (f.s.) || ך־ (f.s.) (responsion/concatenation).
Thematic unity: yes. Zion's state as a woman without a husband will end because the LORD will be her husband again.

CANTICLE iii (54:6–8)

Separation ↑: major division markers in the textual tradition.
Separation ↓: major division markers in the textual tradition.
Canticle parallelism: עזב || עזב (responsion); יהוה || יהוה (inclusion); ך־ (f.s.) || ך־ (f.s.); אמר || אמר (responsion).
Thematic unity: yes. God cannot forsake Zion any longer.
Discussion: The paragraphos after v. 6 in 𝔊^S probably marks the break after v. 5 belatedly.

CANTICLE iv (54:9–10)

Separation ↑: major division markers in the textual tradition.
Separation ↓: major division markers in the textual tradition.
Canticle parallelism: ארץ || הר (responsion); מן || מן (responsion); קצף || חסד (antithetical; responsion); קצף || רחם (antithetical); ך־ (f.s.) || ך־ (f.s.) (responsion).
Thematic unity: yes. Both verses promise Zion mercy and both obviously refer to Gen. 9:9-17, be it in a non-literal way, as is Second Isaiah's custom.

Discussion: The major break after v. 10 is attested in 𝔐, 1Q^{a}, 4Q^{cd} and S^{bce}, but not in 𝔊. However, 𝔊^{A} has major division markers after v. 10bB תמוט and 𝔊^{SB} after נחמה in v. 11, both spots where a major break is impossible. Again the only reasonable explanation is proleptic marking in 𝔊^{A} whereas 𝔊^{SB} are lagging behind. Yet all three must be regarded as witnesses for the break after v.10.

CANTICLE v (54:11–14a)

Separation ↑: major division markers in the textual tradition.
Separation ↓: major division markers in the textual tradition.
Canticle parallelism: יסד || כון (responsion); אבן || אבן (concatenation); ךָ (f.s.) || ךָ (f.s.) (concatenation/responsion); ב || ב (responsion).
Thematic unity: yes. Both strophes describe the restoration of Zion.
Discussion: See our remarks with regard to the preceding canticle. The major division markings in 𝔊^{A} after v. 11 must be regarded as the marking of the strophe end, as is more often the case in this manuscript. 𝔊^{Q} marks the break after v. 14 proleptically after v. 13aA. The Setuma in 1Q^{a} after v. 14bB is probably a belated marking of the same break because 1Q^{a} also indicates the break after v. 15.

CANTICLE vi (54:14b–15)

Separation ↑: major division markers in the textual tradition; change of subject.
Separation ↓: major division markers in the textual tradition.
Canticle parallelism: קרב || גור (unique; responsion); אל || על (responsion); ךָ (f.s.) || ךָ (f.s.) (responsion).
Thematic unity: yes. Both strophes promise protection against enemies.
Discussion: With regard to the Setuma in 1Q^{a} after v. 14 see our comment on the previous canticle. The extreme shortness of this canticle – two strophes of only one verse-line each – is insufficient reason to deviate from the transmitted delimitation. According to the law of expansion and contraction every structural unit, including the canticle, could be condensed or enlarged.[1]

CANTICLE vii (54:16–17)

Separation ↑: major division markers in the textual tradition; change of subject.
Separation ↓: major division markers in the textual tradition.

---

[1]See p. 638.

Canticle parallelism: ברא || יצר (responsion/concatenation); כלי || כלי (responsion); משפט || צדקה (responsion).
Thematic unity: yes. Since God is behind everything, even if Zion is attacked, it is also in his power to prevent the use of weapons against Zion and to punish the attacker for his use of violence.
Discussion: Since the witnesses for a break after v. 17a are also among those who have the break after v. 17b, the former break probably represents a genuine old division point which in view of the shortness of the passage it is marking probably derives from a strophe marker.

14.6 Isaiah 54 – Delimitation of Macrostructure

The coherence of this canto prevents us to subdivide it into subcantos. In all canticles Zion is addressed and often chain-like distant parallelism connects them all:

Canticles i – ii

עקרה לא ילדה (v.1aA – i) || אלמנות (v. 4bB – ii); בן (v. 1bA-B – i) || בן (v. 13aA-B – v); שמם (v. 1bA – i) || עזב (vv. 6aA, 7aA – ii); בעל (v. 1bB – i) || בעל (v. 5aA – ii); אמר (v. 1bC – i) || אמר (v. 6bB – ii) || אמר (v. 10bC – iv).

Canticles ii – iii

עלמים (v. 4bA – ii) || נעורים (v. 6bA – iii) (unique); אלהים (v. 5bB – ii) || אלהים (v. 6bB – iii); קרא (v. 5bB – ii) || קרא (v. 6aB – iii); גאל (v. 5bA – ii) || גאל (v. 8aC – iii)

Canticles iii – iv

רחם (v. 7aB, 8aB – iii) || רחם (v.10bC – iv); קצף (v. 8aA – iii) || קצף (v. 9bA – iv); חסד (v. 8aB – iii) || חסד (v. 10bA – iv).

Canticles iv – v

מוט (vv. 10aB, 10bB – iv) || יסד (v. 11bB – v; antithetical); שלום (v. 10bB – iv) || שלום (v. 13aB – v); רחם (v. 10bC – iv) || נחם (v. 11aA – v).

Canticles v – vi

עני (v. 11aA – v) || עשק (v. 14bA – vi).

Canticles vi – vii

מן (v. 15aA – vi) || מן (v. 17bB – vii); את (prep.) (v. 15aA – vi) || את (prep.) (v. 17bB – vii); גור (v. 15aB – vi) || קום (v. 17aB – vii; unique); את (prep.) (v. 15aB – vi) || את (prep.) (v. 17aB – vii).

As this survey shows, it is impossible to isolate sub-cantos in this chapter without sacrificing some of the parallelistic chaining. Of course there are some other parallelistic bonds, like ארץ (v. 5bB – ii) || ארץ (v. 9aB – iv), ירא (v. 4aA – ii) || ירא (v. 14bA – vi) and צדקה (v. 14aC – v) || צדקה (v. 17bB – vii). But these are far less prominent than the chains enumerated above. Yet we want to underline this final pair – it strongly suggests that the למודי יהוה (v. 13aA) are identical to the עבדי יהוה (v. 17bA). The children of Zion are the servants of the LORD if they learn from his teaching.[1] This is exactly what the servant claims for himself in Isa. 50:4-5 and there too the expectation is that God will justify him (50:8) and that no one will be able to prove him guilty (50:9, compare 54:17). Again our structural analysis lends support to the interpretation of the servant of the LORD as a corporate personality.

The overall structure of the canto appears to be symmetric on the level of the strophes,

SUB-CANTOS	CANTICLES	STROPHES
A	6	14 (3+2+2+2+2+3)

[1]Cf. Ps. 119:124, 135.

Chapter 15

The Structure of Isaiah 55

15.1 Isaiah 55: Text and Translation

𝔐 – 1𝔔^{a} – 4𝔔^{c} – 𝔊^{SBAQ} – 𝔖^{abcde} ________________________________

A.i.1 (Isa. 55:1)

הֹוי כָּל־צָמֵא לְכוּ לַמַּיִם	1aA	Ho,[1] all who are thirsty, come to the waters,
וַאֲשֶׁר אֵין־לֹו כָּסֶף	1aB	and he who has no silver,
לְכוּ שִׁבְרוּ וֶאֱכֹלוּ	1bA	come,[2] buy and eat,[3]
וּלְכוּ שִׁבְרוּ בְּלֹוא־כֶסֶף	1bB	yes, come, buy without silver,
וּבְלֹוא מְחִיר יַיִן וְחָלָב׃	1bC	and without price, wine and milk!

A.i.2 (Isa. 55:2)

לָמָּה תִשְׁקְלוּ־כֶסֶף בְּלֹוא־לֶחֶם	2aA	Why do you weigh out silver for that which is not bread?
{𝔊^{S}𝔖^{b}} וִיגִיעֲכֶם בְּלֹוא לְשָׂבְעָה	2aB	and your labour for that which does not satisfy?
שִׁמְעוּ שָׁמֹועַ אֵלַי וְאִכְלוּ־טֹוב	2bA	Hearken diligently to me, and eat what is good,
{𝔊^{BA}} וְתִתְעַנַּג בַּדֶּשֶׁן נַפְשְׁכֶם׃	2bB	and let your soul[4] delight in fatness.

A.i.3 (Isa. 55:3)

הַטּוּ אָזְנְכֶם וּלְכוּ אֵלַי	3aA	Incline your ear, and come to me;
{𝔊^{Q}} שִׁמְעוּ וּתְחִי נַפְשְׁכֶם	3aB	hear, that your soul may live!
וְאֶכְרְתָה לָכֶם בְּרִית עֹולָם	3bA	And let me make with you an everlasting covenant,
חַסְדֵי דָוִד הַנֶּאֱמָנִים׃	3bB	the steadfast testimonies of loyalty for David.

𝔊^{SA} – 𝔖^{abe} . . . .

---

[1]From the very start the speaker wants to draw the attention of the audience by seemingly contradictory statements. In the mouth of a prophet הוי usually introduced a prophecy of doom, but the sequel immediately disproves this expectation. Cf. W. Janzen, *Mourning Cry and Woe Oracle* (BZAW, 125), Berlin 1972, 20.

[2]BHS proposes to transpose the Atnaḥ, without any justification. Triplets of imperatives are quite normal in Second Isaiah (see our notes on pp. 497, 502, 507.

[3]1𝔔, 𝔊 and 𝔖 shorten the text in different ways. There is insufficient reason, however, for the proposal (e.g. BHS; Whybray, 191; Grimm, Dittert, 91) to delete ולכו שברו, cf. Barthélemy, 409-10; Koole, 321; Oswalt, 432, n. 3.

[4]Up to this moment the audience might still interpret נפש as "throat". Unfortunately this is not a viable option to the translator because of v. 3. Cf. M.C.A. Korpel, "Metaphors in Isaiah LV", *VT* 46 (1996), 43-55 (49).

A.ii.1 (Isa. 55:4)

הֵן עֵד לְאוּמִּים נְתַתִּיו	4aA	Behold, I made him a witness to the nations,
נָגִיד וּמְצַוֵּה לְאֻמִּים׃	4aB	a leader and commander to the peoples.

A.ii.2 (Isa. 55:5)

הֵן גּוֹי לֹא־תֵדַע תִּקְרָא	5aA	Behold, a nation that you know not you shall call,[5]
וְגוֹי לֹא־יְדָעוּךָ אֵלֶיךָ יָרוּצוּ	5aB	and a nation that does not know you shall run to you,
לְמַעַן יְהוָה אֱלֹהֶיךָ	5bA	because of the LORD your God,
וְלִקְדוֹשׁ יִשְׂרָאֵל{𝔊^S}כִּי פֵאֲרָךְ׃	5bB	and of the Holy One of Israel for he has glorified you.

ס<פ> – 1𝔔^ab – 4𝔔^c – 𝔊^SBAQ – 𝔖^bce ______________________________

B.i.1 (Isa. 55:6)

דִּרְשׁוּ יְהוָה	6aA	Seek the LORD,
בְּהִמָּצְאוֹ קְרָאֻהוּ	6aB	call upon him while he may be found,
בִּהְיוֹתוֹ קָרוֹב׃	6aC	while he is near.

B.i.2 (Isa. 55:7)

יַעֲזֹב רָשָׁע דַּרְכּוֹ	7aA	Let the wicked abandon his way
וְאִישׁ אָוֶן מַחְשְׁבֹתָיו	7aB	and the unrighteous man his thoughts.
וְיָשֹׁב אֶל־יְהוָה וִירַחֲמֵהוּ	7bA	Let him return to the LORD and he will have mercy on him,
וְאֶל־אֱלֹהֵינוּ כִּי־יַרְבֶּה לִסְלוֹחַ׃	7bB	and to our God, for he will abundantly pardon.

<ס> – 1𝔔^a – 𝔊^Q ....

B.ii.1 (Isa. 55:8)

כִּי לֹא מַחְשְׁבוֹתַי מַחְשְׁבוֹתֵיכֶם	8aA	For my thoughts are not your thoughts
וְלֹא דַרְכֵיכֶם דְּרָכָי	8aB	neither are your ways my ways,
נְאֻם יְהוָה׃	8aC	declares the LORD.

[5] Our colleague P.C. Beentjes (Catholic Theological University, Utrecht) suggested to us to take קרא in the sense of "to meet" (= קרה). Because the parallel verb is רוץ, this is an attractive option – the two verbs are often combined in the Hebrew Bible.

However, three considerations argue against the proposal. It is not supported by any of the ancient witnesses. Moreover, the function of Israel will be to act as a witness to the nations (v. 4) which makes "to call" the better rendering. Finally, the context requires a more active role of Israel, balancing the running of the peoples.

B.ii.2 (Isa. 55:9)

כִּֽי־גָבְה֤וּ שָׁמַ֙יִם֙ מֵאָ֔רֶץ	9aA	For as[6] the heavens are higher than the earth,
כֵּ֣ן גָּבְה֤וּ דְרָכַי֙ מִדַּרְכֵיכֶ֔ם	9bA	so are my ways higher than your ways,
וּמַחְשְׁבֹתַ֖י מִמַּחְשְׁבֹתֵיכֶֽם׃	9bB	and my thoughts than your thoughts.

<ס> – $1\mathfrak{Q}^{a}$ – $\mathfrak{G}^{AQ}$ ________________________________

C.i.1 (Isa. 55:10a)

כִּ֡י כַּאֲשֶׁר֩ יֵרֵ֨ד הַגֶּ֜שֶׁם {וְהַשֶּׁ֗לֶג} מִן־הַשָּׁמַ֔יִם	10aA	For as the rain comes down {and the snow}[7] from heaven,
וְשָׁ֙מָּה֙ לֹ֣א יָשׁ֔וּב	10aB	and does not return thither,

C.i.2 (Isa. 55:10b-c)

כִּ֚י אִם־הִרְוָ֣ה אֶת־הָאָ֔רֶץ	10bA	but waters the earth
וְהוֹלִידָ֖הּ וְהִצְמִיחָ֑הּ	10bB	making it bear and sprout,
וְנָ֤תַן זֶ֙רַע֙ לַזֹּרֵ֔עַ	10cA	giving seed to the sower
וְלֶ֖חֶם לָאֹכֵֽל׃ {$\mathfrak{G}^{Q}$}	10cB	and bread to the eater,

C.i.3 (Isa. 55:11)

כֵּ֣ן יִהְיֶ֤ה דְבָרִי֙ אֲשֶׁ֣ר יֵצֵ֣א מִפִּ֔י	11aA	so shall my word be that goes forth from my mouth:
לֹֽא־יָשׁ֥וּב אֵלַ֖י רֵיקָ֑ם	11aB	It shall not return to me empty,
כִּ֤י אִם־עָשָׂה֙ אֶת־אֲשֶׁ֣ר חָפַ֔צְתִּי	11bA	but it accomplishes that which I want,
וְהִצְלִ֖יחַ אֲשֶׁ֥ר שְׁלַחְתִּֽיו׃	11bB	and makes succeed what I send it for.

<ס> – $1\mathfrak{Q}^{a}$ – $\mathfrak{S}^{b}$ . . . .

C.ii.1 (Isa. 55:12)

כִּֽי־בְשִׂמְחָ֣ה תֵצֵ֔אוּ	12aA	For you shall go out in joy
וּבְשָׁל֖וֹם תּֽוּבָל֑וּן	12aB	and in peace be led forth.
הֶהָרִ֣ים וְהַגְּבָע֗וֹת	12bA	The mountains and the hills
יִפְצְח֤וּ לִפְנֵיכֶם֙ רִנָּ֔ה	12bB	shall break forth into singing before you,
וְכָל־עֲצֵ֥י הַשָּׂדֶ֖ה יִמְחֲאוּ־כָֽף׃ {$\mathfrak{G}^{A}$}	12bC	and all the trees of the field shall clap their hands.

[6]Cf. J.C.L. Gibson, *Davidson's Introductory Hebrew Grammar: Syntax*, Edinburgh [4]1994, §130.

[7]We regard this as a pseudo-learned gloss. Snow and frost were detrimental to the growth of the vegetation, cf. Gen. R. XIII.12; G. Dalman, *Arbeit und Sitte in Palästina*, Bd. 1,1, Gütersloh 1928, 249-50. This is the opposite of what was meant by the author.

C.ii.2 (Isa. 55:13)

תַּחַת הַנַּעֲצוּץ יַעֲלֶה בְרוֹשׁ	13aA	Instead of a camel thorn[8] shall come up a juniper,
וְתחת הַסִּרְפַּד יַעֲלֶה הֲדַס	13aB	and[9] instead of a nettle[10] shall come up a myrtle.
וְהָיָה לַיהוָה לְשֵׁם	13bA	And it shall be a name for the LORD,
לְאוֹת עוֹלָם לֹא יִכָּרֵת׃	13bB	an everlasting sign which shall not be cut off.

ס <פ> – 1𝔔^{ab} – 𝔊^{SBAQ} – 𝔖^{be} ________________________________

15.2 Isaiah 55 – Delimitation of Cola

COLON 55:1aA:

הוֹי כָּל־צָמֵא לְכוּ לַמַּיִם 1aA Ho, all who are thirsty, come to the waters,

With: 𝔐 (5) – 𝔊^{SQ} – 𝔖^{abcde}
Colon parallelism: צמא || מים.

COLON 55:1aB:

וַאֲשֶׁר אֵין־לוֹ כָּסֶף 1aB and he who has no silver,

With: 𝔐 (2) – 𝔊^{SQ} – 𝔖^{abcd} subordinated punctuation.

COLON 55:1bA:

לְכוּ שִׁבְרוּ וֶאֱכֹלוּ 1bA come, buy and eat,

With: 𝔐 (5)
Colon parallelism: Grammatical parallelism: three times imperative.[1]
Discussion: None of the ancient witnesses supports 𝔐. Instead they have a divider after בלוא־כסף where 𝔐 in turn has a rather weak dividing accent (Tevir, No. 12). However, since both 𝔊 and 𝔖 omit ולכו שברו and as the grammatical colon parallelism supports 𝔐, we decided to accept 𝔐.

[8]Cf. A.E. Rüthy, *Die Pflanze und ihre Teile im biblisch-hebräischen Sprachgebrauch*, Bern 1942, 15-6; J. Feliks, *Plant World of the Bible* (Hebr.), Ramat Gan 1968, 222-3.

[9]With the Qere, 1𝔔^{ab}, and all ancient versions.

[10]Feliks, *Plant World*, 228-9; M. Zohary, *Plants of the Bible*, Cambridge 1982, 162.

[1]Compare M.C.A. Korpel, J.C. de Moor, "Fundamentals of Ugaritic and Hebrew Poetry", in: W. van der Meer, J.C. de Moor (eds.), *The Structural Analysis of Biblical and Canaanite Poetry* (JSOT.S, 74), Sheffield 1988, 1-61 (6-7).

COLON 55:1bB:

וּלְכוּ שִׁבְרוּ בְּלוֹא־כֶסֶף 1bB yes, come, buy without silver,

With: 𝔐 (12) – S^{abcde}
Colon parallelism: See the preceding colon.
Discussion: 𝔐 has a distinctive accent with שברו^{2} (Revia‘, No. 7). Since 𝔊 and S are lacking there, we have no possibility to check 𝔐 at this point. However, the resulting unbalanced colometry argues against 𝔐's division. For this reason we follow S.

COLON 55:1bC:

וּבְלוֹא מְחִיר יַיִן וְחָלָב׃ 1bC and without price, wine and milk!

With: 𝔐 (1) – 𝔊^{S} – S^{abcde}
Colon parallelism: יין || חלב.

COLON 55:2aA:

לָמָּה תִשְׁקְלוּ־כֶסֶף בְּלוֹא־לֶחֶם 2aA Why do you weigh out silver for that which is not bread?

With: 𝔐 (5) – 𝔊^{SQ}; – S^{abcde} subordinate punctuation.
Colon parallelism: כסף || לחם.

COLON 55:2aB:

וִיגִיעֲכֶם בְּלוֹא לְשָׂבְעָה 2aB and your labour for that which does not satisfy?

With: 𝔐 (2) – 𝔊^{SQ}, major division marker in 𝔊^{S} – S^{abcde}, major division marker in S^{b}

COLON 55:2bA:

שִׁמְעוּ שָׁמוֹעַ אֵלַי וְאִכְלוּ־טוֹב 2bA Hearken diligently to me, and eat what is good,

With: 𝔐 (5) – 𝔊^{SQ} – S^{abcde}
Colon parallelism: Grammatical parallelism (two imperatives).

COLON 55:2bB:

וְתִתְעַנַּג בַּדֶּשֶׁן נַפְשְׁכֶם׃ 2bB and let your soul delight in fatness.

With: 𝔐 (1) – 𝔊^{SBAQ}, major division markers in 𝔊^{BA} – S^{abcde}

COLON 55:3aA:

הַטּוּ אָזְנְכֶם וּלְכוּ אֵלַי 3aA Incline your ear, and come to me;

With: 𝔐 (5) – 𝔊^{SQ} – 𝔖^{abde}, cf. Mark 1:3 par.
Discussion: 𝔊^{SQ} have an extra divider after אזנכם (𝔐 Pashṭa, No. 10). 𝔖 does not support 𝔊 and the similar syntactic structure of the next colon argues in favour of 𝔐.

COLON 55:3aB:

שִׁמְעוּ וּתְחִי נַפְשְׁכֶם 3aB hear, that your soul may live!

With: 𝔐 (2) – 𝔊^{SQ}, major division marker in 𝔊^{Q} – 𝔖^{abcde}
Discussion: Again 𝔊^{SQ} have an extra divider, this time after שמעו. Apparently this was based on the decision they took in the preceding colon. 𝔐 deserves confidence because 𝔖 does not support this division and because the resulting colon of only one word is a rare phenomenon.

COLON 55:3bA:

וְאֶכְרְתָה לָכֶם בְּרִית עוֹלָם 3bA And let me make with you an everlasting covenant,

With: 𝔐 (5) – 𝔊^{SQ} – 𝔖^{ce}, and subordinate punctuation in 𝔖^{abd}

COLON 55:3bB:

חַסְדֵי דָוִד הַנֶּאֱמָנִים׃ 3bB the steadfast testimonies of loyalty for David.

With: 𝔐 (1) – 𝔊^{SAQ}, major dision markers in 𝔊^{SA} – 𝔖^{abde}, major division markers in 𝔖^{abe}

COLON 55:4aA:

הֵן עֵד לְאוּמִּים נְתַתִּיו 4aA Behold, I made him a witness to the nations,

With: 𝔐 (2) – 𝔊^{SQ} – 𝔖^{abcde}

COLON 55:4aB:

נָגִיד וּמְצַוֵּה לְאֻמִּים׃ 4aB a leader and commander to the peoples.

With: 𝔐 (1) – 𝔊^{SQ} – 𝔖^{abcde}

COLON 55:5aA:

הֵן גּוֹי לֹא־תֵדַע תִּקְרָא 5aA Behold, a nation that you know not you shall call,

With: 𝔐 (5) – 𝔊^{SQ} – 𝔖^{abcde}

COLON 55:5aB:

וְגוֹי לֹא־יְדָעוּךָ אֵלֶיךָ יָרוּצוּ 5aB and a nation that does not know you shall run to you,

With: 𝔐 (2) – 𝔊[Q] – 𝔖[abcde]
Discussion: 𝔊[SQ] have an extra divider after ולא־ידעוך which is unsupported by 𝔖. 𝔐 has a rather low level accent (Ṭiphḥa, No. 8) at that point.

COLON 55:5bA:

לְמַעַן יְהוָה אֱלֹהֶיךָ 5bA because of the LORD your God,

With: 𝔐 (5) – 𝔖[abe], 𝔖[cd] subordinate punctuation.
Colon parallelism: יהוה || אלהים.

COLON 55:5bB:

וְלִקְדוֹשׁ יִשְׂרָאֵל כִּי פֵאֲרָךְ׃ 5bB and of the Holy One of Israel for he has glorified you.

With: 𝔐 (1), Setuma in many manuscripts, Petuḥa in 1𝔔[a] and 4𝔔[c], indentation in 1𝔔[b] – 𝔊[SBAQ], major division markers in all – 𝔖[abcde], major division markers in 𝔖[bce]
Discussion: 𝔊[SQ] have an extra divider after ישׂראל (𝔐 Ṭiphḥa, No. 8), 𝔊[S] even a Petuḥah and a projecting line. The former is customary before Greek ὅτι and the latter obviously anticipates the major division after v. 5bB, as is indicated by the paragraphos in the same manuscript. Moreover, none of this is supported by 𝔖.

COLON 55:6aA:

דִּרְשׁוּ יְהוָה 6aA Seek the LORD,

With: 𝔐 (8) – 𝔊[SQ] – 𝔖[bde]
Discussion: In this verse 𝔐 and the rest of the ancient witnesses go different ways. Whereas 𝔐 has an Atnaḥ after בהמצאו, indicating a bicolon, 𝔊 and 𝔖 clearly prefer a tricolon. Because of the unanimous nature of their testimony we prefer the latter. It is very likely that the division of 𝔐 was inspired by the rabbinic exegesis of this verse. In bYeb., 59b and yYeb. 5:1 (37b) Isa. 55:6 is read as a bicolon and is applied to the synagogues and study halls. So the Rabbis took the ב in a *local* sense in order to counter Manasseh's purported argument that Isaiah had contradicted Moses (Deut. 4:7). Second Isaiah, however, had to cope with a situation when a common cult place was no longer available and so he explains the experience of God's proximity as a

spiritual process which may happen to a person if he abandons all sinful thoughts (v. 7). So he intended the ב in a *temporal* sense.

COLON 55:6aB:

בְּהִמָּצְאוֹ קְרָאֻהוּ 6aB call upon him while he may be found,

With: $\mathfrak{M}$ (8) – $\mathfrak{G}^{SQ}$ – $\mathfrak{S}^{bcde}$, $\mathfrak{S}^{a}$ subordinated punctuation.
Discussion: $\mathfrak{M}$ stands alone in putting a major incision after בהמצאו. See v. 6aA.

COLON 55:6aC:

בִּהְיוֹתוֹ קָרוֹב׃ 6aC while he is near.

With: $\mathfrak{M}$ (1) – $\mathfrak{G}^{SQ}$ – $\mathfrak{S}^{d}$
Discussion: Part of the $\mathfrak{S}$-tradition connected בהיותו קרוב with the following colon.

COLON 55:7aA:

יַעֲזֹב רָשָׁע דַּרְכּוֹ 7aA Let the wicked abandon his way

With: $\mathfrak{M}$ (5) – $\mathfrak{G}^{SQ}$ – $\mathfrak{S}^{abcde}$ subordinate punctuation.

COLON 55:7aB:

וְאִישׁ אָוֶן מַחְשְׁבֹתָיו 7aB and the unrighteous man his thoughts.

With: $\mathfrak{M}$ (2) – $\mathfrak{G}^{SQ}$ – $\mathfrak{S}^{abcde}$

COLON 55:7bA:

וְיָשֹׁב אֶל־יְהוָה וִירַחֲמֵהוּ 7bA Let him return to the LORD and he will have mercy on him,

With: $\mathfrak{M}$ (5) – $\mathfrak{G}^{SQ}$ – $\mathfrak{S}^{abcde}$
Colon parallelism: שׁוב || רחם.

COLON 55:7bB:

וְאֶל־אֱלֹהֵינוּ כִּי־יַרְבֶּה לִסְלוֹחַ׃ 7bB and to our God, for he will abundantly pardon.

With: $\mathfrak{M}$ (1), Setuma in $_{1}\mathfrak{Q}^{a}$ – $\mathfrak{G}^{SQ}$, major division marker in $\mathfrak{G}^{Q}$ – $\mathfrak{S}^{abcde}$

COLON 55:8aA:

כִּי לֹא מַחְשְׁבוֹתַי מַחְשְׁבוֹתֵיכֶם 8aA For my thoughts are not your thoughts

With: 𝔐 (5) – 𝔊^{SQ} – 𝔖^{abcde}
Colon parallelism: מחשבות || מחשבות.

Colon 55:8aB:

וְלֹ֥א דַרְכֵיכֶ֖ם דְּרָכָ֑י 8aB neither are your ways my ways,

With: 𝔐 (2) – 𝔊^{Q} – 𝔖^{ae}
Colon parallelism: דרך || דרך.
Discussion: 𝔊^{SQ} have an extra divider after דרכיכם (𝔐 Ṭiphḥa, No. 8), but 𝔖 supports 𝔐. Moreover, 𝔊^{Q} also has a dividing point after דרכי.

In most cases 𝔐 and the other ancient witnesses regard this formula not as a separate colon, but as the closing part of a colon.[2] Remarkably enough, however, in this case 𝔐 and some important other witnesses opted for a tricolon.

Colon 55:8aC:

נְאֻ֖ם יְהוָֽה׃ 8aC declares the Lord.

With: 𝔐 (1) – 𝔊^{Q} – 𝔖^{abcde}
Discussion: See our comment on v. 8aB.

Colon 55:9aA:

כִּֽי־גָבְה֥וּ שָׁמַ֖יִם מֵאָ֑רֶץ 9aA For as the heavens are higher than the earth,

With: 𝔐 (2) – 𝔊^{SQ} – 𝔖^{abcde} subordinate punctuation.
Colon parallelism: שמים || ארץ.
Discussion: 𝔐 opts for a unicolon plus a bicolon, in accordance with the parallelism. 𝔖 seems to presuppose a tricolon.

Colon 55:9bA:

כֵּ֣ן גָּבְה֤וּ דְרָכַי֙ מִדַּרְכֵיכֶ֔ם 9bA so are my ways higher than your ways,

With: 𝔐 (5) – 𝔊^{SQ} – 𝔖^{acde} subordinate punctuation.
Colon parallelism: דרך || דרך.
Discussion: See v. 9aA.

Colon 55:9bB:

וּמַחְשְׁבֹתַ֖י מִמַּחְשְׁבֹתֵיכֶֽם׃ 9bB and my thoughts than your thoughts.

With: 𝔐 (1), Setuma in 1𝔔^{a} – 𝔊^{SAQ}, major division markers in 𝔊^{AQ} – 𝔖^{abcde}
Colon parallelism: מחשבות || מחשבות.

[2]See our comments at 41:14bA; 43:10aA, 12bA; 49:18bA; 52:5bA; 54:17bB.

Discussion: 𝔊^{SQ} have a point after ומחשבתי which reflects nothing more than 𝔐's Ṭiphḥah (No. 8).

COLON 55:10aA:

כִּ֠י כַּאֲשֶׁ֩ר יֵרֵ֨ד הַגֶּ֜שֶׁם {וְהַשֶּׁ֙לֶג֙} מִן־הַשָּׁמַ֔יִם 10aA For as the rain comes down {and the snow} from heaven,

With: 𝔐 (7) – 𝔊^{SQ} – 𝔖^{e}

Discussion: In an earlier study one of us suggested that the conjunctive accent Azlah (No. 24) with הגשם in the Codex Leningradensis might be an error for a Pashṭa (No. 10).[3] However, both the Aleppo and Cairo codices support 𝔐^{L}. Moreover, both 𝔊 and 𝔖 support 𝔐. Apparently the resulting extremely long colon was acceptable to all of them. However, sentences running on as well as ellipsis often caused them to adopt such long cola.[4] In this particular case the singular verbs in the rest of v. 10 induce us to assume that והשלג is a hypercorrective gloss. Whereas the verb ירד is used with גשם in Ezek. 34:26 and Joel 2:23, the combination with שלג is unique. Moreover, the Ancients knew that cold halts the growth of the vegetation[5] and therefore snow does not fit in with the sequel. So we accept the colometry of 𝔐, 𝔊 and 𝔖 but omit והשלג.

COLON 55:10aB:

וְשָׁ֔מָּה לֹ֣א יָשׁ֔וּב 10aB and does not return thither,

With: 𝔐 (5) – 𝔊^{S} – 𝔖^{abcde} subordinate punctuation.

COLON 55:10bA:

כִּ֚י אִם־הִרְוָ֣ה אֶת־הָאָ֔רֶץ 10bA but waters the earth

With: 𝔐 (5) – 𝔊^{SQ}

Discussion: 𝔖 balances its very long colon v. 10aA with another long colon. 𝔊 supports 𝔐.

COLON 55:10bB:

וְהוֹלִידָ֖הּ וְהִצְמִיחָ֑הּ 10bB making it bear and sprout,

With: 𝔐 (2) – 𝔊^{S} – 𝔖^{abcde} subordinate punctuation.

Colon parallelism: ילד || צמח (unique).

---

[3]M.C.A. Korpel, "Metaphors in Isaiah lv", *VT* 46 (1996), 43-55 (45, n. 11).

[4]See J.C. de Moor, "Structure and Redaction in Isaiah 60,1–63,6", in: J. van Ruiten, M. Vervenne (eds.), *Studies in the Book of Isaiah: Festschrift Willem A.M. Beuken* (BETL, 132), Leuven 1997, 325-46 (328). Furthermore p. 638.

[5]See p. 608, n. 7.

COLON 55:10cA:

וְנָתַן זֶרַע לַזֹּרֵעַ 10cA giving seed to the sower

With: $\mathfrak{M}$ (5) – $\mathfrak{G}^{SQ}$ – $\mathfrak{S}^{e}$
Colon parallelism: זרע (noun) || זרע (verb).

COLON 55:10cB:

וְלֶחֶם לָאֹכֵל׃ 10cB and bread to the eater,

With: $\mathfrak{M}$ (1) – $\mathfrak{G}^{SQ}$, major division marker in $\mathfrak{G}^{Q}$ – $\mathfrak{S}^{e}$, but subordinate punctuation in $\mathfrak{S}^{abcd}$
Colon parallelism: לחם || אכל.
Discussion: The majority of $\mathfrak{S}$-manuscripts connects with v. 11, but $\mathfrak{M}$ is strongly supported.

COLON 55:11aA:

כֵּן יִהְיֶה דְבָרִי אֲשֶׁר יֵצֵא מִפִּי 11aA so shall my word be that goes forth from my mouth:

With: $\mathfrak{M}$ (5) – $\mathfrak{G}^{SQ}$ – $\mathfrak{S}^{acde}$, $\mathfrak{S}^{b}$ subordinate punctuation.
Colon parallelism: דבר || פה.
Discussion: Although the colon is rather long (six feet), no conclusive objection may be raised against the unanimous testimony of tradition.

COLON 55:11aB:

לֹא־יָשׁוּב אֵלַי רֵיקָם 11aB It shall not return to me empty,

With: $\mathfrak{M}$ (2) – $\mathfrak{G}^{SQ}$ – $\mathfrak{S}^{acde}$, $\mathfrak{S}^{b}$ subordinate punctuation.

COLON 55:11bA:

כִּי אִם־עָשָׂה אֶת־אֲשֶׁר חָפַצְתִּי 11bA but it accomplishes that which I want,

With: $\mathfrak{M}$ (5) – $\mathfrak{G}^{SQ}$
Discussion: $\mathfrak{G}^{SQ}$ both have a divider after כי אם־עשה which should be attributed to the wording in Greek. Both also support $\mathfrak{M}$ at this point, in contrast to $\mathfrak{S}$.

COLON 55:11bB:

וְהִצְלִיחַ אֲשֶׁר שְׁלַחְתִּיו׃ 11bB and makes succeed what I send it for.

With: $\mathfrak{M}$ (1). Setuma in $1\mathfrak{Q}^{a}$ – $\mathfrak{G}^{SQ}$ – $\mathfrak{S}^{abcde}$, major division marker in $\mathfrak{S}^{b}$

COLON 55:12aA:

כִּֽי־בְשִׂמְחָ֣ה תֵצֵ֔אוּ 12aA For you shall go out in joy

With: $\mathfrak{M}$ (5) – $\mathfrak{G}^{SQ}$ – $\mathfrak{S}^{e}$

COLON 55:12aB:

וּבְשָׁל֖וֹם תּֽוּבָל֑וּן 12aB and in peace be led forth.

With: $\mathfrak{M}$ (2) – $\mathfrak{G}^{SQ}$ – $\mathfrak{S}^{abcde}$

COLON 55:12bA:

הֶהָרִ֣ים וְהַגְּבָע֗וֹת 12bA The mountains and the hills

With: $\mathfrak{M}$ (7).
Colon parallelism: הר || גבעה.
Discussion: Even though $\mathfrak{M}$ and the ancient versions apparently read on until רנה, the colon parallelism argues in favour of our division. The circumstance that the sentence continues confused the ancient translators. See our remarks with v. 10aA.

COLON 55:12bB:

יִפְצְח֤וּ לִפְנֵיכֶם֙ רִנָּ֔ה 12bB shall break forth into singing before you,

With: $\mathfrak{M}$ (5) – $\mathfrak{G}^{SQ}$ – $\mathfrak{S}^{abce}$
Discussion: $\mathfrak{G}^{SQ}$ have a dividing point after יפצחו which is not supported by any other witness.

COLON 55:12bC:

וְכָל־עֲצֵ֥י הַשָּׂדֶ֖ה יִמְחֲאוּ־כָֽף׃ 12bC and all the trees of the field shall clap their hands.

With: $\mathfrak{M}$ (1) – $\mathfrak{G}^{SAQ}$, major division marker in $\mathfrak{G}^{A}$ – $\mathfrak{S}^{abcde}$

COLON 55:13aA:

תַּ֤חַת הַנַּֽעֲצוּץ֙ יַעֲלֶ֣ה בְר֔וֹשׁ 13aA Instead of a camel thorn shall come up a juniper,

With: $\mathfrak{M}$ (5) – $\mathfrak{G}^{SQ}$ – $\mathfrak{S}^{abcde}$
Colon parallelism: נעצוץ || ברוש (unique).

COLON 55:13aB:

וְתַ֥חַת הַסִּרְפַּ֖ד יַעֲלֶ֣ה הֲדַ֑ס 13aB and instead of a nettle shall come up a myrtle.

With: 𝔐 (2) – 𝔊^{SQ} – 𝔖^{abcde}
Colon parallelism: סרפד || הדס (unique).

COLON 55:13bA:

וְהָיָה לַיהוָה לְשֵׁם 13bA And it shall be a name for the LORD,

With: 𝔐 (5) – 𝔊^{SQ} – 𝔖^{b}, 𝔖^{acde} subordinate punctuation.

COLON 55:13bB:

לְאוֹת עוֹלָם לֹא יִכָּרֵת׃ 13bB an everlasting sign which shall not be cut off.

With: 𝔐 (1), major division markers, also in 1𝔔^{a} and 1𝔔^{b} – 𝔊^{SBAQ}, major division markers in all four – 𝔖^{abcde}, major division markers in 𝔖^{be}
Discussion: 𝔊^{SQ} have a point after עולם (𝔐 Ṭiphḥa, No. 8) which would seem to be required by the Greek. 𝔖 supports 𝔐.

15.3 Isaiah 55 – Delimitation of Verse-lines

VERSE–LINE: 55:1a:

הוֹי כָּל־צָמֵא לְכוּ לַמַּיִם 1aA Ho, all who are thirsty, come to the waters,
וַאֲשֶׁר אֵין־לוֹ כָּסֶף 1aB and he who has no silver,

𝔐 distinctive accents: 5 – 2 .
Stresses: 4 + 3.
Verse-line parallelism: צמא || אשר אין־לו (unique).
Discussion: The ellipsis of הוי connects v. 1aB with v. 1aA.

VERSE–LINE: 55:1b:

לְכוּ שִׁבְרוּ וֶאֱכֹלוּ 1bA come, buy and eat,
וּלְכוּ שִׁבְרוּ בְּלוֹא־כֶסֶף 1bB yes, come, buy without silver,
וּבְלוֹא מְחִיר יַיִן וְחָלָב׃ 1bC and without price, wine and milk!

𝔐 distinctive accents: 5 – 12 – 1.
Stresses: 3 + 3 + 4.
Verse-line parallelism: צמא || אין; הלך || הלך; שבר || שבר (unique); ב || ב; לוא || לוא; כסף || מחיר; grammatical parallelism; rhyme.
Discussion: Apparently the Masoretes were led astray by the many repetitions and the on-running sentence. The sequence of accents presupposes a division into a bicolon, a unicolon, and finally a bicolon of 2 + 5 stresses again:

הוֹי כָּל־צָמֵא לְכוּ לַמַּיִם
וַאֲשֶׁר אֵין־לוֹ כָּסֶף

לְכוּ שִׁבְרוּ וֶאֱכֹלוּ
וּלְכוּ שִׁבְרוּ
בְּלוֹא־כֶסֶף וּבְלוֹא מְחִיר יַיִן וְחָלָב׃

The reason for this strange colometry is difficult to fathom. It seems as if the Masoretes were not quite happy with the fact that they had to join v. 1bA to vv. 1bB-C – because the Talmud presupposed it.[1] Indeed the option to join v. 1bA to v. 1a is an attractive alternative, because joining it to v. 1bB-C does not resolve the difficulty of the eating.

Our delimitation of this verse-line is mainly based on our delimitation of the cola (see above). The strong parallelism argues in favour of a tricolon. Ellipsis connects vv. 1bB and 1bC.

VERSE–LINE: 55:2a:

לָמָּה תִשְׁקְלוּ־כֶסֶף בְּלוֹא־לֶחֶם	2aA	Why do you weigh out silver for that which is not bread?
וִיגִיעֲכֶם בְּלוֹא לְשָׂבְעָה	2aB	and your labour for that which does not satisfy?

𝔐 distinctive accents: 5 – 2.
Stresses: 3 + 3.
Verse-line parallelism: כסף || יגיע; ב || ב; לוא || לוא; לחם || שׂבע.
Discussion: Vv. 2aA and 2aB are connected by ellipsis.

VERSE–LINE: 55:2b:

שִׁמְעוּ שָׁמוֹעַ אֵלַי וְאִכְלוּ־טוֹב	2bA	Hearken diligently to me, and eat what is good,
וְתִתְעַנַּג בַּדֶּשֶׁן נַפְשְׁכֶם׃	2bB	and let your soul delight in fatness.

𝔐 distinctive accents: 5 – 1.
Stresses: 4 + 3.
Verse-line parallelism: אכל || ענג; טוב || דשן.
Discussion: Ellipsis of שׁמעו שמוע links v. 2bB with v. 2bA.

VERSE–LINE: 55:3a:

הַטּוּ אָזְנְכֶם וּלְכוּ אֵלַי	3aA	Incline your ear, and come to me;
שִׁמְעוּ וּתְחִי נַפְשְׁכֶם	3aB	hear, that your soul may live!

𝔐 distinctive accents: 5 – 2.
Stresses: 4 + 3.
Verse-line parallelism: נטה אזן || שׁמע; ־כם || ־כם; grammatical parallelism.

[1] bBer., 7a; bTaan., 7a.

VERSE–LINE: 55:3b:

וְאֶכְרְתָה לָכֶם֙ בְּרִ֣ית עוֹלָ֔ם 3bA And let me make with you an everlasting covenant,
חַֽסְדֵ֥י דָוִ֖ד הַנֶּאֱמָנִֽים׃ 3bB the steadfast testimonies of loyalty for David.

𝔐 distinctive accents: 5 – 1.
Stresses: 4 + 3.
Verse-line parallelism: ברית || חסד; אמן || עולם.
Discussion: The cola are connected by ellipsis.

VERSE–LINE: 55:4a:

הֵ֥ן עֵ֖ד לְאוּמִּ֣ים נְתַתִּ֑יו 4aA Behold, I made him a witness to the nations,
נָגִ֥יד וּמְצַוֵּ֖ה לְאֻמִּֽים׃ 4aB a leader and commander to the peoples.

𝔐 distinctive accents: 2 – 1.
Stresses: 4 + 3.
Verse-line parallelism: עד || נגיד (unique); עד || צוה (unique); לאם || לאם.
Discussion: Again ellipsis is a binding force.

VERSE–LINE: 55:5a:

הֵ֣ן גּ֤וֹי לֹֽא־תֵדַע֙ תִּקְרָ֔א 5aA Behold, a nation that you know not you shall call,
וְג֥וֹי לֹֽא־יְדָע֛וּךָ אֵלֶ֖יךָ יָר֑וּצוּ 5aB and a nation that you know not shall run to you,

𝔐 distinctive accents: 5 – 2.
Stresses: 4 + 4.
Verse-line parallelism: גוי || גוי; לא || לא; ידע || ידע; קרא || רוץ.

VERSE–LINE: 55:5b:

לְמַ֙עַן֙ יְהוָ֣ה אֱלֹהֶ֔יךָ 5bA because of the LORD your God,
וְלִקְד֥וֹשׁ יִשְׂרָאֵ֖ל כִּ֥י פֵאֲרָֽךְ׃ 5bB and of the Holy One of Israel for he has glorified you.

𝔐 distinctive accents: 5 – 1.
Stresses: 3 + 4.
Verse-line parallelism: למען || ל; יהוה אלהים || קדוש ישראל; ־ך || ־ך.

VERSE–LINE: 55:6a:

דִּרְשׁ֥וּ יְהוָ֖ה 6aA Seek the LORD,
בְּהִמָּצְא֑וֹ קְרָאֻ֖הוּ 6aB call upon him while he may be found,
בִּֽהְיוֹת֥וֹ קָרֽוֹב׃ 6aC while he is near.

𝔐 distinctive accents: 8 – 8 – 1.
Stresses: 2 + 2 + 2.

Verse-line parallelism: דרשׁ || קרא; דרשׁ || מצא; ב || ב; מצא || היה; ־הו || ־ו || ־ו; grammatical parallelism.
Discussion: Our colometry deviates from 𝔐 here.[2] Ellipsis connects the final colon with the preceding ones.

VERSE–LINE: 55:7a:

יַעֲזֹב רָשָׁע דַּרְכּוֹ 7aA Let the wicked abandon his way
וְאִישׁ אָוֶן מַחְשְׁבֹתָיו 7aB and the unrighteous man his thoughts.

𝔐 distinctive accents: 5 – 2.
Stresses: 3 + 3.
Verse-line parallelism: רשׁע || און; דרך || מחשׁבה; ־ו || ־ו.
Discussion: The cola are connected by ellipsis.

VERSE–LINE: 55:7b:

וְיָשֹׁב אֶל־יְהוָה וִירַחֲמֵהוּ 7bA Let him return to the LORD and he will have mercy on him,
וְאֶל־אֱלֹהֵינוּ כִּי־יַרְבֶּה לִסְלוֹחַ׃ 7bB and to our God, for he will abundantly pardon.

𝔐 distinctive accents: 5 – 1.
Stresses: 3 + 3.
Verse-line parallelism: אל (prep.)|| אל (prep.); || אלהים; רחם || סלח.
Discussion: Ellipsis forms a bond between the cola.

VERSE–LINE: 55:8a:

כִּי לֹא מַחְשְׁבוֹתַי מַחְשְׁבוֹתֵיכֶם 8aA For my thoughts are not your thoughts
וְלֹא דַרְכֵיכֶם דְּרָכָי 8aB neither are your ways my ways,
נְאֻם יְהוָה׃ 8aC declares the LORD.

𝔐 distinctive accents: 5 – 2 – 1.
Stresses: 4 + 3 + 2.
Verse-line parallelism: לא || לא; מחשׁבה || דרך (2x); ־י || ־י; ־כם || ־כם.

VERSE–LINE: 55:9a:

כִּי־גָבְהוּ שָׁמַיִם מֵאָרֶץ 9aA For as the heavens are higher than the earth,

𝔐 distinctive accents: 2.
Stresses: 3.
Verse-line parallelism: None (unicolon). Discussion: As mentioned in the discussion on the cola of v. 9,[3] 𝔖 seems to presuppose a tricolon.

[2]See our comments pp. 612-3.
[3]See p. 614.

The parallelism between מחשבה || דרך in v. 9b which also occurred as verse-line parallelism in vv. 7a and 8a, the repetition of the suffixes (all lacking in v. 9a) and the ellipsis in v. 9b all argue in favour of 𝔐's option for a unicolon followed by a bicolon. Probably S wanted to keep the כי ... כן construction in one verse-line. Parallel constructions with כ ... כן do occur in one colon or one verse-line.[4]

VERSE–LINE: 55:9b:

כֵּ֤ן גָּבְה֤וּ דְרָכַי֙ מִדַּרְכֵיכֶ֔ם	9bA	so are my ways higher than your ways,
וּמַחְשְׁבֹתַ֖י מִמַּחְשְׁבֹתֵיכֶֽם׃	9bB	and my thoughts than your thoughts.

𝔐 distinctive accents: 5 – 1.
Stresses: 4 + 2.
Verse-line parallelism: דרך || מחשבה (twice); ־י || ־י; מן || מן; ־כם || ־כם; rhyme.
Discussion: Ellipsis connects the cola.

VERSE–LINE: 55:10a:

כִּ֡י כַּאֲשֶׁר֩ יֵרֵ֨ד הַגֶּ֜שֶׁם {וְהַשֶּׁ֘לֶג} מִן־הַשָּׁמַ֗יִם	10aA	For as the rain comes down {and the snow} from heaven,
וְשָׁ֙מָּה֙ לֹ֣א יָשׁ֔וּב	10aB	and does not return thither,

𝔐 distinctive accents: 7 – 5.
Stresses: 5 + 3.
Verse-line parallelism: ירד || שׁוב.

VERSE–LINE: 55:10b:

כִּ֚י אִם־הִרְוָ֣ה אֶת־הָאָ֔רֶץ	10bA	but waters the earth
וְהוֹלִידָ֖הּ וְהִצְמִיחָ֑הּ	10bB	making it bear and sprout,

𝔐 distinctive accents: 5 – 2.
Stresses: 3 + 2.
Verse-line parallelism: רוה || צמח; grammatical parallelism.

VERSE–LINE: 55:10c:

וְנָ֤תַן זֶ֙רַע֙ לַזֹּרֵ֔עַ	10cA	giving seed to the sower
וְלֶ֖חֶם לָאֹכֵֽל׃	10cB	and bread to the eater,

𝔐 distinctive accents: 5 – 1.
Stresses: 3 + 2.
Verse-line parallelism: זרע || לחם; ל || ל; זרע || אכל.
Discussion: Ellipsis acts as a connecting force.

[4]See the Index of Parallel Words.

VERSE–LINE: 55:11a:

כֵּ֣ן יִהְיֶ֤ה דְבָרִי֙ אֲשֶׁ֣ר יֵצֵ֣א מִפִּ֔י	11aA	so shall my word be that goes forth from my mouth:
לֹֽא־יָשׁ֥וּב אֵלַ֖י רֵיקָ֑ם	11aB	It shall not return to me empty,

𝔐 distinctive accents: 5 – 2.
Stresses: 6 + 3.
Verse-line parallelism: ־י ‖ ־י ‖ ־י; יצא ‖ שׁוב.

VERSE–LINE: 55:11b:

כִּ֤י אִם־עָשָׂה֙ אֶת־אֲשֶׁ֣ר חָפַ֔צְתִּי	11bA	but it accomplishes that which I purpose,
וְהִצְלִ֖יחַ אֲשֶׁ֥ר שְׁלַחְתִּֽיו׃	11bB	and makes succeed what I send it for.

𝔐 distinctive accents: 5 – 1.
Stresses: 4 + 3.
Verse-line parallelism: עשׂה ‖ צלח; אשׁר ‖ אשׁר; חפץ ‖ שׁלח (unique); grammatical parallelism.

VERSE–LINE: 55:12a:

כִּֽי־בְשִׂמְחָ֣ה תֵצֵ֔אוּ	12aA	For you shall go out in joy
וּבְשָׁל֖וֹם תּֽוּבָל֑וּן	12aB	and in peace be led forth.

𝔐 distinctive accents: 5 – 2.
Stresses: 2 + 2.
Verse-line parallelism: ב ‖ ב; שׂמחה ‖ שׁלום; יצא ‖ יבל (unique).

VERSE–LINE: 55:12b:

הֶהָרִ֣ים וְהַגְּבָע֗וֹת	12bA	The mountains and the hills
יִפְצְח֤וּ לִפְנֵיכֶם֙ רִנָּ֔ה	12bB	shall break forth into singing before you,
וְכָל־עֲצֵ֥י הַשָּׂדֶ֖ה יִמְחֲאוּ־כָֽף׃	12bC	and all the trees of the field shall clap their hands.

𝔐 distinctive accents: 7 – 5 – 2.
Stresses: 2 + 3 + 3.
Verse-line parallelism: הר ‖ גבעה ‖ עץ; פצח רנה ‖ מחא כף; grammatical parallelism.

VERSE–LINE: 55:13a:

תַּ֤חַת הַֽנַּעֲצוּץ֙ יַעֲלֶ֣ה בְר֔וֹשׁ	13aA	Instead of a camel thorn shall come up a juniper,
וְתַ֥חַת הַסִּרְפַּ֖ד יַעֲלֶ֣ה הֲדַ֑ס	13aB	and instead of a nettle shall come up a myrtle.

𝔐 distinctive accents: 5 – 2.
Stresses: 4 + 4.

Verse-line parallelism: תחת || תחת; נעצוץ || סרפד (unique); עלה || עלה; ברוש || הדס; grammatical parallelism.

VERSE–LINE: 55:13b:

וְהָיָ֤ה לַֽיהוָה֙ לְשֵׁ֔ם	13bA	And it shall be a name for the LORD,
לְא֥וֹת עוֹלָ֖ם לֹ֥א יִכָּרֵֽת׃	13bB	an everlasting sign which shall not be cut off.

𝔐 distinctive accents: 5 – 1.
Stresses: 3 + 4.
Verse-line parallelism: ל || ל; שׁם || אות עולם.
Discussion: Ellipsis of והיה binds v. 13bA to v. 13bB.

15.4 Isaiah 55 – Delimitation of Strophes

STROPHE A.i.1 (Isa. 55:1)

ה֤וֹי כָּל־צָמֵא֙ לְכ֣וּ לַמַּ֔יִם	1aA	Ho, all who are thirsty, come to the waters,
וַאֲשֶׁ֥ר אֵֽין־ל֖וֹ כָּ֑סֶף	1aB	and he who has no silver,
לְכ֤וּ שִׁבְרוּ֙ וֶֽאֱכֹ֔לוּ	1bA	come, buy and eat,
וּלְכ֣וּ שִׁבְר֗וּ בְּלוֹא־כֶ֛סֶף	1bB	yes, come, buy without silver,
וּבְל֥וֹא מְחִ֖יר יַ֥יִן וְחָלָֽב׃	1bC	and without price, wine and milk!

= Masoretic verse.
Separation ↑: major division markers in the textual tradition; deictic particle(s); imperative(s); vocatives.
Separation ↓: imperative(s); repetitive verse-line parallelism.
Strophe parallelism: הלך || הלך; מים || יין (unique); מים || חלב; כסף || כסף; grammatical parallelism.

STROPHE A.i.2 (Isa. 55:2)

לָ֤מָּה תִשְׁקְלוּ־כֶ֙סֶף֙ בְּלוֹא־לֶ֔חֶם	2aA	Why do you weigh out silver for that which is not bread?
וִיגִיעֲכֶ֖ם בְּל֣וֹא לְשָׂבְעָ֑ה	2aB	and your labour for that which does not satisfy?
שִׁמְע֨וּ שָׁמ֤וֹעַ אֵלַי֙ וְאִכְלוּ־ט֔וֹב	2bA	Hearken diligently to me, and eat what is good,
וְתִתְעַנַּ֥ג בַּדֶּ֖שֶׁן נַפְשְׁכֶֽם׃	2bB	and let your soul delight in fatness.

= Masoretic verse.
Separation ↑: interrogative pronoun; repetitive verse-line parallelism.
Separation ↓: major division markers in the textual tradition; imperative(s); jussive(s); paronomasia; swapping (adjunct).
Strophe parallelism: שׂבעה || אכל; ־כם || ־כם; ב || ב; לחם || דשן.
Discussion: $\mathfrak{G}^S$ and $\mathfrak{S}^b$ seem to testify to a different strophic division which took v. 2a with v. 1 and v. 2b with v. 3. From the viewpoint

of parallelism this is understandable. But both strophes become overloaded and 𝔊[BA] support 𝔐's division.

STROPHE A.i.3 (Isa. 55:3)

הַטּוּ אָזְנְכֶם֙ וּלְכ֣וּ אֵלַ֔י	3aA	Incline your ear, and come to me;
שִׁמְע֖וּ וּתְחִ֣י נַפְשְׁכֶ֑ם	3aB	hear, that your soul may live!
וְאֶכְרְתָ֤ה לָכֶם֙ בְּרִ֣ית עוֹלָ֔ם	3bA	And let me make with you an everlasting covenant,
חַסְדֵ֥י דָוִ֖ד הַנֶּאֱמָנִֽים׃	3bB	the steadfast testimonies of loyalty for David.

= Masoretic verse.
Separation ↑: major division markers in the textual tradition; imperative(s); jussive(s); repetitive verse-line parallelism.
Separation ↓: major division markers in the textual tradition; cohortative(s); swapping (adjunct).
Strophe parallelism: כם- ‖ כם-.
Discussion: Despite the rather weak parallelism the delimitation of the strophe is not in doubt.

STROPHE A.ii.1 (Isa. 55:4)

הֵ֛ן עֵ֥ד לְאוּמִּ֖ים נְתַתִּ֑יו	4aA	Behold, I made him a witness to the nations,
נָגִ֥יד וּמְצַוֵּ֖ה לְאֻמִּֽים׃	4aB	a leader and commander to the peoples.

= Masoretic verse.
Separation ↑: major division markers in the textual tradition; deictic particle(s); swapping (object).
Separation ↓: None (one verse-line).
Strophe parallelism: None (one verse-line).

STROPHE A.ii.2 (Isa. 55:5)

הֵ֣ן גּ֤וֹי לֹֽא־תֵדַע֙ תִּקְרָ֔א	5aA	Behold, a nation that you know not you shall call,
וְג֥וֹי לֹֽא־יְדָע֖וּךָ אֵלֶ֣יךָ יָר֑וּצוּ	5aB	and a nation that does not know you shall run to you,
לְמַ֙עַן֙ יְהוָ֣ה אֱלֹהֶ֔יךָ	5bA	because of the LORD your God,
וְלִקְד֥וֹשׁ יִשְׂרָאֵ֖ל כִּ֥י פֵאֲרָֽךְ׃	5bB	and of the Holy One of Israel for he has glorified you.

= Masoretic verse.
Separation ↑: deictic particle(s); repetitive verse-line parallelism; swapping (subject); swapping (object); swapping (adjunct).
Separation ↓: major division markers in the textual tradition; deictic particle(s); repetitive verse-line parallelism.
Strophe parallelism: ךָ- (m.s.) ‖ ךָ- (m.s.).

Discussion: Despite the rather weak parallelism the delimitation of the strophe is not in doubt.

STROPHE B.i.1 (Isa. 55:6)

דִּרְשׁ֥וּ יְהוָ֖ה	6aA	Seek the LORD,
בְּהִמָּצְא֑וֹ קְרָאֻ֖הוּ	6aB	call upon him while he may be found,
בִּֽהְיוֹת֥וֹ קָרֽוֹב׃	6aC	while he is near.

= Masoretic verse.
Separation ↑: major division markers in the textual tradition; imperative(s); repetitive verse-line parallelism; swapping (adjunct).
Separation ↓: None (one verse-line).
Strophe parallelism: None (one verse-line).

STROPHE B.i.2 (Isa. 55:7)

יַעֲזֹ֤ב רָשָׁע֙ דַּרְכּ֔וֹ	7aA	Let the wicked abandon his way
וְאִ֥ישׁ אָ֖וֶן מַחְשְׁבֹתָ֑יו	7aB	and the unrighteous man his thoughts.
וְיָשֹׁ֤ב אֶל־יְהוָה֙ וִירַחֲמֵ֔הוּ	7bA	Let him return to the LORD and he will have mercy on him,
וְאֶל־אֱלֹהֵ֖ינוּ כִּֽי־יַרְבֶּ֥ה לִסְלֽוֹחַ׃	7bB	and to our God, for he will abundantly pardon.

= Masoretic verse.
Separation ↑: jussive(s); repetitive verse-line parallelism.
Separation ↓: major division markers in the textual tradition; deictic particle(s); jussive(s); repetitive verse-line parallelism.
Strophe parallelism: עזב דרך || שׁוב (unique); און || סלח (unique); grammatical parallelism.

STROPHE B.ii.1 (Isa. 55:8)

כִּ֣י לֹ֤א מַחְשְׁבוֹתַי֙ מַחְשְׁב֣וֹתֵיכֶ֔ם	8aA	For my thoughts are not your thoughts
וְלֹ֥א דַרְכֵיכֶ֖ם דְּרָכָ֑י	8aB	neither are your ways my ways,
נְאֻ֖ם יְהוָֽה׃	8aC	declares the LORD.

= Masoretic verse.
Separation ↑: major division markers in the textual tradition; deictic particle(s); marker of direct speech; repetitive verse-line parallelism.
Separation ↓: None (one verse-line).
Strophe parallelism: None (one verse-line).

STROPHE B.ii.2 (Isa. 55:9)

כִּֽי־גָבְה֥וּ שָׁמַ֖יִם מֵאָ֑רֶץ	9aA	For as the heavens are higher than the earth,
כֵּ֣ן גָּבְה֤וּ דְרָכַי֙ מִדַּרְכֵיכֶ֔ם	9bA	so are my ways higher than your ways,
וּמַחְשְׁבֹתַ֖י מִמַּחְשְׁבֹתֵיכֶֽם׃	9bB	and my thoughts than your thoughts.

= Masoretic verse.

Separation ↑: deictic particle(s).
Separation ↓: major division markers in the textual tradition; deictic particle(s); repetitive verse-line parallelism.
Strophe parallelism: גבה || גבה; מן || מן; grammatical parallelism.

STROPHE C.i.1 (Isa. 55:10a)

כִּי כַּאֲשֶׁר יֵרֵד הַגֶּשֶׁם {וְהַשֶּׁלֶג} מִן־הַשָּׁמַיִם	10aA	For as the rain comes down {and the snow} from heaven,
וְשָׁמָּה לֹא יָשׁוּב	10aB	and does not return thither,

≠ Masoretic verse.
Separation ↑: major division markers in the textual tradition; deictic particle(s); swapping (adjunct).
Separation ↓: None (one verse-line).
Strophe parallelism: None (one verse-line).
Discussion: The Masoretes opted for a quadrocolon plus a bicolon. In our opinion the parallelism between vv. 10b and 10c as well as the inclusion between לא ישוב (v. 10aB) and לא־ישוב (v. 11aB) strongly suggest that the parenthesis is a separate strophe.

STROPHE C.i.2 (Isa. 55:10b-c)

כִּי אִם־הִרְוָה אֶת־הָאָרֶץ	10bA	but waters the earth
וְהוֹלִידָהּ וְהִצְמִיחָהּ	10bB	making it bear and sprout,
וְנָתַן זֶרַע לַזֹּרֵעַ	10cA	giving seed to the sower
וְלֶחֶם לָאֹכֵל׃	10cB	and bread to the eater,

≠ Masoretic verse.
Separation ↑: deictic particle(s).
Separation ↓: major division marker in the textual tradition; repetitive verse-line parallelism.
Strophe parallelism: ילד || זרע; צמח || זרע.
Discussion: See our comment on the previous strophe.

STROPHE C.i.3 (Isa. 55:11)

כֵּן יִהְיֶה דְבָרִי אֲשֶׁר יֵצֵא מִפִּי	11aA	so shall my word be that goes forth from my mouth:
לֹא־יָשׁוּב אֵלַי רֵיקָם	11aB	It shall not return to me empty,
כִּי אִם־עָשָׂה אֶת־אֲשֶׁר חָפַצְתִּי	11bA	but it accomplishes that which I want,
וְהִצְלִיחַ אֲשֶׁר שְׁלַחְתִּיו׃	11bB	and makes succeed what I send it for.

= Masoretic verse.
Separation ↑: major division marker in the textual tradition; deictic particle(s); repetitive verse-line parallelism.

Separation ↓: major division markers in the textual tradition; deictic particle(s); repetitive verse-line parallelism.
Strophe parallelism: אשר || אשר; יצא || שלח; שוב ריקם || צלח (antithetical; unique).

STROPHE C.ii.1 (Isa. 55:12)

כִּֽי־בְשִׂמְחָ֣ה תֵצֵ֔אוּ	12aA	For you shall go out in joy
וּבְשָׁל֖וֹם תּֽוּבָל֑וּן	12aB	and in peace be led forth.
הֶהָרִ֣ים וְהַגְּבָע֗וֹת	12bA	The mountains and the hills
יִפְצְח֤וּ לִפְנֵיכֶם֙ רִנָּ֔ה	12bB	shall break forth into singing before you,
וְכָל־עֲצֵ֥י הַשָּׂדֶ֖ה יִמְחֲאוּ־כָֽף׃	12bC	and all the trees of the field shall clap their hands.

= Masoretic verse.
Separation ↑: major division markers in the textual tradition; deictic particle(s); repetitive verse-line parallelism; swapping (adjunct).
Separation ↓: major division markers in the textual tradition; swapping (subject).
Strophe parallelism: שמחה || רנה.

STROPHE C.ii.2 (Isa. 55:13)

תַּ֤חַת הַֽנַּעֲצוּץ֙ יַעֲלֶ֣ה בְר֔וֹשׁ	13aA	Instead of a camel thorn shall come up a juniper,
וְתַ֥חַת הַסִּרְפַּ֖ד יַעֲלֶ֣ה הֲדַ֑ס	13aB	and instead of a nettle shall come up a myrtle.
וְהָיָ֤ה לַֽיהוָה֙ לְשֵׁ֔ם	13bA	And it shall be a name for the LORD,
לְא֥וֹת עוֹלָ֖ם לֹ֥א יִכָּרֵֽת׃	13bB	an everlasting sign which shall not be cut off.

= Masoretic verse.
Separation ↑: major division markers in the textual tradition; repetitive verse-line parallelism; swapping (adjunct).
Separation ↓: major division markers in the textual tradition; repetitive verse-line parallelism.
Strophe parallelism: עלה || כרת.

15.5 Isaiah 55 – Delimitation of Canticles

CANTICLE A.i (55:1–3)

Separation ↑: major division markers in the textual tradition; thematic discontinuity; change of subject.
Separation ↓: major division markers in the textual tradition.
Canticle parallelism: הלך || הלך (responsion/inclusion); כסף || כסף (responsion/concatenation); יין || לחם (concatenation); חלב || דשן (responsion); אכל || אכל (responsion); שמע || נטה אזן (concatenation); שמע || שמע (concatenation); נפש || נפש (concatenation); ־כם || ־כם (concatenation); טוב || חסד (responsion).
Thematic unity: yes. From an initial attention-drawing performance as a water-seller the prophet gradually uncovers his metaphors: it is the spiritual good of the word of God that Israel should crave for, especially the restoration of the Davidic covenant which is now promised to all those who listen obediently.
Discussion: The major division markers in and after v. 2 indicate the strophic division.[1] $\mathfrak{G}^{Q}$ proleptically marks the boundary after v. 3.

CANTICLE A.ii (55:4–5)

Separation ↑: major division markers in the textual tradition.
Separation ↓: major division markers in the textual tradition.
Canticle parallelism: לאם || גוי (concatenation); נגיד || פאר (unique).
Thematic unity: yes. Just like David,[2] the faithful servants of the

[1]See our comments pp. 624-5.

[2]As David had been a נגיד 'leader' (1 Sam. 9:16; 10:1; 13:14; 25:30; 2 Sam. 5:2; 6:21; 7:8), faithful Israel must now assume leadership in bearing witness to the nations. One might think of David's brave testimony when he confronted Goliath, a testimony which ended with the phrase וידעו כל־הארץ כי יש אלהים לישראל "that all the earth may know that there is a God in Israel" (1 Sam. 17:46). Possibly Second Isaiah connected this with the pre-exilic part of Ps. 89 where the Davidic king is compared to the moon as "a reliable witness in the clouds" (ועד בשחק נאמן, Ps. 89:38; so already $\mathfrak{G}$). The idea of Israel witnessing of its faith among the nations was dear to Second Isaiah who was living among many foreign peoples (see also 43:10, 12; 44:8). Of course, his hope that foreign nations might embrace Israel's monotheistic faith has everything to do with the fact that the Persians were worshipping Ahura Mazda whose henotheistic and aniconic cult (cf. M.A. Dandamaev, *Persien unter den ersten Achämeniden*, Wiesbaden 1976, 215-41) may have appealed to Second Isaiah and may even have encouraged him to hope that the Persians could be converted to the 'monotheistic' faith of Israel. In this sense he expected Cyrus to be a worthy successor of David (Isa. 45:1) if, and only if, he would recognize his vocation by the sole God of Israel (45:3-7).

In 2 Sam. 22:44/Ps. 18:44 David praises God because nations whom he did not know came to serve him, תשמרני לראש גוים עם לא־ידעתי יעבדני "thou didst keep

LORD have to bear witness to the foreign nations.
Discussion: 𝔊^S marks the borderline after v. 5 proleptically and redundantly after ישׂראל.

CANTICLE B.i (55:6–7)

Separation ↑: major division markers in the textual tradition; thematic discontinuity; change of subject.
Separation ↓: major division markers in the textual tradition.
Canticle parallelism: דרשׁ || שׁוב (inclusion); יהוה || יהוה (inclusion); קרא || סלח (inclusion).
Thematic unity: yes. The obvious question after v. 5 was: How can the nations come to worship the LORD when there is no temple? As long as the temple stood on Zion, it was easy to seek and find God there (Ps. 63:2-3; Deut. 4:29; 12:5). Now that the temple has been destroyed, the prophet emphasizes the notion that God can be found in any place by people prepared to abandon their former sinful thoughts.

CANTICLE B.ii (55:8–9)

Separation ↑: major division markers in the textual tradition; change of subject.
Separation ↓: major division markers in the textual tradition.
Canticle parallelism: מחשׁבות || מחשׁבות (inclusion); ־י || ־י (inclusion); ־כם || ־כם (inclusion); דרך || דרך (inclusion).
Thematic unity: yes. The canticle parallelism is obvious enough.

CANTICLE C.i (55:10–11)

Separation ↑: major division markers in the textual tradition; change of subject.
Separation ↓: major division markers in the textual tradition.
Canticle parallelism: כי || כי || כי (responsion/inclusion); ירד || יצא (responsion); שׁמים || ארץ (responsion); שׁוב || שׁוב (responsion).
All three strophes are linked by an on-running sentence (enjambment).

me as the head of the nations; people whom I had not known served me". One may think in this connection of the Cherethites and the Pelethites. However, the adhortation to actively call the unknown nations to the service of the God of Israel would seem to be a new theological approach. This so-called universalism is without parallel and must be the answer to the actual situation of the moment. It is so different from the approximately contemporaneous calls for merciless revenge on the unknown nations (Jer. 10:25; Ps. 79:6) that it might well represent a stance deliberately taken.

Thematic unity: yes. The comparison of the word of God with water which was already anticipated in canticle A.i is now elaborated.
Discussion: The paragraphos in $\mathfrak{G}^{SQ}$ after v. 10 was probably misplaced and belongs to the attested break after v. 11.

CANTICLE C.ii (55:12–13)

Separation ↑: major division markers in the textual tradition; thematic discontinuity; change of subject.
Separation ↓: major division markers in the textual tradition.
Canticle parallelism: שלום || עולם; עץ || ברוש, הדס.
Thematic unity: yes. Fresh trees will welcome the exiles on their Exodus. Cf. Isa. 41:18-19.
Discussion: $\mathfrak{G}^{A}$ marks the end of the first strophe.

15.6 Isaiah 55 – Delimitation of Macrostructure

The coherence of the canto in its present form is impressive, whatever its previous stages of development may have been. Both the first and the last sub-canto make use of the comparison of the word of God with water. Both refer to the reestablishment of the eternal covenant between God and his people (vv. 3bA, 13bB). The wording reminds us of the sabbath which is called a ברית עולם in Exod. 13:16 and an אות עולם in Exod. 31:17.[1] The sabbath came after 6 days of hard labour. It seems not impossible that in this veiled manner Deutero-Isaiah wanted to refer to the period of rest which can start now that the period of forced labour has come to an end (cf. 40:2). At least this veiled allusion was not lost to Trito-Isaiah who obviously picks it up in 56:1-9. The middle sub-canto states the sole condition. Nothing more than repentance is needed to make possible Israel's delivery which from a human point of view seemed unthinkable to the despirited exiles.

The structure of the chapter is symmetric:

SUB-CANTOS	CANTICLES	STROPHES
A	2	5 (3+2)
B	2	4 (2+2)
C	2	5 (3+2)

Distant parallelism connecting the canticles of the three sub-cantos:

[1]The verses belong to an older stratum which was inserted by P at this point, cf. C. Houtman, *Exodus*, deel 3: Exodus 20-40 (COT), Kampen 1996, 571-2.

Sub-canto A:
Though no formal parallelism may be discerned, the mentioning of David in v. 3bB (A.i) has clearly triggered a number of comparisons in A.ii.[2]

Sub-canto B:
יהוה (vv. 6aA, 7bA – B.i) || יהוה (v. 8aC – B.ii); דרך (v. 7aA – B.i) || דרך (vv. 8aB, 9bA – B.ii); מחשבות (v. 7aB – B.i) || מחשבות (vv. 8aA, 9bB – B.ii).

Sub-canto C:
ירד (v. 10aA – C.i) || עלה (v.13A-B – C.ii); *ארץ (v. 10bA – C.i) || שׂדה (v. 12bC – C.ii) *צמח (v. 10bB – C.i) || עלה (vv. 13aA-B – C.ii).

[2]See our comments on p. 629-30, n. 2.

Chapter 16

General Conclusions

16.1 Introductory Remarks

In this study we have tried to place the structural analysis of Classical Hebrew poetry on a firmer basis by making use of data culled from ancient Hebrew, Greek and Syriac manuscripts and by applying a verifiable method of analysis. We want to caution that the conclusions we will draw in this chapter are based on Isaiah 40–55 alone and need not be applicable to all other poetic parts of the Hebrew Bible, though we do expect that a certain number of insights will prove to hold for other poetic Books of the Bible as well.

The kind of research taken up in this work was made possible only by the advent of personal computers. Especially the in-depth research of parallelism, including searches for parallelism between very frequent words or between all derivatives of a given root, was simply impossible only fifteen years ago. One of the more important general results of our study is the observation that the same pairs or triplets of words are not only used in parallelism on the micro-levels of colon, verse-line and strophe, but often also on the macro-levels of canticle, sub-canto and canto. This affords the exegete a precious insight into the personal style of the poet(s) and helps to establish the coherence between extended portions of text. Moreover, the possibility to prove the poetical nature of a given pair by demonstrating that it was used in poetic parallelism elsewhere in the Bible enhances the strength of arguments based on the connecting force of parallelism. It is for this reason that we have appended an index of all parallel words we discussed in this book, with parallels from other books, and for the first time ever divided into colon parallelism, verse-line parallelism, strophe parallelism, canticle parallelism and macro parallelism.

It may well be that many a user of this book will feel overwhelmed by the enormous amount of new data we present here. We believe this is an inevitable consequence of the time we live in. It opens up new vistas in a world too far removed from ours to rely on one's literary 'feeling'. Yet it is a legitimate question whether the ancient poets of Israel really did strive after the high level of sophistication we ascribe to them. Is this sophistication not an artefact of our own imagination? We hope to have presented sufficient evidence to the contrary. In a more general way, however, it may be remarked that in a largely illiterate world people's memory is far more trained to catching allusions and repetitions in large corpora of text than we in our notebook-driven time can imagine. Moreover, it seems absolutely certain now that poets, also prophets, were well-trained for their jobs in schools and had to learn substantial amounts of earlier literature by heart.[1] To a large extent they will have made use of the techniques and examples they had learned in a natural and unconscious manner. But no doubt it was their pride to show their skill for the good cause they were serving. Is it right then to restrict their capabilities to what we deem attainable and tasteful?

16.2 The Colon

16.2.1 Delimiters of Cola

Of the 1295 cola we established in this study 1188 (92%) were delimited by a distinctive Masoretic accent stronger than the Ṭiphḥa (No. 8 on the *Tabula Accentuum* of BHS).[2] In the 107 cases (8%) where the Masoretes had a weaker or even a conjunctive accent it was almost always obvious that they preferred a colometry different from the one we adopted on the basis of the total evidence at our disposal. But the low number of cases where we felt we had to deviate from $\mathfrak{M}$ is significant. We consider this very high rate of reliability of the Masoretic colometric division as one of the major, be it not surprising results of our investigation.

For the first time we made use of the dividing points found in $\mathfrak{G}^S$, $\mathfrak{G}^Q$, and five manuscripts of the Peshiṭta. Of course these points cannot be used uncritically. Normally their position corresponds to the major distinctive accents of $\mathfrak{M}$. But in quite a number of cases the points in the Greek manuscripts correspond to lower accents like Ṭiphḥa (No. 8) and Pashṭa (No. 10) in $\mathfrak{M}$. And so one always has to consider whether or not to interpret these points in the Greek manuscripts as major punctuation or not.[3] Here the combination with points in the $\mathfrak{S}$ manuscripts proved to be an invaluable help.[4] In a

[1]See e.g. N.H. Ridderbos, *Die Psalmen: Stilistische Verfahren und Aufbau mit besonderer Berücksichtigung von Ps 1-41* (BZAW, 117), Berlin 1972, 114-5; A. Lemaire, *Les écoles et la formation de la Bible dans l'ancien Israel* (OBO, 39), Fribourg 1981, esp. 34-71.

[2]In this connection 'stronger' means: having a *lower* number in the *Tabula*. The only exceptions are the Segolta (No. 3) and the Revia' (No. 7) which under relatively rare circumstances may represent a weaker accent. Cf. pp. 31, 144, 235.

[3]We discussed all cases of deviating interpunction in the section dealing with the delimitation of cola.

[4]In $\mathfrak{S}$ the problem of indiscriminate interpunction by points was solved at an early date by the introduction of subordinate punctuation. So a point in a Syriac

considerable number of cases these ancient manuscripts which are centuries older than 𝔐 appear to have preserved the correct division by a dividing point and/or a major division marking. Their individual rates of 'success'[5] are as follows:

$\mathfrak{G}^{S}$ 1051 (81%);
$\mathfrak{G}^{Q}$ 1100 (85%);[6]
$\mathfrak{S}^{a}$ 871 (67%) [including subordinate punctuation at the right places: 1064 (82%)];
$\mathfrak{S}^{b}$ 884 (68%) [including subordinate punctuation at the right places: 1032 (80%)];
$\mathfrak{S}^{c}$ 852 (66%) [including subordinate punctuation at the right places: 1044 (81%)];
$\mathfrak{S}^{d}$ 860 (66%) [including subordinate punctuation at the right places: 1038 (80%)];
$\mathfrak{S}^{e}$ 938 (72%) [including subordinate punctuation at the right places: 1095 (85%)].[7]

There is such a high level of consistency in the placing of punctuation in the Greek and Syriac manuscripts we collated that a more or less haphazard process, allowing individual scribes to insert points wherever they wanted, must be excluded. Just like the text itself, the punctuation must have been part of a fostered tradition. Yet the very fact that the colometric traditions of 𝔐, 𝔊 and 𝔖 are *not* totally identical makes it worthwhile to study them. For they are by no means completely dependent on each other. A case like 51:10b-11a, where 𝔐, 𝔊 and 𝔖 all have different colometric divisions, demonstrates this sufficiently. The following observations may serve to confirm the independency of the Hebrew, Greek and Syriac traditions.

Cases where the punctuation of 𝔊 and 𝔐 agrees against 𝔖:

40:2 צבאה	41:26 אין־מגיד	44:19 אעשׂה
40:9 קולך	43:10 יהוה	44:24 גאלך
40:10 אתו	43:19 תצמח	45:1 מלכים
40:19 צורף	43:22 יעקב	45:12 ארץ
40:20 המסכן	44:1 עבדי	45:15 מסתתר

manuscript is always a major divider.

[5]Defined as: accepted in this study.

[6]It is remarkable that $\mathfrak{G}^{Q}$, which is the younger manuscript, has a somewhat better score.

[7]In this case too the younger manuscript has the best score, confirming its high quality which had already been established for the consonantal text by other researchers. See p. 7, n. 28.

45:16 כלם	48:12 ראשון	51:15 הים
45:16 בכלמה	48:20 מבבל	51:18 בידה
45:21 והגישו	48:21 ויבקע־צור	51:22 חמתי
46:7 תחתיו	50:4 בבקר[1]	52:6 שׁמי
47:1 על־עפר	50:6 למכים	53:9 קברו
47:6 על־עמי	51:2bA קראתיו	53:9 עשׂה
47:9 כשפיך	51:10 דרך	54:2 מיתריך
47:11 הוה	51:11 ישובון	55:10 את־הארץ
48:6 מעתה	51:13 ארץ	55:11 חפצתי

Cases where the punctuation of 𝔖 and 𝔐 agrees against 𝔊:

40:7 חציר[1]	43:18 ראשׁנות	50:5 מריתי
40:8 ודבת־אלהינו	44:15 ויחם	51:11 עולם
40:11 ישׂא	44:17 אליו	51:12 ומבן־אדם
40:14 נועץ	44:17 ויאמר	51:18 בידה
40:16 תרומה	44:17 אתה	51:20 עלפו
40:20 פסל	44:24 מי אתי	52:6bB כי־אני־הוא
40:21 תדעו	45:1 לכורשׁ	52:7 ישועה
40:22 וישביה	45:6 יהוה	52:8 נשׂאו
41:3 ירדפם	45:7 אור	53:2 ונראהו
41:3 שׂלום	45:11 ישׂראל	53:3 מכאבות
41:6 חזק	45:13 עירי	53:7 נענה
41:7 את־צרף	45:23 לשׂון	53:10 אשׁם
41:7 במסמרים	46:1 בל	53:11 נפשׁו
41:8 עבדי	46:4 עשׂיתי	54:3 כי־ימין
41:10 אלהיך	46:5 ותשׁוו	54:9 על־הארץ
41:15 ותדק	46:11 מרחק	54:9 ומגער־בך
41:16 ביהוה	46:13 ותשׁועתי	54:10 שׁלומי
41:16 תהלל	48:1 יהוה	55:3 אזנכם
41:17 והאביונים	48:1 יזכירו	55:3 שׁמעו
41:17 אענם	48:17 להועיל	55:5 לא־ידעוך
41:17 ישׂראל	49:1 קראני	55:5 אלהיך
41:23 ונשׁתעה	49:5 אליו	55:8 דרכיכם
41:24 ופעלכם	49:7 קדושׁו	55:9 ומחשׁבתי
41:24 מאפע	49:7 נאמן	55:11 כי אם־עשׂה
42:1 עבדי	49:25 יקח	55:12 יפצחו
42:1 בחירי	49:26 דמם	55:13 עולם
42:17 אחור	50:1 יהוה	
43:9 לאמים	50:4 כלמודים	

Cases where the punctuation of 𝔊 and 𝔖 agrees against 𝔐:

40:1 עמי	43:2 יעקב	48:20 הגידו
40:2 ירושלם	43:4 נכבת	49:1 מרחוק
40:3 במדבר	44:7 ומי־כמוני	53:4 חשבנו נגוע
40:17 נחשבו־לו	44:19 ולא־תבונה	53:8 מעצר
40:21 הבינתם	44:20 את־נפשו	53:11 יראה ישבע
41:2 צדק	45:3 תדע	53:11 צדיק
41:5 הארץ	45:3 בשמך	55:1 ולכאו
41:11 ויכלמו	45:14 מצרים	55:8 יהוה
41:11 ויאבדו	45:14 וסבאים	55:8 קראהו
41:12 כאין	45:14 יעברו	
42:7 ואצרך	45:18 הארץ	

Cases where 𝔐 does not have any support in 𝔊 and 𝔖 yet has an acceptable division:

40:1aA עמי	42:14aA מעולם	47:5bA יקראו־לך
40:25aA ואשוה	44:9bC יבשו	47:15aA יגעת
41:5aB יחרדו	44:10aA נסך	48:8 לא־שמעת
41:11aA ויכלמו	44:13bB במקצעות	49:18aA ראי
41:11aB ויאבדו	44:13bC יתארהו	49:20aA באזניך
41:12aA תמצאם	44:17aA ושאריתו	50:1bA מנושי
41:12bA וכאפס	44:20aA אפר	50:4bB אזן
41:21aA ריבכם	46:5aA ותשוו	50:10bB גאולים
41:21bA עצמותיכם	46:7bA יענה	51:18aA לה
41:25aA ויאת	46:9aB עוד	55:1bA ואכלו
42:13bA אף־יצריח	47:1bA יקראו־לך	

The evidence collected in these lists demonstrates sufficiently that the traditions on which the punctuation in the Hebrew, Greek and Syriac manuscripts rests are independent.[8] Yet all of them appear to go back on authentic cantillation traditions, not on *ad hoc* inventions. For this reason they deserve to be consulted in all future publications on the colometry of Classical Hebrew poetry. Preferably they should also be made available in future editions of the Hebrew, Greek and Syriac Bible. It is hard to understand why previous scholarship decided to omit this kind of data. We hope to have proved that this information is important to Bible translators and exegetes.[9]

---

[8]In some cases even the testimony of 𝔖 is divided in itself, e.g. in 47:4aA.

[9]Some examples: 41:2a; 44:14; 45:24; 48:16; 50:2, 8; 53:10aC; 54:14aC.

16.2.2 Colon Parallelism

On the level of the colon, parallelism is not an important phenomenon. Of the 1295 cola we identified, only 294 (23%) exhibit colon parallelism. Yet it is one of the arguments that may help to decide cases where the testimony of the ancient witnesses with regard to colon delimitation is divided or difficult to accept.

16.2.3 Length of Cola

According to what we have dubbed the 'Law of Expansion and Contraction' the length of every structural unit of a North-West Semitic poem was flexible and could be expanded or contracted according to the mood and skill of the singers. It was parallelism that allowed them to express the same basic thought in a much more elaborated form, or to reduce it to a smaller unit if they wanted. We have deduced this law from controllable evidence, like added or omitted feet, cola, strophes and even canticles in duplicate manuscripts and parallel passages. The shortest possible form of every structural unit counts only one element of the next lower structural unit.[10]

So the shortest possible colon counted only a single stressed unit (foot).[11] But such an ultra-short colon is a rare phenomenon. In Isaiah 40–55 we accepted only six such cases: 43:12bB; 44:7aA; 45:22aB; 48:16bB, 21bA; 54:9bB (.5% of the total number of cola). Far more common are cola with 2 (316 cases, or 24%), 3 (687 cases, or 53%) or 4 feet (257 cases, or 20%). The longest cola which the Masoretes still found acceptable counted eight feet (47:9a), but in our opinion they were misled by enjambment here. This is also the case in quite a

[10]For all this see J.C. de Moor, "The Art of Versification in Ugarit and Israel", in: Y. Avishur, J. Blau (eds.), *Studies in Bible and the Ancient Near East*, Jeruisalem 1978, 119-39 (127); Idem, "The Art of Versification in Ugarit and Israel II: The Formal Structure", *UF* 10 (1978), 187-217 (200-17); Idem, "The Art of Versification in Ugarit and Israel III: Further Illustrations of the Principle of Expansion", *UF* 12 (1980),311-15; M.C.A. Korpel, J.C. de Moor, "Fundamentals of Ugaritic and Hebrew Poetry", *UF* 18 (1986), 173-212; M.C.A. Korpel, "Exegesis in the Work of Ilimilku of Ugarit", in: J.C. de Moor (ed.), *Intertextuality in Ugarit and Israel* (OTS, 40), Leiden 1998, 86-111 (102-105).

[11]It may be recalled here that we simply counted the number of Masoretic stressed units, so only the Maqqeph gave us reason to count the words connected by it as one foot. We decided to waive the possibility of harmonizing the number of stresses even though there is evidence indicating that this was actually practised in Antiquity.

number of other instances of cola counting seven,[12] six[13] or five[14] feet. In only four cases we accepted a colon of six feet,[15] in twenty cases a colon of five feet,[16] usually because other witnesses supported 𝔐.

16.3 The Verse-Line

16.3.1 Delimiters of Verse-Lines

For the delimitation of verse-lines the only delimiters we could use consistently were the Masoretic distinctive accents.[17] It appears that if we were able to accept 𝔐's division into cola, the verse-lines usually showed a series of accents of increasing weight (decreasing numbers according to the *Tabula Accentuum* of BHS).

In many cases we were able to demonstrate that sentences spilling over into the next colon or verse-line as well as complicated cases of poetic ellipsis created difficulties for the scribes responsible for the punctuation of verse-lines. This was already the case in pre-Masoretic times[18] and so it is small wonder that the same difficulties sometimes confused the Masoretes and ancient translators.[19]

Finally, in a number of cases the Masoretic division appears to rest on rabbinic exegesis. In such cases the Masoretic versification seems to comply with quotations from the Hebrew Bible in the Talmud and other ancient rabbinical writings, even though a different division would have been more logical from the viewpoint of poetic structure.[20] We did not consider it our task to check the exegetical background of the Masoretic structural division systematically, but it would seem worthwhile to check the rabbinic sources whenever the correctness of the Masoretic structural division is in doubt.[21]

---

[12] 42:24aA-aC; 43:10bA; 45:18aA-B; 50:1aB.

[13] 40:28; 42:6a; 43:4aA-aB, 25aA-B; 44:8aB; 45:1a, 14aB-aC, 14d, 20a, 21b, 23aB; 46:7a; 47:2bA-B, 11b; 50:10bA-B, 11a; 51:1a, 6aA, 6aB, 10a, 17bA, 19b; 52:1b, 6a; 54:1b, 6a, 6b.

[14] 40:2a, 9a; 41:22bB; 42:6b; 43:1aA-aB, 14aA-aB; 45:11aA-B; 51:17bB, 20a; 54:9b; 55:12bA-B.

[15] 50:4aA; 54:8aA, 9aB; 55:11aA

[16] 40:7aB, 10aA; 41:15aA; 42:16aA, 16aC; 43:10bA; 44:7bB, 20bB; 45:20bA; 47:1, 5aA, 8aA; 49:6aA, 7bA, 19aA; 51:9aA; 52:1a, 4bA; 53:12bA; 55:10aA.

[17] 1𝔔[a] rarely marks the end of verse-lines with a fractionally wider space.

[18] J.C. de Moor, "Structure and Redaction: Isaiah 60,1–63,6", in: J. van Ruiten, M. Vervenne (eds.), *Studies in the Book of Isaiah: Festschrift Willem A.M. Beuken*, Leuven 1997, 325-46 (328).

[19] Cf. P. Sanders, *The Provenance of Deuteronomy 32* (OTS, 37), Leiden 1996, 117-8, 124-5.

[20] See our discussion of the colometry of 41:2aA, 42:16bC; 43:19aA; 45:1aA; 50:10bA; 55:6aA; the verse-lines 53:9b-10a; 54:1a; 55:1; the strophe 54:12-14a; the canticle 50:2b-3.

[21] Since they are available on CD-ROM this is no longer an extravagant demand.

16.3.2 Verse-line Parallelism

Despite the many problems connected with the identification of parallelism[22] it is still one of the important binding forces on the level of the verse-line. Of the 605 verse-lines we identified, no less than 508 connect the cola by parallelism (84%). This finding certainly corroborates the generally accepted view that parallelism is a most important connecting force on the level of the verse-line.

Yet parallelism was not essential. In 97 cases (16%) we found no parallelism at all, often because the verse-line consisted of only one colon (unicolon). In 65 cases of these verse-lines the lack of parallelism appeared to be caused by the fact that the sentence runs on (enjambment). Yet the Masoretes mostly divided such verse-lines correctly (45 cases, 69%).[23] In other cases, however, enjambment appears to have confused them (20 cases, 31%),[24] often forcing them to accept extremely long cola.

In several cases we were able to observe that lack of parallelism on the level of the verse-line was compensated on the next higher level of the strophe.[25] Mostly it is absolutely clear that such verse-lines with a weak or even lacking parallelism are indispensable in the flow of the text. In other North-West Semitic poetry, like that of Ugarit, one encounters the same phenomenon and this counsels against overly confident statements as to the 'prosaic' nature of certain passages which for that reason can be 'safely' removed.[26]

16.3.3 Ellipsis in Verse-Lines

An often neglected force joining cola into verse-lines is ellipsis – the omission of one or more self-evident words from a parallel colon, mostly the next one, sometimes a previous one. Because such a colon cannot be understood without its supplementing half, this too is an

---

[22]Cf. D. Pardee, *Ugaritic and Hebrew Poetic Parallelism* (VT.S, 39), Leiden 1988.

[23]40:2c, 3b, 20a, 20b, 26bB-C; 41:11a, 12a, 19b, 21b, 22a; 42:4a, 17aA-B; 43:16a, 20b, 21; 44:4a, 7aB-C, 10a, 16aB-C; 45:1a, 6aA-B, 13b, 16aB-C, 17a; 47:1b, 5b, 11b, 13c; 48:9, 21A-B, 22; 50:4a, 6b, 7a, 9a; 51:18a, 18b, 19a; 52:5a, 8b, 9a, 10a, 10b; 53:6b; 55:12A-B.

[24]41:11b, 12b, 13a, 21a; 43:14a; 45:1a, 11a, 17b, 22a, 25; 47:9a, 11b; 48:13b; 50:19b, 20a, 22b; 52:1c; 54:1b, 6a, 6b.

[25]44:7a, 11a; 45:1b; 50:7a; 51:17b, 18, 19a; 54:4, 8a. Sometimes colon parallelism may fulfill this function, e.g. 46:6b; 54:4.

[26]On the problematical nature of the distinction between prose and poetry, see J.C. de Moor, W.G.E. Watson (eds.), *Verse in Ancient Near Eastern Prose* (AOAT, 42), Neukirchen 1993.

argument to combine cola into one and the same verse-line. We found ellipsis in 121 verse-lines, 20% of the total.

16.3.4 Length of Verse-Lines

According to the Law of Expansion and Contraction the shortest possible verse-line should count only one colon. In Isaiah 40-55 we found 38 of these so-called unicola (6% of the total number of verse-lines). Bicola are the most common form of verse-line (75%). Tricola (18%) and quadrocola (1%) are much more rare.

16.3.5 Structural Patterns in Verse-Lines

In the following table we sum up the sequences of major Masoretic distinctive accents delimiting verse-lines we accepted as valid (578 cases, an astounding 95% of the total number of verse-lines). The numbers in the table correspond to the *Tabula Accentuum* of BHS.

SEQUENCES OF ACCENTS PER VERSE-LINE		
SEQUENCE	OCCURRENCES	PERCENTAGE
	UNICOLA	
1	16	3
2	19	3
	BICOLA	
2 – 1	146	25
5 – 1	164	29
5 – 2	151	26
6 – 2	1	0
7 – 1	1	0
7 – 5	11	2
	TRICOLA	
5 – 2 – 1	23	4
5 – 5 – 1	7	1
5 – 5 – 2	9	2
7 – 5 – 1	12	2
7 – 5 – 2	14	2
	QUADROCOLA	
7 – 5 – 5 – 2	4	1

The conclusion can only be that in general the Masoretic division into verse-lines is acceptable and may well serve as the point of departure for any discussion about the meaning of the text. Moreover, the ascending sequences of Masoretic accents (descending according to the *Tabula*) are a reliable guide to determine the limits of a verse-line.

With regard to the rhythmical balance in the verse-line our findings confirm what is well-known by now, namely, that there was no rigid metre or fixed rhythm in Classical Hebrew poetry. We provide a table of the patterns of 1–4 equal and 1–4 unequal numbers of stresses in bicola,

SEQUENCES OF STRESSES PER VERSE-LINE	
SEQUENCE	OCCURRENCES
BICOLA: EQUAL	
1 + 1	0
2 + 2	23
3 + 3	126
4 + 4	18
Total	167
BICOLA: UNEQUAL	
2 + 1	1
2 + 3	29
2 + 4	3
3 + 1	1
3 + 2	88
3 + 4	34
4 + 1	2
4 + 2	56
4 + 3	63
Total	277

Since even this small survey shows that irregularity was the rule and regularity the exception, the number of stresses has some value in discussions of poetical structure only if the number of stresses in the immediate neighbourhood seems to be the same, especially with the pattern of 3+3 stresses, since this is by far the most common type of bicolon.

16.4 The Strophe

16.4.1 Delimiters of Strophes

In most cases strophes are identical to Masoretic verses. Of the 344 strophes which we established 288 (84%) coincided with Masoretic verses. Since the Soph Pasuq was introduced only in the Middle Ages, it is a truly remarkable achievement on the part of the Masoretes that they succeeded in keeping the ancient strophic division intact largely on the basis of oral tradition.

However, not on that basis alone. We noted that 1𝔔^{a}, like the Greek Minor Prophets Scroll from Naḥal Ḥever, sometimes marks the end of a strophe by a small space. It must be assumed that this practice continued to be in use, both in Hebrew and Greek manuscripts, be it not very consistently. Inevitably this became a source of many errors (see below 16.5.1). Yet there is quite a number of cases where major division markers like Petuḥot and Setumot seem to have no other function than indicating the end of a strophe. It must be assumed that they evolved to the status of major dividers through misinterpretation of small spaces meant to indicate strophe ends. We collected the following cases:[27]

𝔐: 41:1, 26; 42:13; 45:9.

1𝔔^{a}: 41:1, 4, 6; 43:7, 26; 44:1, 22; 49:3, 24; 50:1bB, 1cB, 2bB, 2dB, 4bC, 6bB, 7bB; 53:8, 11; 54:1, 17.

𝔊^{S}: 40:27; 41:26; 42:8, 10, 13, 22, 23; 44:1, 6, 7, 22, 24; 45:11, 21; 47:13aC; 48:3, 15; 49:14, 17; 52:4, 5, 7, 8, 9; 53:11; 54:17.

𝔊^{B}: 44:22; 47:13cB; 49:24; 52:4, 5; 55:2.

𝔊^{A}: 40:6, 12, 19, 21; 41:1, 6, 21, 25, 26; 42:5, 7, 22; 43:3, 5, 7, 9, 26; 44:6, 7, 22; 45:11; 47:5, 9, 13aC; 48:3, 7, 13, 15, 21; 49:3, 19, 24; 51:1, 15, 22; 52:5, 8; 53:8; 54:11, 17; 55:2, 12.

𝔊^{Q}: 41:1, 26; 42:5; 43:14; 45:11, 21; 49:17, 19, 24; 52:4, 5, 8; 54:17.

Some manuscripts, like 1𝔔^{a}, 𝔊^{S} and 𝔊^{A}, rest on a tradition which was apparently more liberal in the use of spaces than others and it is often difficult to distinguish between strophic division and canticle division in them. It appears that 𝔖 rests on a manuscriptal tradition which did not make use of this kind of confusing strophic spacing. Possible exceptions are found in 42:13 (all manuscripts) and in 𝔖^{a} 42:22; 44:22.

Of course also the genuine delimiters of canticles (see below) may help to delimit the beginning and/or end of strophes. In total the beginning and/or end of 208 of the 344 strophes we identified was established with the help of major delimiters (60%).

However, major delimitation markers were not the only tool we used. Beginning and end of strophes appear to be marked by certain emphatic grammatical structures meant to capture the attention of the audience.[28] In this respect we booked the following results:[29]

[27]All were discussed in connection with the delimitation of strophes and canticles. We included a number of cases where 1𝔔^{a} still has a smaller space than a normal Setuma. We exclude a number of isolated cases in other manuscripts, like the 4𝔔 fragments, the Codex Reuchlin and the Parma Bible from this survey.

[28]See the general introduction, pp. 14-5.

[29]We counted every phenomenon only once per verse-line, even if it occurred

MARKER START	TOTAL	MARKER END	TOTAL
swapping adjunct	131	swapping adjunct	93
deictic particle	124	deictic particle	70
repetitive parallelism	116	repetitive parallelism	101
swapping subject	72	swapping subject	45
intro direct speech	63	intro direct speech	32
imperative	63	imperative	26
independent pron.	52	independent pron.	42
swapping object	45	swapping object	44
vocative	39	vocative	8
interrogative pron.	28	interrogative pron.	12
jussive	25	jussive	19
demonstr. pronoun	16	demonstr. pronoun	10
paronomasia	5	paronomasia	2
cohortative	4	cohortative	5
precative perfect	3	precative perfect	0
no marking	14	no marking[30]	6

This table shows that hardly any strophe is lacking one or more of these separating emphatic constructs, both upwards and downwards. Another important finding is that the beginning of strophes appears to be better demarcated than their end. And finally, our results warrant repetition of a conclusion one of us drew some years ago with regard to Ugaritic, "It is not possible to describe adequately the syntax of Ugaritic verse without having recourse to the poetic structure. Conversely, the poetic structure cannot be established without paying due attention to the rather special syntax the poets employed."[31] The same appears to be true of Hebrew verse. The function of 'emphatic' constructions that are often not emphatic at all appears to be a structuring force on the level of the strophes.

16.4.2 Strophe Parallelism

Next to the separating delimiters there is also a binding force operative on the level of the strophes. The parallelism functions as a

several times in the same line. However, more than one emphatic structure could be used per verse-line, and so the totals are higher than the number of strophes. Therefore the table only gives an impression of the relative importance of a certain type of emphatic marking.

[30] Of course we discounted the cases where a strophe consists of only one verse-line, without following major division-markers, because it is obvious that one cannot count delimiting markers twice, both upwards and downwards.

[31] J.C. de Moor, "Syntax Peculiar to Ugaritic Poetry", in: J.C. de Moor, W.G.E. Watson (eds.), *Verse in Ancient Near Eastern Prose* (AOAT, 42), Neukirchen 1993, 191-205 (205).

link between verse-lines, even though it often are only small particles, grammatical parallelism or rhyme which establish the link. Yet also in strophes parallelism is not an absolute prerequisite. Strophes without parallelism do occur.[32] Just as lack of parallelism on the level of the verse-line may be compensated for by strophe parallelism, so lack of strophe parallelism may be balanced by canticle parallelism.[33]

16.4.3 Length of Strophes

In accordance with the Law of Expansion and Contraction the smallest strophe counts only one verse-line. We found 83 examples of this in Isaiah 40–55 (24% of the total number of strophes).[34] No strophe in Second Isaiah counts more than two verse-lines. The longest strophe consists of a tricolon followed by a quadrocolon (49:21).

16.4.4 Structural Patterns in Strophes

The variety in strophic patterns is great, but only a few are relatively frequent. The following table lists them in descending order,

STRUCTURAL PATTERNS IN STROPHES		
TYPE	OCCURRENCES	PERCENTAGE
Bicolon – Bicolon	144	42
Single Bicolon	62	18
Tricolon – Bicolon	33	10
Bicolon – Tricolon	30	9
Single Tricolon	20	6

continued on next page

[32] 40:6, 25; 41:16, 20; 42:24; 43:9a-b; 44:2; 45:14, 22, 23; 46:2, 3, 6, 12; 47:1, 7; 48:12, 13; 49:7a-b, 7c-d; 49:18, 20; 51:6, 7, 8, 19; 53:2; 54:11.

[33] E.g. 44:2, 4; 46:3, 12; 49:7c-d.

[34] To those unfamiliar with the flexible nature of North-West Semitic poetry it may seem odd that strophes can have the same length as verse-lines. Therefore we add the specifics here. Strophe consisting of a single verse-line which is at the same time a unicolon: 51:17a. Strophes consisting of a single bicolon which was recognized as a strophe by the Masoretes: 40:16, 17, 23, 25, 29, 30; 41:27; 42:12, 18, 20, 21, 23; 43:8, 11, 15, 18, 21, 22, 27; 44:1, 4, 10, 27; 45:10, 15; 46:5, 12; 47:4; 48:10, 15, 22; 49:3, 14, 24; 50:3; 52:13; 53:1; 54:15; 55:4. Not recognized by the Masoretes: 43:17b; 44:13c; 45:1a; 47:1a; 47:3a, 3b; 48:14a, 14b; 49:23c; 50:1c, 2a, 2b, 8b, 10a, 11c; 51:3c, 6a, 9c, 13a; 52:1c; 54:14b, 17a, 17b; 55:10a. Strophes consisting of a single tricolon which was recognized as a strophe by the Masoretes: 40:21; 41:8; 42:4, 17; 43:7; 45:6, 7; 48:2, 4; 50:5; 51:15; 52:3, 4, 14; 55:6, 8. Not recognized by the Masoretes: 40:9c; 44:12a, 12b; 53:10b-c. Of course the cases deviating from the Masoretes have been discussed at length in our treatment of the delimitation of strophes.

continued from previous page

STRUCTURAL PATTERNS IN STROPHES		
TYPE	OCCURRENCES	PERCENTAGE
Unicolon – Bicolon	20	6
Bicolon – Unicolon	12	3
Tricolon – Tricolon	10	3
Tricolon – Unicolon	5	1
Quadrocolon – Bicolon	3	1
Bicolon – Quadrocolon	2	1
Single Unicolon	1	0
Unicolon – Quadrocolon	1	0
Tricolon – Quadrocolon	1	0

16.5 The Canticle

16.5.1 Delimiters

The most important delimiters for the canticles appear to be

- the Setumot, Petuḥot, indentations and paragraphoi in Hebrew manuscripts;
- the Setumot, Petuḥot, capital letters, protruding lines and paragraphoi in Greek manuscripts;
- the spaces, "diamonds" and paragraphoi in Syriac manuscripts.

Because comparison of these markers shows that they were interchangeable within their own tradition and because there is no functional difference between, say, a Setuma or a Petuḥa, or between one, two or three diamonds, we mostly designated them indiscriminately as 'major division markers', specifying their nature only if this seemed expedient.

Usually these markers are positioned at the end of verses and the circumstance that in the three different traditions they are very often found at exactly the same spot proves that they rest on very ancient common tradition which must have had an important structuring function as early as the second century BCE. It is not excluded that they were already part of the original work as it left the hands of the final editor(s).

However, these dividers are not always placed neatly at the borderline of a verse. Sometimes one finds them at strange places in the middle of verses where they were apparently not intended to mark a new beginning. Some convincing cases are the following:

Isa. 44:8 where $\mathfrak{G}^{SA}$ divide after והגדתי, $\mathfrak{G}^{Q}$ after עדי, and $\mathfrak{G}^{B}$ after מבלעדי. All four divisions are highly unlikely from the viewpoint of content. Therefore we assume them to anticipate the major division marker $1\mathfrak{Q}^{a}$ has after v. 8.

Isa. 45:4 – $\mathfrak{G}^{Q}$ writes Σὺ with a capital in the middle of a line. Capitalization usually indicates a major break and in this case it may safely be assumed to anticipate the break which is attested by $1\mathfrak{Q}^{a}$ and $1\mathfrak{Q}^{b}$ after v. 4.

Isa. 45:25 – $\mathfrak{G}^{A}$ has a Setuma and a protuding capital letter with יצדקו where a break is simply impossible. Since the same manuscript also marks the border between chapters 45 and 46 (with many other witnesses) the former division marking must be proleptic.

Isa. 47:1 – The major division markers $\mathfrak{G}^{Q}$ has after בת־בבל are a typical example of markers lagging behind the actual division point after Isa. 46:13 which has been marked correctly in $\mathfrak{G}^{SBA}$.

Isa. 47:11 – The Petuḥa $1\mathfrak{Q}^{b}$ has after כפרה in v. 11 proleptically indicates the same delimitation which $\mathfrak{G}^{SA}$ mark properly *after* v. 11.

Isa. 48:19 – The protruding capital $\mathfrak{G}^{A}$ has after v. 20aB obviously indicates the well-attested division after v. 19 where a marking in $\mathfrak{G}^{A}$ is conspicuously missing.

Isa. 50:5aA אזן $\mathfrak{G}^{AQ}$ where the nature of $\mathfrak{G}$'s translation excludes the idea that a serious break is made at this point. $1\mathfrak{Q}^{a}$ is consistently marking the beginning of verses here and has a Setuma at the end of v. 4. It is natural to conclude that the position of the major division markers in $\mathfrak{G}^{AQ}$ has shifted.

Isa. 51:16 – The diamond $\mathfrak{S}^{b}$ has after ארץ is apparently a redundant proleptic divider because the same manuscript joins the host of other witnesses testifying to the major break *after* the verse.

Isa. 52:6 – The major division marks $\mathfrak{G}^{S}$ has in the middle of v. 6bB – a highly improbable point – obviously indicate the well-attested break after v. 6 proleptically.

Isa. 52:7-8 – $\mathfrak{G}^{S}$ has a paragraphos marking the end of 52:7 which corresponds to a small Setuma in $1\mathfrak{Q}^{a}$. Obviously the paragraphos goes back to such a marker of the end of a strophe. However, $\mathfrak{G}^{S}$ has a protruding line starting with the second קול in 52:8. Apparently this is a belated marking of the same borderline.

Isa. 54:10 – The major break after v. 10 is attested in $\mathfrak{M}$, $1\mathfrak{Q}^{a}$, $4\mathfrak{Q}^{cd}$ and $\mathfrak{S}^{bce}$, but not in $\mathfrak{G}$. However, $\mathfrak{G}^{A}$ has major division markers after תמוט and $\mathfrak{G}^{SB}$ after נחמה in v. 11, both spots where a major break is impossible. Again the only reasonable explanation is proleptic marking in

𝔊^{A} whereas 𝔊^{SB} are lagging behind. Yet all three must be regarded as witnesses for the break after v.10.

It is possible that the function of the major division markers was no longer understood by all scribes and that this became a source of errors. But even if the scribes did not know the meaning of the major dividers anymore, it is more likely that even in this respect they still tried to faithfully copy their originals.[35] The utmost care devoted to the execution of Bible manuscripts renders any other hypothesis less convincing. However, sometimes the scribes simply picked a suitable point somewhere in the verse which originally ended in a Petuḥa or Setuma. That this is the correct explanation of the phenomenon appears from manuscripts of the Vulgate and from examples of chapter divisions in the middle of verses in the Rabbinic Bible of 1525.[36]

Another source of confusion was the use of small Setumot to mark the end of a strophe. 1𝔔^{a} shows that this was done occasionally and irregularly.[37] As a result, later copyists could easily think that they had to insert a major division marking where their predecessor had simply meant a strophe end. Or the reverse. Even the Hebrew tradition creates the impression that its bearers were not always sure about the correct position of a break. Therefore it is necessary to discuss all major division markers critically.

We have argued that the following 44 markers are erroneous:

𝔐: 40:16; 51:21aB; 52:2bB.

1𝔔^{a}: 40:16; 48:9bA; 49:25aC; 51:21aB.

𝔊^{S}: 41:4aB, 14, 17; 43:9cB, 12aB; 48:9bA; 51:13bB, 21aB; 55:2aB.

𝔊^{B}: 41:12; 42:24aB.

𝔊^{A}: 41:2aB, 4aB, 12, 14, 17; 42:5aB; 43:9cB, 12aB, 19aC; 44:25-28aB; 46:10bA; 48:13aB; 52:2bB, 15aB.

𝔊^{Q}: 44:25-28aB; 48:9bA; 49:25aC; 51:13bB; 52:2bB; 55:10.

𝔖^{a}: 45:18bB.

𝔖^{b}: 41:14; 45:18bB; 49:5aD; 55:2aB.

𝔖^{d}: 45:11aB.

The very fact that many of these presumed errors are found in more than one manuscript seems to indicate that the error must have occurred very early in the chain of tradition and was faithfully perpetuated.

---

[35] Of course they did not always succeed. A very clear case of erroneously placed major dividers is found after Isa. 52:2. See our discussion p. 541 above.

[36] See J.S. Penkower, "Chapter Divisions in the 1525 Rabbinic Bible", *VT* 48 (1998), 350-74 (369-73).

[37] See especially pp. 3-4, 475-9.

Despite all these problems, the attestation of canticle boundaries in the ancient manuscripts is so consistent across largely independent channels of scribal tradition that it is worthwhile to survey the evidence once again here. In the following table

- + indicates that the manuscript has the division marking at the correct position attested in other manuscripts.
- – indicates that the manuscript has no division marking at the position indicated by other manuscripts.
- * indicates that the marking has been placed in an inexact way, anticipating or lagging behind the correct position that has been preserved in other manuscripts.
- ! indicates that the same manuscript has an inexact marking in addition to the correct one.

A double horizontal line in the table indicates a canto boundary, a single horizontal line a sub-canto boundary. We have left out manuscripts which are too incomplete to consider in this general survey ($1\mathfrak{Q}^b$, the $4\mathfrak{Q}$-fragments, the Christian-Palestinian lectionaries). What we enumerate here are the canticle delimiters we accepted as valid in this study. In only two cases we assumed a canticle boundary without having the support of any ancient witness: 43:4 and 44:13.

ATTESTATION OF CANTICLE BORDERS											
AFTER:	$\mathfrak{M}$	$1\mathfrak{Q}^a$	$\mathfrak{G}^S$	$\mathfrak{G}^B$	$\mathfrak{G}^A$	$\mathfrak{G}^Q$	$\mathfrak{S}^a$	$\mathfrak{S}^b$	$\mathfrak{S}^c$	$\mathfrak{S}^d$	$\mathfrak{S}^e$
39:8	+	+	+	+	+	+	+	+	+	+	+
40:2	+	+	+	+	+	+	+	+	+	+	+
40:5	+	+	+	+	+	+	–	+	–	–	+
40:8	+	+	+	+	+	+	+	+	–	+	+
40:9	–	–	–	+	–	–	–	–	–	–	–
40:11	+	+	+	–	+	–	+	+	+	+	+
40:14	–	–	+	–	+	–	–	–	–	–	–
40:17	–	–	+	–	+	–	+	+	–	+	+
40:20	(+)	–	+	–	–	–	–	–	–	–	–
40:22	–	–	–	–	+	–	–	–	–	–	–
40:24	+	+	+	–	+	+	+	+	+	–	+
40:26	+	+	–	–	–	–	–	+	–	–	+
40:28	–	–	–	–	+	–	–	–	–	–	–

continued on next page

continued from previous page

ATTESTATION OF CANTICLE BORDERS											
AFTER:	𝔐	1𝔔ᵃ	$\mathfrak{G}^{S}$	$\mathfrak{G}^{B}$	$\mathfrak{G}^{A}$	$\mathfrak{G}^{Q}$	ς^{a}	ς^{b}	ς^{c}	ς^{d}	ς^{e}
40:31	+	+	+	+	+	+	+	+	+	+	+
41:3	–	–	+	–	*	–	+	–	–	–	+
41:7	+	+	+	+	+	+	–	–	–	+	–
41:10	–	–	+	–	+	+	–	–	–	–	–
41:13	+	+	–	–	–	–	+	–	+	–	–
41:16	+	+	*	–	*	*	–	+	–	+	+
41:20	+	+	+	+	+	+	+	+	–	–	+
41:24	(+)	+	–	–	+	*	+	–	+	–	+
41:29	+	+	+	+	+	+	+	+	+	+	+
42:4	+	+	+	+	+	–	+	+	–	–	+
42:9	+	+	+	+	+	+	+	+	–	+	+
42:12	–	+	+!	–	+!	–	–	–	–	+!	–
42:17	+	+	+!	*	+!	–	+	–	–	–	+
42:20	–	+	–	–	+	–	–	–	–	–	–
42:25	+	+	+	+	+	–	+	+	+	+	+
43:2	–	+	*	–	*	–	–	–	–	–	–
43:4	–	–	–	–	–	–	–	–	–	–	–
43:8	–	+	+	–	–	–	–	–	–	–	–
43:10	+	+	–	–	–	–	+	–	–	–	–
43:13	+	+	+	–	+	*	–	+	+	+	+
43:15	+	+	+	–	+	–	+	+	+	+	+
43:17	(+)	+	+	–	+	+	–	–	–	–	–
43:21	+	+	+	+	+	–	+	+	+	–	+
43:24	+	+	+	–	+	+	–	–	–	–	–
43:28	+	+	+	–	+	–	+	+	–	–	+
44:5	+	+	+	+	+	–	+	+	+	+	+
44:8	–	+	*	*	*	*	–	–	–	–	–
44:11	–	+	*	–	*	–	–	–	–	–	–
44:12	–	+	*	–	*	–	–	–	–	–	–
44:13	–	–	–	–	–	–	–	–	–	–	–
44:15	–	–	–	+	–	–	–	–	–	–	–
44:17	(+)	+	+	–	+	–	–	–	–	–	–
44:20	+	+	+	+	+	–	+	+	–	–	+
44:23	+	+	+!	+	+!	+	+	–	–	–	+
44:28	+	+	+	+	+	+	–	+	–	–	+

continued on next page

continued from previous page

ATTESTATION OF CANTICLE BORDERS

AFTER:	$\mathfrak{M}$	1$\mathfrak{Q}^a$	$\mathfrak{G}^S$	$\mathfrak{G}^B$	$\mathfrak{G}^A$	$\mathfrak{G}^Q$	$\mathfrak{S}^a$	$\mathfrak{S}^b$	$\mathfrak{S}^c$	$\mathfrak{S}^d$	$\mathfrak{S}^e$
45:1	−	−	−	−	+	−	−	−	−	−	−
45:4	−	+	−	−	*	−	−	−	−	−	−
45:7	+	+	+	+	+	+	+	+	−	−	+
45:8	+	+	*	*	*	*	−	+	+	−	+
45:10	+	+	+	+	+	−	+	+	−	−	+
45:13	+	+	+	+	+	+	+	+	+	−	+
45:16	+	+	+	+	+	+	+	+	+	+	+
45:17	+	+	+	+	−	−	−	+	−	−	−
45:19	−	−	+	−	+	−	−	+	−	−	−
45:21	−	−	+	+	*	−	−	−	−	−	−
45:25	+	+	+	+	+!	−	−	−	−	−	−
46:2	+	+	+	+	+	+	+	+	+	+	+
46:4	+	+	+	−	+	*	+	+	−	−	+
46:7	+	+	+	−	+	+	+	+	+	−	+
46:11	+	+	+	+	+	+	+	+	+	+	+
46:13	+	+	+	+	+	*	+	+	−	−	+
47:3	+	+!	*	−	*	−	+	+	−	−	+
47:7	+	+	+!	−	*	−	+	−	−	−	−
47:11	−	−	+	−	+	−	−	−	−	−	−
47:15	+	+	+	+	+!	+	+	+	−	−	+
48:2	+	+	−	−	+	*	−	−	−	−	−
48:5	−	−	+	−	*	*	−	−	−	−	−
48:8	−	*	*	−	−	*	−	−	−	−	−
48:11	+	+	+	+	+	+	+	+	+	+	+
48:14aB	−	−	+	−	+	−	−	−	−	−	−
48:16	+	+	+	−	+	−	+	+	−	−	+
48:19	(+)	+	+	−	*	+	−	+	−	−	+
48:22	+	+	+	+	+	+	+	+	+	+	+
49:4	(+)	+	+	−	+	−	+	+	−	−	+
49:6	+	+	+	+	+!	−	−	+	+	+	+
49:7	(+)	+	+	+	+	−	−	+	−	−	−
49:12	−	+	+	+	+	+	−	−	−	−	−
49:13	+	+	+	+	+	+	+	+	+	−	+
49:15	−	−	+	−	+	+	−	−	−	−	−
49:18	−	−	*	−	+!	−	−	−	−	−	+

continued on next page

continued from previous page

ATTESTATION OF CANTICLE BORDERS

AFTER:	$\mathfrak{M}$	$1\mathfrak{Q}^a$	$\mathfrak{G}^S$	$\mathfrak{G}^B$	$\mathfrak{G}^A$	$\mathfrak{G}^Q$	$\mathfrak{S}^a$	$\mathfrak{S}^b$	$\mathfrak{S}^c$	$\mathfrak{S}^d$	$\mathfrak{S}^e$
49:21	+	+	+	+	+	+	+	+	−	−	+
49:23	+	+	+	−	+	+	−	−	−	−	+
49:26	+	+	+	+	+	+	+	+	+	−	+
50:2aB	−	+	+	−	*	−	−	−	−	−	−
50:3	+	+	+	+	+	−	+	+	+	+	+
50:5	−	+	−	−	*	*	−	−	−	−	−
50:8aC	−	−	+	+	*	−	+	+	−	−	+
50:9	(+)	+!	+	−	+	−	−	−	−	−	−
50:10	+	+	+	−	+	−	−	+	−	−	−
50:11	+	+	+	+	+	+	−	+	+	+	+
51:2	+	−	−	−	+	−	−	−	−	−	−
51:3	+	+	+	+	+	+	+	−	−	+	−
51:5	−	−	+	−	+!	+!	−	−	−	−	−
51:6	+	+	+	+	+	+	−	+	−	−	+
51:8	+	+	+	+	+	+!	+	+	−	+	+
51:11	+	+	+	+	+	−	−	+	+	+	+
51:14	−	+	−	−	+	+	−	+	−	−	−
51:16	+	+	+	−	+	+	+	+!	+	−	+
51:18	−	−	−	−	*	+	−	−	−	−	−
51:20	(+)	+	+	+	+	−	+	+	+	−	+
51:23	+	+	+	−	+	+	+	+	+	+	+
52:3	(+)	+	+	+	+	−	−	+	−	−	−
52:6	(+)	+	*	−	+	−	+	+	+	+	+
52:10	+	+	+	−	+	+	−	+	−	−	−
52:12	+	+	+	+	+	+	+	+	+	+	+
52:15	(+)	+	+	+	+	+	−	−	−	−	−
53:3	−	−	+	−	*	*	−	−	−	−	+
53:6	−	*	*	−	*	+	−	−	−	−	−
53:10a	−	+	*!	−	+	−	−	−	−	−	−
53:12	+	+	+	+	+	+	+	+	+	+	+
54:3	−	−	+	−	+	*	−	−	−	−	−
54:5	−	−	*	+	+	−	−	−	−	−	−
54:8	+	−	−	−	−	−	−	−	−	+	+
54:10	+	+	*	*	*	−	−	+	+	−	+
54:14a	−	*	+	−	+	*	−	−	−	−	−

continued on next page

continued from previous page

ATTESTATION OF CANTICLE BORDERS											
AFTER:	$\mathfrak{M}$	1$\mathfrak{Q}^{a}$	$\mathfrak{G}^{S}$	$\mathfrak{G}^{B}$	$\mathfrak{G}^{A}$	$\mathfrak{G}^{Q}$	$\mathfrak{S}^{a}$	$\mathfrak{S}^{b}$	$\mathfrak{S}^{c}$	$\mathfrak{S}^{d}$	$\mathfrak{S}^{e}$
54:15	–	+	+	–	+	–	–	–	–	–	–
54:17	+	+	+	+	+	+	+	+	+	+	+
55:3	–	–	+	–	+	*	+	+	–	–	+
55:5	+	+	+!	+	+	+	–	+	+	–	+
55:7	–	+	–	–	–	+	–	–	–	–	–
55:9	–	+	–	–	+	+	–	–	–	–	–
55:11	–	+	–	–	–	–	–	+	–	–	–
55:12	+	+	+	+	+	+	–	+	–	–	+

The rate of 'success'[38] of the various witnesses we consulted is as follows: 1. $\mathfrak{G}^{A}$ (fifth century) 91%; 2. $\mathfrak{G}^{S}$ (fourth century) 83%; 3. 1$\mathfrak{Q}^{a}$ (second century BCE) 78%; 4. $\mathfrak{M}$ (tenth century) 65%; 5. $\mathfrak{S}^{b}$ (sixth century) 54%; 6. $\mathfrak{S}^{e}$ (ninth century) 54%; 7. $\mathfrak{G}^{Q}$ (sixth century) 51%; 8. $\mathfrak{G}^{B}$ (fourth century) 44%; 9. $\mathfrak{S}^{a}$ (sixth century) 43%; 10. $\mathfrak{S}^{c}$ (seventh century) 29%; 11. $\mathfrak{S}^{d}$ (eigth century) 26%.

Generally speaking, it looks as if the older manuscripts have preserved more canticle divisions than the younger ones, with $\mathfrak{M}$ and $\mathfrak{S}^{e}$ as the expected good exceptions among the younger manuscripts, and $\mathfrak{G}^{B}$ as a unexpected bad exception among the older ones. One might perhaps object that $\mathfrak{G}^{A}$ also has many erroneous division markers, as we have duly noted above. Is it admissable, then, to invoke it as a sole witness, as we did in 40:9, 22, 28; 45:1? Of course we have given our arguments for doing so in our discussion of the passages involved. Here, however, we want to point out in a more general way that $\mathfrak{G}^{A}$ is sometimes supported by only one other witness, usually also a 'good' witness (42:20; 45:4 1$\mathfrak{Q}^{a}$; 51:2 $\mathfrak{M}$; 47:11; 48:14; 49:18 $\mathfrak{G}^{S}$; 51:18 $\mathfrak{G}^{Q}$). So it is not impossible that under circumstances $\mathfrak{G}^{A}$ is the sole witness to a reliable old tradition.[39]

Generally speaking the boundaries of cantos appear to be attested over the full width of the witnesses we consulted, usually sub-cantos are also well-attested, whereas the boundaries of canticles are sometimes poorly attested. It is for this reason that as many witnesses as possible must be consulted in this respect and that other analytic arguments are necessary to supplement the manuscriptal evidence.

[38] Defined as: accepted as valid in this study.

[39] S. Jellicoe, *The Septuagint and Modern Study*, Oxford 1968, repr. Winona Lake 1993, 187, writes, "The papyrus discoveries of recent years are of special importance as witnessing to the very ancient text which Alexandrinus has preserved in parts despite its assimilation to other recensions".

16.5.2 Thematic Unity

Thematic unity appears to be a significant characteristic of canticles. We found that 120 out of our 125 canticles could be termed thematically coherent (96%). As a corollary to this, discontinuity of theme may be expected to be an indication of the fact that a new canticle has started. We found it in 67 cases (54%). A change of subject at the beginning of a new canticle occurs in 87 cases (70%).

16.5.3 Canticle Parallelism

Pardee was right in calling attention to the phenomenon which he calls 'distant parallelism'.[40] On the level of the canticle too parallelism appears to be a binding force, be it mostly in the form of repetitive parallelism. This is understandable because over a greater distance repetition is more effective than, say, synonymous parallelism which might escape the hearer or reader. We encountered one case of a canticle which has almost no parallelism at all (46:5-7).

Parallelism on the level of the canticle has an embracing function (inclusion), a refrain-like function (responsion) or a chaining function (concatenation). We always noted which of these functions was employed. All three help to highlight certain expressions in connection with the theme of the canticle.

16.5.4 Structural Patterns and Length of Canticles

The smallest canticle consists of only one strophe.[41] Far more frequent are two,[42] three,[43] four,[44] or five[45] strophes per canticle. In many cases strophes within a canticle are linked by an on-running sentence.[46] In

[40] D. Pardee, *Ugaritic and Hebrew Poetic Parallelism* (VT.S, 39), Leiden 1988, esp. 189-91, 197-8.

[41] 45:8, 17; 49:13.

[42] 40:1-2, 6-8, 9a-c, 10-11, 12-14, 18-20, 21-22, 23-24, 25-26, 27-28; 43:1-2, 3-4, 14-15, 16-17; 44:12a-b, 13a-c, 14-15, 16-17; 45:1a-c, 9-10, 18-19; 46:1-2, 3-4, 12-13; 48:1-2; 49:5-6, 7a-d, 14-15, 16-18; 50:4-5, 6-8a, 8b-9, 10a-c, 11a-c; 51:1-2, 3a-c, 4-5, 6a-c, 7-8; 51:15-16, 17-18, 19-20; 52:11-12; 54:4-5, 6-8, 9-10, 11-14a, 14b-15; 55:4-5, 6-7, 8-9, 12-13.

[43] 40:3-5, 15-17, 29-31; 41:1-3, 4-7, 8-10, 11-13, 14-16; 42:1-4, 10-12, 18-20; 43:9-10c, 11-13, 22-24, 25-28; 44:6-8, 9-11, 18-20, 21-23; 45:2-4, 5-7, 11-13, 20-21d, 22-25; 46:5-7, 8-11; 48:3-5, 6-8, 9-11, 12-14a, 14b-16, 17-19, 20-22; 49:19-21, 22-23, 24-26; 50:1-2a, 2b-3; 51:21-23; 52:4-6, 13-15; 53:1-3, 4-6, 7-10aC, 10bA-12; 54:1-3, 16-17; 55:1-3, 10-11.

[44] 41:17-20, 21-24, 25-29; 43:5-8, 18-21; 45:14-16; 47:1-3, 4-7, 8-11, 12-15; 49:1-4, 8-12; 51:9-11, 12-14; 52:1-3, 7-10.

[45] 42:5-9, 13-17, 21-25; 44:1-5, 21-28

[46] 40:2a-2b-c; 40:30a-31a; 41:8-10, 19-20; 42:5-6a, 6b-7; 43:6-7; 43:9c-10, 16-17;

some cases canticles appear to be chained by catchwords (Ch. 44 and 54).

16.6 The Sub–Canto and Canto

16.6.1 Delimiters of Sub-Canto and Canto

As a rule, the boundaries of these large units are better attested by major division markers in the manuscriptal tradition than those of canticles. See above 16.5.1. This is especially true of the manuscripts of the Peshiṭta. Perhaps this points to an early family of Hebrew manuscripts in which only the largest units had been marked.

Unfortunately, this better attestation is hardly sufficient to decide where to begin or end a macro-structural unit. For in certain cases also what we believe to be canticles have a well-attested boundary. So we had to rely largely on conventional arguments derived from content to delimit sub-cantos and cantos.[47] This is unsatisfactory because, as anybody acquainted with our discipline knows, this type of arguments tends to be controversial. However, as we shall see, some additional arguments were emerging from our research and we do hope that in this respect better progress will be made than we were able to achieve here.

16.6.2 Sub-Canto Parallelism

In all sub-cantos we identified the canticles belonging to it have been linked by keywords in distant parallelism. As with the canticles themselves, there appears to have existed a natural preference for repetitive parallelism at this level.

16.6.3 Length of the Macro-Units

The largest structural unit ('cantata') we encountered is found in Ch. 45–46 where three cantos have been brought together in what we regard as one composition ('cantata'). A canto may consist of only one sub-canto,[48] but mostly more sub-cantos are found in Isaiah 40–55,

---

44:19, 24-28; 45:5-7; 46:9aC-11aB, 12-13; 48:4-5, 18-19; 49:5-6, 7; 49:8-9; 50:3a-c; 51:17a-b; 52:14-15a; 55:10-11.

[47] Of course we often looked into the available scholarly literature with regard to the delimitation of these larger units. In many cases our delimitation is far from new.

[48] Ch. 54.

consisting of two,[49] three,[50] four[51] canticles.

16.6.4 Structural Patterns in Sub-Cantos and Cantos

We found a high degree of regularity in the structure of the cantos. The table below may serve to confirm this.

STRUCTURE OF SUB-CANTOS AND CANTOS		
CANTOS	SUB-CANTOS	STROPHES
Isaiah 40		
A	5	11 (2+3+2+2+2)
B	5	11 (2+3+2+2+2)
C	3	7 (2+2+3)
Conclusion: fairly regular.		
Isaiah 41		
A	2	6 (3+3)
B	3	6 (3+3+3)
C	3	12 (4+4+4)
Conclusion: fairly regular.		
Isaiah 42		
A	2	8 (3+5)
B	2	8 (3+5)
C	2	8 (3+5)
Conclusion: completely regular.		
Isaiah 43		
A	3	8 (2+2+4)
B	2	6 (3+3)
C	3	8 (2+2+4)
D	2	6 (3+3)
Conclusion: symmetric.		
Isaiah 44		
A	2	7 (5+3)
B	6	6 (3+2+2+2+2+3)
C	2	7 (3+5)
Conclusion: symmetric.		
Isaiah 45–46: Canto I		
A	2	5 (2+3)
B	2	4 (3+1)
C	2	5 (2+3)
Conclusion: symmetric.		
Isaiah 45–46: Canto II		
A	2	5 (4+1)
B	2	5 (2+3)
C	2	5 (3+2)
Conclusion: completely regular.		

continued on next page

[49]Ch. 45-46 (III); 47; 48.
[50]Ch. 40; 41; 42; 44; 45-46 (I and II); 50:1–51:8; 51:9–52:12; 52:13–53:12; 55.
[51]Ch. 43; 49.

continued from previous page

Structure of Sub-Cantos and Cantos		
Cantos	Sub-Cantos	Strophes
Isaiah 45–46: Canto III		
A	2	5 (2+3)
B	2	5 (3+2)
Conclusion: completely regular.		
Isaiah 47		
A	2	8 (4+4)
B	2	8 (4+4)
Conclusion: completely regular.		
Isaiah 48		
A	4	11 (2+3+3+3)
B	4	12 (3+3+3+3)
Conclusion: fairly regular.		
Isaiah 49		
A	2	6 (4+2)
B	3	7 (2+4+1)
C	3	7 (2+2+3)
D	2	6 (3+3)
Conclusion: symmetric.		
Isaiah 50:1–51:8		
A	2	6 (3+3)
B	5	10 (2+2+2+2+2)
C	5	10 (2+2+2+2+2)
Conclusion: fairly regular.		
Isaiah 51:9–52:12		
A	3	10 (4+4+2)
B	3	8 (3+2+3)
C	4	13 (4+3+4+2)
Conclusion: irregular in its present form.		
Isaiah 52:13–53:12		
A	1	3 (3)
B	3	9 (3+3+3)
C	1	3 (3)
Conclusion: symmetric.		
Isaiah 54		
A	6	14 (3+2+2+2+2+3)
Conclusion: symmetric on the level of strophes.		
Isaiah 55		
A	2	5 (3+2)
B	2	4 (2+2)
C	2	5 (3+2)
Conclusion: symmetric.		

The regularity we found is an interesting result. Of course it is possible that we erred in certain respects, but on the whole it seems likely that whereas Western poetry is characterized by regularity on the level of the smaller units, like metre, rhyme and the number of verse-lines per strophe, ancient Hebrew poetry satisfies its need for order on the level of the higher structural levels.

This is confirmed by an additional observation. From the viewpoint of content all cantos we established show a tendency to return to the point of departure at the end – all but one: Ch. 54 which is at the same time a sub-canto and a canto. One might say therefore that the poetic device of inclusion which operates at the level of the canticles was also applied on the higher level of the canto, at least in Isaiah 40–55.

Both the regularity and the remaining irregularity strongly suggest that our method of analysis also has implications for literary and redactional criticism. The regularity means – at the very least – that the final redactor must have consciously strived after a harmonious result of his editorial work. The irregularity suggests intervention of persons who failed to appreciate the harmony of the work of their predecessor(s). Simple displacement of a major divider at a very early stage of transmission sometimes solves the problem of irregularity.[52] In other cases we tentatively assumed later expansion[53], or contraction for theological reasons.[54] We deliberately did not pursue these highly interesting new avenues because in our opinion structural analysis is a phase in the work of the exegete which should *precede* literary and redactional criticism.

16.7 The Book

It has often been stated that beginning and end of the Book of Second Isaiah link up with each other, creating the impression of a planned composition. Indeed the theme of the Second Exodus is common to both (40:3-5, 10-11, 31 – 55:12). The renewed covenant, implied in the wording of 40:1, is taken up again in 55:3, 13. The word of God has a prominent place in both chapters (40:8 – 55:11).

However, are these parallels sufficient to assume a well-planned composition of the Book as a whole? The Exodus motif recurs in 43:16-17; 48:20-22; 49:8-12; 51:9-11; 52:11-12. So its presence in the last chapter may well be accidental. Better parallels to the renewed covenant are found in 42:6; 49:8; 54:10. The word of God in past and present is a central theme throughout the Book (e.g. 45:19; 48:16; 51:16; 52:6).

---

[52]Examples: the division markers after 44:22 may have moved from their original position after 44:23; those after 45:16 fit better after 45:14; those after 48:9 may have stood after 48:8.

[53]44:12-17; 52:4-6.

[54]A strophe may have been omitted after 45:8.

Emphasizing the similarities between Ch. 40 and Ch. 55 should be balanced by pointing out the differences. David appears for the first time in 55:3. Creation theology, a pivotal theme in Ch. 40 and in many other places, is conspicuously absent in Ch. 55. The witnessing to the nations (55:4) has its closest analogies in 43:9-10, 12; 44:8. The gift of 'water' to the thirsty (55:1–3, 10-11) finds an analogy in 44:3-4. The miraculously growing trees (55:13) have parallels in 41:18-19 and 43:4, hardly in the withering grass of 40:7-8. It would be easy to multiply such examples, but these will suffice. Ch. 55 and Ch. 40 do have a number of similarities, but they have not been planned conciously as beginning and end of the Book.

The following table may serve to demonstrate that no logical order, neither in structure nor in contents, may be discerned in the composition of the Book as a whole:

ISAIAH 40–55					
CHAPTER	CANTO	SUB-CANTOS	CANTICLES	STROPHES	CONTENTS
40	I	A	5	11	God and his people on speaking terms again. Adhortation to have faith in a New Exodus.
		B	5	11	Basis for this faith: in contrast to idols the almighty Creator has the power to topple the rulers of the world.
		C	3	7	The almighty Creator has the power to sustain the weary exiles on their Exodus home.
41	I	A	2	6	Lawsuit: the advent of Cyrus is the work of God.
		B	3	6	God will help Israel whereas its oppressors will be destroyed.
		C	3	12	The nations and their idols will be unable to withstand Cyrus.
42	I	A	2	8	The mission of the servant of God is to liberate the oppressed, trusting in God the Creator.
		B	2	8	All nations have to praise God, even Israel's oppressors.
		C	2	8	The past punishment of God's chosen servant was unavoidable and justified.

continued on next page

continued from previous page

ISAIAH 40–55					
CHAPTER	CANTO	SUB-CANTOS	CANTICLES	STROPHES	CONTENTS
43	I	A	3	8	God will liberate his people and the nations will have to cooperate.
		B	2	6	Lawsuit: Israel has to bear witness of its faith in the Creator.
		C	3	8	The Babylonians will flee, while God will lead out his people on the new Exodus.
		D	2	6	Lawsuit: Israel's past punishment was deserved, but God has forgiven them.
44	I	A	2	7	God's servant Israel has to bear witness of its faith in its incomparable God and Redeemer.
		B	6	6	Denunciation of worshippers of idols who are unable to deliver.
		C	2	7	God will redeem his servant Israel by the hand of Cyrus who will rebuild Jerusalem.
45-46	I	A	2	5	For his servant's sake God will make Cyrus successful.
		B	2	4	All nations and Cyrus himself have to recognize the uniqueness of Israel's God.
		C	2	5	Lawsuit: To the Creator nothing is impossible. He will make Cyrus rebuild Jerusalem.
	II	A	2	5	All nations will be subservient to God and his redeemed people.
		B	2	5	Lawsuit: God decrees what is justice and Israel has known this from the beginning.
		C	2	5	All nations have to recognize the just God of Israel.
	III	A	2	5	The Babylonian idols will bow to Israel's God, unable to help their worshippers.
		B	2	5	Despite Israel's sins God will deliver them by the hand of Cyrus.

continued on next page

continued from previous page

ISAIAH 40–55					
CHAPTER	CANTO	SUB-CANTOS	CANTICLES	STROPHES	CONTENTS
47	I	A	2	8	Lady Babel will have to suffer for her merciless execution of Israel's punishment.
		B	2	8	Babel's magicians will be unable to save her.
48	I	A	4	11	From the beginning God has told sinful Israel what would happen, but it did not believe him and served idols. Therefore God had to punish his people.
		B	4	12	Because God has told the truth from the beginning, sinful Israel should listen to his message of redemption by the hand of Cyrus.
49	I	A	2	6	God's servant Israel gets a message for all nations.
		B	3	7	God will redeem all oppressed ones, but especially his own people which shall embark upon a new Exodus.
		C	3	7	Zion should have faith in the message of her restoration and the return of the exiles.
		D	2	6	Foreign nations will assist in bringing the exiles home.
50f	I	A	2	6	To the almighty Creator nothing is impossible, therefore he is also able to redeem Israel.
		B	5	10	His servant is suffering, but keeps to his faith. He will be proved right whereas the unbelievers will be punished.
		C	5	10	Just as God kept his promise to Abraham and Sarah, so he will keep his promise to the suffering servants.
51f	I	A	3	10	Zion prays to God to deliver her, just as he defeated the sea-monsters in primordial times.
		B	3	8	God admonishes Zion to become active in her own delivery, despite her present sorry state.

continued on next page

continued from previous page					
			ISAIAH 40–55		
CHAPTER	CANTO	SUB-CANTOS	CANTICLES	STROPHES	CONTENTS
		C	4	13 (10)	If she becomes active herself, God will return to her, leading the exiles home on a new Exodus.
52v	I	A	1	3	The suffering servant of God will be exalted.
		B	3	9	His suffering was undeserved, it was inflicted on him because of the sins of others.
		C	1	3	God will accept the servant's suffering as a guilt-offering and will exalt him for his self-sacrifice.
54	I	A	6	14	Zion will be restored and the covenant of peace between God and his people will be restored for ever.
55	I	A	2	5	If Israel listens to the word of God, the Davidic covenant will be restored and foreign nations will come to serve Israel, as in David's days.
		B	2	4	If Israel repents, God will forgive its past sins.
		C	2	5	The word of God will become true: a new Exodus will jubilantly start.

As this table shows, a number of themes recurs several times in the Book and it is certainly possible to create an impression of order by emphasizing certain themes and minimizing the importance of others. But it is better to admit that the composition of the Book as whole is rather chaotic. We believe to have established that up to the level of the canto, or short sequences of cantos as in Ch. 45-46, a much higher degree of order was strived after by the writer or final redactor than we expected up till now. But this kind of order was not a goal on the level of the *Book* anymore, at least not in the case of Second Isaiah. Here more or less haphazard reintroduction of themes must have been thought sufficient to lend coherence to this collection of poems.[55] It is appropriate in this connection to remind ourselves of the fact that books were written on scrolls, a circumstance which made it difficult

[55]For a similar conclusion see Schoors, 297, n. 2: "I am convinced that the collection of the pericopes in Dt.-Is. is secondary, and does not show any structure. The units have been collected according to purely external standards (Catchwords, similarity of subject)". Differently e.g. H. Leene, "Auf der Suche nach einem redaktionskritischen Modell für Jesaja 40–55", *ThLZ* 121 (1996), 803-18.

to survey more than a few columns at the same time.[56]

However, this is not all that has to be said. If the cantos were written as independent poems, the writer or final editor must have decided in what order they would be incorporated into the Book. In the case of Isaiah 40–55, his basic method appears to have been joining poems by catchwords, a method that also played a role in the formation of the Book of the Twelve.[57] Mostly this chaining of cantos is of a purely formal nature and does not have any special meaning. It may be compared with the poetic device of concatenation on the level of strophes or canticles.

CHAINING OF CANTOS IN ISAIAH 40–55			
CANTOS	TEXTS	CATCHWORDS	COMMENTS
40–41	40:31aA 41:1aB	יחליפו כח יחליפו כח	The exhausted Israelites. The foreign nations.
41–42	41:29aC 42:1bA	רוח רוחי	Meaning: wind. Meaning: spirit of God.
42–43	42:25bB 43:2bB	ותבער־בו לא תבער־בך	Fire burns Jacob. Fire burns Jacob *not.*
43–44	43:28bB 44:1aB	ישׂראל ישׂראל	Israel is called בחירי in 43:20. Note בחרתי בו.
44–45f-I	44:28aA 45:1aB	לכורשׁ רעי למשׁיחו לכורשׁ	
45f-I–II	45:13bC 45:14aA	אמר יהוה אמר יהוה	See also v. 13bB מחיר. See also v. 14aC סחר
45f-II–III	46:1bA 46:1bA 46:3bA 46:3bB	נשׂאתיכם עמוסות העמסים הנשׂאים	Idols. Idols. Israelites. Israelites
45f-III–47	46:13b 47:1aA	ציון בת־בבל	 Antithetical parallel.
47–48	47:11bA 48:3bA	ותבא עליך פתאם פתאם עשׂיתי ותבאנה	 Of course also the זאת of 48:1 makes Babel a deterrent example.
48–49	48:29bD 49:3aA-B	עבדו יעקב עבדי־אתה ישׂראל	
49–50f	49:26bC	גאלך	
continued on next page			

[56] Of course coherence and closure were more easily achieved in the case of narrative works, like the Epic of Gilgamesh or the Deuteronomic History, where a grand narrative strand could be developed mentally, lending some sort of coherence to the patchwork of earlier traditions.

[57] Cf. B.A. Jones, *The Formation of the Book of the Twelve: A Study in Text and Canon*, Atlanta 1995, with earlier literature.

continued from previous page

CHAINING OF CANTOS IN ISAIAH 40–55			
CANTOS	TEXTS	CATCHWORDS	COMMENTS
	50:1bB	אשר־מכרתי אתכם	A fixed pair (Lev. 25:25, 48; 27:20, 27, 28) which is also used in 52:3.
50f–51f	51:8bB	לדור דורים	
	51:9bB	דרות עולמים	
51f–52v	52:10aA	חשף יהוה את־זרוע קדשו	
	53:1aB	וזרוע יהוה נגלתה	
52v–54	53:12bC	רבים	
	54:1bA	רבים	
54–55	54:17bA	עבדי יהוה	
	55:1aA	כל־צמא	At first sight this link may seem odd, but it is not from the viewpoint of the redactor of the whole Book of Isaiah. Compare Isa. 65:13 עבדי ישתו ואתם תצמאו, a reversal of Deut. 28:48.

So, although the composition of the Book of Second Isaiah as a whole does not seem to have been planned very rigorously, the redactional arranging of the poems was a well-considered operation. In this respect our investigation calls for a modification of Barton's statement we cited at the end of the first chapter.[58] Moreover, on the lower structural levels, including the larger units we call cantos, regularity was observed so often and consistently that it cannot be ignored. In this study we refrain from expressing an opinion on the question who may have been responsible for this high level of sophistication, the author or the final redactor. We simply wanted to demonstrate that this regularity is not a figment of modern research, but a characteristic of Classical Hebrew poetry attested in the earliest manuscripts we have.

In general, our investigation has confirmed the reliability of the versification of the Tiberian Masoretes. In this respect too their work stands out as a monument of industry which must have made use of the best traditions available in their times. The degree of reliablity is highest with the lower poetic units: colon, verse-line and strophe. With regard to next structural unit, the canticle, the Masoretic Setumot and Petuḥot appear to have been less faithfully copied in the medieval manuscripts. Here the new material from Qumran, the Greek uncials and the five Peshiṭta manuscripts we collated for this study has been a most welcome addition to what was hitherto known.

[58] See p. 16.

The structural analysis of Hebrew poetry along the lines we delineated in this study will take generations to complete. But we believe it is a task biblical scholarship should not shun.[59] In many cases discussions about the exegesis or redactional history of a passage are determined by its correct delimitation. It is of utmost importance to know how it was delimited in Antiquity, because this must be the starting-point of any serious discussion. Admittedly one cannot accept the testimony of the ancient witnesses uncritically, as we have shown time and again. But one cannot afford to ignore this type of verifiable evidence either. Structural analysis is an indispensable step which from a methodical point of view should follow immediately after the philological and textcritical analysis of the text.

[59]Meanwhile the results of partial and provisional investigations like this one may yield methodical insights which can be applied in less detailed studies. For this reason we quantified our findings in this chapter so that one can establish the degree of likelihood of certain structural features appearing in a passage to be analyzed.

Index of Parallel Words

If parallel words occur both in the order X–Y and Y–X, we cite them all under X–Y and under a separate entry Y–X we only give a cross reference. Example: the pair שמים || ארץ has been combined with ארץ || שמים.

Abbreviations:
ColP = Colon parallelism
VrsP = Verse-line parallelism
StrP = Strophe parallelism
CanP = Canticle parallelism
MacP = Parallelism in macrostructure

אב || אשה

DtIsa: VrsP in Isa. 45:10.

Other: VrsP in Jer. 7:18; 44:9.

אב||בן, see also בן || אשה

DtIsa: MacP in Isa. 45:10+11.

Other: ColP in Isa. 38:19. VrsP in Isa. 14:21; Jer. 7:18; 31:29, etc. StrP in Jer. 3:19.

אב || חיל

DtIsa: VrsP in Isa. 51:2. Collocation in Isa. 45:10.

Other: None.

אב || יעקב

DtIsa: CanP in Isa. 43:27+28.

Other: ColP in Isa. 58:14. VrsP in Gen. 49:2.

אב || מליץ

DtIsa: VrsP in Isa. 43:27.

Other: None, but see the collocation of אב and ליץ in Prov. 13:1.

אבד || אין

DtIsa: ColP in Isa. 41:11.

Other: VrsP in Deut. 32:28; Isa. 57:1; Jer. 49:7; Mic. 4:9; 7:2; Ps. 142:5; Qoh. 9:6.

אבד || פוץ

DtIsa: MacP in Isa. 41:11+16.

Other: ColP in Jer. 23:1. VrsP in Jer. 40:15.

אבן || אבן

DtIsa: VrsP in Isa. 54:12. CanP in Isa. 54:11+12.

Other: VrsP in Isa. 27:9; 28:16; Jer. 51:26; Qoh. 3:5.

אברהם || שרה

DtIsa: VrsP in Isa. 51:2.

Other: VrsP in Gen. 49:31.

אגם || מוצא

DtIsa: VrsP in Isa. 41:18.

Other: VrsP in Ps. 107:35 (quotation).

אדון || בעל

DtIsa: VrsP in Isa. 54:4.

Other: None, but see the collocation in Isa. 26:13.

אדם || אל

DtIsa: StrP in Isa. 44:13.

Other: ColP in Isa. 31:3; Ezek. 28:2; Job 27:13. VrsP in Num. 23:19.

אדם || גוי

DtIsa: CanP in Isa. 52:14+15.

Other: ColP in Job 34:29. VrsP in Deut. 32:8; Jer. 49:15; Ps. 94:10; 135:15.

אדם || לאם

DtIsa: VrsP in Isa. 43:4.

Other: None.

אדם || אדמה

DtIsa: MacP in Isa. 45:9+12.

Other: None, but see the collocation in Gen. 2:7; Isa. 6:11.

יהוה || אדני

DtIsa: ColP in Isa. 40:10; 48:16; 49:22; 50:4, 5, 7, 9; 51:22; 52:4. VrsP in Isa. 49:14.

Other: VrsP in Exod. 15:17; Isa. 3:17; Ps. 30:9; 35:22; 38:16. StrP in Amos 7:8.

אדני יהוה || אדני יהוה

DtIsa: CanP in Isa. 50:4+5. MacP in Isa. 50:4+5+7.

Other: VrsP in Amos 7:4. See also the collocation in 2Sam. 7:19; Ezek. 6:3; Ezek. 12:28, etc.

משכן || אהל

VrsP in Isa. 54:2.

Other: ColP in Exod. 39:40; Job 21:28. VrsP in Exod. 39:33; 40:34; Jer. 30:18; Ps. 78:60.

אולי || אולי

DtIsa: VrsP in Isa. 47:12.

Other: None.

און || און

DtIsa: MacP in Isa. 40:26+29.

Other: None.

תהו || רוח || אפס || און

DtIsa: VrsP in Isa. 41:29.

Other: None. See also תהו || אפס, and see the StrP תהו || און in Isa. 59:4.

כח || און

DtIsa: ColP in Isa. 40:26. VrsP in Isa. 40:29.

Other: VrsP in Gen. 49:3; Job 40:16.

סלח || און

DtIsa: StrP in Isa. 55:7.

Other: None.

מטמון || אוצר

DtIsa: VrsP in Isa. 45:3.

Other: None.

זיקות || אור

DtIsa: VrsP in Isa. 50:11.

Other: None.

חשך || אור

DtIsa: ColP in Isa. 45:7.

Other: ColP in Isa. 5:20; 45:7; 58:10; 59:9, etc. VrsP in Isa. 5:30; 9:1, etc.

ישועה || אור

DtIsa: VrsP in Isa. 49:6.

Other: None, but see the VrsP between the roots ישע || אור in Ps. 31:17; 80:4, 8, 20; ColP in Ps. 27:1; cf. Ps. 44:4.

שלום || אור

DtIsa: VrsP in Isa. 45:7.

Other: None.

שמים || אור

DtIsa: MacP in Isa. 45:7+8.

Other: ColP in Jer. 4:23. VrsP in Ps. 104:2; Job 37:3. See also the collocation in Isa. 13:10; Ezek. 32:8.

אז || אז

DtIsa: CanP in Isa. 48:3+5, 7+8. MacP in Isa. 48:3+5+7+8.

Other: VrsP in Lev. 26:41; Josh. 1:8; Ps. 51:21; 126:2. StrP in Lev. 26:34. See also the collocation in 2 Sam. 23:14 (=1 Chron. 11:16).

טרם || אז

DtIsa: VrsP in Isa. 48:5.

Other: None.

עתה || אז

DtIsa: ColP in Isa. 48:7. CanP in Isa. 48:6+7+8.

Other: ColP in Hos. 2:9. StrP in Job 3:13.

אזן || אזן

DtIsa: CanP in Isa. 50:4+5.

Other: VrsP in Jer. 28:1. StrP in Isa. 6:10.

לבב || אזן

DtIsa: CanP in Isa. 49:20+21.

Other: VrsP in Ezek. 3:10. StrP in Isa. 6:10.

קשב || אזן

VrsP in Isa. 42:23; Isa. 51:4.

Other: None. ColP in Isa. 28:23. VrsP in Ps. 86:6; Hos. 5:1; Prov. 17:4. StrP in Ps. 17:1.

שמע || אזן

DtIsa: VrsP in Isa. 42:23.

Other: ColP in Isa. 1:2; 28:23; 64:3; Jer. 13:15. VrsP in Deut. 32:1; Judg. 5:3; Isa. 1:10; Hos. 5:1; Joel 1:2. StrP in Isa. 32:9; Ps. 17:1, etc.

אזן (noun) || שמע, see also
שמע || פתח אזן; שמע || נטה אזן

ColP in Isa. 42:20. VrsP in Isa. 50:4.

Other: ColP in Isa. 6:10; 30:21; 32:3; Jer. 5:21; Ps. 44:2; 94:9; 115:6 VrsP in Ps. 18:7; Job 13:17; 33:8, etc.

פסיל || אחר

DtIsa: VrsP in Isa. 42:8.

Other: None, but see the parallelism between אלהים אחרים and פסל in Exod. 20:3-4; Deut. 5:7-8; 7:4-5.

אחור || אחרית

DtIsa: CanP in Isa. 41:22-23.

Other: None.

בוא || אחרית

DtIsa: VrsP in Isa. 41:22.

Other: None.

אי || אי

DtIsa: CanP in Isa. 42:10+12. MacP in Isa. 41:1+5; 42:10+12+15.

Other: StrP in Ezek. 26:18.

איש || אי

DtIsa: StrP in Isa. 41:5-6.

Other: VrsP in Zeph. 2:11.

Other: None.

לאם || אי

DtIsa: VrsP in Isa. 41:1; 49:1. CanP in Isa. 51:4+5.

Other: None.

קצה הארץ || אי, see also
קצה הארץ || גוי

DtIsa: VrsP in Isa. 41:5. StrP in Isa. 42:10.

Other: None.

אין || אין

DtIsa: VrsP in Isa. 40:16; 41:26 (3x), 28; 42:22; 45:5; 50:2. StrP in Isa. 45:21c-d; 51:18. CanP in Isa. 40:16-17; 41:11-12, 26-28; 43:11+12+13; 45:5+6. MacP in Isa. 41:17+24+26+28; 45:18+21 (3x).

ColP in Isa. 3:7; 5:27; Ps. 19:4, etc. VrsP in Isa. 6:11; 22:22; Prov. 8:24, etc. StrP in Ps. 37:5; 38:4; 142:5, etc.

אפס || אין

ColP in Isa. 41:12. VrsP in Isa. 40:17; 45:14. StrP in Isa. 41:28-29.

Other: VrsP in Isa. 34:12; 46:9; Prov. 26:20.

אפע || אין

DtIsa: VrsP in Isa. 41:24.

Other: None.

בל || אין

DtIsa: ColP in Isa. 44:8.

Other: VrsP in Ps. 10:4. StrP in Ps. 32:9.

קש || אין

DtIsa: StrP in Isa. 47:14. CanP in Isa. 40:23-24.

Other: None.

תהו || אין

DtIsa: VrsP in Isa. 40:17, 23.

Other: None.

אדם || איש, see also בן אדם || איש

DtIsa: VrsP in Isa. 44:13.

Other: ColP in Isa. 2:9; 5:15, etc. VrsP in Isa. 2:11, 17; 31:8; Jer. 10:23; Ps. 140:1; Prov. 24:30, etc. StrP in Jer. 31:30, etc.

איש || איש

DtIsa: VrsP in Isa. 53:3. StrP in Isa. 41:12. CanP in Isa. 41:11-12.

Other: ColP in Isa. 3:5; Jer. 12:15; Ps. 87:5, etc. VrsP in Isa. 13:14; Jer. 50:16;

Ps. 140:12; Prov. 20:5, 6, etc. StrP in Isa. 57:1, etc.

בן אדם || איש

DtIsa: VrsP in Isa. 52:14.

Other: VrsP in Jer. 32:19; 49:18, 33; 50:40; 51:43; Ps. 80:18; Job 35:8; Prov. 8:4.

יועץ (ptc.) || איש

VrsP in Isa. 41:28.

Other: VrsP in Ezek. 11:2.

אכל || אכל

VrsP in Isa. 51:8. CanP in Isa. 55:1+2.

ColP in Jer. 30:16; Ps. 14:4; 53:5; 105:35; Job 18:13; 31:17. VrsP in Jer. 5:17; 10:25; Am. 7:4; Nah. 3:15; Zech. 7:6.

ענג || אכל

DtIsa: VrsP in Isa. 55:2.

Other: StrP in Isa. 58:14.

שׂבע || אכל

DtIsa: VrsP in Isa. 44:16. StrP in Isa. 55:2 (with the noun שׂבעה).

Other: ColP in Lev. 25:19; 26:5, 26; Deut. 6:11; 8:10, etc. VrsP in Exod. 16:8, 12; Isa. 9:19; Ps. 78:25; 81:17; Prov. 1:31; 25:16.

שׁכר || אכל

DtIsa: VrsP in Isa. 49:26.

Other: VrsP in Deut. 32:42; Song 5:1; cf. 2 Sam. 11:13; Hag. 1:6.

אל (neg.) || אל (neg.)

ColP in Isa. 44:8. VrsP in Isa. 41:10; 43:18; 51:7; 54:4. MacP in Isa. 43:1+5

Other: ColP in Ps. 83:2; Prov. 4:5, etc. VrsP in Isa. 6:9; 43:18; 51:7; 54:4; 64:8; Ps. 6:2; 25:2; 27:9; 51:13 (tr.11), Prov. 3:31, etc.

אל (noun) || אל (noun)

DtIsa: StrP in Isa. 44:17. CanP in Isa. 45:20+21.

Other: ColP in Ps. 22:2; 68:21. VrsP in Ps. 81:10; 94:1. StrP in Ezek. 28:2.

אל (prep.) || אל (prep.)

VrsP in Isa. 45:14; 49:22; 51:1, 2, 4, 5; 55:7. StrP in Isa. 51:1. CanP in Isa. 51:4+5. MacP in Isa. 51:1+4+7.

Other: ColP in Jer. 50:35, 37, etc. VrsP in Isa. 2:3; 13:14; 14:15; Jer. 50:35, 36, 45; Ezek. 3:5; Ps. 43:3; 123:2, etc. StrP in Isa. 8:19; Ps. 123:2; Lam. 4:17, etc.

אלהי ישׂראל || אל

DtIsa: VrsP in Isa. 45:15.

Other: VrsP (rev.) of אל ישׂראל || אלהים in Ps. 68:36. See the collocation in Gen. 33:20.

אלהים || אל

DtIsa: VrsP in Isa. 45:14 (cf. 45:15). StrP in Isa. 45:21c-d.

Other: ColP in Ps. 42:3; 63:2. VrsP in Exod. 15:2; Josh. 24:19; 46:9; Ps. 7:12; 43:4; 44:21, etc.

בל || אל (neg.)

DtIsa: StrP in Isa. 44:8.

Other: StrP in Ps. 32:9; 141:4.

יהוה || אל

DtIsa: ColP in Isa. 42:5. VrsP in Isa. 43:12; 45:21. StrP in Isa. 45:21c-d. CanP in Isa. 45:14+15.

Other: ColP in Jer. 51:56; Nah. 1:2; Ps. 10:12, etc. VrsP in Isa. 5:16; 45:21; Jer. 32:18; Ps. 18:31; Ps. 29:3, etc.

לא || אל

DtIsa: ColP in Isa. 54:4 (2x). VrsP in Isa. 44:8.

Other: ColP in Jer. 10:5. VrsP in Judg. 13:14; Jer. 7:6; Amos 5:5; Mic. 2:6; Prov. 27:2; Ruth 2:8. StrP in Isa. 62:6; Jer. 25:6.

על || אל

DtIsa: VrsP in Isa. 40:2. CanP in Isa. 54:14+15.

Other: VrsP in Ps. 42:2; 90:16; Job 22:26; Isa. 17:7, etc. StrP in Ps. 79:6.

פסל || אל (noun)

DtIsa: ColP in Isa. 44:10, 17. VrsP in Isa. 44:15; 45:20. StrP in Isa. 40:18-19.

Other: None.

אלה || אלה || אלה

DtIsa: VrsP in Isa. 49:12, 21. StrP in Isa. 49:21.

Other: ColP in Ps. 20:8. VrsP in Isa. 66:2.

אלהי ישׂראל || אלהי ישׂראל

DtIsa: CanP in Isa. 48:1+2.

Other: None, but see the collocation in 1 Sam. 5:8.

יהוה צבאות || אלהי ישׂראל

DtIsa: VrsP in Isa. 48:2. Cf. Isa. 44:6; 54:5.

Other: ColP in Isa. 37:16; Jer. 7:3, 21; 9:14; 16:9, etc. VrsP in Isa. 21:10. StrP in Ps. 69:7. Cf. 1 Sam. 17:45; 2 Sam. 7:26, 27.

קדוש ישׂראל || אלהי ישׂראל

DtIsa: CanP in Isa. 41:17-20. Compare VrsP in Isa. 43:3; 55:5 and StrP in Isa. 48:17 (with suffixes referring to Israel).

Other: VrsP in Isa. 60:9.

אלהים || אל, see אל || אלהים

אלהים || אלהים

DtIsa: CanP in Isa. 40:27-28; 48:1+2; 52:7+10. MacP in Isa. 40:1+3+8+9; 45:18+21; 54:5+6.

Other: VrsP in Isa. 35:4; 65:16; Jer. 2:11, etc. StrP in Isa. 58:2; Jer. 2:28, etc.

אלוה || אלהים

DtIsa: CanP in Isa. 44:6+8.

Other: VrsP in Deut. 32:17; Ps. 18:32.

יהוה || אלהים

DtIsa: ColP in Isa. 40:28; 48:17; 51:15; 55:5. VrsP in Isa. 40:27; 45:5, 18; 48:1; 49:4, 5; 50:10; 51:20, 22; 55:7. StrP in Isa. 40:3, 7-8; 52:10; 54:5, 6. CanP in Isa. 40:1-2; 42:13+17; 53:4+6.

Other: VrsP in Isa. 1:10; 35:2; 59:13; Jer. 5:4; Ps. 70:2, etc. StrP in Isa. 25:9, etc.

עם || אלהים

DtIsa: VrsP in Isa. 40:1. CanP in Isa. 51:15+16.

Other: VrsP in Exod. 6:7; Lev. 26:12; Deut. 29:12; Jer. 7:23; Ezek. 34:30; Hos. 2:25; Ps. 95:7; Ruth 1:16. Cf. Deut. 7:6.

צור || אלוה

DtIsa: VrsP in Isa. 44:8.

Other: VrsP in Deut. 32:15; Ps. 18:32.

ברא (ptc.) || אל יהוה, see also ברא (ptc.) || יהוה

DtIsa: VrsP in Isa. 42:5.

Other: None, but see the collocation in Mal. 2:10.

פתח פה || אלם

DtIsa: VrsP in Isa. 53:7.

Other: ColP in Ps. 38:14; 39:10; Prov. 31:8. VrsP in Ezek. 24:27. StrP in Ezek. 33:22.

אלמן || אלמנה

DtIsa: CanP in Isa. 47:8+9.

Other: None.

שׁכול || אלמנה, see also שׁכול || אלמון

DtIsa: VrsP in Isa. 47:8.

Other: ColP in Jer. 18:21.

אם (noun) || אם (noun)

DtIsa: CanP in Isa. 50:1.

Other: StrP in Ezek. 16:45; Lam 2:12.

איש || אם

DtIsa: CanP in Isa. 50:1+2a.

Other: ColP in Gen. 2:29; Lev. 19:3; Isa. 66:13. VrsP in Lev. 20:9; Jer. 15:10; Hos. 2:4; Prov. 28:24.

אמן Hiph. || בין

DtIsa: ColP in Isa. 43:10.

Other: VrsP in Prov. 14:15.

ינק || אמן

DtIsa: VrsP in Isa. 49:23.

Other: None, but see the collocation in Num. 11:12.

עולם || אמן

DtIsa: VrsP in Isa. 55:3.

Other: VrsP in Ps. 89:29, 39; and see עולם || אמת in VrsP in Isa. 61:8; Ps. 119:142.

שמע || אמן

DtIsa: ColP in Isa. 53:1.

Other: VrsP in Exod. 4:1, 8, 9; 19:9; Deut. 9:23.

גדל || אמץ

DtIsa: StrP in Isa. 44:14.

Other: None.

עזר || אמץ

DtIsa: ColP in Isa. 41:10.

Other: None.

תמך || עזר || אמץ

DtIsa: VrsP in Isa. 41:10.

Other: None.

אמר || אמר

DtIsa: VrsP in Isa. 40:6. StrP in Isa. 41:21; 26; 44:28; 47:10. CanP in Isa. 44:16+17, 19+20, 24+26+27+28; 45:9+10, 11+13; 45:18+19; 47:8+10; 48:20+22; 49:3+4, 5+6, 8+9, 20+21; 51:22+23; 54:6+8. MacP in Isa. 40:2+6+9; 41:9+13; 54:1+6+10.

Other: VrsP in Isa. 62:4; Ps. 35:25, etc. StrP in Isa. 56:3; Jer. 51:35, etc.

אמר (root) || דבר (root)

DtIsa: VrsP in Isa. 40:27; 45:19. StrP in Isa. 44:26; 51:16. CanP in Isa. 41:26-28; 44:24+26+27+28; 45:18+19; 46:10+11; 52:4+6.

Other: ColP in Ps. 19:4; Job 2:10. VrsP in Ps. 78:19; 89:20; 94:4; 145:11; Prov. 4:20. StrP in Qoh. 2:15.

נאם || אמר

DtIsa: StrP in Isa. 43:9c-10a. CanP in Isa. 52:4+5. MacP in Isa. 41:9+13+14.

Other: ColP in Ezek. 13:6, 7. VrsP in Num. 24:3, 15; Zech. 1:3, 16. StrP in Ezek. 13:8; 30:6; Zech. 8:6; Mal. 1:2, etc.

נגד || אמר

DtIsa: StrP in Isa. 46:10; 48:5, 20. CanP in Isa. 42:5+9; 48:6+7.

Other: VrsP in Deut. 32:7; Jer. 4:5. StrP in Jer. 31:10; 46:14; 50:2.

קרא || אמר

DtIsa: ColP in Isa. 40:6. VrsP in Isa. 44:5. StrP in Isa. 40:1-2a; 54:6. CanP in Isa. 46:10+11; 50:1+2a.

Other: VrsP in Isa. 32:5; 61:6; Prov. 1:21. StrP in Isa. 62:4.

שמע || אמר

DtIsa: StrP in Isa. in Isa. 51:21-22a. CanP in Isa. 42:5+9; 51:21+22.

Other: ColP in Jer. 4:5; 31:7. StrP in Jer. 46:14; Amos 3:9.

בן־אדם || אנוש

DtIsa: VrsP in Isa. 51:12.

Other: VrsP in Isa. 56:2; Ps. 8:4; 90:3; 144:3; Job 25:6.

נחם || אנחה

DtIsa: MacP in Isa. 51:11+12

Other: VrsP in Lam. 1:21.

־י || אני

DtIsa: VrsP in Isa. 43:10, 13; 44:6; 45:5, 21; 49:23. StrP in Isa. 43:10b-c; 45:5; 48:13; 52:6.

Other: VrsP in Deut. 32:39; Ps. 118:7; 143:12, etc.

אני || אני

DtIsa: ColP in Isa. 44:6; 46:4; 48:12, 15. VrsP in Isa. 41:4, 10; 46:4 (2x); 48:12 StrP in Isa. 41:13; 46:4; 49:21. CanP in Isa. 42:6+8+9; 43:3+4, 12+13; 45:2+3, 5+6+7; 47:8+10; 48:12+13, 15+16 MacP in Isa. 43:10+13; 45:5+6+7+8, 21+18.

Other: ColP in Deut. 32:39. VrsP in Isa. 65:24; Job 33:6; Ps. 116:16; Job 32:17; 33:6, etc. StrP in Isa. 66:9, etc.

־ני || אני

DtIsa: ColP in Isa. 52:6. StrP in Isa. 45:5, 19; 47:10.

Other: ColP in Isa. 5:5; 13:3; Jer. 26:14; 40:10, etc. VrsP in Ps. 55:17; 69:14; 109:25, etc. StrP in Deut. 32:21; Isa. 65:18, etc.

אני הוא || אני הוא

DtIsa: MacP in Isa. 43:10+13.

Other: None.

־י || אנכי

DtIsa: VrsP in Isa. 43:11, 25; 44:24; 50:5.

Other: VrsP in Job 12:3; 21:3; Ruth 3:12, etc. StrP in Hos. 13:4, etc.

אני || אנכי

DtIsa: StrP in Isa. 43:12; 45:12. CanP in Isa. 43:11+12+13; 49:25+26.

Other: VrsP in Jon. 1:9; Job 13:2; 33:9. StrP in Jer. 24:7; 25:29; Hos. 5:14.

אנכי || אנכי

DtIsa: ColP in Isa. 43:11, 25 51:12. VrsP in Isa. 49:25. StrP in Isa. 54:16. CanP in Isa. 43:11+12; 45:12+13.

Other: VrsP in Isa. 6:5; Amos 7:14. StrP in Isa. 21:8: Jer. 33:9; Zech. 13:5.

אתה || אנכי

DtIsa: StrP in Isa. 43:25-26.

Other: StrP in Jer. 1:17; Ruth 3:9.

אתם || אנכי

DtIsa: StrP in Isa. 43:12.

Other: VrsP in Jer. 25:29; Hos. 1:9.

־ני || אנכי

DtIsa: VrsP in Isa. 46:9.

Other: VrsP in Ps. 119:19; Job 13:22; 42:4; Ruth 3:12.

ישב חשך || אסיר

DtIsa: VrsP in Isa. 42:7.

Other: VrsP in Ps. 107:10. Compare Ps. 107:14. See also אשר בחשך || אסר.

אשר בחשך || אסר

DtIsa: VrsP in Isa. 49:9.

Other: See ישב חשך || אסיר.

ענִי || אסר

DtIsa: MacP in Isa. 49:9+13.

Other: VrsP (roots) in Job 36:8.

אף || אף

DtIsa: ColP in Isa. 40:24; 46:11. VrsP in Isa. 40:24; 41:10, 26; 46:11. StrP in Isa. 44:15. CanP in Isa. 46:6+7; 48:12+13.

Other: VrsP in Lev. 26:42; Job 32:17; Song 1:16.

גם || אף

DtIsa: StrP in Isa. 40:24.

Other: VrsP in Lev. 26:24. See also the collocation in Lev. 27:44; Est. 5:12.

מלחמה || אף

DtIsa: VrsP in Isa. 42:25.

Other: ColP in Dan. 11:20.

תהו || אפס

DtIsa: ColP in Isa. 40:17. VrsP in Isa. 41:29.

Other: VrsP in Sir. 41:10.

ברוש || ארז

DtIsa: StrP in Isa. 41:19.

Other: VrsP in Isa. 14:8; Ezek. 31:8; Zech. 11:2.

עץ שמן || הדס || שטה || ארז

DtIsa: VrsP in Isa. 41:19.

Other: None, but some of the trees also occur in other enumerations, cf. Isa. 44:14; Ps. 104:16; 148:9; Neh. 8:15.

אלון || תרזה || ארז

VrsP in Isa. 44:14.

Other: None, but see אלון || ארז in Isa. 2:13; Amos 2:9; Zech. 11:2.

דרך || ארח

DtIsa: VrsP in Isa. 40:14.

Other: ColP in Isa. 3:12; Job 6:18. VrsP in Gen. 49:17; Isa. 2:3 (= Mic. 4:2); Isa. 30:11; Joel 2:7; Ps. 25:4; 27:11; 139:3; Prov. 2:8, 13, 20; 4:14; 9:15; 12:28; 15:19.

חזק || ארך

DtIsa: VrsP in Isa. 54:2.

Other: None, but see the parallelism between the roots in Deut. 11:8-9; 2 Chron. 24:12-13.

חטם || ארך

DtIsa: VrsP in Isa. 48:9.

Other: None.

צלח || ארך ימים

DtIsa: VrsP in Isa. 53:10.

Other: None, but the expression ארך ימים is well-known in the context of 'prosperity', cf. Exod. 20:12; Deut. 32:47; Ps. 21:5; 91:16; Prov. 3:2, 16; Qoh. 8:13, etc.

אדם || ארץ

DtIsa: VrsP in Isa. 45:12.

Other: ColP in Jer. 27:5. VrsP in Jer. 32:20; 36:29; Ps. 21:11; Prov. 8:31; 30:14.

אי || ארץ, see also
קצה הארץ || אי

DtIsa: VrsP in Isa. 42:4.

Other: VrsP in Ps. 97:1.

ארץ || ארץ

DtIsa: StrP in Isa. 51:6. CanP in Isa. 40:21-22; 23-24; 45:18+19; 49:8+12; 51:6. MacP in Isa. 40:12+21+22+23+24; 44:23+24; 49:8+13; 54:5+9.

Other: ColP in Isa. 9:1, etc. VrsP in Isa. 24:19; Jer. 2:6, etc. StrP in Isa. 2:7; 11:4; 13:5; 18:6, etc.

הר || ארץ

DtIsa: StrP in Isa. 40:12. CanP in Isa. 42:10+11; 54:9+10.

Other: VrsP in Hag. 1:11; Ps. 90:2; 95:4; 104:13, etc.

חוץ || ארץ

DtIsa: VrsP in Isa. 51:23.

Other: VrsP in 2 Sam. 22:43 (not in Ps. 18:43); Jer. 44:9; Jer. 51:4; Job 5:10; 18:17;. StrP in Isa. 24:11. See the collocation in Lam. 2:21.

ים || ארץ

DtIsa: StrP in Isa. 42:10.

Other: VrsP in Isa. 11:19; Jer. 49:21; Am. 5:8; 9:6; Hab. 2:14; Ps. 69:35; 72:8; 96:11, etc.

כסא || ארץ

DtIsa: ColP in Isa. 47:1.

Other: ColP in Ps. 89:45. StrP in Ezek. 26:16.

שׂדה || ארץ

DtIsa: MacP in Isa. 55:10+12.

Other: VrsP in Jer. 12:4; Ezek. 17:5; 34:27; Qoh. 5:8.

שׁמים || ארץ

DtIsa: ColP in Isa. 49:13; 51:13, 16; 55:9. VrsP in Isa. 42:5; 44:23, 24; 45:18; 48:13; 49:13; 51:6 (2x). StrP in Isa. 40:22; 45:8, 12. CanP in Isa. 40:21-22; 55:10.

Other: VrsP in Deut. 32:1; Isa. 13:13; Jer. 51:15; Hab. 3:3; Hag. 1:10, etc. StrP in Ps. 8:1.

אור || אשׁ

DtIsa: StrP in Isa. 44:16; 47:14; 50:11.

Other: ColP in Isa. 10:17. VrsP in Job 18:5. See also the collocation in Ps. 78:14.

אשׁ || אשׁ

DtIsa: StrP in Isa. 50:11a-b.

Other: ColP in Ezek. 15:7. VrsP in Isa. 64:1; Zech. 12:6. StrP in Isa. 66:15; Ezek. 15:4; Ps. 21:10.

בער || אשׁ

DtIsa: VrsP in Isa. 50:11.

Other: VrsP in Job 1:16. StrP in Isa. 10:17; 30:27, etc. See the collocation in Exod. 3:2; 22:5; 35:3; Lev. 6:5; Num. 11:1, 3, etc.

גחלת || אשׁ

DtIsa: VrsP in Isa. 44:19. StrP in Isa. 47:14.

Other: ColP in Prov. 26:21. VrsP in 2 Sam. 22:9 (= Ps. 18:9). Furthermore both words often occur in the compound גַּחֲלֵי־אֵשׁ (Lev. 16:12; Ezek. 1:13; Ps.18:13, etc.).

זיקות || אשׁ

DtIsa: VrsP in Isa. 50:11.

Other: None.

להבה || אשׁ

DtIsa: VrsP in Isa. 43:2; 47:14.

Other: VrsP in Num. 21:28; Isa. 5:24; 10:17; 47:14; Jer. 48: 45; Joel 1:19; 2:3; Obad. 1:18; Ps. 83:15; 106:18. StrP in

Ezek. 21:3 (tr. 20:47). See the collocation in Lam. 2:3.

אשה || אשה

DtIsa: StrP in Isa. 54:6.

Other: VrsP in Ezek. 23:44; Hos. 12:12, 13; Prov. 6:26. StrP in Jer. 29:6; 44:9; Zech. 12:12.

אשה || בן, see also אב || בן

DtIsa: ColP in Isa. 49:15. MacP in Isa. 45:10+11.

Other: ColP in Jer. 14:16. VrsP in Jer. 7:18; 16:2; Ps. 109:9; Job 19:17, etc. StrP in Ps. 128:3.

אשם || חטא

DtIsa: CanP in Isa. 53:10+12.

Other: None, but cf. Lev. 5:5-7, 15, 17-18; 19:22

אשר || אשר

DtIsa: VrsP in Isa. 52:15; 55:11. StrP in Isa. 50:1; 55:11.

Other: VrsP in Isa. 1:29; Jer. 15:2; Ps. 89:52, etc. StrP in Isa. 7:18; Ps. 79:6, etc.

את (nota acc.) || את (nota acc.)

DtIsa: ColP in Isa. 49:26. VrsP in Isa. 41:7; 49:25. StrP in Isa. 51:17, 22; 52:10; 53:12. MacP in Isa. 51:17+22.

Other: VrsP in Ps. 28:9; 35:1; 47:5; 102:16; 103:1, etc.

את (prep.) || את (prep.)

DtIsa: VrsP in Isa. 45:9; 49:4; 53:9; 54:15. StrP in Isa. 53:12. CanP in Isa. 54:17. MacP in Isa. 54:15+17 (4x).

Other: VrsP in Isa. 28:18; Jer. 2:9; 12:5; 31:31; Ps. 35:1; Prov. 16:19; 22:24, etc. StrP in Isa. 66:10; Jer. 33:21, etc.

אתה || אני

DtIsa: CanP in Isa. 43:1-2.

Other: VrsP in Jer. 46:28; Ezek. 2:8; Ps. 2:7; 31:15, etc. StrP in Jer. 1:11, 13; Hos. 4:6; Zech. 5:2, etc.

אתה || אתה

DtIsa: StrP in Isa. 44:21. MacP in Isa. 41:8+16.

Other: ColP in Ps. 76:8. VrsP in Ps. 74:15, 17; 86:10, etc. StrP in Isa. 63:16; 64:7; Mic. 6:15; Ps. 10:14, etc.

אתה (verb) || אתה (verb)

DtIsa: MacP in Isa. 41:23+25.

Other: StrP in Isa. 21:12. See also the collocation in Dan. 3:13.

אתם || אתם

DtIsa: CanP in Isa. 41:23-24. MacP in Isa. 43:1-+12.

Other: VrsP in Josh. 24:22; Isa. 65:13; Ezek. 20:30; Zech. 7:6; Mal. 3:1, 9. StrP in Isa. 65:13; Jer. 42:16; Joel 4:4.

אתה || בוא

DtIsa: ColP in Isa. 44:7. StrP in Isa. 41:25.

Other: ColP in Mic. 4:8. VrsP in Prov. 1:27.

אתה || ־ך

DtIsa: ColP in Isa. 43:1; 44:21. VrsP in Isa. 43:1; 49:3.

Other: ColP in Prov. 22:19. VrsP in Isa. 63:16; Hab. 2:8; Ps. 2:7; 5:5; 16:12; 22:11; 31:15; 38:16; 69:20; 76:8; 85:7; 86:2, 10; 139:8; 145:15; Job 8:6; 33:33, etc.

אתה || ראשון

DtIsa: VrsP in Isa. 43:9.

Other: None.

אתם || אני

DtIsa: VrsP in Isa. 43:12.

Other: VrsP in Lev. 20:24; Num. 35:34; 1 Sam. 14:40; Ezek. 34:31; Mal. 3:6; Job 32:6; Neh. 1:8; 2 Chron. 12:5. StrP in Jer. 40:10.

אתם || ־כם

VrsP in Isa. 41:24.

Other: VrsP in Isa. 3:14; Jer. 16:12; Mal. 1:5; 3:12; Ps. 82:6; Job 12:2; 13:4. StrP in Josh. 24:13; Jer. 18:6; Hag. 2:3.

ב || ב

DtIsa: VrsP in Isa. 40:11, 12; 41:16; 42:6, 22, 24, 16; 43:2, 14, 16, 19, 20, 23,

24; 44:12, 13; 45:19, 24; 47:12; 48:1, 10; 49:8; 50:1, 10, 11; 52:12; 54:8, 11; 55:1, 2, 6, 12. StrP in Isa. 40:3, 12, 19; 43:2, 24; 44:5; 47:10, 12-13a; 48:1; 49:2, 9; 50:2c-d. CanP in Isa. 44:12a-b; 47:8+10; 49:20+21.

Other: VrsP in Gen. 49:6; Exod. 15:13; Deut. 32:10; Judg. 5:4; Ps. 9:9, etc.

ל || ב

DtIsa: VrsP in Isa. 46:13.

Other: VrsP in Gen. 49:27, etc. StrP in Deut. 33:3; Jer. 32:20; Hos. 6:10, etc.

על || ב

DtIsa: VrsP in Isa. 42:5; 49:22; 53:5; 54:9.

Other: ColP in Judg. 5:5:19; 10:6, 28; 38:16; 49:9; 54:9; Ps. 15:5; 23:2, etc. VrsP in Deut. 32:23.

מות || באשׁ

DtIsa: VrsP in Isa. 50:2.

Other: None, but see the collocation in Exod. 7:18, 21; Qoh. 10:1.

בבל || בבל

DtIsa: MacP in Isa. 48:14+20.

Other: VrsP in Jer. 20:4. StrP in Jer. 51:49.

כשׂדים || בבל

DtIsa: VrsP in Isa. 43:14; 47:1; 48:14, 20. MacP in Isa. 48:14+20.

ColP in Jer. 21:4; 22:25; 32:4, etc. VrsP in Isa. 13:19; Jer. 50:8, 35, 45.

בבקר || בבקר

DtIsa: ColP in Isa. 50:4.

Other: ColP in Isa. 28:19; Ezek. 46:13, 14, 15; Zeph. 3:5.

בגד || בגד

DtIsa: MacP in Isa. 51:6+8.

Other: None.

פשׁע || בגד

DtIsa: VrsP in Isa. 48:8.

Other: None.

צמר || בגד

DtIsa: VrsP in Isa. 51:8.

Other: None. See, however, the collocation in Lev. 13:47, 52, 59; Ezek. 44:17.

קסם || בד

DtIsa: VrsP in Isa. 44:25.

Other: None.

עיפה || בהמה

DtIsa: StrP in Isa. 46:1.

Other: None.

בוא || בוא

DtIsa: StrP in Isa. 47:9, 11. CanP in Isa. 47:9+11(4x); 48:3+5. MacP in Isa. 41:22+25; 47:9+11+13 (5x).

Other: VrsP in Isa. 35:4; 37:34; 60:17; Jer. 9:16; Ps. 96:13; Job 30:26, etc. StrP in Isa. 60:4; Jer. 2:7, etc.

בוא Hiph. || בוא Hiph.

DtIsa: CanP in Isa. 43:5+6.

Other: VrsP in Isa. 60:17; Jer. 17:6; Ezek. 14:22; Mal. 1:13.

נגשׁ || בוא

DtIsa: VrsP in Isa. 45:20.

Other: VrsP in Gen. 27:25; Exod. 28:43; 30:20; Lev. 21:23. StrP in Judg. 9:52. See also the parallelism in Lev. 2:8.

בוא Hiph. || יצא Hiph.

DtIsa: CanP in Isa. 43:6+8.

Other: VrsP in Ezek. 20:10.

נפל || בוא

DtIsa: VrsP in Isa. 47:11.

Other: VrsP in Job 1:16. StrP in Jer. 15:8.

בוא Hif. || נשׂא

DtIsa: VrsP in Isa. 49:22.

Other: VrsP in Exod. 19:4; Jer. 17:21; Ezek. 11:1, 24; 43:5. See also the paired roots in 2 Sam. 23:16; 1 Kgs 10:11; 2 Kgs 4:20; 1 Chron. 10:12; 11:18.

עשׂה || בוא

DtIsa: ColP in Isa. 48:3. VrsP in Isa. 46:11. CanP in Isa. 48:14+15.

Other: ColP in Isa. 16:3; Jer. 40:3; Ezek. 24:14; Hag. 1:14?.

צמח || בוא

DtIsa: StrP in Isa. 42:9.

Other: None.

בוא Hif. || קבץ

DtIsa: ColP in Isa. 45:20; 49:18. VrsP in Isa. 43:5.

Other: ColP in 60:4; 66:18; Jer. 49:14, etc. VrsP in Jer. 31:8; Ezek. 34:13, etc. StrP in Jer. 49:5, etc.

קרא || בוא

DtIsa: VrsP in Isa. 48:15; 50:2.

Other: VrsP in Prov. 18:6. StrP in Isa. 1:13; Jer. 1:15; Ps. 18:7.

רדף || בוא

DtIsa: VrsP in Isa. 41:3.

Other: VrsP in Deut. 28:45.

רמס || בוא

DtIsa: VrsP in Isa. 41:25.

Other: ColP in Nah. 3:14. See the collocation in Isa. 1:12.

שמע || בוא

DtIsa: ColP in Isa. 41:22; 48:5.

Other: ColP of the same roots in Isa. 48:5; Ezek. 33:30. VrsP in Ps. 18:7; 102:2; Job 27:9.

אבד || בוש

DtIsa: StrP in Isa. 41:11.

Other: VrsP in Ps. 83:18. StrP in Joel 1:11.

בוש || בוש

DtIsa: StrP in Isa. 44:11. CanP in Isa. 44:9+11.

Other: ColP in Jer. 17:18. VrsP in Jer. 2:36; 48:1; Ps. 6:11; 25:3; 31:18. StrP in Jer. 6:15; 8:12; 48:13; 50:2.

בטח || בוש

DtIsa: VrsP in Isa. 42:17.

Other: ColP in Ps. 22:6; 25:2; Job 6:20.

בשת || בוש

DtIsa: ColP in Isa. 42:17. StrP in Isa. 54:4.

Other: VrsP in Jer. 2:26. StrP in Isa. 30:5; Ps. 55:26.

חפר || בוש

DtIsa: VrsP in Isa. 54:4.

Other: ColP in Jer. 15:9; Ps. 35:26; 40:15; 70:13. VrsP in Isa. 1:29 (ignoring Zaqeph, otherwise: StrP); 24:23; Jer. 50:12; Mic. 3:7; Ps. 35:4.

כלם || בוש

DtIsa: ColP in Isa. 41:11; 45:16, 17. VrsP in Isa.54:4. StrP in Isa. 45:16; 50:7.

Other: ColP in Jer. 14:3; 31:19; Ps. 35:4. VrsP in Jer. 8:12; 22:22; Ez. 36:32. StrP in Ps. 40:15; 69:7.

צדק || בוש

DtIsa: VrsP in Isa. .50:7b-8a.

Other: None, but see the collocation in Ezek. 16:52.

משסה || בז

DtIsa: VrsP in Isa. 42:22.

Other: VrsP inJer. 30:16 . See the collocation 2 Kgs 21:14.

בזה || בזה

DtIsa: StrP in Isa. 53:3.

Other: VrsP in Mal. 1:6.

בזה Nif. || חדל אישים

DtIsa: ColP in Isa. 53:3.

Other: None.

לא חשב || בזה

DtIsa: ColP in Isa. 53:3.

Other: None.

תעב || בזה

DtIsa: ColP in Isa. 49:7.

Other: None.

בזז || בז, see also בזז || בזז

DtIsa: StrP in Isa. 42:22.

Other: ColP in Isa. 10:6; 33:23; Jer. 30:16; Ezek. 29:9; 38:12, 13.

בז || בזז, see also בזז || בזז

DtIsa: CanP in Isa. 42:22+24.

Other: ColP in Ezek. 39:10; Nah. 2:10.

בזז || משׁוסה

משׁסה || בזז

DtIsa: VrsP in Isa. 42:24. StrP in Isa. 42:22.

Other: VrsP (roots) in Jer. 30:16.

אהב || בחר

DtIsa: VrsP in Isa. 41:8.

Other: VrsP in Deut. 4:37; Ps. 47:5, 78:68. Cf. the parallelism in Deut. 10:15.

בחר || בחר

DtIsa: CanP in Isa. 41:8+9; 44:1+2.

Other: StrP in Isa. 66:4.

מאס || בחר

DtIsa: ColP in Isa. 41:9.

Other: ColP in Isa. 7:15, 16. VrsP in Ps. 78:67; Job 34:33.

בחר (root) || קרא

DtIsa: VrsP in Isa. 41:9. StrP in Isa. 45:4.

Other: VrsP in Isa. 65:15.

בטח || בטח

DtIsa: CanP in Isa. 47:8+10.

Other: VrsP in Ezek. 28:26; Ps. 22:4; Job 11:18. See also the collocation in 2 Kgs 18:21 (= Isa. 36:6).

שׁען || בטח

DtIsa: VrsP in Isa. 50:10.

Other: ColP in Job 24:23. VrsP in Isa. 30:12; Prov. 3:5. StrP in Isa. 31:1.

זקנה || בטן

DtIsa: CanP in Isa. 46:3+4.

Other: None.

מעים || בטן

DtIsa: VrsP in Isa. 49:1.

Other: ColP in Ezek. 33:3. VrsP in Ps. 71:6.

רחם || בטן

DtIsa: VrsP in Isa. 46:3.

Other: VrsP in Jer. 1:5; Ps. 22:10; 58:4; Job 3:11; 31:15.

בין || בין

DtIsa: MacP in Isa. 40:14+21.

Other: VrsP in Prov. 8:5; 19:25; 28:5.

ידע || בין

DtIsa: ColP in Isa. 43:10; 44:18. CanP in Isa. 43:18+19.

Other: ColP in Isa. 56:11; Ps. 82:5; 119:125. VrsP in Mic. 4:12; Ps. 92:7; 139:2; Job 14:21, etc.

שׂכל || בין

DtIsa: VrsP in Isa. 44:18.

Other: VrsP in Deut. 32:9; Ps. 94:8.

תבונה || בין

DtIsa: VrsP in Isa. 40:14. StrP in Isa. 44:18-19a.

Other: None.

בית || בית, see also
בית || בת and ישׂראל || יעקב

VrsP in Isa. 46:3.

Other: ColP in Isa. 5:8; Jer. 3:18; 5:11; 11:10, etc. VrsP in Isa. 22:10; 27:21; Ps. 115:12; 135:19, etc.

בית ישׂראל || בית יעקב

DtIsa: VrsP in Isa. 46:3.

Other: VrsP in Jer. 2:4; Mi. 3:9.

בל || בל

DtIsa: ColP in Isa. 40:24. VrsP in Isa. 40:24. StrP in Isa. 44:9.

Other: VrsP in Isa. 26:10, 14, 28; 33:20, 23; 44:9; Ps. 16:4; 17:3; 104:9; Prov. 23:35.

בלתי || בל

DtIsa: CanP in Isa. 44:9+10.

Other: None.

נבו || בל

DtIsa: ColP in Isa. 45:1aA.

Other: None.

עצב || בל

DtIsa: VrsP in Isa. 46:1.

Other: VrsP in Jer. 50:2.

אכל || בלה

DtIsa: VrsP in Isa. 50:9. MacP in Isa. 51:6+8.

Other: VrsP in Job 13:28. StrP in 65:22.

בלעדי || בלעדי

DtIsa: CanP in Isa. 44:6+8.

Other: VrsP in 2 Sam. 22:32 (= Ps. 18:32).

זולת || בלעדי

DtIsa: StrP in Isa. 45:21c-d. CanP in Isa. 45:5+6.

Other: VrsP in Ps. 18:32.

במו || ב, see ב || ב

DtIsa: VrsP in Isa. 43:2. StrP in Isa. 43:2.

במו || על, see ב || על

DtIsa: VrsP in Isa. 44:19.

אמן || בן

DtIsa: CanP in Isa. 49:22+23.

Other: None.

בן || בן

DtIsa: VrsP in Isa. 54:1, 13. MacP in Isa. 49:15+20, 22+25; 51:18+20; 54:1+13.

Other: VrsP in Gen. 49:22; Isa. 54:13; Prov. 10:1, 5, etc. StrP in Deut. 32:8; Ps. 132:12.

בנה || בן

DtIsa: MacP in Isa. 49:15+17+20.

Other: None, but compare the use of בנה in Gen. 2:22.

בת || בן

DtIsa: VrsP in Isa. 43:6; 49:22.

Other: ColP in Deut. 32:19; Isa. 56:5; Jer. 3:25; 5:17. VrsP in Isa. 49:22; 60:4; Jer. 48:46; Mic. 7:6; Ps. 106:37; 144:12.[1]

פעל יד || בן

DtIsa: VrsP in Isa. 45:11.

Other: None. See, however, the semantic VrsP ילד || פעל יד in Isa. 29:23 and מעשׂה יד || בן in Lam. 4:2.

זרע || בת, בן

DtIsa: CanP in Isa. 43:5+6; 54:1+3.

Other: ColP in Isa. 1:4; 57:3. VrsP in Ps. 102:29; 105:6.

בנה || בנה

DtIsa: CanP in Isa. 44:26+28.

Other: VrsP in Jer. 31:4; Ps. 127:1. StrP in Mal. 1:4.

הרס || בנה

DtIsa: ColP in Isa. 49:17.

Other: ColP in Jer. 1:10; 24:6; 42:10; 45:4; Ezek. 36:36; Mal. 1:4; Ps. 28:5; Job 12:14. VrsP in Prov. 14:1. StrP in Jer. 31:28.

חרב || בנה

DtIsa: VrsP in Isa. 49:17.

Other: None, but see the collocation in Isa. 61:4; Neh. 2:17.

יסד || בנה

DtIsa: VrsP in Isa. 44:28.

VrsP in Am. 9:6; Zech. 8:9; Ps. 78:69. StrP in 1 Kgs 16:34. Cf. collocation in Josh. 6:26; Ezra 3:10; 2 Chron. 3:3.

בעל || בעל

DtIsa: MacP in Isa. 54:1+5.

Other: VrsP in Isa. 62:5. StrP in Isa. 62:4.

נשׂק || חמם || בער

VrsP in Isa. 44:15.

Other: None. For the wordpair בער || חמם see the VrsP in Ps. 39:4.

עולה || בער

DtIsa: VrsP in Isa. 40:16.

[1] VrsP in Gen. 49:22 in our opinion has to be ignored because the word בנות in this particular case has to be interpreted as "in the meadows". See Korpel, *A Rift in the Clouds*, 532-4.

Other: None, but see the collocation in Lev. 6:12, and the StrP of the two roots in 2 Sam. 22:9 (= Ps. 18:9).

מצא || בקש

DtIsa: ColP in Isa. 41:12.

Other: ColP in Isa. 65:1; Hos. 2:9; Ps. 37:36; Song 3:1-2; 5:6; Qoh. 12:10. VrsP in Jer. 2:24; 5:1; Qoh. 7:28. StrP in Ezek. 22:30; Qoh. 8:17.

עזב || בקש

DtIsa: StrP in Isa. 41:17.

Other: VrsP in Ps. 37:25.

ברא || ברא

DtIsa: VrsP in Isa. 45:7. StrP in Isa 45:18; 54:16. MacP in Isa. 40:26+28; 43:1+7; 45:7+8.

Other: VrsP in Gen. 1:27. StrP in Isa. 65:18.

ברא (ptc.) || יהוה

DtIsa: VrsP in Isa. 40:28; 43:15; 45:18.

Other: None.

גאל || ברא

DtIsa: StrP in Isa. 43:1. CanP in Isa. 43:14+15.

Other: None.

יצר || ברא

DtIsa: ColP in Isa. 43:1; 45:7. VrsP in Isa. 43:7; 45:7, 18 (2x). CanP in Isa. 45:11+12; 54:16+17. MacP in Isa. 43:15+21.

ColP in Amos 4:13.

עשׂה || יצר || ברא

DtIsa: VrsP in Isa. 43:7; 45:7, 18.

Other: VrsP in Amos 4:13.

נטה || ברא

DtIsa: ColP in Isa. 42:5. StrP in Isa. 45:12.

Other: None.

עשׂה || ברא

DtIsa: VrsP in Isa. 41:20; 43:7; 45:7, 12, 18; 54:16.

Other: VrsP in Amos 4:13. Cf. Gen. 5:1; 2:3, 4; 6:7.

צוה || ברא

DtIsa: StrP in Isa. 45:12.

Other: ColP in Ps. 148:5.

רקע || ברא

DtIsa: VrsP in Isa. 42:5.

Other: None. See the collocation of the noun רקיע and the verb ברא in Gen. 1:20-21.

עתה || בראשון

DtIsa: CanP in Isa. 52:5.

Other: None in this form, but cf. Hos. 2:9; Hag. 2:3; Zech. 8:11.

הדס || ברוש, see also עץ || ברוש, הדס

DtIsa: VrsP in Isa. 55:13. StrP in Isa. 41:19.

Other: None.

תאשור || תדהר || ברוש

DtIsa: ColP in Isa. 41:19.

Other: ColP in Isa. 60:13.

כסף || ברזל, see also כסף || נחושה

DtIsa: MacP in Isa. 48:4+10.

Other: ColP in Isa. 60:17. See also the collocation in Num. 31:22; Josh. 6:19, 24; 22:8; Ezek. 22:18, 20; 27:12; 1Chron. 22:14, etc.

נחשת, נחושה || ברזל

VrsP in Isa. 45:2; 48:4.

VrsP in Lev. 26:19; Deut. 8:9; 28:23; Isa. 48:4; 60:17; Jer. 1:18; Ps. 107:16; Mic. 4:13; Job 20:24; 28:2; 40:18; 41:19 (tr. 27).

אור || ברית

DtIsa: VrsP in Isa. 42:6.

Other: None.

חסד || ברית

DtIsa: VrsP in Isa. 54:10; 55:3.

Other: ColP in Deut. 7:9, 12; 1 Kgs 8:23; Dan. 9:4; Neh. 1:5; 9:32; 2 Chron. 6:14. VrsP in Ps. 25:10; 89:29; 106:45.

לשון || ברך

DtIsa: VrsP in Isa. 45:23.

Other: None, but compare the parallism between the verb ברך and the noun לשון in Judg. 7:5.

רבה Hif. || ברך

ColP in Isa. 51:2.

Other: ColP in Gen. 26:24; Deut. 7:13; Ps. 107:38. VrsP in Gen. 17:20; 22:17; 28:3.

בשׂר (noun) || בשׂר (noun)

DtIsa: StrP in Isa. 49:26

Other: ColP in Gen. 2:23. VrsP in Lev. 26:29; Jer. 19:9; Ezek. 11:19.

בשׂר (verb) || בשׂר (verb)

VrsP in Isa. 52:7. StrP in Isa. 40:9.

Other: None, but cf. 2 Sam. 18:20.

דם || בשׂר

DtIsa: VrsP in Isa. 49:26.

Other: ColP in Ezek. 39:17. VrsP in Deut. 32:42; Ezek. 39:18; Ps. 50:13.

שמע Hif. || בשׂר

ColP in Isa. 52:7 (2x). CanP in Isa. 41:26-27.

Other: ColP in Nah. 2:1.

הרפה || בשת

DtIsa: VrsP in Isa. 54:4.

Other: VrsP in Isa. 30:5; Ps. 69:20.

בת || בת

DtIsa: VrsP in Isa. 47:1. MacP in Isa. 47:1+5.

Other: VrsP in Ezek. 16:48; Zech. 9:9. StrP in Isa. 37:22; Mic. 4:8; Zeph. 3:14; Lam. 2:13; 4:22.

ינק || בת

DtIsa: CanP in Isa. 49:22+23.

Other: None.

בת || בתולה

DtIsa: ColP in Isa. 47:1.

ColP in Isa. 23:12; 37:22; Jer. 14:17; 46:11; Lam. 1:15. StrP in Lam. 2:10.

אביר || גאל

DtIsa: ColP in Isa. 49:26.

Other: ColP in Isa. 60:16 (quotation).

אלהים || גאל, see also יהוה || גאל

DtIsa: VrsP in Isa. 54:5. StrP in Isa. 48:17.

Other: VrsP in Ps. 78:35.

גאל || גאל

DtIsa: CanP in Isa. 44:22+23. MacP in Isa. 44:22+23+24; 48:17+20; 52:3+9; 54:5+8.

Other: ColP in Ruth 3:13; 4:4, 6. VrsP in Ps. 107:2; Ruth 3:12, 13; 4:4, 6.

יהוה || גאל

DtIsa: ColP in Isa. 44:24; 48:17; 54:8. VrsP in Isa. 41:14; 43:14; 49:7, 26.

Other: ColP in Ps. 19:15. VrsP in Isa. 59:20; 60:16; 63:16; Jer. 50:34.

ישׁע || גאל

DtIsa: VrsP in Isa. 49:26. MacP in Isa. 43:1+3.

Other: VrsP in Isa. 60:16; 63:9; Ps. 106:10.

נחם || גאל

DtIsa: VrsP in Isa. 52:9. MacP in Isa. 49:7+13

Other: StrP in Hos. 13:14.

עזר || גאל

DtIsa: VrsP in Isa. 41:14. CanP in Isa. 49:7-8. MacP in Isa. 44:2+6.

Other: None.

עשׂה || גאל

DtIsa: StrP in Isa. 44:23, 24; 54:5.

Other: None.

פאר || גאל

DtIsa: VrsP in Isa. 44:23.

Other: None.

פדה || גאל

DtIsa: CanP in Isa. 51:10+11.

Other: VrsP in Jer. 31:11; Hos. 13:14; Ps. 69:19.

קדוש ישׂראל || גאל

DtIsa: ColP in Isa. 41:14; 43:14; 49:7; 54:5. VrsP in Isa. 47:4; 48:17.

Other: None.

קרא בשׁם || גאל

DtIsa: VrsP in Isa. 43:1.

Other: None.

גבה || גבה

DtIsa: StrP in Isa. 55:9.

Other: ColP (roots) in 1 Sam. 2:3; Amos 2:9; Qoh. 5:7. VrsP in Ezek. 17:24; 19:11; 31:10, 14.

אביר || גבור

DtIsa: CanP in Isa. 49:24+26.

Other: None.

אישׁ מלחמה || גבור

DtIsa: VrsP in Isa. 42:13.

ColP in 1 Sam. 16:8; Isa. 3:2; Ezek. 39:20; 2 Chron. 17:13. VrsP in Jer. 48:14; Joel 2:7; 4:9 (tr. 3:9). See the collocation in Josh. 8:3; 1 Sam. 14:52; 2 Sam. 17:8; 2 Kgs 24:16, etc.

גבור || גבור

DtIsa: CanP in Isa. 49:24+25.

Other: ColP in Jer. 46:12. VrsP in Ps. 24:8; Song 3:7. StrP in Ezek. 32:27.

גבר Hitpa. || גבור

DtIsa: StrP in Isa. 42:13.

Other: None.

עריץ || גבור

DtIsa: VrsP in Isa. 49:25.

Other: VrsP in Ezek. 32:12. See the stereotyped phrase in Jer. 20:11.

צדיק || גבור

DtIsa: VrsP in Isa. 49:24.

Other: None.

גבירה || גבירה

DtIsa: CanP in Isa. 47:5+7.

Other: None.

מישׁור || גבעה

DtIsa: StrP in Isa. 40:4.

Other: None.

אדר Hiph. || גדל Hiph.

ColP in Isa. 42:21.

Other: StrP in Ps. 136:17-18.

לחי || גו

DtIsa: VrsP in Isa. 50:6.

Other: None.

פנים || גו

DtIsa: StrP in Isa. 50:6.

Other: None.

אי || גוי

DtIsa: StrP in Isa. 40:15. CanP in Isa. 42:1+4.

Other: None. VrsP in Jer. 31:10. See also the parallelism in Isa. 66:19, and the collocation in Zeph. 2:11.

עיר || גוי

DtIsa: VrsP in Isa. 54:3.

Other: ColP in 2 Chron. 15:6. VrsP in Deut. 9:1. StrP in Jer. 4:7; Zeph. 3:6.

גוי || גוי

DtIsa: VrsP in Isa. 55:5. CanP in Isa. 40:15-17. MacP in Isa. 42:1+6

Other: ColP in Ps. 105:13. VrsP in Isa. 26:15; 60:12; Jer. 51:7; Job 12:23, etc.

לאם || גוי

DtIsa: VrsP in Isa. 43:9. CanP in Isa. 41:1+2; 55:4+5. MacP in Isa. 49:1+6.

Other: VrsP in Gen. 25:23; Isa. 34:1; Ps. 2:1; 44:3; 105:44; Prov. 14:34.

מלך || גוי

DtIsa: VrsP in Isa. 41:2; 45:1; 52:15. CanP in Isa. 49:22+23, cf. 49:7.

Other: VrsP in Isa. 60:3, 11, 16; 62:2; Ps. 72:11; 102:15; 135:10. See also the collocation in Jer. 25:14; 27:7, 8, etc.

משׁל || גוי

DtIsa: ColP in Isa. 49:7.

Other: ColP in Deut. 15:6; Ps. 22:29. VrsP in Ps. 66:7; 106:41.

עם || גוי

DtIsa: VrsP in Isa. 42:6; 49:22. CanP in Isa. 52:9+10.

VrsP in Deut. 32:21; Isa. 1:4; 2:4; 10:6; 11:10; 25:3; 33:3; 61:9; Ps. 96:3. StrP in Isa. 14:6; Jer. 2:11; Ezek. 20:41, etc.

קצה הארץ || גוי, see also קצה הארץ || אי

DtIsa: VrsP in Isa. 49:6.

Other: VrsP in Isa. 5:26; Jer. 25:31. See also the collocation in Deut. 28:49.

בנים || גוים

DtIsa: StrP in Isa. 49:22.

Other: VrsP in Deut. 32:8; Jer. 3:19.

אפסי־ארץ || גוים

DtIsa: StrP in Isa. 51:10.

Other: ColP in Jer. 16:19. VrsP in Ps. 2:8; 22:28.

קום || גור II

DtIsa: MacP in Isa. 54:15+17.

Other: None.

גור II || גור II,

VrsP in Isa. 54:15.

Other: None.

נגע || גזר

DtIsa: VrsP in Isa. 53:8.

Other: None, but see the collocation in 2 Chron. 26:20-21.

אור || גחלת

DtIsa: VrsP in Isa. 47:14.

Other: None.

הר וגבעה || גיא

DtIsa: VrsP in Isa. 40:4.

Other: ColP in Ezek. 6:3; 36:4, 6. StrP in Ezek. 35:8.

מישור || גיא

DtIsa: StrP in Isa. 40:4.

Other: None.

הלל || גיל

DtIsa: VrsP in Isa. 41:16.

Other: StrP in Ps. 149:2–3. See the collocation of the roots in Ps. 9:15; Ps. 48:11-12.

פצח רנה || גיל

DtIsa: VrsP in Isa. 49:13.

Other: None, but see the collocation of גיל and רנה in Zeph. 3:17.

גלה || גלה

DtIsa: VrsP in Isa. 47:2. CanP in Isa. 47:2+3.

Other: VrsP in Ezek. 23:18. Cf. the parallelism in Lev. 18:7, 15, 17; 20:18; 1 Sam. 22:8; 2 Sam. 6:20.

חשף || גלה

DtIsa: ColP in Isa. . VrsP in Isa. 47:2.

Other: VrsP in Jer. 49:10.

סור || גלה

DtIsa: ColP in Isa. 49:21.

Other: VrsP in Amos 6:7.

ראה || גלה

DtIsa: VrsP in Isa. 47:3. StrP in Isa. 40:5.

Other: ColP in Prov. 27:25. VrsP in Num. 22:31; 1 Sam. 3:21; 2 Sam. 22:16 (= Ps. 18:16); Ezek. 16:37; 21:29; Job 38:17. StrP in Nah. 3:5.

גם || גם

DtIsa: ColP in Isa. 48:8. VrsP in Isa. 48:8.

Other: ColP in Deut. 32:25; Jer. 14:18; 23:11; Ps. 49:3; Job 15:10. VrsP in Judg. 5:4; Jer. 6:15; 12:2, 6.

אמר || דבר, see אמר || דבר

בוא Hiph. || דבר

DtIsa: ColP in Isa. 46:11. VrsP in Isa. 48:15.

Other: None, but see the collocation of the roots in 2 Sam. 14:10; Jer. 25:13.

דבר (root) || דבר (root)

DtIsa: StrP in Isa. 45:19 CanP in Isa. 48:15+16. MacP in Isa. 40:2+5+8.

Other: VrsP in Num. 23:5; Ezek. 12:25; Ps. 73:8, etc. StrP in Jer. 26:2; Job 42:7, etc.

יצר || דבר

DtIsa: VrsP in Isa. 46:11.

Other: None.

נגד || דבר

DtIsa: VrsP in Isa. 45:19.

Other: ColP in Ps. 40:6. See also the collocation in Jer. 9:11; 16:10; 38:25.

עצה || דבר

DtIsa: VrsP in Isa. 44:26.

Other: See the collocation in Judg. 20:7; 2 Sam. 16:23; 2 Kgs 18:20; Isa. 36:5.

פה || (noun) דבר

DtIsa: ColP in Isa. 55:11. VrsP in Isa. 45:23.

Other: VrsP in Ezek. 35:13; Ps. 33:6; Prov. 12:6, etc. StrP in Ps. 55:22.

קרא || דבר

DtIsa: ColP in Isa. 48:15. VrsP in Isa. 40:2. StrP in Isa. 46:11. CanP in Isa. 40:3-5; 41:1-3.

Other: VrsP in Isa. 65:12, 24; 66:4; Jer. 7:13, 27; 20:8; 35:17; Ps. 50:1; Job 13:22.

שלח || דבר

DtIsa: StrP in Isa. 48:16.

Other: ColP in Jer. 14:14. StrP in Jer. 24:10 (both said of the mission of prophets).

חשך || דומם

DtIsa: ColP in Isa. 47:5.

Other: ColP (roots) in 1 Sam. 2:9.

שים כמץ || דקק || דוש

DtIsa: VrsP in Isa. 41:15.

Other: None.

אי || דור

DtIsa: CanP in Isa. 41:4+5.

Other: None.

עם || דור

DtIsa: StrP in Isa. 53:8.

Other: StrP in Ps. 95:10; 102:19.

זרה || דוש

DtIsa: CanP in Isa. 41:15+16.

Other: None.

די || די

DtIsa: VrsP in Isa. 40:16.

Other: VrsP in Isa. 66:23; Jer. 51:58; Hab. 2:13. Frequently in Dan. and Ezra.

דכא || דכא

DtIsa: MacP in Isa. 53:5+10.

Other: None.

חלה || דכא

DtIsa: ColP in Isa. 53:10.

Other: None.

מאזנים || דלי

DtIsa: VrsP in Isa. 40:15.

Other: None.

בריח || דלת

DtIsa: VrsP in Isa. 45:2.

Other: ColP in Jer. 49:31; Job 38:10. VrsP in Ps. 107:16 (possibly a quotation). See also the collocation in Deut. 3:5; Judg. 16:3; 1 sam. 23:7; Ezek. 38:11; Neh. 3:3, 6, 13, 14, 15; 2 Chron. 8:5; 14:6.

דלת || דלת

DtIsa: MacP in Isa. 45:1+2.

Other: None.

שער || דלת

DtIsa: VrsP in Isa. 45:1.

Other: None. See, however, the collocation in Judg. 16:3; 1 Sam. 21:14; Nah. 3:1, 3, etc.

בשר || דם

DtIsa: StrP in Isa. 49:26.

Other: ColP in Ezek. 39:17. VrsP in Deut. 32:42; Ezek. 39:18; Ps. 50:13.

דמה || דמה

DtIsa: VrsP in Isa. 46:5.

Other: StrP in Ezek. 31:8.

דמות || דמה

DtIsa: VrsP in Isa. 40:18.

Other: None.

שוה || דמה

DtIsa: ColP in Isa. 40:25; 46:5.

Other: StrP in Lam. 2:13.

כבה || דעך

DtIsa: ColP in Isa. 43:17.

Other: None.

ידע || דעת

DtIsa: VrsP in Isa. 40:14. StrP in Isa. 44:18-19a. CanP in Isa. 47:8+10+11.

Other: ColP in Num. 24:16; Job 13:2; Prov. 17:27; 30:3. VrsP in Prov. 14:7; 29:7. StrP in Job 42:3.

עצה || דעת

DtIsa: CanP in Isa. 44:25+26.

Other: ColP in Job 42:3. VrsP in Isa. 11:2; Job 38:2.

תבונה || דעת

DtIsa: ColP in Isa. 44:19.

Other: VrsP in Prov. 17:27.

אהל || דק

DtIsa: VrsP in Isa. 40:22.

Other: None.

דרך || דרך

DtIsa: ColP in Isa. 55:8. CanP in Isa. 49:9+11; 55:8+9. MacP in Isa. 43:16+19; 48:15+17; 55:7+8+9.

Other: VrsP in Isa. 35:8; 57:14; Jer. 18:11; 21:8; 32:19; Ps. 1:6; 139:24, etc.

הלך || דרך

DtIsa: ColP in Isa. 48:17. VrsP in Isa. 42:16.

Other: VrsP in Ps. 58:8; 107:7.

מחשבה || דרך

DtIsa: VrsP in Isa. 55:7, 8, 9. CanP in Isa. 55:8-9.

Other: VrsP in Isa. 65:2.

מסלה || דרך

DtIsa: VrsP in Isa. 49:11. StrP in Isa. 40:3.

Other: VrsP in Jer. 31:21 (probably the Zaqeph Qaṭon, No. 5, is misplaced. Otherwise colon par.). StrP in Isa. 62:10. See also the collocation in 1 Sam. 6:12.

משפט || דרך

DtIsa: VrsP in Isa. 40:27.

Other: ColP in Deut. 32:4. VrsP in Jer. 5:4, 5; Ezek. 7:27; Ps. 10:5; 25:9. StrP in Isa. 59:2; Jer. 7:5.

נתיבה || דרך

DtIsa: VrsP in Isa. 42:16; 43:16, 19.

Other: ColP in Lam. 3:9. VrsP in Jer. 6:16; 18:15; Hos. 2:6; Job 24:13; Prov. 1:15; 3:17; 7:25; 8:2. StrP in Isa. 59:8.

עיר || דרך

DtIsa: StrP in Isa. 45:13.

Other: VrsP in Ps. 107:4, 7.

שפי || דרך

DtIsa: VrsP in Isa. 49:9.

Other: VrsP in Jer. 3:2. See also the collocation in Jer.3:21; 4:11.

תורה || דרך

DtIsa: VrsP in Isa. 42:24.

Other: VrsP in Mal. 2:8,9; Ps. 119:1. StrP in Exod. 18:20; Isa. 2:3; Mic. 4:2. See also the parallelism in Josh. 22:5.

מצא || דרש

DtIsa: VrsP in Isa. 55:6.

Other: VrsP in Isa. 65:1; Jer. 29:13; Ps.10:15. See also the collocation in Deut. 4:29.

קרא || דרש

DtIsa: VrsP in Isa. 55:6.

Other: ColP in Isa. 34:16. VrsP in Jer. 29:12-13.

שוב || דרש

DtIsa: CanP in Isa. 55:6+7.

Other: VrsP in Isa. 9:12; Ps. 78:34.

ה- || ה-

DtIsa: ColP in Isa. 44:7. VrsP in 40:2; 42:5; 45:18; 49:15; 51:3. StrP in 40:2b-c; 51:18. CanP in Isa. 40:1-2.

Other: ColP in Ps. 65:11; Job 28:27; Lam. 1:9, etc. VrsP in Ps. 24:1; 45:15;

46:6; Job 9:6; Prov. 31:28; Lam. 1:5; 4:13, etc. StrP in Isa. 14:23; 27:3; Lam. 2:9, etc.

חזה || הבר

DtIsa: VrsP in Isa. 47:13.

Other: None.

חמד || הדר

DtIsa: VrsP in Isa. 53:2.

Other: None. See, however, the CanP parallelism between כל־הדרה || כל־מחמדיה in Lam. 1:6-7.

־הו || ־הו

DtIsa: VrsP in 40:14; 46:7. StrP in Isa. 44:12; 46:7. CanP in Isa. 44:13a-c.

Other: ColP in Isa. 5:2. VrsP in Deut. 32:10.

־ו || ־הו

DtIsa: VrsP in Isa. 42:25; 45:13; 46:7; 52:14; Isa. 53:3; 55:6.

Other: ColP in Isa. 5:25. StrP in Isa. 5:2.

הוא || הוא

DtIsa: VrsP in Isa. 45:18; 52:6. CanP in Isa. 53:4+5. MacP in Isa. 43:10+13.

Other: VrsP in Deut. 32:6; Isa. (8:13); 9:14; 34:16; Jer. 5:15; Ps. 33:9, etc. StrP in Hos. 7:9.

שואה || הוה

DtIsa: StrP in Isa. 47:11.

Other: None.

הוי || הוי

DtIsa: CanP in Isa. 45:9+10.

Other: ColP in Jer. 22:18; Zech. 2:10. VrsP in Jer. 22:18.

היא || היא

DtIsa: CanP in Isa. 51:9+10.

Other: ColP in Ezek. 21:16. VrsP in Ezek. 21:17; 46:16; Amos 5:13; Song 6:9; Qoh. 3:21. StrP in Song 8:9.

היה || היה

DtIsa: StrP in Isa. 49:6. CanP in Isa. 47:14+15; 49:5+6. MacP in Isa. 51:6+8.

Other: ColP in Gen. 1:3, 5, etc. VrsP in Lev. 26:12, 33; Num. 24:18; Ps. 109:12, etc. StrP in Isa. 1:18; 5:5; Mic. 5:1, etc.

לא חתת || היה לעולם

DtIsa: VrsP in Isa. 51:6.

Other: None.

אם־לא || הלוא

DtIsa: ColP in Isa. 40:28.

Other: VrsP in Gen. 4:7; Isa. 10:8.

ה־ || הלוא

DtIsa: StrP in Isa. 44:8.

Other: StrP in Deut. 32:6; Jer. 14:22; Ezek. 17:10; Mic. 2:7, etc.

הלוא || הלוא

DtIsa: StrP in Isa. 40:21 (4x) CanP in Isa. 51:9+10.

Other: VrsP in Mal. 2:10, Ps. 94:9. StrP in Amos 9:7; Mic. 1:5.

לא || הלוא

DtIsa: VrsP in Isa. 44:20. StrP in Isa. 42:24; 48:6.

Other: VrsP in Jer. 38:15; Ps. 14:4; 53:5; 60:12; 108:12; Job 4:21; 21:29. StrP in Isa. 57:11; 58:7; Jer. 5:3.

דרך || הלך, see הלך || דרך

הלך || הלך

DtIsa: VrsP in Isa. 55:1. StrP in Isa. 52:12. CanP in Isa. 45:14+16; 55:1+3.

Other: ColP in Isa. 2:5; Prov. 10:9; Ruth 1:16. VrsP in Judg. 5:6; Qoh. 7:2. StrP in Jer. 18:18; Mic. 4:5.

יעף || הלך

DtIsa: ColP in Isa. 40:31.

Other: None.

אסף Pi. || הלך לפנים

DtIsa: VrsP in Isa. 52:12.

Other: None, VrsP in but see the collocation in Josh. 6:13.

ישר || הלך לפנים

DtIsa: VrsP in Isa. 45:2.

Other: None.

חכם || הלל

DtIsa: StrP in Isa. 44:25.

Other: None.

-הם || -הם

DtIsa: VrsP in 41:29. StrP in 44:9.

Other: ColP in Isa. 56:7, etc. VrsP in Isa. 5:21; 13:16; 14:2; 59:6; Ps. 81:15. StrP in 49:10.

המה || המה

DtIsa: CanP in Isa. 44:9+11.

Other: None. ColP in Isa. 57:6. VrsP in Jer. 12:6; Ezek. 44:16; Ps. 95:10, etc. StrP in Jer. 4:22; 5:5, etc.

הן || הן

DtIsa: StrP in Isa. 40:4; 50:9.

Other: None.

הנה || הנה

DtIsa: VrsP in Isa. 49:12. StrP in Isa. 40:10.

Other: ColP in Isa. 65:1. VrsP in Isa. 5:7; Ps. 92:10, etc. StrP in Isa. 29:8; 40:10; 62:11; 65:13, etc.

בקעה || הר

DtIsa: StrP in Isa. 40:4.

Other: ColP in Deut. 8:7; 11:1. VrsP in Ps. 104:8. See also the collocation in Josh. 11:17.

גבעה || הר

DtIsa: ColP in Isa. 40:4; 42:15; 55:12. VrsP in Isa. 41:15; 54:10.

Other: ColP in Ezek. 36:4, 6; Ps. 148:9. VrsP in Jer. 4:24; Ezek. 34:6; Hos. 4:13; Ps. 72:4; 114:4, 6, etc.

עץ || גבעה || הר, see also עץ || הר

DtIsa: VrsP in Isa. 55:12.

Other: VrsP in Deut. 12:2; Ezek. 6:13; Ps. 148:9.

הר || הר

DtIsa: MacP in Isa. 42:11+15; 49:11+13.

Other: ColP in Mic. 7:12; Ps. 68:16. VrsP in Isa. 2:2 (= Mic. 4:1); Ps. 68:16. StrP in Jer. 50:6; 51:25; Ps. 68:16, 17.

יער || הר

DtIsa: VrsP in Isa. 44:23.

Other: VrsP in Ps. 50:10; 83:15.

נהר || הר

DtIsa: StrP in Isa. 42:15.

Other: VrsP in Ps. 98:8.

עץ || הר

DtIsa: VrsP in Isa. 44:23; 55:12.

Other: VrsP in Jer. 3:6; Ps. 148:9. Compare the VrsP of עץ || גבעה in Jer. 17:2.

עקב || הר

DtIsa: StrP in Isa. 40:4.

Other: None.

עשב || הר

DtIsa: VrsP in Isa. 42:15.

Other: None, but see the collocation in Ps. 72:16; Prov. 27:25.

ציון || הר

DtIsa: VrsP in Isa. 40:9. StrP in Isa. 52:7.

Other: ColP in Ps. 2:6. VrsP in Jer. 26:18; Joel 2:1; Mic. 3:12. StrP in Zech. 8:3. See also the stereotyped phrase in 2 Kgs 19:31; Isa. 4:5; 8:18; 10:12; Ps. 125:1; Lam. 5:18, etc. and the collocation in Isa. 2:3; Mic. 4:2.

בלע || הריסות

DtIsa: CanP in Isa. 49:17+19.

Other: StrP (roots) in Lam. 2:2.

הריסות || הרס

DtIsa: MacP in Isa. 49:17+19.

Other: None.

חרב || הרס

DtIsa: VrsP in Isa. 49:17.

Other: ColP in Ezek. 36:35. VrsP in Mal. 1:4.

-ו || -ו

DtIsa: VrsP in Isa. 40:10; 41:2; 42:24; 43:7; 44:14, 16, 17, 19, 26; 45:9, 24; 48:14, 15; 49:5, 13; 53:5, 9; 55:7; StrP in Isa. 40:10, 13-14; 42:1; 53:10b-c.

Other: VrsP in Gen. 49:24; Deut. 32:4; Ps. 135:14, etc.

־הו || ־הו || ־ו

DtIsa: VrsP in Isa. 51:2; 53:2.

Other: See ־הו || ־ו.

־ה || זאת

DtIsa: VrsP in Isa. 41:20; 45:21; 48:20.

Other: VrsP in Isa. 56:2; Jer. 5:20; 9:11; Ps. 109:27; 132:14.

זבח (noun) || זבח (noun)

DtIsa: CanP in Isa. 43:23+24.

Other: None.

זבח (noun) || לבנה

DtIsa: StrP in Isa. 43:23.

Other: None.

זה || זה

DtIsa: VrsP in Isa. 44:5. StrP in Isa. 44:5 (3x).

Other: ColP in Isa. 6:3; Ps. 75:8, etc. VrsP in Isa. 63:1; 66:1; Job 38:19, etc. StrP in Isa. 25:9; 58:5, etc.

כסף || זהב

DtIsa: VrsP in Isa. 40:19; 46:6.

Other: ColP in Isa. 2:7; Ps. 105:37; 115:4; 119:72; Prov. 22:1; 25:11; 27:21, etc. VrsP in Isa. 2:20; 13:17; 30:22; 31:7; 60:17; Song 1:11; 3:10, etc.

שקל || זול

DtIsa: VrsP in Isa. 46:6.

Other: None.

זולת || בלעדי, see בלעדי || זולת

זיקה || זיקה

DtIsa: StrP in Isa. 50:11a-b.

Other: None.

בין || זכר

DtIsa: VrsP in Isa. 43:18.

Other: VrsP in Deut. 32:7.

זכר || זכר

DtIsa: StrP in Isa. 46:8-9.

Other: VrsP in Lev. 26:42. StrP in Ps. 25:7.

זכר Qal || זכר Hiph.

DtIsa: StrP in Isa. 43:25-26.

Other: VrsP in Ps. 77:12.

מחה || זכר

DtIsa: VrsP in Isa. 43:25. CanP in Isa. 44:21+22.

Other: VrsP in Ps. 109:14, compare Neh. 13:14. See also the collocation in Exod. 7:14; Deut. 25:19.

ספר || זכר

DtIsa: VrsP in Isa. 43:26.

Other: VrsP (roots) in Isa. 36:3.

שוב על לב || זכר, see also
שים על לב || זכר

DtIsa: VrsP in Isa. 46:8.

Other: StrP in Lam. 3:20-21.

קרא || זכר שם, see also קרא בשם || זכר

DtIsa: VrsP in Isa. 49:1.

Other: None, but see the collocation in 2 Sam. 18:18.

שיבה || זקן

DtIsa: VrsP in Isa. 46:4.

Other: ColP in Ps. 71:18.

זרוע || זרוע

DtIsa: StrP in Isa. 51:5. CanP in Isa. 40:10-11.

Other: VrsP in 1 Sam. 2:31; Ezek. 30:25. StrP in Ezek. 30:24; Zech. 11:17; Ps. 44:4.

יד || זרוע

DtIsa: MacP in Isa. 53:1+10.

Other: ColP in Gen. 49:24; Jer. 21:5; Ps. 136:12. VrsP in Ps. 18:35; 89:14, 22. StrP in Gen. 49:24.

עין || זרוע

DtIsa: VrsP in Isa. 52:10.

Other: ColP and VrsP in Zech. 11:17.

אכל || זרע

DtIsa: VrsP in Isa. 55:10.

Other: ColP (roots) in Job 31:8. VrsP in Lev. 26:16; and see Hag. 1:6 (roots). See also the parallelism in Gen. 47:24 and the collocation of roots in Lev. 25:20, 22; 2 Kgs 19:29, etc.

זרע || בן, בת, see בן, בת || זרע

זרע (noun) || זרע (verb)

DtIsa: ColP in Isa. 55:10.

Other: ColP in Gen. 1:29; Lev. 26:26; Jer. 35:7. VrsP in Isa. 30:23. StrP in Jer. 31:27; Ps. 126:5-6.

זרע (noun) || לחם (verb)

DtIsa: VrsP in Isa. 55:10.

Other: VrsP in Isa. 30:23. StrP in Lev. 26:5. See the parallelism in Gen. 47:19 and the collocation in

זרע || צאצא

DtIsa: VrsP in Isa. 44:3; 48:19.

Other: VrsP in Isa. 61:9; 65:23; Job 21:8; 31:8.

זרע || שם

DtIsa: StrP in Isa. 48:19.

Other: ColP. in Isa. 66:22. VrsP in 1 Sam. 24:22; Ps. 69:37.

זרע || שרש

DtIsa: VrsP in Isa. 40:24.

Other: VrsP (roots) in Job 31:8.

חבא || סתר

DtIsa: StrP in Isa. 49:2.

Other: StrP in Amos 9:3.

חבר || כשפים

DtIsa: VrsP in Isa. 47:9, 12.

Other: None.

חד || ברור

DtIsa: StrP in Isa. 49:2.

Other: None.

חדש || נצר

DtIsa: VrsP in Isa. 48:6.

Other: None.

חדש || צמח

DtIsa: VrsP in Isa. 42:9; 43:19.

Other: None.

חול || מעה

DtIsa: VrsP in Isa. 48:19.

Other: None.

חור || בת כלא

DtIsa: VrsP in Isa. 42:22.

Other: None.

חזה || ידע

DtIsa: StrP in Isa. 47:13b-c.

Other: StrP in Num. 24:16.

חזק || זרוע

DtIsa: VrsP in Isa. 40:10.

Other: None. See the standard phrases in Deut. 4:34; Jer. 21:5; Ezek. 20:33; Ps. 136:12, etc.

חזק || חזק

DtIsa: StrP in Isa. 41:7. CanP in Isa. 41:6-7.

Other: VrsP in Hag. 2:4. StrP in Nah. 3:14; Zech. 8:23.

חזק || ירא

DtIsa: StrP in Isa. 41:5-6, 13. CanP in Isa. 41:9-10.

Other: ColP in Isa. 35:4; Zech. 8:13. VrsP in Deut. 31:6; Josh. 10:25.

חזק || נצר

DtIsa: ColP in Isa. 42:6.

Other: VrsP in Nah. 2:2; Prov. 4:13.

חזק || עזר

DtIsa: VrsP in Isa. 41:6. StrP in Isa. 41:13.

Other: None.

חזק || קרא

DtIsa: VrsP in Isa. 41:9; 42:6.

Other: VrsP in Isa. 64:6.

חזק || תמך

DtIsa: CanP in Isa. 41:9+10. MacP in Isa. 41:10+13; 42:1+6.

Other: VrsP in Prov. 3:18.

חטא || לא הלך || לא שמע

DtIsa: VrsP in Isa. 42:24.

Other: VrsP in Jer. 44:23 . See also the collocation of the roots in Lev. 26:21.

חטא || פשע

DtIsa: VrsP in Isa. 43:27; and of both roots in 53:12.

Other: ColP in Isa. 1:28. VrsP in 1 Kgs 8:50; Jer. 33:8. For both roots: Ps. 51:15; Job 8:4; 35:6 StrP (roots) in Ezek. 33:12; 37:23. See also the parallelism (roots) in 1 Sam. 24:12.

חטאת || חטא (verb)

DtIsa: CanP in Isa. 43:25+27.

Other: ColP in Jer. 16:10; Ezek. 16:51; 18:24; 33:16.

חטאת || חטאת

DtIsa: MacP in Isa. 43:24+25.

Other: ColP in Isa. 30:1. VrsP in Job 13:23. StrP in Ps. 32:5.

חטאת || עון, see also חטא || עון

DtIsa: VrsP in Isa. 43:24. StrP in Isa. 40:2b-c.

Other: ColP in Jer. 16:10, 18, etc. VrsP in Isa. 6:7; 27:9; Jer. 5:25; 14:10; Ps. 51:4; 85:3; Prov. 5:22, etc. StrP in Isa. 59:2, 12, etc.

חיה || בהמה

DtIsa: ColP in Isa. 46:1.

Other: ColP in Ps. 148:10. VrsP in Ps. 50:10. StrP in Lev. 26:22. Often in collocation, Gen. 1:24-25, etc.

חיה || גוי

DtIsa: CanP in Isa. 40:15-17.

Other: VrsP in Ezek. 31:6; 34:28.

חיה || יענה

DtIsa: VrsP in Isa. 43:20.

Other: None.

חיה || תן

DtIsa: VrsP in Isa. 43:20.

Other: None.

חיים || מות

DtIsa: CanP in Isa. 53:8+9.

Other: ColP in Deut. 30:19; 2 Sam. 1:23; 15:21; Jer. 8:3; Jon. 4:3, 8. VrsP in Jer. 21:8; Prov. 11:19; 12:28; 13:14; 14:27; Qoh. 9:3.

חיל || עזוז

DtIsa: ColP in Isa. 43:17.

Other: None.

חכם || דעת, see also חכמה || דעת

DtIsa: VrsP in Isa. 44:25.

Other: VrsP in Prov. 22:17; 24:5; Eccl. 12:9.

חכם || סכל

DtIsa: VrsP in Isa. 44:25.

Other: ColP in Qoh. 2:19. StrP in Jer. 4:22.

חכמה || דעת, see also חכם || דעת

DtIsa: ColP in Isa. 47:10.

Other: ColP in Isa. 33:6; Prov. 1:7; Qoh. 1:16; 7:12; 9:10. VrsP in Prov. 2:10; 8:12; 9:10; 14:6; 30:3; Qoh. 2:21; 7:12. StrP in Isa. 11:2.

חלב || דשן

DtIsa: CanP in Isa. 55:1+2.

Other: ColP in Ps. 63:6.

חלי || חלה

DtIsa: MacP in Isa. 53:3+4+10.

Other: VrsP in Isa. 38:9 and see the collocation in Jer. 10:19.

חלי || מכאב

DtIsa: ColP in Isa. 53:3. VrsP in Isa. 53:4.

Other: ColP (roots) in Isa. 17:11.

חלי || נכה

DtIsa: StrP in Isa. 53:4.

Other: StrP in Isa. 1:5.

חלי || עון

DtIsa: CanP in Isa. 53:4+5+6.

Other: None, but see the collocation in Isa. 33:24.

חלי || רפא

DtIsa: CanP in Isa. 53:4+5.

Other: ColP and VrsP of the verbs in Ezek. 34:4.

דכא || חלל

DtIsa: VrsP in Isa. 53:5.

Other: ColP in Ps. 89:11.

נתן לחרם || חלל

DtIsa: StrP in Isa. 43:28.

Other: None.

יעל || חלף

DtIsa: VrsP in Isa. 40:31.

Other: None, but see the collocation in 1 Sam. 10:3.

יגע || חלף כח

DtIsa: StrP in Isa. 40:31.

Other: None.

יעף || חלף כח, see also יעף || כח

DtIsa: StrP in Isa. 40:31.

Other: None.

חלק Hiph. || הלם Qal

DtIsa: ColP in Isa. 41:7.

Other: None. ColP in Isa. 33:6; Prov. 1:7; Qoh. 1:16; 7:12; 9:10. VrsP in Prov. 2:10; 8:12; 9:10; 14:6; 30:3; Qoh. 2:21; 7:12. StrP in Isa. 11:2.

חלק || חלק

DtIsa: VrsP in Isa. 53:12.

Other: VrsP (roots) in 1 Sam. 30:24. StrP (roots) in Num. 18:20; Mic. 2:4.

בער || חמה

DtIsa: StrP in Isa. 42:25.

Other: ColP in Ps. 89:47. VrsP in Jer. 21:12; 44:6. StrP in Jer. 7:20.

גערה || חמה

DtIsa: VrsP in Isa. 51:20.

Other: None, VrsP in but see the collocation in Isa. 66:15.

חמה || חמה

DtIsa: StrP in Isa. 51:13b-c.

Other: VrsP in Ezek. 13:13; Ps. 76:11. StrP in Jer. 42:18; Ezek. 5:13.

עזוז || חמה

DtIsa: VrsP in Isa. 42:25.

Other: None.

שחת || חמה

DtIsa: VrsP in Isa. 51:13.

Other: ColP in Ps. 106:23. VrsP in Ezek. 9:8; Ps. 78:38. StrP in 2 Chron. 12:7.

חמם || חמם

DtIsa: VrsP in Isa. 44:16.

Other: VrsP in Qoh. 4:11.

שרף || חמם

DtIsa: StrP in Isa. 44:16; 47:14.

Other: None.

דכא || חמס

DtIsa: VrsP in Isa. 53:9-10.

Other: None.

חלי || חמס

DtIsa: VrsP in Isa. 53:9-10.

Other: VrsP in Jer. 6:7.

רמה || חמס

DtIsa: VrsP in Isa. 53:9-10.

Other: ColP (roots) in Zeph. 1:9. VrsP (roots) in Mic. 6:12. See also the collocation of roots in 1 Chron. 12:18.

טיט || חמר

DtIsa: VrsP in Isa. 41:25.

Other: ColP in Nah. 3:14.

פעל || חמר

DtIsa: VrsP in Isa. 45:9.

Other: None.

חנם || חנם

DtIsa: MacP in Isa. 52:3+5.

Other: VrsP in Ps. 35:7.

כסף || חנם

DtIsa: VrsP in Isa. 52:3.

Other: ColP in Exod. 21:11. See also the parallelism in 2 Sam. 24:24; 1 Chron. 21:24.

ברית || חסד, see חסד || ברית

חסד || חסד

DtIsa: MacP in Isa. 54:8+10.

Other: VrsP in Josh. 2:12; 2 Sam. 10:2; Prov. 20:28.

רחם || חסד (root)

DtIsa: ColP in Isa. 54:8 VrsP in Isa. 54:10.

Other: ColP in Hos. 2:21; Zech. 7:9; Ps. 25:6; 103:4; Dan. 1:9. VrsP in Exod. 34:6; Isa. 63:7; Joel 2:13; Jon. 4:2; Ps. 40:12; 51:3; 69:17; 86:15; 103:8; 145:8; Lam. 3:22, 32; Neh. 9:17.

רחם || שלום || חסד

DtIsa: VrsP in Isa. 54:10.

Other: VrsP in Jer. 16:5.

שלום || חסד

DtIsa: VrsP in Isa. 54:10.

Other: VrsP in Jer. 16:5; Ps. 85:11.

נוס || חפז

DtIsa: VrsP in Isa. 52:12.

Other: VrsP in Ps. 104:7. See also the collocation in 2 Sam. 4:4.

שלח || חפץ

DtIsa: VrsP in Isa. 55:11.

Other: None.

חרפה || חפר

DtIsa: StrP in Isa. 54:4.

Other: None.

אשפה || חץ

DtIsa: VrsP in Isa. 49:2.

Other: None, but see the parallelism in in Ps. 127:4-5; Lam. 3:12-13.

חלל || חצב

DtIsa: VrsP in Isa. 51:9.

Other: None.

נקר || חצב

DtIsa: VrsP in Isa. 51:1.

Other: None.

חצי || חצי

DtIsa: VrsP in Isa. 44:16.

Other: VrsP in Zech. 14:8. See also the parallelism in Exod. 24:6; Neh. 4:16.

יתר || חצי

DtIsa: StrP in Isa. 44:19b-c.

Other: VrsP in Zech. 14:2.

שארית || חצי

DtIsa: CanP in Isa. 44:16+17.

Other: None.

חציר || חציר

DtIsa: StrP in Isa. 40:7-8. CanP in Isa. 40:6-8.

Other: None.

ציץ || חציר

DtIsa: ColP in Isa. 40:7, 8. VrsP in Isa. 40:6.

Other: VrsP in Ps. 103:15.

כתף || חצן

DtIsa: VrsP in Isa. 49:22.

Other: None.

בין || חקר

DtIsa: VrsP in Isa. 40:28.

Other: VrsP in Job 32:11; Prov. 28:11.

חץ || חרב

DtIsa: StrP in Isa. 49:2.

Other: ColP in Prov. 25:10. VrsP in Deut. 32:42; Ps. 57:5; 64:4.

חרבה || חרב

DtIsa: MacP in Isa. 49:17+19.

Other: None.

יבש || חרב

DtIsa: VrsP in Isa. 42:15; 44:27. StrP in Isa. 42:15.

Other: ColP in Isa. 19:5; Jer. 50:38; Job 14:11. VrsP in Jer. 51:36; Nah. 1:4.

ים || חרב DtIsa: ColP in Isa. 50:2.

Other: ColP in Isa. 51:10, 36; Ps. 106:9.

מדבר || חרב, see also מדבר || חרבה

DtIsa: VrsP in Isa. 50:2.

Other: VrsP in Ps. 106:9.

קשׁת || חרב

DtIsa: VrsP in Isa. 41:2.

Other: ColP in Josh. 24:12; Hos. 1:7; 2:20, etc. VrsP in 2 Sam. 1:22; Isa. 21:15; Zech. 9:13; Ps. 7:13; 37:14, 15; 44:7; 76:4. StrP in Hos. 7:16. See also the parallelism in Gen. 48:22; 2 Kgs 6:22; Neh. 4:7; 1 Chron. 5:18.

שׁלום || חרב

DtIsa: StrP in Isa. 41:2c-3.

Other: VrsP in Jer. 4:10. StrP in Lev. 26:6; Jer. 12:12; 14:13.

הרס || שׁמם || חרב

DtIsa: ColP in Isa. 49:19.

Other: ColP in Ezek. 36:35.

ישׁב || חרבה

DtIsa: VrsP in Isa. 44:26. StrP in Isa. 49:19.

Other: ColP in Ezek. 32:24; 38:12. VrsP in Jer. 44;2, 22; Ezek. 26:20. StrP in Isa. 58:12; Ezek. 38:8.

מדבר || חרבה, see also מדבר || חרב

DtIsa: StrP in Isa. 51:3a-b.

Other: VrsP in Ps. 102:7.

ריב || חרה

DtIsa: StrP in Isa. 41:11.

Other: VrsP in Gen. 31:36.

גדוף || חרם

DtIsa: VrsP in Isa. 43:28.

Other: None.

גדוף || חרפה

DtIsa: VrsP in Isa. 51:7.

Other: ColP (roots) in Ezek. 5:14. VrsP in Zeph. 2:8.

בעל פיפיות || חרץ

DtIsa: VrsP in Isa. 41:15.

Other: None.

חמר || חרשׂ

DtIsa: StrP in Isa. 45:9.

Other: None.

חרשׁ Hiph. || אפק Hitpa.

DtIsa: ColP in Isa. 42:14.

Other: None.

דבר || חרשׁ

DtIsa: StrP in Isa. 41:1.

Other: ColP in Job 33:31. VrsP in Job 13:13.

חרשׁ || חרשׁ

DtIsa: CanP in Isa. 40:19+20; 42:18 +19.

Other: None, but see the collocation in 2 Sam. 5:11; 1Chron. 14:1; 2Chron. 24:12.

הולם פעם || מחליק פטישׁ || חרשׁ

DtIsa: VrsP in Isa. 41:7.

Other: None.

מעשׂה || חרשׁ

DtIsa: VrsP in Isa. 54:16.

Other: None, but see the collocation of roots in Hos. 8:6; 13:2 and the stereotyped phrase מעשׂה חרשׁ in Exod. 28:11; Deut. 27:15; Jer. 10:9 (cf. 10:3); Hos. 13:2.

נשׁם || חרשׁ

DtIsa: StrP in Isa. 42:14.

Other: None.

עור || חרשׁ

DtIsa: VrsP in Isa. 42:18, 19; 43:8.

Other: VrsP in Exod. 4:11; Lev. 19:14; Isa. 29:18; 35:5.

יצר || פעל || חרשׁ, see also פעל || יצר

DtIsa: VrsP in Isa.44:12 .

Other: None.

צרף || חרשׁ

DtIsa: ColP in Isa. 41:7. VrsP in Isa. 40:19.

Other: ColP in Jer. 10:9.

חשׁב || חשׁב

DtIsa: CanP in Isa. 40:15-17. MacP in Isa. 53:3+4.

Other: None, but see the parallelism in Gen. 50:20.

אפק || חשה

DtIsa: VrsP in Isa. 42:14.

Other: VrsP in sa. 64:12.

חרש || חשה

DtIsa: VrsP in Isa. 42:14.

Other: VrsP in Ps. 28:1.

פעה || חשה

DtIsa: StrP in Isa. 42:14.

Other: None.

מסתר || חשך, see also סתר || חשך

DtIsa: VrsP in Isa. 45:3.

Other: None.

סתר || חשך, see also מסתר || חשך

DtIsa: VrsP in Isa. 45:19.

Other: VrsP in Isa. 29:15; Job 34:22. See also the collocation in Ps. 18:12; Dan. 2:22.

רע || חשך

DtIsa: VrsP in Isa. 45:7.

Other: StrP in Isa. 5:20.

תהו || חשך

DtIsa: VrsP in Isa. 45:19.

Other: VrsP in Gen. 1:2.

נגה || חשכה

DtIsa: VrsP in Isa. 50:10.

Other: ColP (roots) in 2 Sam. 22:29; Ps. 18:28. VrsP (roots) in Isa. 13:10; 59:9; Amos 5:20. StrP (roots) in Isa. 9:1.

גזז || טבח

DtIsa: VrsP in Isa. 53:7.

Other: None, but see the collocation in 1 Sam. 25:11.

דשן || טוב

DtIsa: VrsP in Isa. 55:2.

Other: ColP in Prov. 15:30. VrsP in Jer. 31:14; Ps. 65:12.

חזק || טוב

DtIsa: VrsP in Isa. 41:7.

Other: None, but compare the collocation in Ezra 9:12; Neh. 2:18; 2 Chron. 19:11.

חסד || טוב

DtIsa: CanP in Isa. 55:2+3.

Other: ColP in Ps. 23:6; 63:4; 69:17. VrsP in Isa. 63:6; Jer. 33:11; Ps. 25:7; 86:5; 100:5; 106:1; 107:1, etc. StrP in Isa, 63:6; Mic. 6:8.

ישועה || טוב

DtIsa: ColP in Isa. 52:7.

Other: None.

ברר || טמא

DtIsa: StrP in Isa. 52:11.

Other: None.

טמא || טמא

DtIsa: MacP in Isa. 52:1+11.

Other: VrsP in Isa. 6:5. StrP in Ezek. 23:17.

־י || ־י

DtIsa: ColP in Isa. 49:1, 5; 51:5; 52:6. VrsP in Isa. 40:27; 41:8; 42:1, 8, 19; 43:7, 10 (2x), 21, 22, 23; 44:24, 28; 45:11, 23, 24; 46:10, 13; 47:6; 48:4, 5, 9, 12, 13, 20, 22; 50:2, 6, 7-8; 51:4 (2x), 5, 6, 7, 8, 16; 54:10; 55:8, 9, 11. StrP in Isa. 42:1, 8; 44:21; 45:23; 46:13; 48:11; 49:21; 51:5. CanP in Isa. 45:11+12; 48:9+11 (6x); 49:1+2+3+4, 5+6; 50: 8+9; 51:4+5; 52:4+5+6; 55:8+9. MacP in Isa. 50:7+9; 51:1+4+7.

Other: ColP in Isa. 21:10; Ps. 71:3, etc. VrsP in Gen. 49:6; Deut. 32:2; Isa. 10:5; 26:9; 28:23; etc. StrP in Isa. 12:2, etc.

אני || ־י, see ־י || אני

אנכי || ־י, see ־י || אנכי

־ני || ־י

DtIsa: VrsP in Isa. 43:24; 44:7, 17, 21; 49:1, 2, 21. StrP in Isa. 45:5. CanP in Isa. 48:18+19.

Other: ColP in Job 7:8. VrsP in Ps. 139:24; 142:5; 143:11.

לקח || יבל

DtIsa: CanP in Isa. 53:7+8.

Other: StrP in Hos. 10:6.

יבש || יבש

DtIsa: StrP in Isa. 40:7-8; 42:15.

Other: VrsP in Ezek. 17:9. StrP in Ezek. 19:12; Joel 1:12. See also the parallelism in Josh. 4:23.

נבל || יבש

DtIsa: ColP in Isa. 40:7, 8.

Other: None.

אנחה || יגון

DtIsa: ColP in Isa. 51:11.

Other: VrsP in Isa. 35:10 (quotation). StrP in Jer. 45:3; Ps. 31:10.

סחר || יגיע, see also סחר || יגע

DtIsa: VrsP in Isa. 45:14.

Other: None.

יגע || יגע

DtIsa: CanP in Isa. 40:30+31; 43:22+23+24; 47:12+15. MacP in Isa. 40:28+30+31.

Other: VrsP in Mal. 2:17.

כלה || יגע

DtIsa: VrsP in Isa. 49:4.

Other: StrP in Ps. 69:4.

כשל || יגע

DtIsa: VrsP in Isa. 40:30.

Other: None.

לאה || יגע

DtIsa: StrP in Isa. 47:12.

Other: None.

סחר || יגע, see also סחר || יגיע

DtIsa: VrsP in Isa. 47:15.

Other: None.

זרע || יד

DtIsa: MacP in Isa. 48:13+14.

Other: ColP in Deut. 4:34; 5:15; 7:19, etc. VrsP in Gen. 49:24; 2 Sam. 22:35 (= Ps. 18:35); Ezek. 30:24; Ps. 89:14, 22.

יד || יד

DtIsa: StrP in Isa. 45:11+12. CanP in Isa. 51:17+18, 22+23. MacP in Isa. 45:9+11; 51:17+18+22+23.

Other: VrsP in Isa. 36:20; Jer. 18:6; Ps. 90:17; 106:10, etc. StrP in Gen. 49:24; Isa. 25:11; Lam. 1:14, etc.

ימין || יד

DtIsa: VrsP in Isa. 48:13.

Other: VrsP in Judg. 5:26; Ps. 21:9; 26:10; 74:11; 89:14, 26; 138:7; 139:10; 144:11.

כח || יד

DtIsa: VrsP in Isa. 50:2.

Other: ColP in Exod. 32:11; Deut. 8:17. VrsP in Qoh. 9:10; Neh. 1:10.

נס || יד

DtIsa: VrsP in Isa. 49:22.

Other: StrP in Isa. 13:2.

נפש || יד

DtIsa: VrsP in Isa. 51:23. StrP in Isa. 53:10b-c.

Other: VrsP in Exod. 15:9 (rev.); Ps. 77:3; 143:6. StrP in Jer. 11:21. See also the collocation in Jer. 19:7; 20:13; 21:7; 22:25; Ps. 97;10, etc.

זמר || ידה Hif.

DtIsa: ColP in Isa. 51:3.

Other: VrsP in 2 Sam. 22:50 (=Ps. 18:50); Ps. 7:18; 30:5; 33:2; 57:10; 92:2; 95:2; 108:4; 138:1; 147:7. StrP in Ps. 71:22.

בין || אמן Hiph. || ידע, see also בין || אמן and בין || ידע

DtIsa: ColP in Isa. 43:10.

Other: None.

אמר || ידע

DtIsa: VrsP in Isa. 41:26. CanP in Isa. 40:.

Other: VrsP in Jer. 2:8; see also Ezek. 17:12; Ps. 32:5; 79:10.

בין || ידע, see ידע || בין

ידע || בין || ראה || שׂכל, see also ידע || ראה, שׂכל || בין and בין || ראה, שׂכל || ראה

DtIsa: VrsP in Isa. 44:18.

Other: None.

ידע || דעת, see ידע || דעת

ידע || ידע

DtIsa: VrsP in Isa. 42:16; 55:5.
StrP in Isa. 40:13-14; 47:11; 48:8. CanP in Isa. 41:22-23; 45:3+4, 5+6; 48:6+7+8. MacP in Isa. 40:13+14+21; 41:20+ 22+26; 44:9+18; 48:4+6+7+8; 49:23+26.

Other: ColP in Job 15:9. VrsP in Isa. 19:21; Ps. 39:5; 119:79. StrP in Isa. 1:3.

ידע || יכל

DtIsa: VrsP in Isa. 47:11.

Other: VrsP in Isa. 56:10.

ידע || לב

DtIsa: ColP, see Isa. 41:22. VrsP in Isa. 51:7, see also 42:25; 44:18, 19.

Other: VrsP in Ps. 36:11; Prov. 27:23.

ידע || נגד

DtIsa: ColP in Isa. 41:26. VrsP in Isa. 40:21; 41:22, 23. StrP in Isa. 48:6. CanP in Isa. 45:20+21.

Other: VrsP in Isa. 19:12. See also the collocation in Gen. 21:26; Lev. 5:1; 1 Sam. 20:9; 2 Sam. 1:5; 19:6.

ידע || קרא בשם

DtIsa: VrsP in Isa. 45:3, 4. CanP in Isa. 41:25-26.

Other: VrsP in Isa. 12:4; Ps. 79:6; 105:1; Qoh. 6:10; 1 Chron. 16:8. StrP in Jer. 10:25.

ידע || ראה

DtIsa: ColP in Isa. 41:20; 44:9. VrsP in Isa. 44:18.

Other: ColP in Isa. 6:9; Jer. 5:1, etc. VrsP in Jer. 2:23, etc. StrP in Isa. 58:3, etc.

ידע || שׂים לב

DtIsa: ColP in Isa. 41:22. VrsP in Isa. 42:25.

Other: None.

ידע || שׂכל

DtIsa: VrsP in Isa. 41:20; 44:18.

Other: ColP in Jer. 9:23.

ידע || שׁמע

DtIsa: ColP in Isa. 40:28; 48:8. VrsP in Isa. 48:6. StrP in Isa. 48:7. CanP in Isa. 42:(23+)24+25.

Other: ColP in 40:28; 48:8; Ps. 78:3; Ps. 81:6. VrsP in Isa. 33:13; Jer. 5:15; Ps. 143:8.

יהודה || אלהים

DtIsa: VrsP in Isa. 40:9.

Other: None, but see the collocation in Hos. 1:7; Zech. 10:6; Ps. 76:1, etc.

יהוה || אדני, see יהוה || אדני

יהוה || אל, see יהוה || אל

יהוה || אלהי ישׂראל

DtIsa: VrsP in Isa. 41:17; 45:3; 48:1; 52:12.

Other: None, but see the stereotyped phrase in Josh. 24:2, 23; Judg. 5:3, 5; Isa. 17:6; 21:17; 24:15; 37:21; Jer. 13:12; 21:4; 23:2; 24:5; 25:15; 30:2; Ezek. 44:2; Mal. 2:16; Ps. 41:14; Ruth 2:12.

יהוה || אלהים, see יהוה || אלהים

יהוה || גאל, see יהוה || גאל

יהוה || הוא

DtIsa: VrsP in Isa. 41:4.

Other: VrsP in Ps. 99:2, 5; 115:9; 148:5.

יהוה || יהוה

DtIsa: VrsP in Isa. 54:17. StrP in Isa. 40:5; 44:5, 23, 24; 45:18, 24-25; 51:3a-b. CanP in Isa. 40:3+5; 42:10+12; 43:14+15; 44:2+5;
45:5+6 +7, 18+19; 48:1+2, 14+16, 20+22; 49:7, 22+23, 25+26; 51:9+11; 52:11+12; 54:6+8; 55:6+7. MacP in Isa. 44:5+6; 45:5+6+7+8, 19+2; 49:23+26 (+ כי אני); 51:10; 55:6+7+8.

Other: VrsP in Exod. 15:3; Ps. 29:1, etc.

יהוה || יהוה צבאות, see also יהוה צבאות || יהוה אלהים

DtIsa: VrsP in Isa. 44:6.

Other: StrP in Isa. 14:22; Jer. 50:25, etc. See also the collocation in 1 Sam. 1:3; Jer. 19:3; 23:16, etc.

יעקב || יהוה

DtIsa: VrsP in Isa. 43:1; 44:5; 49:5. StrP in Isa. 40:27; 41:14, 21; 44:2.

Other: VrsP in Isa 2:5; Mal. 3:6. See also the collocation in Am. 8:7; Mal. 1:2; Ps. 20:2; 46:12; 84:9; 85:2; 132:2, 5; 146:5, etc.

ישׂראל || יעקב || יהוה, see also יעקב || יהוה and ישׂראל || יהוה

DtIsa: VrsP in Isa. 42:24; 43:1; 49:5. For StrP see also Isa. 40:27; 41:14; 44:5; 48:1.

Other: VrsP in Jer. 2:4; Nah. 2:3; Ps. 14:7; 22:23; 78:21. StrP in Jer. 31:7.

ישׂראל || יהוה

DtIsa: VrsP in Isa. 44:5; 45:25. StrP in Isa. 48:1.

Other: VrsP in Isa. 5:7; 30:29, etc. StrP in Isa. 4:2.

מושיע || יהוה

DtIsa: ColP in Isa. 49:26. VrsP in Isa. 43:3, 11. StrP in Isa. 45:21.

Other: ColP in Isa. 60:16. VrsP in 2 Sam. 22:42 (= Ps. 18:42). StrP in Hos. 13:4. See also the collocation in 1 Sam. 14:39.

מלך || יהוה

DtIsa: VrsP in Isa. 43:15. StrP in Isa. 41:21.

Other: ColP in Isa. 33:22; Ps. 10:16; 24:8; 29:10; 98:6, etc. VrsP in Ps. 47:2; 95:3, etc.

עבדו || יהוה

DtIsa: VrsP in Isa. 50:10.

Other: VrsP in Ezek. 34:24.

ציון || יהוה

DtIsa: ColP in Isa. 49:14; 51:3; 52:8. VrsP in Isa. 51:11.

Other: It is questionable whether this is a parallel pair in the strict sense of the word. See, however, Isa. 4:5; 14:32; 24:23; 51:3; 52:8; Jer. 50:28; 51:10; Joel 4:16, 21; Amos 1:2; Ps. 9:12; 87:2; 99:2; 102:17, 22; 110:2; 125:1; 126:1; 132:13, etc.

קדוש ישׂראל || יהוה

DtIsa: ColP in Isa. 43:15 (the suffix refers to Israel). VrsP in Isa. 41:14, 16, 20; 43:14; 45:11; 48:17; 49:7 (2x).

Other: VrsP in Isa. 1:4; 29:19; 60:9, 14; Jer. 50:29; Ps. 89:19.

יהוה צבאות || יהוה אלהים

DtIsa: VrsP in Isa. 51:15.

Other: StrP in Jer. 2:19. See the stereotyped phrase in Jer. 5:14; Amos 5:16; Ps. 80:5; 84:9, etc.

קדוש ישׂראל || יהוה אלהים, see also קדוש ישׂראל || יהוה and קדוש ישׂראל || אלהים

DtIsa: VrsP in Isa. 43:3; 55:5. StrP in Isa. 48:17.

Other: VrsP in Isa. 55:5; 60:9.

קדוש ישׂראל || יהוה צבאות

DtIsa: VrsP in Isa. 47:4. StrP in Isa. 54:5. CanP in Isa. 45:11+13.

Other: VrsP in Isa. 5:24. StrP in Jer. 51:5.

שׁרשׁ || יונק

DtIsa: VrsP in Isa. 53:2.

Other: StrP in Hos. 14:6-7; Job 8:16-17. See also the parallelism in Job 14:7-8 and compare Ps. 80:10 and 12.

יחדו || יחדו

DtIsa: CanP in Isa. 45:20+21; 52:8+9.

Other: None.

יטב Hiph. || רעע Hiph.

DtIsa: ColP in Isa. 41:23.

Other: ColP in Jer. 13:23. VrsP in Jer. 4:22; 10:5; Zeph. 1:12.

חלב || יין

DtIsa: ColP in Isa. 55:1.

Other: ColP in Song 5:1. VrsP in Gen. 49:12; Deut. 32:38.

לחם || יין

DtIsa: CanP in Isa. 55:1+2.

Other: VrsP in Deut. 29:5; Ps. 104:15; Prov. 4:17; 9:5; Qoh. 9:7; 10:19. StrP in Hos. 9:4. Often collocated in prose, cf. Gen. 14:18; Judg. 19:19; 1 Sam. 10:3, etc.

לאה || יכל

DtIsa: VrsP in Isa. 12b-13a.

Other: ColP in Jer. 20:9. VrsP in Job 4:2. StrP in Isa. 16:12.

גדל || ילד

DtIsa: StrP in Isa. 49:21; 51:18.

Other: VrsP in Judg. 13:24; Isa. 23:4. See also the collocation in Judg. 11:2; 1 Sam. 2:21.

גלמוד || ילד

DtIsa: VrsP in Isa. 49:21.

Other: StrP in Job 15:34-35.

זרע || ילד

DtIsa: StrP in Isa. 55:10b-c.

Other: VrsP (roots) in Isa. 57:4. StrP in Isa. 65:23; Ruth 4:12.

חיל || ילד

DtIsa: VrsP in Isa. 45:10; 54:1.

Other: ColP in Isa. 23:4; 66:7, 8; Mic. 4:10. VrsP in Deut. 32:18; Isa. 26:18; 66:8; Ps. 90:2. StrP in Isa. 66:8. See also the collocation in Isa. 13:8; 26:17.

צמח || ילד

DtIsa: ColP in Isa. 55:10.

Other: None.

שׁכולה || ילד

DtIsa: VrsP in Isa. 49:21.

Other: None, but see the collocation in Hos. 9:11-12.

נאץ שׁם || ילל

DtIsa: VrsP in Isa. 52:5.

Other: None.

אי || ים

DtIsa: VrsP in Isa. 42:10.

Other: VrsP in Ezek. 27:3. See also the collocation in Isa. 11:11; 23:2; 24:15; Jer. 25:11; Ezek. 27:3; Est. 10:1.

גל || ים

DtIsa: ColP in Isa. 51:15.

Other: ColP in Jer. 31:35; Ezek. 26:3. VrsP in Jer. 51:42; Zech. 10:11; 65:8; 89:10. StrP in Jer. 5:22; Jonah 2:4.

חול || ים

DtIsa: CanP in Isa. 48:18+19.

Other: VrsP in Deut. 33:19. Apparently break-up of the standard expression חול הים, cf. Gen. 32:13; Isa. 10:22; Jer. 33:22; Hos. 2:1.

ים || ים

DtIsa: StrP in Isa. 51:10. MacP in Isa. 51:10+15.

Other: ColP in Amos 8:12; Mic. 7:12; Ps. 72:8. VrsP in Exod. 15:4, 19; Isa. 23:4; Zech. 14:8. StrP in Josh. 24:6.

מדבר || ים

DtIsa: MacP in Isa. 43:16+19.

Other: VrsP in Num. 33:11; Ps. 106:9, etc. StrP in Isa. 16:8.

מים || ים

DtIsa: VrsP in Isa. 43:16; 51:10. StrP in Isa. 50:2c-d.

Other: VrsP in Exod. 15:10; Isa. 51:10; Ps. 77:20; 78:13; 93:4, etc. StrP in Isa. 17:12; 57:20; Ezek. 27:26, etc.

נהר || ים

DtIsa: VrsP in Isa. 48:18; 50:2.

Other: VrsP in Isa. 11:15; 19:5; 50:2; Ezek. 32:2; Nah. 1:4; Hab. 3:8; Zech. 9:10; Ps. 24:2; 66:6; 72:8; 80:12; 89:26; Job 14:11.

שׁמים || ים

DtIsa: CanP in Isa. 50:2+3; 51:15+16.

Other: ColP in Ezek. 38:20; Zeph. 1:3; Ps. 8:9, etc. VrsP in Jer. 33:22; Hos. 4:3; Hag. 2:6; Ps. 69:35; 96:11, etc.

ארץ || שׁמים || ים, see also שׁמים || ים

DtIsa: VrsP in Isa. 40:12

Other: VrsP in Gen. 1:26 (par.); Amos 9:6 (also with מי־הים); Hos. 4:3; Hag. 2:6; Ps. 69:35; 96:11; 135:6; 146:6. See also the collocation in Exod. 20:11; Neh. 9:6.

תהום || ים

DtIsa: VrsP in Isa. 51:10.

Other: ColP in Ps. 135:6. VrsP in Ps. 33:7; 106:9; Job 28:14; 38:16.

ימין || ימין

DtIsa: MacP in Isa. 41:10+13.

Other: ColP in Ps. 144:8, 11. VrsP in Exod. 15:6; Ps. 118:16. StrP in Zech. 11:17. See also the collocation in Gen. 48:13.

פנה || ימין

DtIsa: CanP in Isa. 45:1.

Other: VrsP in Zech. 3:1; Ps. 16:11; 44:4; Lam. 2:3.

שׂמאל || ימין

DtIsa: ColP in Isa. 54:3.

Other: ColP in Zech. 12:6; Prov. 4:27. VrsP in Isa. 9:19; Ezek. 16:46; 39:3; Zech. 4:3, 11; Job 23:9; Prov. 3:16; Song 2:6; 8:3; Qoh. 10:2.

טפח || יסד

DtIsa: VrsP in Isa. 48:13.

Other: None.

כון || יסד

DtIsa: CanP in Isa. 54:11+14.

Other: VrsP in Ps. 24:2; Prov. 3:19.

נטע || יסד

DtIsa: ColP in Isa. 51:16. MacP in Isa. 51:13+16.

Other: None, but see the collocation of the nouns מטע and יסד in Mic. 1:6.

יסף || יסף

DtIsa: MacP in Isa. 47:1+5.

Other: ColP in Qoh. 1:18. VrsP in Isa. 26:15. StrP in Gen. 8:21.

יעל || יעל

DtIsa: CanP in Isa. 44:9+10.

Other: VrsP in Isa. 30:5.

עור || יעף

DtIsa: StrP in Isa. 50:4.

Other: None.

אין אונים || יעף

DtIsa: VrsP in Isa. 40:29.

Other: None.

יגע || יעף

DtIsa: ColP in Isa. 40:28, 30. VrsP in Isa. 40:31.

Other: VrsP in Jer. 51:58; Hab. 2:13.

יעף || יעף

DtIsa: CanP in Isa. 40:29-31. MacP in Isa. 40:28+29+30+31.

Other: None, but. see the collocation of roots in Dan. 9:21.

כח || יעף

DtIsa: ColP in Isa. 40:29. VrsP in Isa. 44:12. StrP in Isa. 40:31.

Other: None.

כשל || יעף

DtIsa: VrsP in Isa. 40:30.

Other: None.

בין || יעץ

DtIsa: ColP in Isa. 40:14.

Other: ColP (roots) in Mic. 4:12; Job 12:13. VrsP (roots) in Isa. 3:3; Job 42:3; Prov. 8:14; 20:5; 21:30.

ידע || למד || יעץ, see also ידע || למד

DtIsa: VrsP in Isa. 40:14.

Other: None. For verse-line parallelism of ידע || יעץ see Job 26:3 and the collocation in Isa. 19:12.

יהוה || יעקב, see יעקב || יהוה

יעקב || יעקב

DtIsa: CanP in Isa. 44:1+2+5, 21+23; 49:5+6. MacP in Isa. 41:8+14; 48:12+20.

Other: VrsP in Mal. 1:2. StrP in Num. 23:23; Isa. 14:1; 29:22; Jer. 30:10; 46:27; Mic. 1:5.

ישׂראל || יעקב

DtIsa: ColP in Isa. 43:1. VrsP in Isa. 40:27; 41:14; 43:22, 28; 44:1, 21; 44:23; 46:3; 48:12; 49:6. StrP in Isa. 44:5. CanP in Isa. 49:5+6.

Other: VrsP in Gen. 49:24; Isa. 9:7; 27:6; 41:8, 14; 43:1, 22, 28; 44:1; Ps. 22:24; 78:5; 105:10, etc.

יהודה || ישׂראל || יעקב

DtIsa: VrsP in Isa. 48:1.

Other: StrP in Mic. 1:5.

יהוה || ישׂראל || יעקב,
see ישׂראל || יעקב || יהוה

ישרון || יעקב

DtIsa: VrsP in Isa. 44:2.

Other: None. Verse-line parallelism, however, is attested in S in Deut. 32:14-15.

עץ || יער

DtIsa: ColP in Isa. 40:23.

Other: ColP in Jer. 10:3. VrsP in Ezek. 39:10; Qoh. 2:6.

ברח || יצא

DtIsa: ColP in Isa. 48:20.

Other: VrsP in Job 14:2. See also the collocation in Jer. 39:4; 52:7.

גלה || יצא

DtIsa: VrsP in Isa. 49:9.

Other: VrsP in Job 12:22. StrP in Isa. 26:21.

הלך || יצא

DtIsa: VrsP in Isa. 52:12.

Other: VrsP in Jer. 6:25; Hab. 3:5. StrP in Exod. 15:22.

יבל || יצא

DtIsa: VrsP in Isa. 55:12.

Other: None.

יצא || יצא

DtIsa: StrP in Isa. 48:20; 52:11. CanP in Isa. 42:1+3; 52:11+12.

Other: ColP in 2 Sam. 16:7. VrsP in Judg. 14:14; Zech. 2:7; Prov. 30:33. StrP in 1 Kgs 20:18; Amos 5:3; Hab. 1:4.

יצא Hiph. || יצא Hiph.

DtIsa: MacP in Isa. 42:1+3+7.

Other: VrsP in Prov. 30:33.

מהר || יצא

DtIsa: VrsP in Isa. 49:17.

Other: None. See the collocation in Josh. 8:14.

עור || יצא

DtIsa: VrsP in Isa. 42:13.

Other: StrP in Jer. 25:32.

רעה || יצא

DtIsa: StrP in Isa. 49:9.

Other: VrsP in Song 1:8. StrP in Num. 27:17; 2 Sam. 5:2; Ezek. 34:13.

שׁוב || יצא

DtIsa: VrsP in Isa. 45:23; 55:11.

Other: ColP in Ps. 146:4; Job 39:4. VrsP in Ezek. 21:10; Job 15:13. See also the collocation in Gen. 8:7; 24:5; 31:13; Exod. 4:7, etc.

שׁלח || יצא

DtIsa: StrP in Isa. 55:11.

Other: None, but see the collocation in 1 Sam. 18:5.

עשׂה || יצא מפה

DtIsa: StrP in Isa. 48:3.

Other: ColP in Num. 30:3; 32:24. StrP in Isa. 55:11. See also the collocation in Judg. 11:36; Jer. 44:17.

שׁמע || יצא מפה

DtIsa: ColP in Isa. 48:3.

Other: VrsP in Josh. 6:10; Job 37:2.

יצק || יצק

DtIsa: StrP in Isa. 44:3.

Other: None.

אב || יצר

DtIsa: CanP in Isa. 45:9+10.

Other: VrsP in Isa. 64:8.

ברא || יצר, see יצר || ברא

חרשׁ || יצר

DtIsa: VrsP in Isa. 45:9.

Other: None, but see the collocation in Lam. 4:2; Isa. 30:14; Jer. 19:1.

יצר || יצר

DtIsa: StrP in Isa. 45:9, 18. CanP in Isa. 44:9+10. MacP in Isa. 43:1+7; 44:9+10+12, 21+24; 45:9+11.

Other: StrP in Hab. 2:18.

כון || יצר

DtIsa: VrsP in Isa. 45:18.

Other: None, but see the collocation in Jer. 33:2.

עשׂה || יצר

DtIsa: ColP in Isa. 43:7; 45:7, 9; 46:11. VrsP in Isa. 44:2; 45:7. StrP in Isa. 44:24. CanP in Isa. 44:21+23; 45:11+12.

Other: VrsP in Isa. 27:11; 29:16; 37:26, etc.

פעל || יצר

DtIsa: VrsP in Isa. 44:12; 45:9. StrP in Isa. 45:9, 11. MacP in Isa. 43:10+13.

Other: None.

אהב || יקר בעינים

DtIsa: VrsP in Isa. 43:4.

Other: None.

אמץ || ירא

DtIsa: StrP in Isa. 41:10.

Other: VrsP in Deut. 31:6; Josh. 10:25.

בטח || ירא

DtIsa: CanP in Isa. 50:10.

Other: ColP in Ps. 115:11; VrsP in Ps. 27:3; 40:4; 56:4, 11; 112:7; Prov. 14:16.

גיל || ירא

DtIsa: CanP in Isa. 41:14+16. MacP in Isa. 41:10+16.

Other: StrP in Joel 2:21.

חזק || ירא, see ירא || חזק

ירא || ירא

DtIsa: MacP in Isa. 43:1+5; 54:4+14.

Other: VrsP in Ezek. 2:6; Ps. 34:10; Qoh. 8:12. StrP in Isa. 57:11; Jer. 42:11; Mal. 3:16.

חרד || ירא

DtIsa: VrsP in Isa. 41:5.

Other: StrP in Jer. 30:10; 46:27.

חתת || ירא

DtIsa: VrsP in Isa. 51:7.

Other: ColP in Deut. 1:21; 31:8; Josh. 8:1; 10:25; 1 Sam. 17:11; Jer. 23:8; Ezek. 2:6; 3:9; 1 Chron. 22:13; 28:20; 2 Chron. 20:15, 17; 32:7. VrsP in Jer. 30:10; 46:27; Mal. 2:5.

כלם || ירא

DtIsa: VrsP in Isa. 54:4. MacP in Isa. 41:10+11+13

Other: None.

עזר || ירא

DtIsa: ColP in Isa. 41:13. StrP in Isa. 41:5-6, 10, 14; 44:2.

Other: None, but compare the parallelism in Ps. 115:11.

פחד || ירא

DtIsa: CanP in Isa. 51:12+13. MacP in Isa. 44:2+8.

Other: ColP in Ps. 91:5; Prov. 3:25. VrsP in Mic. 7:17; Ps. 27:1; 119:120.

קרב || ירא

DtIsa: VrsP in Isa. ad 41:5; 54:14.

Other: VrsP in Lam. 3:57. See also Exod. 14:10.

שׁמע || ירא

DtIsa: VrsP in Isa. 50:10.

Other: ColP in Deut. 19:20, etc. VrsP in 1 Sam. 12:14; 15:24; Hab. 3:2, etc. StrP in Deut. 13:5 (with parallels).

שׁעה || ירא

DtIsa: ColP in Isa. 41:23. VrsP in Isa. 41:10.

Other: None.

יצא || ירד

DtIsa: CanP in Isa. 55:10+11.

Other: VrsP in Ezek. 47:8; Mic. 1:3; Ps. 78:16. StrP in Ezek. 47:1.

ישב || ירד

DtIsa: ColP in Isa. 47:1. VrsP in Isa. 42:10.

Other: VrsP in Jer. 48:18; Ezek. 26:20. See also the canticle parallelism in Ezek. 26:16.

שוב || ירד

DtIsa: VrsP in Isa. 55:10.

Other: VrsP in Ps. 7:17. StrP in Deut. 1:25. See also the collocation in Josh. 2:23; 2 Kgs 20:11; Isa. 38:8.

היכל || ירושלם

DtIsa: VrsP in Isa. 44:28.

Other: VrsP in Ps. 79:1. See also the collocation in Ps. 68:30.

יהודה || ירושלם

DtIsa: VrsP in Isa. 44:26. CanP in Isa. 40:9.

Other: ColP in Isa. 1:1; Jer. 11:12, etc. VrsP in Isa. 3:8; 5:3; Jer. 1:15; 7:17, 34; 9:10; 11:6, etc. StrP in 40:9; Jer. 4:16. See also the collocation in 2 Kgs 21:12; 23:1, etc.

ירושלם || ירושלם

DtIsa: StrP in Isa. 52:9. CanP in Isa. 44:26+28; 52:1+2. MacP in Isa. 40:2+9; 52:1+2+9.

Other: VrsP in Zech. 12:6. StrP in Isa. 4:3; Jer. 3:17; 17:27; Zech. 1:16; 8:3; 12:2.

ציון || ירושלם

DtIsa: VrsP in Isa. 41:27. StrP in Isa. 40:9; 52:1a-b, 2. CanP in Isa. 52:7+8+9.

Other: VrsP in Isa. 2:3; 4:3, 4; 10:32; 62:1; 64:9; Ps. 51:20; 102:22. StrP in Jer. 51:35.

מיתר || יריעה

DtIsa: StrP in Isa. 54:2.

Other: StrP in Jer. 10:20.

ישב || ירש

DtIsa: VrsP in Isa. 54:3.

Other: ColP in Num. 33:53; Deut. 2:21; Deut. 19:1, etc. VrsP in Jer. 49:1; Ps. 69:36.

אלהים || ישראל

DtIsa: StrP in Isa. 40:27.

Other: VrsP in Jer. 3:23; Hos. 3:5; 14:2; Ps. 50:7, etc. See also the collocation in Jer. 31:33; Ezek. 14:11; 20:5, etc.

בבל || ישראל

DtIsa: StrP in Isa. 43:14.

Other: ColP in Jer. 51:49. VrsP in Jer. 28:2.

בנים || ישראל

DtIsa: StrP in Isa. 45:11.

Other: None, but see the VrsP of ישראל || בן in Hos. 11:1.

יהוה || ישראל, see ישראל || יהוה

אברהם || יעקב || ישראל

DtIsa: VrsP in Isa. 41:8.

Other: None, but see the collocation in Exod. 3:15, 16.

ישראל || ישראל

DtIsa: StrP in Isa. 41:14; 44:21; 48:1. CanP in Isa. 43:14+15; 44:1+5, 21+23; 45:3+4; 48:1+2; 49:7. MacP in Isa. 41:8+14+16; 44:1+5+6; 48:12+17.

Other: VrsP in Judg. 6:6. StrP in Deut. 32:51; Jer. 18:6; 32:30; 51:5; Hos. 5:3; Amos 4:12; Ps. 14:7; 53:7, etc.

ישרון || ישראל

DtIsa: CanP in Isa. 44:1+2.

Other: None.

כל־הארץ || ישראל

DtIsa: VrsP in Isa. 54:5.

Other: VrsP in Jer. 51:49.

מצרים || ישראל

DtIsa: StrP in Isa. 43:3. CanP in Isa. 45:14+15.

Other: ColP in Isa. 19:24; Ps. 105:23; 114:1, etc. VrsP in Isa. 19:25; Jer. 32:20; Hos. 11:1, etc.

עם || ישׂראל

DtIsa: CanP in Isa. 47:4+6.

Other: VrsP in Deut. 33:29; Isa. 1:3; Mic. 6:2; Ps. 50:7, etc. StrP in Isa. 11:16.

אין || ישׁ

DtIsa: VrsP in Isa. 44:8. CanP in Isa. 44:6+8.

Other: ColP in Prov. 13:7. See also the parallelism in Num. 13:20; Deut. 29:15; Judg. 4:20; 2 Kgs 4:2.

בוא || ישׁב

DtIsa: ColP in Isa. 47:5.

Other: ColP in 2 Kgs 19:27 (= Isa. 37:28) . VrsP in Ps. 26:4.

קום || בנה || ישׁב

DtIsa: VrsP in Isa. 44:26.

Other: StrP in Isa. 58:12. See also the collocation in 1 Kgs 8:20; 2 Chron. 6:10. VrsP of קום || בנה in Isa. 58:12; Isa. 61:4; Amos 9:11. ColP of בנה || ישׁב in Isa. 65:21, 22; Jer. 29:5, etc. and VrsP in Ps. 69:36.

חרבה || ישׁב, see ישׁב || חרבה

ישׁב || ישׁב

DtIsa: VrsP in Isa. 40:22; 47:1. StrP in Isa. 40:22; 42:11; 47:8. CanP in Isa. 42:10+11. MacP in Isa. 47:8+14; 49:19+20.

Other: VrsP in Ps. 29:10; 33:14; Jer. 50:39, etc.

ישׁועה || ישׁועה, see also
ישׁע (root) || ישׁע (root)

DtIsa: CanP in Isa. 52:7+10.

Other: VrsP in Isa. 12:2.

צדקה || ישׁועה, see also צדקה || ישׁע and
תשׁועה || צדקה

DtIsa: VrsP in Isa. 51:6, 8.

Other: VrsP in Isa. 56:1; 59:17; Ps. 98:2.

קום||ישׁועה Hiph.

DtIsa: StrP in Isa. 49:6, 8.

Other: None.

ישׁימון || ישׁימון

DtIsa: CanP in Isa. 43:19+20.

Other: None.

אביר || ישׁע

DtIsa: VrsP in Isa. 49:26.

Other: VrsP in Isa. 60:16 (quotation).

גאל || ישׁע, see ישׁע || גאל

זרוע || ישׁע

DtIsa: VrsP in Isa. 51:5. StrP (root) in Isa. 52:10.

Other: VrsP in Isa. 33:2. See also the collocation in Isa. 59:16; 63:5; Ps. 44:4; Ps. 98:1.

ישׁע || ישׁועה

DtIsa: MacP in Isa. 51:5+6+8.

Other: None.

ישׁע (root) || ישׁע (root), see also
תשׁועה || תשׁועה, ישׁועה || ישׁועה

DtIsa: VrsP in Isa. 45:17. StrP in Isa. 46:13. CanP in Isa. 43:11+12; [45:15-17, see our remarks Ch. 7.6]; 45:20+21; 47:13+15; 49:25+26. MacP in Isa. 51:5+6+8.

Other: ColP in Jer. 17:14. VrsP in Hab. 3:13; Ps. 20:7. StrP in Isa. 12:2; 25:9; Hos. 1:7.

מלט || ישׁע

DtIsa: StrP in Isa. 49:25. MacP in Isa. 45:22+46:2; 46:4+7.

Other: None.

נצל || ישׁע

DtIsa: CanP in Isa. 43:11+12+13; 47:13+14.

Other: ColP in Jer. 15:20; Ps. 7:2. VrsP in Isa. 19:20; Jer. 42:11; Ps. 31:3; 33:16, etc.

צדקה || ישׁע

DtIsa: VrsP in Isa. 45:8.

Other: ColP in Ps. 24:5, etc. VrsP in Isa. 59:17; 61:10; 62:1; Ps. 98:2l.

מישׁור || ישׁר

DtIsa: CanP in Isa. 40:3-4.

Other: None.

ך־ (f.s.) || ך־ (f.s.)

DtIsa: ColP in Isa. 54:5. VrsP in Isa. 41:14; 45:14; 47:3, 9, 10, 11, 12, 15; 49:16, 17, 18, 19, 20, 22, 23, 25; 51:19, 22, 23; 54:2 (2x), 7, 8, 9, 10, 11, 12, 13-14, 17. StrP in Isa. 40:9a-b; 45:14c-d; 47:9, 10, 11, 12-13a; 49:16-17, 19, 23a-b; 51:19; 52:1a-b; 54:2, 5, 6, 7-8, 12-14a. CanP in Isa. 41:14+15; 45:14 (6x); 47:12+13+15 (9x); 49:16+17+18 (8x); 51:19+20, 22+23 (6x); 54:2+3, 4+5, 6+7+8, 9+10, 11+12+13, 14+15.

Other: VrsP in Isa. 1:22, 26; 3:25; 29:3; Ps. 122:7; 147:13; etc. StrP in Lam. 4:22, etc.

ך־ (m.s.) || ך־ (m.s.)

DtIsa: VrsP in Isa. 41:9 (2x), 10 (2x), 13 (2x); 43:1, 2, 3 (2x), 4, 5, 23, 24, 25, 27; 44:2, 3, 22, 24; 45:4; 48:4, 5, 8, 10, 17, 18, 19; 51:16; 55:5. StrP in Isa. 41:9, 10, 11, 12, 13; 42:6; 43:1, 2, 3, 4, 5, 24; 45:4; 48:8, 9, 17; 55:5. CanP in Isa. 41:11-13; 43:1+2 (4x), 3+4 (4x); 45:2+3+4 (6x); 48:9+10, 17+18+19 (8x); 51:15+16.

Other: VrsP in Deut. 32:18; Judg. 5:4; Isa. 25:3; 26:20; Ps. 2:8; 5:8; 6:2; 21:2, etc.

אתה || ך־, see ך־ || אתה

כ || כ

DtIsa: VrsP in Isa. 40:15, 22; 41:2; 42:13, 19; 44:13, 22; 48:18, 19; 49:18; 51:3, 6, 8, 23; 53:2, 7. StrP in Isa. 40:15, 22; 42:19. CanP in Isa. 40:15-17; 41:11-12. MacP in Isa. 51:6+8.

Other: ColP in Gen. 49:9. VrsP in Deut. 32:2; Isa. 1:26; Ps. 18:21; Job 10:10, etc. StrP in Isa. 5:24; 17:5, etc.

כן || כ, see also כן || כאשר

DtIsa: StrP in Isa. 54:9.

Other: ColP in Isa. 38:13, 14. VrsP in Isa. 31:5; 66:13; Jer. 2:26. StrP in Isa. 61:11; 63:14.

כן || כאשר, see also כן || כ

DtIsa: VrsP in Isa. 52:14.

Other: ColP in Isa. 14:24; Ezek. 12:11; Ps. 48:9; Prov. 24:29. VrsP in Isa. 10:11; Jer, 13:11. StrP in Isa. 29:8; 31:4; 65:8; 66:13, 22; Jer. 31:28; Ezek. 20:36; Amos 3:12; Zech. 7:13, etc.

אהב || כבד

DtIsa: VrsP in Isa. 43:4.

Other: None.

כבד Pi. || ספר תהלה, see also תהלה || כבוד

DtIsa: CanP in Isa. 43:20+21.

Other: None.

עז || כבד

DtIsa: VrsP in Isa. 49:5.

Other: ColP in Isa. 25:3.

בשׂר || כבוד

DtIsa: StrP in Isa. 40:5.

Other: VrsP in Isa. 10:18; 17:4; Ps. 16:9.

תהלה || כבוד

DtIsa: VrsP in Isa. 42:8, 12. CanP in Isa. 48:9+11.

Other: VrsP in Ps. 66:2. See also the collocation in Neh. 9:5.

חפץ || אקדח || כדכד

DtIsa: VrsP in Isa. 54:12.

Other: None.

כה אמר יהוה || כה אמר יהוה

DtIsa: MacP in Isa. 43:14+16; 49:7+8, 22+25.*

Other: Frequent in distant parallelism.

כהה || כהה

DtIsa: CanP in Isa. 42:3+4.

Other: StrP in Qoh. 12:6.

בער || כוה

DtIsa: VrsP in Isa. 43:2.

Other: None.

שׁמים || כוכבים

DtIsa: VrsP in Isa. 47:13.

Other: VrsP in Isa. 14:13; Ezek. 32:7; Ps. 8:4; Job 22:12.

מוט || כון

DtIsa: ColP in Isa. 40:20.

Other: ColP in Ps. 93:1 par. VrsP of the roots in Ps. 104:5; Prov. 12:3.

כוס || כוס

DtIsa: StrP in Isa. 51:17b-c. MacP in Isa. 51:17+22.

Other: VrsP in Ezek. 23:33.

כוס חמה || כוס חמה

DtIsa: MacP in Isa. 51:17+22.

Other: None.

קבעת || כוס

DtIsa: ColP in Isa. 51:17, 22. StrP in Isa. 51:22b-c.

Other: None.

שתה || כוס

DtIsa: VrsP in Isa. 51:17, 22.

Other: StrP in Jer. 51:7; Hab. 2:16; Ps. 75:9. See also the collocation in Jer. 25:28; 35:5; 49:12; Ezek. 23:32.

כח || און, see און || כח

כח || כח

DtIsa: VrsP in Isa. 44:12. MacP in Isa. 40:26+29.

Other: ColP in Job 6:12. See also the collocation in Josh. 14:11; Dan. 8:24; 10:8.

עז || כח

DtIsa: MacP in Isa. 49:4+5.

Other: VrsP in Gen. 49:3; Job 26:2; Prov. 24:5.

עצמה || כח

DtIsa: VrsP in Isa. 40:29.

Other: ColP (roots) in Ps. 31:11 . See also the root parallelism in Deut. 8:17 and the collocation of the verb עצם and כח in Dan. 8:24.

כי || כי

DtIsa: VrsP in Isa. 40:2; 41:10; 54:4, 14. StrP in Isa. 40:2b-c; 43:2; 44:23; 49:19; 52:12. CanP in Isa. 43:1+2; 54:4+5; 55:10+11 (3x).

Other: VrsP in Gen. 49:7, 15; Isa. 59:16; Ps. 8:5, etc.

איש || כל

DtIsa: VrsP in Isa. 53:6.

Other: VrsP in Isa. 14:18; 56:11; Jer. 31:30; 32:19, etc.

כל || כל

DtIsa: VrsP in Isa. 40:4, 6; 45:23; 54:17. StrP in Isa. 44:11; 45:24-25; 49:18; 51:18; 52:10; 53:6; 54:12-14a. 17a. CanP in Isa. 40:4+5; 44:9+11; 45:12+13, 22+23+24.

Other: VrsP in Isa. 1:5; 2:12; 25:7; 56:9; Ps. 49:1, etc. StrP in Isa. 22:3; Lam. 2:15, etc.

בוא || כלא Hiph.

DtIsa: StrP in Isa. 43:6.

Other: None, but see the collocation in Exod. 36:6.

כל־ברך || כל־אפסי־ארץ

DtIsa: CanP in Isa. 45:22+23.

Other: None.

כלי || כלי

DtIsa: CanP in Isa. 54:16+17.

Other: ColP in Jer. 48:11. VrsP in Isa. 22:24.

לשון || כלי

DtIsa: VrsP in Isa. 54:17.

Other: None.

כלם || בוש, see בוש || כלם

כלם || הלך בכלמה, see also כלמה || כלם

DtIsa: StrP in Isa. 45:16.

Other: None, but see VrsP of כלמה || כלם in Ezek. 16:54.

חפר || כלם

DtIsa: ColP in Isa. 54:4.

Other: VrsP in Ps. 35:4. StrP in Ps. 40:14; 70:3.

יחד || כלם

DtIsa: VrsP in Isa. 44:11.

Other: ColP in Isa. 22:3 (2x); 31:3; 40:5; 43:9; Jer. 31:24; Ps. 14:3; 41:8; 53:4; Job 34:15; Zech. 10:4. VrsP in Ps. 33:15; 74:8; 88:18; Job 38:7, see also Josh. 11:5

StrP in Isa. 18:6; 45:16; Jer. 50:33; Mic. 2:12.

כלמה || כלם, see also הלך בכלמה || כלם

DtIsa: StrP in Isa. 45:16.

Other: ColP in Ezek. 16:54.

רקק || כלמה

DtIsa: ColP in Isa. 50:6.

Other: None.

־כם || ־כם

DtIsa: VrsP in 41:24; 43:15; 50:1; 51:2; 52:12; 55:3, 8, 9. StrP in Isa. 41:21, 24; 43:14; 50:1; 55:2, 3. CanP in 50:1; 55:2+3, 8+9.

Other: VrsP in Isa. 59:2; Ps. 115:14, etc.

כמו || כמו, see also כ || כ

DtIsa: VrsP in Isa. 41:25.

Other: ColP in Ps. 58:10. VrsP in Exod. 15:11; Ps. 29:6; 58:8 (?); Job 10:22. StrP in Job 12:3.

כן || כן

DtIsa: CanP in Isa. 52:14+15.

Other: VrsP in Isa. 10:7; Hag. 2:14.

יגיע || כסף

DtIsa: VrsP in Isa. 55:2.

Other: None.

כסף || כסף

DtIsa: StrP in Isa. 55:1. CanP in Isa. 55:1+2.

Other: VrsP in Qoh. 5:9. StrP in Ezek. 7:19; Mal. 3:3.

לחם || כסף

DtIsa: ColP in Isa. 55:2.

Other: VrsP in Qoh. 10:19. See also the parallelism in 1 Sam. 2:36.

מחיר || כסף

DtIsa: VrsP in Isa. 55:1.

Other: ColP in Job 28:15. VrsP in Mic. 3:11; Lam. 5:4. See also the collocation in 2 Sam. 24:24; 1 Kgs 21:2.

תחת || כפר

DtIsa: VrsP in Isa. 43:3.

Other: VrsP in Prov. 21:18.

שׁלח || כריתות

DtIsa: VrsP in Isa. 50:1 .

Other: VrsP (roots) in Ezek. 14:13. StrP (roots) in Ezek. 14:19, 21. See the collocation in Deut. 24:1, 3; Jer. 3:8 and the parallelism of roots in 1 Kgs 9:7.

כרע || כרע

DtIsa: CanP in Isa. 46:1+2. MacP in Isa. 45:23+46:1-2.

Other: VrsP in Judg. 5:27.

קרס || כרע

DtIsa: ColP in Isa. 46:1, 2.

Other: None.

שׁבע || כרע

DtIsa: VrsP in Isa. 45:23.

Other: None.

נטע || כרת

DtIsa: StrP in Isa. 44:14.

Other: None.

שׁמד || כרת

DtIsa: VrsP in Isa. 48:19.

Other: VrsP in Lev. 26:30; 1 Sam. 24:22; Isa. 10:17; Ezek. 25:7; Ps. 37:38.

כשׂדים || כשׂדים

DtIsa: MacP in Isa. 47:1+5; 48:14+20.

Other: None.

ממלכות || כשׂדים

DtIsa: StrP in Isa. 47:5.

Other: VrsP in Isa. 13:19.

רוץ || כשׁל

DtIsa: CanP in Isa. 40:29-31.

Other: ColP in Prov. 4:12.

כשׁפים || חבר, see חבר || כשׁפים

כשׁפים || כשׁפים

DtIsa: MacP in Isa. 47:9+12.

Other: StrP in Nah. 3:4.

כנה || כתב

DtIsa: VrsP in Isa. 44:5.

Other: None.

ל || אל

DtIsa: VrsP in Isa. 51:6.

Other: VrsP in Ps. 143:6; 145:15; Job 21:19; 34:18, etc.

ל || ל

DtIsa: ColP in Isa. 50:4. VrsP in Isa. 40:4, 29; 41:18, 27; 42:5, 6, 8, 16, 24; 43:6, 28; 44:14, 19, 26; 45:10; 449:4, 9, 20; 50:4, 6, 11; 51:8; 53:7; 54:12; 55:10, 13. StrP in Isa. 42:7; 44:28; 45:1b-c; 48:9, 11; 49:6, 21; 50:4; 51:14; 54:16. CanP in Isa. 49:5+6. MacP in Isa. 50:7+9; 51:6+8.

Other: VrsP in Gen. 49:11; Deut. 32:41; Judg. 5:26; Ps. 7:6; 75:5, etc. StrP in Isa. 2:7, etc.

לא || אין

DtIsa: VrsP in Isa. 40:28. StrP in Isa. 41:12; 45:5.

Other: VrsP in Isa. 5:27. StrP in Isa. 34:10; 41:12, 17.

לא || לא

DtIsa: ColP in Isa. 40:21, 28; 44:19aB; 49:10. VrsP in Isa. 40:31; 42:2, 3, 16, 20, 24, 25; 43:2, 10, 23 (2x), 24; 44:19; 45:19, 20; 46:7, 13; 47:7, 8, 11; 48:7, 19; 49:10; 50:5; 51:14; 52:12; 52:15; 53:2, 10; 54:1, 4, 5, 8, 10, 14; 55:1, 2. StrP in Isa. 40:28; 42:2-3 (4x), 16; 43:23; 44:18-19a; 46:7; 47:11; 50:7; 53:7. CanP in Isa. 43:22+23+24 (4x); 44:18+19+20 (8x); 47:5+6+7; 48:6+7+8 (7x); 53:2+3.

Other: ColP in Isa. 5:6, 27, 7:7; 11:9; Ps. 82:5, 121:5, etc. VrsP in Isa. 1:3, 7:9; Ps. 15:3, 60:2, 131:1, etc. StrP in Deut. 32:21.

לא || לא || לוא, see לא || לא

DtIsa: VrsP in Isa. 44:20. StrP in Isa. 42:24.

לא || לא || מן || מן

DtIsa: VrsP in Isa. 44:18.

Other: None.

לאם || אי, see אי || לאם

לאם || גוי, see גוי || לאם

לאם || לאם

DtIsa: VrsP in Isa. 55:4.

Other: See also the collocation in Gen. 25:23.

לב || יד

DtIsa: CanP in Isa. 40:1-2.

Other: VrsP in Ezek. 13:22; 21:12; 22:14; Ps. 58:3; 76:6; Job 31:27; Prov. 16:5; 17:16; 21:1.

לב || ידע || בין

DtIsa: VrsP in Isa. 44:19.

Other: ColP in Prov. 15:14; 18:15. VrsP in Prov. 14:33; 24:12. See also the collocation in Exod. 36:1.

לב || לב

DtIsa: StrP in Isa. 44:18-19a. CanP in Isa. 44:18+19+20.

Other: VrsP in Isa. 65:14; Jer. 4:9; 23:26, etc.

לב || נפש

DtIsa: StrP in Isa. 44:20.

Other: ColP in Deut. 28:65; Jer. 32:41; Prov. 14:10; 19:8. VrsP in Ps. 84:3; Prov. 2:10; 6:32; 27:9.

לבב || לב

DtIsa: CanP in Isa. 47:8+10.

Other: VrsP in Ezek. 28:6. StrP in Isa. 6:10. See also the collocation in 1 Sam. 6:6; Qoh. 9:3.

לבדי || מי אתי

DtIsa: VrsP in Isa. 44:24. See also the similar use of לבדי and מי in Isa. 49:21.

Other: None.

לבש || כסה

DtIsa: VrsP in Isa. 50:3.

Other: StrP in Ezek. 16:10.

לבש || לבש

DtIsa: StrP in Isa. 52:1a-b.

Other: ColP in Job 29:14. VrsP in Ps. 93:1. StrP in Isa. 59:17.

לבש || קשר

DtIsa: VrsP in Isa. 49:18.

Other: None.

בער || להט

DtIsa: VrsP in Isa. 42:25.

Other: VrsP in Ps. 83:14; 106:18. StrP in Mal. 3:19 (tr. 4:1).

פנים || לחי

DtIsa: StrP in Isa. 50:6.

Other: None.

אכל || לחם

DtIsa: ColP in Isa. 55:10. See also the collocation in Isa. 44:19.

Other: ColP in Gen. 3:19; Lev. 26:5; Am. 7:12; Ps. 14:4; 41:10; 53:5, etc.

דשן || לחם

DtIsa: StrP in Isa. 55:2.

Other: None, but derivatives of the same roots occur in VrsP in Isa. 30:23.

שׂבע || לחם

DtIsa: VrsP in Isa. 55:2.

Other: ColP in Exod. 16:3, 8, 12; Lev. 26:5; Ps. 78:25; 105:40; 132:15; Lam. 5:6, etc. StrP in Lev. 26:26.

לכן || לכן

DtIsa: StrP in Isa. 52:6.

Other: VrsP in Isa. 30:18; Ezek. 22:19.

דרך Hif. || למד

DtIsa: VrsP in Isa. 48:17.

Other: VrsP in Ps. 25:5, 9.

ידע || למד, see also ידע || למוד

DtIsa: VrsP in Isa. 40:14.

Other: VrsP in Judg. 3:2; 29:24; Ps. 25:4; Prov. 30:3. See also the collocation in Jer. 31:34.

ידע || למוד, see also ידע || למד

DtIsa: VrsP in Isa. 50:4.

Other: None.

למוד || למוד

DtIsa: StrP in Isa. 50:4.

Other: None.

ל || למען

DtIsa: VrsP in Isa. 55:5.

Other: VrsP in Ps. 8:3; 106:8.

למען || למען

DtIsa: ColP in Isa. 48:11. StrP in Isa. 43:25-26. CanP in Isa. 45:3+4; 48:9+11.

Other: VrsP in Isa. 37:35; 62:1; Jer. 44:8. StrP in Isa. 66:11; Ezek. 20:26.

אחרי || לפנים

DtIsa: VrsP in Isa. 43:10.

Other: VrsP in Gen. 32:21; Exod. 34:19; 1 Sam. 25:19.

לקח || לקח

DtIsa: CanP in Isa. 44:14+15; 47:2+3; 49:24+25.

Other: VrsP in Jer. 29:6. StrP in Ezek. 15:3.

מלט || לקח

DtIsa: VrsP in Isa. 49:24, 25.

Other: StrP in Job 1:15, 17.

שׂים || לקח

DtIsa: CanP in Isa. 51:22.

Other: VrsP in Ezek. 14:5; Job 22:22.

אזן || לשון

DtIsa: StrP in Isa. 50:4.

Other: None.

דבר || לשון

DtIsa: VrsP in Isa. 50:4.

Other: VrsP in 2 Sam. 23:2; Jer. 5:15; 9:7; 18:18; Mic. 6:12; Zeph. 3:13; Ps. 52:6; 64:4. See also the collocation in Exod. 4:10.

־ם || ־ם

DtIsa: ColP in Isa. 42:16. VrsP in Isa. 41:16, 17; 43:14; 47:14; 48:5; 49:10, 26; 50:9. StrP in Isa. 40:24, 26.

Other: VrsP in Gen. 49:7; Deut. 32:17, Isa. 5:24; 20:5; 41:17; Ps. 18:15, 38, 43; 37:40; 44:3, etc.

־מו || ־ם

DtIsa: VrsP in Isa. 48:21.

Other: ColP in Ps. 49:12. VrsP in Deut. 32:23, 38; Ps. 5:11; 21:10, 11; 55:16; 59:12; 80:6.

ארץ ציה || מדבר

DtIsa: VrsP in Isa. 41:18.

Other: VrsP in Ezek. 19:13; Hos. 2:5; Ps. 107:35. StrP in Jer. 2:6.

הר || מדבר

DtIsa: StrP in Isa. 42:11. CanP in Isa. 40:3+4.

Other: VrsP in Isa. 16:1; Lam. 4:19.

ישמון || מדבר

DtIsa: VrsP in Isa. 43:19, 20.

Other: ColP in Ps. 107:4. VrsP in Deut. 32:10; Isa. 43:20; Ps. 78:40; 106:14.

מדבר || מדבר
vspace0.1cm
DtIsa: CanP in Isa. 41:18-19; 43:19+20.

Other: VrsP in Ps. 29:8. StrP in Isa. 21:1; 64:9. See also the collocation in Exod. 15:22.

מים || מדבר

DtIsa: ColP in Isa. 41:18; 43:20 StrP in Isa. 50:2.

Other: ColP in Exod. 15:22; Isa. 35:6. VrsP in Ps. 107:35.

עדן || מדבר

DtIsa: ColP in Isa. 51:3.

Other: VrsP in Joel 2:3.

עיר || מדבר

DtIsa: ColP in Isa. 42:11.

Other: ColP in sa. 64:9. VrsP in Isa. 14:17; Jer. 4:26; 22:6; Ps. 107:4.

ערבה || מדבר

DtIsa: VrsP in Isa. 51:3. StrP in Isa. 40:3; 41:19.

Other: ColP in Jer. 50:12. VrsP in Isa. 35:1, 6; Jer. 2:6. StrP in Jer. 17:6; Job 24:5.

צמא || מדבר

DtIsa: StrP in Isa.50:2c-d .

Other: VrsP in Ezek. 19:13. StrP in Hos. 2:5.

קדר || מדבר

DtIsa: VrsP in Isa. 42:11.

Other: None.

שקל || מדד

DtIsa: StrP in Isa. 40:12.

Other: ColP (roots) in Lev. 19:35. VrsP (roots) in Job 28:25.

כול || תכן || מדד

DtIsa: VrsP in Isa. 40:12.

Other: None, but see the collocation of the roots תכן and מדד in Job 28:25.

מה || מה

DtIsa: VrsP in Isa. 45:10. CanP in Isa. 45:9+10.

Other: ColP in Zech. 9:17; Ps. 133:1. VrsP in Isa. 22:11; Hos. 6:4; Ps. 42:12; 43:5; 120:3; 139:17; Job 6:11, 25. StrP in Jer. 2:18, etc.

בוא || מהר

DtIsa: CanP in Isa. 49:17+18.

Other: VrsP in Jer. 48:16. StrP in Isa 5:19.

יסד || מוט

DtIsa: MacP in Isa. 54:10+11.

Other: VrsP in Ps. 104:5.

מוט || מוט

DtIsa: StrP in Isa. 54:10.

Other: None.

חבורה || מוסר

DtIsa: VrsP in Isa. 53:5.

Other: None.

שביה || מוסר

DtIsa: VrsP in Isa. 52:2.

Other: VrsP in Isa. 61:1.

מוט || מוש

DtIsa: VrsP in Isa. 54:10 (2x).

Other: None.

מוש || מוש

DtIsa: StrP in Isa. 54:10.

Other: None.

דכא || מות

DtIsa: StrP in Isa. 53:9-10a.

Other: VrsP in Ps. 143:3.

חלה || מות

DtIsa: StrP in Isa. 53:9-10a.

Other: None, but see the collocation in 2 Kgs 13:14; 20:1 (= Isa. 38:1; 2 Chron. 32:41).

חסר לחם || מות

DtIsa: VrsP in Isa. 51:14.

Other: None, but see antithetical connection between לחם || מות in Gen. 47:15, 19; Num. 21:5; 2 Kgs 18:32; Jer. 38:9.

מות || מות

DtIsa: CanP in Isa. 51:12+14.

Other: VrsP in Jer. 11:22; Ezek. 6:12.

פשע || מות

DtIsa: VrsP in Isa. 53:12.

Other: None, but see the connection between both words in Ezek. 18:31.

ארץ מרחוק || מזרח

DtIsa: VrsP in Isa. 46:11.

Other: None.

מערב || מזרח

DtIsa: ColP in Isa. 45:6. VrsP in Isa. 43:5.

Other: ColP in Ps. 103:12; 107:3. VrsP in Isa. 59:19. See also the collocation in 1 Chron. 7:28; 12:16.

מזרח, מערב || צפון || תימן || רחוק, see also רחוק || צפון

DtIsa: CanP in Isa. 43:5+6.

Other: None.

מחה || זכר, see זכר || מחה

גאל || מחה פשע

DtIsa: StrP in Isa. 44:22.

Other: None.

מחשבה || מחשבה

DtIsa: ColP in Isa. 55:8, 9. CanP in Isa. 55:8+9. MacP in Isa. 55:7+8+9.

Other: ColP in Isa. 59:7.

אור || מחשך

DtIsa: VrsP in Isa. 42:16.

Other: ColP in Isa. 5:20; Isa. 45:7; Ps. 112:4. VrsP in Isa. 5:30. See also the collocation in Gen. 1:4, 5, etc.

מעקש || מחשך

DtIsa: VrsP in Isa. 42:16.

Other: Compare the canticle parallelism in Isa. 59:8-9.

איפה || מי

DtIsa: VrsP in Isa. 49:21.

Other: VrsP in Job 4:7. StrP in Job 38:4-5.

מה || מי

DtIsa: VrsP in Isa. 40:18.

Other: ColP in Isa. 22:16. VrsP in Judg. 18:3; Job 38:6, etc. StrP in Isa. 10:3; Prov. 30:4, etc.

מי || מי

DtIsa: VrsP in Isa. 50:8; 53:1. StrP in Isa. 40:13-14; 42:19; 49:21; 51:19. CanP in Isa. 40:12+13+1414; 25+26. MacP in Isa. 41:2+4.

Other: ColP in Isa. 6:8; Prov. 23:29, etc. VrsP in Exod. 15:1; Isa. 14:27; 28:9; 53:1; 57:4; Ps. 15:1, etc.

אש || מים

DtIsa: StrP in Isa. 43:2.

Other: ColP in Isa. 64:1; Ps. 66:12. VrsP in Isa. 30:14; Joel 1:20; Prov. 30:16.

חלב || מים

DtIsa: StrP in Isa. 55:1.

Other: VrsP in Judg. 5:25; Joel 4:18; Song 5:12.

יין || מים

DtIsa: StrP in Isa. 55:1.

Other: None.

מים || מדבר, see מדבר || מים

מים || מים

DtIsa: VrsP in Isa. 41:18. StrP in Isa. 48:21. CanP in Isa. 41:17-18; 44:3+4. MacP in Isa. 43:16+20.

Other: VrsP in Exod. 15:27; Isa. 58:11; Ps. 29:3; 77:17; 107:35; 114:8, etc. StrP in Jer. 2:13, 18; Ezek. 19:10, etc.

נהר || מים

DtIsa: VrsP in Isa. 43:2, 20. MacP in Isa. 48:18+21.

Other: VrsP in Isa. 19:5. StrP in Num. 24:6.

נזל || מים

DtIsa: VrsP in Isa. 44:3.

Other: ColP in Jer. 18:14. VrsP in Exod. 15:8; Ps. 78:16; Prov. 5:15.

צמא || מים

DtIsa: ColP in Isa. 44:3; 55:1. VrsP in Isa. 41:17; 48:21; 50:2. StrP in Isa. 49:10.

Other: StrP in Ps. 63:1. See also the collocation in Exod. 17:3; Judg. 4:19; Isa. 21:14; 49:10; Amos 8:11; Prov. 25:21; Neh. 9:15, 20.

רוח || מים

DtIsa: StrP in Isa. 44:3.

Other: None.

בקעה || מישור

DtIsa: VrsP in Isa. 40:4.

Other: None.

יתד || מיתר

DtIsa: VrsP in Isa. 54:2.

Other: VrsP in Exod. 35:18; Num. 3:37. See also the collocation in Exod. 39:40; Num. 3:37; 4:32.

חלי || מכאב, see מכאב || חלי

נגע || מכאב

DtIsa: StrP in Isa. 53:4.

Other: None, but see the collocation of nouns in 2 Chron. 6:29.

גאל || מכר

DtIsa: VrsP in Isa. 52:3.

Other: ColP in Lev. 27:28. See also the parallelism in Lev. 25:25, 48; 27:20, 27.

מכר || מכר

DtIsa: CanP in Isa. 50:1.

Other: StrP in Joel 4:8.

פדות || מכר

DtIsa: MacP in Isa. 50:1+2.

Other: None, but see the collocation of verbs in Exod. 21:8; Lev. 27:27.

שׁלח || מכר

DtIsa: VrsP in Isa. 50:1. StrP in Isa. 50:1.

Other: VrsP (roots) in Ps. 105:17. See also the collocation in Gen 45:5; Deut. 15:12; 21:14; Jer. 34:14.

ישב || מלא

DtIsa: VrsP in Isa. 42:10.

Other: VrsP in Jer. 8:16; 47:2; Ezek. 12:19; 32:15; Ps. 24:1; 98:7.

לקח || מלא

DtIsa: StrP in Isa. 40:2b-c.

Other: None, but see the collocation of roots in Exod. 9:8; 16:33; Lev. 16:12.

רצה || מלא

DtIsa: VrsP in Isa. 40:2.

Other: None, but see the collocation of both verbs in 2 Chron. 36:21.

מות || בלה || מלח

DtIsa: VrsP in Isa. 51:6. The parallelism is comparable to that of Isa. 50:9.

Other: None.

ישׁע || מלט, see ישׁע || מלט

מלט || מלט

DtIsa: CanP in Isa. 49:24+25.

Other: VrsP in Ezek. 17:15; Am. 2:15; Ps. 124:7; Job 22:30. StrP in 1 Kgs 19:17.

גאל || מלך

DtIsa: VrsP in Isa. 44:6.

Other: None.

יועץ || מלך

DtIsa: MacP in Isa. 41:21+28.

Other: ColP in Job 3:14. VrsP in Mic. 4:9.

סגן || מלך

DtIsa: MacP in Isa. 41:21+25.

Other: VrsP in Jer. 51:28, 57.

שׂר || מלך

DtIsa: VrsP in Isa. 49:7.

Other: ColP in Isa. 10:8; Jer. 1:18; 2:26; 4:9. VrsP in Isa. 32:1; Hos. 7:3; Amos 1:15; Ps. 148:11.

שׂרה || מלך, see also שׂר || מלך

DtIsa: VrsP in Isa. 49:23.

Other: None.

מלקוח || מלקוח

DtIsa: CanP in Isa. 49:24+25.

Other: None.

שׁבי || מלקוח

DtIsa: VrsP in Isa. 49:24, 25.

Other: None, but see the collocation in Num. 31:12, 26.

מן || מן

DtIsa: VrsP in Isa. 41:9, 24, 25, 26; 42:7; 43:5, 6, 13, 21; 46:3, 10, 11; 48:3, 16, 20; 49:1, 12; 51:12; 52:14; 53:5, 8; 54:9, 14; 55:9. StrP in Isa. 49:1; 51:18; 52:11; 53:8; 55:9. CanP in Isa. 42:10+11; 43:5+6; 44:6+7+8; 46:9+10+11; 47:12+15; 48:3+5, 6+7+8; 54:9+10. MacP in Isa. 48:3+5+7+8 (all with אז); 54:15+17.

Other: VrsP in Ps. 114:1; 120:2; Job 18:16; Prov. 30:14; Lam. 5:14, etc.

עד || מן

DtIsa: CanP in Isa. 46:3+4.

Other: ColP in Isa. 9:6; 10:18; 38:12, 13; 59:21; Jer. 12:12; Ps. 41:14, etc. VrsP in Isa. 22:24; Ps. 71:17. etc.

לבונה || מנחה

DtIsa: VrsP in Isa. 43:23.

Other: VrsP in Isa. 66:3. See also the collocation in Lev. 2:1, 15; 6:8; Num. 5:15; Jer. 17:26; 41:5; Neh. 13:5, 9.

בית כלא || מסגר

DtIsa: VrsP in Isa. 42:7.

Other: None.

רב || מספר

DtIsa: StrP in Isa. 40:26.

Other: ColP in Job 38:21. VrsP in Ps. 147:5 . See also the parallelism in Lev. 25:16; Judg. 6:5; 7:12.

מוצא מים || מעין

DtIsa: StrP in Isa. 41:18.

Other: None.

מקבת || מעצד

DtIsa: VrsP in Isa. 44:12.

Other: None.

נסך || מעשׂה

DtIsa: VrsP in Isa. 41:29.

Other: None.

אין || מצא

DtIsa: StrP in Isa. 41:12.

Other: VrsP in Ezek. 26:21; Ps. 37:36; 69:20.

היה || מצא

DtIsa: VrsP in Isa. 55:6. StrP Isa. 41:12.

Other: VrsP in Isa. 35:9; Mal. 2:6.

צדקה || מצוה

DtIsa: StrP in Isa. 48:18.

Other: ColP (roots) in Ps. 119:172. VrsP in Deut. 6:25.

מלחמה || מצות

DtIsa: StrP in Isa. 41:12.

Other: None.

אשׁור || מצרים

DtIsa: VrsP in Isa. 52:4.

Other: ColP in Isa. 11:11; 19:23 (4x), 24; Hos. 7:11; 9:3; 11:5; VrsP in Isa. 7:18; 19:25; 27:13; Jer. 2:36; Hos. 11:11; 12:2; Zech. 10:10, 11. StrP in Isa. 10:24; 11:16; Jer. 2:18.

ישׂראל || מצרים, see ישׂראל || מצרים

סבא || כושׁ||מצרים

DtIsa: VrsP in Isa. 43:3; 45:14.

Other: None, but ColP of כוש || מצרים in Isa. 20:4; Nah. 3:9 and VrsP in Isa. 20:5; Ezek. 30:4; Ps. 68:32.

ישב || מקום

DtIsa: VrsP in Isa. 49:20.

Other: ColP in Jer. 19:2. VrsP in Isa. 5:8; Jer. 32:37; 51:62.

משכן || מקום

DtIsa: VrsP in Isa. 54:2.

Other: VrsP in Ps. 132:5; Job 18:21.

שחק || מר

DtIsa: VrsP in Isa. 40:15.

Other: None.

תאר || מראה

DtIsa: VrsP in Isa. 52:14; 53:2.

Other: ColP in Gen. 29:17; 39:6; Est. 2:7.

סוג || מרה

DtIsa: VrsP in Isa. 50:5.

Other: StrP in Ps. 78:56-57.

צבא || מרום

DtIsa: VrsP in Isa. 40:26.

Other: None, but see also the collocation in Isa. 24:21.

רחק || רחוק || מרחק, see also רחק || רחוק

DtIsa: MacP in Isa. 46:11+12+13.

Other: None.

נשא || משא, see also נשא || משא

DtIsa: CanP in Isa. 46:1+2.

Other: VrsP in Jer. 23:36. StrP in Jer. 23:33, 38.

עבד || משיח

DtIsa: MacP in Isa. 45:1+4.

Other: VrsP in Ps. 132:10.

דמה || משל

DtIsa: ColP in Isa. 46:5.

Other: None.

מלך || משל

DtIsa: CanP in Isa. 49:7.

Other: VrsP in Gen. 37:8; Josh. 12:2; Ps. 105:20.

רעה || משל

DtIsa: CanP in Isa. 40:10-11.

Other: CanP in Mic. 5:1-3.

עבד יהוה || משלם, see שלם Pu.

בזז || משסה, see בזז || משסה

משסה || משסה, see also שסה || משסה

DtIsa: CanP in Isa. 42:22+24.

Other: None.

ישועה || משפט

DtIsa: MacP in Isa. 49:4+6.

Other: VrsP in Isa. 56:1; 59:11.

משפט || משפט

DtIsa: CanP in Isa. 42:1-4 (3x).

Other: VrsP in Isa. 28:6; 58:2. StrP in Hab. 1:4; Ps. 99:4.

פעלה || משפט

DtIsa: VrsP in Isa. 49:4.

Other: StrP in Isa. 61:8.

צדק || משפט (noun)

DtIsa: CanP in Isa. 41:1-3; 51:4+5.

Other: ColP in Deut. 16:18; Isa. 16:15; 58:2. VrsP in Lev. 19:15; Isa. 1:21; 26:9; 32:1; Jer. 22:13; Hos. 2:21; Ps. 9:5, etc.

צדק || משפט (verb)

DtIsa: StrP in Isa. 50:8.

Other: ColP in Isa. 16:5; 58:2; Hos. 2:21; Ps. 89:15; 94:15; 97:2, etc. VrsP in Isa. 26:9; 32:1; Jer. 22:13; Ps. 9:5; 37:6; 72:2, etc. StrP in Isa. 1:21.

צדקה || משפט

DtIsa: CanP in Isa. 54:16+17.

Other: ColP in Isa. 9:6; Ps. 33:5, etc. VrsP in Deut. 33:21; Isa. 1:27; 28:17; Amos 5:7; Mic. 7:9; Ps. 36:7, etc. StrP in Isa. 5:7, etc.

תבונה || משפט

DtIsa: VrsP in Isa. 40:14.

Other: None, but see the collocation in of roots in 1 Kgs 3:9.

משפט || תורה

DtIsa: VrsP in Isa. 42:4; 51:4.

Other: ColP in Ps. 89:31. VrsP in Hab. 1:4; Mal. 3:22.

נא־ || נא־

DtIsa: CanP in Isa. 47:12+13.

Other: VrsP in Ps. 118:25. StrP in Gen. 50:17; Isa. 37:20.

נאם || נאם

DtIsa: StrP in Isa. 52:5.

Other: VrsP in Num. 24:3, 15; 2 Sam. 23:1; Isa. 14:22; Hag. 2:23, etc. StrP in Jer. 3:12; 23:24, 32; Zech. 2:10, etc.

נבט || נבט

DtIsa: CanP in Isa. 51:1+2.

Other: StrP in Hab. 1:13.

נבט Hiph. || ראה

DtIsa: ColP in Isa. 42:18.

Other: ColP in Isa. 63:15; Ps. 22:18; 80:15, etc. VrsP in Isa. 5:12; 22:11; 38:11; Hab. 1:3, 13; Ps. 10:14, etc.

נבל || נבל

DtIsa: StrP in Isa. 40:7-8.

Other: VrsP in Isa. 34:4.

נגד || אמר, see אמר || נגד

נגד || בשׂר

DtIsa: CanP in Isa. 41:26-27.

Other: VrsP in 2 Sam. 1:20.

נגד || ידע, see ידע || נגד

נגד || ידע || שׁמע

DtIsa: VrsP in Isa. 41:22.

Other: StrP in Gen. 21:26.

נגד || יעץ

DtIsa: VrsP in Isa. 45:21.

Other: StrP in Jer. 38:15.

נגד || ישׁע || שׁמע, see also נגד || שׁמע

DtIsa: ColP in Isa. 43:12.

Other: None.

נגד || נגד

DtIsa: StrP in Isa. 41:22, 26; 44:7; 45:21a-b. CanP in Isa. 41:22-23; 44:7+8; 48:3+5. MacP in Isa. 41:22+23+26; 43:9+12; 45:19+21 (3x).

Other: ColP in Jer. 20:10; 51:31. VrsP in Judg. 14:16. StrP in Gen. 24:49; Jer. 51:31.

נגד || נגשׁ

DtIsa: ColP in Isa. 41:22; 45:21.

Other: None.

נגד || עד (noun)

DtIsa: StrP in Isa. 43:12; 44:8.

Other: None. but see the collocation in Prov. 12:17.

נגד || ערך

DtIsa: ColP in Isa. 44:7.

Other: StrP in Ps. 40:6.

נגד || שׂים

DtIsa: ColP in Isa. 41:22. VrsP in Isa. 42:12.

Other: See also the collocation in Josh. 7:19; Ezek. 40:4.

נגד || שׁמע

DtIsa: ColP in Isa. 43:12; 44:8. VrsP in Isa. 40:21; 41:26; 42:9; 43:9; 45:21; 48:3, 6, 5, 14, 20. StrP in Isa. 45:21a-b.

Other: VrsP in Gen. 21:26; 41:22, 26; 42:9; 43:9; 45:21; 48:3, 5, 6, 14, 20.

נגד || שׁמע Hiph. || יצא Hiph. || אמר, see also נגד || שׁמע

DtIsa: VrsP in Isa. 48:20, cf. 48:3.

Other: None, but but VrsP of נגד || שׁמע Hif. || אמר in Jer. 4:5; 5:20 and StrP in Jer. 31:10; 46:14; 50:2.

נגד || שׁמע Hiph. || שׁמע Qal., see נגד || שׁמע

DtIsa: VrsP in Isa. 41:26.

נגה || יהוה

DtIsa: StrP in Isa. 50:10.

Other: ColP (roots) in 2 Sam. 22:29; Ps. 18:29. StrP in Isa. 60:19.

נגיד || פאר

DtIsa: CanP in Isa. 55:4+5.

Other: None.

נגע || נגע

DtIsa: MacP in Isa. 53:4+8.

Other: VrsP in Zech. 2:12. StrP in Isa. 6:7.

נגע || נכה

DtIsa: VrsP in Isa. 53:4.

Other: None.

נגע || ענה

DtIsa: VrsP in Isa. 53:4.

Other: None.

נגש || נגד, see נגד || נגש

נגש || דבר

DtIsa: ColP in Isa. 41:1.

Other: None, but see the collocation in Gen. 43:19; Deut. 20:2; 2 Kgs 5:13.

נגש || נגש

DtIsa: CanP in Isa. 45:20+21.

Other: VrsP in Mal. 1:8.

נגש || קרב

DtIsa: VrsP in Isa. 41:1. StrP in Isa. 41:21. CanP in Isa. 41:21-22. MacP in: Isa. 41:1+5.

Other: ColP in Jer. 30:21. VrsP in Isa. 65:5. See also the collocation in Lev. 2:8; Mal. 1:8.

נדף || רדף

DtIsa: StrP in Isa. 41:2c-3.

Other: None, but see the collocation in Lev. 26:36; Job 13:25.

־נה || ־נה

DtIsa: VrsP in Isa. 46:11.

Other: VrsP in Judg. 15:2; Isa. 7:6; Ps. 80:14; Prov. 2:4; 12:25. StrP in Isa. 27:3; Jer. 2:24; Ezek. 4:12.

נהג || נהל

DtIsa: VrsP in Isa. 49:10.

Other: None.

נהר || אגם

DtIsa: VrsP in Isa. 42:15. StrP in Isa. 41:18.

Other: None, but see the collocation in in Exod. 7:19; 8:1.

נהר || גל

DtIsa: VrsP in Isa. 48:18.

Other: VrsP in Isa. 11:15; 19:5; 50:2; Ezek. 32:2; Nah. 1:4; Hab. 3:8; Zech. 9:10; Ps. 24:2; 66:6; 72:8; 80:12; 89:26; Job 14:11.

נהר || ישימון

DtIsa: ColP in Isa. 43:20.

Other: None.

נהר || מדבר

DtIsa: ColP in Isa. 50:2. StrP in Isa. 41:18.

Other: ColP in Ps. 107:33.

נהר || מים, see מים || נהר

נהר || מעין

DtIsa: VrsP in Isa. 41:18.

Other: VrsP in Ps. 74:15.

־נו || ־נו

DtIsa: VrsP in Isa. 53:4, 5 (2x). StrP in Isa. 41:22; 53:5, 6. CanP in Isa. 53:4+5+6 (8x).

Other: VrsP in Deut. 32:31; Isa. 4:1; 17:14; 26:12; Ps. 4:7, etc.

נוד || נחם

DtIsa: StrP in Isa. 51:19.

Other: VrsP in Nah. 3:7; Ps. 69:21.

נוח Hiph. || עמד

DtIsa: ColP in Isa. 46:7.

Other: None.

נזל || יבשה

DtIsa: ColP in Isa. 44:3.

Other: None.

נח || נח

DtIsa: VrsP in Isa. 54:9.

Other: VrsP in Gen. 5:32; 7:9. See also Gen. 6:9; 7:13.

כסף || נחושה, see also כסף || ברזל

DtIsa: MacP in Isa. 48:4+10.

Other: VrsP in Isa. 60:17. See also the collocation in Exod. 25:3; Ezek. 22:18, 20, etc.

צדקה || נחלה

DtIsa: VrsP in Isa. 54:17.

Other: None.

גאל || נחם

DtIsa: VrsP in Isa. 52:9.

Other: StrP in Hos. 13:14.

דבר על לב || נחם

DtIsa: StrP in Isa 40:1-2a.

Other: ColP in Jer. 4:10, 11. VrsP in Isa. 65:18, 19; Jer. 8:5; 39:8; Ps. 125:2.

ירא || נחם

DtIsa: StrP in Isa. 51:12.

Other: StrP in Ps. 23:4.

נחם || נחם

DtIsa: ColP in Isa. 40:1. VrsP in Isa. 51:3.

Other: VrsP in Isa. 66:13.

רחם || נחם

DtIsa: VrsP in Isa. 49:13. MacP in Isa. 54:10+11

Other: StrP in Ps. 119:76, and of נחם Nif. || רחם in Ps. 106:45-46. See also the collocation of roots in Joel 2:13; Jon. 4:2.

שׂמח || נחם

DtIsa: CanP in Isa. 51:3.

Other: ColP in Jer. 31:13. StrP in Jer. 31:13.

שׂשׂון || נחם

DtIsa: CanP in Isa. 51:3.

Other: VrsP in Jer. 31:13.

נטע || נטה

DtIsa: MacP in Isa. 51:13+16.

Other: None, but see the collocation in Num. 24:6.

יסד || נטה

DtIsa: ColP in Isa. 51:13. MacP in Isa. 51:13+16.

Other: ColP in Zech. 12:1.

מתח || נטה

DtIsa: VrsP in Isa. 40:22.

Other: None.

עשׂה || נטה

DtIsa: VrsP in Isa. 44:24; 51:13. StrP in Isa. 44:13; 45:12 .

Other: VrsP in Jer. 10:12; 51:15.

צוה || נטה

DtIsa: VrsP in Isa. 45:12.

Other: StrP in Isa. 23:11.

רקע || נטה

DtIsa: VrsP in Isa. 42:5; 44:24.

Other: None.

שׁמע || נטה אזן

DtIsa: VrsP in Isa. 55:3. CanP in Isa. 55:2+3.

Other: ColP in Isa. 37:17; Jer. 7:24; 11:8; 44:5; Ps. 17:6; 45:11; Prov. 22:17. VrsP in Jer. 7:26; 17:23; 25:4; 34:14; 35:15; Prov. 5:13.

גדל || נטע

DtIsa: VrsP in Isa. 44:14.

Other: VrsP in Qoh. 2:4. See also the collocation in Ezek. 31:4.

זרע || נטע

DtIsa: ColP in Isa. 40:24.

Other: VrsP in 2 Kgs 19:29 = Isa. 37:30; Isa. 17:10; Jer. 35:7; Ps. 107:37.

יסד || נטע, see נטע || יסד

שׁרשׁ || נטע

DtIsa: VrsP in Isa. 40:24.

Other: ColP in Jer. 12:2.

אני || ־ני, see ־ני || אני

־י || ־ני, see ־ני || ־י

ני־ || ני־

DtIsa: VrsP in Isa. 43:24; 45:11; 46:5; 49:2, 14. StrP in Isa. 43:24; 49:2.

Other: ColP in Isa. 6:8; 65:1; Job 19:21.etc. VrsP in Judg. 14:13; 16:28; Deut. 32:21; Isa. 29:13; 38:12; 61:10; Jer. 10:24; 11:18; Job 6:9, etc. StrP in Isa. 22:4; 38:12; 65:1; Ps. 143:8, etc.

נכה || חלל

DtIsa: CanP in Isa. 53:4+5.

Other: VrsP (roots) in Ps. 69:27.

נכה || מרט

DtIsa: VrsP in Isa. 50:6.

Other: ColP in Neh. 13:25.

נכה || ענה

DtIsa: ColP in Isa. 53:4.

Other: ColP in Isa. 66:2.

נכה || רחם

DtIsa: StrP in Isa. 49:10.

Other: VrsP in Isa. 60:10; Jer. 21:7.

נסך || רקע

DtIsa: VrsP in Isa. 40:19.

Other: None.

נעורים || נעורים

DtIsa: CanP in Isa. 47:12+15.

Other: StrP in Ezek. 23:21.

נעצוץ || ברוש

DtIsa: ColP in Isa. 55:13.

Other: None.

נעצוץ || סרפד

DtIsa: VrsP in Isa. 55:13.

Other: None.

נער || בחור

DtIsa: VrsP in Isa. 40:30.

Other: VrsP in Jer. 51:22; Ps. 148:12; Lam. 2:21; 5:13. StrP in Lam. 5:13-14.

נפשׁ || יד, see יד || נפשׁ

נפשׁ || נפשׁ

DtIsa: CanP in Isa. 53:10+11+12; 55:2+3.

Other: ColP in Lev. 24:18; Deut. 19:21; Job 33:28. VrsP in Lev. 24:18; Isa. 58:10; Jer. 31:25; Ezek. 13:19; 18:4; Zech. 11:8; Ps. 86:4; 107:9; 131:2; Job 10:1; Prov. 13:4; 27:7.

נפשׁ || רוח

DtIsa: StrP in Isa. 42:1.

Other: VrsP in Isa. 26:9; Job 7:11; 12:10.

נצל || שׁוב Hiph.

DtIsa: VrsP in Isa. 42:22. StrP in Isa. 43:13.

Other: None, but see the collocation in Gen. 37:22; Num. 35:25.

נצר || קום

DtIsa: VrsP in Isa. 49:6, 8.

Other: None, but see the collocation of roots in Jer. 3:16.

נשׂא || גבה

DtIsa: ColP in Isa. 52:13.

Other: ColP in Isa. 57:7;. VrsP in Isa. 30:25.

נשׂא || משׁה

DtIsa: VrsP in Isa. 46:1.

Other: None, but see the collocation in Num. 4:15; 11:17; Deut. 1:12; 2 Kgs 9:25; Jer. 17:4, 27.

נשׂא || נשׂא, see also משׂא || משׂא

DtIsa: CanP in Isa. 46:3+4. MacP in Isa. 46:3+7

Other: VrsP in Ezek. 1:19, 21; Ps. 24:7; 93:3, etc. StrP in Ps. 126:6, etc.

נשׂא || סבל

DtIsa: ColP in Isa. 46:7. VrsP in Isa. 46:4; 53:4a. CanP in Isa. 53:11+12.

Other: None, but see the collocation in 1 Kgs 5:29; Neh. 4:11.

נשׂא || עמס

DtIsa: ColP in Isa. 46:1. VrsP in Isa. 46:3.

Other: See the collocation of roots in Neh. 4:11; 13:15.

פגע || נשׂא

DtIsa: VrsP in Isa. 53:12.

Other: VrsP in Jer. 7:16.

פוץ || נשׂא

DtIsa: VrsP in Isa. 41:16.

Other: None, but see the collocation in Ezek. 20:23.

רום || נשׂא

DtIsa: ColP in Isa. 52:13. VrsP in Isa. 49:22.

Other: ColP in Isa. 2:13; 6:1; 57:15; Hab. 3:10. VrsP in Isa. 2:12, 14; 13:2; 33:10; Prov. 30:13. StrP in Isa. 37:23.

שׁמע Hiph. קול || נשׂא

DtIsa: VrsP in Isa. 42:2.

Other: None, but see the collocation in Judg. 9:7.

שׁפל || נשׂא

DtIsa: VrsP in Isa. 40:4.

Other: VrsP in Ezek. 17:14; 29:15. See also the collocation in Isa. 2:12; 57:15.

נבט || נשׂא עינים

DtIsa: VrsP in Isa. 51:6.

Other: None.

ראה || נשׂא עינים

DtIsa: ColP in Isa. 40:26; 49:18. Other:

ColP in Isa. 60:4; Jer. 3:2; 13:20; Zech. 2:1, 5; 5:1, 5; 6:1.

רנן || (קול) נשׂא

DtIsa: VrsP in Isa. 52:8. StrP in Isa. 42:11.

Other: ColP in Isa. 24:14.

מכר || נשׁה

DtIsa: VrsP in Isa. 50:1.

Other: VrsP in Isa. 24:2.

שׁאף || נשׁם

DtIsa: ColP in Isa. 42:14.

Other: None.

רוח || נשׁמה

DtIsa: VrsP in Isa. 42:5.

Other: ColP in Job 34:14. VrsP in Isa. 57:16; Job 4:9; 27:3; 32:8; 33:4.

סערה || נשׁף

DtIsa: VrsP in Isa. 40:24.

Other: None.

יצא Hiph. || נתן

DtIsa: VrsP in Isa. 42:1.

Other: VrsP in Ezek. 11:9; 38:4. StrP in Ezek. 28:18

כלא || נתן

DtIsa: VrsP in Isa. 43:6.

Other: None.

נתן || נתן

DtIsa: CanP in Isa. 41:2; 42:5+6+8.

Other: VrsP in Ezek. 11:19; 16:34; Hos. 9:14; Zech. 8:12; Ps. 85:13. StrP in Isa. 56:5; Jer. 9:10; 26:6; Ezek. 4:2; 15:6, etc.

עשׂה || נתן

DtIsa: VrsP in Isa. 40:23. StrP in Isa. 48:11.

Other: VrsP in Ezek. 11:9; 36:27; Ps. 146:7.

רבה || נתן

DtIsa: VrsP in Isa. 40:29.

Other: ColP in Ezek. 37:26. VrsP in 2 Sam. 22:36; Ps. 18:36; Prov. 22:16. StrP in Hos. 2:10. See also the parallelism in Gen. 17:2; 26:4; 34:12; 48:4; Exod. 30:15, etc.

שׂים || נתן

DtIsa: StrP in Isa. 41:19. CanP in Isa. 49:8+11.

Other: VrsP in Isa. 61:3 (?); Ps. 66:9.

ירד Hiph. || נתן לפניו

DtIsa: VrsP in Isa. 41:2.

Other: None, but see the parallelism between ירד || נתן in Ezek. 31:14: 34:26; Joel 2:23 and the collocation in 1 Kgs 17:23; 2 Kgs 16:17.

שׁקה Hiph. || נתן מים

DtIsa: VrsP in Isa. 43:20.

Other: None, but see the collocation in Num. 20:8; 1 Sam. 30:11.

רוח/נתן נשמה || נתן רוח

DtIsa: MacP in Isa. 42:1+5.

Other: None.

סבל || נשׂא, see נשׂא || סבל

סבל || סבל

DtIsa: StrP in Isa. 46:4. MacP in Isa. 46:4+7.

Other: None.

שׁחה || סגד

DtIsa: ColP in Isa. 44:17; 46:6. VrsP in Isa. 44:15.

Other: None.

בושׁ || סוג אחור

DtIsa: ColP in Isa. 42:17.

Other: ColP in Ps. 129:5. VrsP in Ps. 35:4; 40:15; 70:3.

אל נגע || סור

DtIsa: VrsP in Isa. 52:11.

Other: VrsP in Lam. 4:15.

טמא || סור

DtIsa: VrsP in Isa. 52:11.

Other: ColP in Lam. 4:15.

יצא || סור

DtIsa: ColP in Isa. 52:11.

Other: None.

לבד || סור

DtIsa: VrsP in Isa. 49:21.

Other: None, but see the collocation in 2 Kgs 17:18.

סור || סור

DtIsa: ColP in Isa. 52:11.

Other: VrsP in Judg. 4:18; Isa. 14:25; Lam. 4:15. StrP in Job 15:30.

חרשׁ || סכן

DtIsa: StrP in Isa. 40:20.

Other: None.

הר || סלע

DtIsa: VrsP in Isa. 42:11.

Other: VrsP in 1 Kgs. 19:11; Jer. 16:16; Ps. 104:18.

נחם || סער

DtIsa: ColP in Isa. 54:11.

Other: None.

ראה || ספר

DtIsa: ColP in Isa. 52:15.

Other: VrsP (roots) in Job 31:4.

שׁמע || ספר

DtIsa: VrsP in Isa. 52:15.

Other: ColP in Ps. 66:16. VrsP in Ps. 26:7; 44:2; 78:3; Job 15:17.

הדס || סרפד

DtIsa: ColP in Isa. 55:13.

Other: None.

ישׁע || סתר

DtIsa: VrsP in Isa. 45:15.

Other: StrP (roots) in Ps. 27:9.

עבר || סתר

DtIsa: VrsP in Isa. 40:27.

Other: VrsP in Prov. 22:3: 27:14. See also the collocation in Isa. 28:15.

סתר פנים || בזה, see also עזב || סתר פנים

DtIsa: VrsP in Isa. 53:3.

Other: VrsP in Ps. 22:25.

רחם || סתר פנים

DtIsa: VrsP in Isa. 54:8.

Other: None.

ענן || עב

DtIsa: VrsP in Isa. 44:22.

Other: VrsP in Job 26:8; 37:11; probably also Qoh. 11:3 (cf. Avishur, *Stylistic Studies*, 682).

אהב || עבד

DtIsa: VrsP in Isa. 41:8.

Other: ColP in Jer. 8:2; Ps. 119:140. VrsP in Isa. 56:6; Ps. 69:36 .

עבד || בחר (root)

DtIsa: ColP in Isa. 43:10. VrsP in Isa. 41:8, 9; 42:1; 44:1, 2; 45:4.

Other: ColP in Ps. 78:70. VrsP in Isa. 65:9; Ps. 89:4; 105:6, 26; 1 Chron. 16:13. StrP in Hag. 2:23.

יגע || עבד

DtIsa: VrsP in Isa. 43:23, 24.

Other: None.

כבד || עבד

DtIsa: StrP in Isa. 49:5.

Other: None, but see the collocation in 1 Sam. 22:14.

מלאך || עבד

DtIsa: VrsP in Isa. 42:19; 44:26.

Other: VrsP in Job 4:18. See also the parallelism in 1 Chron. 19:2.

עבד (noun) || עבד (noun)

DtIsa: StrP in Isa. 42:19; 44:21. CanP in Isa. 41:8-9; 44:1+2(+5); 49:5+6. MacP in Isa. 44:21+26; 49:3+6.

Other: VrsP in Lev. 25:42; Isa. 65:13; Ps. 116:16; Qoh. 10:7. StrP in Isa. 65:13.

עבד (verb) || עבד (verb)

DtIsa: CanP in Isa. 43:23+24.

Other: VrsP in Josh. 24:15; Jer. 5:19; Mal. 3:18. StrP in Josh. 24:14; Jer. 27:7.

פעלה || עבד

DtIsa: CanP in Isa. 49:3+4.

Other: None, but see the collocation in Ezek. 29:20.

תולעת || עבד

DtIsa: MacP in Isa. 41:8+14.

Other: None.

בוא || עבר

DtIsa: VrsP in Isa. 41:3. CanP in Isa. 51:10+11.

Other: ColP in Isa. 10:28; 28:15. VrsP in Ezek. 20:37; Am. 5:5. See also the collocation in Josh. 24:11.

הלך || עבר

DtIsa: VrsP in Isa. 45:14. StrP in Isa. 43:2.

Other: VrsP in Josh. 24:17; Isa. 33:21; 35:8; Amos 6:2.

עבר || עבר

DtIsa: VrsP in Isa. 45:14. StrP in Isa. 51:23.

Other: ColP in Isa. 62:10; Ezek. 39:15. VrsP in Gen. 31:52; Exod. 15:16; Isa. 28:19; Ezek. 14:15; 29:11; 39:14; Mic. 2:13; Prov. 4:15; 26:17 StrP in Jer. 5:22; Ezek. 39:11.

שחה || עבר

DtIsa: CanP in Isa. 45:14.

Other: None, but for the combination in prose, see 2 Sam. 24:20 .

שטף || עבר

DtIsa: VrsP in Isa. 43:2.

ColP in Isa. 8:8. VrsP in Ps. 124:4. See also the collocation in Isa. 28:15, 18; Nah. 1:8; paired roots in Dan. 11:10, 40.

ידע || עד

DtIsa: VrsP in Isa. 44:9.

Other: ColP in Jer. 29:23.

נגיד || עד

DtIsa: VrsP in Isa. 55:4.

Other: VrsP (roots) in Prov. 12:17. See also the collocation of roots in Isa. 43:9, 12; 44:8; 45;21; Ps. 119:46.

עבד || עד

DtIsa: VrsP in Isa. 43:10.

Other: None.

עד (noun) || עד (noun)

DtIsa: StrP in Isa. 43:9c-10a. MacP in Isa. 43:9+10+12.

Other: VrsP in 1 Sam. 12:5; Prov. 14:5.

עד (prep.) || עד (prep.)

DtIsa: VrsP in Isa. 46:4.

Other: ColP in Isa. 62:7. VrsP in Exod. 15:16; Isa. 25:5; 57:9; Amos 8:12; Zech. 9:10; Ps. 13:2, 3; 57:11, etc. StrP in Isa. 6:11.

צוה || עד

DtIsa: VrsP in Isa. 55:4.

Other: None.

שמע || עד

DtIsa: VrsP in Isa. 43:9; 44:8. StrP in Isa. 43:12.

Other: ColP (perhaps) in Lev. 5:1. VrsP in Prov. 21:28.

ישב לבטח || עדין

DtIsa: ColP in Isa. 47:8.

Other: None.

גן־יהוה || עדן

DtIsa: VrsP in Isa. 51:3.

Other: None. ColP גן־אלהים || עדן in Ezek. 28:13. VrsP גן־אלהים || עדן in Ezek. 31:9.

טלה || עדר

DtIsa: VrsP in Isa. 40:11.

Other: None.

עוד || עוד

DtIsa: CanP in Isa. 45:5+6; 47:8+10.

Other: VrsP in Isa. 62:4; Jer. 31:4; Ezek. 14:11; 36:14, 15; 37:22; Job 7:10. StrP in Jer. 3:16.

שמע || עוד

DtIsa: StrP in Isa. 50:4.

Other: ColP in Jer. 6:10; Amos 3:13. VrsP in Jer. 11:7; Ps. 81:9. StrP in Ps. 50:7.

בטן || עול

DtIsa: VrsP in Isa. 49:15.

Other: None.

טלה || עול

DtIsa: StrP in Isa. 40:11.

Other: None.

זבח || עולה

DtIsa: VrsP in Isa. 43:23.

Other: VrsP in Jer. 6:20. Cf. Exod. 18:12; Lev. 17:8; Jer. 7:21; Ezek. 44:11, etc.

מנחה || עולה

DtIsa: StrP in Isa. 43:23.

Other: ColP in Jer. 14:12. See also the collocation in Exod. 30:9; 40:29, etc.

אז || עולם

DtIsa: CanP in Isa. 44:7+8.

Other: VrsP in Ps. 93:2.

אתה || עולם

DtIsa: StrP in Isa. 44:7.

Other: None.

דור דורים || עולם

DtIsa: VrsP in Isa. 51:8.

Other: None, but see the comparable VrsP דור ודור || עולם resp. דור || עולם לדור, in Deut. 32:7; Isa. 34:17; 58:12; 60:15; Ps. 33:11; 45:18; 49:12; 79:13; 85:6; 89:2, 5; 100:5; 102:13; 105:8; ColP in Ps. 106:31; 135:13; 145:13; 146:10; Prov. 27:24; StrP in Isa. 34:10; 61:4.

עולם || עולם

DtIsa: StrP in Isa. 45:17. CanP in Isa. 51:9+11. MacP in Isa. 50:6+8.

Other: ColP in Jer. 7:7; 25:5; Ps. 41:14; 90:2; 103:17; 106:48. VrsP in 2 Sam. 7:16; Jer. 23:40; Hab. 3:6; Ps. 112:6. See also the collocation in Num. 18:19; Ezek. 37:25, 26.

קדם || עולם

DtIsa: VrsP in Isa. 51:9. CanP in Isa. 46:9+10.

Other: VrsP in Deut. 33:15, 27; Ps. 77:6; 119:52; Prov. 8:23; Mic. 5:1.

חטא || עון, see also חטאת || עון

DtIsa: CanP in Isa. 53:11+12.

Other: ColP in Hos. 12:9. VrsP in Ps. 51:7, 11; 103:10.

חטאת || עון, see חטאת || עון

פשע || עון

DtIsa: VrsP in Isa. 50:1; 53:5. MacP in Isa. 43:24+25

VrsP in Isa. 59:12; Jer. 3:13; 33:8; Ezek. 18:30; 21:29; Ps. 32:5; 65:4; 89:33; 107:17; Job 7:21; 13:23; 14:17; 31:33; 33:9. StrP in Ps. 51:3-4 .

אור || עור

DtIsa: StrP in Isa. 42:16.

Other: None.

עור || חרש, see חרש || עור

עור || חשך, see also עור || מחשך

DtIsa: StrP in Isa. 42:7.

Other: ColP in Isa. 29:18.

עור || מחשך, see also עור || חשך

DtIsa: StrP in Isa. 42:16.

Other: None.

עור (adj.) || עור (adj.),

VrsP in Isa. 42:19. StrP in Isa. 42:19. CanP in Isa. 42:18+19 (4x).

Other: None.

עור (verb) || עור (verb)

ColP in Isa. 51:9, 17; 52:1. VrsP in Isa. 50:4. StrP in Isa. 51:9.

Other: ColP in Zech. 4:1; Song 2:7; 3:5; 8:4. VrsP in Judg. 5:12; Ps. 57:9; 108:3.

קום || עור

DtIsa: ColP in Isa. 51:17. CanP in Isa. 52:1+2.

Other: StrP in Judg. 5:12; Isa. 14:9; Ps. 7:7; Job 14:12.

קרא || עור

DtIsa: VrsP in Isa. 41:2, 25.

Other: ColP in Ps. 59:5. VrsP in Isa. 64:6.

ישועה || עז

DtIsa: CanP in Isa. 49:5+6.

Other: ColP in Ps. 140:8. VrsP in Exod. 15:2; Ps. 21:2; 28:8; 118:14. StrP in Isa. 12:2.

עזוז || עז

DtIsa: StrP in Isa. 43:16-17a.

Other: None.

תפארת || עז

DtIsa: StrP in Isa. 52:1a-b.

Other: ColP in Ps. 96:6 (see also Ps. 89:18). VrsP in Ps. 78:61.

נעורים || עזב

DtIsa: StrP in Isa. 54:6.

Other: ColP in Prov. 2:17.

עזב || סתר פנים, see also בזה || סתר פנים

DtIsa: StrP in Isa. 54:7-8.

Other: ColP in Deut. 31:17. StrP in Ps. 27:9.

עזב || עזב

DtIsa: CanP in Isa. 54:6+7.

Other: StrP in Jer. 16:11; 17:13.

עצב || עזב

DtIsa: ColP in Isa. 54:6.

Other: None.

קבץ || עזב

DtIsa: VrsP in Isa. 54:7.

Other: None, but cf. Neh. 13:11.

שאר לבד || עזב

DtIsa: MacP in Isa. 49:14+21.

Other: None.

שכח || עזב

DtIsa: VrsP in Isa. 49:14.

Other: VrsP in Isa. 65:11; Job 9:27; Prov. 2:17; Lam. 5:20.

שוב || עזב דרך

DtIsa: StrP in Isa. 55:7.

Other: None.

עזר || גאל, see גאל || עזר

עזר || חזק, see חזק || עזר

עזר || ירא, see ירא || עזר

עזר || עזר

DtIsa: MacP in Isa. 41:10+13+14; 50:7+9.

Other: ColP in Isa. 31:3. See also the collocation of roots in Dan. 11:34; 1 Chron. 12:19.

צדק Hiph. || עזר

DtIsa: StrP in Isa. 50:7-8a.

Other: None.

איש עצתו || עיט

VrsP in Isa. 46:11.

Other: None.

אזן || עין

DtIsa: VrsP in Isa. 43:8.

Other: ColP in Isa. 6:10 (2x); Ezek. 44:5; Prov. 20:12, etc. VrsP in Isa. 11:3; 32:3; 33:15; 35:5; 37:17; Jer. 5:21; Ps. 34;16; Ps. 92:12; 94:9; Job 13:1; 29:11; 42:5, etc.

לב || עין

DtIsa: VrsP in Isa. 44:18.

Other: ColP in Jer. 22:17; Ezek. 40:4; 44:5, etc. VrsP in Isa. 6:10; Ezek. 6:9; Ps. 36:2; 38:11, etc. StrP in Ps. 19:9, etc.

עין || עין

DtIsa: ColP in Isa. 52:8. CanP in Isa. 52:8+10.

Other: ColP in Lam. 1:16. VrsP in Isa. 6:10; Jer. 16:17; Ps. 123:2; Job 7:8; 24:15. StrP in Zech. 11:17.

ראה || עין

DtIsa: StrP in Isa. 52:10.

Other: None, but see the collocation in Isa. 40:26; 44:18; 49:18; 52:8, etc.

חצר || עיר

DtIsa: VrsP in Isa. 42:11.

Other: None. But see the parallelism in 1 Chron. 4:32. Collocation in Josh. 13:23, 28; 15:32; 16:9; 18:28; 19:6; 21:12, etc.; 1 Chron. 4:33; 6:56.

אל || על, see על || אל

את || על

DtIsa: VrsP in Isa. 54:17.

Other: ColP in Jer. 32:41. VrsP in Ps. 109:2. StrP in Jer. 21:2.

ב || על, see על || ב

ל || על

DtIsa: VrsP in Isa. 47:1.

Other: VrsP in Ps. 16:6; 33:22; 37:4; 103:10, etc.

על || על

DtIsa: VrsP in Isa. 44:3; 45:11; 47:11. StrP in Isa. 44:3 (4x); 47:11. CanP in Isa. 52:14+15.

Other: VrsP in Ps. 113:4; 133:2; Job 26:7; Prov. 7:3; 26:14.

תחת || על

DtIsa: VrsP in Isa. 46:7.

Other: VrsP in Gen. 1:7; 49:25; Job 37:3.

ירד || עלה

DtIsa: MacP in Isa. 55:10+13.

Other: ColP in Job 7:9; Prov. 30:4. VrsP in Deut. 28:43; Jer. 48:15; Amos 9:2; Jon. 2:7; Ps. 30:4; 104:8; 107:26; Prov. 21:22; Qoh. 3:21. StrP in Jer. 48:18.

כרת || עלה

DtIsa: StrP in Isa. 55:13.

Other: In this sense unique.

עלה || עלה

DtIsa: VrsP in Isa. 55:13.

VrsP in Judg. 13:20. StrP in Exod. 40:37; Jer. 46:8; Ezek. 26:3, etc.

רום || עלה

DtIsa: StrP in Isa. 40:9a-b.

Other: VrsP in Isa. 14:13.

אלמנות || עלומים

DtIsa: VrsP in Isa. 54:4.

Other: None.

על־כן || על־כן

DtIsa: StrP in Isa. 50:7.

Other: StrP in Isa. 24:6.

נעורים || עלמים

DtIsa: MacP in Isa. 54:4+6.

Other: None.

שׂכב || עלף

DtIsa: ColP in Isa. 51:20.

Other: None.

אי || עם

DtIsa: StrP in Isa. 51:5.

Other: ColP in Ezek. 21:3.

אלהים || עם, see עם || אלהים

זקן || עם

DtIsa: StrP in Isa. 47:6.

Other: VrsP in Ps. 107:32. StrP in Joel 2:16.

ירושלם || עם

DtIsa: VrsP in Isa. 52:9. StrP in Isa. 40:1-2.

Other: ColP in Jer. 4:10, 11. VrsP in Isa. 65:18, 19; Jer. 8:5; 39:8; Ps. 125:2.

לאם || עם

DtIsa: VrsP in Isa. 51:4.

Other: VrsP in Jer. 51:58; Hab. 2:13; Ps. 47:4; 67:5; Prov. 14:28; 24:24. StrP in Isa. 17:12.

נחלה || עם

DtIsa: VrsP in Isa. 47:6; 49:8.

Other: ColP in Ps. 33:12. VrsP in Deut. 32:9; Isa. 19:25; Ps. 28:9; 78:62, 71; 94:5, 14; 106:40.

עם (noun) || עם (noun)

DtIsa: StrP in Isa. 51:4. CanP in Isa. 42:5+6; 43:20+21; 51:4+5; 52:4+5+6. MacP in Isa. 40:1+7; 49:8+13; 52:4+5+6+9.

Other: VrsP in Exod. 15:16; 2 Sam. 22:44 (= Ps. 18:44); Isa. 18:7; 33:19; Ps. 29:11; 67:4, 6, etc. StrP in Deut. 32:43; Isa. 3:12, etc.

עני || עם

DtIsa: VrsP in Isa. 49:13.

Other: VrsP in Isa. 3:15; Ps. 72:2. Cf. collocation in Exod. 3:7; 4:31; Isa. 10:2; 14:32; Zeph. 3:12; Ps. 18:28; Ps. 72:4.

ישע || עמד

DtIsa: ColP in Isa. 47:13.

VrsP in Ps. 109:31.

מוש || עמד

DtIsa: VrsP in Isa. 46:7.

Other: None.

נגש || עמד

DtIsa: VrsP in Isa. 50:8.

Other: VrsP in Exod. 20:21.

עמד || עמד

DtIsa: CanP in Isa. 47:12+13.

Other: ColP in Ezek. 1:21; 10:17; Nah. 2:9. VrsP in Zech. 3:1; Ps. 38:12. StrP in Isa. 66:22.

קבץ || עמד

DtIsa: ColP in Isa. 40:11. CanP in Isa. 48:13+14.

Other: None.

משׂא || עמס, see also נשׂא || עמס

DtIsa: VrsP in Isa. 46:1.

Other: None, but see the collocation in Neh. 13:15.

נשׂא || עמס, see נשׂא || עמס

דכא || ענה

DtIsa: CanP in Isa. 53:4+5.

Other: VrsP in Ps. 94:5.

חלה || ענה

DtIsa: CanP in Isa. 53:7+10.

Other: None, but see the collocation in Ps. 35:13.

ישע || ענה

DtIsa: VrsP in Isa. 46:7.

Other: ColP in Ps. 65:6; 108:7. VrsP in Ps. 69:14; rev. in Ps. 18:42; 20:7, 10; 60:7. StrP in Zech. 10:6.

לא עזב || ענה

DtIsa: VrsP in Isa. 41:17.

Other: None.

עזר || ענה

DtIsa: VrsP in Isa. 49:8.

Other: StrP in Ps. 20:2-3.

ענה || ענה

DtIsa: MacP in Isa. 53:4+7.

Other: ColP in Num. 24:24. VrsP in Nah. 1:12.

אביון || עני

DtIsa: ColP in Isa. 41:17.

Other: ColP in Ezek. 18:12; 22:29; Ps. 12:6; 35:10; 37:14, etc. VrsP in Amos 8:4; Ps. 9:19; 35:10, etc.

עשק || עני

DtIsa: MacP in Isa. 54:11+14.

Other: ColP in Zech. 7:10. VrsP in Ezek. 22:29; Ps. 72:4.

ארץ || עפר

DtIsa: VrsP in Isa. 47:1; 49:23.

Other: ColP in Isa. 25:12. VrsP in Isa. 26:5; 29:4; 34:7; Ps. 7:6; 44:26; Job 14:8; 39:14;Prov. 8:26.

קש || עפר

DtIsa: VrsP in Isa. 41:2.

Other: None.

ברוש, הדס || עץ, see also ברוש || הדס

DtIsa: CanP in Isa. 55:12+13.

Other: None, but see the collocation in 2 Sam. 6:5; 1 Kgs 5:22, 24; 6:34, etc.; see also Isa. 41:19.

פסל || עץ

DtIsa: StrP in Isa. 40:20.

Other: None.

נסך || עצב

DtIsa: VrsP in Isa. 48:5.

ColP in 2 Chron. 34:3, 4.

נשואה || עצב

DtIsa: StrP in Isa. 46:1.

Other: None.

פסל || עצב

DtIsa: VrsP in Isa. 48:5.

Other: VrsP in Mic. 1:7. StrP in Isa. 10:10-11.

חפץ || עצה

DtIsa: StrP in Isa. 40:13-14. VrsP in Isa. 46:10.

Other: None.

יעץ || עצה

DtIsa:

Other: ColP in Isa. 14:26; Jer. 49:30; Ezek. 11:2. VrsP in Isa. 19:11, 17; Jer. 49:20; 50:45. See also the collocation in 2Sam. 16:23; 17:7; 1Kings 1:12; 12:8, 13; 2 Chron. 10:8.

עצה || עצה

DtIsa: CanP in Isa. 46:10+11.

Other: None.

תבונה || עצה

DtIsa: StrP in Isa. 40:13-14.

Other: ColP in Job. 12:13. VrsP in Deut. 32:28; Prov. 20:5; 21:30.

פשע || עצום

DtIsa: StrP in Isa. 53:12.

Other: None, but see the collocation in Amos 5:12.

שיח || עצר

DtIsa: VrsP in Isa. 53:8.

Other: None.

מישור || עקב

DtIsa: ColP in Isa. 40:4.

Other: None.

רכס || עקב

DtIsa: VrsP in Isa. 40:4.

Other: None.

שמם || עקר

DtIsa: StrP in Isa. 54:1.

Other: VrsP (roots) in Zeph. 2:4.

ילד || עקרה

DtIsa: ColP in Isa. 54:1.

Other: ColP in Judg. 13:2, 3; 1 Sam. 2:5; Job 24:21.

אלמנות || עקרה לא ילדה

DtIsa: MacP in Isa. 54:1+4.

Other: Almost identical VrsP of אלמנה || עקרה לא תלד in Job 24:21.

ישר || עקש

DtIsa: ColP in Isa. 42:16.

Other: ColP in Mic. 3:9.

נשא || ערה

DtIsa: VrsP in Isa. 53:12.

Other: VrsP in Isa. 22:6.

חרפה || ערוה

DtIsa: VrsP in Isa. 47:3.

Other: None.

טמא || ערל

DtIsa: ColP in Isa. 52:1.

Other: None.

מצח || ערף

DtIsa: VrsP in Isa. 48:4.

Other: None.

קשה || ערף

DtIsa: VrsP in Isa. 48:4.

Other: None. See, however, the stereotyped phrase in Exod. 32:9; 33:3, 5; 34:9; Deut. 9:6; 10:16; 31:27; 2 Kgs 17:14; Jer. 7:26; 17:23; 19:15; Prov. 29:1; Neh. 9:16, 17, 291 2 Chron. 30:8; 36:13.

בוא || עשה, see עשה || בוא

ברא || עשה, see עשה || ברא

גאל || עשה, see עשה || גאל

חלל || עשה

DtIsa: VrsP in Isa. 48:11.

Other: VrsP in Isa. 56:2; Ezek. 20:14, 22; 23:39. StrP in Mal. 2:11.

יסד || עשה

DtIsa: VrsP in Isa. 51:13.

Other: None.

יצר || עשה, see עשה || יצר

כון || עשה

DtIsa: ColP in Isa. 45:18. StrP in Isa. 51:13.

ColP in Deut. 32:6; Ps. 119:73 . VrsP in Jer. 10:12; 33:2; 51:15; Job 31:15; Prov. 20:8. StrP in Ps. 99:4.

נטה || עשה, see עשה || נטה

נתן || עשה, see עשה || נתן

עזב || עשה

DtIsa: ColP in Isa. 42:16.

Other: VrsP in Isa. 58:2; Jer. 2:13, 17. See also Gen. 28:15.

עשה || עשה

DtIsa: StrP in Isa. 46:10. CanP in Isa. 44:13a-c; 46:10+11; 48:3+5. MacP in Isa. 44:13+15+17, 23+24; 46:4+6.

Other: VrsP in Isa. 5:2, 4; 27:5; Prov. 24:29, etc. StrP in Isa. 5:10; 10:11, etc.

פעל || עשה

DtIsa: ColP in Isa. 41:4. VrsP in Isa. 44:15; 45:9.

Other: VrsP in Jer. 50:29; Job 35:6; Prov. 21:15; 24:29. StrP in Mic. 2:1.

צוה || עשה

DtIsa: VrsP in Isa. 48:5. StrP in Isa. 45:12.

Other: None, but often in collocation.

צלח || עשה

DtIsa: VrsP in Isa. 55:11.

Other: ColP in Ps. 1:3; Dan. 8:12, etc. VrsP in Gen. 39:3; Ps. 37:7; Dan. 11:36, etc.

שים || עשה

DtIsa: StrP in Isa. 43:19.

Other: VrsP in Ezek. 39:21. StrP in Jer. 7:30.

סס || עש

DtIsa: VrsP in Isa. 51:8.

Other: None.

מרמה || עשיר

DtIsa: StrP in Isa. 53:9-10a.

Other: VrsP (roots) in Jer. 5:27.

כן || בגד || עשן

DtIsa: VrsP in Isa. 51:6.

Other: None.

מחתה || עשק

DtIsa: VrsP in Isa. 54:14.

Other: None.

יום || עת

DtIsa: VrsP in Isa. 49:8.

Other: ColP in Jer. 33:15; 50:4, 20. VrsP in Isa. 13:22; Jer. 46:21; 50:31; Ezek. 7:7, 12; 12:27; 21:30; 30:3; Ps. 37:19; Job 24:1; 38:23; Prov. 8:30. StrP in Jer. 30:7; Zech. 14:7.

עתה || עת

DtIsa: StrP in Isa. 48:16.

Other: None.

אז || עתה, see עתה || אז

יום || עתה

VrsP in Isa. 48:7.

Other: ColP in Jer. 40:4. VrsP in Ezek. 26:18; Hag. 2:15.

עתה || עתה

DtIsa: CanP in Isa. 48:6+7.

Other: VrsP in Isa. 29:22; 33:10.

נצל || פדה

DtIsa: VrsP in Isa. 50:2.

Other: VrsP in Jer. 15:21.

יד || פה

DtIsa: VrsP in Isa. 49:2; 51:16.

Other: ColP in Prov. 8:3; 12:14; 26:9. VrsP in Isa. 51:16; Jer. 1:9; 44:25; Ps. 144:11; Job 5:15. See also the collocation in Ezek. 33:22.

פה || פה

DtIsa: StrP in Isa. 53:7. CanP in Isa. 53:7+9.

Other: None. ColP in Ps. 109:2; Isa. 59:21. VrsP in Exod. 4:15; Prov. 6:2; 10:11; Qoh. 10:13, etc.

ספיר || פוך

DtIsa: VrsP in Isa. 54:11.

Other: None.

בוש || פחד

DtIsa: ColP in Isa. 44:11.

Other: None.

רהה || פחד

DtIsa: ColP in Isa. 44:8.

Other: None.

פעם || פטיש

DtIsa: ColP in Isa. 41:7.

Other: None.

ישע || פליט

DtIsa: StrP in Isa. 45:20.

Other: None, but see the VrsP of the verbs in Ps. 37:40; 71:2.

אמר || פלל

DtIsa: VrsP in Isa. 44:17.

Other: None, but see the collocation in Jon. 4:2.

שחה || פלל

DtIsa: ColP in Isa. 44:17. VrsP in Isa. 45:14.

Other: None.

מאזנים || פלס

DtIsa: VrsP in Isa. 40:12.

Other: ColP in Prov. 16:11.

ישע || פנה (root)

DtIsa: ColP in Isa. 45:22.

Other: StrP in Ps. 86:16.

ישר || פנה

DtIsa: StrP in Isa. 40:3. Compare Isa. 45:2.

Other: None.

מתנים || פנים

DtIsa: VrsP in Isa. 45:1.

Other: VrsP in Nah. 2:11.

פנים || פנים

DtIsa: StrP in Isa. 45:1b-c. CanP in Isa. 50:6+7.

Other: ColP in Prov. 27:9. VrsP in Deut. 28:50; Judg. 5:5; Isa. 21:15; 30:17; Jer. 1:17; Ps. 142:3; Job 23:7, etc. StrP in Isa. 21:15; Ezek. 15:7; Mic. 2:13; Ps. 68:9; Lam. 4:16, etc.

אל || פסל (noun), see אל (noun) || פסל

אלהים || פסל

DtIsa: VrsP in Isa. 42:17. CanP in Isa. 45:20+21.

Other: StrP in Ps. 79:7. See also the collocation in Nah. 1:14.

מסכה || פסל

DtIsa: VrsP in Isa. 42:17.

Other: ColP in Nah. 1:14. VrsP in Hab. 2:18. See also the collocation in Deut. 27:15; Judg. 17:3, 4; 18:14, 17, 18.

נסך || פסל

DtIsa: ColP in Isa. 48:5. See also the collocation of roots in Isa. 40:19; 44:10.

Other: StrP in Jer. 10:14 (= 51:17).

פסל || פסל

DtIsa: CanP in Isa. 40:18-20; 44:9+10. MacP in Isa. 44:9+10+15+17.

Other: None, but see the collocation of roots in Hab. 2:18.

נשם || פעה

DtIsa: VrsP in Isa. 42:14.

Other: None.

פעל || פעל

DtIsa: CanP in Isa. 44:12a-b. MacP in Isa. 44:12+15; 45:9+11.

Other: None.

שאף || פעה

DtIsa: VrsP in Isa. 42:14.

Other: None.

פעל || עשה, see עשה || פעל

פצח || רנן, see רנן || פצח רנה

DtIsa: ColP in Isa. 52:9.

Other: ColP in Ps. 98:4.

מחא כף || פצח רנה

DtIsa: VrsP in Isa. 55:12.

Other: None, but see VrsP of (מחא) כף || רנה in Ps. 47:2; 98:8.

צהל || פצח רנה

DtIsa: ColP in Isa. 54:1.

Other: None.

רנן || פצח רנה

DtIsa: VrsP in Isa. 44:23; 49:13; 54:1.

Other: None.

שמע || פקח אזן

DtIsa: ColP in Isa. 42:20.

Other: None, but see he collocation in 2 Kgs 19:16; Isa. 37:17; Dan. 9:18.

צמח || פרה

DtIsa: VrsP in Isa. 45:8.

Other: VrsP (roots) in Isa. 4:2. See also the collocation in Ezek. 17:9.

הלל || פרר

DtIsa: VrsP in Isa. 44:25.

Other: None.

שוב || פרר

DtIsa: StrP in Isa. 44:25.

Other: VrsP in Isa. 14:27; Ps. 85:5.

אביר לב || פשע

DtIsa: MacP in Isa. 46:8+12.

Other: None.

פשע || חטא, see חטא || פשע

חטאת || פשע

DtIsa: VrsP in Isa. 43:25; 44:22.

Other: ColP in Josh. 24:19; Ps. 25:7, etc. VrsP in Isa. 58:1; 59:12; Ps. 32:5; 51:3, etc. StrP in Isa. 59:2, 12, etc.

פשע || עון, see עון || פשע

פשע (root) || פשע (root)

DtIsa: CanP in Isa. 43:25+27. MacP in Isa. 53:5+8.

Other: ColP in 1 Kgs 8:50; Ezek. 18:31.

רשע || פשע

DtIsa: CanP in Isa. 53:8+9.

Other: ColP in Ps. 36:2; Prov. 29:16. VrsP in Ps. 37:38. StrP in Ezek. 33:12.

גאל || פתח

DtIsa: CanP in Isa. 52:2+3.

Other: None.

סגר || פתח

DtIsa: VrsP in Isa. 45:1.

Other: ColP in Isa. 22:22; Ezek. 44:2. VrsP in Isa. 60:11; Jer. 13:19. See also the collocation in Ezek. 46:10.

פתח || פתח

DtIsa: StrP in Isa. 45:1b-c; 53:7.

Other: VrsP in Isa. 22:22.

פתח אזן || מרה (לא), see also שמע || מרה

DtIsa: VrsP in Isa. 50:5.

Other: None.

צמח || צאצא

DtIsa: StrP in Isa. 42:5+9.

Other: None.

עון || צבא

DtIsa: VrsP in Isa. 40:2.

Other: None.

צבא || צבא

DtIsa: CanP in Isa. 45:12+13.

Other: ColP in Isa. 13:4. StrP in Isa. 34:4.

צדיק || ישע (root)

DtIsa: ColP in Isa. 45:21.

Other: ColP in Zech. 9:9.

צדק || אמת

DtIsa: VrsP in Isa. 43:9.

Other: ColP in Ps. 45:5. VrsP in Ps. 15:2; 19:10; 85:11, 12; 89:15; 119:142, 160.

צדק || יהוה

DtIsa: VrsP in Isa. 51:1. See also the collocation in Isa. 42:6, 21; 45:19.

Other: ColP in Jer. 50:7. VrsP in Isa. 58:8; 61:3. StrP in Zeph. 2:3.

צדק (noun) || ישע (noun)

DtIsa: ColP in Isa. 51:5a. StrP in Isa. 45:8.

Other: VrsP in Ps. 65:6.

צדק || ישר, see צדק || מישרים

DtIsa: VrsP in Isa. 45:13.

Other: None.

צדק || מישרים

DtIsa: VrsP in Isa. 45:19.

Other: ColP in Prov. 1:3, and of roots in Isa. 26:7; Deut. 32:4. VrsP in Ps. 9:9; 58:2; 98:9; Prov. 2:9, and of roots in Isa. 11:4; 33:15; Ps. 9:9; 32:11; 33:1; Prov. 16:13.

צדק || סבל עון

DtIsa: VrsP in Isa. 53:11.

Other: None.

צדק (verb) || צדקה

DtIsa: StrP in Isa. 45:24-25. CanP in Isa. 23+25; 51:7+8. MacP in Isa. 45:13+46:13; 51:1+5+6+8.

Other: None, VrsP in Isa. 5:23. and see the collocation in 1Kgs 8:32; 2 Chron. 6:23.

צדק Hiph. || רשע Hiph.

DtIsa: MacP in Isa. 50:8+9.

Other: ColP in Prov. 17:15. VrsP in Deut. 25:1; 1 Kgs 8:32.

צדק || שחד

DtIsa: StrP in Isa. 45:13.

Other: None, but see the collocation of roots in Isa. 5:23.

צדק || שפט. See also צדק, צדקה || משפט.

DtIsa: VrsP in Isa. 43:26; 51:5.

Other: VrsP in Ps. 82:3.

צדק || תורה

DtIsa: VrsP in Isa. 42:21; 51:7.

Other: None, but see the collocation in Ps. 119:142.

צדקה || עז

DtIsa: VrsP in Isa. 45:24.

Other: None.

צדקה || צדק (verb) see צדק (verb) || צדקה

צדקה || צדקה

DtIsa: CanP in Isa. 45:22+23; 46:12+ 13. MacP in Isa. 54:14+17.

Other: VrsP in Judg. 5:11; Isa. 32:17; Jer. 33:15; Prov. 21:21. StrP in Isa. 56:1; Ezek. 18:24; 33:13.

צדקה || תפארת

DtIsa: StrP in Isa. 46:13.

Other: VrsP in Prov. 16:31.

צדקה || תשועה, see also צדקה || ישע

DtIsa: VrsP in Isa. 46:13.

Other: VrsP in Ps. 40:11; 51:16; 71:15.

צוה || צוה

DtIsa: CanP in Isa. 45:11+12.

Other: None.

צולה || נהר

DtIsa: VrsP in Isa. 44:27.

Other: None, but compare the VrsP of מצולה || נהר in Jon. 2:4.

צוק || צוק

DtIsa: StrP in Isa. 51:13b-c.

Other: None.

מים || צור

DtIsa: VrsP in Isa. 48:21.

Other: ColP in Ps. 78:20; 105:41; 114:8. See also the collocation in Exod. 17:6; Deut. 8:15; Ps. 78:15-16 and compare Num 20:8, 10, 11; Neh. 9:15 with סלע instead of צור.

מקבת בור || צור

DtIsa: VrsP in Isa. 51:1.

Other: None, but see the antithetical StrP between צור || בור in Ps. 28:1.

צור || צור

DtIsa: StrP in Isa. 48:21.

Other: ColP in Deut. 32:31. VrsP in 2 Sam. 22:47.

מים || ציה

DtIsa: ColP in Isa. 41:18.

Other: None.

אלהים || ציון

DtIsa: ColP in Isa. 52:7.

Other: ColP in Ps. 65:2; 69:36; 84:8; 146:10; 147:12. VrsP in Jer. 31:6; 51:10; Joel 2:23; 4:17; Ps. 50:2.

יהוה || ציון, see ציון || יהוה

ירושלם || ציון, see ציון || ירושלם

ישׂראל || ציון

DtIsa: VrsP in Isa. 46:13.

Other: VrsP in Isa. 12:6; Mi. 1:13; Zeph. 3:14; 149:2; Lam. 2:1.

עדן || ציון

DtIsa: StrP in Isa. 51:3a-b.

Other: None.

ציון || ציון

DtIsa: CanP in Isa. 52:1+2, 7+8. MacP in Isa. 51:11+16; 52:1+2+7+8.

Other: None.

ציץ || ציץ

DtIsa: StrP in Isa. 40:7-8. CanP in Isa. 40:6-8.

Other: ColP (roots) in Num. 17:23; Ps. 103:15.

אכל || צלה

DtIsa: ColP in Isa. 44:19. VrsP in Isa. 44:16.

Other: None.

רשׁע || צלח

DtIsa: VrsP in Isa. 54:17.

Other: None, but see the collocation in Jer. 12:1.

מים || צמא, see צמא || מים

שׁבל || צמה

DtIsa: ColP in Isa. 47:2.

Other: None.

אשׁר אין־לו || צמא

DtIsa: VrsP in Isa. 55:1.

Other: None.

יבשׁה || צמא

DtIsa: VrsP in Isa. 44:3.

Other: None.

זרע || צמח

DtIsa: StrP in Isa. 55:10b-c.

Other: ColP in Deut. 29:22.

עלה || צמח

DtIsa: MacP in Isa. 55:10+13.

Other: VrsP in Deut. 29:22.

נשׂא || צעק

DtIsa: ColP in Isa. 42:2.

Other: None.

ענה || צעק

DtIsa: ColP in Isa. 46:7.

Other: ColP in Job 19:7; 35:12. Semantically close Colp in 2 Sam. 22:42 (= Ps. 18:42).

צרה || צעק

DtIsa: VrsP in Isa. 46:7.

Other: VrsP in Ps. 34:18. See also the collocation in Neh. 9:27.

שׁמע קול || צעק

DtIsa: VrsP in Isa. 42:2.

Other: None.

ראה || צפה

DtIsa: StrP in Isa. 52:8.

Other: None.

ים || צפון

DtIsa: ColP in Isa. 49:12.

Other: ColP in Ps. 107:3. VrsP in Amos 8:12.

מזרח || צפון

DtIsa: VrsP in Isa. 41:25.

Other: ColP in Amos 8:12 . VrsP in Ps. 107:3. StrP in Zech. 14:4.

רחוק || צפון

DtIsa: VrsP in Isa. 49:12. StrP in Isa. 43:6.

Other: VrsP in Jer. 25:26.

תימן || צפון

DtIsa: VrsP in Isa. 43:6.

Other: VrsP in Song 4:16. StrP in Zech. 6:6. See also the collocation in Exod. 26:35; Deut. 3:27.

חרש || צרח

DtIsa: CanP in Isa. 42:13+14.

Other: None.

בחר || צרף

DtIsa: VrsP in Isa. 48:10.

Other: None.

צר || צרר

DtIsa: CanP in Isa. 49:19+20.

Other: StrP (roots) in Deut. 28:52; Isa. 11:13.

קבעת || קבעת

DtIsa: MacP in Isa. 51:17+22.

Other: None.

שתה || קבעת

DtIsa: VrsP in Isa. 51:17, 22.

Other: None.

קבץ || בוא Hif., see בוא Hif. || קבץ

יחד || קבץ

DtIsa: VrsP in Isa. 45:20.

Other: None, but see the pleonastic expression 'to gather together', cf. Josh. 9:2; Isa. 43:9; Hos. 2:2; Ps. 102:23.

קבץ || עמד, see עמד || קבץ

רחם || קבץ

DtIsa: StrP in Isa. 54:7-8.

Other: VrsP in Deut. 30:3.

שמע || קבץ

DtIsa: ColP in Isa. 48:14.

Other: None.

מות || קבר

DtIsa: VrsP in Isa. 53:9.

Other: ColP in Jer. 20:6. VrsP in Jer. 16:4; 20:17; Ps. 88:6; Ruth 1:17.

איש || קדוש

DtIsa: CanP in Isa. 40:25-26.

Other: VrsP in Hos. 11:9.

ברא || קדוש

DtIsa: VrsP in Isa. 43:15. See also the collocation in Isa. 41:20.

Other: None.

קדוש || קדוש

DtIsa: CanP in Isa. 43:14+15; 49:7.

Other: ColP in Isa. 6:3. VrsP in Lev. 11:44, 45; 19:2; 20:26; 21:8. StrP in Lev. 21:8; Isa. 57:15.

אלהים || קדוש ישראל

DtIsa: VrsP in Isa. 54:5.

Other: VrsP in Ps. 71:22. StrP in Jer. 51:5.

יהוה אלהים || קדוש ישראל see יהוה אלהים || קדוש ישראל

יהוה צבאות || קדוש ישראל see יהוה צבאות || קדוש ישראל

קדוש ישראל || קדוש ישראל

DtIsa: CanP in Isa. 41:14-16.

Other: See the concatenation in Isa. 30:11-12, and in 30:12-15.

בער || קדח

DtIsa: StrP in Isa. 50:11a-b.

Other: None.

אז || קדם

DtIsa: VrsP in Isa. 45:21.

Other: None, but see the collocation in Prov. 8:22.

עולם || קדם, see קדם || עולם

כסות || קדרות

DtIsa: VrsP in Isa. 50:3.

Other: VrsP (roots) in Ezek. 32:7.

טמא || קדש

DtIsa: CanP in Isa. 52:1.

Other: ColP in Ps. 79:1 (allusion?). Also VrsP in Lev. 10:10; Ezek. 22:26; 44:23. StrP in Isa. 35:8.

תפארת || קדש

DtIsa: VrsP in Isa. 52:1.

Other: ColP in Isa. 63:15; 64:10. See also the collocation in Exod. 28:2; Deut. 26:19.

שׂרד || קו

DtIsa: StrP in Isa. 44:13.

Other: None.

יחל || קוה

DtIsa: VrsP in Isa. 51:5.

Other: VrsP in Mi. 5:6; Ps. 130:5; Job 30:26.

רוץ || קוה

DtIsa: StrP in Isa. 40:31.

Other: None.

דבר || קול

DtIsa: CanP in Isa. 40:6-8.

Other: ColP in Ps. 103:20; Qoh. 5:2. VrsP in Joel 2:11; Ps. 19:4; Qoh. 10:20.

פה || קול

DtIsa: CanP in Isa. 40:3-5.

Other: VrsP in Ezek. 21:27; Job 37:2.

קול || קול

DtIsa: ColP in Isa. 52:8. MacP in Isa. 40:3+6+9.

Other: ColP in Gen. 27:22; Exod. 4:8; Isa. 65:19; 66:6; Jer. 7:34; 16:9; 25:10; 33:11; Ezek. 43:2; Nah. 3:2; Ps. 68:34. VrsP in Jer. 49:21; Ezek. 1:24; 3:13; Ps. 29:4; 77:2; 130:2; 142:2; Job 37:4; Song 2:14. StrP in Isa. 13:4; Jer. 4:31; 42:6; 51:55; Ezek. 1:24; 10:5; Joel 2:5; Zech. 11:3.

ישׁב || קום

DtIsa: ColP in Isa. 52:2.

Other: StrP in 1 Sam. 2:8.

ישועה || קום Hiph., see קום Hiph. ||ישועה

נצר || קום, see קום || נצר

עשׂה || קום

DtIsa: VrsP in Isa. 46:10.

Other: ColP in Jer. 23:20; 30:24. See also the parallelism in Jer. 28:6.

קום || קום

DtIsa: StrP in Isa. 44:26.

Other: VrsP in Deut. 33:11; Judg. 5:7; Am. 5:7. StrP in Am. 9:11; Qoh. 4:10.

שׁוב || קום

DtIsa: VrsP in Isa. 49:6.

Other: VrsP in Jer. 23:20; Ps. 89:44. StrP in 2 Kgs 21:3; 2 Chron. 33:3. Cf. Gen. 31:13; 43:13; Num. 24:25.

שׁחה || קום

DtIsa: MacP in Isa. 51:17+23.

Other: None.

שׁלם || קום

DtIsa: VrsP in Isa. 44:26.

Other: VrsP in Ps. 41:11. StrP in Ps. 35:11-12.

גדל || קטן

DtIsa: VrsP in Isa. 54:7.

Other: ColP in Gen. 48:19; Jer. 16:6; Amos 8:5; Ps. 105:25; 115:13, etc. VrsP in Gen. 1:16; Amos 6:11.

זבח || קנה

DtIsa: VrsP in Isa. 43:24.

Other: StrP in Jer. 6:20.

חלב || קנה

DtIsa: VrsP in Isa. 43:24.

Other: None.

קנה || פשתה

DtIsa: VrsP in Isa. 42:3.

Other: None, but see the collocation in Ezek. 40:3.

קנה || רוה

DtIsa: VrsP in Isa. 43:24.

Other: None.

קסם || חכם

DtIsa: StrP in Isa. 44:25.

Other: None.

קפץ פה || ספר

DtIsa: StrP in Isa. 52:15.

Other: None.

קצה הארץ || אי, see אי || קצה הארץ

קצה הארץ || אציל

DtIsa: VrsP in Isa. 41:9.

Other: None.

קצף || גער

DtIsa: VrsP in Isa. 54:9.

Other: None.

קצף || חלל

DtIsa: VrsP in Isa. 47:6.

Other: None, but see the collocation of roots in Num. 17:11.

קצף || חסד, see also שצף קצף || חסד עולמים

DtIsa: CanP in Isa. 54:9.

Other: None.

קצף || קצף

DtIsa: MacP in Isa. 54:8+9.

Other: ColP in Zech. 1:2, 5. VrsP in Isa 57:17.

קצף (verb) || רחם (verb), see also רחמים || קצף

DtIsa: CanP in Isa. 54:9.

Other: None.

קצף (verb) || רחמים (noun), see also רחמים || קצף (noun)

DtIsa: StrP in Isa. 47:6.

Other: None.

קרא || אמר, see אמר || קרא

קרא || בוא, see בוא || קרא

קרא || בחר (root), see בחר (root) || קרא

קרא || ברך

DtIsa: VrsP in Isa. 51:2.

Other: None, but see the collocation in Gen. 28:1; 48:1.

קרא || חזק, see חזק || קרא

קרא || יגע

DtIsa: VrsP in Isa. 43:22.

Other: None, but see the collocation in Ps. 69:4.

קרא || נגד

DtIsa: ColP in Isa. 44:7.

Other: StrP in Isa. 58:1; Jer. 4:5; 33:3.

קרא || סלח

DtIsa: CanP in Isa. 55:6+7.

Other: VrsP in Ps. 86:5.

קרא || ענה

DtIsa: ColP in Isa. 50:2.

Other: ColP in Isa. 58:6; 65:12, 24; 66:4; Jer. 7:13, 27; 33:3; 35:17; Jon. 2:3; Ps. 4:2, etc. VrsP in Zech. 13:9; Ps. 3:5, etc.

קרא || קרא

DtIsa: VrsP in Isa. 40:6. CanP in Isa. 48:1+2, 12+13. MacP in Isa. 40:3+6 (2x); 41:2+4; 44:5+7; 45:3+46:11; 47:1+5; 54:5+6.

Other: VrsP in Zech. 7:13; 11:7; Ps. 141:1; 145:18. StrP in Isa. 62:16; Ps. 99:6; Ruth 1:20; 4:17.

קרא || קרב

DtIsa: CanP in Isa. 41:4+5.

Other: ColP in Lam. 3:57.

קרא || רוץ

DtIsa: VrsP in Isa. 55:5.

Other: VrsP in Gen. 41:14; 1 Sam. 3:5.

קרא || שׂם

DtIsa: StrP in Isa. 54:5.

Other: None, but often in collocation in קרא בשם.

זכר || קרא בשם

DtIsa: StrP in Isa. 48:1.

Other: StrP in Isa. 12:4.

ידע || קרא בשם, see ידע || קרא בשם

כנה || קרא בשם

קרא בשם || קרא בשם

DtIsa: CanP in Isa. 45:3+4. MacP in Isa. 43:1+7.

Other: None, but see the collocation in Ruth 4:17.

אתה || קרב

DtIsa: ColP in Isa. 41:5.

Other: None.

גור || קרב

DtIsa: CanP in Isa. 54:14+15.

Other: None.

נגש || קרב, see נגש || קרב

שמע || קרב

DtIsa: ColP in Isa. 48:16.

Other: ColP in Isa. 34:1; Qoh. 4:17.

בוא || קרה

DtIsa: StrP in Isa. 41:22.

Other: None.

כרע || קרס, see כרע || קרס

קרס || קרס

DtIsa: CanP in Isa. 46:1+2.

Other: None.

אזן || קשב, see אזן || קשב

שמע || קשב

DtIsa: ColP in Isa. 42:23. VrsP in Isa. 49:1. MacP in Isa. 51:1+4+7.

Other: ColP in Isa. 28:23; 32:3; Jer. 8:6; 23:18; Zech. 1:4; Mal. 3:16, etc. VrsP in Isa. 34:1; 49:1; Jer. 18:19; Hos. 5:1; Mic. 1:2, etc.

בין || ראה

DtIsa: VrsP in Isa. 52:15.

Other: ColP in Job 11:11. VrsP in Isa. 6:10 (cf. 6:9); 14:16; 44:18; Jer. 2:10; Ps. 94:7; Job 9:11; 13:1; Prov. 7:7.

הנה || ראה

DtIsa: StrP in Isa. 41:28-29.

Other: ColP in Jer. 7:11; Ezek. 1:4, 15; 2:9, etc. VrsP in Jer. 4:23, 24, etc.

ירא || ראה

DtIsa: ColP in Isa. 41:5.

Other: ColP in Zech. 9:5; Ps. 40:4; 52:8; 119:74; Job 6:21. VrsP in Ps. 112:8; Job 37:24. See also the parallelism in 1 Sam. 28:5, 13.

פקח || ראה

DtIsa: VrsP in Isa. 42:20.

Other: None, but see the collocation in Gen. 21:19; 2 Kon. 6:17, 20; 19:16; Isa. 37:17; Dan. 9:18, with פקח connected to עין 'eye', instead of אזן 'ear'.

קום || ראה

DtIsa: ColP in Isa. 49:7.

Other: VrsP in Job 29:8.

שחה Hitpa., || קום || ראה

DtIsa: VrsP in Isa. 49:7.

Other: None, but see the collocation in Gen. 19:1; Exod. 33:10, see also Gen. 18:2; Num. 22:31; Deut. 4:19; 1 Sam. 25:23; 2 Sam. 24:20; 2 Kgs. 2:15; 1 Chron. 21:21; 2 Chron. 7:3.

ראה || ראה

DtIsa: CanP in Isa. 42:18+20; 52:8+10. MacP in Isa. 44:9+18.

Other: Very often in collocation, but definitely ColP in Isa. 30:10; Ps. 77:17; Job 10:4; Song 6:11. StrP in Jer. 20:12; Mic. 7:10.

שים || ראה

DtIsa: VrsP in Isa. 41:20.

Other: None, but see the parallelism of ראה and שים לב in Ezek. 40:4; 44:5.

שכל || ראה

DtIsa: VrsP in Isa. 41:20; 44:18.

Other: None.

שבע || ראה

DtIsa: VrsP in Isa. 53:11.

Other: ColP in Job 10:15. VrsP in Jer. 44:17; Ps. 91:16.

שמע || ראה

DtIsa: VrsP in Isa. 42:18, 20.

Other: ColP in Ps. 45:11; 48:9. VrsP in Isa. 6:9; 21:3; 29:18; 30:30; 32:3; 33:15; 37:17; 38:5; 42:20; Jer. 4:21; 5:21; Ps.66:18; Lam. 1:18, etc. StrP in Isa. 33:19.

שמר || ראה

DtIsa: ColP in Isa. 42:20.

Other: ColP in Ps. 37:37. VrsP in Qoh. 11:4.

צלח || ראה זרע

DtIsa: VrsP in Isa. 53:10.

Other: None, but see the collocation of זרע and צלח in Jer. 22:30.

לפנים || ראש

DtIsa: VrsP in Isa. 41:26.

Other: ColP in Isa. 9:15. VrsP in Ezek. 7:18; Mic. 2:13; Ps. 23:5.

עת || ראש

DtIsa: VrsP in Isa. 48:16.

Other: None.

ראשון || ראש, see also ראשית || ראשון

DtIsa: StrP in Isa. 41:4. CanP in Isa. 41:26-27.

Other: StrP in Exod. 12:2.

אחרון || ראשון

DtIsa: ColP in Isa. 44:6. VrsP in Isa. 41:4; 48:12.

Other: ColP in Hag. 2:9; Ruth 3:10. VrsP in Jer. 50:17. StrP in Isa. 8:23. See also Exod. 4:8; Neh. 8:18; 1 Chron. 29:29; 2 Chron. 9:29; 12:15; 16:11; 20:34; 25:26: 26:22; 28:26; 35:27.

אל || ראשון

DtIsa: VrsP in Isa. 46:9.

Other: None. Often, however, God is called ראשון in Second Isaiah, cf. Isa. 41:4, 27; 44:6; 48:12.

בוא || ראשון

DtIsa: ColP in Isa. 42:9. VrsP in Isa. 41:22. StrP in Isa. 48:3.

Other: VrsP in Prov. 18:17.

חדש || ראשון

DtIsa: StrP in Isa. 42:9. CanP in Isa. 43:18+19. MacP in Isa. 48:3+6.

Other: VrsP in Isa. 65:17.

עולם || ראשון

DtIsa: ColP in Isa. 46:9. CanP in Isa. 44:6+7.

Other: VrsP in Isa. 61:4.

קדמני || ראשון

DtIsa: VrsP in Isa. 43:18.

Other: None, but see the VrsP of ראש || קדם in Prov. 8:23.

ראשית || ראשון, see also ראש || ראשון

DtIsa: CanP in Isa. 46:9+10.

Other: None.

אחרית || ראשית

DtIsa: ColP in Isa. 46:10.

Other: ColP in Qoh. 7:8. VrsP in Num. 24:10; Job 8:7. See also the collocation in Deut. 11:12; Job 42:12.

קדם || ראשית

DtIsa: VrsP in Isa. 46:10.

Other: VrsP in Prov. 8:22, 23.

אתיות || באות || ראשנות

DtIsa: CanP in Isa. 41:22-23.

Other: None.

אמיץ || רב

DtIsa: ColP in Isa. 40:26.

Other: None.

עצום || רב

DtIsa: VrsP in Isa. 53:12.

Other: ColP in Exod. 1:9; Deut. 7:1; 9:14; 25:5; Isa. 8:7; Joel 2:2; Zech. 8:22. VrsP in Num. 32:1; Joel 2:11; Amos 5:12; Mic. 4:3; Ps. 35:18; 135:10; Prov. 7:26.

רב (noun) || רב (noun)

DtIsa: StrP in Isa. 47:12-13a. MacP in Isa. 47:9+12+13.

Other: ColP in Qoh. 1:18. VrsP in Ps. 33:16; Qoh. 5:2.

רבה || רב

DtIsa: MacP in Isa. 40:26+29.

Other: VrsP in Ezek. 28:5; Hos. 10:1; Qoh. 5:6.

רבים || רבים

DtIsa: StrP in Isa. 53:12. CanP in Isa. 52:14+15; 53:11+12 (3x).

Other: VrsP in Exod. 23:2. StrP in Deut. 15:6; Jer. 16:16.

יסד || רבץ

DtIsa: VrsP in Isa. 54:11.

Other: None.

ירד || רגל

DtIsa: StrP in Isa. 41:2a-b.

Other: ColP in Prov. 5:5. VrsP in 2 Sam. 22:10 (= Ps. 18:10).

רגל || רגל

DtIsa: CanP in Isa. 41:2+3.

Other: ColP in Ezek. 1:7. VrsP in Isa. 26:6; Ezek. 29:11; 34:19. StrP in Ezek. 34:19; Job 13:27.

יום || רגע

DtIsa: VrsP in Isa. 47:9.

Other: VrsP in Job 21:13.

עולם || רגע

DtIsa: VrsP in Isa. 54:8.

Other: None.

פתאם || רגע

DtIsa: CanP in Isa. 47:9+11.

Other: VrsP in Jer. 4:20.

רגע || רגע

DtIsa: StrP in Isa. 54:7-8.

Other: None.

בקשׁ || רדף

DtIsa: VrsP in Isa. 51:1.

Other: ColP in Ps. 34:15; Qoh. 3:15. VrsP in 1 Sam. 25:29; 26:20; Hos. 2:9. See also the collocation in Josh. 2:22; 1 Sam. 23:25.

ים || רהב

DtIsa: CanP in Isa. 51:9+10.

Other: VrsP in Job 26:12.

תנין || רהב

DtIsa: VrsP in Isa. 51:9.

Other: None.

צמח || רוה

DtIsa: VrsP in Isa. 55:10 .

Other: StrP in Ps. 65:11.

ברכה || רוח

DtIsa: VrsP in Isa. 44:3.

Other: None.

משׁפט || רוח

DtIsa: VrsP in Isa. 42:1.

Other: See also the collocation in Isa. 4:4; 28:6; Jer. 4:12; Ezek. 36:27 and Isa. 11:2-4 where the רוח of YHWH and the root שׁפט are related.

סערה || רוח

DtIsa: VrsP in Isa. 41:16.

Other: None, but see the collocation in Ezek. 1:4; 13:11, 13: Ps. 107:25; 148:8.

עצה || רוח

DtIsa: VrsP in Isa. 40:13.

Other: VrsP in Isa. 19:3. See also the collocation in Isa. 11:2; 30:1.

רום || נשׂא, see נשׂא || רום

רום Hiph. || רום Hiph.

DtIsa: CanP in Isa. 40:9.

Other: VrsP in Isa. 10:15. See also the parallelism in Num. 15:20; 2 Chron. 30:24.

חשׁה || רוע

DtIsa: CanP in Isa. 42:13+14.

Other: None.

רוע Hiph. || צרח Hiph.

DtIsa: ColP in Isa. 42:13.

Other: None.

פעה || רוע

DtIsa: CanP in Isa. 42:13+14.

Other: None.

יגע || רוץ

DtIsa: ColP in Isa. 40:31.

Other: None.

שפט || רזן

DtIsa: VrsP in Isa. 40:23.

Other: None.

ארך || רחב

DtIsa: StrP in Isa. 54:2.

Other: VrsP in Isa. 57:4.

נטה || רחב

DtIsa: VrsP in Isa. 54:2.

Other: VrsP in Isa. 8:8.

פרץ || רחב

DtIsa: CanP in Isa. 54:2+3.

Other: None.

קצה הארץ || רחוק

DtIsa: VrsP in Isa. 43:6.

Other: VrsP in Isa. 5:26; Ps. 65:6. See also the collocation in Deut. 13:8; 29:49.

צפון || רחוק, see רחוק || צפון

ארץ סינים || ים || צפון || רחוק, see also רחוק || צפון and ים || צפון

DtIsa: VrsP in Isa. 49:12.

Other: None.

רחק (verb) || רחוק, see also רחק || רחוק || מרחק

DtIsa: CanP in Isa. 46:12+13.

Other: None.

נחם || רחם, see רחם || נחם

סלח || רחם

DtIsa: VrsP in Isa. 55:7.

Other: VrsP in 1 Kgs 8:50.

רחם || רחם

DtIsa: MacP in Isa. 54:7+8+10.

Other: ColP in Exod. 33:19; Hos. 2:25. VrsP in Ps. 103:13.

שיבה || רחם

DtIsa: CanP in Isa. 46:3+4.

Other: None.

חסד || רחמים

DtIsa: StrP in Isa. 54:7-8.

Other: ColP in Jer. 16:5; Hos. 2:21; Zech. 7:9; Ps. 103:4. VrsP in Isa. 63:7; Ps. 25:6; 40:12; 51:3; 69:17; Lam. 3:22.

רחמים (noun) || קצף (noun), see also רחמים || קצף and רחם || קצף

DtIsa: StrP in Isa. 54:7-8.

Other: None.

רחם || רחמים

DtIsa: StrP in Isa. 54:7-8.

Other: VrsP in Deut. 13:18; 1 Kgs 8:50; Jer. 42:12.

אחר || רחק

DtIsa: VrsP in Isa. 46:13.

Other: VrsP (roots) in Isa. 59:14. See also the collocation of roots in Jer. 2:5.

ישע || ריב

DtIsa: VrsP in Isa. 49:25.

Other: ColP in Isa. 19:20. VrsP in Judg. 6:31. See also the collocation in Judg. 12:2.

מצות || ריב

DtIsa: CanP in Isa. 41:11-12.

Other: None.

משפט || ריב

DtIsa: VrsP in Isa. 50:8.

Other: ColP in Mi. 7:9. VrsP in Ezek. 44:24; Ps. 35:23; Job 31:13. StrP in Isa. 1:17; Jer. 12:1.

עצום || ריב

DtIsa: StrP in Isa. 41:21.

Other: None.

ריב || ריב

DtIsa: ColP in Isa. 49:25.

Other: ColP in Jer. 51:36; Hos. 2:4; Mic. 7:9; Ps. 43:1; 74:22; 119:154; Prov.

23:11; Lam. 3:58. VrsP in Jer. 2:9. StrP in Mic. 6:2.

הבל || ריק

DtIsa: VrsP in Isa. 49:4.

Other: ColP in Isa. 30:7.

עזר || ריב

DtIsa: CanP in Isa. 50:8+9.

Other: VrsP (roots) in Deut. 33:7.

פעולה || ריק

DtIsa: StrP in Isa. 49:4.

Other: None.

תהו || ריק

DtIsa: VrsP in Isa. 49:4.

Other: None.

ענג || רך

DtIsa: ColP in Isa. 47:1.

Other: ColP in Deut. 28:54. VrsP in Deut. 28:56.

חיל || סוס || רכב

DtIsa: VrsP in Isa. 43:17.

Other: None, but see the collocation in Exod. 14:9, Deut. 11:4; 1 Kgs. 20:1, 25; 2 Kgs. 6:14, 15; 7:6 and compare Exod. 14:17, 28; Ezek. 38:15 and see סוס || רכב in ColP in Isa. 66:20; Jer. 17:25; 22:4; 50:37; Ezek. 26:7; 39:20; Ps. 20:8; 76:7; VrsP Jer. 46:9; 51:21; Zech. 9:10; StrP in Isa. 31:1.

בקעה || רכס

DtIsa: ColP in Isa. 40:4.

Other: None.

חלה || רמה (root)

DtIsa: VrsP in Isa. 53:9-10a.

Other: StrP in Mic. 6:12-13.

שמחה || רנה

DtIsa: VrsP in Isa. 51:11. StrP in Isa. 55:12.

Other: VrsP in Isa. 35:10; Zeph. 3:17.

ששון || רנה

DtIsa: StrP in Isa. 51:11.

Other: VrsP in Ps. 105:43. See also the quotation of Isa. 53:11 in Isa. 35:10.

תהלה || רנה

DtIsa: MacP in Isa. 43:14+21.

Other: None, but see the collocation in 2 Chron. 20:22.

גיל || רנן

DtIsa: ColP in Isa. 49:13.

Other: VrsP in Isa. 16:10; 35:2; Ps. 32:11.

נחם || רנן

DtIsa: VrsP in Isa. 52:9. StrP in Isa. 49:13.

Other: None.

פצח רנה || רנן, see רנן || פצח רנה

צהל || רנן

DtIsa: VrsP in Isa. 54:1.

Other: ColP in Isa. 12:6. VrsP in Isa. 24:14; Jer. 31:7.

צוח || רנן

DtIsa: VrsP in Isa. 42:11.

Other: None.

רוע || רנן

DtIsa: MacP in Isa. 42:11+13.

Other: ColP in Isa. 16:10. VrsP in Zeph. 3:14; Ps. 81:2; 95:1; Job 38:7.

פצח רנה || רוע || רנן, see also רוע || רנן

DtIsa: VrsP in Isa. 44:23.

Other: None, but see VrsP of פצח || רוע || רנן in Ps. 98:4.

רנן || רנן

DtIsa: CanP in Isa. 52:8+9.

Other: None.

אח || רע

DtIsa: VrsP in Isa. 41:6.

Other: ColP in Isa. 19:2; Jer. 23:35, 34:17; Ps. 35:14; 122:8. VrsP in Jer. 9:4; 31:34; Job 30:29; Prov. 17:17; 18:24; 27:10.

חרב || רעב

DtIsa: ColP in Isa. 51:19.

Other: ColP in Jer. 5:12; 14:12, 15, 16; 27:8, 13; 29:17, 18; 32: 24, 36; 34:17; 38:2; 42:22; 44:12, 13, 18, 27; Ezek. 6:12; 14:21. VrsP in Jer. 11:22; 14:13; 16:4; 18:21; 21:7; Ezek. 12:16; Job 5:20; Lam. 4:9. StrP in Jer. 14:18; Ezek. 5:12, 17.

(לא) שתה || רעב

DtIsa: VrsP in Isa. 44:12.

Other: StrP in Isa. 65:13.

צמא || רעב

DtIsa: ColP in Isa. 49:10.

Other: ColP (roots) in Deut. 8:48; Ps. 107:5. VrsP (roots) in Isa 5:13; 32:6; Amos 8:11. StrP (roots) in .Isa. 29:8; 65:13; Prov. 25:21.

הוה || רעה

DtIsa: VrsP in Isa. 47:11.

Other: ColP in Ps. 38:12.

מרעית || רעה, see also רעה || רעה

DtIsa: VrsP in Isa. 49:9.

Other: None, but see the collocation in Jer. 10:21; 23:1; 25:36.

נהג || רעה

DtIsa: CanP in Isa. 49:9+10.

Other: VrsP in Ps. 80:1.

נהל || רעה

DtIsa: StrP in Isa. 40:11. CanP in Isa. 49:9+10.

Other: StrP in Ps. 23:1-2.

קבץ || רעה

DtIsa: VrsP in Isa. 40:11.

Other: VrsP in Jer. 31:10. StrP in Ezek. 34:13. See also the collocation in Nah. 3:18.

רעה || רעה

DtIsa: ColP in Isa. 40:11. CanP in Isa. 47:10+11.

Other: VrsP in Jer. 3:15; 23:4; Ezek. 34:2, 8, 10; Song 1:8.

ירא || רעע

DtIsa: VrsP in Isa. 41:23.

Other: ColP in Ps. 23:4; 49:6; 112:7; Prov. 3:7; 14:16. VrsP in Jer. 10:5. StrP in Qoh. 8:12.

פעל || רעע

DtIsa: CanP in Isa. 41:23-24.

Other: VrsP in Isa. 31:2; Ps. 64:3; 94:16.

נזל || רעף

DtIsa: VrsP in Isa. 45:8.

Other: VrsP in Job 36:28.

ישועה || רצון

DtIsa: VrsP in Isa. 49:8.

Other: VrsP in Ps. 106:4.

רצץ || רצץ

DtIsa: CanP in Isa. 42:3+4.

Other: StrP in Prov. 30:33.

שבר || רצץ

DtIsa: ColP in Isa. 42:3.

Other: VrsP in Qoh. 12:6.

און || רשע

DtIsa: VrsP in Isa. 55:7.

Other: ColP in Prov. 19:28. VrsP in Ps. 28:3; 92:8; 101:8; 141:4; Job 34:8; Prov. 11:7; 12:21.

חמס || רשע

DtIsa: StrP in Isa. 53:9-10a.

Other: ColP in Ezek. 7:11; Prov. 10:6, 11. VrsP in Ps. 11:5; 140:5; Prov. 4:17.

עשיר || רשע

DtIsa: VrsP in Isa. 53:9.

Other: None, but note the assonance between the two words and see the parallelism (roots) in the announcements of doom in Jer. 5:26-27; Mic. 6:11-12.

אכל || שׂבעה, see אכל || שׂבע

מדבר || שׂדה

DtIsa: StrP in Isa. 43:20.

Other: VrsP in Joel 1:19, 20.

רחל || שׂה

DtIsa: VrsP in Isa. 53:7.

Other: None.

כון || שׂים

DtIsa: StrP in Isa. 54:12-14a.

Other: ColP in Isa. 62:7.

נטע || שׂים

DtIsa: StrP in Isa. 51:16.

Other: VrsP in 2 Sam. 7:10.

נגד || שׂים, see שׂים || נגד

שׂים || שׂים

DtIsa: StrP in Isa. 41:15; 49:2; 51:23. CanP in Isa. 41:18-20; 47:6+7.

Other: VrsP in Exod. 4:11; Mic. 4:13. StrP in Isa. 5:20; Jer. 12:11; Ezek. 21:27.

זכר || שׂים על־לב, see also שוב על לב || זכר

DtIsa: VrsP in Isa. 47:7.

Other: VrsP in Isa. 57:11. See also the collocation in 2 Sam. 19:20.

ידע || שׂים לב, see לב || ידע

שׂמח || שׂישׂ

DtIsa: ColP in Isa. 51:3.

Other: ColP in Isa. 22:13; 24:11; 35:10; 51:11; Jer. 7:34; 15:16; 16:9; 25:10; 33:1; Zeph. 3:17; Zech. 8:19; Ps. 40:17; 51:10; 68:10; 70:5; Lam. 4:21. VrsP in Jer. 31:13; Ps. 68:10. StrP in Isa. 66:10.

גבה || שׂכל

DtIsa: VrsP in Isa. 52:13.

Other: None.

נשׂא || שׂכל

DtIsa: VrsP in Isa. 52:13.

Other: None.

רום || שׂכל

DtIsa: VrsP in Isa. 52:13.

Other: VrsP in Job 17:4.

פעלה || שׂכר

DtIsa: VrsP in Isa. 40:10.

Other: VrsP in Isa. 62:11 (quoted). See also the collocation in Jer. 31:16; Prov. 11:18, and collocation of roots in Ruth 2:12.

זמרה || שׂמחה

DtIsa: VrsP in Isa. 51:3.

Other: VrsP (roots) in Ps. 9:3. StrP (roots) in Ps. 149:2-3.

יגון || שׂמחה

DtIsa: VrsP in Isa. 51:11.

Other: ColP in Est. 9:22; (roots) in Jer. 31:13. VrsP in Isa. 35:10.

רנה || שׂמחה, see שׂמחה || רנה

שׂמחה || שׂמחה

DtIsa: StrP in Isa. 51:11.

Other: StrP in Isa. 9:2; quotation of Isa. 53:11 in Isa. 35:10. See also the collocation in Est. 9:22; Neh. 12:43.

שׁלום || שׂמחה

DtIsa: VrsP in Isa. 55:12.

Other: ColP in Prov. 12:20. VrsP in Zech. 8:19.

מחוגה || מקצועה || שׂרד

DtIsa: VrsP in Isa. 44:13.

Other: None.

צלה || אפה || שׂרף, see also צלה || שׂרף

DtIsa: VrsP in Isa. 44:19.

Other: None.

צלה || שׂרף

DtIsa: VrsP in Isa. 44:16, 19.

Other: None.

חמם || שׂרף, see שׂרף || חמם

יגון || שׂשׂון

DtIsa: VrsP in Isa. 51:11.

Other: VrsP in Isa. 35:10; Jer. 31:13.

שׂמחה || שׂשׂון

DtIsa: ColP in Isa. 51:3, 11.

Other: ColP in Isa. 22;13; 35:10. StrP in Isa. 35:10.

תודה || שׂשׂון

DtIsa: VrsP in Isa. 51:3.

Other: None, but see the collocation in Jer. 33:11.

צוה || שׁאל

DtIsa: VrsP in Isa. 45:11.

Other: None.

שבי || מלקוח, מלקוח || שבי

שבי || שבי

DtIsa: CanP in Isa. 49:24+25.

ColP in Jer. 15:2; 43:11.

זכר || שבע

DtIsa: VrsP in Isa. 48:1.

Other: ColP in Josh. 23:7. See also the collocation in Exod. 32:13.

דבר || יצא מפה || שבע

DtIsa: VrsP in Isa. 45:23.

Other: None, but see the collocation in Num. 30:3.

שבע || שבע

DtIsa: StrP in Isa. 45:23; 54:9.

Other: VrsP in Isa. 65:16; Zech. 1:5. StrP in Jer. 12:16.

גדע || שבר

DtIsa: VrsP in Isa. 45:2.

Other: ColP in Jer. 50:23; Ps. 107:16. VrsP in Deut. 12:3; Jer. 48:25; Ezek. 6:6; 2 Chron. 14:3. StrP in Deut. 7:5; 2 Chron. 34:4. See also the collocation in 2 Chron. 31:1.

כבה || שבר

DtIsa: VrsP in Isa. 42:3.

Other: None.

שבר || שבר

DtIsa: VrsP in Isa. 55:1.

Other: None.

נחם || שד

DtIsa: VrsP in Isa. 51:19.

Other: VrsP in Isa. 22:4.

שבר || שד

DtIsa: ColP in Isa. 51:19.

Other: ColP in Isa. 59:7; 60:18; Jer. 48:3.

אסף || שוב

DtIsa: VrsP in Isa. 49:5.

Other: VrsP in Ps. 85:4. See also the collocation in Deut. 22:2; Ps. 104:29; 2 Chron. 24:11.

בוא || שוב

DtIsa: VrsP in Isa. 51:11.

Other: ColP in Isa. 37:34. VrsP in Exod. 15:19; Isa. 35:10; 37:29; Jer. 40:12. StrP in Jer. 3:14; Ezek. 39:2.

רחם || שוב

DtIsa: ColP in Isa. 55:7.

Other: ColP in Jer. 12:15; Mic. 7:19. VrsP in Jer. 30:18.

שוב || שוב

DtIsa: CanP in Isa. 49:5+6.

Other: ColP in Jer. 15:19; 31:18, etc. VrsP in Jer. 31:21; 34:11, 16; Mal. 3:7; Ps. 90:3; StrP in Jer. 8:5; 12:15, etc

צלח || שוב ריקם

DtIsa: StrP in Isa. 55:11.

Other: None.

משל || שוה

DtIsa: VrsP in Isa. 46:5.

Other: None.

לחך || שחה

DtIsa: VrsP in Isa. 49:23.

Other: None.

סגד || שחה, see שחה || סגד

דק || שחק

DtIsa: StrP in Isa. 40:15.

Other: None.

שחת (verb) || שחת

DtIsa: CanP in Isa. 51:13+14.

Other: None.

רנן || שיר

DtIsa: CanP in Isa. 42:10+11.

Other: VrsP in Ps. 59:16.

תהלה || שיר

DtIsa: VrsP in Isa. 42:10.

Other: VrsP in Ps. 40:3; 149:1. See also the collocation in Ps. 106:12; Neh. 12:46.

כבה, דעך || בל קום, שכב

DtIsa: VrsP in Isa. 43:17.

Other: None.

קום || שכב

DtIsa: ColP in Isa. 43:17.

Other: ColP in Deut. 6:7; 11:19; Ps. 41:9; Job 14:12. VrsP in Num. 24:9; Judg. 16:3; Job 7:4; Prov. 6:9; Ruth 3:14. StrP in Num. 23:24.

אלמון || שכול, see also אלמנה || שכול

DtIsa: ColP in Isa. 47:9.

Other: ColP (roots) in Jer. 18:21.

שכול || שכול

DtIsa: CanP in Isa. 47:8+9.

Other: None. VrsP (roots) in 1 Sam. 15:33. See also the collocation of the verb in Gen. 43:14.

גלמודה || שכולה

DtIsa: ColP in Isa. 49:21.

Other: None.

זכר || שכח

DtIsa: VrsP in Isa. 54:4.

Other: ColP in Gen. 40:23; Deut. 9:7; 1 Sam. 1:11. VrsP in Isa. 17:10; 23:16; Ps. 9:13; Job 11:16; 24:20; Prov. 31:7. See also the collocation in Deut. 25:19; Qoh. 9:5.

רחם || שכח,

DtIsa: VrsP in Isa. 49:15.

Other: VrsP in Ps. 77:10. See also the collocation in Deut. 4:31; Job 24:20.

שכח || שכח

DtIsa: VrsP in Isa. 49:15. StrP in Isa. 49:15. CanP in Isa. 49:14+15.

Other: VrsP in Hos. 4:6; Ps. 137:5. StrP in Jer. 2:32; 23:27.

שכולה || שכלים

DtIsa: CanP in Isa. 49:20+21.

Other: VrsP (roots) in 1 Sam. 15:33.

ישועה || שלום, see also ישע || שלום

DtIsa: VrsP in Isa. 52:7.

Other: CanP in Isa. 60:17-18; Ps. 85:10-11; 119:165-166.

ישע || שלום, see also ישועה || שלום

DtIsa: MacP in Isa. 45:7+8.

Other: None.

עולם || שלום

DtIsa: CanP in Isa. 55:12+13.

Other: VrsP in Ezek. 37:26.

צדקה || שלום

DtIsa: VrsP in Isa. 48:18; 54:13a-14a.

Other: ColP in Isa. 32:17; Ps. 85:11. VrsP in Isa. 60:17; Ps. 72:3.

רע || שלום

DtIsa: ColP in Isa. 45:7.

Other: VrsP in 1 Sam. 29:7; Ps. 34:15; Prov. 12:20.

רפא || שלום

DtIsa: VrsP in Isa. 53:5.

Other: VrsP in Isa. 57:19; Jer. 6:14; 8:11. StrP in Jer. 33:6.

רשע || שלום

DtIsa: VrsP in Isa. 48:22.

Other: ColP in Ps. 73:3. VrsP in Isa. 57:21. StrP in Ps. 28:3. See also the collocation of roots in Ps. 37:21.

שלום || שלום

DtIsa: MacP in Isa. 48:18+22; 54:10 +13.

Other: ColP in Isa. 26:3; 57:19; Jer. 6:14; 8:11; 29:7; Ezek. 13:10. VrsP in 1 Sam. 25:6; Isa. 27:5; Ezek. 13:16. StrP in Isa. 59:8; Jer. 29:7.

מכר || שלח, see מכר || שלח

שלח || שלח

DtIsa: CanP in Isa. 50:1.

Other: VrsP in Ezek. 5:16. StrP in Gen. 32:26; Isa. 6:8; Ps. 57:3.

עבד יהוה || שלם Pu.

DtIsa: VrsP in Isa. 42:19.

Other: None.

שלם Hiph. || שלם Hiph.

DtIsa: CanP in Isa. 44:26+28.

Other: None.

אות עולם || שם

DtIsa: VrsP in Isa. 55:13.

Other: None, but compare the parallelism between שם עולם || שם || יד in Isa. 56:5.

כבוד || שם

DtIsa: VrsP in Isa. 43:7. StrP in Isa. 42:8. CanP in Isa. 48:9+11.

Other: VrsP in Isa. 59:19; Jer. 14:21; Ps. 102:16. StrP in Isa. 62:2. See also the collocation in Mal. 1:6; 2:2; Ps. 29:2; 66:2; 72:19; 79:9; 96:8; Ps. 115:1.

שם (noun) || שם (noun)

DtIsa: StrP in Isa. 44:5; 48:1. CanP in Isa. 48:1+2. MacP in Isa. 48:1+2+9.

Other: VrsP in Isa. 12:4; 65:15; Jer. 23:27; Ps. 68:5; 72:17; 148:13, etc. StrP in Isa. 56:5; Ps. 79:9, etc.

תהלה || שם

DtIsa: VrsP in Isa. 48:9. StrP in Isa. 42:8.

Other: ColP in Jer. 13:11; 33:9. VrsP in Ps. 48:11; 66:2; 102:22; 106:47; 145:21.

אלהים || שם יהוה

DtIsa: VrsP in Isa. 48:1; 50:10.

Other: VrsP in Deut. 32:3. See also the collocation in Deut. 18:7; 1 Sam. 17:45; 1 Kgs 18:24; 2 Kgs 5:11; Isa. 24:15; Jer. 26:16; Mi. 4:5; 5:3; Ps. 20:8; 2 Chron. 33:18.

ארץ || שמים, see שמים || ארץ

הר || ארץ || שמים, see also שמים || ארץ || הר

DtIsa: VrsP in Isa. 44:23; 49:13. StrP in Isa. 40:12.

Other: VrsP in Ps. 147:8. See also the collocation in Gen. 7:19; Ezek. 38:20; Hab. 3:3.

ישביה || ארץ || שמים

DtIsa: VrsP in Isa. 51:6. See also the collocation in Isa. 40:22.

Other: None, but see the collocation in Hos. 4:3.

מעל || שמים

DtIsa: ColP in Isa. 45:8.

Other: ColP in Exod. 20:4; Deut. 4:39; 5:8; 1 Kgs 8:23; Jer. 4:28; 31:37. VrsP in Isa. 14:13; Ps. 78:23.

צבא || שמים

DtIsa: VrsP in Isa. 45:12.

Other: ColP in Gen. 2:1. VrsP in Ps. 33:6; 80:15. StrP in Isa. 34:4. See also the well-known expression צבא השמים, e.g. 1 Kgs 22:19; Jer. 8:22; Zeph. 1:5.

שחקים || שמים

DtIsa: VrsP in Isa. 45:8.

Other: VrsP in Deut. 33:26; Jer. 51:9; Ps. 36:6; 57:11; 78:23; 108:5; Job 35:5; 38:37.

שמים || שמים

DtIsa: CanP in Isa. 51:6. MacP in Isa. 40:12+22; 44:23+24; 51:13+16.

Other: ColP in Ps. 68:34; 115:16. VrsP in Isa. 34:4; Ps. 148:4.

יער וכל־עץ || הרים || תחתיות ארץ || שמים

DtIsa: VrsP in Isa. 44:23.

Other: None.

בעל || שמם

DtIsa: VrsP in Isa. 54:1.

Other: None.

עזב || שמם

DtIsa: MacP in Isa. 54:1+6+7.

Other: ColP in Ezek. 36:4. VrsP in Lev. 26:43.

שחת || שמם

DtIsa: VrsP in Isa. 52:14.

Other: StrP (roots) in Jer. 4:7; 12:10. CanP in Jer. 51:25-26. See also the collocation in Dan. 9:26.

שמם || שמם

DtIsa: CanP in Isa. 54:1+3.

Other: StrP in Isa. 61:4; Ezek. 36:35.

אמר || שמע, see שמע || אמר

בין || שמע

DtIsa: ColP in Isa. 52:15. VrsP in Isa. 40:21.

Other: ColP in Isa. 6:9; Job 13:1. VrsP in Isa. 6:10; Job 26:14; Prov. 1:5.

גלה || שמע

DtIsa: VrsP in Isa. 53:1.

Other: StrP in Prov. 25:9-10; Job 36:10-11.

דבר || שמע

DtIsa: VrsP in Isa. 48:16.

Other: ColP in Isa. 65:12, 24; 66:4; Jer. 5:15; 6:10; 7:13; Ps. 50:7, etc. VrsP in Isa. 1:2; 36:11; Jer. 7:27; Ps. 62:12; Job 33:31, etc.

חזה || שמע

DtIsa: ColP in Isa. 48:6.

Other: VrsP in Num. 24:4. StrP in Num. 24:16.

ידע || שמע, see ידע || שמע

מרה || שמע, see also פתח אזן || מרה (לא)

DtIsa: CanP in Isa. 50:4+5.

Other: VrsP in Deut. 9:23; 21:18, 20; Josh. 1:18; 1 Sam. 12:14, etc.

נבט || שמע

DtIsa: VrsP in Isa. 42:18. StrP in Isa. 51:1.

Other: VrsP in Ps. 92:11; 94:9.

נגד || שמע, see נגד || שמע

נטה אזן || שמע, see נטה אזן || שמע

פתח אזן || שמע, see also פקח אזן || שמע

DtIsa: VrsP in Isa. 48:8. CanP in Isa. 50:4+5.

Other: None, but see the collocation in 2 Chron. 6:39-40; Neh. 1:6.

קרא || שמע

DtIsa: VrsP in Isa. 48:1, 12. StrP in Isa. 48:8; 49:1.

Other: ColP in 1 Kgs. 8:52; Zech. 7:13; Ps. 4:4; 27:7; etc. VrsP in 2 Sam. 22:7 (= Ps. 18:7); 1 Kgs. 8:43; Isa. 65:24; Ps. 34:7. StrP in Isa. 65:12; 66:4.

קשב || שמע, see קשב || שמע

ראה || שמע, see ראה || שמע

שמע || שמע

DtIsa: VrsP in Isa. 41:26; 52:7. StrP in Isa. 48:6. CanP in Isa. 42:18+20; 43:9; 48:3+5, 6+7+8, 12+14; 55:2+3. MacP in Isa. 41:22+26; 42:18+20+23+24; 43:9+12; 44:1+8.

Other: ColP in 2 Sam. 20:16; Isa. 6:9, etc. VrsP in Gen. 49:2; Isa. 23:5; 28:23, etc.

שמע || שמר

DtIsa: VrsP in Isa. 42:20.

Other: ColP in Exod. 23:21; Deut. 6:3; 12:28. VrsP in Gen. 26:5; Ex. 19:5; Deut. 7:12; Prov. 8:34. StrP in Josh. 22:2; Jer. 35:18.

תורה || שמר

DtIsa: MacP in Isa. 42:20+21+24.

Other: None, but see the collocation in Deut. 32:46; Ps. 78:10; 105:45; 119:34, 44, 55, 136; Prov. 7:2; 28:4; 29:18.

אור || שמש

DtIsa: CanP in Isa. 45:6+7.

Other: VrsP in 2 Sam. 23:4; Am. 8:9; Qoh. 11:7. StrP in Isa. 60:20.

גבול || שער || שמש

DtIsa: VrsP in Isa. 54:12.

Other: None, but see StrP of גבול || שער in Isa. 60:18; Ps. 147:13-14 and the collocation in Deut. 12:20-21; 16:4-5.

בזז || שסה

DtIsa: ColP in Isa. 42:22.

Other: VrsP in Isa. 17:14.

משסה || שסה, see also משסה || משסה

DtIsa: StrP in Isa. 42:22.

Other: None.

בריח || שער

DtIsa: MacP in Isa. 45:1+2.

Other: VrsP in Nah. 3:13; Lam. 2:9.

צדק || שפט (verb). See also משפט.

DtIsa: VrsP in Isa. 43:26.

Other: VrsP in Ps. 82:3.

בקעה || שפי

DtIsa: VrsP in Isa. 41:18.

Other: None.

מדבר || שפי

DtIsa: StrP in Isa. 41:18.

Other: ColP in Jer. 4:11; 12:12. StrP in Jer. 3:2.

מרעית || שפי

DtIsa: ColP in Isa. 49:9.

Other: None.

רגע || שצף

DtIsa: StrP in Isa. 54:7-8.

Other: None.

שצף קצף || חסד עולם, see also חסד || קצף

DtIsa: VrsP in Isa. 54:8.

Other: None.

שרב || שמש

DtIsa: ColP in Isa. 49:10.

Other: None.

מצה || שתה

DtIsa: ColP in Isa. 51:17.

Other: ColP in Ezek. 23:34; Ps. 75:9.

שתה || שתה

DtIsa: StrP in Isa. 51:17b-c. MacP in Isa. 51:17+22.

Other: VrsP in Isa. 24:9; Ob. 1:16; Zech. 7:6; StrP in Isa. 22:13; Jer. 2:18; Song 5:1.

הדר || תאר

DtIsa: ColP in Isa. 53:2.

Other: None.

תאר || עשה || תאר

DtIsa: VrsP in Isa. 44:13.

Other: None.

תבונה || ידע, see also בין || ידע

DtIsa: ColP in Isa. 40:14.

Other: VrsP in Prov. 17:27.

תפארת || תבנית

DtIsa: VrsP in Isa. 44:13.

Other: None.

בל יעל || תהו

DtIsa: VrsP in Isa. 44:9.

Other: None, but see the collocation in 1 Sam. 12:21.

הבל || תהו

DtIsa: ColP in Isa. 49:4.

Other: None.

ישב || תהו

DtIsa: VrsP in Isa. 45:18.

Other: None.

צדק || תהו

DtIsa: StrP in Isa. 45:19.

Other: StrP in Isa. 59:4.

תהו || תהו

DtIsa: CanP in Isa. 45:18+19.

Other: None, but see the collocation in 1 Sam. 12:21.

תהלה || כבוד, see כבוד || תהלה

תהלה || תהלה

DtIsa: CanP in Isa. 42:10+12.

Other: None.

מורג || תולעת

DtIsa: CanP in Isa. 41:14-15.

Other: None.

רמה || תולעת

DtIsa: VrsP in Isa. 41:14.

Other: VrsP in Isa. 14:11; Job 25:6.

בול עץ || תועבה

DtIsa: VrsP in Isa. 44:19.

Other: None.

אור || תורה

DtIsa: VrsP in Isa. 51:4.

Other: ColP in Prov. 6:23.

תורה || ישועה, see also ישע || תורה

DtIsa: CanP in Isa. 51:7+8.

Other: VrsP in Ps. 119:174.

תורה || ישע, see also ישועה || תורה

DtIsa: CanP in Isa. 51:4+5.

Other: None.

משפט || תורה, see תורה || משפט

תורה || תורה

DtIsa: CanP in Isa. 42:21+24.

Other: VrsP in Ps. 1:2; Prov. 28:4.

תחת || תחת

DtIsa: VrsP in Isa. 43:4; 55:13. CanP in Isa. 43:3+4.

Other: VrsP in Isa. 3:24; 10:4; 60:17; 61:3. StrP in Isa. 57:5.

ידע || תכן

DtIsa: VrsP in Isa. 40:13.

Other: None, but see the collocation of roots in 1 Sam. 2:3; Prov. 24:12.

תכן || תכן

DtIsa: CanP in Isa. 40:12-14.

Other: StrP in Ezek. 18:25, 29; 33:17.

תלל Hoph. || נטה Hiph.

DtIsa: ColP in Isa. 44:20.

Other: None.

מאד || רב || תם

DtIsa: VrsP in Isa. 47:9.

Other: None, but see the parallelism between רב || מאד in Isa. 31:1; Ps. 109:30 and see the collocation in Gen. 30:43; Exod. 12;38; Josh. 22:8; 1 Ki. 10;10; Ezek. 37:2; 47:7; Zech. 4:14.

כל־היום || תמיד

DtIsa: ColP in Isa. 51:13; 52:5.

Other: ColP in Isa. 52:5; Ps. 72:15, comparable ColP in Jer. 52:33. VrsP in Isa. 62:6.

חזק || תמך, see תמך || חזק

יענה || תן

DtIsa: ColP in Isa. 43:20.

Other: VrsP in Isa. 34:13; Mic. 1:8; Job 30:29.

תהום || תנין

DtIsa: CanP in Isa. 51:9+10.

Other: ColP in Ps. 148:7.

פנה לדרכו || תעה

DtIsa: VrsP in Isa. 53:6.

Other: None.

ארן || תרזה

DtIsa: StrP in Isa. 44:14.

Other: None.

תפארת || תשועה

DtIsa: VrsP in Isa. 46:13.

Other: None.

תשועה || תשועה, see also ישע (root) || ישע (root)

DtIsa: StrP in Isa. 46:13.

Other: ColP in 2 Kgs 13:17.

Abbreviations

For common abbreviations of periodicals we refer the reader to S.M. Schwertner, *Internationales Abkürzungsverzeichnis für Theologie und Grenzgebiete*, Berlin ^{2}1992.

α	Aquila.
AHw	W. VON SODEN, *Akkadisches Handwörterbuch*, 3 Bde., Wiesbaden 1965–1981.
AOAT	*Alte Orient und Altes Testament* (Neukirchen).
ARTU	J.C. DE MOOR, *An Anthology of Religious Texts from Ugarit*, Leiden 1987.
ATD	*Das Alte Testament Deutsch* (Göttingen).
b	Babylonian Talmud.
Barthélemy	D. Barthélemy, *Critique textuelle de l'Ancien Testament*, t. 2, Fribourg 1986.
Berges	U. Berges, *Das Buch Jesaja: Komposition und Endgestalt*, Freiburg 1998.
Beuken	W.A.M. Beuken, *Jesaja* II^{A-B} (POT), 2 dln, Nijkerk 1979–1983.
BHS	*Biblia Hebraica Stuttgartensia.*
Bibl	*Biblica* (Roma).
BK	*Biblischer Kommentar Altes Testament* (Neukirchen).
CAD	*The Assyrian Dictionary of the Oriental Institute of the University of Chicago.*
CARTU	J.C. DE MOOR, K. SPRONK, *A Cuneiform Anthology of Religious Texts from Ugarit*, Leiden 1987.
CB	*Calwer Bibelkommentare* (Stuttgart).
CBQ	*Catholic Biblical Quarterly* (Washington, DC).
COT	*Commentaar op het Oude Testament* (Kampen).
"Consistency with Regard to Tenses"	M.C.A. Korpel, J.C. de Moor, F. Sepmeijer, "Consistency with Regard to Tenses: Targum and Peshiṭta in Two Samples from Deutero-Isaiah", in: *Proceedings of the Fifth International Colloquium Bible and Computer: Translation and Transmission, Aix-en-Provence, 1–4 September 1997*, Paris 1998, 195-220.
DCH	D.J.A. Clines (ed.), *The Dictionary of Classical Hebrew*, vol. 1–4, Sheffield 1993-1998.
Delitzsch	F. Delitzsch, *Commentar über das Buch Jesaia* (BCAT, 3/1), Leipzig ^{4}1889.

De Waard	J. de Waard, *A Handbook on Isaiah*, Winona Lake 1997.
DtIsa	Deutero-Isaiah (Second Isaiah, Isaiah 40–55).
Elliger	K. Elliger, *Deuterojesaja*, 1.Teilband: Jesaja 40,1–45,7 (BK, 11/1), Neukirchen 1978.
Franke	C. Franke, *Isaiah 46, 47, and 48: A New Literary-Critical Reading*, Winona Lake 1994.
𝔊	Septuaginta.
$𝔊^A$	Codex Alexandrinus, cf. p. 5.
$𝔊^B$	Codex Vaticanus, cf. p. 5.
$𝔊^Q$	Codex Marchialianus, cf. p. 5.
$𝔊^S$	Codex Sinaiticus, cf. p. 5.
Gen. R.	Genesis Rabba.
GK	W. Gesenius, E. Kautzsch, A.E. Cowley, *Hebrew Grammar*, Oxford ^{2}1910.
Grimm, Dittert	W. Grimm, K. Dittert, *Deuterojesaja: Deutung – Wirkung – Gegenwart* (CB), Stuttgart 1990.
HAHAT	H. Donner *et al.* (eds.), *Wilhem Gesenius Hebräisches und Aramäisches Handwörterbuch über das Alte Testament*, Lief. 1–2, Heidelberg ^{18}1987–1995.
HALAT	W. BAUMGARTNER *et al.*, *Hebräisches und aramäisches Lexikon zum Alten Testament*, Leiden 1967-1995.
HCOT	*The Historical Commentary on the Old Testament* (Kampen).
Hermisson	H.-J. Hermisson, *Deuterojesaja* (BK, 11/Lief. 7-9), Neukirchen 1987-1992.
Holter	K. Holter, *Second Isaiah's Idol-Fabrication Passages*, Frankfurt a.M. 1995.
Hulst	A.R. Hulst, *Old Testament Translation Problems*, Leiden 1960.
ICC	*The International Critical Commentary* (Edinburgh).
j	Palestinian (Jerusalem) Talmud.
Joüon, Muraoka	P. Joüon, T. Muraoka, *A Grammar of Biblical Hebrew*, 2 vols., Roma 1991.
JPS	*Jewish Publication Society Version.*
JSOT	*Journal for the Study of the Old Testament* (Sheffield).
KAI	H. DONNER, W. RÖLLIG, *Kanaanäische und aramäische Inschriften*, Bd.1–3, Wiesbaden 1966–1969.
KJV	*King James Version.*
Knight	G.A.F. Knight, *Servant Theology: A Commentary on the Book of Isaiah 40–55*, rev. ed. Grand Rapids, 1984.
König, *Syntax*	E. König, *Historisch-comparative Syntax der hebräischen Sprache*, Leipzig 1897.

Koole	J.L. Koole, *Jesaja II vertaald en verklaard* (COT), 2 dln, Kampen 1985–1990 (the first volume now also available in English: J.L. Koole, *Isaiah III* (HCOT), vol. 1, Kampen 1997).
Kooij	See: Van der Kooij.
KTU	M. DIETRICH, O. LORETZ, J. SANMARTÍN, *The Cuneiform Alphabetic Texts from Ugarit, Ras Ibn Hani and Other Places* (KTU: second, enlarged edition), Neukirchen 1976.
LÄ	*Lexikon der Ägyptologie*, 7 Bde., Wiesbaden 1975–1992.
Luther	*Luther Bibel.*
𝔐	Masoretic Text, after BHS.
Melugin	R.F. Melugin, *The Formation of Isaiah 40–55* (BZAW, 141), Berlin 1976.
Merendino	R.P. Merendino, *Der Erste und der Letzte: Eine Untersuchung von Jes 40–48* (SVT, 31), Leiden 1981.
Naz.	Nazir.
NCBC	*The New Century Bible Commentary* (LOndon/Grand Rapids).
NEB	*New English Bible.*
NICOT	*The New International Commentary on the Old Testament* (Grand Rapids).
NIV	*New International Version.*
NJB	*New Jerusalem Bible.*
OBO	*Orbis Biblicus et Orientalis* (Freiburg).
Oorschot	See: Van Oorschot.
Oswalt	J.N. Oswalt, *The Book of Isaiah, Chapters 40–66* (NICOT), Grand Rapids 1998.
OTL	*Old Testament Library* (London).
OTS	*Oudtestamentische Studiën* (Leiden).
POT	*De Prediking van het Oude Testament* (Nijkerk).
𝔔	Manuscript of Qumran.
REB	*Revised English Bible.*
RSV	*Revised Standard Version.*
Schoors	A. Schoors, *I Am God Your Saviour: A Form-Critical Study of the Main Genres in Is. XL–LV* (VT.S, 24), Leiden 1973.
Segond	*Traduction de la Bible* par L. Segond, rev. ed.
σ	Symmachus.
S^{abcde}	Manuscripts of the Peshiṭta, cf. p. 7.
Spykerboer	H.C. Spykerboer, *The Structure and Composition of Deutero-Isaiah*, Meppel 1976.

Steck	O.H. Steck, *Gottesknecht und Zion*, Tübingen 1991.
𝔗	Targum.
θ	Theodotion.
ThWAT	*Theologisches Wörterbuch zum Alten Testament* (Stuttgart).
v., vv.	If the number is followed by a, b, c, d: verse-line(s), if not: verse(s).
Van der Kooij	A. van der Kooij, *Die alten Textzeugen des Jesajabuches* (OBO, 35), Freiburg 1981.
Van Oorschot	J. van Oorschot, *Von Babel zum Zion: Eine literarkritische und redaktionsgeschichtliche Untersuchung* (BZAW, 206), Berlin 1993.
𝔙	Vulgate.
Waard	See: De Waard.
Waltke, O'Connor	B.K. Waltke, M. O'Connor, *An Introduction to Biblical Hebrew Syntax*, Winona Lake 1990.
Watts	J.D.W. Watts, *Isaiah 34–66* (WBC), Waco 1987.
Westermann	C. Westermann, *Das Buch Jesaja, Kapitel 40–66* (ATD), Göttingen ^{5}1986.
Whybray	R.N. Whybray, *Isaiah 40–66* (NCBC), London 1981, repr. Grand Rapids 1996.
Young	E.J. Young, *The Book of Isaiah*, vol. 3, Grand Rapids 1972, repr. 1996.

Index of Biblical Texts

(excluding Isa. 40–55 and Index of Parallel Words)

OUDTESTAMENTISCHE STUDIËN

Edited by Johannes C. de Moor

15. *The Priestly Code and Seven Other Studies.* 1969. ISBN 90 04 03099 9
17. *The Witness of Tradition.* Papers Read at the Joint British-Dutch Old Testament Conference Held at Woudschoten (Holland), September 1970. 1972. ISBN 90 04 03343 2
18. LABUSCHAGNE, C.J.; LEEUWEN, C. VAN; MULDER, M.J.; BRONGERS, H.A.; JONGELING, B.; DEQUEKER, L.; BOER, P.A.H. DE. *Syntax and meaning.* Studies in Hebrew Syntax and Biblical Exegesis. 1973. ISBN 90 04 03785 3
19. *Language and Meaning.* Studies in Hebrew Language and Biblical Exegesis. Papers Read at the Joint British-Dutch Old Testament Conference Held at London, 1973. 1974. ISBN 90 04 03943 0
20. *Instruction and Interpretation.* Studies in Hebrew Language, Palestinian Archaeology and Biblical Exegesis. Papers Read at the Joint British-Dutch Old Testament Conference Held at Louvain, 1976. 1977. ISBN 90 04 05433 2
21. ALBREKTSON, B.; et al. *Remembering All the Way...* A Collection of Old Testament Studies Published on the Occasion of the Fortieth Anniversary of the Oudtestamentisch Werkgezelschap in Nederland. 1981. ISBN 90 04 06305 6
22. WILDE, A. DE (ed.). *Das Buch Hiob.* Eingeleitet, übersetzt und erläutert. 1981. ISBN 90 04 06372 2
23. *Prophets, worship and theodicy.* Studies in Prophetism, Biblical Theology and Structural and Rhetorical Analysis, and the Place of Music in Worship. Papers Read at the Joint British-Dutch Old Testament Conference Held at Woudschoten, 1982. 1984. ISBN 90 04 07035 4
24. *Crises and Perspectives.* Studies in Ancient Near Eastern Polytheism, Biblical Theology, Palestinian Archaeology and Intertestamental Literature. Papers Read at the Joint British-Dutch Old Testament Conference Held at Cambridge, U.K., 1985. 1986. ISBN 90 04 07873 8
25. WOUDE, A.S. VAN DER (ed.). *New Avenues in the Study of the Old Testament.* A Collection of Old Testament Studies Published on the Occasion of the Fiftieth Anniversary of the Oudtestamentisch Werkgezelschap and the Retirement of Prof. Dr. M.J. Mulder. 1989. ISBN 90 04 09125 4
26. WOUDE, A.S. VAN DER (ed.). *In Quest of the Past.* Studies in Israelite Religion, Literature and Prophetism. Papers Read at the Joint British-Dutch Old Testament Conference, Held at Elspeet, 1988. 1990. ISBN 90 04 09192 0
27. BOER, P.A.H. DE; DUIN, C. VAN. *Selected Studies in Old Testament Exegesis.* 1991. ISBN 90 04 09342 7
28. SMELIK, K.A.D. *Converting the Past.* Studies in Ancient Israelite and Moabite Historiography. 1992. ISBN 90 04 09480 6
29. DIRKSEN, P.B.; VAN DER KOOIJ, A. (eds.). *Abraham Kuenen (1828-1891). His Major Contributions to the Study of the Old Testament.* A Collection of Old Testament Studies Published on the Occasion of the Centenary of Abraham Kuenen's Death (10 December 1991). 1993. ISBN 90 04 09732 5
30. HOUTMAN, C. *Der Himmel im Alten Testament.* Israels Weltbild und Weltanschauung. 1993. ISBN 90 04 09690 6
31. PEELS, H.G.L. *The Vengeance of God.* The Meaning of the Root NQM and the Function of the NQM-Texts in the Context of Divine Revelation in the Old Testament. 1995. ISBN 90 04 10164 0

32. LUGT, P. VAN DER. *Rhetorical Criticism and the Poetry of the Book of Job.* 1995. ISBN 90 04 10326
33. EYNIKEL, E. *The Reform of King Josiah and the Composition of the Deuteronomistic History.* 1996. ISBN 90 04 10266 3
34. MOOR, J.C. DE (ed.). *Synchronic or Diachronic?* A Debate on Method in Old Testament Exegesis 1995. ISBN 90 04 10342 2
35. TIGCHELAAR, E.J.C. *Prophets of Old and The Day of the End.* Zechariah, the Book of Watchers and Apocalyptic. 1995. ISBN 90 04 10356 2
36. SMELIK, W.F. *The Targum of Judges.* 1995. ISBN 90 04 10365 1
37. SANDERS, P. *The Provenance of Deuteronomy 32.* 1996. ISBN 90 04 10648 0
38. KEULEN, P.S.F. VAN, *Manasseh through the Eyes of the Deuteronomists.* The Manasseh Account (2 Kings 21:1-18) and the Final Chapters of the Deuteronomistic History. 1996. ISBN 90 04 10666 9
39. HOOP, R. DE, *Genesis 49 in its Literary and Historical Context.* 1998. ISBN 90 04 10913 7 (*In Preparation*)
40. MOOR, J.C. DE (ed.). *Intertextuality in Ugarit and Israel.* Papers Read at The Tenth Joint Meeting of The Society for Old Testament Study and Het Oudtestamentisch Werkgezelschap in Nederland en België Held at Oxford, 1997. 1998. ISBN 90 04 11154 9
41. KORPEL, M.C.A.; DE MOOR, J.C. *The Structure of Classical Hebrew Poetry: Isaiah 40 -55.* 1998. ISBN 90 04 11261 8

Marjo C. A. Korpel, D. D. (1990), Theological University Kampen, The Netherlands, is Lecturer of Old Testament at Utrecht University, The Netherlands. Her major publications concern Ugaritic and Hebrew poetry.

Johannes C. de Moor, Ph. D. (1971), Free University, Amsterdam, is Professor of Semitic languages at the Theological University Kampen, The Netherlands. He has published extensively on Ugaritic, Hebrew and Targumic Aramaic. He is editor of several international series and journals.